W9-CCI-980

PUBLISHER	Susan Elbe
ASSOCIATE PUBLISHER	Jay O'Callaghan
ACQUISITIONS EDITOR	Mark Bonadeo
SENIOR MARKETING MANAGER	Steven Herdegen
OUTSIDE DEVELOPMENT EDITOR	Ann Torbert
PRODUCTION SERVICES MANAGER	Jeanine Furino
SUPPLEMENTS EDITOR	Ed Brislin
PROJECT EDITOR	Brian Kamins
MEDIA EDITOR	Allison Morris
SENIOR DESIGNER	Karin Kincheloe
ILLUSTRATION EDITOR	Anna Melhorn
COVER PHOTOS	© www.danheller.com

This book was set in Palatino by Techbooks and printed and bound by Von Hoffmann Press. The cover was printed by Lehigh Press.

This book is printed on acid-free paper. ∞

Main Update:	ISBN 0-471-66180-5
Volume I Update:	ISBN 0-471-71757-6
Volume II Update:	ISBN 0-471-71838-6
WIE Update:	ISBN 0-471-66184-8

Printed in the United States of America

10 9 8 7 6 5 4 3 2 1

Intermediate Accounting

ELEVENTH EDITION 2005 FASB UPDATE

INTERMEDIATE ACCOUNTING

Donald E. Kieso Ph.D., C.P.A.
KPMG Emeritus Professor of Accounting
Northern Illinois University
DeKalb, Illinois

Jerry J. Weygandt Ph.D., C.P.A.
Arthur Anderson Alumni Professor of Accounting
University of Wisconsin
Madison, Wisconsin

Terry D. Warfield Ph.D.
Associate Professor of Accounting
University of Wisconsin
Madison, Wisconsin

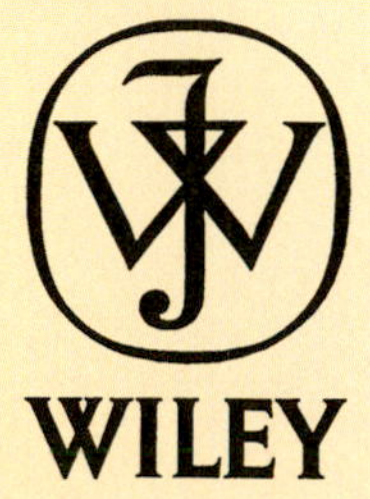

WILEY
John Wiley & Sons, Inc.

Contents

This update booklet contains discussions of key accounting standards that have been issued since the publication of *Intermediate Accounting* 11e, by Kieso, Weygandt, and Warfield. In addition, it provides an update on major standards likely to be issued next year that are presently in exposure draft format. These standards are discussed, by topic, in seven sections, as outlined below. See the following page for a visual display of how these sections relate to the textbook chapters.

OTHER WAYS TO STAY UP-TO-DATE

A **quarterly eNewsletter** is distributed to users of *Intermediate Accounting*, 11th Edition, to provide information that updates and complements material in the textbook. Each newsletter contains four parts: (1) ***Updates*** provide the latest information about new accounting standards. (2) ***Financial Reporting Challenges*** address a contemporary issue being debated by accounting professionals and standard setters. (3) "***By the Way***" provides a "heads-up" to instructors on topics that have implications for the intermediate accounting course. (4) ***CPA Exam Update***, prepared by Debra R. Hopkins, CPA, CIA, Director of the Northern Illinois University CPA Review, shares information useful for preparing student for the new CPA exam.

FARS Online (Educational Version) gives students six complete infobases: Original Pronouncements, Current Text, EITF Abstracts, Staff Implementation Guides (Q&A), Derivative Instruments and Hedging Activities, and a Comprehensive Topical Index. To learn more or to access FARS Online, visit www.wiley.com/college/farsonline.

Key to Using this Update

The following chapters in *Intermediate Accounting* 11e are affected by the update information described in the callout boxes below.

4 Income Statement and Related Information

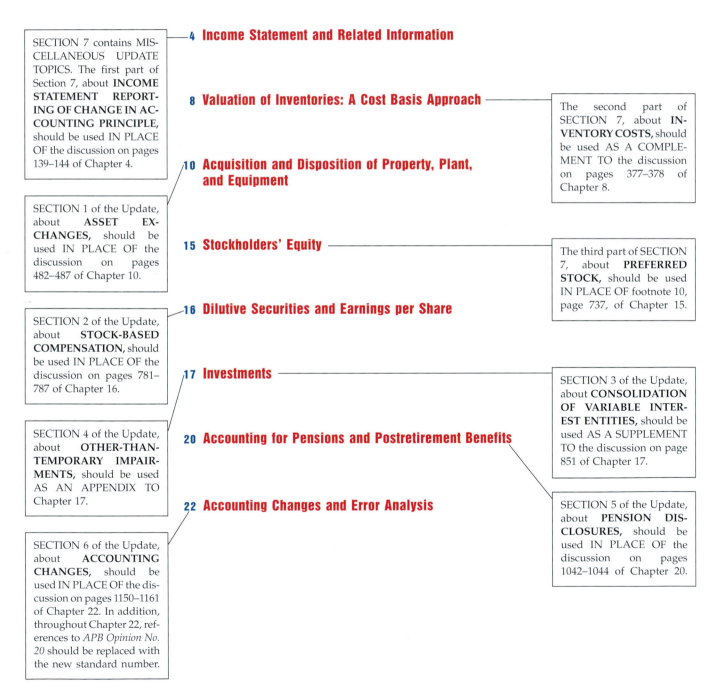

SECTION 7 contains MISCELLANEOUS UPDATE TOPICS. The first part of Section 7, about **INCOME STATEMENT REPORTING OF CHANGE IN ACCOUNTING PRINCIPLE,** should be used IN PLACE OF the discussion on pages 139–144 of Chapter 4.

8 Valuation of Inventories: A Cost Basis Approach

The second part of SECTION 7, about **INVENTORY COSTS,** should be used AS A COMPLEMENT TO the discussion on pages 377–378 of Chapter 8.

10 Acquisition and Disposition of Property, Plant, and Equipment

SECTION 1 of the Update, about **ASSET EXCHANGES,** should be used IN PLACE OF the discussion on pages 482–487 of Chapter 10.

15 Stockholders' Equity

The third part of SECTION 7, about **PREFERRED STOCK,** should be used IN PLACE OF footnote 10, page 737, of Chapter 15.

16 Dilutive Securities and Earnings per Share

SECTION 2 of the Update, about **STOCK-BASED COMPENSATION,** should be used IN PLACE OF the discussion on pages 781–787 of Chapter 16.

17 Investments

SECTION 3 of the Update, about **CONSOLIDATION OF VARIABLE INTEREST ENTITIES,** should be used AS A SUPPLEMENT TO the discussion on page 851 of Chapter 17.

SECTION 4 of the Update, about **OTHER-THAN-TEMPORARY IMPAIRMENTS,** should be used AS AN APPENDIX TO Chapter 17.

20 Accounting for Pensions and Postretirement Benefits

SECTION 5 of the Update, about **PENSION DISCLOSURES,** should be used IN PLACE OF the discussion on pages 1042–1044 of Chapter 20.

22 Accounting Changes and Error Analysis

SECTION 6 of the Update, about **ACCOUNTING CHANGES,** should be used IN PLACE OF the discussion on pages 1150–1161 of Chapter 22. In addition, throughout Chapter 22, references to *APB Opinion No. 20* should be replaced with the new standard number.

SECTION 1 ASSET EXCHANGES

In 2004, the FASB issued a new standard addressing the accounting for exchanges of productive assets. This new standard, "Exchanges of Productive Assets: An Amendment of *APB Opinion No. 29," Statement of Financial Accounting Standard* (Stamford, Conn.: FASB, 2004), is part of the FASB's short-term international convergence project and amends *APB Opinion No. 29*.

The following material should be used **in place of** the discussion in Chapter 10, pages 482–487, of *Intermediate Accounting*, 11th Edition.

Exchanges of Nonmonetary Assets

The proper accounting for exchanges of nonmonetary assets (such as inventories and property, plant, and equipment) is controversial.[1] Some argue that the accounting for these types of exchanges should be based on the fair value of the asset given up or the fair value of the asset received, with a gain or loss recognized. Others believe that the accounting should be based on the recorded amount (book value) of the asset given up, with no gain or loss recognized. Still others favor an approach that would recognize losses in all cases, but defer gains in special situations.

Ordinarily accounting for the exchange of **nonmonetary assets** should be based on **the fair value of the asset given up or the fair value of the asset received, whichever is clearly more evident**.[2] Thus, any gains or losses on the exchange **should be recognized immediately**. The rationale for this approach is that the transaction has **commercial substance** and therefore should be recognized.

Meaning of Commercial Substance

As indicated above, fair value is the basis for measuring an asset acquired in a nonmonetary exchange, **only if the transaction has commercial substance**. An exchange has commercial substance if the future cash flows change as a result of the transaction. That is, if the two parties' economic positions change, the transaction has commercial substance. For example, Andrew Co. exchanges some of its equipment for land held by Roddick Inc. It is likely that the timing and amount of the cash flows arising from the land received in the exchange will be significantly different from the cash flows from the equipment. As a result, both Andrew Co. and Roddick Inc. are in **different economic positions**. Therefore the exchange has commercial substance.

Even if similar assets are exchanged (e.g., an exchange of a truck for another truck), a change in the economic position of the company can result. For example, let's say the useful life of the truck received is significantly longer than the truck given up. In this case the cash flows for the trucks can be significantly different. As a result, the transaction has commercial substance and fair value should be used as a basis for measuring the asset received in the exchange. However, if the difference in cash flows is not

[1]Nonmonetary assets are items whose price in terms of the monetary unit may change over time. Monetary assets—cash and short- or long-term accounts and notes receivable—are fixed in terms of units of currency by contract or otherwise.

[2]"Accounting for Nonmonetary Transactions," *Opinions of the Accounting Principles Board No. 29* (New York: AICPA, 1973), par 18, and "Exchanges of Productive Assets: An Amendment of *APB Opinion No. 29," Statement of Financial Accounting Standard* (Stamford, Conn.: FASB, 2004).

significant, then the company is in the same economic position as before the exchange **and no gain or loss should be recorded.**[3]

As we will see in the examples below, use of fair value generally results in recognition of a gain or loss at the time of the exchange. Consequently companies must carefully evaluate the cash flow characteristics of the assets exchanged to determine if the transaction has commercial substance.[4] Asset exchange situations and the related accounting are summarized in Illustration U10-1.

ILLUSTRATION U10-1
Accounting for Exchanges

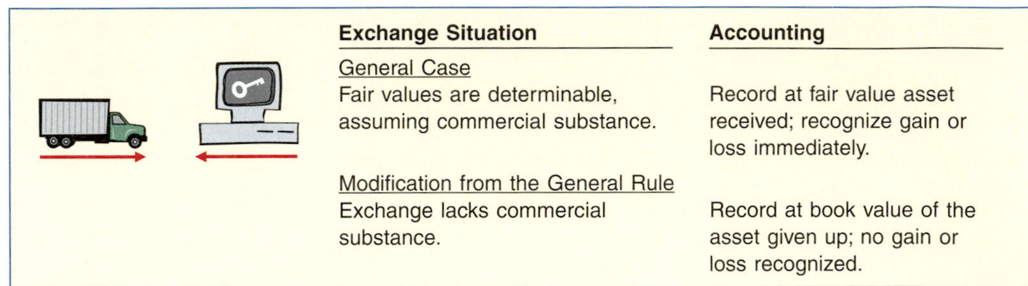

Exchange Situation	Accounting
General Case Fair values are determinable, assuming commercial substance.	Record at fair value asset received; recognize gain or loss immediately.
Modification from the General Rule Exchange lacks commercial substance.	Record at book value of the asset given up; no gain or loss recognized.

To summarize, fair value is used to record an asset acquired in a nonmonetary exchange, if the transaction **has commercial substance**. A gain or loss is recorded on the exchange based on the difference between the carrying value of the asset relinquished and the fair value of the asset received. If the exchange **lacks commercial substance**, the exchange is recorded based on book values. In that case, no gains or losses are recognized on the exchange.

To illustrate the accounting for exchange transactions, we examine the following situations:

1. Exchange with commercial substance—gain.
2. Exchange with commercial substance—loss.
3. Exchange lacks commercial substance.

Exchange with Commercial Substance—Gain

The cost of a nonmonetary asset acquired in exchange for another nonmonetary asset is usually recorded at the **fair value of the asset given up**, and a gain or loss is recognized. The **fair value of the asset received** should be used only if it is more clearly evident than the fair value of the asset given up.

To illustrate, Interstate Transportation Company exchanged a number of used trucks plus cash for vacant land that might be used for a future plant site. The trucks have a combined book value of $42,000 (cost $64,000 less $22,000 accumulated depreciation). Interstate's purchasing agent, who has had previous dealings in the secondhand market, indicates that the trucks have a fair market value of $49,000. In addition

[3]According to previous accounting standards, the primary factor in determining whether to recognize gains on exchanges was based on whether the assets exchanged were "similar" in nature. This approach was criticized due to the subjectivity of determining similarity in the assets being exchanged. Adopting the commercial substance condition addresses this concern and contributes to international accounting convergence. The FASB and the IASB are collaborating on a project in which they have agreed to converge around high-quality solutions to resolve differences between U.S. GAAP and International Financial Reporting Standards (IFRS). By adopting the commercial substance approach, U.S. GAAP and IFRS are now in agreement.

[4]The determination of the commercial substance of a transaction requires significant judgment. In determining whether future cash flows change, it is necessary to either (1) determine whether the risk, timing, and amount of cash flows arising for the asset received is different from the cash flows associated with the outbound asset, or (2) evaluate whether cash flows are affected with the exchange versus without the exchange.

to the trucks, Interstate must pay $17,000 cash for the land. The cost of the land to Interstate is $66,000 computed as follows.

Fair value of trucks exchanged	$49,000
Cash paid	17,000
Cost of land	$66,000

ILLUSTRATION U10-2
Computation of Land Cost

The journal entry to record the exchange transaction is:

Land	66,000	
Accumulated Depreciation—Trucks	22,000	
Trucks		64,000
Gain on Disposal of Trucks		7,000
Cash		17,000

The gain is the difference between the fair value of the trucks and their book value. It is verified as follows.

Fair value of trucks		$49,000
Cost of trucks	$64,000	
Less: Accumulated depreciation	22,000	
Book value of trucks		42,000
Gain on disposal of used trucks		$ 7,000

ILLUSTRATION U10-3
Computation of Gain on Disposal of Used Trucks

It follows that if the fair value of the trucks was $39,000 instead of $49,000, a loss on the exchange of $3,000 ($42,000 − $39,000) would be reported. In either case, the company is in a different economic position and therefore the transaction has commercial substance. Thus, **a gain or loss should be recognized**.

Exchange with Commercial Substance—Loss

To illustrate a loss situation, assume that Information Processing, Inc. trades its used machine for a new model. The machine given up has a book value of $8,000 (original cost $12,000 less $4,000 accumulated depreciation) and a fair value of $6,000. It is traded for a new model that has a list price of $16,000. In negotiations with the seller, a trade-in allowance of $9,000 is agreed on for the used machine. Based on an evaluation of cash flows arising from the assets exchanged, management determines that this transaction has commercial substance. The cash payment that must be made for the new asset and the cost of the new machine are computed as follows.

List price of new machine	$16,000
Less: Trade-in allowance for used machine	9,000
Cash payment due	7,000
Fair value of used machine	6,000
Cost of new machine	$13,000

ILLUSTRATION U10-4
Computation of Cost of New Machine

The journal entry to record this transaction is:

Equipment	13,000	
Accumulated Depreciation—Equipment	4,000	
Loss on Disposal of Equipment	2,000	
Equipment		12,000
Cash		7,000

The loss on the disposal of the used machine can be verified as follows.

ILLUSTRATION U10-5
Computation of Loss on Disposal of Used Machine

Fair value of used machine	$6,000
Book value of used machine	8,000
Loss on disposal of used machine	$2,000

Why was the trade-in allowance or the book value of the old asset not used as a basis for the new equipment? The trade-in allowance is not used because it included a price concession (similar to a price discount) to the purchaser. For example, few individuals pay list price for a new car. Trade-in allowances on the used car are often inflated so that actual selling prices are below list prices. To record the car at list price would state it at an amount in excess of its cash equivalent price because the new car's list price is usually inflated. Similarly, use of book value in this situation would overstate the value of the new machine by $2,000. Because assets should not be valued at more than their cash equivalent price, the loss should be recognized immediately rather than added to the cost of the newly acquired asset.

Exchange Lacks Commercial Substance

The accounting treatment for exchanges that lack commercial substance is illustrated in the real estate industry. In this industry, it is common practice for companies to "swap" real estate holdings. Assume that Landmark Company and Hillfarm, Inc. each had undeveloped land on which it intended to build shopping centers. Appraisals indicated that the land of both companies had increased significantly in value, but the cash flows arising from the land parcels to be exchanged are not significantly different. Although the companies may wish to exchange (swap) their undeveloped land, record a gain, and report their new parcels of land at current fair values, they are precluded from recognizing gains because the exchange lacks commercial substance. That is, the companies remain in the same economic position after the swap as before. Therefore, the asset acquired should be recorded at book value with **no gain recognized**.[5]

Let's look at another example of an exchange that lacks commercial substance. Davis Rent-A-Car has a rental fleet of automobiles consisting primarily of Ford Motor Company products. Davis's management wants to increase the variety of automobiles in its rental fleet by adding numerous General Motors models. Davis arranges with Nertz Rent-A-Car to exchange a group of Ford automobiles that are essentially identical to the General Motors models. The Ford vehicles to be exchanged have a fair value of $160,000 and a book value of $135,000 (cost $150,000 less accumulated depreciation $15,000). The GM models in the exchange have a fair value of $170,000. Davis pays $10,000 in cash in addition to the Ford automobiles exchanged. The total gain to Davis Rent-A-Car is computed as shown in Illustration U10-6.

ILLUSTRATION U10-6
Computation of Gain (Unrecognized)

Fair value of Ford automobiles exchanged	$160,000
Book value of Ford automobiles exchanged	135,000
Total gain (unrecognized)	$ 25,000

In this case, Davis Rent-A-Car still has a fleet of cars with essentially the same cash flows as the cars given up although different models. Therefore, the transaction lacks commercial substance. As a result, the total gain is deferred, and the basis of the General

[5]Note that the asset given up may be impaired. As a result, if the book value exceeds the fair value, an impairment is recorded, if the impairment test is met. For homework purposes, assume that the impairment test is not met.

Motors automobiles is reduced via two different but acceptable computations as shown below.

ILLUSTRATION U10-7
Basis of New Automobiles—Fair Value vs. Book Value

Fair value of GM automobiles	$170,000	OR	Book value of Ford automobiles	$135,000
Less: Gain deferred	(25,000)		Cash paid	10,000
Basis of GM automobiles	$145,000		Basis of GM automobiles	$145,000

The entry by Davis to record this transaction is as follows.

Automobiles (GM)	145,000	
Accumulated Depreciation—Automobiles	15,000	
Automobiles (Ford)		150,000
Cash		10,000

The gain that reduced the basis of the new automobiles will be recognized when those automobiles are sold to an outside party. While these automobiles are held, depreciation charges will be lower, and net income will be higher in subsequent periods because of the reduced basis.

To summarize, fair value is the basis for measuring an asset acquired in a nonmonetary exchange, if the transaction has commercial substance. A gain or loss is recorded on the exchange based on the difference between the carrying value of the asset relinquished and the fair value of the asset received. One other exception to the general rules must be noted: If fair values for either the asset received or the asset given up in the exchange are not determinable within reasonable limits, the book value of the asset relinquished (plus any cash paid) will be recorded as the cost of the asset received.[6]

For example, due to a change in its meat packing process, Jones Meat Locker Co. trades its specialty meat-packing equipment for new equipment that can be used in its new packing process. Because of the specialty nature of the equipment being exchanged, the fair values of the assets being exchanged cannot be reliably determined. The used equipment has a book value of $9,000 (original cost of $17,000 less $8,000 accumulated depreciation). The list price of the new equipment is $21,000. The equipment vendor gives Jones an $11,000 trade-in allowance on its old equipment. The cash payment made for the new machine and the cost to be recorded are computed as follows.

ILLUSTRATION U10-8
Computation of Cost of New Machine

List price of new equipment	$21,000
Less: Trade-in allowance for used equipment	11,000
Cash payment due	10,000
Book value of old equipment	9,000
Cost of new equipment	$19,000

The journal entry to record the exchange is:

Equipment	19,000	
Accumulated Depreciation—Equipment	8,000	
Equipment		17,000
Cash		10,000

As indicated, in the absence of fair values (for either the asset received or the asset relinquished), the company uses the book value of the asset added to cash paid in the exchange to measure the cost of the new equipment.

[6] Yet another exception to the fair value rule is for an exchange that facilitates sales to customers. An example of this situation is when a company exchanges its inventory items with inventory of another company because of color, size, etc. to facilitate sale to an outside customer. In this case, the earnings process for the inventory is not considered complete, and a gain is not recognized.

An enterprise that engages in one or more nonmonetary exchanges during a period should disclose in financial statements for the period the nature of the transactions, the method of accounting for the assets transferred, and gains or losses recognized on transfers.[7]

WHAT DO THE NUMBERS MEAN?

ABOUT THOSE SWAPS

In a press release, Roy Olofson, former vice president of finance for **Global Crossing**, accused company executives of improperly describing the company's revenue to the public. Olofson said Global Crossing had improperly recorded long-term sales immediately rather than over the term of the contract, that the company improperly booked swaps of capacity with other carriers as cash transactions, and that Global Crossing fired him when he blew the whistle.

The accounting for the swaps is of particular interest here. The accounting for swaps involves exchanges of similar network capacity. Companies engaged in such deals, they have said, because it was less costly and quicker than building segments that their own networks lacked, or because such pacts provided redundancies to make their own networks more reliable to customers. In one expert's view, an exchange of similar network capacity is the equivalent of trading a blue truck for a red truck—it shouldn't boost a company's revenue.

But Global Crossing and **Qwest**, among others, used the transactions to do just that, counting as revenue the money received from the company on the other end of the deal. (In general, in transactions involving leased capacity, the companies booked the revenue over the life of the contract.) Some of these companies then treated their own purchases as capital expenditures, which weren't run through the income statement. Instead, the spending led to the addition of assets on the balance sheet.

Both congressional and Securities and Exchange Commission investigators are seeking to determine whether some of these capacity exchanges may have been a device to pad revenue. Revenue growth was a key factor in the valuation of some of these companies, such as Global Crossing and Qwest, throughout the craze for tech stocks in the late 1990s and 2000.

Source: Adapted from Henny Sender, "Telecoms Draw Focus for Moves in Accounting," *Wall Street Journal* (March 26, 2002), p. C7.

EXERCISES

UE10-1 (Nonmonetary Exchange) Cannondale Company purchased an electric wax melter on April 30, 2005, by trading in its old gas model and paying the balance in cash. The following data relate to the purchase.

List price of new melter	$15,800
Cash paid	10,000
Cost of old melter (5-year life, $700 residual value)	11,200
Accumulated depreciation—old melter (straight-line)	6,300
Second-hand market value of old melter	5,200

Instructions

Prepare the journal entry(ies) necessary to record this exchange, assuming that the exchange **(a)** has commercial substance, and **(b)** lacks commercial substance. Cannondale's fiscal year ends on December 31, and depreciation has been recorded through December 31, 2004.

UE10-2 (Nonmonetary Exchange) Carlos Arruza Company exchanged equipment used in its manufacturing operations plus $3,000 in cash for similar equipment used in the operations of Tony LoBianco Company. The following information pertains to the exchange.

[7] "Accounting for Nonmonetary Transactions," op. cit., par. 28.

	Carlos Arruza Co.	Tony LoBianco Co.
Equipment (cost)	$28,000	$28,000
Accumulated depreciation	19,000	10,000
Fair value of equipment	12,500	15,500
Cash given up	3,000	

Instructions

(a) Prepare the journal entries to record the exchange on the books of both companies. Assume that the exchange lacks commercial substance.

(b) Prepare the journal entries to record the exchange on the books of both companies. Assume that the exchange has commercial substance.

UE10-3 (Nonmonetary Exchange) Busytown Corporation, which manufactures shoes, hired a recent college graduate to work in its accounting department. On the first day of work, the accountant was assigned to total a batch of invoices with the use of an adding machine. Before long, the accountant, who had never before seen such a machine, managed to break the machine. Busytown Corporation gave the machine plus $340 to Dick Tracy Business Machine Company (dealer) in exchange for a new machine. Assume the following information about the machines. (The difference in expected cash flows between the exchanged machines is significant.)

	Busytown Corp. (Old Machine)	Dick Tracy Co. (New Machine)
Machine cost	$290	$270
Accumulated depreciation	140	–0–
Fair value	85	425

Instructions

For each company, prepare the necessary journal entry to record the exchange.

UE10-4 (Nonmonetary Exchange) Dana Ashbrook Inc. has negotiated the purchase of a new piece of equipment at a price of $8,000 plus trade-in, f.o.b. factory. Dana Ashbrook Inc. paid $8,000 cash and traded in used equipment. The used equipment had originally cost $62,000; it had a book value of $42,000 and a secondhand market value of $47,800, as indicated by recent transactions involving similar equipment. Freight and installation charges for the new equipment required a cash payment of $1,100.

Instructions

(a) Prepare the general journal entry to record this transaction, assuming that the exchange has commercial substance.

(b) Assume the same facts as in (a) except that fair value information for the assets exchanged is *not* determinable. Prepare the general journal entry to record this transaction.

PROBLEMS

UP10-1 (Nonmonetary Exchanges) Susquehanna Corporation wishes to exchange a machine used in its operations. Susquehanna has received the following offers from other companies in the industry.

1. Choctaw Company offered to exchange a similar machine plus $23,000 (exchange has commercial substance).
2. Powhatan Company offered to exchange a similar machine (exchange lacks commercial substance).
3. Shawnee Company offered to exchange a similar machine, but wanted $8,000 in addition to Susquehanna's machine (exchange has commercial substance).

	Susquehanna	Choctaw	Powhatan	Shawnee
Machine cost	$160,000	$120,000	$147,000	$160,000
Accumulated depreciation	50,000	45,000	71,000	75,000
Fair value	92,000	69,000	92,000	100,000

Instructions

For each of the three independent situations, prepare the journal entries to record the exchange on the books of each company.

UP10-2 (Nonmonetary Exchanges) On August 1, Arna, Inc. exchanged productive assets with Bontemps, Inc. Arna's asset is referred to below as "Asset A," and Bontemps' is referred to as "Asset B." The following facts pertain to these assets.

	Asset A	Asset B
Original cost	$96,000	$110,000
Accumulated depreciation (to date of exchange)	45,000	52,000
Fair market value at date of exchange	60,000	75,000
Cash paid by Arna, Inc.	15,000	
Cash received by Bontemps, Inc.		15,000

Instructions

(a) Assuming that the exchange of Assets A and B has commercial substance, record the exchange for both Arna, Inc. and Bontemps, Inc. in accordance with generally accepted accounting principles.

(b) Assuming that the exchange of Assets A and B lacks commercial substance, record the exchange for both Arna, Inc. and Bontemps, Inc. in accordance with generally accepted accounting principles.

UP10-3 (Nonmonetary Exchanges) During the current year, Garrison Construction trades an old crane that has a book value of $80,000 (original cost $140,000 less accumulated depreciation $60,000) for a new crane from Keillor Manufacturing Co. The new crane cost Keillor $165,000 to manufacture and is classified as inventory. The following information is also available.

	Garrison Const.	Keillor Mfg. Co.
Fair market value of old crane	$ 72,000	
Fair market value of new crane		$190,000
Cash paid	118,000	
Cash received		118,000

Instructions

(a) Assuming that this exchange is considered to have commercial substance, prepare the journal entries on the books of (1) Garrison Construction and (2) Keillor Manufacturing.

(b) Assuming that this exchange lacks commercial substance for Garrison, prepare the journal entries on the books of Garrison Construction.

(c) Assuming the same facts as those in (a), except that the fair market value of the old crane is $98,000 and the cash paid is $92,000, prepare the journal entries on the books of (1) Garrison Construction and (2) Keillor Manufacturing.

(d) Assuming the same facts as those in (b), except that the fair market value of the old crane is $87,000 and the cash paid $103,000. Prepare the journal entries on the books of Garrison Construction.

SECTION 2 STOCK-BASED COMPENSATION

Presented below is a discussion of a *proposed* standard on stock compensation plans. The FASB announced in mid-October 2004 a six-month delay in passage of the standard. Thus, mandatory expensing of stock-based compensation would not begin until the third quarter of 2005. Many attribute the delay to questions related to the valuation models used to value stock options.

The following material provides information necessary to understand the new standard and can be used **in place of** the discussion in Chapter 16, pages 781–787, of *Intermediate Accounting*, 11th Edition.

STOCK COMPENSATION PLANS

Another form of warrant arises in stock compensation plans used to pay and motivate employees. This warrant is a **stock option**, which gives selected employees the option to purchase common stock at a given price over an extended period of time. As indicated in the opening story, stock options are very popular. For example, the following chart shows stock options as a percentage of total compensation for 1999–2000 given to the top 200 CEOs and to 100 dot-com company CEOs.

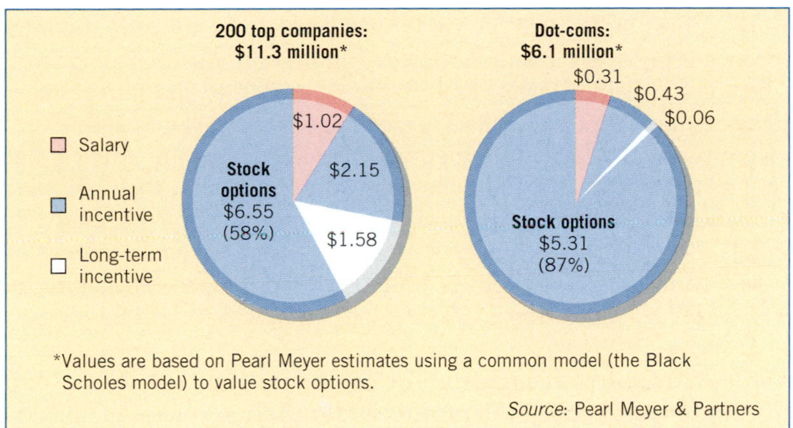

ILLUSTRATION U16-1
Stock Options as a Portion of Total Compensation

These figures show the dramatic change in the way many top executives (and for that matter, regular employees) are compensated.

Effective compensation has been a subject of considerable interest lately. A consensus of opinion is that effective compensation programs are ones that (1) motivate employees to high levels of performance, (2) help retain executives and allow for recruitment of new talent, (3) base compensation on employee and company performance, (4) maximize the employee's after-tax benefit and minimize the employee's after-tax cost, and (5) use performance criteria over which the employee has control. Although straight cash compensation plans (salary and, perhaps, bonus) are an important part of any compensation program, they are oriented to the short run. Many companies recognize that a more long-run compensation plan is often needed in addition to a cash component.

Long-term compensation plans attempt to develop in key employees a strong loyalty toward the company. An effective way to accomplish this goal is to give the employees "a piece of the action"—that is, an equity interest based on changes in long-term measures such as increases in earnings per share, revenues, stock price, or market share. These plans, generally referred to as **stock option plans**, come in many different forms. Essentially, they provide the employee with the opportunity to receive stock or cash in the future if the performance of the company (by whatever measure) is satisfactory.

The Major Reporting Issue

Suppose that you are an employee for Hurdle Inc. and you are granted options to purchase 10,000 shares of the firm's common stock as part of your compensation. The date you receive the options is referred to as the **grant date**. The options are good for 10 years. The market price and the exercise price for the stock are both $20 at the grant date. **What is the value of the compensation you just received?**

Some believe you have not received anything: That is, the difference between the market price and the exercise price is zero, and therefore no compensation results. Others argue these options have value: If the stock price goes above $20 any time over the next 10 years and you exercise these options, substantial compensation results. For example, if at the end of the fourth year, the market price of the stock is $30 and you exercise your options, you will have earned $100,000 [10,000 options × ($30 − $20)], ignoring income taxes.

How should the granting of these options be reported by Hurdle Inc.? In the past, GAAP required that compensation cost be measured by the excess of the market price of the stock over its exercise price at the grant date. This approach is referred to as the **intrinsic value method** because the computation is not dependent on external circumstances: **The compensation cost is the difference between the market price of the**

stock and the exercise price of the options at the grant date. Hurdle would therefore not recognize any compensation expense related to your options because at the grant date the market price and exercise price were the same.

Under previous accounting standards, companies could use **either** the intrinsic or fair value methods for recognizing stock-based compensation. Fair value represents the market value of the option at the date of grant. Most companies adopted the intrinsic value approach because it generally results in lower compensation expense. However, during 2002 a number of companies began voluntarily to switch to the fair value method for recording compensation expense related to stock options. By March 2004 over 500 public companies were using the fair value method. A major reason for this change was that these companies wanted to show the investing community that they believe in fair and transparent financial reporting, particularly in the aftermath of the many financial reporting scandals. Because some companies included stock-based compensation expense in income based on fair value and others only disclosed the pro-forma effects, comparability concerns were raised, and the FASB developed a new standard for stock-based compensation.

The FASB now **requires recognition of compensation cost for the fair value of stock-based compensation paid to employees for their services.**[1] The FASB position is that the accounting for the cost of employee services should be based on the value of compensation paid, which is presumed to be a measure of the value of the services received. Accordingly, the compensation cost arising from employee stock options should be measured based on the fair value of the stock options granted.[2] To determine this value, acceptable option pricing models are used to value options at the date of grant. This approach is referred to as the **fair value method** because the option value is estimated based on the many factors that determine its underlying value.[3]

Accounting for Stock Compensation

OBJECTIVE U1
Describe the accounting for stock compensation plans under generally accepted accounting principles.

Stock option plans involve two main accounting issues:

1. How should compensation expense be determined?
2. Over what periods should compensation expense be allocated?

Determining Expense

Under the fair value method, total compensation expense is computed based on the fair value of the options expected to vest[4] on the date the options are granted to the employee(s) (i.e., the **grant date**). Fair value for public companies is to be estimated using an option pricing model, with some adjustments for the unique factors of employee stock options. No adjustments are made after the grant date, in response to subsequent changes in the stock price—either up or down.

[1]"Accounting for Stock-Based Compensation," *Statement of Financial Accounting Standards No. 123* (Norwalk, Conn.: FASB, 1995). "Share-Based Payment: An Amendment of FASB Statements No. 123 and 95," *Statement of Financial Accounting Standard* (Stamford, Conn.: FASB, 2004).

Note that in 2004 the International Accounting Standards Board (IASB) also issued a statement, titled "Share-Based Payment," which requires the expensing of stock-based compensation based on fair values. Thus the FASB's new standard contributes to international accounting convergence.

[2]Stock options issued to non-employees in exchange for other goods or services must be recognized according to the fair value method in *SFAS 123*.

[3]These factors include the volatility of the underlying stock, the expected life of the options, the risk-free rate during the option life, and expected dividends during the option life.

[4]"To vest" means "to earn the rights to." An employee's award becomes vested at the date that the employee's right to receive or retain shares of stock or cash under the award is no longer contingent on remaining in the service of the employer.

A LITTLE HONESTY GOES A LONG WAY

WHAT DO THE NUMBERS MEAN?

You might think investors would punish companies that have decided to expense stock options. After all, most of corporate America has been battling for years to avoid such a fate, worried that accounting for those perks would destroy earnings. And indeed, Merrill Lynch estimates that if all S&P 500 companies were to expense options [in 2002], reported profits would fall 10 percent.

And yet, as a small but growing band of big-name companies makes the switch, investors have for the most part showered them with love. With a few exceptions, the stock prices of the expensers, from **Cinergy** to **Fannie Mae**, have outpaced the market since they announced the change.

The few, the brave

	Estimated 2002 EPS		% change since announcement**
	Without options	With options expensed*	Company stock price
Cinergy	$ 2.80	$ 2.77	22.4%
Washington Post	20.48	20.10	16.4
Computer Associates	−0.46	−0.62	11.1
Fannie Mae	6.15	6.02	6.7
Bank One	2.77	2.61	2.6
General Motors	5.84	5.45	2.6
Procter & Gamble	3.57	3.35	−2.3
Coca-Cola	1.79	1.70	−6.2
General Electric	1.65	1.61	−6.2
Amazon	0.04	−0.99	−11.4

*Assumes options expenses for 2002 are the same as 2001 and that all outstanding grants are counted.

**As of 8/6/02.

Data sources: Merrill Lynch; company reports.

Source: David Stires, "A Little Honesty Goes a Long Way," *Fortune* (September 2, 2002), p. 186. Reprinted by permission.

Allocating Compensation Expense

In general, compensation expense is recognized in the periods in which the employee performs the service—the **service period**. Unless otherwise specified, the service period is the vesting period—the time between the grant date and the vesting date. Thus, total compensation cost is determined at the grant date and allocated to the periods benefited by the employees' services.

Illustration

To illustrate the accounting for a stock option plan, assume that on November 1, 2002, the stockholders of Chen Company approve a plan that grants the company's five executives options to purchase 2,000 shares each of the company's $1 par value common stock. The options are granted on January 1, 2003, and may be exercised at any time within the next 10 years. The option price per share is $60, and the market price of the stock at the date of grant is $70 per share.

Under the fair value method, total compensation expense is computed by applying an acceptable fair value option pricing model (such as the Black-Scholes option pricing model). To keep this illustration simple, we will assume that the fair value option pricing model determines total compensation expense to be $220,000.

Basic Entries. The value of the options is recognized as an expense in the periods in which the employee performs services. In the case of Chen Company, assume that the expected period of benefit is 2 years, starting with the grant date. The journal entries to record the transactions related to this option contract are shown below.

At date of grant (January 1, 2003)

No entry

To record compensation expense for 2003 (December 31, 2003)

Compensation Expense	110,000	
Paid-in Capital—Stock Options ($220,000 ÷ 2)		110,000

To record compensation expense for 2004 (December 31, 2004)

Compensation Expense	110,000	
Paid-in Capital—Stock Options		110,000

As indicated, compensation expense is allocated evenly over the 2-year service period.

Exercise. If 20 percent, or 2,000, of the 10,000 options were exercised on June 1, 2006 (3 years and 5 months after date of grant), the following journal entry would be recorded.

June 1, 2006

Cash (2,000 × $60)	120,000	
Paid-in Capital—Stock Options (20% × $220,000)	44,000	
Common Stock (2,000 × $1)		2,000
Paid-in Capital in Excess of Par		162,000

Expiration. If the remaining stock options are not exercised before their expiration date, the balance in the Paid-in Capital—Stock Options account should be transferred to a more properly titled paid-in capital account, such as Paid-in Capital from Expired Stock Options. The entry to record this transaction at the date of expiration would be as follows.

January 1, 2013 (expiration date)

Paid-in Capital—Stock Options	176,000	
Paid-in Capital from Expired Stock Options (80% × $220,000)		176,000

Adjustment. The fact that a stock option is not exercised does not nullify the propriety of recording the costs of services received from executives and attributable to the stock option plan. Under GAAP, compensation expense is, therefore, not adjusted upon expiration of the options.

However, if a stock option is forfeited because **an employee fails to satisfy a service requirement** (e.g., leaves employment), the estimate of compensation expense recorded in the current period should be adjusted (as a change in estimate). This change in estimate would be recorded by debiting Paid-in Capital—Stock Options and crediting Compensation Expense, thereby decreasing compensation expense in the period of forfeiture.

Types of Plans

Many different types of plans are used to compensate key employees. In all these plans the amount of the reward depends upon future events. Consequently, continued employment is a necessary element in almost all types of plans. The popularity of a given plan usually depends on the firm's prospects in the stock market and on tax considerations. For example, if it appears that appreciation will occur in a company's stock, a plan that offers the option to purchase stock is attractive. Conversely, if it appears that price appreciation is unlikely, then compensation might be tied to some performance measure such as an increase in book value or earnings per share.

Three common compensation plans that illustrate different objectives are:

1. Stock option plans (incentive or nonqualified).
2. Stock appreciation rights plans.
3. Performance-type plans.

Most plans follow the general guidelines for reporting established in the previous sections.

Noncompensatory Plans

In some companies, employee share purchase plans permit all employees to purchase stock at a discounted price for a short period of time. These plans are usually classified as noncompensatory. Noncompensatory means that the primary purpose of the plan is not to compensate the employees but, rather, to enable the employer to secure equity capital or to induce widespread ownership of an enterprise's common stock among employees. Thus, compensation expense is not reported for these plans. **Noncompensatory plans** have three characteristics:

1. Substantially all full-time employees may participate on an equitable basis.
2. The discount from market price is small. That is, it does not exceed the greater of a per share discount reasonably offered to stockholders or the per share amount of costs avoided by not having to raise cash in a public offering.
3. The plan offers no substantive option feature.

For example, Masthead Company had a stock purchase plan under which employees who meet minimal employment qualifications are entitled to purchase Masthead stock at a 5 percent reduction from market price for a short period of time. The reduction from market price is not considered compensatory because the per share amount of the costs avoided by not having to raise the cash in a public offering is equal to 5 percent. **Plans that do not possess all of the above mentioned three characteristics are classified as compensatory.**

Disclosure of Compensation Plans

Full disclosure should be made about the status of these plans at the end of the periods presented, including the number of shares under option, options exercised and forfeited, the weighted average option prices for these categories, the weighted average fair value of options granted during the year, and the average remaining contractual life of the options outstanding.[5] In addition to information about the status of the stock option plans, companies must also disclose the method and significant assumptions used to estimate the fair values of the stock options.

Illustration U16-2 (page UP-14) shows the types of information to be disclosed related to stock-based compensation.

Debate over Stock Option Accounting

OBJECTIVE U2
Explain the controversy involving stock compensation plans.

The FASB faced considerable opposition when it proposed the fair value method for accounting for stock options. This is not surprising, given that use of the fair value approach results in greater compensation costs relative to the intrinsic value model. As indicated in the story on page UP-11, a study of the companies in the Standard & Poor's 500 stock index documented that, on average, earnings in 2002 could be overstated by 10 percent through the use of the intrinsic value method. However, a number of companies, such as **Coca-Cola**, **General Electric**, **Wachovia**, **Bank One**, and **The Washington Post**, decided to use the fair value method. As the CFO of Coke stated, "There is no doubt that stock options are compensation. If they weren't, none of us would want them."

Even given the exemplary behavior of certain companies, many in corporate America resist the fair value method. Many small high-technology companies are particularly vocal in their opposition, arguing that only through offering stock options can they attract top professional management. They contend that if they are forced to recognize large amounts of compensation expense under these plans, they will be at a competitive disadvantage with larger companies that can withstand higher compensation

[5]These data should be reported separately for each different type of plan offered to employees.

ILLUSTRATION U16-2
Stock Option Plan Disclosure

The Company has a share-based compensation plan. The compensation cost that has been charged against income for the plan was $29.4 million, and $28.7 million for 2004 and 2003, respectively.

The Company's 2004 Employee Share Option Plan (the Plan), which is shareholder-approved, permits the grant of share options and shares to its employees for up to 8 million shares of common stock. The Company believes that such awards better align the interests of its employees with those of its shareholders. Option awards are generally granted with an exercise price equal to the market price of the Company's stock at the date of grant; those option awards generally vest based on 5 years of continuous service and have 10-year contractual terms. Share awards generally vest over five years. Certain option and share awards provide for accelerated vesting if there is a change in control (as defined by the Plan).

The fair value of each option award is estimated on the date of grant using an option valuation model based on the assumptions noted in the following table.

	2004	2003
Expected volatility	25%–40%	24%–38%
Weighted-average volatility	33%	30%
Expected dividends	1.5%	1.5%
Expected term (in years)	5.3–7.8	5.5–8.0
Risk-free rate	6.3%–11.2%	6.0%–10.0%

A summary of option activity under the Plan as of December 31, 2004, and changes during the year then ended are presented below.

Options	Shares (000)	Weighted-Average Exercise Price	Weighted-Average Remaining Contractual Term	Aggregate Intrinsic Value ($000)
Outstanding at January 1, 2004	4,660	42		
Granted	950	60		
Exercised	(800)	36		
Forfeited or expired	(80)	59		
Outstanding at December 31, 2004	4,730	47	6.5	85,140
Exercisable at December 31, 2004	3,159	41	4.0	75,816

The weighted-average grant-date fair value of options granted during the years 2004 and 2003 was $19.57 and $17.46, respectively. The total intrinsic value of options exercised during the years ended December 31, 2004 and 2003, was $25.2 million, and $20.9 million, respectively.

As of December 31, 2004, there was $25.9 million of total unrecognized compensation cost related to nonvested share-based compensation arrangements granted under the Plan. That cost is expected to be recognized over a weighted-average period of 4.9 years. The total fair value of shares vested during the years ended December 31, 2004 and 2003, was $22.8 million and $21 million, respectively.

charges. As one high-tech executive stated, "If your goal is to attack fat-cat executive compensation in multi-billion dollar firms, then please do so! But not at the expense of the people who are 'running lean and mean,' trying to build businesses and creating jobs in the process."

The stock option controversy involves economic consequence issues. The FASB believes the neutrality concept should be followed. Others disagree, noting that factors other than accounting theory should be considered.

The stock option saga is a classic example of the difficulty the FASB faces in issuing an accounting standard. Many powerful interests aligned against the Board; even some who initially appeared to support the Board's actions later reversed themselves. These efforts are unfortunate because they undermine the authority of the FASB at a time when it is essential that we restore faith in our financial reporting system. It must be emphasized that transparent financial reporting—including recognizing stock-based compensation expense—should not be criticized because companies will report lower income. We may not like what the financial statements say, but we are always better off when the statements are representationally faithful to the underlying economic substance of transactions.

By leaving stock-based compensation expense out of income, reported income is biased. It may be in the interests of managers of some companies to report biased income numbers, but doing so does not serve financial reporting or our capital markets well. Biased reporting not only raises concerns about the credibility of companies' reports, but also of financial reporting in general. Consider companies that do not use stock options. Why should they be made to look worse because they use a different form of compensation? As we have learned from **Enron**, **WorldCom**, **Xerox**, **MicroStrategy**, **Lucent**, and other recent failures, credibility of financial reporting is fundamental to the efficient operation of our capital markets. Even good companies get tainted by biased reporting of a few "bad apples."[6] If we continue to write standards so that some social, economic, or public policy goal is achieved, financial reporting will lose its credibility.

SECTION 3 CONSOLIDATION OF VARIABLE INTEREST ENTITIES

Late in 2003, the FASB issued an interpretation of *ARB No. 51*. That document, *FASB Interpretation No. 46 (Revised)*, "Consolidation of Variable Interest Entities," addresses the concern that some companies were not reporting the risks and rewards of certain investments and other financial arrangements in their consolidated financial statements. While preparation of consolidated financial statements is generally beyond the scope of most intermediate accounting courses, many of the investments and arrangements addressed in the interpretation are topics in intermediate accounting.

The following discussion can be used **as a supplement** to the section "Holdings of More than 50%" in Chapter 17, on page 851, of *Intermediate Accounting*, 11th Edition.

CONSOLIDATED FINANCIAL STATEMENTS: ADDITIONAL REPORTING ISSUES

As one analyst noted, **Enron** showed the world the power of the idea that "if investors can't see it, they can't ask you about it—the 'it' being assets and liabilities." What exactly did Enron do? For starters, it created a number of entities whose purpose was to hide debt, avoid taxes, and enrich certain management personnel to the detriment of the company and its stockholders. In effect, these entities, often dubbed **special purpose entities (SPEs)**, appeared to be separate entities for which Enron had a limited economic interest. Unfortunately, for many of these arrangements, Enron actually had a substantial economic interest because the risks and rewards of ownership were not shifted to the entities but remained with Enron. In short, Enron was obligated to repay investors in these SPEs when they were unsuccessful. Once Enron's problems were discovered, it soon became apparent that many other companies had similar problems.

What About GAAP?

A reasonable question to ask with regard to SPEs is, "Why didn't GAAP prevent companies from hiding SPE debt and other risks, by forcing companies to include these obligations in their consolidated financial statements?" To understand why, we have to look at the basic rules of consolidation. The GAAP rules indicate that consolidated financial statements are "usually necessary for a fair presentation when one of the companies in the group directly or indirectly has a controlling financial interest in other

[6]Congress reacted to these events with passage of the **Sarbanes-Oxley Act of 2002**. The Act affirmed the role of the FASB as an independent private sector accounting standard-setter. However, recent actions by Congress in the stock option controversy have undermined the Act's support for independent accounting standard-setting by the FASB.

companies." It further notes that "the usual condition for a controlling financial interest is ownership of a majority voting interest." In other words, if a company like **Intel** owns more than 50 percent of the voting stock of another company, Intel consolidates that company. GAAP also indicates that controlling financial interest may be achieved through arrangements that do not involve voting interests. However, applying these guidelines in practice is difficult.

Whenever a clear line, like "greater than 50 percent" is used, the criterion is sometimes exploited. For example, some companies set up joint ventures in which each party owns exactly 50 percent. In that case, neither party consolidates. Or the company owns less than 50 percent of the voting stock, but maintains effective control through board of director relationships or supply relationships, or through some other type of financial arrangement.

So the FASB realized that changes had to be made to GAAP for consolidations, and it issued *SFAS Interpretation No. 46 (Revised),* "Consolidation of Variable Interest Entities." This interpretation (*FIN No. 46R*) defines when a company should use factors other than voting interest to determine controlling financial interest. In this interpretation, the FASB created a new risk-and-reward model to be used in situations where voting interests were unclear. The risk-and-reward model answers the basic question of who stands to gain or lose the most from ownership in an SPE when ownership is uncertain.

In other words, we now have two models for consolidation:

1. **Voting-interest model**—If a company owns more than 50 percent of another company, then consolidate in most cases.
2. **Risk-and-reward model**—If a company is involved substantially in the economics of another company, then consolidate.

Operationally, the voting-interest model is easily applied: It sets a "bright line" ownership standard of more than 50 percent of the voting stock. However, if control can not be determined based on voting interest, the risk-and-reward model may be used.

A Closer Look at the New GAAP

To answer the question of who gains or loses when voting rights do not determine consolidation, the FASB developed a risk-and-reward model. In this model, the FASB introduced the notion of a variable interest entity. A **variable interest entity (VIE)** is an entity that has **one** of the following characteristics:

1. **Insufficient equity investment at risk**. Stockholders are assumed to have sufficient capital investment to support the entity's operations. If thinly capitalized, the entity is considered a VIE and is subject to the risk-and-reward model.
2. **Stockholders lack decision-making rights**. In some cases, stockholders do not have the influence to control the company's destiny.
3. **Stockholders do not absorb the losses or receive the benefits of a normal stockholder**. In some entities, stockholders are shielded from losses related to their primary risks, or their returns are capped or must be shared by other parties.

Once it is determined that an entity is a variable interest entity, the voting-interest model is no longer appropriate. The question that must then be asked is, "What party is exposed to the majority of the risks and rewards associated with the VIE?" This party is called the **primary beneficiary** and must consolidate the VIE. The decision model for the VIE consolidation model is shown in Illustration U17-1.

Note that the primary beneficiary may have the risks and rewards of ownership through use of a variety of instruments and financial arrangements, such as equity investments, loans to the VIE, leases, derivatives, and guarantees. Potential VIEs include the following: corporations, partnerships, limited liability companies, and majority-owned subsidiaries.

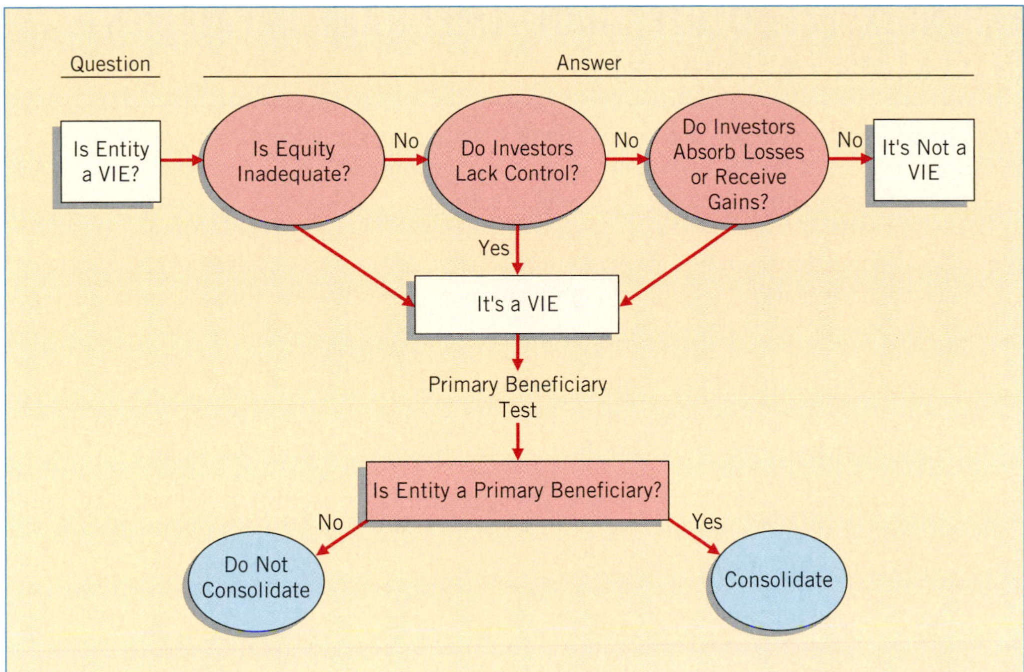

ILLUSTRATION U17-1
VIE Consolidation Model

WHAT IS HAPPENING IN PRACTICE?

As shown in Illustration U17-2, one study of 509 companies with total market values over $500 million found that 17 percent of the companies reviewed have a material impact from *FIN No. 46R*.

Of the material VIEs disclosed, the most common types (42%) were related to joint-venture equity investments, followed by off-balance-sheet lease arrangements (22%). In some cases, companies are restructuring transactions to avoid consolidation. For example, **Pep Boys**, **Choice Point, Inc.**, and **Anadarko** all appear to have restructured their lease transactions to avoid consolidation. On the other hand, companies like **eBay**, **Kimberly-Clark**, and **Williams-Sonoma Inc.** intend to or have consolidated their VIEs.

In summary, *FIN No. 46R* introduces a new model for determining if certain investments or other financial arrangements should be included in consolidated financial statements. As a result, financial statements should be more complete in reporting the risks and rewards of these transactions.

ILLUSTRATION U17-2
Impact of *FIN No. 46 R*

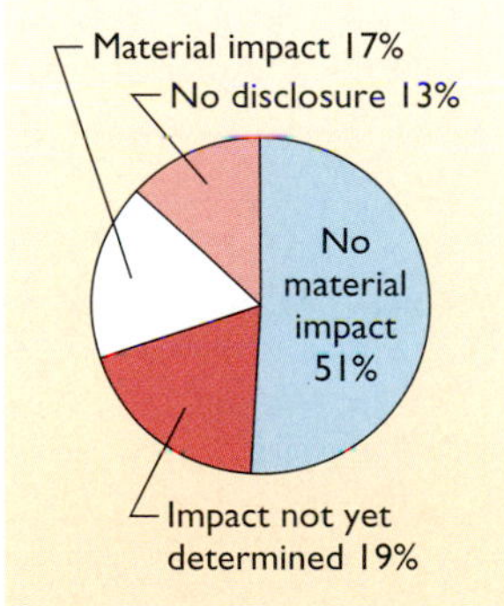

SOURCE: Company Reports, *Glass, Lewis, & Co. Research Report* (November 6, 2003).

SECTION 4 OTHER-THAN-TEMPORARY IMPAIRMENTS

Since publication of *Intermediate Accounting*, 11th Edition, the Emerging Issues Task Force (EITF) reached a consensus on "Other-Than-Temporary Impairment" of debt and equity investments (*EITF Issue No. 03-1*, "The Meaning of Other-Than-Temporary Impairment and Its Application to Certain Investments"). This new standard is described below.

This discussion should be considered **an appendix to Chapter 17**. It provides additional analysis as to the recognition of impairments.

APPENDIX 17B: OTHER-THAN-TEMPORARY IMPAIRMENTS OF CERTAIN INVESTMENTS

As discussed in the chapter, determination of whether an equity or debt investment is impaired is predicated on the notion of "other than temporary." However, conflicting guidance in the accounting literature about the meaning of "other than temporary" has resulted in inconsistent application in practice. Consequently, the EITF addressed this issue to develop a common approach for evaluating other-than-temporary impairments. In brief, the EITF provides guidance based on application of the following three-step model:

- **Step 1:** Determine whether an investment is impaired.
- **Step 2:** Evaluate whether an impairment is other than temporary.
- **Step 3:** If the impairment is other than temporary, recognize an impairment loss equal to the difference between the investment's cost and its fair value.

Also addressed in the consensus is the accounting subsequent to the recognition of the impairment and required disclosures about unrealized losses not recognized as other-than-temporary impairments.

Three-Step Model

Recall that **debt investments** are classified into three categories: (1) held-to-maturity, (2) trading securities, and (3) available-for-sale securities. **Investments in equity securities** are classified into four categories: (1) available-for-sale, (2) trading, (3) equity method, and (4) full consolidation. The general guidelines in accounting for investments in securities are that available-for-sale or trading securities are adjusted to fair value, and the related income or loss amount is reported as part of income or as part of comprehensive income.

Every investment should be evaluated at each reporting date to determine if it has suffered an **impairment**—a loss in value that is other-than-temporary. If the decline is judged to be other-than-temporary, the cost basis of the individual security is written down to a new cost basis. The amount of the write-down is accounted for as a realized loss and, therefore, is included in net income.

In practice, the notion of "other-than-temporary" has been interpreted in different ways, and inconsistencies in accounting for impairments have developed. The accounting now is based on the application of a three-step model.

Step 1: Determine Whether an Investment Is Impaired

Consistent with other authoritative literature, an investment is **impaired if the fair value of the investment is less than its cost.** This assessment should be performed each reporting period. Because the fair value of most cost method investments is not readily determinable, impairment evaluation may be triggered by **impairment indicators**. Examples of such indicators are a significant deterioration in the earnings performance, credit rating, asset quality, business prospects of the investee, or a significant adverse change in the regulatory, economic, or technological environment of the investee. If an impairment indicator is present, the investor should estimate the fair value of the investment.

Step 2: Evaluate Whether an Impairment Is Other-Than-Temporary

In general, an **impairment should be recorded** unless:

a. The investor has the ability and intent to hold an investment for a reasonable period of time sufficient for a forecasted recovery of fair value up to (or beyond) the cost of the investment,

and

b. Evidence indicating that the cost of the investment is recoverable within a reasonable period of time outweighs evidence to the contrary.

The "ability and intent" to hold an investment is assessed based on a couple of guidelines. The first is whether the investor's cash or working capital requirements and contractual or regulatory obligations indicate that the investment may need to be sold before the forecasted recovery of fair value occurs. The second guideline is whether the issuer has the ability to settle the security during the forecasted recovery period.

To evaluate the amount of the impairment, the investor should assess (a) the extent to which fair value is below cost, and (b) the nature of the event (or events) that gave rise to the impairment. Thus, an other-than-temporary impairment may occur if, based on all available evidence, the cost of the investment is not recoverable within a reasonable period of time.

Step 3: Recognize an Impairment Loss

If it is determined in Step 2 that the impairment is other-than-temporary, then an impairment loss should be recognized in earnings equal to the difference between the investment's cost and its fair value at the balance sheet date for which the assessment is made. The **fair value of the investment would then become the new cost basis** of the investment. That amount **should not be adjusted for subsequent recoveries in fair value**.

Here is an example that illustrates the above points.

Example

Amclone Company is developing a product that is highly anticipated by the market. On January 1, 2004, Costello Inc. purchased 200,000 shares of Amclone stock at a cost of $20 per share. On May 1, 2004, a regulatory body informed Amclone that the product did not meet certain regulatory requirements and therefore would not receive the regulatory approval required to sell the product.

On May 2, 2004, Amclone issued a press release announcing the regulator's decision. The company also reiterated its belief that it will ultimately obtain regulatory approval. However, no evidence exists to support its assertion at this time. Amclone's share price immediately declined from $34 per share to $10 per share, and it traded in the $10 to $12 range through June 30, 2004. At June 30, 2004, the price was $11. No information is available to support a recovery of fair value up to (or beyond) the cost of the investment. Costello has the ability and intent to hold the investment for an indefinite period.

Solution

If we use the three-step model for assessing impairments, we have the following:

Step 1: Determine whether Costello's investment in Amclone is impaired. The investment is impaired because the cost of the investment, $4,000,000 (200,000 × $20) is higher than its fair value of $2,200,000 (200,000 × $11) on June 30, 2004.

Step 2: Determine whether Costello's investment is other-than-temporary. Even though Costello has the ability and intent to hold the investment for an indefinite period, Costello should deem the investment as other-than-temporarily impaired, given:

1. The severity of the decline.
2. The cause of the decline (that is, failure to obtain regulatory approval of a product).
3. The absence of evidence to support a recovery of fair value up to (or beyond) the cost of the investment within a reasonable period of time.

Consequently, at June 30, 2004, Costello would record an impairment of $1,800,000 ($4,000,000 − $2,200,000) for the Amclone stock held.

Step 3: If the impairment is other-than-temporary, recognize an impairment loss equal to the difference between the investment's cost and its fair value. As noted above, Costello would report a loss on the impairment of $1,800,000. Once the investment is recognized as impaired, the investment now has a new cost basis. The entry to record this loss will depend on classification of the investment (e.g., as trading or available for sale). **This cost basis cannot be adjusted upward** even if the fair value of Amclone stock increases in the next reporting period.

DISCLOSURES RELATED TO INVESTMENTS

Also addressed by the EITF is the topic of additional disclosures related to investments. These additional disclosures were mandated due to concerns expressed regarding the lack of transparency involving unrealized losses on investment accounts. There are three major requirements related to the disclosures of unrealized losses, discussed below.

Tabular Information

Investments with an unrealized loss should be reported in a table, which provides fair value information and the amount of the unrealized loss. In addition, investments should be segregated between investments that have had continuous losses for fewer than 12 months, and those for 12 months or more.

By providing this disclosure, users of the financial statements can better understand how many securities have unrealized losses and how long the fair value of these securities have been below cost. The longer the time the company has this loss, the greater the likelihood the investment is impaired. That is, the greater the likelihood that the loss is other-than-temporary.

Narrative

In addition to the tabular summary, the company is required to explain why the unrealized losses are considered temporary. The disclosure might include a discussion of the nature of the investment, the causes for the unrealized losses, the severity and duration of the unrealized losses, the number of investments in this position, and other substantial evidence used by management in making its impairment judgment.

Cost-Method Investments

Also required is a disclosure of the aggregate carrying amount of cost-method investments and an explanation as to why any cost-based investment was not evaluated for impairment. In other words, the disclosure indicates whether impairment was not considered because estimating fair values was not practical, or because there were no significant adverse effects on the investment.

SECTION 5 PENSION DISCLOSURES

In 2003, the FASB issued a new standard addressing pension disclosures, *Statement of Financial Accounting Standard No. 132* (Stamford, Conn.: FASB, revised 2003) entitled "Employers' Disclosures about Pensions and other Postretirement Benefits." This new standard provides for enhanced financial disclosures related to defined benefit plans.

The following material should be used **in place of** the discussion in Chapter 20, pages 1042–1045, of *Intermediate Accounting*, 11th Edition.

OBJECTIVE U1
Describe the reporting requirements for pension plans in financial statements.

REPORTING PENSION PLANS IN FINANCIAL STATEMENTS

One might suspect that a phenomenon as significant and complex as pensions would involve extensive reporting and disclosure requirements. We will cover these requirements in two categories: (1) those within the financial statements, and (2) those within the notes to the financial statements.

Within the Financial Statements

If the amount funded (credit to Cash) by the employer to the pension trust is **less than the annual expense** (debit to Pension Expense), a credit balance accrual of the difference arises in the long-term liabilities section. It might be described as Accrued Pension Cost, Liability for Pension Expense Not Funded, or Pension Liability. A liability is classified as current when it requires the disbursement of cash within the next year.

If the amount funded to the pension trust during the period is **greater than the amount charged to expense**, an asset equal to the difference arises. This asset is reported as Prepaid Pension Cost, Deferred Pension Expense, or Prepaid Pension Expense in the current assets section if it is current in nature, and in the other assets section if it is long-term in nature.

If the **accumulated benefit obligation exceeds the fair value of pension plan assets**, an additional liability is recorded. The debit is either to an Intangible Asset—Deferred Pension Cost or to a contra account to stockholders' equity entitled Excess of Additional Pension Liability Over Unrecognized Prior Service Cost. If the debit is less than unrecognized prior service cost, it is reported as an intangible asset. If the debit is greater than unrecognized prior service cost, the excess debit is reported as part of other comprehensive income and the accumulated balance as a component of accumulated other comprehensive income.

Within the Notes to the Financial Statements

Pension plans are frequently important to an understanding of financial position, results of operations, and cash flows of a company. Therefore, the following information, if not disclosed in the body of the financial statements, should be disclosed in the notes.[1]

1. A schedule showing all the major components of pension expense should be reported.
   Rationale: Information provided about the components of pension expense helps users better understand how pension expense is determined and is useful in forecasting a company's net income.
2. A **reconciliation** showing how the projected benefit obligation and the fair value of the plan assets changed from the beginning to the end of the period is required.
   Rationale: Disclosing the projected benefit obligation, the fair value of the plan assets, and changes in them helps users understand the economics underlying the obligations and resources of these plans. The Board believes that explaining the changes in the projected benefit obligation and fair value of plan assets in the form of a reconciliation provides a more complete disclosure and makes the financial statements more understandable.
3. The **funded status** of the plan (difference between the projected benefit obligation and fair value of the plan assets) and the amounts recognized and not recognized in the financial statements must be disclosed.
   Rationale: Providing a reconciliation of the plan's funded status to the amount reported in the balance sheet highlights the difference between the funded status and the balance sheet presentation.[2]

---

[1]"Employers' Disclosures about Pensions and Other Postretirement Benefits," *Financial Accounting Standard No. 132* (Stamford, Conn.: FASB, 1998; revised 2003). This statement and its revision modify the disclosure requirements of *SFAS No. 87.* The revised statement was issued because concerns were raised recently about the lack of transparency in pension information. This new standard amends the existing disclosure requirements related to pensions by (1) continuing the existing disclosure requirements, while (2) requiring companies to provide more details about their plan assets, benefit obligations, cash flows, benefit costs, and other relevant information.

[2]The vested benefit obligation does not need to be disclosed, since it is not used in the accounting for the fund. The accumulated benefit obligation (ABO) under *FAS 87* for all plans combined should be disclosed. Information on the ABO is useful because it is relevant to assessing the minimum liability (whether the company has recognized the minimum liability or not). In addition, it provides another measure for assessing the overall funded status of the plan.

4. A disclosure of the rates used in measuring the benefit amounts (discount rate, expected return on plan assets, rate of compensation increases) should be disclosed. *Rationale:* Disclosure of these rates permits the reader to determine the reasonableness of the assumptions applied in measuring the pension liability and pension expense.
5. A table is required indicating the allocation of pension plan assets by category (equity securities, debt securities, real estate, and other assets), and showing the percentage of the fair value to total plan assets. In addition, a narrative description of investment policies and strategies, including the target allocation percentages (if used by the company), must be disclosed.
Rationale: Such information is useful to users of the financial statements in evaluating the pension plan's exposure to market risk and possible cash flow demands on the company. In addition, it will help users to better understand and assess the reasonableness of the company's expected rate of return assumption.
6. The company must disclose the **expected benefit payments** to be paid to current plan participants for each of the next five fiscal years and in the aggregate for the five fiscal years thereafter, based on the same assumptions used to measure the company's benefit obligation at the end of the year. Also required is disclosure of a company's best **estimate of expected contributions** to be paid to the plan during the next year. *Rationale:* These disclosures provide information related to the cash outflows of the company. With this information, financial statement users can better understand the potential cash outflows related to the pension plan. As a result, users can better assess the liquidity and solvency of the company, which helps in assessing the company's overall financial flexibility.

In summary, the disclosure requirements are extensive, and purposely so. One factor that has been a challenge for useful pension reporting in the past has been the lack of consistency in terminology. Furthermore, a substantial amount of offsetting is inherent in the measurement of pension expense and the pension liability. These disclosures are designed to address these concerns and take some of the mystery out of pension reporting.

Illustration of Pension Note Disclosure

In the following sections we provide illustrations and explain the key pension disclosure elements.

Components of Pension Expense

The FASB requires disclosure of the individual pension expense components—(1) service cost, (2) interest cost, (3) expected return on assets, (4) other deferrals and amortization—so that more sophisticated readers can understand how pension expense is determined. Providing information on the components should also be useful in predicting future pension expense. Using the information from the Zarle Company illustration—specifically, the expense component information taken from the left-hand column of the work sheet in Illustration U20-1—an example of this part of the disclosure in presented in the following schedule.

ILLUSTRATION U20-1
Summary of Expense Components—2003, 2004, 2005

ZARLE COMPANY

	2003	2004	2005
Components of Net Periodic Pension Expense			
Service cost	$ 9,000	$ 9,500	$13,000
Interest cost	10,000	19,200	$21,270
Expected return on plan assets	(10,000)	(11,100)	(13,410)*
Amortization of prior service cost	–0–	27,200	20,800
Net periodic pension expense	$ 9,000	$44,800	$41,660

*Note that the expected return must be disclosed, not the actual. In 2005, the expected return is $13,410, which is the actual gain ($12,000) adjusted by the unrecognized loss ($1,410).

Reconciliation and Funded Status of Plan

A reconciliation of the changes in the assets and liabilities from the beginning of the year to the end of the year is provided to enable statement readers to better understand the underlying economics of the plan. In essence, this disclosure (reconciliation) contains the information in the pension work sheet for the projected benefit obligation and plan asset columns.

In addition, the FASB also requires a disclosure of the funded status of the plan. That is, the off-balance-sheet assets, liabilities, and unrecognized gains and losses must be reconciled with the on-balance-sheet liability or asset. Many believe this is the key to understanding the accounting for pensions. Why is such a disclosure important? The FASB acknowledged that the delayed recognition of some pension elements may exclude the most current and the most relevant information about the pension plan from the financial statements. This important information, however, is provided within this disclosure.

UNDERLYING CONCEPTS

This represents another compromise between relevance and reliability. The disclosure of the unrecognized items attempts to balance these objectives.

Using the information for Zarle Company, the following schedule provides an example of the reconciliation.

ILLUSTRATION U20-2
Pension Disclosure for Zarle Company—2003, 2004, 2005

ZARLE COMPANY
PENSION DISCLOSURE

	2003	2004	2005
Change in benefit obligation			
Benefit obligation at beginning of year	$100,000	$112,000	$212,700
Service cost	9,000	9,500	13,000
Interest cost	10,000	19,200	21,270
Amendments (Prior service cost)	–0–	80,000	–0–
Actuarial loss	–0–	–0–	28,530
Benefits paid	(7,000)	(8,000)	(10,500)
Benefit obligation at end of year	112,000	212,700	265,000
Change in plan assets			
Fair value of plan assets at beginning of year	100,000	111,000	134,100
Actual return on plan assets	10,000	11,100	12,000
Contributions	8,000	20,000	24,000
Benefits paid	(7,000)	(8,000)	(10,500)
Fair value of plan assets at end of year	111,000	134,100	159,600
Funded status	(1,000)	(78,600)	(105,400)
Unrecognized net actuarial loss	–0–	–0–	29,940
Unrecognized prior service cost	–0–	52,800	32,000
Prepaid (accrued) benefit cost	**(1,000)**	**(25,800)**	**(43,460)**
Minimum liability adjustment included in:			
Intangible assets	–0–	(4,100)	(32,000)
Stockholders' equity	–0–	–0–	(5,540)
Accrued pension cost liability in the balance sheet	$ (1,000)	$ (29,900)	$ (81,000)

UNDERLYING CONCEPTS

Does it make a difference to users of financial statements whether pension information is recognized in the financial statements or disclosed only in the notes? The FASB was not sure, so in accord with the full disclosure principle, it decided to provide extensive pension plan disclosures.

The 2003 column reveals that the projected benefit obligation is underfunded by $1,000. The 2004 column reveals that the underfunded liability of $78,600 is reported in the balance sheet at $29,900, due to the unrecognized prior service cost of $52,800 and the $4,100 additional liability. Finally, the 2005 column indicates that underfunded liability of $105,400 is recognized in the balance sheet at only $81,000 because of $32,000 in unrecognized prior service costs, $29,940 of unrecognized net loss, and $37,540 additional liability (with $5,540 of the minimum liability recorded in stockholders' equity).

Illustration U20-3 provides a representative postretirement benefit disclosure for **Gillette Company**.[3] This disclosure shows how companies are providing information on the rates used in measuring the benefit amounts.

[3]Note that the Gillette disclosure combines the disclosures for pensions and other postretirement benefits in one disclosure. This is one way the new standard streamlined the reporting on benefit plans. The accounting for other postretirement benefits is discussed in Appendix 20A.

ILLUSTRATION U20-3
Gillette Company
Pension Disclosure

Gillette Company

Pensions and Other Retiree Benefits. The Company has various retirement programs, including defined benefit, defined contribution, and other plans, that cover most employees worldwide. Other retiree benefits are health care and life insurance benefits provided to eligible retired employees, principally in the United States. The components of defined benefit expense for continuing operations follow.

	Pensions			Other Retiree Benefits		
Years ended December 31, (millions)	2001	2000	1999	2001	2000	1999
Components of net benefit expense:						
Service cost-benefits earned	$ 61	$ 64	$ 67	$ 6	$ 6	$ 6
Interest cost on benefit obligation	130	122	112	18	19	16
Estimated return on assets	(166)	(171)	(159)	(4)	(4)	(4)
Net amortization	9	5	13	(5)	(7)	(7)
Plan curtailments and other	—	(3)	(7)	—	—	—
	34	17	26	15	14	11
Other	12	9	9	–	—	—
Net defined benefit expense	$ 46	$ 26	$ 35	$15	$14	$11

The funded status of the Company's principal defined benefit and other retiree benefit plans and the amounts recognized in the balance sheet follow.

	Pension Benefits		Other Retiree Benefits	
Years ended December 31, (millions)	2001	2000	2001	2000
Change in benefit obligation:				
Balance at beginning of year	$1,961	$1,956	$ 259	$ 261
Benefit payments	(113)	(111)	(21)	(17)
Service and interest costs	191	185	24	24
Amendments	12	26	(14)	—
Actuarial (gains) losses	(57)	78	135	(7)
Plan curtailments	(3)	(33)	—	—
Divestitures	—	(71)	—	—
Currency translation adjustment	(41)	(69)	(3)	(2)
Balance at end of year	$1,950	$1,961	$ 380	$ 259
Change in fair value of plan assets:				
Balance at beginning of year	$1,878	$2,052	$ 40	$ 41
Actual return on plan assets	(168)	42	(2)	(1)
Employer contribution	35	31	—	—
Benefit payments	(92)	(91)	—	—
Divestitures	—	(87)	—	—
Currency translation adjustment	(35)	(69)	—	—
Balance at end of year	$1,618	$1,878	$ 38	$ 40
Benefit obligations in excess of plan assets	$ (332)	$ (83)	$(342)	$(219)
Unrecognized prior service cost and transition obligation	41	44	2	18
Unrecognized net loss (gain)	399	128	57	(90)
Minimum liability adjustment included in:				
Intangible assets	(12)	(6)	—	—
Stockholders' equity	(87)	(34)	—	—
Net prepaid (accrued) benefit cost	$ 9	$ 49	$(283)	$(291)

Additional Postretirement Benefit Disclosures

The values for pension plans with accumulated benefit obligations in excess of plan assets follow.

At December 31, (millions)	2001	2000
Projected benefit obligation	$550	$513
Accumulated benefit obligation	490	445
Fair value of plan assets	276	277

The weighted average assumptions used in determining related obligations of pension benefit plans are shown below.

At December 31, (percent)	2001	2000	1999
Discount rate	6.8	7.0	6.8
Long-term rate of return on assets	8.6	9.1	9.1
Rate of compensation increases	4.2	4.7	4.7

The weighted average assumptions used in determining related obligations of other retiree benefit plans are shown below.

At December 31, (percent)	2001	2000	1999
Discount rate	7.2	7.2	7.5
Long-term rate of return on assets	9.0	10.0	10.0

The assumed health care cost trend rate for 2002 is 12%, decreasing to 5% by 2007. A one percentage point increase in the trend rate would have increased the accumulated postretirement benefit obligation by 14%, and interest and service cost by 21%. A one percentage point decrease in the trend rate would have decreased the accumulated postretirement benefit obligation by 12%, and interest and service cost by 17%. . . . In addition to the defined benefit and other retiree benefit plans, the Company also sponsors defined contribution plans, primarily covering U.S. employees. The Company's expense for defined contribution plans in 2001, 2000 and 1999 totaled $34 million, $35 million and $36 million, respectively.

Illustration U20-4 provides an example of the disclosures on pension plan asset allocations and expected cash flows for the pension plan, as reported by **Procter & Gamble**. These disclosures, mandated by the revision of *SFAS No. 132*, should help users compare the riskiness of companies' pension plan investments and the future cash requirements for the pension plan.

ILLUSTRATION U20-4
Procter & Gamble Co. Pension Disclosure of Asset Allocation and Expected Cash Flows

PROCTER & GAMBLE COMPANY

Plan Assets. The Company's target asset allocation for the year ending June 30, 2005, and actual asset allocation by asset category as of June 30, 2004, and 2003, are as follows:

	Target Allocation	
	Pension Benefits	Other Retiree Benefits
Asset Category	2005	2005
Equity securities[1]	64%	99%
Debt securities	32%	1%
Real estate	4%	0%
Total	100%	100%

	Plan Asset Allocation at June 30			
	Pension Benefits		Other Retiree Benefits	
Asset Category	**2004**	2003	**2004**	2003
Equity securities[1]	**64%**	62%	**99%**	99%
Debt securities	**32%**	35%	**1%**	1%
Real estate	**4%**	3%	**0%**	0%
Total	**100%**	100%	**100%**	100%

The Company's investment objective for defined benefit plan assets is to meet the plans' benefit obligations, while minimizing the potential for future required Company plan contributions. The investment strategies focus on asset class diversification, liquidity to meet benefit payments, and an appropriate balance of long-term investment return and risk. Target ranges for asset allocations are determined by matching the actuarial projections of the plans' future liabilities and benefit payments with expected long-term rates of return on the assets, taking into account investment return volatility and correlations across asset classes.

Cash Flows ($ millions). Management's best estimate of its cash requirements for the defined benefit plans and other retiree benefit plans for the year ending June 30, 2005 is $237 and $20, respectively.

Total benefit payments expected to be paid to participants, which include payments funded from the Company's assets, as discussed above, as well as payments paid from the plans are as follows:

	Years ended June 30	
	Pension Benefits	Other Retiree Benefits
Expected benefit payments		
2005	$ 191	$ 144
2006	177	152
2007	193	166
2008	207	176
2009	207	185
2010–2014	1,180	1,058

SECTION 6 ACCOUNTING CHANGES

In 2005, the FASB issued a new standard addressing accounting changes and error corrections. This new standard, "Accounting Changes and Error Corrections," *Statement of Financial Accounting Standard* (Stamford, Conn.: FASB, 2005), is part of the FASB's short-term international convergence project and replaces *APB Opinion No. 20 and FASB Statement No. 3.*

The following material should be used **in place of** the discussion in Chapter 22, pages 1150–1161, of *Intermediate Accounting*, 11th Edition. Throughout Chapter 22, references to *APB Opinion No. 20* should be replaced with this new standard.

OBJECTIVE U1
Identify the types of accounting changes.

UNDERLYING CONCEPTS

While the qualitative characteristic of *usefulness* may be enhanced by changes in accounting, the characteristics of *comparability* and *consistency* may be adversely affected.

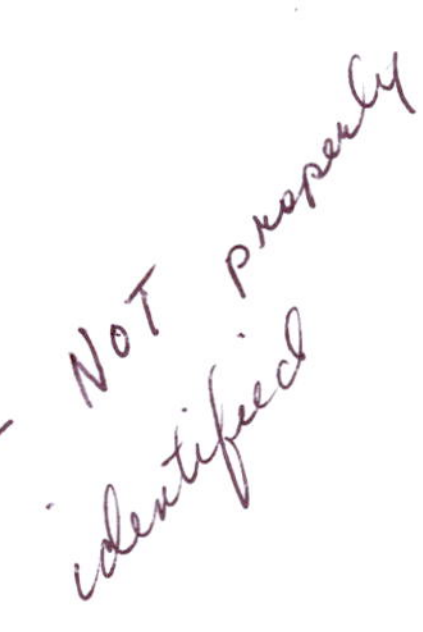

When accounting alternatives exist, comparability of the statements between periods and between companies is diminished and useful historical trend data are obscured. For example, if **Ford** revises its estimates for equipment useful lives, depreciation expense for the current year will not be comparable to depreciation expense reported by Ford in prior years. Similarly, if **Best Buy** changes to FIFO inventory pricing while **Circuit City** uses LIFO, it will be difficult to compare these companies' reported results. Thus a reporting framework is needed to preserve the usefulness of accounting when there is an accounting change. The first step in this area, then, is to establish categories for the different types of changes and corrections that occur in practice.[1] The three types of accounting changes are:

1. *Change in Accounting Principle*. A change from one generally accepted accounting principle to another generally accepted accounting principle. Example: A change in the basis of inventory pricing from average cost to FIFO.
2. *Change in Accounting Estimate*. A change that occurs as the result of new information or as additional experience is acquired. Example: A change in the estimate of the useful lives of depreciable assets.
3. *Change in Reporting Entity*. A change from reporting as one type of entity to another type of entity. Example: changing specific subsidiaries that constitute the group of companies for which consolidated financial statements are prepared.[2]

A fourth category necessitates changes in the accounting, though it is not classified as an accounting change.

4. ***Errors in Financial Statements.*** Errors occur as a result of mathematical mistakes, mistakes in the application of accounting principles, or oversight or misuse of facts that existed at the time financial statements were prepared. Example: the incorrect application of the retail inventory method for determining the final inventory value.

Changes are classified in these four categories because the individual characteristics of each category necessitate different methods of recognizing these changes in the

[1] "Accounting Changes and Error Corrections," *Statement of Financial Accounting Standard* (Stamford, Conn.: FASB, 2005).

[2] *Accounting Trends and Techniques—2003* in its survey of 600 annual reports identified the following specific types of accounting changes reported.

Goodwill and intangibles	465	Derivatives	29
Impairments	156	Costs of exit or disposal activities	18
Business combinations	54	Stock compensation	16
Debt extinguishments	54	Other	44
Revenue recognition and income reporting	60		

financial statements. Each of these items is discussed separately, to investigate its unusual characteristics and to determine how each item should be reported in the accounts and how the information should be disclosed in comparative statements.

CHANGES IN ACCOUNTING PRINCIPLE

OBJECTIVE U2
Describe the accounting for changes in accounting principles.

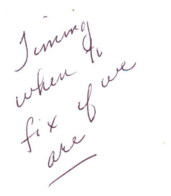

A change in accounting principle involves a change from one generally accepted accounting principle to another. For example, a company might change the basis of inventory pricing from average cost to LIFO. Or it might change from the completed-contract to percentage-of-completion method of accounting for construction contracts.

A careful examination must be made in each circumstance to ensure that a change in principle has actually occurred. **A change in accounting principle is not considered to result from the adoption of a new principle in recognition of events that have occurred for the first time or that were previously immaterial.** For example, when an inventory pricing method that is adopted for a new line of products is different from the method or methods used for **previously recorded** inventories, a change in accounting principle has **not occurred**. As another example, certain marketing expenditures that were previously immaterial and expensed in the period incurred may become material and acceptably deferred and amortized without a change in accounting principle occurring.

Finally, **if the accounting principle previously followed was not acceptable, or if the principle was applied incorrectly, a change to a generally accepted accounting principle is considered a correction of an error**. A switch from the cash or income tax basis of accounting to the accrual basis is considered a correction of an error. If the company deducted salvage value when computing double-declining depreciation on plant assets and later recomputed depreciation without deduction of estimated salvage value, an error is corrected.

Three approaches have been suggested for reporting changes in accounting principles in the accounts:

Currently. The **cumulative effect** of the change, which measures the cumulative difference in prior years' income between the newly adopted and prior accounting method, is reported in the current year's income statement as a special item. Under this approach, the effect of change on prior years' income is reported on the current-year income statement; **prior-year financial statements are not restated.**

Advocates of this position argue that restating financial statements for prior years results in a loss of confidence by investors in financial reports. Restatement, if permitted, also might upset many contractual and other arrangements that were based on the old figures. For example, profit-sharing arrangements computed on the old basis might have to be recomputed and completely new distributions made, which might create numerous legal problems. Many practical difficulties also exist; the cost of restatement may be excessive, or restatement may be impossible on the basis of data available.

Retrospectively. Under this approach, a **retroactive adjustment** of the financial statements is made such that the **prior years' statements are recast** on a basis consistent with the newly adopted principle. Any cumulative effect of the change for periods prior to those presented is recorded as an adjustment to beginning retained earnings of the earliest year presented.

Advocates of this position argue that only by restatement of prior periods can changes in accounting principles lead to comparable financial statements. If this approach is not used, the year previous to the change will be on the old method; the year of the change will report the entire cumulative adjustment in income; and the following year will present financial statements on the new basis without the cumulative effect of the change. Consistency is considered essential in providing meaningful earnings-trend data and other financial relationships necessary to evaluate the business.

Prospectively (in the future). Previously reported results remain; no change is made. Opening balances are not adjusted, and no attempt is made to allocate charges or credits for prior events.

Advocates of this position argue that once management presents financial statements based on acceptable accounting principles, they are final; management cannot change prior periods by adopting a new principle. According to this line of reasoning, the cumulative adjustment in the current year is not appropriate, because such an approach includes amounts that have little or no relationship to the current year's income or economic events.

INTERNATIONAL INSIGHT

IAS 8 generally requires restatement of prior years for accounting changes. However, *IAS 8* permits the cumulative-effect method or prospective method if the amounts to restate prior periods are not reasonably determinable.

The FASB now believes that the retrospective approach provides financial statement users with more useful information than the current or prospective approaches.[3] The rationale? First, through restatement, the retrospective approach results in greater consistency across accounting periods. As a result, users can better compare results from one period to the next. Furthermore, reporting the cumulative adjustment in the period of the change might have such a large effect on net income that the income figure would be misleading. A perfect illustration is the experience of **Chrysler Corporation** (now **DaimlerChrysler**) when it changed its inventory accounting from LIFO to FIFO. If the change had been handled on a current basis, Chrysler would have had to report a $53,500,000 adjustment to net income, which would have resulted in net income of $45,900,000 instead of a net loss of $7,600,000.

As another illustration, in the early 1980s the railroad industry switched from the retirement-replacement method of depreciating railroad equipment to a more generally used method such as straight-line depreciation. Cumulative-effect treatment meant that a substantial adjustment would be made to income in the period of change. Many in the railroad industry argued that the adjustment was so large that to include the cumulative effect in the current year instead of restating prior years would distort the information and make it less useful. Such situations lend support to restatement so that comparability is not seriously affected.[4]

In the following sections we illustrate application of the retrospective approach for accounting changes and how the prospective approach is applied to changes in accounting estimates.

Retrospective Accounting Change Approach

OBJECTIVE U3
Understand how to apply the retrospective accounting approach.

Under the retrospective approach, the cumulative effect of the new method on the financial statements at the beginning of the period is computed. A retroactive adjustment of the financial statements presented is made by **recasting prior years on a basis consistent with the newly adopted accounting principle**. We first illustrate application of the retrospective approach followed by a situation when it is impracticable to apply the retrospective approach—the change to the LIFO method.

Illustration

To illustrate the retrospective approach, assume that Denson Construction Co. has accounted for its income from long-term construction contracts using the completed-contract method. In 2005 the company changed to the percentage-of-completion method

[3]The new standard carries forward many of the provisions in the previous accounting change standard (*APB Opinion No. 20*), including the accounting for errors, changes in estimates, and the disclosures related to accounting changes.

[4]Adoption of the retrospective approach contributes to international accounting convergence. The FASB and the IASB are collaborating on a project in which they have agreed to converge around high-quality solutions to resolve differences between U.S. GAAP and International Financial Reporting Standards (IFRS). By adopting the retrospective approach, which is the method used in IFRS, the FASB agreed that this approach is superior to the current approach.

because management believes that this approach provides a more appropriate measure of the income earned. For tax purposes (assume a 40 percent enacted tax rate), the company has employed the completed-contract method and plans to continue using this method in the future.

Illustration U22-1 provides the information for analysis.

	Pretax Income from		Difference in Income		
Year	Percentage-of-Completion	Completed-Contract	Difference	Tax Effect 40%	Income Effect (net of tax)
Prior to 2004	$600,000	$400,000	$200,000	$80,000	$120,000
In 2004	180,000	160,000	20,000	8,000	12,000
Total at beginning of 2005	$780,000	$560,000	$220,000	$88,000	$132,000
Total in 2005	$200,000	$190,000	$ 10,000	$ 4,000	$ 6,000

ILLUSTRATION U22-1
Data for Change in Accounting for Long-Term Construction Contracts

The entry to record the change in 2005 would be:

Construction in Process	220,000	
Deferred Tax Liability		88,000
Retained Earnings		132,000

The Construction in Process account is increased by $220,000 (as indicated in the first column under "Difference in Income" in Illustration U22-1). The credit to Retained Earnings of $132,000 reflects the cumulative income effects prior to 2005 (third column under "Difference in Income" in Illustration U22-1). Retained Earnings is credited because prior years' income is closed to this account each year. The credit to Deferred Tax Liability represents the adjustment to prior years' tax expense, which is now recognized as a tax liability for future taxable amounts. That is, in future periods taxable income will be higher than book income as a result of current temporary differences, and therefore a deferred tax liability must be reported in the current year.

Income Statement Presentation

The bottom portion of the income statement for Denson Construction Co., **before giving effect to the change in accounting principle**, would be as follows.

Income Statement	2005	2004
Net income	$114,000[a]	$96,000[a]
Per Share Amounts		
Earnings per share (100,000 shares)	$1.14	$0.96

[a]The net income for the two periods is computed as follows:
2005 $190,000 − .40($190,000) = $114,000
2004 $160,000 − .40($160,000) = $96,000

ILLUSTRATION U22-2
Income Statement before Retroactive Change

The bottom portion of the income statement for Denson Construction Co., **after giving effect to the change in accounting principle,** would be as follows.

Income Statement	2005	2004
Net income	$120,000[a]	$108,000[a]
Per Share Amounts		
Earnings per share (100,000 shares)	$1.20	$1.08

[a]The net income for the two periods is computed as follows:
2005 $200,000 − .40($200,000) = $120,000
2004 $180,000 − .40($180,000) = $108,000

ILLUSTRATION U22-3
Income Statement after Retroactive Change

Retained Earnings Statement

Assuming a retained earnings balance of $1,600,000 at the beginning of 2004, the retained earnings statement **before giving effect to the change in accounting principle**, would appear as follows.

ILLUSTRATION U22-4
Retained Earnings Statement before Retroactive Change

RETAINED EARNINGS STATEMENT

	2005	2004
Balance at beginning of year	$1,696,000	$1,600,000
Net income	114,000	96,000
Balance at end of year	$1,810,000	$1,696,000

To develop a comparative retained earnings statement, after giving effect to the change in accounting principle, the beginning retained earnings for earliest period presented must be adjusted for the cumulative prior years' effects, as indicated in Illustration U22-5.

ILLUSTRATION U22-5
Retained Earnings Statement after Retroactive Change

RETAINED EARNINGS STATEMENT

	2005	2004
Balance at beginning of year, as previously reported		$1,600,000
Add: Adjustment for the cumulative effect on prior years of applying retrospectively the new method of accounting for long-term contracts (Note A)		120,000
Balance at beginning of year, as adjusted	$1,828,000	1,720,000
Net income	120,000	108,000
Balance at end of year	$1,948,000	$1,828,000

Note A: Change in Method of Accounting for Long-Term Contracts. The company has accounted for revenue and costs for long-term construction contracts by the percentage-of-completion method in 2005, whereas in all prior years revenue and costs were determined by the completed-contract method. The new method of accounting for long-term contracts was adopted to recognize . . . [state justification for change in accounting principle] . . . and financial statements of prior years have been restated to apply the new method retroactively. For income tax purposes, the completed-contract method has been continued. The effect of the accounting change on income of 2005 was an increase of $6,000 net of related taxes and on income of 2004 as previously reported was an increase of $12,000 net of related taxes. The balances of retained earnings for 2004 and 2005 have been adjusted for the effect of applying retrospectively the new method of accounting.

In 2004, the beginning balance was adjusted for the excess of the percentage-of-completion income over the completed-contract income prior to 2004 ($120,000). Under the newly adopted method, income for 2004 ($108,000) is added to the adjusted beginning balance, resulting in the ending retained earnings for 2004 ($1,828,000). This amount is also the beginning Retained Earnings for 2005. Adding 2005 income of $120,000 (as measured under the newly adopted method) results in the 2005 ending Retained Earnings balance. Thus, after adjusting beginning 2004 for the cumulative effect from prior periods, and recording income based on the newly adopted method, comparable Retained Earnings amounts are reported for 2004 and 2005.

OBJECTIVE U4
Understand how to account for changes to LIFO.

Change to LIFO Method

As indicated above, **unless it is impracticable to do so, changes in accounting principles should be reported by retrospective application.** Three conditions are considered in assessing impracticality:

1. The effects of the retrospective application are not determinable.
2. Retrospective application requires assumptions about management's intent in a prior period.
3. Retrospective application requires significant estimates for a prior period, and the availability of the necessary information to develop these estimates cannot be objectively verified.

If any of the above conditions exists, it is deemed impracticable to apply the retrospective approach. In this case, the new accounting principle is **applied prospectively** as of the earliest date it is practicable to do so.

CHANGE MANAGEMENT

WHAT DO THE NUMBERS MEAN?

The recent experience at **Halliburton** offers a case study in the importance of good reporting of an accounting change. Recall from Chapter 18 that Halliburton uses percentage-of-completion accounting for its long-term construction services contracts. Recently, the SEC questioned the company about its change in accounting for disputed claims.

Prior to 1998 Halliburton took a very conservative approach to its accounting for disputed claims. That is, the company waited until all disputes were resolved before recognizing associated revenues. In contrast, in 1998 the company recognized revenue for disputed claims before their resolution, using estimates of amounts expected to be recovered. Such revenue and its related profit are more tentative and subject to possible later adjustment. The accounting method in 1998 is more aggressive than the company's former policy but is still within the boundaries of GAAP.

It appears that the problem with Halliburton's accounting stems more from the way it handled its accounting change than from the new accounting method itself. That is, an overt reference to the company's change in accounting method was not provided in its 1998 annual report. In fact, rather than stating its new policy, the company simply deleted the sentence that described how it accounted for disputed claims. Then later, in its 1999 annual report, the new accounting policy was stated.

When such changes in accounting are made, investors need to be apprised of them and their effects on the company's financial results and position. With such information, current results can be compared with those of prior periods and a more informed assessment can be made about the company's future prospects.

Source: Adapted from "Accounting Ace Charles Mulford Answers Accounting Questions," *Wall Street Journal Online* (June 7, 2002).

An example of the impracticable condition is the change to the LIFO method. In such a situation, **the base-year inventory for all subsequent LIFO calculations is the opening inventory in the year the method is adopted. There is no restatement of prior years' income because it is just too impractical.** A restatement to LIFO would be subject to assumptions as to the different years that the layers were established, and these assumptions would ordinarily result in the computation of a number of different earnings figures. The only adjustment necessary may be to restate the beginning inventory to a cost basis from a lower of cost or market approach.

Disclosure then is limited to showing the effect of the change on the results of operations in the period of change. Also, the reasons for omitting the computations of the cumulative effect and the pro forma amounts for prior years should be explained. Finally, the company should disclose the justification for the change to LIFO. As shown in Illustration U22-6 on the next page, the Annual Report of **Quaker Oats Company** indicates the type of disclosure necessary.

In practice, many companies defer the formal adoption of LIFO until year-end. Management thus has an opportunity to assess the impact that a change to LIFO will have on the financial statements and to evaluate the desirability of a change for tax purposes. As indicated in Chapter 8, many companies use LIFO because of the advantages of this inventory valuation method in a period of inflation.

ILLUSTRATION U22-6
Disclosure of Change to LIFO

The Quaker Oats Company

Note 1 (In Part): Summary of Significant Accounting Policies

Inventories. Inventories are valued at the lower of cost or market, using various cost methods, and include the cost of raw materials, labor and overhead. The percentage of year-end inventories valued using each of the methods is as follows:

June 30	1989	1988	1987
Average quarterly cost	21%	54%	52%
Last-in, first-out (LIFO)	65%	29%	31%
First-in, first-out (FIFO)	14%	17%	17%

Effective July 1, 1988, the Company adopted the LIFO cost flow assumption for valuing the majority of remaining U.S. Grocery Products inventories. The Company believes that the use of the LIFO method better matches current costs with current revenues. The cumulative effect of this change on retained earnings at the beginning of the year is not determinable, nor are the pro-forma effects of retroactive application of LIFO to prior years. The effect of this change on fiscal 1989 was to decrease net income by $16.0 million, or $.20 per share.

If the LIFO method of valuing certain inventories were not used, total inventories would have been $60.1 million, $24.0 million and $14.6 million higher than reported at June 30, 1989, 1988, and 1987, respectively.

CHANGES IN ACCOUNTING ESTIMATE

OBJECTIVE U5
Describe the accounting for changes in estimates.

The preparation of financial statements requires estimating the effects of future conditions and events. The following are examples of items that require estimates:

1. Uncollectible receivables.
2. Inventory obsolescence.
3. Useful lives and salvage values of assets.
4. Periods benefited by deferred costs.
5. Liabilities for warranty costs and income taxes.
6. Recoverable mineral reserves.

Future conditions and events and their effects cannot be perceived with certainty; therefore, estimating requires the exercise of judgment. Accounting estimates will change as new events occur, as more experience is acquired, or as additional information is obtained.

Changes in estimates must be handled prospectively. That is, no changes should be made in previously reported results. Opening balances are not adjusted, and no attempt is made to "catch-up" for prior periods. Financial statements of prior periods are not restated. Instead, the effects of all changes in estimate are accounted for in (1) the period of change if the change affects that period only, or (2) the period of change and future periods if the change affects both. As a result, changes in estimates are viewed as **normal recurring corrections and adjustments**, the natural result of the accounting process. Retrospective treatment is prohibited.

INTERNATIONAL INSIGHT

In most nations, changes in accounting estimates are treated prospectively. International differences occur in the degree of disclosure required.

The circumstances related to a change in estimate are different from those surrounding a change in accounting principle. If changes in estimates were handled on a retrospective basis, continual adjustments of prior years' income would occur. It seems proper to accept the view that because new conditions or circumstances exist, the revision fits the new situation and should be handled in the current and future periods.

To illustrate, Underwriters Labs Inc. purchased a building for $300,000 which was originally estimated to have a useful life of 15 years and no salvage value. Depreciation has been recorded for 5 years on a straight-line basis. On January 1, 2005, the estimate of the useful life is revised so that the asset is considered to have a total life of 25 years. Assume that the useful life for financial reporting and tax purposes is the same. The accounts at the beginning of the sixth year are as follows.

Building	$300,000
Less: Accumulated depreciation—building (5 × $20,000)	100,000
Book value of building	$200,000

ILLUSTRATION U22-7
Book Value after Five Years' Depreciation

The entry to record depreciation for the year 2005 is:

Depreciation Expense	10,000	
Accumulated Depreciation—Building		10,000

The $10,000 depreciation charge is computed as follows.

$$\text{Depreciation charge} = \frac{\text{Book value of asset}}{\text{Remaining service live}} = \frac{\$200{,}000}{25\text{ years} - 5\text{ years}} = \$10{,}000$$

ILLUSTRATION U22-8
Depreciation after Change in Estimate

The disclosure of a change in estimated useful lives appeared in the Annual Report of **Ampco–Pittsburgh Corporation**.

Ampco–Pittsburgh Corporation

Note 11: Change in Accounting Estimate. The Corporation revised its estimate of the useful lives of certain machinery and equipment. Previously, all machinery and equipment, whether new when placed in use or not, were in one class and depreciated over 15 years. The change principally applies to assets purchased new when placed in use. Those lives are now extended to 20 years. These changes were made to better reflect the estimated periods during which such assets will remain in service. The change had the effect of reducing depreciation expense and increasing net income by approximately $991,000 ($.10 per share).

ILLUSTRATION U22-9
Disclosure of Change in Estimated Useful Lives

Differentiating between a change in an estimate and a change in an accounting principle is sometimes difficult. Is it a change in principle or a change in estimate when a company changes from deferring and amortizing certain marketing costs to recording them as an expense as incurred because future benefits of these costs have become doubtful? In such a case, **whenever it is impossible to determine whether a change in principle or a change in estimate has occurred, the change should be considered a change in estimate.**

The FASB relied on this rationale for "...a change in estimate that is effected by a change in accounting principle." An example of this type of change is a change in depreciation (as well as amortization or depletion) methods. Because changes in depreciation methods are made based on changes in estimates about future benefits arising from long-lived assets, it is not possible to separate the effect of the accounting principle change from that of the estimates. **As a result, the FASB decided to account for a change in depreciation methods as a change in estimate.**[5]

A similar problem occurs in differentiating between a change in estimate and a correction of an error, although the answer is more clear cut. How do we determine whether the information was overlooked in earlier periods (an error) or whether the information is now available for the first time (change in estimate)? Proper classification is important because corrections of errors have a different accounting treatment from that given changes in estimates. The general rule is that **careful estimates that**

[5] "Accounting Changes and Error Corrections," Statement of Financial Accounting Standards (Stamford, Conn.: FASB. 2005).

later prove to be incorrect should be considered changes in estimate. Only when the estimate was obviously computed incorrectly because of lack of expertise or in bad faith should the adjustment be considered an error. There is no clear demarcation line here, and good judgment must be used in light of all the circumstances.[6]

EXERCISES

UE22-1 (Change in Principle—Long-term Contracts) Pam Erickson Construction Company changed from the completed-contract to the percentage-of-completion method of accounting for long-term construction contracts during 2005. For tax purposes, the company employs the completed-contract method and will continue this approach in the future. (*Hint:* Adjust all tax consequences through the Deferred Tax Liability account.) The appropriate information related to this change is as follows.

	Pretax Income from:		
	Percentage-of-Completion	Completed-Contract	Difference
2004	$780,000	$590,000	$190,000
2005	700,000	480,000	220,000

Instructions

(a) Assuming that the tax rate is 35%, what is the amount of net income that would be reported in 2005?

(b) What entry(ies) are necessary to adjust the accounting records for the change in accounting principle?

UE22-2 (Change in Principle—Inventory Methods) Holder-Webb Company began operations on January 1, 2002, and uses the average cost method of pricing inventory. Management is contemplating a change in inventory methods for 2005. The following information is available for the years 2002–2004.

	Net Income Computed Using		
	Average Cost Method	FIFO Method	LIFO Method
2002	$15,000	$19,000	$12,000
2003	18,000	23,000	14,000
2004	20,000	25,000	17,000

Instructions

(a) Prepare the journal entry necessary to record a change from the average cost method to the FIFO method in 2005.

(b) Determine net income to be reported for 2002, 2003, and 2004, after giving effect to the change in accounting principle.

(c) Assume Holder-Webb Company used the LIFO method instead of the average cost method during the years 2002–2004. In 2005, Holder-Webb changed to the FIFO method. Prepare the journal entry necessary to record the change in principle.

UE22-3 (Accounting Changes—Depreciation) Kathleen Cole Inc. acquired the following assets in January of 2002.

Equipment, estimated service life, 5 years; salvage value, $15,000	$525,000
Building, estimated service life, 30 years; no salvage value	$693,000

The equipment has been depreciated using the sum-of-the-years'-digits method for the first 3 years for financial reporting purposes. In 2005, the company decided to change the method of computing depreciation to the straight-line method for the equipment, but no change was made in the estimated service life or salvage value. It was also decided to change the total estimated service life of the building from 30

[6]In evaluating reasonableness, the auditor should use one or a combination of the following approaches:

(a) Review and test the process used by management to develop the estimate.

(b) Develop an independent expectation of the estimate to corroborate the reasonableness of management's estimate.

(c) Review subsequent events or transactions occurring prior to completion of fieldwork.

"Auditing Accounting Estimates," *Statement on Auditing Standards No. 57* (New York: AICPA, 1988).

years to 40 years, with no change in the estimated salvage value. The building is depreciated on the straight-line method.

Instructions

(a) Prepare the general journal entry to record depreciation expense for the equipment in 2005.

(b) Prepare the journal entry to record depreciation expense for the building in 2005. (Round all computations to two decimal places.)

UE22-4 (Change in Principle and Error; Financial Statements) Presented below are the comparative statements for Denise Habbe Inc.

	2005	2004
Sales	$340,000	$270,000
Cost of sales	200,000	142,000
Gross profit	140,000	128,000
Expenses	88,000	50,000
Net income	$ 52,000	$ 78,000
Retained earnings (Jan. 1)	$125,000	$ 72,000
Net income	52,000	78,000
Dividends	(30,000)	(25,000)
Retained earnings (Dec. 31)	$147,000	$125,000

The following additional information is provided:

1. In 2005, Denise Habbe Inc. decided to switch its depreciation method from sum-of-the-years'-digits to the straight-line method. The assets were purchased at the beginning of 2004 for $100,000 with an estimated useful life of 4 years and no salvage value. (The 2005 income statement contains depreciation expense of $30,000.)
2. In 2005, the company discovered that the ending inventory for 2004 was overstated by $24,000; ending inventory for 2005 is correctly stated.

Instructions

Prepare the revised income and retained earnings statement for 2004 and 2005, assuming comparative statements.

UE22-5 (Accounting for Accounting Changes and Errors) Listed below are various types of accounting changes and errors.

_____ 1. Change in a plant asset's salvage value.
_____ 2. Change due to overstatement of inventory.
_____ 3. Change from sum-of-the-years'-digits to straight-line method of depreciation.
_____ 4. Change from presenting unconsolidated to consolidated financial statements.
_____ 5. Change from LIFO to FIFO inventory method.
_____ 6. Change in the rate used to compute warranty costs.
_____ 7. Change from an unacceptable accounting principle to an acceptable accounting principle.
_____ 8. Change in a patent's amortization period.
_____ 9. Change from completed-contract to percentage-of-completion method on construction contracts.
_____ 10. Change from FIFO to average-cost inventory method.

Instructions

For each change or error, indicate how it would be accounted for using the following code letters:

a. Accounted for prospectively.
b. Accounted for retrospectively.
c. Neither of the above.

PROBLEMS

UP22-1 (Change in Estimate, Principle, and Error Correction) Brueggen Company is in the process of preparing its financial statements for 2004. Assume that no entries for depreciation have been recorded in 2004. The following information related to depreciation of fixed assets is provided to you:

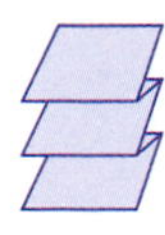

1. Brueggen purchased equipment on January 2, 2001, for $65,000. At that time, the equipment had an estimated useful life of 10 years with a $5,000 salvage value. The equipment is depreciated

on a straight-line basis. On January 2, 2004, as a result of additional information, the company determined that the equipment has a remaining useful life of 4 years with a $3,000 salvage value.

2. During 2004 Brueggen changed from the double-declining balance method for its building to the straight-line method. The building originally cost $300,000. It had a useful life of 10 years and a salvage value of $30,000. The following computations present depreciation on both bases for 2002 and 2003.

	2003	2002
Straight-line	$27,000	$27,000
Declining-balance	48,000	60,000

3. Brueggen purchased a machine on July 1, 2002, at a cost of $80,000. The machine has a salvage value of $8,000 and a useful life of 8 years. Brueggen's bookkeeper recorded straight-line depreciation in 2002 and 2003 but failed to consider the salvage value.

Instructions

(a) Prepare the journal entries to record depreciation expense for 2004 and correct any errors made to date related to the information provided. (Round all computations to two decimal places.)

(b) Show comparative net income for 2003 and 2004. Income before depreciation expense was $300,000 in 2004, and was $310,000 in 2003. Ignore taxes.

UP22-2 (Comprehensive Accounting Change and Error Analysis Problem) Larry Kingston Inc. was organized in late 2002 to manufacture and sell hosiery. At the end of its fourth year of operation, the company has been fairly successful, as indicated by the following reported net incomes.

2002	$140,000[a]	2004	$205,000
2003	160,000[b]	2005	276,000

[a]Includes a $12,000 increase because of change in bad debt experience rate.
[b]Includes extraordinary gain of $40,000.

The company has decided to expand operations and has applied for a sizable bank loan. The bank officer has indicated that the records should be audited and presented in comparative statements to facilitate analysis by the bank. Larry Kingston Inc. therefore hired the auditing firm of Check & Doublecheck Co. and has provided the following additional information.

1. In early 2003, Larry Kingston Inc. changed its estimate from 2% to 1% on the amount of bad debt expense to be charged to operations. Bad debt expense for 2002, if a 1% rate had been used, would have been $12,000. The company therefore restated its net income for 2002.
2. In 2005, the auditor discovered that the company had changed its method of inventory pricing from LIFO to FIFO. The effect on the income statements for the previous years is as follows.

	2002	2003	2004	2005
Net income unadjusted—LIFO basis	$140,000	$160,000	$205,000	$276,000
Net income unadjusted—FIFO basis	155,000	165,000	215,000	260,000
	$ 15,000	$ 5,000	$ 10,000	($ 16,000)

3. In 2005, the auditor discovered that:
   a. The company incorrectly overstated the ending inventory by $11,000 in 2004.
   b. A dispute developed in 2003 with the Internal Revenue Service over the deductibility of entertainment expenses. In 2002, the company was not permitted these deductions, but a tax settlement was reached in 2005 that allowed these expenses. As a result of the court's finding, tax expenses in 2005 were reduced by $60,000.

Instructions

(a) Indicate how each of these changes or corrections should be handled in the accounting records. Ignore income tax considerations.

(b) Present comparative income statements for the years 2002 to 2005, starting with income before extraordinary items. Ignore income tax considerations.

UP22-3 (Error Corrections and Accounting Changes) Patricia Voga Company is in the process of adjusting and correcting its books at the end of 2005. In reviewing its records, the following information is compiled.

1. Voga has failed to accrue sales commissions payable at the end of each of the last 2 years, as follows.

December 31, 2004	$4,000
December 31, 2005	$2,500

2. In reviewing the December 31, 2005, inventory, Voga discovered errors in its inventory-taking procedures that have caused inventories for the last 3 years to be incorrect, as follows.

December 31, 2003	Understated	$16,000
December 31, 2004	Understated	$21,000
December 31, 2005	Overstated	$ 6,700

Voga has already made an entry that established the incorrect December 31, 2005, inventory amount.

3. At December 31, 2005, Voga decided to change the depreciation method on its office equipment from double-declining balance to straight-line. The equipment has an original cost of $100,000 when purchased on January 1, 2003. It has a 10-year useful life and no salvage value. Depreciation expense recorded prior to 2005 under the double-declining balance method was $36,000. Voga has already recorded 2005 depreciation expense of $12,800 using the double-declining balance method.
4. Before 2005, Voga accounted for its income from long-term construction contracts on the completed-contract basis. Early in 2005, Voga changed to the percentage-of-completion basis for both accounting and tax purposes. Income for 2005 has been recorded using the percentage-of-completion method. The income tax rate is 40%. The following information is available.

	Pretax Income	
	Percentage-of-Completion	Completed-Contract
Prior to 2005	$150,000	$95,000
2005	60,000	20,000

Instructions

Prepare the journal entries necessary at December 31, 2005, to record the above corrections and changes. The books are still open for 2005. Voga has not yet recorded its 2005 income tax expense and payable amounts so current year-tax effects may be ignored. Prior-year tax effects must be considered in item 4.

UP22-4 (Change in Principle) Plato Corporation performs year-end planning in November of each year before their calendar year ends in December. The preliminary estimated net income is $3 million. The CFO, Mary Sheets, meets with the company president, S. A. Plato, to review the projected numbers. She presents the following projected information.

PLATO CORPORATION
PROJECTED INCOME STATEMENT
FOR THE YEAR ENDED DECEMBER 31, 2004

Sales		$29,000,000
Cost of goods sold	$14,000,000	
Depreciation	2,600,000	
Operating expenses	6,400,000	23,000,000
Income before income taxes		$ 6,000,000
Provision for income taxes		3,000,000
Net income		$ 3,000,000

PLATO CORPORATION
SELECTED BALANCE SHEET INFORMATION
AT DECEMBER 31, 2004

Estimated cash balance	$ 5,000,000
Available-for-sale securities (at cost)	10,000,000
Security fair value adjustment account (1/1/04)	200,000

Estimated market value at December 31, 2004:

Security	Cost	Estimated Market
A	$ 2,000,000	$ 2,200,000
B	4,000,000	3,900,000
C	3,000,000	3,000,000
D	1,000,000	2,800,000
Total	$10,000,000	$11,900,000

Other information at December 31, 2004:

Equipment	$3,000,000
Accumulated depreciation (5-year SL)	1,200,000
New robotic equipment (purchased 1/1/04)	5,000,000
Accumulated depreciation (5-year DDB)	2,000,000

The corporation has never used robotic equipment before, and Sheets assumed an accelerated method because of the rapidly changing technology in robotic equipment. The company normally uses straight-line depreciation for production equipment.

Plato explains to Sheets that it is important for the corporation to show an $8,000,000 net income before taxes because Plato receives a $1,000,000 bonus if the income before taxes and bonus reaches $8,000,000. He also cautions that he will not pay more than $3,000,000 in income taxes to the government.

Instructions

(a) What can Sheets do within GAAP to accommodate the president's wishes to achieve $8,000,000 income before taxes and bonus? Present the revised income statement based on your decision.

(b) Are the actions ethical? Who are the stakeholders in this decision, and what effect does Sheets' actions have on their interests?

SECTION 7 MISCELLANEOUS UPDATE TOPICS

Income Statement Reporting of Change in Accounting Principle

In 2005, the FASB issued a new standard addressing accounting changes and error corrections. This new standard, "Accounting Changes and Error Corrections," *Statement of Financial Accounting Standard* (Stamford, Conn.: FASB, 2005), is part of the FASB's short-term international convergence project and replaces *APB Opinion No. 20* and *FASB Statement No. 3*.

The following material should be used **in place of** the discussion in Chapter 4, pages 139–144, of *Intermediate Accounting*, 11th *Edition*.

UNDERLYING CONCEPTS

Companies can change principles, but it must be demonstrated that the newly adopted principle is preferable to the old one. Such changes mean that consistency from period to period is lost.

Changes in Accounting Principle

Changes in accounting occur frequently in practice, because important events or conditions may be in dispute or uncertain at the statement date. One type of accounting change, therefore, comprises the normal recurring corrections and adjustments that are made by every business enterprise. Another accounting change results when an accounting principle is adopted that is different from the one previously used. Changes in accounting principle would include a change in the method of inventory pricing from FIFO to average cost or a change in accounting for construction contracts from percentage of completion to completed contract.[1]

Changes in accounting principle are recognized by making a **retroactive adjustment** of the financial statements such that the **prior years' statements are recast** on a basis consistent with the newly adopted principle. Any cumulative effect of the change

[1]"Accounting Changes and Error Corrections," *Statement of Financial Accounting Standard* (Stamford, Conn.: FASB, 2005). In Chapter 22, we examine in greater detail the problems related to accounting changes.

for periods prior to those presented is recorded as an adjustment to beginning retained earnings of the earliest year presented.

To illustrate, Gaubert Inc. decided in March 2004 to change from FIFO to weighted-average inventory pricing. Gaubert's income before taxes, using the new weighted-average method in 2004, is $30,000. The pretax income data for 2002 and 2003 for this example are shown in Illustration U4-1.

ILLUSTRATION U4-1
Calculation of a Change in Accounting Principle

Year	FIFO	Weighted-Average Method	Excess of FIFO over Weighted-Average Method
2002	$40,000	$35,000	$5,000
2003	30,000	27,000	3,000
Total			$8,000

The information presented in the 2004 financial statements is shown in Illustration U4-2. (The tax rate was 30 percent.)

ILLUSTRATION U4-2
Income Statement Presentation of a Change in Accounting Principle

	2004	2003	2002
Income before taxes	$30,000	$27,000	$35,000
Income tax	9,000	8,100	10,500
Net income	$21,000	$18,900	$24,500

Thus, under the retrospective approach, the prior year's income numbers are restated under the newly adopted method in the current year; comparability across years is preserved.

Changes in Estimates

Estimates are inherent in the accounting process. Estimates are made, for example, of useful lives and salvage values of depreciable assets, of uncollectible receivables, of inventory obsolescence, and of the number of periods expected to benefit from a particular expenditure. Not infrequently, as time passes, as circumstances change, or as additional information is obtained, even estimates originally made in good faith must be changed. Such **changes in estimates** are accounted for in the period of change if they affect only that period, or in the period of change and future periods if the change affects both.

To illustrate a change in estimate that affects only the period of change, assume that DuPage Materials Corp. has consistently estimated its bad debt expense at 1 percent of credit sales. In 2003, however, DuPage's controller determines that the estimate of bad debts for the current year's credit sales must be revised upward to 2 percent, or double the prior years' percentage. Using 2 percent results in a bad debt charge of $240,000, or double the amount using the 1 percent estimate for prior years. The 2 percent rate is necessary to reduce accounts receivable to net realizable value. The provision is recorded at December 31, 2003, as follows.

Bad Debt Expense	240,000	
Allowance for Doubtful Accounts		240,000

The entire change in estimate is included in 2003 income because no future periods are affected by the change. **Changes in estimate are not handled retrospectively.** That is, they are not carried back to adjust prior years. (Changes in estimate that affect both the current and future periods are examined in greater detail in Chapter 22.) **Changes in estimate are not considered errors (prior period adjustments) or extraordinary items.**

Summary of Irregular Items

UNDERLYING CONCEPTS

The AICPA Special Committee on Financial Reporting indicates a company's core activities—usual and recurring events—provide the best historical data from which users determine trends and relationships and make their predictions about the future. Therefore, the effects of core and non-core activities should be separately displayed.

The modified all-inclusive income concept is accepted in practice. Except for a couple of items (discussed later in this chapter) that are charged or credited directly to retained earnings, all other irregular gains or losses or nonrecurring items are closed to Income Summary and are included in the income statement. Of these, **discontinued operations of a component** of a business is classified as a separate item in the income statement after continuing operations. The **unusual, material, nonrecurring items** that are significantly different from the typical or customary business activities are shown in a separate section for "**Extraordinary items**" below discontinued operations. Other items of a material amount that are of an **unusual or nonrecurring** nature and are **not considered extraordinary** are separately disclosed.

Because of the numerous intermediate income figures that are created by the reporting of these irregular items, careful evaluation of earnings information reported by the financial press is needed. Illustration U4-3 summarizes the basic concepts previously discussed. Although the chart is simplified, it provides a useful framework for determining the treatment of special items affecting the income statement.

ILLUSTRATION U4-3
Summary of Irregular Items in the Income Statement

Type of Situation[a]	Criteria	Examples	Placement on Financial Statements
Discontinued operations	Disposal of a component of a business for which the operations and cash flows can be clearly distinguished from the rest of the company's operations.	Sale by diversified company of major division that represents only activities in electronics industry. Food distributor that sells wholesale to supermarket chains and through fast-food restaurants decides to discontinue the division that sells to one of two classes of customers.	Shown in separate section of the income statement after continuing operations but before extraordinary items. (Shown net of tax.)
Extraordinary items	Material, and both unusual and infrequent (nonrecurring).	Gains or losses resulting from casualties, an expropriation, or a prohibition under a new law.	Separate section in the income statement entitled "Extraordinary items." (Shown net of tax.)
Unusual gains or losses, not considered extraordinary	Material; character typical of the customary business activities; unusual or infrequent but not both.	Write-downs of receivables, inventories; adjustments of accrued contract prices; gains or losses from fluctuations of foreign exchange; gains or losses from sales of assets used in business.	Separate section in income statement above income before extraordinary items. Often reported in "Other revenues and gains" or "Other expenses and losses" section. (Not shown net of tax.)
Changes in principle	Change from one generally accepted principle to another.	Change in the basis of inventory pricing from FIFO to average cost.	Prior years' income statements are restated on the same basis as the newly adopted principle.
Changes in estimates	Normal, recurring corrections and adjustments.	Changes in the realizability of receivables and inventories; changes in estimated lives of equipment, intangible assets; changes in estimated liability for warranty costs, income taxes, and salary payments.	Change in income statement only in the account affected. (Not shown net of tax.)

[a]This summary provides only the general rules to be followed in accounting for the various situations described above. Exceptions do exist in some of these situations.

SPECIAL REPORTING ISSUES

Intraperiod Tax Allocation

OBJECTIVE U1
Explain intraperiod tax allocation.

We noted that certain irregular items are shown on the income statement net of tax. Many believe that the resulting income tax effect should be directly associated with that event or item. In other words, the tax expense for the year should be related, where possible, to **specific items** on the income statement to provide a more informative disclosure to statement users. This procedure is called **intraperiod tax allocation**, that is, allocation within a period. Its main purpose is to relate the income tax expense of the period to the items that affect the amount of the tax expense. Intraperiod tax allocation is used for the following items: (1) income from continuing operations, (2) discontinued operations, (3) extraordinary items, and (4) changes in accounting principle. The general concept is, "**Let the tax follow the income.**"

The income tax expense attributable to "income from continuing operations" is computed by finding the income tax expense related to revenue and to expense transactions used in determining this income. In this tax computation, no effect is given to the tax consequences of the items excluded from the determination of "income from continuing operations." A separate tax effect is then associated with each irregular item.

Extraordinary Gains

In applying the concept of intraperiod tax allocation, assume that Schindler Co. has income before income tax and extraordinary item of $250,000 and an extraordinary gain from the sale of a single stock investment of $100,000. If the income tax rate is assumed to be 30 percent, the following information is presented on the income statement.

ILLUSTRATION U4-4
Intraperiod Tax Allocation, Extraordinary Gain

Income before income tax and extraordinary item		$250,000
Income tax		75,000
Income before extraordinary item		175,000
Extraordinary gain—sale of investment	$100,000	
Less: Applicable income tax	30,000	70,000
Net income		$245,000

The income tax of $75,000 ($250,000 × 30%) attributable to "Income before income tax and extraordinary item" is determined from revenue and expense transactions related to this income. In this income tax computation, the tax consequences of items excluded from the determination of "Income before income tax and extraordinary item" are not considered. The "Extraordinary gain—sale of investment" then shows a separate tax effect of $30,000.

Extraordinary Losses

To illustrate the reporting of an extraordinary loss, assume that Schindler Co. has income before income tax and extraordinary item of $250,000 and an extraordinary loss from a major casualty of $100,000. Assuming a 30 percent tax rate, the presentation of income tax on the income statement would be as shown in Illustration U4-5. In this case, the loss provides a positive tax benefit of $30,000 and, therefore, is subtracted from the $100,000 loss.

ILLUSTRATION U4-5
Intraperiod Tax Allocation, Extraordinary Loss

Income before income tax and extraordinary item		$250,000
Income tax		75,000
Income before extraordinary item		175,000
Extraordinary item—loss from casualty	$100,000	
Less: Applicable income tax reduction	30,000	70,000
Net income		$105,000

An extraordinary item may be reported "net of tax" with note disclosure, as shown in Illustration U4-6.

ILLUSTRATION U4-6
Note Disclosure of Intraperiod Tax Allocation

Income before income tax and extraordinary item	$250,000
Income tax	75,000
Income before extraordinary item	175,000
Extraordinary item, less applicable income tax reduction (Note 1)	70,000
Net income	$105,000

Note 1: During the year the Company suffered a major casualty loss of $70,000, net of applicable income tax reduction of $30,000.

OBJECTIVE U2
Explain where earnings per share information is reported.

Earnings per Share

The results of a company's operations are customarily summed up in one important figure: net income. As if this condensation were not enough of a simplification, the financial world has widely accepted an even more distilled and compact figure as its most significant business indicator—**earnings per share (EPS)**.

The computation of earnings per share is usually straightforward. **Net income minus preferred dividends (income available to common stockholders) is divided by the weighted average of common shares outstanding to arrive at earnings per share.**[2] To illustrate, assume that Lancer, Inc. reports net income of $350,000 and declares and pays preferred dividends of $50,000 for the year. The weighted average number of common shares outstanding during the year is 100,000 shares. Earnings per share is $3, as computed in Illustration U4-7.

ILLUSTRATION U4-7
Equation Illustrating Computation of Earnings per Share

$$\frac{\text{Net Income} - \text{Preferred Dividends}}{\text{Weighted Average of Common Shares Outstanding}} = \text{Earnings per Share}$$

$$\frac{\$350{,}000 - \$50{,}000}{100{,}000} = \$3$$

Note that the EPS figure measures the number of dollars earned by each share of common stock—not the dollar amount paid to stockholders in the form of dividends.

"Net income per share" or "earnings per share" is a ratio commonly used in prospectuses, proxy material, and annual reports to stockholders. It is also highlighted in the financial press, by statistical services like Standard & Poor's, and by Wall Street securities analysts. Because of its importance, **earnings per share is required to be disclosed on the face of the income statement**. A company that reports a discontinued operation or an extraordinary item must report per share amounts for these line items either on the face of the income statement or in the notes to the financial statements.[3]

To illustrate the income statement order of presentation and the earnings per share data, we present an income statement for Poquito Industries Inc. in Illustration U4-8 on page UP-43. Notice the order in which data are shown. In addition, per share information is shown at the bottom. Assume that the company had 100,000 shares outstanding for the entire year. The Poquito Industries Inc. income statement, in Illustration U4-8, is highly condensed. Items such as "Unusual charge," "Discontinued operations," and "Extraordinary item" would have to be described fully and appropriately in the statement or related notes.

---

[2]In the calculation of earnings per share, preferred dividends are deducted from net income if declared or if cumulative though not declared.

[3]"Earnings Per Share," *Statement of Financial Accounting Standards No. 128* (Norwalk, Conn.: FASB, 1996).

ILLUSTRATION U4-8
Income Statement

POQUITO INDUSTRIES INC. INCOME STATEMENT FOR THE YEAR ENDED DECEMBER 31, 2004		
Sales revenue		$1,420,000
Cost of goods sold		600,000
Gross profit		820,000
Selling and administrative expenses		320,000
Income from operations		500,000
Other revenues and gains		
Interest revenue		10,000
Other expenses and losses		
Loss on disposal of part of Textile Division	$ (5,000)	
Unusual charge—loss on sale of investments	(45,000)	(50,000)
Income from continuing operations before income tax		460,000
Income tax		208,000
Income from continuing operations		252,000
Discontinued operations		
Income from operations of Pizza Division, less applicable income tax of $24,800	54,000	
Loss on disposal of Pizza Division, less applicable income tax of $41,000	(90,000)	(36,000)
Income before extraordinary item		216,000
Extraordinary item—loss from earthquake, less applicable income tax of $23,000		(45,000)
Net income		$ 171,000
Per share of common stock		
Income from continuing operations		$3.12
Income from operations of discontinued division, net of tax		0.54
Loss on disposal of discontinued operation, net of tax		(0.90)
Income before extraordinary item		2.76
Extraordinary loss, net of tax		(0.45)
Net income		$1.71

Many corporations have simple capital structures that include only common stock. For these companies, a presentation such as "earnings per common share" is appropriate on the income statement. In many instances, however, companies' earnings per share are subject to dilution (reduction) in the future because existing contingencies permit the issuance of additional common shares.[4]

In summary, the simplicity and availability of figures for per share earnings lead inevitably to their widespread use. Because of the undue importance that the public, even the well-informed public, attaches to earnings per share, the EPS figure must be made as meaningful as possible.

INVENTORY COSTS

In 2004, the FASB issued a new standard addressing the accounting for inventory costs. This new standard is titled "Inventory Costs: An Amendment of *ARB No. 43*, Chapter 4," *Statement of Financial Accounting Standard* (Stamford, Conn.: FASB, 2004). It is part of the FASB's short-term international convergence project.

The following material **complements** the discussion on product and period costs in Chapter 8, pages 377–378, of *Intermediate Accounting*, 11th Edition.

[4]Ibid. The computational problems involved in accounting for these dilutive securities in earnings per share computations are discussed in Chapter 16.

COSTS INCLUDED IN INVENTORY

U.S. GAAP has not required that certain abnormal inventory costs, such as those related to idle capacity and spoilage, double freight, and re-handling, be excluded from the cost of inventory. As a result, companies following U.S. GAAP may include such costs in inventory, whereas companies following International Financial Reporting Standards would treat these items as period costs.

The FASB has now decided to be consistent with the IASB position, to require that these costs, when abnormal, should be **excluded from the cost of inventory**. This change should improve the comparability of financial statements prepared under U.S. and international GAAP.

PREFERRED STOCK

Late in 2003, the FASB issued a new standard that affects the accounting for certain "hybrid" financial instruments, which have characteristics of both liabilities and equity. This standard, "Accounting for Certain Financial Instruments with Characteristics of Both Liabilities and Equity," *Statement of Financial Accounting Standards No. 150,* is one part of the FASB Debt-Equity Project.

The following discussion **replaces** the discussion in Chapter 15, page 737, footnote 10, in *Intermediate Accounting,* 11th Edition.

REDEEMABLE PREFERRED STOCK

Recently, more and more issuances of preferred stock have features that make the security more like debt (a legal obligation to pay) than an equity instrument. For example, **redeemable preferred stock** is a preferred stock that has a mandatory redemption period or redemption feature that is outside the control of the issuer. Previously, public companies were not permitted to report these debt-like preferreds in equity, but they were not required to report them as a liability either. There were concerns about classification of these debt-like securities, which may have been reported as equity or in the "mezzanine" section of balance sheets between debt and equity. There also was diversity in practice as to how dividends on these securities were reported. The new standard addresses these concerns by requiring that such instruments be **classified as liabilities** and be measured and accounted for similar to liabilities.

Note that *SFAS No. 150* represents completion of the first phase in a broader project on liabilities and equity. In phase two of the project, the FASB will deal with the accounting for compound financial instruments (e.g., convertible debt covered in Chapter 16) that have characteristics of liabilities and equity, the definition of an ownership relationship, and the definition of liabilities (an amendment to FASB Concepts Statement No. 6, *Elements of Financial Statements*.)

0-555-02018-5

ELEVENTH EDITION

INTERMEDIATE ACCOUNTING

Volume II

Donald E. Kieso Ph.D., C.P.A.
KPMG Peat Marwick Emeritus Professor of Accounting
Northern Illinois University
DeKalb, Illinois

Jerry J. Weygandt Ph.D., C.P.A.
Arthur Andersen Alumni Professor of Accounting
University of Wisconsin
Madison, Wisconsin

Terry D. Warfield Ph.D.
Associate Professor
University of Wisconsin
Madison, Wisconsin

WILEY

John Wiley & Sons, Inc.

Dedicated to our parents,
Lester and Mildred, Adolph and Sylvia, and Donald and Helen;
and to our fathers- and mothers-in-law,
William and Mathilda, Sigurd and Maxyne, and Mike and Flo,
for their love, support, and encouragement

PUBLISHER:	Susan Elbe
ACQUISITIONS EDITOR:	Mark Bonadeo
MARKETING MANAGER:	Keari Bedford
PROJECT EDITOR:	David B. Kear
MEDIA EDITOR:	Allison Keim
DEVELOPMENTAL EDITOR:	Ann Torbert
PRODUCTION SERVICES MANAGER:	Jeanine Furino
SENIOR DESIGNER:	Karin Kincheloe
ILLUSTRATION EDITOR:	Anna Melhorn
ASSOCIATE EDITOR:	Ed Brislin
TEXT DESIGNER:	Lee Goldstein
COVER DESIGNER:	David Levy
PROJECT MANAGEMENT:	Elm Street Publishing Services, Inc.
COVER PHOTOS:	© www.danheller.com

This book was set in Palatino by Techbooks and printed and bound by Von Hoffmann.
The cover was printed by Von Hoffmann.

This book is printed on acid-free paper. ∞

0-471-42638-5
Printed in the United States of America
10 9 8 7 6 5 4 3 2 1

About the Authors

Donald E. Kieso, Ph.D., C.P.A., received his bachelor's degree from Aurora University and his doctorate in accounting from the University of Illinois. He has served as chairman of the Department of Accountancy and is currently the KPMG Peat Marwick Emeritus Professor of Accounting at Northern Illinois University. He has public accounting experience with Price Waterhouse & Co. (San Francisco and Chicago) and Arthur Andersen & Co. (Chicago) and research experience with the Research Division of the American Institute of Certified Public Accountants (New York). He has done postdoctorate work as a Visiting Scholar at the University of California at Berkeley and is a recipient of NIU's Teaching Excellence Award and four Golden Apple Teaching Awards. Professor Kieso is the author of other accounting and business books and is a member of the American Accounting Association, the American Institute of Certified Public Accountants, and the Illinois CPA Society. He has served as a member of the Board of Directors of the Illinois CPA Society, the AACSB's Accounting Accreditation Committees, the State of Illinois Comptroller's Commission, as Secretary-Treasurer of the Federation of Schools of Accountancy, and as Secretary-Treasurer of the American Accounting Association. Professor Kieso served as a charter member of the national Accounting Education Change Commission. He is the recipient of the Outstanding Accounting Educator Award from the Illinois CPA Society, the FSA's Joseph A. Silvoso Award of Merit, and the NIU Foundation's Humanitarian Award for Service to Higher Education.

Jerry J. Weygandt, Ph.D., C.P.A., is Arthur Andersen Alumni Professor of Accounting at the University of Wisconsin—Madison. He holds a Ph.D. in accounting from the University of Illinois. Articles by Professor Weygandt have appeared in the *Accounting Review, Journal of Accounting Research, Accounting Horizons, Journal of Accountancy,* and other academic and professional journals. These articles have examined such financial reporting issues as accounting for price-level adjustments, pensions, convertible securities, stock option contracts, and interim reports. Professor Weygandt is author of other accounting and financial reporting books and is a member of the American Accounting Association, the American Institute of Certified Public Accountants, and the Wisconsin Society of Certified Public Accountants. He has served on numerous committees of the American Accounting Association and as a member of the editorial board of the *Accounting Review*; he also has served as President and Secretary-Treasurer of the American Accounting Association. In addition, he has been actively involved with the American Institute of Certified Public Accountants and has been a member of the Accounting Standards Executive Committee (AcSEC) of that organization. He has served on the FASB task force that examined the reporting issues related to accounting for income taxes and is presently a trustee of the Financial Accounting Foundation. Professor Weygandt has received the Chancellor's Award for Excellence in Teaching and the Beta Gamma Sigma Dean's Teaching Award. He is on the board of directors of M & I Bank of Southern Wisconsin and the Dean Foundation. He is the recipient of the Wisconsin Institute of CPA's Outstanding Educator's Award and the Lifetime Achievement Award. In 2001 he received the American Accounting Association's Outstanding Accounting Educator Award.

Terry D. Warfield, Ph.D., is associate professor of accounting at the University of Wisconsin—Madison. He received a B.S. and M.B.A. from Indiana University and a Ph.D. in accounting from the University of Iowa. Professor Warfield's area of expertise is financial reporting, and prior to his academic career, he worked for five years in the banking industry. He served as the Academic Accounting Fellow in the Office of the Chief Accountant at the U.S. Securities and Exchange Commission in Washington, D.C. from 1995–1996. Professor Warfield's primary research interests concern financial accounting standards and disclosure policies. He has published scholarly articles in *The Accounting Review, Journal of Accounting and Economics, Research in Accounting Regulation,* and *Accounting Horizons,* and he has served on the editorial boards of *The Accounting Review, Accounting Horizons,* and *Issues in Accounting Education.* He has served on the Financial Accounting Standards Committee of the American Accounting Association (Chair 1995–1996) and on the AAA-FASB Research Conference Committee. Professor Warfield has received teaching awards at both the University of Iowa and the University of Wisconsin, and he was named to the Teaching Academy at the University of Wisconsin in 1995. Professor Warfield has developed and published several case studies based on his research for use in accounting classes. These cases have been selected for the AICPA Professor-Practitioner Case Development Program and have been published in *Issues in Accounting Education.*

Preface

As we wrote this edition of *Intermediate Accounting*, the importance of financial accounting and reporting has never been more apparent. Recent failures of major corporations, such as **Enron**, **WorldCom**, and **Global Crossing**, have highlighted the need for relevant and reliable financial information to ensure that our capital market system functions efficiently. Although we are saddened by these failures and their negative consequences for companies, employees, investors, and creditors, we believe that much good can come from a renewed commitment to provide high-quality financial information to users of financial statements.

The Sarbanes-Oxley Act of 2002 will provide a framework that can be used to enhance the quality of financial information. For example, the Act mandates that managements and auditors meet higher standards in accounting and financial reporting in response to the recent business and accounting failures. Business executives must understand and certify to the accuracy of their company's financial statements. Consequently, it is imperative that every student of business understands the fundamentals of accounting and financial reporting.

In this edition of *Intermediate Accounting*, we continue a tradition begun nearly 30 years ago of helping students understand, prepare, and use financial information. As indicated above, the importance of students' understanding the role of financial information in capital markets has never been more important. For example, a recent *Wall Street Journal* ran the following headlines:

"The SEC Checks Whether Microsoft Was Too Conservative in Booking Revenues"

"Qwest Communications Acknowledges Some Off-Balance-Sheet Transactions"

"SEC Reviews Allegations That EMC Improperly Accounted for Some Sales"

"Krispy Kreme Makes Changes After an Accounting Technique Is Questioned"

"Marriott Is Set to Disclose Details of Write-Offs Related to Developer Franchising"

An important feature of *Intermediate Accounting*, therefore, is an enhanced effort to provide more perspective on the information available in financial reporting. As a result, special boxed insights titled "What Do the Numbers Mean?" illustrate how reporting methods affect the decisions of financial statement users. By means of these boxes, we hope to convey the excitement and ever-changing nature of accounting, illuminating its significance and highlighting its importance. During our years of teaching, we have found that many students, when introduced to the issues involved in financial reporting, genuinely enjoy the subject area.

A second key feature of this edition is the introduction of the *Take Action!* CD-ROM, which can be packaged with the text. The *Take-Action!* CD is an electronic gateway to a comprehensive set of materials that supplement the already comprehensive coverage of accounting topics in the textbook. Major elements of the *Take Action!* CD build on those contained in the *Gateway to the Profession Digital Tool* of the 10th Edition of *Intermediate Accounting*. In addition to updating the well-accepted material on the *Digital Tool*, the *Take Action!* CD has several new and enhanced features. These new features include self-assessment quizzes and interactive tutorials, which provide expanded discussion and explanation in a visual, audio, and narrative context. (Elements of the *Take Action!* CD are described in more detail later in the preface.)

The 11th Edition of *Intermediate Accounting* also introduces a new element to the "Using Your Judgment" section of the end-of-chapter material: A "Professional

Simulation" in each chapter provides students with a new and integrative context for applying the concepts introduced in the chapter. This new element is patterned after the new computerized CPA exam. It expands the focus of many of the elements of the *Take Action!* CD (writing, working in teams, using the analyst's toolkit) to help students learn how to use accounting facts and procedures in various business contexts.

We continue to strive for a balanced discussion of conceptual and procedural presentations so that these elements are mutually reinforcing. In addition, text discussions focus on explaining the rationale behind business transactions before addressing the accounting and reporting for those transactions. As in prior editions, we have thoroughly revised and updated the text to include all the latest developments in the accounting profession and practice. For example, the chapter on intangibles has been completely revised to reflect new accounting standards for intangible assets. Benefiting from the comments and recommendations of adopters of the 10th Edition, we have made significant revisions. Explanations have been expanded where necessary; complicated discussions and illustrations have been simplified; realism has been integrated to heighten interest and relevancy; and new topics and coverage have been added to maintain currency. We have deleted some 10th Edition coverage from the text. For example, the two chapters related to stockholders' equity have been combined and streamlined. Finally, to provide the instructor with flexibility of use and no loss in topic coverage, discussions of less commonly used methods and more complex or specialized topics have been moved to the *Take Action!* CD.

NEW FEATURES

Based on extensive reviews, focus groups, and interactions with other intermediate accounting instructors and students, we have developed a number of new pedagogical features and content changes designed both to help students learn more effectively and to answer the changing needs of the course.

New Chapters

As discussed, we have completely updated the chapter on intangibles, and we have streamlined the coverage of stockholders' equity by combining Chapters 15 and 16 of the 10th Edition.

New Pedagogy

With the introduction of the "What Do the Numbers Mean?" boxed insights and the Professional Simulations, we have enhanced the pedagogy in the book to better engage students in the material and to provide new opportunities for students to apply accounting concepts to various business contexts.

Take Action! CD

As described above, the *Take Action!* CD is a major resource of the 11th Edition, which can be packaged with the text or is available separately for purchase. Key elements of the *Take Action!* CD are described below.

Analyst's Toolkit

"Tools" in the Analyst's Toolkit consist of the following items.

Database of Real Companies. More than 20 annual reports of well-known companies, including three international companies, are provided on the *Take Action!* CD. These annual reports can be used in a variety of ways. For example, they can be used for illustrating different presentations of financial information or for comparing note disclosures across companies. In addition, these reports can be used to analyze a company's financial condition and compare its prospects with those of other companies in the same industry. Assignment material provides some examples of different types of analysis that can be performed.

Company Web Links. Each of the companies in the database of real companies is identified by a Web address to facilitate the gathering of additional information, if desired.

Additional Enrichment Material. A chapter on Financial Statement Analysis is provided on the CD, along with related assignment material. This chapter can also be used in conjunction with the database of annual reports of real companies.

Spreadsheet Tools. Present value templates are provided which can be used to solve time value of money problems.

Additional Internet Links. A number of useful links related to financial analysis are provided to expand expertise in this area.

Professional Toolkit

Consistent with expanding beyond technical accounting knowledge, the *Take Action!* CD emphasizes certain skills necessary to become a successful accountant and financial manager.

Writing Materials. A primer on professional communications gives students a framework for writing professional materials. This primer discusses issues such as the top ten writing problems, strategies for rewriting, how to do revisions, and tips on clarity. This primer has been class-tested and is effective in helping students enhance their writing skills.

Group Work Materials. Recent evaluations of accounting education have identified the need to develop more skills in group problem solving. The *Take Action!* CD provides a second primer dealing with the role that groups play in organizations. Information is included on what makes a successful group, how you can participate effectively in the group, and do's and don'ts of group formation.

Ethics. The Professional Toolkit contains expanded materials on the role of ethics in the profession, including references to:

Speeches and articles on ethics in accounting.
Codes of ethics for major professional bodies.
Examples and additional case studies on ethics.

Career Professional Spotlights. Every student should have a good understanding of the profession he or she is entering. Career vignettes on the *Take Action!* CD indicate the types of work that accountants do. Other aspects of the spotlights on careers are included on the *Take Action!* CD to help students make successful career choices. These include professional Web links—important links to Web sites that can provide useful career information to facilitate the student's efforts in this area.

Student Toolkit

Also included on the *Take Action!* CD are features that help students process and understand the course materials. They are:

Interactive Tutorials. To help students better understand some of the more difficult topics in intermediate accounting, we have developed several interactive tutorials that provide expanded discussion and explanation in a visual and narrative context. Topics addressed include the accounting cycle; inventory methods, including dollar-value LIFO; depreciation and impairment of long-lived assets; and interest capitalization.

Note that these tutorials are for the benefit of the student and should require no use of class time on the part of instructors.

Expanded Discussions and Illustrations. The Expanded Discussion section provides additional topics not covered in depth in the textbook. The *Take Action!* CD gives the flexibility to enrich or expand the course by discussion of additional topics such as those listed below.

International Accounting. The *Take Action!* CD provides an expanded discussion of international accounting institutions, the evolution of international accounting standards, and a framework for understanding the differences in accounting practice. This discussion is designed to complement the International Reporting Cases in the "Using Your Judgment" sections.

Take Action! CD Topics. Topics included on the *Take Action!* CD are as follows (with appropriate chapter linkage identified).

Chapter 1

- Expanded discussion of international accounting.
- Expanded discussion of ethical issues in financial accounting.

Chapter 2

- Discussion of accounting for changing prices.

Chapter 3

- Presentation of work sheet using the periodic inventory method.
- Specialized journals and methods of processing accounting data.
- Tutorial on the accounting cycle.

Chapter 6

- Present-value-based measurements, including an expanded discussion of spreadsheet tools for solving present value problems.

Chapter 7

- Discussion of how a four-column bank reconciliation (the proof of cash) can be used for control purposes.
- Expanded example of transfers of receivables without recourse, with accounting entries.
- Tutorials on the accounting for bad debts and transfer of receivables.

Chapter 8

- Tutorial on inventory cost flow assumptions.
- Tutorial on LIFO issues, including dollar-value LIFO.

Chapter 10

- Tutorial on interest capitalization.

Chapter 11

- Discussion of lesser-used depreciation methods, such as the retirement and replacement methods.
- Tutorial on depreciation methods.
- Tutorial on impairments.

Chapter 12

- Expanded discussion on valuing goodwill.

Chapter 13

- Expanded discussion on property taxes.

Chapter 15

- Expanded discussion on the par value method for treasury stock.
- Expanded discussion on quasi-reorganizations.

Chapter 16

- Comprehensive earnings per share illustration.

Chapter 17

- Illustration of accounting entries for transfers of investment securities.
- Expanded discussion of special issues related to investments.

Chapter 19

- Discussion of the conceptual aspects of interperiod tax allocation, including the deferred and net of tax methods.
- Discussion of accounting for intraperiod tax allocation, with examples.

Chapter 21

- Discussion of real estate leases and leveraged leases.

Chapter 23

- Discussion of the T-account method for preparing a statement of cash flows. A detailed example is provided.

Chapter 24

- Discussion of accounting for changing prices both for general and specific price level changes.
- Financial analysis primer.

In addition to these materials, illustrative disclosures of financial reporting practices are provided.

Self-Study Tests and Additional Self-Tests. Each chapter on the *Take Action!* CD includes two sets of self-tests to allow students to check their understanding of key concepts from the chapter.

Glossary. A complete glossary of all the key terms used in the text is provided, in alphabetical order. Page numbers where these key terms appear in the text are also shown.

Learning Style Survey. Research on left brain/right brain differences and also on learning and personality differences suggests that each person has preferred ways to receive and communicate information. After taking this quiz, students will be able to pinpoint the study aids in the text that will help them learn the material based on their particular learning styles.

In summary, the *Take Action!* CD is a comprehensive complement to the 11th Edition of *Intermediate Accounting*, providing new materials as well as a new way to communicate that material.

ENHANCED FEATURES

We have continued and enhanced many of the features of the 10th Edition of *Intermediate Accounting*, including the following.

Chapter-Opening Vignettes

We have updated and introduced new chapter-opening vignettes to provide an even better real-world context that helps motivate student interest in the chapter topic.

"Using Your Judgment" Section

The "Using Your Judgment" section at the end of each chapter has been revised and updated. Elements in this section include a Financial Reporting Problem (featuring **3M Company**), Financial Statement Analysis Case, Comparative Analysis Case (featuring **The CocaCola Company** and **PepsiCo, Inc.**), Research Case(s), International Reporting Case, and the new Professional Simulation. Explicit writing and group assignments and ethics cases have been moved out of the Using Your Judgment sections and are instead integrated into the Exercises, Problems, and Conceptual Cases. Exercises, problems, and cases that are especially suited for group or writing assignments and those that specifically address ethics are identified with special icons, as shown here in the margin.

Real-World Emphasis

We believe that one of the goals of the intermediate accounting course is to orient students to the application of accounting principles and techniques in practice. Accordingly, we have continued our practice of using numerous examples from real corporations throughout the text. The names of these real companies are highlighted in red. Illustrations and exhibits marked by the icon shown here in the margin or by company logos are excerpts from actual financial statements of existing firms. In addition, the 2001 report of **3M Company** is included in Appendix 5B, and many real-company financial reports appear in the database on the *Take Action!* CD.

International Insights

International Insight paragraphs that describe or compare IASB standards and the accounting practices in other countries with U.S. GAAP are provided in the margin. We have continued this feature to help students understand that other countries sometimes use different recognition and measurement principles to report financial information. These insights are marked with the icon shown here in the margin.

Currency and Accuracy

Accounting continually changes as its environment changes; an up-to-date book is therefore a necessity. As in past editions, we have strived to make this edition the most up-to-date and accurate text available.

Streamlined Presentation

We have continued our efforts to keep the topical coverage of *Intermediate Accounting* in line with the way instructors are currently teaching the course. Accordingly, we have moved some optional topics into appendixes and have omitted altogether some topics that formerly were covered in appendixes, moving them to the *Take Action!* CD. Details are noted in the list of specific content changes below and in the earlier CD-content list.

CONTENT CHANGES

The following list outlines the revisions and improvements made in chapters of the 11th Edition.

Chapter 1 Financial Accounting and Accounting Standards

- New vignette.
- Discussion of Sarbanes-Oxley Act of 2002.
- Updated international discussion.

Chapter 2 Conceptual Framework Underlying Financial Accounting

- New vignette.
- Enhanced discussion of the new concepts statement on present values and cash flows.

Chapter 3 The Accounting Information System

- Updated vignette.
- Presentation of work sheet in spreadsheet format.
- The accounting equation analyses in the margin next to key journal entries now include indication of the cash flow effect.

Chapter 4 Income Statement and Related Information

- New vignette.
- Updated discussion of quality of earnings. Updated discussion of irregular items.
- Deleted appendix on discontinued operations, given changes in accounting standards.

Chapter 5 Balance Sheet and Statement of Cash Flows

- New vignette.
- New featured company.

Chapter 6 Accounting and the Time Value of Money

- Introduced new concepts statement on present values and expected cash flows.
- Moved appendix on spreadsheets to *Take Action!* CD.

Chapter 7 Cash and Receivables

- Updated vignette.
- Added new graphic on uncollectible accounts.

Chapter 8 Valuation of Inventories: A Cost Basis Approach

- New vignette on usefulness of inventory disclosures.
- Streamlined discussion of manufacturing costs and absorption costing.

Chapter 9 Inventories: Additional Valuation Issues

- Updated vignette.

Chapter 10 Acquisition and Disposition of Property, Plant, and Equipment

- New vignette on the significance of property, plant, and equipment.
- Updated discussion on capital additions and repairs.

Chapter 11 Depreciation, Impairments, and Depletion

- New vignette on impairments.
- Introduced component depreciation.

Chapter 12 Intangible Assets

- New chapter, given new standard on intangible assets.

Chapter 13 Current Liabilities and Contingencies

- Streamlined discussion of current liabilities.
- Moved property taxes payable to *Take Action!* CD.
- Introduced new standard on asset retirement obligations.
- Updated discussion on guarantees.

Chapter 14 Long-Term Liabilities

- New vignette on the impact of debt levels on equity markets.
- Streamlined discussion on types of bonds and bond ratings. Updated discussion on reporting of gains and losses on extinguishment of debt.
- Updated discussion of off-balance-sheet financing.

Chapter 15 Stockholders' Equity

- New combined chapter on stockholders' equity.

Chapter 16 Dilutive Securities and Earnings Per Share

- New vignette.
- Updated discussion of hybrid securities.
- New graphic on components of compensation.
- Updated discussion of stock options.

Chapter 17 Investments

- Updated vignette on equity method.
- Updated discussion on equity method and goodwill.
- Moved appendix on special issues related to investments to *Take Action!* CD.

Chapter 18 Revenue Recognition

- Updated discussion of regulatory environment related to revenue recognition.
- Introduced new International Insights.

Chapter 19 Accounting for Income Taxes

- Updated vignette.
- Streamlined discussion of alternative minimum tax.
- Streamlined discussion of multiple tax rates.

Chapter 20 Accounting for Pensions and Postretirement Benefits

- New vignette on pension funding.
- New graphic on magnitude of pension plans.
- Streamlined discussion of capitalization.

Chapter 21 Accounting for Leases

- Updated vignette and graphic on airline leases.
- Streamlined discussion of leasing advantages.
- Streamlined journal entries for lessor accounting.
- Moved summary lease illustrations to appendix.

Chapter 22 Accounting Changes and Error Analysis

- New vignette on restatements.
- Streamlined discussion on accounting change framework.
- Added spreadsheet presentation of accounting error work sheet.
- Updated appendix for equity method goodwill.

Chapter 23 Statement of Cash Flows

- Updated vignette on usefulness of cash flows.
- Introduced spreadsheet presentation of cash flow work sheet.

Chapter 24 Full Disclosure in Financial Reporting

- New vignette on quality financial reporting.
- New accounting policy illustration.
- Updated discussion of related party transactions.
- Updated discussion of fraudulent financial reporting.

END-OF-CHAPTER ASSIGNMENT MATERIAL

At the end of each chapter we have provided a comprehensive set of review and homework material consisting of Questions, Brief Exercises, Exercises, Problems, and short Conceptual Cases. For this edition, many of the exercises and problems have been revised or updated. In addition, the Using Your Judgment sections, which (as described earlier) include Financial Reporting Problems, Financial Statement Analysis Cases, Comparative Analysis Cases, Research Cases, International Reporting Cases, and Professional Simulations, have all been updated. All of the assignment materials have been class-tested and/or double-checked for accuracy and clarity.

The Questions are designed for review, self-testing, and classroom discussion purposes as well as for homework assignments. Typically, a Brief Exercise covers one topic, an Exercise one or two topics. Exercises require less time and effort to solve than do Problems. The Problems are designed to develop a professional level of achievement and are more challenging and time-consuming to solve than the Exercises. Those Exercises and Problems that are contained in the *Excel Problems* supplements are identified by the icon shown here in the margin.

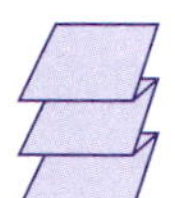

The Conceptual Cases generally require an essay as opposed to quantitative solutions. They are intended to confront the student with situations calling for conceptual analysis and the exercise of judgment in identifying problems and evaluating alternatives. The "Using Your Judgment" assignments, described earlier, are designed to develop students' critical thinking, analytical, research, and communication skills.

Probably no more than one-fourth of the total exercise, problem, and case material must be used to cover the subject matter adequately. Consequently, problem assignments may be varied from year to year without repetition.

SUPPLEMENTARY MATERIALS

Accompanying this textbook is an improved and expanded package of student learning aids and instructor teaching aids.

The *Intermediate Accounting,* 11th Edition, *Take Action!* CD, described in detail on pages vii–x and available for packaging with the textbook, provides additional tools for students and instructors. Its three parts consist of the Analyst's Toolkit, the Professional Toolkit, and the Student Toolkit. Other teaching and learning aids are described below. In addition, other resources for students and instructors can be found at the book's companion Web site at www.wiley.com/college/kieso.

Instructor Teaching Aids

Instructor's Resource System on CD-ROM (IRCD)

- Resource manager with friendly interface for course development and presentation.
- Includes all instructor supplements, text art, and transparencies.

Instructor's Manual: Vol. 1: Chs. 1–14

Instructor's Manual: Vol. 2: Chs. 15–24

- Lecture outlines keyed to text learning objectives.
- Chapter reviews.
- Also available on the Kieso Web site and IRCD.

Solutions Manual, Vol. 1: Chs. 1–14

Solutions Manual, Vol. 2: Chs. 15–24

- Answers to all Brief Exercises, Exercises, Problems, and Case material provided.
- Classification Tables categorize the end-of-chapter material by topic to assist in assigning homework.
- Also available on the Kieso Web site and IRCD.
- Assignment Tables (of characteristics) describe the end-of-chapter material, its difficulty level, and estimated completion time.
- All solutions have been triple-checked to ensure accuracy.

Test Bank, Vol. 1: Chs. 1–14

Test Bank, Vol. 2: Chs. 15–24

- Essay questions with solutions for true-false, multiple choice, short answer, and essays help you test students' communication skills.
- Estimated completion times facilitate test planning.
- Computations for multiple-choice problems assist you in giving partial credit.
- Also available on the Kieso Web site and IRCD.

Computerized Test Bank IBM

- A large collection of objective questions and exercises with answers for each chapter in the text.
- Enables you to generate questions randomly or manually and modify/customize tests with your own material.
- Enables you to create versions of the same test by scrambling by type, character, number, or learning objective.
- Also available on the Kieso Web site and IRCD.

Test Preparation Service

- Simply call Wiley's Accounting Hotline (800-541-5602) with the questions you have selected for an exam. Wiley will provide a master within 24 hours.

Solutions Transparencies, Vol. 1: Chs. 1–14

Solutions Transparencies, Vol. 2: Chs. 15–24

- Provided in organizer box with chapter file folders.
- Large, bold type size for easier class presentation.
- Provided for all exercises, problems, and brief exercises.

PowerPoint Presentations

- Designed to enhance presentation of chapter topics and examples.
- Separate presentation for each chapter, available on the Kieso Web site and IRCD.

Teaching Transparencies

- More than 100 color figure illustrations and exhibits.

Checklist of Key Figures

- Available at the Kieso Web site to both students and instructors, and on the Instructor's Resource System CD (IRCD).

Solutions to Rockford Practice Set

- Available for download from the Kieso Web site, this supplement provides solutions to the *Rockford Practice Set.*

Solutions to Excel Templates

- Available for download from the Kieso Web site and IRCD, these are solutions to the *Solving Problems Using Excel Workbook* templates.

Course Management Resources

- Course content cartridges are available for both WebCT and Blackboard.

CPA Connection

The CPA Connection is a new resource developed for the 11th Edition. This booklet provides instructors with information about the computerized uniform Certified Public Accountant (CPA) examination scheduled to be administered for the first time in 2004. It provides knowledge about the changes in the exam and gives instuctors ideas to assist their students in practicing the type of skills necessary to pass the Financial Accounting and Reporting section of the exam. Many of the ideas and tips included in the booklet are directly linked to *Intermediate Accounting*. Specifically, *The CPA Connection*: (1) develops awareness of the changed exam format, delivery, and content as it affects the financial accounting area, and (2) presents ideas and testing formats that instructors may choose to incorporate into their intermediate accounting classes. *The CPA Connection* should be viewed as a reference source, from which instructors can easily select and use the information that fits into their classroom situation. In addition, *The CPA Connection* booklet will be supplemented by an e-mail newsletter.

Student Learning Aids

Student Study Guide, Vol. 1: Chs. 1–14

Student Study Guide, Vol. 2: Chs. 15–24

- Chapter Learning Objectives
- Chapter Outline—a broad overview of general chapter content with space for note-taking in class.
- Chapter Review with summary of key concepts.
- Glossary of key terms.
- Review Questions and Exercises—self-test items with supporting computations.

Working Papers, Vol. 1: Chs. 1–14

Working Papers, Vol. 2: Chs. 15–24

- Solution forms and partially completed solutions forms for all end-of-chapter problems and exercises.
- Demonstrates how to correctly set up solution formats.

Excel Working Papers, Vol. 1: Chs. 1–14

Excel Working Papers, Vol. 2: Chs. 15–24

- Solution forms and partially completed solutions forms for all end-of-chapter problems and exercises; solution forms are available as Excel templates.
- Solutions can be typed directly into the templates, which are saved onto a hard drive or written manually after forms are printed.
- Students enter data electronically, enabling them to paste homework to a new file and e-mail the work sheet to their instructor.

Problem Solving Survival Guide, Vol. 1: Chs. 1–14

Problem Solving Survival Guide, Vol. 2: Chs. 15–24

- Provides additional questions and problems to develop students' problem-solving skills.
- Explanations assist in the approach, set-up, and completion of problems.
- Tips alert students to common pitfalls and misconceptions.

Solving Problems Using Excel Workbook

- Review of intermediate accounting and Excel concepts.
- Spreadsheet requirements range in difficulty (from data entry to developing spreadsheets).
- Each chapter consists of a basic tutorial, a more advanced tutorial, and two or three problems from the text.
- Each problem is followed by "what-if" questions to build students' analytical skills.

Rockford Corporation: An Accounting Practice Set

Rockford Corporation: A Computerized Accounting Practice Set

- Practice set that has been designed as a students' review and update of the accounting cycle and the preparation of financial statements.
- Available in a print version and in an updated computerized version.

Business Extra Web Site at www.wiley.com/college/businessextra

BUSINESS EXTRA

- Gives you instant access to a wealth of current articles dealing with all aspects of accounting.
- Articles are organized to correspond with the chapters of this text.
- To access Business Extra, you will need to purchase the "Doing Business in Turbulent Times" booklet.

ACKNOWLEDGMENTS

We thank the many users of our 10th Edition who contributed to the revision through their comments and instructive criticism. Special thanks are extended to the focus group participants and the primary reviewers of and contributors to our 11th Edition manuscript.

Janice Bell
California State University at Northridge

Larry Bergin
Winona State University

Robert Bloom
John Carroll University

Phillip Buchanan
George Mason University

Tom Buchman
University of Colorado, Boulder

Tom Carment
Northeastern State University

Joanne Duke
San Francisco State University

William Foster
New Mexico State University

Clyde Galbraith
West Chester University

Harold Goedde
SUNY Oneonta

Julia Higgs
Florida Atlantic University

Judy Hora
University of San Diego

Kathy Hsu
University of Louisiana, Lafayette

Daniel Ivancevich
University of North Carolina at Wilmington

Susan Ivancevich
University of North Carolina at Wilmington

James Johnston
Louisiana Tech University

Lisa Koonce
University of Texas at Austin

Steve Lafave
Augsburg College

Patsy Lee
University of Texas—Arlington

Gary Luoma
University of South Carolina

Joan Monnin-Callahan
University of Cincinnati

Patricia Parker
Columbus State Community College

Richard Parker
Olivet College

Marlene Plumlee
University of Utah

Debbie Rankin
Lincoln University

Paul Robertson
New Mexico State University

Larry Roman
Cuyahoga Community College

John Rossi
Moravian College

George Sanders
Western Washington University

Jerry Siebel
University of South Florida

Pamela Stuerke
Case Western Reserve University

Ron Stunda
Birmingham Southern College

Gary Taylor
University of Alabama

Gary Testa
Brooklyn College

Lynn Thomas
Kansas State University

Lynn Turner
Colorado State University

Elizabeth Venuti
Hofstra University

Jeannie Welsh
La Salle University

We would also like to thank other colleagues who provided helpful criticism and made valuable suggestions as members of focus groups or as adopters and reviewers of previous editions.

Charlene Abendroth
California State University—Hayward

Diana Adcox
University of North Florida

Noel Addy
Mississippi State University

Roberta Allen
Texas Tech University

James Bannister
University of Hartford

Kathleen Bauer
Midwestern State University

Jon A. Booker
Tennessee Technological University

John C. Borke
University of Wisconsin—Platteville

Suzanne M. Busch
California State University—Hayward

Eric Carlsen
Kean College of New Jersey

Robert Cluskey
Tennessee State University

Edwin Cohen
DePaul University

W. Terry Dancer
Arkansas State University

Lee Dexter
Moorhead State University

Judith Doing
University of Arizona

Dean S. Eiteman
Indiana University—Pennsylvania

Larry R. Falcetto
Emporia State University

Richard Fern
Eastern Kentucky University

Richard Fleischman
John Carroll University

Stephen L. Fogg
Temple University

Clyde Galbraith
West Chester University

Susan Gill
Washington State University

Lynford E. Graham
Rutgers University

Donald J. Griffin
Cayuga Community College

Marcia I. Halvorsen
University of Cincinnati

Garry Heesacker
Central Washington University

Wayne M. Higley
Buena Vista University

Geoffrey R. Horlick
St. Francis College

M. Zafar Iqbal
California Polytechnic State University—San Luis Obispo

Cynthia Jeffrey
Iowa State University

Jeff Jones
Auburn University

Celina Jozsi
University of South Florida

Douglas W. Kieso
University of California—Irvine

Paul D. Kimmel
University of Wisconsin—Milwaukee

Martha King
Emporia State University

Florence Kirk
State University of New York at Oswego

Mark Kohlbeck
University of Wisconsin—Madison

Lisa Koonce
University of Texas—Austin

David B. Law
Youngstown State University

Henry LeClerc
Suffolk Community College—Selden Campus

Barbara Leonard
Loyola University—Chicago

Brian Leventhal
University of Illinois—Chicago

Timothy Lindquist
University of Northern Iowa

Tom Linsmeier
Michigan State University

Daphne Main
University of New Orleans

Mostafa Maksy
Northeastern Illinois University

Danny Matthews
Midwestern State University

Robert J. Matthews
New Jersey City University

Robert Milbrath
University of Houston

John Mills
University of Nevada—Reno

Mohamed E. Moustafa
California State University—Long Beach

Siva Nathan
Georgia State University

Kermit Natho
Georgia State University

Obeau S. Persons
Rider University

Ray Pfeiffer
University of Massachusetts—Amherst

Tom Porter
Georgia State University

Robert Rambo
University of New Orleans

Vernon Richardson
University of Kansas

Richard Riley
West Virginia University

Jeffrey D. Ritter
St. Norbert College

Paul Robertson
New Mexico State University

Steven Rock
University of Colorado

Victoria Rymer
University of Maryland

James Sander
Butler University

John Sander
University of Southern Maine

Douglas Sharp
Wichita State University

John R. Simon
Northern Illinois University

Keith Smith
George Washington University

Pam Smith
Northern Illinois University

Billy S. Soo
Boston College

Carlton D. Stolle
Texas A & M University

William Stout
University of Louisville

Iris Stuart
California State University—Fullerton

Eric Sussman
University of California, Los Angeles

Diane L. Tanner
University of North Florida

Paula B. Thomas
Middle Tennessee State University

James D. Waddington, Jr.
Hawaii Pacific University

Dick Wasson
Southwestern College

Frank F. Weinberg
Golden Gate University

Shari H. Wescott
Houston Baptist University

Michael Willenborg
University of Connecticut

William H. Wilson
Oregon Health University

Kenneth Wooling
Hampton University

Joni Young
University of New Mexico

Paul Zarowin
New York University

Stephen A. Zeff
Rice University

We would also like to thank the following colleagues who contributed to several of the unique features of this edition.

Take Action! CD:

Andrew Prewitt, *KPMG, Chicago*
Jeff Seymour, *KPMG, Minneapolis*
Matt Sullivan, *Deloitte and Touche, Milwaukee*
Erin Viel, *PricewaterhouseCoopers, Milwaukee*

"Working in Teams" Materials:

Edward Wertheim, *Northeastern University*

The Writing Handbook:

Michelle Ephraim, *Worcester Polytechnic Institute*

Self-Test Materials:

Dick Wasson, *Southwestern College*

Perspectives and "From Classroom to Career" Interviews:

Stuart Weiss, *Stuart Weiss Business Writing, Inc.*

Ancillary Authors, Contributors, and Accuracy Checkers:

Shiela Ammons
Austin Community College

Maryann Benson
John C. Borke
University of Wisconsin—Platteville

Larry Falcetto
Emporia State University

Clyde Galbraith
West Chester University

Marc Giullian
Montana State University

Edwin Hackleman and Don Newell
Delta Software

Debra R. Hopkins
Northern Illinois University

Marilyn F. Hunt
University of Central Florida

Heather Johnson
Elm Street Publishing Services

Douglas W. Kieso
University of California—Irvine

Jennifer Laudermilch
Gary Lubin
Rex A. Schildhouse
University of Phoenix—San Diego

Barbara Muller
Arizona State University

Paul Jep Robertson
New Mexico State University

Alice Sineath
Forsyth Technical Community College

Dick D. Wasson
Southwestern College

Practicing Accountants and Business Executives

From the fields of corporate and public accounting, we owe thanks to the following practitioners for their technical advice and for consenting to interviews.

Tracy Barber
Deloitte & Touche

Ron Bernard
NFL Enterprises

Penelope Flugger
J.P. Morgan & Co.

John Gribble
PricewaterhouseCoopers

Darien Griffin
S.C. Johnson & Son Wax

Michael Lehman
Sun Microsystems, Inc.

Michele Lippert
Evoke.com

Sue McGrath
Vision Capital Management

David Miniken
Sweeney Conrad

Robert Sack
University of Virgina

Claire Schulte
Deloitte & Touche

Willie Sutton
Mutual Community Savings Bank, Durham, NC

Gary Valenzuela
Yahoo!

Rachel Woods
PricewaterhouseCoopers

Arthur Wyatt
Arthur Andersen & Co., and the University of Illinois—Urbana

In addition, we appreciate the exemplary support and professional commitment given us by the development, marketing, production, and editorial staffs of John Wiley & Sons, including Susan Elbe, Jay O'Callaghan, Mark Bonadeo, Keari Bedford, David Kear, Brian Kamins, Ed Brislin, Allie Keim, Jeanine Furino, Karen Kincheloe, Anna Melhorn, Lenore Belton, and Cynthia Taylor and to the management and staff at TechBooks. A special note of thanks also to Ann Torbert (editorial and content assistance) and Elm Street Publishing Services (Martha Beyerlein and Heather Johnson) for facilitating the production of the manuscript and the book. We also wish to thank Dick Wasson of Southwestern College for coordinating the efforts of the supplements authors and checkers. Finally, thanks to Maris Technologies for developing the format of the *Take Action!* CD. We appreciate the cooperation of the American Institute of Certified Public Accountants and the Financial Accounting Standards Board in permitting us to quote from their pronouncements. We thank 3M Company for permitting us to use its 2001 Annual Report for our specimen financial statements. We also acknowledge permission from the American Institute of Certified Public Accountants, the Institute of Management Accountants, and the Institute of Internal Auditors to adapt and use material from the Uniform CPA Examinations, the CMA Examinations, and the CIA Examination, respectively.

If this book helps teachers instill in their students an appreciation for the challenges, worth, and limitations of accounting, if it encourages students to evaluate critically and understand financial accounting theory and practice, and if it prepares students for advanced study, professional examinations, and the successful and ethical pursuit of their careers in accounting or business, then we will have attained our objective.

Suggestions and comments from users of this book will be appreciated.

Donald E. Kieso
Somonauk, Illinois

Jerry J. Weygandt
Madison, Wisconsin

Terry D. Warfield
Madison, Wisconsin

Brief Contents

Contents

Intermediate Accounting

CHAPTER 15

Stockholders' Equity

LEARNING OBJECTIVES

After studying this chapter, you should be able to:

1. **Discuss the characteristics of the corporate form of organization.**
2. **Explain the key components of stockholders' equity.**
3. **Explain the accounting procedures for issuing shares of stock.**
4. **Explain the accounting for treasury stock.**
5. **Explain the accounting for and reporting of preferred stock.**
6. **Describe the policies used in distributing dividends.**
7. **Identify the various forms of dividend distributions.**
8. **Explain the accounting for small and large stock dividends, and for stock splits.**
9. **Indicate how stockholders' equity is presented and analyzed.**

Stocking Up

Quick—how did the market do yesterday? If asked this question, you probably responded that the market went up or down, based on the change in the Dow Jones Industrial Average. And just what is the Dow Jones Industrial Average (DJIA)? It is the average of 30 U.S. "blue-chip" (high-quality) stocks which represent the various sectors of the U.S. economy and have broad public ownership. **AT&T**, **American Express**, **Coca-Cola**, **ExxonMobil**, **General Electric**, **Merck**, and **McDonald's** are examples of the type of companies found in this index.

The DJIA and other stock market indexes are becoming of increasing importance to most Americans. The reason: More and more of the country's wealth is tied up in the stock market.

The following two tables list the ten most active stocks by dollar and share volume (in round lots) in 2001 on the New York Stock Exchange. (A round lot is a unit of 100 shares of stock.)

Ten most active stocks by dollar volume, 2001
(millions of dollars)

Issue	Reported dollar volume
IBM Corporation	$189,407
General Electric	187,414
AOL Time Warner	143,769
Citigroup Inc.	136,829
Pfizer Inc.	114,141
EMC Corp.	111,481
Tyco International Ltd.	106,576
American International Group Inc.	99,890
ExxonMobil Corp.	98,421
Johnson & Johnson	95,479

Ten most active stocks, 2001
(millions of shares) (round lots)

Issue	Reported share volume
General Electric	4,363.4
Lucent Technologies Inc.	4,264.1
EMC Corp.	3,864.1
Nortel Networks	3,541.8
AOL Time Warner	3,444.8
Nokia Corp.	2,950.8
Citigroup Inc.	2,836.6
Pfizer Inc.	2,759.3
Compaq Computer	2,743.6
AT&T Corp.	2,649.4

Source: Courtesy of the New York Stock Exchange.

Although the late 1990s were great for investing in the stock market, the early 2000s have been miserable ones for investors. An interesting question is whether dollar and share volume will continue to increase, given the uncertainties present today. In addition, the percentage of Americans owning stock has increased dramatically over the last 25 years. Will stock ownership continue, given the recent dismal market performance? One certainty: The presentation of relevant and reliable financial information on a company's performance will lead to more stable markets in the future.

PREVIEW OF CHAPTER 15

As indicated from the opening story, the stock market is of substantial importance in any economy that functions on private ownership. It provides a market where prices are established to serve as signals and incentives to guide the allocation of the economy's financial resources. The purpose of this chapter is to explain the various accounting issues for various transactions related to the stockholders' equity section of a corporation. The content and organization of this chapter are as follows.

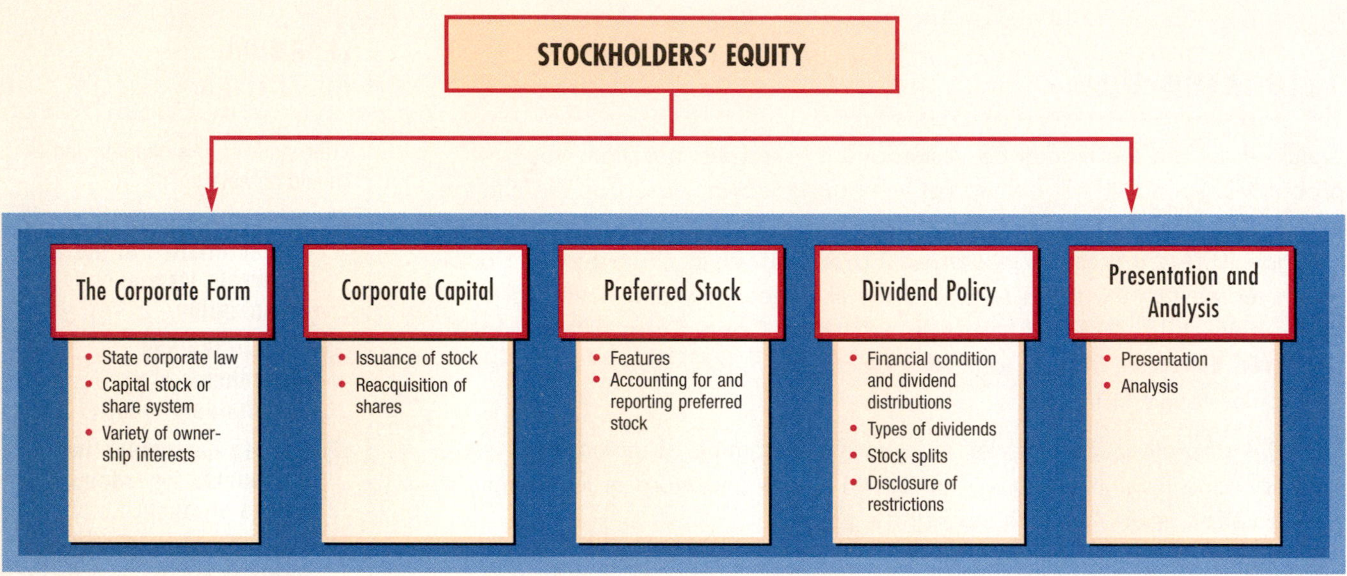

THE CORPORATE FORM

OBJECTIVE 1
Discuss the characteristics of the corporate form of organization.

Of the three **primary forms of business organization—the proprietorship, the partnership, and the corporation**—the dominant form of business is the corporate form. In terms of the aggregate amount of resources controlled, goods and services produced, and people employed, the corporation is by far the leader. All of the "Fortune 500" largest industrial firms are corporations. Although the corporate form has a number of advantages (as well as disadvantages) over the other two forms, its principal advantage is its facility for attracting and accumulating large amounts of capital.

Among the special characteristics of the corporate form that affect accounting are:

1. Influence of state corporate law.
2. Use of the capital stock or share system.
3. Development of a variety of ownership interests.

State Corporate Law

Anyone who wishes to establish a corporation must submit **articles of incorporation** to the state in which incorporation is desired. Assuming the requirements are properly fulfilled, the corporation charter is issued, and the corporation is recognized as a legal entity subject to state law. Regardless of the number of states in which a corporation has operating divisions, it is incorporated in only one state.

It is to the company's advantage to incorporate in a state whose laws are favorable to the corporate form of business organization. General Motors, for example, is incorporated in Delaware; **United States Steel Corp.** is a New Jersey corporation. Some corporations have increasingly been incorporating in states with laws favorable to existing management. For example, to thwart possible unfriendly takeovers, **Gulf Oil** changed its state of incorporation to Delaware. There, certain tactics against takeovers can be approved by the board of directors alone, without a vote of the shareholders.

Each state has its own business incorporation act, and the accounting for stockholders' equity follows the provisions of this act. In many cases states have adopted the principles contained in the Model Business Corporate Act prepared by the American Bar Association. State laws are complex and vary both in their provisions and in their definitions of certain terms. Some laws fail to define technical terms, and so terms often mean one thing in one state and another thing in a different state. These problems may be further compounded because legal authorities often interpret the effects and restrictions of the laws differently.

INTERNATIONAL INSIGHT

In the United States, stockholders are treated equally as far as access to financial information. That is not always the case in other countries. For example, in Mexico, foreign investors as well as minority investors often have difficulty obtaining financial data. These restrictions are rooted in the habits of companies that for many years have been tightly controlled by a few stockholders and managers.

Capital Stock or Share System

Stockholders' equity in a corporation is generally made up of a large number of units or shares. Within a given class of stock each share is exactly equal to every other share. Each owner's interest is determined by the number of shares he or she possesses. If a company has but one class of stock divided into 1,000 shares, a person owning 500 shares controls one-half of the ownership interest of the corporation; one holding 10 shares has a one-hundredth interest.

Each share of stock has certain rights and privileges that can be restricted only by special contract at the time the shares are issued. One must examine the articles of incorporation, stock certificates, and the provisions of the state law to ascertain such restrictions on or variations from the standard rights and privileges. In the absence of restrictive provisions, each share carries the following rights:

1. To share proportionately in profits and losses.
2. To share proportionately in management (the right to vote for directors).
3. To share proportionately in corporate assets upon liquidation.
4. To share proportionately in any new issues of stock of the same class—called the **preemptive right**.[1]

The first three rights are to be expected in the ownership of any business. The last may be used in a corporation to protect each stockholder's proportional interest in the enterprise. **The preemptive right protects an existing stockholder from involuntary dilution of ownership interest.** Without this right, stockholders with a given percentage interest might find their interest reduced by the issuance of additional stock without their knowledge and at prices that were not favorable to them. The preemptive right that attaches to existing shares has been eliminated by many corporations. The reason is that this right makes it inconvenient for corporations to make large issuances of additional stock, as they frequently do in acquiring other companies.

The great advantage of the share system is the ease with which an interest in the business may be transferred from one individual to another. **Individuals owning shares in a corporation may sell them to others at any time and at any price without obtaining the consent of the company or other stockholders.** Each share is personal property of the owner and may be disposed of at will. All that is required of the corporation is that it maintain a list or subsidiary ledger of stockholders as a guide to dividend payments, issuance of stock rights, voting proxies, and the like. Because shares are

[1]This privilege is referred to as a **stock right** or **warrant**. The warrants issued in these situations are of short duration, unlike the warrants issued with other securities.

freely and frequently transferred, it is necessary for the corporation to revise the subsidiary ledger of stockholders periodically, generally in advance of every dividend payment or stockholders' meeting. Also, the major stock exchanges require controls that the typical corporation finds uneconomic to provide. Thus **registrars** and **transfer agents** who specialize in providing services for recording and transferring stock are usually used. The negotiability of stock certificates is governed by the Uniform Stock Transfer Act and the Uniform Commercial Code.

INTERNATIONAL INSIGHT

The American and British systems of corporate governance and finance depend to a large extent on equity financing and the widely dispersed ownership of shares traded in highly liquid markets. The German and Japanese systems have relied more on debt financing, interlocking stock ownership, banker/directors, and worker/shareholder rights.

Variety of Ownership Interests

In every corporation one class of stock must represent the basic ownership interest. That class is called common stock. **Common stock** is the residual corporate interest that bears the ultimate risks of loss and receives the benefits of success. It is guaranteed neither dividends nor assets upon dissolution. But common stockholders generally control the management of the corporation and tend to profit most if the company is successful. In the event that a corporation has only one authorized issue of capital stock, that issue is by definition common stock, whether so designated in the charter or not.

In an effort to appeal to all types of investors, corporations may offer two or more classes of stock, each with different rights or privileges. The preceding section pointed out that each share of stock of a given issue has the same rights as other shares of the same issue and that there are four rights inherent in every share. By special stock contracts between the corporation and its stockholders, certain of these rights may be sacrificed by the stockholder in return for other special rights or privileges. Thus special classes of stock are created. Because they have certain preferential rights, they are usually called **preferred stock**. In return for any special preference, the preferred stockholder is always called on to sacrifice some of the inherent rights of capital stock interests.

A common type of preference is to give the preferred stockholders a prior claim on earnings. They are assured a dividend, usually at a stated rate, before any amount may be distributed to the common stockholders. In return for this preference the preferred stock may sacrifice its right to a voice in management or its right to share in profits beyond the stated rate.

WHAT DO THE NUMBERS MEAN?

CLASSY STOCK

Some companies grant preferences to different shareholders by issuing different classes of common stock. And sometimes these different classes of shares trade at dramatically different prices. For example, **Molex** has issued both common shares and Class A common stock, with the common shares trading at up to a 15 percent premium over the Class A shares. Why the difference in price? The most common explanation is voting rights. In the Molex case, the common shareholders get one vote per share; Class A shares don't get to vote.

For most retail investors, voting rights are not that important. But for family-controlled companies, issuing newer classes of lower or non-voting stock is an effective way to create currency for acquisitions, increase liquidity, or put a public value on the company without diluting the family's voting control. Thus, investors must be careful when comparing the apparent bargain prices for some classes of stock—they may end up as second-class citizens with no voting rights.

Source: Adapted from Lauren Rublin, "Separate but Equal," *Barons On-Line* (August 16, 1999).

CORPORATE CAPITAL

Owner's equity in a corporation is defined as stockholders' equity, shareholders' equity, or corporate capital. The following three categories normally appear as part of stockholders' equity:

1. Capital stock.
2. Additional paid-in capital.
3. Retained earnings.

OBJECTIVE 2 Explain the key components of stockholders' equity.

The first two categories, capital stock and additional paid-in capital, constitute contributed (paid-in) capital. **Retained earnings** represents the earned capital of the enterprise. **Contributed capital (paid-in capital)** is the total amount paid in on capital stock—the amount provided by stockholders to the corporation for use in the business. Contributed capital includes items such as the par value of all outstanding stock and premiums less discounts on issuance. **Earned capital** is the capital that develops if the business operates profitably; it consists of all undistributed income that remains invested in the enterprise.

Stockholders' equity is the difference between the assets and the liabilities of the enterprise. **Therefore, the owners' or stockholders' interest in a business enterprise is a residual interest.**[2] **Stockholders' (owners') equity** represents the cumulative net contributions by stockholders plus earnings that have been retained. As a residual interest, stockholders' equity has no existence apart from the assets and liabilities of the enterprise—stockholders' equity equals net assets. Stockholders' equity is not a claim to specific assets but a claim against a portion of the total assets. Its amount is not specified or fixed; it depends on the enterprise's profitability. Stockholders' equity grows if the enterprise is profitable. It shrinks, or may disappear entirely, if the enterprise is unprofitable.

Issuance of Stock

OBJECTIVE 3 Explain the accounting procedures for issuing shares of stock.

In issuing stock, the following procedures are followed: First, the stock must be authorized by the state, generally in a certificate of incorporation or charter. Next, shares are offered for sale, and contracts to sell stock are entered into. Then, amounts to be received for the stock are collected and the shares issued.

The accounting problems involved in the issuance of stock are discussed under the following topics.

1. Accounting for par value stock.
2. Accounting for no-par stock.
3. Accounting for stock issued in combination with other securities (lump-sum sales).
4. Accounting for stock issued in noncash transactions.
5. Accounting for costs of issuing stock.

Par Value Stock

The par value of a stock has no relationship to its fair market value. At present, the par value associated with most capital stock issuances is very low ($1, $5, $10), Such values contrast dramatically with the situation in the early 1900s, when practically all stock issued had a par value of $100. The reason for this change is to permit the original sale

[2] "Elements of Financial Statements," *Statement of Financial Accounting Concepts No. 6* (Stamford, Conn.: FASB, 1985), par. 60.

of stock at low amounts per share and to avoid the contingent liability associated with stock sold below par.[3]

To show the required information for issuance of par value stock, accounts must be kept for each class of stock as follows.

1. ***Preferred Stock or Common Stock.*** Reflects the par value of the corporation's issued shares. These accounts are credited when the shares are originally issued. No additional entries are made in these accounts unless additional shares are issued or shares are retired.
2. ***Paid-in Capital in Excess of Par or Additional Paid-in Capital.*** Indicates any excess over par value paid in by stockholders in return for the shares issued to them. Once paid in, the excess over par becomes a part of the corporation's additional paid-in capital, and the individual stockholder has no greater claim on the excess paid in than all other holders of the same class of shares.

No entry is generally made in the general ledger accounts at the time the corporation receives its stock authorization from the state of incorporation.

No-Par Stock

Many states permit the issuance of capital stock without par value. **No-par stock** is shares issued with no per-share amount printed on the stock certificate. The reasons for issuance of no-par stock are twofold: First, issuance of no-par stock **avoids the contingent liability** that might occur if par value stock were issued at a discount. Second, some confusion exists over the relationship (or rather the absence of a relationship) between the par value and fair market value. If shares have no par value, **the questionable treatment of using par value as a basis for fair value never arises**. This circumstance is particularly advantageous whenever stock is issued for property items such as tangible or intangible fixed assets. The major disadvantages of no-par stock are that some states levy a high tax on these issues, and the total may be considered legal capital.

No-par shares, like par value shares, are sold for whatever price they will bring, but unlike par value shares, they are issued without a premium or a discount. The exact amount received represents the credit to common or preferred stock. For example, Video Electronics Corporation is organized with authorized common stock of 10,000 shares without par value. No entry, other than a memorandum entry, need be made for the authorization, inasmuch as no amount is involved. If 500 shares are then issued for cash at $10 per share, the entry would be:

Cash	5,000	
Common Stock—No-Par Value		5,000

If another 500 shares are issued for $11 per share, the entry would be:

Cash	5,500	
Common Stock—No-Par Value		5,500

True no-par stock should be carried in the accounts at issue price without any complications due to additional paid-in capital or discount. But some states permit the issuance of no-par stock and then either require or, in some cases, permit such stock to have a **stated value**, that is, a minimum value below which it cannot be issued. Thus, instead of becoming no-par stock, it becomes, in effect, stock with a very low par value, open to all the criticism and abuses that first encouraged the development of no-par stock.[4]

---

[3]Stock with a low par value is rarely, if ever, issued below par value. If stock is issued below par, the discount is recorded as a debit to Additional Paid-in Capital. In addition, the original purchaser or the current holder of the shares issued below par may be called on to pay in the amount of the discount to prevent creditors from sustaining a loss upon liquidation of the corporation.

[4]*Accounting Trends and Techniques—2001* indicates that its 600 surveyed companies reported 644 issues of outstanding common stock, 580 par value issues, and 57 no-par issues; 7 of the no-par issues were shown at their stated (assigned) values.

If no-par stock is required to have a minimum issue price of $5 per share and no provision is made as to how amounts in excess of $5 per share are to be handled, the board of directors usually declares all such amounts to be additional paid-in capital, which in many states is fully or partially available for dividends. Thus, no-par value stock with either a minimum stated value or a stated value assigned by the board of directors permits a new corporation to commence its operations with additional paid-in capital that may be in excess of its stated capital. For example, if 1,000 of the shares with a $5 stated value were issued at $15 per share for cash, the entry could be either of the following:

Cash	15,000	
Common Stock		15,000

or

Cash	15,000	
Common Stock		5,000
Paid-in Capital in Excess of Stated Value		10,000

In most instances the obvious advantages to the corporation of setting up an initial Additional Paid-in Capital account will influence the board of directors to require the latter entry. Whether for this or for other reasons, the prevailing tendency is to account for no-par stock with stated value as if it were par value stock with par equal to the stated value.

Stock Issued with Other Securities (Lump-Sum Sales)

Generally, corporations sell classes of stock separately from one another so that the proceeds relative to each class, and ordinarily even relative to each lot, are known. Occasionally, two or more classes of securities are issued for a single payment or lump sum. It is not uncommon, for example, for more than one type or class of security to be issued in the acquisition of another company. The accounting problem in such **lump-sum sales** is the allocation of the proceeds among the several classes of securities. The two methods of allocation available are (1) the proportional method and (2) the incremental method.

Proportional Method. If the fair market value or other sound basis for determining relative value is available for each class of security, **the lump sum received is allocated among the classes of securities on a proportional basis**—that is, the ratio that each is to the total. For instance, if 1,000 shares of $10 stated value common stock having a market value of $20 a share and 1,000 shares of $10 par value preferred stock having a market value of $12 a share are issued for a lump sum of $30,000, the allocation of the $30,000 to the two classes would be as shown in Illustration 15-1.

ILLUSTRATION 15-1
Allocation in Lump-Sum Securities Issuance—Proportional Method

Fair market value of common (1,000 × $20) =	$20,000
Fair market value of preferred (1,000 × $12) =	12,000
Aggregate fair market value	$32,000
Allocated to common: $\frac{\$20,000}{\$32,000} \times \$30,000$ =	$18,750
Allocated to preferred: $\frac{\$12,000}{\$32,000} \times \$30,000$ =	11,250
Total allocation	$30,000

Incremental Method. In instances where the fair market value of all classes of securities is not determinable, the incremental method may be used. The market value of the securities is used as a basis for those classes that are known, and the remainder of the lump sum is allocated to the class for which the market value is not known. For instance, if 1,000 shares of $10 stated value common stock having a market value of $20 and 1,000 shares of $10 par value preferred stock having no established market value are issued for a lump sum of $30,000, the allocation of the $30,000 to the two classes would be as follows.

ILLUSTRATION 15-2
Allocation in Lump-Sum Securities Issuance—Incremental Method

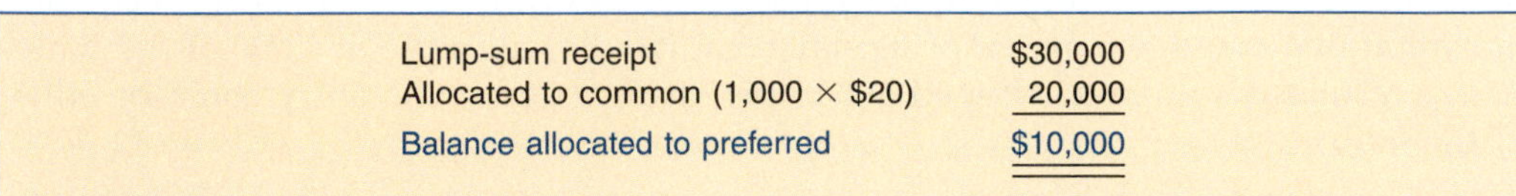

Lump-sum receipt	$30,000
Allocated to common (1,000 × $20)	20,000
Balance allocated to preferred	$10,000

If no fair value is determinable for any of the classes of stock involved in a lump-sum exchange, the allocation may have to be arbitrary. An expert's appraisal may be used. Or, if it is known that one or more of the classes of securities issued will have a determinable market value in the near future, the arbitrary basis may be used with the intent to make an adjustment when the future market value is established.

Stock Issued in Noncash Transactions

Accounting for the issuance of shares of stock for property or services involves an issue of valuation. **The general rule is: Stock issued for services or property other than cash should be recorded at either the fair value of the stock issued or the fair value of the noncash consideration received, whichever is more clearly determinable.**

If both are readily determinable and the transaction is the result of an arm's-length exchange, there will probably be little difference in their fair values. In such cases it should not matter which value is regarded as the basis for valuing the exchange.

If the fair value of the stock being issued and the property or services being received are not readily determinable, the value to be assigned is generally established by the board of directors or management at an amount that they consider fair and that is not controverted by available evidence. Independent appraisals usually serve as dependable bases. The use of the book, par, or stated values as a basis of valuation for these transactions should be avoided.

Unissued stock or treasury stock (issued shares that have been reacquired but not retired) may be exchanged for the property or services. If treasury shares are used, their cost should not be regarded as the decisive factor in establishing the fair value of the property or services. Instead, the fair value of the treasury stock, if known, should be used to value the property or services. If the fair value of the treasury stock is not known, the fair value of the property or services should be used, if determinable.

The following series of transactions illustrates the procedure for recording the issuance of 10,000 shares of $10 par value common stock for a patent, in various circumstances.

1. The fair value of the patent is not readily determinable, but the fair value of the stock is known to be $140,000.

Patent	140,000	
Common Stock (10,000 shares × $10 per share)		100,000
Paid-in Capital in Excess of Par		40,000

2. The fair value of the stock is not readily determinable, but the fair value of the patent is determined to be $150,000.

Patent	150,000	
Common Stock (10,000 shares × $10 per share)		100,000
Paid-in Capital in Excess of Par		50,000

3. Neither the fair value of the stock nor the fair value of the patent is readily determinable. An independent consultant values the patent at $125,000, and the board of directors agrees with that valuation.

Patent	125,000	
Common Stock (10,000 shares × $10 share)		100,000
Paid-in Capital in Excess of Par		25,000

In corporate law, the board of directors is granted the power to set the value of noncash transactions. This power has been abused. The issuance of stock for property or services has resulted in cases of overstated corporate capital through intentional overvaluation of the property or services received. The overvaluation of the stockholders' equity resulting from inflated asset values creates what is referred to as **watered stock.** The "water" can be eliminated from the corporate structure by simply writing down the overvalued assets.

If as a result of the issuance of stock for property or services the recorded assets are undervalued, **secret reserves** are created. An understated corporate structure or secret reserve may also be achieved by other methods: excessive depreciation or amortization charges, expensing capital expenditures, excessive write-downs of inventories or receivables, or any other understatement of assets or overstatement of liabilities. An example of a liability overstatement is an excessive provision for estimated product warranties that ultimately results in an understatement of owners' equity, thereby creating a secret reserve.

Costs of Issuing Stock

Direct costs incurred to sell stock, such as underwriting costs, accounting and legal fees, printing costs, and taxes, should be reported as a reduction of the amounts paid in. Issue costs are therefore debited to Additional Paid-in Capital because they are unrelated to corporate operations. In effect, **issue costs are a cost of financing** and should reduce the proceeds received from the sale of the stock.

Management salaries and other indirect costs related to the stock issue should be expensed as incurred because it is difficult to establish a relationship between these costs and the proceeds received upon sale. In addition, corporations annually incur costs for maintaining the stockholders' records and handling ownership transfers. These recurring costs, primarily registrar and transfer agents' fees, are normally charged to expense in the period in which incurred.

THE CASE OF THE DISAPPEARING RECEIVABLE

WHAT DO THE NUMBERS MEAN?

Sometimes companies issue stock but do not receive any cash in return. As a result, a company records a receivable. Controversy exists regarding the presentation of this receivable on the balance sheet. Some argue that the receivable should be reported as an asset similar to other receivables. Others argue that the receivable should be reported as a deduction from stockholders' equity (similar to the treatment of treasury stock). The SEC settled this issue: It requires companies to use the contra-equity approach because the risk of collection in this type of transaction is often very high.

Unfortunately this accounting issue surfaced in examining **Enron**'s accounting. Starting in early 2000, Enron issued shares of its common stock to four "special-purpose entities" in exchange for which it received a note receivable. Enron then increased its assets (recording a receivable) and stockholders' equity, a move the company now calls an accounting error. As a result, Enron's 2000 audited financial statements overstated assets and stockholders' equity by $172 million. And Enron's 2001 unaudited statements overstated them by $828 million. The $1 billion overstatement is 8.5 percent of Enron's previously reported stockholders' equity as of June 30. As Lynn Turner, former chief accountant of the SEC, noted, "It is a basic accounting principle that you don't record equity until you get cash, and a note doesn't count as cash." Situations like this led investors, creditors, and suppliers to lose faith in the creditability of Enron, which eventually caused its bankruptcy.

Source: Adapted from Jonathan Weil, "Basic Accounting Tripped Up Enron—Financial Statements Didn't Add Up—Auditors Overlook a Simple Rule," *Wall Street Journal* (November 11, 2001), p. C1.

Reacquisition of Shares

OBJECTIVE 4
Explain the accounting for treasury stock.

It is not unusual for companies to buy back their own shares. In fact, share buybacks now exceed dividends as a form of distribution to stockholders.[5] **Merrill Lynch & Co.** estimated that in a recent year more than 1,400 corporations announced buyback programs totaling over $80 billion and 2.4 billion shares. Two of the biggest stock buyback programs were **General Motors**' purchase of 20 percent (64 million shares) of its stock for $4.8 billion, and **Santa Fe Southern Pacific**'s buyback of 38 percent (60 million shares) of its stock for $3.4 billion in the mid-1990s. Data on recent corporate buybacks indicate that companies are continuing to spend millions of dollars to repurchase shares. For example, during one week in 2001, over 70 companies announced buybacks of as much as $12 billion of their own shares. As a result of buybacks, **Boeing** reduced its shares outstanding by 11 percent, and outstanding shares of **Rex Stores** declined by 24 percent during 2001.

The reasons corporations purchase their outstanding stock are varied. Some major reasons are:

1. ***To provide tax efficient distributions of excess cash to shareholders.*** Capital gain rates on sales of stock to the company by the stockholders are approximately half of what ordinary tax rates are. As a result, most stockholders will pay less tax if they receive cash in a buyback versus receiving a cash dividend.
2. ***To increase earnings per share and return on equity.*** By reducing shares outstanding and by reducing stockholders' equity, certain performance ratios often are enhanced.
3. ***To provide stock for employee stock compensation contracts or to meet potential merger needs.*** **Honeywell Inc.** reported that part of its purchase of one million common shares was to be used for employee stock option contracts. Other companies acquire shares to have them available for business acquisitions.
4. ***To thwart takeover attempts or to reduce the number of stockholders.*** By reducing the number of shares held by the public, existing owners and managements can keep "outsiders" from gaining control or significant influence. When Ted Turner attempted to acquire **CBS**, CBS started a substantial buyback of its stock. Stock purchases may also be used to eliminate dissident stockholders.
5. ***To make a market in the stock.*** As one company executive noted, "Our company is trying to establish a floor for the stock." By purchasing stock in the marketplace, a demand is created which may stabilize the stock price or, in fact, increase it.

Some publicly held corporations have chosen to "go private," that is, to eliminate public (outside) ownership entirely by purchasing all of their outstanding stock. Such a procedure is often accomplished through a **leveraged buyout (LBO)**, as discussed in Chapter 14.

Once shares are reacquired, they may either be retired or held in the treasury for reissue. If not retired, such shares are referred to as **treasury shares** or **treasury stock**. Technically, treasury stock is a corporation's own stock that has been reacquired after having been issued and fully paid.

UNDERLYING CONCEPTS

As indicated in Chapter 2, an asset should have probable future economic benefits. Treasury stock simply reduces common stock outstanding.

Treasury stock is not an asset. When treasury stock is purchased, a reduction occurs in both assets and stockholders' equity. It is inappropriate to imply that a corporation can own a part of itself. Treasury stock may be sold to obtain funds, but that possibility does not make treasury stock a balance sheet asset. When a corporation buys back some of its own outstanding stock, it has reduced its capitalization, but it has not

[5] At the beginning of the 1990s the situation was just the opposite—that is, share buybacks were less than half the level of dividends. Companies are extremely reluctant to reduce or eliminate their dividends, because they believe that this action would be viewed negatively by the market. On the other hand, many companies are no longer raising their dividends per share at the same percentage rate as increases in earnings per share, thus effectively reducing the dividend payout over time.

acquired an asset. The possession of treasury stock does not give the corporation the right to vote, to exercise preemptive rights as a stockholder, to receive cash dividends, or to receive assets upon corporate liquidation. **Treasury stock is essentially the same as unissued capital stock**, and no one advocates classifying unissued capital stock as an asset in the balance sheet.[6]

SIGNALS TO BUY?

WHAT DO THE NUMBERS MEAN?

Market analysts sometimes look to stock buybacks as a buy signal for a stock. That strategy is not that surprising if you look at the performance of companies that did buybacks. For example, in one study, buyback companies outperformed similar companies without buybacks by an average of 23 percent. In 2001, companies followed by **Buybackletter.com** over a 3-year period were up 16.4 percent, while the S&P 500 Stock Index was up just 7.1 percent in that period. Why the premium? Well, the conventional wisdom is that companies who buy back shares believe their shares are undervalued. Thus, the buyback announcement is viewed as an important piece of inside information about future company prospects.

One warning for traders following buybacks: Research shows that the biggest market gains accrue to companies that report the biggest reduction in shares outstanding following the buyback. Thus, you want to be certain that an announced buyback actually results in a net reduction in shares outstanding. For example, when companies, such as **Microsoft**, bought back shares to meet share demands for stock option exercises, net shares outstanding actually increased, when the repurchased shares were reissued to the option holders upon exercise. In this case the buyback was not a signal to buy, but an indication that share ownership in the buyback company will be further diluted.

Source: Adapted from Ann Tergesen, "When Buybacks Are Signals to Buy," *Business Week Online* (October 1, 2001).

Purchase of Treasury Stock

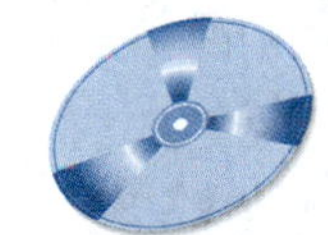

Discussion of Using Par or Stated Value for Treasury Stock Transactions

Two general methods of handling treasury stock in the accounts are the cost method and the par value method. Both methods are generally acceptable. The **cost method** enjoys more widespread use.[7] It results in debiting the Treasury Stock account for the reacquisition cost and in reporting this account as a deduction from the total paid-in capital **and** retained earnings on the balance sheet. The **par** or **stated value method** records all transactions in treasury shares at their par value and reports the treasury stock as a deduction from capital stock only. No matter which method is used, the cost of the treasury shares acquired is considered a restriction on retained earnings in most states.

The cost method is generally used in accounting for treasury stock. This method derives its name from the fact that the Treasury Stock account is maintained at the cost of the shares purchased.[8] Under the cost method, the Treasury Stock account is

[6]The possible justification for classifying these shares as assets is that they will be used to liquidate a specific liability that appears on the balance sheet. *Accounting Trends and Techniques—2001* reported that out of 600 companies surveyed, 410 disclosed treasury stock, but none classified it as an asset.

[7]*Accounting Trends and Techniques—2001* indicates that of its selected list of 600 companies, 384 carried common stock in treasury at cost and only 23 at par or stated value; 3 companies carried preferred stock in treasury at cost and 1 at par or stated value.

[8]If numerous acquisitions of blocks of treasury shares are made at different prices, inventory costing methods—such as specific identification, average, or FIFO—may be used to identify the cost at date of reissuance.

debited for the cost of the shares acquired and upon reissuance of the shares is credited for this same cost. The price received for the stock when it was originally issued does not affect the entries to record the acquisition and reissuance of the treasury stock.

To illustrate, assume that Ho Company has issued 100,000 shares of $1 par value common stock at a price of $10 per share. In addition, it has retained earnings of $300,000. The stockholders' equity section on December 31, 2003, before purchase of treasury stock is as follows.

ILLUSTRATION 15-3
Stockholders' Equity with No Treasury Stock

Stockholders' equity	
Paid-in capital	
Common stock, $1 par value, 100,000 shares issued and outstanding	$ 100,000
Additional paid-in capital	900,000
Total paid-in capital	1,000,000
Retained earnings	300,000
Total stockholders' equity	$1,300,000

On January 20, 2004, Ho Company acquires 10,000 shares of its stock at $11 per share. The entry to record the reacquisition is:

January 20, 2004		
Treasury Stock	110,000	
Cash		110,000

Note that Treasury Stock is debited for the cost of the shares purchased. The original paid-in capital account, Common Stock, is not affected because the number of issued shares does not change. The same is true for the Additional Paid-in Capital account. Treasury stock is deducted from total paid-in capital and retained earnings in the stockholders' equity section.

The stockholders' equity section for Ho Company after purchase of the treasury stock is as follows.

ILLUSTRATION 15-4
Stockholders' Equity with Treasury Stock

Stockholders' equity	
Paid-in capital	
Common stock, $1 par value, 100,000 shares issued and 90,000 outstanding	$ 100,000
Additional paid-in capital	900,000
Total paid-in capital	1,000,000
Retained earnings	300,000
Total paid-in capital and retained earnings	1,300,000
Less: Cost of treasury stock (10,000 shares)	110,000
Total stockholders' equity	$1,190,000

The cost of the treasury stock is subtracted from the total of common stock, additional paid-in capital, and retained earnings. It therefore reduces stockholders' equity. Many states require a corporation to restrict retained earnings for the cost of treasury stock purchased. The restriction serves to keep intact the corporation's legal capital that is temporarily being held as treasury stock. When treasury stock is sold, the restriction is lifted.

Both the number of shares issued (100,000) and the number in the treasury (10,000) are disclosed. The difference is the number of shares of stock outstanding (90,000). The term **outstanding stock** means the number of shares of issued stock that are being held by stockholders.

Sale of Treasury Stock

Treasury stock is usually sold or retired. When treasury shares are sold, the accounting for the sale depends on the price. If the selling price of the treasury stock is equal to cost, the sale of the shares is recorded by a debit to Cash and a credit to Treasury Stock. In cases where the selling price of the treasury stock is not equal to cost, then accounting for treasury stock sold **above cost** differs from the accounting for treasury stock sold **below cost**. However, the sale of treasury stock either above or below cost increases both total assets and stockholders' equity.

Sale of Treasury Stock Above Cost. When the selling price of shares of treasury stock is greater than cost, the difference is credited to Paid-in Capital from Treasury Stock. To illustrate, assume that 1,000 shares of treasury stock of Ho Company previously acquired at $11 per share are sold at $15 per share on March 10. The entry is as follows.

March 10, 2004

Cash	15,000	
Treasury Stock		11,000
Paid-in Capital from Treasury Stock		4,000

There are two reasons why the $4,000 credit in the entry would not be made to Gain on Sale of Treasury Stock: (1) Gains on sales occur when **assets** are sold, and treasury stock is not an asset. (2) A corporation does not realize a gain or suffer a loss from stock transactions with its own stockholders. Thus, paid-in capital arising from the sale of treasury stock should not be included in the measurement of net income. Paid-in capital from treasury stock is listed separately on the balance sheet as a part of paid-in capital.

Sale of Treasury Stock Below Cost. When treasury stock is sold below its cost, the excess of the cost over selling price is usually debited to Paid-in Capital from Treasury Stock. Thus, if Ho Company sells an additional 1,000 shares of treasury stock on March 21 at $8 per share, the entry is as follows.

March 21, 2004

Cash	8,000	
Paid-in Capital from Treasury Stock	3,000	
Treasury Stock		11,000

Observe from the two sale entries (sale above cost and sale below cost) that (1) Treasury Stock is credited at cost in each entry, (2) Paid-in Capital from Treasury Stock is used for the difference between the cost and the resale price of the shares, and (3) the original paid-in capital account, Common Stock, is not affected.

When the credit balance in Paid-in Capital from Treasury Stock is eliminated, any additional excess of cost over selling price is debited to Retained Earnings. To illustrate, assume that Ho Company sells an additional 1,000 shares at $8 per share on April 10. The balance in the Paid-in Capital from Treasury Stock account is:

ILLUSTRATION 15-5
Treasury Stock Transactions in Paid-in Capital Account

Paid-in Capital from Treasury Stock

Mar. 21	3,000	Mar. 10	4,000
		Balance	1,000

In this case, $1,000 of the excess is debited to Paid-in Capital from Treasury Stock, and the remainder is debited to Retained Earnings. The entry is:

April 10, 2004

Cash	8,000	
Paid-in Capital from Treasury Stock	1,000	
Retained Earnings	2,000	
Treasury Stock		11,000

Retiring Treasury Stock

The board of directors may approve the retirement of treasury shares. This decision results in cancellation of the treasury stock and a reduction in the number of shares of issued stock. Retired treasury shares have the status of authorized and unissued shares. The accounting effects are similar to the sale of treasury stock except that debits are made to the **paid-in capital accounts applicable to the retired shares** instead of to cash. For example, if the shares are originally sold at par, Common Stock is debited for the par value per share. If the shares are originally sold at $3 above par value, a debit to Paid-in Capital in Excess of Par Value for $3 per share is also required.

PREFERRED STOCK

OBJECTIVE 5
Explain the accounting for and reporting of preferred stock.

Preferred stock is a special class of shares that is designated "preferred" because it possesses certain preferences or features not possessed by the common stock.[9] The following features are those most often associated with preferred stock issues.

1. Preference as to dividends.
2. Preference as to assets in the event of liquidation.
3. Convertible into common stock.
4. Callable at the option of the corporation.
5. Nonvoting.

The features that distinguish preferred from common stock may be of a more restrictive and negative nature than preferences. For example, the preferred stock may be nonvoting, noncumulative, and nonparticipating.

Preferred stock is usually issued with a par value, and the dividend preference is expressed as a **percentage of the par value**. Thus, holders of 8 percent preferred stock with a $100 par value are entitled to an annual dividend of $8 per share. This stock is commonly referred to as 8 percent preferred stock. In the case of no-par preferred stock, a dividend preference is expressed as a **specific dollar amount** per share, for example, $7 per share. This stock is commonly referred to as $7 preferred stock.

A preference as to dividends is not assurance that dividends will be paid. It is merely assurance that the stated dividend rate or amount applicable to the preferred stock must be paid before any dividends can be paid on the common stock.

Features of Preferred Stock

A corporation may attach whatever preferences or restrictions in whatever combination it desires to a preferred stock issue, so long as it does not specifically violate its state incorporation law. Also, it may issue more than one class of preferred stock. The most common features attributed to preferred stock are discussed below.

1. ***Cumulative Preferred Stock.*** Dividends not paid in any year must be made up in a later year before any profits can be distributed to common stockholders. If the directors fail to declare a dividend at the normal date for dividend action, the dividend is said to have been "passed." Any passed dividend on cumulative preferred stock constitutes a **dividend in arrears**. Because no liability exists until the board

[9]*Accounting Trends and Techniques—2001* reports that of its 600 surveyed companies, 86 had preferred stock outstanding, 71 had one class of preferred, and 10 had two classes.

of directors declares a dividend, a dividend in arrears is not recorded as a liability but is disclosed in a note to the financial statements. Noncumulative preferred stock is seldom issued because a passed dividend is lost forever to the preferred stockholder, and so this stock issue would be less marketable.

2. ***Participating Preferred Stock.*** Holders of participating preferred stock share ratably with the common stockholders in any profit distributions beyond the prescribed rate. That is, 5 percent preferred stock, if fully participating, will receive not only its 5 percent return, but also dividends at the same rates as those paid to common stockholders if amounts in excess of 5 percent of par or stated value are paid to common stockholders. Also, participating preferred stock may not always be fully participating, but may be partially participating. Although participating preferreds are not used extensively (unlike the cumulative provision), examples of companies that have used participating preferreds are **Southern California Edison** and **Allied Products Corporation**.

3. ***Convertible Preferred Stock.*** The stockholders may at their option exchange preferred shares for common stock at a predetermined ratio. The convertible preferred stockholder not only enjoys a preferred claim on dividends but also has the option of converting into a common stockholder with unlimited participation in earnings.

4. ***Callable Preferred Stock.*** The issuing corporation at its option can call or redeem the outstanding preferred shares at specified future dates and at stipulated prices. Many preferred issues are callable. The call or redemption price is ordinarily set slightly above the original issuance price and is commonly stated in terms related to the par value. The callable feature permits the corporation to use the capital obtained through the issuance of such stock until the need has passed or it is no longer advantageous. The existence of a call price or prices tends to set a ceiling on the market value of the preferred shares unless they are convertible into common stock. When a preferred stock is called for redemption, any dividends in arrears must be paid.

Preferred stock is often issued (instead of debt) because a company's debt-to-equity ratio has become too high. In other instances, issuances are made through private placements with other corporations at a lower-than-market dividend rate because the acquiring corporation receives dividends that are largely tax free (owing to the IRS's 70 percent or 80 percent dividends received deduction).[10]

Accounting for and Reporting Preferred Stock

The accounting for preferred stock at issuance is similar to that for common stock, with proceeds allocated between the par value of the preferred stock and additional paid-in capital. To illustrate, assume that Bishop Co. issues 10,000 shares of $10 par value preferred stock for $12 cash per share. The entry to record the issuance is:

Cash	120,000	
Preferred Stock		100,000
Paid-in Capital in Excess of Par		20,000

Thus, separate accounts are maintained for these different classes of shares.

Preferred stock generally has no maturity date, and therefore no legal obligation exists to pay the preferred stockholder. As a result, preferred stock is classified as part

[10]Recently, more and more issuances of preferred stock have features that make the security more like debt (legal obligation to pay) than an equity instrument. For example, **redeemable preferred stock** is preferred stock that has a mandatory redemption period or a redemption feature that is outside the control of the issuer. Under current accounting standards, most companies report redeemable preferred stock between debt and equity classifications (the so-called **mezzanine**). Under a recent standard, "Accounting for Certain Financial Liabilities with Characteristics of Liabilities and Equity," *Statement of Financial Accounting Standards No. 149* (Norwalk, Conn.: FASB, 2003), companies are required to report redeemable preferred stock as debt.

of stockholders' equity. Preferred stock is generally reported at par value as the first item in the stockholders' equity section. Any excess over par value is reported as part of additional paid-in capital. Dividends on preferred stock are considered a distribution of income and not an expense of the corporation. Companies must disclose the pertinent rights of the preferred stock outstanding.[11]

DIVIDEND POLICY

OBJECTIVE 6
Describe the policies used in distributing dividends.

Determining the proper amount of dividends to pay is a difficult financial management decision. Companies that are paying dividends are extremely reluctant to reduce or eliminate their dividend, because they believe that this action could be viewed negatively by the securities market. As a consequence, companies that have been paying cash dividends will make every effort to continue to do so. In addition, the type of shareholder the company has (taxable or nontaxable, retail investor or institutional investor) plays a large role in determining dividend policy. For example, a nontaxable entity will probably prefer cash dividends rather than a share buyback because tax considerations are not as important. As indicated earlier, more companies are becoming involved in share buyback programs and are either not starting or not increasing their present dividend program significantly.

Very few companies pay dividends in amounts equal to their legally available retained earnings. The major reasons are as follows.

1. Agreements (bond covenants) with specific creditors to retain all or a portion of the earnings, in the form of assets, to build up additional protection against possible loss.
2. Some state corporation laws require that earnings equivalent to the cost of treasury shares purchased be restricted against dividend declarations.
3. Desire to retain assets that would otherwise be paid out as dividends, to finance growth or expansion. This is sometimes called internal financing, reinvesting earnings, or "plowing" the profits back into the business.
4. Desire to smooth out dividend payments from year to year by accumulating earnings in good years and using such accumulated earnings as a basis for dividends in bad years.
5. Desire to build up a cushion or buffer against possible losses or errors in the calculation of profits.

The reasons above are probably self-explanatory except for the second. The laws of some states require that the corporation's legal capital be restricted from distribution to stockholders so that it may serve as a protection against loss for creditors.[12] The legality of a dividend can be determined only by reviewing the applicable state law.

Financial Condition and Dividend Distributions

Good management of a business requires attention to more than the legality of dividend distributions. Consideration must be given to economic conditions, most importantly, liquidity. Assume an extreme situation as shown on the next page.

[11]"Disclosure of Information about Capital Structure," *Statement of Financial Accounting Standards No. 129* (Norwalk, Conn.: FASB, 1997).

[12]If the corporation buys its own outstanding stock, it has reduced its legal capital and distributed assets to stockholders. If this were permitted, the corporation could, by purchasing treasury stock at any price desired, return to the stockholders their investments and leave creditors with little or no protection against loss.

ILLUSTRATION 15-6
Balance Sheet, Showing a Lack of Liquidity

BALANCE SHEET

Plant assets	$500,000	Capital stock	$400,000
		Retained earnings	100,000
	$500,000		$500,000

The depicted company has a retained earnings credit balance and generally, unless it is restricted, can declare a dividend of $100,000. But because all its assets are plant assets and used in operations, payment of a cash dividend of $100,000 would require the sale of plant assets or borrowing.

Even if we assume a balance sheet showing current assets, as shown below, the question remains as to whether those cash assets are needed for other purposes.

ILLUSTRATION 15-7
Balance Sheet, Showing Cash but Minimal Working Capital

BALANCE SHEET

Cash	$100,000	Current liabilities		$ 60,000
Plant assets	460,000	Capital stock	$400,000	
	$560,000	Retained earnings	100,000	500,000
				$560,000

The existence of current liabilities implies very strongly that some of the cash is needed to meet current debts as they mature. In addition, day-by-day cash requirements for payrolls and other expenditures not included in current liabilities also require cash.

Thus, before a dividend is declared, management must consider **availability of funds to pay the dividend**. Other demands for cash should perhaps be investigated by preparing a cash forecast. A dividend should not be paid unless both the present and future financial position appear to warrant the distribution.

The SEC encourages companies to disclose their dividend policy in their annual report. Those that (1) have earnings but fail to pay dividends, or (2) do not expect to pay dividends in the forseeable future are encouraged to report this information. In addition, companies that have had a consistent pattern of paying dividends are encouraged to indicate whether they intend to continue this practice in the future.

Types of Dividends

OBJECTIVE 7
Identify the various forms of dividend distributions.

Dividend distributions generally are based either on accumulated profits (that is, retained earnings) or on some other capital item such as additional paid-in capital. The natural expectation of any stockholder who receives a dividend is that the corporation has operated successfully and that he or she is receiving a share of its profits. A **liquidating dividend**—that is, a dividend not based on retained earnings—should be adequately described in the accompanying message to the stockholders so that there will be no misunderstanding about its source. Dividends are of the following types.

1. Cash dividends.
2. Property dividends.
3. Liquidating dividends.
4. Stock dividends.

Dividends are commonly paid in cash but occasionally are paid in stock or some other asset.[13] **All dividends, except for stock dividends, reduce the total stockhold-**

[13] *Accounting Trends and Techniques—2001* reported that of its 600 surveyed companies, 403 paid a cash dividend on common stock, 69 paid a cash dividend on preferred stock, 12 issued stock dividends, and 7 issued or paid dividends in kind. Some companies declare more than one type of dividend in a given year.

ers' equity in the corporation, because the equity is reduced either through an immediate or promised future distribution of assets. When a stock dividend is declared, the corporation does not pay out assets or incur a liability. It issues additional shares of stock to each stockholder and nothing more.

Cash Dividends

The board of directors votes on the declaration of **cash dividends**, and if the resolution is properly approved, the dividend is declared. Before it is paid, a current list of stockholders must be prepared. For this reason there is usually a time lag between declaration and payment. A resolution approved at the January 10 (**date of declaration**) meeting of the board of directors might be declared payable February 5 (**date of payment**) to all stockholders of record January 25 (**date of record**).[14]

In this example, the period from January 10 to January 25 gives time for any transfers in process to be completed and registered with the transfer agent. The time from January 25 to February 5 provides an opportunity for the transfer agent or accounting department, depending on who does this work, to prepare a list of stockholders as of January 25 and to prepare and mail dividend checks.

A declared cash dividend is a liability, and because payment is generally required very soon, is usually a current liability. The following entries are required to record the declaration and payment of an ordinary dividend payable in cash. For example, Roadway Freight Corp. on June 10 declared a cash dividend of 50 cents a share on 1.8 million shares payable July 16 to all stockholders of record June 24.

At date of declaration (June 10)		
Retained Earnings (Cash Dividends Declared)	900,000	
Dividends Payable		900,000
At date of record (June 24)		
No entry		
At date of payment (July 16)		
Dividends Payable	900,000	
Cash		900,000

To set up a ledger account that shows the amount of dividends declared during the year, Cash Dividends Declared might be debited instead of Retained Earnings at the time of declaration. This account is then closed to Retained Earnings at year-end.

INTERNATIONAL INSIGHT

As a less preferred but still allowable treatment, international accounting standards permit firms to reduce equity by the amount of proposed dividends prior to their legal declaration.

Dividends may be declared either as a certain percent of par, such as a 6 percent dividend on preferred stock, or as an amount per share, such as 60 cents per share on no-par common stock. In the first case, the rate is multiplied by the par value of outstanding shares to get the total dividend. In the second, the amount per share is multiplied by the number of shares outstanding. **Cash dividends are not declared and paid on treasury stock.**

Dividend policies vary among corporations. Some older, well-established firms take pride in a long, unbroken string of quarterly dividend payments. They would lower or pass the dividend only if forced to do so by a sustained decline in earnings or a critical shortage of cash.

"Growth" companies, on the other hand, pay little or no cash dividends because their policy is to expand as rapidly as internal and external financing permit. Neither **Quest Medical, Inc.**, a small growth company, nor **Federal Express Corporation**, a large growth company, has ever paid cash dividends to their common stockholders. These investors hope that the price of their shares will appreciate in value and that they will

[14]Theoretically, the ex-dividend date is the day after the date of record. However, to allow time for transfer of the shares, the stock exchanges generally advance the ex-dividend date 2 to 4 days. Therefore, the party who owns the stock on the day prior to the expressed ex-dividend date receives the dividends, and the party who buys the stock on and after the ex-dividend date does not receive the dividend. Between the declaration date and the ex-dividend date, the market price of the stock includes the dividend.

realize a profit when they sell their shares. As indicated earlier, many companies are less concerned with dividend payout, and more focused on increasing share price, stock repurchase programs, and corporate earnings.

Property Dividends

Dividends payable in assets of the corporation other than cash are called **property dividends** or **dividends in kind**. Property dividends may be merchandise, real estate, or investments, or whatever form the board of directors designates. **Ranchers Exploration and Development Corp.** reported one year that it would pay a fourth-quarter dividend in gold bars instead of cash. Because of the obvious difficulties of divisibility of units and delivery to stockholders, the usual property dividend is in the form of securities of other companies that the distributing corporation holds as an investment.

For example, when **DuPont**'s 23 percent stock interest in **General Motors** was held by the Supreme Court to be in violation of antitrust laws, DuPont was ordered to divest itself of the GM stock within 10 years. The stock represented 63 million shares of GM's 281 million shares then outstanding. DuPont couldn't sell the shares in one block of 63 million, nor could it sell 6 million shares annually for the next 10 years without severely depressing the value of the GM stock. At that time the entire yearly trading volume in GM stock did not exceed 6 million shares. DuPont solved its problem by declaring a property dividend and distributing the GM shares as a dividend to its own stockholders.

When the property dividend is declared, the corporation should **restate at fair value the property to be distributed, recognizing any gain or loss** as the difference between the property's fair value and carrying value at date of declaration. The declared dividend may then be recorded as a debit to Retained Earnings (or Property Dividends Declared) and a credit to Property Dividends Payable, at an amount equal to the fair value of the property to be distributed. Upon distribution of the dividend, Property Dividends Payable is debited, and the account containing the distributed asset (restated at fair value) is credited.

For example, Trendler, Inc. transferred to stockholders some of its investments in marketable securities costing $1,250,000 by declaring a property dividend on December 28, 2002, to be distributed on January 30, 2003, to stockholders of record on January 15, 2003. At the date of declaration the securities have a market value of $2,000,000. The entries are as follows.

At date of declaration (December 28, 2002)		
Investments in Securities	750,000	
Gain on Appreciation of Securities		750,000
Retained Earnings (Property Dividends Declared)	2,000,000	
Property Dividends Payable		2,000,000
At date of distribution (January 30, 2003)		
Property Dividends Payable	2,000,000	
Investments in Securities		2,000,000

Liquidating Dividends

Some corporations use paid-in capital as a basis for dividends. Without proper disclosure of this fact, stockholders may erroneously believe the corporation has been operating at a profit. A further result could be subsequent sale of additional shares at a higher price than is warranted. This type of deception, intentional or unintentional, can be avoided by requiring that a clear statement of the source of every dividend accompany the dividend check.

Dividends based on other than retained earnings are sometimes described as **liquidating dividends**, thus implying that they are a return of the stockholder's investment rather than of profits. In other words, **any dividend not based on earnings is a reduction of corporate paid-in capital and to that extent, it is a liquidating dividend**. Companies in the extractive industries may pay dividends equal to the total of accumulated income and depletion. The portion of these dividends in excess of accumulated income represents a return of part of the stockholder's investment.

For example, McChesney Mines Inc. issued a "dividend" to its common stockholders of $1,200,000. The cash dividend announcement noted that $900,000 should be considered income and the remainder a return of capital. The entries are:

At date of declaration		
Retained Earnings	900,000	
Additional Paid-in Capital	300,000	
Dividends Payable		1,200,000
At date of payment		
Dividends Payable	1,200,000	
Cash		1,200,000

In some cases, management may simply decide to cease business and declare a liquidating dividend. In these cases, liquidation may take place over a number of years to ensure an orderly and fair sale of assets. For example, when **Overseas National Airways** was dissolved, it agreed to pay a liquidating dividend to its stockholders over a period of years equivalent to $8.60 per share. Each liquidating dividend payment in such cases reduces paid-in capital.

Stock Dividends

If the management wishes to "capitalize" part of the earnings (i.e., reclassify amounts from earned to contributed capital), and thus retain earnings in the business on a permanent basis, it may issue a stock dividend. In this case, **no assets are distributed**, and each stockholder has exactly the same proportionate interest in the corporation and the same total book value after the stock dividend was issued as before it was declared. Of course, the book value per share is lower because an increased number of shares is held.

A **stock dividend** therefore is the nonreciprocal issuance by a corporation of its own stock to its stockholders on a pro rata basis. In recording a stock dividend, some believe that the **par value** of the stock issued as a dividend should be transferred from retained earnings to capital stock. Others believe that the **fair value** of the stock issued —its market value at the declaration date—should be transferred from retained earnings to capital stock and additional paid-in capital.

If, by requiring fair value, the intent of the CAP was to punish companies that used stock dividends, it violated the neutrality concept (that is, that standards-setting should be even-handed).

The fair value position was originally adopted in this country, at least in part, in order to influence the stock dividend policies of corporations. Evidently in 1941 both the New York Stock Exchange and a majority of the Committee on Accounting Procedure (CAP) regarded periodic stock dividends as objectionable. The CAP therefore acted to make it more difficult for corporations to sustain a series of such stock dividends out of their accumulated earnings, by requiring the use of fair market value when it was substantially in excess of book value.[15]

OBJECTIVE 8
Explain the accounting for small and large stock dividends, and for stock splits.

When the stock dividend is less than 20–25 percent of the common shares outstanding at the time of the dividend declaration, the accounting profession requires that the **fair market value** of the stock issued be transferred from retained earnings. Stock dividends of less than 20–25 percent are often referred to as **small (ordinary) stock dividends**. This method of handling stock dividends is justified on the grounds that "many recipients of stock dividends look upon them as distributions of corporate earnings and usually in an amount equivalent to the fair value of the additional shares

[15]This represented perhaps the earliest instance of an accounting pronouncement being affected by "economic consequences," because the Committee on Accounting Procedure described its action as being required by "proper accounting and corporate policy." See Stephen A. Zeff, "The Rise of 'Economic Consequences,'" *The Journal of Accountancy* (December 1978), pp. 53–66.

received."[16] We do not consider this a convincing argument. It is generally agreed that stock dividends are not income to the recipients, and therefore sound accounting should not recommend procedures simply because some recipients think they are income.

To illustrate a small stock dividend, assume that a corporation has outstanding 1,000 shares of $100 par value capital stock and retained earnings of $50,000. If the corporation declares a 10 percent stock dividend, it issues 100 additional shares to current stockholders. If it is assumed that the fair value of the stock at the time of the stock dividend is $130 per share, the entry is:

At date of declaration

Retained Earnings (Stock Dividend Declared)	13,000	
Common Stock Dividend Distributable		10,000
Paid-in Capital in Excess of Par		3,000

Note that no asset or liability has been affected. The entry merely reflects a reclassification of stockholders' equity. If a balance sheet is prepared between the dates of declaration and distribution, the common stock dividend distributable should be shown in the stockholders' equity section as an addition to capital stock (whereas cash or property dividends payable are shown as current liabilities).

When the stock is issued, the entry is:

At date of distribution

Common Stock Dividend Distributable	10,000	
Common Stock		10,000

No matter what the fair value is at the time of the stock dividend, each stockholder retains the same proportionate interest in the corporation.

Some state statutes specifically prohibit the issuance of stock dividends on treasury stock. In those states that permit treasury shares to participate in the distribution accompanying a stock dividend or stock split, practice is influenced by the planned use of the treasury shares. For example, if the treasury shares are intended for issuance in connection with employee stock options, the treasury shares may participate in the distribution because the number of shares under option is usually adjusted for any stock dividends or splits. But unless there are specific uses for the treasury stock, no useful purpose is served by issuing additional shares to the treasury stock since they are essentially equivalent to authorized but unissued shares.

To continue with our example of the effect of the small stock dividend, note in Illustration 15-8 (on page 744) that the total stockholders' equity has not changed as a result of the stock dividend. Also note that the proportion of the total shares outstanding held by each stockholder is unchanged.

Stock Splits

If a company has undistributed earnings over several years and a sizable balance in retained earnings has accumulated, the market value of its outstanding shares is likely to increase. Stock that was issued at prices less than $50 a share can easily attain a market value in excess of $200 a share. The higher the market price of a stock, the less readily it can be purchased by some investors.

---

[16]American Institute of Certified Public Accountants, *Accounting Research and Terminology Bulletins*, No. 43 (New York: AICPA, 1961), Ch. 7, par. 10. One study concluded that *small* stock dividends do not always produce significant amounts of extra value on the date after issuance (ex date) and that *large* stock dividends almost always fail to generate extra value on the ex-dividend date. Taylor W. Foster III and Don Vickrey, "The Information Content of Stock Dividend Announcements," *The Accounting Review*, Vol. LIII, No. 2 (April 1978), pp. 360–370.

ILLUSTRATION 15-8
Effects of a Small (10%) Stock Dividend

Before dividend	
Capital stock, 1,000 shares of $100 par	$100,000
Retained earnings	50,000
Total stockholders' equity	$150,000
Stockholders' interests:	
A. 400 shares, 40% interest, book value	$ 60,000
B. 500 shares, 50% interest, book value	75,000
C. 100 shares, 10% interest, book value	15,000
	$150,000
After declaration but before distribution of 10% stock dividend	
If fair value ($130) is used as basis for entry:	
Capital stock, 1,000 shares at $100 par	$100,000
Common stock distributable, 100 shares at $100 par	10,000
Paid-in capital in excess of par	3,000
Retained earnings ($50,000 − $13,000)	37,000
Total stockholders' equity	$150,000
After declaration and distribution of 10% stock dividend	
If fair value ($130) is used as basis for entry:	
Capital stock, 1,100 shares at $100 par	$110,000
Paid-in capital in excess of par	3,000
Retained earnings ($50,000 − $13,000)	37,000
Total stockholders' equity	$150,000
Stockholders' interest:	
A. 440 shares, 40% interest, book value	$ 60,000
B. 550 shares, 50% interest, book value	75,000
C. 110 shares, 10% interest, book value	15,000
	$150,000

The managements of many corporations believe that for better public relations, wider ownership of the corporation stock is desirable. They wish, therefore, to have a market price sufficiently low to be within range of the majority of potential investors. To reduce the market value of shares, the common device of a **stock split** is employed. For example, after its stock price increased by 25-fold during 1999, **Qualcomm Inc.** split its stock 4-for-1. Qualcomm's stock had risen above $500 per share, raising concerns that Qualcomm could not meet an analyst target of $1,000 per share. The split reduced the analysts' target to $250, which could better be met with wider distribution of shares at lower trading prices.

From an accounting standpoint, **no entry is recorded for a stock split**. A memorandum note, however, is made to indicate that the par value of the shares has changed, and that the number of shares has increased. The lack of change in stockholders' equity is portrayed in Illustration 15-9 of a 2-for-1 stock split on 1,000 shares of $100 par value stock with the par being halved upon issuance of the additional shares.

ILLUSTRATION 15-9
Effects of a Stock Split

Stockholders' Equity before 2-for-1 Split		Stockholders' Equity after 2-for-1 Split	
Common stock, 1,000 shares at $100 par	$100,000	Common stock, 2,000 shares at $50 par	$100,000
Retained earnings	50,000	Retained earnings	50,000
	$150,000		$150,000

SPLITSVILLE

WHAT DO THE NUMBERS MEAN?

Stock splits were all the rage in the booming stock market of the 1990s. Of major companies on the New York Stock Exchange, fewer than 80 companies split shares in 1990; by 1998, with stock prices soaring, over 200 companies split shares. Although the split does not increase a stockholder's proportionate ownership of the company, studies have shown that split shares usually outperform those that don't split, as well as the market as a whole, for several years after the split. In addition, the splits help the company keep the shares in more attractive price ranges.

What about when the market "turns south"? A number of companies who split their shares in the boom markets of the 1990s have since then seen their share prices decline to the point that they are considered too low. For example, since **Ameritrade**'s 12-for-1 split in 1999, its stock price has declined over 74 percent, so that it was trading around $6 per share in March 2002. And **Lucent** is trading at less than $5 a share following a 4-for-1 split. For some investors, these low price stocks are unattractive because some brokerage commissions are based on the number of shares traded, not the dollar amount. Others are concerned that low-priced shares are easier for would-be scamsters to manipulate.

Some companies are considering reverse stock splits in which, say, 5 shares are consolidated into one. Thus, a stock previously trading at $5 per share would be part of an unsplit share trading at $25. By unsplitting, some of the negative consequences of a low trading price can be avoided. The downside to this strategy is that reverse splits might be viewed as additional bad news about the direction of the stock price. For example, **Webvan**, a failed Internet grocer, did a 1-for-25 reverse split just before it entered bankruptcy.

Source: Adapted from David Henry, "Stocks: The Case for Unsplitting," *BusinessWeek Online* (April 1, 2002).

Stock Split and Stock Dividend Differentiated

From a legal standpoint, a stock split is distinguished from a stock dividend because a stock split results in an increase in the number of shares outstanding and a corresponding decrease in the par or stated value per share. **A stock dividend, although it results in an increase in the number of shares outstanding, does not decrease the par value. Thus it increases the total par value of outstanding shares.**

The reasons for issuing a stock dividend are numerous and varied. Stock dividends can be primarily a publicity gesture, **because they are considered by many as dividends**. Consequently, the corporation is not criticized for retention of profits. More defensible perhaps, the corporation may simply wish to retain profits in the business by capitalizing a part of retained earnings. In such a situation, a transfer is made on declaration of a stock dividend from earned capital to contributed or permanent capital.

A stock dividend, like a stock split, also may be used to increase the marketability of the stock, although marketability is often a secondary consideration. If the stock dividend is large, it has the same effect on market price as a stock split. The profession has taken the position that **whenever additional shares are issued for the purpose of reducing the unit market price, then the distribution more closely resembles a stock split than a stock dividend. This effect usually results only if the number of shares issued is more than 20–25 percent of the number of shares previously outstanding.**[17] A stock dividend of more than 20–25 percent of the number of shares previously

[17]*Accounting Research and Terminology Bulletin No. 43*, par. 13.

outstanding is called a **large stock dividend**.[18] The profession also recommends that such a distribution not be called a stock dividend, but it might properly be called "a split-up effected in the form of a dividend" or "stock split."

Also, since the par value of the outstanding shares is not altered, the transfer from retained earnings is only in the amount required by statute. Ordinarily this means a transfer from retained earnings to capital stock **for the par value of the stock issued**, as opposed to a transfer of the market value of the shares issued as in the case of a small stock dividend.[19] For example, **Brown Group, Inc.** at one time authorized a 2-for-1 split, effected in the form of a stock dividend. As a result of this authorization, approximately 10.5 million shares were distributed, and more than $39 million representing the par value of the shares issued was transferred from Retained Earnings to the Common Stock account.

To illustrate a large stock dividend (stock split-up effected in the form of a dividend), Rockland Steel, Inc. declared a 30 percent stock dividend on November 20, payable December 29 to stockholders of record December 12. At the date of declaration, 1,000,000 shares, par value $10, are outstanding and with a fair market value of $200 per share. The entries are:

At date of declaration (November 20)

Retained Earnings	3,000,000	
Common Stock Dividend Distributable		3,000,000

Computation: 1,000,000 shares × 30% = 300,000; 300,000 Additional shares × $10 Par value = $3,000,000

At date of distribution (December 29)

Common Stock Dividend Distributable	3,000,000	
Common Stock		3,000,000

Illustration 15-10 summarizes and compares the effects of various types of dividends and stock splits on various elements of the financial statements.

ILLUSTRATION 15-10
Effects of Dividends and Stock Splits on Financial Statement Elements

			Declaration and Distribution of		
Effect on:	Declaration of Cash Dividend	Payment of Cash Dividend	Small Stock Dividend	Large Stock Dividend	Stock Split
Retained earnings	Decrease	-0-	Decrease[a]	Decrease[b]	-0-
Capital stock	-0-	-0-	Increase[b]	Increase[b]	-0-
Additional paid-in capital	-0-	-0-	Increase[c]	-0-	-0-
Total stockholders' equity	Decrease	-0-	-0-	-0-	-0-
Working capital	Decrease	-0-	-0-	-0-	-0-
Total assets	-0-	Decrease	-0-	-0-	-0-
Number of shares outstanding	-0-	-0-	Increase	Increase	Increase

[a]Market value of shares. [b]Par or stated value of shares. [c]Excess of market value over par.

INTERNATIONAL INSIGHT

In Switzerland, companies are allowed to create income reserves. That is, they reduce income in years with good profits by allocating it to reserves on the balance sheet. In less profitable years, they are able to reallocate from the reserves to improve income. This "smoothes" income across years.

[18]The SEC has added more precision to the 20–25 percent rule. Specifically, the SEC indicates that distributions of 25 percent or more should be considered a "split-up effected in the form of a dividend." Distributions of less than 25 percent should be accounted for as a stock dividend. The SEC more precisely defined GAAP here, and as a result the SEC rule is followed by public companies.

[19]Often, a split-up effected in the form of a dividend is debited to Paid-in Capital instead of Retained Earnings to indicate that this transaction should affect only paid-in capital accounts. No reduction of retained earnings is required except as indicated by legal requirements. For homework purposes, assume that the debit is to Retained Earnings. See, for example, Taylor W. Foster III and Edmund Scribner, "Accounting for Stock Dividends and Stock Splits: Corrections to Textbook Coverage," *Issues in Accounting Education* (February 1998).

Disclosure of Restrictions on Retained Earnings

In many corporations restrictions on retained earnings or dividends exist, but no formal journal entries are made. Such restrictions are **best disclosed by note**. Parenthetical notations are sometimes used, but restrictions imposed by bond indentures and loan agreements commonly require an extended explanation. Notes provide a medium for more complete explanations and free the financial statements from abbreviated notations. The note disclosure should reveal the source of the restriction, pertinent provisions, and the amount of retained earnings subject to restriction, or the amount not restricted.

Restrictions may be based on the retention of a certain retained earnings balance, the corporation's ability to observe certain working capital requirements, additional borrowing, and on other considerations. The following example from the annual report of Alberto-Culver Company illustrates a note disclosing potential restrictions on retained earnings and dividends.

Alberto-Culver Company

Note 3 (in part): The $200 million revolving credit facility, the term note due September 2000, and the receivables agreement impose restrictions on such items as total debt, working capital, dividend payments, treasury stock purchases, and interest expense. At September 30, 1998, the company was in compliance with these arrangements, and $220 million of consolidated retained earnings was not restricted as to the payment of dividends.

ILLUSTRATION 15-11
Disclosure of Restrictions on Retained Earnings and Dividends

PRESENTATION AND ANALYSIS OF STOCKHOLDERS' EQUITY

Presentation

OBJECTIVE 9
Indicate how stockholders' equity is presented and analyzed.

Balance Sheet

Illustration 15-12 (on page 748) shows a comprehensive stockholders' equity section from a balance sheet that includes most of the equity items discussed in this chapter. Frost Corporation should also disclose the pertinent rights and privileges of the various securities outstanding. For example, all of the following must be disclosed: dividend and liquidation preferences, participation rights, call prices and dates, conversion or exercise prices and pertinent dates, sinking fund requirements, unusual voting rights, and significant terms of contracts to issue additional shares. The disclosure related to liquidation preferences should be made in the equity section of the balance sheet, rather than in the notes to the financial statements, to emphasize the possible effect of this restriction on future cash flows.[20]

Statement of Stockholders' Equity

Statements of stockholders' equity are frequently presented in the following basic format.

1. Balance at the beginning of the period.
2. Additions.
3. Deductions.
4. Balance at the end of the period.

Reporting of Stockholders' Equity in Kodak's Annual Report

[20]"Disclosure of Information about Capital Structure," *Statement of Financial Accounting Standards No. 129* (Norwalk, Conn.: FASB, February 1997), par. 4.

ILLUSTRATION 15-12
Comprehensive Stockholders' Equity Presentation

FROST CORPORATION STOCKHOLDERS' EQUITY DECEMBER 31, 2002		
Capital stock		
Preferred stock, $100 par value, 7% cumulative, 100,000 shares authorized, 30,000 shares issued and outstanding		$ 3,000,000
Common stock, no par, stated value $10 per share, 500,000 shares authorized, 400,000 shares issued		4,000,000
Common stock dividend distributable, 20,000 shares		200,000
Total capital stock		7,200,000
Additional paid-in capital[21]		
Excess over par—preferred	$150,000	
Excess over stated value—common	840,000	990,000
Total paid-in capital		8,190,000
Retained earnings		4,360,000
Total paid-in capital and retained earnings		12,550,000
Less: Cost of treasury stock (2,000 shares, common)		(190,000)
Accumulated other comprehensive loss[22]		(360,000)
Total stockholders' equity		$12,000,000

The disclosure of changes in the separate accounts comprising stockholders' equity is required to make the financial statements sufficiently informative.[23] Disclosure of such changes may take the form of separate statements or may be made in the basic financial statements or notes thereto.[24]

A **columnar format** for the presentation of changes in stockholders' equity items in published annual reports is commonly used. An example is **Hewlett-Packard Company**'s statement of stockholders' equity shown in Illustration 15-13.

[21]*Accounting Trends and Techniques—2001* reports that of its 600 surveyed companies, 522 had additional paid-in capital, 281 used the caption "Additional paid-in capital," 123 used "Capital in excess of par or stated value" as the caption, 86 used "Paid-in capital" or "Additional capital," and 32 used other captions.

[22]A number of items may be included in the "Accumulated other comprehensive loss." Among these items are "Foreign currency translation adjustments" (covered in advanced accounting), "Unrealized holding gains and losses for available-for-sale securities" (covered in Chapter 17), "Excess of additional pension liability over unrecognized prior service cost" (covered in Chapter 20), "Guarantees of employee stock option plan (ESOP) debt," "Unearned or deferred compensation related to employee stock award plans," and others.

Accounting Trends and Techniques—2001 reports that of its 600 surveyed companies reporting other items in the equity section, 93 reported cumulative translation adjustments, 31 reported minimum pension liability adjustments, 38 reported unrealized losses/gains on certain investments, 145 reported unearned compensation, and 37 reported guarantees of ESOP debt. A number of companies had more than one item.

[23]If a company has other comprehensive income, and total comprehensive income is computed only in the statement of stockholders' equity, the statement of stockholders' equity must be displayed with the same prominence as other financial statements. "Reporting Comprehensive Income," *Statement of Financial Accounting Standards No. 130* (Norwalk, Conn.: FASB, June 1997).

[24]*Accounting Trends and Techniques—2001* reports that of the 600 companies surveyed, 577 presented statements of stockholders' equity, 7 presented separate statements of retained earnings only, 10 presented combined statements of income and retained earnings, and 6 presented changes in equity items in the notes only.

Hewlett-Packard Company and Subsidiaries
Consolidated Statement of Stockholders' Equity

(in millions, except number of shares in thousands)	Common Stock Number of Shares	Common Stock Par Value	Additional Paid-in Capital	Retained Earnings	Accumulated Other Comprehensive Income	Total
Balance October 31, 2000	1,947,312	$19	—	$14,097	$ 93	$14,209
Net earnings	—	—	—	408	—	408
Net unrealized loss on available-for-sale securities	—	—	—	—	(74)	(74)
Net unrealized gain on derivative instruments	—	—	—	—	22	22
Comprehensive income						356
Issuance of common stock	36,552	—	$ 1,233	—	—	1,233
Repurchase of common stock	(45,036)	—	(1,049)	(191)	—	(1,240)
Tax benefit from employee stock plans	—	—	16	—	—	16
Dividends	—	—	—	(621)	—	(621)
Balance October 31, 2001	1,938,828	$19	$ 200	$13,693	$ 41	$13,953

ILLUSTRATION 15-13
Columnar Format for Statement of Stockholders' Equity

Analysis

Several ratios use stockholders' equity related amounts to evaluate a company's profitability and long-term solvency. The following three ratios are discussed and illustrated below.

1. Rate of return on common stock equity.
2. Payout ratio.
3. Book value per share.

Rate of Return on Common Stock Equity

A widely used ratio that measures profitability from the common stockholders' viewpoint is **rate of return on common stock equity**. This ratio shows how many dollars of net income were earned for each dollar invested by the owners. It is computed by dividing net income less preferred dividends by average common stockholders' equity. For example, assume that Gerber's Inc. had net income of $360,000, declared and paid preferred dividends of $54,000, and average common stockholders' equity of $2,550,000. Gerber's ratio is computed as shown in Illustration 15-14.

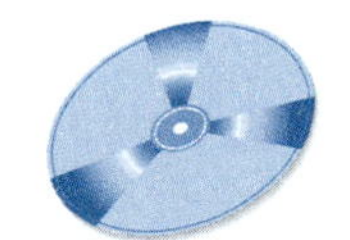
Financial Analysis Primer

$$\text{Rate of Return on Common Stock Equity} = \frac{\text{Net income} - \text{Preferred dividends}}{\text{Average common stockholders' equity}}$$

$$= \frac{\$360{,}000 - \$54{,}000}{\$2{,}550{,}000}$$

$$= 12\%$$

ILLUSTRATION 15-14
Computation of Rate of Return on Common Stock Equity

When preferred stock is present, preferred dividends are deducted from net income to compute income available to common stockholders. Similarly, the par value of preferred stock is deducted from total stockholders' equity to arrive at the amount of common stock equity used in this ratio.

When the rate of return on total assets is lower than the rate of return on the common stockholders' investment, the company is said to be trading on the equity at a gain. **Trading on the equity** describes the practice of using borrowed money at fixed interest rates or issuing preferred stock with constant dividend rates in hopes of obtaining a higher rate of return on the money used. These issues must be given a prior claim on some or all of the corporate assets. Thus, the advantage to common stockholders of trading on the equity must come from borrowing at a lower rate of interest than the rate of return obtained on the assets borrowed. If this can be done, the capital obtained from bondholders or preferred stockholders earns enough to pay the interest or preferred dividends and to leave a margin for the common stockholders. When this condition exists, trading on the equity is profitable.

Payout Ratio

Another measure of profitability is the **payout ratio**, which is the ratio of cash dividends to net income. If preferred stock is outstanding, this ratio is computed for common stockholders by dividing cash dividends paid to common stockholders by net income available to common stockholders. Assuming that Troy Co. has cash dividends of $100,000 and net income of $500,000, and no preferred stock outstanding, the payout ratio is computed in the following manner.

ILLUSTRATION 15-15
Computation of Payout Ratio

$$\text{Payout Ratio} = \frac{\text{Cash dividends}}{\text{Net income} - \text{Preferred dividends}}$$

$$= \frac{\$100{,}000}{\$500{,}000}$$

$$= 20\%$$

It is important to some investors that the payout be sufficiently high to provide a good yield on the stock.[25] However, payout ratios have declined for many companies because many investors view appreciation in the value of the stock as more important than the amount of the dividend.

Book Value Per Share

A much-used basis for evaluating net worth is found in the **book value** or **equity value per share** of stock. Book value per share of stock is the amount each share would receive if the company were liquidated **on the basis of amounts reported on the balance sheet**. However, the figure loses much of its relevance if the valuations on the balance sheet do not approximate fair market value of the assets. **Book value per share** is computed by dividing common stockholders' equity by outstanding common shares. Assuming that Chen Corporation's common stockholders' equity is $1,000,000 and it has 100,000 shares of common stock outstanding, its book value per share is computed as follows.

ILLUSTRATION 15-16
Computation of Book Value Per Share

$$\text{Book Value Per Share} = \frac{\text{Common stockholders' equity}}{\text{Outstanding shares}}$$

$$= \frac{\$1{,}000{,}000}{100{,}000}$$

$$= \$10 \text{ per share}$$

[25] Another closely watched ratio is the **dividend yield**—the cash dividend per share divided by the market price of the stock. This ratio affords investors some idea of the rate of return that will be received in cash dividends from their investment.

SUMMARY OF LEARNING OBJECTIVES

1 Discuss the characteristics of the corporate form of organization. Among the specific characteristics of the corporate form that affect accounting are: (1) influence of state corporate law; (2) use of the capital stock or share system; and (3) development of a variety of ownership interests. In the absence of restrictive provisions, each share of stock carries the following rights: (1) to share proportionately in profits and losses; (2) to share proportionately in management (the right to vote for directors); (3) to share proportionately in corporate assets upon liquidation; (4) to share proportionately in any new issues of stock of the same class (called the preemptive right).

2 Explain the key components of stockholders' equity. Stockholders' or owners' equity is classified into two categories: contributed capital, and earned capital. Contributed capital (paid-in capital) is the term used to describe the total amount paid in on capital stock. Put another way, it is the amount advanced by stockholders to the corporation for use in the business. Contributed capital includes items such as the par value of all outstanding capital stock and premiums less any discounts on issuance. Earned capital is the capital that develops if the business operates profitably; it consists of all undistributed income that remains invested in the enterprise.

3 Explain the accounting procedures for issuing shares of stock. Accounts required to be kept for different types of stock are: *Par value stock:* (a) preferred stock or common stock; (b) paid-in capital in excess of par or additional paid-in capital; and (c) discount on stock. *No-par stock:* common stock or common stock and additional paid-in capital, if stated value used. *Stock issued in combination with other securities (lump-sum sales):* The two methods of allocation available are (a) the proportional method; and (b) the incremental method. *Stock issued in noncash transactions:* When stock is issued for services or property other than cash, the property or services should be recorded at either the fair market value of the stock issued, or the fair market value of the noncash consideration received, whichever is more clearly determinable.

4 Explain the accounting for treasury stock. The cost method is generally used in accounting for treasury stock. This method derives its name from the fact that the Treasury Stock account is maintained at the cost of the shares purchased. Under the cost method, the Treasury Stock account is debited for the cost of the shares acquired and is credited for this same cost upon reissuance. The price received for the stock when originally issued does not affect the entries to record the acquisition and reissuance of the treasury stock.

5 Explain the accounting for and reporting of preferred stock. Preferred stock is a special class of shares that possesses certain preferences or features not possessed by the common stock. The features that are most often associated with preferred stock issues are: (1) preference as to dividends; (2) preference as to assets in the event of liquidation; (3) convertible into common stock; (4) callable at the option of the corporation; (5) nonvoting. At issuance, the accounting for preferred stock is similar to that for common stock.

6 Describe the policies used in distributing dividends. The state incorporation laws normally provide information concerning the legal restrictions related to the payment of dividends. Corporations rarely pay dividends in an amount equal to the legal limit. This is due, in part, to the fact that assets represented by undistributed earnings are used to finance future operations of the business. If a company is considering declaring a dividend, two preliminary questions must be asked: (1) Is the condition of the corporation such that the dividend is **legally permissible**? (2) Is the condition of the corporation such that a dividend is **economically sound**?

KEY TERMS

additional paid-in capital, 728
book value per share, 750
callable preferred stock, 737
cash dividends, 740
common stock, 726
contributed (paid-in) capital, 727
convertible preferred stock, 737
cost method, 733
cumulative preferred stock, 736
earned capital, 727
large stock dividend, 746
liquidating dividends, 739, 741
lump-sum sales, 729
no-par stock, 728
par (stated) value method, 733
participating preferred stock, 737
payout ratio, 750
preemptive right, 725
preferred stock, 726, 736
property dividends, 741
rate of return on common stock equity, 749
redeemable preferred stock, 737n
residual interest, 727
retained earnings, 727
small (ordinary) stock dividends, 742
stated value, 728
statement of stockholders' equity, 747
stock dividend, 742
stock split, 744
stockholders' (owners') equity, 727
trading on the equity, 750
treasury stock, 732

7 Identify the various forms of dividend distributions. Dividends are of the following types: (1) cash dividends, (2) property dividends, (3) liquidating dividends (dividends based on other than retained earnings), (4) stock dividends (the nonreciprocal issuance by a corporation of its own stock to its stockholders on a pro rata basis).

Expanded Discussion of Quasi-Reorganization

8 Explain the accounting for small and large stock dividends, and for stock splits. Generally accepted accounting principles require that the accounting for small stock dividends (less than 20 or 25%) be based on the fair market value of the stock issued. When a stock dividend is declared, Retained Earnings is debited at the fair market value of the stock to be distributed. The entry includes a credit to Common Stock Dividend Distributable at par value times the number of shares, with any excess credited to Paid-in Capital in Excess of Par. If the number of shares issued exceeds 20 to 25% of the shares outstanding (large stock dividend), Retained Earnings is debited at par value, and there is no additional paid-in capital.

A stock dividend is a capitalization of retained earnings that results in a reduction in retained earnings and a corresponding increase in certain contributed capital accounts. The par value and total stockholders' equity remain unchanged with a stock dividend, and all stockholders retain their same proportionate share of ownership. A stock split results in an increase or decrease in the number of shares outstanding, with a corresponding decrease or increase in the par or stated value per share. No accounting entry is required for a stock split.

9 Indicate how stockholders' equity is presented and analyzed. The stockholders' equity section of a balance sheet includes capital stock, additional paid-in capital, and retained earnings. Additional items that might also be presented are treasury stock and accumulated other comprehensive income. A statement of stockholders' equity is often provided. Common ratios that use stockholders' equity amounts are: rate of return on common stock equity, payout ratio, and book value per share.

APPENDIX 15A

Dividend Preferences and Book Value Per Share

OBJECTIVE 10
Explain the different types of preferred stock dividends and their effect on book value per share.

DIVIDEND PREFERENCES

Illustrations 15A-1 to 15A-4 indicate the **effects of** various **dividend preferences** on dividend distributions to common and preferred stockholders. Assume that in a given year, $50,000 is to be distributed as cash dividends, outstanding common stock has a par value of $400,000, and 6 percent preferred stock has a par value of $100,000. Dividends would be distributed to each class, employing the assumptions given.

1 If the preferred stock is noncumulative and nonparticipating:

	Preferred	Common	Total
6% of $100,000	$6,000		$ 6,000
The remainder to common		$44,000	44,000
Totals	$6,000	$44,000	$50,000

ILLUSTRATION 15A-1
Dividend Distribution, Noncumulative and Nonparticipating Preferred

2 If the preferred stock is cumulative and nonparticipating, and dividends were not paid on the preferred stock in the preceding 2 years:

	Preferred	Common	Total
Dividends in arrears, 6% of $100,000 for 2 years	$12,000		$12,000
Current year's dividend, 6% of $100,000	6000		6,000
The remainder to common		$32,000	32,000
Totals	$18,000	$32,000	$50,000

ILLUSTRATION 15A-2
Dividend Distribution, Cumulative and Nonparticipating Preferred, with Dividends in Arrears

3 If the preferred stock is noncumulative and is fully participating:[1]

	Preferred	Common	Total
Current year's dividend, 6%	$ 6,000	$24,000	$30,000
Participating dividend of 4%	4,000	16,000	20,000
Totals	$10,000	$40,000	$50,000

The participating dividend was determined as follows:		
Current year's dividend:		
Preferred, 6% of $100,000 =	$ 6,000	
Common, 6% of $400,000 =	24,000	$ 30,000
Amount available for participation ($50,000 − $30,000)		$ 20,000
Par value of stock that is to participate ($100,000 + $400,000)		$500,000
Rate of participation ($20,000 ÷ $500,000)		4%
Participating dividend:		
Preferred, 4% of $100,000		$ 4,000
Common, 4% of $400,000		16,000
		$ 20,000

ILLUSTRATION 15A-3
Dividend Distribution, Noncumulative and Fully Participating Preferred

[1]When preferred stock is participating, there may be different agreements as to how the participation feature is to be executed. However, in the absence of any specific agreement the following procedure is recommended:

a. After the preferred stock is assigned its current year's dividend, the common stock will receive a "like" percentage of par value outstanding. In example (3), this amounts to 6 percent of $400,000.

b. If there is a remainder of declared dividends for participation by the preferred and common stock, this remainder will be shared in proportion to the par value dollars outstanding in each class of stock. In example (3) this proportion is:

$$\text{Preferred } \frac{\$100{,}000}{\$500{,}000} \times \$20{,}000 = \$4{,}000$$

$$\text{Common } \frac{\$400{,}000}{\$500{,}000} \times \$20{,}000 = \$16{,}000$$

4 If the preferred stock is cumulative and is fully participating, and if dividends were not paid on the preferred stock in the preceding 2 years (the same procedure as described in example (3) is used in this example to effect the participation feature):

ILLUSTRATION 15A-4
Dividend Distribution, Cumulative and Fully Participating Preferred, with Dividends in Arrears

	Preferred	Common	Total
Dividends in arrears, 6% of $100,000 for 2 years	$12,000		$12,000
Current year's dividend, 6%	6,000	$24,000	30,000
Participating dividend, 1.6% ($8,000 ÷ $500,000)	1,600	6,400	8,000
Totals	$19,600	$30,400	$50,000

BOOK VALUE PER SHARE

The computation of book value per share becomes more complicated if a company has preferred stock in its capital structure. For example, if preferred dividends are in arrears, the preferred stock is participating, or if preferred stock has a redemption or liquidating value higher than its carrying amount, retained earnings must be allocated between the preferred and common stockholders in computing book value.

To illustrate, assume that the following situation exists.

ILLUSTRATION 15A-5
Computation of Book Value Per Share—No Dividends in Arrears

Stockholders' equity	Preferred	Common
Preferred stock, 5%	$300,000	
Common stock		$400,000
Excess of issue price over par of common stock		37,500
Retained earnings		162,582
Totals	$300,000	$600,082
Shares outstanding		4,000
Book value per share		$150.02

In Illustration 15A-5 it is assumed that no preferred dividends are in arrears and that the preferred is not participating. Now assume that the same facts exist except that the 5 percent preferred is cumulative, participating up to 8 percent, and that dividends for 3 years before the current year are in arrears. The book value of the common stock is then computed as follows, assuming that no action has yet been taken concerning dividends for the current year.

ILLUSTRATION 15A-6
Computation of Book Value Per Share—With Dividends in Arrears

Stockholders' equity	Preferred	Common
Preferred stock, 5%	$300,000	
Common stock		$400,000
Excess of issue price over par of common stock		37,500
Retained earnings:		
Dividends in arrears (3 years at 5% a year)	45,000	
Current year requirement at 5%	15,000	20,000
Participating—additional 3%	9,000	12,000
Remainder to common		61,582
Totals	$369,000	$531,082
Shares outstanding		4,000
Book value per share		$132.77

In connection with the book value computation, the analyst must know how to handle the following items: the number of authorized and unissued shares; the number of treasury shares on hand; any commitments with respect to the issuance of unissued shares or the reissuance of treasury shares; and the relative rights and privileges of the various types of stock authorized.

SUMMARY OF LEARNING OBJECTIVE FOR APPENDIX 15A

10 Explain the different types of preferred stock dividends and their effect on book value per share. Dividends paid to stockholders are affected by the dividend preferences of the preferred stock. Preferred stock can be (1) cumulative or noncumulative, and (2) fully participating, partially participating, or nonparticipating. If preferred dividends are in arrears, if the preferred stock is participating, or if preferred stock has a redemption or liquidation value higher than its carrying amount, retained earnings must be allocated between preferred and common stockholders in computing book value per share.

Note: All **asterisked** Questions, Brief Exercises, and Exercises relate to material contained in the appendix to the chapter.

QUESTIONS

1. In the absence of restrictive provisions, what are the basic rights of stockholders of a corporation?
2. Why is a preemptive right important?
3. Distinguish between common and preferred stock.
4. Why is the distinction between paid-in capital and retained earnings important?
5. Explain each of the following terms: authorized capital stock, unissued capital stock, issued capital stock, outstanding capital stock, and treasury stock.
6. What is meant by par value, and what is its significance to stockholders?
7. Describe the accounting for the issuance for cash of no-par value common stock at a price in excess of the stated value of the common stock.
8. Explain the difference between the proportional method and the incremental method of allocating the proceeds of lump sum sales of capital stock.
9. What are the different bases for stock valuation when assets other than cash are received for issued shares of stock?
10. Explain how underwriting costs and accounting and legal fees associated with the issuance of stock should be recorded.
11. For what reasons might a corporation purchase its own stock?
12. Discuss the propriety of showing:
    (a) Treasury stock as an asset.
    (b) "Gain" or "loss" on sale of treasury stock as additions to or deductions from income.
    (c) Dividends received on treasury stock as income.
13. What features or rights may alter the character of preferred stock?
14. Little Texas Inc. recently noted that its 4% preferred stock and 4% participating second preferred stock, which are both cumulative, have priority as to dividends up to 4% of their par value. Its participating preferred stock participates equally with the common stock in any dividends in excess of 4%. What is meant by the term participating? Cumulative?
15. Where in the financial statements is preferred stock normally reported?
16. List possible sources of additional paid-in capital.
17. Goo Goo Dolls Inc. purchases 10,000 shares of its own previously issued $10 par common stock for $290,000. Assuming the shares are held in the treasury with intent to reissue, what effect does this transaction have on (a) net income, (b) total assets, (c) total paid-in capital, and (d) total stockholders' equity?
18. Indicate how each of the following accounts should be classified in the stockholders' equity section.
    (a) Common Stock
    (b) Retained Earnings
    (c) Paid-in Capital in Excess of Par Value
    (d) Treasury Stock
    (e) Paid-in Capital from Treasury Stock
    (f) Paid-in Capital in Excess of Stated Value
    (g) Preferred Stock
19. What factors influence the dividend policy of a company?
20. What are the characteristics of state incorporation laws relative to the legality of dividend payments?
21. What are the principal considerations of a board of directors in making decisions involving dividend declarations? Discuss briefly.

22. Dividends are sometimes said to have been paid "out of retained earnings." What is the error in that statement?

23. Distinguish among: cash dividends, property dividends, liquidating dividends, and stock dividends.

24. Describe the accounting entry for a stock dividend, if any. Describe the accounting entry for a stock split, if any.

25. Stock splits and stock dividends may be used by a corporation to change the number of shares of its stock outstanding.

(a) What is meant by a stock split effected in the form of a dividend?

(b) From an accounting viewpoint, explain how the stock split effected in the form of a dividend differs from an ordinary stock dividend.

(c) How should a stock dividend that has been declared but not yet issued be classified in a statement of financial position? Why?

26. The following comment appeared in the notes of Belinda Alvarado Corporation's annual report: "Such distributions, representing proceeds from the sale of James Buchanan, Inc. were paid in the form of partial liquidating dividends and were in lieu of a portion of the Company's ordinary cash dividends." How would a partial liquidating dividend be accounted for in the financial records?

27. This comment appeared in the annual report of Rodriguez Lopez Inc.: "The Company could pay cash or property dividends on the Class A common stock without paying cash or property dividends on the Class B common stock. But if the Company pays any cash or property dividends on the Class B common stock, it would be required to pay at least the same dividend on the Class A common stock." How is a property dividend accounted for in the financial records?

28. For what reasons might a company restrict a portion of its retained earnings?

29. How are restrictions of retained earnings reported?

***30.** Aaron Burr Corp. had $100,000 of 10%, $20 par value preferred stock and 12,000 shares of $25 par value common stock outstanding throughout 2003.

(a) Assuming that total dividends declared in 2003 were $88,000, and that the preferred stock is not cumulative but is fully participating, each common share should receive 2003 dividends of what amount?

(b) Assuming that total dividends declared in 2003 were $88,000, and that the preferred stock is fully participating and cumulative with preferred dividends in arrears for 2002, preferred stockholders should receive 2003 dividends totaling what amount?

(c) Assuming that total dividends declared in 2003 were $30,000, that cumulative nonparticipating preferred stock was issued on January 1, 2002, and that $5,000 of preferred dividends were declared and paid in 2002, the common stockholders should receive 2003 dividends totaling what amount?

BRIEF EXERCISES

BE15-1 Lost Vikings Corporation issued 300 shares of $10 par value common stock for $4,100. Prepare Lost Vikings' journal entry.

BE15-2 Shinobi Corporation issued 600 shares of no-par common stock for $10,200. Prepare Shinobi's journal entry if (a) the stock has no stated value, and (b) the stock has a stated value of $2 per share.

BE15-3 Lufia Corporation has the following account balances at December 31, 2003.

Common stock, $5 par value	$ 210,000
Treasury stock	90,000
Retained earnings	2,340,000
Paid-in capital in excess of par	1,320,000

Prepare Lufia's December 31, 2003, stockholders' equity section.

BE15-4 Primal Rage Corporation issued 300 shares of $10 par value common stock and 100 shares of $50 par value preferred stock for a lump sum of $14,200. The common stock has a market value of $20 per share, and the preferred stock has a market value of $90 per share. Prepare the journal entry to record the issuance.

BE15-5 On February 1, 2003, Mario Andretti Corporation issued 2,000 shares of its $5 par value common stock for land worth $31,000. Prepare the February 1, 2003, journal entry.

BE15-6 Powerdrive Corporation issued 2,000 shares of its $10 par value common stock for $70,000. Powerdrive also incurred $1,500 of costs associated with issuing the stock. Prepare Powerdrive's journal entry to record the issuance of the company's stock.

BE15-7 Maverick Inc. has outstanding 10,000 shares of $10 par value common stock. On July 1, 2003, Maverick reacquired 100 shares at $85 per share. On September 1, Maverick reissued 60 shares at $90 per share. On November 1, Maverick reissued 40 shares at $83 per share. Prepare Maverick's journal entries to record these transactions using the cost method.

BE15-8 Power Rangers Corporation has outstanding 20,000 shares of $5 par value common stock. On August 1, 2003, Power Rangers reacquired 200 shares at $75 per share. On November 1, Power Rangers reissued the 200 shares at $70 per share. Power Rangers had no previous treasury stock transactions. Prepare Power Rangers' journal entries to record these transactions using the cost method.

BE15-9 Popeye Corporation issued 450 shares of $100 par value preferred stock for $61,500. Prepare Popeye's journal entry.

BE15-10 Micro Machines Inc. declared a cash dividend of $1.50 per share on its 2 million outstanding shares. The dividend was declared on August 1, payable on September 9 to all stockholders of record on August 15. Prepare all journal entries necessary on those three dates.

BE15-11 Ren Inc. owns shares of Stimpy Corporation stock classified as available-for-sale securities. At December 31, 2003, the available-for-sale securities were carried in Ren's accounting records at their cost of $875,000, which equals their market value. On September 21, 2004, when the market value of the securities was $1,400,000, Ren declared a property dividend whereby the Stimpy securities are to be distributed on October 23, 2004, to stockholders of record on October 8, 2004. Prepare all journal entries necessary on those three dates.

BE15-12 Radical Rex Mining Company declared, on April 20, a dividend of $700,000 payable on June 1. Of this amount, $125,000 is a return of capital. Prepare the April 20 and June 1 entries for Radical Rex.

BE15-13 Mike Holmgren Football Corporation has outstanding 200,000 shares of $10 par value common stock. The corporation declares a 5% stock dividend when the fair value of the stock is $65 per share. Prepare the journal entries for Mike Holmgren Football Corporation for both the date of declaration and the date of distribution.

BE15-14 Use the information from BE15-13, but assume Mike Holmgren Football Corporation declared a 100% stock dividend rather than a 5% stock dividend. Prepare the journal entries for both the date of declaration and the date of distribution.

***BE15-15** Minnesota Fats Corporation has outstanding 10,000 shares of $100 par value, 8% preferred stock and 60,000 shares of $10 par value common stock. The preferred stock was issued in January 2003, and no dividends were declared in 2003 or 2004. In 2005, Minnesota Fats declares a cash dividend of $300,000. How will the dividend be shared by common and preferred if the preferred is (a) noncumulative and (b) cumulative?

EXERCISES

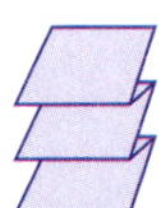

E15-1 (Recording the Issuances of Common Stock) During its first year of operations, Collin Raye Corporation had the following transactions pertaining to its common stock.

Jan. 10	Issued 80,000 shares for cash at $6 per share.
Mar. 1	Issued 5,000 shares to attorneys in payment of a bill for $35,000 for services rendered in helping the company to incorporate.
July 1	Issued 30,000 shares for cash at $8 per share.
Sept. 1	Issued 60,000 shares for cash at $10 per share.

Instructions

(a) Prepare the journal entries for these transactions, assuming that the common stock has a par value of $5 per share.

(b) Prepare the journal entries for these transactions, assuming that the common stock is no par with a stated value of $3 per share.

E15-2 (Recording the Issuance of Common and Preferred Stock) Kathleen Battle Corporation was organized on January 1, 2003. It is authorized to issue 10,000 shares of 8%, $100 par value preferred stock, and 500,000 shares of no par common stock with a stated value of $1 per share. The following stock transactions were completed during the first year.

Jan. 10	Issued 80,000 shares of common stock for cash at $5 per share.
Mar. 1	Issued 5,000 shares of preferred stock for cash at $108 per share.

Apr. 1	Issued 24,000 shares of common stock for land. The asking price of the land was $90,000; the fair market value of the land was $80,000.
May 1	Issued 80,000 shares of common stock for cash at $7 per share.
Aug. 1	Issued 10,000 shares of common stock to attorneys in payment of their bill of $50,000 for services rendered in helping the company organize.
Sept. 1	Issued 10,000 shares of common stock for cash at $9 per share.
Nov. 1	Issued 1,000 shares of preferred stock for cash at $112 per share.

Instructions

Prepare the journal entries to record the above transactions.

E15-3 (Stock Issued for Land) Twenty-five thousand shares reacquired by Elixir Corporation for $53 per share were exchanged for undeveloped land that has an appraised value of $1,700,000. At the time of the exchange the common stock was trading at $62 per share on an organized exchange.

Instructions

(a) Prepare the journal entry to record the acquisition of land assuming the stock was originally recorded using the cost method.

(b) Briefly identify the possible alternatives (including those that are totally unacceptable) for quantifying the cost of the land and briefly support your choice.

E15-4 (Lump-Sum Sale of Stock with Bonds) Faith Evans Corporation is a regional company which is an SEC registrant. The corporation's securities are thinly traded through the NASDAQ (National Association of Securities Dealers Quotes). Faith Evans Corp. has issued 10,000 units. Each unit consists of a $500 par, 12% subordinated debenture and 10 shares of $5 par common stock. The investment banker has retained 400 units as the underwriting fee. The other 9,600 units were sold to outside investors for cash at $880 per unit. Prior to this sale the 2-week ask price of common stock was $40 per share. Twelve percent is a reasonable market yield for the debentures.

Instructions

(a) Prepare the journal entry to record the previous transaction, under the following conditions.

  (1) Employing the incremental method, assuming the interest rate on the debentures is the best market measure.

  (2) Employing the proportional method, using the recent price quotes on the common stock.

(b) Briefly explain which method is, in your opinion, the better method.

E15-5 (Lump-Sum Sales of Stock with Preferred Stock) Dave Matthew Inc. issues 500 shares of $10 par value common stock and 100 shares of $100 par value preferred stock for a lump sum of $100,000.

Instructions

(a) Prepare the journal entry for the issuance when the market value of the common shares is $165 each and market value of the preferred is $230 each.

(b) Prepare the journal entry for the issuance when only the market value of the common stock is known and it is $170 per share.

E15-6 (Stock Issuances and Repurchase) Lindsey Hunter Corporation is authorized to issue 50,000 shares of $5 par value common stock. During 2003, Lindsey Hunter took part in the following selected transactions.

1. Issued 5,000 shares of stock at $45 per share, less costs related to the issuance of the stock totaling $7,000.
2. Issued 1,000 shares of stock for land appraised at $50,000. The stock was actively traded on a national stock exchange at approximately $46 per share on the date of issuance.
3. Purchased 500 shares of treasury stock at $43 per share. The treasury shares purchased were issued in 2000 at $40 per share.

Instructions

(a) Prepare the journal entry to record item 1.

(b) Prepare the journal entry to record item 2.

(c) Prepare the journal entry to record item 3 using the cost method.

E15-7 (Effect of Treasury Stock Transactions on Financials) Joe Dumars Company has outstanding 40,000 shares of $5 par common stock which had been issued at $30 per share. Joe Dumars then entered into the following transactions.

1. Purchased 5,000 treasury shares at $45 per share.
2. Resold 2,000 of the treasury shares at $49 per share.
3. Resold 500 of the treasury shares at $40 per share.

Instructions
Use the following code to indicate the effect each of the four transactions has on the financial statement categories listed in the table below, assuming Joe Dumars Company uses the cost method: (I = Increase; D = Decrease; NE = No effect).

#	Assets	Liabilities	Stockholders' Equity	Paid-in Capital	Retained Earnings	Net Income
1						
2						
3						

*E15-8 **(Preferred Stock Entries and Dividends)** Otis Thorpe Corporation has 10,000 shares of $100 par value, 8%, preferred stock and 50,000 shares of $10 par value common stock outstanding at December 31, 2003.

Instructions
Answer the questions in each of the following independent situations.

(a) If the preferred stock is cumulative and dividends were last paid on the preferred stock on December 31, 2000, what are the dividends in arrears that should be reported on the December 31, 2003, balance sheet? How should these dividends be reported?

(b) If the preferred stock is convertible into seven shares of $10 par value common stock and 4,000 shares are converted, what entry is required for the conversion assuming the preferred stock was issued at par value?

(c) If the preferred stock was issued at $107 per share, how should the preferred stock be reported in the stockholders' equity section?

E15-9 (Correcting Entries for Equity Transactions) Pistons Inc. recently hired a new accountant with extensive experience in accounting for partnerships. Because of the pressure of the new job, the accountant was unable to review what he had learned earlier about corporation accounting. During the first month, he made the following entries for the corporation's capital stock.

May 2	Cash	192,000	
	Capital Stock		192,000
	(Issued 12,000 shares of $5 par value common stock at $16 per share)		
10	Cash	600,000	
	Capital Stock		600,000
	(Issued 10,000 shares of $30 par value preferred stock at $60 per share)		
15	Capital Stock	15,000	
	Cash		15,000
	(Purchased 1,000 shares of common stock for the treasury at $15 per share)		
31	Cash	8,500	
	Capital Stock		5,000
	Gain on Sale of Stock		3,500
	(Sold 500 shares of treasury stock at $17 per share)		

Instructions
On the basis of the explanation for each entry, prepare the entries that should have been made for the capital stock transactions.

E15-10 (Analysis of Equity Data and Equity Section Preparation) For a recent 2-year period, the balance sheet of Santana Dotson Company showed the following stockholders' equity data in millions.

	2004	2003
Additional paid-in capital	$ 931	$ 817
Common stock—par	545	540
Retained earnings	7,167	5,226
Treasury stock	1,564	918
Total stockholders' equity	$7,079	$5,665
Common stock shares issued	218	216
Common stock shares authorized	500	500
Treasury stock shares	34	27

Instructions

(a) Answer the following questions.
   (1) What is the par value of the common stock?
   (2) Was the cost per share of acquiring treasury stock higher in 2004 or in 2003?
(b) Prepare the stockholders' equity section for 2004.

E15-11 (Equity Items on the Balance Sheet) The following are selected transactions that may affect stockholders' equity.

1. Recorded accrued interest earned on a note receivable.
2. Declared a cash dividend.
3. Declared and distributed a stock split.
4. Recorded a retained earnings restriction.
5. Recorded the expiration of insurance coverage that was previously recorded as prepaid insurance.
6. Paid the cash dividend declared in item 2 above.
7. Recorded accrued interest expense on a note payable.
8. Declared a stock dividend.
9. Distributed the stock dividend declared in item 8.

Instructions

In the table below, indicate the effect each of the nine transactions has on the financial statement elements listed. Use the following code:

I = Increase   D = Decrease   NE = No effect

Item	Assets	Liabilities	Stockholders' Equity	Paid-in Capital	Retained Earnings	Net Income

E15-12 (Cash Dividend and Liquidating Dividend) Lotoya Davis Corporation has ten million shares of common stock issued and outstanding. On June 1 the board of directors voted an 80 cents per share cash dividend to stockholders of record as of June 14, payable June 30.

Instructions

(a) Prepare the journal entry for each of the dates above assuming the dividend represents a distribution of earnings.
(b) How would the entry differ if the dividend were a liquidating dividend?
(c) Assume Lotoya Davis Corporation holds 300,000 common shares in the treasury and as a matter of administrative convenience dividends are paid on treasury shares. How should this cash receipt be recorded?

E15-13 (Stock Split and Stock Dividend) The common stock of Alexander Hamilton Inc. is currently selling at $120 per share. The directors wish to reduce the share price and increase share volume prior to a new issue. The per share par value is $10; book value is $70 per share. Nine million shares are issued and outstanding.

Instructions

Prepare the necessary journal entries assuming the following.

(a) The board votes a 2-for-1 stock split.
(b) The board votes a 100% stock dividend.
(c) Briefly discuss the accounting and securities market differences between these two methods of increasing the number of shares outstanding.

E15-14 (Entries for Stock Dividends and Stock Splits) The stockholders' equity accounts of G.K. Chesterton Company have the following balances on December 31, 2004.

Common stock, $10 par, 300,000 shares issued and outstanding	$3,000,000
Paid-in capital in excess of par	1,200,000
Retained earnings	5,600,000

Shares of G.K. Chesterton Company stock are currently selling on the Midwest Stock Exchange at $37.

Instructions

Prepare the appropriate journal entries for each of the following cases.

(a) A stock dividend of 5% is declared and issued.
(b) A stock dividend of 100% is declared and issued.
(c) A 2-for-1 stock split is declared and issued.

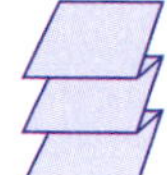

E15-15 (Dividend Entries) The following data were taken from the balance sheet accounts of John Masefield Corporation on December 31, 2003.

Current assets	$540,000
Investments	624,000
Common stock (par value $10)	500,000
Paid-in capital in excess of par	150,000
Retained earnings	840,000

Instructions

Prepare the required journal entries for the following unrelated items.

(a) A 5% stock dividend is declared and distributed at a time when the market value of the shares is $39 per share.
(b) The par value of the capital stock is reduced to $2 with a 5-for-1 stock split.
(c) A dividend is declared January 5, 2004, and paid January 25, 2004, in bonds held as an investment. The bonds have a book value of $100,000 and a fair market value of $135,000.

E15-16 (Computation of Retained Earnings) The following information has been taken from the ledger accounts of Isaac Stern Corporation.

Total income since incorporation	$317,000
Total cash dividends paid	60,000
Proceeds from sale of donated stock	40,000
Total value of stock dividends distributed	30,000
Gains on treasury stock transactions	18,000
Unamortized discount on bonds payable	32,000

Instructions

Determine the current balance of retained earnings.

E15-17 (Stockholders' Equity Section) Bruno Corporation's post-closing trial balance at December 31, 2003, was as follows.

BRUNO CORPORATION
POST-CLOSING TRIAL BALANCE
DECEMBER 31, 2003

	Dr.	Cr.
Accounts payable		$ 310,000
Accounts receivable	$ 480,000	
Accumulated depreciation—building and equipment		185,000
Additional paid-in capital—common		
In excess of par value		1,300,000
From sale of treasury stock		160,000
Allowance for doubtful accounts		30,000
Bonds payable		300,000
Building and equipment	1,450,000	
Cash	190,000	
Common stock ($1 par value)		200,000
Dividends payable on preferred stock—cash		4,000
Inventories	560,000	
Land	400,000	
Preferred stock ($50 par value)		500,000
Prepaid expenses	40,000	
Retained earnings		301,000
Treasury stock—common at cost	170,000	
Totals	$3,290,000	$3,290,000

At December 31, 2003, Bruno had the following number of common and preferred shares.

	Common	Preferred
Authorized	600,000	60,000
Issued	200,000	10,000
Outstanding	190,000	10,000

The dividends on preferred stock are $4 cumulative. In addition, the preferred stock has a preference in liquidation of $50 per share.

Instructions

Prepare the stockholders' equity section of Bruno's balance sheet at December 31, 2003.

(AICPA adapted)

E15-18 (Dividends and Stockholders' Equity Section) Anne Cleves Company reported the following amounts in the stockholders' equity section of its December 31, 2002, balance sheet.

Preferred stock, 10%, $100 par (10,000 shares authorized, 2,000 shares issued)	$200,000
Common stock, $5 par (100,000 shares authorized, 20,000 shares issued)	100,000
Additional paid-in capital	125,000
Retained earnings	450,000
Total	$875,000

During 2003, Cleves took part in the following transactions concerning stockholders' equity.

1. Paid the annual 2002 $10 per share dividend on preferred stock and a $2 per share dividend on common stock. These dividends had been declared on December 31, 2002.
2. Purchased 1,700 shares of its own outstanding common stock for $40 per share. Cleves uses the cost method.
3. Reissued 700 treasury shares for land valued at $30,000.
4. Issued 500 shares of preferred stock at $105 per share.
5. Declared a 10% stock dividend on the outstanding common stock when the stock is selling for $45 per share.
6. Issued the stock dividend.
7. Declared the annual 2003 $10 per share dividend on preferred stock and the $2 per share dividend on common stock. These dividends are payable in 2004.

Instructions

(a) Prepare journal entries to record the transactions described above.

(b) Prepare the December 31, 2003, stockholders' equity section. Assume 2003 net income was $330,000.

E15-19 (Comparison of Alternative Forms of Financing) Shown below is the liabilities and stockholders' equity section of the balance sheet for Jana Kingston Company and Mary Ann Benson Company. Each has assets totaling $4,200,000.

Jana Kingston Co.		Mary Ann Benson Co.	
Current liabilities	$ 300,000	Current liabilities	$ 600,000
Long-term debt, 10%	1,200,000	Common stock ($20 par)	2,900,000
Common stock ($20 par)	2,000,000	Retained earnings (Cash dividends, $328,000)	700,000
Retained earnings (Cash dividends, $220,000)	700,000		
	$4,200,000		$4,200,000

For the year each company has earned the same income before interest and taxes.

	Jana Kingston Co.	Mary Ann Benson Co.
Income before interest and taxes	$1,200,000	$1,200,000
Interest expense	120,000	–0–
	1,080,000	1,200,000
Income taxes (45%)	486,000	540,000
Net income	$ 594,000	$ 660,000

At year end, the market price of Kingston's stock was $101 per share, and Benson's was $63.50.

Instructions

(a) Which company is more profitable in terms of return on total assets?
(b) Which company is more profitable in terms of return on stockholders' equity?
(c) Which company has the greater net income per share of stock? Neither company issued or reacquired shares during the year.
(d) From the point of view of net income, is it advantageous to the stockholders of Jana Kingston Co. to have the long-term debt outstanding? Why?
(e) What is the book value per share for each company?

E15-20 (Trading on the Equity Analysis) Presented below is information from the annual report of Emporia Plastics, Inc.

Operating income	$ 532,150
Bond interest expense	135,000
	397,150
Income taxes	183,432
Net income	$ 213,718
Bonds payable	$1,000,000
Common stock	875,000
Retained earnings	375,000

Instructions

Is Emporia Plastics Inc. trading on the equity successfully? Explain.

***E15-21 (Preferred Dividends)** The outstanding capital stock of Edna Millay Corporation consists of 2,000 shares of $100 par value, 8% preferred, and 5,000 shares of $50 par value common.

Instructions

Assuming that the company has retained earnings of $90,000, all of which is to be paid out in dividends, and that preferred dividends were not paid during the 2 years preceding the current year, state how much each class of stock should receive under each of the following conditions.

(a) The preferred stock is noncumulative and nonparticipating.
(b) The preferred stock is cumulative and nonparticipating.
(c) The preferred stock is cumulative and participating.

***E15-22 (Preferred Dividends)** Archibald MacLeish Company's ledger shows the following balances on December 31, 2004.

7% Preferred stock—$10 par value, outstanding 20,000 shares	$ 200,000
Common stock—$100 par value, outstanding 30,000 shares	3,000,000
Retained earnings	630,000

Instructions

Assuming that the directors decide to declare total dividends in the amount of $366,000, determine how much each class of stock should receive under each of the conditions stated below. One year's dividends are in arrears on the preferred stock.

(a) The preferred stock is cumulative and fully participating.
(b) The preferrred stock is noncumulative and nonparticipating.
(c) The preferred stock is noncumulative and is participating in distributions in excess of a 10% dividend rate on the common stock.

***E15-23 (Preferred Stock Dividends)** Cajun Company has outstanding 2,500 shares of $100 par, 6% preferred stock and 15,000 shares of $10 par value common. The schedule on the next page shows the amount of dividends paid out over the last 4 years.

Instructions

Allocate the dividends to each type of stock under assumptions (a) and (b). Express your answers in per-share amounts using the format shown on the next page.

		Assumptions			
		(a) Preferred, noncumulative, and nonparticipating		(b) Preferred, cumulative, and fully participating	
Year	Paid-out	Preferred	Common	Preferred	Common
2002	$13,000				
2003	$26,000				
2004	$57,000				
2005	$76,000				

***E15-24 (Computation of Book Value per Share)** Morgan Sondgeroth Inc. began operations in January 2002 and reported the following results for each of its 3 years of operations.

2002 $260,000 net loss 2003 $40,000 net loss 2004 $800,000 net income

At December 31, 2004, Morgan Sondgeroth Inc. capital accounts were as follows.

8% cumulative preferred stock, par value $100; authorized, issued, and outstanding 5,000 shares	$500,000
Common stock, par value $1.00; authorized 1,000,000 shares; issued and outstanding 750,000 shares	$750,000

Morgan Sondgeroth Inc. has never paid a cash or stock dividend. There has been no change in the capital accounts since Sondgeroth began operations. The state law permits dividends only from retained earnings.

Instructions

(a) Compute the book value of the common stock at December 31, 2004.

(b) Compute the book value of the common stock at December 31, 2004, assuming that the preferred stock has a liquidating value of $106 per share.

PROBLEMS

P15-1 (Equity Transactions and Statement Preparation) On January 5, 2003, Drabek Corporation received a charter granting the right to issue 5,000 shares of $100 par value, 8% cumulative and nonparticipating preferred stock, and 50,000 shares of $5 par value common stock. It then completed these transactions.

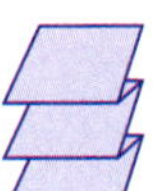

Jan.	11	Issued 20,000 shares of common stock at $16 per share.
Feb.	1	Issued to Robb Nen Corp. 4,000 shares of preferred stock for the following assets: machinery with a fair market value of $50,000; a factory building with a fair market value of $110,000; and land with an appraised value of $270,000.
July	29	Purchased 1,800 shares of common stock at $19 per share. (Use cost method.)
Aug.	10	Sold the 1,800 treasury shares at $14 per share.
Dec.	31	Declared a $0.25 per share cash dividend on the common stock and declared the preferred dividend.
Dec.	31	Closed the Income Summary account. There was a $175,700 net income.

Instructions

(a) Record the journal entries for the transactions listed above.

(b) Prepare the stockholders' equity section of Drabek Corporation's balance sheet as of December 31, 2003.

P15-2 (Treasury Stock Transactions and Presentation) Jodz Company had the following stockholders' equity as of January 1, 2004.

Common stock, $5 par value, 20,000 shares issued	$100,000
Paid-in capital in excess of par	300,000
Retained earnings	320,000
Total stockholders' equity	$720,000

During 2004, the following transactions occurred.

Feb.	1	Jodz repurchased 2,000 shares of treasury stock at a price of $18 per share.
Mar.	1	800 shares of treasury stock repurchased above were reissued at $17 per share.
Mar.	18	500 shares of treasury stock repurchased above were reissued at $14 per share.
Apr.	22	600 shares of treasury stock repurchased above were reissued at $20 per share.

Instructions

(a) Prepare the journal entries to record the treasury stock transactions in 2004, assuming Jodz uses the cost method.

(b) Prepare the stockholders' equity section as of April 30, 2004. Net income for the first 4 months of 2004 was $110,000.

P15-3 (Equity Transactions and Statement Preparation) Amado Company has two classes of capital stock outstanding: 8%, $20 par preferred and $5 par common. At December 31, 2002, the following accounts were included in stockholders' equity.

Preferred Stock, 150,000 shares	$ 3,000,000
Common Stock, 2,000,000 shares	10,000,000
Paid-in Capital in Excess of Par—Preferred	200,000
Paid-in Capital in Excess of Par—Common	27,000,000
Retained Earnings	4,500,000

The following transactions affected stockholders' equity during 2003.

Jan. 1	25,000 shares of preferred stock issued at $22 per share.
Feb. 1	40,000 shares of common stock issued at $20 per share.
June 1	2-for-1 stock split (par value reduced to $2.50).
July 1	30,000 shares of common treasury stock purchased at $9 per share. Amado uses the cost method.
Sept. 15	10,000 shares of treasury stock reissued at $11 per share.
Dec. 31	Net income is $2,100,000.
Dec. 31	The preferred dividend is declared, and a common dividend of 50¢ per share is declared.

Instructions

Prepare the stockholders' equity section for Amado Company at December 31, 2003. Show all supporting computations.

P15-4 (Stock Transactions—Assessment and Lump Sum) Shikai Corporation's charter authorized issuance of 100,000 shares of $10 par value common stock and 50,000 shares of $50 preferred stock. The following transactions involving the issuance of shares of stock were completed. Each transaction is independent of the others.

1. Issued a $10,000, 9% bond payable at par and gave as a bonus one share of preferred stock, which at that time was selling for $106 a share.
2. Issued 500 shares of common stock for machinery. The machinery had been appraised at $7,100; the seller's book value was $6,200. The most recent market price of the common stock is $15 a share.
3. Issued 375 shares of common and 100 shares of preferred for a lump sum amounting to $11,300. The common had been selling at $14 and the preferred at $65.
4. Issued 200 shares of common and 50 shares of preferred for furniture and fixtures. The common had a fair market value of $16 per share and the furniture and fixtures were appraised at $6,200.

Instructions

Record the transactions listed above in journal entry form.

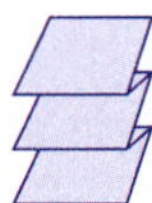

P15-5 (Treasury Stock—Cost Method) Before Polska Corporation engages in the treasury stock transactions listed below, its general ledger reflects, among others, the following account balances (par value of its stock is $30 per share).

Paid-in Capital in Excess of Par	Common Stock	Retained Earnings
Balance $99,000	Balance $270,000	Balance $80,000

Instructions

Record the treasury stock transactions (given below) under the cost method of handling treasury stock; use the FIFO method for purchase-sale purposes.

(a) Bought 380 shares of treasury stock at $39 per share.
(b) Bought 300 shares of treasury stock at $43 per share.
(c) Sold 350 shares of treasury stock at $42 per share.
(d) Sold 120 shares of treasury stock at $38 per share.

P15-6 (Treasury Stock—Cost Method—Equity Section Preparation) Constantine Company has the following stockholders' equity accounts at December 31, 2002.

Common Stock—$100 par value, authorized 8,000 shares	$480,000
Retained Earnings	294,000

Instructions

(a) Prepare entries in journal form to record the following transactions, which took place during 2003.
   (1) 240 shares of outstanding stock were purchased at $97 per share. (These are to be accounted for using the cost method.)
   (2) A $20 per share cash dividend was declared.
   (3) The dividend declared in No. 2 above was paid.
   (4) The treasury shares purchased in No. 1 above were resold at $102 per share.
   (5) 500 shares of outstanding stock were purchased at $103 per share.
   (6) 330 of the shares purchased in No. 5 above were resold at $96 per share.

(b) Prepare the stockholders' equity section of Constantine Company's balance sheet after giving effect to these transactions, assuming that the net income for 2003 was $94,000.

P15-7 (Cash Dividend Entries) The books of John Dos Passos Corporation carried the following account balances as of December 31, 2003.

Cash	$ 195,000
Preferred stock, 6% cumulative, nonparticipating, $50 par	750,000
Common stock, no par value, 300,000 shares issued	1,500,000
Paid-in capital in excess of par (preferred)	150,000
Treasury stock (common 4,200 shares at cost)	33,600
Retained earnings	105,000

The preferred stock has dividends in arrears for the past year (2003)—to be settled by issuance of treasury stock.

The board of directors, at their annual meeting on December 21, 2004, declared the following: "The current year dividends shall be 6% on the preferred and $.30 per share on the common. The dividends in arrears shall be paid by issuing one share of treasury stock for each ten shares of preferred held."

The preferred is currently selling at $80 per share, and the common at $8 per share. Net income for 2004 is estimated at $77,000.

Instructions

(a) Prepare the journal entries required for the dividend declaration and payment, assuming that they occur simultaneously.

(b) Could John Dos Passos Corporation give the preferred stockholders 2 years' dividends and common stockholders a 30 cents per share dividend, all in cash?

P15-8 (Dividends and Splits) Gutsy Company provides you with the following condensed balance sheet information.

Assets		Liabilities and Stockholders' Equity		
Current assets	$ 40,000	Current and long-term liabilities		$100,000
Investments in ABC stock		Stockholders' equity		
(10,000 shares at cost)	60,000	Common stock ($2 par)	$ 20,000	
Equipment (net)	250,000	Paid-in capital in excess of par	110,000	
Intangibles	60,000	Retained earnings	180,000	310,000
Total assets	$410,000	Total liabilities and stockholders' equity		$410,000

Instructions

For each transaction below, indicate the dollar impact (if any) on the following five items: (1) total assets, (2) common stock, (3) paid-in capital in excess of par, (4) retained earnings, and (5) stockholders' equity. (Each situation is independent.)

(a) Gutsy declares and pays a $0.50 per share cash dividend.
(b) Gutsy declares and issues a 10% stock dividend when the market price of the stock is $14 per share.
(c) Gutsy declares and issues a 40% stock dividend when the market price of the stock is $15 per share.
(d) Gutsy declares and distributes a property dividend. Gutsy gives one share of ABC stock for every two shares of Gutsy Company stock held. ABC is selling for $10 per share on the date the property dividend is declared.
(e) Gutsy declares a 2-for-1 stock split and issues new shares.

P15-9 (Stockholders' Equity Section of Balance Sheet) The following is a summary of all relevant transactions of Jadzia Dax Corporation since it was organized in 2004.

In 2004, 15,000 shares were authorized and 7,000 shares of common stock ($50 par value) were issued at a price of $57. In 2005, 1,000 shares were issued as a stock dividend when the stock was selling for $62. Three hundred shares of common stock were bought in 2006 at a cost of $66 per share. These 300 shares are still in the company treasury.

In 2002, 10,000 preferred shares were authorized and the company issued 4,000 of them ($100 par value) at $113. Some of the preferred stock was reacquired by the company and later reissued for $4,700 more than it cost the company.

The corporation has earned a total of $610,000 in net income after income taxes and paid out a total of $312,600 in cash dividends since incorporation.

Instructions

Prepare the stockholders' equity section of the balance sheet in proper form for Jadzia Dax Corporation as of December 31, 2003. Account for treasury stock using the cost method.

P15-10 (Stock Dividends and Stock Split) Jenny Durdil Inc. $10 par common stock is selling for $120 per share. Five million shares are currently issued and outstanding. The board of directors wishes to stimulate interest in Jenny Durdil common stock before a forthcoming stock issue but does not wish to distribute capital at this time. The board also believes that too many adjustments to the stockholders' equity section, especially retained earnings, might discourage potential investors.

The board has considered three options for stimulating interest in the stock:

1. A 20% stock dividend.
2. A 100% stock dividend.
3. A 2-for-1 stock split.

Instructions

Acting as financial advisor to the board, you have been asked to report briefly on each option and, considering the board's wishes, make a recommendation. Discuss the effects of each of the foregoing options.

P15-11 (Stock and Cash Dividends) Gul Ducat Corporation has outstanding 2,000,000 shares of common stock of a par value of $10 each. The balance in its retained earnings account at January 1, 2003, was $24,000,000, and it then had Additional Paid-in Capital of $5,000,000. During 2003, the company's net income was $5,700,000. A cash dividend of $0.60 a share was paid June 30, 2003, and a 6% stock dividend was distributed to stockholders of record at the close of business on December 31, 2003. You have been asked to advise on the proper accounting treatment of the stock dividend.

The existing stock of the company is quoted on a national stock exchange. The market price of the stock has been as follows.

October 31, 2003	$31
November 30, 2003	$33
December 31, 2003	$38
Average price over the 2-month period	$35

Instructions

(a) Prepare the journal entry to record the cash dividend.
(b) Prepare the journal entry to record the stock dividend.
(c) Prepare the stockholders' equity section (including schedules of retained earnings and additional paid-in capital) of the balance sheet of Gul Ducat Corporation for the year 2003 on the basis of the foregoing information. Draft a note to the financial statements setting forth the basis of the accounting for the stock dividend, and add separately appropriate comments or explanations regarding the basis chosen.

P15-12 (Analysis and Classification of Equity Transactions) Ohio Company was formed on July 1, 2000. It was authorized to issue 300,000 shares of $10 par value common stock and 100,000 shares of 8% $25 par value, cumulative and nonparticipating preferred stock. Ohio Company has a July 1–June 30 fiscal year.

The following information relates to the stockholders' equity accounts of Ohio Company.

Common Stock

Prior to the 2002–03 fiscal year, Ohio Company had 110,000 shares of outstanding common stock issued as follows.

1. 95,000 shares were issued for cash on July 1, 2000, at $31 per share.
2. On July 24, 2000, 5,000 shares were exchanged for a plot of land which cost the seller $70,000 in 1994 and had an estimated market value of $220,000 on July 24, 2000.
3. 10,000 shares were issued on March 1, 2000, for $42 per share.

During the 2002–03 fiscal year, the following transactions regarding common stock took place.

November 30, 2002	Ohio purchased 2,000 shares of its own stock on the open market at $39 per share. Ohio uses the cost method for treasury stock.
December 15, 2002	Ohio declared a 5% stock dividend for stockholders of record on January 15, 2001, to be issued on January 31, 2003. Ohio was having a liquidity problem and could not afford a cash dividend at the time. Ohio's common stock was selling at $52 per share on December 15, 2002.
June 20, 2003	Ohio sold 500 shares of its own common stock that it had purchased on November 30, 2002, for $21,000.

Preferred Stock
Ohio issued 50,000 shares of preferred stock at $44 per share on July 1, 2001.

Cash Dividends
Ohio has followed a schedule of declaring cash dividends in December and June, with payment being made to stockholders of record in the following month. The cash dividends which have been declared since inception of the company through June 30, 2003, are shown below.

Declaration Date	Common Stock	Preferred Stock
12/15/01	$0.30 per share	$1.00 per share
6/15/02	$0.30 per share	$1.00 per share
12/15/02	—	$1.00 per share

No cash dividends were declared during June 2003 due to the company's liquidity problems.

Retained Earnings
As of June 30, 2002, Ohio's retained earnings account had a balance of $690,000. For the fiscal year ending June 30, 2003, Ohio reported net income of $40,000.

Instructions
Prepare the stockholders' equity section of the balance sheet, including appropriate notes, for Ohio Company as of June 30, 2003, as it should appear in its annual report to the shareholders.

(CMA adapted)

CONCEPTUAL CASES

C15-1 (Preemptive Rights and Dilution of Ownership) Alvarado Computer Company is a small, closely held corporation. Eighty percent of the stock is held by Eduardo Alvarado, president. Of the remainder, 10% is held by members of his family and 10% by Shaunda Jones, a former officer who is now retired. The balance sheet of the company at June 30, 2003, was substantially as shown below.

Assets		Liabilities and Stockholders' Equity	
Cash	$ 22,000	Current liabilities	$ 50,000
Other	450,000	Capital stock	250,000
	$472,000	Retained earnings	172,000
			$472,000

Additional authorized capital stock of $300,000 par value had never been issued. To strengthen the cash position of the company, Eduardo Alvarado issued capital stock with a par value of $100,000 to himself at par for cash. At the next stockholders' meeting, Jones objected and claimed that her interests had been injured.

Instructions

(a) Which stockholder's right was ignored in the issue of shares to Eduardo Alvarado?
(b) How may the damage to Jones' interests be repaired most simply?
(c) If Eduardo Alvarado offered Jones a personal cash settlement and they agreed to employ you as an impartial arbitrator to determine the amount, what settlement would you propose? Present your calculations with sufficient explanation to satisfy both parties.

C15-2 (Issuance of Stock for Land) Hopee Corporation is planning to issue 3,000 shares of its own $10 par value common stock for 2 acres of land to be used as a building site.

Instructions

(a) What general rule should be applied to determine the amount at which the land should be recorded?

(b) Under what circumstances should this transaction be recorded at the fair market value of the land?

(c) Under what circumstances should this transaction be recorded at the fair market value of the stock issued?

(d) Assume Hopee intentionally records this transaction at an amount greater than the fair market value of the land and the stock. Discuss this situation.

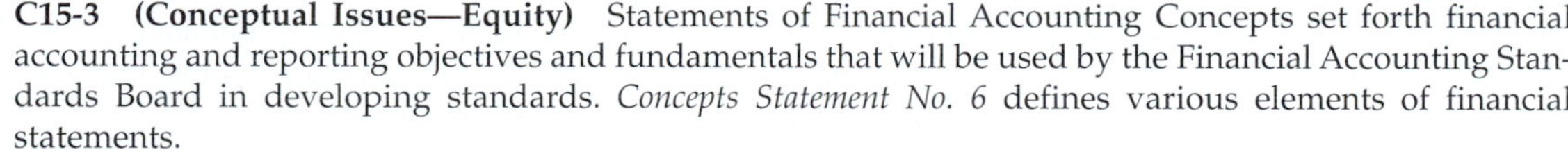

C15-3 (Conceptual Issues—Equity) Statements of Financial Accounting Concepts set forth financial accounting and reporting objectives and fundamentals that will be used by the Financial Accounting Standards Board in developing standards. *Concepts Statement No. 6* defines various elements of financial statements.

Instructions

Answer the following questions based on *SFAC No. 6.*

(a) Define and discuss the term "equity."

(b) What transactions or events change owners' equity?

(c) Define "investments by owners" and provide examples of this type of transaction. What financial statement element other than equity is typically affected by owner investments?

(d) Define "distributions to owners" and provide examples of this type of transaction. What financial statement element other than equity is typically affected by distributions?

(e) What are examples of changes within owners' equity that do not change the total amount of owners' equity?

C15-4 (Stock Dividends and Splits) The directors of Amman Corporation are considering the issuance of a stock dividend. They have asked you to discuss the proposed action by answering the following questions.

Instructions

(a) What is a stock dividend? How is a stock dividend distinguished from a stock split (1) from a legal standpoint, and (2) from an accounting standpoint?

(b) For what reasons does a corporation usually declare a stock dividend? A stock split?

(c) Discuss the amount, if any, of retained earnings to be capitalized in connection with a stock dividend.

(AICPA adapted)

C15-5 (Stock Dividends) Kitakyushu Inc., a client, is considering the authorization of a 10% common stock dividend to common stockholders. The financial vice president of Kitakyushu wishes to discuss the accounting implications of such an authorization with you before the next meeting of the board of directors.

Instructions

(a) The first topic the vice president wishes to discuss is the nature of the stock dividend to the recipient. Discuss the case against considering the stock dividend as income to the recipient.

(b) The other topic for discussion is the propriety of issuing the stock dividend to all "stockholders of record" or to "stockholders of record exclusive of shares held in the name of the corporation as treasury stock." Discuss the case against issuing stock dividends on treasury shares.

(AICPA adapted)

C15-6 (Stock Dividend, Cash Dividend, and Treasury Stock) Hsuchou Company has 30,000 shares of $10 par value common stock authorized and 20,000 shares issued and outstanding. On August 15, 2003, Hsuchou purchased 1,000 shares of treasury stock for $16 per share. Hsuchou uses the cost method to account for treasury stock. On September 14, 2003, Hsuchou sold 500 shares of the treasury stock for $20 per share.

In October 2003, Hsuchou declared and distributed 1,950 shares as a stock dividend from unissued shares when the market value of the common stock was $21 per share.

On December 20, 2003, Hsuchou declared a $1 per share cash dividend, payable on January 10, 2004, to shareholders of record on December 31, 2003.

Instructions

(a) How should Hsuchou account for the purchase and sale of the treasury stock, and how should the treasury stock be presented in the balance sheet at December 31, 2003?

(b) How should Hsuchou account for the stock dividend, and how would it affect the stockholders' equity at December 31, 2003? Why?

(c) How should Hsuchou account for the cash dividend, and how would it affect the balance sheet at December 31, 2003? Why?

(AICPA adapted)

C15-7 (Treasury Stock) Jean Loptien, president of Sycamore Corporation, is concerned about several large stockholders who have been very vocal lately in their criticisms of her leadership. She thinks they might mount a campaign to have her removed as the corporation's CEO. She decides that buying them out by purchasing their shares could eliminate them as opponents, and she is confident they would accept a "good" offer. Loptien knows the corporation's cash position is decent, so it has the cash to complete the transaction. She also knows the purchase of these shares will increase earnings per share, which should make other investors quite happy. (Earnings per share is calculated by dividing net income available for the common shareholders by the weighted average number of shares outstanding. Therefore, if the number of shares outstanding is decreased by purchasing treasury shares, earnings per share increases.)

Instructions

Answer the following questions.

(a) Who are the stakeholders in this situation?

(b) What are the ethical issues involved?

(c) Should Loptien authorize the transaction?

USING YOUR JUDGMENT

FINANCIAL REPORTING PROBLEM

3M Company

The financial statements of 3M are presented in Appendix 5B or can be accessed on the Take Action! CD.

Instructions

Refer to these financial statements and the accompanying notes to answer the following questions.

(a) What is the par or stated value of 3M's preferred stock?

(b) What is the par or stated value of 3M's common stock?

(c) What percentage of 3M's authorized common stock was issued at December 31, 2001?

(d) How many shares of common stock were outstanding at December 31, 2001, and December 31, 2000?

(e) What amount of cash dividends per share was declared by 3M in 2001? What was the dollar amount effect of the cash dividends on 3M's stockholders' equity?

(f) What is 3M's rate of return on common stock equity for 2001 and 2000?

(g) What is 3M's payout ratio for 2001 and 2000?

(h) What was the market price range (high/low) of 3M's common stock during the quarter ended December 31, 2001?

FINANCIAL STATEMENT ANALYSIS CASE

Case 1: Kellogg Corporation

Kellogg Corporation is the world's leading producer of ready-to-eat cereal products. In recent years the company has taken numerous steps aimed at improving its profitability and earnings per share. Presented on the next page are some basic facts for Kellogg Corporation.

(all dollars in millions)	2001	2000
Net sales	$8,853	$6,955
Net earnings	474	588
Total assets	10,369	4,886
Total liabilities	9,497	4,349
Common stock, $0.25 par value	104	104
Capital in excess of par value	92	102
Retained earnings	1,565	1,501
Treasury stock, at cost	337	374
Number of shares outstanding (in millions)	406	406

Instructions

(a) What are some of the reasons that management purchases its own stock?

(b) Explain how earnings per share might be affected by treasury stock transactions.

(c) Calculate the ratio of debt to total assets for 2000 and 2001, and discuss the implications of the change.

Case 2: Wiebold, Incorporated

The following note related to stockholders' equity was reported in Wiebold, Inc.'s annual report.

On February 1, 2000, the Board of Directors declared a 3-for-2 stock split, distributed on February 22, 2000, to shareholders of record on February 10, 2000. Accordingly, all numbers of common shares, except unissued shares and treasury shares, and all per share data have been restated to reflect this stock split in addition to the 3-for-2 stock split declared on January 27, 1999, distributed on February 26, 1999, to shareholders of record on February 10, 1999.

On the basis of amounts declared and paid, the annualized quarterly dividends per share were $0.80 in 1999, $0.75 in 1998, and $0.71 in 1997.

Instructions

(a) What is the significance of the date of record and the date of distribution?

(b) Why might Weibold have declared a 3-for-2 for stock split?

(c) What impact does Wiebold's stock split have on (1) total stockholders' equity, (2) total par value, (3) outstanding shares, and (4) book value per share?

COMPARATIVE ANALYSIS CASE

The Coca-Cola Company and PepsiCo, Inc.

Instructions

Go to the Take Action! CD and use information found there to answer the following questions related to The Coca-Cola Company and PepsiCo, Inc.

(a) What is the par or stated value of Coca-Cola's and PepsiCo's common or capital stock?

(b) What percentage of authorized shares was issued by Coca-Cola at December 31, 2001, and by PepsiCo at December 29, 2001?

(c) How many shares are held as treasury stock by Coca-Cola at December 31, 2001, and by PepsiCo at December 29, 2001?

(d) How many Coca-Cola common shares are outstanding at December 31, 2001? How many PepsiCo shares of capital stock are outstanding at December 29, 2001?

(e) What amounts of cash dividends per share were declared by Coca-Cola and PepsiCo in 2001? What were the dollar amount effects of the cash dividends on each company's stockholders' equity?

(f) What are Coca-Cola's and PepsiCo's rate of return on common/capital stock equity for 2001 and 2000? Which company gets the higher return on the equity of its shareholders?

(g) What are Coca-Cola's and PepsiCo's payout ratios for 2001?

(h) What was the market price range (high/low) for Coca-Cola's common stock and PepsiCo's capital stock during the fourth quarter of 2001? Which company's (Coca-Cola's or PepsiCo's) stock price increased more (%) during 2001?

RESEARCH CASE

The article "Leading the News: **AT&T Corp.** Resorts to Unusual Motion: Reverse Stock Split—Market Capitalization Stays Constant, but Measure Would Boost Share Price," by Deborah Solomon, was published in the *Wall Street Journal* on April 11, 2002. (Subscribers to **Business Extra** can access the article at that site.)

Instructions

Read the article and answer the following questions.

(a) Why is AT&T doing a reverse stock split? What advantage does it expect?

(b) Why are reverse stock splits seen as a sign of weakness? How is a reverse stock split recorded, and how is it reported in the financial statements?

(c) Why are share buybacks considered "a sign of strength"? How are they recorded, and how are they reported in the financial statements?

(d) If you were an AT&T stockholder, would you agree to this reverse stock split? Why or why not?

PROFESSIONAL SIMULATION

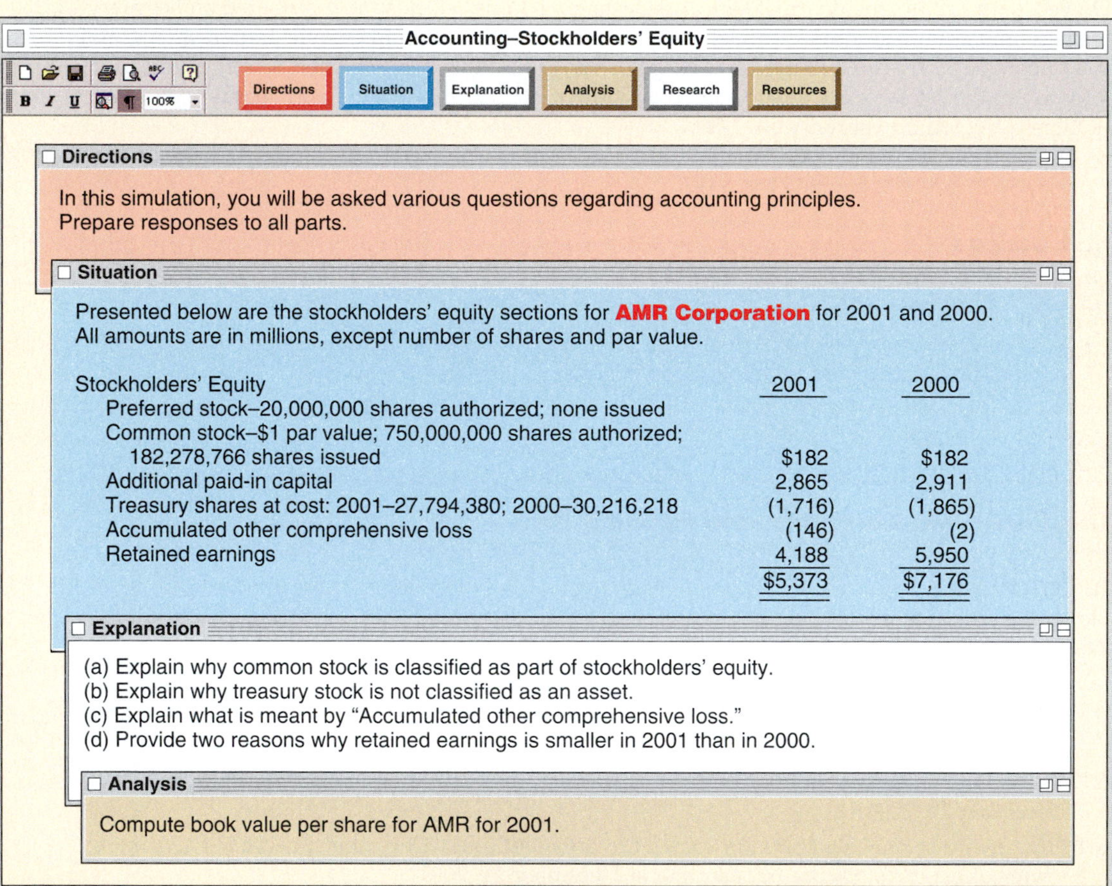

Accounting–Stockholders' Equity

Directions | Situation | Explanation | Analysis | Research | Resources

Directions

In this simulation, you will be asked various questions regarding accounting principles. Prepare responses to all parts.

Situation

Presented below are the stockholders' equity sections for **AMR Corporation** for 2001 and 2000. All amounts are in millions, except number of shares and par value.

Stockholders' Equity	2001	2000
Preferred stock–20,000,000 shares authorized; none issued		
Common stock–$1 par value; 750,000,000 shares authorized; 182,278,766 shares issued	$182	$182
Additional paid-in capital	2,865	2,911
Treasury shares at cost: 2001–27,794,380; 2000–30,216,218	(1,716)	(1,865)
Accumulated other comprehensive loss	(146)	(2)
Retained earnings	4,188	5,950
	$5,373	$7,176

Explanation

(a) Explain why common stock is classified as part of stockholders' equity.
(b) Explain why treasury stock is not classified as an asset.
(c) Explain what is meant by "Accumulated other comprehensive loss."
(d) Provide two reasons why retained earnings is smaller in 2001 than in 2000.

Analysis

Compute book value per share for AMR for 2001.

Remember to check the **Take Action! CD** and the book's **companion Web site** to find additional resources for this chapter.

CHAPTER 16

Dilutive Securities and Earnings per Share

Just Like Candy Kisses

What do President George Bush, Federal Reserve Board Chair Alan Greenspan, Senators Joseph Lieberman and John McCain, and the guru of investing Warren Buffet all have in common? Each of them has a strong opinion on whether stock options should be reported as an expense in corporate income statements.

You might wonder why such important individuals are interested in such an arcane dispute about how to account for these options. The reason: CEOs now get over 60 percent of their total pay from stock options—with only minimal performance standards for most. The punishing bear market in which many investors have lost considerable wealth, coupled with the accounting scandals at **Enron**, **WorldCom**, **Global Crossing**, and a host of other companies, has transformed once-blessed stock options into potent symbols of executive abuse and a compensation system gone haywire.

As the excesses of the 1990s are laid bare, it's becoming clear that options played a central role at numerous companies. Options were touted as a way to align the interests of corporate managers with those of stockholders. But, option grants that promised to turn caretaker corporate managers into multimillionaires in just a few years encouraged some to ignore the basics of management in favor of pumping up stock prices, exercising options, and cashing out.

As disenchantment with greedy managers has grown, investors, regulators, and politicians believe that more regulation is needed in this area. One area under intense scrutiny is the accounting for stock options. Presently most companies are generally not required to expense options. Although under current accounting standards, the potential dilution from stock options is reflected in earnings per share, many believe that not recording option grants as an expense gives the impression that options are free. As a result, options tend to be given out like candy kisses. Stay tuned. Worse may be yet to come. Companies are still issuing options at a furious pace. In fact, in recent years 200 of the largest companies have handed out amounts approaching 3 percent of their outstanding shares every year, more than double the pace of a decade ago.[1]

[1]Adapted from David Henry, Michelle Conlin, Nanette Byrnes, Michael Mandel, Stanley Holmes, and Stanley Reed, "Too Much of a Good Incentive?" *Business Week Online* (March 4, 2002).

LEARNING OBJECTIVES

After studying this chapter, you should be able to:

1. **Describe the accounting for the issuance, conversion, and retirement of convertible securities.**
2. **Explain the accounting for convertible preferred stock.**
3. **Contrast the accounting for stock warrants and for stock warrants issued with other securities.**
4. **Describe the accounting for stock compensation plans under generally accepted accounting principles.**
5. **Explain the controversy involving stock compensation plans.**
6. **Compute earnings per share in a simple capital structure.**
7. **Compute earnings per share in a complex capital structure.**

PREVIEW OF CHAPTER 16

As indicated in the opening story, the widespread use of options and other dilutive securities has led the accounting profession to examine the area closely. Specifically, the profession has directed its attention to accounting for these securities at date of issuance and to the presentation of earnings per share figures that recognize their effect. The first section of this chapter discusses convertible securities, warrants, stock options, and contingent shares. These securities are called **dilutive securities** because a reduction—dilution—in earnings per share often results when these securities become common stock. The second section indicates how these securities are used in earnings per share computations. The content and organization of the chapter are as follows.

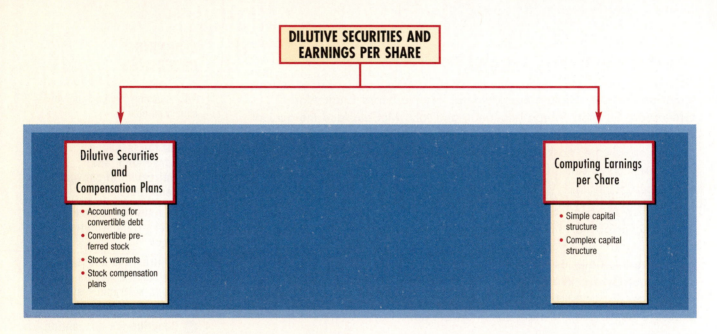

SECTION 1 *DILUTIVE SECURITIES AND COMPENSATION PLANS*

ACCOUNTING FOR CONVERTIBLE DEBT

OBJECTIVE 1
Describe the accounting for the issuance, conversion, and retirement of convertible securities.

If bonds can be converted into other corporate securities during some specified period of time after issuance, they are called **convertible bonds**. **A convertible bond combines the benefits of a bond with the privilege of exchanging it for stock at the holder's option.** It is purchased by investors who desire the security of a bond holding—guaranteed interest—plus the added option of conversion if the value of the stock appreciates significantly.

Corporations issue convertibles for two main reasons. One is the desire **to raise equity capital** without giving up more ownership control than necessary. To illustrate, assume that a company wants to raise $1,000,000 at a time when its common stock is selling at $45 per share. Such an issue would require sale of 22,222 shares (ignoring issue costs). By selling 1,000 bonds at $1,000 par, each convertible into 20 shares of common stock, the enterprise may raise $1,000,000 by committing only 20,000 shares of its common stock.

A second reason why companies issue convertible securities is **to obtain debt financing at cheaper rates**. Many enterprises could issue debt only at high interest rates unless a convertible covenant were attached. The conversion privilege entices the investor to accept a lower interest rate than would normally be the case on a straight debt issue. For example, **Amazon.com** at one time issued convertible bonds that pay interest at an effective yield of 4.75 percent, a rate much lower than Amazon.com would have had to pay if it had issued straight debt. For this lower interest rate, the investor receives the right to buy Amazon.com's common stock at a fixed price until maturity.[2]

Accounting for convertible debt involves reporting issues at the time of (1) issuance, (2) conversion, and (3) retirement.

At Time of Issuance

The method for recording convertible bonds **at the date of issue follows the method used to record straight debt issues** (with none of the proceeds recorded as equity). Any discount or premium that results from the issuance of convertible bonds is amortized to its maturity date because it is difficult to predict when, if at all, conversion will occur. However, the accounting for convertible debt as a straight debt issue is controversial; we discuss it more fully later in this chapter.

At Time of Conversion

If bonds are converted into other securities, the principal accounting problem is to determine the amount at which to record the securities exchanged for the bond. Assume Hilton, Inc. issued at a premium of $60 a $1,000 bond convertible into 10 shares of common stock (par value $10). At the time of conversion the unamortized premium is $50, the market value of the bond is $1,200, and the stock is quoted on the market at $120. **The book value method of recording the conversion of the bonds is the method most commonly used in practice and is considered GAAP.** To illustrate the specifics of this approach, the entry for the conversion of the Hilton, Inc. bonds would be:

Bonds Payable	1,000	
Premium on Bonds Payable	50	
Common Stock		100
Paid-in Capital in Excess of Par		950

Support for the book value approach is based on the argument that an agreement was established at the date of the issuance either to pay a stated amount of cash at maturity or to issue a stated number of shares of equity securities. Therefore, when the debt is converted to equity in accordance with the preexisting contract terms, no gain or loss should be recognized upon conversion.

Induced Conversions

Sometimes the issuer wishes to encourage prompt conversion of its convertible debt to equity securities in order to reduce interest costs or to improve its debt to equity ratio. As a result, the issuer may offer some form of additional consideration (such as cash or common stock), called a "sweetener," to **induce conversion**. The sweetener should be reported as an expense of the current period at an amount equal to the fair value of the additional securities or other consideration given.

---

[2]As with any investment, a buyer has to be careful. For example, **Wherehouse Entertainment Inc.**, which had 6¼ percent convertibles outstanding, was taken private in a leveraged buyout. As a result, the convertible was suddenly as risky as a junk bond of a highly leveraged company with a coupon of only 6¼ percent. As one holder of the convertibles noted, "What's even worse is that the company will be so loaded down with debt that it probably won't have enough cash flow to make its interest payments. And the convertible debt we hold is subordinated to the rest of Wherehouse's debt." These types of situations have made convertibles less attractive and have led to the introduction of takeover protection covenants in some convertible bond offerings. Or, sometimes convertibles are permitted to be called at par and therefore the conversion premium may be lost.

Assume that Helloid, Inc. has outstanding $1,000,000 par value convertible debentures convertible into 100,000 shares of $1 par value common stock. Helloid wishes to reduce its annual interest cost. To do so, Helloid agrees to pay the holders of its convertible debentures an additional $80,000 if they will convert. Assuming conversion occurs, the following entry is made.

Debt Conversion Expense	80,000	
Bonds Payable	1,000,000	
Common Stock		100,000
Additional Paid-in Capital		900,000
Cash		80,000

The additional $80,000 is recorded as **an expense of the current period** and not as a reduction of equity. Some argue that the cost of a conversion inducement is a cost of obtaining equity capital. As a result, they contend, it should be recognized as a cost of—a reduction of—the equity capital acquired and not as an expense. However, the FASB indicated that when an additional payment is needed to make bondholders convert, the payment is for a service (bondholders converting at a given time) and should be reported as an expense. This expense is not reported as an extraordinary item.[3]

Retirement of Convertible Debt

As indicated earlier, the method for recording the **issuance** of convertible bonds follows that used in recording straight debt issues. Specifically this means that no portion of the proceeds should be attributable to the conversion feature and credited to Additional Paid-in Capital. Although theoretical objections to this approach can be raised, to be consistent, a gain or loss on **retiring convertible debt needs to be recognized in the same way as a gain or loss on retiring debt** that is not convertible. For this reason, differences between the cash acquisition price of debt and its carrying amount should be reported **currently in income as a gain or loss.**

CONVERTIBLE PREFERRED STOCK

OBJECTIVE 2
Explain the accounting for convertible preferred stock.

The major difference between accounting for a convertible bond and a **convertible preferred stock** at the date of issue is that convertible bonds are considered liabilities, whereas convertible preferreds (unless mandatory redemption exists) are considered a part of stockholders' equity.

In addition, when convertible preferred stocks are exercised, there is no theoretical justification for recognition of a gain or loss. No gain or loss is recognized when the entity deals with stockholders in their capacity as business owners. The **book value method is employed**: Preferred Stock, along with any related Additional Paid-in Capital, is debited; Common Stock and Additional Paid-in Capital (if an excess exists) are credited.

A different treatment develops when the par value of the common stock issued exceeds the book value of the preferred stock. In that case, Retained Earnings is usually debited for the difference.

Assume Host Enterprises issued 1,000 shares of common stock (par value $2) upon conversion of 1,000 shares of preferred stock (par value $1) that was originally issued for a $200 premium. The entry would be:

Convertible Preferred Stock	1,000	
Paid-in Capital in Excess of Par (Premium on Preferred Stock)	200	
Retained Earnings	800	
Common Stock		2,000

[3]"Induced Conversions of Convertible Debt," *Statement of Financial Accounting Standards No. 84* (Stamford, Conn.: FASB, 1985).

The rationale for the debit to Retained Earnings is that the preferred stockholders are offered an **additional return** to facilitate their conversion to common stock. In this example, the additional return is charged to retained earnings. Many states, however, require that this charge simply reduce additional paid-in capital from other sources.

DESPERATE DEAL

WHAT DO THE NUMBERS MEAN?

When you're in dire straits, you do what you have to do.

So it is now with **Corning**, the once great company that provided the glass for Edison's first light bulb. It was a steady company until it fell for the great fiber optic bubble. It sold profitable divisions that seemed less exciting and spent billions on overpriced fiber optic acquisitions.

Recently, needing cash to finance operating losses and with the credit rating agencies having determined that its bonds are junk and its commercial paper unsalable, Corning came up with a glorified common stock offering that devastated an already depressed share price, which fell 50 percent in just three days.

Formally, this is a convertible preferred offering. But that is fiction. Of the $500 million put up by investors, $102 million was used to buy Treasury bonds that will pay the promised 7 percent dividends for three years, after which the preferred must be converted into common. If Corning goes bankrupt before then, the preferred holders are supposed to get the dividends immediately.

This is a bear market vehicle. In three years, the preferred shares will be converted into somewhere between 214 million and 312 million common shares. For a company that now has 952 million shares outstanding, that means dilution of at least a quarter, and maybe a third, depending on where the stock is by then.

Why not just issue common now? Why should buyers pay Corning to manage a portfolio of Treasuries? Corning's investment bankers figured they could attract a different class of investors. People now want income, so Wall Street will give it to them, even if in reality it is nothing more than common stock in drag.

Source: Adapted from Floyd Norris, "Corning's Desperate Deal Destroys Value," *New York Times* (August 2, 2002), p. C1. Reprinted with permission.

STOCK WARRANTS

OBJECTIVE 3
Contrast the accounting for stock warrants and for stock warrants issued with other securities.

Warrants are certificates entitling the holder to acquire shares of stock at a certain price within a stated period. This option is similar to the conversion privilege: Warrants, if exercised, become common stock and usually have a dilutive effect (reduce earnings per share) similar to that of the conversion of convertible securities. However, a substantial difference between convertible securities and stock warrants is that upon exercise of the warrants, the holder has to pay a certain amount of money to obtain the shares.

The issuance of warrants or options to buy additional shares normally arises under three situations:

1. When issuing different types of securities, such as bonds or preferred stock, warrants are often included **to make the security more attractive**—to provide an "equity kicker."
2. Upon the issuance of additional common stock, existing stockholders have a **preemptive right to purchase common stock** first. Warrants may be issued to evidence that right.
3. Warrants, often referred to as stock options, are given as **compensation to executives and employees**.

The problems in accounting for stock warrants are complex and present many difficulties—some of which remain unresolved.

Stock Warrants Issued with Other Securities

Warrants issued with other securities are basically long-term options to buy common stock at a fixed price. Although some perpetual warrants are traded, generally their life is 5 years, occasionally 10.

A warrant works like this: **Tenneco Automotive Inc.** offered a unit comprising one share of stock and one detachable warrant exercisable at $24.25 per share and good for 5 years. The unit sold for $22.75. Since the price of the common the day before the sale was $19.88, the difference suggests a price of $2.87 for the warrants.

In this situation, the warrants had an apparent value of $2.87, even though it would not be profitable at present for the purchaser to exercise the warrant and buy the stock, because the price of the stock is much below the exercise price of $24.25.[4] The investor pays for the warrant in order to receive a possible future call on the stock at a fixed price when the price has risen significantly. For example, if the price of the stock rises to $30, the investor has gained $2.88 ($30 minus $24.25 minus $2.87) on an investment of $2.87, a 100 percent increase! But, if the price never rises, the investor loses the full $2.87.[5]

The proceeds from the sale of debt with **detachable stock warrants** should be allocated between the two securities.[6] The reason: Two separable instruments are involved—that is, (1) a bond and (2) a warrant giving the holder the right to purchase common stock at a certain price. Warrants that are detachable can be traded separately from the debt, and therefore a market value can be determined. The two methods of allocation available are:

1. The proportional method.
2. The incremental method.

Proportional Method

AT&T's offering of detachable 5-year warrants to buy one share of common stock (par value $5) at $25, at a time when a share was selling for approximately $50, enabled it to price its offering of bonds at par with a moderate 8¾ percent yield. To place a value on the two securities, one would determine (1) the value of the bonds without the warrants and (2) the value of the warrants.

For example, assume that AT&T's bonds (par $1,000) sold for 99 without the warrants soon after they were issued. The market value of the warrants at that time was $30. (Prior to sale the warrants will not have a market value.) The allocation is based on an estimate of market value, generally as established by an investment banker, or on the relative market value of the bonds and the warrants soon after they are issued and traded. The price paid for 10,000, $1,000 bonds with the warrants attached was par, or $10,000,000. The allocation between the bonds and warrants is shown in Illustration 16-1.

---

[4]Later in this discussion it will be shown that the value of the warrant is normally determined on the basis of a relative market value approach because of the difficulty of imputing a warrant value in any other manner.

[5]From the illustration, it is apparent that buying warrants can be an "all or nothing" proposition.

[6]A detachable warrant means that the warrant can sell separately from the bond. *APB Opinion No. 14* makes a distinction between detachable and nondetachable warrants because nondetachable warrants must be sold with the security as a complete package; thus, no allocation is permitted.

ILLUSTRATION 16-1
Proportional Allocation of Proceeds between Bonds and Warrants

Fair market value of bonds (without warrants) ($10,000,000 × .99)	$ 9,900,000
Fair market value of warrants (10,000 × $30)	300,000
Aggregate fair market value	$10,200,000

Allocated to bonds:	$\frac{\$9,900,000}{\$10,200,000}$ × $10,000,000 =	$ 9,705,882
Allocated to warrants:	$\frac{\$300,000}{\$10,200,000}$ × $10,000,000 =	294,118
Total allocation		$10,000,000

In this situation the bonds sell at a discount and are recorded as follows.

Cash	9,705,882	
Discount on Bonds Payable	294,118	
Bonds Payable		10,000,000

In addition, the company sells warrants that are credited to paid-in capital. The entry is as follows.

Cash	294,118	
Paid-in Capital—Stock Warrants		294,118

The entries may be combined if desired; they are shown separately here to indicate that the purchaser of the bond is buying not only a bond, but also a possible future claim on common stock.

Assuming that all 10,000 warrants are exercised (one warrant per one share of stock), the following entry would be made.

Cash (10,000 × $25)	250,000	
Paid-in Capital—Stock Warrants	294,118	
Common Stock (10,000 × $5)		50,000
Paid-in Capital in Excess of Par		494,118

What if the warrants are not exercised? In that case, Paid-in Capital—Stock Warrants is debited for $294,118, and Paid-in Capital from Expired Warrants is credited for the same amount. The additional paid-in capital reverts to the existing stockholders.

Incremental Method

In instances where the fair value of either the warrants or the bonds is not determinable, the incremental method used in lump-sum security purchases (explained in Chapter 15, page 729) may be used. That is, the security for which the market value is determinable is used, and the remainder of the purchase price is allocated to the security for which the market value is not known.

For example, assume that the market price of the **AT&T** warrants was known to be $300,000, but the market price of the bonds without the warrants could not be determined. In this case, the amount allocated to the warrants and the stock would be as follows.

ILLUSTRATION 16-2
Incremental Allocation of Proceeds between Bonds and Warrants

Lump-sum receipt	$10,000,000
Allocated to the warrants	300,000
Balance allocated to bonds	$ 9,700,000

Conceptual Questions

The question arises whether the allocation of value to the warrants is consistent with the handling accorded convertible debt, in which no value is allocated to the conversion privilege. The FASB has concluded that the features of a convertible security are **inseparable** in the sense that choices are mutually exclusive: the holder either converts

Reporting a convertible bond solely as debt is not representationally faithful. However, the cost-benefit constraint is used to justify the failure to allocate between debt and equity.

or redeems the bonds for cash, but cannot do both. No basis, therefore, exists for recognizing the conversion value in the accounts. The FASB, however, indicates that the issuance of bonds with **detachable warrants** involves two securities, one a debt security, which will remain outstanding until maturity, and the other a warrant to purchase common stock. At the time of issuance, separable instruments exist, and therefore separate treatment is justified. **Nondetachable warrants**, however, **do not require an allocation of the proceeds between the bonds and the warrants**. The entire proceeds are recorded as debt.

Many argue that the conversion feature is not significantly different in nature from the call represented by a warrant. The question is whether, although the legal forms are different, sufficient similarities of substance exist to support the same accounting treatment. Some contend that inseparability per se is not a sufficient basis for restricting allocation between identifiable components of a transaction. Examples of allocation between assets of value in a single transaction are not uncommon, such as allocation of values in basket purchases and separation of principal and interest in capitalizing long-term leases. Critics of the current accounting for convertibles say that to deny recognition of value to the conversion feature merely looks to the form of the instrument and does not deal with the substance of the transaction.

INTERNATIONAL INSIGHT

International accounting standards require that the issuer of convertible debt record the liability and equity components separately.

The authors disagree with the FASB as well. In both situations (convertible debt and debt issued with warrants), the investor has made a payment to the firm for an equity feature—the right to acquire an equity instrument in the future. The only real distinction between them is that the additional payment made when the equity instrument is formally acquired takes different forms. The warrant holder pays additional cash to the issuing firm; the convertible debt holder pays for stock by forgoing the receipt of interest from conversion date until maturity date and by forgoing the receipt of the maturity value itself. Thus, it is argued that the difference is one of method or form of payment only, rather than one of substance. **Until the profession officially reverses its stand in regard to accounting for convertible debt, however, only bonds issued with detachable stock warrants will result in accounting recognition of the equity feature.**[7]

Rights to Subscribe to Additional Shares

If the directors of a corporation decide to issue new shares of stock, the old stockholders generally have the right (preemptive privilege) to purchase newly issued shares in proportion to their holdings. The privilege, referred to as a **stock right**, saves existing stockholders from suffering a dilution of voting rights without their consent. Also, it may allow them to purchase stock somewhat below its market value. The warrants issued in these situations are of short duration, unlike the warrants issued with other securities.

The certificate representing the stock right states the number of shares the holder of the right may purchase, as well as the price at which the new shares may be purchased. Each share owned ordinarily gives the owner one stock right. The price is normally less than the current market value of such shares, which gives the rights a value in themselves. From the time they are issued until they expire, stock rights may be purchased and sold like any other security.

No entry is required when rights are issued to existing stockholders. Only a memorandum entry is needed to indicate the number of rights issued to existing stockholders and to ensure that the company has additional unissued stock registered for

[7]Recent research indicates that estimates of the debt and equity components of convertible bonds are subject to considerable measurement error. See Mary Barth, Wayne Landsman, and Richard Rendleman, Jr., "Option Pricing–Based Bond Value Estimates and a Fundamental Components Approach to Account for Corporate Debt," *The Accounting Review* (January 1998). The FASB is currently working on a standard that will address the accounting for securities with both debt and equity features, such as convertible bonds. In its exposure draft, the Board requires that the issuer classify separately the liability and equity components of a financial instrument. As a result, it now appears likely that financial instruments such as convertible debt will be divided into liability and equity components for accounting and reporting purposes in the near future.

issuance in case the rights are exercised. No formal entry is made at this time because no stock has been issued and no cash has been received.

If the rights are exercised, usually a cash payment of some type is involved. If the cash received is equal to the par value, an entry crediting Common Stock at par value is made. If it is in excess of par value, a credit to Paid-in Capital in Excess of Par develops. If it is less than par value, a charge to Paid-in Capital is appropriate.

STOCK COMPENSATION PLANS

Another form of warrant arises in stock compensation plans used to pay and motivate employees. This warrant is a **stock option**, which gives selected employees the option to purchase common stock at a given price over an extended period of time. As indicated in the opening story, stock options are very popular. For example, the following chart shows stock options as a percentage of total compensation for 1999–2000 given to the top 200 CEOs and to 100 dot-com company CEOs.

ILLUSTRATION 16-3
Stock Options as a Portion of Total Compensation

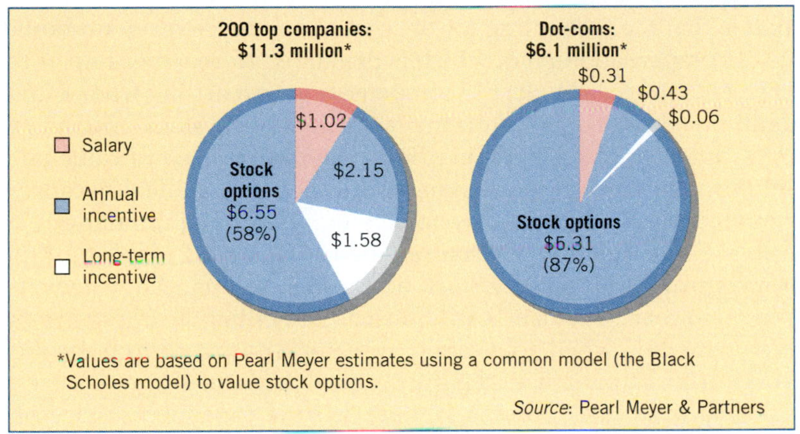

These figures show the dramatic change in the way many top executives (and for that matter, regular employees) are compensated.

Effective compensation has been a subject of considerable interest lately. A consensus of opinion is that effective compensation programs are ones that (1) motivate employees to high levels of performance, (2) help retain executives and allow for recruitment of new talent, (3) base compensation on employee and company performance, (4) maximize the employee's after-tax benefit and minimize the employee's after-tax cost, and (5) use performance criteria over which the employee has control. Although straight cash compensation plans (salary and, perhaps, bonus) are an important part of any compensation program, they are oriented to the short run. Many companies recognize that a more long-run compensation plan is often needed in addition to a cash component.

Long-term compensation plans attempt to develop in key employees a strong loyalty toward the company. An effective way to accomplish this goal is to give the employees "a piece of the action"—that is, an equity interest based on changes in long-term measures such as increases in earnings per share, revenues, stock price, or market share. These plans, generally referred to as **stock option plans**, come in many different forms. Essentially, they provide the employee with the opportunity to receive stock or cash in the future if the performance of the company (by whatever measure) is satisfactory.

The Major Reporting Issue

Suppose that you are an employee for Hurdle Inc. and you are granted options to purchase 10,000 shares of the firm's common stock as part of your compensation. The date you receive the options is referred to as the **grant date**. The options are good for 10 years. The market price and the exercise price for the stock are both $20 at the grant date. **What is the value of the compensation you just received?**

Some believe you have not received anything: That is, the difference between the market price and the exercise price is zero, and therefore no compensation results. Others argue these options have value: If the stock price goes above $20 any time over the next 10 years and you exercise these options, substantial compensation results. For example, if at the end of the fourth year, the market price of the stock is $30 and you exercise your options, you will have earned $100,000 [10,000 options × ($30 − $20)], ignoring income taxes.

How should the granting of these options be reported by Hurdle Inc.? In the past, GAAP required that compensation cost be measured by the excess of the market price of the stock over its exercise price at the grant date. This approach is referred to as the **intrinsic value method** because the computation is not dependent on external circumstances: **The compensation cost is the difference between the market price of the stock and the exercise price of the options at the grant date**. Hurdle would therefore not recognize any compensation expense related to your options because at the grant date the market price and exercise price were the same.

The FASB **encourages but does not require recognition of compensation cost for the fair value of stock-based compensation paid to employees for their services.**[8] The FASB position is that the accounting for the cost of employee services should be based on the value of compensation paid, which is presumed to be a measure of the value of the services received. Accordingly, the compensation cost arising from employee stock options should be measured based on the fair value of the stock options granted.[9] To determine this value, acceptable option pricing models are used to value options at the date of grant. This approach is referred to as the **fair value method** because the option value is estimated based on the many factors that determine its underlying value.[10]

The FASB met considerable resistance when it proposed requiring the fair value method for recognizing the costs of stock options in the financial statements. As a result, it was decided that a company **can choose** to use **either** the intrinsic value method **or** the fair value method when accounting for compensation cost on the income statement. However, if a company uses the intrinsic value method to recognize compensation costs for employee stock options, it must provide expanded disclosures on these costs. Specifically, companies that choose the intrinsic value method are required to disclose in a note to the financial statements pro-forma net income and earnings per share (if presented by the company), **as if it had used the fair value method**.

Accounting for Stock Compensation

OBJECTIVE 4
Describe the accounting for stock compensation plans under generally accepted accounting principles.

A company is given a choice in the recognition method for stock compensation. However, **the FASB encourages adoption of the fair value method**. Our discussion in this section illustrates both methods. Stock option plans involve two main accounting issues:

1. How should compensation expense be determined?
2. Over what periods should compensation expense be allocated?

Determining Expense

Under the fair value method, total compensation expense is computed based on the fair value of the options expected to vest[11] on the date the options are granted to the employee(s) (i.e., the **grant date**). Fair value for public companies is to be estimated us-

[8]"Accounting for Stock-Based Compensation," *Statement of Financial Accounting Standards No. 123* (Norwalk, Conn.: FASB, 1995).

[9]Stock options issued to non-employees in exchange for other goods or services must be recognized according to the fair value method in *SFAS 123*.

[10]These factors include the volatility of the underlying stock, the expected life of the options, the risk-free rate during the option life, and expected dividends during the option life.

[11]"To vest" means "to earn the rights to." An employee's award becomes vested at the date that the employee's right to receive or retain shares of stock or cash under the award is no longer contingent on remaining in the service of the employer.

ing an option pricing model, with some adjustments for the unique factors of employee stock options. No adjustments are made after the grant date, in response to subsequent changes in the stock price—either up or down.[12]

Under the intrinsic value method, total compensation cost is computed as the excess of the market price of the stock over the option price on the date when both the number of shares to which employees are entitled and the option or purchase price for those shares are known. This date is called the **measurement date**. For many plans, the measurement date is the **grant date**. However, the measurement date may be later for plans with variable terms (either number of shares and/or option price are not known) that depend on events after the date of grant. For such variable plans, compensation expense may have to be estimated on the basis of assumptions as to the final number of shares and the option price (usually at the exercise date).

A LITTLE HONESTY GOES A LONG WAY

WHAT DO THE NUMBERS MEAN?

You might think investors would punish companies that have decided to expense stock options. After all, most of corporate America has been battling for years to avoid such a fate, worried that accounting for those perks would destroy earnings. And indeed, Merrill Lynch estimates that if all S&P 500 companies were to expense options [in 2002], reported profits would fall 10 percent.

And yet, as a small but growing band of big-name companies makes the switch, investors have for the most part showered them with love. With a few exceptions, the stock prices of the expensers, from Cinergy to Fannie Mae, have outpaced the market since they announced the change.

The few, the brave

	Estimated 2002 EPS		% change since announcement**
	Without options	With options expensed*	Company stock price
Cinergy	$ 2.80	$ 2.77	22.4%
Washington Post	20.48	20.10	16.4
Computer Associates	−0.46	−0.62	11.1
Fannie Mae	6.15	6.02	6.7
Bank One	2.77	2.61	2.6
General Motors	5.84	5.45	2.6
Procter & Gamble	3.57	3.35	−2.3
Coca-Cola	1.79	1.70	−6.2
General Electric	1.65	1.61	−6.2
Amazon	0.04	−0.99	−11.4

*Assumes options expenses for 2002 are the same as 2001 and that all outstanding grants are counted.

**As of 8/6/02.

Data sources: Merrill Lynch; company reports.

Source: David Stires, "A Little Honesty Goes a Long Way," *Fortune* (September 2, 2002), p. 186. Reprinted by permission.

[12]Nonpublic companies frequently do not have data with which to estimate the fair-value element. Therefore, nonpublic companies are permitted to use a minimum value method to estimate the value of the options. The minimum value method does not consider the volatility of the stock price when estimating option value.

Allocating Compensation Expense

In general, under both the fair and intrinsic value methods, compensation expense is recognized in the periods in which the employee performs the service—the **service period**. Unless otherwise specified, the service period is the vesting period—the time between the grant date and the vesting date. Thus, total compensation cost is determined at the grant date and allocated to the periods benefited by the employees' services.

Illustration

To illustrate the accounting for a stock option plan, assume that on November 1, 2002, the stockholders of Chen Company approve a plan that grants the company's five executives options to purchase 2,000 shares each of the company's $1 par value common stock. The options are granted on January 1, 2003, and may be exercised at any time within the next 10 years. The option price per share is $60, and the market price of the stock at the date of grant is $70 per share. **Under the intrinsic value method**, the total compensation expense is computed below.

ILLUSTRATION 16-4
Computation of Compensation Expense—Intrinsic Value Method

Market value of 10,000 shares at date of grant ($70 per share)	$700,000
Option price of 10,000 shares at date of grant ($60 per share)	600,000
Total compensation expense (intrinsic value)	$100,000

Under the fair value method, total compensation expense is computed by applying an acceptable fair value option pricing model (such as the Black-Scholes option pricing model). To keep this illustration simple, we will assume that the fair value option pricing model determines total compensation expense to be $220,000.

Basic Entries. The value of the options under either method is recognized as an expense in the periods in which the employee performs services. In the case of Chen Company, assume that the expected period of benefit is 2 years, starting with the grant date. The journal entries to record the transactions related to this option contract using both the intrinsic value and fair value method are shown below.

ILLUSTRATION 16-5
Comparison of Entries for Option Contract—Intrinsic Value and Fair Value Methods

Intrinsic Value			Fair Value		
At date of grant (January 1, 2003)					
No entry			No entry		
To record compensation expense for 2003 (December 31, 2003)					
Compensation Expense	50,000		Compensation Expense	110,000	
Paid-in Capital—Stock Options			Paid-in Capital—Stock Options		
($100,000 ÷ 2)		50,000	($220,000 ÷ 2)		110,000
To record compensation expense for 2004 (December 31, 2004)					
Compensation Expense	50,000		Compensation Expense	110,000	
Paid-in Capital—Stock Options		50,000	Paid-in Capital—Stock Options		110,000

Under both methods, compensation expense is allocated evenly over the 2-year service period. The only difference between the two methods is the amount of compensation recognized.

Exercise. If 20 percent, or 2,000, of the 10,000 options were exercised on June 1, 2006 (3 years and 5 months after date of grant), the following journal entry would be recorded using the **intrinsic value method**.

June 1, 2006		
Cash (2,000 × $60)	120,000	
Paid-in Capital—Stock Options (20% × $100,000)	20,000	
Common Stock (2,000 × $1)		2,000
Paid-in Capital in Excess of Par		138,000

Under the **fair value approach**, the entry would be:

June 1, 2006		
Cash (2,000 × $60)	120,000	
Paid-in Capital—Stock Options (20% × $220,000)	44,000	
Common Stock (2,000 × $1)		2,000
Paid-in Capital in Excess of Par		162,000

Expiration. If the remaining stock options are not exercised before their expiration date, the balance in the Paid-in Capital—Stock Options account should be transferred to a more properly titled paid-in capital account, such as Paid-in Capital from Expired Stock Options. The entry to record this transaction at the date of expiration would be as follows.

ILLUSTRATION 16-6
Comparison of Entries for Stock Option Expiration—Intrinsic Value and Fair Value Methods

Intrinsic Value			Fair Value		
January 1, 2013 (expiration date)					
Paid-in Capital—Stock Options	80,000		Paid-in Capital—Stock Options	176,000	
Paid-in Capital from Expired Stock Options (80% × $100,000)		80,000	Paid-in Capital from Expired Stock Options (80% × $220,000)		176,000

Adjustment. The fact that a stock option is not exercised does not nullify the propriety of recording the costs of services received from executives and attributable to the stock option plan. Under GAAP, compensation expense is, therefore, not adjusted upon expiration of the options.

However, if a stock option is forfeited because **an employee fails to satisfy a service requirement** (e.g., leaves employment), the estimate of compensation expense recorded in the current period should be adjusted (as a change in estimate). This change in estimate would be recorded by debiting Paid-in Capital—Stock Options and crediting Compensation Expense, thereby decreasing compensation expense in the period of forfeiture.

Types of Plans

Many different types of plans are used to compensate key employees. In all these plans the amount of the reward depends upon future events. Consequently, continued employment is a necessary element in almost all types of plans. The popularity of a given plan usually depends on the firm's prospects in the stock market and on tax considerations. For example, if it appears that appreciation will occur in a company's stock, a plan that offers the option to purchase stock is attractive. Conversely, if it appears that price appreciation is unlikely, then compensation might be tied to some performance measure such as an increase in book value or earnings per share.

Three common compensation plans that illustrate different objectives are:

1. Stock option plans (incentive or nonqualified).
2. Stock appreciation rights plans.
3. Performance-type plans.

Most plans follow the general guidelines for reporting established in the previous sections. An expanded discussion of these types of plans and their accounting is provided in Appendix 16A.

Noncompensatory Plans

In some companies, stock purchase plans permit all employees to purchase stock at a discounted price for a short period of time. These plans are usually classified as noncompensatory. Noncompensatory means that the primary purpose of the plan is not to compensate the employees but, rather, to enable the employer to secure equity capital or to induce widespread ownership of an enterprise's common stock among employees. Thus, compensation expense is not reported for these plans. **Noncompensatory plans** have three characteristics:

1. Substantially all full-time employees may participate on an equitable basis.
2. The discount from market price is small. That is, it does not exceed the greater of a per share discount reasonably offered to stockholders or the per share amount of costs avoided by not having to raise cash in a public offering.
3. The plan offers no substantive option feature.

For example, Masthead Company had a stock purchase plan under which employees who meet minimal employment qualifications are entitled to purchase Masthead stock at a 5 percent reduction from market price for a short period of time. The reduction from market price is not considered compensatory because the per share amount of the costs avoided by not having to raise the cash in a public offering is equal to 5 percent. **Plans that do not possess all of the above mentioned three characteristics are classified as compensatory.**

Disclosure of Compensation Plans

To comply with *SFAS No. 123*, companies offering stock-based compensation plans must determine the fair value of the options. Companies must then decide whether to use the fair value method and recognize expense in the income statement, or to use the intrinsic value approach and disclose in the notes the pro forma impact on net income and earnings per share (if presented), as if the fair value method had been used.

Regardless of whether the intrinsic value or fair value method is used, full disclosure should be made about the status of these plans at the end of the periods presented, including the number of shares under option, options exercised and forfeited, the weighted average option prices for these categories, the weighted average fair value of options granted during the year, and the average remaining contractual life of the options outstanding.[13] In addition to information about the status of the stock option plans, companies must also disclose the method and significant assumptions used to estimate the fair values of the stock options.

[13]These data should be reported separately for each different type of plan offered to employees.

If the intrinsic value method is used in the financial statements, companies must still disclose the pro forma net income and pro forma earnings per share (if presented), as if the fair value method had been used to account for the stock-based compensation cost. Illustration 16-7 illustrates this disclosure, as provided by **Gateway, Inc.**

Gateway, Inc.

Had compensation expense for employee and director stock options been determined based on the fair value of the options on the date of grant, net income (loss) and net income (loss) per share would have resulted in the pro forma amounts indicated below (in thousands, except per share amounts):

	2001	2000	1999
Net income (loss)—as reported	$(1,033,915)	$241,483	$427,944
Net income (loss)—pro forma	(1,106,376)	(53,675)	319,494
Net income (loss) per share—as reported			
Basic	$ (3.20)	$ 0.75	$ 1.36
Diluted	$ (3.20)	$ 0.73	$ 1.32
Net income (loss) per share—pro forma			
Basic	$ (3.42)	$ (0.17)	$ 1.02
Diluted	$ (3.42)	$ (0.17)	$ 0.98

The pro forma effect on net income (loss) for 2001, 2000, and 1999 is not fully representative of the pro forma effect on net income (loss) in future years because it does not take into consideration pro forma compensation expense related to the vesting of grants made prior to 1997.

ILLUSTRATION 16-7
Disclosure of Pro Forma Effect of Stock Option Plans

Debate over Stock Option Accounting

OBJECTIVE 5
Explain the controversy involving stock compensation plans.

In general, use of the fair value approach results in greater compensation costs relative to the intrinsic value model. As indicated in the story on page 783, a study of the companies in the Standard & Poor's 500 stock index documented that, on average, earnings in 2002 could be overstated by 10 percent through the use of the intrinsic value method. Until recently, only two major companies, **Boeing Co.** and **Winn-Dixie Stores**, used the fair value method in recording compensation expense. However, a number of companies, such as **Coca-Cola**, **General Electric**, **Wachovia**, **Bank One**, and **The Washington Post**, have decided to use the fair value method. As the CFO of Coke stated, "There is no doubt that stock options are compensation. If they weren't, none of us would want them."

Even given the exemplary behavior of certain companies, many in corporate America are fighting hard not to use the fair value method. Many small high-technology companies are particularly vocal in their opposition, arguing that only through offering stock options can they attract top professional management. They contend that if they are forced to recognize large amounts of compensation expense under these plans, they will be at a competitive disadvantage with larger companies that can withstand higher compensation charges. As one high-tech executive stated, "If your goal is to attack fat-cat executive compensation in multi-billion dollar firms, then please do so! But not at the expense of the people who are 'running lean and mean,' trying to build businesses and creating jobs in the process."

The stock option controversy involves economic consequence issues. The FASB believes the neutrality concept should be followed. Others disagree, noting that factors other than accounting theory should be considered.

The stock option saga is a classic example of the difficulty the FASB faces in issuing an accounting standard. Many powerful interests aligned against the Board; even some who initially appeared to support the Board's actions later reversed themselves. The whole incident is troubling because the debate for the most part is not about the **proper accounting** but more about the **economic consequences** of the standards. If we continue to write standards so that some social, economic, or public policy goal is achieved, financial reporting will lose its credibility.

We are hopeful that many companies will decide to follow the **Coca-Cola** and **General Electric** examples and use the fair value method to record option expense. The fiction that options are free has led to abuse at many companies. Providing a faithful representation of the cost of these options on the income statement will lead to a better understanding of a company's financial performance.[14]

SECTION 2 COMPUTING EARNINGS PER SHARE

Earnings per share data are frequently reported in the financial press and are widely used by stockholders and potential investors in evaluating the profitability of a company. **Earnings per share (EPS)** indicates the income earned by each share of common stock. Thus, **earnings per share is reported only for common stock**. For example, if Oscar Co. has net income of $300,000 and a weighted average of 100,000 shares of common stock outstanding for the year, earnings per share is $3 ($300,000 ÷ 100,000).

Because of the importance of earnings per share information, most companies are required to report this information on the face of the income statement.[15] The exception is nonpublic companies: because of cost-benefit considerations they do not have to report this information.[16] Generally, earnings per share information is reported below net income in the income statement. For Oscar Co. the presentation would be as follows.

ILLUSTRATION 16-8
Income Statement Presentation of EPS

Net income	$300,000
Earnings per share	$3.00

INTERNATIONAL INSIGHT

In many nations (e.g., Switzerland, Sweden, Spain, and Mexico) there is no legal requirement to disclose earnings per share.

When the income statement contains intermediate components of income, earnings per share should be disclosed for each component. Illustration 16-9 shows the income statement presentation of EPS components.

[14]Recently, the FASB has indicated that companies that voluntarily switch to the fair value method will be provided one of three transition methods for initial adoption. In addition, the Board has tentatively concluded that all companies will have to disclose the following in their accounting policy note to the financial statements: (1) the method of accounting for stock options, (2) total stock compensation cost recognized in the income statement, (3) total stock compensation that would have been recorded had *FASB 123* been adopted as of its effective date, and (4) pro forma net income and earnings per share that would have been reported had *FASB 123* been adopted as of its effective date.

[15]"Earnings per Share," *Statement of Financial Accounting Standards No. 128* (Norwalk, Conn.: FASB, 1997). For an article on the usefulness of EPS reported data and the application of the qualitative characteristics of accounting information to EPS data, see Lola W. Dudley, "A Critical Look at EPS," *Journal of Accountancy* (August 1985), pp. 102–11.

[16]A nonpublic enterprise is an enterprise (1) whose debt or equity securities are not traded in a public market on a foreign or domestic stock exchange or in the over-the-counter market (including securities quoted locally or regionally) or (2) that is not required to file financial statements with the SEC. An enterprise is no longer considered a nonpublic enterprise when its financial statements are issued in preparation for the sale of any class of securities in a public market.

Earnings per share:	
Income from continuing operations	$4.00
Loss from discontinued operations, net of tax	0.60
Income before extraordinary item and cumulative effect of change in accounting principle	3.40
Extraordinary gain, net of tax	1.00
Cumulative effect of change in accounting principle, net of tax	0.50
Net income	$4.90

ILLUSTRATION 16-9
Income Statement Presentation of EPS Components

These disclosures enable the user of the financial statements to recognize the effects of income from continuing operations on EPS, as distinguished from income or loss from irregular items.[17]

EARNINGS PER SHARE—SIMPLE CAPITAL STRUCTURE

OBJECTIVE 6
Compute earnings per share in a simple capital structure.

A corporation's capital structure is considered **simple** if it consists only of common stock or includes no **potential common stock** that upon conversion or exercise could dilute earnings per common share. (A capital structure is considered **complex** if it includes securities that could have a dilutive effect on earnings per common share.) The computation of earnings per share for a simple capital structure involves two items (other than net income)—preferred stock dividends and weighted average number of shares outstanding.

Preferred Stock Dividends

As indicated earlier, earnings per share relates to earnings per common share. When a company has both common and preferred stock outstanding, **the current-year preferred stock dividend is subtracted from net income to arrive at income available to common stockholders**. The formula for computing earnings per share is as follows.

$$\text{Earnings per Share} = \frac{\text{Net Income} - \text{Preferred Dividends}}{\text{Weighted Average Number of Shares Outstanding}}$$

ILLUSTRATION 16-10
Formula for Computing Earnings per Share

In reporting earnings per share information, dividends on preferred stock should be subtracted from each of the intermediate components of income (income from continuing operations and income before extraordinary items) and finally from net income to arrive at income available to common stockholders. If dividends on preferred stock are declared and a net loss occurs, **the preferred dividend is added to the loss** in order to compute the loss per share. If the preferred stock is cumulative and the dividend is not declared in the current year, **an amount equal to the dividend that should have been declared for the current year only** should be subtracted from net income or added to the net loss. Dividends in arrears for previous years should have been included in the previous years' computations.

[17]Per share amounts for discontinued operations, an extraordinary item, or the cumulative effect of an accounting change in a period should be presented either on the face of the income statement or in the notes to the financial statements.

Weighted Average Number of Shares Outstanding

In all computations of earnings per share, the **weighted average number of shares outstanding** during the period constitutes the basis for the per share amounts reported. Shares issued or purchased during the period affect the amount outstanding and must be **weighted by the fraction of the period they are outstanding**. The rationale for this approach is to find the equivalent number of **whole shares** outstanding for the year.

To illustrate, assume that Stallone Inc. has the following changes in its common stock shares outstanding for the period.

ILLUSTRATION 16-11
Shares Outstanding, Ending Balance—Stallone Inc.

Date	Share Changes	Shares Outstanding
January 1	Beginning balance	90,000
April 1	Issued 30,000 shares for cash	30,000
		120,000
July 1	Purchased 39,000 shares	39,000
		81,000
November 1	Issued 60,000 shares for cash	60,000
December 31	Ending balance	141,000

To compute the weighted average number of shares outstanding, the following computation is made.

ILLUSTRATION 16-12
Weighted Average Number of Shares Outstanding

Dates Outstanding	(A) Shares Outstanding	(B) Fraction of Year	(C) Weighted Shares (A × B)
Jan. 1–Apr. 1	90,000	3/12	22,500
Apr. 1–July 1	120,000	3/12	30,000
July 1–Nov. 1	81,000	4/12	27,000
Nov. 1–Dec. 31	141,000	2/12	23,500
Weighted average number of shares outstanding			103,000

INTERNATIONAL INSIGHT

Where EPS disclosure is prevalent, it is usually based on the weighted average of shares outstanding.

As illustrated, 90,000 shares were outstanding for 3 months, which translates to 22,500 whole shares for the entire year. Because additional shares were issued on April 1, the shares outstanding change, and these shares must be weighted for the time outstanding. When 39,000 shares were purchased on July 1, the shares outstanding were reduced, and again a new computation must be made to determine the proper weighted shares outstanding.

Stock Dividends and Stock Splits

When **stock dividends** or **stock splits** occur, computation of the weighted average number of shares requires restatement of the shares outstanding before the stock dividend or split. For example, assume that a corporation had 100,000 shares outstanding on January 1 and issued a 25 percent stock dividend on June 30. For purposes of computing a weighted average for the current year, the additional 25,000 shares outstanding as a result of the stock dividend are assumed to have been **outstanding since the beginning of the year**. Thus the weighted average for the year would be 125,000 shares.

The issuance of a stock dividend or stock split is restated, but the issuance or repurchase of stock for cash is not. Why? The reason is that stock splits and stock dividends do not increase or decrease the net assets of the enterprise; only additional shares of stock are issued, and therefore the weighted average shares must be restated. By restating, valid comparisons of earnings per share can be made between periods before and after the stock split or stock dividend. Conversely, the issuance or purchase of stock for cash changes the amount of net assets. As a result, the company either earns more or less in the future as a result of this change in net assets. Stated another way, **a stock dividend or split does not change the shareholders' total investment**—it only increases (unless it is a reverse stock split) the number of common shares representing this investment.

To illustrate how a stock dividend affects the computation of the weighted average number of shares outstanding, assume that Rambo Company has the following changes in its common stock shares during the year.

ILLUSTRATION 16-13
Shares Outstanding, Ending Balance—Rambo Company

Date	Share Changes	Shares Outstanding
January 1	Beginning balance	100,000
March 1	Issued 20,000 shares for cash	20,000
		120,000
June 1	60,000 additional shares (50% stock dividend)	60,000
		180,000
November 1	Issued 30,000 shares for cash	30,000
December 31	Ending balance	210,000

The computation of the weighted average number of shares outstanding would be as follows.

ILLUSTRATION 16-14
Weighted Average Number of Shares Outstanding—Stock Issue and Stock Dividend

Dates Outstanding	(A) Shares Outstanding	(B) Restatement	(C) Fraction of Year	(D) Weighted Shares (A × B × C)
Jan. 1–Mar. 1	100,000	1.50	2/12	25,000
Mar. 1–June 1	120,000	1.50	3/12	45,000
June 1–Nov. 1	180,000		5/12	75,000
Nov. 1–Dec. 31	210,000		2/12	35,000
Weighted average number of shares outstanding				180,000

The shares outstanding prior to the stock dividend must be restated. The shares outstanding from January 1 to June 1 are adjusted for the stock dividend, so that these shares are stated on the same basis as shares issued subsequent to the stock dividend. Shares issued after the stock dividend do not have to be restated because they are on the new basis. The stock dividend simply restates existing shares. **The same type of treatment applies to a stock split.**

If a stock dividend or stock split occurs after the end of the year, but before the financial statements are issued, the weighted average number of shares outstanding for the year (and for any other years presented in comparative form) must be restated. For example, assume that Hendricks Company computes its weighted average number of shares to be 100,000 for the year ended December 31, 2004. On January 15, 2005, before the financial statements are issued, the company splits its stock 3 for 1. In this case, the weighted average number of shares used in computing earnings per share for 2004 would be 300,000 shares. If earnings per share information for 2003 is provided as comparative information, it also must be adjusted for the stock split.

Comprehensive Illustration

Sylvester Corporation has income before extraordinary item of $580,000 and an extraordinary gain, net of tax, of $240,000. In addition, it has declared preferred dividends of $1 per share on 100,000 shares of preferred stock outstanding. Sylvester Corporation also has the following changes in its common stock shares outstanding during 2004.

ILLUSTRATION 16-15
Shares Outstanding, Ending Balance—Sylvester Corp.

Dates	Share Changes	Shares Outstanding
January 1	Beginning balance	180,000
May 1	Purchased 30,000 treasury shares	30,000
		150,000
July 1	300,000 additional shares (3-for-1 stock split)	300,000
		450,000
December 31	Issued 50,000 shares for cash	50,000
December 31	Ending balance	500,000

To compute the earnings per share information, the weighted average number of shares outstanding is determined as follows.

ILLUSTRATION 16-16
Weighted Average Number of Shares Outstanding

Dates Outstanding	(A) Shares Outstanding	(B) Restatement	(C) Fraction of Year	(D) Weighted Shares (A × B × C)
Jan. 1–May 1	180,000	3	4/12	180,000
May 1–Dec. 31	150,000	3	8/12	300,000
Weighted average number of shares outstanding				480,000

In computing the weighted average number of shares, the shares sold on December 31, 2004, are ignored because they have not been outstanding during the year. The weighted average number of shares is then divided into income before extraordinary item and net income to determine earnings per share. Sylvester Corporation's preferred dividends of $100,000 are subtracted from income before extraordinary item ($580,000) to arrive at income before extraordinary item available to common stockholders of $480,000 ($580,000 − $100,000).

Deducting the preferred dividends from the income before extraordinary item has the effect of also reducing net income without affecting the amount of the extraordinary item. The final amount is referred to as **income available to common stockholders**.

ILLUSTRATION 16-17
Computation of Income Available to Common Stockholders

	(A) Income Information	(B) Weighted Shares	(C) Earnings per Share (A ÷ B)
Income before extraordinary item available to common stockholders	$480,000*	480,000	$1.00
Extraordinary gain (net of tax)	240,000	480,000	0.50
Income available to common stockholders	$720,000	480,000	$1.50

*$580,000 − $100,000

Disclosure of the per share amount for the extraordinary item (net of tax) must be reported either on the face of the income statement or in the notes to the financial statements. Income and per share information reported on the face of the income statement would be as follows.

ILLUSTRATION 16-18
Earnings per Share, with Extraordinary Item

Income before extraordinary item	$580,000
Extraordinary gain, net of tax	240,000
Net income	$820,000
Earnings per share:	
Income before extraordinary item	$1.00
Extraordinary item, net of tax	0.50
Net income	$1.50

EARNINGS PER SHARE—COMPLEX CAPITAL STRUCTURE

OBJECTIVE 7
Compute earnings per share in a complex capital structure.

One problem with a **basic EPS** computation is that it fails to recognize the potentially dilutive impact on outstanding stock when a corporation has dilutive securities in its capital structure. **Dilutive securities** are securities that can be converted to common stock and that upon conversion or exercise reduce—dilute—earnings per share. Dilutive securities present a serious problem because conversion or exercise often has an adverse effect on earnings per share. This adverse effect can be significant and, more important, unexpected, unless financial statements call attention to the potential dilutive effect in some manner.[18]

A complex capital structure exists when a corporation has convertible securities, options, warrants or other rights that upon conversion or exercise could dilute earnings per share. Therefore when a company has a complex capital structure, both a basic and diluted earnings per share are generally reported.

The computation of **diluted EPS** is similar to the computation of basic EPS. The difference is that diluted EPS includes the effect of all dilutive potential common shares that were outstanding during the period. The formula in Illustration 16-19 shows the relationship between basic EPS and diluted EPS.

ILLUSTRATION 16-19
Relation between Basic and Diluted EPS

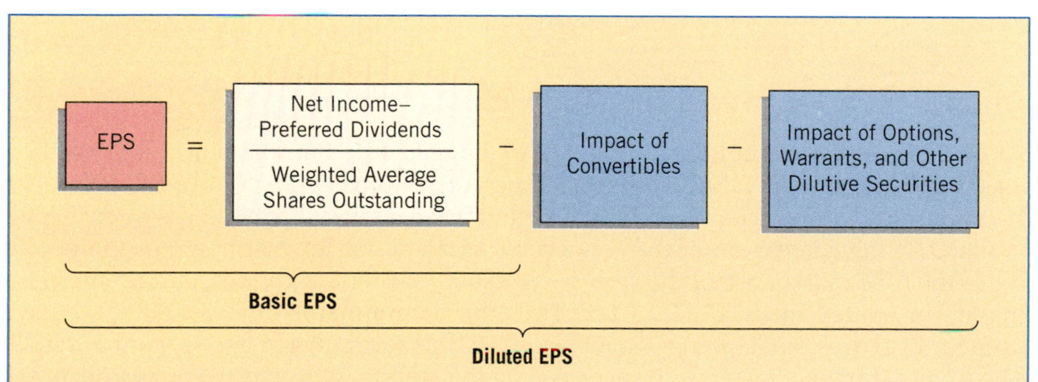

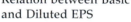

INTERNATIONAL INSIGHT

The provisions in U.S. GAAP are substantially the same as those in International Accounting Standard No. 33, *Earnings per Share*, issued by the IASB.

Note that companies with complex capital structures will not report diluted EPS if the securities in their capital structure are antidilutive. **Antidilutive securities** are securities that upon conversion or exercise increase earnings per share (or reduce the

[18]Issuance of these types of securities is typical in mergers and compensation plans.

loss per share). The purpose of the dual presentation is to inform financial statement users of situations that will likely occur and to provide "worst case" dilutive situations. If the securities are antidilutive, the likelihood of conversion or exercise is considered remote. Thus, companies that have only antidilutive securities are not permitted to increase earnings per share and are required to report only the basic EPS number.

The computation of basic EPS was illustrated in the prior section. The discussion in the following sections addresses the effects of convertible and other dilutive securities on EPS calculations.

WHAT DO THE NUMBERS MEAN?

THE SOURCE OF MY DILUTION

What is the source of dilutive securities, which give rise to complex capital structures? Merger activity is a major source.

Typical mergers in the 1990s were combinations of information, entertainment, or financial (banking) companies. For example, **Bell Atlantic Corp.** and **Nynex Corp.** combined in a $22.7 billion deal, **Time** acquired **Warner Communications** for $10.1 billion, and **Walt Disney Co.** purchased **Capital Cities/ABC, Inc.** Even larger were the mergers of **Nations Bank** and **BankAmerica** ($62 billion), and **Bell Atlantic** and **GTE** ($71 billion) in 1998.

One consequence of heavy merger activity is an increase in the use of securities such as convertible bonds, convertible preferred stocks, stock warrants, and contingent shares to structure these deals. Although not common stock in form, these securities enable their holders to obtain common stock upon exercise or conversion.

Although merger and acquisition activity has declined in the recent bear market, the presence of dilutive securities on corporate balance sheets is still very prevalent. As discussed in the prior section, the use of stock option plans, which also are dilutive in nature, is increasing. In addition, as noted in the story related to **Corning** earlier in the chapter (page 777), companies that have difficulty selling common stock at a reasonable price often use some form of convertible preferred or bond to help finance their operations.

Source: Farrell Kramer, "Mergers Have Been in Fashion in 1996, With Seven Big Ones," *St. Louis Post-Dispatch* (December 16, 1996), p. A7; and Geoffrey Colvin, "The Year of the Mega Merger," *Fortune* (January 11, 1999), p. 62.

Diluted EPS—Convertible Securities

At conversion, convertible securities are exchanged for common stock. The method used to measure the dilutive effects of potential conversion on EPS is called the **if-converted method**. The if-converted method for a convertible bond assumes the following: (1) the conversion of the convertible securities at the beginning of the period (or at the time of issuance of the security, if issued during the period), and (2) the elimination of related interest, net of tax. Thus the **denominator**—the weighted average number of shares outstanding—is increased by the additional shares assumed issued. The **numerator**—net income—is increased by the amount of interest expense, net of tax associated with those convertible securities.

Comprehensive Illustration—If-Converted Method

As an example, Marshy Field Corporation has net income for the year of $210,000 and a weighted average number of common shares outstanding during the period of 100,000 shares. The basic earnings per share is, therefore, $2.10 ($210,000 ÷ 100,000). The company has two convertible debenture bond issues outstanding. One is a 6 percent issue sold at 100 (total $1,000,000) in a prior year and convertible into 20,000 common shares.

The other is a 10 percent issue sold at 100 (total $1,000,000) on April 1 of the current year and convertible into 32,000 common shares. The tax rate is 40 percent.

As shown in Illustration 16-20, to determine the numerator, we add back the interest on the if-converted securities, less the related tax effect. Because the if-converted method assumes conversion as of the beginning of the year, no interest on the convertibles is assumed to be paid during the year. The interest on the 6 percent convertibles is $60,000 for the year ($1,000,000 × 6%). The increased tax expense is $24,000 ($60,000 × .40), and the interest added back net of taxes is **$36,000** [$60,000 − $24,000 or simply $60,000 × (1 − .40)].

Because 10 percent convertibles are issued subsequent to the beginning of the year, the shares assumed to have been issued on that date, April 1, are weighted as outstanding from April 1 to the end of the year. In addition, the interest adjustment to the numerator for these bonds would reflect the interest for only 9 months. Thus the interest added back on the 10 percent convertible would be **$45,000** [$1,000,000 × 10% × 9/12 year × (1 − .40)]. The computation of earnings (the numerator) for diluted earnings per share is shown in Illustration 16-20.

ILLUSTRATION 16-20
Computation of Adjusted Net Income

Net income for the year	$210,000
Add: Adjustment for interest (net of tax)	
6% debentures ($60,000 × [1 − .40])	36,000
10% debentures ($100,000 × 9/12 × [1 − .40])	45,000
Adjusted net income	$291,000

The computation for shares adjusted for dilutive securities (the denominator) for diluted earnings per share is shown in Illustration 16-21.

ILLUSTRATION 16-21
Computation of Weighted Average Number of Shares

Weighted average number of shares outstanding	100,000
Add: Shares assumed to be issued:	
6% debentures (as of beginning of year)	20,000
10% debentures (as of date of issue, April 1; 9/12 × 32,000)	24,000
Weighted average number of shares adjusted for dilutive securities	144,000

Marshy Field would then report earnings per share based on a dual presentation on the face of the income statement; basic and diluted earnings per share are reported.[19] The presentation is shown in Illustration 16-22.

ILLUSTRATION 16-22
Earnings per Share Disclosure

Net income for the year	$210,000
Earnings per Share (Note X)	
Basic earnings per share ($210,000 ÷ 100,000)	$2.10
Diluted earnings per share ($291,000 ÷ 144,000)	$2.02

Other Factors

The example above assumed that Marshy Field's bonds were sold at the face amount. If the bonds are sold at a premium or discount, interest expense must be adjusted each period to account for this occurrence. Therefore, the amount of interest expense added

[19]Conversion of bonds is dilutive because EPS with conversion ($2.02) is less than basic EPS ($2.10).

back, net of tax, to net income is the interest expense reported on the income statement, not the interest paid in cash during the period.

In addition, the conversion rate on a dilutive security may change over the period during which the dilutive security is outstanding. In this situation, for the diluted EPS computation, the **most advantageous conversion rate available to the holder is used**. For example, assume that a convertible bond was issued January 1, 2003, with a conversion rate of 10 common shares for each bond starting January 1, 2005. Beginning January 1, 2008, the conversion rate is 12 common shares for each bond, and beginning January 1, 2012, it is 15 common shares for each bond. In computing diluted EPS in 2003, the conversion rate of 15 shares to one bond is used.

Finally, if the 6 percent convertible debentures were instead 6 percent convertible preferred stock, the convertible preferred would be considered potential common shares and included in shares outstanding in diluted EPS calculations. Preferred dividends are not subtracted from net income in computing the numerator. Why not? Because it is assumed that the convertible preferreds are converted and are outstanding as common stock for purposes of computing EPS. Net income is used as the numerator—**no tax effect** is computed because preferred dividends generally are not deductible for tax purposes.

Diluted EPS—Options and Warrants

Stock options and warrants outstanding (whether or not presently exercisable) are included in diluted earnings per share unless they are antidilutive. Options and warrants and their equivalents are included in earnings per share computations through the **treasury stock method**.

The treasury stock method assumes that the options or warrants are exercised at the beginning of the year (or date of issue if later) and that the proceeds from the exercise of options and warrants are used to purchase common stock for the treasury. If the exercise price is lower than the market price of the stock, then the proceeds from exercise are not sufficient to buy back all the shares. The incremental shares remaining are added to the weighted average number of shares outstanding for purposes of computing diluted earnings per share.

For example, if the exercise price of a warrant is $5 and the fair market value of the stock is $15, the treasury stock method would increase the shares outstanding. Exercise of the warrant would result in one additional share outstanding, but the $5 received for the one share issued is not sufficient to purchase one share in the market at $15. Three warrants would have to be exercised (and three additional shares issued) to produce enough money ($15) to acquire one share in the market. Thus, a net increase of two shares outstanding would result.

To see this computation using larger numbers, assume 1,500 options outstanding at an exercise price of $30 for a common share and a common stock market price per share of $50. Through application of the treasury stock method there would be 600 **incremental shares** outstanding, computed as follows.[20]

ILLUSTRATION 16-23
Computation of Incremental Shares

Proceeds from exercise of 1,500 options (1,500 × $30)	$45,000
Shares issued upon exercise of options	1,500
Treasury shares purchasable with proceeds ($45,000 ÷ $50)	900
Incremental shares outstanding (potential common shares)	600

[20]The incremental number of shares may be more simply computed:

$$\frac{\text{Market price} - \text{Option price}}{\text{Market price}} \times \text{Number of options} = \text{Number of shares}$$

$$\frac{\$50 - \$30}{\$50} \times 1{,}500 \text{ options} = 600 \text{ shares}$$

Thus, if the exercise price of the option or warrant is **lower than** the market price of the stock, dilution occurs. If the exercise price of the option or warrant is **higher than** the market price of the stock, common shares are reduced. In this case, the options or warrants are **antidilutive** because their assumed exercise leads to an increase in earnings per share.

For both options and warrants, exercise is not assumed unless the average market price of the stock is above the exercise price during the period being reported.[21] As a practical matter, a simple average of the weekly or monthly prices is adequate, so long as the prices do not fluctuate significantly.

Comprehensive Illustration—Treasury Stock Method

To illustrate application of the treasury stock method, assume that Kubitz Industries, Inc. has net income for the period of $220,000. The average number of shares outstanding for the period was 100,000 shares. Hence, basic EPS—ignoring all dilutive securities—is $2.20. The average number of shares under outstanding options (although not exercisable at this time), at an option price of $20 per share, is 5,000 shares. The average market price of the common stock during the year was $28. The computation is shown below.

ILLUSTRATION 16-24
Computation of Earnings per Share—Treasury Stock Method

	Basic Earnings per Share	Diluted Earnings per Share
Average number of shares under option outstanding:		5,000
Option price per share		× $20
Proceeds upon exercise of options		$100,000
Average market price of common stock		$28
Treasury shares that could be repurchased with proceeds ($100,000 ÷ $28)		3,571
Excess of shares under option over the treasury shares that could be repurchased (5,000 − 3,571)—potential common incremental shares		1,429
Average number of common shares outstanding	100,000	100,000
Total average number of common shares outstanding and potential common shares	100,000 (A)	101,429 (C)
Net income for the year	$220,000 (B)	$220,000 (D)
Earnings per share	$2.20 (B ÷ A)	$2.17 (D ÷ C)

Contingent Issue Agreement

In business combinations, the acquirer may promise to issue additional shares—referred to as **contingent shares**—if certain conditions are met. If these shares are issuable upon the **mere passage of time or upon the attainment of a certain earnings or market price level, and this level is met at the end of the year**, the contingent shares should be considered as outstanding for the computation of diluted earnings per share.[22]

[21]Options and warrants have essentially the same assumptions and computational problems, although the warrants may allow or require the tendering of some other security, such as debt, in lieu of cash upon exercise. In such situations, the accounting becomes quite complex. *SFAS No. 128* explains the proper disposition in this situation.

[22]In addition to contingent issuances of stock, other types of situations that might lead to dilution are the issuance of participating securities and two-class common shares. The reporting of these types of securities in EPS computations is beyond the scope of this textbook.

For example, assume that Walz Corporation purchased Cardella Company and agreed to give Cardella's stockholders 20,000 additional shares in 2007 if Cardella's net income in 2006 is $90,000. In 2005 Cardella Company's net income is $100,000. Because the 2006 stipulated earnings of $90,000 are already being attained, diluted earnings per share of Walz for 2005 would include the 20,000 contingent shares in the shares outstanding computation.

Antidilution Revisited

In computing diluted EPS, the aggregate of all dilutive securities must be considered. But first we must determine which potentially dilutive securities are in fact individually dilutive and which are antidilutive. **Any security that is antidilutive should be excluded** and cannot be used to offset dilutive securities.

Recall that antidilutive securities are securities whose inclusion in earnings per share computations would increase earnings per share (or reduce net loss per share). Convertible debt is antidilutive if the addition to income of the interest (net of tax) causes a greater percentage increase in income (numerator) than conversion of the bonds causes a percentage increase in common and potentially dilutive shares (denominator). In other words, convertible debt is antidilutive if conversion of the security causes common stock earnings to increase by a greater amount per additional common share than earnings per share was before the conversion.

To illustrate, assume that Kohl Corporation has a 6 percent, $1,000,000 debt issue that is convertible into 10,000 common shares. Net income for the year is $210,000, the weighted average number of common shares outstanding is 100,000 shares, and the tax rate is 40 percent. In this case, assumed conversion of the debt into common stock at the beginning of the year requires the following adjustments of net income and the weighted average number of shares outstanding.

ILLUSTRATION 16-25
Test for Antidilution

Net income for the year	$210,000	Average number of shares outstanding	100,000
Add: Adjustment for interest (net of tax) on 6% debentures $60,000 × (1 − .40)	36,000	Add: Shares issued upon assumed conversion of debt	10,000
Adjusted net income	$246,000	Average number of common and potential common shares	110,000

Basic EPS = $210,000 ÷ 100,000 = $2.10
Diluted EPS = $246,000 ÷ 110,000 = $2.24 = **Antidilutive**

As a shortcut, the convertible debt also can be identified as antidilutive by comparing the EPS resulting from conversion, $3.60 ($36,000 additional earnings ÷ 10,000 additional shares), with EPS before inclusion of the convertible debt, $2.10.

With options or warrants, whenever the exercise price is higher than the market price, the security is antidilutive. **Antidilutive securities should be ignored in all calculations and should not be considered in computing diluted earnings per share.** This approach is reasonable because the profession's intent was to inform the investor of the **possible dilution** that might occur in reported earnings per share. The intent was not to highlight securities that, if converted or exercised, would result in an increase in earnings per share. Appendix 16B to this chapter provides an extended example of how antidilution is considered in a complex situation with multiple securities.

PRO FORMA EPS CONFUSION

WHAT DO THE NUMBERS MEAN?

Many companies are reporting pro forma EPS numbers along with U.S. GAAP-based EPS numbers in the financial information provided to investors. Pro forma earnings generally exceed GAAP earnings because the pro forma numbers exclude such items as restructuring charges, impairments of assets, R&D expenditures, and stock compensation expense. Here are some examples.

Company	U.S. GAAP EPS	Pro Forma EPS
Adaptec, Inc.	$(0.62)	$ 0.05
Corning Inc.	(0.24)	0.09
General Motors Corp.	(0.41)	0.85
Honeywell International Inc.	(0.38)	0.44
International Paper Co.	(0.57)	0.14
QUALCOMM Inc.	(0.06)	0.20
Broadcom Corp.	(6.36)	(0.13)
Lucent Technologies Inc.	(2.16)	(0.27)

Source: Company press releases.

The SEC has expressed concern that pro forma earnings may be misleading. For example, **Trump Hotels & Casino Resorts Inc.** (DJT) was cited for abuses related to its 1999 third-quarter pro forma EPS release. The SEC noted that the firm misrepresented its operating results by excluding a material, one-time $81.4 million charge in its pro forma EPS statement and including an undisclosed nonrecurring gain of $17.2 million. The gain enabled DJT to post a profit in the quarter. The SEC emphasized that DJT's pro forma EPS statement deviated from conservative U.S. GAAP reporting. Therefore, it was "fraudulent" because it created a "false and misleading impression" that DJT had actually (1) recorded a profit in the third quarter of 1999 and (2) exceeded consensus earnings expectations by enhancing its operating fundamentals.

The Sarbanes-Oxley Act of 2002 requires the SEC to develop regulations on pro forma reporting. As a consequence, the SEC now requires companies that provide pro forma financial information to make sure that the information is not misleading. In addition, a reconciliation between pro forma and GAAP information is required.

Sources: SEC Accounting and Enforcement Release No. 1499 (January 16, 2002); "SEC Proposes Rules to Implement Sarbanes-Oxley Act Reforms," SEC Press Release 2002-155 (October 30, 2002).

EPS Presentation and Disclosure

If a company's capital structure is complex, the EPS presentation would be as follows.

ILLUSTRATION 16-26
EPS Presentation—Complex Capital Structure

Earnings per common share	
Basic earnings per share	$3.30
Diluted earnings per share	$2.70

When the earnings of a period include irregular items, per share amounts (where applicable) should be shown for income from continuing operations, income before extraordinary items, income before accounting change, and net income. Companies that report a discontinued operation, an extraordinary item, or the cumulative effect of an accounting change should present per share amounts for those line items either on the face of the income statement or in the notes to the financial statements. A presentation reporting extraordinary items only is presented in Illustration 16-27.

ILLUSTRATION 16-27
EPS Presentation, with Extraordinary Item

Basic earnings per share	
Income before extraordinary item	$3.80
Extraordinary item	0.80
Net income	$3.00
Diluted earnings per share	
Income before extraordinary item	$3.35
Extraordinary item	0.65
Net income	$2.70

Earnings per share amounts must be shown for all periods presented. Also, all prior period earnings per share amounts presented should be restated for stock dividends and stock splits. If diluted EPS data are reported for at least one period, they should be reported for all periods presented, even if they are the same as basic EPS. When results of operations of a prior period have been restated as a result of a prior period adjustment, the earnings per share data shown for the prior periods should also be restated. The effect of the restatement should be disclosed in the year of the restatement.

Complex capital structures and dual presentation of earnings per share require the following additional disclosures in note form.

1. Description of pertinent rights and privileges of the various securities outstanding.
2. A reconciliation of the numerators and denominators of the basic and diluted per share computations, including individual income and share amount effects of all securities that affect EPS.
3. The effect given preferred dividends in determining income available to common stockholders in computing basic EPS.
4. Securities that could potentially dilute basic EPS in the future that were not included in the computation because they would be antidilutive.
5. Effect of conversions subsequent to year-end, but before statements have been issued.

Illustration 16-28 presents the reconciliation and the related disclosure that is needed to meet disclosure requirements for EPS.

ILLUSTRATION 16-28
Reconciliation for Basic and Diluted EPS

	For the Year Ended 2005		
	Income (Numerator)	Shares (Denominator)	Per Share Amount
Income before extraordinary item and accounting change	$7,500,000		
Less: Preferred stock dividends	(45,000)		
Basic EPS			
Income available to common stockholders	7,455,000	3,991,666	$1.87
Warrants		30,768	
Convertible preferred stock	45,000	308,333	
4% convertible bonds (net of tax)	60,000	50,000	
Diluted EPS			
Income available to common stockholders + assumed conversions	$7,560,000	4,380,767	$1.73

Stock options to purchase 1,000,000 shares of common stock at $85 per share were outstanding during the second half of 2005 but were not included in the computation of diluted EPS because the options' exercise price was greater than the average market price of the common shares. The options were still outstanding at the end of year 2005 and expire on June 30, 2015.[23]

[23]Note that *Statement No. 123* has specific disclosure requirements as well regarding stock option plans and earnings per share disclosures.

Summary

As you can see, computation of earnings per share is a complex issue. It is a controversial area because many securities, although technically not common stock, have many of its basic characteristics. Some companies have issued these types of securities rather than common stock in order to avoid an adverse dilutive effect on earnings per share.

Illustrations 16-29 and 16-30 show the elementary points of calculating earnings per share in a simple capital structure and in a complex capital structure.

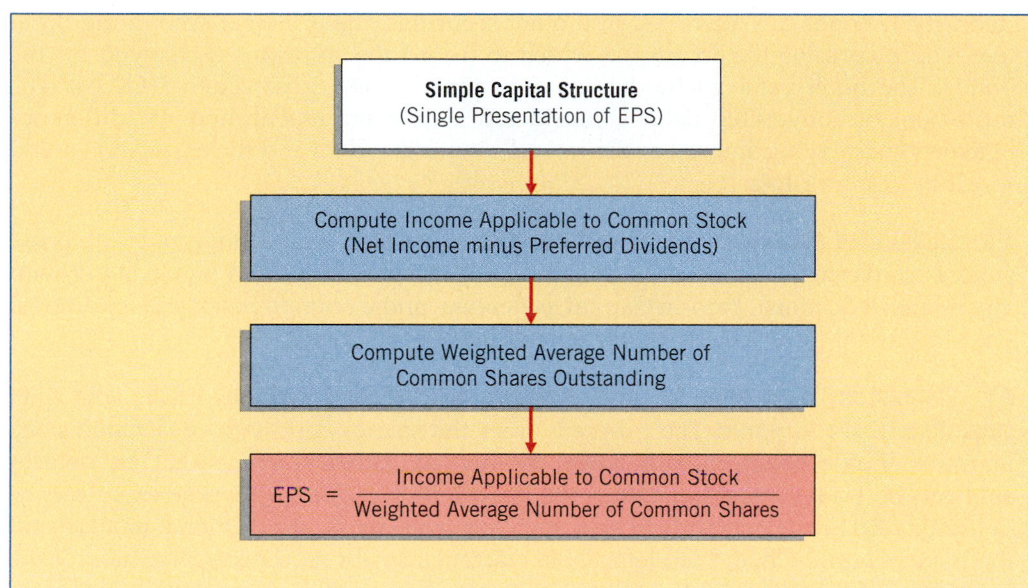

ILLUSTRATION 16-29
Calculating EPS, Simple Capital Structure

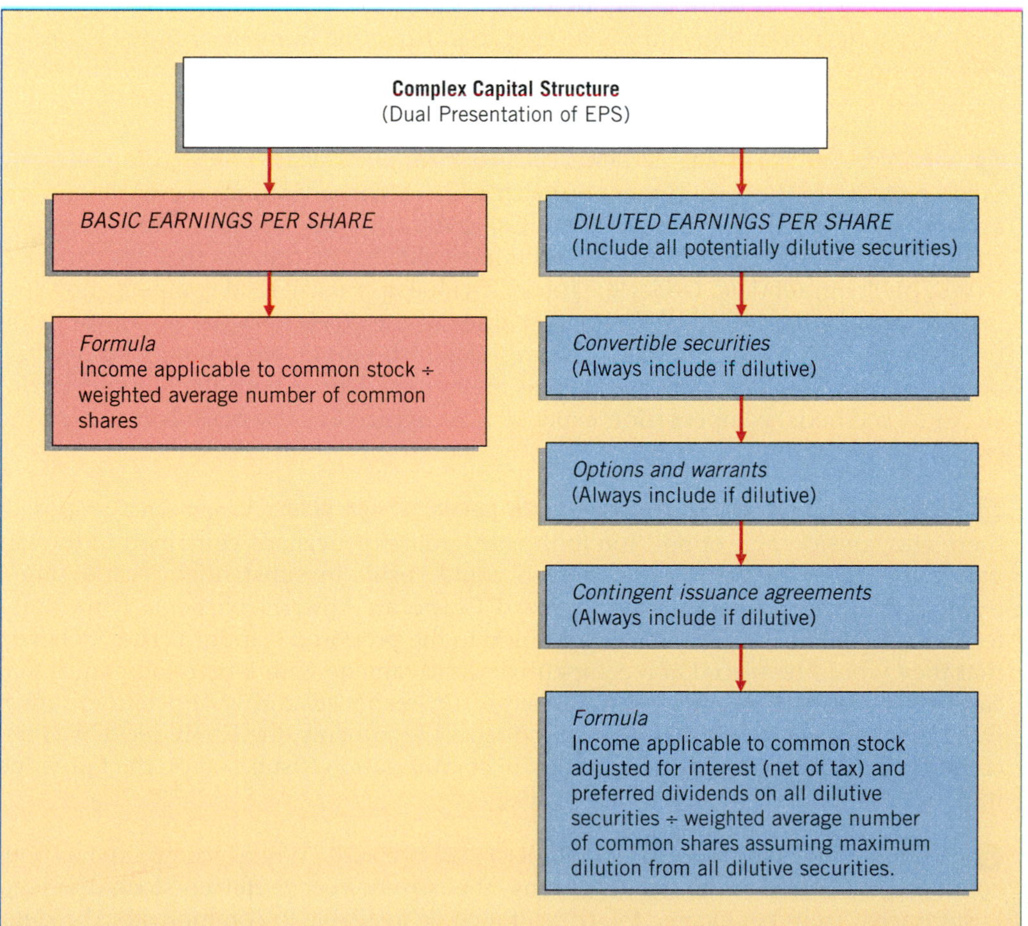

ILLUSTRATION 16-30
Calculating EPS, Complex Capital Structure

KEY TERMS

antidilutive securities, *793*
basic EPS, *793*
complex capital structure, *789*
convertible bonds, *774*
convertible preferred stock, *776*
detachable stock warrants, *778*
diluted EPS, *793*
dilutive securities, *793*
earnings per share, *788*
fair value method, *782*
grant date, *781*
if-converted method, *794*
income available to common stockholders, *789*
induced conversion, *775*
intrinsic value method, *782*
measurement date, *783*
noncompensatory plans, *786*
service period, *784*
simple capital structure, *789*
stock option, *781*
stock option plans, *781*
stock right, *780*
treasury stock method, *796*
warrants, *777*
weighted average number of shares outstanding, *790*

SUMMARY OF LEARNING OBJECTIVES

1 Describe the accounting for the issuance, conversion, and retirement of convertible securities. The method for recording convertible bonds at the date of issuance follows that used to record straight debt issues. Any discount or premium that results from the issuance of convertible bonds is amortized assuming the bonds will be held to maturity. If bonds are converted into other securities, the principal accounting problem is to determine the amount at which to record the securities exchanged for the bonds. The book value method is used in practice and is considered GAAP. The retirement of convertible debt is considered a debt retirement, and the difference between the carrying amount of the retired convertible debt and the cash paid should result in a gain or loss.

2 Explain the accounting for convertible preferred stock. When convertible preferred stock is converted, the book value method is employed: Preferred Stock, along with any related Additional Paid-in Capital, is debited, and Common Stock and Additional Paid-in Capital (if an excess exists) are credited.

3 Contrast the accounting for stock warrants and for stock warrants issued with other securities. *Stock warrants:* The proceeds from the sale of debt with detachable stock warrants should be allocated between the two securities. Warrants that are detachable can be traded separately from the debt, and therefore, a market value can be determined. The two methods of allocation available are the proportional method and the incremental method. Nondetachable warrants do not require an allocation of the proceeds between the bonds and the warrants. The entire proceeds are recorded as debt. *Stock rights:* No entry is required when rights are issued to existing stockholders. Only a memorandum entry is needed to indicate the number of rights issued to existing stockholders and to ensure that the company has additional unissued stock registered for issuance in case the rights are exercised.

4 Describe the accounting for stock compensation plans under GAAP. Companies are given a choice in the recognition approach to stock compensation; the FASB encourages adoption of the fair value method. Using the fair value approach, total compensation expense is computed based on the fair value of the options that are expected to vest on the grant date. Under the intrinsic value approach, total compensation cost is computed as the excess of the market price of the stock over the option price on the date when both the number of shares to which employees are entitled and the option or purchase price for those shares are known. Under both the fair and intrinsic value methods, compensation expense is recognized in the periods in which the employee performs the services.

5 Explain the controversy involving stock compensation plans. When first proposed, there was considerable opposition to the recognition provisions contained in the fair value approach, because that approach could result in substantial compensation expense that was not previously recognized. Corporate America, particularly the high-tech sector, was quite vocal in its opposition to the proposed standard. They believed that they would be placed at a competitive disadvantage with larger companies that can withstand higher compensation charges. In response to this opposition, which was based primarily on economic consequences arguments, the FASB decided to encourage, rather than require, recognition of compensation cost based on the fair value method and require expanded disclosures.

6 Compute earnings per share in a simple capital structure. When a company has both common and preferred stock outstanding, the current-year preferred stock dividend is subtracted from net income to arrive at income available to common stockholders. The formula for computing earnings per share is net income less preferred stock dividends divided by the weighted average of shares outstanding.

7 Compute earnings per share in a complex capital structure. A complex capital structure requires a dual presentation of earnings per share, each with equal prominence on the face of the income statement. These two presentations are referred to as basic earnings per share and diluted earnings per share. Basic earnings per share is based on the number of weighted average common shares outstanding (i.e., equivalent to EPS for a simple capital structure). Diluted earnings per share indicates the dilution of earnings per share that would have occurred if all potential issuances of common stock that would have reduced earnings per share had taken place.

APPENDIX 16A

Stock Options— Additional Complications

Before 1995, accounting for stock options was governed by the provisions in *APB Opinion No. 25*. This appendix discusses the provisions of *APB Opinion No. 25* because many companies have not adopted the recognition guidelines provided in *SFAS No. 123*. In addition, an expanded discussion of the types of plans used to compensate key executives is provided.

OBJECTIVE 8
Explain the accounting for various stock option plans under APB Opinion No. 25.

DETERMINING COMPENSATION EXPENSE

Under *APB Opinion No. 25*, total compensation expense is computed as the excess of the market price of the stock **over the option price on the measurement date**.[1] The measurement date is the first date on which are known both (1) the number of shares that an individual employee is entitled to receive, and (2) the option or purchase price. The measurement date for many plans is the date an **option is granted to an employee** (i.e., the grant date). The measurement date may be later than the grant date in plans with variable terms (either number of shares or option price, or both, not known) that depend on events after date of grant. Usually the measurement date for plans with variable terms is the **date of exercise**.

UNDERLYING CONCEPTS

GAAP is often characterized as misleading when compensation is measured at the grant date, using the excess of the market price of the stock over the exercise price. GAAP in this case is reliable, but many question the relevance of the compensation reported.

If the number of shares or the option price, or both, are unknown, compensation expense may have to be estimated on the basis of assumptions about the final number of shares and the option price.

Three common plans that illustrate different accounting issues are:

1. Stock option plans (incentive or nonqualified).
2. Stock appreciation rights plans.
3. Performance-type plans.

[1]"Accounting for Stock Issued to Employees," *Opinions of the Accounting Principles Board No. 25* (New York: AICPA, 1972).

Stock Option Plans

A stock option plan can be either an incentive stock option plan or a nonqualified (or nonstatutory) stock option plan. The distinction between an incentive and a nonqualified stock option plan is based on the IRS Code and relates to the tax treatment afforded the plan.

From the perspective of the executive, the **incentive stock option** provides a greater tax advantage. In these plans, an executive pays no tax on the difference between the market price of the stock and the option price when the stock is purchased. Subsequently, when the shares are sold, the executive pays tax on that difference at either capital gains rates (20 percent) or ordinary income tax rates (usually higher than capital gains rates), depending upon the executive's holding period.[2] Conversely, an executive who receives a nonqualified stock option must pay taxes, at ordinary income tax rates, on the difference between the market price of the stock and the option price at the time the stock is purchased. Thus, under an incentive stock option, the payment of the tax is deferred and may be less.

From the perspective of the company, the **nonqualified option plan** provides greater tax advantages. No tax deduction is received in an incentive stock option plan. In contrast, in a nonqualified stock option plan the company receives a tax deduction equal to the difference between the market price and option price at the date the employee purchases the stock. To illustrate, assume that Hubbard, Inc. grants options to purchase 10,000 shares at an option price of $10 when the current market price of the stock is $10; the shares are purchased at a time when the market price is $20; and the executive sells the shares one year later at $20. A comparison of the effect of both plans on the executive and on the company is shown in Illustration 16A-1.

ILLUSTRATION 16A-1
Comparison of Incentive and Nonqualified Stock Option Plans

	Incentive Stock Option[3]	Nonqualified Stock Option
Effect on Executive:		
(assuming 36% tax bracket)		
Profit on exercise [10,000 × ($20 − $10)]	$100,000	$100,000
Tax on exercise ($100,000 × 36%)	–0–	$ 36,000
Tax on sale ($100,000 × 20%)	$ 20,000	–0–
After-tax benefit	$ 80,000	$ 64,000
Effect on Company:		
(assuming 34% corporate rate)	Zero tax deduction resulting in no tax benefit.	$100,000 tax deduction resulting in a $34,000 tax benefit.

In effect, the executive in Hubbard, Inc.'s case would incur an $80,000 benefit under the incentive stock option plan and a $64,000 benefit under the nonqualified stock option plan. The tax is also deferred until the stock is sold under the incentive stock option plan. The company receives no benefit from an incentive stock option but a $100,000 tax deduction (which becomes a $34,000 tax benefit) for the nonqualified stock option.

Incentive Stock Option Plan

Why would companies want to issue incentive stock options? The major reason is to attract high-quality personnel, and many companies believe that incentive stock options are a greater attraction than nonqualified plans. Incentive stock options are particularly helpful to smaller higher-technology enterprises that have little cash and perhaps so little taxable income that the tax deduction is not important. Granting such

[2]Capital gains are now taxed at rates not to exceed 18 percent, as long as the stock is held for more than 5 years.

[3]For an ISO, the executive has an alternative minimum tax (AMT) preference upon exercise, which may lead to tax payments under AMT rules. The illustration also assumes that the executive receiving an ISO receives favorable capital gains treatment.

options helps them attract and retain key personnel for whom they must compete against larger, established companies.

In an incentive stock option plan the tax laws require that the market price of the stock and the option price at the date of grant be equal. The tax laws do not require this equality in nonqualified plans. **No compensation expense is, therefore, recorded for an incentive stock option** because no excess of market price over the option price exists at the date of grant (the measurement date in this case).[4]

Nonqualified Stock Option Plans

Nonqualified stock option plans usually involve compensation expense because the market price exceeds the option price **at the date of grant** (the measurement date). Total compensation cost is measured by this difference and then allocated to the periods benefited. The option price is set by the terms of the grant and generally remains the same throughout the option period. The market price of the shares under option, however, may vary materially in the extended period during which the option is outstanding.

The options in the Chen Company illustration on pages 784–785 were nonqualified stock options. Recall that under the fair value approach (*SFAS No. 123*), the total compensation expense is measured at the grant date based on the fair value of the options that are expected to vest. Under the intrinsic value approach, compensation expense is recorded for the excess of the market price over the exercise price at the grant date.

Stock Appreciation Rights

One of the main advantages of a **nonqualified stock option** plan is that an executive may acquire shares of stock having a market price substantially above the option price. A major disadvantage is that an executive must pay income tax on the difference between the market price of the stock and the option price at the **date of exercise**. This can be a financial hardship for an executive who wishes to keep the stock (rather than sell it immediately) because he or she would have to pay not only income tax but the option price as well. For **incentive stock options**, much the same problem exists. That is, the executive may have to borrow to finance the exercise price, which leads to related interest costs.

One solution to this problem was the creation of **stock appreciation rights (SARs)**. In this type of plan, the executive is given the right to receive compensation equal to the **share appreciation**, which is defined as the excess of the market price of the stock at the date of exercise over a pre-established price. This share appreciation may be paid in cash, shares, or a combination of both. The major advantage of SARs is that the executive often does not have to make a cash outlay at the date of exercise, but receives a payment for the share appreciation. Unlike shares acquired under a stock option plan, the shares that constitute the basis for computing the appreciation in a SARs plan are not issued. The executive is awarded only cash or stock having a market value equivalent to the appreciation.

As indicated earlier, the usual date for measuring compensation related to stock compensation plans is the date of grant. However, with SARs, the final amount of cash or shares (or a combination of the two) to be distributed is not known until the date of exercise—the measurement date. Therefore total compensation cannot be measured until this date.

How then should compensation expense be recorded during the interim periods from the date of grant to the date of exercise? Such a determination is not easy because

---

[4]The FASB has developed rules under which expense may be recorded on stock options that are re-priced after the original grant. See "Accounting for Certain Transactions Involving Stock Compensation (an interpretation of *APB Opinion No. 25*)," *FASB Interpretation No. 44* (Norwalk, Conn.: FASB, 2000). Repricing occurs when, following a decline in the stock price, a company resets the option price to a lower level, thereby making it more likely that the option will be "in the money" and valuable to the executive.

it is impossible to know what total compensation cost will be until the date of exercise, and the service period will probably not coincide with the exercise date. The best estimate of total compensation cost for the plan at any interim period is the difference between the **current market price** of the stock and the **option price** multiplied by the number of stock appreciation rights outstanding. This total estimated compensation cost is then allocated over the service period, to record an expense (or a decrease in expense if market price falls) in each period.[5] At the end of each interim period, total compensation expense reported to date should equal the percentage of the total service period that has elapsed multiplied by the estimated compensation cost.

For example, if at the end of an interim period the service period is 40 percent complete and total estimated compensation is $100,000, then cumulative compensation expense reported to date should equal $40,000 ($100,000 × .40). As another illustration, in the first year of a 4-year plan, the company charges one-fourth of the appreciation to date. In the second year, it charges off two-fourths or 50 percent of the appreciation to date less the amount already recognized in the first year. In the third year, it charges off three-fourths of the appreciation to date less the amount recognized previously, and in the fourth year it charges off the remaining compensation expense. We will refer to this method as the **percentage approach** for allocating compensation expense.

A special problem arises when the exercise date is later than the service period. In the previous example, if the SARs were not exercised at the end of 4 years it would be necessary to account for the difference in the market price and the option price in the fifth year. In this case, compensation expense is adjusted whenever a change in the market price of the stock **occurs in subsequent reporting periods, until the rights expire or are exercised, whichever comes first**.

Increases or decreases in the market value of those shares between the date of grant and the exercise date, therefore, result in a change in the measure of compensation. Some periods will have credits to compensation expense if the quoted market price of the stock falls from one period to the next. The credit to compensation expense, however, cannot exceed previously recognized compensation expense. In other words, **cumulative compensation expense cannot be negative**.

To illustrate, assume that American Hotels, Inc. establishes a SARs program on January 1, 2004, which entitles executives to receive cash at the date of exercise (anytime in the next 5 years) for the difference between the market price of the stock and the preestablished price of $10 on 10,000 SARs. The market price of the stock on December 31, 2004, is $13, and the service period runs for 2 years (2004–2005). Illustration 16A-2 indicates the amount of compensation expense to be recorded each period, assuming that the executives hold the SARs for 3 years, at which time the rights are exercised.

ILLUSTRATION 16A-2
Compensation Expense, Stock Appreciation Rights

STOCK APPRECIATION RIGHTS
SCHEDULE OF COMPENSATION EXPENSE

(1) Date	(2) Market Price	(3) Pre-established Price (10,000 SARs)	(4) Cumulative Compensation Recognizable[a]	(5) Percentage Accrued[b]	(6) Cumulative Compensation Accrued to Date	Expense 2004	Expense 2005	Expense 2006
12/31/04	$13	$10	$30,000	50%	$ 15,000	$15,000		
					55,000		$55,000	
12/31/05	17	10	70,000	100%	70,000			
					(20,000)			$(20,000)
12/31/06	15	10	50,000	100%	$ 50,000			

[a]Cumulative compensation for unexercised SARs to be allocated to periods of service.
[b]The percentage accrued is based upon a 2-year service period (2004–2005).

[5]"Accounting for Stock Appreciation Rights and Other Variable Stock Option or Award Plans," *FASB Interpretation No. 28* (Stamford, Conn.: FASB, 1978), par. 2.

In 2004 American Hotels would record compensation expense of $15,000 because 50 percent of the $30,000 total of compensation cost estimated at December 31, 2004, is allocable to 2004.

In 2005 the market price increased to $17 per share; therefore, the additional compensation expense of $55,000 ($70,000 minus $15,000) was recorded. The SARs were held through 2006, during which time the stock decreased to $15. The decrease is recognized by recording a $20,000 credit to compensation expense and a debit to Liability under Stock Appreciation Plan. Note that after the service period ends, since the rights are still outstanding, the rights are adjusted to market at December 31, 2006. Any such credit to compensation expense cannot exceed previous charges to expense attributable to that plan.

As the compensation expense is recorded each period, the corresponding credit should be to a liability account if the stock appreciation is to be paid in cash. If stock is to be issued, then a more appropriate credit would be to Paid-in Capital. The entry to record compensation expense in the first year, assuming that the SARs ultimately will be paid in cash, is as follows.

Compensation Expense	15,000	
Liability under Stock Appreciation Plan		15,000

The liability account would be credited again in 2005 for $55,000 and debited for $20,000 in 2006 when the negative compensation expense is recorded. The entry to record the negative compensation expense is as follows.

Liability under Stock Appreciation Plan	20,000	
Compensation Expense		20,000

At December 31, 2006, the executives receive $50,000. The entry removing the liability is as follows.

Liability under Stock Appreciation Plan	50,000	
Cash		50,000

Because compensation expense is measured by the difference between market prices of the stock from period to period, multiplied by the number of SARs, compensation expense can increase or decrease substantially from one period to the next.

For this reason, companies with substantial stock appreciation rights plans that settle in shares may choose to use *SFAS No. 123* guidelines because the total compensation expense is determined at the date of grant. Subsequent changes in market price are therefore ignored. Total compensation expense may be lower under *SFAS No. 123.*

SARs are often issued in combination with compensatory stock options (referred to as **tandem** or **combination plans**), and the executive must then select which of the two sets of terms to exercise, thereby canceling the other. The existence of alternative plans running concurrently poses additional problems. You must determine, on the basis of the facts available each period, which of the two plans has the higher probability of exercise and then account for this plan and ignore the other.

Performance-Type Plans

Some executives have become disenchanted with stock compensation plans whose ultimate payment depends on an increase in the market price of the common stock. They do not like having their compensation and judgment of performance at the mercy of the stock market's erratic behavior. As a result, there has been a substantial increase in the use of plans whereby executives receive common stock (or cash) if specified performance criteria are attained during the performance period (generally 3 to 5 years). Most of the 200 largest companies now have some type of plan that does not rely on stock price appreciation.

The **performance criteria** employed usually are increases in return on assets or equity, growth in sales, growth in earnings per share (EPS), or a combination of these factors. A good illustration of this type of plan is that of **Atlantic Richfield** (now part of **BP PLC**) which at one time offered performance units valued in excess of $700,000 to the chairman of the board. These performance units are payable in 5 years, contingent upon the company's meeting certain levels of return on stockholders' equity and cash dividends.

As another example, **Honeywell** has used growth in EPS or free cash flow as its performance criteria. For example, when certain levels of EPS are achieved, executives receive shares of stock. If the company achieves an average annual EPS growth of 13 percent, the executive will earn 100 percent of the shares. The maximum allowable is 130 percent, which would require a 17 percent growth rate; below 9 percent the executives receive nothing.

A performance-type plan's measurement date is the date of exercise because the number of shares that will be issued or the cash that will be paid out when performance is achieved are not known at the date of grant. The compensation cost is allocated to the periods involved in the same manner as with stock appreciation rights. That is, the **percentage approach** is used.

Tandem or combination awards are popular with these plans. The executive has the choice of selecting between a performance or stock option award. Companies such as **General Electric** and **Xerox** have adopted plans of this nature. In these cases the executive has the best of both worlds: If either the stock price increases or the performance goal is achieved, the executive gains. Sometimes, the executive receives both types of plans, so that the monies received from the performance plan can finance the exercise price on the stock option plan.

Summary of Compensation Plans

A summary of compensation plans and their major characteristics is provided in Illustration 16A-3.

ILLUSTRATION 16A-3
Summary of Compensation Plans

Type of Plan	Measurement Date	Measurement of Compensation	Allocation Period	Allocation Method
Incentive stock option				
APB Opinion No. 25	Grant	Market price less exercise price	N/A (no compensation expense)	N/A (no compensation expense)
SFAS No. 123	Grant	Option pricing model	Service	Straight-line
Nonqualified stock option				
APB Opinion No. 25	Grant	Market price less exercise price	Service	Straight-line
SFAS No. 123	Grant	Option pricing model	Service	Straight-line
Stock appreciation rights				
APB Opinion No. 25	Exercise	Market price less exercise price	Service	Percentage approach for service period, then mark to market
SFAS No. 123	Grant	Option pricing model	Service	Straight-line
Performance-type Plan				
APB Opinion No. 25	Exercise	Market value of shares issued	Service	Percentage approach for service period, then mark to market
SFAS No. 123	Exercise	Market value of shares issued	Service	Percentage approach for service period, then mark to market

SUMMARY OF LEARNING OBJECTIVE FOR APPENDIX 16A

8 Explain the accounting for various stock option plans under APB Opinion No. 25. (1) *Incentive stock option plans*: The market price and exercise price on the grant date must be equal. Because there is no compensation expense, there is no allocation problem. (2) *Nonqualified stock option plans*: Compensation is the difference between the market price and the exercise price on the grant date. Compensation expense is allocated by the straight-line method during the service period. (3) *Stock appreciation rights:* The compensation is measured by the difference between market price and exercise price on the exercise date. The compensation expense is allocated by the percentage approach over the service period, then is marked to market. (4) *Performance-type plan:* Compensation is measured by the market value of shares issued on the exercise date. Compensation expense is allocated by the percentage approach over the service period, then is marked to market. See also Illustration 16A-3.

KEY TERMS

date of exercise, *803*
incentive stock option plan, *804*
nonqualified stock option plan, *804*
percentage approach, *806*
share appreciation, *805*
stock appreciation rights (SARs), *805*
tandem (combination) plans, *807*

APPENDIX 16B

Comprehensive Earnings per Share Illustration

The purpose of this appendix is to illustrate the method of computing dilution when many securities are involved. The following section of the balance sheet of Webster Corporation is presented for analysis. Assumptions related to the capital structure follow the balance sheet.

OBJECTIVE 9
Compute earnings per share in a complex situation.

ILLUSTRATION 16B-1
Balance Sheet for Comprehensive Illustration

WEBSTER CORPORATION
BALANCE SHEET (PARTIAL)
AT DECEMBER 31, 2004

Long-term debt	
Notes payable, 14%	$ 1,000,000
8% convertible bonds payable	2,500,000
10% convertible bonds payable	2,500,000
Total long-term debt	$ 6,000,000
Stockholders' equity	
10% cumulative, convertible preferred stock, par value $100; 100,000 shares authorized, 25,000 shares issued and outstanding	$ 2,500,000
Common stock, par value $1, 5,000,000 shares authorized, 500,000 shares issued and outstanding	500,000
Additional paid-in capital	2,000,000
Retained earnings	9,000,000
Total stockholders' equity	$14,000,000

Notes and Assumptions
December 31, 2004

1. Options were granted in July 2002 to purchase 50,000 shares of common stock at $20 per share. The average market price of Webster's common stock during 2004 was $30 per share. No options were exercised during 2004.
2. Both the 8 percent and 10 percent convertible bonds were issued in 2003 at face value. Each convertible bond is convertible into 40 shares of common stock. (Each bond has a face value of $1,000.)
3. The 10 percent cumulative, convertible preferred stock was issued at the beginning of 2004 at par. Each share of preferred is convertible into four shares of common stock.
4. The average income tax rate is 40 percent.
5. The 500,000 shares of common stock were outstanding during the entire year.
6. Preferred dividends were not declared in 2004.
7. Net income was $1,750,000 in 2004.
8. No bonds or preferred stock were converted during 2004.

The computation of basic earnings per share for 2004 starts with the amount based upon the weighted average of common shares outstanding, as shown in Illustration 16B-2.

ILLUSTRATION 16B-2
Computation of Earnings per Share—Simple Capital Structure

Net income	$1,750,000
Less: 10% cumulative, convertible preferred stock dividend requirements	250,000
Income applicable to common stockholders	$1,500,000
Weighted average number of common shares outstanding	500,000
Earnings per common share	$3.00

Note the following points concerning the calculation above.

1. When preferred stock is cumulative, the preferred dividend is subtracted to arrive at income applicable to common stock whether the dividend is declared or not.
2. The earnings per share of $3 must be computed as a starting point, because it is the per share amount that is subject to reduction due to the existence of convertible securities and options.

DILUTED EARNINGS PER SHARE

The steps for computing diluted earnings per share are:

1. Determine, for each dilutive security, the per share effect assuming exercise/conversion.
2. Rank the results from step 1 from smallest to largest earnings effect per share. That is, rank the results from most dilutive to least dilutive.
3. Beginning with the earnings per share based upon the weighted average of common shares outstanding ($3), recalculate earnings per share by adding the smallest per share effects from step 2. If the results from this recalculation are less than $3, proceed to the next smallest per share effect and recalculate earnings per share. Continue this process so long as each recalculated earnings per share is smaller than the previous amount. The process will end either because there are no more securities to test or a particular security maintains or increases earnings per share (is antidilutive).

We'll now apply the three steps to Webster Corporation. (Note that net income and income available to common stockholders are not the same if preferred dividends are declared or cumulative.) Webster Corporation has four securities (options, 8 percent and 10 percent convertible bonds, and the convertible preferred stock) that could reduce EPS.

The first step in the computation of diluted earnings per share is to determine a per share effect for each potentially dilutive security. Illustrations 16B-3 through 16B-6 illustrate these computations.

ILLUSTRATION 16B-3
Per Share Effect of Options (Treasury Stock Method), Diluted Earnings per Share

Number of shares under option	50,000
Option price per share	× $20
Proceeds upon assumed exercise of options	$1,000,000
Average 2004 market price of common	$30
Treasury shares that could be acquired with proceeds ($1,000,000 ÷ $30)	33,333
Excess of shares under option over treasury shares that could be repurchased (50,000 − 33,333)	16,667
Per share effect:	
$\frac{\text{Incremental Numerator Effect}}{\text{Incremental Denominator Effect}} = \frac{\text{None}}{\text{16,667 shares}} =$	$0

ILLUSTRATION 16B-4
Per Share Effect of 8% Bonds (If-Converted Method), Diluted Earnings per Share

Interest expense for year (8% × $2,500,000)	$200,000
Income tax reduction due to interest (40% × $200,000)	80,000
Interest expense avoided (net of tax)	$120,000
Number of common shares issued assuming conversion of bonds (2,500 bonds × 40 shares)	100,000
Per share effect:	
$\frac{\text{Incremental Numerator Effect}}{\text{Incremental Denominator Effect}} = \frac{\text{\$120,000}}{\text{100,000 shares}} =$	$1.20

ILLUSTRATION 16B-5
Per Share Effect of 10% Bonds (If-Converted Method), Diluted Earnings per Share

Interest expense for year (10% × $2,500,000)	$250,000
Income tax reduction due to interest (40% × $250,000)	100,000
Interest expense avoided (net of tax)	$150,000
Number of common shares issued assuming conversion of bonds (2,500 bonds × 40 shares)	100,000
Per share effect:	
$\frac{\text{Incremental Numerator Effect}}{\text{Incremental Denominator Effect}} = \frac{\text{\$150,000}}{\text{100,000 shares}} =$	$1.50

ILLUSTRATION 16B-6
Per Share Effect of 10% Convertible Preferred (If-Converted Method), Diluted Earnings per Share

Dividend requirement on cumulative preferred (25,000 shares × $10)	$250,000
Income tax effect (dividends not a tax deduction)	none
Dividend requirement avoided	$250,000
Number of common shares issued assuming conversion of preferred (4 × 25,000 shares)	100,000
Per share effect:	
$\frac{\text{Incremental Numerator Effect}}{\text{Incremental Denominator Effect}} = \frac{\text{\$250,000}}{\text{100,000 shares}} =$	$2.50

Illustration 16B-7 shows the ranking of all four potentially dilutive securities.

ILLUSTRATION 16B-7
Ranking of per Share Effects (Smallest to Largest), Diluted Earnings per Share

	Effect per Share
1. Options	$ 0
2. 8% convertible bonds	1.20
3. 10% convertible bonds	1.50
4. 10% convertible preferred	2.50

The next step is to determine earnings per share giving effect to the ranking in Illustration 16B-7. Starting with the earnings per share of $3 computed previously, add the incremental effects of the options to the original calculation, as follows.

ILLUSTRATION 16B-8
Recomputation of EPS Using Incremental Effect of Options

Options	
Income applicable to common stockholders	$1,500,000
Add: Incremental numerator effect of options	none
Total	$1,500,000
Weighted average number of common shares outstanding	500,000
Add: Incremental denominator effect of options (Illustration 16B-3)	16,667
Total	516,667
Recomputed earnings per share ($1,500,000 ÷ 516,667 shares)	$2.90

Since the recomputed earnings per share is reduced (from $3 to $2.90), the effect of the options is dilutive. Again, this effect could have been anticipated because the average market price ($30) exceeded the option price ($20).

Recomputed earnings per share, assuming the 8 percent bonds are converted, is as follows.

ILLUSTRATION 16B-9
Recomputation of EPS Using Incremental Effect of 8% Convertible Bonds

8% Convertible Bonds	
Numerator from previous calculation	$1,500,000
Add: Interest expense avoided (net of tax)	120,000
Total	$1,620,000
Denominator from previous calculation (shares)	516,667
Add: Number of common shares assumed issued upon conversion of bonds	100,000
Total	616,667
Recomputed earnings per share ($1,620,000 ÷ 616,667 shares)	$2.63

Since the recomputed earnings per share is reduced (from $2.90 to $2.63), the effect of the 8 percent bonds is dilutive.

Next, earnings per share is recomputed assuming the conversion of the 10 percent bonds. This is shown below.

ILLUSTRATION 16B-10
Recomputation of EPS Using Incremental Effect of 10% Convertible Bonds

10% Convertible Bonds	
Numerator from previous calculation	$1,620,000
Add: Interest expense avoided (net of tax)	150,000
Total	$1,770,000
Denominator from previous calculation (shares)	616,667
Add: Number of common shares assumed issued upon conversion of bonds	100,000
Total	716,667
Recomputed earnings per share ($1,770,000 ÷ 716,667 shares)	$2.47

Since the recomputed earnings per share is reduced (from $2.63 to $2.47), the effect of the 10 percent convertible bonds is dilutive.

The final step is the recomputation that includes the 10 percent preferred stock. This is shown below.

ILLUSTRATION 16B-11
Recomputation of EPS Using Incremental Effect of 10% Convertible Preferred

10% Convertible Preferred	
Numerator from previous calculation	$1,770,000
Add: Dividend requirement avoided	250,000
Total	$2,020,000
Denominator from previous calculation (shares)	716,667
Add: Number of common shares assumed issued upon conversion of preferred	100,000
Total	816,667
Recomputed earnings per share ($2,020,000 ÷ 816,667 shares)	$2.47

Since the recomputed earnings per share is not reduced, the effect of the 10 percent convertible preferred is not dilutive. Diluted earnings per share is $2.47, and the per share effects of the preferred are not used in the computation.

Finally, the disclosure of earnings per share on the income statement for Webster Corporation is shown below.

ILLUSTRATION 16B-12
Income Statement Presentation, EPS

Net income	$1,750,000
Basic earnings per common share (Note X)	$3.00
Diluted earnings per common share	$2.47

A company uses **income from continuing operations (adjusted for preferred dividends) to determine whether potential common stock is dilutive or antidilutive**. (Some refer to this measure as the **control number**.) To illustrate, assume that Barton Company provides the following information.

ILLUSTRATION 16B-13
Barton Company Data

Income from continuing operations	$2,400,000
Loss from discontinued operations	3,600,000
Net loss	$1,200,000
Weighted average shares of common stock outstanding	1,000,000
Potential common stock	200,000

The computation of basic and dilutive earnings per share is as follows.

ILLUSTRATION 16B-14
Basic and Diluted EPS

Basic earnings per share	
Income from continuing operations	$2.40
Loss from discontinued operations	3.60
Net loss	$1.20
Diluted earnings per share	
Income from continuing operations	$2.00
Loss from discontinued operations	3.00
Net loss	$1.00

As shown in Illustration 16B-14, basic earnings per share from continuing operations is higher than the diluted earnings per share from continuing operations. The reason: The diluted earnings per share from continuing operations includes an additional 200,000 shares of potential common stock in its denominator.[1]

EPS Illustration with Multiple Dilutive Securities

Income from continuing operations is used as the control number because many companies will show income from continuing operations (or a similar line item above net income if it appears on the income statement), but report a final net loss due to a loss on discontinued operations. If the final net loss is used as the control number, basic and diluted earnings per share would be the same because the potential common shares are antidilutive.[2]

KEY TERMS

control number, *813*

SUMMARY OF LEARNING OBJECTIVE FOR APPENDIX 16B

9 Compute earnings per share in a complex situation. For diluted EPS, make the following computations: (1) Determine, for each potentially dilutive security, the per share effect assuming exercise/conversion. (2) Rank the results from most dilutive to least dilutive. (3) Recalculate EPS starting with the most dilutive, and continue adding securities until EPS increases (is antidilutive).

Note: All **asterisked** Questions, Brief Exercises, Exercises, and Conceptual Cases relate to material contained in the appendix to the chapter.

QUESTIONS

1. What is meant by a dilutive security?
2. Briefly explain why corporations issue convertible securities.
3. Discuss the similarities and the differences between convertible debt and debt issued with stock warrants.
4. Plantagenet Corp. offered holders of its 1,000 convertible bonds a premium of $160 per bond to induce conversion into shares of its common stock. Upon conversion of all the bonds, Plantagenet Corp. recorded the $160,000 premium as a reduction of paid-in capital. Comment on Plantagenet's treatment of the $160,000 "sweetener."
5. Explain how the conversion feature of convertible debt has a value (a) to the issuer and (b) to the purchaser.
6. What are the arguments for giving separate accounting recognition to the conversion feature of debentures?
7. Four years after issue, debentures with a face value of $1,000,000 and book value of $960,000 are tendered for conversion into 80,000 shares of common stock immediately after an interest payment date. At that time the market price of the debentures is 104, and the common stock is selling at $14 per share (par value $10). The company records the conversion as follows.

Bonds Payable	1,000,000	
Discount on Bonds Payable		40,000
Common Stock		800,000
Paid-in Capital in Excess of Par		160,000

Discuss the propriety of this accounting treatment.

8. On July 1, 2004, Roberts Corporation issued $3,000,000 of 9% bonds payable in 20 years. The bonds include detachable warrants giving the bondholder the right to purchase for $30 one share of $1 par value common stock at any time during the next 10 years. The bonds were sold for $3,000,000. The value of the warrants at the time of issuance was $200,000. Prepare the journal entry to record this transaction.
9. What are stock rights? How does the issuing company account for them?
10. Briefly explain the accounting requirements for stock compensation plans under *Statement of Financial Accounting Standards No. 123.*

[1]A company that does not report a discontinued operation but reports an extraordinary item or the cumulative effect of a change in accounting principle should use that line item (for example, income before extraordinary items) as the control number.

[2]If a loss from continuing operations is reported, basic and diluted earnings per share will be the same because potential common stock will be antidilutive, even if the company reports final net income. The FASB believes that comparability of EPS information will be improved by using income from continuing operations as the control number.

11. Weiland Corporation has an employee stock purchase plan which permits all full-time employees to purchase 10 shares of common stock on the third anniversary of their employment and an additional 15 shares on each subsequent anniversary date. The purchase price is set at the market price on the date purchased and no commission is charged. Discuss whether this plan would be considered compensatory.

12. What date or event does the profession believe should be used in determining the value of a stock option? What arguments support this position?

13. Over what period of time should compensation cost be allocated?

14. How is compensation expense computed using the fair value approach?

15. At December 31, 2004, Amad Company had 600,000 shares of common stock issued and outstanding, 400,000 of which had been issued and outstanding throughout the year and 200,000 of which were issued on October 1, 2004. Net income for 2004 was $3,000,000, and dividends declared on preferred stock were $400,000. Compute Amad's earnings per common share. (Round to the nearest penny.)

16. What effect do stock dividends or stock splits have on the computation of the weighted average number of shares outstanding?

17. Define the following terms.

(a) Basic earnings per share.

(b) Potentially dilutive security.

(c) Diluted earnings per share.

(d) Complex capital structure.

(e) Potential common stock.

18. What are the computational guidelines for determining whether a convertible security is to be reported as part of diluted earnings per share?

19. Discuss why options and warrants may be considered potentially dilutive common shares for the computation of diluted earnings per share.

20. Explain how convertible securities are determined to be potentially dilutive common shares and how those convertible securities that are not considered to be potentially dilutive common shares enter into the determination of earnings per share data.

21. Explain the treasury stock method as it applies to options and warrants in computing dilutive earnings per share data.

22. Earnings per share can affect market prices of common stock. Can market prices affect earnings per share? Explain.

23. What is meant by the term antidilution? Give an example.

24. What type of earnings per share presentation is required in a complex capital structure?

***25.** How is antidilution determined when multiple securities are involved?

BRIEF EXERCISES

BE16-1 Faital Inc. issued $5,000,000 par value, 7% convertible bonds at 99 for cash. If the bonds had not included the conversion feature, they would have sold for 95. Prepare the journal entry to record the issuance of the bonds.

BE16-2 Sasha Verbitsky Corporation has outstanding 1,000 $1,000 bonds, each convertible into 50 shares of $10 par value common stock. The bonds are converted on December 31, 2005, when the unamortized discount is $30,000 and the market price of the stock is $21 per share. Record the conversion using the book value approach.

BE16-3 Malik Sealy Corporation issued 2,000 shares of $10 par value common stock upon conversion of 1,000 shares of $50 par value preferred stock. The preferred stock was originally issued at $55 per share. The common stock is trading at $26 per share at the time of conversion. Record the conversion of the preferred stock.

BE16-4 Divac Corporation issued 1,000 $1,000 bonds at 101. Each bond was issued with one detachable stock warrant. After issuance, the bonds were selling in the market at 98, and the warrants had a market value of $40. Use the proportional method to record the issuance of the bonds and warrants.

BE16-5 Ceballos Corporation issued 1,000 $1,000 bonds at 101. Each bond was issued with one detachable stock warrant. After issuance, the bonds were selling separately at 98. The market price of the warrants without the bonds cannot be determined. Use the incremental method to record the issuance of the bonds and warrants.

BE16-6 On January 1, 2005, Johnson Corporation granted 5,000 options to executives. Each option entitles the holder to purchase one share of Johnson's $5 par value common stock at $50 per share at any time during the next 5 years. The market price of the stock is $65 per share on the date of grant. The period of benefit is 2 years. Prepare Johnson's journal entries for January 1, 2005, and December 31, 2005 and 2006, using the intrinsic value method.

BE16-7 Use the information given for Johnson Corporation in BE16-6. Assume the fair value option pricing model determines that total compensation expense is $140,000. Prepare Johnson's journal entries for January 1, 2005, and December 31, 2005 and 2006, using the fair value method.

BE16-8 Haley Corporation had 2005 net income of $1,200,000. During 2005, Haley paid a dividend of $2 per share on 100,000 shares of preferred stock. During 2005, Haley had outstanding 250,000 shares of common stock. Compute Haley's 2005 earnings per share.

BE16-9 Barkley Corporation had 120,000 shares of stock outstanding on January 1, 2005. On May 1, 2005, Barkley issued 45,000 shares. On July 1, Barkley purchased 10,000 treasury shares, which were reissued on October 1. Compute Barkley's weighted average number of shares outstanding for 2005.

BE16-10 Green Corporation had 200,000 shares of common stock outstanding on January 1, 2005. On May 1, Green issued 30,000 shares. (a) Compute the weighted average number of shares outstanding if the 30,000 shares were issued for cash. (b) Compute the weighted average number of shares outstanding if the 30,000 shares were issued in a stock dividend.

BE16-11 Strickland Corporation earned net income of $300,000 in 2005 and had 100,000 shares of common stock outstanding throughout the year. Also outstanding all year was $400,000 of 10% bonds, which are convertible into 16,000 shares of common. Strickland's tax rate is 40 percent. Compute Strickland's 2005 diluted earnings per share.

BE16-12 Sabonis Corporation reported net income of $400,000 in 2005 and had 50,000 shares of common stock outstanding throughout the year. Also outstanding all year were 5,000 shares of cumulative preferred stock, each convertible into 2 shares of common. The preferred stock pays an annual dividend of $5 per share. Sabonis' tax rate is 40%. Compute Sabonis' 2005 diluted earnings per share.

BE16-13 Sarunas Corporation reported net income of $300,000 in 2005 and had 200,000 shares of common stock outstanding throughout the year. Also outstanding all year were 30,000 options to purchase common stock at $10 per share. The average market price of the stock during the year was $15. Compute diluted earnings per share.

BE16-14 The 2005 income statement of Schrempf Corporation showed net income of $480,000 and an extraordinary loss of $120,000. Schrempf had 50,000 shares of common stock outstanding all year. Prepare Schrempf's income statement presentation of earnings per share.

***BE16-15** Sam Perkins, Inc. established a stock appreciation rights (SAR) program on January 1, 2004, which entitles executives to receive cash at the date of exercise for the difference between the market price of the stock and the preestablished price of $20 on 5,000 SARs. The required service period is 2 years. The market price of the stock is $22 on December 31, 2004, and $29 on December 31, 2005. The SARs are exercised on January 1, 2006. Compute Perkins' compensation expense for 2004 and 2005.

EXERCISES

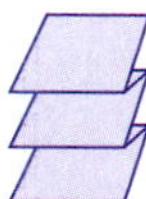

E16-1 (Issuance and Conversion of Bonds) For each of the unrelated transactions described below, present the entry(ies) required to record each transaction.

1. Grand Corp. issued $20,000,000 par value 10% convertible bonds at 99. If the bonds had not been convertible, the company's investment banker estimates they would have been sold at 95. Expenses of issuing the bonds were $70,000.
2. Hoosier Company issued $20,000,000 par value 10% bonds at 98. One detachable stock purchase warrant was issued with each $100 par value bond. At the time of issuance, the warrants were selling for $4.
3. On July 1, 2004, Trady Company called its 11% convertible debentures for conversion. The $10,000,000 par value bonds were converted into 1,000,000 shares of $1 par value common stock. On July 1, there was $55,000 of unamortized discount applicable to the bonds, and the company paid an additional $75,000 to the bondholders to induce conversion of all the bonds. The company records the conversion using the book value method.

E16-2 (Conversion of Bonds) Aubrey Inc. issued $4,000,000 of 10%, 10-year convertible bonds on June 1, 2004, at 98 plus accrued interest. The bonds were dated April 1, 2004, with interest payable April 1 and October 1. Bond discount is amortized semiannually on a straight-line basis.

On April 1, 2005, $1,500,000 of these bonds were converted into 30,000 shares of $20 par value common stock. Accrued interest was paid in cash at the time of conversion.

Instructions

(a) Prepare the entry to record the interest expense at October 1, 2004. Assume that accrued interest payable was credited when the bonds were issued. (Round to nearest dollar.)

(b) Prepare the entry(ies) to record the conversion on April 1, 2005. (Book value method is used.) Assume that the entry to record amortization of the bond discount and interest payment has been made.

E16-3 (Conversion of Bonds) Vargo Company has bonds payable outstanding in the amount of $500,000, and the Premium on Bonds Payable account has a balance of $7,500. Each $1,000 bond is convertible into 20 shares of preferred stock of par value of $50 per share. All bonds are converted into preferred stock.

Instructions

Assuming that the book value method was used, what entry would be made?

E16-4 (Conversion of Bonds) On January 1, 2003, when its $30 par value common stock was selling for $80 per share, Plato Corp. issued $10,000,000 of 8% convertible debentures due in 20 years. The conversion option allowed the holder of each $1,000 bond to convert the bond into five shares of the corporation's common stock. The debentures were issued for $10,800,000. The present value of the bond payments at the time of issuance was $8,500,000, and the corporation believes the difference between the present value and the amount paid is attributable to the conversion feature. On January 1, 2004, the corporation's $30 par value common stock was split 2 for 1, and the conversion rate for the bonds was adjusted accordingly. On January 1, 2005, when the corporation's $15 par value common stock was selling for $135 per share, holders of 30% of the convertible debentures exercised their conversion options. The corporation uses the straight-line method for amortizing any bond discounts or premiums.

Instructions

(a) Prepare in general journal form the entry to record the original issuance of the convertible debentures.

(b) Prepare in general journal form the entry to record the exercise of the conversion option, using the book value method. Show supporting computations in good form.

E16-5 (Conversion of Bonds) The December 31, 2004, balance sheet of Kepler Corp. is as follows.

10% callable, convertible bonds payable (semiannual interest dates April 30 and October 31; convertible into 6 shares of $25 par value common stock per $1,000 of bond principal; maturity date April 30, 2010)	$500,000	
Discount on bonds payable	10,240	$489,760

On March 5, 2005, Kepler Corp. called all of the bonds as of April 30 for the principal plus interest through April 30. By April 30 all bondholders had exercised their conversion to common stock as of the interest payment date. Consequently, on April 30, Kepler Corp. paid the semiannual interest and issued shares of common stock for the bonds. The discount is amortized on a straight-line basis. Kepler uses the book value method.

Instructions

Prepare the entry(ies) to record the interest expense and conversion on April 30, 2005. Reversing entries were made on January 1, 2005. (Round to the nearest dollar.)

E16-6 (Conversion of Bonds) On January 1, 2004, Gottlieb Corporation issued $4,000,000 of 10-year, 8% convertible debentures at 102. Interest is to be paid semiannually on June 30 and December 31. Each $1,000 debenture can be converted into eight shares of Gottlieb Corporation $100 par value common stock after December 31, 2005.

On January 1, 2006, $400,000 of debentures are converted into common stock, which is then selling at $110. An additional $400,000 of debentures are converted on March 31, 2006. The market price of the common stock is then $115. Accrued interest at March 31 will be paid on the next interest date.

Bond premium is amortized on a straight-line basis.

Instructions

Make the necessary journal entries for:

(a) December 31, 2005. **(c)** March 31, 2006.
(b) January 1, 2006. **(d)** June 30, 2006.

Record the conversions using the book value method.

E16-7 (Issuance of Bonds with Warrants) Illiad Inc. has decided to raise additional capital by issuing $170,000 face value of bonds with a coupon rate of 10%. In discussions with investment bankers, it was determined that to help the sale of the bonds, detachable stock warrants should be issued at the rate of one warrant for each $100 bond sold. The value of the bonds without the warrants is considered to be $136,000, and the value of the warrants in the market is $24,000. The bonds sold in the market at issuance for $152,000.

Instructions

(a) What entry should be made at the time of the issuance of the bonds and warrants?
(b) If the warrants were nondetachable, would the entries be different? Discuss.

E16-8 (Issuance of Bonds with Detachable Warrants) On September 1, 2004, Sands Company sold at 104 (plus accrued interest) 4,000 of its 9%, 10-year, $1,000 face value, nonconvertible bonds with detachable stock warrants. Each bond carried two detachable warrants. Each warrant was for one share of common stock at a specified option price of $15 per share. Shortly after issuance, the warrants were quoted on the market for $3 each. No market value can be determined for the Sands Company bonds. Interest is payable on December 1 and June 1. Bond issue costs of $30,000 were incurred.

Instructions

Prepare in general journal format the entry to record the issuance of the bonds.

(AICPA adapted)

E16-9 (Issuance of Bonds with Stock Warrants) On May 1, 2004, Friendly Company issued 2,000 $1,000 bonds at 102. Each bond was issued with one detachable stock warrant. Shortly after issuance, the bonds were selling at 98, but the market value of the warrants cannot be determined.

Instructions

(a) Prepare the entry to record the issuance of the bonds and warrants.
(b) Assume the same facts as part (a), except that the warrants had a fair value of $30. Prepare the entry to record the issuance of the bonds and warrants.

E16-10 (Issuance and Exercise of Stock Options) On November 1, 2004, Columbo Company adopted a stock option plan that granted options to key executives to purchase 30,000 shares of the company's $10 par value common stock. The options were granted on January 2, 2005, and were exercisable 2 years after the date of grant if the grantee was still an employee of the company. The options expired 6 years from date of grant. The option price was set at $40, and the fair value option pricing model determines the total compensation expense to be $450,000.

All of the options were exercised during the year 2007: 20,000 on January 3 when the market price was $67, and 10,000 on May 1 when the market price was $77 a share.

Instructions

Prepare journal entries relating to the stock option plan for the years 2005, 2006, and 2007 under the fair value method. Assume that the employee performs services equally in 2005 and 2006.

E16-11 (Issuance, Exercise, and Termination of Stock Options) On January 1, 2005, Titania Inc. granted stock options to officers and key employees for the purchase of 20,000 shares of the company's $10 par common stock at $25 per share. The options were exercisable within a 5-year period beginning January 1, 2007, by grantees still in the employ of the company, and expiring December 31, 2011. The service period for this award is 2 years. Assume that the fair value option pricing model determines total compensation expense to be $350,000.

On April 1, 2006, 2,000 option shares were terminated when the employees resigned from the company. The market value of the common stock was $35 per share on this date.

On March 31, 2007, 12,000 option shares were exercised when the market value of the common stock was $40 per share.

Instructions

Prepare journal entries using the fair value method to record issuance of the stock options, termination of the stock options, exercise of the stock options, and charges to compensation expense, for the years ended December 31, 2005, 2006, and 2007.

E16-12 (Issuance, Exercise, and Termination of Stock Options) On January 1, 2003, Nichols Corporation granted 10,000 options to key executives. Each option allows the executive to purchase one share of Nichols' $5 par value common stock at a price of $20 per share. The options were exercisable within a 2-year period beginning January 1, 2005, if the grantee is still employed by the company at the time of the exercise. On the grant date, Nichols' stock was trading at $25 per share, and a fair value option-pricing model determines total compensation to be $400,000.

On May 1, 2005, 8,000 options were exercised when the market price of Nichols' stock was $30 per share. The remaining options lapsed in 2007 because executives decided not to exercise their options.

Instructions

Prepare the necessary journal entries related to the stock option plan for the years 2003 through 2007. Nichols uses the fair value approach to account for stock options.

***E16-13 (Stock Appreciation Rights)** On December 31, 2000, Beckford Company issues 150,000 stock appreciation rights to its officers entitling them to receive cash for the difference between the market price of its stock and a preestablished price of $10. The market price fluctuates as follows: 12/31/01—$14; 12/31/02—$8; 12/31/03—$20; 12/31/04—$19. The service period is 4 years and the exercise period is 7 years. The company elects to use *APB Opinion No. 25* accounting for this transaction.

Instructions

(a) Prepare a schedule that shows the amount of compensation expense allocable to each year affected by the stock appreciation rights plan.

(b) Prepare the entry at December 31, 2004, to record compensation expense, if any, in 2004.

(c) Prepare the entry on December 31, 2004, assuming that all 150,000 SARs are exercised.

***E16-14 (Stock Appreciation Rights)** Capulet Company establishes a stock appreciation rights program that entitles its new president Ben Davis to receive cash for the difference between the market price of the stock and a preestablished price of $30 (also market price) on December 31, 2001, on 30,000 SARs. The date of grant is December 31, 2001, and the required employment (service) period is 4 years. President Davis exercises all of the SARs in 2007. The market value of the stock fluctuates as follows: 12/31/02—$36; 12/31/03—$39; 12/31/04—$45; 12/31/05—$36; 12/31/06—$48. The company elects to use *APB Opinion No. 25* accounting for this transaction.

Instructions

(a) Prepare a 5-year (2002–2006) schedule of compensation expense pertaining to the 30,000 SARs granted president Davis.

(b) Prepare the journal entry for compensation expense in 2002, 2005, and 2006 relative to the 30,000 SARs.

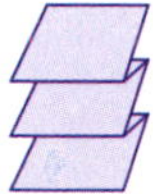

E16-15 (Weighted Average Number of Shares) Newton Inc. uses a calendar year for financial reporting. The company is authorized to issue 9,000,000 shares of $10 par common stock. At no time has Newton issued any potentially dilutive securities. Listed below is a summary of Newton's common stock activities.

1. Number of common shares issued and outstanding at December 31, 2002	2,000,000
2. Shares issued as a result of a 10% stock dividend on September 30, 2003	200,000
3. Shares issued for cash on March 31, 2004	2,000,000
Number of common shares issued and outstanding at December 31, 2004	4,200,000

4. A 2-for-1 stock split of Newton's common stock took place on March 31, 2005.

Instructions

(a) Compute the weighted average number of common shares used in computing earnings per common share for 2003 on the 2004 comparative income statement.

(b) Compute the weighted average number of common shares used in computing earnings per common share for 2004 on the 2004 comparative income statement.

(c) Compute the weighted average number of common shares to be used in computing earnings per common share for 2004 on the 2005 comparative income statement.

(d) Compute the weighted average number of common shares to be used in computing earnings per common share for 2005 on the 2005 comparative income statement.

(CMA adapted)

E16-16 (EPS: Simple Capital Structure) On January 1, 2005, Wilke Corp. had 480,000 shares of common stock outstanding. During 2005, it had the following transactions that affected the common stock account.

February 1	Issued 120,000 shares
March 1	Issued a 10% stock dividend
May 1	Acquired 100,000 shares of treasury stock
June 1	Issued a 3-for-1 stock split
October 1	Reissued 60,000 shares of treasury stock

Instructions

(a) Determine the weighted average number of shares outstanding as of December 31, 2005.

(b) Assume that Wilke Corp. earned net income of $3,456,000 during 2005. In addition, it had 100,000 shares of 9%, $100 par nonconvertible, noncumulative preferred stock outstanding for the entire year. Because of liquidity considerations, however, the company did not declare and pay a preferred dividend in 2005. Compute earnings per share for 2005, using the weighted-average number of shares determined in part (a).

(c) Assume the same facts as in part (b), except that the preferred stock was cumulative. Compute earnings per share for 2005.

(d) Assume the same facts as in part (b), except that net income included an extraordinary gain of $864,000 and a loss from discontinued operations of $432,000. Both items are net of applicable income taxes. Compute earnings per share for 2005.

E16-17 (EPS: Simple Capital Structure) Ace Company had 200,000 shares of common stock outstanding on December 31, 2005. During the year 2006 the company issued 8,000 shares on May 1 and retired 14,000 shares on October 31. For the year 2006 Ace Company reported net income of $249,690 after a casualty loss of $40,600 (net of tax).

Instructions

What earnings per share data should be reported at the bottom of its income statement, assuming that the casualty loss is extraordinary?

E16-18 (EPS: Simple Capital Structure) Flagstad Inc. presented the following data.

Net income	$2,500,000
Preferred stock: 50,000 shares outstanding, $100 par, 8% cumulative, not convertible	5,000,000
Common stock: Shares outstanding 1/1	750,000
Issued for cash, 5/1	300,000
Acquired treasury stock for cash, 8/1	150,000
2-for-1 stock split, 10/1	

Instructions

Compute earnings per share.

E16-19 (EPS: Simple Capital Structure) A portion of the combined statement of income and retained earnings of Seminole Inc. for the current year follows.

Income before extraordinary item		$15,000,000
Extraordinary loss, net of applicable income tax (Note 1)		1,340,000
Net income		13,660,000
Retained earnings at the beginning of the year		83,250,000
		96,910,000
Dividends declared:		
On preferred stock—$6.00 per share	$ 300,000	
On common stock—$1.75 per share	14,875,000	15,175,000
Retained earnings at the end of the year		$81,735,000

Note 1. During the year, Seminole Inc. suffered a major casualty loss of $1,340,000 after applicable income tax reduction of $1,200,000.

At the end of the current year, Seminole Inc. has outstanding 8,500,000 shares of $10 par common stock and 50,000 shares of 6% preferred.

On April 1 of the current year, Seminole Inc. issued 1,000,000 shares of common stock for $32 per share to help finance the casualty.

Instructions

Compute the earnings per share on common stock for the current year as it should be reported to stockholders.

E16-20 (EPS: Simple Capital Structure) On January 1, 2005, Lennon Industries had stock outstanding as follows.

6% Cumulative preferred stock, $100 par value, issued and outstanding 10,000 shares	$1,000,000
Common stock, $10 par value, issued and outstanding 200,000 shares	2,000,000

To acquire the net assets of three smaller companies, Lennon authorized the issuance of an additional 160,000 common shares. The acquisitions took place as shown on page 821.

Date of Acquisition	Shares Issued
Company A April 1, 2005	50,000
Company B July 1, 2005	80,000
Company C October 1, 2005	30,000

On May 14, 2005, Lennon realized a $90,000 (before taxes) insurance gain on the expropriation of investments originally purchased in 1994.

On December 31, 2005, Lennon recorded net income of $300,000 before tax and exclusive of the gain.

Instructions

Assuming a 50% tax rate, compute the earnings per share data that should appear on the financial statements of Lennon Industries as of December 31, 2005. Assume that the expropriation is extraordinary.

E16-21 (EPS: Simple Capital Structure) At January 1, 2005, Langley Company's outstanding shares included the following.

280,000 shares of $50 par value, 7% cumulative preferred stock
900,000 shares of $1 par value common stock

Net income for 2005 was $2,530,000. No cash dividends were declared or paid during 2005. On February 15, 2006, however, all preferred dividends in arrears were paid, together with a 5% stock dividend on common shares. There were no dividends in arrears prior to 2005.

On April 1, 2005, 450,000 shares of common stock were sold for $10 per share, and on October 1, 2005, 110,000 shares of common stock were purchased for $20 per share and held as treasury stock.

Instructions

Compute earnings per share for 2005. Assume that financial statements for 2005 were issued in March 2006.

E16-22 (EPS with Convertible Bonds, Various Situations) In 2003 Bonaparte Enterprises issued, at par, 60 $1,000, 8% bonds, each convertible into 100 shares of common stock. Bonaparte had revenues of $17,500 and expenses other than interest and taxes of $8,400 for 2004. (Assume that the tax rate is 40%.) Throughout 2004, 2,000 shares of common stock were outstanding; none of the bonds was converted or redeemed.

Instructions

(a) Compute diluted earnings per share for 2004.

(b) Assume the same facts as those assumed for part (a), except that the 60 bonds were issued on September 1, 2004 (rather than in 2003), and none have been converted or redeemed.

(c) Assume the same facts as assumed for part (a), except that 20 of the 60 bonds were actually converted on July 1, 2004.

E16-23 (EPS with Convertible Bonds) On June 1, 2002, Mowbray Company and Surrey Company merged to form Lancaster Inc. A total of 800,000 shares were issued to complete the merger. The new corporation reports on a calendar-year basis.

On April 1, 2004, the company issued an additional 400,000 shares of stock for cash. All 1,200,000 shares were outstanding on December 31, 2004.

Lancaster Inc. also issued $600,000 of 20-year, 8% convertible bonds at par on July 1, 2004. Each $1,000 bond converts to 40 shares of common at any interest date. None of the bonds have been converted to date.

Lancaster Inc. is preparing its annual report for the fiscal year ending December 31, 2004. The annual report will show earnings per share figures based upon a reported after-tax net income of $1,540,000. (The tax rate is 40%.)

Instructions

Determine the following for 2004.

(a) The number of shares to be used for calculating:
  (1) Basic earnings per share.
  (2) Diluted earnings per share.

(b) The earnings figures to be used for calculating:
  (1) Basic earnings per share.
  (2) Diluted earnings per share.

(CMA adapted)

E16-24 (EPS with Convertible Bonds and Preferred Stock) The Simon Corporation issued 10-year, $5,000,000 par, 7% callable convertible subordinated debentures on January 2, 2004. The bonds have a par value of $1,000, with interest payable annually. The current conversion ratio is 14:1, and in 2 years it will increase to 18:1. At the date of issue, the bonds were sold at 98. Bond discount is amortized on a straight-line basis. Simon's effective tax was 35%. Net income in 2004 was $9,500,000, and the company had 2,000,000 shares outstanding during the entire year.

Instructions

(a) Prepare a schedule to compute both basic and diluted earnings per share.
(b) Discuss how the schedule would differ if the security was convertible preferred stock.

E16-25 (EPS with Convertible Bonds and Preferred Stock) On January 1, 2004, Crocker Company issued 10-year, $2,000,000 face value, 6% bonds, at par. Each $1,000 bond is convertible into 15 shares of Crocker common stock. Crocker's net income in 2004 was $300,000, and its tax rate was 40%. The company had 100,000 shares of common stock outstanding throughout 2004. None of the bonds were converted in 2004.

Instructions

(a) Compute diluted earnings per share for 2004.
(b) Compute diluted earnings per share for 2004, assuming the same facts as above, except that $1,000,000 of 6% convertible preferred stock was issued instead of the bonds. Each $100 preferred share is convertible into 5 shares of Crocker common stock.

E16-26 (EPS with Options, Various Situations) Venzuela Company's net income for 2004 is $50,000. The only potentially dilutive securities outstanding were 1,000 options issued during 2003, each exercisable for one share at $6. None has been exercised, and 10,000 shares of common were outstanding during 2004. The average market price of Venzuela's stock during 2004 was $20.

Instructions

(a) Compute diluted earnings per share. (Round to nearest cent.)
(b) Assume the same facts as those assumed for part (a), except that the 1,000 options were issued on October 1, 2004 (rather than in 2003). The average market price during the last 3 months of 2004 was $20.

E16-27 (EPS with Contingent Issuance Agreement) Winsor Inc. recently purchased Holiday Corp., a large midwestern home painting corporation. One of the terms of the merger was that if Holiday's income for 2004 was $110,000 or more, 10,000 additional shares would be issued to Holiday's stockholders in 2005. Holiday's income for 2003 was $120,000.

Instructions

(a) Would the contingent shares have to be considered in Winsor's 2003 earnings per share computations?
(b) Assume the same facts, except that the 10,000 shares are contingent on Holiday's achieving a net income of $130,000 in 2004. Would the contingent shares have to be considered in Winsor's earnings per share computations for 2003?

E16-28 (EPS with Warrants) Howat Corporation earned $360,000 during a period when it had an average of 100,000 shares of common stock outstanding. The common stock sold at an average market price of $15 per share during the period. Also outstanding were 15,000 warrants that could be exercised to purchase one share of common stock for $10 for each warrant exercised.

Instructions

(a) Are the warrants dilutive?
(b) Compute basic earnings per share.
(c) Compute diluted earnings per share.

PROBLEMS

P16-1 (Entries for Various Dilutive Securities) The stockholders' equity section of McLean Inc. at the beginning of the current year appears below.

Common stock, $10 par value, authorized 1,000,000 shares, 300,000 shares issued and outstanding	$3,000,000
Paid-in capital in excess of par	600,000
Retained earnings	570,000

During the current year the following transactions occurred.

1. The company issued to the stockholders 100,000 rights. Ten rights are needed to buy one share of stock at $32. The rights were void after 30 days. The market price of the stock at this time was $34 per share.
2. The company sold to the public a $200,000, 10% bond issue at par. The company also issued with each $100 bond one detachable stock purchase warrant, which provided for the purchase of common stock at $30 per share. Shortly after issuance, similar bonds without warrants were selling at 96 and the warrants at $8.
3. All but 10,000 of the rights issued in (1) were exercised in 30 days.
4. At the end of the year, 80% of the warrants in (2) had been exercised, and the remaining were outstanding and in good standing.
5. During the current year, the company granted stock options for 5,000 shares of common stock to company executives. The company using a fair value option pricing model determines that each option is worth $10. The option price is $30. The options were to expire at year-end and were considered compensation for the current year.
6. All but 1,000 shares related to the stock option plan were exercised by year-end. The expiration resulted because one of the executives failed to fulfill an obligation related to the employment contract.

Instructions

(a) Prepare general journal entries for the current year to record the transactions listed above.

(b) Prepare the stockholders' equity section of the balance sheet at the end of the current year. Assume that retained earnings at the end of the current year is $750,000.

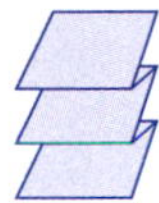

P16-2 (Entries for Conversion, Amortization, and Interest of Bonds) Counter Inc. issued $1,500,000 of convertible 10-year bonds on July 1, 2004. The bonds provide for 12% interest payable semiannually on January 1 and July 1. The discount in connection with the issue was $34,000, which is being amortized monthly on a straight-line basis.

The bonds are convertible after one year into 8 shares of Counter Inc.'s $100 par value common stock for each $1,000 of bonds.

On August 1, 2005, $150,000 of bonds were turned in for conversion into common. Interest has been accrued monthly and paid as due. At the time of conversion any accrued interest on bonds being converted is paid in cash.

Instructions

(Round to nearest dollar)

Prepare the journal entries to record the conversion, amortization, and interest in connection with the bonds as of the following dates.

(a) August 1, 2005. (Assume the book value method is used.)

(b) August 31, 2005.

(c) December 31, 2005, including closing entries for end-of-year.

(AICPA adapted)

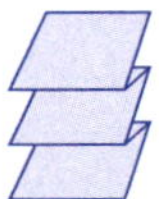

P16-3 (Stock Option Plan) ISU Company adopted a stock option plan on November 30, 2002, that provided that 70,000 shares of $5 par value stock be designated as available for the granting of options to officers of the corporation at a price of $8 a share. The market value was $12 a share on November 30, 2002.

On January 2, 2003, options to purchase 28,000 shares were granted to president Don Pedro—15,000 for services to be rendered in 2003 and 13,000 for services to be rendered in 2004. Also on that date, options to purchase 14,000 shares were granted to vice president Beatrice Leonato—7,000 for services to be rendered in 2003 and 7,000 for services to be rendered in 2004. The market value of the stock was $14 a share on January 2, 2003. The options were exercisable for a period of one year following the year in which the services were rendered.

In 2004 neither the president nor the vice president exercised their options because the market price of the stock was below the exercise price. The market value of the stock was $7 a share on December 31, 2004, when the options for 2003 services lapsed.

On December 31, 2005, both president Pedro and vice president Leonato exercised their options for 13,000 and 7,000 shares, respectively, when the market price was $16 a share.

Instructions

Prepare the necessary journal entries in 2002 when the stock option plan was adopted, in 2003 when options were granted, in 2004 when options lapsed, and in 2005 when options were exercised. The company elects to use the intrinsic value method following *APB Opinion No. 25.*

P16-4 (EPS with Complex Capital Structure) Diane Leto, controller at Dewey Yaeger Pharmaceutical Industries, a public company, is currently preparing the calculation for basic and diluted earnings per share and the related disclosure for Yaeger's external financial statements. Below is selected financial information for the fiscal year ended June 30, 2005.

DEWEY YAEGER PHARMACEUTICAL INDUSTRIES
SELECTED STATEMENT OF FINANCIAL POSITION INFORMATION
JUNE 30, 2005

Long-term debt	
Notes payable, 10%	$ 1,000,000
7% convertible bonds payable	5,000,000
10% bonds payable	6,000,000
Total long-term debt	$12,000,000
Shareholders' equity	
Preferred stock, 8.5% cumulative, $50 par value, 100,000 shares authorized, 25,000 shares issued and outstanding	$ 1,250,000
Common stock, $1 par, 10,000,000 shares authorized, 1,000,000 shares issued and outstanding	1,000,000
Additional paid-in capital	4,000,000
Retained earnings	6,000,000
Total shareholders' equity	$12,250,000

The following transactions have also occurred at Yaeger.

1. Options were granted in 2003 to purchase 100,000 shares at $15 per share. Although no options were exercised during 2005, the average price per common share during fiscal year 2005 was $20 per share.
2. Each bond was issued at face value. The 7% convertible debenture will convert into common stock at 50 shares per $1,000 bond. It is exercisable after 5 years and was issued in 2004.
3. The 8.5% preferred stock was issued in 2003.
4. There are no preferred dividends in arrears; however, preferred dividends were not declared in fiscal year 2005.
5. The 1,000,000 shares of common stock were outstanding for the entire 2005 fiscal year.
6. Net income for fiscal year 2005 was $1,500,000, and the average income tax rate is 40%.

Instructions

For the fiscal year ended June 30, 2005, calculate the following for Dewey Yaeger Pharmaceutical Industries.

(a) Basic earnings per share.
(b) Diluted earnings per share.

P16-5 (Basic EPS: Two-Year Presentation) Hillel Corporation is preparing the comparative financial statements for the annual report to its shareholders for fiscal years ended May 31, 2003, and May 31, 2004. The income from operations for each year was $1,800,000 and $2,500,000, respectively. In both years, the company incurred a 10% interest expense on $2,400,000 of debt, an obligation that requires interest-only payments for 5 years. The company experienced a loss of $500,000 from a fire in its Scotland facility in February 2004, which was determined to be an extraordinary loss. The company uses a 40% effective tax rate for income taxes.

The capital structure of Hillel Corporation on June 1, 2002, consisted of 2 million shares of common stock outstanding and 20,000 shares of $50 par value, 8%, cumulative preferred stock. There were no preferred dividends in arrears, and the company had not issued any convertible securities, options, or warrants.

On October 1, 2002, Hillel sold an additional 500,000 shares of the common stock at $20 per share. Hillel distributed a 20% stock dividend on the common shares outstanding on January 1, 2003. On December 1, 2003, Hillel was able to sell an additional 800,000 shares of the common stock at $22 per share. These were the only common stock transactions that occurred during the two fiscal years.

Instructions

(a) Identify whether the capital structure at Hillel Corporation is a simple or complex capital structure, and explain why.

(b) Determine the weighted average number of shares that Hillel Corporation would use in calculating earnings per share for the fiscal year ended
 (1) May 31, 2003.
 (2) May 31, 2004.

(c) Prepare, in good form, a comparative income statement, beginning with income from operations, for Hillel Corporation for the fiscal years ended May 31, 2003, and May 31, 2004. This statement will be included in Hillel's annual report and should display the appropriate earnings per share presentations.

(CMA adapted)

P16-6 (EPS Computation of Basic and Diluted EPS) Edmund Halvor of the controller's office of East Aurora Corporation was given the assignment of determining the basic and diluted earnings per share values for the year ending December 31, 2004. Halvor has compiled the information listed below.

1. The company is authorized to issue 8,000,000 shares of $10 par value common stock. As of December 31, 2003, 3,000,000 shares had been issued and were outstanding.
2. The per share market prices of the common stock on selected dates were as follows.

	Price per Share
July 1, 2003	$20.00
January 1, 2004	21.00
April 1, 2004	25.00
July 1, 2004	11.00
August 1, 2004	10.50
November 1, 2004	9.00
December 31, 2004	10.00

3. A total of 700,000 shares of an authorized 1,200,000 shares of convertible preferred stock had been issued on July 1, 2003. The stock was issued at its par value of $25, and it has a cumulative dividend of $3 per share. The stock is convertible into common stock at the rate of one share of convertible preferred for one share of common. The rate of conversion is to be automatically adjusted for stock splits and stock dividends. Dividends are paid quarterly on September 30, December 31, March 31, and June 30.
4. East Aurora Corporation is subject to a 40% income tax rate.
5. The after-tax net income for the year ended December 31, 2004 was $13,550,000.

The following specific activities took place during 2004.

1. January 1—A 5% common stock dividend was issued. The dividend had been declared on December 1, 2003, to all stockholders of record on December 29, 2003.
2. April 1—A total of 200,000 shares of the $3 convertible preferred stock was converted into common stock. The company issued new common stock and retired the preferred stock. This was the only conversion of the preferred stock during 2004.
3. July 1—A 2-for-1 split of the common stock became effective on this date. The board of directors had authorized the split on June 1.
4. August 1—A total of 300,000 shares of common stock were issued to acquire a factory building.
5. November 1—A total of 24,000 shares of common stock were purchased on the open market at $9 per share. These shares were to be held as treasury stock and were still in the treasury as of December 31, 2004.
6. Common stock cash dividends—Cash dividends to common stockholders were declared and paid as follows.
 April 15—$0.30 per share
 October 15—$0.20 per share
7. Preferred stock cash dividends—Cash dividends to preferred stockholders were declared and paid as scheduled.

Instructions

(a) Determine the number of shares used to compute basic earnings per share for the year ended December 31, 2004.

(b) Determine the number of shares used to compute diluted earnings per share for the year ended December 31, 2004.

(c) Compute the adjusted net income to be used as the numerator in the basic earnings per share calculation for the year ended December 31, 2004.

P16-7 (Computation of Basic and Diluted EPS) The information on page 826 pertains to Prancer Company for 2004.

Net income for the year	$1,200,000
8% convertible bonds issued at par ($1,000 per bond). Each bond is convertible into 40 shares of common stock.	2,000,000
6% convertible, cumulative preferred stock, $100 par value. Each share is convertible into 3 shares of common stock.	3,000,000
Common stock, $10 par value	6,000,000
Common stock options (granted in a prior year) to purchase 50,000 shares of common stock at $20 per share	500,000
Tax rate for 2004	40%
Average market price of common stock	$25 per share

There were no changes during 2004 in the number of common shares, preferred shares, or convertible bonds outstanding. There is no treasury stock.

Instructions

(a) Compute basic earnings per share for 2004.
(b) Compute diluted earnings per share for 2004.

P16-8 (EPS with Stock Dividend and Extraordinary Items) Cordelia Corporation is preparing the comparative financial statements to be included in the annual report to stockholders. Cordelia employs a fiscal year ending May 31.

Income from operations before income taxes for Cordelia was $1,400,000 and $660,000, respectively, for fiscal years ended May 31, 2004 and 2003. Cordelia experienced an extraordinary loss of $500,000 because of an earthquake on March 3, 2004. A 40% combined income tax rate pertains to any and all of Cordelia Corporation's profits, gains, and losses.

Cordelia's capital structure consists of preferred stock and common stock. The company has not issued any convertible securities or warrants and there are no outstanding stock options.

Cordelia issued 50,000 shares of $100 par value, 6% cumulative preferred stock in 2000. All of this stock is outstanding, and no preferred dividends are in arrears.

There were 1,500,000 shares of $1 par common stock outstanding on June 1, 2002. On September 1, 2002, Cordelia sold an additional 400,000 shares of the common stock at $17 per share. Cordelia distributed a 20% stock dividend on the common shares outstanding on December 1, 2003. These were the only common stock transactions during the past 2 fiscal years.

Instructions

(a) Determine the weighted average number of common shares that would be used in computing earnings per share on the current comparative income statement for:
 (1) The year ended May 31, 2003.
 (2) The year ended May 31, 2004.

(b) Starting with income from operations before income taxes, prepare a comparative income statement for the years ended May 31, 2004 and 2003. The statement will be part of Cordelia Corporation's annual report to stockholders and should include appropriate earnings per share presentation.

(c) The capital structure of a corporation is the result of its past financing decisions. Furthermore, the earnings per share data presented on a corporation's financial statements is dependent upon the capital structure.
 (1) Explain why Cordelia Corporation is considered to have a simple capital structure.
 (2) Describe how earnings per share data would be presented for a corporation that has a complex capital structure.

(CMA adapted)

CONCEPTUAL CASES

C16-1 (Warrants Issued with Bonds and Convertible Bonds) Incurring long-term debt with an arrangement whereby lenders receive an option to buy common stock during all or a portion of the time the debt is outstanding is a frequent corporate financing practice. In some situations the result is achieved through the issuance of convertible bonds; in others, the debt instruments and the warrants to buy stock are separate.

Instructions

(a) **(1)** Describe the differences that exist in current accounting for original proceeds of the issuance of convertible bonds and of debt instruments with separate warrants to purchase common stock.

(2) Discuss the underlying rationale for the differences described in (a)1 above.
(3) Summarize the arguments that have been presented in favor of accounting for convertible bonds in the same manner as accounting for debt with separate warrants.

(b) At the start of the year Biron Company issued $18,000,000 of 12% bonds along with warrants to buy 1,200,000 shares of its $10 par value common stock at $18 per share. The bonds mature over the next 10 years, starting one year from date of issuance, with annual maturities of $1,800,000. At the time, Biron had 9,600,000 shares of common stock outstanding, and the market price was $23 per share. The company received $20,040,000 for the bonds and the warrants. For Biron Company, 12% was a relatively low borrowing rate. If offered alone, at this time, the bonds would have been issued at a 22% discount. Prepare the journal entry (or entries) for the issuance of the bonds and warrants for the cash consideration received.

(AICPA adapted)

C16-2 (Ethical Issues—Compensation Plan) The executive officers of Coach Corporation have a performance-based compensation plan. The performance criteria of this plan is linked to growth in earnings per share. When annual EPS growth is 12%, the Coach executives earn 100% of the shares; if growth is 16%, they earn 125%. If EPS growth is lower than 8%, the executives receive no additional compensation.

In 2003, Joanna Becker, the controller of Coach, reviews year-end estimates of bad debt expense and warranty expense. She calculates the EPS growth at 15%. Peter Reiser, a member of the executive group, remarks over lunch one day that the estimate of bad debt expense might be decreased, increasing EPS growth to 16.1%. Becker is not sure she should do this because she believes that the current estimate of bad debts is sound. On the other hand, she recognizes that a great deal of subjectivity is involved in the computation.

Instructions

Answer the following questions.

(a) What, if any, is the ethical dilemma for Becker?
(b) Should Becker's knowledge of the compensation plan be a factor that influences her estimate?
(c) How should Becker respond to Reiser's request?

C16-3 (Stock Warrants—Various Types) For various reasons a corporation may issue warrants to purchase shares of its common stock at specified prices that, depending on the circumstances, may be less than, equal to, or greater than the current market price. For example, warrants may be issued:

1. To existing stockholders on a pro rata basis.
2. To certain key employees under an incentive stock option plan.
3. To purchasers of the corporation's bonds.

Instructions

For each of the three examples of how stock warrants are used:

(a) Explain why they are used.
(b) Discuss the significance of the price (or prices) at which the warrants are issued (or granted) in relation to (1) the current market price of the company's stock, and (2) the length of time over which they can be exercised.
(c) Describe the information that should be disclosed in financial statements, or notes thereto, that are prepared when stock warrants are outstanding in the hands of the three groups listed above.

(AICPA adapted)

***C16-4 (Stock Options and Stock Appreciation Rights—Intrinsic Value Model)** In 2002 Sanford Co. adopted a plan to give additional incentive compensation to its dealers to sell its principal product, fire extinguishers. Under the plan Sanford transferred 9,000 shares of its $1 par value stock to a trust with the provision that Sanford would have to forfeit interest in the trust and no part of the trust fund could ever revert to Sanford. Shares were to be distributed to dealers on the basis of their shares of fire extinguisher purchases from Sanford (above certain minimum levels) over the 3-year period ending June 30, 2005.

In 2002 the stock was closely held. The book value of the stock was $7.90 per share as of June 30, 2002, and in 2002 additional shares were sold to existing stockholders for $8 per share. On the basis of this information, market value of the stock was determined to be $8 per share.

In 2002 when the shares were transferred to the trust, Sanford charged prepaid expenses for $72,000 ($8 per share market value) and credited capital stock for $9,000 and additional paid-in capital for $63,000. The prepaid expense was charged to operations over a 3-year period ended June 30, 2005.

Sanford sold a substantial number of shares of its stock to the public in 2004 at $60 per share.

In July 2005 all shares of the stock in the trust were distributed to the dealers. The market value of the shares at date of distribution of the stock from the trust had risen to $110 per share. Sanford obtained a tax deduction equal to that market value for the tax year ended June 30, 2006.

Instructions

(Note: Use *APB Opinion No. 25* to solve this problem.)

(a) How much should be reported as selling expense in each of the years noted above, assuming that the company uses the intrinsic value model?

(b) Sanford is also considering other types of option plans. One such plan is a stock appreciation right (SAR) plan. What is a stock appreciation right plan? What is a potential disadvantage of a SAR plan from the viewpoint of the company?

C16-5 (Stock Compensation Plans) Presented below is an excerpt from a speech given by former SEC commissioner J. Carter Beese, Jr.

> ...I believe investors will be far better off if the value of stock options is reported in a footnote rather than on the face of the income statement. By allowing footnote disclosures, we will protect shareholders' current and future investments by not raising the cost of capital for the innovative, growth companies that depend on stock options to attract and retain key employees. I've said it before and I'll say it again: The stock option accounting debate essentially boils down to one thing—the cost of capital. And as long as we can adequately protect investors without raising the cost of capital to such a vital segment of our economy, why would we want to do it any other way?
>
> The FASB has made the assertion that when it comes to public policy, they lack the competence to weigh various national goals. I also agree with the sentiment that, as a general matter, Congress should not be in the business of writing accounting standards.
>
> But the SEC has the experience and the capability to determine exactly where to draw the regulatory lines to best serve investors and our capital markets. That is our mandate, and that is what we do, day in and day out.
>
> But we may have to act sooner rather than later. As we speak, the FASB's proposals are raising the cost of venture capital. That's because venture capitalists are pricing deals based on their exit strategies, which usually include cashing out in public offerings. The FASB's proposals, however, provide incentives for companies to stay private longer—they are able to use options more freely to attract and retain key employees, and they avoid the earnings hit that going public would entail. Even worse, as venture capital deals become less profitable because of the FASB's proposed actions, venture capitalists are starting to look overseas for alternative investment opportunities that lack the investment drag now associated with certain American ventures.
>
> I acknowledge that the FASB deserves some degree of freedom to determine what they believe is the best accounting approach. At the same time, however, I cannot stand by idly for long and watch venture capital increase in price or even flee this country because of a myopic search for an accounting holy grail. At some point, I believe that the SEC must inject itself into this debate, and help the FASB determine what accounting approach is ultimately in the best interests of investors as a whole.
>
> We owe it to shareholders, issuers and all market participants, and indeed our country, to make the best decision in accordance with the public good, not just technical accounting theory.

Instructions

(a) What are the major recommendations of *SFAS No. 123* on "Accounting for Stock-Based Compensation Plans"?

(b) Write a response to commissioner Beese, defending the use of the concept of neutrality in financial accounting and reporting.

C16-6 (EPS: Preferred Dividends, Options, and Convertible Debt) "Earnings per share" (EPS) is the most featured single financial statistic about modern corporations. Daily published quotations of stock prices have recently been expanded to include for many securities a "times earnings" figure that is based on EPS. Stock analysts often focus their discussions on the EPS of the corporations they study.

Instructions

(a) Explain how dividends or dividend requirements on any class of preferred stock that may be outstanding affect the computation of EPS.

(b) One of the technical procedures applicable in EPS computations is the "treasury stock method." Briefly describe the circumstances under which it might be appropriate to apply the treasury stock method.

(c) Convertible debentures are considered potentially dilutive common shares. Explain how convertible debentures are handled for purposes of EPS computations.

(AICPA adapted)

C16-7 (EPS Concepts and Effect of Transactions on EPS) Fernandez Corporation, a new audit client of yours, has not reported earnings per share data in its annual reports to stockholders in the past. The treasurer, Angelo Balthazar, requested that you furnish information about the reporting of earnings per share data in the current year's annual report in accordance with generally accepted accounting principles.

Instructions

(a) Define the term "earnings per share" as it applies to a corporation with a capitalization structure composed of only one class of common stock. Explain how earnings per share should be computed and how the information should be disclosed in the corporation's financial statements.

(b) Discuss the treatment, if any, that should be given to each of the following items in computing earnings per share of common stock for financial statement reporting.

(1) Outstanding preferred stock issued at a premium with a par value liquidation right.

(2) The exercise at a price below market value but above book value of a common stock option issued during the current fiscal year to officers of the corporation.

(3) The replacement of a machine immediately prior to the close of the current fiscal year at a cost 20% above the original cost of the replaced machine. The new machine will perform the same function as the old machine that was sold for its book value.

(4) The declaration of current dividends on cumulative preferred stock.

(5) The acquisition of some of the corporation's outstanding common stock during the current fiscal year. The stock was classified as treasury stock.

(6) A 2-for-1 stock split of common stock during the current fiscal year.

(7) A provision created out of retained earnings for a contingent liability from a possible lawsuit.

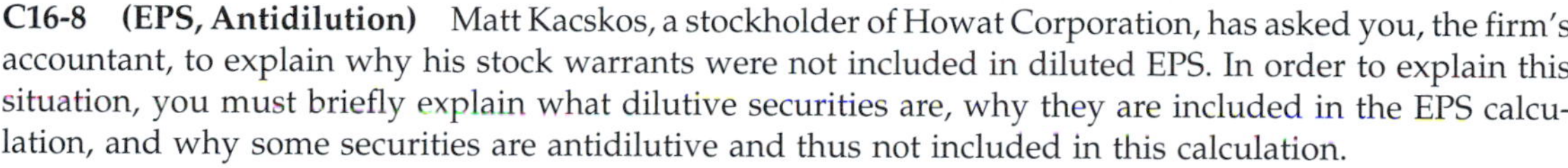

C16-8 (EPS, Antidilution) Matt Kacskos, a stockholder of Howat Corporation, has asked you, the firm's accountant, to explain why his stock warrants were not included in diluted EPS. In order to explain this situation, you must briefly explain what dilutive securities are, why they are included in the EPS calculation, and why some securities are antidilutive and thus not included in this calculation.

Instructions

Write Mr. Kacskos a 1–1.5 page letter explaining why the warrants are not included in the calculation. Use the following data to help you explain this situation.

Howat Corporation earned $228,000 during the period, when it had an average of 100,000 shares of common stock outstanding. The common stock sold at an average market price of $25 per share during the period. Also outstanding were 15,000 warrants that could be exercised to purchase one share of common stock at $30 per warrant.

USING YOUR JUDGMENT

FINANCIAL REPORTING PROBLEM

3M Company

The financial statements of 3M are presented in Appendix 5B or can be accessed on the Take Action! CD.

Instructions

Refer to 3M's financial statements and accompanying notes to answer the following questions.

(a) Under 3M's general employee stock purchase plan, eligible employees may purchase shares of 3M's common stock at 85% of fair market value. (1) How many shares are authorized to be issued under the plan? (2) How many were available for issuance at December 31, 2001? (3) How many shares were purchased by employees in 2001 under the plan, and how much was paid for those shares?

(b) 3M has a stock option plan (referred to as the Management Stock Ownership Program, MSOP) under which officers, key employees, and directors may be granted options to purchase 3M common stock. (1) What is the range of exercise prices for options outstanding under MSOP at December 31, 2001? (2) How many years from the grant date do these MSOP options expire? (3) To what accounts are the proceeds from these option exercises credited? (4) What is the number of shares of outstanding options at December 31, 2001 under MSOP, and at what weighted average exercise price? (5) How many options are exercisable under MSOP at December 31, 2001, and at what price?

(c) What number of weighted average common shares outstanding was used by 3M in computing earnings per share for 2001, 2000, and 1999? What was 3M's diluted earnings per share in 2001, 2000, and 1999?

(d) What would be the amount of compensation expense reported in 2001 for 3M if it had used the fair value method? (*Hint*: See Note 19.)

FINANCIAL STATEMENT ANALYSIS CASE

Kellogg Company

Kellogg Company in its 2001 Annual Report in Note 1—Accounting Policies made the following comment about its accounting for employee stock options and other stock-based compensation.

> **Stock compensation.** The Company follows Accounting Principles Board Opinion (APB) No. 25, "Accounting for Stock Issued to Employees," in accounting for its employee stock options and other stock-based compensation. Under APB No. 25, because the exercise price of the Company's employee stock options equals the market price of the underlying stock on the date of the grant, no compensation expense is recognized. As permitted, the Company has elected to adopt the disclosure provisions only of Statement of Financial Accounting Standards (SFAS) No. 123, "Accounting for Stock-Based Compensation." Refer to Note 8 for further information.

Instructions

In electing to adopt only the disclosure provisions of *FASB Statement No. 123*, what minimum disclosures was Kellogg Company required to make in its notes to the financial statements about its employee stock options and other stock-based compensation?

COMPARATIVE ANALYSIS CASE

The Coca-Cola Company and PepsiCo, Inc.

Instructions

Go to the Take Action! CD and use information found there to answer the following questions related to The Coca-Cola Company and PepsiCo, Inc.

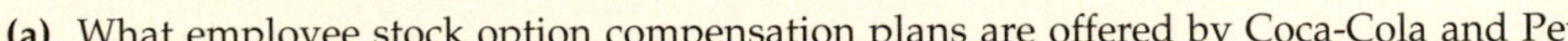

(a) What employee stock option compensation plans are offered by Coca-Cola and PepsiCo?

(b) How many options are outstanding at year-end 2001 for both Coca-Cola and PepsiCo?

(c) How many options were granted by Coca-Cola and PepsiCo to officers and employees during 2001?

(d) How many options were exercised during 2001?

(e) What was the range of option prices exercised by Coca-Cola and PepsiCo employees during 2001?

(f) What are the weighted average number of shares used by Coca-Cola and PepsiCo in 2001, 2000, and 1999 to compute diluted earnings per share?

(g) What was the diluted net income per share for Coca-Cola and PepsiCo for 2001, 2000, and 1999?

RESEARCH CASES

Case 1

Instructions

Examine a copy of *Statement of Financial Accounting Standards No. 123*, "Accounting for Stock-Based Compensation," and answer the following questions.

(a) As indicated in Chapter 1, the passage of a new Financial Accounting Standards Board statement requires the support of four of the seven members of the Board. What was the vote with regard to *SFAS 123*? Which members of the Board dissented?

(b) What was the major objection cited by the dissenters? What reasoning was used to support this objection?

(c) The dissenters expressed a preference for measuring the fair value of stock options at the vesting date instead of the grant date. Under what circumstances would they have accepted the modified grant method? Why?

Case 2

An article by Martha Brannigan titled "Questioning the Books: **AES** Seeks to Reassure Investors Worried over Dilution of Equity" appeared in the *Wall Street Journal* on February 22, 2002. (Subscribers to **Business Extra** can access the article at that site.)

Instructions

Read this article and answer the following questions.

(a) Where does AES get additional unregistered shares to secure its loans? How are these shares reported in its financial statements?

(b) Exactly how does a company "register shares"? How does registering shares affect the company's accounts?

(c) The article says registering the shares would dilute earnings per share. What is dilution? Why would registering the shares cause dilution?

(d) Why is measurement of dilution in earnings per share a problem for investors?

INTERNATIONAL REPORTING CASE

Clearly Canadian Beverage is a Canadian company engaged in the manufacturing and distribution of its Clearly Canadian line of carbonated mineral water and natural fruit-flavored sparkling beverages, non-carbonated beverages, and bottled water. Its shares are traded on the Nasdaq exchange. Because its shares trade on a U.S. exchange, Clearly Canadian Beverage must either prepare its financial statements in accordance with U.S. GAAP or prepare a reconciliation of its financial statements (based on Canadian standards) to how they would be reported under U.S. GAAP. As a result of this requirement, Clearly Canadian presented the following information in its financial statements to meet the U.S. GAAP reconciliation requirement.

Clearly Canadian Beverage Corporation

Notes to Consolidated Financial Statements

December 31, 2001, 2000 and 1999 (figures in tables are in thousands of United States dollars, except where indicated)

Note 22 Reconciliation to accounting principles generally accepted in the United States of America. As disclosed in the summary of significant accounting policies, these consolidated financial statements are prepared in accordance with Canadian GAAP which differs in certain respects from those principles and practices the Company would have followed had its consolidated financial statements been prepared in accordance with U.S. GAAP.

Under U.S. GAAP, the Company would report its consolidated statements of operations as follows:

	2001	2000	1999
Loss under Canadian GAAP	$(8,753)	$(6,449)	$(9,945)
Incremental costs (d)	51	9	39
Loss under U.S. GAAP	(8,702)	(6,440)	(9,906)
Unrealized holding gains (losses) (b)	(38)	847	187
Foreign currency translation adjustments (note 14)	(38)	(355)	1,018
Comprehensive loss under U.S. GAAP (c)	$(8,778)	$(5,948)	$(8,701)
Basic and diluted loss per share before comprehensive income (loss) adjustments (expressed in dollars)	$ (1.31)	$ (1.06)	$ (1.55)

(b) **Unrealized holding gains (losses).** Under U.S. GAAP, the long-term investments in publicly traded companies would be shown at fair market value. Unrealized holding gains or losses are recorded in other comprehensive income. Under Canadian GAAP, such long-term investments are recorded at cost less any impairment in value that is other than temporary.

(c) **Comprehensive income (loss).** Comprehensive income is defined as the change in equity from transactions and other events and circumstances other than those resulting from investments by owners and distributions to owners. Comprehensive income (loss) consists of net loss and other comprehensive income (loss). The accumulated balance of other comprehensive income is included in the equity section of the balance sheets. The Company's other comprehensive income consists of foreign exchange adjustments.

(d) **Incremental costs.** Under U.S. GAAP consultants' fees would be considered incremental costs and would not be capitalized, as Canadian GAAP permits, but would be recorded as a period expense.

In addition, Clearly Canadian provided the following disclosure related to its stock compensation plans:

Under Canadian GAAP, the Company does not measure compensation expense in connection with the granting or repricing of options.

Under U.S. GAAP, the Company applies APB Opinion 25, "Accounting for Stock Issued to Employees," and related interpretations in accounting for stock compensation to employees and directors. Under APB 25, because the exercise price of the Company's employee stock options equals the market price of the underlying stock on the date of the grant, no compensation is recognized at the time of the initial grant. If the exercise price of a fixed stock option award is reduced after December 15, 1998, FASB Interpretation No. 44 (FIN 44) requires that the option award be accounted for as variable from the date of the modification to the date the award is exercised, is forfeited or expires unexercised. Accordingly, the Company records compensation expense or recovery for such modified options calculated as the amount of the change in the intrinsic value of the options from the time of the modification to the date the modified option is exercised, is forfeited or expires.

Statement of Financial Accounting Standards No. 123, "Accounting for Stock-Based Compensations," (SFAS 123) requires the Company to provide pro forma information regarding net income and earnings per share as if compensation for the Company's stock option plans had been determined in accordance with the fair value based method prescribed in SFAS 123. The Company estimates the fair value of each stock option at the grant date or measures variable compensation for options subject to modification and requiring variable accounting from the date of modification by using the Black-Scholes option-pricing model with the following weighted average assumptions used for grants in the year ended December 31, 2001: dividend yield of $0: expected volatility of 85% (2000—85%; 1999—70%); risk-free interest rate of 4.99% (2000—5.3%; 1999—4.7%); and expected life of 6.6 years (2000—6.2 years; 1999—7.1 years).

During the year ended December 31, 2000, the Company repriced its options. The Company is now required to use the variable compensation method of accounting for stock options. Since the exercise price exceeded the market value of shares at the end of the year, the Company has not recorded a stock-based compensation charge.

Instructions

Use the information in the Clearly Canadian disclosure to respond to the following questions.

(a) What are the major differences between earnings reported by Clearly Canadian Beverage and earnings under U.S. GAAP?

(b) What are the major differences between earnings reported by Clearly Canadian Beverage and comprehensive income under U.S. GAAP?

(c) What do you think are some reasons why Clearly Canadian Beverage might not want to prepare its financial statements in accordance with U.S. GAAP?

(d) What is the impact of U.S. GAAP on Clearly Canadian's profit? Why isn't this adjustment reflected in the reconciliation schedule?

PROFESSIONAL SIMULATION

Earnings per Share

Directions | Situation | Explanation | Financial Statements | Research | Resources

Directions

In this simulation, you will be asked various questions concerning the accounting for stock options and earnings per share computations. Prepare responses to all parts.

Situation

As auditor for Banquo & Associates, you have been assigned to check Duncan Corporation's computation of earnings per share for the current year. The controller, Mac Beth, has supplied you with the following computations.

Net income	$3,374,960
Common shares issued and outstanding:	
Beginning of year	1,285,000
End of year	1,200,000
Average	1,242,500
Earnings per share:	

$$\frac{\$3{,}374{,}960}{1{,}242{,}500} = \$2.72 \text{ per share}$$

You have developed the following additional information.

1. There are no other equity securities in addition to the common shares.
2. There are no options or warrants outstanding to purchase common shares.
3. There are no convertible debt securities.
4. Activity in common shares during the year was as follows.

Outstanding, Jan. 1	1,285,000
Treasury shares acquired, Oct. 1	(250,000)
	1,035,000
Shares reissued, Dec. 1	165,000
Outstanding, Dec. 31	1,200,000

Explanation

On the basis of the information above, do you agree with the controller's computation of earnings per share for the year? If you disagree, prepare a revised computation of earnings per share.

Financial Statements

Assume the same facts as those presented above, except that options had been issued to purchase 140,000 shares of common stock at $10 per share. These options were outstanding at the beginning of the year and none had been exercised or canceled during the year. The average market price of the common shares during the year was $25, and the ending market price was $35. What earnings per share amounts will be reported?

Remember to check the **Take Action! CD** and the book's **companion Web site** to find additional resources for this chapter.

CHAPTER 17

Investments

Who's in Control Here?

The Coca-Cola Company owns 42 percent of the shares of **Coca-Cola Enterprises** (a U.S. bottling business) and 43 percent of **Coca-Cola Amatil** (a European and Asian bottling business). And **PepsiCo Inc.** owns 42 percent of **The Pepsi Bottling Group** (PBG) and 37 percent of **PepsiAmericas**. These bottling businesses are very important to Coca-Cola and PepsiCo, because they are the primary distributors of Coke and Pepsi products. Furthermore, the bottlers are very dependent on Coca-Cola and PepsiCo, which provide significant marketing and distribution development support. Indeed, an argument can be made that the bottling companies are controlled by Coca-Cola and PepsiCo, because they would not exist without their support.

However, because The Coca-Cola Company and PepsiCo do not own more than 50 percent of the shares in these companies, they do not prepare consolidated financial statements. Instead, these investments are accounted for using the *equity method*. For example, under the equity method, Coca-Cola reports a single income item for its profits from the bottlers, and only the net amount of its investment is reported in the balance sheet.

Equity method accounting gives Coca-Cola and PepsiCo pristine balance sheets and income statements, by keeping the assets and liabilities and the profit margins of these bottlers separate from the beverage-making business. What's more, as summarized in the following table, many countries allow *proportional consolidation*, an accounting method that includes part of the assets, liabilities, and income of investees in the financial statements of the investor company.

International Reporting of Less than 50% Equity Investments

Countries/Standards	Method(s) Allowed
U.S. GAAP: United Kingdom, Brazil, Mexico	Equity
IASB: France, Germany, Netherlands, Italy, Japan	Proportional consolidation or equity

This variation in practice makes it difficult to compare Coca-Cola and PepsiCo to other international beverage companies. Such lack of comparability is part of the reason why U.S. and international accounting standards-setters are studying the accounting rules for equity investments like Coca-Cola's and PepsiCo's.[1]

[1]Based on Morgan Stanley Dean Witter, "Apples to Apples, Global Beverage: Thirst for Knowledge" (May 25, 1999).

LEARNING OBJECTIVES

After studying this chapter, you should be able to:

1. **Identify the three categories of debt securities and describe the accounting and reporting treatment for each category.**
2. **Understand the procedures for discount and premium amortization on bond investments.**
3. **Identify the categories of equity securities and describe the accounting and reporting treatment for each category.**
4. **Explain the equity method of accounting and compare it to the fair value method for equity securities.**
5. **Describe the disclosure requirements for investments in debt and equity securities.**
6. **Discuss the accounting for impairments of debt and equity investments.**
7. **Describe the accounting for transfer of investment securities between categories.**

PREVIEW OF CHAPTER 17

As indicated in the opening story, the measurement, recognition, and disclosure for certain investments are under study by U.S. and international standards-setters. This chapter addresses the accounting for debt and equity investments. The appendix to this chapter discusses the accounting for derivative instruments. The content and organization of this chapter are as follows.

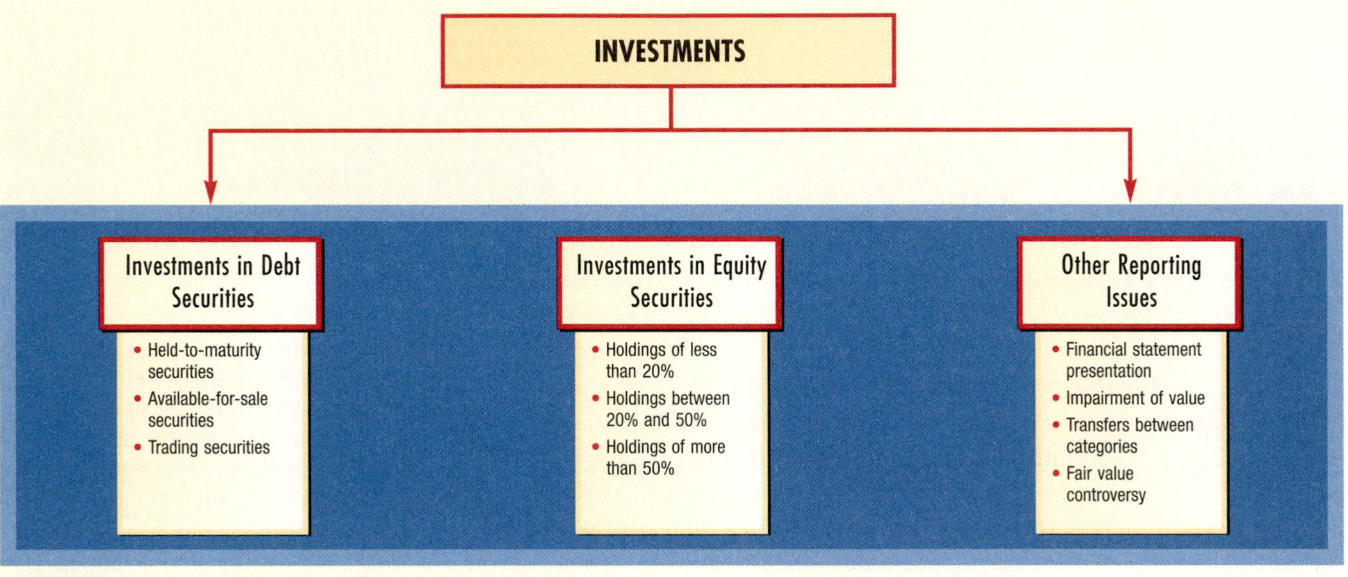

Companies have different motivations for investing in securities issued by other companies.[2] **One motivation is to earn a high rate of return.** A company can receive interest revenue from a debt investment or dividend revenue from an equity investment. In addition, capital gains on both types of securities can be realized. **Another motivation for investing (in equity securities) is to secure certain operating or financing arrangements with another company.** As in the opening story, **Coca-Cola** and **PepsiCo** are able to exercise some control over bottling companies based on their significant (but not controlling) equity investments.

To provide useful information, the accounting for investments is based on the type of security (debt or equity) and management's intent with respect to the investment. As indicated in Illustration 17-1, our study of investments is organized by type of security. Within each section, we explain how the accounting for investments in debt and equity securities varies according to management intent.

[2]A **security** is a share, participation, or other interest in property or in an enterprise of the issuer or an obligation of the issuer that: (a) either is represented by an instrument issued in bearer or registered form or, if not represented by an instrument, is registered in books maintained to record transfers by or on behalf of the issuer; (b) is of a type commonly dealt in on securities exchanges or markets or, when represented by an instrument, is commonly recognized in any area in which it is issued or dealt in as a medium for investment; and (c) either is one of a class or series or by its terms is divisible into a class or series of shares, participations, interests, or obligations. From "Accounting for Certain Investments in Debt and Equity Securities," *Statement of Financial Accounting Standards No. 115* (Norwalk, Conn.: FASB, 1993), p. 48, par. 137.

Types of Security	Management Intent	Valuation Approach
Debt (Section 1)	No plans to sell	Amortized cost
	Plan to sell	Fair value
Equity (Section 2)	Plan to sell	Fair value
	Exercise some control	Equity method

ILLUSTRATION 17-1
Summary of Investment Accounting Approaches

INVESTMENTS IN DEBT SECURITIES — SECTION 1

Debt securities are instruments representing a creditor relationship with an enterprise. Debt securities include U.S. government securities, municipal securities, corporate bonds, convertible debt, commercial paper, and all securitized debt instruments. Trade accounts receivable and loans receivable are not debt securities because they do not meet the definition of a security.

Investments in debt securities are grouped into three separate categories for accounting and reporting purposes. These categories are as follows:

OBJECTIVE 1
Identify the three categories of debt securities and describe the accounting and reporting treatment for each category.

> **Held-to-maturity:** Debt securities that the enterprise has the positive intent and ability to hold to maturity.
>
> **Trading:** Debt securities bought and held primarily for sale in the near term to generate income on short-term price differences.
>
> **Available-for-sale:** Debt securities not classified as held-to-maturity or trading securities.

Illustration 17-2 identifies these categories, along with the accounting and reporting treatments required for each.

Category	Valuation	Unrealized Holding Gains or Losses	Other Income Effects
Held-to-maturity	Amortized cost	Not recognized	Interest when earned; gains and losses from sale.
Trading securities	Fair value	Recognized in net income	Interest when earned; gains and losses from sale.
Available-for-sale	Fair value	Recognized as other comprehensive income and as separate component of stockholders' equity	Interest when earned; gains and losses from sale.

ILLUSTRATION 17-2
Accounting for Debt Securities by Category

Amortized cost is the acquisition cost adjusted for the amortization of discount or premium, if appropriate. **Fair value** is the amount at which a financial instrument could be exchanged in a current transaction between willing parties, other than in a forced or liquidation sale.[3]

UNDERLYING CONCEPTS
Debt securities are reported at fair value not only because the information is relevant but also because it is reliable.

[3]Ibid., pp. 47–48. The fair value is **readily determinable** if its sale price or other quotations are available on SEC registered exchanges, or, for over-the-counter securities, are published by recognized national publication systems.

HELD-TO-MATURITY SECURITIES

Only debt securities can be classified as held-to-maturity because, by definition, equity securities have no maturity date. A debt security should be classified as **held-to-maturity** only if the reporting entity has **both (1) the positive intent** and **(2) the ability to hold those securities to maturity**. A company should not classify a debt security as held-to-maturity if the company intends to hold the security for an indefinite period of time. Likewise, if the enterprise anticipates that a sale may be necessary due to changes in interest rates, foreign currency risk, liquidity needs, or other asset-liability management reasons, the security should not be classified as held-to-maturity.[4]

OBJECTIVE 2
Understand the procedures for discount and premium amortization on bond investments.

Held-to-maturity securities are accounted for **at amortized cost**, not fair value. If management intends to hold certain investment securities to maturity and has no plans to sell them, fair values (selling prices) are not relevant for measuring and evaluating the cash flows associated with these securities. Finally, because held-to-maturity securities are not adjusted to fair value, they do not increase the volatility of either reported earnings or reported capital as do trading securities and available-for-sale securities.

To illustrate the accounting for held-to-maturity debt securities, assume that Robinson Company purchased $100,000 of 8% bonds of Evermaster Corporation on January 1, 2003, paying $92,278. The bonds mature January 1, 2008, and interest is payable each July 1 and January 1. The entry to record the investment is:

Calculator Solution for Bond Price

	Inputs	Answer
N	10	
I	5	
PV	?	–92,278
PMT	4,000	
FV	100,000	

January 1, 2003

Held-to-Maturity Securities	92,278	
Cash		92,278

A Held-to-Maturity Securities account is used to indicate the type of debt security purchased.

As indicated in Chapter 14, the **effective-interest method** is required to amortize premium or discount unless some other method—such as the straight-line method—yields a similar result. The effective-interest method is applied to bond investments in a fashion similar to that described for bonds payable. The effective-interest rate or yield is computed at the time of investment and is applied to its beginning carrying amount (book value) for each interest period to compute interest revenue. The investment carrying amount is increased by the amortized discount or decreased by the amortized premium in each period.

Illustration 17-3 (on page 839) shows the effect of the discount amortization on the interest revenue recorded each period for the investment in Evermaster Corporation bonds. The journal entry to record the receipt of the first semiannual interest payment on July 1, 2003 (using the data in Illustration 17-3) is:

UNDERLYING CONCEPTS

The use of some simpler method which yields results similar to the effective-interest method is an application of the materiality concept.

July 1, 2003

Cash	4,000	
Held-to-Maturity Securities	614	
Interest Revenue		4,614

Because Robinson Company is on a calendar-year basis, it accrues interest and amortizes the discount at December 31, 2003, as follows.

December 31, 2003

Interest Receivable	4,000	
Held-to-Maturity Securities	645	
Interest Revenue		4,645

Again, the interest and amortization amounts are provided in Illustration 17-3.

[4]The FASB defines situations where, even though a security is sold before maturity, it has constructively been held to maturity, and thus does not represent a violation of the held-to-maturity requirement. These include selling a security close enough to maturity (such as 3 months) so that interest rate risk is no longer an important pricing factor.

ILLUSTRATION 17-3
Schedule of Interest Revenue and Bond Discount Amortization—Effective-Interest Method

8% BONDS PURCHASED TO YIELD 10%

Date	Cash Received	Interest Revenue	Bond Discount Amortization	Carrying Amount of Bonds
1/1/03				$ 92,278
7/1/03	$ 4,000[a]	$ 4,614[b]	$ 614[c]	92,892[d]
1/1/04	4,000	4,645	645	93,537
7/1/04	4,000	4,677	677	94,214
1/1/05	4,000	4,711	711	94,925
7/1/05	4,000	4,746	746	95,671
1/1/06	4,000	4,783	783	96,454
7/1/06	4,000	4,823	823	97,277
1/1/07	4,000	4,864	864	98,141
7/1/07	4,000	4,907	907	99,048
1/1/08	4,000	4,952	952	100,000
	$40,000	$47,722	$7,722	

[a]$4,000 = $100,000 × .08 × 6/12
[b]$4,614 = $92,278 × .10 × 6/12
[c]$614 = $4,614 − $4,000
[d]$92,892 = $92,278 + $614

Evermaster bonds are presented in the company's December 31, 2003, financial statements as follows.

ILLUSTRATION 17-4
Reporting of Held-to-Maturity Securities

Balance Sheet

Current assets	
Interest receivable	$ 4,000
Long-term investments	
Held-to-maturity securities, at amortized cost	$93,537

Income Statement

Other revenues and gains	
Interest revenue	$ 9,259

The sale of a held-to-maturity debt security close enough to its maturity date that a change in the market interest rates would not significantly affect the security's fair value may be considered a sale at maturity. If Robinson Company sells its investment in Evermaster bonds on November 1, 2007, for example, at 99¾ plus accrued interest, the following computations and entries would be made. The discount amortization from July 1, 2007, to November 1, 2007, is $635 (4/6 × $952). The entry to record this discount amortization is as follows.

November 1, 2007

Held-to-Maturity Securities	635	
Interest Revenue		635

The computation of the realized gain on the sale is shown in Illustration 17-5.

ILLUSTRATION 17-5
Computation of Gain on Sale of Bonds

Selling price of bonds (exclusive of accrued interest)		$99,750
Less: Book value of bonds on November 1, 2007:		
Amortized cost, July 1, 2007	$99,048	
Add: Discount amortized for the period July 1, 2007, to November 1, 2007	635	
		99,683
Gain on sale of bonds		$ 67

The entry to record the sale of the bonds is:

November 1, 2007

Cash	102,417	
Interest Revenue (4/6 × $4,000)		2,667
Held-to-Maturity Securities		99,683
Gain on Sale of Securities		67

The credit to Interest Revenue represents accrued interest for 4 months, for which the purchaser pays cash. The debit to Cash represents the selling price of the bonds, $99,750, plus accrued interest of $2,667. The credit to the Held-to-Maturity Securities account represents the book value of the bonds on the date of sale. The credit to Gain on Sale of Securities represents the excess of the selling price over the book value of the bonds.

AVAILABLE-FOR-SALE SECURITIES

UNDERLYING CONCEPTS

Recognizing unrealized gains and losses is an application of the concept of comprehensive income.

Investments in debt securities that are in the **available-for-sale** category are reported at fair value. The unrealized gains and losses related to changes in the fair value of available-for-sale debt securities are recorded in an unrealized holding gain or loss account. This account is reported as other comprehensive income and as a separate component of stockholders' equity until realized. Thus, **changes in fair value are not reported as part of net income until the security is sold**. This approach reduces the volatility of net income.

Illustration: Single Security

To illustrate the accounting for available-for-sale securities, assume that Graff Corporation purchases $100,000, 10 percent, 5-year bonds on January 1, 2003, with interest payable on July 1 and January 1. The bonds sell for $108,111 which results in a bond premium of $8,111 and an effective-interest rate of 8 percent.

The entry to record the purchase of the bonds is as follows.[5]

January 1, 2003

Available-for-Sale Securities	108,111	
Cash		108,111

Illustration 17-6 discloses the effect of the premium amortization on the interest revenue recorded each period using the effective-interest method. The entry to record interest revenue on July 1, 2003, would be as follows.

July 1, 2003

Cash	5,000	
Available-for-Sale Securities		676
Interest Revenue		4,324

At December 31, 2003, Graff would make the following entry to recognize interest revenue.

December 31, 2003

Interest Receivable	5,000	
Available-for-Sale Securities		703
Interest Revenue		4,297

As a result, Graff would report interest revenue for 2003 of $8,621 ($4,324 + $4,297).

[5]Investments acquired at par, at a discount, or at a premium are generally recorded in the accounts at cost, including brokerage and other fees but excluding the accrued interest; generally they are not recorded at maturity value. The use of a separate discount or premium account as a valuation account is acceptable procedure for investments, but in practice it has not been widely used.

ILLUSTRATION 17-6
Schedule of Interest Revenue and Bond Premium Amortization—Effective-Interest Method

10% Bonds Purchased to Yield 8%

Date	Cash Received	Interest Revenue	Bond Premium Amortization	Carrying Amount of Bonds
1/1/03				$108,111
7/1/03	$ 5,000[a]	$ 4,324[b]	$ 676[c]	107,435[d]
1/1/04	5,000	4,297	703	106,732
7/1/04	5,000	4,269	731	106,001
1/1/05	5,000	4,240	760	105,241
7/1/05	5,000	4,210	790	104,451
1/1/06	5,000	4,178	822	103,629
7/1/06	5,000	4,145	855	102,774
1/1/07	5,000	4,111	889	101,885
7/1/07	5,000	4,075	925	100,960
1/1/08	5,000	4,040	960	100,000
	$50,000	$41,889	$8,111	

[a]$5,000 = $100,000 × .10 × 6/12
[b]$4,324 = $108,111 × .08 × 6/12
[c]$676 = $5,000 − $4,324
[d]$107,435 = $108,111 − $676

Calculator Solution for Bond Price

	Inputs	Answer
N	10	
I	4	
PV	?	−108,111
PMT	5,000	
FV	100,000	

To apply the fair value method to these debt securities, assume that at year-end the fair value of the bonds is $105,000 and that the carrying amount of the investments is $106,732. Comparing this fair value with the carrying amount (amortized cost) of the bonds at December 31, 2003, Graff recognizes an unrealized holding loss of $1,732 ($106,732 − $105,000). This loss is reported as other comprehensive income and as a separate component of stockholders' equity. The entry is as follows.

December 31, 2003

Unrealized Holding Gain or Loss—Equity	1,732	
Securities Fair Value Adjustment (Available-for-Sale)		1,732

A valuation account is used instead of crediting the Available-for-Sale Securities account. The use of the **Securities Fair Value Adjustment (Available-for-Sale) account** enables the company to maintain a record of its amortized cost. Because the adjustment account has a credit balance in this case, it is subtracted from the balance of the Available-for-Sale Securities account to arrive at fair value. The fair value is the amount reported on the balance sheet. At each reporting date, the bonds would be reported at fair value with an adjustment to the Unrealized Holding Gain or Loss—Equity account.

Illustration: Portfolio of Securities

To illustrate the accounting for a portfolio of securities, assume that Webb Corporation has two debt securities that are classified as available-for-sale. Illustration 17-7 provides information on amortized cost, fair value, and the amount of the unrealized gain or loss.

ILLUSTRATION 17-7
Computation of Securities Fair Value Adjustment—Available-for-Sale Securities (2004)

Available-for-Sale Debt Security Portfolio
December 31, 2004

Investments	Amortized Cost	Fair Value	Unrealized Gain (Loss)
Watson Corporation 8% bonds	$ 93,537	$103,600	$ 10,063
Anacomp Corporation 10% bonds	200,000	180,400	(19,600)
Total of portfolio	$293,537	$284,000	(9,537)
Previous securities fair value adjustment balance			–0–
Securities fair value adjustment—Cr.			$ (9,537)

The total fair value of Webb's available-for-sale portfolio is $284,000. The gross unrealized gains are $10,063, and the gross unrealized losses are $19,600, resulting in a net unrealized loss of $9,537. That is, the fair value of available-for-sale securities is $9,537 lower than its amortized cost. An adjusting entry is made to a valuation allowance to record the decrease in value and to record the loss as follows.

December 31, 2004		
Unrealized Holding Gain or Loss—Equity	9,537	
Securities Fair Value Adjustment (Available-for-Sale)		9,537

The unrealized holding loss of $9,537 is reported as other comprehensive income and a reduction of stockholders' equity. As indicated earlier, unrealized holding gains and losses related to investments that are classified in the available-for-sale category are not included in net income.

Sale of Available-for-Sale Securities

If bonds carried as investments in available-for-sale securities are sold before the maturity date, entries must be made to remove from the Available-for-Sale Securities account the amortized cost of bonds sold. To illustrate, assume that Webb Corporation sold the Watson bonds (from Illustration 17-7) on July 1, 2005, for $90,000, at which time it had an amortized cost of $94,214. The computation of the realized loss is as follows.

ILLUSTRATION 17-8
Computation of Loss on Sale of Bonds

Amortized cost (Watson bonds)	$94,214
Less: Selling price of bonds	90,000
Loss on sale of bonds	$ 4,214

The entry to record the sale of the Watson bonds is as follows.

July 1, 2005		
Cash	90,000	
Loss on Sale of Securities	4,214	
Available-for-Sale Securities		94,214

This realized loss is reported in the "Other expenses and losses" section of the income statement. Assuming no other purchases and sales of bonds in 2005, Webb Corporation on December 31, 2005, prepares the information shown in Illustration 17-9.

ILLUSTRATION 17-9
Computation of Securities Fair Value Adjustment—Available-for-Sale (2005)

AVAILABLE-FOR-SALE DEBT SECURITY PORTFOLIO
DECEMBER 31, 2005

Investments	Amortized Cost	Fair Value	Unrealized Gain (Loss)
Anacomp Corporation 10% bonds (total portfolio)	$200,000	$195,000	$(5,000)
Previous securities fair value adjustment balance—Cr.			(9,537)
Securities fair value adjustment—Dr.			$ 4,537

Webb Corporation has an unrealized holding loss of $5,000. However, the Securities Fair Value Adjustment account already has a credit balance of $9,537. To reduce the adjustment account balance to $5,000, it is debited for $4,537, as follows.

December 31, 2005		
Securities Fair Value Adjustment (Available-for-Sale)	4,537	
Unrealized Holding Gain or Loss—Equity		4,537

Financial Statement Presentation

Webb Corporation's December 31, 2005, balance sheet and the 2005 income statement would contain the following items and amounts. (The Anacomp bonds are long-term investments but are not intended to be held to maturity.)

ILLUSTRATION 17-10
Reporting of Available-for-Sale Securities

Balance Sheet	
Current assets	
Interest receivable	$ xxx
Investments	
Available-for-sale securities, at fair value	$195,000
Stockholders' equity	
Accumulated other comprehensive loss	$ 5,000
Income Statement	
Other revenues and gains	
Interest revenue	$ xxx
Other expenses and losses	
Loss on sale of securities	$ 4,214

Should the unrealized holding gain or loss be reported in net income rather than in other comprehensive income?[6] Some companies, particularly financial institutions, note that recognizing unrealized gains and losses on assets, but not liabilities, introduces substantial volatility in net income. They argue that often hedges exist between assets and liabilities so that gains in assets are offset by losses in liabilities, and vice versa. In short, to recognize unrealized gains and losses only on the asset side is unfair and not representative of the economic activities of the company.

This argument was convincing to the FASB. As a result, unrealized gains and losses on available-for-sale securities are **not included in net income**. However, even this approach does not solve all of the problems, because **volatility of capital** still results. This is of concern to financial institutions because regulators restrict financial institutions' operations based upon their level of capital. In addition, companies can still manage their net income by engaging in **gains trading** (i.e., selling the winners and holding the losers).

MARK-TO-MARKET EVERYWHERE

WHAT DO THE NUMBERS MEAN?

While many companies, particularly banks, opposed implementation of fair value accounting for investments, other companies have embraced the use of mark-to-market accounting. Energy companies, such as **Dynergy**, **Williams Companies**, and **Enron** use fair value methods to account for energy contracts, a type of derivative whose value depends on expected energy prices. (The accounting for derivative instruments is discussed in Appendix 17A at the end of the chapter.)

However, there is concern that use of fair value methods for energy contracts may not be appropriate.[7] This is because determining fair value of these contracts requires estimation of energy prices 15 to 20 years in the future, based on changes in current market prices. If current prices increase, companies can record gains on the contract; under mark-to-market accounting these gains are recorded in income. Whether energy companies use unreasonable assumptions in their valuation models in order to book paper gains is subject to debate. However, most agree that companies need to disclose the models used to value energy contracts so that investors can compare the results of energy company trading operations.

[6]In Chapter 4, we discussed the reporting of other comprehensive income and the concept of comprehensive income. "Reporting Comprehensive Income," *Statement of Financial Accounting Standards No. 130* (Norwalk, Conn.: FASB, 1997).

[7]The EITF has ruled that energy contracts that do not meet the definition of a derivative may not be marked to market. J. Weil, "Energy Traders to Feel Effects of FASB's Reporting Changes," *Wall Street Journal Online* (October 28, 2002).

TRADING SECURITIES

Trading securities are held with the intention of selling them in a short period of time. "Trading" in this context means frequent buying and selling, and trading securities are used to generate profits from short-term differences in price. The holding period for these securities is generally less than 3 months, and more probably is measured in days or hours. **These securities are reported at fair value, with unrealized holding gains and losses reported as part of net income. Any discount or premium is not amortized.** A **holding gain or loss** is the net change in the fair value of a security from one period to another, exclusive of dividend or interest revenue recognized but not received. In short, the FASB says to adjust the trading securities to fair value, at each reporting date. In addition, the change in value is reported as part of net income, not other comprehensive income.

To illustrate, assume that on December 31, 2004, Western Publishing Corporation determined its trading securities portfolio to be as shown in Illustration 17-11 (Assume that 2004 is the first year that Western Publishing held trading securities.) At the date of acquisition, these trading securities were recorded at cost, including brokerage commissions and taxes, in the account entitled Trading Securities. This is the first valuation of this recently purchased portfolio.

ILLUSTRATION 17-11
Computation of Securities Fair Value Adjustment—Trading Securities Portfolio (2004)

TRADING DEBT SECURITY PORTFOLIO
DECEMBER 31, 2004

Investments	Cost	Fair Value	Unrealized Gain (Loss)
Burlington Northern 10% bonds	$ 43,860	$ 51,500	$ 7,640
GM Corporation 11% bonds	184,230	175,200	(9,030)
AOL Time Warner 8% bonds	86,360	91,500	5,140
Total of portfolio	$314,450	$318,200	3,750
Previous securities fair value adjustment balance			–0–
Securities fair value adjustment—Dr.			$ 3,750

INTERNATIONAL INSIGHT

IAS provide for classification as trading, available-for-sale, or held-to-maturity for all types of financial assets. U.S. GAAP applies these classifications only to securities.

The total cost of Western's trading portfolio is $314,450. The gross unrealized gains are $12,780 ($7,640 + $5,140), and the gross unrealized losses are $9,030, resulting in a net unrealized gain of $3,750. The fair value of trading securities is $3,750 greater than its cost.

At December 31, an adjusting entry is made to a valuation allowance, referred to as Securities Fair Value Adjustment (Trading), to record the increase in value and to record the unrealized holding gain.

December 31, 2004

Securities Fair Value Adjustment (Trading)	3,750	
Unrealized Holding Gain or Loss—Income		3,750

Because the Securities Fair Value Adjustment account balance is a debit, it is added to the cost of the Trading Securities account to arrive at a fair value for the trading securities. The fair value of the securities is the amount reported on the balance sheet.

When securities are actively traded, the FASB believes that financial reporting is improved when the economic events affecting the company (changes in fair value) and related unrealized gains and losses are reported in the same period. Including changes in fair value in income provides more relevant information to current stockholders whose composition may be different next period.

INVESTMENTS IN EQUITY SECURITIES — SECTION 2

OBJECTIVE 3
Identify the categories of equity securities and describe the accounting and reporting treatment for each category.

Equity securities are securities representing ownership interests such as common, preferred, or other capital stock. They also include rights to acquire or dispose of ownership interests at an agreed-upon or determinable price, such as in warrants, rights, and call or put options. Convertible debt securities and redeemable preferred stocks are not treated as equity securities. When equity securities are purchased, their cost includes the purchase price of the security plus broker's commissions and other fees incidental to the purchase.

The degree to which one corporation (**investor**) acquires an interest in the common stock of another corporation (**investee**) generally determines the accounting treatment for the investment subsequent to acquisition. Investments by one corporation in the common stock of another can be classified according to the percentage of the voting stock of the investee held by the investor:

1. Holdings of less than 20 percent (**fair value method**)—investor has passive interest.
2. Holdings between 20 percent and 50 percent (**equity method**)—investor has significant influence.
3. Holdings of more than 50 percent (**consolidated statements**)—investor has controlling interest.

These levels of interest or influence and the corresponding valuation and reporting method that must be applied to the investment are graphically displayed in Illustration 17-12.

ILLUSTRATION 17-12
Levels of Influence Determine Accounting Methods

Percentage of Ownership	0% ⟷ 20%	20% ⟷ 50%	50% ⟷ 100%
Level of Influence	Little or None	Significant	Control
Valuation Method	Fair Value Method	Equity Method	Consolidation

The accounting and reporting for equity securities therefore depends upon the level of influence and the type of security involved, as shown in Illustration 17-13.

ILLUSTRATION 17-13
Accounting and Reporting for Equity Securities by Category

Category	Valuation	Unrealized Holding Gains or Losses	Other Income Effects
Holdings less than 20%			
1. Available-for-sale	Fair value	Recognized in "Other comprehensive income" and as separate component of stockholders' equity	Dividends declared; gains and losses from sale.
2. Trading	Fair value	Recognized in net income	Dividends declared; gains and losses from sale.
Holdings between 20% and 50%	Equity	Not recognized	Proportionate shares of investee's net income
Holdings more than 50%	Consolidation	Not recognized	Not applicable

HOLDINGS OF LESS THAN 20%

As mentioned earlier, equity securities are recorded at cost. In some cases, cost is difficult to determine. For example, equity securities acquired in **exchange for noncash consideration** (property or services) should be recorded at (1) the fair value of the consideration given, or (2) the fair value of the security received, whichever is more clearly determinable. The absence of clearly determinable values for the property or services or a market price for the security acquired may require the use of appraisals or estimates to arrive at a cost.

If market prices are not available at the date of acquisition of several securities, it may be necessary to defer cost apportionment until evidence of at least one value becomes available. In some instances cost apportionment may have to wait until one of the securities is sold. In such cases, the proceeds from the sale of the one security may be subtracted from the lump sum cost, leaving the residual cost to be assigned as the cost of the other.[8]

When an investor has an interest of less than 20 percent, it is presumed that the investor has little or no influence over the investee. In such cases, if market prices are available, the investment is valued and reported subsequent to acquisition using the **fair value method**.[9] The fair value method requires that companies classify equity securities at acquisition as **available-for-sale securities** or **trading securities**. Because equity securities have no maturity date, they cannot be classified as held-to-maturity.

Available-for-Sale Securities

Available-for-sale securities when acquired are recorded at cost. To illustrate, assume that on November 3, 2004, Republic Corporation purchased common stock of three companies, each investment representing less than a 20 percent interest.

	Cost
Northwest Industries, Inc.	$259,700
Campbell Soup Co.	317,500
St. Regis Pulp Co.	141,350
Total cost	$718,550

These investments would be recorded as follows.

November 3, 2004		
Available-for-Sale Securities	718,550	
Cash		718,550

On December 6, 2004, Republic receives a cash dividend of $4,200 on its investment in the common stock of Campbell Soup Co. The cash dividend is recorded as follows.

December 6, 2004		
Cash	4,200	
Dividend Revenue		4,200

[8]Accounting for numerous purchases of securities requires that information regarding the cost of individual purchases be preserved, as well as the dates of purchases and sales. If **specific identification** is not possible, the use of an **average cost** may be used for multiple purchases of the same class of security. The **first-in, first-out method** (FIFO) of assigning costs to investments at the time of sale is also acceptable and is normally employed.

[9]When market prices are not available, the investment is valued and reported at cost in periods subsequent to acquisition. This approach is often referred to as the **cost method**. Dividends are recognized as dividend revenue when received, and the portfolio is valued and reported at acquisition cost. No gains or losses are recognized until the securities are sold.

All three of the investee companies reported net income for the year, but only Campbell Soup declared and paid a dividend to Republic. But, as indicated before, when an investor owns less than 20 percent of the common stock of another corporation, it is presumed that the investor has relatively little influence on the investee. As a result, **net income earned by the investee is not considered a proper basis for recognizing income from the investment by the investor**. The reason is that the investee may choose to retain for use in the business increased net assets resulting from profitable operations. Therefore, **net income is not considered earned by the investor until cash dividends are declared by the investee**.

At December 31, 2004, Republic's available-for-sale equity security portfolio has the following cost and fair value.

ILLUSTRATION 17-14
Computation of Securities Fair Value Adjustment—Available-for-Sale Equity Security Portfolio (2004)

AVAILABLE-FOR-SALE EQUITY SECURITY PORTFOLIO
DECEMBER 31, 2004

Investments	Cost	Fair Value	Unrealized Gain (Loss)
Northwest Industries, Inc.	$259,700	$275,000	$ 15,300
Campbell Soup Co.	317,500	304,000	(13,500)
St. Regis Pulp Co.	141,350	104,000	(37,350)
Total of portfolio	$718,550	$683,000	(35,550)
Previous securities fair value adjustment balance			–0–
Securities fair value adjustment—Cr.			$(35,550)

For Republic's available-for-sale equity securities portfolio, the gross unrealized gains are $15,300, and the gross unrealized losses are $50,850 ($13,500 + $37,350), resulting in a net unrealized loss of $35,550. The fair value of the available-for-sale securities portfolio is $35,550 less than its cost. As with available-for-sale **debt** securities, the net unrealized gains and losses related to changes in the fair value of available-for-sale **equity** securities are recorded in an Unrealized Holding Gain or Loss—Equity account that is reported as a **part of other comprehensive income and as a component of stockholders' equity until realized**. In this case, Republic prepares an adjusting entry debiting the Unrealized Holding Gain or Loss—Equity account and crediting the Securities Fair Value Adjustment account to record the decrease in fair value and to record the loss as follows.

December 31, 2004

Unrealized Holding Gain or Loss—Equity	35,550	
Securities Fair Value Adjustment (Available-for-Sale)		35,550

On January 23, 2005, Republic sold all of its Northwest Industries, Inc. common stock receiving net proceeds of $287,220. The realized gain on the sale is computed as follows.

ILLUSTRATION 17-15
Computation of Gain on Sale of Stock

Net proceeds from sale	$287,220
Cost of Northwest shares	259,700
Gain on sale of stock	$ 27,520

The sale is recorded as follows.

January 23, 2005

Cash	287,220	
Available-for-Sale Securities		259,700
Gain on Sale of Stock		27,520

In addition, assume that on February 10, 2005, Republic purchased 20,000 shares of Continental Trucking at a market price of $12.75 per share plus brokerage commissions of $1,850 (total cost, $256,850).

On December 31, 2005, Republic's portfolio of available-for-sale securities is as follows.

ILLUSTRATION 17-16
Computation of Securities Fair Value Adjustment—Available-for-Sale Equity Security Portfolio (2005)

AVAILABLE-FOR-SALE EQUITY SECURITY PORTFOLIO
DECEMBER 31, 2005

Investments	Cost	Fair Value	Unrealized Gain (Loss)
Continental Trucking	$256,850	$278,350	$ 21,500
Campbell Soup Co.	317,500	362,550	45,050
St. Regis Pulp Co.	141,350	139,050	(2,300)
Total of portfolio	$715,700	$779,950	64,250
Previous securities fair value adjustment balance—Cr.			(35,550)
Securities fair value adjustment—Dr.			$ 99,800

At December 31, 2005, the fair value of Republic's available-for-sale equity securities portfolio exceeds cost by $64,250 (unrealized gain). The Securities Fair Value Adjustment account had a credit balance of $35,550 at December 31, 2004. To adjust Republic's December 31, 2005, available-for-sale portfolio to fair value requires that the Securities Fair Value Adjustment account be debited for $99,800 ($35,550 + $64,250). The entry to record this adjustment is as follows.

December 31, 2005

Securities Fair Value Adjustment (Available-for-Sale)	99,800	
Unrealized Holding Gain or Loss—Equity		99,800

Trading Securities

The accounting entries to record trading equity securities are the same as for available-for-sale equity securities, except for recording the unrealized holding gain or loss. For trading equity securities, the unrealized holding gain or loss is **reported as part of net income**. Thus, the account title Unrealized Holding Gain or Loss—Income is used. When a sale is made, the remainder of the gain or loss is recognized in income.

HOLDINGS BETWEEN 20% AND 50%

An investor corporation may hold an interest of less than 50 percent in an investee corporation and thus not possess legal control. However, as shown in the opening story about **Coca-Cola** and **PepsiCo**, an investment in voting stock of less than 50 percent can still give Coke (the investor) the ability to exercise significant influence over the operating and financial policies of its bottlers.[10] To provide a guide for accounting for investors when 50 percent or less of the common voting stock is held and to develop an operational definition of "**significant influence**," the APB in *Opinion No. 18* noted that ability to exercise influence may be indicated in several ways. Examples would be: representation on the board of directors, participation in policy-making processes, material intercompany transactions, interchange of managerial personnel, or technological dependency. Another important consideration is the extent of ownership by an investor in relation to the concentration of other shareholdings. To achieve a reasonable degree of

[10]"The Equity Method of Accounting for Investments in Common Stock," *Opinions of the Accounting Principles Board No. 18* (New York: AICPA, 1971), par. 17.

uniformity in application of the "significant influence" criterion, the profession concluded that an investment (direct or indirect) of 20 percent or more of the voting stock of an investee should lead to a presumption that in the absence of evidence to the contrary, an investor has the ability to exercise significant influence over an investee.[11]

In instances of "significant influence" (generally an investment of 20 percent or more), the investor is required to account for the investment using the **equity method**.

WHAT'S IN IT FOR ME?

WHAT DO THE NUMBERS MEAN?

The extent of control or influence for an equity investor, given a level of investment, can vary internationally. This was illustrated when **DaimlerChrysler** made a 33.4 percent investment in **Mitsubishi Motors**. Under Japanese commercial law, that level of investment gives DaimlerChrysler regular seats on the board and gives it the power to veto board decisions. Whether this is a good deal for Mitsubishi will depend on whether and how DaimlerChrysler exercises its control over Mitsubishi operations. Mitsubishi is said to have pushed for assurances that DaimlerChrysler would not push for job cuts, but may have been willing to give DaimlerChrysler more control in exchange for the financial boost it provided and for access to the German-American carmaker's engineering and production expertise.

Source: S. Miller and N. Shirouzu, "DaimlerChrysler to Acquire a Stake in Mitsubishi Motors for $1.94 Billion," *Wall Street Journal Online* (March 27, 2000).

Equity Method

OBJECTIVE 4
Explain the equity method of accounting and compare it to the fair value method for equity securities.

Under the **equity method**, a substantive economic relationship is acknowledged between the investor and the investee. The investment is originally recorded at the cost of the shares acquired but is subsequently adjusted each period for changes in the net assets of the investee. That is, the **investment's carrying amount is periodically increased (decreased) by the investor's proportionate share of the earnings (losses) of the investee and decreased by all dividends received by the investor from the investee**. The equity method recognizes that investee's earnings increase investee's net assets, and that investee's losses and dividends decrease these net assets.

To illustrate the equity method and compare it with the fair value method, assume that Maxi Company purchases a 20 percent interest in Mini Company. To apply the fair value method in this example, assume that Maxi does not have the ability to exercise significant influence and the securities are classified as available-for-sale. Where the equity method is applied in this example, assume that the 20 percent interest permits Maxi to exercise significant influence. The entries are shown in Illustration 17-17 on page 850.

Note that under the fair value method only the cash dividends received from Mini Company are reported as revenue by Maxi Company. **The earning of net income by the investee is not considered a proper basis for recognition of income from the investment by the investor.** The reason is that increased net assets resulting from the

[11]Examples of cases in which an investment of 20 percent or more might not enable an investor to exercise significant influence are:

(1) The investee opposes the investor's acquisition of its stock.

(2) The investor and investee sign an agreement under which the investor surrenders significant shareholder rights.

(3) The investor's ownership share does not result in "significant influence" because majority ownership of the investee is concentrated among a small group of shareholders who operate the investee without regard to the views of the investor.

(4) The investor tries and fails to obtain representation on the investee's board of directors.

"Criteria for Applying the Equity Method of Accounting for Investments in Common Stock," *Interpretations of the Financial Accounting Standards Board No. 35* (Stamford, Conn.: FASB, 1981).

ILLUSTRATION 17-17 Comparison of Fair Value Method and Equity Method

ENTRIES BY MAXI COMPANY

Fair Value Method			Equity Method		
On January 2, 2004, Maxi Company acquired 48,000 shares (20% of Mini Company common stock) at a cost of $10 a share.					
Available-for-Sale-Securities	480,000		Investment in Mini Stock	480,000	
Cash		480,000	Cash		480,000
For the year 2004, Mini Company reported net income of $200,000; Maxi Company's share is 20%, or $40,000.					
No entry			Investment in Mini Stock	40,000	
			Revenue from Investment		40,000
At December 31, 2004, the 48,000 shares of Mini Company have a fair value (market price) of $12 a share, or $576,000.					
Securities Fair Value Adjustment (Available-for-Sale)	96,000		No entry		
Unrealized Holding Gain or Loss—Equity		96,000			
On January 28, 2005, Mini Company announced and paid a cash dividend of $100,000; Maxi Company received 20%, or $20,000.					
Cash	20,000		Cash	20,000	
Dividend Revenue		20,000	Investment in Mini Stock		20,000
For the year 2005, Mini reported a net loss of $50,000; Maxi Company's share is 20%, or $10,000.					
No entry			Loss on Investment	10,000	
			Investment in Mini Stock		10,000
At December 31, 2005, the Mini Company 48,000 shares have a fair value (market price) of $11 a share, or $528,000.					
Unrealized Holding Gain or Loss—Equity	48,000		No entry		
Securities Fair Value Adjustment (Available-for-Sale)		48,000			

investee's profitable operation may be permanently retained in the business by the investee. Therefore, revenue is not considered earned by the investor until dividends are received from the investee.

INTERNATIONAL INSIGHT

IAS permit significant-influence investments to be measured using the equity, cost, or fair value methods.

Under the equity method, Maxi Company reports as revenue its share of the net income reported by Mini Company; the cash dividends received from Mini Company are recorded as a decrease in the investment carrying value. As a result, the investor records its share of the net income of the investee in the year when it is earned. In this case, the investor can ensure that any net asset increases of the investee resulting from net income will be paid in dividends if desired. To wait until a dividend is received ignores the fact that the investor is better off if the investee has earned income.

Using dividends as a basis for recognizing income poses an additional problem. For example, assume that the investee reports a net loss, but the investor exerts influence to force a dividend payment from the investee. In this case, the investor reports income, even though the investee is experiencing a loss. **In other words, if dividends are used as a basis for recognizing income, the economics of the situation are not properly reported.**

Investee Losses Exceed Carrying Amount

UNDERLYING CONCEPTS

Revenue to be recognized should be earned and realized or realizable. A low level of ownership indicates that the income from an investee should be deferred until cash is received.

If an investor's share of the investee's losses exceeds the carrying amount of the investment, should the investor recognize additional losses? Ordinarily the investor should discontinue applying the equity method and not recognize additional losses.

If the investor's potential loss is not limited to the amount of its original investment (by guarantee of the investee's obligations or other commitment to provide further financial support), or if imminent return to profitable operations by the investee appears to be assured, it is appropriate for the investor to recognize additional losses.[12]

[12]"The Equity Method of Accounting for Investments in Common Stock," op. cit., par. 19(i).

FROM BAD TO WORSE

WHAT DO THE NUMBERS MEAN?

Amazon.com, the pioneer of Internet retailing, has struggled to turn a profit. Furthermore, some of Amazon's equity investments have resulted in Amazon's recent earnings performance going from bad to worse. In 2001, Amazon.com disclosed equity stakes in such companies as **Altera International**, **Basis Technology**, **drugstore.com**, and **Eziba.com**. Apparently, these companies are not faring any better than Amazon, as indicated in Amazon's income statement.

(in thousands)	2001	2000	1999
Net income (loss)	$(567,227)	$(1,411,273)	$(719,968)
Equity in losses of equity method investees	(30,327)	(304,596)	(76,769)
% of total loss	5.3	21.6	10.7

Because these companies operate in the same depressed Internet economy as Amazon, under the equity method of accounting, their negative results can make Amazon's already bad bottom line even worse.

HOLDINGS OF MORE THAN 50%

INTERNATIONAL INSIGHT

In contrast to U.S. firms, financial statements of non-U.S. companies often include both consolidated (group) statements and parent company financial statements.

When one corporation acquires a voting interest of more than 50 percent—**controlling interest**—in another corporation, the investor corporation is referred to as the **parent** and the investee corporation as the **subsidiary**. The investment in the common stock of the subsidiary is presented as a long-term investment on the separate financial statements of the parent.

When the parent treats the subsidiary as an investment, **consolidated financial statements** are generally prepared instead of separate financial statements for the parent and the subsidiary. Consolidated financial statements disregard the distinction between separate legal entities and treat the parent and subsidiary corporations as a single economic entity. The subject of when and how to prepare consolidated financial statements is discussed extensively in advanced accounting. Whether or not consolidated financial statements are prepared, the investment in the subsidiary is generally accounted for on the parent's books **using the equity method** as explained in this chapter.

CONSOLIDATE THIS!

WHAT DO THE NUMBERS MEAN?

Presently the rules for consolidation seem very straightforward: If a company owns more than 50 percent of another company, it generally should be consolidated. If it owns less than 50 percent, it is generally not consolidated. However the FASB recognizes that the present test is too artificial, and determination of who really has control is often based on factors other than stock ownership.

In fact, specific guidelines have been developed that force consolidation even though stock ownership is not above 50 percent in certain limited situations. For example, **Enron**'s failure to consolidate three special purpose entities that were effectively controlled by Enron led to an overstatement of income of $569 million and overstatement of equity of $1.2 billion. In these three cases, the GAAP answer would have led to consolidation. That is, the following factors indicate that consolidation should have occurred: the majority owner of the special purpose entity (SPE) made only a modest investment, the activities of the SPE were virtually to benefit Enron, and the substantive risks and rewards related to the assets or debt of the SPE rested directly or indirectly with Enron.

The FASB now indicates it will issue new guidelines related to SPEs, given all the reporting problems that have surfaced related to SPEs as a result of the Enron bankruptcy.[13]

[13]*Proposed Interpretation*: "Consolidation of Certain Special Purpose Entities" (Norwalk, Conn.: FASB, June 28, 2002).

SECTION 3 OTHER REPORTING ISSUES

We have identified the basic issues involved in accounting for investments in debt and equity securities. In addition, the following issues relate to both of these types of securities.

1. Financial statement presentation
2. Impairment of value
3. Transfers between categories
4. Fair value controversy

FINANCIAL STATEMENT PRESENTATION OF INVESTMENTS

OBJECTIVE 5
Describe the disclosure requirements for investments in debt and equity securities.

Companies are required to present individual amounts for the three categories of investments either on the balance sheet or in the related notes. Trading securities should be reported at aggregate fair value as current assets. Individual held-to-maturity and available-for-sale securities are classified as current or noncurrent depending upon the circumstances.

Held-to-maturity securities should be classified as current or noncurrent, based on the maturity date of the individual securities. Debt securities identified as available-for-sale should be classified as current or noncurrent, based on maturities and expectations as to sales and redemptions in the following year. Equity securities identified as available-for-sale should be classified as current if these securities are available for use in current operations. Thus, if the invested cash used to purchase the equity securities is considered a contingency fund to be used whenever a need arises, then the securities should be classified as current.

For securities classified as available-for-sale and separately for securities classified as held-to-maturity, a company should describe:

Actual Company Disclosures Related to Investments and Comprehensive Income

1. Aggregate fair value, gross unrealized holding gains, gross unrealized losses, and amortized cost basis by major security type (debt and equity).
2. Information about the contractual maturities of debt securities. Maturity information may be combined in appropriate groupings such as (a) within 1 year, (b) after 1 year through 5 years, (c) after 5 years through 10 years, and (d) after 10 years.

In classifying investments, management's expressed intent should be supported by evidence, such as the history of the company's investment activities, events subsequent to the balance sheet date, and the nature and purpose of the investment.

Companies have to be extremely careful with debt securities held to maturity. If a debt security in this category is sold prematurely, the sale may "taint" the entire held-to-maturity portfolio. That is, a management's statement regarding "intent" is no longer as credible, and therefore the securities might have to be reclassified. This could lead to unfortunate consequences. An interesting by-product of this situation is that companies that wish to retire their debt securities early are finding it difficult to do so; the holder will not sell because the securities are classified as held-to-maturity.

Disclosures Required Under the Equity Method

The significance of an investment to the investor's financial position and operating results should determine the extent of disclosures. The following disclosures in the investor's financial statements generally apply to the equity method.

Disclosures Related to Equity Investments

1. The name of each investee and the percentage of ownership of common stock.
2. The accounting policies of the investor with respect to investments in common stock.

3. The difference, if any, between the amount in the investment account and the amount of underlying equity in the net assets of the investee.
4. The aggregate value of each identified investment based on quoted market price (if available).
5. When investments of 20 percent or more interest are, in the aggregate, material in relation to the financial position and operating results of an investor, it may be necessary to present summarized information concerning assets, liabilities, and results of operations of the investees, either individually or in groups, as appropriate.

In addition, the investor is expected to disclose the reasons for **not** using the equity method in cases of 20 percent or more ownership interest and **for** using the equity method in cases of less than 20 percent ownership interest.

UNDERLYING CONCEPTS

The consolidation of financial results of different companies follows the economic entity assumption and disregards legal entities. The key objective is to provide useful information to financial statement users.

Reclassification Adjustments

As indicated in Chapter 4, changes in unrealized holding gains and losses related to available-for-sale securities are reported as part of other comprehensive income. Companies have the option to display the components of other comprehensive income in one of three ways: (1) in a combined statement of income and comprehensive income, (2) in a separate statement of comprehensive income that begins with net income, or (3) in a statement of stockholders' equity.

The reporting of changes in unrealized gains or losses in comprehensive income is straightforward unless securities are sold during the year. In that case, double counting results when realized gains or losses are reported as part of net income but also are shown as part of other comprehensive income in the current period or in previous periods.

To ensure that gains and losses are not counted twice when a sale occurs, a **reclassification adjustment** is necessary. To illustrate, assume that Open Company has the following two available-for-sale securities in its portfolio at the end of 2003 (its first year of operations).

ILLUSTRATION 17-18
Available-for-Sale Security Portfolio (2003)

Investments	Cost	Fair Value	Unrealized Holding Gain (Loss)
Lehman Inc. common stocks	$ 80,000	$105,000	$25,000
Woods Co. common stocks	120,000	135,000	15,000
Total of portfolio	$200,000	$240,000	40,000
Previous securities fair value adjustment balance			–0–
Securities fair value adjustment—Dr.			$40,000

If Open Company reports net income in 2003 of $350,000, a statement of comprehensive income would be reported as follows.

ILLUSTRATION 17-19
Statement of Comprehensive Income (2003)

OPEN CO. STATEMENT OF COMPREHENSIVE INCOME FOR THE YEAR ENDED DECEMBER 31, 2003	
Net income	$350,000
Other comprehensive income	
Holding gains arising during period	40,000
Comprehensive income	$390,000

During 2004, Open Company sold the Lehman Inc. common stock for $105,000 and realized a gain on the sale of $25,000 ($105,000 − $80,000). At the end of 2004, the fair value of the Woods Co. common stock increased an additional $20,000, to $155,000. The computation of the change in the securities fair value adjustment account is computed as follows.

ILLUSTRATION 17-20
Available-for-Sale Security Portfolio (2004)

Investments	Cost	Fair Value	Unrealized Holding Gain (Loss)
Woods Co. common stocks	$120,000	$155,000	$35,000
Previous securities fair value adjustment balance—Dr.			(40,000)
Securities fair value adjustment—Cr.			$ (5,000)

Illustration 17-20 indicates that an unrealized holding loss of $5,000 should be reported in comprehensive income in 2004. In addition, Open Company realized a gain of $25,000 on the sale of the Lehman common stock. Comprehensive income includes both realized and unrealized components, and therefore the total holding gain (loss) recognized in 2004 is $20,000, computed as follows.

ILLUSTRATION 17-21
Computation of Total Holding Gain (Loss)

Unrealized holding gain (loss)	$ (5,000)
Realized holding gain	25,000
Total holding gain recognized	$20,000

Open Company reports net income of $720,000 in 2004, which includes the realized gain on sale of the Lehman securities. A statement of comprehensive income for 2004 is shown in Illustration 17-22, indicating how the components of holding gains (losses) are reported.

ILLUSTRATION 17-22
Statement of Comprehensive Income (2004)

OPEN COMPANY
STATEMENT OF COMPREHENSIVE INCOME
FOR THE YEAR ENDED DECEMBER 31, 2004

Net income (includes $25,000 realized gain on Lehman shares)		$720,000
Other comprehensive income		
Holding gains arising during period ($155,000 − $135,000)	$20,000	
Less: Reclassification adjustment for gains included in net income	(25,000)	(5,000)
Comprehensive income		$715,000

In 2003, the unrealized gain on the Lehman Co. common stock was included in comprehensive income. In 2004, it was sold, and the realized gain reported in net income increases comprehensive income again. To avoid double counting this gain, a reclassification adjustment is made to eliminate the realized gain from the computation of comprehensive income.

A company has the option to display reclassification adjustments on the face of the financial statement in which comprehensive income is reported, or it may disclose these reclassification adjustments in the notes to the financial statements.

Comprehensive Illustration

To illustrate the reporting of investment securities and related gain or loss on available-for-sale securities, assume that on January 1, 2003, Hinges Co. had cash and common stock of $50,000.[14] At that date the company had no other asset, liability, or equity balance. On January 2, Hinges Co. purchased for cash $50,000 of equity securities that are classified as available-for-sale. On June 30, Hinges Co. sold part of the available-for-sale security portfolio, realizing a gain as follows.

ILLUSTRATION 17-23
Computation of Realized Gain

Fair value of securities sold	$22,000
Less: Cost of securities sold	20,000
Realized gain	$ 2,000

Hinges Co. did not purchase or sell any other securities during 2003. It received $3,000 in dividends during the year. At December 31, 2003, the remaining portfolio is:

ILLUSTRATION 17-24
Computation of Unrealized Gain

Fair value of portfolio	$34,000
Less: Cost of portfolio	30,000
Unrealized gain	$ 4,000

The company's income statement for 2003 is shown in Illustration 17-25.

ILLUSTRATION 17-25
Income Statement

HINGES CO.
INCOME STATEMENT
FOR THE YEAR ENDED DECEMBER 31, 2003

Dividend revenue	$3,000
Realized gains on investment in securities	2,000
Net income	$5,000

The company decides to report its change in the unrealized holding gain in a statement of comprehensive income as follows.

ILLUSTRATION 17-26
Statement of Comprehensive Income

HINGES CO.
STATEMENT OF COMPREHENSIVE INCOME
FOR THE YEAR ENDED DECEMBER 31, 2003

Net income		$5,000
Other comprehensive income:		
Holding gains arising during the period	$6,000	
Less: Reclassification adjustment for gains included in net income	2,000	4,000
Comprehensive income		$9,000

[14]This example adapted from Dennis R. Beresford, L. Todd Johnson, and Cheri L. Reither, "Is a Second Income Statement Needed?" *Journal of Accountancy* (April 1996), p. 71.

Its statement of stockholders' equity would show the following.

ILLUSTRATION 17-27
Statement of Stockholders' Equity

HINGES CO.
STATEMENT OF STOCKHOLDERS' EQUITY
FOR THE YEAR ENDED DECEMBER 31, 2003

	Common Stock	Retained Earnings	Accumulated Other Comprehensive Income	Total
Beginning balance	$50,000	$-0-	$-0-	$50,000
Add: Net income		5,000		5,000
Other comprehensive Income			4,000	4,000
Ending balance	$50,000	$5,000	$4,000	$59,000

A comparative balance sheet is shown below.

ILLUSTRATION 17-28
Comparative Balance Sheet

HINGES CO.
COMPARATIVE BALANCE SHEET

	1/1/03	12/31/03
Assets		
Cash	$50,000	$25,000
Available-for-sale securities		34,000
Total assets	$50,000	$59,000
Stockholders' equity		
Common stock	$50,000	$50,000
Retained earnings		5,000
Accumulated other comprehensive income		4,000
Total stockholders' equity	$50,000	$59,000

This example indicates how an unrealized gain or loss on available-for-sale securities affects all the financial statements. It should be noted that the components that comprise accumulated comprehensive income must be disclosed.

IMPAIRMENT OF VALUE

OBJECTIVE 6
Discuss the accounting for impairments of debt and equity investments.

Every investment should be evaluated at each reporting date to determine if it has suffered **impairment**—a loss in value that is other than temporary. A bankruptcy or a significant liquidity crisis being experienced by an investee are examples of situations in which a loss in value to the investor may be permanent. **If the decline is judged to be other than temporary, the cost basis of the individual security is written down to a new cost basis.** The amount of the write-down is accounted for as a realized loss and, therefore, included in net income.

For debt securities, the impairment test is to determine whether "it is probable that the investor will be unable to collect all amounts due according to the contractual terms." **For equity securities**, the guideline is less precise. Any time realizable value is lower than the carrying amount of the investment, an impairment must be considered. Factors involved are the following: the length of time and the extent to which the fair value has been less than cost; the financial condition and near-term prospects of the issuer; and the intent and ability of the investor company to retain its investment to allow for any anticipated recovery in fair value.

To illustrate an impairment, assume that Strickler Company holds available-for-sale bond securities with a par value and amortized cost of $1 million. The fair value of these securities is $800,000. Strickler has previously reported an unrealized loss on these securities of $200,000 as part of other comprehensive income. In evaluating the securities, Strickler now determines it probable that it will not be able to collect all amounts due. In this case, the unrealized loss of $200,000 will be reported as a loss on impairment of $200,000 and included in income, with the bonds stated at their new cost basis. The journal entry to record this impairment would be as follows.

Loss on Impairment	200,000	
Securities Fair Value Adjustment (Available-for-Sale)	200,000	
Unrealized Holding Gain or Loss—Equity		200,000
Available-for-Sale Securities		200,000

The new cost basis of the investment in debt securities is $800,000. Subsequent increases and decreases in the fair value of impaired available-for-sale securities are included as other comprehensive income.[15]

The impairment test used for debt and equity securities is based on a fair value test. This test is slightly different from the impairment test for loans discussed in Appendix 14A. The FASB rejected the discounted cash flow alternative for securities because of the availability of market price information.

TRANSFERS BETWEEN CATEGORIES

OBJECTIVE 7
Describe the accounting for transfer of investment securities between categories.

Transfers between any of the categories are accounted for at fair value. Thus, if available-for-sale securities are transferred to held-to-maturity investments, the new investment (held-to-maturity) is recorded at the date of transfer at **fair value** in the new category. Similarly, if held-to-maturity investments are transferred to available-for-sale investments, the new investments (available-for-sale) are recorded at **fair value**. This **fair value rule** assures that a company cannot escape recognition of fair value simply by transferring securities to the held-to-maturity category. Illustration 17-29 (on page 858) summarizes the accounting treatment for transfers. **This illustration assumes that adjusting entries to report changes in fair value for the current period are not yet recorded.**

FAIR VALUE CONTROVERSY

FASB Statement No. 115 leaves many issues unresolved. Many parties are dissatisfied with its results: some think it goes too far, others think it does not go far enough. In this section we look at some of the major unresolved issues.

Measurement Based on Intent

Debt securities can be classified as held-to-maturity, available-for-sale, or trading. As a result, three identical debt securities could be reported in three different ways in the financial statements. Some argue such treatment is confusing. Furthermore, the held-to-maturity category is based solely on intent, which is a subjective evaluation. What is not subjective is the market price of the debt instrument, which is observable in the marketplace. In other words, the three classifications are subjective, and therefore arbitrary classifications will result.

Gains Trading

Certain debt securities can be classified as held-to-maturity and therefore reported at amortized cost. Other debt and equity securities can be classified as available-for-sale and reported at fair value with the unrealized gain or loss reported as other

[15]Amortization of any discount related to the debt securities is not permitted after recording the impairment. The new cost basis of impaired held-to-maturity securities would not change unless additional impairment occurred.

ILLUSTRATION 17-29
Accounting for Transfers

Type of Transfer	Measurement Basis	Impact of Transfer on Stockholders' Equity	Impact of Transfer on Net Income
Transfer from trading to available-for-sale	Security transferred at fair value at the date of transfer, which is the new cost basis of the security.	The unrealized gain or loss at the date of transfer increases or decreases stockholders' equity.	The unrealized gain or loss at the date of transfer is recognized in income.
Transfer from available-for-sale to trading	Security transferred at fair value at the date of transfer, which is the new cost basis of the security.	The unrealized gain or loss at the date of transfer increases or decreases stockholders' equity.	The unrealized gain or loss at the date of transfer is recognized in income.
Transfer from held-to-maturity to available-for-sale*	Security transferred at fair value at the date of transfer.	The separate component of stockholders' equity is increased or decreased by the unrealized gain or loss at the date of transfer.	None
Transfer from available-for-sale to held-to-maturity	Security transferred at fair value at the date of transfer.	The unrealized gain or loss at the date of transfer carried as a separate component of stockholders' equity is amortized over the remaining life of the security.	None

**Statement No. 115* states that these types of transfers should be rare.

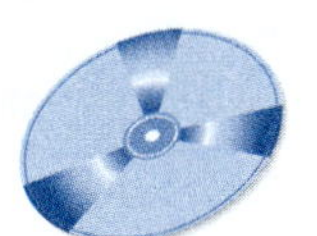

Examples of Entries for Recording Transfers Between Categories

comprehensive income. In either case, a company can become involved in "gains trading" (also referred to as "cherry picking"). In **gains trading**, companies sell their "winners," reporting the gains in income, and hold on to the losers.

Liabilities Not Fairly Valued

Many argue that if investment securities are going to be reported at fair value, so also should liabilities. They note that by recognizing changes in value on only one side of the balance sheet (the asset side), a high degree of volatility can occur in the income and stockholders' equity amounts. It is further argued that financial institutions are involved in asset and liability management (not just asset management) and that viewing only one side may lead managers to make uneconomic decisions as a result of the accounting. Although the Board was sympathetic with this view, it noted that certain debt securities were still reported at amortized cost and that other types of securities were excluded from the scope of this standard. In addition, serious valuation issues arose in relation to some types of liabilities. As a result, liabilities were excluded from consideration.[16]

[16]In a recent preliminary report concerning valuation of financial instruments, the FASB indicated its support for valuing liabilities at fair value. "Reporting Financial Instruments and Certain Related Assets and Liabilities at Fair Value," *FASB Preliminary Views* (Norwalk, Conn.: FASB, 1999).

Subjectivity of Fair Values

Some people question the relevance of fair value measures for investments in securities, arguing in favor of reporting based on amortized cost. They believe that amortized cost provides relevant information: it focuses on the decision to acquire the asset, the earning effects of that decision that will be realized over time, and the ultimate recoverable value of the asset. They argue that fair value ignores those concepts. Instead, fair value focuses on the effects of transactions and events that do not involve the enterprise, reflecting opportunity gains and losses whose recognition in the financial statements is, in their view, not appropriate until they are realized.

SUMMARY

The major debt and equity securities and their reporting treatment are summarized in Illustration 17-30.

ILLUSTRATION 17-30
Summary of Treatment of Major Debt and Equity Securities

Category	Balance Sheet	Income Statement
Trading (debt and equity securities)	Investments shown at fair value. Current assets.	Interest and dividends are recognized as revenue. Unrealized holding gains and losses are included in net income.
Available-for-sale (debt and equity securities)	Investments shown at fair value. Current or long-term assets. Unrealized holding gains and losses are a separate component of stockholders' equity.	Interest and dividends are recognized as revenue. Unrealized holding gains and losses are **not** included in net income but in other comprehensive income.
Held-to-maturity (debt securities)	Investments shown at amortized cost. Current or long-term assets.	Interest is recognized as revenue.
Equity method and/or consolidation (equity securities)	Investments originally are carried at cost, are periodically adjusted by the investor's share of the investee's earnings or losses, and are decreased by all dividends received from the investee. Classified as long-term.	Revenue is recognized to the extent of the investee's earnings or losses reported subsequent to the date of investment.

Expanded Discussion—Special Issues Related to Investments

SUMMARY OF LEARNING OBJECTIVES

1 Identify the three categories of debt securities and describe the accounting and reporting treatment for each category. (1) *Held-to-maturity debt securities* are carried and reported at amortized cost. (2) *Trading debt securities* are valued for reporting purposes at fair value, with unrealized holding gains or losses included in net income. (3) *Available-for-sale debt securities* are valued for reporting purposes at fair value, with unrealized holding gains or losses reported as other comprehensive income and as a separate component of stockholders' equity.

2 Understand the procedures for discount and premium amortization on bond investments. Similar to bonds payable, discount or premium on bond investments should be amortized using the effective-interest method. The effective-interest rate or yield is applied to the beginning carrying value of the investment for each interest period in order to compute interest revenue.

KEY TERMS

amortized cost, *837*
available-for-sale securities, *840*
consolidated financial statements, *851*
controlling interest, *851*
debt securities, *837*
effective-interest method, *838*
equity method, *849*
equity securities, *845*
exchange for noncash consideration, *846*

fair value, *837*
fair value method, *846*
gains trading, *858*
held-to-maturity securities, *838*
holding gain or loss, *844*
impairment, *856*
investee, *845*
investor, *845*
parent, *851*
reclassification adjustment, *853*
Securities Fair Value Adjustment account, *841*
security, *836(n)*
significant influence, *848*
subsidiary, *851*
trading securities, *844*

3 Identify the categories of equity securities and describe the accounting and reporting treatment for each category. The degree to which one corporation (investor) acquires an interest in the common stock of another corporation (investee) generally determines the accounting treatment for the investment. Long-term investments by one corporation in the common stock of another can be classified according to the percentage of the voting stock of the investee held by the investor.

4 Explain the equity method of accounting and compare it to the fair value method for equity securities. Under the equity method, a substantive economic relationship is acknowledged between the investor and the investee. The investment is originally recorded at cost but is subsequently adjusted each period for changes in the net assets of the investee. That is, the investment's carrying amount is periodically increased (decreased) by the investor's proportionate share of the earnings (losses) of the investee, and is decreased by all dividends received by the investor from the investee. Under the fair value method, the equity investment is reported by the investor at fair value each reporting period irrespective of the investee's earnings or dividends paid to the investor. The equity method is applied to investment holdings between 20 percent and 50 percent of ownership. The fair value method is applied to holdings below 20 percent.

5 Describe the disclosure requirements for investments in debt and equity securities. Trading securities should be reported at aggregate fair value as current assets. Individual held-to-maturity and available-for-sale securities are classified as current or noncurrent depending upon the circumstances. For available-for-sale and held-to-maturity securities, a company should describe: aggregate fair value, gross unrealized holding gains, gross unrealized losses, amortized cost basis by type (debt and equity), and information about the contractual maturity of debt securities. A reclassification adjustment is necessary when realized gains or losses are reported as part of net income but also are shown as part of other comprehensive income in the current or in previous periods. Unrealized holding gains or losses related to available-for-sale securities should be reported in other comprehensive income and the aggregate balance as accumulated comprehensive income on the balance sheet.

6 Discuss the accounting for impairments of debt and equity investments. Impairments of debt and equity securities are losses in value that are determined to be other than temporary, are based on a fair value test, and are charged to income.

7 Describe the accounting for transfer of investment securities between categories. Transfers of securities between categories of investments are accounted for at fair value, with unrealized holding gains or losses treated in accordance with the nature of the transfer.

APPENDIX 17A

Accounting for Derivative Instruments

It has been said that until the early 1970s most financial managers worked in a cozy, if unthrilling world. Since then, however, constant change caused by volatile markets, new technology, and deregulation has increased the risks to businesses. The response from the financial community was to develop products to manage the risks due to changes in market prices.

These products—called **derivative financial instruments** or, simply, **derivatives**—are useful for risk management because the fair values or cash flows of these instruments can be used to offset the changes in fair values or cash flows of the assets that are at risk. The growth in use of derivatives has been aided by the development of powerful computing and communication technology, which provides new ways to analyze information about markets as well as the power to process high volumes of payments.

UNDERSTANDING DERIVATIVES

In order to understand derivatives, consider the following examples.

Illustration 1—Forward Contract. Let's assume that you believe that the price of **Microsoft**'s stock will increase substantially in the next 3 months. Unfortunately, you do not have the cash resources to purchase the stock today. You therefore enter into a contract with your broker for delivery of 100 shares of Microsoft stock in 3 months at the price of $110 per share. As a result of the contract, you **have received the right** to receive 100 shares of Microsoft stock in 3 months and you **have an obligation** to pay $110 per share at that time. You have entered into a **forward contract**, a type of derivative. The benefit of this derivative contract to you is that you are able to buy Microsoft stock today and take delivery in 3 months. If the price goes up, as you expect, you win. If the price goes down, you lose.

Illustration 2—Option Contract. Let's suppose that instead of entering into the forward contract for delivery of the stock in 3 months, you tell your broker that you are undecided about whether to purchase Microsoft stock and need 2 weeks to decide. You enter into a different type of contract with your broker, one that gives you the right to purchase Microsoft stock at its current price any time within the next 2 weeks. As part of the contract, the broker charges you $300 for holding the contract open for 2 weeks at a set price. You have entered into an **option contract**, another type of derivative. As a result of this contract, **you have received the right, but not the obligation** to purchase this stock. If the price of the Microsoft stock increases in the next 2 weeks, you exercise your option. In this case, the cost of the stock to you is the price of the stock stated in the contract plus the cost of the option contract. If the price does not increase, you do not exercise the contract, but you incur a cost for the option.

For both the forward contract and the option contract, the delivery of the stock was for a future date, and the value of the contract was based on the underlying asset—the Microsoft stock. These financial instruments are referred to as **derivatives** because their value **is derived from** values of other assets (for example, stocks, bonds, or commodities) or is related to a market-determined indicator (for example, interest rates or the Standard and Poor's 500 stock composite index).

In this appendix, we will discuss the accounting for three different types of derivatives:

1. Financial forwards or financial futures.
2. Options.
3. Swaps.

Who Uses Derivatives, and Why?

OBJECTIVE 8
Explain who uses derivatives and why.

Whether it is protection from changes in interest rates, the weather, stock prices, oil prices, or foreign currencies, derivative contracts can be used to smooth the fluctuations caused by various types of risks. Any individual or company that wants to ensure against certain types of business risks often can use derivative contracts to achieve this objective.

Producers and Consumers

To illustrate who might use derivatives, assume that Heartland Ag is a large producer of potatoes for the consumer market. The present price for potatoes is excellent, but unfortunately it will take Heartland 2 months to harvest its potatoes and deliver them to the market. Because Heartland is concerned that the price of potatoes will drop, it signs a contract agreeing to sell its potatoes today at the current market price for delivery in 2 months.

Who would buy this contract? Suppose on the other side of the contract is McDonald's Corporation who wants to have potatoes (for French fries) in 2 months and is worried that prices will increase. McDonald's is therefore agreeable to delivery in 2 months at current prices. McDonald's knows that it will need potatoes in 2 months and that it can make an acceptable profit at this price level.

In this situation, if the price of potatoes increases before delivery, you might conclude that Heartland loses and McDonald's wins. Conversely, if prices decrease, Heartland wins and McDonald's loses. However the objective is not to gamble on the outcome. Regardless of which way the price moves, both Heartland and McDonald's should be pleased because both have received a price at which an acceptable profit is obtained. In this case, Heartland is a **producer** and McDonald's is a **consumer**. Both companies are referred to as **hedgers** because they are hedging their positions to ensure an acceptable financial result.

Commodity prices are volatile and depend on weather, crop disasters, and general economic conditions. For the producer and the consumer to plan effectively, it makes good sense to lock in specific future revenues or costs in order to run their businesses successfully.

Speculators and Arbitrageurs

In some cases, instead of McDonald's taking a position in the forward contract, a speculator may purchase the contract from Heartland. The **speculator** is betting that the price of potatoes will increase and therefore the value of the forward contract will increase. The speculator, who may be in the market for only a few hours, will then sell the forward contract to another speculator or to a company like McDonald's.

Another user of derivatives is **arbitrageurs**. These market players attempt to exploit inefficiencies in various derivative markets. They seek to lock in profits by simultaneously entering into transactions in two or more markets. For example, an arbitrageur might trade in a futures contract and at the same time in the commodity underlying the futures contract, hoping to achieve small price gains on the difference between the two. Speculators and arbitrageurs are very important to the derivatives market because they keep it liquid on a daily basis.

In these illustrations, we explained why Heartland Ag (the producer) and McDonald's (the consumer) would become involved in a derivative contract. Consider other types of situations that companies face.

1. Airlines, like **Delta**, **Southwest**, and **United**, are affected by changes in the price of jet fuel.
2. Financial institutions, such as **Citigroup**, **Bankers Trust**, and **M&I Bank**, are involved in borrowing and lending funds which are affected by changes in interest rates.
3. Multinational corporations, like **Cisco Systems**, **Coca-Cola**, and **General Electric**, are subject to changes in foreign exchange rates.

It is not surprising that you find most corporations involved in some form of derivatives transactions. Here are some reasons given by companies in their annual reports as to why they use derivatives.

1. **ExxonMobil** uses derivative instruments primarily to hedge its exposure to fluctuations in interest rates, foreign currency exchange rates, and hydrocarbon prices.
2. **Caterpillar** uses derivative financial instruments to manage foreign currency exchange rates, interest rates, and commodity price exposure.
3. **Johnson & Johnson** uses derivative financial instruments to manage the impact of interest rate and foreign exchange rate changes on earnings and cash flows.

Many corporations use derivatives extensively and successfully. However, derivatives can be dangerous, and it is critical that all parties involved understand the risks and rewards associated with these contracts.[1]

BASIC PRINCIPLES IN ACCOUNTING FOR DERIVATIVES

OBJECTIVE 9
Understand the basic guidelines for accounting for derivatives.

In *SFAS No. 133*, the FASB concluded that derivatives such as forwards and options are assets and liabilities and should be reported in the balance sheet at **fair value**.[2] The Board believes that fair value will provide statement users the best information about derivative financial instruments.[3] Relying on some other basis of valuation for derivatives, such as historical cost, does not make sense because many derivatives have a historical cost of zero. Furthermore, given the well-developed markets for derivatives and for the assets upon which derivatives' values are based, the Board believed that reliable fair value amounts could be determined for derivative instruments.

Any unrealized gain or loss should be recognized in income if the derivative is used for speculation purposes. If the derivative is used for hedging purposes, the accounting for any gain or loss depends on the type of hedge used. The accounting for hedged transactions is discussed later in the appendix.

---

[1]There are some well-publicized examples of companies that have suffered considerable losses using derivatives. For example, companies such as **Enron** (U.S.), **Showa Shell Sekiyu** (Japan), **Metallgesellschaft** (Germany), **Procter & Gamble** (U.S.), and **Air Products & Chemicals** (U.S.) have incurred significant losses from investments in derivative instruments.

[2]"Accounting for Derivative Instruments and Hedging Activities," *Statement of Financial Accounting Standards No. 133* (Stamford, Conn.: FASB, 1998). All derivative instruments, whether financial or not, are covered under this standard. Our discussion in this chapter focuses on derivative financial instruments because of their widespread use in practice.

[3]*Fair value* is defined as the amount at which an asset (or liability) could be bought (incurred) or sold (settled) between two willing parties (i.e., not forced or in liquidation). Quoted market prices in active markets are the best evidence of fair value and should be used if available. In the absence of market prices, the prices of similar assets or liabilities or accepted present value techniques can be used. "Disclosures About Fair Value of Financial Instruments," *Statement of Financial Accounting Standards No. 107* (Stamford, Conn.: FASB, 1991) paras. 5–6, 11. The Board's long-term objective is to require fair value measurement and recognition for all financial instruments (*SFAS No. 133*, para. 216).

In summary, the following guidelines are used in accounting for derivatives.

1. Derivatives should be recognized in the financial statements as assets and liabilities.
2. Derivatives should be reported at fair value.
3. Gains and losses resulting from speculation in derivatives should be recognized immediately in income.
4. Gains and losses resulting from hedge transactions are reported in different ways, depending upon the type of hedge.

Illustration of Derivative Financial Instrument—Speculation

OBJECTIVE 10
Describe the accounting for derivative financial instruments.

To illustrate the measurement and reporting of a derivative financial instrument for speculative purposes, we examine a derivative whose value is related to the market price of Laredo Inc. common stock. As in the previous Microsoft example, you could realize a gain from the increase in the value of the Laredo shares with the use of a derivative financial instrument, such as a call option.[4] A **call option** gives the holder the right, but not the obligation, to buy shares at a preset price (often referred to as the **strike price** or the **exercise price**).

For example, assume you enter into a call option contract with Baird Investment Co., which gives you the option to purchase Laredo stock at $100 per share.[5] If the price of Laredo stock increases above $100, you can exercise this option and purchase the shares for $100 per share. If Laredo's stock never increases above $100 per share, the call option is worthless and you recognize a loss.

Accounting Entries

To illustrate the accounting for a call option, assume that you purchased a call option contract on January 2, 2003, when Laredo shares are trading at $100 per share. The terms of the contract give you the option to purchase 1,000 shares (referred to as the **notional amount**) of Laredo stock at an option price of $100 per share. The option expires on April 30, 2003. You purchase the call option for $400 and make the following entry.

January 2, 2003

Call Option	400	
Cash		400

This payment, referred to as the **option premium**, is generally much less than the cost of purchasing the shares directly. The option premium is comprised of two amounts: (1) intrinsic value and (2) time value. The formula to compute the option premium is shown in Illustration 17A-1.

ILLUSTRATION 17A-1
Option Premium Formula

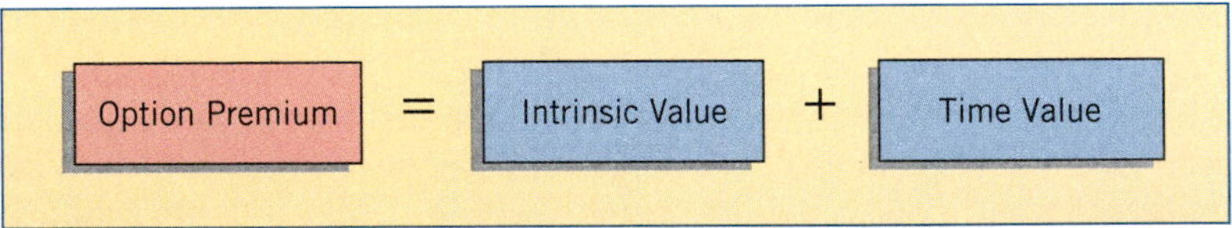

Intrinsic value is the difference between the market price and the preset strike price at any point in time. It represents the amount realized by the option holder if the option were exercised immediately. On January 2, 2003, the intrinsic value is zero because the market price is equal to the preset strike price.

---

[4]You could use a different type of option contract—a **put option**—to realize a gain if you speculate that the Laredo stock will decline in value. A put option gives the holder the option to sell shares at a preset price. Thus, a put option **increases** in value when the underlying asset **decreases** in value.

[5]Baird Investment Company is referred to as the **counterparty**. Counterparties frequently are investment bankers or other entities that hold inventories of financial instruments.

Time value refers to the option's value over and above its intrinsic value. Time value reflects the possibility that the option has a fair value greater than zero because there is some expectation that the price of Laredo shares will increase above the strike price during the option term. As indicated, the time value for the option is $400.[6]

On March 31, 2003, the price of Laredo shares has increased to $120 per share. The intrinsic value of the call option contract is now $20,000. That is, you could exercise the call option and purchase 1,000 shares from Baird Co. for $100 per share and then sell the shares in the market for $120 per share. This gives you a gain of $20,000 ($120,000 − $100,000) on the option contract.[7] The entry to record the increase in the intrinsic value of the option is as follows.

March 31, 2003

Call Option	20,000	
Unrealized Holding Gain or Loss—Income		20,000

A market appraisal indicates that the time value of the option at March 31, 2003, is $100.[8] The entry to record this change in value of the option is as follows.

March 31, 2003

Unrealized Holding Gain or Loss—Income	300	
Call Option ($400 − $100)		300

At March 31, 2003, the call option is reported in your balance sheet at fair value of $20,100.[9] The unrealized holding gain increases net income for the period, and the loss on the time value of the option decreases net income.

On April 1, 2003, the entry to record the settlement of the call option contract with Baird Investment Co. is as follows.

April 1, 2003

Cash	20,000	
Loss on Settlement of Call Option	100	
Call Option		20,100

Illustration 17A-2 summarizes the effects of the call option contract on net income.

ILLUSTRATION 17A-2
Effect on Income—Derivative Financial Instrument

Date	Transaction	Income (Loss) Effect
March 31, 2003	Net increase in value of call option ($20,000 − $300)	$19,700
April 1, 2003	Settle call option	(100)
	Total net income	$19,600

The accounting summarized in Illustration 17A-2 is in accord with *SFAS No. 133.* That is, because the call option meets the definition of an asset, it is recorded in the balance sheet on March 31, 2003. Furthermore, the call option is reported at fair value, with any gains or losses reported in income.

[6]This cost is estimated using option-pricing models, such as the Black-Scholes model. The fair value estimate is affected by the volatility of the underlying stock, the expected life of the option, the risk-free rate of interest, and expected dividends on the underlying stock during the option term.

[7]In practice, you generally do not have to actually buy and sell the Laredo shares to settle the option and realize the gain. This is referred to as the **net settlement** feature of option contracts.

[8]The decline in value reflects both the decreased likelihood that the Laredo shares will continue to increase in value over the option period and the shorter time to maturity of the option contract.

[9]As indicated earlier, the total value of the option at any point in time is equal to the intrinsic value plus the time value.

Differences between Traditional and Derivative Financial Instruments

What is the difference between a traditional and derivative financial instrument? A derivative financial instrument has three basic characteristics.[10]

1. **The instrument has (1) one or more underlyings and (2) an identified payment provision.** An **underlying** is a specified interest rate, security price, commodity price, index of prices or rates, or other market-related variable. Payment is determined by the interaction of the underlying with the face amount or the number of units specified in the derivative contract (the notional amounts). For example, the value of the call option increased in value when the value of the Laredo stock increased. In this case, the underlying was the stock price. The change in the stock price is multiplied by the number of shares (notional amount) to arrive at the payment provision.
2. **The instrument requires little or no investment at the inception of the contract.** To illustrate, you paid a small premium to purchase the call option—an amount much less than if the Laredo shares were purchased as a direct investment.
3. **The instrument requires or permits net settlement.** As indicated in the call option example, you could realize a profit on the call option without taking possession of the shares. This **net settlement** feature serves to reduce the transaction costs associated with derivatives.

Illustration 17A-3 summarizes the differences between traditional and derivative financial instruments. We use a trading security for the traditional financial instrument and a call option as an example of a derivative financial instrument.

ILLUSTRATION 17A-3
Features of Traditional and Derivative Financial Instruments

Feature	Traditional Financial Instrument (Trading Security)	Derivative Financial Instrument (Call Option)
Payment provision	Stock price times the number of shares.	Change in stock price (underlying) times number of shares (notional amount).
Initial investment	Investor pays full cost.	Initial investment is much less than full cost.
Settlement	Deliver stock to receive cash.	Receive cash equivalent, based on changes in stock price times the number of shares.

These distinctions between traditional and derivative financial instruments explain in part the popularity of derivatives but also suggest that the accounting might be different.

DERIVATIVES USED FOR HEDGING

Flexibility in use and the low-cost features of derivatives relative to traditional financial instruments explain why derivatives have become so popular in recent years. An additional use for derivatives is in risk management. For example, companies such as **Coca-Cola**, **ExxonMobil**, and **General Electric**, which borrow and lend substantial amounts in credit markets are exposed to significant **interest rate risk**. That is, they face substantial risk that the fair values or cash flows of interest-sensitive assets or liabilities will change if interest rates increase or decrease. These same companies also have significant international operations and so are exposed to **exchange rate risk**—the risk that changes in foreign currency exchange rates will negatively impact the profitability of their international businesses.

[10]In *SFAS No. 133*, the FASB identifies these same features as the key characteristics of derivatives. The FASB used these broad characteristics so that the definitions and hence the standard could be applied to yet-to-be-developed derivatives (par. 249).

Derivatives can be used to offset the risks that a firm's fair values or cash flows will be negatively impacted by changes in interest rates or foreign currency exchange rates. This use of derivatives is referred to as **hedging**.

SFAS No. 133 established accounting and reporting standards for derivative financial instruments used in hedging activities.[11] Special accounting is allowed for two types of hedges—fair value and cash flow hedges.[12]

RISKY BUSINESS

WHAT DO THE NUMBERS MEAN?

As shown in the graph below, use of derivatives has grown steadily in the past several years. Over $3 trillion in derivative contracts were in play at the end of 2001. The primary players in the market for derivatives—large companies and various financial institutions—continue to find new uses for derivatives for speculation and risk management.

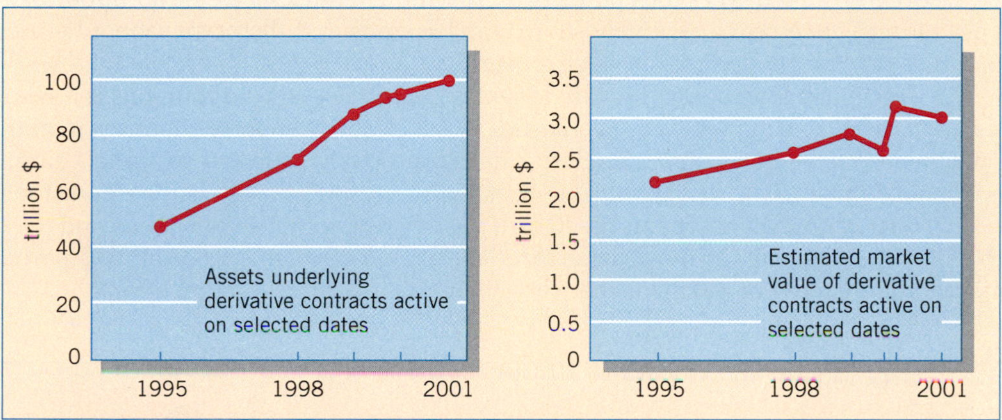

Source: Bank for International Settlements

However, as financial engineers develop new uses for derivatives, many times through the use of increasingly complex webs of transactions, spanning a number of markets, the financial system as a whole can be dramatically affected. As a result, some market-watchers are concerned about the risk that a crisis in one company or sector could bring the entire financial system to its knees.

This concern was illustrated recently when **Long-Term Capital Management**, a venerable hedge fund, experienced big losses on some of its derivative investments and had to be bailed out by a consortium of large banks. In cases like this, there is the possibility that even big market players would rush to cut their losses, resulting in a shortage of cash that could paralyze the system. Stock markets could tumble and banks could close, thereby putting even the savings of households at risk. And if that were to happen, even people with no money directly invested in the derivatives markets could be negatively affected. Thus the growing use of derivatives and their potential impact on the entire financial system highlights the need for transparency in the accounting and reporting of derivative transactions.

Source: Adapted from Daniel Altman, "Contracts So Complex They Imperil the System," *New York Times on the Web* (February 24, 2002).

[11]The hedge accounting provisions of *SFAS No. 133* are the major new elements in the standard and contain some of the more difficult accounting issues. The provisions were needed because of growth in the quantity and variety of derivative financial instruments used for hedging and due to the lack of, and inconsistency in, existing accounting standards for derivatives used in hedging transactions.

[12]*SFAS No. 133* also addresses the accounting for certain foreign currency hedging transactions. In general, these transactions are special cases of the two hedges discussed here. Understanding of foreign currency hedging transactions requires knowledge of consolidation of multinational entities, which is beyond the scope of this textbook.

Fair Value Hedge

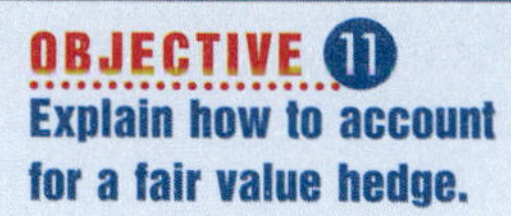

OBJECTIVE 11
Explain how to account for a fair value hedge.

In a **fair value hedge**, a derivative is used to hedge (offset) the exposure to changes in the fair value of a recognized asset or liability or of an unrecognized commitment. In a perfectly hedged position, the gain or loss on the fair value of the derivative and that of the hedged asset or liability should be equal and offsetting. A common type of fair value hedge is the use of interest rate swaps to hedge the risk that changes in interest rates will impact the fair value of debt obligations. Another typical fair value hedge is the use of put options to hedge the risk that an equity investment will decline in value.

Interest Rate Swap—A Fair Value Hedge

Options and futures have certain disadvantages. First, because they are traded on organized securities exchanges, options and futures have standardized terms and lack the flexibility needed to tailor contracts to specific circumstances. In addition, most types of derivatives have relatively short time horizons and therefore cannot be used to reduce any type of long-term risk exposure.

As a result, a very popular type of derivative used by many corporations is a swap. A **swap** is a transaction between two parties in which the first party promises to make a payment to the second party. Similarly, the second party promises to make a simultaneous payment to the first party. The most common type of swap is the **interest rate swap**: one party makes payments based on a fixed or floating rate, and the second party does just the opposite. In most cases, large money-center banks find the two parties and handle the flow of payments between the two parties, as shown below.

ILLUSTRATION 17A-4
Swap Transaction

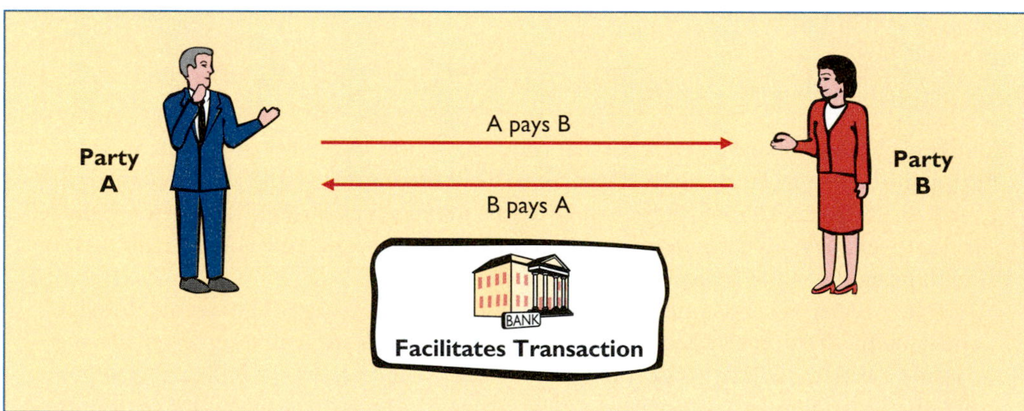

Accounting Entries

To illustrate the accounting for a fair value hedge, assume that Jones Company issues $1,000,000 of 5-year, 8 percent fixed-rate bonds on January 2, 2003. The entry to record this transaction is as follows.

January 2, 2003		
Cash	1,000,000	
Bonds Payable		1,000,000

A fixed interest rate was offered to appeal to investors. But Jones is concerned that if market interest rates decline, the fair value of the liability will increase and the company will suffer an economic loss.[13] To protect against the risk of loss, Jones decides to hedge the risk of a decline in interest rates by entering into a 5-year interest rate swap contract. The terms of the swap contract to Jones are:

[13]This economic loss arises because Jones is locked into the 8 percent interest payments even if rates decline.

1. Jones will receive fixed payments at 8 percent (based on the $1,000,000 amount).
2. Jones will pay variable rates, based on the market rate in effect for the life of the swap contract. The variable rate at the inception of the contract is 6.8 percent.

As depicted in Illustration 17A-5, by using this swap Jones can change the interest on the bonds payable from a fixed rate to a variable rate.

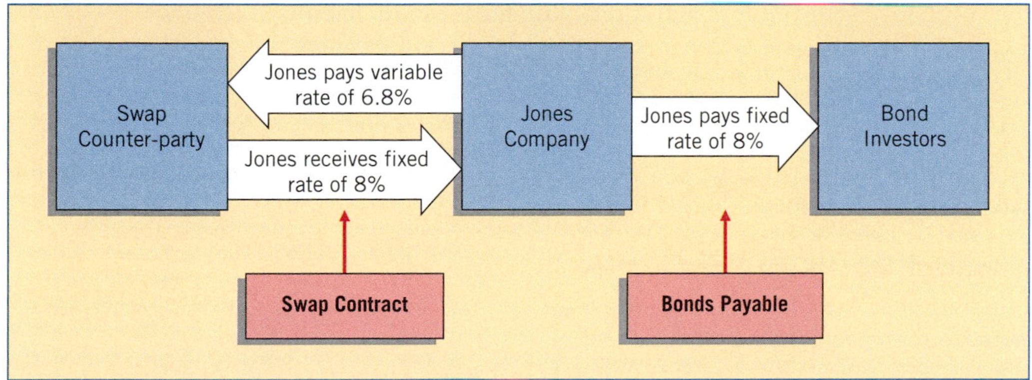

ILLUSTRATION 17A-5
Interest Rate Swap

The settlement dates for the swap correspond to the interest payment dates on the debt (December 31). On each interest payment (settlement) date, Jones and the counterparty will compute the difference between current market interest rates and the fixed rate of 8 percent and determine the value of the swap.[14] If interest rates decline, the value of the swap contract to Jones increases (Jones has a gain), while at the same time Jones's fixed-rate debt obligation increases (Jones has an economic loss). The swap is an effective risk-management tool in this setting. Its value is related to the same underlying (interest rates) that will affect the value of the fixed-rate bond payable. Thus, if the value of the swap goes up, it offsets the loss related to the debt obligation.

Assuming that the swap was entered into on January 2, 2003 (the same date as the issuance of the debt), the swap at this time has no value. Therefore no entry is necessary.

January 2, 2003

No entry required. Memorandum to indicate that the swap contract is signed.

At the end of 2003, the interest payment on the bonds is made. The journal entry to record this transaction is as follows.

December 31, 2003

Interest Expense	80,000	
Cash (8% × $1,000,000)		80,000

At the end of 2003, market interest rates have declined substantially. Therefore the value of the swap contract has increased. Recall (see Illustration 17A-5) that in the swap, Jones is to receive a fixed rate of 8 percent, or $80,000 ($1,000,000 × 8%), and pay a variable rate (which in this case is 6.8 percent), or $68,000. Jones therefore receives $12,000 ($80,000 − $68,000) as a settlement payment on the swap contract on the first interest payment date. The entry to record this transaction is as follows.

December 31, 2003

Cash	12,000	
Interest Expense		12,000

[14]The underlying for an interest rate swap is some index of market interest rates. The most commonly used index is the London Interbank Offer Rate, or LIBOR. In this example, we assumed the LIBOR is 6.8 percent.

In addition, a market appraisal indicates that the value of the interest rate swap has increased $40,000. This increase in value is recorded as follows.[15]

December 31, 2003		
Swap Contract	40,000	
Unrealized Holding Gain or Loss—Income		40,000

This swap contract is reported in the balance sheet, and the gain on the hedging transaction is reported in the income statement. Because interest rates have declined, the company records a loss and a related increase in its liability as follows.

December 31, 2003		
Unrealized Holding Gain or Loss—Income	40,000	
Bonds Payable		40,000

The loss on the hedging activity is reported in net income, and bonds payable in the balance sheet is adjusted to fair value.

Financial Statement Presentation

Illustration 17A-6 indicates how the asset and liability related to this hedging transaction are reported on the balance sheet.

ILLUSTRATION 17A-6
Balance Sheet Presentation of Fair Value Hedge

JONES COMPANY
BALANCE SHEET (PARTIAL)
DECEMBER 31, 2003

Current assets	
Swap contract	$40,000
Long-term liabilities	
Bonds payable	$1,040,000

The effect on the Jones Company balance sheet is the addition of the swap asset and an increase in the carrying value of the bonds payable. Illustration 17A-7 indicates how the effects of this swap transaction are reported in the income statement.

ILLUSTRATION 17A-7
Income Statement Presentation of Fair Value Hedge

JONES COMPANY
INCOME STATEMENT (PARTIAL)
FOR THE YEAR ENDED DECEMBER 31, 2003

Interest expense ($80,000 − $12,000)		$68,000
Other income		
Unrealized holding gain—swap contract	$40,000	
Unrealized holding loss—bonds payable	(40,000)	
Net gain (loss)		$-0-

On the income statement, interest expense of $68,000 is reported. Jones has effectively changed the debt's interest rate from fixed to variable. That is, by receiving a fixed rate and paying a variable rate on the swap, the fixed rate on the bond payable is converted to variable, which results in an effective interest rate of 6.8 percent in 2003.[16]

[15]Theoretically, this fair value change reflects the present value of expected future differences in variable and fixed interest rates.

[16]Similar accounting and measurement will be applied at future interest payment dates. Thus, if interest rates increase, Jones will continue to receive 8 percent on the swap (records a loss) but will also be locked into the fixed payments to the bondholders at an 8 percent rate (records a gain).

Also, the gain on the swap offsets the loss related to the debt obligation. Therefore the net gain or loss on the hedging activity is zero.

The overall impact of the swap transaction on the financial statements is shown in Illustration 17A-8.

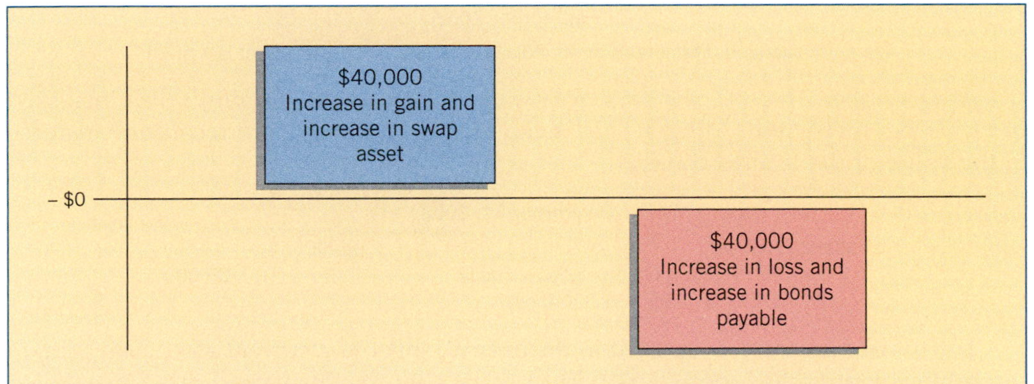

ILLUSTRATION 17A-8
Impact on Financial Statements of Fair Value Hedge

In summary, the accounting for fair value hedges (as illustrated in the Jones example) **records the derivative at its fair value in the balance sheet with any gains and losses recorded in income**. Thus, the gain on the swap offsets or hedges the loss on the bond payable, due to the decline in interest rates. By adjusting the hedged item (the bond payable in the Jones case) to fair value, with the gain or loss recorded in earnings, the accounting for the Jones bond payable deviates from amortized cost. This special accounting is justified in order to report accurately the nature of the hedging relationship between the swap and the bond payable in the balance sheet (both the swap and the debt obligation are recorded at fair value) and in the income statement (offsetting gains and losses are reported in the same period).

Cash Flow Hedge

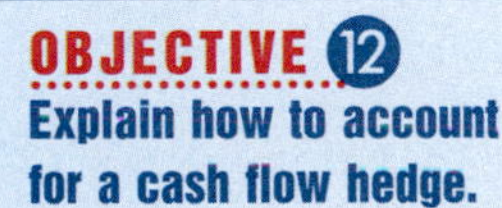

OBJECTIVE 12
Explain how to account for a cash flow hedge.

Cash flow hedges are used to hedge exposures to **cash flow risk**, which is exposure to the variability in cash flows. Special accounting is allowed for cash flow hedges. Generally, derivatives are measured and reported at fair value on the balance sheet, and gains and losses are reported directly in net income. However, derivatives used in cash flow hedges are accounted for at fair value on the balance sheet, but **gains or losses are recorded in equity, as part of other comprehensive income**.

To illustrate the accounting for cash flow hedges, assume that in September 2002 Allied Can Co. anticipates purchasing 1,000 metric tons of aluminum in January 2003. Allied is concerned that prices for aluminum will increase in the next few months, and it wants to protect against possible price increases for aluminum inventory. To hedge the risk that it might have to pay higher prices for inventory in January 2003, Allied enters into an aluminum futures contract.

INTERNATIONAL INSIGHT

Under IAS, unrealized holding gains or losses on cash flow hedges are recorded as adjustments to the value of the hedged item, not in other comprehensive income.

A **futures contract** gives the holder the right and the obligation to purchase an asset at a preset price for a specified period of time.[17] In this case, the aluminum futures contract gives Allied the right and the obligation to purchase 1,000 metric tons of aluminum for $1,550 per ton. This contract price is good until the contract expires in January 2003. The underlying for this derivative is the price of aluminum. If the price of aluminum

[17]A **futures contract** is a firm contractual agreement between a buyer and seller for a specified asset on a fixed date in the future. The contract also has a standard specification so both parties know exactly what is being traded. A **forward** is similar but is not traded on an exchange and does not have standardized conditions.

rises above \$1,550, the value of the futures contract to Allied increases, because Allied will be able to purchase the aluminum at the lower price of \$1,550 per ton.[18]

Assuming that the futures contract was entered into on September 1, 2002, and that the price to be paid today for inventory to be delivered in January—the **spot price**—was equal to the contract price, the futures contract has no value. Therefore no entry is necessary.

September 2002

No entry required. Memorandum to indicate that the futures contract is signed.

At December 31, 2002, the price for January delivery of aluminum has increased to \$1,575 per metric ton. Allied would make the following entry to record the increase in the value of the futures contract.

December 31, 2002

Futures Contract	25,000	
Unrealized Holding Gain or Loss—Equity ([\$1,575 − \$1,550] × 1,000 tons)		25,000

The futures contract is reported in the balance sheet as a current asset. The gain on the futures contract is reported as part of other comprehensive income. Since Allied has not yet purchased and sold the inventory, this is an **anticipated transaction**. In this type of transaction, gains or losses on the futures contract are accumulated in equity as part of other comprehensive income until the period in which the inventory is sold and earnings is affected.

In January 2003, Allied purchases 1,000 metric tons of aluminum for \$1,575 and makes the following entry.[19]

January 2003

Aluminum Inventory	1,575,000	
Cash (\$1,575 × 1,000 tons)		1,575,000

At the same time, Allied makes final settlement on the futures contract and makes the following entry.

January 2003

Cash	25,000	
Futures Contract (\$1,575,000 − \$1,550,000)		25,000

Through use of the futures contract derivative, Allied has been able to fix the cost of its inventory. The \$25,000 futures contract settlement offsets the amount paid to purchase the inventory at the prevailing market price of \$1,575,000. The result is that the net cash outflow is at \$1,550 per metric ton, as desired. In this way, Allied has hedged the cash flow for the purchase of inventory, as depicted in Illustration 17A-9.

ILLUSTRATION 17A-9
Effect of Hedge on Cash Flows

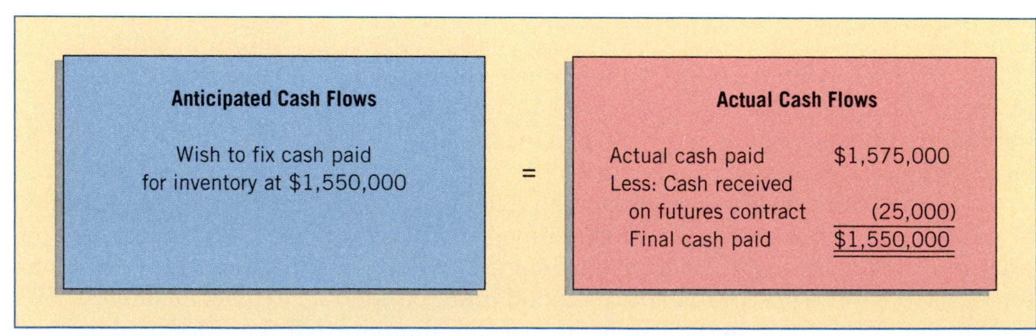

[18]As with the earlier call option example, the actual aluminum does not have to be exchanged. Rather, the parties to the futures contract settle by paying the cash difference between the futures price and the price of aluminum on each settlement date.

[19]In practice, futures contracts are settled on a daily basis; for our purposes we show only one settlement for the entire amount.

There are no income effects at this point. The gain on the futures contract is accumulated in equity as part of other comprehensive income until the period when the inventory is sold and earnings is affected through cost of goods sold.

For example, assume that the aluminum is processed into finished goods (cans). The total cost of the cans (including the aluminum purchases in January 2003) is $1,700,000. Allied sells the cans in July 2003 for $2,000,000. The entry to record this sale is as follows.

July 2003		
Cash	2,000,000	
Sales Revenue		2,000,000
Cost of Goods Sold	1,700,000	
Inventory (Cans)		1,700,000

Since the effect of the anticipated transaction has now affected earnings, Allied makes the following entry related to the hedging transaction.

July 2003		
Unrealized Holding Gain or Loss—Equity	25,000	
Cost of Goods Sold		25,000

The gain on the futures contract, which was reported as part of other comprehensive income, now reduces cost of goods sold. As a result, the cost of aluminum included in the overall cost of goods sold is $1,550,000. The futures contract has worked as planned to manage the cash paid for aluminum inventory and the amount of cost of goods sold.

OTHER REPORTING ISSUES

The preceding examples illustrate the basic reporting issues related to the accounting for derivatives. Additional issues of importance are as follows.

1. The accounting for embedded derivatives.
2. Qualifying hedge criteria.
3. Disclosures about financial instruments and derivatives.

OBJECTIVE 13
Identify special reporting issues related to derivative financial instruments that cause unique accounting problems.

Embedded Derivatives

As indicated at the beginning of this appendix, a major impetus for unifying and improving the accounting standards for derivatives was the rapid innovation in the development of complex financial instruments. In recent years, this innovation has led to the development of **hybrid securities**. These securities have characteristics of both debt and equity, and they often are a combination of traditional and derivative financial instruments. For example, a convertible bond (as discussed in Chapter 16) is a hybrid instrument because it is comprised of a debt security, referred to as the **host security**, combined with an option to convert the bond to shares of common stock, the **embedded derivative**.

To provide consistency in accounting for similar derivative instruments, embedded derivatives are required to be accounted for similarly to other derivative instruments. Therefore, a derivative that is embedded in a hybrid security should be **separated from the host security** and accounted for using the accounting for derivatives. This separation process is referred to as **bifurcation**.[20] Thus, an investor in a convertible bond is required to separate the stock option component of the instrument. He

[20]Such a derivative can also be designated as a hedging instrument, and the hedge accounting provisions outlined earlier in the chapter would be applied.

or she then accounts for the derivative (the stock option) at fair value and the host instrument (the debt) according to GAAP, as if there were no embedded derivative.[21]

Qualifying Hedge Criteria

INTERNATIONAL INSIGHT

IAS qualifying hedge criteria are similar to those used in *SFAS No. 133.*

The FASB identified certain criteria that hedging transactions must meet before the special accounting for hedges is required. These criteria are designed to ensure that hedge accounting is used in a consistent manner across different hedge transactions. The general criteria relate to the following areas.

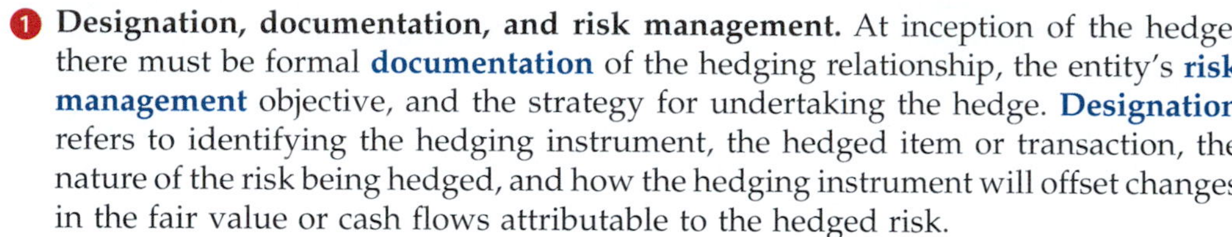

1. **Designation, documentation, and risk management.** At inception of the hedge, there must be formal **documentation** of the hedging relationship, the entity's **risk management** objective, and the strategy for undertaking the hedge. **Designation** refers to identifying the hedging instrument, the hedged item or transaction, the nature of the risk being hedged, and how the hedging instrument will offset changes in the fair value or cash flows attributable to the hedged risk.

   The FASB decided that designation and documentation are critical to the implementation of the special hedge accounting model. Without these requirements, there was concern that companies would try to apply the hedge accounting provisions retroactively only in response to negative changes in market conditions, in order to offset the negative impact of a transaction on the financial statements. Allowing special hedge accounting in such a setting could mask the speculative nature of the original transaction.

2. **Effectiveness of the hedging relationship.** At inception and on an ongoing basis, the hedging relationship is expected to be **highly effective** in achieving offsetting changes in fair value or cash flows. Assessment of effectiveness is required whenever financial statements are prepared. The general guideline for effectiveness is that the fair values or cash flows of the hedging instrument (the derivative) and the hedged item exhibit a high degree of correlation. In practice, high effectiveness is assumed when the correlation is close to one (for example, within plus or minus .10). In our earlier hedging examples (interest rate swap and the futures contract on aluminum inventory), the fair values and cash flows were exactly correlated. That is, when the cash payment for the inventory purchase increased, it was offset dollar for dollar by the cash received on the futures contract.

   If the effectiveness criterion is not met, either at inception or because of changes following inception of the hedging relationship, special hedge accounting is no longer allowed, and the derivative should be accounted for as a free-standing derivative.[22]

3. **Effect on reported earnings of changes in fair values or cash flows.** A change in the fair value of a hedged item or variation in the cash flow of a hedged forecasted transaction must have the potential to change the amount recognized in reported earnings. There is no need for special hedge accounting if both the hedging instrument and the hedged item are accounted for at fair value under existing GAAP. In this case, the offsetting gains and losses will be properly reflected in earnings. For example, special accounting is not needed for a fair value hedge of a trading security, because both the investment and the derivative are accounted for at fair value on the balance sheet with gains or losses reported in earnings. Thus, "spe-

[21]The **issuer** of the convertible bonds would not bifurcate the option component of the convertible bonds payable. *SFAS No. 133* explicitly precludes embedded derivative accounting for an embedded derivative that is indexed to an entity's own common stock. If the conversion feature was tied to **another company**'s stock, this derivative would be bifurcated.

[22]The accounting for the part of a derivative that is not effective in a hedge is at fair value with gains and losses recorded in income.

cial" hedge accounting is necessary only when there is a mismatch of the accounting effects for the hedging instrument and the hedged item under GAAP.[23]

Disclosure Provisions

OBJECTIVE 14
Describe the disclosure requirements for traditional and derivative financial instruments.

Because *SFAS No. 133* provides comprehensive accounting guidance for derivatives, this standard replaces the disclosure provisions in *SFAS No. 105* and *SFAS No. 119* and amends the disclosure rules in *SFAS No. 107*.[24] Thus, *SFAS No. 107* provides general guidance for traditional financial instrument disclosures, and *SFAS No. 133* addresses the disclosures for derivative financial instruments.

As a consequence of these two pronouncements, the primary requirements for disclosures related to financial instruments are as follows.

1. A company should disclose the fair value and related carrying value of its financial instruments in the body of the financial statements, in a note, or in a summary table form that makes it clear whether the amounts represent assets or liabilities.
2. The fair value disclosures should distinguish between financial instruments held or issued for purposes other than trading. For derivative financial instruments, the firm should disclose its objectives for holding or issuing those instruments (speculation or hedging), the hedging context (fair value or cash flow), and its strategies for achieving risk management objectives.
3. In disclosing fair values of financial instruments, a company should not combine, aggregate, or net the fair value of separate financial instruments, even if those instruments are considered to be related.
4. A company should display as a separate classification of other comprehensive income the net gain or loss on derivative instruments designated in cash flow hedges.
5. Companies are encouraged, but not required, to provide quantitative information about market risks of derivative financial instruments, and also of its other assets and liabilities. Such information should be consistent with the way the company manages and adjusts risks, and it should be useful for comparing the results of its use of derivative financial instruments.

While these additional disclosures of fair value provide useful information to financial statement users, they are generally provided as supplemental information only. The balance sheet continues to rely primarily on historical cost. Exceptions to this general rule are the fair value requirements for certain investment securities and derivative financial instruments, as illustrated earlier. Illustration 17A-10 (on page 876) provides a fair value disclosure for **The Gillette Company**.

UNDERLYING CONCEPTS
Providing supplemental information on the fair values of financial instruments illustrates application of the full disclosure principle.

The fair values of cash and cash equivalents, short-term investments, and short-term debt approximate cost because of the immediate and short-term maturities of these financial instruments. The fair value of long-term investments (and some derivatives) is based on quoted market prices at the reporting date. The fair value of long-term debt and some derivatives is based on market prices for similar instruments or by discounting expected cash flows at rates currently available to the company for instruments with similar risks and maturities.

---

[23] An important criterion specific to cash flow hedges is that the forecasted transaction in a cash flow hedge "is likely to occur." This probability (defined as significantly greater than the term "more likely than not") should be supported by observable facts such as frequency of similar past transactions and the firm's financial and operational ability to carry out the transaction.

[24] *SFAS No. 105* refers to "Disclosure of Information about Financial Instruments with Off-Balance Sheet Risk and Financial Instruments with Concentrations of Credit Risk," *Statement of Financial Accounting Standards No. 105* (Stamford, Conn.: FASB, 1990). *SFAS No. 119* refers to "Disclosure about Derivative Financial Instruments and Fair Value of Financial Instruments," *Statement of Financial Accounting Standards No. 119* (Stamford, Conn.: FASB, 1994).

ILLUSTRATION 17A-10 The Gillette Company Fair Value Disclosure

The Gillette Company

Notes to the Financial Statements

Financial Instruments. The estimated fair values of the Company's financial instruments are summarized below.

(in millions)	December 31, 2000 Carrying Amount	December 31, 2000 Fair Value	December 31, 1999 Carrying Amount	December 31, 1999 Fair Value
Long-term investments	$ 186	$ 187	$ 188	$ 188
Long-term debt	(2,281)	(2,308)	(3,289)	(3,186)
Derivative instruments				
Debt-related contracts	(28)	(19)	140	93
Other currency forwards				
Purchase contracts	23	27	—	—
Sell contracts	(1)	(5)	—	—
Currency options	—	—	1	1
Equity contracts	7	7	1	1
Commodity contracts	—	(2)	—	5

If a company is unable to arrive at an estimate of fair value, it must disclose information relevant to the estimate of fair value (such as the terms of the instrument) and the reason why it is unable to arrive at an estimate of fair value.[25]

Summary of *SFAS No. 133*

Illustration 17A-11 provides a summary of the accounting provisions for derivatives and hedging transactions.

ILLUSTRATION 17A-11 Summary of Derivative Accounting Under *SFAS 133*

Derivative Use	Accounting for Derivative	Accounting for Hedged Item	Common Example
Speculation	At fair value with unrealized holding gains and losses recorded in income.	Not applicable	Call or put option on an equity security.
Hedging			
Fair value	At fair value with holding gains and losses recorded in income.	At fair value with gains and losses recorded in income.	Interest rate swap hedge of a fixed-rate debt obligation.
Cash flow	At fair value with unrealized holding gains and losses from the hedge recorded in other comprehensive income, and reclassified in income when the hedged transaction's cash flows affect earnings.	Use other generally accepted accounting principles for the hedged item.	Use of a futures contract to hedge a forecasted purchase of inventory.

[25]*SFAS No. 107* lists a number of exceptions to this requirement; most of these exceptions are covered in other standards. The exception list includes such items as: pension and post-retirement benefits; employee stock options; insurance contracts; lease contracts; warranties, rights, and obligations; purchase obligations; equity method investments; minority interests; and instruments classified as stockholders' equity in the entity's balance sheet.

As indicated, the general accounting for derivatives is based on fair values. *SFAS No. 133* also establishes **special accounting guidance** when derivatives are used **for hedging purposes**. For example, when an interest rate swap was used to hedge the bonds payable in a fair value hedge (see Jones Co. earlier), unrealized losses on the bonds payable were recorded in earnings, which is not GAAP for bonds issued without such a hedge. This special accounting is justified in order to accurately report the nature of the hedging relationship in the balance sheet (both the swap and the liability are recorded at fair value) and in the income statement (offsetting gains and losses are reported in the same period).

Special accounting also is used for cash flow hedges. Derivatives used in qualifying cash flow hedges are accounted for at fair value on the balance sheet, but unrealized holding gains or losses are recorded in other comprehensive income until the hedged item is sold or settled. In a cash flow hedge, the hedged item continues to be recorded at its historical cost.

COMPREHENSIVE HEDGE ACCOUNTING EXAMPLE

To demonstrate a comprehensive example of the hedge accounting provisions, using a fair value hedge, let's assume that on April 1, 2002, Hayward Co. purchased 100 shares of Sonoma stock at a market price of $100 per share. Hayward does not intend to actively trade this investment and consequently classifies the Sonoma investment as available-for-sale. Hayward makes the following entry to record this available-for-sale investment.

April 1, 2002		
Available-for-Sale Securities	10,000	
Cash		10,000

Available-for-sale securities are recorded at fair value on the balance sheet, and unrealized gains and losses are reported in equity as part of other comprehensive income.[26] Fortunately for Hayward, the value of the Sonoma shares increases to $125 per share during 2002. Hayward makes the following entry to record the gain on this investment.

December 31, 2002		
Security Fair Value Adjustment (Available-for-Sale)	2,500	
Unrealized Holding Gain or Loss—Equity		2,500

Illustration 17A-12 indicates how the Sonoma investment is reported in Hayward's balance sheet.

ILLUSTRATION 17A-12
Balance Sheet Presentation of Available-for-Sale Securities

HAYWARD CO. BALANCE SHEET (PARTIAL) DECEMBER 31, 2002	
Assets	
Available-for-sale securities (at fair value)	$12,500
Stockholders' Equity	
Accumulated other comprehensive income	
Unrealized holding gain	$2,500

While Hayward has benefited from an increase in the price of Sonoma shares, it is exposed to the risk that the price of the Sonoma stock will decline. To hedge this risk, Hayward locks in its gain on the Sonoma investment by purchasing a put option on 100 shares of Sonoma stock.

[26]The distinction between trading and available-for-sale investments is discussed earlier in the chapter.

Hayward enters into the put option contract on January 2, 2003, and designates the option as a fair value hedge of the Sonoma investment. This put option (which expires in 2 years) gives Hayward the option to sell Sonoma shares at a price of $125. Since the exercise price is equal to the current market price, no entry is necessary at inception of the put option.[27]

January 2, 2003

No entry required. Memorandum to indicate that put option contract is signed and is designated as a fair value hedge for the Sonoma investment.

At December 31, 2003, the price of the Sonoma shares has declined to $120 per share. Hayward records the following entry for the Sonoma investment.

December 31, 2003

Unrealized Holding Gain or Loss—Income	500	
Security Fair Value Adjustment (Available-for-Sale)		500

Note that upon designation of the hedge, the accounting for the available-for-sale security changes from regular GAAP in that the unrealized holding loss is recorded in income, not in equity. If Hayward had not followed this accounting, a mismatch of gains and losses in the income statement would result. Thus, special accounting for the hedge item (in this case, an available-for-sale security) is necessary in a fair value hedge.

The following journal entry records the increase in value of the put option on Sonoma shares.

December 31, 2003

Put Option	500	
Unrealized Holding Gain or Loss—Income		500

The decline in the price of Sonoma shares results in an increase in the fair value of the put option. That is, Hayward could realize a gain on the put option by purchasing 100 shares in the open market for $120 and then exercise the put option, selling the shares for $125. This results in a gain to Hayward of $500 (100 shares × [$125 − $120]).[28]

Illustration 17A-13 indicates how the amounts related to the Sonoma investment and the put option are reported.

ILLUSTRATION 17A-13
Balance Sheet Presentation of Fair Value Hedge

HAYWARD CO.
BALANCE SHEET (PARTIAL)
DECEMBER 31, 2003

Assets	
Available-for-sale securities (at fair value)	$12,000
Put option	500

The increase in fair value on the option offsets or hedges the decline in value on Hayward's available-for-sale security. By using fair value accounting for both financial instruments, the financial statements reflect the underlying substance of Hayward's net exposure to the risks of holding Sonoma stock. By using fair value accounting for both these financial instruments, the balance sheet reports the amount that Hayward would receive on the investment and the put option contract if they were sold and settled respectively.

[27]To simplify the example, we assume no premium is paid for the option.

[28]In practice, Hayward generally does not have to actually buy and sell the Sonoma shares to realize this gain. Rather, unless the counterparty wants to hold Hayward shares, the contract can be "closed out" by having the counterparty pay Hayward $500 in cash. This is an example of the net settlement feature of derivatives.

Illustration 17A-14 illustrates the reporting of the effects of the hedging transaction on income for the year ended December 31, 2003.

ILLUSTRATION 17A-14
Income Statement Presentation of Fair Value Hedge

HAYWARD CO. INCOME STATEMENT (PARTIAL) FOR THE YEAR ENDED DECEMBER 31, 2003	
Other Income	
Unrealized holding gain—put option	$ 500
Unrealized holding loss—available-for-sale securities	(500)

The income statement indicates that the gain on the put option offsets the loss on the available-for-sale securities.[29] The reporting for these financial instruments, even when they reflect a hedging relationship, illustrates why the FASB argued that fair value accounting provides the most relevant information about financial instruments, including derivatives.

CONTROVERSY AND CONCLUDING REMARKS

SFAS No. 133 represents the FASB's effort to develop accounting guidance for derivatives. Many believe that these new rules are needed to properly measure and report derivatives in financial statements. Others argue that reporting derivatives at fair value results in unrealized gains and losses that are difficult to interpret. Concerns also were raised about the complexity and cost of implementing the standard, since prior to *SFAS No. 133*, many derivatives were not recognized in financial statements.

The FASB, as part of its due process, worked to respond to these concerns. From the beginning of the project in 1992, the FASB held over 100 meetings and received comments from over 400 constitutents or constituent groups. In response to these comments, the FASB revised the original proposal to make the provisions easier to apply. The FASB also delayed the effective date for *SFAS No. 133*, to give preparers more time to understand the standard and to develop the information systems necessary to implement the standard. More than 120 companies requested the delay, arguing that the rule could complicate companies' efforts to deal with the year 2000 (Y2K) problem.[30]

The authors believe that the long-term benefits of this standard will far outweigh any short-term implementation costs. As the volume and complexity of derivatives and hedging transactions continue to grow, the risk that investors and creditors will be exposed to unexpected losses arising from derivative transactions also increases. Without this standard, statement readers do not have comprehensive information in financial statements concerning many derivative financial instruments and the effects of hedging transactions using derivatives.

[29]Note that the fair value changes in the option contract will not offset **increases** in the value of the Hayward investment. Should the price of Sonoma stock increase above $125 per share, Hayward would have no incentive to exercise the put option.

[30]Interestingly, some companies adopted the standard early because the rules provide better accounting for some derivatives relative to the rules in place before *SFAS No. 133*. Paula Froelich, "U.S. Companies Find New Accounting Rule Costly, Inefficient," Dow Jones News Service (March 2, 1999). In June 2000, the FASB issued guidance to ease implementation of the provisions of *SFAS No. 133*: "Accounting for Certain Derivative Hedging Instruments and Certain Hedging Activities—An Amendment to FASB Statement No. 133," *Statement of Financial Accounting Standards No. 138* (Stamford, Conn.: FASB, 2000).

KEY TERMS

anticipated transaction, *872*
bifurcation, *873*
call option, *864*
cash flow hedge, *871*
counterparty, *864(n)*
derivative financial instrument, derivative, *861*
designation, *874*
documentation, *874*
embedded derivative, *873*
fair value, *863*
fair value hedge, *868*
futures contract, *871*
hedging, *867*
highly effective, *874*
host security, *873*
hybrid security, *873*
interest rate swap, *868*
intrinsic value, *864*
net settlement, *865(n)*
notional amount, *864*
option premium, *864*
put option, *864(n)*
risk management, *874*
security, *836(n)*
spot price, *872*
strike (exercise) price, *864*
swap, *868*
time value, *865*
underlying, *866*

SUMMARY OF LEARNING OBJECTIVES FOR APPENDIX 17A

8 **Explain who uses derivatives and why.** Any company or individual that wants to ensure against different types of business risks may use derivative contracts to achieve this objective. In general, these transactions involve some type of hedge. Speculators also use derivatives, attempting to find an enhanced return. Speculators are very important to the derivatives market because they keep it liquid on a daily basis. Arbitrageurs attempt to exploit inefficiencies in various derivative markets. Derivatives are used primarily for purposes of hedging a company's exposure to fluctuations in interest rates, foreign currency exchange rates, and commodity prices.

9 **Understand the basic guidelines for accounting for derivatives.** Derivatives should be recognized in the financial statements as assets and liabilities and reported at fair value. Gains and losses resulting from speculation should be recognized immediately in income. Gains and losses resulting from hedge transactions are reported in different ways, depending upon the type of hedge.

10 **Describe the accounting for derivative financial instruments.** Derivative financial instruments are reported in the balance sheet and recorded at fair value. Except for derivatives used in hedging, realized and unrealized gains and losses on derivative financial instruments are recorded in income.

11 **Explain how to account for a fair value hedge.** The derivative used in a qualifying fair value hedge is recorded at its fair value in the balance sheet, with any gains and losses recorded in income. In addition, the item being hedged with the derivative is also accounted for at fair value. By adjusting the hedged item to fair value, with the gain or loss recorded in earnings, the accounting for the hedged item may deviate from GAAP in the absence of a hedge relationship. This special accounting is justified in order to report accurately the nature of the hedging relationship between the derivative hedging instruments and the hedged item. Both are reported in the balance sheet at fair value, with offsetting gains and losses reported in income in the same period.

12 **Explain how to account for a cash flow hedge.** Derivatives used in qualifying cash flow hedges are accounted for at fair value on the balance sheet, but gains or losses are recorded in equity as part of other comprehensive income. These gains or losses are accumulated and reclassified in income when the hedged transaction's cash flows affect earnings. Accounting is according to GAAP for the hedged item.

13 **Identify special reporting issues related to derivative financial instruments that cause unique accounting problems.** A derivative that is embedded in a hybrid security should be separated from the host security and accounted for using the accounting for derivatives. This separation process is referred to as bifurcation. Special hedge accounting is allowed only for hedging relationships that meet certain criteria. The main criteria are: (1) There is formal documentation of the hedging relationship, the entity's risk management objective, the strategy for undertaking the hedge, and that the derivative is designated as either a cash flow or fair value hedge. (2) The hedging relationship is expected to be highly effective in achieving offsetting changes in fair value or cash flows. (3) "Special" hedge accounting is necessary only when there is a mismatch of the accounting effects for the hedging instrument and the hedged item under GAAP.

14 **Describe the disclosure requirements for traditional and derivative financial instruments.** Companies must disclose the fair value and related carrying value of its financial instruments, and these disclosures should distinguish between amounts that represent assets or liabilities. The disclosures should distinguish between financial instruments held or issued for purposes other than trading. For derivative financial instruments, the firm should disclose whether the instruments are used for speculation

or hedging. In disclosing fair values of financial instruments, a company should not combine, aggregate, or net the fair value of separate financial instruments, even if those instruments are considered to be related. A company should display as a separate classification of other comprehensive income the net gain or loss on derivative instruments designated in cash flow hedges. Companies are encouraged, but not required, to provide quantitative information about market risks of derivative financial instruments.

Note: All **asterisked** Questions, Exercises, and Problems relate to material contained in the appendix to the chapter.

QUESTIONS

1. Distinguish between a debt security and an equity security.

2. What purpose does the variety in bond features (types and characteristics) serve?

3. What is the cost of a long-term investment in bonds?

4. Identify and explain the three types of classifications for investments in debt securities.

5. When should a debt security be classified as held-to-maturity?

6. Explain how trading securities are accounted for and reported.

7. At what amount should trading, available-for-sale, and held-to-maturity securities be reported on the balance sheet?

8. On July 1, 2004, Ingalls Company purchased $2,000,000 of Wilder Company's 8% bonds, due on July 1, 2011. The bonds, which pay interest semiannually on January 1 and July 1, were purchased for $1,750,000 to yield 10%. Determine the amount of interest revenue Ingalls should report on its income statement for year ended December 31, 2004.

9. If the bonds in question 8 are classified as available-for-sale and they have a fair value at December 31, 2004, of $1,802,000, prepare the journal entry (if any) at December 31, 2004, to record this transaction.

10. Indicate how unrealized holding gains and losses should be reported for investment securities classified as trading, available-for-sale, and held-to-maturity.

11. (a) Assuming no Securities Fair Value Adjustment (Available-for-Sale) account balance at the beginning of the year, prepare the adjusting entry at the end of the year if Laura Company has an unrealized holding loss of $70,000 on its available-for-sale securities. (b) Assume the same information as part (a), except that Laura Company has a debit balance in its Securities Fair Value Adjustment (Available-for-Sale) account of $10,000 at the beginning of the year. Prepare the adjusting entry at year-end.

12. How is the premium or discount handled relative to a trading debt security?

13. On what basis should stock acquired or exchanged for noncash consideration be recorded?

14. Identify and explain the different types of classifications for investment in equity securities.

15. Why are held-to-maturity investments applicable only to debt securities?

16. Emily Company sold 10,000 shares of Dickinson Co. common stock for $27.50 per share, incurring $1,770 in brokerage commissions. These securities were classified as trading and originally cost $250,000. Prepare the entry to record the sale of these securities.

17. Distinguish between the accounting treatment for available-for-sale equity securities and trading equity securities.

18. What constitutes "significant influence" when an investor's financial interest is below the 50% level?

19. Explain how the investment account is affected by investee activities under the equity method.

20. When the equity method is applied, what disclosures should be made in the investor's financial statements?

21. Molly Pitcher Co. uses the equity method to account for investments in common stock. What accounting should be made for dividends received in excess of Pitcher's share of investee's earnings subsequent to the date of investment?

22. Elizabeth Corp. has an investment carrying value (equity method) on its books of $170,000 representing a 40% interest in Dole Company, which suffered a $620,000 loss this year. How should Elizabeth Corp. handle its proportionate share of Dole's loss?

23. Where on the asset side of the balance sheet are trading securities, available-for-sale securities, and held-to-maturity securities reported? Explain.

24. Explain why reclassification adjustments are necessary.

25. Briefly discuss how a transfer of securities from the available-for-sale category to the trading category affects stockholders' equity and income.

26. When is a debt security considered impaired? Explain how to account for the impairment of an available-for-sale debt security.

***27.** What is meant by the term underlying as it relates to derivative financial instruments?

***28.** What are the main distinctions between a traditional financial instrument and a derivative financial instrument?

***29.** What is the purpose of a fair value hedge?

***30.** In what situation will bonds payable carrying amounts not be reported at cost or amortized cost?

***31.** Why might a company become involved in an interest rate swap contract to receive fixed interest payments and pay variable?

***32.** What is the purpose of a cash flow hedge?

***33.** Where are gains and losses related to cash flow hedges involving anticipated transactions reported?

***34.** What are hybrid securities? Give an example of a hybrid security.

BRIEF EXERCISES

BE17-1 Moonwalker Company purchased, as a held-to-maturity investment, $50,000 of the 9%, 5-year bonds of Prime Time Corporation for $46,304, which provides an 11% return. Prepare Moonwalker's journal entries for (a) the purchase of the investment, and (b) the receipt of annual interest and discount amortization. Assume effective interest amortization is used.

BE17-2 Use the information from BE17-1, but assume the bonds are purchased as an available-for-sale security. Prepare Moonwalker's journal entries for (a) the purchase of the investment, (b) the receipt of annual interest and discount amortization, and (c) the year-end fair value adjustment. The bonds have a year-end fair value of $47,200.

BE17-3 Mask Corporation purchased, as a held-to-maturity investment, $40,000 of the 8%, 5-year bonds of Phantasy Star, Inc. for $43,412, which provides a 6% return. The bonds pay interest semiannually. Prepare Masks' journal entries for (a) the purchase of the investment, and (b) the receipt of semiannual interest and premium amortization. Assume effective-interest amortization is used.

BE17-4 Pete Sampras Corporation purchased for $22,500 as a trading investment bonds with a face value of $20,000. At December 31, Sampras received annual interest of $2,000, and the fair value of the bonds was $20,900. Prepare Sampras' journal entries for (a) the purchase of the investment, (b) the interest received, and (c) the fair value adjustment.

BE17-5 Pacman Corporation purchased 300 shares of Galaga Inc. common stock as an available-for-sale investment for $9,900. During the year, Galaga paid a cash dividend of $3.25 per share. At year-end, Galaga stock was selling for $34.50 per share. Prepare Pacman's journal entries to record (a) the purchase of the investment, (b) the dividends received, and (c) the fair value adjustment.

BE17-6 Use the information from BE17-5 but assume the stock was purchased as a trading security. Prepare Pacman's journal entries to record (a) the purchase of the investment, (b) the dividends received, and (c) the fair value adjustment.

BE17-7 Penn Corporation purchased for $300,000 a 25% interest in Teller, Inc. This investment enables Penn to exert significant influence over Teller. During the year Teller earned net income of $180,000 and paid dividends of $60,000. Prepare Penn's journal entries related to this investment.

BE17-8 Swartentruber Company has a stock portfolio valued at $4,000. Its cost was $3,500. If the Securities Fair Value Adjustment (Available-for-Sale) has a debit balance of $200, prepare the journal entry at year-end.

BE17-9 The following information relates to Cargill Co. for 2003: net income $800,000; unrealized holding gain of $20,000 related to available-for-sale securities during the year; accumulated other comprehensive income of $60,000 on January 1, 2003. Determine (a) other comprehensive income for 2003, (b) comprehensive income for 2003, and (c) accumulated other comprehensive income at December 31, 2003.

EXERCISES

E17-1 (Investment Classifications) For the following investments identify whether they are:

1. Trading Securities
2. Available-for-Sale Securities
3. Held-to-Maturity Securities

Each case is independent of the other.

(a) A bond that will mature in 4 years was bought 1 month ago when the price dropped. As soon as the value increases, which is expected next month, it will be sold.
(b) 10% of the outstanding stock of Farm-Co was purchased. The company is planning on eventually getting a total of 30% of its outstanding stock.
(c) 10-year bonds were purchased this year. The bonds mature at the first of next year.
(d) Bonds that will mature in 5 years are purchased. The company would like to hold them until they mature, but money has been tight recently and they may need to be sold.
(e) Preferred stock was purchased for its constant dividend. The company is planning to hold the preferred stock for a long time.
(f) A bond that matures in 10 years was purchased. The company is investing money set aside for an expansion project planned 10 years from now.

E17-2 (Entries for Held-to-Maturity Securities) On January 1, 2003, Dagwood Company purchased at par 12% bonds having a maturity value of $300,000. They are dated January 1, 2003, and mature January 1, 2008, with interest receivable December 31 of each year. The bonds are classified in the held-to-maturity category.

Instructions

(a) Prepare the journal entry at the date of the bond purchase.
(b) Prepare the journal entry to record the interest received for 2003.
(c) Prepare the journal entry to record the interest received for 2004.

E17-3 (Entries for Held-to-Maturity Securities) On January 1, 2003, Hi and Lois Company purchased 12% bonds, having a maturity value of $300,000, for $322,744.44. The bonds provide the bondholders with a 10% yield. They are dated January 1, 2003, and mature January 1, 2008, with interest receivable December 31 of each year. Hi and Lois Company uses the effective-interest method to allocate unamortized discount or premium. The bonds are classified in the held-to-maturity category.

Instructions

(a) Prepare the journal entry at the date of the bond purchase.
(b) Prepare a bond amortization schedule.
(c) Prepare the journal entry to record the interest received and the amortization for 2003.
(d) Prepare the journal entry to record the interest received and the amortization for 2004.

E17-4 (Entries for Available-for-Sale Securities) Assume the same information as in E17-3 except that the securities are classified as available-for-sale. The fair value of the bonds at December 31 of each year-end is as follows.

2003	$320,500	2006	$310,000
2004	$309,000	2007	$300,000
2005	$308,000		

Instructions

(a) Prepare the journal entry at the date of the bond purchase.
(b) Prepare the journal entries to record the interest received and recognition of fair value for 2003.
(c) Prepare the journal entry to record the recognition of fair value for 2004.

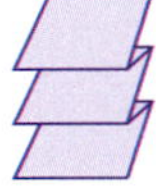

E17-5 (Effective-Interest versus Straight-Line Bond Amortization) On January 1, 2003, Phantom Company acquires $200,000 of Spiderman Products, Inc., 9% bonds at a price of $185,589. The interest is payable each December 31, and the bonds mature December 31, 2005. The investment will provide Phantom Company a 12% yield. The bonds are classified as held-to-maturity.

Instructions

(a) Prepare a 3-year schedule of interest revenue and bond discount amortization, applying the straight-line method.
(b) Prepare a 3-year schedule of interest revenue and bond discount amortization, applying the effective-interest method.
(c) Prepare the journal entry for the interest receipt of December 31, 2004, and the discount amortization under the straight-line method.
(d) Prepare the journal entry for the interest receipt of December 31, 2004, and the discount amortization under the effective-interest method.

E17-6 (Entries for Available-for-Sale and Trading Securities) The information on the following page is available for Barkley Company at December 31, 2003, regarding its investments.

Securities	Cost	Fair Value
3,000 shares of Myers Corporation Common Stock	$40,000	$48,000
1,000 shares of Cole Incorporated Preferred Stock	25,000	22,000
	$65,000	$70,000

Instructions

(a) Prepare the adjusting entry (if any) for 2003, assuming the securities are classified as trading.
(b) Prepare the adjusting entry (if any) for 2003, assuming the securities are classified as available-for-sale.
(c) Discuss how the amounts reported in the financial statements are affected by the entries in (a) and (b).

E17-7 (Trading Securities Entries) On December 21, 2003, Tiger Company provided you with the following information regarding its trading securities.

December 31, 2003

Investments (Trading)	Cost	Fair Value	Unrealized Gain (Loss)
Clemson Corp. stock	$20,000	$19,000	$(1,000)
Colorado Co. stock	10,000	9,000	(1,000)
Buffaloes Co. stock	20,000	20,600	600
Total of portfolio	$50,000	$48,600	(1,400)
Previous securities fair value adjustment balance			–0–
Securities fair value adjustment—Cr.			$(1,400)

During 2004, Colorado Company stock was sold for $9,400. The fair value of the stock on December 31, 2004, was: Clemson Corp. stock—$19,100; Buffaloes Co. stock—$20,500.

Instructions

(a) Prepare the adjusting journal entry needed on December 31, 2003.
(b) Prepare the journal entry to record the sale of the Colorado Company stock during 2004.
(c) Prepare the adjusting journal entry needed on December 31, 2004.

E17-8 (Available-for-Sale Securities Entries and Reporting) Rams Corporation purchases equity securities costing $73,000 and classifies them as available-for-sale securities. At December 31, the fair value of the portfolio is $65,000.

Instructions

Prepare the adjusting entry to report the securities properly. Indicate the statement presentation of the accounts in your entry.

E17-9 (Available-for-Sale Securities Entries and Financial Statement Presentation) At December 31, 2003, the available-for-sale equity portfolio for Steffi Graf, Inc. is as follows.

Security	Cost	Fair Value	Unrealized Gain (Loss)
A	$17,500	$15,000	($2,500)
B	12,500	14,000	1,500
C	23,000	25,500	2,500
Total	$53,000	$54,500	1,500
Previous securities fair value adjustment balance—Dr.			400
Securities fair value adjustment—Dr.			$1,100

On January 20, 2004, Steffi Graf, Inc. sold security A for $15,100. The sale proceeds are net of brokerage fees.

Instructions

(a) Prepare the adjusting entry at December 31, 2003, to report the portfolio at fair value.
(b) Show the balance sheet presentation of the investment related accounts at December 31, 2003. (Ignore notes presentation.)
(c) Prepare the journal entry for the 2004 sale of security A.

E17-10 (Comprehensive Income Disclosure) Assume the same information as E17-9 and that Steffi Graf Inc. reports net income in 2003 of $120,000 and in 2004 of $140,000. Total unrealized holding gains (including any realized holding gain or loss) arising during 2004 totals $40,000.

Instructions

(a) Prepare a statement of comprehensive income for 2003 starting with net income.
(b) Prepare a statement of comprehensive income for 2004 starting with net income.

E17-11 (Equity Securities Entries) Arantxa Corporation made the following cash purchases of securities during 2003, which is the first year in which Arantxa invested in securities.

1. On January 15, purchased 10,000 shares of Sanchez Company's common stock at $33.50 per share plus commission $1,980.
2. On April 1, purchased 5,000 shares of Vicario Co.'s common stock at $52.00 per share plus commission $3,370.
3. On September 10, purchased 7,000 shares of WTA Co.'s preferred stock at $26.50 per share plus commission $4,910.

On May 20, 2003, Arantxa sold 4,000 shares of Sanchez Company's common stock at a market price of $35 per share less brokerage commissions, taxes, and fees of $3,850. The year-end fair values per share were: Sanchez $30, Vicario $55, and WTA $28. In addition, the chief accountant of Arantxa told you that Arantxa Corporation holds these securities with the intention of selling them in order to earn profits from appreciation in prices.

Instructions

(a) Prepare the journal entries to record the above three security purchases.
(b) Prepare the journal entry for the security sale on May 20.
(c) Compute the unrealized gains or losses and prepare the adjusting entries for Arantxa on December 31, 2003.

E17-12 (Journal Entries for Fair Value and Equity Methods) Presented below are two independent situations.

Situation 1

Conchita Cosmetics acquired 10% of the 200,000 shares of common stock of Martinez Fashion at a total cost of $13 per share on March 18, 2003. On June 30, Martinez declared and paid a $75,000 cash dividend. On December 31, Martinez reported net income of $122,000 for the year. At December 31, the market price of Martinez Fashion was $15 per share. The securities are classified as available-for-sale.

Situation 2

Monica, Inc. obtained significant influence over Seles Corporation by buying 30% of Seles's 30,000 outstanding shares of common stock at a total cost of $9 per share on January 1, 2003. On June 15, Seles declared and paid a cash dividend of $36,000. On December 31, Seles reported a net income of $85,000 for the year.

Instructions

Prepare all necessary journal entries in 2003 for both situations.

E17-13 (Equity Method) Parent Co. invested $1,000,000 in Sub Co. for 25% of its outstanding stock. At the time of the purchase, Sub Co. had a book value of $3,200,000. Sub Co. pays out 40% of net income in dividends each year.

Instructions

Use the information in the following T-account for the investment in Sub to answer the following questions.

Investment in Sub Co.	
1,000,000	
110,000	
	44,000

(a) How much was Parent Co.'s share of Sub Co.'s net income for the year?
(b) How much was Parent Co.'s share of Sub Co.'s dividends for the year?
(c) What was Sub Co.'s total net income for the year?
(d) What was Sub Co.'s total dividends for the year?

E17-14 (Equity Investment—Trading) Oregon Co. had purchased 200 shares of Washington Co. for $40 each this year and classified the investment as a trading security. Oregon Co. sold 100 shares of the stock for $45 each. At year end the price per share of the Washington Co. had dropped to $35.

Instructions

Prepare the journal entries for these transactions.

E17-15 (Securities Entries—Buy and Sell) Buddy Lazier Company has the following securities in its trading portfolio of securities on December 31, 2003.

Investments (Trading)	Cost	Fair Value
1,500 shares of Davy Jones, Inc., Common	$ 73,500	$ 69,000
5,000 shares of Richie Hearn Corp., Common	180,000	175,000
400 shares of Alessandro Zampedri, Inc., Preferred	60,000	61,600
	$313,500	$305,600

All of the securities were purchased in 2003.
In 2004, Lazier completed the following securities transactions.

March 1 Sold the 1,500 shares of Davy Jones, Inc., Common, @ $45 less fees of $1,200.
April 1 Bought 700 shares of Roberto Guerrero Corp., Common, @ $75 plus fees of $1,300.

Lazier Company's portfolio of trading securities appeared as follows on December 31, 2004.

Investments (Trading)	Cost	Fair Value
5,000 shares of Richie Hearn Corp., Common	$180,000	$175,000
700 shares of Guerrero Corp., Common	53,800	50,400
400 shares of Zampedri Preferred	60,000	58,000
	$293,800	$283,400

Instructions

Prepare the general journal entries for Lazier Company for:

(a) The 2003 adjusting entry.
(b) The sale of the Davy Jones stock.
(c) The purchase of the Roberto Guerrero stock.
(d) The 2004 adjusting entry for the trading portfolio.

E17-16 (Fair Value and Equity Method Compared) Jaycie Phelps Inc. acquired 20% of the outstanding common stock of Theresa Kulikowski Inc. on December 31, 2002. The purchase price was $1,200,000 for 50,000 shares. Kulikowski Inc. declared and paid an $0.85 per share cash dividend on June 30 and on December 31, 2003. Kulikowski reported net income of $730,000 for 2003. The fair value of Kulikowski's stock was $27 per share at December 31, 2003.

Instructions

(a) Prepare the journal entries for Jaycie Phelps Inc. for 2003, assuming that Phelps cannot exercise significant influence over Kulikowski. The securities should be classified as available-for-sale.
(b) Prepare the journal entries for Jaycie Phelps Inc. for 2003, assuming that Phelps can exercise significant influence over Kulikowski.
(c) At what amount is the investment in securities reported on the balance sheet under each of these methods at December 31, 2003? What is the total net income reported in 2003 under each of these methods?

E17-17 (Equity Method) On January 1, 2003, Warner Corporation purchased 30% of the common shares of Martz Company for $180,000. During the year, Martz earned net income of $80,000 and paid dividends of $20,000.

Instructions

Prepare the entries for Warner to record the purchase and any additional entries related to this investment in Martz Company in 2003.

E17-18 (Impairment of Debt Securities) Dominique Moceanu Corporation has municipal bonds classified as available-for-sale at December 31, 2003. These bonds have a par value of $800,000, an amortized cost of $800,000, and a fair value of $720,000. The unrealized loss of $80,000 previously recognized as other comprehensive income and as a separate component of stockholders' equity is now determined to be other than temporary. That is, the company believes that impairment accounting is now appropriate for these bonds.

Instructions

(a) Prepare the journal entry to recognize the impairment.
(b) What is the new cost basis of the municipal bonds? Given that the maturity value of the bonds is $800,000, should Moceanu Corporation accrete the difference between the carrying amount and the maturity value over the life of the bonds?

(c) At December 31, 2004, the fair value of the municipal bonds is $760,000. Prepare the entry (if any) to record this information.

*E17-19 **(Derivative Transaction)** On January 2, 2002, Jones Company purchases a call option for $300 on Merchant common stock. The call option gives Jones the option to buy 1,000 shares of Merchant at a strike price of $50 per share. The market price of a Merchant share is $50 on January 2, 2002 (the intrinsic value is therefore $0). On March 31, 2002, the market price for Merchant stock is $53 per share, and the time value of the option is $200.

Instructions

(a) Prepare the journal entry to record the purchase of the call option on January 2, 2002.
(b) Prepare the journal entry(ies) to recognize the change in the fair value of the call option as of March 31, 2002.
(c) What was the effect on net income of entering into the derivative transaction for the period January 2 to March 31, 2002?

*E17-20 **(Fair Value Hedge)** On January 2, 2003, MacCloud Co. issued a 4-year, $100,000 note at 6% fixed interest, interest payable semiannually. MacCloud now wants to change the note to a variable-rate note.

As a result, on January 2, 2003, MacCloud Co. enters into an interest rate swap where it agrees to receive 6% fixed and pay LIBOR of 5.7% for the first 6 months on $100,000. At each 6-month period, the variable rate will be reset. The variable rate is reset to 6.7% on June 30, 2003.

Instructions

(a) Compute the net interest expense to be reported for this note and related swap transaction as of June 30, 2003.
(b) Compute the net interest expense to be reported for this note and related swap transaction as of December 31, 2003.

*E17-21 **(Cash Flow Hedge)** On January 2, 2002, Parton Company issues a 5-year, $10,000,000 note at LIBOR, with interest paid annually. The variable rate is reset at the end of each year. The LIBOR rate for the first year is 5.8%.

Parton Company decides it prefers fixed-rate financing and wants to lock in a rate of 6%. As a result, Parton enters into an interest rate swap to pay 6% fixed and receive LIBOR based on $10 million. The variable rate is reset to 6.6% on January 2, 2003.

Instructions

(a) Compute the net interest expense to be reported for this note and related swap transactions as of December 31, 2002.
(b) Compute the net interest expense to be reported for this note and related swap transactions as of December 31, 2003.

*E17-22 **(Fair Value Hedge)** Sarazan Company issues a 4-year, 7.5% fixed-rate interest only, nonprepayable $1,000,000 note payable on December 31, 2002. It decides to change the interest rate from a fixed rate to variable rate and enters into a swap agreement with M&S Corp. The swap agreement specifies that Sarazan will receive a fixed rate at 7.5% and pay variable with settlement dates that match the interest payments on the debt. Assume that interest rates have declined during 2003 and that Sarazan received $13,000 as an adjustment to interest expense for the settlement at December 31, 2003. The loss related to the debt (due to interest rate changes) was $48,000. The value of the swap contract increased $48,000.

Instructions

(a) Prepare the journal entry to record the payment of interest expense on December 31, 2003.
(b) Prepare the journal entry to record the receipt of the swap settlement on December 31, 2003.
(c) Prepare the journal entry to record the change in the fair value of the swap contract on December 31, 2003.
(d) Prepare the journal entry to record the change in the fair value of the debt on December 31, 2003.

*E17-23 **(Fair Value Hedge)** Using the same information from *E17-22, consider the effects of the swap on M&S Corp. The $1,000,000 nonprepayable note is classified as an available-for-sale security by M&S Corp.

Instructions

(a) Prepare the journal entry to record the receipt of interest revenue on December 31, 2003.
(b) Prepare the journal entry to record the payment of the swap settlement on December 31, 2003.
(c) Prepare the journal entry to record the change in the fair value of the swap contract on December 31, 2003.
(d) Prepare the journal entry to record the change in the fair value of the available-for-sale debt security on December 31, 2003.

PROBLEMS

P17-1 (Debt Securities) Presented below is an amortization schedule related to Kathy Baker Company's 5-year, $100,000 bond with a 7% interest rate and a 5% yield, purchased on December 31, 2001, for $108,660.

Date	Cash Received	Interest Revenue	Bond Premium Amortization	Carry Amount of Bonds
12/31/01				$108,660
12/31/02	$7,000	$5,433	$1,567	107,093
12/31/03	7,000	5,354	1,646	105,447
12/31/04	7,000	5,272	1,728	103,719
12/31/05	7,000	5,186	1,814	101,905
12/31/06	7,000	5,095	1,905	100,000

The following schedule presents a comparison of the amortized cost and fair value of the bonds at year-end.

	12/31/02	12/31/03	12/31/04	12/31/05	12/31/06
Amortized cost	$107,093	$105,447	$103,719	$101,905	$100,000
Fair value	$106,500	$107,500	$105,650	$103,000	$100,000

Instructions

(a) Prepare the journal entry to record the purchase of these bonds on December 31, 2001, assuming the bonds are classified as held-to-maturity securities.
(b) Prepare the journal entry(ies) related to the held-to-maturity bonds for 2002.
(c) Prepare the journal entry(ies) related to the held-to-maturity bonds for 2004.
(d) Prepare the journal entry(ies) to record the purchase of these bonds, assuming they are classified as available-for-sale.
(e) Prepare the journal entry(ies) related to the available-for-sale bonds for 2002.
(f) Prepare the journal entry(ies) related to the available-for-sale bonds for 2004.

P17-2 (Debt Securities Available-for-Sale) On January 1, 2004, Bon Jovi Company purchased $200,000, 8% bonds of Mercury Co. for $184,557. The bonds were purchased to yield 10% interest. Interest is payable semiannually on July 1 and January 1. The bonds mature on January 1, 2009. Bon Jovi Company uses the effective interest method to amortize discount or premium. On January 1, 2006, Bon Jovi Company sold the bonds for $185,363 after receiving interest to meet its liquidity needs.

Instructions

(a) Prepare the journal entry to record the purchase of bonds on January 1. Assume that the bonds are classified as available-for-sale.
(b) Prepare the amortization schedule for the bonds.
(c) Prepare the journal entries to record the semiannual interest on July 1, 2004, and December 31, 2004.
(d) If the fair value of Mercury bonds is $186,363 on December 31, 2005, prepare the necessary adjusting entry. (Assume the securities fair value adjustment balance on January 1, 2005, is a debit of $3,375.)
(e) Prepare the journal entry to record the sale of the bonds on January 1, 2006.

P17-3 (Entries for Long-Term Investments) Octavio Paz Corp. carries an account in its general ledger called Investments, which contained the following debits for investment purchases, and no credits.

Feb. 1, 2003	Chiang Kai-Shek Company common stock, $100 par, 200 shares	$ 37,400
April 1	U.S. government bonds, 11%, due April 1, 2013, interest payable April 1 and October 1, 100 bonds of $1,000 par each	100,000
July 1	Claude Monet Company 12% bonds, par $50,000, dated March 1, 2003 purchased at 104 plus accrued interest, interest payable annually on March 1, due March 1, 2023	54,000

Instructions

(a) Prepare entries necessary to classify the amounts into proper accounts, assuming that all the securities are classified as available-for-sale.
(b) Prepare the entry to record the accrued interest and the amortization of premium on December 31, 2003, using the straight-line method.

(c) The fair values of the securities on December 31, 2003, were:

Chiang Kai-shek Company common stock	$ 33,800
U.S. government bonds	124,700
Claude Monet Company bonds	58,600

What entry or entries, if any, would you recommend be made?

(d) The U.S. government bonds were sold on July 1, 2004, for $119,200 plus accrued interest. Give the proper entry.

P17-4 (Available-for-Sale Debt Securities) Presented below is information taken from a bond investment amortization schedule with related fair values provided. These bonds are classified as available-for-sale.

	12/31/03	12/31/04	12/31/05
Amortized cost	$491,150	$519,442	$550,000
Fair value	$499,000	$506,000	$550,000

Instructions

(a) Indicate whether the bonds were purchased at a discount or at a premium.
(b) Prepare the adjusting entry to record the bonds at fair value at December 31, 2003. The Securities Fair Value Adjustment account has a debit balance of $1,000 prior to adjustment.
(c) Prepare the adjusting entry to record the bonds at fair value at December 31, 2004.

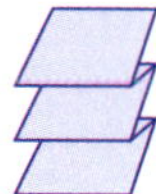

P17-5 (Equity Securities Entries and Disclosures) Incognito Company has the following securities in its investment portfolio on December 31, 2003 (all securities were purchased in 2003): (1) 3,000 shares of Bush Co. common stock which cost $58,500, (2) 10,000 shares of David Sanborn Ltd. common stock which cost $580,000, and (3) 6,000 shares of Abba Company preferred stock which cost $255,000. The Securities Fair Value Adjustment account shows a credit of $10,100 at the end of 2003.

In 2004, Incognito completed the following securities transactions.

1. On January 15, sold 3,000 shares of Bush's common stock at $23 per share less fees of $2,150.
2. On April 17, purchased 1,000 shares of Tractors' common stock at $31.50 per share plus fees of $1,980.

On December 31, 2004, the market values per share of these securities were: Bush $20, Sanborn $62, Abba $40, and Tractors $29. In addition, the accounting supervisor of Incognito told you that, even though all these securities have readily determinable fair values, Incognito will not actively trade these securities because the top management intends to hold them for more than one year.

Instructions

(a) Prepare the entry for the security sale on January 15, 2004.
(b) Prepare the journal entry to record the security purchase on April 17, 2004.
(c) Compute the unrealized gains or losses and prepare the adjusting entry for Incognito on December 31, 2004.
(d) How should the unrealized gains or losses be reported on Incognito's balance sheet?

P17-6 (Trading and Available-for-Sale Securities Entries) Gypsy Kings Company has the following portfolio of investment securities at September 30, 2003, its last reporting date.

Trading Securities	Cost	Fair Value
Dan Fogelberg, Inc. common (5,000 shares)	$225,000	$200,000
Petra, Inc. preferred (3,500 shares)	133,000	140,000
Tim Weisberg Corp. common (1,000 shares)	180,000	179,000

On October 10, 2003, the Fogelberg shares were sold at a price of $54 per share. In addition, 3,000 shares of Los Tigres common stock were acquired at $59.50 per share on November 2, 2003. The December 31, 2003, fair values were: Petra $96,000, Los Tigres $132,000, and the Weisberg common $193,000. All the securities are classified as trading.

Instructions

(a) Prepare the journal entries to record the sale, purchase, and adjusting entries related to the trading securities in the last quarter of 2003.
(b) How would the entries in part (a) change if the securities were classified as available-for-sale?

P17-7 (Available-for-Sale and Held-to-Maturity Debt Securities Entries) The information on the next page relates to the debt securities investments of Yellowjackets Company.

1. On February 1, the company purchased 12% bonds of Vanessa Williams Co. having a par value of $500,000 at 100 plus accrued interest. Interest is payable April 1 and October 1.
2. On April 1, semiannual interest is received.
3. On July 1, 9% bonds of Chieftains, Inc. were purchased. These bonds with a par value of $200,000 were purchased at 100 plus accrued interest. Interest dates are June 1 and December 1.
4. On September 1, bonds with a par value of $100,000, purchased on February 1, are sold at 99 plus accrued interest.
5. On October 1, semiannual interest is received.
6. On December 1, semiannual interest is received.
7. On December 31, the fair value of the bonds purchased February 1 and July 1 are 95 and 93, respectively.

Instructions

(a) Prepare any journal entries you consider necessary, including year-end entries (December 31), assuming these are available-for-sale securities.

(b) If Yellowjackets classified these as held-to-maturity securities, explain how the journal entries would differ from those in part (a).

P17-8 (Applying Fair Value Method) Pacers Corp. is a medium-sized corporation specializing in quarrying stone for building construction. The company has long dominated the market, at one time achieving a 70% market penetration. During prosperous years, the company's profits, coupled with a conservative dividend policy, resulted in funds available for outside investment. Over the years, Pacers has had a policy of investing idle cash in equity securities. In particular, Pacers has made periodic investments in the company's principal supplier, Ricky Pierce Industries. Although the firm currently owns 12% of the outstanding common stock of Pierce Industries, Pacers does not have significant influence over the operations of Pierce Industries.

Cheryl Miller has recently joined Pacers as assistant controller, and her first assignment is to prepare the 2004 year-end adjusting entries for the accounts that are valued by the "fair value" rule for financial reporting purposes. Miller has gathered the following information about Pacers' pertinent accounts.

1. Pacers has trading securities related to Dale Davis Motors and Rik Smits Electric. During this fiscal year, Pacers purchased 100,000 shares of Davis Motors for $1,400,000; these shares currently have a market value of $1,600,000. Pacers' investment in Smits Electric has not been profitable; the company acquired 50,000 shares of Smits in April 2004 at $20 per share, a purchase that currently has a value of $620,000.
2. Prior to 2004, Pacers invested $22,500,000 in Ricky Pierce Industries and has not changed its holdings this year. This investment in Ricky Pierce Industries was valued at $21,500,000 on December 31, 2003. Pacers' 12% ownership of Ricky Pierce Industries has a current market value of $22,275,000.

Instructions

(a) Prepare the appropriate adjusting entries for Pacers as of December 31, 2004, to reflect the application of the "fair value" rule for both classes of securities described above.

(b) For both classes of securities presented above, describe how the results of the valuation adjustments made in (a) would be reflected in the body of and/or notes to Pacers' 2004 financial statements.

P17-9 (Financial Statement Presentation of Available-for-Sale Investments) Woolford Company has the following portfolio of available-for-sale securities at December 31, 2003.

			Per Share	
Security	Quantity	Percent Interest	Cost	Market
Favre, Inc.	2,000 shares	8%	$11	$16
Walsh Corp.	5,000 shares	14%	23	17
Dilfer Company	4,000 shares	2%	31	24

Instructions

(a) What should be reported on Woolford's December 31, 2003, balance sheet relative to these long-term available-for-sale securities?

On December 31, 2004, Woolford's portfolio of available-for-sale securities consisted of the following common stocks.

			Per Share	
Security	Quantity	Percent Interest	Cost	Market
Walsh Corp.	5,000 shares	14%	$23	$30
Dilfer Company	4,000 shares	2%	31	23
Dilfer Company	2,000 shares	1%	25	23

At the end of year 2004, Woolford Company changed its intent relative to its investment in Favre, Inc. and reclassified the shares to trading securities status when the shares were selling for $9 per share.

(b) What should be reported on the face of Woolford's December 31, 2004, balance sheet relative to available-for-sale securities investments? What should be reported to reflect the transactions above in Woolford's 2004 income statement?

(c) Assuming that comparative financial statements for 2003 and 2004 are presented, draft the footnote necessary for full disclosure of Woolford's transactions and position in equity securities.

P17-10 (Gain on Sale of Securities and Comprehensive Income) On January 1, 2003, Enid Inc. had the following balance sheet.

ENID INC.
BALANCE SHEET
AS OF JANUARY 1, 2003

Assets		Equity	
Cash	$ 50,000	Common stock	$250,000
Available-for-sale securities	240,000	Accumulated other comprehensive income	40,000
Total	$290,000	Total	$290,000

The accumulated other comprehensive income related to unrealized holding gains on available-for-sale securities. The fair value of Enid Inc.'s available-for-sale securities at December 31, 2003, was $190,000; its cost was $120,000. No securities were purchased during the year. Enid Inc.'s income statement for 2003 was as follows. (Ignore income taxes.)

ENID INC.
INCOME STATEMENT
FOR THE YEAR ENDED DECEMBER 31, 2003

Dividend revenue	$15,000
Gain on sale of available-for-sale securities	20,000
Net income	$35,000

Instructions

(Assume all transactions during the year were for cash.)

(a) Prepare the journal entry to record the sale of the available-for-sale securities in 2003.
(b) Prepare a statement of comprehensive income for 2003.
(c) Prepare a balance sheet as of December 31, 2003.

P17-11 (Equity Investments—Available for Sale) Big Brother Holdings, Inc. had the following available-for-sale investment portfolio at January 1, 2002.

Earl Company	1,000 shares @ $15 each	$15,000
Josie Company	900 shares @ $20 each	18,000
David Company	500 shares @ $9 each	4,500
Available-for sale securities @ cost		37,500
Securities fair value adjustment—Available-for-sale		(7,500)
Available-for-sale securities @ fair value		$30,000

During 2002, the following transactions took place.

1. On March 1, Josie Company paid a $2 per share dividend.
2. On April 30, Big Brother Holdings, Inc. sold 300 shares of David Company for $10 per share.
3. On May 15, Big Brother Holdings, Inc. purchased 50 more shares of Earl Co. stock at $16 per share.
4. At December 31, 2002, the stocks had the following price per share values: Earl $17, Josie $19, and David $8.

During 2003, the following transactions took place.

5. On February 1, Big Brother Holdings, Inc. sold the remaining David shares for $7 per share.
6. On March 1, Josie Company paid a $2 per share dividend.
7. On December 21, Earl Company declared a cash dividend of $3 per share to be paid in the next month.
8. At December 31, 2003, the stocks had the following price per shares values: Earl $19 and Josie $21.

Instructions

(a) Prepare journal entries for each of the above transactions.
(b) Prepare a partial balance sheet showing the Investments account at December 31, 2002 and 2003.

P17-12 (Available-for-Sale Securities—Statement Presentation) Maryam Alvarez Corp. invested its excess cash in available-for-sale securities during 2002. As of December 31, 2002, the portfolio of available-for-sale securities consisted of the following common stocks.

Security	Quantity		Cost	Fair Value
Keesha Jones, Inc.	1,000 shares		$ 15,000	$ 21,000
Eola Corp.	2,000 shares		50,000	42,000
Yevette Aircraft	2,000 shares		72,000	60,000
		Totals	$137,000	$123,000

Instructions

(a) What should be reported on Alvarez's December 31, 2002, balance sheet relative to these securities? What should be reported on Alvarez's 2002 income statement?

On December 31, 2003, Alvarez's portfolio of available-for-sale securities consisted of the following common stocks.

Security	Quantity		Cost	Fair Value
Keesha Jones, Inc.	1,000 shares		$ 15,000	$20,000
Keesha Jones, Inc.	2,000 shares		38,000	40,000
King Company	1,000 shares		16,000	12,000
Yevette Aircraft	2,000 shares		72,000	22,000
		Totals	$141,000	$94,000

During the year 2003, Alvarez Corp. sold 2,000 shares of Eola Corp. for $38,200 and purchased 2,000 more shares of Keesha Jones, Inc. and 1,000 shares of King Company.

(b) What should be reported on Alvarez's December 31, 2003, balance sheet? What should be reported on Alvarez's 2003 income statement?

On December 31, 2004, Alvarez's portfolio of available-for-sale securities consisted of the following common stocks.

Security	Quantity		Cost	Fair Value
Yevette Aircraft	2,000 shares		$72,000	$82,000
King Company	2,500 shares		8,000	6,000
		Totals	$80,000	$88,000

During the year 2004, Alvarez Corp. sold 3,000 shares of Keesha Jones, Inc. for $39,900 and 500 shares of King Company at a loss of $2,700.

(c) What should be reported on the face of Alvarez's December 31, 2004, balance sheet? What should be reported on Alvarez's 2004 income statement?

(d) What would be reported in a statement of comprehensive income at (1) December 31, 2002, and (2) December 31, 2003?

***P17-13 (Derivative Financial Instrument)** The treasurer of Miller Co. has read on the Internet that the stock price of Ewing Inc. is about to take off. In order to profit from this potential development, Miller Co. purchased a call option on Ewing common shares on July 7, 2002, for $240. The call option is for 200 shares (notional value), and the strike price is $70. The option expires on January 31, 2003. The following data are available with respect to the call option.

Date	Market Price of Ewing Shares	Time Value of Call Option
September 30, 2002	$77 per share	$180
December 31, 2002	75 per share	65
January 4, 2003	76 per share	30

Instructions

Prepare the journal entries for Miller Co. for the following dates.

(a) July 7, 2002—Investment in call option on Ewing shares.
(b) September 30, 2002—Miller prepares financial statements.
(c) December 31, 2002—Miller prepares financial statements.
(d) January 4, 2003—Miller settles the call option on the Ewing shares.

***P17-14 (Derivative Financial Instrument)** Johnstone Co. purchased a put option on Ewing common shares on July 7, 2002, for $240. The put option is for 200 shares, and the strike price is $70. The option expires on January 31, 2003. The following data are available with respect to the put option.

Date	Market Price of Ewing Shares	Time Value of Put Option
September 30, 2002	$77 per share	$125
December 31, 2002	75 per share	50
January 31, 2003	78 per share	0

Instructions

Prepare the journal entries for Johnstone Co. for the following dates.

(a) January 7, 2002—Investment in put option on Ewing shares.
(b) September 30, 2002—Johnstone prepares financial statements.
(c) December 31, 2002—Johnstone prepares financial statements.
(d) January 31, 2003—Put option expires.

***P17-15 (Free-standing Derivative)** Warren Co. purchased a put option on Echo common shares on January 7, 2003, for $360. The put option is for 400 shares, and the strike price is $85. The option expires on July 31, 2003. The following data are available with respect to the put option.

Date	Market Price of Echo Shares	Time Value of Put Option
March 31, 2003	$80 per share	$200
June 30, 2003	82 per share	90
July 6, 2003	77 per share	25

Instructions

Prepare the journal entries for Warren Co. for the following dates.

(a) January 7, 2003—Investment in put option on Echo shares.
(b) March 31, 2003—Warren prepares financial statements.
(c) June 30, 2003—Warren prepares financial statements.
(d) July 6, 2003—Warren settles the call option on the Echo shares.

***P17-16 (Fair Value Hedge Interest Rate Swap)** On December 31, 2002, Mercantile Corp. had a $10,000,000, 8% fixed-rate note outstanding, payable in 2 years. It decides to enter into a 2-year swap with Chicago First Bank to convert the fixed-rate debt to variable-rate debt. The terms of the swap indicate that Mercantile will receive interest at a fixed rate of 8.0% and will pay a variable rate equal to the 6-month LIBOR rate, based on the $10,000,000 amount. The LIBOR rate on December 31, 2002, is 7%. The LIBOR rate will be reset every 6 months and will be used to determine the variable rate to be paid for the following 6-month period.

Mercantile Corp. designates the swap as a fair value hedge. Assume that the hedging relationship meets all the conditions necessary for hedge accounting. The 6-month LIBOR rate and the swap and debt fair values are as follows.

Date	6-Month LIBOR Rate	Swap Fair Value	Debt Fair Value
December 31, 2002	7.0%	—	$10,000,000
June 30, 2003	7.5%	(200,000)	9,800,000
December 31, 2003	6.0%	60,000	10,060,000

Instructions

(a) Present the journal entries to record the following transactions.
  (1) The entry, if any, to record the swap on December 31, 2002.
  (2) The entry to record the semiannual debt interest payment on June 30, 2003.
  (3) The entry to record the settlement of the semiannual swap amount receivables at 8%, less amount payable at LIBOR, 7%.
  (4) The entry to record the change in the fair value of the debt on June 30, 2003.
  (5) The entry to record the change in the fair value of the swap at June 30, 2003.

(b) Indicate the amount(s) reported on the balance sheet and income statement related to the debt and swap on December 31, 2002.

(c) Indicate the amount(s) reported on the balance sheet and income statement related to the debt and swap on June 30, 2003.

(d) Indicate the amount(s) reported on the balance sheet and income statement related to the debt and swap on December 31, 2003.

***P17-17 (Cash Flow Hedge)** LEW Jewelry Co. uses gold in the manufacture of its products. LEW anticipates that it will need to purchase 500 ounces of gold in October 2002, for jewelry that will be shipped for the holiday shopping season. However, if the price of gold increases, LEW's cost to produce its jewelry will increase, which would reduce its profit margins.

To hedge the risk of increased gold prices, on April 1, 2002, LEW enters into a gold futures contract and designates this futures contract as a cash flow hedge of the anticipated gold purchase. The notional amount of the contract is 500 ounces, and the terms of the contract give LEW the option to purchase gold at a price of $300 per ounce. The price will be good until the contract expires on October 31, 2002.

Assume the following data with respect to the price of the call options and the gold inventory purchase.

Date	Spot Price for October Delivery
April 1, 2002	$300 per ounce
June 30, 2002	310 per ounce
September 30, 2002	315 per ounce

Instructions

Prepare the journal entries for the following transactions.

(a) April 1, 2002—Inception of the futures contract, no premium paid.

(b) June 30, 2002—LEW Co. prepares financial statements.

(c) September 30, 2002—LEW Co. prepares financial statements.

(d) October 10, 2002—LEW Co. purchases 500 ounces of gold at $315 per ounce and settles the futures contract.

(e) December 20, 2002—LEW sells jewelry containing gold purchased in October 2002 for $350,000. The cost of the finished goods inventory is $200,000.

(f) Indicate the amount(s) reported on the balance sheet and income statement related to the futures contract on June 30, 2002.

(g) Indicate the amount(s) reported in the income statement related to the futures contract and the inventory transactions on December 31, 2002.

***P17-18 (Fair Value Hedge)** On November 3, 2003, Sprinkle Co. invested $200,000 in 4,000 shares of the common stock of Johnstone Co. Sprinkle classified this investment as available-for-sale. Sprinkle Co. is considering making a more significant investment in Johnstone Co. at some point in the future but has decided to wait and see how the stock does over the next several quarters.

To hedge against potential declines in the value of Johnstone stock during this period, Sprinkle also purchased a put option on the Johnstone stock. Sprinkle paid an option premium of $600 for the put option, which gives Sprinkle the option to sell 4,000 Johnstone shares at a strike price of $50 per share. The option expires on July 31, 2004. The following data are available with respect to the values of the Johnstone stock and the put option.

Date	Market Price of Johnstone Shares	Time Value of Put Option
December 31, 2003	$50 per share	$375
March 31, 2004	45 per share	175
June 30, 2004	43 per share	40

Instructions

(a) Prepare the journal entries for Sprinkle Co. for the following dates.

- **(1)** November 3, 2003—Investment in Johnstone stock and the put option on Johnstone shares.
- **(2)** December 31, 2003—Sprinkle Co. prepares financial statements.
- **(3)** March 31, 2004—Sprinkle prepares financial statements.
- **(4)** June 30, 2004—Sprinkle prepares financial statements.
- **(5)** July 1, 2004—Sprinkle settles the put option and sells the Johnstone shares for $43 per share.

(b) Indicate the amount(s) reported on the balance sheet and income statement related to the Johnstone investment and the put option on December 31, 2003.

(c) Indicate the amount(s) reported on the balance sheet and income statement related to the Johnstone investment and the put option on June 30, 2004.

CONCEPTUAL CASES

C17-1 (Issues Raised about Investment Securities) You have just started work for Andre Love Co. as part of the controller's group involved in current financial reporting problems. Jackie Franklin, controller for Love, is interested in your accounting background because the company has experienced a series of financial reporting surprises over the last few years. Recently, the controller has learned from the company's auditors that an FASB *Statement* may apply to its investment in securities. She assumes that you are familiar with this pronouncement and asks how the following situations should be reported in the financial statements.

Situation 1
Trading securities in the current assets section have a fair value of $4,200 lower than cost.

Situation 2
A trading security whose fair value is currently less than cost is transferred to the available-for-sale category.

Situation 3
An available-for-sale security whose fair value is currently less than cost is classified as noncurrent but is to be reclassified as current.

Situation 4
A company's portfolio of available-for-sale securities consists of the common stock of one company. At the end of the prior year the fair value of the security was 50% of original cost, and this reduction in market value was reported as an other than temporary impairment. However, at the end of the current year the fair value of the security had appreciated to twice the original cost.

Situation 5
The company has purchased some convertible debentures that it plans to hold for less than a year. The fair value of the convertible debenture is $7,700 below its cost.

Instructions

What is the effect upon carrying value and earnings for each of the situations above? Assume that these situations are unrelated.

C17-2 (Equity Securities) James Joyce Co. has the following available-for-sale securities outstanding on December 31, 2002 (its first year of operations).

	Cost	Fair Value
Anna Wickham Corp. Stock	$20,000	$19,000
D. H. Lawrence Company Stock	10,000	8,800
Edith Sitwell Company Stock	20,000	20,600
	$50,000	$48,400

During 2003 D. H. Lawrence Company stock was sold for $9,200, the difference between the $9,200 and the "fair value" of $8,800 being recorded as a "Gain on Sale of Securities." The market price of the stock on December 31, 2003, was: Anna Wickham Corp. stock $19,900; Edith Sitwell Company stock $20,500.

Instructions

(a) What justification is there for valuing available-for-sale securities at fair value and reporting the unrealized gain or loss as part of stockholders' equity?
(b) How should James Joyce Company apply this rule on December 31, 2002? Explain.
(c) Did James Joyce Company properly account for the sale of the D. H. Lawrence Company stock? Explain.
(d) Are there any additional entries necessary for James Joyce Company at December 31, 2003, to reflect the facts on the financial statements in accordance with generally accepted accounting principles? Explain.

(AICPA adapted)

C17-3 (Financial Statement Effect of Equity Securities) Presented below are three unrelated situations involving equity securities.

Situation 1
An equity security, whose market value is currently less than cost, is classified as available-for-sale but is to be reclassified as trading.

Situation 2
A noncurrent portfolio with an aggregate market value in excess of cost includes one particular security whose market value has declined to less than one-half of the original cost. The decline in value is considered to be other than temporary.

Situation 3
The portfolio of trading securities has a cost in excess of fair value of $13,500. The available-for-sale portfolio has a fair value in excess of cost of $28,600.

Instructions

What is the effect upon carrying value and earnings for each of the situations above? Complete your response to each situation before proceeding to the next situation.

C17-4 (Equity Securities) The Financial Accounting Standards Board issued its *Statement No. 115* to clarify accounting methods and procedures with respect to certain debt and all equity securities. An important part of the statement concerns the distinction between held-to-maturity, available-for-sale, and trading securities.

Instructions

(a) Why does a company maintain an investment portfolio of held-to-maturity, available-for-sale, and trading securities?

(b) What factors should be considered in determining whether investments in securities should be classified as held-to-maturity, available-for-sale, and trading? How do these factors affect the accounting treatment for unrealized losses?

C17-5 (Investment Accounted for under the Equity Method) On July 1, 2004, Sylvia Warner Company purchased for cash 40% of the outstanding capital stock of Robert Graves Company. Both Sylvia Warner Company and Robert Graves Company have a December 31 year-end. Graves Company, whose common stock is actively traded in the over-the-counter market, reported its total net income for the year to Warner Company and also paid cash dividends on November 15, 2004, to Warner Company and its other stockholders.

Instructions

How should Warner Company report the above facts in its December 31, 2004, balance sheet and its income statement for the year then ended? Discuss the rationale for your answer.

(AICPA adapted)

C17-6 (Equity Investment) On July 1, 2003, Cheryl Munns Company purchased for cash 40% of the outstanding capital stock of Huber Corporation. Both Munns and Huber have a December 31 year-end. Huber Corporation, whose common stock is actively traded on the American Stock Exchange, paid a cash dividend on November 15, 2003, to Munns Company and its other stockholders. It also reported its total net income for the year of $920,000 to Munns Company.

Instructions

Prepare a one-page memorandum of instructions on how Cheryl Munns Company should report the above facts in its December 31, 2003, balance sheet and its 2003 income statement. In your memo, identify and describe the method of valuation you recommend. Provide rationale where you can. Address your memo to the chief accountant at Cheryl Munns Company.

C17-7 (Fair Value) Addison Manufacturing holds a large portfolio of debt and equity securities as an investment. The fair value of the portfolio is greater than its original cost, even though some securities have decreased in value. Ted Abernathy, the financial vice president, and Donna Nottebart, the controller, are near year-end in the process of classifying for the first time this securities portfolio in accordance with *FASB Statement No. 115.* Abernathy wants to classify those securities that have increased in value during the period as trading securities in order to increase net income this year. He wants to classify all the securities that have decreased in value as available-for-sale (the equity securities) and as held-to-maturity (the debt securities).

Nottebart disagrees. She wants to classify those securities that have decreased in value as trading securities and those that have increased in value as available-for-sale (equity) and held-to-maturity (debt). She contends that the company is having a good earnings year and that recognizing the losses will help to smooth the income this year. As a result, the company will have built-in gains for future periods when the company may not be as profitable.

Instructions

Answer the following questions.

(a) Will classifying the portfolio as each proposes actually have the effect on earnings that each says it will?

(b) Is there anything unethical in what each of them proposes? Who are the stakeholders affected by their proposals?

(c) Assume that Abernathy and Nottebart properly classify the entire portfolio into trading, available-for-sale, and held-to-maturity categories. But then each proposes to sell just before year-end the securities with gains or with losses, as the case may be, to accomplish their effect on earnings. Is this unethical?

USING YOUR JUDGMENT

FINANCIAL REPORTING PROBLEM

3M Company

The financial statements of 3M are presented in Appendix 5B or can be accessed on the Take Action! CD.

Instructions

Refer to 3M's financial statements and the accompanying notes to answer the following questions.

(a) What investments does 3M report in 2001, and where are these investments reported in its financial statements?

(b) How are 3M's investments valued? How does 3M determine fair value?

(c) How does 3M use derivative financial instruments?

FINANCIAL STATEMENT ANALYSIS CASE

Union Planters

Union Planters is a Tennessee bank holding company. (That is, it is a corporation that owns banks.) It manages $32 billion in assets, the largest of which is its loan portfolio of $19 billion. In addition to its loan portfolio, however, like other banks it has significant debt investments. The nature of these investments varies from short-term in nature to long-term in nature. As a consequence, consistent with the requirements of accounting rules, Union Planters reports its investments in two different categories—trading and available-for-sale. The following facts were found in a recent Union Planters' Annual Report.

(all dollars in millions)	Amortized Cost	Gross Unrealized Gains	Gross Unrealized Losses	Fair Value
Trading account assets	$ 275	—	—	$ 275
Securities available for sale	8,209	$108	$15	8,302
Net income				224
Net securities gains (losses)				(9)

Instructions

(a) Why do you suppose Union Planters purchases investments, rather than simply making loans? Why does it purchase investments that vary in nature both in terms of their maturities and in type (debt versus stock)?

(b) How must Union Planters account for its investments in each of the two categories?

(c) In what ways does classifying investments into two different categories assist investors in evaluating the profitability of a company like Union Planters?

(d) Suppose that the management of Union Planters was not happy with its net income for the year. What step could it have taken with its investment portfolio that would have definitely increased reported profit? How much could it have increased reported profit? Why do you suppose it chose not to do this?

COMPARATIVE ANALYSIS CASE

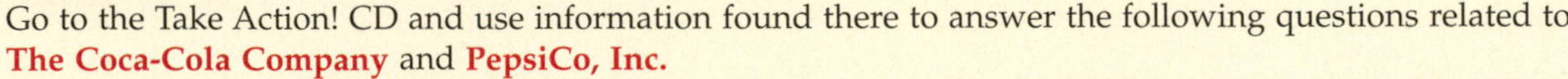

The Coca-Cola Company and PepsiCo, Inc.

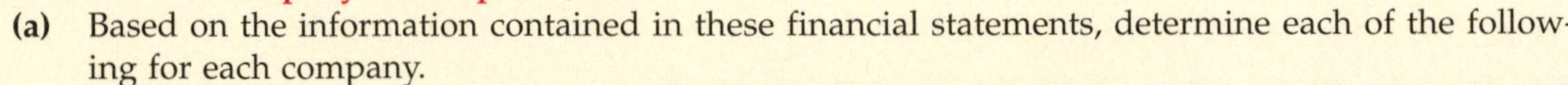

Instructions

Go to the Take Action! CD and use information found there to answer the following questions related to **The Coca-Cola Company** and **PepsiCo, Inc.**

(a) Based on the information contained in these financial statements, determine each of the following for each company.

(1) Cash used in (for) investing activities during 2001 (from the Statement of Cash Flows).

(2) Cash used for acquisitions and investments in unconsolidated affiliates (or principally bottling companies) during 2001.

(3) Total investment in unconsolidated affiliates (or investments and other assets) at December 31, 2001.

(4) What conclusions concerning the management of investments can be drawn from these data?

(b) (1) Briefly identify from Coca-Cola's December 31, 2001, balance sheet the investments it reported as being accounted for under the equity method. (2) What is the amount of investments that Coca-Cola reported in its 2001 balance sheet as "cost method investments," and what is the nature of these investments?

(c) In its note number 8 on Financial Instruments, what total amounts did Coca-Cola report at December 31, 2001, as: (1) trading securities, (2) available-for-sale securities, and (3) held-to-maturity securities?

RESEARCH CASE

The March 6, 2002, edition of the *Wall Street Journal* includes an article by Susan Pulliam and Carrick Mollenkamp entitled "Investors Turn Attention to **Bank One** for Its Accounting of Securitizations." (Subscribers to **Business Extra** can access the article at that site.)

Instructions

Read the article and answer the following questions.

(a) Explain the questions that analysts are raising about Bank One's accounting for credit-card securitizations. Why does the accounting for these securities matter?

(b) Bank One treats these securities as "available-for-sale." What are the criteria for classifying securities as available-for-sale? Based on the information in the article, do you think Bank One is classifying these securities properly? Justify your answer.

(c) How should an investment in available-for-sale securities be reported in the balance sheet? How are unrealized gains and losses on these securities reported?

(d) What is materiality, and how does it affect Bank One's financial statements? Would you consider $900 million immaterial for Bank One? Why or why not?

PROFESSIONAL SIMULATION

Investments

Directions | Situation | Journal Entries | Explanation | Research | Resources

Directions

In this simulation, you will be asked several questions related to investments. Be sure to answer all parts.

Situation

Powerpuff Corp. carries an account in its general ledger called Investments, which contained the following debits for investment purchases and no credits.

Feb. 1, 2003	Blossom Company common stock, $100 par, 200 shares	$ 37,400
April 1	U.S. Government bonds, 11%, due April 1, 2013, interest payable April 1 and October 1, 100 bonds of $1,000 par each	100,000
July 1	Buttercup Company 12% bonds, par $50,000, dated March 1, 2003, purchased at par plus accrued interest, interest payable annually on March 1, due March 1, 2023	52,000

Journal Entries

(a) Assuming that all the securities are classified as available-for-sale, prepare the journal entries necessary to classify the amounts into the proper accounts.

(b) Prepare the entry to record the accrued interest on December 31, 2003.

Resources

The fair values of the securities on December 31, 2003, were:

Blossom Company common stock	$ 33,800 (1% interest)
U.S. Government bonds	124,700
Buttercup Company bonds	58,600

Use a computer spreadsheet to prepare a schedule indicating any fair value adjustment needed at December 31, 2003.

Explanation

Now assume Powerpuff's investment in Blossom Company represents 30% of Blossom's shares. In 2003, Blossom declared and paid dividends of $9,000 (on September 30) and reported net income of $30,000. Prepare a brief memorandum explaining how the accounting for the Blossom investment will change, and discuss the impact on the financial statements of Powerpuff Corp.

Remember to check the **Take Action! CD** and the book's **companion Web site** to find additional resources for this chapter.

CHAPTER 18

Revenue Recognition

Cyberspace Trading for Revenues

Since the time when early man traded tools for animal skins and frontier farmers traded cows for horses, barter has been an accepted form of commerce. Today, the practice of trading for goods and services appears to have caught on in a big way on the Internet. Consider **Sportsline, USA**. Its sports-related Internet advertising address is constantly being promoted on **CBS** telecasts of sporting events. This is not surprising, since CBS is part owner of this dot-com venture. How does Sportsline make money? Looking at the cash flow, it is not clear. For example, in the first half of 1999, none of Sportsline's revenue of $24 million was received in cash. Instead Sportsline sold advertising on its site in exchange for advertising and other services on its customers' Internet sites.

A lot of commerce is being transacted on such virtual trading posts, and much of the reported revenue comes from barter. For example, in a recent quarter, barter revenue comprised more than 10 percent of the revenues at Internet companies such as **iVillage**, **Salon.com**, **Earthweb**, **Verticalnet**, and **Edgar Online**. However, the growth in these types of exchanges has raised concerns that the financial picture for the Internet industry is being distorted. Because these companies rarely report positive net incomes, reported revenues (without deducting expenses) have become a key valuation indicator, with strong revenue growth leading to higher stock prices. As one expert noted, "Valuations for these companies are being driven by revenues, and barter creates the potential for distortion in a company's revenues."

This potential distortion caught the attention of accounting regulators. Lynn Turner, the former Securities and Exchange Commission's chief accountant, says he was concerned about the proportion of dot-com revenues coming from barter. According to Mr. Turner, "We want to make sure that the information being reported gives investors a true notion of what is really going on with revenues and that they are reliable numbers. . . . We're always concerned that someone will push the envelope too far." Some bartering dot-coms may be pushing the financial reporting envelope too far by trading relevant and reliable numbers for higher reported revenues.[1]

LEARNING OBJECTIVES

After studying this chapter, you should be able to:

1. **Apply the revenue recognition principle.**
2. **Describe accounting issues involved with revenue recognition at point of sale.**
3. **Apply the percentage-of-completion method for long-term contracts.**
4. **Apply the completed-contract method for long-term contracts.**
5. **Identify the proper accounting for losses on long-term contracts.**
6. **Describe the installment-sales method of accounting.**
7. **Explain the cost-recovery method of accounting.**

[1]Based on Edward Wyatt, "A Whole Other Type of E-Trade," *New York Times* (October 20, 1999).

PREVIEW OF CHAPTER 18

As indicated in the opening story about barter transactions on the Internet, "When should revenue be recognized?" is a complex question. In some cases, the many methods of marketing products and services make it difficult to develop guidelines that will apply to all situations. The purpose of this chapter is to provide you with general guidelines used in most business transactions. The content and organization of the chapter are as follows.

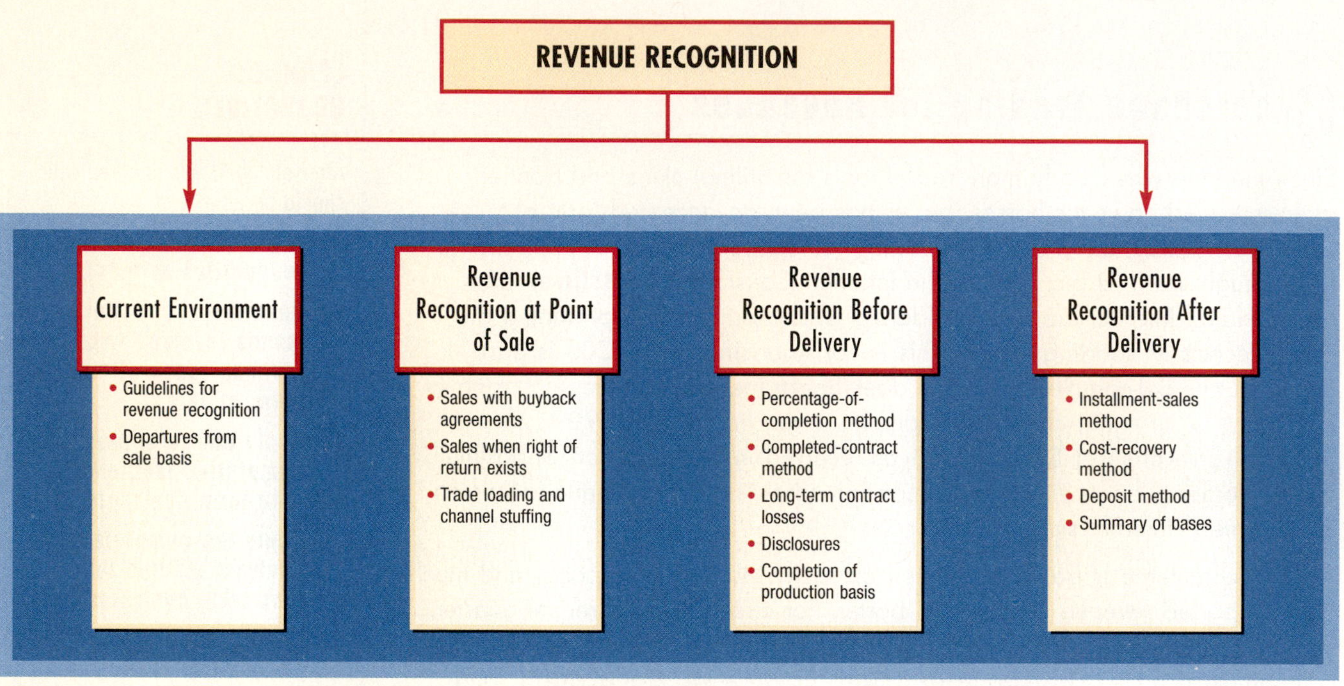

THE CURRENT ENVIRONMENT

According to one study, the area of revenue recognition has been the largest single source of public-company restatements over the past decade. The study noted the following:

1. Restatements for improper revenue recognition result in larger drops in market capitalization than any other type of restatement.
2. Eight of the top ten market value losses in 2000 were caused by revenue problems.
3. Of the ten companies, the leading three lost $20 billion in market value in just 3 days following disclosure of revenue recognition problems.[2]

As a result of these revenue recognition problems, the SEC has increased its enforcement actions in this area. In some of these cases significant adjustments to previously issued financial statements were made. As indicated by Lynn Turner, former chief accountant of the SEC, "When people cross over the boundaries of legitimate reporting, the Commission will take appropriate action to ensure the fairness and integrity that investors need and depend on every day."[3]

[2]PricewaterhouseCoopers, "Current Developments for Audit Committees 2002" (Florham Park, N.J.: PricewaterhouseCoopers, 2002), p. 65.

[3]The Sarbanes-Oxley Act of 2002 also makes it clear that Congress will not tolerate abuses of the financial reporting process and that those who fail to adhere to "certain standards" will be prosecuted.

Inappropriate recognition of revenue can occur in any industry. Products that are sold to distributors for resale pose different risks than products or services that are sold directly to customers. Sales in high-technology industries where rapid product obsolescence is a significant issue pose different risks than sale of inventory with a longer life, such as farm or construction equipment, automobiles, trucks, and appliances.[4]

The opening story indicates the difficulties often associated with revenue recognition in new industries. A number of dot-com companies, such as **L90 Inc.**, **Homestead.com**, and **Hi Speed Media**, have turned themselves into virtual trading posts, swapping ad space with one another. In these situations, an equal amount of revenue and expense is reported, so there is no effect on cash flows and net income. But, Internet stocks often trade on revenue multiples, not earnings multiples, and therefore reporting of higher revenue amounts may affect stock valuations. The swapping has related not only to ad space. As indicated in Chapter 10, telecom companies such as **Global Crossing** and **Qwest Communications** swapped fiber optic capacity to increase revenue.

In addition, the SEC has expressed concern that dot-com companies are increasing their revenue by including product sales in their revenue even though they are acting only as the distributor (intermediary) on behalf of other companies. In other words, dot-com companies should be reporting only a distribution (brokerage) fee for selling another company's products.[5]

GROSSED OUT

WHAT DO THE NUMBERS MEAN?

Consider **Priceline.com**, the company made famous by those William Shatner ads about "naming your own price" for airline tickets and hotel rooms. In its third-quarter 1999 quarterly SEC filings, Priceline reported that it earned $152 million in revenues. But that includes the full amount customers paid for tickets, hotel rooms, and rental cars. Traditional travel agencies call that amount "gross bookings," not revenues. And much like regular travel agencies, Priceline keeps only a small portion of gross bookings—namely, the spread between the customers' accepted bids and the price it paid for the merchandise. The rest, which Priceline calls "product costs," are paid to the airlines and hotels that supply the tickets and rooms. In the most recent quarter, those costs came to $134 million, leaving Priceline just $18 million of what it calls "gross profit" and what most other companies would call revenues. And that's before all of Priceline's other costs—like advertising and salaries—which netted out to a loss of $102 million. The difference isn't academic: Priceline stock traded at about 23 times its reported revenues but at a mind-boggling 214 times its "gross profit."

Source: Jeremy Kahn, "Presto Chango! Sales Are Huge," *Fortune* (March 20, 2000), p. 44.

Guidelines for Revenue Recognition

OBJECTIVE 1
Apply the revenue recognition principle.

In general, the guidelines for revenue recognition are quite broad. In addition, certain industries have very specific guidelines that provide additional insight into when revenue should be recognized. The **revenue recognition principle** provides that revenue

[4]Adapted from American Institute of Certified Public Accountants, Inc., *Audit Issues in Revenue Recognition* (New York: AICPA, 1999).

[5]The SEC noted that if a company performs as an agent or broker without assuming the risks and rewards of ownership of the goods, sales should be reported on a net (fee) basis ("Revenue Recognition in Financial Statements," *SEC Staff Accounting Bulletin No. 101*, December 3, 1999).

is recognized[6] (1) when it is realized or realizable and (2) when it is earned.[7] Revenues are **realized** when goods and services are exchanged for cash or claims to cash (receivables). Revenues are **realizable** when assets received in exchange are readily convertible to known amounts of cash or claims to cash. Revenues are **earned** when the entity has substantially accomplished what it must do to be entitled to the benefits represented by the revenues—that is, when the earnings process is complete or virtually complete.[8]

Four revenue transactions are recognized in accordance with this principle.

UNDERLYING CONCEPTS

Revenues are inflows of assets and/or settlements of liabilities from delivering or producing goods, rendering services, or other earning activities that constitute an enterprise's ongoing major or central operations during a period.

1. Revenue from selling products is recognized at the date of sale, usually interpreted to mean the date of delivery to customers.
2. Revenue from services rendered is recognized when services have been performed and are billable.
3. Revenue from permitting others to use enterprise assets, such as interest, rent, and royalties, is recognized as time passes or as the assets are used.
4. Revenue from disposing of assets other than products is recognized at the date of sale.

These revenue transactions are diagrammed in Illustration 18-1.

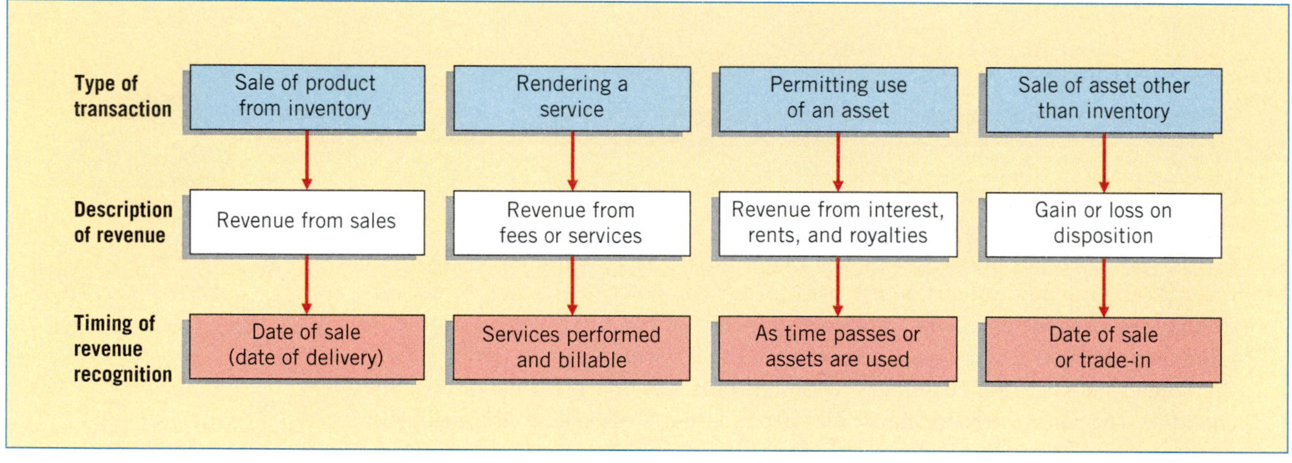

ILLUSTRATION 18-1
Revenue Recognition Classified by Nature of Transaction

The preceding statements describe the conceptual nature of revenue and are the basis of accounting for revenue transactions. Yet, in practice, there are departures from the revenue recognition principle (e.g., the full accrual method). Revenue is sometimes recognized at other points in the earning process, owing in great measure to the considerable variety of revenue transactions.

[6]Recognition is "the process of formally recording or incorporating an item in the accounts and financial statements of an entity" (*SFAC No. 3*, par. 83). "Recognition includes depiction of an item in both words and numbers, with the amount included in the totals of the financial statements" (*SFAC No. 5*, par. 6). For an asset or liability, recognition involves recording not only acquisition or incurrence of the item but also later changes in it, including removal from the financial statements previously recognized.

Recognition is not the same as realization, although the two are sometimes used interchangeably in accounting literature and practice. *Realization* is "the process of converting noncash resources and rights into money and is most precisely used in accounting and financial reporting to refer to sales of assets for cash or claims to cash" (*SFAC No. 3*, par. 83).

[7]"Recognition and Measurement in Financial Statements of Business Enterprises," *Statement of Financial Accounting Concepts No. 5* (Stamford, Conn.: FASB, 1984), par. 83.

[8]Gains (as contrasted to revenues) commonly result from transactions and other events that do not involve an "earning process." For gain recognition, being earned is generally less significant than being realized or realizable. Gains are commonly recognized at the time of sale of an asset, disposition of a liability, or when prices of certain assets change.

Departures from the Sale Basis

An FASB study found some common **reasons for departures from the sale basis.**[9] One reason is a desire to **recognize earlier** in the earning process than the time of sale the effect of earning activities (revenue) if there is a high degree of certainty about the amount of revenue earned. A second reason is a desire to **delay recognition** of revenue beyond the time of sale if the degree of uncertainty concerning the amount of either revenue or costs is sufficiently high or if the sale does not represent substantial completion of the earnings process.

This chapter is devoted exclusively to the discussion and illustration of two of the four general types of revenue transactions described earlier, namely, (1) selling products and (2) rendering services—both of which are **sales transactions**. The other two types of revenue transactions—(3) revenue from permitting others to use enterprise assets and (4) revenue from disposing of assets other than products—are discussed in several other sections of the textbook. Our discussion of product sales transactions is organized around the following topics:

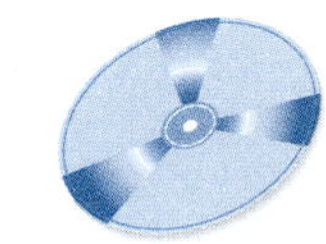

Examples of Revenue Recognition Policies

1. Revenue recognition at point of sale (delivery).
2. Revenue recognition before delivery.
3. Revenue recognition after delivery.
4. Revenue recognition for special sales transactions—franchises and consignments.

This organization of revenue recognition topics is depicted graphically in Illustration 18-2.

ILLUSTRATION 18-2
Revenue Recognition Alternatives

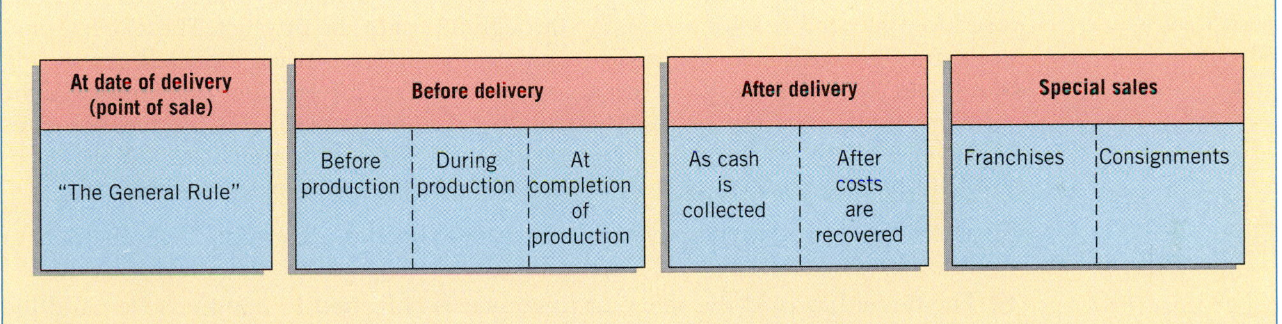

REVENUE RECOGNITION AT POINT OF SALE (DELIVERY)

OBJECTIVE 2
Describe accounting issues involved with revenue recognition at point of sale.

According to the FASB in *Concepts Statement No. 5*, the two conditions for recognizing revenue (being realized or realizable and being earned) are usually met by the time that product or merchandise is delivered or services are rendered to customers.[10] Revenues from manufacturing and selling activities are commonly recognized at **point of sale** (usually meaning delivery).[11] Problems of implementation, however, can arise.

[9]Henry R. Jaenicke, *Survey of Present Practices in Recognizing Revenues, Expenses, Gains, and Losses*, A Research Report (Stamford, Conn.: FASB, 1981), p. 11.

[10]It should be noted that the SEC believes that revenue is realized or realizable and earned when **all** of the following criteria are met: (1) Persuasive evidence of an arrangement exists; (2) delivery has occurred or services have been rendered; (3) the seller's price to the buyer is fixed or determinable; and (4) collectibility is reasonably assured. See "Revenue Recognition in Financial Statements," *SEC Staff Accounting Bulletin No. 101* (December 3, 1999). The SEC provided more specific guidance because the general criteria were difficult to interpret. In an effort to provide better and more comprehensive guidance as to when companies should record revenues, the FASB has added to its agenda a project on revenue recognition.

[11]*Statement of Financial Accounting Concepts No. 5*, op. cit., par. 84.

Three such situations are discussed below: (1) sales with buyback agreements, (2) sales when right of return exists, and (3) trade loading and channel stuffing.

Sales with Buyback Agreements

If a company sells a product in one period and agrees to buy it back in the next accounting period, has the company sold the product? As indicated in Chapter 8, legal title has transferred in this situation, but the economic substance of the transaction is that retention of risks of ownership are retained by the seller. Recognition of revenue using this practice has been curtailed. When a repurchase agreement exists at a set price and this price covers all costs of the inventory plus related holding costs, the inventory and related liability remain on the seller's books.[12] In other words, no sale.

Sales When Right of Return Exists

UNDERLYING CONCEPTS

This is an example of *realized* but *unearned revenue.* When high rates of return exist and cannot be reasonably estimated, a question arises as to whether the earnings process has been substantially completed.

Whether cash or credit sales are involved, a special problem arises with claims for returns and allowances. In Chapter 7, the accounting treatment for normal returns and allowances was presented. However, certain companies experience such a **high rate of returns**—a high ratio of returned merchandise to sales—that they find it necessary to postpone reporting sales until the return privilege has substantially expired. For example, in the publishing industry the rate of return approaches 25 percent for hardcover books and 65 percent for some magazines. Other types of companies that experience high return rates are perishable food dealers, rack jobbers or distributors who sell to retail outlets, record and tape companies, and some toy and sporting goods manufacturers. Returns in these industries are frequently made either through a right of contract or as a matter of practice involving "guaranteed sales" agreements or consignments.

Three alternative revenue recognition methods are available when the seller is exposed to continued risks of ownership through return of the product. These are: (1) not recording a sale until all return privileges have expired; (2) recording the sale, but reducing sales by an estimate of future returns; and (3) recording the sale and accounting for the returns as they occur. The FASB concluded that if a company sells its product but gives the buyer the right to return it, then revenue from the sales transaction shall be recognized at the time of sale **only if all of the following** six conditions have been met.[13]

1. The seller's price to the buyer is substantially fixed or determinable at the date of sale.
2. The buyer has paid the seller, or the buyer is obligated to pay the seller, and the obligation is not contingent on resale of the product.
3. The buyer's obligation to the seller would not be changed in the event of theft or physical destruction or damage of the product.
4. The buyer acquiring the product for resale has economic substance apart from that provided by the seller.
5. The seller does not have significant obligations for future performance to directly bring about resale of the product by the buyer.
6. The amount of future returns can be reasonably estimated.

What if revenue cannot be recognized at the time of sale because the six conditions are not met? In that case sales revenue and cost of sales that are not recognized at the time of sale should be recognized either when the return privilege has substantially expired or when those six conditions subsequently are met, whichever occurs first. Sales revenue and cost of sales reported in the income statement should be reduced by the amount of the estimated returns.

[12] "Accounting for Product Financing Arrangements," *Statement of Financial Accounting Standards No. 49* (Stamford, Conn.: FASB, 1981).

[13] "Revenue Recognition When Right of Return Exists," *Statement of Financial Accounting Standards No. 48* (Stamford, Conn.: FASB, 1981), par. 6.

Trade Loading and Channel Stuffing

Some companies record revenues at date of delivery with neither buyback nor unlimited return provisions. Although they appear to be following acceptable point-of-sale revenue recognition practices, they are recognizing revenues and earnings prematurely. The domestic cigarette industry at one time engaged in a distribution practice known as **trade loading**. Said one commentator about this practice, "Trade loading is a crazy, uneconomic, insidious practice through which manufacturers—trying to show sales, profits, and market share they don't actually have—induce their wholesale customers, known as the trade, to buy more product than they can promptly resell."[14] In total, the cigarette industry appears to have exaggerated a couple years' operating profits by as much as $600 million by taking the profits from future years.

INTERNATIONAL INSIGHT

General revenue recognition principles are provided by IAS that are consistent with U.S. GAAP but contain limited detailed or industry-specific guidance.

In the computer software industry this same practice is referred to as **channel stuffing**. When a software maker needed to make its financial results look good, it offered deep discounts to its distributors to overbuy, and then recorded revenue when the software left the loading dock.[15] Of course, the distributors' inventories become bloated and the marketing channel gets stuffed, but the software maker's financials are improved—to the detriment of future periods' results, unless the process is repeated.

Trade loading and channel stuffing hype sales, distort operating results, and "window dress" financial statements. If used without an appropriate allowance for sales returns, channel stuffing is a classic example of booking tomorrow's revenue today. **The practices of trade loading and channel stuffing need to be discouraged.** Business managers need to be aware of the ethical dangers of misleading the financial community by engaging in such practices to improve their financial statements.

NO TAKE-BACKS, REVISITED

WHAT DO THE NUMBERS MEAN?

You may recall from an earlier discussion in Chapter 2 (page 40) that investors in **Lucent Technologies** were negatively affected when Lucent violated one of the fundamental criteria for revenue recognition—the "no take-back" rule, which holds that revenue should not be booked on inventory that is shipped if the customer can return it at some point in the future. In this particular case, Lucent agreed to take back shipped inventory from its distributors, if the distributors were unable to sell the items to their customers.

In essence, Lucent was "stuffing the channel." By booking sales when goods were shipped, even though they most likely would get them back, Lucent was able to report continued sales growth. However, Lucent investors got a nasty surprise when distributors returned those goods and Lucent was forced to restate its financial results. The restatement erased $679 million in revenues, turning an operating profit into a loss. In response to this bad news, Lucent's stock price declined $1.31 per share, or 8.5 percent. Lucent is not alone in this practice. **Sunbeam** got caught stuffing the sales channel with barbecue grills and other outdoor items, which contributed to its troubles when it was forced to restate its earnings.

Additional Disclosures of Revenue Recognition Policies

Investors can be tipped off to potential channel stuffing by carefully reviewing a company's revenue recognition policy for generous return policies and by watching inventory and receivable levels. When sales increase along with receivables, that's one sign that customers are not paying for goods shipped on credit. And growing inventory levels are an indicator that customers have all the goods they need. Both scenarios suggest a higher likelihood of goods being returned and revenues and income being restated. So remember, no take-backs!

Source: Adapted from S. Young, "Lucent Slashes First Quarter Outlook, Erases Revenue from Latest Quarter," *Wall Street Journal Online* (December 22, 2000), and Tracey Byrnes, "Too Many Thin Mints: Spotting the Practice of Channel Stuffing," *Wall Street Journal Online* (February 7, 2002).

---

[14]"The $600 Million Cigarette Scam," *Fortune* (December 4, 1989), p. 89.

[15]"Software's Dirty Little Secret," *Forbes* (May 15, 1989), p. 128.

REVENUE RECOGNITION BEFORE DELIVERY

For the most part, recognition at the point of sale (delivery) is used because most of the uncertainties concerning the earning process are removed and the exchange price is known. Under certain circumstances, however, revenue is recognized prior to completion and delivery. The most notable example is long-term construction contract accounting, where the percentage-of-completion method is applicable.

Long-term contracts such as construction-type contracts, development of military and commercial aircraft, weapons delivery systems, and space exploration hardware frequently provide that the seller (builder) may bill the purchaser at intervals, as various points in the project are reached. When the project consists of separable units such as a group of buildings or miles of roadway, passage of title and billing may take place at stated stages of completion, such as the completion of each building unit or every 10 miles of road. Such contract provisions provide for delivery in installments, and the accounting records should report this by recording sales when installments are "delivered."[16]

Two distinctly different methods of accounting for long-term construction contracts are recognized.[17] They are:

1. **Percentage-of-Completion Method.** Revenues and gross profit are recognized each period based upon the progress of the construction—that is, the percentage of completion. Construction costs **plus gross profit earned to date** are accumulated in an inventory account (Construction in Process), and progress billings are accumulated in a contra inventory account (Billings on Construction in Process).
2. **Completed-Contract Method.** Revenues and gross profit are recognized only when the contract is completed. Construction costs are accumulated in an inventory account (Construction in Process), and progress billings are accumulated in a contra inventory account (Billings on Construction in Process).

The rationale for using percentage-of-completion accounting is that under most of these contracts the buyer and seller have obtained enforceable rights. The buyer has the legal right to require specific performance on the contract. The seller has the right to require progress payments that provide evidence of the buyer's ownership interest. As a result, a continuous sale occurs as the work progresses, and revenue should be recognized accordingly.

The percentage-of-completion method must be used when estimates of progress toward completion, revenues, and costs are reasonably dependable and **all of the following conditions** exist.[18]

UNDERLYING CONCEPTS

The percentage-of-completion method recognizes revenue from long-term contracts in the periods that the revenue is earned. The firm contract fixes the selling price. And, if costs are estimable and collection reasonably assured, the revenue recognition concept is not violated.

1. The contract clearly specifies the enforceable rights regarding goods or services to be provided and received by the parties, the consideration to be exchanged, and the manner and terms of settlement.
2. The buyer can be expected to satisfy all obligations under the contract.
3. The contractor can be expected to perform the contractual obligations.

The completed-contract method should be used only under the following conditions: (1) when an entity has primarily short-term contracts, or (2) when the conditions for using the percentage-of-completion method cannot be met, or (3) when there are inherent hazards in the contract beyond the normal, recurring business risks. The presumption is that **percentage-of-completion is the better method and that the com-**

[16]*Statement of Financial Accounting Concepts No. 5*, par. 84, item c.

[17]*Accounting Trends and Techniques—2001* reports that, of the 95 of its 600 sample companies that referred to long-term construction contracts, 90 used the percentage-of-completion method and 5 used the completed-contract method.

[18]"Accounting for Performance of Construction-Type and Certain Production-Type Contracts," *Statement of Position 81-1* (New York: AICPA, 1981), par. 23.

pleted-contract method should be used only when the percentage-of-completion method is inappropriate.

Percentage-of-Completion Method

OBJECTIVE 3
Apply the percentage-of-completion method for long-term contracts.

The **percentage-of-completion method** recognizes revenues, costs, and gross profit as progress is made toward completion on a long-term contract. To defer recognition of these items until completion of the entire contract is to misrepresent the efforts (costs) and accomplishments (revenues) of the interim accounting periods. In order to apply the percentage-of-completion method, one must have some basis or standard for measuring the progress toward completion at particular interim dates.

Measuring the Progress toward Completion

As one practicing accountant wrote, "The big problem in applying the percentage-of-completion method that cannot be demonstrated in an example has to do with the ability to make reasonably accurate estimates of completion and the final gross profit."[19] Various methods are used in practice to determine the **extent of progress toward completion**. The most common are "cost-to-cost method," "efforts-expended methods," and "units of work performed method."

The objective of all the methods is to measure the extent of progress in terms of costs, units, or value added. The various measures (costs incurred, labor hours worked, tons produced, stories completed, etc.) are identified and classified as input and output measures. **Input measures** (costs incurred, labor hours worked) are made in terms of efforts devoted to a contract. **Output measures** (tons produced, stories of a building completed, miles of a highway completed) are made in terms of results. Neither are universally applicable to all long-term projects. Their use requires careful tailoring to the circumstances and the exercise of judgment.

Both input and output measures have certain disadvantages. The input measure is based on an established relationship between a unit of input and productivity. If inefficiencies cause the productivity relationship to change, inaccurate measurements result. Another potential problem, called "front-end loading," produces higher estimates of completion by virtue of incurring significant costs up front. Some early-stage construction costs should be disregarded if they do not relate to contract performance—for example, costs of uninstalled materials or costs of subcontracts not yet performed.

Output measures can result in inaccurate measures if the units used are not comparable in time, effort, or cost to complete. For example, using stories completed can be deceiving. Completing the first story of an eight-story building may require more than one-eighth the total cost because of the substructure and foundation construction.

One of the more popular input measures used to determine the progress toward completion is the **cost-to-cost basis**. Under the cost-to-cost basis, the percentage of completion is measured by comparing costs incurred to date with the most recent estimate of the total costs to complete the contract, as shown in the following formula.

$$\frac{\text{Costs incurred to date}}{\text{Most recent estimate of total costs}} = \text{Percent complete}$$

ILLUSTRATION 18-3
Formula for Percentage of Completion, Cost-to-Cost Basis

The percentage that costs incurred bear to total estimated costs is applied to the total revenue or the estimated total gross profit on the contract. The amount determined is the revenue or the gross profit to be recognized to date.

[19]Richard S. Hickok, "New Guidance for Construction Contractors: 'A Credit Plus,'" *The Journal of Accountancy* (March 1982), p. 46.

ILLUSTRATION 18-4
Formula for Total Revenue to Be Recognized to Date

Percent complete	×	Estimated total revenue (or gross profit)	=	Revenue (or gross profit) to be recognized to date

To find the amounts of revenue and gross profit recognized each period, we subtract total revenue or gross profit recognized in prior periods, as shown in Illustration 18-5.

ILLUSTRATION 18-5
Formula for Amount of Current-Period Revenue, Cost-to-Cost Basis

Revenue (or gross profit) to be recognized to date	−	Revenue (or gross profit) recognized in prior periods	=	Current-period revenue (or gross profit)

Because **the profession specifically recommends the cost-to-cost method** (without excluding other bases for measuring progress toward completion), we have adopted it for use in our illustrations.[20]

Illustration of Percentage-of-Completion Method—Cost-to-Cost Basis

To illustrate the percentage-of-completion method, assume that Hardhat Construction Company has a contract starting July 2004 to construct a $4,500,000 bridge that is expected to be completed in October 2006 at an estimated cost of $4,000,000. The following data pertain to the construction period. (Note that by the end of 2005 the estimated total cost has increased from $4,000,000 to $4,050,000.)

	2004	2005	2006
Costs to date	$1,000,000	$2,916,000	$4,050,000
Estimated costs to complete	3,000,000	1,134,000	—
Progress billings during the year	900,000	2,400,000	1,200,000
Cash collected during the year	750,000	1,750,000	2,000,000

The percentage complete would be computed as follows.

ILLUSTRATION 18-6
Application of Percentage-of-Completion Method, Cost-to-Cost Basis

	2004	2005	2006
Contract price	$4,500,000	$4,500,000	$4,500,000
Less estimated cost:			
Costs to date	1,000,000	2,916,000	4,050,000
Estimated costs to complete	3,000,000	1,134,000	—
Estimated total costs	4,000,000	4,050,000	4,050,000
Estimated total gross profit	$ 500,000	$ 450,000	$ 450,000
Percent complete	25%	72%	100%
	($1,000,000 / $4,000,000)	($2,916,000 / $4,050,000)	($4,050,000 / $4,050,000)

[20]Committee on Accounting Procedure, "Long-Term Construction-Type Contracts," *Accounting Research Bulletin No. 45* (New York: AICPA, 1955), p. 7.

On the basis of the data above, the following entries would be prepared to record (1) the costs of construction, (2) progress billings, and (3) collections. These entries appear as summaries of the many transactions that would be entered individually as they occur during the year.

ILLUSTRATION 18-7
Journal Entries—Percentage-of-Completion Method, Cost-to-Cost Basis

	2004		2005		2006	
To record cost of construction:						
Construction in Process	1,000,000		1,916,000		1,134,000	
Materials, Cash, Payables, etc.		1,000,000		1,916,000		1,134,000
To record progress billings:						
Accounts Receivable	900,000		2,400,000		1,200,000	
Billings on Construction in Process		900,000		2,400,000		1,200,000
To record collections:						
Cash	750,000		1,750,000		2,000,000	
Accounts Receivable		750,000		1,750,000		2,000,000

In this illustration, the costs incurred to date as a proportion of the estimated total costs to be incurred on the project are a measure of the extent of progress toward completion. The estimated revenue and gross profit to be recognized for each year are calculated as follows.

ILLUSTRATION 18-8
Percentage-of-Completion, Revenue and Gross Profit, by Year

	2004	2005	2006
Revenue recognized in:			
2004 $4,500,000 × 25%	$1,125,000		
2005 $4,500,000 × 72%		$3,240,000	
Less: Revenue recognized in 2004		1,125,000	
Revenue in 2005		$2,115,000	
2006 $4,500,000 × 100%			$4,500,000
Less: Revenue recognized in 2004 and 2005			3,240,000
Revenue in 2006			$1,260,000
Gross profit recognized in:			
2004 $500,000 × 25%	$ 125,000		
2005 $450,000 × 72%		$ 324,000	
Less: Gross profit recognized in 2004		125,000	
Gross profit in 2005		$ 199,000	
2006 $450,000 × 100%			$ 450,000
Less: Gross profit recognized in 2004 and 2005			324,000
Gross profit in 2006			$ 126,000

The entries to recognize revenue and gross profit each year and to record completion and final approval of the contract are shown in Illustration 18-9.

ILLUSTRATION 18-9
Journal Entries to Recognize Revenue and Gross Profit and to Record Contract Completion—Percentage-of-Completion Method, Cost-to-Cost Basis

	2004		2005		2006	
To recognize revenue and gross profit:						
Construction in Process (gross profit)	125,000		199,000		126,000	
Construction Expenses	1,000,000		1,916,000		1,134,000	
Revenue from Long-Term Contract		1,125,000		2,115,000		1,260,000
To record completion of the contract:						
Billings on Construction in Process					4,500,000	
Construction in Process						4,500,000

Note that gross profit as computed in Illustration 18-8 is debited to Construction in Process. Similarly, Revenue from Long-Term Contract is credited for the amounts computed in Illustration 18-8. The difference between the amounts recognized each year for revenue and gross profit is debited to a nominal account, Construction Expenses (similar to cost of goods sold in a manufacturing enterprise), which is reported in the income statement. That amount is the actual cost of construction incurred in that period. For example, in the Hardhat Construction Company cost-to-cost illustration the actual costs of $1,000,000 in 2004 are used to compute both the gross profit of $125,000 and the percent complete (25 percent).

Costs must continue to be accumulated in the Construction in Process account in order to maintain a record of total costs incurred (plus recognized profit) to date. Although theoretically a series of "sales" takes place using the percentage-of-completion method, the inventory cost cannot be removed until the construction is completed and transferred to the new owner. The Construction in Process account would include the following summarized entries over the term of the construction project.

ILLUSTRATION 18-10
Content of Construction in Process Account—Percentage-of-Completion Method

Construction in Process				
2004 construction costs	$1,000,000	12/31/06	to close completed project	$4,500,000
2004 recognized gross profit	125,000			
2005 construction costs	1,916,000			
2005 recognized gross profit	199,000			
2006 construction costs	1,134,000			
2006 recognized gross profit	126,000			
Total	$4,500,000	Total		$4,500,000

The Hardhat Construction Company illustration contained a **change in estimate** in the second year, 2005, when the estimated total costs increased from $4,000,000 to $4,050,000. The change in estimate is accounted for in a **cumulative catch-up manner**. This is done by adjusting the percent completed to the new estimate of total costs and then deducting the amount of revenues and gross profit recognized in prior periods from revenues and gross profit computed for progress to date. That is, the change in estimate is accounted for **in the period of change** so that the balance sheet at the end of the period of change and the accounting in subsequent periods are as they would have been if the revised estimate had been the original estimate.

Financial Statement Presentation—Percentage of Completion

Generally when a receivable from a sale is recorded, the Inventory account is reduced. Under the percentage-of-completion method, however, both the receivable and the inventory continue to be carried. Subtracting the balance in the **Billings account** from Construction in Process avoids double-counting the inventory. During the life of the contract, the difference between the Construction in Process and the Billings on Construction in Process accounts is reported in the balance sheet **as a current asset if a debit, or as a current liability if a credit.**

When the costs incurred plus the gross profit recognized to date (the balance in Construction in Process) exceed the billings, this excess is reported as a current asset entitled "Cost and recognized profit in excess of billings." The unbilled portion of revenue recognized to date can be calculated at any time by subtracting the billings to date from the revenue recognized to date, as illustrated below for 2004 for Hardhat Construction.

ILLUSTRATION 18-11
Computation of Unbilled Contract Price at 12/31/04

Contract revenue recognized to date: $4,500,000 × $\frac{\$1,000,000}{\$4,000,000}$	$1,125,000
Billings to date	900,000
Unbilled revenue	$ 225,000

When the billings exceed costs incurred and gross profit to date, this excess is reported as a current liability entitled "Billings in excess of costs and recognized profit."

When a company has a number of projects, and costs exceed billings on some contracts and billings exceed costs on others, the contracts should be segregated. The asset side should include only those contracts on which costs and recognized profit exceed billings, and the liability side should include only those on which billings exceed costs and recognized profit. Separate disclosures of the dollar volume of billings and costs are preferable to a summary presentation of the net difference.

Using data from the previous illustration, Hardhat Construction Company would report the status and results of its long-term construction activities under the percentage-of-completion method as follows.

ILLUSTRATION 18-12
Financial Statement Presentation—Percentage-of-Completion Method

HARDHAT CONSTRUCTION COMPANY

		2004	2005	2006
Income Statement				
Revenue from long-term contracts		$1,125,000	$2,115,000	$1,260,000
Costs of construction		1,000,000	1,916,000	1,134,000
Gross profit		$ 125,000	$ 199,000	$ 126,000
Balance Sheet (12/31)				
Current assets				
Accounts receivable		$ 150,000	$ 800,000	
Inventories				
Construction in process	$1,125,000			
Less: Billings	900,000			
Costs and recognized profit in excess of billings		225,000		
Current liabilities				
Billings ($3,300,000) in excess of costs and recognized profit ($3,240,000)			$ 60,000	

Note 1. Summary of significant accounting policies.
Long-Term Construction Contracts. The company recognizes revenues and reports profits from long-term construction contracts, its principal business, under the percentage-of-completion method of accounting. These contracts generally extend for periods in excess of one year. The amounts of revenues and profits recognized each year are based on the ratio of costs incurred to the total estimated costs. Costs included in construction in process include direct materials, direct labor, and project-related overhead. Corporate general and administrative expenses are charged to the periods as incurred and are not allocated to construction contracts.

Completed-Contract Method

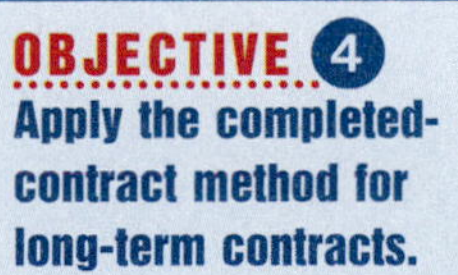

OBJECTIVE 4
Apply the completed-contract method for long-term contracts.

Under the **completed-contract method**, revenue and gross profit are recognized only at point of sale—that is, when the contract is completed. Costs of long-term contracts in process and current billings are accumulated, but there are **no interim**

The completed-contract method does not violate the *matching concept* because the costs are also deferred until the completion of the contract.

charges or credits to income statement accounts for revenues, costs, and gross profit.

The principal advantage of the completed-contract method is that reported revenue is based on final results rather than on estimates of unperformed work. Its major disadvantage is that it does not reflect current performance when the period of a contract extends into more than one accounting period. Although operations may be fairly uniform during the period of the contract, revenue is not reported until the year of completion, creating a distortion of earnings.

The **annual entries** to record costs of construction, progress billings, and collections from customers would be identical to those illustrated under the percentage-of-completion method with the significant exclusion of the recognition of revenue and gross profit. For the bridge project of Hardhat Construction Company illustrated on the preceding pages, the following entries are made in 2006 under the completed-contract method to recognize revenue and costs and to close out the inventory and billing accounts.

Billings on Construction in Process	4,500,000	
Revenue from Long-Term Contracts		4,500,000
Costs of Construction	4,050,000	
Construction in Process		4,050,000

Comparing the two methods in relation to the same bridge project, the Hardhat Construction Company would have recognized gross profit as follows.

ILLUSTRATION 18-13
Comparison of Gross Profit Recognized under Different Methods

	Percentage-of-Completion	Completed-Contract
2004	$125,000	$ 0
2005	199,000	0
2006	126,000	450,000

Hardhat Construction would report its long-term construction activities as follows:

ILLUSTRATION 18-14
Financial Statement Presentation—Completed-Contract Method

HARDHAT CONSTRUCTION COMPANY

		2004	2005	2006
Income Statement				
Revenue from long-term contracts		—	—	$4,500,000
Costs of construction		—	—	4,050,000
Gross profit		—	—	$ 450,000

		2004	2005	2006
Balance Sheet (12/31)				
Current assets				
Accounts receivable		$150,000	$800,000	
Inventories				
Construction in process	$1,000,000			
Less: Billings	900,000			
Unbilled contract costs		100,000		
Current liabilities				
Billings ($3,300,000) in excess of contract costs ($2,916,000)			$384,000	

Note 1. Summary of significant accounting policies.
Long-Term Construction Contracts. The company recognizes revenues and reports profits from long-term construction contracts, its principal business, under the completed-contract method. These contracts generally extend for periods in excess of one year. Contract costs and billings are accumulated during the periods of construction, but no revenues or profits are recognized until completion of the contract. Costs included in construction in process include direct material, direct labor, and project-related overhead. Corporate general and administrative expenses are charged to the periods as incurred.

Long-Term Contract Losses

OBJECTIVE 5
Identify the proper accounting for losses on long-term contracts.

Two types of losses can become evident under long-term contracts:[21]

1. ***Loss in the Current Period on a Profitable Contract.*** This condition arises when, during construction, there is a significant increase in the estimated total contract costs but the increase does not eliminate all profit on the contract. Under the percentage-of-completion method only, the estimated cost increase requires a current-period adjustment of excess gross profit recognized on the project in prior periods. This adjustment is recorded as a loss in the current period because it is a **change in accounting estimate** (discussed in Chapter 22).
2. ***Loss on an Unprofitable Contract.*** Cost estimates at the end of the current period may indicate that a loss will result on completion of the entire contract. Under both the percentage-of-completion and the completed-contract methods, the entire expected contract loss must be recognized in the current period.

UNDERLYING CONCEPTS

Conservatism justifies recognizing the losses immediately. Loss recognition does not require *realization;* it only requires evidence that an impairment of asset value has occurred.

The treatment described for unprofitable contracts is consistent with the accounting custom of anticipating foreseeable losses to avoid overstatement of current and future income (conservatism).

Loss in Current Period

To illustrate a loss in the current period on a contract expected to be profitable upon completion, assume that on December 31, 2005, Hardhat Construction Company estimates the costs to complete the bridge contract at $1,468,962 instead of $1,134,000 (refer to page 910). Assuming all other data are the same as before, Hardhat would compute the percentage complete and recognize the loss as shown in Illustration 18-15. Compare these computations with those for 2005 in Illustration 18-6. The "percent complete" has dropped from 72 percent to 66½ percent due to the increase in estimated future costs to complete the contract.

ILLUSTRATION 18-15
Computation of Recognizable Loss, 2005—Loss in Current Period

Cost to date (12/31/05)	$2,916,000
Estimated costs to complete (revised)	1,468,962
Estimated total costs	$4,384,962
Percent complete ($2,916,000 ÷ $4,384,962)	66½%
Revenue recognized in 2005	
($4,500,000 × 66½%) − $1,125,000	$1,867,500
Costs incurred in 2005	1,916,000
Loss recognized in 2005	$ 48,500

The 2005 loss of $48,500 is a cumulative adjustment of the "excessive" gross profit recognized on the contract in 2004. **Instead of restating the prior period, the prior period misstatement is absorbed entirely in the current period.** In this illustration, the adjustment was large enough to result in recognition of a loss.

Hardhat Construction would record the loss in 2005 as follows.

Construction Expenses	1,916,000	
Construction in Process (loss)		48,500
Revenue from Long-Term Contract		1,867,500

[21]Sak Bhamornsiri, "Losses from Construction Contracts," *The Journal of Accountancy* (April 1982), p. 26.

The loss of $48,500 will be reported on the 2005 income statement as the difference between the reported revenues of $1,867,500 and the costs of $1,916,000.[22] **Under the completed-contract method, no loss is recognized in 2005 because the contract is still expected to result in a profit** to be recognized in the year of completion.

Loss on an Unprofitable Contract

To illustrate the accounting for an overall loss on a long-term contract, assume that at December 31, 2005, Hardhat Construction Company estimates the costs to complete the bridge contract at $1,640,250 instead of $1,134,000. Revised estimates relative to the bridge contract appear as follows.

	2004	2005
	Original Estimates	Revised Estimates
Contract price	$4,500,000	$4,500,000
Estimated total cost	4,000,000	4,556,250*
Estimated gross profit	$ 500,000	
Estimated loss		$ (56,250)

*($2,916,000 + $1,640,250)

Under the percentage-of-completion method, $125,000 of gross profit was recognized in 2004 (see Illustration 18-8). This $125,000 must be offset in 2005 because it is no longer expected to be realized. In addition, the total estimated loss of $56,250 must be recognized in 2005 since losses must be recognized as soon as estimable. Therefore, a total loss of $181,250 ($125,000 + $56,250) must be recognized in 2005.

The revenue recognized in 2005 is computed as follows.

ILLUSTRATION 18-16
Computation of Revenue Recognizable, 2005—Unprofitable Contract

Revenue recognized in 2005:		
Contract price		$4,500,000
Percent complete		× 64%*
Revenue recognizable to date		2,880,000
Less: Revenue recognized prior to 2005		1,125,000
Revenue recognized in 2005		$1,755,000
*Cost to date (12/31/05)	$2,916,000	
Estimated cost to complete	1,640,250	
Estimated total costs	$4,556,250	
Percent complete: $2,916,000 ÷ $4,556,250 = 64%		

To compute the construction costs to be expensed in 2005, we add the total loss to be recognized in 2005 ($125,000 + $56,250) to the revenue to be recognized in 2005. This computation is shown in Illustration 18-17.

[22]In 2006 Hardhat Construction will recognize the remaining 33½ percent of the revenue, $1,507,500, with costs of $1,468,962 as expected, and will report a gross profit of $38,538. The total gross profit over the 3 years of the contract would be $115,038 [$125,000 (2004) − $48,500 (2005) + $38,538 (2006)]. This amount is the difference between the total contract revenue of $4,500,000 and the total contract costs of $4,384,962.

Revenue recognized in 2005 (computed above)		$1,755,000
Total loss recognized in 2005:		
Reversal of 2004 gross profit	$125,000	
Total estimated loss on the contract	56,250	181,250
Construction cost expensed in 2005		$1,936,250

ILLUSTRATION 18-17
Computation of Construction Expense, 2005—Unprofitable Contract

Hardhat Construction would record the long-term contract revenues, expenses, and loss in 2005 as follows.

Construction Expenses	1,936,250	
Construction in Process (Loss)		181,250
Revenue from Long-Term Contracts		1,755,000

At the end of 2005, Construction in Process has a balance of $2,859,750 as shown below.[23]

Construction in Process			
2004 Construction costs	1,000,000		
2004 Recognized gross profit	125,000		
2005 Construction costs	1,916,000	2005 Recognized loss	181,250
Balance	**2,859,750**		

ILLUSTRATION 18-18
Content of Construction in Process Account at End of 2005—Unprofitable Contract

Under the completed-contract method, the contract loss of $56,250 is also recognized, in the year in which it first became evident, through the following entry in 2005.

Loss from Long-Term Contracts	56,250	
Construction in Process (Loss)		56,250

Just as the Billings account balance cannot exceed the contract price, neither can the balance in Construction in Process exceed the contract price. In circumstances where the Construction in Process balance exceeds the billings, the recognized loss may be deducted on the balance sheet from such accumulated costs. That is, under both the percentage-of-completion and the completed-contract methods, the provision for the loss (the credit) may be combined with Construction in Process, thereby reducing the inventory balance. In those circumstances, however (as in the 2005 illustration above), where the billings exceed the accumulated costs, the amount of the estimated loss must be reported separately on the balance sheet as a current liability. That is, under both the percentage-of-completion and the completed-contract methods, the amount of the loss of $56,250, as estimated in 2005, would be taken from the Construction in Process account and reported separately as a current liability entitled "Estimated liability from long-term contracts."[24]

Disclosures in Financial Statements

In addition to making the financial statement disclosures required of all businesses, construction contractors usually make some unique disclosures. Generally these additional disclosures are made in the notes to the financial statements. For example, a

[23]If the costs in 2006 are $1,640,250 as projected, at the end of 2006 the Construction in Process account will have a balance of $1,640,250 + $2,859,750, or $4,500,000, equal to the contract price. When the revenue remaining to be recognized in 2006 of $1,620,000 [$4,500,000 (total contract price) − $1,125,000 (2004) − $1,755,000 (2005)] is matched with the construction expense to be recognized in 2006 of $1,620,000 [total costs of $4,556,250 less the total costs recognized in prior years of $2,936,250 (2004, $1,000,000; 2005, $1,936,250)], a zero profit results. Thus the total loss has been recognized in 2005, the year in which it first became evident.

[24]*Construction Contractors*, Audit and Accounting Guide (New York: AICPA, 1981), pp. 148–149.

construction contractor should disclose the following: the method of recognizing revenue,[25] the basis used to classify assets and liabilities as current (the nature and length of the operating cycle), the basis for recording inventory, the effects of any revision of estimates, the amount of backlog on uncompleted contracts, and the details about receivables (billed and unbilled, maturity, interest rates, retainage provisions, and significant individual or group concentrations of credit risk).

WHAT DO THE NUMBERS MEAN?

LESS CONSERVATIVE

Halliburton provides engineering- and construction-related services. Much of the company's work is completed under contract over long periods of time. As such, the company uses percentage-of-completion accounting.

Recently the SEC has questioned the company about its accounting for contract claims and disagreements with customers, including those arising from changed orders and disputes about billable amounts and costs associated with a construction delay.

Prior to 1998 Halliburton took a very conservative approach to its accounting for disputed claims. As stated in the company's 1997 annual report, "Claims for additional compensation are recognized during the period such claims are resolved." That is, the company waited until all disputes were resolved before recognizing associated revenues. In contrast, in 1998 the company recognized revenue for disputed claims before their resolution, using estimates of amounts expected to be recovered. Such revenue and its related profit are more tentative and are subject to possible later adjustment than revenue and profit recognized when all claims have been resolved. As a case in point, the company noted that it incurred losses of $99 million in 1998 related to customer claims.

The accounting method put in place in 1998 is more aggressive than the company's former policy, but it is still within the boundaries of generally accepted accounting principles. The Halliburton situation illustrates the difficulty of using estimates in percentage-of-completion accounting and the impact of those estimates on the financial statements.

Source: Adapted from "Accounting Ace Charles Mulford Answers Accounting Questions," *Wall Street Journal Online* (June 7, 2002).

Completion-of-Production Basis

UNDERLYING CONCEPTS

This is not an exception to the revenue recognition principle. At the completion of production, realization is virtually assured and the earning process is substantially completed.

In certain cases revenue is recognized at the completion of production even though no sale has been made. Examples of such situations involve precious metals or agricultural products with assured prices. Under the **completion-of-production basis**, revenue is recognized when these metals are mined or agricultural crops harvested because the sales price is reasonably assured, the units are interchangeable, and no significant costs are involved in distributing the product (see discussion in Chapter 9, page 429, "Valuation at Net Realizable Value").[26] When sale or cash receipt precedes production and delivery, as in the case of magazine subscriptions, revenues may be recognized as earned by production and delivery.[27]

---

[25]Ibid., p. 30.

[26]Such revenue satisfies the criteria of *Concepts Statement No. 5* since the assets are readily realizable and the earning process is virtually complete (see par. 84, item c).

[27]*Statement of Financial Accounting Concepts No. 5*, par. 84, item b.

REVENUE RECOGNITION AFTER DELIVERY

In some cases, the collection of the sales price is not reasonably assured and revenue recognition is deferred. One of two methods is generally employed to defer revenue recognition until the cash is received: the **installment-sales method** or the **cost-recovery method**. In some situations cash is received prior to delivery or transfer of the property and is recorded as a deposit because the sale transaction is incomplete. This is referred to as the **deposit method**.

Installment-Sales Accounting Method

OBJECTIVE 6
Describe the installment-sales method of accounting.

The installment-sales method emphasizes collection rather than sale. It recognizes income in the periods of collection rather than in the period of sale. This method is justified on the basis that when there is no reasonable approach for estimating the degree of collectibility, revenue should not be recognized until cash is collected.

The expression "installment sales" is generally used to describe any type of sale for which payment is required in periodic installments over an extended period of time. It is used in retailing where all types of farm and home equipment and furnishings are sold on an installment basis. It is also sometimes used in the heavy equipment industry in which machine installations are paid for over a long period. A more recent application of the method is in land development sales.

Because payment for the product or property sold is spread over a relatively long period, the risk of loss resulting from uncollectible accounts is greater in installment-sales transactions than in ordinary sales. Consequently, various devices are used to protect the seller. In merchandising, the two most common are: (1) the use of a conditional sales contract that provides that title to the item sold does not pass to the purchaser until all payments have been made, and (2) use of notes secured by a chattel (personal property) mortgage on the article sold. Either of these permits the seller to "repossess" the goods sold if the purchaser defaults on one or more payments. The repossessed merchandise is then resold at whatever price it will bring to compensate the seller for the uncollected installments and the expense of repossession.

UNDERLYING CONCEPTS

Realization is a critical part of revenue recognition. Thus, if a high degree of uncertainty exists about collectibility, revenue recognition must be deferred.

INTERNATIONAL INSIGHT

In Japan, installment method accounting is frequently used whenever the collection period exceeds 2 years, whether or not there is any uncertainty with regard to the collectibility of cash.

Under the installment-sales method of accounting, income recognition is deferred until the period of cash collection. Both revenues and costs of sales are recognized in the period of sale, but the related gross profit is deferred to those periods in which cash is collected. Thus, **instead of the sale being deferred to the future periods of anticipated collection and then related costs and expenses being deferred, only the proportional gross profit is deferred**. This approach is equivalent to deferring both sales and cost of sales. Other expenses, that is, selling expense, administrative expense, and so on, are not deferred.

Thus, the theory that cost and expenses should be matched against sales is applied in installment-sales transactions through the gross profit figure but no further. Companies using the installment-sales method of accounting generally record operating expenses without regard to the fact that some portion of the year's gross profit is to be deferred. This practice is often justified on the basis that (1) these expenses do not follow sales as closely as does the cost of goods sold, and (2) accurate apportionment among periods would be so difficult that it could not be justified by the benefits gained.[28]

Acceptability of the Installment-Sales Method

The use of the installment-sales method for revenue recognition has fluctuated widely. At one time it was widely used and accepted for installment-sales transactions. As installment-sales transactions increased in popularity, somewhat paradoxically,

[28]In addition, other theoretical deficiencies of the installment-sales method could be cited. For example, see Richard A. Scott and Rita K. Scott, "Installment Accounting: Is It Inconsistent?" *The Journal of Accountancy* (November 1979).

acceptance and application of the installment-sales method for financial accounting purposes decreased. Finally, it was concluded that except in special circumstances, "the installment method of recognizing revenue is not acceptable."[29]

The rationale for this position is that because the installment-sales method of accounting recognizes no income until cash is collected, it is not in accordance with the accrual accounting concept. On the other hand, the installment-sales method is frequently justified on the grounds that the risk of not collecting an account receivable may be so great that the sale itself is not sufficient evidence that recognition should occur. In some cases, this reasoning may be valid but not in a majority of cases. The general approach is that if a sale has been completed, it should be recognized; if bad debts are expected, they should be recorded as separate estimates of uncollectibles. Although collection expenses, repossession expenses, and bad debts are an unavoidable part of installment-sales activities, the incurrence of these costs and the collectibility of the receivables are reasonably predictable.

We study this topic in financial accounting because the method is acceptable in cases where a reasonable basis of estimating the degree of collectibility is deemed not to exist. In addition, weaknesses in the sales method of revenue recognition became very apparent when the franchise and land development booms of the 1960s and 1970s produced many failures and disillusioned investors. Application of the sales method to **franchise and license operations** resulted in the abuse described earlier as "front-end loading" (recognizing revenue prematurely, such as when the franchise is granted or the license issued, rather than as it is earned or as the cash is received). Many **land development** ventures were susceptible to the same abuses. As a result, the FASB prescribes application of the installment-sales method of accounting for sales of real estate under certain circumstances.[30]

WHAT DO THE NUMBERS MEAN?

THE CHECK IS IN THE MAIL

Datapoint Corp. encouraged its customers to load up with large shipments at the end of the year, allowing Datapoint to report these shipments as revenues, even though payment hadn't been collected. Unfortunately, some of the customers went broke before paying for the equipment received. As a result, the company had to record substantial bad debts or in some cases reverse previously recorded sales. If Datapoint had used a less aggressive revenue recognition method, such as the installment-sales method, this revenue would not have been reported. As a result, revenue recognition practices that are cash-basis oriented, such as the installment-sales method, are becoming more acceptable as it becomes difficult to tell when a sale is a sale.

Procedure for Deferring Revenue and Cost of Sales of Merchandise

One could easily work out a procedure that deferred both the uncollected portion of the sales price and the proportionate part of the cost of the goods sold. Instead of apportioning both sales price and cost over the period of collection, however, **only the**

[29]"Omnibus Opinion," *Opinions of the Accounting Principles Board No. 10* (New York: AICPA, 1966), par. 12.

[30]"Accounting for Sales of Real Estate," *Statement of Financial Accounting Standards No. 66* (Norwalk, Conn.: FASB, 1982), pars. 45–47. The installment-sales method of accounting must be applied to a retail land sale that meets **all** of the following criteria: (1) the period of cancellation of the sale with refund of the down payment and any subsequent payments has expired; (2) cumulative cash payments equal or exceed 10 percent of the sales value; and (3) the seller is financially capable of providing all promised contract representations (e.g., land improvements, off-site facilities).

gross profit is deferred. This procedure has exactly the same effect as deferring both sales and cost of sales but requires only one deferred account rather than two.

The steps to be used are as follows.

For the sales in any one year:

1. During the year, record both sales and cost of sales in the regular way, using the special accounts described later, and compute the rate of gross profit on installment-sales transactions.
2. At the end of the year, apply the rate of gross profit to the cash collections of the current year's installment sales to arrive at the realized gross profit.
3. Defer to future years the gross profit not realized.

For sales made in prior years:

1. The gross profit rate of each year's sales must be applied against cash collections of accounts receivable resulting from that year's sales to arrive at the realized gross profit.

From the preceding discussion of the general practice followed in taking up income from installment sales, it is apparent that special accounts must be used. These accounts provide certain special information required to determine the realized and unrealized gross profit in each year of operations. The requirements for special accounts are as follows.

1. Installment sales transactions must be kept separate in the accounts from all other sales.
2. Gross profit on sales sold on installment must be determinable.
3. The amount of cash collected on installment-sales accounts receivable must be known, and, further, the total collected on the current year's and on each preceding year's sales must be determinable.
4. Provision must be made for carrying forward each year's deferred gross profit.

In each year, ordinary operating expenses are charged to expense accounts. These expenses are closed to the Income Summary account as under customary accounting procedure. Thus, the only peculiarity in computing net income under the installment-sales method as generally applied is **the deferral of gross profit until realized by accounts receivable collection**.

To illustrate the installment-sales method in accounting for the sales of merchandise, assume the following data.

	2004	2005	2006
Installment sales	$200,000	$250,000	$240,000
Cost of installment sales	150,000	190,000	168,000
Gross profit	$ 50,000	$ 60,000	$ 72,000
Rate of gross profit on sales	25%[a]	24%[b]	30%[c]
Cash receipts			
2004 sales	$ 60,000	$100,000	$ 40,000
2005 sales		100,000	125,000
2006 sales			80,000

[a] $\frac{\$50,000}{\$200,000}$ [b] $\frac{\$60,000}{\$250,000}$ [c] $\frac{\$72,000}{\$240,000}$

To simplify the illustration, interest charges have been excluded. Summary entries in general journal form for year 2004 are shown on the next page.

2004

Account	Debit	Credit
Installment Accounts Receivable, 2004	200,000	
Installment Sales		200,000
(To record sales made on installment in 2004)		
Cash	60,000	
Installment Accounts Receivable, 2004		60,000
(To record cash collected on installment receivables)		
Cost of Installment Sales	150,000	
Inventory (or Purchases)		150,000
(To record cost of goods sold on installment in 2004 on either a perpetual or a periodic inventory basis)		
Installment Sales	200,000	
Cost of Installment Sales		150,000
Deferred Gross Profit, 2004		50,000
(To close installment sales and cost of installment sales for the year)		
Deferred Gross Profit, 2004	15,000	
Realized Gross Profit on Installment Sales		15,000
(To remove from deferred gross profit the profit realized through cash collections; $60,000 × 25%)		
Realized Gross Profit on Installment Sales	15,000	
Income Summary		15,000
(To close profits realized by collections)		

The realized and deferred gross profit is computed for the year 2004 as follows.

ILLUSTRATION 18-19
Computation of Realized and Deferred Gross Profit, Year 1

2004	
Rate of gross profit current year	25%
Cash collected on current year's sales	$60,000
Realized gross profit (25% of $60,000)	15,000
Gross profit to be deferred ($50,000 − $15,000)	35,000

Summary entries in journal form for year 2 (2005) are shown below.

2005

Account	Debit	Credit
Installment Accounts Receivable, 2005	250,000	
Installment Sales		250,000
(To record sales made on installment in 2005)		
Cash	200,000	
Installment Accounts Receivable, 2004		100,000
Installment Accounts Receivable, 2005		100,000
(To record cash collected on installment receivables)		
Cost of Installment Sales	190,000	
Inventory (or Purchases)		190,000
(To record cost of goods sold on installment in 2005)		
Installment Sales	250,000	
Cost of Installment Sales		190,000
Deferred Gross Profit, 2005		60,000
(To close installment sales and cost of installment sales for the year)		
Deferred Gross Profit, 2004 ($100,000 × 25%)	25,000	
Deferred Gross Profit, 2005 ($100,000 × 24%)	24,000	
Realized Gross Profit on Installment Sales		49,000
(To remove from deferred gross profit the profit realized through collections)		
Realized Gross Profit on Installment Sales	49,000	
Income Summary		49,000
(To close profits realized by collections)		

The realized and deferred gross profit is computed for the year 2005 as shown in Illustration 18-20.

ILLUSTRATION 18-20
Computation of Realized and Deferred Gross Profit, Year 2

2005	
Current year's sales	
Rate of gross profit	24%
Cash collected on current year's sales	$100,000
Realized gross profit (24% of $100,000)	24,000
Gross profit to be deferred ($60,000 − $24,000)	36,000
Prior year's sales	
Rate of gross profit—2004	25%
Cash collected on 2004 sales	$100,000
Gross profit realized in 2005 on 2004 sales (25% of $100,000)	25,000
Total gross profit realized in 2005	
Realized on collections of 2004 sales	$ 25,000
Realized on collections of 2005 sales	24,000
Total	$ 49,000

The entries in 2006 would be similar to those of 2005, and the total gross profit taken up or realized would be $64,000, as shown by the following computations.

ILLUSTRATION 18-21
Computation of Realized and Deferred Gross Profit, Year 3

2006	
Current year's sales	
Rate of gross profit	30%
Cash collected on current year's sales	$ 80,000
Gross profit realized on 2006 sales (30% of $80,000)	24,000
Gross profit to be deferred ($72,000 − $24,000)	48,000
Prior years' sales	
2004 sales	
Rate of gross profit	25%
Cash collected	$ 40,000
Gross profit realized in 2006 on 2004 sales (25% of $40,000)	10,000
2005 sales	
Rate of gross profit	24%
Cash collected	$125,000
Gross profit realized in 2006 on 2005 sales (24% of $125,000)	30,000
Total gross profit realized in 2006	
Realized on collections of 2004 sales	$ 10,000
Realized on collections of 2005 sales	30,000
Realized on collections of 2006 sales	24,000
Total	$ 64,000

Additional Problems of Installment-Sales Accounting

In addition to computing realized and deferred gross profit currently, other problems are involved in accounting for installment-sales transactions. These problems are related to:

1. Interest on installment contracts.
2. Uncollectible accounts.
3. Defaults and repossessions.

Interest on Installment Contracts. Because the collection of installment receivables is spread over a long period, it is customary to charge the buyer interest on the unpaid balance. A schedule of equal payments consisting of interest and principal is set up. Each successive payment is attributable to a smaller amount of interest and a correspondingly larger amount attributable to principal, as shown in Illustration 18-22. This illustration assumes that an asset costing $2,400 is sold for $3,000 with interest of 8 percent included in the three installments of $1,164.10.

ILLUSTRATION 18-22
Installment Payment Schedule

Date	Cash (Debit)	Interest Earned (Credit)	Installment Receivables (Credit)	Installment Unpaid Balance	Realized Gross Profit (20%)
1/2/04	—	—	—	$3,000.00	—
1/2/05	$1,164.10[a]	$240.00[b]	$ 924.10[c]	2,075.90[d]	$184.82[e]
1/2/06	1,164.10	166.07	998.03	1,077.87	199.61
1/2/07	1,164.10	86.23	1,077.87	–0–	215.57
					$600.00

[a]Periodic payment = Original unpaid balance ÷ PV of an annuity of $1.00 for three periods at 8%; $1,164.10 = $3,000 ÷ 2.57710.
[b]$3,000.00 × .08 = $240.
[c]$1,164.10 − $240.00 = $924.10.
[d]$3,000.00 − $924.10 = $2,075.90.
[e]$924.10 × .20 = $184.82.

Interest should be accounted for separately from the gross profit recognized on the installment-sales collections during the period. It is recognized as interest revenue at the time of the cash receipt.

Uncollectible Accounts. The problem of bad debts or uncollectible accounts receivable is somewhat different for concerns selling on an installment basis because of a repossession feature commonly incorporated in the sales agreement. This feature gives the selling company an opportunity to recoup any uncollectible accounts through repossession and resale of repossessed merchandise. If the experience of the company indicates that repossessions do not, as a rule, compensate for uncollectible balances, it may be advisable to provide for such losses through charges to a special bad debt expense account, just as is done for other credit sales.

Defaults and Repossessions. Depending on the terms of the sales contract and the policy of the credit department, the seller can repossess merchandise sold under an installment arrangement if the purchaser fails to meet payment requirements. Repossessed merchandise may be reconditioned before being offered for sale. It may be resold for cash or installment payments.

The accounting for **repossessions** recognizes that the related installment receivable account is not collectible and that it should be written off. Along with the account receivable, the applicable deferred gross profit must be removed from the ledger using the following entry:

Repossessed Merchandise (an inventory account)	xx	
Deferred Gross Profit	xx	
Installment Accounts Receivable		xx

The entry above assumes that the repossessed merchandise is to be recorded on the books at exactly the amount of the uncollected account less the deferred gross profit applicable. This assumption may or may not be proper. The condition of the merchandise repossessed, the cost of reconditioning, and the market for second-hand merchandise of that particular type must all be considered. **The objective should be to put any asset acquired on the books at its fair value or, when fair value is not ascertainable, at the best possible approximation of fair value.** If the fair value of the merchandise repossessed is less than the uncollected balance less the deferred gross profit, a "loss on repossession" should be recorded at the date of repossession.

Some contend that repossessed merchandise should be entered at a valuation that will permit the company to make its regular rate of gross profit on resale. If it is entered at its approximated cost to purchase, the regular rate of gross profit could be provided for upon its ultimate sale, but that is completely a secondary consideration. **It is more**

important that the asset acquired by repossession be recorded at fair value in accordance with the general practice of carrying assets at acquisition price, as represented by the fair market value at the date of acquisition.

To illustrate the required entry, assume that a refrigerator was sold to Marilyn Hunt for $500 on September 1, 2004. Terms require a down payment of $200 and $20 on the first of every month for 15 months, starting October 1, 2004. It is further assumed that the refrigerator cost $300 and that it is sold to provide a 40 percent rate of gross profit on selling price. At the year-end, December 31, 2004, a total of $60 should have been collected in addition to the original down payment.

If Hunt makes her January and February payments in 2005 and then defaults, the account balances applicable to Hunt at time of default would be:

Installment Account Receivable ($500 − $200 − $20 − $20 − $20 − $20 − $20)	200 (dr.)
Deferred Gross Profit [40% × ($500 − $200 − $20 − $20 − $20)]	96 (cr.)

The deferred gross profit applicable to the Hunt account still has the December 31, 2004, balance, because no entry has yet been made to take up gross profit realized by 2005 cash collections. The regular entry at the end of 2005, however, will take up the gross profit realized by all cash collections including amounts received from Hunt. Hence, the balance of deferred gross profit applicable to Hunt's account may be computed by applying the gross profit rate for the year of sale to the 2005 balance of Hunt's account receivable, 40 percent of $200, or $80. The account balances should therefore be considered as:

Installment Account Receivable (Hunt)	200 (dr.)
Deferred Gross Profit (applicable to Hunt after recognition of $8 of profit in both January and February)	80 (cr.)

If the estimated fair value of the article repossessed is set at $70, the following entry would be required to record the repossession.

Deferred Gross Profit	80	
Repossessed Merchandise	70	
Loss on Repossession	50	
Installment Account Receivable (Hunt)		200

The amount of the loss is determined by (1) subtracting the deferred gross profit from the amount of the account receivable, to determine the unrecovered cost (or book value) of the merchandise repossessed, and (2) subtracting the estimated fair value of the merchandise repossessed from the unrecovered cost, to get the amount of the loss on repossession. The loss on the refrigerator in our example is computed as shown in Illustration 18-23.

ILLUSTRATION 18-23
Computation of Loss on Repossession

Balance of account receivable (representing uncollected selling price)	$200
Less: Deferred gross profit	80
Unrecovered cost	120
Less: Estimated fair value of merchandise repossessed	70
Loss (Gain) on repossession	$50

As pointed out earlier, the loss on repossession may be charged to Allowance for Doubtful Accounts if such an account is carried.

Financial Statement Presentation of Installment-Sales Transactions

If installment-sales transactions represent a significant part of total sales, full disclosure of installment sales, the cost of installment sales, and any expenses allocable to installment sales is desirable. If, however, installment-sales transactions constitute an insignificant part of total sales, it may be satisfactory to include only the realized gross profit in the income statement as a special item following the gross profit on sales. This presentation is shown in Illustration 18-24.

ILLUSTRATION 18-24
Disclosure of Installment-Sales Transactions—Insignificant Amount

HEALTH MACHINE COMPANY
INCOME STATEMENT
FOR THE YEAR ENDED DECEMBER 31, 2005

Sales	$620,000
Cost of goods sold	490,000
Gross profit on sales	130,000
Gross profit realized on installment sales	51,000
Total gross profit on sales	$181,000

If more complete disclosure of installment-sales transactions is desired, a presentation similar to the following may be used.

ILLUSTRATION 18-25
Disclosure of Installment-Sales Transactions—Significant Amount

HEALTH MACHINE COMPANY
INCOME STATEMENT
FOR THE YEAR ENDED DECEMBER 31, 2005

	Installment Sales	Other Sales	Total
Sales	$248,000	$620,000	$868,000
Cost of goods sold	182,000	490,000	672,000
Gross profit on sales	66,000	130,000	196,000
Less: Deferred gross profit on installment sales of this year	47,000		47,000
Realized gross profit on this year's sales	19,000	130,000	149,000
Add: Gross profit realized on installment sales of prior years	32,000		32,000
Gross profit realized this year	$ 51,000	$130,000	$181,000

The apparent awkwardness of this method of presentation is difficult to avoid if full disclosure of installment-sales transactions is to be provided in the income statement. One solution, of course, is to prepare a separate schedule showing installment-sales transactions, with only the final figure carried into the income statement.

In the balance sheet it is generally considered desirable to classify installment accounts receivable by year of collectibility. There is some question as to whether installment accounts that are not collectible for two or more years should be included in current assets. If installment sales are part of normal operations, they may be considered as current assets because they are collectible within the operating cycle of the business. Little confusion should result from this practice if maturity dates are fully disclosed, as illustrated in the following example.

ILLUSTRATION 18-26
Disclosure of Installment Accounts Receivable, by Year

Current assets		
Notes and accounts receivable		
Trade customers	$78,800	
Less: Allowance for doubtful accounts	3,700	
	75,100	
Installment accounts collectible in 2005	22,600	
Installment accounts collectible in 2006	47,200	$144,900

On the other hand, receivables from an installment contract, or contracts, resulting from a transaction **not** related to normal operations should be reported in the "Other assets" section if due beyond one year.

Repossessed merchandise is a part of inventory and should be included as such in the "Current assets" section of the balance sheet. Any gain or loss on repossessions should be included in the income statement in the "Other revenues and gains or other expenses and losses" section.

Deferred gross profit on installment sales is generally treated as unearned revenue and is classified as a current liability. Theoretically, deferred gross profit consists of three elements: (1) income tax liability to be paid when the sales are reported as realized revenue (current liability); (2) allowance for collection expense, bad debts, and repossession losses (deduction from installment accounts receivable); and (3) net income (retained earnings, restricted as to dividend availability). Because of the difficulty in allocating deferred gross profit among these three elements, however, the whole amount is frequently reported as unearned revenue.

In contrast, the FASB in *SFAC No. 6* states that "no matter how it is displayed in financial statements, deferred gross profit on installment sales is conceptually an asset valuation—that is, a reduction of an asset."[31] We support the FASB position, but we recognize that until an official standard on this topic is issued, financial statements will probably continue to report such deferred gross profit as a current liability.

Cost-Recovery Method

OBJECTIVE 7
Explain the cost-recovery method of accounting.

Under the cost-recovery method, no profit is recognized until cash payments by the buyer exceed the seller's cost of the merchandise sold. After all costs have been recovered, any additional cash collections are included in income. The income statement for the period of sale reports sales revenue, the cost of goods sold, and the gross profit—both the amount (if any) that is recognized during the period and the amount that is deferred. The deferred gross profit is offset against the related receivable—reduced by collections—on the balance sheet. Subsequent income statements report the gross profit as a separate item of revenue when it is recognized as earned.

APB Opinion No. 10 allows a seller to use the cost-recovery method to account for sales in which "there is no reasonable basis for estimating collectibility." This method is required under *FASB Statements No. 45* (franchises) and *No. 66* (real estate) where a high degree of uncertainty exists related to the collection of receivables.[32]

To illustrate the cost-recovery method, assume that early in 2004, Fesmire Manufacturing sells inventory with a cost of $25,000 to Higley Company for $36,000 with payments receivable of $18,000 in 2004, $12,000 in 2005, and $6,000 in 2006. If the cost-recovery method applies to this sales transaction and the cash is collected as scheduled, cash collections, revenue, cost, and gross profit are recognized as follows.[33]

ILLUSTRATION 18-27
Computation of Gross Profit—Cost-Recovery Method

	2004	2005	2006
Cash collected	$18,000	$12,000	$6,000
Revenue	$36,000	–0–	–0–
Cost of goods sold	25,000	–0–	–0–
Deferred gross profit	11,000	$11,000	$6,000
Recognized gross profit	–0–	5,000*	6,000
Deferred gross profit balance (end of period)	$11,000	$ 6,000	$ –0–

*$25,000 − $18,000 = $7,000 of unrecovered cost at the end of 2004; $12,000 − $7,000 = $5,000, the excess of cash received in 2005 over unrecovered cost.

[31]See *Statement of Financial Accounting Concepts No. 6*, pars. 232–234.

[32]"Omnibus Opinion—1966," *Opinions of the Accounting Principles Board No. 10* (New York: AICPA, 1969), footnote 8, page 149; "Accounting for Franchise Fee Revenue," *Statement of Financial Accounting Standards No. 45* (Stamford, Conn.: FASB, 1981), par. 6; "Accounting for Sales of Real Estate," *Statement of Financial Accounting Standards No. 66*, pars. 62 and 63.

[33]An alternative format for computing the amount of gross profit recognized annually is shown below.

Year	Cash Received	Original Cost Recovered	Balance of Unrecovered Cost	Gross Profit Realized
Beginning balance	—	—	$25,000	—
12/31/04	$18,000	$18,000	7,000	$ –0–
12/31/05	12,000	7,000	–0–	5,000
12/31/06	6,000	–0–	–0–	6,000

INTERNATIONAL INSIGHT

Using international standards, construction contracts under which the percentage of completion can be determined, use the cost-recovery method.

Under the cost-recovery method, total revenue and cost of goods sold are reported in the period of sale, similar to the installment-sales method. However, unlike the installment-sales method, which recognizes income as cash is collected, the cost-recovery method recognizes profit only when cash collections exceed the total cost of the goods sold.

The journal entry to record the deferred gross profit on this transaction (after the sale and the cost of sale were recorded in the normal manner) at the end of 2004 is as follows.

2004		
Sales	36,000	
Cost of Sales		25,000
Deferred Gross Profit		11,000
(To close sales and cost of sales and to record deferred gross profit on sales accounted for under the cost-recovery method)		

In 2005 and 2006, the deferred gross profit becomes realized gross profit as the cumulative cash collections exceed the total costs, by recording the following entries.

2005		
Deferred Gross Profit	5,000	
Realized Gross Profit		5,000
(To recognize gross profit to the extent that cash collections in 2005 exceed costs)		
2006		
Deferred Gross Profit	6,000	
Realized Gross Profit		6,000
(To recognize gross profit to the extent that cash collections in 2006 exceed costs)		

Deposit Method

In some cases, cash is received from the buyer before transfer of the goods or property. There is not sufficient transfer of the risks and rewards of ownership for a sale to be recorded. In such cases the seller has not performed under the contract and has no claim against the purchaser. The method of accounting for these incomplete transactions is the **deposit method**. Under the deposit method the seller reports the cash received from the buyer as a deposit on the contract and classifies it as a liability (refundable deposit or customer advance) on the balance sheet. The seller continues to report the property as an asset on its balance sheet, along with any related existing debt. Also, the seller continues to charge depreciation expense as a period cost for the property. **No revenue or income should be recognized until the sale is complete.**[34] At that time, the deposit account is closed and one of the revenue recognition methods discussed in this chapter is applied to the sale.

The **major difference between the installment-sales and cost-recovery methods and the deposit method** is that in the installment-sales and cost-recovery methods it is assumed that the seller has performed on the contract, but cash collection is highly uncertain. In the deposit method, the seller has not performed and no legitimate claim exists. The **deposit method** postpones recognizing a sale until it can be determined whether a sale has occurred for accounting purposes. Revenue recognition is delayed until a future event occurs. If there has not been sufficient transfer of risks and rewards of ownership, even if a deposit has been received, recognition of the sale should be postponed until sufficient transfer has occurred. In that sense, the deposit method is not a revenue recognition method as are the installment-sales and cost-recovery methods.

[34]*Statement of Financial Accounting Standards No. 66*, par. 65.

Summary of Product Revenue Recognition Bases

The revenue recognition bases or methods, the criteria for their use, and the reasons for departing from the sale basis are summarized in Illustration 18-28.

ILLUSTRATION 18-28
Revenue Recognition Bases Other Than the Sale Basis for Products[35]

Recognition Basis (or Method of Applying a Basis)	Criteria for Use	Reason(s) for Departing from Sale Basis
Percentage-of-completion method	Long-term construction of property; dependable estimates of extent of progress and cost to complete; reasonable assurance of collectibility of contract price; expectation that both contractor and buyer can meet obligations; and absence of inherent hazards that make estimates doubtful.	Availability of evidence of ultimate proceeds; better measure of periodic income; avoidance of fluctuations in revenues, expenses, and income; performance is a "continuous sale" and therefore not a departure from the sale basis.
Completed-contract method	Use on short-term contracts, and whenever percentage-of-completion cannot be used on long-term contracts.	Existence of inherent hazards in the contract beyond the normal, recurring business risks; conditions for using the percentage-of-completion method are absent.
Completion-of-production basis	Immediate marketability at quoted prices; unit interchangeability; difficulty of determining costs; and no significant distribution costs.	Known or determinable revenues; inability to determine costs and thereby defer expense recognition until sale.
Installment-sales method and cost-recovery method	Absence of reasonable basis for estimating degree of collectibility and costs of collection.	Collectibility of the receivable is so uncertain that gross profit (or income) is not recognized until cash is actually received.
Deposit method	Cash received before the sales transaction is completed.	No recognition of revenue and income because there is not sufficient transfer of the risks and rewards of ownership.

CONCLUDING REMARKS

As indicated, revenue recognition principles are sometimes difficult to apply and often vary by industry. Recently the SEC has attempted to provide more guidance in this area because of the concern that the revenue recognition principle is sometimes being incorrectly applied. In some cases there has even been intentional misstatement of revenue to achieve better financial results. The latter practice is fraudulent financial reporting, and the SEC is vigorously prosecuting these situations.

For our capital markets to be efficient, investors must have confidence that the financial information provided is both relevant and reliable. As a result, it is imperative that aggressive revenue recognition practices be eliminated. It is our hope that recent efforts by the SEC and the accounting profession will lead to higher-quality reporting in this area.

[35]Adapted from *Survey of Present Practices in Recognizing Revenues, Expenses, Gains, and Losses,* op. cit., pp. 12 and 13.

KEY TERMS

SUMMARY OF LEARNING OBJECTIVES

1 Apply the revenue recognition principle. The revenue recognition principle provides that revenue is recognized (1) when it is realized or realizable and (2) when it is earned. Revenues are realized when goods and services are exchanged for cash or claims to cash. Revenues are realizable when assets received in exchanges are readily convertible to known amounts of cash or claims to cash. Revenues are earned when the entity has substantially accomplished what it must do to be entitled to the benefits represented by the revenues—that is, when the earnings process is complete or virtually complete.

2 Describe accounting issues involved with revenue recognition at point of sale. The two conditions for recognizing revenue are usually met by the time products or merchandise are delivered or services are rendered to customers. Revenues from manufacturing and selling activities are commonly recognized at time of sale. Problems of implementation can arise because of (1) sales with buyback agreements, (2) revenue recognition when right of return exists, and (3) trade loading and channel stuffing.

3 Apply the percentage-of-completion method for long-term contracts. To apply the percentage-of-completion method to long-term contracts, one must have some basis for measuring the progress toward completion at particular interim dates. One of the most popular input measures used to determine the progress toward completion is the cost-to-cost basis. Using this basis, the percentage of completion is measured by comparing costs incurred to date with the most recent estimate of the total costs to complete the contract. The percentage that costs incurred bear to total estimated costs is applied to the total revenue or the estimated total gross profit on the contract in arriving at the revenue or the gross profit amounts to be recognized to date.

4 Apply the completed-contract method for long-term contracts. Under this method, revenue and gross profit are recognized only at point of sale, that is, when the contract is completed. Costs of long-term contracts in process and current billings are accumulated, but there are no interim charges or credits to income statement accounts for revenues, costs, and gross profit. The annual entries to record costs of construction, progress billings, and collections from customers would be identical to those for the percentage-of-completion method with the significant exclusion of the recognition of revenue and gross profit.

5 Identify the proper accounting for losses on long-term contracts. Two types of losses can become evident under long-term contracts: (1) *Loss in current period on a profitable contract:* Under the percentage-of-completion method only, the estimated cost increase requires a current-period adjustment of excess gross profit recognized on the project in prior periods. This adjustment is recorded as a loss in the current period because it is a change in accounting estimate. (2) *Loss on an unprofitable contract:* Under both the percentage-of-completion and the completed-contract methods, the entire expected contract loss must be recognized in the current period.

6 Describe the installment-sales method of accounting. The installment-sales method recognizes income in the periods of collection rather than in the period of sale. The installment-sales method of accounting is justified on the basis that when there is no reasonable approach for estimating the degree of collectibility, revenue should not be recognized until cash is collected.

7 Explain the cost-recovery method of accounting. Under the cost-recovery method, no profit is recognized until cash payments by the buyer exceed the seller's cost of the merchandise sold. After all costs have been recovered, any additional cash collections are included in income. The income statement for the period of sale reports sales revenue, the cost of goods sold, and the gross profit—both the amount that is recognized during the period and the amount that is deferred. The deferred gross profit is offset against the related receivable on the balance sheet. Subsequent income statements report the gross profit as a separate item of revenue when it is recognized as earned.

APPENDIX 18A

Revenue Recognition for Special Sales Transactions

To supplement our presentation of revenue recognition, we have chosen to cover two common yet unique types of business transactions—**franchises** and **consignments**.

FRANCHISES

OBJECTIVE 8
Explain revenue recognition for franchises and consignment sales.

Accounting for franchise sales was chosen because of its popularity, complexity, and applicability to many of the previously discussed revenue recognition bases. In accounting for franchise sales, the accountant must analyze the transaction and, considering all the circumstances, must use judgment in selecting and applying one or more of the revenue recognition bases and then, possibly, monitor the situation over a long period of time.

As indicated throughout this chapter, revenue is recognized on the basis of two criteria: (1) when it is realized or realizable (occurrence of an exchange for cash or claims to cash), and (2) when it is earned (completion or virtual completion of the earnings process). These criteria are appropriate for most business activities. For some sales transactions, though, they simply do not adequately define when revenue should be recognized. The fast-growing franchise industry has given accountants special concern and challenge.

Four types of franchising arrangements have evolved: (1) manufacturer-retailer, (2) manufacturer-wholesaler, (3) service sponsor-retailer, and (4) wholesaler-retailer. The fastest-growing category of franchising, and the one that caused a reexamination of appropriate accounting, has been the third category, **service sponsor-retailer**. Included in this category are such industries and businesses as:

Soft ice cream/frozen yogurt stores (**Tastee Freeze, TCBY, Dairy Queen**)
Food drive-ins (**McDonald's, KFC, Burger King**)
Restaurants (**TGI Friday's, Pizza Hut, Denny's**)
Motels (**Holiday Inn, Marriott, Best Western**)
Auto rentals (**Avis, Hertz, National**)
Others (**H & R Block, Meineke Mufflers, 7-Eleven Stores, Kelly Services**)

Franchise companies derive their revenue from one or both of two sources: (1) from the sale of initial franchises and related assets or services, and (2) from continuing fees based on the operations of franchises. The **franchisor** (the party who grants business rights under the franchise) normally provides the **franchisee** (the party who operates the franchised business) with the following services.

1. Assistance in site selection: (a) analyzing location and (b) negotiating lease.
2. Evaluation of potential income.
3. Supervision of construction activity: (a) obtaining financing, (b) designing building, and (c) supervising contractor while building.
4. Assistance in the acquisition of signs, fixtures, and equipment.
5. Bookkeeping and advisory services: (a) setting up franchisee's records; (b) advising on income, real estate, and other taxes; and (c) advising on local regulations of the franchisee's business.
6. Employee and management training.
7. Quality control.
8. Advertising and promotion.[1]

During the 1960s and early 1970s it was standard practice for franchisors to recognize the entire franchise fee at the date of sale whether the fee was received then or was collectible over a long period of time. Frequently, franchisors recorded the entire amount as revenue in the year of sale, even though many of the services were yet to be performed and uncertainty existed regarding the collection of the entire fee.[2] In effect, the franchisors were counting their fried chickens before they were hatched.

However, a **franchise agreement** may provide for refunds to the franchisee if certain conditions are not met, and franchise fee profit can be reduced sharply by future costs of obligations and services to be rendered by the franchisor. To curb the abuses in revenue recognition that existed and to standardize the accounting and reporting practices in the franchise industry, the FASB issued *Statement No. 45*.

Initial Franchise Fees

The **initial franchise fee** is consideration for establishing the franchise relationship and providing some initial services. Initial franchise fees are to be recorded as revenue only when and as the franchisor makes "substantial performance" of the services it is obligated to perform and collection of the fee is reasonably assured. **Substantial performance** occurs when the franchisor has no remaining obligation to refund any cash received or excuse any nonpayment of a note and has performed all the initial services required under the contract. According to *FASB No. 45* "commencement of operations by the franchisee shall be presumed to be the earliest point at which substantial performance has occurred, unless it can be demonstrated that substantial performance of all obligations, including services rendered voluntarily, has occurred before that time."[3]

Illustration of Entries for Initial Franchise Fee

To illustrate, assume that Tum's Pizza Inc. charges an initial franchise fee of $50,000 for the right to operate as a franchisee of Tum's Pizza. Of this amount, $10,000 is payable when the agreement is signed, and the balance is payable in five annual payments of $8,000 each. In return for the initial franchise fee, the franchisor will help locate the site, negotiate the lease or purchase of the site, supervise the construction activity, and provide the bookkeeping services. The credit rating of the franchisee indicates that money

---

[1]Archibald E. MacKay, "Accounting for Initial Franchise Fee Revenue," *The Journal of Accountancy* (January 1970), pp. 66–67.

[2]In 1987 and 1988 the SEC ordered a half-dozen fast-growing startup franchisors, including **Jiffy Lube International**, **Moto Photo, Inc.**, **Swensen's, Inc.**, and **LePeep Restaurants, Inc.**, to defer their initial franchise fee recognition until earned. See "Claiming Tomorrow's Profits Today," *Forbes* (October 17, 1988), p. 78.

[3]"Accounting for Franchise Fee Revenue," *Statement of Financial Accounting Standards No. 45* (Stamford, Conn.: FASB, 1981), par. 5.

can be borrowed at 8 percent. The present value of an ordinary annuity of five annual receipts of $8,000 each discounted at 8 percent is $31,941.68. The discount of $8,058.32 represents the interest revenue to be accrued by the franchisor over the payment period.

1. If there is reasonable expectation that the down payment may be refunded and if substantial future services remain to be performed by Tum's Pizza Inc., the entry should be:

Cash	10,000.00	
Notes Receivable	40,000.00	
Discount on Notes Receivable		8,058.32
Unearned Franchise Fees		41,941.68

2. If the probability of refunding the initial franchise fee is extremely low, the amount of future services to be provided to the franchisee is minimal, collectibility of the note is reasonably assured, and substantial performance has occurred, the entry should be:

Cash	10,000.00	
Notes Receivable	40,000.00	
Discount on Notes Receivable		8,058.32
Revenue from Franchise Fees		41,941.68

3. If the initial down payment is not refundable, represents a fair measure of the services already provided, with a significant amount of services still to be performed by the franchisor in future periods, and collectibility of the note is reasonably assured, the entry should be:

Cash	10,000.00	
Notes Receivable	40,000.00	
Discount on Notes Receivable		8,058.32
Revenue from Franchise Fees		10,000.00
Unearned Franchise Fees		31,941.68

4. If the initial down payment is not refundable and no future services are required by the franchisor, but collection of the note is so uncertain that recognition of the note as an asset is unwarranted, the entry should be:

Cash	10,000	
Revenue from Franchise Fees		10,000

5. Under the same conditions as those listed in case 4 above, except that the down payment is refundable or substantial services are yet to be performed, the entry should be:

Cash	10,000	
Unearned Franchise Fees		10,000

In cases 4 and 5—where collection of the note is extremely uncertain—cash collections may be recognized using the installment-sales method or the cost-recovery method.[4]

Continuing Franchise Fees

Continuing franchise fees are received in return for the continuing rights granted by the franchise agreement and for providing such services as management training, advertising and promotion, legal assistance, and other support. Continuing fees should

[4]A study that compared four revenue recognition procedures—installment-sales basis, spreading recognition over the contract life, percentage-of-completion basis, and substantial performance—for franchise sales concluded that the percentage-of-completion method is the most acceptable revenue recognition method; the substantial-performance method was found sometimes to yield ultra-conservative results. See Charles H. Calhoun III, "Accounting for Initial Franchise Fees: Is It a Dead Issue?" *The Journal of Accountancy* (February 1975), pp. 60–67.

be reported as revenue when they are earned and receivable from the franchisee, unless a portion of them has been designated for a particular purpose, such as providing a specified amount for building maintenance or local advertising. In that case, the portion deferred shall be an amount sufficient to cover the estimated cost in excess of continuing franchise fees and provide a reasonable profit on the continuing services.

Bargain Purchases

In addition to paying continuing franchise fees, franchisees frequently purchase some or all of their equipment and supplies from the franchisor. The franchisor would account for these sales as it would for any other product sales.

Sometimes, however, the franchise agreement grants the franchisee the right to make **bargain purchases** of equipment or supplies after the initial franchise fee is paid. If the bargain price is lower than the normal selling price of the same product, or if it does not provide the franchisor a reasonable profit, then a portion of the initial franchise fee should be deferred. The deferred portion would be accounted for as an adjustment of the selling price when the franchisee subsequently purchases the equipment or supplies.

Options to Purchase

A franchise agreement may give the franchisor an **option to purchase** the franchisee's business. As a matter of management policy, the franchisor may reserve the right to purchase a profitable franchised outlet, or to purchase one that is in financial difficulty. If it is probable at the time the option is given that the franchisor will ultimately purchase the outlet, then the initial franchise fee should not be recognized as revenue but should be recorded as a liability. When the option is exercised, the liability would reduce the franchisor's investment in the outlet.

Franchisor's Cost

Franchise accounting also involves proper accounting for the **franchisor's cost**. The objective is to match related costs and revenues by reporting them as components of income in the same accounting period. Franchisors should ordinarily defer **direct costs** (usually incremental costs) relating to specific franchise sales for which revenue has not yet been recognized. Costs should not be deferred, however, without reference to anticipated revenue and its realizability.[5] **Indirect costs** of a regular and recurring nature, such as selling and administrative expenses that are incurred irrespective of the level of franchise sales, should be expensed as incurred.

Disclosures of Franchisors

Disclosure of all significant commitments and obligations resulting from franchise agreements, including a description of services that have not yet been substantially performed, is required. Any resolution of uncertainties regarding the collectibility of franchise fees should be disclosed. Initial franchise fees should be segregated from other franchise fee revenue if they are significant. Where possible, revenues and costs related to franchisor-owned outlets should be distinguished from those related to franchised outlets.

CONSIGNMENTS

In some arrangements the delivery of the goods by the manufacturer (or wholesaler) to the dealer (or retailer) is not considered to be full performance and a sale because the manufacturer retains title to the goods. This specialized method of marketing cer-

[5]"Accounting for Franchise Fee Revenue," p. 17.

tain types of products makes use of a device known as a **consignment**. Under this arrangement, the **consignor** (manufacturer or wholesaler) ships merchandise to the **consignee** (dealer), who is to act as an agent for the consignor in selling the merchandise. Both consignor and consignee are interested in selling—the former to make a profit or develop a market, the latter to make a commission on the sales.

The consignee accepts the merchandise and agrees to exercise due diligence in caring for and selling it. Cash received from customers is remitted to the consignor by the consignee, after deducting a sales commission and any chargeable expenses.

A modified version of the sale basis of revenue recognition is used by the consignor. That is, revenue is recognized only after the consignor receives notification of sale and the cash remittance from the consignee. The merchandise is carried throughout the consignment as the inventory of the consignor, separately classified as Merchandise on Consignment. **It is not recorded as an asset on the consignee's books.** Upon sale of the merchandise, the consignee has **a liability for the net amount due the consignor**. The consignor periodically receives from the consignee a report called **account sales** that shows the merchandise received, merchandise sold, expenses chargeable to the consignment, and the cash remitted. Revenue is then recognized by the consignor.

To illustrate consignment accounting entries, assume that Nelba Manufacturing Co. ships merchandise costing $36,000 on consignment to Best Value Stores. Nelba pays $3,750 of freight costs, and Best Value pays $2,250 for local advertising costs that are reimbursable from Nelba. By the end of the period, two-thirds of the consigned merchandise has been sold for $40,000 cash. Best Value notifies Nelba of the sales, retains a 10 percent commission, and remits the cash due Nelba. The following journal entries would be made by the consignor (Nelba) and the consignee (Best Value) as follows.

ILLUSTRATION 18A-1
Entries for Consignment Sales

NELBA MFG. CO. (CONSIGNOR)			BEST VALUE STORES (CONSIGNEE)		
Shipment of consigned merchandise					
Inventory on Consignment	36,000		No entry (record memo of merchandise		
Finished Goods Inventory		36,000	received).		
Payment of freight costs by consignor					
Inventory on Consignment	3,750		No entry.		
Cash		3,750			
Payment of advertising by consignee					
No entry until notified.			Receivable from Consignor	2,250	
			Cash		2,250
Sales of consigned merchandise					
No entry until notified.			Cash	40,000	
			Payable to Consignor		40,000
Notification of sales and expenses and remittance of amount due					
Cash	33,750		Payable to Consignor	40,000	
Advertising Expense	2,250		Receivable from		
Commission Expense	4,000		Consignor		2,250
Revenue from			Commission Revenue		4,000
Consignment Sales		40,000	Cash		33,750
Adjustment of inventory on consignment for cost of sales					
Cost of Goods Sold	26,500		No entry.		
Inventory on Consignment		26,500			
[2/3 ($36,000 + $3,750) = $26,500]					

Under the consignment arrangement, the consignor accepts the risk that the merchandise might not sell and relieves the consignee of the need to commit part of its working capital to inventory. A variety of different systems and account titles are used to record consignments, but they all share the common goal of postponing the recognition of revenue until it is known that a sale to a third party has occurred.

KEY TERMS

account sales, *935*
consignee, *935*
consignment, *935*
consignor, *935*
continuing franchise fees, *933*
franchisee, *932*
franchisor, *932*
initial franchise fee, *932*
substantial performance, *932*

SUMMARY OF LEARNING OBJECTIVE FOR APPENDIX 18A

8 Explain revenue recognition for franchises and consignment sales. In a franchise arrangement, the initial franchise fee is recorded as revenue only when and as the franchisor makes substantial performance of the services it is obligated to perform and collection of the fee is reasonably assured. Continuing franchise fees are recognized as revenue when they are earned and receivable from the franchisee. Revenue is recognized by the consignor when an account sales and the cash are received from the consignee.

Note: All **asterisked** Questions, Brief Exercises, Exercises, and Conceptual Cases relate to material contained in the appendix to the chapter.

QUESTIONS

1. Explain the current environment regarding revenue recognition.

2. When is revenue conventionally recognized? What conditions should exist for the recognition at date of sale of all or part of the revenue and income of any sale transaction?

3. When is revenue recognized in the following situations: (a) Revenue from selling products? (b) Revenue from services rendered? (c) Revenue from permitting others to use enterprise assets? (d) Revenue from disposing of assets other than products?

4. Identify several types of sales transactions and indicate the types of business for which that type of transaction is common.

5. What are the three alternative accounting methods available to a seller that is exposed to continued risks of ownership through return of the product?

6. Under what conditions may a seller who is exposed to continued risks of a high rate of return of the product sold recognize sales transactions as current revenue?

7. What are the two basic methods of accounting for long-term construction contracts? Indicate the circumstances that determine when one or the other of these methods should be used.

8. F. Scott Fitzgerald Construction Co. has a $60 million contract to construct a highway overpass and cloverleaf. The total estimated cost for the project is $50 million. Costs incurred in the first year of the project are $9 million. F. Scott Fitzgerald Construction Co. appropriately uses the percentage-of-completion method. How much revenue and gross profit should F. Scott Fitzgerald recognize in the first year of the project?

9. For what reasons should the percentage-of-completion method be used over the completed-contract method whenever possible?

10. What methods are used in practice to determine the extent of progress toward completion? Identify some "input measures" and some "output measures" that might be used to determine the extent of progress.

11. What are the two types of losses that can become evident in accounting for long-term contracts? What is the nature of each type of loss? How is each type accounted for?

12. Under the percentage-of-completion method, how are the Construction in Process and the Billings on Construction in Process accounts reported in the balance sheet?

13. Explain the differences between the installment-sales method and the cost-recovery method.

14. Identify and briefly describe the two methods generally employed to account for the cash received in situations where the collection of the sales price is not reasonably assured.

15. What is the deposit method and when might it be applied?

16. What is the nature of an installment sale? How do installment sales differ from ordinary credit sales?

17. Describe the installment-sales method of accounting.

18. How are operating expenses (not included in cost of goods sold) handled under the installment-sales method of accounting? What is the justification for such treatment?

19. Jack London sold his condominium for $500,000 on September 14, 2003; he had paid $310,000 for it in 1995. London collected the selling price as follows: 2003, $80,000; 2004, $320,000; and 2005, $100,000. London appropriately uses the installment-sales method. Prepare a schedule to determine the gross profit for 2003, 2004, and 2005 from the installment sale.

20. When interest is involved in installment-sales transactions, how should it be treated for accounting purposes?

21. How should the results of installment sales be reported on the income statement?

22. At what time is it proper to recognize income in the following cases: (a) Installment sales with no reasonable basis for estimating the degree of collectibility? (b) Sales for future delivery? (c) Merchandise shipped on consignment? (d) Profit on incomplete construction contracts? (e) Subscriptions to publications?

23. When is revenue recognized under the cost-recovery method?

24. When is revenue recognized under the deposit method? How does the deposit method differ from the installment-sales and cost-recovery methods?

***25.** Why in franchise arrangements may it not be proper to recognize the entire franchise fee as revenue at the date of sale?

***26.** How does the concept of "substantial performance" apply to accounting for franchise sales?

***27.** How should a franchisor account for continuing franchise fees and routine sales of equipment and supplies to franchisees?

***28** What changes are made in the franchisor's recording of the initial franchise fee when the franchise agreement:

(a) Contains an option allowing the franchisor to purchase the franchised outlet, and it is likely that the option will be exercised?

(b) Allows the franchisee to purchase equipment and supplies from the franchisor at bargain prices?

***29** What is the nature of a sale on consignment? When is revenue recognized from a consignment sale?

BRIEF EXERCISES

BE18-1 Scooby Doo Music sold CDs to retailers and recorded sales revenue of $800,000. During 2005, retailers returned CDs to Scooby Doo and were granted credit of $78,000. Past experience indicates that the normal return rate is 15%. Prepare Scooby Doo's entries to record (a) the $78,000 of returns and (b) estimated returns at December 31, 2005.

BE18-2 Shock Wave, Inc. began work on a $7,000,000 contract in 2005 to construct an office building. During 2005, Shock Wave, Inc. incurred costs of $1,715,000, billed their customers for $1,200,000, and collected $960,000. At December 31, 2005, the estimated future costs to complete the project total $3,185,000. Prepare Shock Wave's 2005 journal entries using the percentage-of-completion method.

BE18-3 Shadow Blasters, Inc. began work on a $7,000,000 contract in 2005 to construct an office building. Shadow Blasters uses the percentage-of-completion method. At December 31, 2005, the balances in certain accounts were: construction in process $2,450,000; accounts receivable $240,000; and billings on construction in process $1,200,000. Indicate how these accounts would be reported in Shadow Blasters' December 31, 2005, balance sheet.

BE18-4 Use the information from BE18-2, but assume Shock Wave uses the completed-contract method. Prepare the company's 2005 journal entries.

BE18-5 Cordero, Inc. began work on a $7,000,000 contract in 2005 to construct an office building. Cordero uses the completed-contract method. At December 31, 2005, the balances in certain accounts were construction in process $1,715,000; accounts receivable $240,000; and billings on construction in process $1,200,000. Indicate how these accounts would be reported in Cordero's December 31, 2005, balance sheet.

BE18-6 Shaq Fu Construction Company began work on a $420,000 construction contract in 2005. During 2005, Shaq Fu incurred costs of $288,000, billed its customer for $215,000, and collected $175,000. At December 31, 2005, the estimated future costs to complete the project total $162,000. Prepare Shaq Fu's journal entry to record profit or loss using (a) the percentage-of-completion method and (b) the completed-contract method, if any.

BE18-7 Thunder Paradise Corporation began selling goods on the installment basis on January 1, 2005. During 2005, Thunder Paradise had installment sales of $150,000; cash collections of $54,000; cost of installment sales of $105,000. Prepare the company's entries to record installment sales, cash collected, cost of installment sales, deferral of gross profit, and gross profit recognized, using the installment-sales method.

BE18-8 Shinobi, Inc. sells goods on the installment basis and uses the installment-sales method. Due to a customer default, Shinobi repossessed merchandise that was originally sold for $800, resulting in a gross profit rate of 40%. At the time of repossession, the uncollected balance is $560, and the fair value of the repossessed merchandise is $275. Prepare Shinobi's entry to record the repossession.

BE18-9 At December 31, 2005, Soul Star Corporation had the following account balances.

Installment Accounts Receivable, 2004	$ 65,000
Installment Accounts Receivable, 2005	110,000
Deferred Gross Profit, 2004	23,400
Deferred Gross Profit, 2005	40,700

Most of Soul Star's sales are made on a 2-year installment basis. Indicate how these accounts would be reported in Soul Star's December 31, 2005, balance sheet. The 2004 accounts are collectible in 2006, and the 2005 accounts are collectible in 2007.

BE18-10 Yogi Bear Corporation sold equipment to Magilla Company for $20,000. The equipment is on Yogi's books at a net amount of $14,000. Yogi collected $10,000 in 2004, $5,000 in 2005, and $5,000 in 2006. If Yogi uses the cost-recovery method, what amount of gross profit will be recognized in each year?

***BE18-11** Speed Racer, Inc. charges an initial franchise fee of $75,000 for the right to operate as a franchisee of Speed Racer. Of this amount, $25,000 is collected immediately. The remainder is collected in 4 equal annual installments of $12,500 each. These installments have a present value of $39,623. There is reasonable expectation that the down payment may be refunded and substantial future services be performed by Speed Racer, Inc. Prepare the journal entry required by Speed Racer to record the franchise fee.

***BE18-12** Tom and Jerry Corporation shipped $20,000 of merchandise on consignment to Toons Company. Tom and Jerry paid freight costs of $2,000. Toons Company paid $500 for local advertising which is reimbursable from Tom and Jerry. By year-end, 60% of the merchandise had been sold for $22,300. Toons notified Tom and Jerry, retained a 10% commission, and remitted the cash due to Tom and Jerry. Prepare Tom and Jerry's entry when the cash is received.

EXERCISES

E18-1 (Revenue Recognition on Book Sales with High Returns) Justin Huish Publishing Co. publishes college textbooks that are sold to bookstores on the following terms. Each title has a fixed wholesale price, terms f.o.b. shipping point, and payment is due 60 days after shipment. The retailer may return a maximum of 30% of an order at the retailer's expense. Sales are made only to retailers who have good credit ratings. Past experience indicates that the normal return rate is 12%, and the average collection period is 72 days.

Instructions

(a) Identify alternative revenue recognition tests that Huish could employ concerning textbook sales.

(b) Briefly discuss the reasoning for your answers in (a) above.

(c) In late July, Huish shipped books invoiced at $16,000,000. Prepare the journal entry to record this event that best conforms to generally accepted accounting principles and your answer to part (b).

(d) In October, $2 million of the invoiced July sales were returned according to the return policy, and the remaining $14 million was paid. Prepare the entry recording the return and payment.

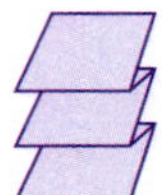

E18-2 (Sales Recorded Both Gross and Net) On June 3, David Reid Company sold to Kim Rhode merchandise having a sale price of $5,000 with terms of 2/10, n/60, f.o.b. shipping point. An invoice totaling $120, terms n/30, was received by Rhode on June 8 from the Olympic Transport Service for the freight cost. Upon receipt of the goods, June 5, Rhode notified Reid Company that merchandise costing $400 contained flaws that rendered it worthless. The same day Reid Company issued a credit memo covering the worthless merchandise and asked that it be returned at company expense. The freight on the returned merchandise was $24, paid by Reid Company on June 7. On June 12, the company received a check for the balance due from Rhode.

Instructions

(a) Prepare journal entries on Reid Company books to record all the events noted above under each of the following bases.

- **(1)** Sales and receivables are entered at gross selling price.
- **(2)** Sales and receivables are entered net of cash discounts.

(b) Prepare the journal entry under basis 2, assuming that Kim Rhode did not remit payment until August 5.

E18-3 (Revenue Recognition on Marina Sales with Discounts) Brooke Bennett Marina has 300 available slips that rent for $900 per season. Payments must be made in full at the start of the boating season,

April 1. Slips for the next season may be reserved if paid for by December 31. Under a new policy, if payment is made by December 31, a 5% discount is allowed. The boating season ends October 31, and the marina has a December 31 year-end. To provide cash flow for major dock repairs, the marina operator is also offering a 25% discount to slip renters who pay for the second season following the current December 31.

For the fiscal year ended December 31, 2004, all 300 slips were rented at full price. Two hundred slips were reserved and paid for for the 2005 boating season, and 60 slips were reserved and paid for for the 2006 boating season.

Instructions

(a) Prepare the appropriate journal entries for fiscal 2004.

(b) Assume the marina operator is unsophisticated in business. Explain the managerial significance of the accounting above to this person.

E18-4 (Recognition of Profit on Long-Term Contracts) During 2004 Pierson Company started a construction job with a contract price of $1,500,000. The job was completed in 2006. The following information is available.

	2004	2005	2006
Costs incurred to date	$400,000	$935,000	$1,070,000
Estimated costs to complete	600,000	165,000	–0–
Billings to date	300,000	900,000	1,500,000
Collections to date	270,000	810,000	1,425,000

Instructions

(a) Compute the amount of gross profit to be recognized each year assuming the percentage-of-completion method is used.

(b) Prepare all necessary journal entries for 2005.

(c) Compute the amount of gross profit to be recognized each year assuming the completed-contract method is used.

E18-5 (Analysis of Percentage-of-Completion Financial Statements) In 2004, Beth Botsford Construction Corp. began construction work under a 3-year contract. The contract price was $1,000,000. Beth Botsford uses the percentage-of-completion method for financial accounting purposes. The income to be recognized each year is based on the proportion of cost incurred to total estimated costs for completing the contract. The financial statement presentations relating to this contract at December 31, 2004, follow.

Balance Sheet

Accounts receivable—construction contract billings		$21,500
Construction in progress	$65,000	
Less: Contract billings	61,500	
Cost of uncompleted contract in excess of billings		3,500

Income Statement

Income (before tax) on the contract recognized in 2004	$18,200

Instructions

(a) How much cash was collected in 2004 on this contract?

(b) What was the initial estimated total income before tax on this contract?

(AICPA adapted)

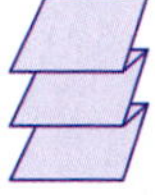

E18-6 (Gross Profit on Uncompleted Contract) On April 1, 2004, Brad Bridgewater Inc. entered into a cost-plus-fixed-fee contract to construct an electric generator for Tom Dolan Corporation. At the contract date, Bridgewater estimated that it would take 2 years to complete the project at a cost of $2,000,000. The fixed fee stipulated in the contract is $450,000. Bridgewater appropriately accounts for this contract under the percentage-of-completion method. During 2004 Bridgewater incurred costs of $700,000 related to the project. The estimated cost at December 31, 2004, to complete the contract is $1,300,000. Dolan was billed $600,000 under the contract.

Instructions

Prepare a schedule to compute the amount of gross profit to be recognized by Bridgewater under the contract for the year ended December 31, 2004. Show supporting computations in good form.

(AICPA adapted)

E18-7 (Recognition of Profit, Percentage-of-Completion) In 2004 Jeff Rouse Construction Company agreed to construct an apartment building at a price of $1,000,000. The information relating to the costs and billings for this contract is shown on the next page.

	2004	2005	2006
Costs incurred to date	$280,000	$600,000	$ 785,000
Estimated costs yet to be incurred	520,000	200,000	–0–
Customer billings to date	150,000	400,000	1,000,000
Collection of billings to date	120,000	320,000	940,000

Instructions

(a) Assuming that the percentage-of-completion method is used, (1) compute the amount of gross profit to be recognized in 2004 and 2005, and (2) prepare journal entries for 2005.

(b) For 2005, show how the details related to this construction contract would be disclosed on the balance sheet and on the income statement.

E18-8 (Recognition of Revenue on Long-Term Contract and Entries) Amy Van Dyken Construction Company uses the percentage-of-completion method of accounting. In 2004, Van Dyken began work under contract #E2-D2, which provided for a contract price of $2,200,000. Other details follow:

	2004	2005
Costs incurred during the year	$ 480,000	$1,425,000
Estimated costs to complete, as of December 31	1,120,000	–0–
Billings during the year	420,000	1,680,000
Collections during the year	350,000	1,500,000

Instructions

(a) What portion of the total contract price would be recognized as revenue in 2004? In 2005?

(b) Assuming the same facts as those above except that Van Dyken uses the completed-contract method of accounting, what portion of the total contract price would be recognized as revenue in 2005?

(c) Prepare a complete set of journal entries for 2004 (using percentage-of-completion).

E18-9 (Recognition of Profit and Balance Sheet Amounts for Long-Term Contracts) Andre Agassi Construction Company began operations January 1, 2004. During the year, Andre Agassi Construction entered into a contract with Lindsey Davenport Corp. to construct a manufacturing facility. At that time, Agassi estimated that it would take 5 years to complete the facility at a total cost of $4,500,000. The total contract price for construction of the facility is $6,300,000. During the year, Agassi incurred $1,185,800 in construction costs related to the construction project. The estimated cost to complete the contract is $4,204,200. Lindsey Davenport Corp. was billed and paid 30% of the contract price.

Instructions

Prepare schedules to compute the amount of gross profit to be recognized for the year ended December 31, 2004, and the amount to be shown as "cost of uncompleted contract in excess of related billings" or "billings on uncompleted contract in excess of related costs" at December 31, 2004, under each of the following methods.

(a) Completed-contract method.

(b) Percentage-of-completion method.

Show supporting computations in good form.

(AICPA adapted)

E18-10 (Long-Term Contract Reporting) Derrick Adkins Construction Company began operations in 2004. Construction activity for the first year is shown below. All contracts are with different customers, and any work remaining at December 31, 2004, is expected to be completed in 2005.

Project	Total Contract Price	Billings through 12/31/04	Cash Collections through 12/31/04	Contract Costs Incurred through 12/31/04	Estimated Additional Costs to Complete
1	$ 560,000	$ 360,000	$340,000	$450,000	$140,000
2	670,000	220,000	210,000	126,000	504,000
3	500,000	500,000	440,000	330,000	–0–
	$1,730,000	$1,080,000	$990,000	$906,000	$644,000

Instructions

Prepare a partial income statement and balance sheet to indicate how the above information would be reported for financial statement purposes. Derrick Adkins Construction Company uses the completed-contract method.

E18-11 (Installment-Sales Method Calculations, Entries) Austin Corporation appropriately uses the installment-sales method of accounting to recognize income in its financial statements. The following information is available for 2004 and 2005.

	2004	2005
Installment sales	$900,000	$1,000,000
Cost of installment sales	630,000	680,000
Cash collections on 2004 sales	370,000	350,000
Cash collections on 2005 sales	–0–	475,000

Instructions

(a) Compute the amount of realized gross profit recognized in each year.
(b) Prepare all journal entries required in 2005.

E18-12 (Analysis of Installment-Sales Accounts) Charles Austin Co. appropriately uses the installment-sales method of accounting. On December 31, 2006, the books show balances as follows.

Installment Receivables		Deferred Gross Profit		Gross Profit on Sales	
2004	$11,000	2004	$ 7,000	2004	35%
2005	40,000	2005	26,000	2005	34%
2006	80,000	2006	95,000	2006	32%

Instructions

(a) Prepare the adjusting entry or entries required on December 31, 2006 to recognize 2006 realized gross profit. (Installment receivables have already been credited for cash receipts during 2006.)
(b) Compute the amount of cash collected in 2006 on accounts receivable each year.

E18-13 (Gross Profit Calculations and Repossessed Merchandise) Randy Barnes Corporation, which began business on January 1, 2004, appropriately uses the installment-sales method of accounting. The following data were obtained for the years 2004 and 2005.

	2004	2005
Installment sales	$750,000	$840,000
Cost of installment sales	525,000	604,800
General & administrative expenses	70,000	84,000
Cash collections on sales of 2004	310,000	300,000
Cash collections on sales of 2005	–0–	400,000

Instructions

(a) Compute the balance in the deferred gross profit accounts on December 31, 2004, and on December 31, 2005.
(b) A 2004 sale resulted in default in 2006. At the date of default, the balance on the installment receivable was $12,000, and the repossessed merchandise had a fair value of $8,000. Prepare the entry to record the repossession.

(AICPA adapted)

E18-14 (Interest Revenue from Installment Sale) Gail Devers Corporation sells farm machinery on the installment plan. On July 1, 2004, Devers entered into an installment-sale contract with Gwen Torrence Inc. for a 10-year period. Equal annual payments under the installment sale are $100,000 and are due on July 1. The first payment was made on July 1, 2004.

Additional information

1. The amount that would be realized on an outright sale of similar farm machinery is $676,000.
2. The cost of the farm machinery sold to Gwen Torrence Inc. is $500,000.
3. The finance charges relating to the installment period are $324,000 based on a stated interest rate of 10%, which is appropriate.
4. Circumstances are such that the collection of the installments due under the contract is reasonably assured.

Instructions

What income or loss before income taxes should Devers record for the year ended December 31, 2004, as a result of the transaction above?

(AICPA adapted)

E18-15 (Installment-Sales Method and Cost Recovery) Kenny Harrison Corp., a capital goods manufacturing business that started on January 4, 2004, and operates on a calendar-year basis, uses the installment-sales method of profit recognition in accounting for all its sales. The following data were taken from the 2004 and 2005 records.

	2004	2005
Installment sales	$480,000	$620,000
Gross profit as a percent of costs	25%	28%
Cash collections on sales of 2004	$140,000	$240,000
Cash collections on sales of 2005	–0–	$180,000

The amounts given for cash collections exclude amounts collected for interest charges.

Instructions

(a) Compute the amount of realized gross profit to be recognized on the 2005 income statement, prepared using the installment-sales method.

(b) State where the balance of Deferred Gross Profit would be reported on the financial statements for 2005.

(c) Compute the amount of realized gross profit to be recognized on the income statement, prepared using the cost-recovery method.

(CIA adapted)

E18-16 (Installment-Sales Method and Cost-Recovery Method) On January 1, 2004, Barkly Company sold property for $200,000. The note will be collected as follows: $100,000 in 2004, $60,000 in 2005, and $40,000 in 2006. The property had cost Barkly $150,000 when it was purchased in 2002.

Instructions

(a) Compute the amount of gross profit realized each year, assuming Barkly uses the cost-recovery method.

(b) Compute the amount of gross profit realized each year, assuming Barkly uses the installment-sales method.

E18-17 (Cost-Recovery Method) On January 1, 2005, Allen Johnson Company sold real estate that cost $110,000 to Carl Lewis for $120,000. Lewis agreed to pay for the purchase over 3 years by making three end-of-year equal payments of $52,557 that include 15% interest. Shortly after the sale, Allen Johnson Company learns distressing news about Lewis's financial circumstances and because collection is so uncertain decides to account for the sale using the cost-recovery method.

Instructions

Applying the cost-recovery method, prepare a schedule showing the amounts of cash collected, the increase (decrease) in deferred interest revenue, the balance of the receivable, the balance of the unrecovered cost, the gross profit realized, and the interest revenue realized for each of the 3 years assuming the payments are made as agreed.

E18-18 (Installment Sales—Default and Repossession) Michael Johnson Imports Inc. was involved in two default and repossession cases during the year:

1. A refrigerator was sold to Merlene Ottey for $1,800, including a 35% markup on selling price. Ottey made a down payment of 20%, four of the remaining 16 equal payments, and then defaulted on further payments. The refrigerator was repossessed, at which time the fair value was determined to be $800.
2. An oven that cost $1,200 was sold to Donovan Bailey for $1,600 on the installment basis. Bailey made a down payment of $240 and paid $80 a month for six months, after which he defaulted. The oven was repossessed and the estimated value at time of repossession was determined to be $750.

Instructions

Prepare journal entries to record each of these repossessions. (Ignore interest charges.)

E18-19 (Installment Sales—Default and Repossession) Kurt Angle Company uses the installment-sales method in accounting for its installment sales. On January 1, 2005, Angle Company had an installment account receivable from Kay Bluhm with a balance of $1,800. During 2005, $400 was collected from Bluhm. When no further collection could be made, the merchandise sold to Bluhm was repossessed. The merchandise had a fair market value of $650 after the company spent $60 for reconditioning of the merchandise. The merchandise was originally sold with a gross profit rate of 40%.

Instructions

Prepare the entries on the books of Angle Company to record all transactions related to Bluhm during 2005. (Ignore interest charges.)

E18-20 (Cost-Recovery Method) On January 1, 2005, Tom Brands sells 200 acres of farmland for $600,000, taking in exchange a 10% interest-bearing note. Tom Brands purchased the farmland in 1990 at a cost of $500,000. The note will be paid in three installments of $241,269 each on December 31, 2005, 2006, and 2007. Collectibility of the note is uncertain; Tom, therefore, uses the cost-recovery method.

Instructions

Prepare for Tom a 3-year installment payment schedule (under the cost-recovery method) that shows cash collections, deferred interest revenue, installment receivable balances, unrecovered cost, realized gross profit, and realized interest revenue by year.

***E18-21 (Franchise Entries)** Kendall Crossburgers Inc. charges an initial franchise fee of $70,000. Upon the signing of the agreement, a payment of $40,000 is due. Thereafter, three annual payments of $10,000 are required. The credit rating of the franchisee is such that it would have to pay interest at 10% to borrow money.

Instructions

Prepare the entries to record the initial franchise fee on the books of the franchisor under the following assumptions.

(a) The down payment is not refundable, no future services are required by the franchisor, and collection of the note is reasonably assured.

(b) The franchisor has substantial services to perform, the down payment is refundable, and the collection of the note is very uncertain.

(c) The down payment is not refundable, collection of the note is reasonably certain, the franchisor has yet to perform a substantial amount of services, and the down payment represents a fair measure of the services already performed.

***E18-22 (Franchise Fee, Initial Down Payment)** On January 1, 2004, Svetlana Masterkova signed an agreement to operate as a franchisee of Short-Track Inc. for an initial franchise fee of $50,000. The amount of $20,000 was paid when the agreement was signed, and the balance is payable in five annual payments of $6,000 each, beginning January 1, 2005. The agreement provides that the down payment is not refundable and that no future services are required of the franchisor. Svetlana Masterkova's credit rating indicates that she can borrow money at 11% for a loan of this type.

Instructions

(a) How much should Short-Track record as revenue from franchise fees on January 1, 2004? At what amount should Svetlana record the acquisition cost of the franchise on January 1, 2004?

(b) What entry would be made by Short-Track on January 1, 2004, if the down payment is refundable and substantial future services remain to be performed by Short-Track?

(c) How much revenue from franchise fees would be recorded by Short-Track on January 1, 2004, if:

(1) The initial down payment is not refundable, it represents a fair measure of the services already provided, a significant amount of services is still to be performed by Short-Track in future periods, and collectibility of the note is reasonably assured?

(2) The initial down payment is not refundable and no future services are required by the franchisor, but collection of the note is so uncertain that recognition of the note as an asset is unwarranted?

(3) The initial down payment has not been earned and collection of the note is so uncertain that recognition of the note as an asset is unwarranted?

***E18-23 (Consignment Computations)** On May 3, 2004, Michelle Smith Company consigned 70 freezers, costing $500 each, to Angel Martino Company. The cost of shipping the freezers amounted to $840 and was paid by Smith Company. On December 30, 2004, an account sales was received from the consignee, reporting that 40 freezers had been sold for $700 each. Remittance was made by the consignee for the amount due, after deducting a commission of 6%, advertising of $200, and total installation costs of $320 on the freezers sold.

Instructions

(a) Compute the inventory value of the units unsold in the hands of the consignee.

(b) Compute the profit for the consignor for the units sold.

(c) Compute the amount of cash that will be remitted by the consignee.

PROBLEMS

P18-1 (Comprehensive Three-Part Revenue Recognition) Simona Amanar Industries has three operating divisions—Gina Construction Division, Gogean Publishing Division, and Chorkina Securities Division. Each division maintains its own accounting system and method of revenue recognition.

Gina Construction Division

During the fiscal year ended November 30, 2004, Gina Construction Division had one construction project in process. A $30,000,000 contract for construction of a civic center was granted on June 19, 2004, and construction began on August 1, 2004. Estimated costs of completion at the contract date were $25,000,000 over a 2-year time period from the date of the contract. On November 30, 2004, construction costs of $7,800,000 had been incurred and progress billings of $9,500,000 had been made. The construction costs to complete the remainder of the project were reviewed on November 30, 2004, and were estimated to amount to only $16,200,000 because of an expected decline in raw materials costs. Revenue recognition is based upon a percentage-of-completion method.

Gogean Publishing Division

The Gogean Publishing Division sells large volumes of novels to a few book distributors, which in turn sell to several national chains of bookstores. Gogean allows distributors to return up to 30% of sales, and distributors give the same terms to bookstores. While returns from individual titles fluctuate greatly, the returns from distributors have averaged 20% in each of the past 5 years. A total of $8,000,000 of paperback novel sales were made to distributors during fiscal 2004. On November 30, 2004, $2,500,000 of fiscal 2004 sales were still subject to return privileges over the next 6 months. The remaining $5,500,000 of fiscal 2004 sales had actual returns of 21%. Sales from fiscal 2003 totaling $2,000,000 were collected in fiscal 2004 less 18% returns. This division records revenue according to the method referred to as revenue recognition when the right of return exists.

Chorkina Securities Division

Chorkina Securities Division works through manufacturers' agents in various cities. Orders for alarm systems and down payments are forwarded from agents, and the Division ships the goods f.o.b. factory directly to customers (usually police departments and security guard companies). Customers are billed directly for the balance due plus actual shipping costs. The company received orders for $6,000,000 of goods during the fiscal year ended November 30, 2004. Down payments of $600,000 were received, and $5,200,000 of goods were billed and shipped. Actual freight costs of $100,000 were also billed. Commissions of 10% on product price are paid to manufacturing agents after goods are shipped to customers. Such goods are warranted for 90 days after shipment, and warranty returns have been about 1% of sales. Revenue is recognized at the point of sale by this division.

Instructions

(a) There are a variety of methods of revenue recognition. Define and describe each of the following methods of revenue recognition, and indicate whether each is in accordance with generally accepted accounting principles.
  (1) Point of sale.
  (2) Completion-of-production.
  (3) Percentage-of-completion.
  (4) Installment-sales contract.

(b) Compute the revenue to be recognized in fiscal year 2004 for each of the three operating divisions of Simona Amanar Industries in accordance with generally accepted accounting principles.

P18-2 (Recognition of Profit on Long-Term Contract) Jenny Thompson Construction Company has entered into a contract beginning January 1, 2004, to build a parking complex. It has been estimated that the complex will cost $600,000 and will take 3 years to construct. The complex will be billed to the purchasing company at $900,000. The following data pertain to the construction period.

	2004	2005	2006
Costs to date	$270,000	$420,000	$600,000
Estimated costs to complete	330,000	180,000	–0–
Progress billings to date	270,000	550,000	900,000
Cash collected to date	240,000	500,000	900,000

Instructions

(a) Using the percentage-of-completion method, compute the estimated gross profit that would be recognized during each year of the construction period.

(b) Using the completed-contract method, compute the estimated gross profit that would be recognized during each year of the construction period.

P18-3 (Recognition of Profit and Entries on Long-Term Contract) On March 1, 2004, Winter Company entered into a contract to build an apartment building. It is estimated that the building will cost $2,000,000 and will take 3 years to complete. The contract price was $3,000,000. The information on the next page pertains to the construction period.

	2004	2005	2006
Costs to date	$ 600,000	$1,560,000	$2,100,000
Estimated costs to complete	1,400,000	390,000	–0–
Progress billings to date	1,050,000	2,100,000	3,000,000
Cash collected to date	950,000	1,950,000	2,750,000

Instructions

(a) Compute the amount of gross profit to be recognized each year assuming the percentage-of-completion method is used.

(b) Prepare all necessary journal entries for 2006.

(c) Prepare a partial balance sheet for December 31, 2005, showing the balances in the receivables and inventory accounts.

P18-4 (Recognition of Profit and Balance Sheet Presentation, Percentage-of-Completion) On February 1, 2004, Amanda Beard Construction Company obtained a contract to build an athletic stadium. The stadium was to be built at a total cost of $5,400,000 and was scheduled for completion by September 1, 2006. One clause of the contract stated that Beard was to deduct $15,000 from the $6,600,000 billing price for each week that completion was delayed. Completion was delayed 6 weeks, which resulted in a $90,000 penalty. Below are the data pertaining to the construction period.

	2004	2005	2006
Costs to date	$1,782,000	$3,850,000	$5,500,000
Estimated costs to complete	3,618,000	1,650,000	–0–
Progress billings to date	1,200,000	3,100,000	6,510,000
Cash collected to date	1,000,000	2,800,000	6,510,000

Instructions

(a) Using the percentage-of-completion method, compute the estimated gross profit recognized in the years 2004–2006.

(b) Prepare a partial balance sheet for December 31, 2005, showing the balances in the receivable and inventory accounts.

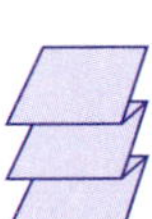

P18-5 (Completed Contract and Percentage of Completion with Interim Loss) Gold Medal Custom Builders (GMCB) was established in 1975 by Whitney Hedgepeth and initially built high-quality customized homes under contract with specific buyers. In the 1980s, Hedgepeth's two sons joined the firm and expanded GMCB's activities into the high-rise apartment and industrial plant markets. Upon the retirement of GMCB's long-time financial manager, Hedgepeth's sons recently hired Le Jingyi as controller for GMCB. Jingyi, a former college friend of Hedgepeth's sons, has been associated with a public accounting firm for the last 6 years.

Upon reviewing GMCB's accounting practices, Jingyi observed that GMCB followed the completed-contract method of revenue recognition, a carryover from the years when individual home building was the majority of GMCB's operations. Several years ago, the predominant portion of GMCB's activities shifted to the high-rise and industrial building areas. From land acquisition to the completion of construction, most building contracts cover several years. Under the circumstances, Jingyi believes that GMCB should follow the percentage-of-completion method of accounting. From a typical building contract, Jingyi developed the following data.

DAGMAR HAZE TRACTOR PLANT

Contract price: $8,000,000

	2003	2004	2005
Estimated costs	$2,010,000	$3,015,000	$1,675,000
Progress billings	1,000,000	2,500,000	4,500,000
Cash collections	800,000	2,300,000	4,900,000

Instructions

(a) Explain the difference between completed-contract revenue recognition and percentage-of-completion revenue recognition.

(b) Using the data provided for the Dagmar Haze Tractor Plant and assuming the percentage-of-completion method of revenue recognition is used, calculate GMCB's revenue and gross profit for 2003, 2004, and 2005, under **each** of the following circumstances.

(1) Assume that all costs are incurred, all billings to customers are made, and all collections from customers are received within 30 days of billing, as planned.

(2) Further assume that, as a result of unforeseen local ordinances and the fact that the building site was in a wetlands area, GMCB experienced cost overruns of $800,000 in 2003 to bring

the site into compliance with the ordinances and to overcome wetlands barriers to construction.

(3) Further assume that, in addition to the cost overruns of $800,000 for this contract incurred under part (b)2, inflationary factors over and above those anticipated in the development of the original contract cost have caused an additional cost overrun of $540,000 in 2004. It is not anticipated that any cost overruns will occur in 2005.

(CMA adapted)

P18-6 (Long-Term Contract with Interim Loss) On March 1, 2004, Franziska van Almsick Construction Company contracted to construct a factory building for Sandra Volker Manufacturing Inc. for a total contract price of $8,400,000. The building was completed by October 31, 2006. The annual contract costs incurred, estimated costs to complete the contract, and accumulated billings to Volker for 2004, 2005, and 2006 are given below.

	2004	2005	2006
Contract costs incurred during the year	$3,200,000	$2,600,000	$1,450,000
Estimated costs to complete the contract at 12/31	3,200,000	1,450,000	–0–
Billings to Volker during the year	3,200,000	3,500,000	1,700,000

Instructions

(a) Using the percentage-of-completion method, prepare schedules to compute the profit or loss to be recognized as a result of this contract for the years ended December 31, 2004, 2005, and 2006. (Ignore income taxes.)

(b) Using the completed-contract method, prepare schedules to compute the profit or loss to be recognized as a result of this contract for the years ended December 2004, 2005, and 2006. (Ignore incomes taxes.)

P18-7 (Long-Term Contract with an Overall Loss) On July 1, 2004, Kim Kyung-wook Construction Company Inc. contracted to build an office building for Fu Mingxia Corp. for a total contract price of $1,950,000. On July 1, Kyung-wook estimated that it would take between 2 and 3 years to complete the building. On December 31, 2006, the building was deemed substantially completed. Following are accumulated contract costs incurred, estimated costs to complete the contract, and accumulated billings to Mingxia for 2004, 2005, and 2006.

	At 12/31/04	At 12/31/05	At 12/31/06
Contract costs incurred to date	$ 150,000	$1,200,000	$2,100,000
Estimated costs to complete the contract	1,350,000	800,000	–0–
Billings to Mingxia	300,000	1,100,000	1,850,000

Instructions

(a) Using the percentage-of-completion method, prepare schedules to compute the profit or loss to be recognized as a result of this contract for the years ended December 31, 2004, 2005, and 2006. (Ignore income taxes.)

(b) Using the completed-contract method, prepare schedules to compute the profit or loss to be recognized as a result of this contract for the years ended December 2004, 2005, and 2006. (Ignore income taxes.)

P18-8 (Installment Sales Computations and Entries) Presented below is summarized information for Deng Yaping Co., which sells merchandise on the installment basis.

	2004	2005	2006
Sales (on installment plan)	$250,000	$260,000	$280,000
Cost of sales	150,000	163,800	182,000
Gross profit	$100,000	$ 96,200	$ 98,000
Collections from customers on:			
2004 installment sales	$ 75,000	$100,000	$ 50,000
2005 installment sales		100,000	120,000
2006 installment sales			110,000

Instructions

(a) Compute the realized gross profit for each of the years 2004, 2005, and 2006.

(b) Prepare in journal form all entries required in 2006, applying the installment-sales method of accounting. (Ignore interest charges.)

P18-9 (Installment-Sales Income Statements) Laura Flessel Stores sells merchandise on open account as well as on installment terms.

	2004	2005	2006
Sales on account	$385,000	$426,000	$525,000
Installment sales	320,000	275,000	380,000
Collections on installment sales			
Made in 2004	110,000	90,000	40,000
Made in 2005		110,000	140,000
Made in 2006			125,000
Cost of sales			
Sold on account	270,000	277,000	341,000
Sold on installment	214,400	167,750	224,200
Selling expenses	77,000	87,000	92,000
Administrative expenses	50,000	51,000	52,000

Instructions

From the data above, which cover the 3 years since Laura Flessel Stores commenced operations, determine the net income for each year, applying the installment-sales method of accounting. (Ignore interest charges.)

P18-10 (Installment-Sales Computations and Entries) Isabell Werth Stores sell appliances for cash and also on the installment plan. Entries to record cost of sales are made monthly.

ISABELL WERTH STORES
TRIAL BALANCE
DECEMBER 31, 2006

	Dr.	Cr.
Cash	$153,000	
Installment Accounts Receivable, 2005	48,000	
Installment Accounts Receivable, 2006	91,000	
Inventory—New Merchandise	123,200	
Inventory—Repossessed Merchandise	24,000	
Accounts Payable		$98,500
Deferred Gross Profit, 2005		45,600
Capital Stock		170,000
Retained Earnings		93,900
Sales		343,000
Installment Sales		200,000
Cost of Sales	255,000	
Cost of Installment Sales	128,000	
Gain or Loss on Repossessions	800	
Selling and Administrative Expenses	128,000	
	$951,000	$951,000

The accounting department has prepared the following analysis of cash receipts for the year.

Cash sales (including repossessed merchandise)	$424,000
Installment accounts receivable, 2005	104,000
Installment accounts receivable, 2006	109,000
Other	36,000
Total	$673,000

Repossessions recorded during the year are summarized as follows.

	2005
Uncollected balance	$8,000
Loss on repossession	800
Repossessed merchandise	4,800

Instructions

From the trial balance and accompanying information:

(a) Compute the rate of gross profit for 2005 and 2006.
(b) Prepare closing entries as of December 31, 2006, under the installment-sales method of accounting.

(c) Prepare a statement of income for the year ended December 31, 2006. Include only the realized gross profit in the income statement.

P18-11 (Installment-Sales Entries) The following summarized information relates to the installment-sales activity of Lisa Jacob Stores Inc. for the year 2004.

Installment sales during 2004	$500,000
Costs of goods sold on installment basis	330,000
Collections from customers	200,000
Unpaid balances on merchandise repossessed	24,000
Estimated value of merchandise repossessed	9,200

Instructions

(a) Prepare journal entries at the end of 2004 to record on the books of Lisa Jacob Stores, Inc. the summarized data above.

(b) Prepare the entry to record the gross profit realized during 2004.

P18-12 (Installment-Sales Computation and Entries—Periodic Inventory) Catherine Fox Inc. sells merchandise for cash and also on the installment plan. Entries to record cost of goods sold are made at the end of each year.

Repossessions of merchandise (sold in 2005) were made in 2006 and were recorded correctly as follows.

Deferred Gross Profit, 2005	7,200	
Repossessed Merchandise	8,000	
Loss on Repossessions	2,800	
Installment Accounts Receivable, 2005		18,000

Part of this repossessed merchandise was sold for cash during 2006, and the sale was recorded by a debit to Cash and a credit to Sales.

The inventory of repossessed merchandise on hand December 31, 2006, is $4,000; of new merchandise, $127,400. There was no repossessed merchandise on hand January 1, 2006.

Collections on accounts receivable during 2006 were:

Installment Accounts Receivable, 2005	$80,000
Installment Accounts Receivable, 2006	50,000

The cost of the merchandise sold under the installment plan during 2006 was $117,000.

The rate of gross profit on 2005 and on 2006 installment sales can be computed from the information given above.

CATHERINE FOX INC.
TRIAL BALANCE
DECEMBER 31, 2006

	Dr.	Cr.
Cash	$ 98,400	
Installment Accounts Receivable, 2005	80,000	
Installment Accounts Receivable, 2006	130,000	
Inventory, Jan. 1, 2006	120,000	
Repossessed Merchandise	8,000	
Accounts Payable		$ 47,200
Deferred Gross Profit, 2005		64,000
Capital Stock, Common		200,000
Retained Earnings		40,000
Sales		400,000
Installment Sales		180,000
Purchases	380,000	
Loss on Repossessions	2,800	
Operating Expenses	112,000	
	$931,200	$931,200

Instructions

(a) From the trial balance and other information given above, prepare adjusting and closing entries as of December 31, 2006.

(b) Prepare an income statement for the year ended December 31, 2006. Include only the realized gross profit in the income statement.

P18-13 (Installment Repossession Entries) Selected transactions of Marie-Jose Perec TV Sales Company are presented below.

1. A television set costing $560 is sold to Wang Junxia on November 1, 2005, for $800. Junxia makes a down payment of $200 and agrees to pay $30 on the first of each month for 20 months thereafter.
2. Junxia pays the $30 installment due December 1, 2005.
3. On December 31, 2005, the appropriate entries are made to record profit realized on the installment sales.
4. The first seven 2006 installments of $30 each are paid by Junxia. (Make one entry.)
5. In August 2006 the set is repossessed, after Junxia fails to pay the August 1 installment and indicates that he will be unable to continue the payments. The estimated fair value of the repossessed set is $100.

Instructions

Prepare journal entries to record on the books of Marie-Jose Perec TV Sales Company the transactions above. Closing entries should not be made.

P18-14 (Installment-Sales Computations and Schedules) Valentina Vezzali Company, on January 2, 2004, entered into a contract with a manufacturing company to purchase room-size air conditioners and to sell the units on an installment plan with collections over approximately 30 months with no carrying charge.

For income tax purposes Vezzali Company elected to report income from its sales of air conditioners according to the installment-sales method.

Purchases and sales of new units were as follows.

	Units Purchased		Units Sold	
Year	Quantity	Price Each	Quantity	Price Each
2004	1,400	$130	1,100	$200
2005	1,200	112	1,500	170
2006	900	136	800	182

Collections on installment sales were as follows.

	Collections Received		
	2004	2005	2006
2004 sales	$42,000	$88,000	$ 80,000
2005 sales		51,000	100,000
2006 sales			34,600

In 2006, 50 units from the 2005 sales were repossessed and sold for $80 each on the installment plan. At the time of repossession, $1,440 had been collected from the original purchasers, and the units had a fair value of $3,000.

General and administrative expenses for 2006 were $60,000. No charge has been made against current income for the applicable insurance expense from a 3-year policy expiring June 30, 2007, costing $7,200, and for an advance payment of $12,000 on a new contract to purchase air conditioners beginning January 2, 2007.

Instructions

Assuming that the weighted-average method is used for determining the inventory cost, including repossessed merchandise, prepare schedules computing for 2004, 2005, and 2006:

(a) **(1)** The cost of goods sold on installments.
(2) The average unit cost of goods sold on installments for each year.
(b) The gross profit percentages for 2004, 2005, and 2006.
(c) The gain or loss on repossessions in 2006.
(d) The net income from installment sales for 2006. (Ignore income taxes.)

(AICPA adapted)

P18-15 (Completed-Contract Method) Renata Mauer Construction Company, Inc., entered into a firm fixed-price contract with Giovanna Trillini Clinic on July 1, 2002, to construct a four-story office building. At that time, Mauer estimated that it would take between 2 and 3 years to complete the project. The total contract price for construction of the building is $4,500,000. Mauer appropriately accounts for this contract under the completed-contract method in its financial statements and for income tax reporting. The building was deemed substantially completed on December 31, 2004. Estimated percentage of completion, accumulated contract costs incurred, estimated costs to complete the contract, and accumulated billings to the Trillini Clinic under the contract are shown on the next page.

	At December 31, 2002	At December 31, 2003	At December 31, 2004
Percentage of completion	30%	65%	100%
Contract costs incurred	$1,140,000	$3,055,000	$4,800,000
Estimated costs to complete the contract	$2,660,000	$1,645,000	–0–
Billings to Trillini Clinic	$1,500,000	$2,500,000	$4,300,000

Instructions

(a) Prepare schedules to compute the amount to be shown as "Cost of uncompleted contract in excess of related billings" or "Billings on uncompleted contract in excess of related costs" at December 31, 2002, 2003, and 2004. Ignore income taxes. Show supporting computations in good form.

(b) Prepare schedules to compute the profit or loss to be recognized as a result of this contract for the years ended December 31, 2002, 2003, and 2004. Ignore income taxes. Show supporting computations in good form.

(AICPA adapted)

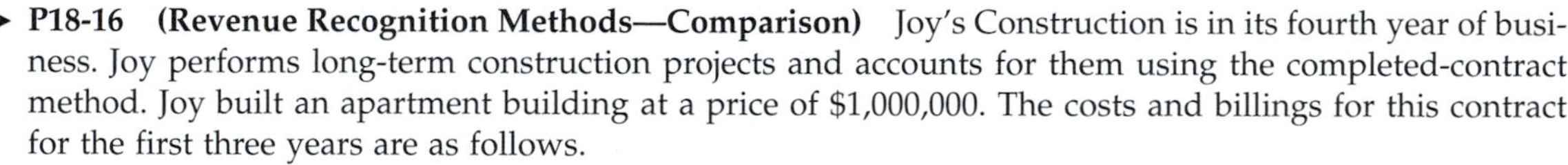

P18-16 (Revenue Recognition Methods—Comparison) Joy's Construction is in its fourth year of business. Joy performs long-term construction projects and accounts for them using the completed-contract method. Joy built an apartment building at a price of $1,000,000. The costs and billings for this contract for the first three years are as follows.

	2003	2004	2005
Costs incurred to date	$320,000	$600,000	$ 790,000
Estimated costs yet to be incurred	480,000	200,000	–0–
Customer billings to date	150,000	410,000	1,000,000
Collection of billings to date	120,000	340,000	950,000

Joy has contacted you, a certified public accountant, about the following concern. She would like to attract some investors, but she believes that in order to recognize revenue she must first "deliver" the product. Therefore, on her balance sheet, she did not recognize any gross profits from the above contract until 2005, when she recognized the entire $210,000. That looked good for 2005, but the preceding years looked grim by comparison. She wants to know about an alternative to this completed-contract revenue recognition.

Instructions

Draft a letter to Joy, telling her about the percentage-of-completion method of recognizing revenue. Compare it to the completed-contract method. Explain the idea behind the percentage-of-completion method. In addition, illustrate how much revenue she could have recognized in 2003, 2004, and 2005 if she had used this method.

P18-17 (Comprehensive Problem—Long-Term Contracts) You have been engaged by Rich Mathre Construction Company to advise it concerning the proper accounting for a series of long-term contracts. Rich Mathre Construction Company commenced doing business on January 1, 2004. Construction activities for the first year of operations are shown below. All contract costs are with different customers, and any work remaining at December 31, 2004, is expected to be completed in 2005.

Project	Total Contract Price	Billings Through 12/31/04	Cash Collections Through 12/31/04	Contract Costs Incurred Through 12/31/04	Estimated Additional Costs to Complete
A	$ 300,000	$200,000	$180,000	$248,000	$ 67,000
B	350,000	110,000	105,000	67,800	271,200
C	280,000	280,000	255,000	186,000	–0–
D	200,000	35,000	25,000	123,000	87,000
E	240,000	205,000	200,000	185,000	15,000
	$1,370,000	$830,000	$765,000	$809,800	$440,200

Instructions

(a) Prepare a schedule to compute gross profit (loss) to be reported, unbilled contract costs and recognized profit, and billings in excess of costs and recognized profit using the percentage-of-completion method.

(b) Prepare a partial income statement and balance sheet to indicate how the information would be reported for financial statement purposes.

(c) Repeat the requirements for part (a) assuming Rich Mathre uses the completed-contract method.

(d) Using the responses above for illustrative purposes, prepare a brief report comparing the conceptual merits (both positive and negative) of the two revenue recognition approaches.

CONCEPTUAL CASES

C18-1 (Revenue Recognition—Alternative Methods) Alexsandra Isosev Industries has three operating divisions—Falilat Mining, Mourning Paperbacks, and Osygus Protection Devices. Each division maintains its own accounting system and method of revenue recognition.

Falilat Mining
Falilat Mining specializes in the extraction of precious metals such as silver, gold, and platinum. During the fiscal year ended November 30, 2004, Falilat entered into contracts worth $2,250,000 and shipped metals worth $2,000,000. A quarter of the shipments were made from inventories on hand at the beginning of the fiscal year, and the remainder were made from metals that were mined during the year. Mining totals for the year, valued at market prices, were: silver at $750,000, gold at $1,300,000, and platinum at $490,000. Falilat uses the completion-of-production method to recognize revenue, because its operations meet the specified criteria—i.e., reasonably assured sales prices, interchangeable units, and insignificant distribution costs.

Mourning Paperbacks
Mourning Paperbacks sells large quantities of novels to a few book distributors that in turn sell to several national chains of bookstores. Mourning allows distributors to return up to 30% of sales, and distributors give the same terms to bookstores. While returns from individual titles fluctuate greatly, the returns from distributors have averaged 20% in each of the past 5 years. A total of $8,000,000 of paperback novel sales were made to distributors during the fiscal year. On November 30, 2004, $3,200,000 of fiscal 2004 sales were still subject to return privileges over the next 6 months. The remaining $4,800,000 of fiscal 2004 sales had actual returns of 21%. Sales from fiscal 2004 totaling $2,500,000 were collected in fiscal 2004, with less than 18% of sales returned. Mourning records revenue according to the method referred to as revenue recognition when the right of return exits, because all applicable criteria for use of this method are met by Mourning's operations.

Osygus Protection Devices
Osygus Protection Devices works through manufacturers' agents in various cities. Orders for alarm systems and down payments are forwarded from agents, and Osygus ships the goods f.o.b. shipping point. Customers are billed for the balance due plus actual shipping costs. The firm received orders for $6,000,000 of goods during the fiscal year ended November 30, 2004. Down payments of $600,000 were received, and $5,000,000 of goods were billed and shipped. Actual freight costs of $100,000 were also billed. Commissions of 10% on product price were paid to manufacturers' agents after the goods were shipped to customers. Such goods are warranted for 90 days after shipment, and warranty returns have been about 1% of sales. Revenue is recognized at the point of sale by Osygus.

Instructions

(a) There are a variety of methods for revenue recognition. Define and describe each of the following methods of revenue recognition, and indicate whether each is in accordance with generally accepted accounting principles.
  (1) Completion-of-production method.
  (2) Percentage-of-completion method.
  (3) Installment-sales method.

(b) Compute the revenue to be recognized in the fiscal year ended November 30, 2004, for
  (1) Falilat Mining.
  (2) Mourning Paperbacks.
  (3) Osygus Protection Devices.

(CMA adapted)

C18-2 (Recognition of Revenue—Theory) Revenue is usually recognized at the point of sale. Under special circumstances, however, bases other than the point of sale are used for the timing of revenue recognition.

Instructions

(a) Why is the point of sale usually used as the basis for the timing of revenue recognition?

(b) Disregarding the special circumstances when bases other than the point of sale are used, discuss the merits of each of the following objections to the sales basis of revenue recognition:
  (1) It is too conservative because revenue is earned throughout the entire process of production.
  (2) It is not conservative enough because accounts receivable do not represent disposable funds, sales returns and allowances may be made, and collection and bad debt expenses may be incurred in a later period.

(c) Revenue may also be recognized (1) during production and (2) when cash is received. For each of these two bases of timing revenue recognition, give an example of the circumstances in which it is properly used and discuss the accounting merits of its use in lieu of the sales basis.

(AICPA adapted)

C18-3 (Recognition of Revenue—Theory) The earning of revenue by a business enterprise is recognized for accounting purposes when the transaction is recorded. In some situations, revenue is recognized approximately as it is earned in the economic sense. In other situations, however, accountants have developed guidelines for recognizing revenue by other criteria, such as at the point of sale.

Instructions

(Ignore income taxes.)

(a) Explain and justify why revenue is often recognized as earned at time of sale.

(b) Explain in what situations it would be appropriate to recognize revenue as the productive activity takes place.

(c) At what times, other than those included in (a) and (b) above, may it be appropriate to recognize revenue? Explain.

C18-4 (Recognition of Revenue—Bonus Dollars) Alexei & Nemov Inc. was formed early this year to sell merchandise credits to merchants who distribute the credits free to their customers. For example, customers can earn additional credits based on the dollars they spend with a merchant (e.g., airlines and hotels). Accounts for accumulating the credits and catalogs illustrating the merchandise for which the credits may be exchanged are maintained online. Centers with inventories of merchandise premiums have been established for redemption of the credits. Merchants may not return unused credits to Alexei & Nemov.

The following schedule expresses Alexei & Nemov's expectations as to percentages of a normal month's activity that will be attained. For this purpose, a "normal month's activity" is defined as the level of operations expected when expansion of activities ceases or tapers off to a stable rate. The company expects that this level will be attained in the third year and that sales of credits will average $6,000,000 per month throughout the third year.

Month	Actual Credit Sales Percent	Merchandise Premium Purchases Percent	Credit Redemptions Percent
6th	30%	40%	10%
12th	60	60	45
18th	80	80	70
24th	90	90	80
30th	100	100	95

Alexei & Nemov plans to adopt an annual closing date at the end of each 12 months of operation.

Instructions

(a) Discuss the factors to be considered in determining when revenue should be recognized in measuring the income of a business enterprise.

(b) Discuss the accounting alternatives that should be considered by Alexei & Nemov Inc. for the recognition of its revenues and related expenses.

(c) For each accounting alternative discussed in (b), give balance sheet accounts that should be used and indicate how each should be classified.

(AICPA adapted)

C18-5 (Recognition of Revenue from Subscriptions) *Cutting Edge* is a monthly magazine that has been on the market for 18 months. It currently has a circulation of 1.4 million copies. Negotiations are underway to obtain a bank loan in order to update the magazine's facilities. They are producing close to capacity and expect to grow at an average of 20% per year over the next 3 years.

After reviewing the financial statements of *Cutting Edge*, Gary Hall, the bank loan officer, had indicated that a loan could be offered to *Cutting Edge* only if it could increase its current ratio and decrease its debt to equity ratio to a specified level.

Alexander Popov, the marketing manager of *Cutting Edge*, has devised a plan to meet these requirements. Popov indicates that an advertising campaign can be initiated to immediately increase circulation. The potential customers would be contacted after the purchase of another magazine's mailing list. The campaign would include:

1. An offer to subscribe to *Cutting Edge* at 3/4 the normal price.
2. A special offer to all new subscribers to receive the most current world atlas whenever requested at a guaranteed price of $2.

3. An unconditional guarantee that any subscriber will receive a full refund if dissatisfied with the magazine.

Although the offer of a full refund is risky, Popov claims that few people will ask for a refund after receiving half of their subscription issues. Popov notes that other magazine companies have tried this sales promotion technique and experienced great success. Their average cancellation rate was 25%. On average, each company increased its initial circulation threefold and in the long run increased circulation to twice that which existed before the promotion. In addition, 60% of the new subscribers are expected to take advantage of the atlas premium. Popov feels confident that the increased subscriptions from the advertising campaign will increase the current ratio and decrease the debt to equity ratio.

You are the controller of *Cutting Edge* and must give your opinion of the proposed plan.

Instructions

(a) When should revenue from the new subscriptions be recognized?
(b) How would you classify the estimated sales returns stemming from the unconditional guarantee?
(c) How should the atlas premium be recorded? Is the estimated premium claims a liability? Explain.
(d) Does the proposed plan achieve the goals of increasing the current ratio and decreasing the debt to equity ratio?

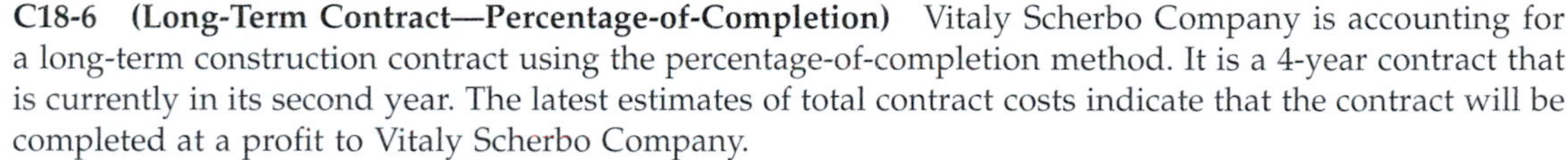

C18-6 (Long-Term Contract—Percentage-of-Completion) Vitaly Scherbo Company is accounting for a long-term construction contract using the percentage-of-completion method. It is a 4-year contract that is currently in its second year. The latest estimates of total contract costs indicate that the contract will be completed at a profit to Vitaly Scherbo Company.

Instructions

(a) What theoretical justification is there for Vitaly Scherbo Company's use of the percentage-of-completion method?
(b) How would progress billings be accounted for? Include in your discussion the classification of progress billings in Vitaly Scherbo Company financial statements.
(c) How would the income recognized in the second year of the 4-year contract be determined using the cost-to-cost method of determining percentage of completion?
(d) What would be the effect on earnings per share in the second year of the 4-year contract of using the percentage-of-completion method instead of the completed-contract method? Discuss.

(AICPA adapted)

C18-7 (Revenue Recognition—Real Estate Development) Pankratov Lakes is a new recreational real estate development which consists of 500 lake-front and lake-view lots. As a special incentive to the first 100 buyers of lake-view lots, the developer is offering 3 years of free financing on 10-year, 12% notes, no down payment, and one week at a nearby established resort—"a $1,200 value." The normal price per lot is $12,000. The cost per lake-view lot to the developer is an estimated average of $2,000. The development costs continue to be incurred; the actual average cost per lot is not known at this time. The resort promotion cost is $700 per lot. The notes are held by Davis Corp., a wholly owned subsidiary.

Instructions

(a) Discuss the revenue recognition and gross profit measurement issues raised by this situation.
(b) How would the developer's past financial and business experience influence your decision concerning the recording of these transactions?
(c) Assume 50 persons have accepted the offer, signed 10-year notes, and have stayed at the local resort. Prepare the journal entries that you believe are proper.
(d) What should be disclosed in the notes to the financial statements?

C18-8 (Revenue Recognition) Nimble Health and Racquet Club (NHRC), which operates eight clubs in the Chicago metropolitan area, offers one-year memberships. The members may use any of the eight facilities but must reserve racquetball court time and pay a separate fee before using the court. As an incentive to new customers, NHRC advertised that any customers not satisfied for any reason could receive a refund of the remaining portion of unused membership fees. Membership fees are due at the beginning of the individual membership period. However, customers are given the option of financing the membership fee over the membership period at a 9% interest rate.

Some customers have expressed a desire to take only the regularly scheduled aerobic classes without paying for a full membership. During the current fiscal year, NHRC began selling coupon books for aerobic classes to accommodate these customers. Each book is dated and contains 50 coupons that may be redeemed for any regularly scheduled aerobics class over a one-year period. After the one-year period, unused coupons are no longer valid.

During 2001, NHRC expanded into the health equipment market by purchasing a local company that manufactures rowing machines and cross-country ski machines. These machines are used in NHRC's facilities and are sold through the clubs and mail order catalogs. Customers must make a 20% down payment when placing an equipment order; delivery is 60–90 days after order placement. The machines are sold with a 2-year unconditional guarantee. Based on past experience, NHRC expects the costs to repair machines under guarantee to be 4% of sales.

NHRC is in the process of preparing financial statements as of May 31, 2004, the end of its fiscal year. James Hogan, corporate controller, expressed concern over the company's performance for the year and decided to review the preliminary financial statements prepared by Barbara Hardy, NHRC's assistant controller. After reviewing the statements, Hogan proposed that the following changes be reflected in the May 31, 2004, published financial statements.

1. Membership revenue should be recognized when the membership fee is collected.
2. Revenue from the coupon books should be recognized when the books are sold.
3. Down payments on equipment purchases and expenses associated with the guarantee on the rowing and cross-country machines should be recognized when paid.

Hardy indicated to Hogan that the proposed changes are not in accordance with generally accepted accounting principles, but Hogan insisted that the changes be made. Hardy believes that Hogan wants to manipulate income to forestall any potential financial problems and increase his year-end bonus. At this point, Hardy is unsure what action to take.

Instructions

(a) **(1)** Describe when Nimble Health and Racquet Club (NHRC) should recognize revenue from membership fees, court rentals, and coupon book sales.

(2) Describe how NHRC should account for the down payments on equipment sales, explaining when this revenue should be recognized.

(3) Indicate when NHRC should recognize the expense associated with the guarantee of the rowing and cross-country machines.

(b) Discuss why James Hogan's proposed changes and his insistence that the financial statement changes be made is unethical. Structure your answer around or to include the following aspects of ethical conduct: competence, confidentiality, integrity, and/or objectivity.

(c) Identify some specific actions Barbara Hardy could take to resolve this situation.

(CMA adapted)

C18-9 (Revenue Recognition—Membership Fees) Midwest Health Club offers one-year memberships. Membership fees are due in full at the beginning of the individual membership period. As an incentive to new customers, MHC advertised that any customers not satisfied for any reason could receive a refund of the remaining portion of unused membership fees. As a result of this policy, Stanley Hack, corporate controller, recognized revenue ratably over the life of the membership.

MHC is in the process of preparing its year-end financial statements. Phyllis Cavaretta, MHC's treasurer, is concerned about the company's lackluster performance this year. She reviews the financial statements Hack prepared and tells Hack to recognize membership revenue when the fees are received.

Instructions

Answer the following questions.

(a) What are the ethical issues involved?

(b) What should Hack do?

***C18-10 (Franchise Revenue)** Chou Foods Inc. sells franchises to independent operators throughout the northwestern part of the United States. The contract with the franchisee includes the following provisions.

1. The franchisee is charged an initial fee of $80,000. Of this amount, $30,000 is payable when the agreement is signed, and a $10,000 non-interest-bearing note is payable at the end of each of the 5 subsequent years.
2. All of the initial franchise fee collected by Chou Foods Inc. is to be refunded and the remaining obligation canceled if, for any reason, the franchisee fails to open his or her franchise.
3. In return for the initial franchise fee, Chou Foods Inc. agrees to (a) assist the franchisee in selecting the location for the business, (b) negotiate the lease for the land, (c) obtain financing and assist with building design, (d) supervise construction, (e) establish accounting and tax records, and (f) provide expert advice over a 5-year period relating to such matters as employee and management training, quality control, and promotion.
4. In addition to the initial franchise fee, the franchisee is required to pay to Chou Foods Inc. a monthly fee of 2% of sales for menu planning, receipt innovations, and the privilege of purchasing ingredients from Chou Foods Inc. at or below prevailing market prices.

Management of Chou Foods Inc. estimates that the value of the services rendered to the franchisee at the time the contract is signed amounts to at least $30,000. All franchisees to date have opened their locations at the scheduled time, and none have defaulted on any of the notes receivable.

The credit ratings of all franchisees would entitle them to borrow at the current interest rate of 10%. The present value of an ordinary annuity of five annual receipts of $10,000 each discounted at 10% is $37,908.

Instructions

(a) Discuss the alternatives that Chou Foods Inc. might use to account for the initial franchise fees, evaluate each by applying generally accepted accounting principles, and give illustrative entries for each alternative.

(b) Given the nature of Chou Foods Inc.'s agreement with its franchisees, when should revenue be recognized? Discuss the question of revenue recognition for both the initial franchise fee and the additional monthly fee of 2% of sales, and give illustrative entries for both types of revenue.

(c) Assume that Chou Foods Inc. sells some franchises for $100,000, which includes a charge of $20,000 for the rental of equipment for its useful life of 10 years; that $50,000 of the fee is payable immediately and the balance on non-interest-bearing notes at $10,000 per year; that no portion of the $20,000 rental payment is refundable in case the franchisee goes out of business; and that title to the equipment remains with the franchisor. Under those assumptions, what would be the preferable method of accounting for the rental portion of the initial franchise fee? Explain.

(AICPA adapted)

USING YOUR JUDGMENT

FINANCIAL REPORTING PROBLEM

3M Company

The financial statements of 3M are presented in Appendix 5B or can be accessed on the Take Action! CD.

Instructions

Refer to 3M's financial statements and the accompanying notes to answer the following questions.

(a) What were 3M's sales for 2001?

(b) What was the percentage of increase or decrease in 3M's sales from 2000 to 2001? From 1999 to 2001? From 1996 to 2001?

(c) In its notes to the financial statements, what criteria does 3M use to recognize revenue?

(d) Explain what happened to 3M in 2000 regarding its revenue recognition policies.

FINANCIAL STATEMENT ANALYSIS CASE

Westinghouse Electric Corporation

The following note appears in the "Summary of Significant Accounting Policies" section of the Annual Report of Westinghouse Electric Corporation.

> **Note 1 (in part): Revenue Recognition.** Sales are primarily recorded as products are shipped and services are rendered. The percentage-of-completion method of accounting is used for nuclear steam supply system orders with delivery schedules generally in excess of five years and for certain construction projects where this method of accounting is consistent with industry practice.
>
> WFSI revenues are generally recognized on the accrual method. When accounts become delinquent for more than two payment periods, usually 60 days, income is recognized only as payments are received. Such delinquent accounts for which no payments are received in the current month, and other accounts on which income is not being recognized because the receipt of either principal or interest is questionable, are classified as nonearning receivables.

Instructions

(a) Identify the revenue recognition methods used by Westinghouse Electric as discussed in its note on significant accounting policies.

(b) Under what conditions are the revenue recognition methods identified in the first paragraph of Westinghouse's note above acceptable?

(c) From the information provided in the second paragraph of Westinghouse's note, identify the type of operation being described and defend the acceptability of the revenue recognition method.

COMPARATIVE ANALYSIS CASE

The Coca-Cola Company and PepsiCo, Inc.

Instructions

Go to the Take Action! CD and use information found there to answer the following questions related to **The Coca-Cola Company** and **PepsiCo, Inc.**

(a) What were Coca-Cola's and PepsiCo's net revenues (sales) for the year 2001? Which company increased its revenues more (dollars and percentage) from 2000 to 2001?

(b) In which foreign countries (geographic areas) did Coca-Cola and PepsiCo experience significant revenues in 2001? Compare the amounts of foreign revenues to U.S. revenues for both Coca-Cola and PepsiCo.

RESEARCH CASES

Case 1

Companies registered with the Securities and Exchange Commission are required to file a current report on Form 8-K upon the occurrence of certain events.

Instructions

Use EDGAR or some other source to identify 8-Ks recently filed by two companies of your choice. Examine the 8-Ks and answer the following questions with regard to each.

(a) What corporate event or transaction triggered the filing of the Form 8-K?

(b) Identify any financial statements or exhibits included in the filing. How might these items help investors in evaluating the event/transaction?

Case 2

An article titled "SEC Broadens Investigation in Revenue-Boosting Tricks; Fearing Bogus Numbers Are Widespread, Agency Probes **Lucent** and Others," by Susan Pulliam and Rebecca Blumenstein, appeared in the May 16, 2002, *Wall Street Journal*. (Subscribers to **Business Extra** can access the article at that site.)

Instructions

Read this article and answer the following questions.

(a) The article predicts that, "Probing revenue promises to be a much broader inquiry than the earlier investigations of **Enron** and other companies accused of using accounting tricks to boost their profits." What is the difference between inflating profits and inflating revenues?

(b) What are the ways in which accounting information is used (both in general and in ways specifically cited in this article)? What are the concerns about using accounting information that has been manipulated to increase revenues? To increase profits?

(c) Describe the specific techniques that may be used to inflate revenues that are enumerated in this article. Why would a practice of inflating revenues be of particular concern during the "dot-com boom"?

(d) The article says that **L90 Inc.** "lopped $8.3 million, or just over 10%, off revenue previously reported for 2000 and 2001," while booking the $250,000 net difference in the amount of wire transfers that had been used in one of these transactions as "Other income" rather than revenue. What is the difference between revenues and other income? Where might these items be found in a multi-step income statement? In a single-step income statement?

(e) What are "vendor allowances"? How might these allowances be used to inflate revenues? Consider the case of Lucent Technologies described in the article. Might Lucent's techniques also have been used to boost profits?

PROFESSIONAL SIMULATION

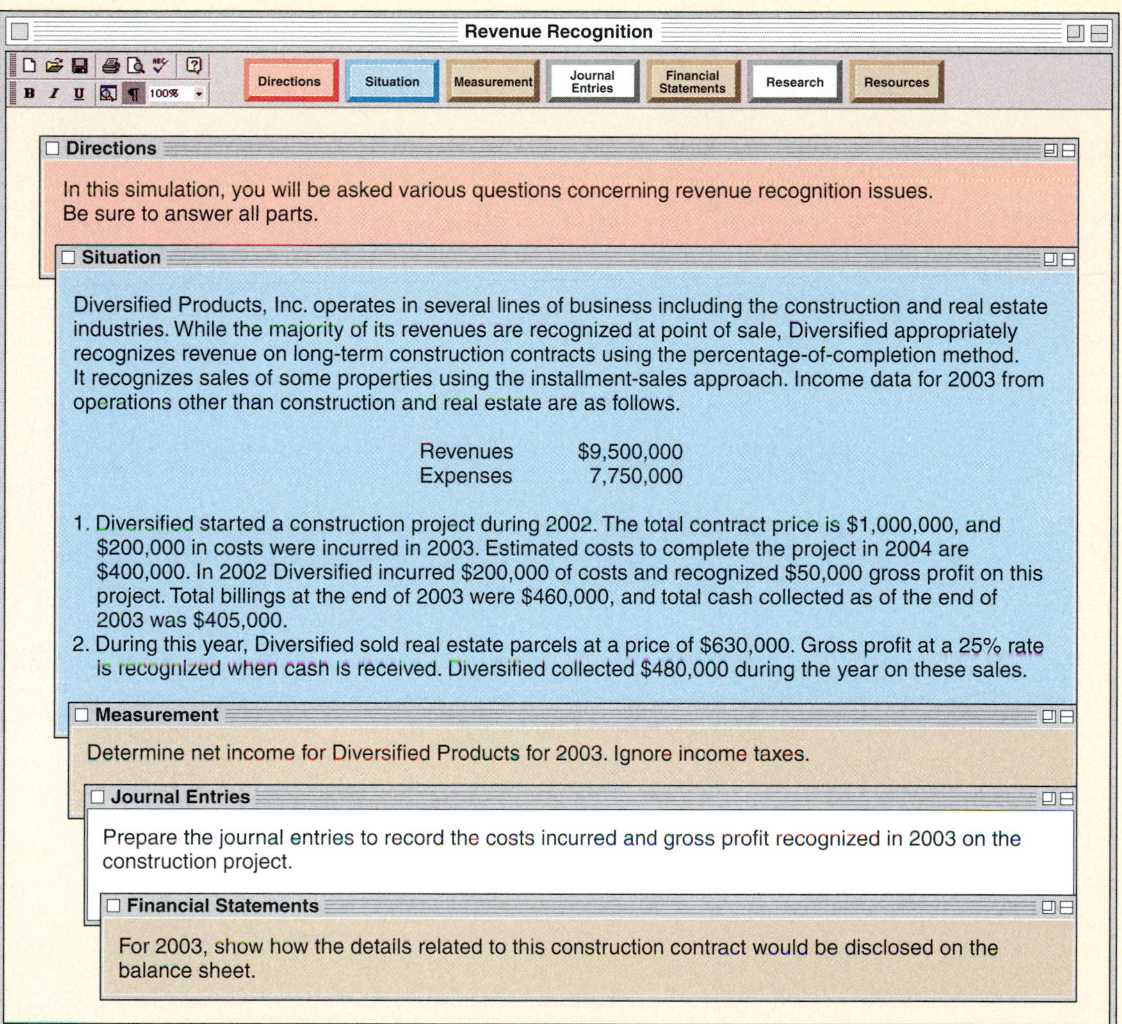

Revenue Recognition
Directions
Situation
Measurement
Journal Entries
Financial Statements
Research
Resources
Directions
In this simulation, you will be asked various questions concerning revenue recognition issues. Be sure to answer all parts.
Situation
Diversified Products, Inc. operates in several lines of business including the construction and real estate industries. While the majority of its revenues are recognized at point of sale, Diversified appropriately recognizes revenue on long-term construction contracts using the percentage-of-completion method. It recognizes sales of some properties using the installment-sales approach. Income data for 2003 from operations other than construction and real estate are as follows.
Revenues $9,500,000
Expenses 7,750,000
1. Diversified started a construction project during 2002. The total contract price is $1,000,000, and $200,000 in costs were incurred in 2003. Estimated costs to complete the project in 2004 are $400,000. In 2002 Diversified incurred $200,000 of costs and recognized $50,000 gross profit on this project. Total billings at the end of 2003 were $460,000, and total cash collected as of the end of 2003 was $405,000.
2. During this year, Diversified sold real estate parcels at a price of $630,000. Gross profit at a 25% rate is recognized when cash is received. Diversified collected $480,000 during the year on these sales.
Measurement
Determine net income for Diversified Products for 2003. Ignore income taxes.
Journal Entries
Prepare the journal entries to record the costs incurred and gross profit recognized in 2003 on the construction project.
Financial Statements
For 2003, show how the details related to this construction contract would be disclosed on the balance sheet.

Remember to check the **Take Action! CD** and the book's **companion Web site** to find additional resources for this chapter.

CHAPTER 19

Accounting for Income Taxes

Use It, But Don't Abuse It

One set of costs that companies manage are those related to taxes. For example, by using accelerated depreciation methods for fixed assets, companies reduce their tax bills. With faster tax write-offs on fixed assets, companies report lower taxable income and pay lower taxes in the early years of the assets' lives, thereby managing tax costs.

Also, companies such as **GAP Inc.** and **Stanley Works** are managing state tax costs by locating part of their businesses in low-tax-rate states while operating retail outlets elsewhere. For example, **Limited Brands Inc.** based a subsidiary (which does nothing more than hold the trademarks for Bath and Body Works and Victoria's Secret) in the state of Delaware and was able to transfer hundreds of millions of dollars away from Limited's retail outlets in high-tax states and into Delaware, which has a state tax rate of zero.

As shown in the nearby graph, these location strategies are working: In 2000, states collected about 5 percent of their taxes from corporations, compared to over 9 percent in 1980.

However, the IRS and some states have been increasing their scrutiny of transactions that are done only to avoid taxes and that do not serve a legitimate business purpose. In one case, an attorney for North Carolina alleged that **Limited Brands Inc.** ". . . engaged in hocus pocus bookkeeping and deceptive accounting," the sole purpose of which was to reduce its state tax bill. The court agreed, and Limited must now pay millions of dollars in back taxes dating back to 1994. Thus, companies can manage their tax costs as long as they do not abuse the state and federal tax codes.[1]

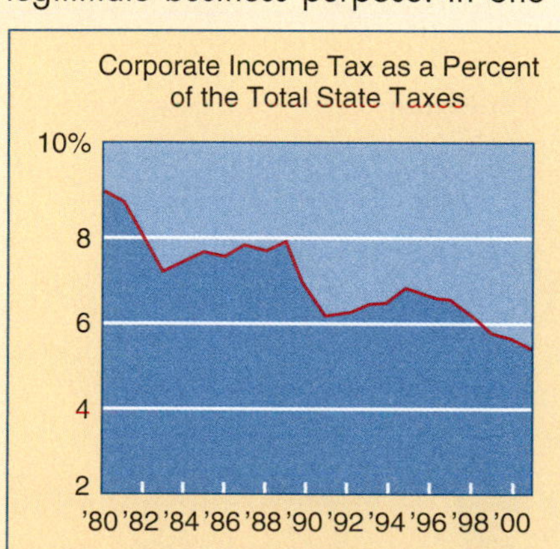

Source: U.S. Census Bureau

[1]Based on Howard Gleckman and Lorraine Woellert, "Kiss that Tax Shelter Good-bye? The Courts Crack Down on Egregious Corporate Tax Avoidance," *Business Week* (November 15, 1999), p. 50, and Glenn Simpson, "A Tax Maneuver in Delaware Puts Squeeze on States," *Wall Street Journal* (August 9, 2002), p. A1.

LEARNING OBJECTIVES

After studying this chapter, you should be able to:

1. **Identify differences between pretax financial income and taxable income.**
2. **Describe a temporary difference that results in future taxable amounts.**
3. **Describe a temporary difference that results in future deductible amounts.**
4. **Explain the purpose of a deferred tax asset valuation allowance.**
5. **Describe the presentation of income tax expense in the income statement.**
6. **Describe various temporary and permanent differences.**
7. **Explain the effect of various tax rates and tax rate changes on deferred income taxes.**
8. **Apply accounting procedures for a loss carryback and a loss carryforward.**
9. **Describe the presentation of deferred income taxes in financial statements.**
10. **Indicate the basic principles of the asset-liability method.**

PREVIEW OF CHAPTER 19

Income taxes are a major cost of business to most corporations. As a result, companies spend a considerable amount of time and effort to minimize their tax payments. The purpose of this chapter is to discuss the basic guidelines that companies must follow in reporting income taxes. The content and organization of the chapter are as follows.

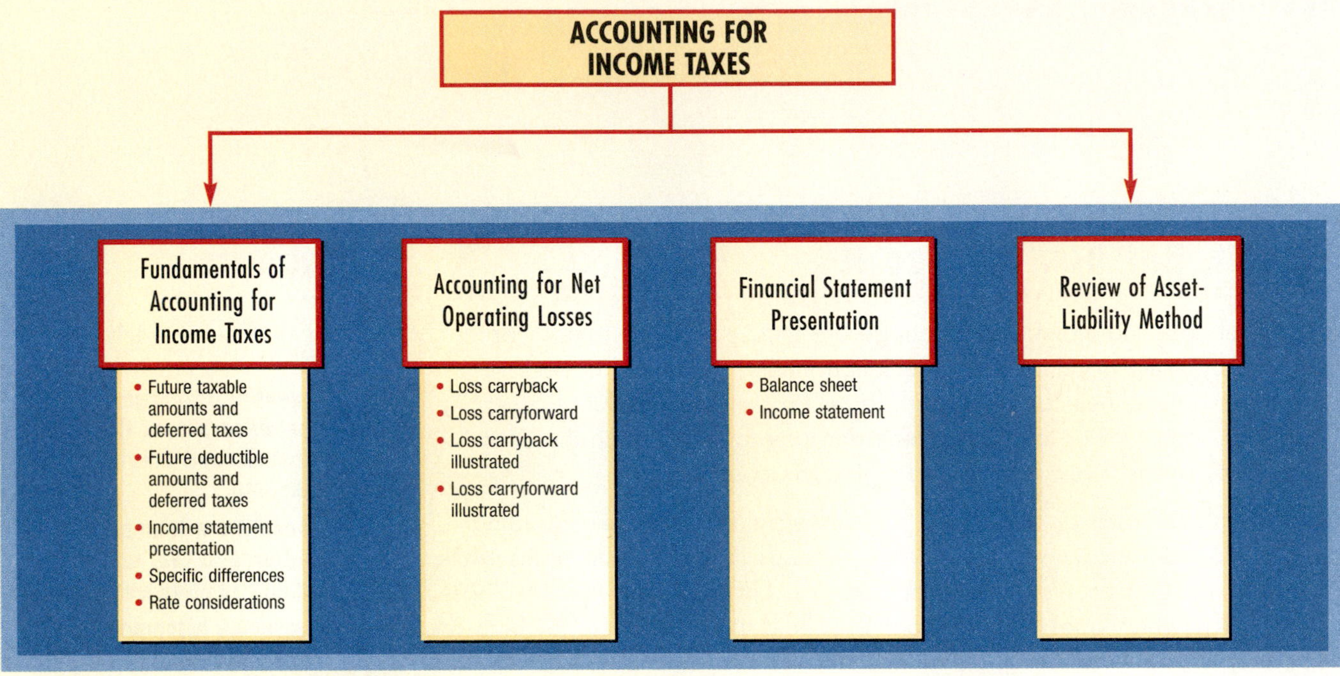

FUNDAMENTALS OF ACCOUNTING FOR INCOME TAXES

Because GAAP and tax regulations differ, pretax financial income and taxable income frequently differ, and the amount that a company reports as tax expense will differ from the amount of taxes payable to the IRS. Illustration 19-1 highlights these differences.

ILLUSTRATION 19-1
Fundamental Differences between Financial and Tax Reporting

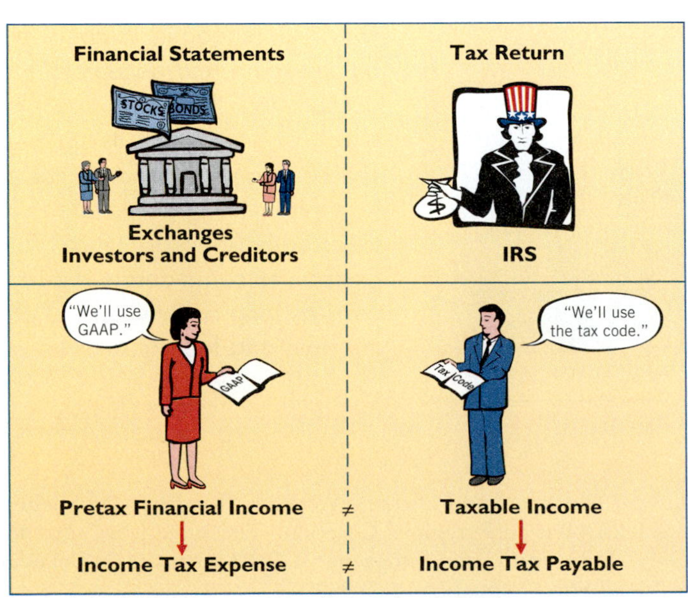

OBJECTIVE 1
Identify differences between pretax financial income and taxable income.

Pretax financial income is a financial reporting term often referred to as income before taxes, income for financial reporting purposes, or income for book purposes. Pretax financial income is determined according to GAAP and is measured with the objective of providing useful information to investors and creditors. **Taxable income** (income for tax purposes) is a tax accounting term used to indicate the amount upon which income tax payable is computed. Taxable income is determined according to the Internal Revenue Code (the tax code), which is designed to raise money to support government operations.

To illustrate how differences in GAAP and IRS rules affect financial reporting and taxable income, assume that Chelsea Inc. reported revenues of $130,000 and expenses of $60,000 in each of its first 3 years of operations. Illustration 19-2 shows the (partial) income statement over these 3 years.

ILLUSTRATION 19-2
Financial Reporting Income

CHELSEA INC.
GAAP REPORTING

	2004	2005	2006	Total
Revenues	$130,000	$130,000	$130,000	
Expenses	60,000	60,000	60,000	
Pretax financial income	$ 70,000	$ 70,000	$ 70,000	$ 210,000
Income tax expense (40%)	$ 28,000	$ 28,000	$ 28,000	$ 84,000

For tax purposes (following the tax code), Chelsea reported the same expenses to the IRS in each of the years. But taxable revenues were $100,000 in 2004, $150,000 in 2005, and $140,000 in 2006 as shown in Illustration 19-3.

ILLUSTRATION 19-3
Tax Reporting Income

CHELSEA INC.
TAX REPORTING

	2004	2005	2006	Total
Revenues	$100,000	$150,000	$140,000	
Expenses	60,000	60,000	60,000	
Taxable income	$ 40,000	$ 90,000	$ 80,000	$ 210,000
Income tax payable (40%)	$ 16,000	$ 36,000	$ 32,000	$ 84,000

Income tax expense and income tax payable differ over the 3 years, but **in total** they are the same, as shown in Illustration 19-4.

ILLUSTRATION 19-4
Comparison of Income Tax Expense to Income Tax Payable

CHELSEA INC.
INCOME TAX EXPENSE AND
INCOME TAX PAYABLE

	2004	2005	2006	Total
Income tax expense	$28,000	$28,000	$28,000	$84,000
Income tax payable	16,000	36,000	32,000	84,000
Difference	$12,000	$ (8,000)	$ (4,000)	$ 0

INTERNATIONAL INSIGHT

In some countries, taxable income and pretax financial income are the same. As a consequence, accounting for differences between tax and book income is not significant.

The differences between income tax expense and income tax payable arise for a simple reason: For financial reporting, the full accrual method is used to report revenues, whereas for tax purposes a modified cash basis is used. As a result, Chelsea reports pretax financial income of $70,000 and income tax expense of $28,000 for each of the 3 years. However, taxable income fluctuates. For example, in 2004 taxable income is only $40,000, which means that just $16,000 is owed to the IRS that year. The income tax payable is classified as a current liability on the balance sheet.

As indicated in Illustration 19-4, for Chelsea the $12,000 ($28,000 − $16,000) difference between income tax expense and income tax payable in 2004 reflects taxes that will be paid in future periods. This $12,000 difference is often referred to as a **deferred tax amount**. In this case it is a **deferred tax liability**. In cases where taxes will be lower in the future, Chelsea would record a **deferred tax asset**. We explain the measurement and accounting for deferred tax liabilities and assets in the following two sections.

Future Taxable Amounts and Deferred Taxes

OBJECTIVE 2
Describe a temporary difference that results in future taxable amounts.

The example summarized in Illustration 19-4 shows how income tax payable can differ from income tax expense. One way that this can happen is when there are temporary differences between the amounts reported for tax purposes and those reported for book purposes. A **temporary difference** is the difference between the tax basis of an asset or liability and its reported (carrying or book) amount in the financial statements that will result in taxable amounts or deductible amounts in future years. **Taxable amounts** increase taxable income in future years, and **deductible amounts** decrease taxable income in future years.

In Chelsea Inc.'s situation, the only difference between the book basis and tax basis of the assets and liabilities relates to accounts receivable that arose from revenue recognized for book purposes. Illustration 19-5 indicates that accounts receivable are reported at $30,000 in the December 31, 2004, GAAP-basis balance sheet, but the receivables have a zero tax basis.

ILLUSTRATION 19-5
Temporary Difference, Sales Revenue

Per Books	12/31/04	Per Tax Return	12/31/04
Accounts receivable	$30,000	Accounts receivable	$-0-

What will happen to this $30,000 temporary difference that originated in 2004 for Chelsea Inc.? Assuming that Chelsea expects to collect $20,000 of the receivables in 2005 and $10,000 in 2006, this collection will result in future taxable amounts of $20,000 in 2005 and $10,000 in 2006. These future taxable amounts will cause taxable income to exceed pretax financial income in both 2005 and 2006.

An assumption inherent in a company's GAAP balance sheet is that the assets and liabilities will be recovered and settled at their reported amounts (carrying amounts). This assumption creates a requirement under accrual accounting to recognize currently the deferred tax consequences of temporary differences—that is, the amount of income taxes that would be payable (or refundable) when the reported amounts of the assets are recovered and the liabilities are settled, respectively. The diagram in Illustration 19-6 shows the reversal or turn-around of the temporary difference described in Illustration 19-5 and the resulting taxable amounts in future periods.

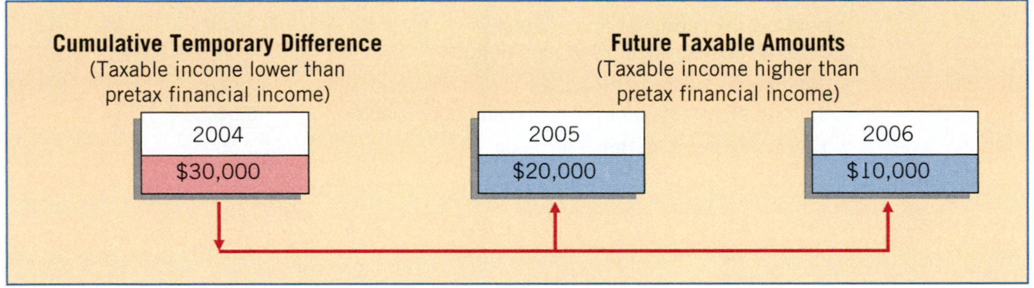

ILLUSTRATION 19-6
Reversal of Temporary Difference, Chelsea Inc.

We have assumed that Chelsea will collect the accounts receivable and report the $30,000 collection as taxable revenues in future tax returns. A payment of income tax in both 2005 and 2006 will occur. We therefore should record in Chelsea's books in 2004 the deferred tax consequences of the revenue and related receivables reflected in the 2004 financial statements. This necessitates the recording of a deferred tax liability.

Deferred Tax Liability

A **deferred tax liability** is the deferred tax consequences attributable to taxable temporary differences. In other words, **a deferred tax liability represents the increase in taxes payable in future years as a result of taxable temporary differences existing at the end of the current year.** Recall from the Chelsea example that income tax payable is $16,000 ($40,000 × 40%) in 2004 (Illustration 19-4). In addition, a temporary difference exists at year-end because the revenue and related accounts receivable are reported differently for book and tax purposes. The book basis of accounts receivable is $30,000, and the tax basis is zero. Thus, the total deferred tax liability at the end of 2004 is $12,000, computed as follows.

Book basis of accounts receivable	$30,000
Tax basis of accounts receivable	–0–
Cumulative temporary difference at the end of 2004	30,000
Tax rate	40%
Deferred tax liability at the end of 2004	$12,000

ILLUSTRATION 19-7
Computation of Deferred Tax Liability, End of 2004

Another way to compute the deferred tax liability is to prepare a schedule that indicates the taxable amounts scheduled for the future as a result of existing temporary differences. Such a schedule (see Illustration 19-8, below) is particularly useful when the computations become more complex.

	Future Years		
	2005	2006	Total
Future taxable amounts	$20,000	$10,000	$30,000
Tax rate	40%	40%	
Deferred tax liability at the end of 2004	$ 8,000	$ 4,000	$12,000

ILLUSTRATION 19-8
Schedule of Future Taxable Amounts

Because it is the first year of operations for Chelsea, there is no deferred tax liability at the beginning of the year. The income tax expense for 2004 is computed as shown in Illustration 19-9.

ILLUSTRATION 19-9
Computation of Income Tax Expense, 2004

Deferred tax liability at end of 2004	$12,000
Deferred tax liability at beginning of 2004	–0–
Deferred tax expense for 2004	12,000
Current tax expense for 2004 (Income tax payable)	16,000
Income tax expense (total) for 2004	$28,000

This computation indicates that income tax expense has two components—current tax expense (which is the amount of income tax payable for the period) and deferred tax expense. **Deferred tax expense** is the increase in the deferred tax liability balance from the beginning to the end of the accounting period.

Taxes due and payable are credited to Income Tax Payable, and the increase in deferred taxes is credited to Deferred Tax Liability. The sum of those two items is debited to Income Tax Expense. For Chelsea Inc. the following entry is made at the end of 2004.

Income Tax Expense	28,000	
Income Tax Payable		16,000
Deferred Tax Liability		12,000

At the end of 2005 (the second year), the difference between the book basis and the tax basis of the accounts receivable is $10,000. This difference is multiplied by the applicable tax rate to arrive at the deferred tax liability of $4,000 ($10,000 × 40%) to be reported at the end of 2005. Income tax payable for 2005 is $36,000 (Illustration 19-3), and the income tax expense for 2005 is as follows.

ILLUSTRATION 19-10
Computation of Income Tax Expense, 2005

Deferred tax liability at end of 2005	$ 4,000
Deferred tax liability at beginning of 2005	12,000
Deferred tax expense (benefit) for 2005	(8,000)
Current tax expense for 2005 (Income tax payable)	36,000
Income tax expense (total) for 2005	$28,000

The journal entry to record income tax expense, the change in the deferred tax liability, and income tax payable for 2005 is as follows.

Income Tax Expense	28,000	
Deferred Tax Liability	8,000	
Income Tax Payable		36,000

In the entry to record income taxes at the end of 2006, the Deferred Tax Liability is reduced by $4,000. The Deferred Tax Liability account appears as follows at the end of 2006.

ILLUSTRATION 19-11
Deferred Tax Liability Account after Reversals

Deferred Tax Liability			
2005	8,000	2004	12,000
2006	4,000		

The Deferred Tax Liability account has a zero balance at the end of 2006.

WHAT DO THE NUMBERS MEAN?

"REAL LIABILITIES"

Some analysts dismiss deferred tax liabilities when assessing the financial strength of a company. But the FASB indicates that the deferred tax liability meets the definition of a liability established in *Statement of Financial Accounting Concepts No. 6*, "Elements of Financial Statements" because:

1. ***It results from a past transaction.*** In the Chelsea example, services were performed for customers and revenue was recognized in 2004 for financial reporting purposes but was deferred for tax purposes.
2. ***It is a present obligation.*** Taxable income in future periods will be higher than pretax financial income as a result of this temporary difference. Thus, a present obligation exists.
3. ***It represents a future sacrifice.*** Taxable income and taxes due in future periods will result from events that have already occurred. The payment of these taxes when they come due is the future sacrifice.

A study by B. Ayers[2] indicates that the market views deferred tax assets and liabilities similarly to other assets and liabilities, and that *SFAS No. 109* increased the usefulness of deferred tax amounts in financial statements.

Summary of Income Tax Accounting Objectives

One objective of accounting for income taxes is to recognize the amount of taxes payable or refundable for the current year. In Chelsea's case, income tax payable is $16,000 for 2004.

A **second objective** is to recognize deferred tax liabilities and assets for the future tax consequences of events that have already been recognized in the financial statements or tax returns. Chelsea sold services to customers that resulted in accounts receivable of $30,000 in 2004. That amount was reported on the 2004 income statement, but it was not reported on the tax return as income. It will appear on future tax returns as income for the period **when it is collected**. As a result, a $30,000 temporary difference exists at the end of 2004, which will cause future taxable amounts. A deferred tax liability of $12,000 is reported on the balance sheet at the end of 2004, which represents the increase in taxes payable in future years ($8,000 in 2005 and $4,000 in 2006) as a result of a temporary difference existing at the end of the current year. The related deferred tax liability is reduced by $8,000 at the end of 2005 and by another $4,000 at the end of 2006.

In addition to affecting the balance sheet, deferred taxes have an impact on income tax expense in each of the 3 years affected. In 2004, taxable income ($40,000) is less than pretax financial income ($70,000). Income tax payable for 2004 is therefore $16,000 (based on taxable income). Deferred tax expense of $12,000 is caused by the increase in the Deferred Tax Liability account on the balance sheet. Income tax expense is then $28,000 for 2004.

In 2005 and 2006, however, taxable income will be more than pretax financial income, due to the reversal of the temporary difference ($20,000 in 2005 and $10,000 in 2006). Income tax payable will therefore be higher than income tax expense in 2005 and 2006. The Deferred Tax Liability account will be debited for $8,000 in 2005 and $4,000 in 2006. Credits for these amounts are recorded in Income Tax Expense (often referred to as a **deferred tax benefit**).

[2]B. Ayers, "Deferred Tax Accounting Under *SFAS No. 109*: An Empirical Investigation of Its Incremental Value-Relevance Relative to *APB No. 11*," *The Accounting Review* (April 1998).

OBJECTIVE 3
Describe a temporary difference that results in future deductible amounts.

Future Deductible Amounts and Deferred Taxes

Assume that during 2004, Cunningham Inc. estimated its warranty costs related to the sale of microwave ovens to be $500,000, paid evenly over the next 2 years. For book purposes, in 2004 Cunningham reported warranty expense and a related estimated liability for warranties of $500,000 in its financial statements. For tax purposes, **the warranty tax deduction is not allowed until paid**. Therefore, no warranty liability is recognized on a tax-basis balance sheet. Thus, the balance sheet difference at the end of 2004 is as follows.

ILLUSTRATION 19-12
Temporary Difference, Warranty Liability

Per Books	12/31/04	Per Tax Return	12/31/04
Estimated liability for warranties	$500,000	Estimated liability for warranties	$–0–

When the warranty liability is paid, an expense (deductible amount) will be reported for tax purposes. Because of this temporary difference, Cunningham Inc. should recognize in 2004 the tax benefits (positive tax consequences) for the tax deductions that will result from the future settlement of the liability. This future tax benefit is reported in the December 31, 2004, balance sheet as a **deferred tax asset**.

Another way to think about this situation is as follows: Deductible amounts will occur in future tax returns. These **future deductible amounts** will cause taxable income to be less than pretax financial income in the future as a result of an existing temporary difference. Cunningham's temporary difference originates (arises) in one period (2004) and reverses over two periods (2005 and 2006). This situation is diagrammed as follows.

ILLUSTRATION 19-13
Reversal of Temporary Difference, Cunningham Inc.

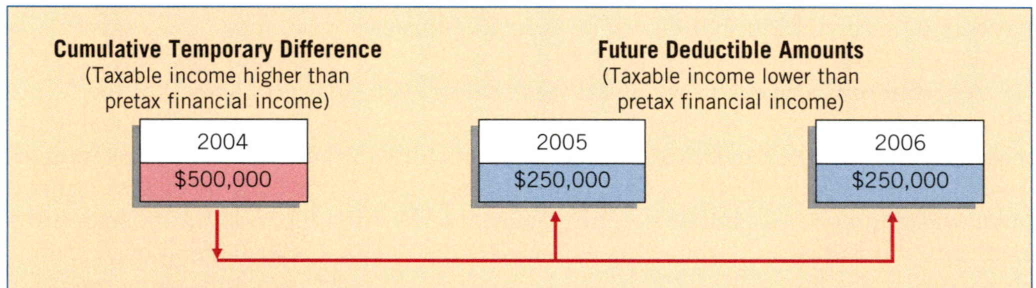

Deferred Tax Asset

A **deferred tax asset** is the deferred tax consequence attributable to deductible temporary differences. In other words, a **deferred tax asset represents the increase in taxes refundable (or saved) in future years as a result of deductible temporary differences existing at the end of the current year**.

To illustrate, assume that Hunt Co. accrues a loss and a related liability of $50,000 in 2004 for financial reporting purposes because of pending litigation. This amount is not deductible for tax purposes until the period the liability is paid, which is expected to be 2005. As a result, a deductible amount will occur in 2005 when the liability (Estimated Litigation Liability) is settled, causing taxable income to be lower than pretax financial income. The computation of the deferred tax asset at the end of 2004 (assuming a 40% tax rate) is as follows.

ILLUSTRATION 19-14
Computation of Deferred Tax Asset, End of 2004

Book basis of litigation liability	$50,000
Tax basis of litigation liability	–0–
Cumulative temporary difference at the end of 2004	50,000
Tax rate	40%
Deferred tax asset at the end of 2004	$20,000

Another way to compute the deferred tax asset is to prepare a schedule that indicates the deductible amounts scheduled for the future as a result of deductible temporary differences. This schedule is shown in Illustration 19-15.

ILLUSTRATION 19-15
Schedule of Future Deductible Amounts

	Future Years
Future deductible amounts	$50,000
Tax rate	40%
Deferred tax asset at the end of 2004	$20,000

Assuming that 2004 is Hunt's first year of operations, and income tax payable is $100,000, the income tax expense is computed as follows.

ILLUSTRATION 19-16
Computation of Income Tax Expense, 2004

Deferred tax asset at end of 2004	$ 20,000
Deferred tax asset at beginning of 2004	–0–
Deferred tax expense (benefit) for 2004	(20,000)
Current tax expense for 2004 (Income tax payable)	100,000
Income tax expense (total) for 2004	$ 80,000

The **deferred tax benefit** results from the increase in the deferred tax asset from the beginning to the end of the accounting period. The deferred tax benefit is a negative component of income tax expense. The total income tax expense of $80,000 on the income statement for 2004 is thus comprised of two elements—current tax expense of $100,000 and deferred tax benefit of $20,000. For Hunt Co. the journal entry that is made at the end of 2004 to record income tax expense, deferred income taxes, and income tax payable is as follows.

Income Tax Expense	80,000	
Deferred Tax Asset	20,000	
Income Tax Payable		100,000

At the end of 2005 (the second year), the difference between the book value and the tax basis of the litigation liability is zero. Therefore, there is no deferred tax asset at this date. Assuming that income tax payable for 2005 is $140,000, the computation of income tax expense for 2005 is as follows.

ILLUSTRATION 19-17
Computation of Income Tax Expense, 2005

Deferred tax asset at the end of 2005	$ –0–
Deferred tax asset at the beginning of 2005	20,000
Deferred tax expense (benefit) for 2005	20,000
Current tax expense for 2005 (Income tax payable)	140,000
Income tax expense (total) for 2005	$160,000

The journal entry to record income taxes for 2005 is as follows.

Income Tax Expense	160,000	
Deferred Tax Asset		20,000
Income Tax Payable		140,000

The total income tax expense of $160,000 on the income statement for 2005 is thus comprised of two elements—current tax expense of $140,000 and deferred tax expense of $20,000.

The Deferred Tax Asset account at the end of 2005 is shown in Illustration 19-18.

ILLUSTRATION 19-18
Deferred Tax Asset Account after Reversals

Deferred Tax Asset			
2004	20,000	2005	20,000

WHAT DO THE NUMBERS MEAN?

"REAL ASSETS"

A key issue in accounting for income taxes is whether a deferred tax asset should be recognized in the financial records. Based on the conceptual definition of an asset, a deferred tax asset meets the three main conditions for an item to be recognized as an asset:

1. ***It results from a past transaction.*** In the Hunt Co. example, the accrual of the loss contingency is the past event that gives rise to a future deductible temporary difference.
2. ***It gives rise to a probable benefit in the future.*** Taxable income is higher than pretax financial income in the current year (2004). However, in the next year the exact opposite occurs; that is, taxable income is lower than pretax financial income. Because this deductible temporary difference reduces taxes payable in the future, a probable future benefit exists at the end of the current period.
3. ***The entity controls access to the benefits.*** Hunt Co. has the ability to obtain the benefit of existing deductible temporary differences by reducing its taxes payable in the future. Hunt Co. has the exclusive right to that benefit and can control others' access to it.

Market analysts' reaction to the **write-off** of deferred tax assets also supports their treatment as assets. When **Bethlehem Steel** reported a $1 billion charge in 2001 to write off a deferred tax asset, analysts believed that Bethlehem was signaling that it would be unable to realize the future benefits of the tax deductions; thus, the asset should be written down like other assets.[3]

Deferred Tax Asset—Valuation Allowance

OBJECTIVE 4
Explain the purpose of a deferred tax asset valuation allowance.

A deferred tax asset is recognized for all deductible temporary differences. However, a deferred tax asset should be reduced by a **valuation allowance** if, based on all available evidence, **it is more likely than not** that some portion or all of the deferred tax asset **will not be realized**. "More likely than not" means a level of likelihood that is at least slightly more than 50 percent.

Assume that Jensen Co. has a deductible temporary difference of $1,000,000 at the end of its first year of operations. Its tax rate is 40 percent, which means a deferred tax asset of $400,000 ($1,000,000 × 40%) is recorded. Assuming that income taxes payable are $900,000, the journal entry to record income tax expense, the deferred tax asset, and income tax payable is as follows.

Income Tax Expense	500,000	
Deferred Tax Asset	400,000	
Income Tax Payable		900,000

After careful review of all available evidence, it is determined that it is more likely than not that $100,000 of this deferred tax asset will not be realized. The journal entry to record this reduction in asset value is as follows.

Income Tax Expense	100,000	
Allowance to Reduce Deferred Tax Asset to Expected Realizable Value		100,000

In this journal entry, income tax expense is increased in the current period because a favorable tax benefit is not expected to be realized for a portion of the deductible tempo-

[3]J. Weil and S. Liesman, "Stock Gurus Disregard Most Big Write-offs But They Often Hold Vital Clues to Outlook," *Wall Street Journal Online* (December 31, 2001).

rary difference. **A valuation allowance is simultaneously established to recognize the reduction in the carrying amount of the deferred tax asset.** This valuation account is a contra account and may be reported on the financial statements in the following manner.

Deferred tax asset	$400,000
Less: Allowance to reduce deferred tax asset to expected realizable value	100,000
Deferred tax asset (net)	$300,000

ILLUSTRATION 19-19
Balance Sheet Presentation of Valuation Allowance Account

This allowance account is evaluated at the end of each accounting period. If, at the end of the next period, the deferred tax asset is still $400,000, but now $350,000 of this asset is expected to be realized, then the following entry is made to adjust the valuation account.

Allowance to Reduce Deferred Tax Asset to Expected Realizable Value	50,000	
Income Tax Expense		50,000

All available evidence, both positive and negative, should be carefully considered to determine whether, based on the weight of available evidence, a valuation allowance is needed. For example, if the company has been experiencing a series of loss years, a reasonable assumption is that these losses will continue and the benefit of the future deductible amounts will be lost. The use of a valuation account under other conditions will be discussed later in the chapter.

Income Statement Presentation

OBJECTIVE 5
Describe the presentation of income tax expense in the income statement.

Whether the change in deferred income taxes should be added to or subtracted from income tax payable in computing income tax expense depends on the circumstances. For example, an increase in a deferred tax liability would be added to income tax payable. On the other hand, an increase in a deferred tax asset would be subtracted from income tax payable. The formula to compute income tax expense (benefit) is as follows.

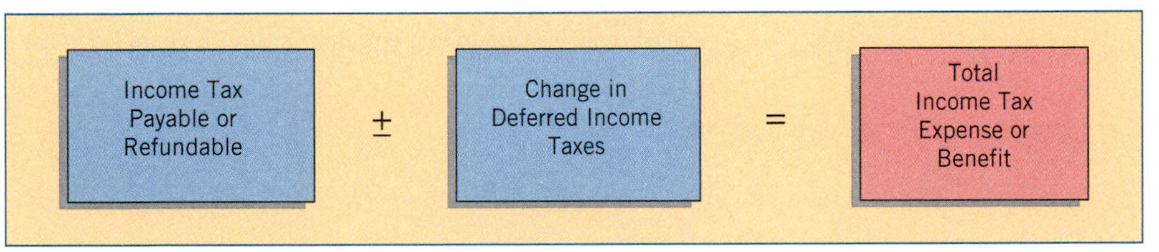

ILLUSTRATION 19-20
Formula to Compute Income Tax Expense

In the income statement or in the notes to the financial statements, the significant components of income tax expense attributable to continuing operations should be disclosed. Given the information related to Chelsea Inc. on page 961, Chelsea's income statement is reported as follows.

CHELSEA INC.
INCOME STATEMENT
FOR THE YEAR ENDING DECEMBER 31, 2004

Revenues		$130,000
Expenses		60,000
Income before income taxes		70,000
Income tax expense		
Current	$16,000	
Deferred	12,000	28,000
Net income		$ 42,000

ILLUSTRATION 19-21
Income Statement Presentation of Income Tax Expense

As illustrated, both the current portion (amount of income tax payable for the period) and the deferred portion of income tax expense are reported. Another option is to simply report the total income tax expense on the income statement, and then in the notes to the financial statements indicate the current and deferred portions. Income tax expense is often referred to as "Provision for income taxes." Using this terminology, the current provision is $16,000, and the provision for deferred taxes is $12,000.

Specific Differences

OBJECTIVE 6
Describe various temporary and permanent differences.

Numerous items create differences between pretax financial income and taxable income. For purposes of accounting recognition, these differences are of two types: (1) temporary, and (2) permanent.

Temporary Differences

Temporary differences that will result in taxable amounts in future years when the related assets are recovered are often called **taxable temporary differences**. Temporary differences that will result in deductible amounts in future years when the related book liabilities are settled are often called **deductible temporary differences**. Taxable temporary differences give rise to recording deferred tax liabilities; deductible temporary differences give rise to recording deferred tax assets. Examples of temporary differences are provided in Illustration 19-22.[4]

ILLUSTRATION 19-22
Examples of Temporary Differences

A. **Revenues or gains are taxable after they are recognized in financial income.**
An asset (e.g., accounts receivable or investment) may be recognized for revenues or gains that will result in **taxable amounts in future years** when the asset is recovered. Examples:
1. Sales accounted for on the accrual basis for financial reporting purposes and on the installment (cash) basis for tax purposes.
2. Contracts accounted for under the percentage-of-completion method for financial reporting purposes and a portion of related gross profit deferred for tax purposes.
3. Investments accounted for under the equity method for financial reporting purposes and under the cost method for tax purposes.
4. Gain on involuntary conversion of nonmonetary asset which is recognized for financial reporting purposes but deferred for tax purposes.

B. **Expenses or losses are deductible after they are recognized in financial income.**
A liability (or contra asset) may be recognized for expenses or losses that will result in **deductible amounts in future years** when the liability is settled. Examples:
1. Product warranty liabilities.
2. Estimated liabilities related to discontinued operations or restructurings.
3. Litigation accruals.
4. Bad debt expense recognized using the allowance method for financial reporting purposes; direct write-off method used for tax purposes.

C. **Revenues or gains are taxable before they are recognized in financial income.**
A liability may be recognized for an advance payment for goods or services to be provided in future years. For tax purposes, the advance payment is included in taxable income upon the receipt of cash. Future sacrifices to provide goods or services (or future refunds to those who cancel their orders) that settle the liability will result in **deductible amounts in future years**. Examples:
1. Subscriptions received in advance.
2. Advance rental receipts.
3. Sales and leasebacks for financial reporting purposes (income deferral) and reported as sales for tax purposes.
4. Prepaid contracts and royalties received in advance.

D. **Expenses or losses are deductible before they are recognized in financial income.**
The cost of an asset may have been deducted for tax purposes faster than it was expensed for financial reporting purposes. Amounts received upon future recovery of the amount of the asset for financial reporting (through use or sale) will exceed the remaining tax basis of the asset and thereby result in **taxable amounts in future years**. Examples:
1. Depreciable property, depletable resources, and intangibles.
2. Deductible pension funding exceeding expense.
3. Prepaid expenses that are deducted on the tax return in the period paid.

[4]*SFAS No. 109* gives more examples of temporary differences. We have presented the most common types.

Determining a company's temporary differences may prove difficult. A company should prepare a balance sheet for tax purposes that can be compared with its GAAP balance sheet; many of the differences between the two balance sheets would be temporary differences.

Originating and Reversing Aspects of Temporary Differences. An **originating temporary difference** is the initial difference between the book basis and the tax basis of an asset or liability, regardless of whether the tax basis of the asset or liability exceeds or is exceeded by the book basis of the asset or liability. A **reversing difference**, on the other hand, occurs when a temporary difference that originated in prior periods is eliminated and the related tax effect is removed from the deferred tax account.

For example, assume that Sharp Co. has tax depreciation in excess of book depreciation of $2,000 in 2000, 2001, and 2002, and that it has an excess of book depreciation over tax depreciation of $3,000 in 2003 and 2004 for the same asset. Assuming a tax rate of 30 percent for all years, the Deferred Tax Liability account is as follows.

ILLUSTRATION 19-23
Tax Effects of Originating and Reversing Differences

	Deferred Tax Liability				
Tax Effects of Reversing Differences	2003	900	2000	600	Tax Effects of Originating Differences
	2004	900	2001	600	
			2002	600	

The originating differences for Sharp in each of the first 3 years would be $2,000, and the related tax effect of each originating difference would be $600. The reversing differences in 2003 and 2004 would each be $3,000, and the related tax effect of each would be $900.

Permanent Differences

Permanent differences are caused by items that (1) enter into pretax financial income but **never** into taxable income, or (2) enter into taxable income but **never** into pretax financial income.

Congress has enacted a variety of tax law provisions in an effort to achieve certain political, economic, and social objectives. Some of these provisions exclude certain revenues from taxation, limit the deductibility of certain expenses, and permit the deduction of certain other expenses in excess of costs incurred. A corporation that has tax-free income, nondeductible expenses, or allowable deductions in excess of cost has an effective tax rate that is different from the statutory (regular) tax rate.

Since permanent differences affect only the period in which they occur, they do not give rise to future taxable or deductible amounts. As a result, **there are no deferred tax consequences to be recognized**. Examples of permanent differences are shown in Illustration 19-24.

ILLUSTRATION 19-24
Examples of Permanent Differences

A. **Items are recognized for financial reporting purposes but not for tax purposes.**
Examples:
1. Interest received on state and municipal obligations.
2. Expenses incurred in obtaining tax-exempt income.
3. Proceeds from life insurance carried by the company on key officers or employees.
4. Premiums paid for life insurance carried by the company on key officers or employees (company is beneficiary).
5. Fines and expenses resulting from a violation of law.
6. Compensation expense associated with certain employee stock options.

B. **Items are recognized for tax purposes but not for financial reporting purposes.**
Examples:
1. "Percentage depletion" of natural resources in excess of their cost.
2. The deduction for dividends received from U.S. corporations, generally 70% or 80%.

Temporary and Permanent Differences Illustrated

To illustrate the computations used when both temporary and permanent differences exist, assume that Bio-Tech Company reports pretax financial income of $200,000 in each of the years 2002, 2003, and 2004. The company is subject to a 30 percent tax rate, and has the following differences between pretax financial income and taxable income.

1. An installment sale of $18,000 in 2002 is reported for tax purposes over an 18-month period at a constant amount per month beginning January 1, 2003. The entire sale is recognized for book purposes in 2002.
2. Premium paid for life insurance carried by the company on key officers is $5,000 in 2003 and 2004. This is not deductible for tax purposes, but is expensed for book purposes.

The installment sale is a temporary difference, and the life insurance premium is a permanent difference. The reconciliation of Bio-Tech Company's pretax financial income to taxable income and the computation of income tax payable is shown in Illustration 19-25.

ILLUSTRATION 19-25
Reconciliation and Computation of Income Taxes Payable

	2002	2003	2004
Pretax financial income	$200,000	$200,000	$200,000
Permanent difference			
Nondeductible expense		5,000	5,000
Temporary difference			
Installment sale	(18,000)	12,000	6,000
Taxable income	182,000	217,000	211,000
Tax rate	30%	30%	30%
Income tax payable	$ 54,600	$ 65,100	$ 63,300

Note that differences causing pretax financial income to exceed taxable income are **deducted** from pretax financial income when determining taxable income. Conversely, differences causing pretax financial income to be less than taxable income are **added to** pretax financial income in determining taxable income.

Both permanent and temporary differences are considered in reconciling pretax financial income to taxable income. Since the permanent difference (nondeductible expense) does not result in future taxable or deductible amounts, deferred income taxes are not recorded for this difference.

The journal entries to record income taxes for Bio-Tech for 2002, 2003, and 2004 are as follows.

December 31, 2002		
Income Tax Expense ($54,600 + $5,400)	60,000	
Deferred Tax Liability ($18,000 × 30%)		5,400
Income Tax Payable ($182,000 × 30%)		54,600
December 31, 2003		
Income Tax Expense ($65,100 − $3,600)	61,500	
Deferred Tax Liability ($12,000 × 30%)	3,600	
Income Tax Payable ($217,000 × 30%)		65,100
December 31, 2004		
Income Tax Expense ($63,300 − $1,800)	61,500	
Deferred Tax Liability ($6,000 × 30%)	1,800	
Income Tax Payable ($211,000 × 30%)		63,300

Bio-Tech has one temporary difference, which originates in 2002 and reverses in 2003 and 2004. A deferred tax liability is recognized at the end of 2002 because the temporary difference causes future taxable amounts. As the temporary difference reverses, the deferred tax liability is reduced. There is no deferred tax amount associated with the difference caused by the nondeductible insurance expense because it is a permanent difference.

Although a statutory (enacted) tax rate of 30 percent applies for all 3 years, the effective rate is different. The **effective tax rate** is computed by dividing total income tax expense for the period by pretax financial income. The effective rate is 30 percent for 2002 (\$60,000 ÷ \$200,000 = 30%) and 30.75 percent for 2003 and 2004 (\$61,500 ÷ \$200,000 = 30.75%).

Tax Rate Considerations

OBJECTIVE 7
Explain the effect of various tax rates and tax rate changes on deferred income taxes.

In our previous illustrations, the enacted tax rate did not change from one year to the next. Thus, to compute the deferred income tax amount to be reported on the balance sheet, the cumulative temporary difference is simply multiplied by the current tax rate. Using Bio-Tech as an example, the cumulative temporary difference of \$18,000 is multiplied by the enacted tax rate, 30 percent in this case, to arrive at a deferred tax liability of \$5,400 (\$18,000 × 30%) at the end of 2002.

Future Tax Rates

What happens if tax rates are different for future years? In this case, the **enacted tax rate** expected to apply should be used. Therefore, presently enacted changes in the tax rate that become effective for a particular future year(s) must be considered when determining the tax rate to apply to existing temporary differences. For example, assume that Warlen Co. at the end of 2001 has the following cumulative temporary difference of \$300,000, computed as follows.

ILLUSTRATION 19-26
Computation of Cumulative Temporary Difference

Book basis of depreciable assets	\$1,000,000
Tax basis of depreciable assets	700,000
Cumulative temporary difference	\$ 300,000

Furthermore, assume that the \$300,000 will reverse and result in taxable amounts in the following years when the enacted tax rates are as follows.

ILLUSTRATION 19-27
Deferred Tax Liability Based on Future Rates

	2002	2003	2004	2005	2006	Total
Future taxable amounts	\$80,000	\$70,000	\$60,000	\$50,000	\$40,000	\$300,000
Tax rate	40%	40%	35%	30%	30%	
Deferred tax liability	\$32,000	\$28,000	\$21,000	\$15,000	\$12,000	\$108,000

The total deferred tax liability at the end of 2001 is \$108,000. Tax rates other than the current rate may be used only when the future tax rates have been enacted into law, as is apparently the case in this example. **If new rates are not yet enacted into law for future years, the current rate should be used.**

In determining the appropriate enacted tax rate for a given year, companies are required to use the **average tax rate**. The Internal Revenue Service and other taxing jurisdictions tax income on a graduated tax basis. For a U.S. corporation, the first \$50,000 of taxable income is taxed at 15 percent, the next \$25,000 at 25 percent, with higher incremental levels of income being taxed at rates as high as 39 percent. In computing deferred income taxes, companies for which graduated tax rates are a significant factor are therefore required to **determine the average tax rate and use that rate**.

Revision of Future Tax Rates

When a change in the tax rate is enacted into law, its effect on the existing deferred income tax accounts should be recorded immediately. **The effect is reported as an adjustment to income tax expense in the period of the change.**

Assume that on December 10, 2001, a new income tax act is signed into law that lowers the corporate tax rate from 40 percent to 35 percent, effective January 1, 2003. If Hostel Co. has one temporary difference at the beginning of 2001 related to $3 million of excess tax depreciation, then it has a Deferred Tax Liability account with a balance of $1,200,000 ($3,000,000 × 40%) at January 1, 2001. If taxable amounts related to this difference are scheduled to occur equally in 2002, 2003, and 2004, the deferred tax liability at the end of 2001 should be $1,100,000, computed as follows.

ILLUSTRATION 19-28
Schedule of Future Taxable Amounts and Related Tax Rates

	2002	2003	2004	Total
Future taxable amounts	$1,000,000	$1,000,000	$1,000,000	$3,000,000
Tax rate	40%	35%	35%	
Deferred tax liability	$ 400,000	$ 350,000	$ 350,000	$1,100,000

An entry, therefore, would be made at the end of 2001 to recognize the decrease of $100,000 ($1,200,000 − $1,100,000) in the deferred tax liability as follows.

Deferred Tax Liability	100,000	
Income Tax Expense		100,000

Corporate tax rates do not change often and, therefore, the current rate will usually be employed. However, state and foreign tax rates change more frequently and they require adjustments in deferred income taxes accordingly.[5]

ACCOUNTING FOR NET OPERATING LOSSES

OBJECTIVE 8
Apply accounting procedures for a loss carryback and a loss carryforward.

A **net operating loss (NOL)** occurs for tax purposes in a year when tax-deductible expenses exceed taxable revenues. An inequitable tax burden would result if companies were taxed during profitable periods without receiving any tax relief during periods of net operating losses. Under certain circumstances, therefore, the federal tax laws permit taxpayers to use the losses of one year to offset the profits of other years. This income-averaging provision is accomplished through the **carryback and carryforward of net operating losses**. Under this provision, a company pays no income taxes for a year in which it incurs a net operating loss. In addition, it may select one of the two options discussed below.

Loss Carryback

Through use of a **loss carryback**, a company may carry the net operating loss back 2 years and receive refunds for income taxes paid in those years. The loss must be applied to the earlier year first and then to the second year. Any loss remaining after the 2-year carryback may be **carried forward** up to 20 years to offset future taxable in-

[5]Tax rate changes nearly always will have a substantial impact on income numbers and the reporting of deferred income taxes on the balance sheet. As a result, you can expect to hear an economic consequences argument every time that Congress decides to change the tax rates. For example, when Congress raised the corporate rate from 34 percent to 35 percent in 1993, companies took an additional "hit" to earnings if they were in a deferred tax liability position.

come.[6] The following diagram illustrates the loss carryback procedure, assuming a loss in 2004.

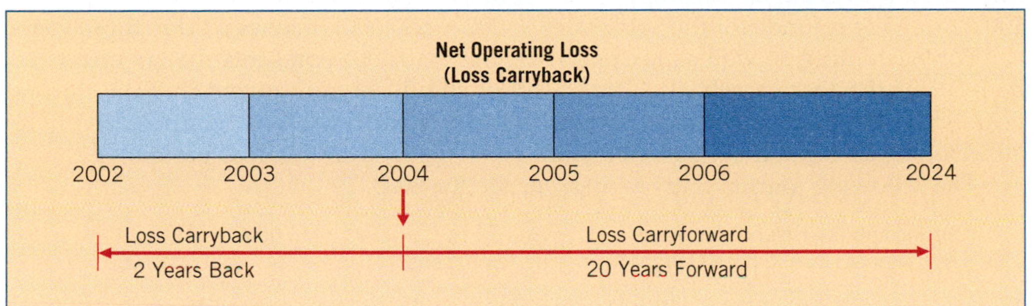

ILLUSTRATION 19-29
Loss Carryback Procedure

Loss Carryforward

A company may elect to forgo the loss carryback and use only the **loss carryforward** option, offsetting future taxable income for up to 20 years. Illustration 19-30 shows this approach.

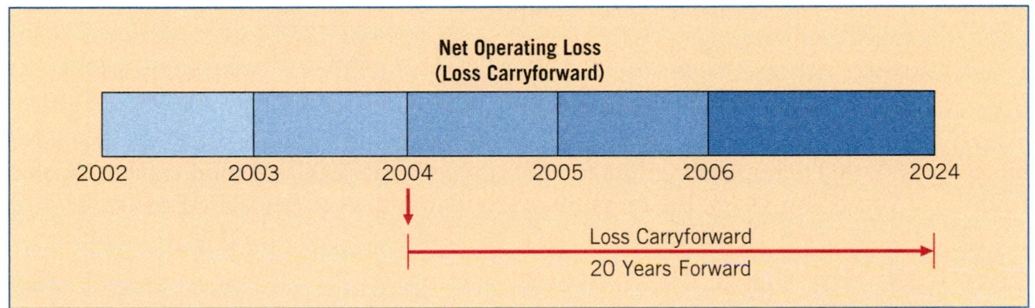

ILLUSTRATION 19-30
Loss Carryforward Procedure

Operating losses can be substantial. **PepsiCo, Inc.** had losses of $2.9 billion in 2000, representing millions of dollars in potential tax savings. Companies that have suffered substantial losses are often attractive merger candidates because in certain cases the acquirer may use these losses to reduce its own income taxes.

Loss Carryback Illustrated

To illustrate the accounting procedures for a net operating loss carryback, assume that Groh Inc. has no temporary or permanent differences. Groh experiences the following.

Year	Taxable Income or Loss	Tax Rate	Tax Paid
2000	$ 50,000	35%	$17,500
2001	100,000	30%	30,000
2002	200,000	40%	80,000
2003	(500,000)	—	–0–

[6]For net operating losses arising in tax years 2001 and 2002, companies can carry back up to 5 years. This temporary change was designed to stimulate the economy in the wake of the terrorist attacks on 9/11/2001. For homework purposes, we will use a 2-year carryback period.

In 2003, Groh Inc. incurs a net operating loss that it decides to carry back. Under the law, the carryback must be applied first to the **second year preceding the loss year**. Therefore, the loss would be carried back first to 2001. Any unused loss would then be carried back to 2002. Accordingly, Groh would file amended tax returns for 2001 and 2002, receiving refunds for the $110,000 ($30,000 + $80,000) of taxes paid in those years.

For accounting as well as tax purposes, the $110,000 represents the **tax effect (tax benefit) of the loss carryback**. This tax effect should be recognized in 2003, the loss year. Since the tax loss gives rise to a refund that is both measurable and currently realizable, the associated tax benefit should be recognized in this loss period.

The following journal entry is appropriate for 2003.

Income Tax Refund Receivable	110,000	
Benefit Due to Loss Carryback (Income Tax Expense)		110,000

The account debited, **Income Tax Refund Receivable**, is reported on the balance sheet as a current asset at December 31, 2003. The account credited is reported on the income statement for 2003 as follows.

ILLUSTRATION 19-31
Recognition of Benefit of the Loss Carryback in the Loss Year

GROH INC.
INCOME STATEMENT (PARTIAL) FOR 2003

Operating loss before income taxes	$(500,000)
Income tax benefit	
Benefit due to loss carryback	110,000
Net loss	$(390,000)

Since the $500,000 net operating loss for 2003 exceeds the $300,000 total taxable income from the 2 preceding years, the remaining $200,000 loss is to be carried forward.

Loss Carryforward Illustrated

If a net operating loss is not fully absorbed through a carryback, or if the company decides not to carry the loss back, then it can be carried forward for up to 20 years.[7] Because carryforwards are used to offset future taxable income, the **tax effect of a loss carryforward** represents **future tax savings**. Realization of the future tax benefit depends upon future earnings, the prospect of which may be highly uncertain.

The key accounting issue is whether there should be different requirements for recognition of a deferred tax asset for (a) deductible temporary differences, and (b) operating loss carryforwards. The FASB's position is that in substance these items are the same—both are amounts that are deductible on tax returns in future years. As a result, the Board concluded that there **should not be different requirements** for recognition of a deferred tax asset from deductible temporary differences and operating loss carryforwards.[8]

Carryforward without Valuation Allowance

To illustrate the accounting for an operating loss carryforward, return to the Groh Inc. example from the preceding section. In 2003 the company would record the tax effect of the $200,000 loss carryforward as a deferred tax asset of $80,000 ($200,000 × 40%)

[7]The length of the carryforward period has varied. It has increased from 7 years to 20 years over a period of time.

[8]This requirement is controversial because many do not believe it is appropriate to recognize deferred tax assets except when they are assured beyond a reasonable doubt. Others argue that deferred tax assets for loss carryforwards should never be recognized until income is realized in the future.

assuming that the enacted future tax rate is 40 percent. The journal entries to record the benefits of the carryback and the carryforward in 2003 would be as follows.

To recognize benefit of loss carryback		
Income Tax Refund Receivable	110,000	
Benefit Due to Loss Carryback (Income Tax Expense)		110,000

To recognize benefit of loss carryforward		
Deferred Tax Asset	80,000	
Benefit Due to Loss Carryforward (Income Tax Expense)		80,000

The income tax refund receivable of $110,000 will be realized immediately as a refund of taxes paid in the past. A Deferred Tax Asset is established for the benefits of future tax savings. The two accounts credited are contra income tax expense items, which would be presented on the 2003 income statement as follows.

ILLUSTRATION 19-32
Recognition of the Benefit of the Loss Carryback and Carryforward in the Loss Year

GROH INC.
INCOME STATEMENT (PARTIAL) FOR 2003

Operating loss before income taxes		$(500,000)
Income tax benefit		
Benefit due to loss carryback	$110,000	
Benefit due to loss carryforward	80,000	190,000
Net loss		$(310,000)

The $110,000 **current tax benefit** is the income tax refundable for the year, which is determined by applying the carryback provisions of the tax law to the taxable loss for 2003. The $80,000 is the **deferred tax benefit** for the year, which results from an increase in the deferred tax asset.

For 2004, assume that Groh Inc. returns to profitable operations and has taxable income of $250,000 (prior to adjustment for the NOL carryforward) subject to a 40 percent tax rate. Groh Inc. would then realize the benefits of the carryforward for tax purposes in 2004 which were recognized for accounting purposes in 2003. The income tax payable for 2004 is computed as follows.

ILLUSTRATION 19-33
Computation of Income Tax Payable with Realized Loss Carryforward

Taxable income prior to loss carryforward	$ 250,000
Loss carryforward deduction	(200,000)
Taxable income for 2004	50,000
Tax rate	40%
Income tax payable for 2004	$ 20,000

The journal entry to record income taxes in 2004 would be as follows.

Income Tax Expense	100,000	
Deferred Tax Asset		80,000
Income Tax Payable		20,000

The Deferred Tax Asset account is reduced because the benefits of the NOL carryforward are realized in 2004.

The 2004 income statement that appears in Illustration 19-34 would **not report** the tax effects of either the loss carryback or the loss carryforward, because both had been reported previously.

ILLUSTRATION 19-34
Presentation of the Benefit of Loss Carryforward Realized in 2004, Recognized in 2003

GROH INC. INCOME STATEMENT (PARTIAL) FOR 2004		
Income before income taxes		$250,000
Income tax expense		
Current	$20,000	
Deferred	80,000	100,000
Net income		$150,000

Carryforward with Valuation Allowance

Return to the Groh Inc. example. Assume that it is more likely than not that the entire NOL carryforward will not be realized in future years. In this situation, Groh Inc. records the tax benefits of $110,000 associated with the $300,000 NOL carryback, as previously described. In addition, it records a deferred tax asset of $80,000 ($200,000 × 40%) for the potential benefits related to the loss carryforward, and an allowance to reduce the deferred tax asset by the same amount. The journal entries in 2003 are as follows.

To recognize benefit of loss carryback		
Income Tax Refund Receivable	110,000	
Benefit Due to Loss Carryback (Income Tax Expense)		110,000
To recognize benefit of loss carryforward		
Deferred Tax Asset	80,000	
Benefit Due to Loss Carryforward (Income Tax Expense)		80,000
To record allowance amount		
Benefit Due to Loss Carryforward (Income Tax Expense)	80,000	
Allowance to Reduce Deferred Tax Asset to Expected Realizable Value		80,000

The latter entry indicates that because positive evidence of sufficient quality and quantity is not available to counteract the negative evidence, a valuation allowance is needed.

The presentation in the 2003 income statement would be as follows.

ILLUSTRATION 19-35
Recognition of Benefit of Loss Carryback Only

GROH INC. INCOME STATEMENT (PARTIAL) FOR 2003	
Operating loss before income taxes	$(500,000)
Income tax benefit	
Benefit due to loss carryback	110,000
Net loss	$(390,000)

In 2004, assuming that the company has taxable income of $250,000 (before considering the carryforward) subject to a tax rate of 40 percent, the deferred tax asset is realized and the allowance is no longer needed. The following entries would be made.

To record current and deferred income taxes		
Income Tax Expense	100,000	
Deferred Tax Asset		80,000
Income Tax Payable		20,000
To eliminate allowance and recognize loss carryforward		
Allowance to Reduce Deferred Tax Asset to Expected Realizable Value	80,000	
Benefit Due to Loss Carryforward (Income Tax Expense)		80,000

The $80,000 benefit due to the loss carryforward is computed by multiplying the $200,000 loss carryforward by the 40 percent tax rate. This amount is reported on the

2004 income statement because it was not recognized in 2003. Assuming that the income for 2004 is derived from continuing operations, the income statement would be:

ILLUSTRATION 19-36
Recognition of Benefit of Loss Carryforward When Realized

GROH INC.
INCOME STATEMENT (PARTIAL) FOR 2004

Income before income taxes		$250,000
Income tax expense		
Current	$ 20,000	
Deferred	80,000	
Benefit due to loss carryforward	(80,000)	20,000
Net income		$230,000

Another method is to report only one line for total income tax expense of $20,000 on the face of the income statement and disclose the components of income tax expense in the notes to the financial statements.

Valuation Allowance Revisited

All positive and negative information should be considered in determining whether a valuation allowance is needed. Whether a deferred tax asset will be realized depends on whether sufficient taxable income exists or will exist within the carryback or carryforward period available under tax law. The following possible sources of taxable income may be available under the tax law to realize a tax benefit for deductible temporary differences and carryforwards.

ILLUSTRATION 19-37
Possible Sources of Taxable Income

Taxable Income Sources

a. Future reversals of existing taxable temporary differences

b. Future taxable income exclusive of reversing temporary differences and carryforwards

c. Taxable income in prior carryback year(s) if carryback is permitted under the tax law

d. **Tax-planning strategies** that would, if necessary, be implemented to:
(1) Accelerate taxable amounts to utilize expiring carryforwards
(2) Change the character of taxable or deductible amounts from ordinary income or loss to capital gain or loss
(3) Switch from tax-exempt to taxable investments.[9]

If any one of these sources is sufficient to support a conclusion that a valuation allowance is not necessary, other sources need not be considered.

Forming a conclusion that a valuation allowance is not needed is difficult when there is negative evidence such as cumulative losses in recent years. Companies may also cite positive evidence indicating that a valuation allowance is not needed. Examples (not prerequisites) of evidence to consider when determining the need for a valuation allowance are presented in Illustration 19-38.

[9]"Accounting for Income Taxes," *Statement of Financial Accounting Standards No. 109* (Norwalk, Conn.: FASB, 1992). A tax-planning strategy is an action that would be implemented to realize a tax benefit for an operating loss or tax credit carryforward before it expires. Tax-planning strategies are considered when assessing the need for and amount of a valuation allowance for deferred tax assets.

ILLUSTRATION 19-38
Evidence to Consider in Evaluating the Need for a Valuation Account

Negative Evidence

a. A history of operating loss or tax credit carryforwards expiring unused
b. Losses expected in early future years (by a presently profitable entity)
c. Unsettled circumstances that, if unfavorably resolved, would adversely affect future operations and profit levels on a continuing basis in future years
d. A carryback, carryforward period that is so brief that it would limit realization of tax benefits if (1) a significant deductible temporary difference is expected to reverse in a single year or (2) the enterprise operates in a traditionally cyclical business.

Positive Evidence

a. Existing contracts or firm sales backlog that will produce more than enough taxable income to realize the deferred tax asset based on existing sale prices and cost structures
b. An excess of appreciated asset value over the tax basis of the entity's net assets in an amount sufficient to realize the deferred tax asset
c. A strong earnings history exclusive of the loss that created the future deductible amount (tax loss carryforward or deductible temporary difference) coupled with evidence indicating that the loss (for example, an unusual, infrequent, or extraordinary item) is an aberration rather than a continuing condition.[10]

INTERNATIONAL INSIGHT

Under international accounting standards *(IAS 12)*, a deferred tax asset may not be recognized unless realization is "probable." However, "probable" is not defined in the standard, leading to diversity in the recognition of deferred tax assets.

The use of a valuation allowance provides management with an opportunity to manage its earnings. As one accounting expert notes, "The 'more likely than not' provision is perhaps the most judgmental clause in accounting." What some companies might do is set up valuation accounts and then use the valuation account to increase income as needed. Others could take the income immediately to increase capital or to offset large negative charges to income.

WHAT DO THE NUMBERS MEAN?

READ THOSE NOTES

A recent study of companies' valuation allowances indicates that the allowances are related to the factors identified as positive and negative evidence. And though there is little evidence that the valuation allowance is used to manage earnings,[11] the press sometimes understates the impact of reversing the deferred tax valuation allowance. For example, Verity, Inc. eliminated its entire valuation allowance of $18.9 million in 2000 but focused on a net deferred tax gain of $2.9 million in its press release. Why the difference? As revealed in Verity's financial statement notes, other deferred tax expense amounts totaled over $16 million. Thus, the one-time valuation reversal gave an $18.9 million bump to income, not the net $2.9 million reported in the press. The lesson: After you read the morning paper, read the financial statement notes.

Not on Exam

FINANCIAL STATEMENT PRESENTATION

Balance Sheet Presentation

OBJECTIVE 9
Describe the presentation of deferred income taxes in financial statements.

Deferred tax accounts are reported on the balance sheet as assets and liabilities. They should be classified as a net current amount and a net noncurrent amount. **An individual deferred tax liability or asset is classified as current or noncurrent based on the classification of the related asset or liability for financial reporting purposes.** A deferred tax asset or liability is considered to be related to an asset or liability if reduction of the asset or liability will cause the temporary difference to reverse or turn around. A deferred tax liability or asset that is not related to an asset or liability for

[10]Ibid., par. 23 and 24.

[11]G. S. Miller and D. J. Skinner, "Determinants of the Valuation Allowance for Deferred Tax Assets under *SFAS No. 109*," *The Accounting Review* (April 1998)

financial reporting, including a deferred tax asset related to a loss carryforward, should be classified according to the expected reversal date of the temporary difference.

To illustrate, assume that Morgan Inc. records bad debt expense using the allowance method for accounting purposes and the direct write-off method for tax purposes. The company currently has Accounts Receivable and Allowance for Doubtful Accounts balances of $2 million and $100,000, respectively. In addition, given a 40 percent tax rate, it has a debit balance in the Deferred Tax Asset account of $40,000 (40% × $100,000). The $40,000 debit balance in the Deferred Tax Asset account is considered to be related to the Accounts Receivable and the Allowance for Doubtful Accounts balances because collection or write-off of the receivables will cause the temporary difference to reverse. Therefore, the Deferred Tax Asset account is classified as current, the same as the Accounts Receivable and Allowance for Doubtful Accounts balances.

In practice, most companies engage in a large number of transactions that give rise to deferred taxes. The balances in the deferred tax accounts should be analyzed and classified on the balance sheet in two categories: one for the **net current amount**, and one for the **net noncurrent amount**. This procedure is summarized as follows.

1. ***Classify the amounts as current or noncurrent.*** If they are related to a specific asset or liability, the amounts should be classified in the same manner as the related asset or liability. If not so related, they should be classified on the basis of the expected reversal date of the temporary difference.
2. ***Determine the net current amount*** by summing the various deferred tax assets and liabilities classified as current. If the net result is an asset, report it on the balance sheet as a current asset; if a liability, report it as a current liability.
3. ***Determine the net noncurrent amount*** by summing the various deferred tax assets and liabilities classified as noncurrent. If the net result is an asset, report it on the balance sheet as a noncurrent asset; if a liability, report it as a long-term liability.

To illustrate, assume that K. Scott Company has four deferred tax items at December 31, 2004. An analysis reveals the following.

ILLUSTRATION 19-39
Classification of Temporary Differences as Current or Noncurrent

Temporary Difference	Resulting Deferred Tax (Asset)	Resulting Deferred Tax Liability	Related Balance Sheet Account	Classification
1. Rent collected in advance: recognized when earned for accounting purposes and when received for tax purposes.	$(42,000)		Unearned Rent	Current
2. Use of straight-line depreciation for accounting purposes and accelerated depreciation for tax purposes.		$214,000	Equipment	Noncurrent
3. Recognition of profits on installment sales during period of sale for accounting purposes and during period of collection for tax purposes.		45,000	Installment Accounts Receivable	Current
4. Warranty liabilities: recognized for accounting purposes at time of sale; for tax purposes at time paid.	(12,000)		Estimated Liability under Warranties	Current
Totals	$(54,000)	$259,000		

The deferred taxes to be classified as current net to a $9,000 asset ($42,000 + $12,000 − $45,000). The deferred taxes to be classified as noncurrent net to a $214,000 liability. Consequently, deferred income taxes would appear on K. Scott's December 31, 2004, balance sheet, as shown in Illustration 19-40.

ILLUSTRATION 19-40
Balance Sheet Presentation of Deferred Income Taxes

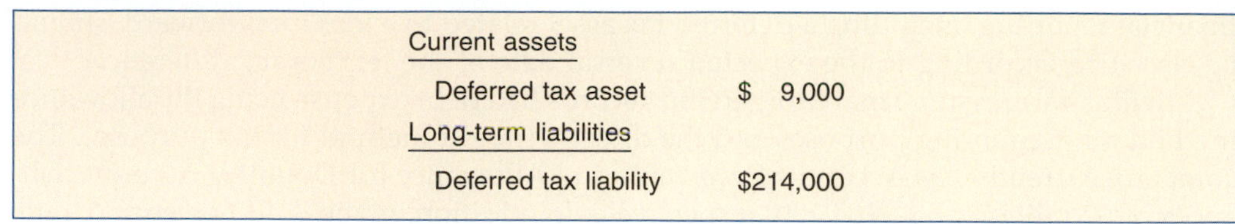

Current assets	
Deferred tax asset	$ 9,000
Long-term liabilities	
Deferred tax liability	$214,000

As indicated earlier, a deferred tax asset or liability **may not be related** to an asset or liability for financial reporting purposes. One example is an operating loss carryforward. In this case, a deferred tax asset is recorded, but there is no related, identifiable asset or liability for financial reporting purposes. In these limited situations, deferred income taxes should be classified according to the **expected reversal date** of the temporary difference. That is, the tax effect of any temporary difference reversing next year should be reported as current, and the remainder should be reported as noncurrent. If a deferred tax asset is noncurrent, it should be classified in the "Other assets" section.

The total of all deferred tax liabilities, the total of all deferred tax assets, and the total valuation allowance should be disclosed. In addition, the following should be disclosed: (1) any net change during the year in the total valuation allowance, and (2) the types of temporary differences, carryforwards, or carrybacks that give rise to significant portions of deferred tax liabilities and assets.

Income tax payable is shown as a current liability on the balance sheet. Corporations are required to make estimated tax payments to the Internal Revenue Service quarterly. These estimated payments are recorded by a debit to Prepaid Income Taxes. As a result, the balance of the Income Tax Payable is offset by the balance of the Prepaid Income Taxes account when reporting income taxes on the balance sheet.

Income Statement Presentation

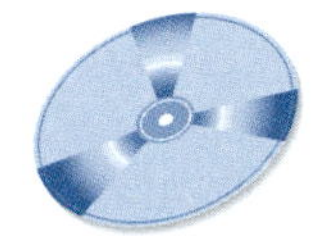

Expanded Discussion of Intraperiod Tax Allocation

Income tax expense (or benefit) should be allocated to continuing operations, discontinued operations, extraordinary items, the cumulative effect of accounting changes, and prior period adjustments. This approach is referred to as intraperiod tax allocation.

In addition, the significant components of income tax expense attributable to continuing operations should be disclosed:

1. Current tax expense or benefit.
2. Deferred tax expense or benefit, exclusive of other components listed below.
3. Investment tax credits.
4. Government grants (to the extent they are recognized as a reduction of income tax expense).
5. The benefits of operating loss carryforwards (resulting in a reduction of income tax expense).
6. Tax expense that results from allocating certain tax benefits either directly to paid-in capital or to reduce goodwill or other noncurrent intangible assets of an acquired entity.
7. Adjustments of a deferred tax liability or asset for enacted changes in tax laws or rates or a change in the tax status of an enterprise.
8. Adjustments of the beginning-of-the-year balance of a valuation allowance because of a change in circumstances that causes a change in judgment about the realizability of the related deferred tax asset in future years.

In the notes, companies are also required to reconcile (using percentages or dollar amounts) income tax expense attributable to continuing operations with the amount that results from applying domestic federal statutory tax rates to pretax income from continuing operations. The estimated amount and the nature of each significant reconciling item should be disclosed. An example from the 2000 Annual Report of **PepsiCo, Inc.** is presented in Illustration 19-41.

ILLUSTRATION 19-41
Disclosure of Income Taxes—PepsiCo, Inc.

PepsiCo, Inc.
(in millions)

Note 13: Income Taxes

U.S. and foreign income before income taxes:

	2000	1999
U.S.	$2,126	$2,771
Foreign	1,084	885
	$3,210	$3,656

Provision for income taxes:

		2000	1999
Current:	Federal	$ 771	$ 730
	Foreign	157	306
	State	36	40
		964	1,076
Deferred:	Federal	60	519
	Foreign	(10)	(12)
	State	13	23
		63	530
		$1,027	$1,606

Reconciliation of the U.S. Federal statutory tax rate to our effective tax rate:

	2000	1999
U.S. Federal statutory tax rate	35.0%	35.0%
State income tax, net of Federal tax benefit	1.0	1.1
Lower taxes on foreign results	(3.0)	(2.7)
Bottling transactions	–	10.6
Other, net	(1.0)	(0.1)
Effective tax rate	32.0%	43.9%

Deferred taxes are recorded to give recognition to temporary differences between the tax bases of assets or liabilities and their reported amounts in the financial statements. We record the tax effect of these temporary differences as deferred tax assets or deferred tax liabilities. Deferred tax assets generally represent items that can be used as a tax deduction or credit in future years. Deferred tax liabilities generally represent items that we have taken a tax deduction for, but have not yet recorded in the Consolidated Statement of income.

Deferred tax liabilities (assets):

	2000	1999
Investments in unconsolidated affiliates	$ 672	$ 667
Property, plant, and equipment	576	545
Safe harbor leases	94	101
Zero-coupon notes	73	76
Intangible assets other than nondeductible goodwill	54	47
Other	404	328
Gross deferred tax liabilities	1,873	1,764
Net operating loss carryforwards	(443)	(450)
Postretirement benefits	(187)	(179)
Various current liabilities and other	(640)	(626)
Gross deferred tax assets	(1,270)	(1,255)
Deferred tax assets valuation allowances	464	461
Deferred tax assets, net of valuation allowances	(806)	(794)
Net deferred tax liabilities	$ 1,067	$ 970
Included in:		
Prepaid expenses and other current assets	$ (294)	$ (239)
Deferred income taxes	1,361	1,209
	$ 1,067	$ 970

Net operating loss carryforwards totaling $2.9 billion at year-end 2000 are being carried forward and are available to reduce future taxable income of certain subsidiaries in a number of foreign and state jurisdictions. These net operating losses will expire as follows: $0.1 billion in 2001, $2.5 billion between 2002 and 2016, and $0.3 billion may be carried forward indefinitely.

Valuation allowances have been established primarily for deferred tax assets related to net operating losses in certain state and foreign tax jurisdictions where the amount of expected future taxable income from operations does not support the recognition of these deferred tax assets.

Additional Examples of Deferred Tax Disclosures

These income tax disclosures are required for several reasons. Three of these reasons are:

1. ***Assessing Quality of Earnings.*** Many investors seeking to assess the quality of a company's earnings are interested in the reconciliation of pretax financial income to taxable income. Earnings that are enhanced by a favorable tax effect should be examined carefully, particularly if the tax effect is nonrecurring. For example, the tax disclosure in Illustration 19-41 indicates that **PepsiCo**'s effective tax rate declined from 43.9 percent in 1999 to 32 percent in 2000. The decline translates into a tax savings of $579 million. That savings offset the decline in income before taxes and allowed PepsiCo to report a slight increase in bottom-line income from 1999 to 2000.
2. ***Making Better Predictions of Future Cash Flows.*** Examination of the deferred portion of income tax expense provides information as to whether taxes payable are likely to be higher or lower in the future. In **PepsiCo**'s case, significant future taxable amounts and higher tax payments are expected, due to lower depreciation in the future and realization of gains on equity investments. As a result, it may be possible to predict future reductions in deferred tax liabilities leading to a loss of liquidity because actual tax payments will be higher than the tax expense reported on the income statement.[12]
3. ***Predicting Future Cash Flows from Operating Loss Carryforwards.*** The amounts and expiration dates of any operating loss carryforwards for tax purposes should be disclosed. From this disclosure, the reader can determine the amount of income that may be recognized in the future on which no income tax will be paid. For example, the **PepsiCo** disclosure in Illustration 19-41 indicates that PepsiCo has $2.9 billion in net operating loss carryforwards that can be used to reduce future taxes up to the year 2016 and beyond.

   Loss carryforwards can be extremely valuable to a potential acquirer. At one time, **Dalfort Company** received nearly $360 million in operating loss carryforwards and other credits as a result of its ownership of **Braniff Airlines**. Many speculate that Dalfort bought **Levitz Furniture Corp.** (a large discounter of quality furniture) so that it could offset its carryforward losses from Braniff against Levitz's earnings. Companies that have suffered substantial losses may find themselves worth more "dead" than alive because their tax losses have little value to themselves but great value to other enterprises. In short, substantial tax carryforwards can have real economic value.[13]

REVIEW OF THE ASSET-LIABILITY METHOD

OBJECTIVE 10
Indicate the basic principles of the asset-liability method.

The FASB believes that the **asset-liability method** (sometimes referred to as the liability approach) is the most consistent method for accounting for income taxes. One objective of this approach is to recognize the amount of taxes payable or refundable for the current year. A second objective is to recognize **deferred tax liabilities and assets** for the **future tax consequences** of events that have been recognized in the financial statements or tax returns.

[12]An article by R. P. Weber and J. E. Wheeler, "Using Income Tax Disclosures to Explore Significant Economic Transactions," *Accounting Horizons* (September 1992), discusses how deferred tax disclosures can be used to assess the quality of earnings and to predict future cash flows.

[13]The IRS frowns on acquisitions done solely to obtain operating loss carryforwards. If the merger is determined to be solely tax motivated, then the deductions will be disallowed. But because it is very difficult to determine whether a merger is or is not tax motivated, the "purchase of operating loss carryforwards" continues.

SHELTERED

WHAT DO THE NUMBERS MEAN?

As mentioned in the opening story, companies employ various tax strategies to reduce their tax bills. The following table reports some recent high-profile cases in which profitable companies during the 1996–2000 time period paid little income tax, and in some cases got tax refunds.

Company	Pre-Tax Income ($ millions)	Federal Tax Paid (Refund) ($ millions)	Tax Rate (%)
Enron	$ 1,785	$(381)	(21.34)%
El Paso Energy	1,638	(254)	(15.51)
Goodyear	442	(23)	(5.20)
Navistar	1,368	28	2.05
General Motors	12,468	740	5.94

These companies used various tools to lower their tax bills, including off-shore tax shelters, tax deferrals, and hefty use of stock options, the cost of which reduce taxable income but do not affect pretax financial income.[14] Thus, companies can use various provisions in the tax code to reduce their effective tax rate well below the statutory rate of 35 percent.

One IRS provision designed to curb excessive tax avoidance is the **alternative minimum tax (AMT)**, in which companies compute their potential tax liability, after adjusting for various preference items that reduce their tax bills under the regular tax code. (Examples of such preference items are accelerated depreciation methods and the installment method for revenue recognition.) Companies must pay the higher of the two tax obligations computed under the AMT and the regular tax code. But, as indicated by the cases above, some profitable companies are able to avoid high tax bills, even in the presence of the AMT. Maybe we are in for some more tax reform?

To implement the objectives, the following basic principles are applied in accounting for income taxes at the date of the financial statements.

ILLUSTRATION 19-42
Basic Principles of the Asset-Liability Method

Basic Principles

a. A current tax liability or asset is recognized for the estimated taxes payable or refundable on the tax return for the current year.
b. A deferred tax liability or asset is recognized for the estimated future tax effects attributable to temporary differences and carryforwards.
c. The measurement of current and deferred tax liabilities and assets is based on provisions of the enacted tax law; the effects of future changes in tax laws or rates are not anticipated.
d. The measurement of deferred tax assets is reduced, if necessary, by the amount of any tax benefits that, based on available evidence, are not expected to be realized.[15]

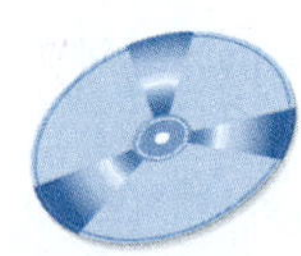

Discussion of Conceptual Approaches to Interperiod Tax Allocation

The procedures for implementing the asset-liability method are shown in Illustration 19-43.

[14]H. Gleckman, D. Foust, M. Arndt, and K. Kerwin, "Tax Dodging: Enron Isn't Alone," *Business Week* (March 4, 2002), 40–41.

[15]"Accounting for Income Taxes" par. 6 and 8, 1992.

ILLUSTRATION 19-43
Procedures for Computing and Reporting Deferred Income Taxes

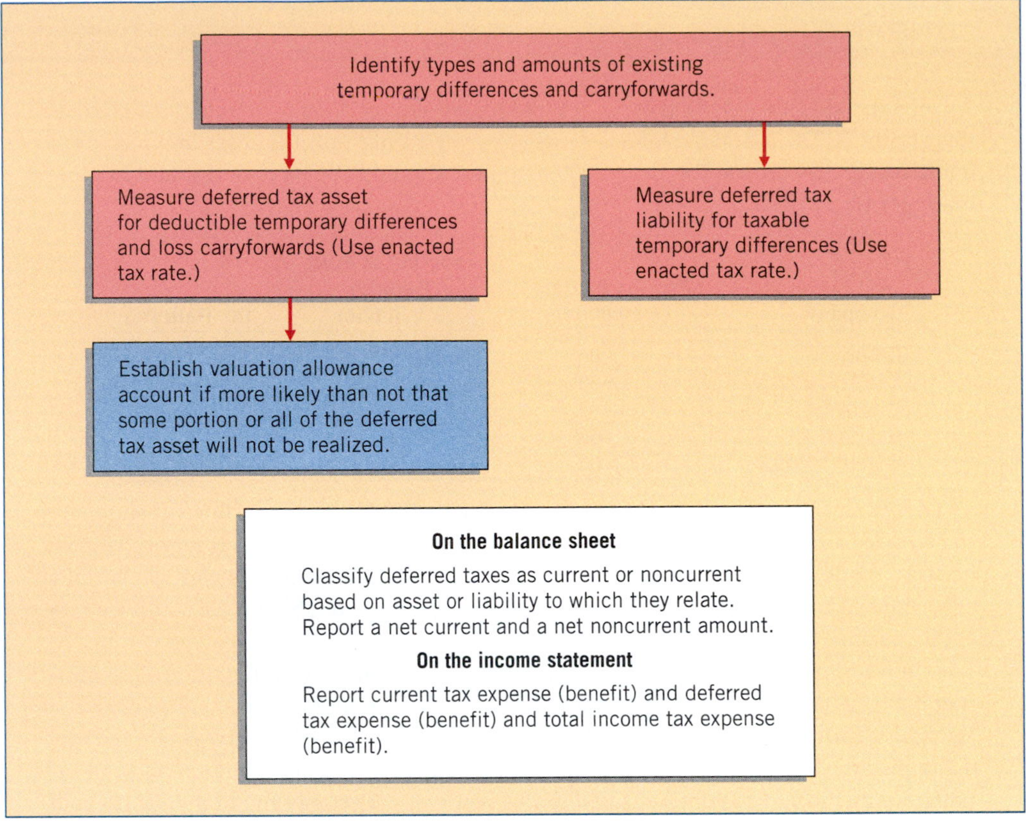

INTERNATIONAL INSIGHT

Nations that recognize deferred taxes using the liability method include, among others, Australia, Germany, the United Kingdom, and Spain. IASB standards for taxes also use the liability method. The European Directives do not specify the accounting for deferred taxes.

As an aid to understanding deferred income taxes, we provide the following glossary.[16]

KEY DEFERRED INCOME TAX TERMS

CARRYBACKS. Deductions or credits that cannot be utilized on the tax return during a year and that may be carried back to reduce taxable income or taxes paid in a prior year. An **operating loss carryback** is an excess of tax deductions over gross income in a year; a **tax credit carryback** is the amount by which tax credits available for utilization exceed statutory limitations.

CARRYFORWARDS. Deductions or credits that cannot be utilized on the tax return during a year and that may be carried forward to reduce taxable income or taxes payable in a future year. An **operating loss carryforward** is an excess of tax deductions over gross income in a year; a **tax credit carryforward** is the amount by which tax credits available for utilization exceed statutory limitations.

CURRENT TAX EXPENSE (BENEFIT). The amount of income taxes paid or payable (or refundable) for a year as determined by applying the provisions of the enacted tax law to the taxable income or excess of deductions over revenues for that year.

DEDUCTIBLE TEMPORARY DIFFERENCE. Temporary differences that result in deductible amounts in future years when the related asset or liability is recovered or settled, respectively.

[16]"Accounting for Income Taxes," Appendix E.

DEFERRED TAX ASSET. The deferred tax consequences attributable to deductible temporary differences and carryforwards.

DEFERRED TAX CONSEQUENCES. The future effects on income taxes as measured by the enacted tax rate and provisions of the enacted tax law resulting from temporary differences and carryforwards at the end of the current year.

DEFERRED TAX EXPENSE (BENEFIT). The change during the year in an enterprise's deferred tax liabilities and assets.

DEFERRED TAX LIABILITY. The deferred tax consequences attributable to taxable temporary differences.

INCOME TAXES. Domestic and foreign federal (national), state, and local (including franchise) taxes based on income.

INCOME TAXES CURRENTLY PAYABLE (REFUNDABLE). Refer to current tax expense (benefit).

INCOME TAX EXPENSE (BENEFIT). The sum of current tax expense (benefit) and deferred tax expense (benefit).

TAXABLE INCOME. The excess of taxable revenues over tax deductible expenses and exemptions for the year as defined by the governmental taxing authority.

TAXABLE TEMPORARY DIFFERENCE. Temporary differences that result in taxable amounts in future years when the related asset or liability is recovered or settled, respectively.

TAX-PLANNING STRATEGY. An action that meets certain criteria and that would be implemented to realize a tax benefit for an operating loss or tax credit carryforward before it expires. Tax-planning strategies are considered when assessing the need for and amount of a valuation allowance for deferred tax assets.

TEMPORARY DIFFERENCE. A difference between the tax basis of an asset or liability and its reported amount in the financial statements that will result in taxable or deductible amounts in future years when the reported amount of the asset or liability is recovered or settled, respectively.

VALUATION ALLOWANCE. The portion of a deferred tax asset for which it is more likely than not that a tax benefit will not be realized.

SUMMARY OF LEARNING OBJECTIVES

1 Identify differences between pretax financial income and taxable income. Pretax financial income (or income for book purposes) is computed in accordance with generally accepted accounting principles. Taxable income (or income for tax purposes) is computed in accordance with prescribed tax regulations. Because tax regulations and GAAP are different in many ways, pretax financial income and taxable income frequently differ. Differences may exist, for example, in the timing of revenue recognition and the timing of expense recognition.

2 Describe a temporary difference that results in future taxable amounts. A credit sale that is recognized as revenue for book purposes in the period it is earned but is deferred and reported as revenue for tax purposes in the period it is collected will result in future taxable amounts. The future taxable amounts will occur in the periods the receivable is recovered and the collections are reported as revenue for tax purposes. This results in a deferred tax liability.

KEY TERMS

alternative minimum tax, *985*
asset-liability method, *984*
average tax rate, *973*
current tax benefit (expense), *977*
deductible amounts, *962*
deductible temporary difference, *970*
deferred tax asset, *966*
deferred tax expense (benefit), *964*, *967*

3 **Describe a temporary difference that results in future deductible amounts.** An accrued warranty expense that is paid for and is deductible for tax purposes in a period later than the period in which it is incurred and recognized for book purposes will result in future deductible amounts. The future deductible amounts will occur in the periods during which the related liability for book purposes is settled. This results in a deferred tax asset.

4 **Explain the purpose of a deferred tax asset valuation allowance.** A deferred tax asset should be reduced by a valuation allowance if, based on all available evidence, it is more likely than not (a level of likelihood that is at least slightly more than 50 percent) that some portion or all of the deferred tax asset will not be realized. All available evidence, both positive and negative, should be carefully considered to determine whether, based on the weight of available evidence, a valuation allowance is needed.

5 **Describe the presentation of income tax expense in the income statement.** The significant components of income tax expense should be disclosed in the income statement or in the notes to the financial statements. The most commonly encountered components are the current expense (or benefit) and the deferred expense (or benefit).

6 **Describe various temporary and permanent differences.** Examples of temporary differences are: (1) revenue or gains that are taxable after they are recognized in financial income; (2) expenses or losses that are deductible after they are recognized in financial income; (3) revenues or gains that are taxable before they are recognized in financial income; (4) expenses or losses that are deductible before they are recognized in financial income. Examples of permanent differences are: (1) items recognized for financial reporting purposes but not for tax purposes, and (2) items recognized for tax purposes but not for financial reporting purposes.

7 **Explain the effect of various tax rates and tax rate changes on deferred income taxes.** Tax rates other than the current rate may be used only when the future tax rates have been enacted into law. When a change in the tax rate is enacted into law, its effect on the deferred income tax accounts should be recognized immediately. The effects are reported as an adjustment to income tax expense in the period of the change.

8 **Apply accounting procedures for a loss carryback and a loss carryforward.** A company may carry a net operating loss back 2 years and receive refunds for income taxes paid in those years. The loss must be applied to the earlier year first and then to the second year. Any loss remaining after the 2-year carryback may be carried forward up to 20 years to offset future taxable income. A company may forgo the loss carryback and use the loss carryforward, offsetting future taxable income for up to 20 years.

9 **Describe the presentation of deferred income taxes in financial statements.** Deferred tax accounts are reported on the balance sheet as assets and liabilities. They should be classified as a net current and a net noncurrent amount. An individual deferred tax liability or asset is classified as current or noncurrent based on the classification of the related asset or liability for financial reporting. A deferred tax liability or asset that is not related to an asset or liability for financial reporting, including a deferred tax asset related to a loss carryforward, should be classified according to the expected reversal date of the temporary difference.

10 **Indicate the basic principles of the asset-liability method.** The following basic principles are applied in accounting for income taxes at the date of the financial statements: (1) A current tax liability or asset is recognized for the estimated taxes payable or refundable on the tax return for the current year. (2) A deferred tax liability or asset is recognized for the estimated future tax effects attributable to temporary differences and carryforwards using the enacted tax rate. (3) The measurement of current and deferred tax liabilities and assets is based on provisions of the enacted tax law. (4) The measurement of deferred tax assets is reduced, if necessary, by the amount of any tax benefits that, based on available evidence, are not expected to be realized.

APPENDIX 19A

Comprehensive Illustration of Interperiod Tax Allocation

OBJECTIVE 11
Understand and apply the concepts and procedures of interperiod tax allocation.

This appendix presents a comprehensive illustration of a deferred income tax problem with several temporary and permanent differences. The illustration follows one company through two complete years (2003 and 2004). **Study it carefully.** It should help you understand the concepts and procedures presented in the chapter.

FIRST YEAR—2003

Allman Company, which began operations at the beginning of 2003, produces various products on a contract basis. Each contract generates a gross profit of $80,000. Some of Allman's contracts provide for the customer to pay on an installment basis whereby one-fifth of the contract revenue is collected in each of the following four years. Gross profit is recognized in the year of completion for financial reporting purposes (accrual basis) and in the year cash is collected for tax purposes (installment basis).

Presented below is information related to Allman's operations for 2003.

1. In 2003, the company completed seven contracts that allow for the customer to pay on an installment basis. The related gross profit amount of $560,000 was recognized for financial reporting purposes. Only $112,000 of gross profit on installment sales was reported on the 2003 tax return. The future collections on the related installment receivables are expected to result in taxable amounts of $112,000 in each of the next 4 years.
2. At the beginning of 2003, Allman Company purchased depreciable assets with a cost of $540,000. For financial reporting purposes, Allman depreciates these assets using the straight-line method over a 6-year service life. For tax purposes, the assets fall in the 5-year recovery class and Allman uses the MACRS system. The depreciation schedules for both financial reporting and tax purposes follow.

Year	Depreciation for Financial Reporting Purposes	Depreciation for Tax Purposes	Difference
2003	$ 90,000	$108,000	$(18,000)
2004	90,000	172,800	(82,800)
2005	90,000	103,680	(13,680)
2006	90,000	62,208	27,792
2007	90,000	62,208	27,792
2008	90,000	31,104	58,896
	$540,000	$540,000	$ –0–

3. The company warrants its product for 2 years from the date of completion of a contract. During 2003 product warranty liability accrued for financial reporting purposes was $200,000, and the amount paid for the satisfaction of warranty liability

was $44,000. The remaining $156,000 is expected to be settled by expenditures of $56,000 in 2004 and $100,000 in 2005.

4. In 2003 nontaxable municipal bond interest revenue was $28,000.
5. During 2003 nondeductible fines and penalties of $26,000 were paid.
6. Pretax financial income for 2003 amounts to $412,000.
7. Tax rates enacted before the end of 2003 were:

2003	50%
2004 and later years	40%

8. The accounting period is the calendar year.
9. The company is expected to have taxable income in all future years.

Taxable Income and Income Tax Payable—2003

The first step is to determine Allman Company's income tax payable for 2003 by calculating its taxable income. This computation is as follows.

ILLUSTRATION 19A-1
Computation of Taxable Income, 2003

Pretax financial income for 2003	$412,000
Permanent differences:	
Nontaxable revenue—municipal bond interest	(28,000)
Nondeductible expenses—fines and penalties	26,000
Temporary differences:	
Excess gross profit per books ($560,000 − $112,000)	(448,000)
Excess depreciation per tax ($108,000 − $90,000)	(18,000)
Excess warranty expense per books ($200,000 − $44,000)	156,000
Taxable income for 2003	$100,000

Income tax payable is computed on taxable income for $100,000 as follows.

ILLUSTRATION 19A-2
Computation of Income Tax Payable, End of 2003

Taxable income for 2003	$100,000
Tax rate	50%
Income tax payable (current tax expense) for 2003	$ 50,000

Computing Deferred Income Taxes—End of 2003

The following schedule is helpful in summarizing the temporary differences and the resulting future taxable and deductible amounts.

ILLUSTRATION 19A-3
Schedule of Future Taxable and Deductible Amounts, End of 2003

	Future Years					
	2004	2005	2006	2007	2008	Total
Future taxable (deductible) amounts:						
Installment sales	$112,000	$112,000	$112,000	$112,000		$448,000
Depreciation	(82,800)	(13,680)	27,792	27,792	$58,896	18,000
Warranty costs	(56,000)	(100,000)				(156,000)

The amounts of deferred income taxes to be reported at the end of 2003 are computed as shown in Illustration 19A-4.

ILLUSTRATION 19A-4
Computation of Deferred Income Taxes, End of 2003

Temporary Difference	Future Taxable (Deductible) Amounts	Tax Rate	Deferred Tax (Asset)	Deferred Tax Liability
Installment sales	$448,000	40%		$179,200
Depreciation	18,000	40%		7,200
Warranty costs	(156,000)	40%	$(62,400)	
Totals	$310,000		$(62,400)	$186,400*

*Because only a single tax rate is involved in all relevant years, these totals can be reconciled: $310,000 × 40% = ($62,400) + $186,400.

The temporary difference caused by the use of the accrual basis for financial reporting purposes and the installment method for tax purposes will result in future taxable amounts; hence, a deferred tax liability will arise. Because of the installment contracts completed in 2003, a temporary difference of $448,000 originates that will reverse in equal amounts over the next 4 years. The company is expected to have taxable income in all future years, and there is only one enacted tax rate applicable to all future years. Therefore, that rate (40%) is used to compute the entire deferred tax liability resulting from this temporary difference.

The temporary difference caused by different depreciation policies for books and for tax purposes originates over 3 years and then reverses over 3 years. This difference will cause deductible amounts in 2004 and 2005 and taxable amounts in 2006, 2007, and 2008, which sum to a net future taxable amount of $18,000 (which is the cumulative temporary difference at the end of 2003). Because the company is expected to have taxable income in all future years and because there is only one tax rate enacted for all of the relevant future years, that rate is applied to the net future taxable amount to determine the related net deferred tax liability.

The third temporary difference, caused by different methods of accounting for warranties, will result in deductible amounts in each of the 2 future years it takes to reverse. Because the company expects to report a positive income on all future tax returns and because there is only one tax rate enacted for each of the relevant future years, that 40 percent rate is used to calculate the resulting deferred tax asset.

Deferred Tax Expense (Benefit) and the Journal Entry to Record Income Taxes—2003

To determine the deferred tax expense (benefit), the beginning and ending balances of the deferred income tax accounts must be compared.

ILLUSTRATION 19A-5
Computation of Deferred Tax Expense (Benefit), 2003

Deferred tax asset at the end of 2003	$ 62,400
Deferred tax asset at the beginning of 2003	–0–
Deferred tax expense (benefit)	$ (62,400)
Deferred tax liability at the end of 2003	$186,400
Deferred tax liability at the beginning of 2003	–0–
Deferred tax expense (benefit)	$186,400

The $62,400 increase in the deferred tax asset causes a deferred tax benefit to be reflected in the income statement. The $186,400 increase in the deferred tax liability during 2003 results in a deferred tax expense. These two amounts **net** to a deferred tax expense of $124,000 for 2003.

ILLUSTRATION 19A-6
Computation of Net Deferred Tax Expense, 2003

Deferred tax expense (benefit)	$ (62,400)
Deferred tax expense (benefit)	186,400
Net deferred tax expense for 2003	$124,000

The total income tax expense is then computed as follows.

ILLUSTRATION 19A-7
Computation of Total Income Tax Expense, 2003

Current tax expense for 2003	$ 50,000
Deferred tax expense for 2003	124,000
Income tax expense (total) for 2003	$174,000

The journal entry to record income tax payable, deferred income taxes, and income tax expense is as follows.

Income Tax Expense	174,000	
Deferred Tax Asset	62,400	
Income Tax Payable		50,000
Deferred Tax Liability		186,400

Financial Statement Presentation—2003

Deferred tax assets and liabilities are to be classified as current and noncurrent on the balance sheet based on the classifications of related assets and liabilities. When there is more than one category of deferred taxes, they are classified into a net current amount and a net noncurrent amount. The classification of Allman's deferred tax accounts at the end of 2003 is as follows.

ILLUSTRATION 19A-8
Classification of Deferred Tax Accounts, End of 2003

Temporary Difference	Resulting Deferred Tax (Asset)	Resulting Deferred Tax Liability	Related Balance Sheet Account	Classification
Installment sales		$179,200	Installment Receivable	Current
Depreciation		7,200	Plant Assets	Noncurrent
Warranty costs	$(62,400)		Warranty Obligation	Current
Totals	$(62,400)	$186,400		

For the first temporary difference, there is a related asset on the balance sheet, installment accounts receivable. That asset is classified as a current asset because the company has a trade practice of selling to customers on an installment basis. Therefore, the resulting deferred tax liability is classified as a current liability. There are assets on the balance sheet that are related to the depreciation difference—the property, plant, and equipment being depreciated. The plant assets are classified as noncurrent. Therefore, the resulting deferred tax liability is to be classified as noncurrent. Since Allman's operating cycle is at least 4 years in length, the entire $156,000 warranty obligation is classified as a current liability. Thus, the related deferred tax asset of $62,400 is classified as current.[1]

[1]If Allman's operating cycle were less than one year in length, $56,000 of the warranty obligation would be expected to be settled within one year of the December 31, 2003, balance sheet and would require the use of current assets to settle it; thus $56,000 of the warranty obligation would be a current liability and the remaining $100,000 warranty obligation would be classified as a long-term (noncurrent) liability. This would mean $22,400 ($56,000 × 40%) of the related deferred tax asset would be classified as a current asset, and $40,000 ($100,000 × 40%) of the deferred tax asset would be classified as a noncurrent asset. In doing homework problems, unless it is evident otherwise, assume a company's operating cycle is not longer than a year.

The balance sheet at the end of 2003 reports the following amounts.

ILLUSTRATION 19A-9
Balance Sheet Presentation of Deferred Taxes, 2003

Current liabilities	
Income tax payable	$ 50,000
Deferred tax liability ($179,200 − $62,400)	116,800
Long-term liabilities	
Deferred tax liability	$ 7,200

The income statement for 2003 reports the following.

ILLUSTRATION 19A-10
Income Statement Presentation of Income Tax Expense, 2003

Income before income taxes		$412,000
Income tax expense		
Current	$ 50,000	
Deferred	124,000	174,000
Net income		$238,000

SECOND YEAR—2004

1. During 2004 the company collected $112,000 from customers for the receivables arising from contracts completed in 2003. Recovery of the remaining receivables is expected to result in taxable amounts of $112,000 in each of the following 3 years.
2. In 2004 the company completed four new contracts that allow for the customer to pay on an installment basis. These installment sales created new installment receivables. Future collections of these receivables will result in reporting gross profit of $64,000 for tax purposes in each of the next 4 years.
3. During 2004 Allman continued to depreciate the assets acquired in 2003 according to the depreciation schedules appearing on page 989. Thus, depreciation amounted to $90,000 for financial reporting purposes and $172,800 for tax purposes.
4. An analysis at the end of 2004 of the product warranty liability account showed the following details.

Balance of liability at beginning of 2004	$156,000
Expense for 2004 income statement purposes	180,000
Amount paid for contracts completed in 2003	(56,000)
Amount paid for contracts completed in 2004	(50,000)
Balance of liability at end of 2004	$230,000

The balance of the liability is expected to require expenditures in the future as follows.

$100,000	in 2005 due to 2003 contracts
$ 50,000	in 2005 due to 2004 contracts
$ 80,000	in 2006 due to 2004 contracts
$230,000	

5. During 2004 nontaxable municipal bond interest revenue was $24,000.
6. A loss of $172,000 was accrued for financial reporting purposes because of pending litigation. This amount is not tax-deductible until the period the loss is realized, which is estimated to be 2012.
7. Pretax financial income for 2004 amounts to $504,800.
8. The enacted tax rates still in effect are:

2003	50%
2004 and later years	40%

Taxable Income and Income Tax Payable—2004

The computation of taxable income for 2004 is as follows.

ILLUSTRATION 19A-11
Computation of Taxable Income, 2004

Pretax financial income for 2004	$504,800
Permanent difference:	
Nontaxable revenue—municipal bond interest	(24,000)
Reversing temporary differences:	
Collection on 2003 installment sales	112,000
Payments on warranties from 2003 contracts	(56,000)
Originating temporary differences:	
Excess gross profit per books—2004 contracts	(256,000)
Excess depreciation per tax	(82,800)
Excess warranty expense per books—2004 contracts	130,000
Loss accrual per books	172,000
Taxable income for 2004	$500,000

Income tax payable for 2004 is computed as follows.

ILLUSTRATION 19A-12
Computation of Income Tax Payable, End of 2004

Taxable income for 2004	$500,000
Tax rate	40%
Income tax payable (current tax expense) for 2004	$200,000

Computing Deferred Income Taxes—End of 2004

ILLUSTRATION 19A-13
Schedule of Future Taxable and Deductible Amounts, End of 2004

The following schedule is helpful in summarizing the temporary differences existing at the end of 2004 and the resulting future taxable and deductible amounts.

	Future Years					
	2005	2006	2007	2008	2012	Total
Future taxable (deductible) amounts:						
Installment sales—2003	$112,000	$112,000	$112,000			$336,000
Installment sales—2004	64,000	64,000	64,000	$64,000		256,000
Depreciation	(13,680)	27,792	27,792	58,896		100,800
Warranty costs	(150,000)	(80,000)				(230,000)
Loss accrual					$(172,000)	(172,000)

The amounts of deferred income taxes to be reported at the end of 2004 are computed as follows.

ILLUSTRATION 19A-14
Computation of Deferred Income Taxes, End of 2004

Temporary Difference	Future Taxable (Deductible) Amounts	Tax Rate	Deferred Tax (Asset)	Deferred Tax Liability
Installment sales	$592,000*	40%		$236,800
Depreciation	100,800	40%		40,320
Warranty costs	(230,000)	40%	$ (92,000)	
Loss accrual	(172,000)	40%	(68,800)	
Totals	$290,800		$(160,800)	$277,120**

*Cumulative temporary difference = $336,000 + $256,000
**Because of a flat tax rate, these totals can be reconciled: $290,800 × 40% = $(160,800) + $277,120

Deferred Tax Expense (Benefit) and the Journal Entry to Record Income Taxes—2004

To determine the deferred tax expense (benefit), the beginning and ending balances of the deferred income tax accounts must be compared.

ILLUSTRATION 19A-15
Computation of Deferred Tax Expense (Benefit), 2004

Deferred tax asset at the end of 2004	$160,800
Deferred tax asset at the beginning of 2004	62,400
Deferred tax expense (benefit)	$ (98,400)
Deferred tax liability at the end of 2004	$277,120
Deferred tax liability at the beginning of 2004	186,400
Deferred tax expense (benefit)	$ 90,720

The deferred tax expense (benefit) and the total income tax expense for 2004 are, therefore, as follows.

ILLUSTRATION 19A-16
Computation of Total Income Tax Expense, 2004

Deferred tax expense (benefit)	$ (98,400)
Deferred tax expense (benefit)	90,720
Deferred tax benefit for 2004	(7,680)
Current tax expense for 2004	200,000
Income tax expense (total) for 2004	$192,320

The deferred tax expense of $90,720 and the deferred tax benefit of $98,400 net to a deferred tax benefit of $7,680 for 2004.

The journal entry to record income taxes for 2004 is as follows.

Income Tax Expense	192,320	
Deferred Tax Asset	98,400	
Income Tax Payable		200,000
Deferred Tax Liability		90,720

Financial Statement Presentation—2004

The classification of Allman's deferred tax accounts at the end of 2004 is shown in Illustration 19A-17.

ILLUSTRATION 19A-17
Classification of Deferred Tax Accounts, End of 2004

Temporary Difference	Resulting Deferred Tax (Asset)	Resulting Deferred Tax Liability	Related Balance Sheet Account	Classification
Installment sales		$236,800	Installment Receivables	Current
Depreciation		40,320	Plant Assets	Noncurrent
Warranty costs	$ (92,000)		Warranty Obligation	Current
Loss accrual	(68,800)		Litigation Obligation	Noncurrent
Totals	$(160,800)	$277,120		

The new temporary difference introduced in 2004 (due to the litigation loss accrual) results in a litigation obligation that is classified as a long-term liability. Thus, the related deferred tax asset is noncurrent.

The balance sheet at the end of 2004 reports the following amounts.

ILLUSTRATION 19A-18
Balance Sheet Presentation of Deferred Taxes, End of 2004

Other assets (noncurrent)	
Deferred tax asset ($68,800 − $40,320)	$ 28,480
Current liabilities	
Income tax payable	$200,000
Deferred tax liability ($236,800 − $92,000)	144,800

The income statement for 2004 reports the following.

ILLUSTRATION 19A-19
Income Statement Presentation of Income Tax Expense, 2004

Income before income taxes		$504,800
Income tax expense		
Current	$200,000	
Deferred	(7,680)	192,320
Net income		$312,480

SUMMARY OF LEARNING OBJECTIVE FOR APPENDIX 19A

11 Understand and apply the concepts and procedures of interperiod tax allocation. Accounting for deferred taxes includes calculating taxable income and income tax payable for the year, computing deferred income taxes at the end of the year, determining deferred tax expense (benefit) and making the journal entry to record income taxes, and classifying deferred tax assets and liabilities as current or noncurrent in the financial statements.

QUESTIONS

1. Explain the difference between pretax financial income and taxable income.
2. What are the two objectives of accounting for income taxes?
3. Interest on municipal bonds is referred to as a permanent difference when determining the proper amount to report for deferred taxes. Explain the meaning of permanent differences, and give two other examples.
4. Explain the meaning of a temporary difference as it relates to deferred tax computations, and give three examples.
5. Differentiate between an originating temporary difference and a reversing difference.

6. The book basis of depreciable assets for Guinan Co. is $900,000, and the tax basis is $700,000 at the end of 2004. The enacted tax rate is 34% for all periods. Determine the amount of deferred taxes to be reported on the balance sheet at the end of 2004.

7. Borg Inc. has a deferred tax liability of $68,000 at the beginning of 2004. At the end of 2004, it reports accounts receivable on the books at $80,000 and the tax basis at zero (its only temporary difference). If the enacted tax rate is 34% for all periods, and income tax payable for the period is $230,000, determine the amount of total income tax expense to report for 2004.

8. What is the difference between a future taxable amount and a future deductible amount? When is it appropriate to record a valuation account for a deferred tax asset?

9. Pretax financial income for Mott Inc. is $300,000, and its taxable income is $100,000 for 2004. Its only temporary difference at the end of the period relates to a $90,000 difference due to excess depreciation for tax purposes. If the tax rate is 40% for all periods, compute the amount of income tax expense to report in 2004. No deferred income taxes existed at the beginning of the year.

10. How are deferred tax assets and deferred tax liabilities reported on the balance sheet?

11. Describe the procedures involved in segregating various deferred tax amounts into current and noncurrent categories.

12. How is it determined whether deferred tax amounts are considered to be "related" to specific assets or liability amounts?

13. At the end of the year, North Carolina Co. has pretax financial income of $550,000. Included in the $550,000 is $70,000 interest income on municipal bonds, $30,000 fine for dumping hazardous waste, and depreciation of $60,000. Depreciation for tax purposes is $45,000. Compute income taxes payable, assuming the tax rate is 30% for all periods.

14. Raleigh Co. has one temporary difference at the beginning of 2004 of $500,000. The deferred tax liability established for this amount is $150,000, based on a tax rate of 30%. The temporary difference will provide the following taxable amounts: $100,000 in 2005; $200,000 in 2006, and $200,000 in 2007. If a new tax rate for 2007 of 25% is enacted into law at the end of 2004, what is the journal entry necessary in 2004 (if any) to adjust deferred taxes?

15. What are some of the reasons that the components of income tax expense should be disclosed and a reconciliation between the effective tax rate and the statutory tax rate be provided?

16. Differentiate between "loss carryback" and "loss carryforward." Which can be accounted for with the greater certainty when it arises? Why?

17. What are the possible treatments for tax purposes of a net operating loss? What are the circumstances that determine the option to be applied? What is the proper treatment of a net operating loss for financial reporting purposes?

18. What controversy relates to the accounting for net operating loss carryforwards?

BRIEF EXERCISES

BE19-1 In 2004, Speedy Gonzalez Corporation had pretax financial income of $168,000 and taxable income of $110,000. The difference is due to the use of different depreciation methods for tax and accounting purposes. The effective tax rate is 40%. Compute the amount to be reported as income taxes payable at December 31, 2004.

BE19-2 Murphy Corporation began operations in 2004 and reported pretax financial income of $225,000 for the year. Murphy's tax depreciation exceeded its book depreciation by $30,000. Murphy's tax rate for 2004 and years thereafter is 30%. In its December 31, 2004 balance sheet, what amount of deferred tax liability should be reported?

BE19-3 Using the information from BE19-2, assume this is the only difference between Murphy's pretax financial income and taxable income. Prepare the journal entry to record the income tax expense, deferred income taxes, and income tax payable, and show how the deferred tax liability will be classified on the December 31, 2004, balance sheet.

BE19-4 At December 31, 2003, Yserbius Corporation had a deferred tax liability of $25,000. At December 31, 2004, the deferred tax liability is $42,000. The corporation's 2004 current tax expense is $43,000. What amount should Yserbius report as total 2004 tax expense?

BE19-5 At December 31, 2004, Deep Space Nine Corporation had an estimated warranty liability of $125,000 for accounting purposes and $0 for tax purposes. (The warranty costs are not deductible until paid.) The effective tax rate is 40%. Compute the amount Deep Space Nine should report as a deferred tax asset at December 31, 2004.

BE19-6 At December 31, 2003, Next Generation Inc. had a deferred tax asset of $35,000. At December 31, 2004, the deferred tax asset is $59,000. The corporation's 2004 current tax expense is $61,000. What amount should Next Generation report as total 2004 tax expense?

BE19-7 At December 31, 2004, Stargate Corporation has a deferred tax asset of $200,000. After a careful review of all available evidence, it is determined that it is more likely than not that $80,000 of this deferred tax asset will not be realized. Prepare the necessary journal entry.

BE19-8 Steven Seagal Corporation had income before income taxes of $175,000 in 2004. Seagal's current income tax expense is $40,000, and deferred income tax expense is $30,000. Prepare Seagal's 2004 income statement, beginning with income before income taxes.

BE19-9 Tazmania Inc. had pretax financial income of $154,000 in 2004. Included in the computation of that amount is insurance expense of $4,000 which is not deductible for tax purposes. In addition, depreciation for tax purposes exceeds accounting depreciation by $14,000. Prepare Tazmania's journal entry to record 2004 taxes, assuming a tax rate of 45%.

BE19-10 Terminator Corporation has a cumulative temporary difference related to depreciation of $630,000 at December 31, 2004. This difference will reverse as follows: 2005, $42,000; 2006, $294,000; and 2007, $294,000. Enacted tax rates are 34% for 2005 and 2006, and 40% for 2007. Compute the amount Terminator should report as a deferred tax liability at December 31, 2004.

BE19-11 At December 31, 2003, Tick Corporation had a deferred tax liability of $680,000, resulting from future taxable amounts of $2,000,000 and an enacted tax rate of 34%. In May 2004, a new income tax act is signed into law that raises the tax rate to 38% for 2004 and future years. Prepare the journal entry for Tick to adjust the deferred tax liability.

BE19-12 Valis Corporation had the following tax information.

Year	Taxable Income	Tax Rate	Taxes Paid
2001	$300,000	35%	$105,000
2002	$325,000	30%	$ 97,500
2003	$400,000	30%	$120,000

In 2004 Valis suffered a net operating loss of $450,000, which it elected to carry back. The 2004 enacted tax rate is 29%. Prepare Valis's entry to record the effect of the loss carryback.

BE19-13 Zoop Inc. incurred a net operating loss of $500,000 in 2004. Combined income for 2002 and 2003 was $400,000. The tax rate for all years is 40%. Prepare the journal entries to record the benefits of the loss carryback and the loss carryforward.

BE19-14 Use the information for Zoop Inc. given in BE19-13. Assume that it is more likely than not that the entire net operating loss carryforward will not be realized in future years. Prepare all the journal entries necessary at the end of 2004.

BE19-15 Vectorman Corporation has temporary differences at December 31, 2004, that result in the following deferred taxes.

Deferred tax liability—current	$38,000
Deferred tax asset—current	$(52,000)
Deferred tax liability—noncurrent	$96,000
Deferred tax asset—noncurrent	$(27,000)

Indicate how these balances would be presented in Vectorman's December 31, 2004, balance sheet.

EXERCISES

E19-1 (One Temporary Difference, Future Taxable Amounts, One Rate, No Beginning Deferred Taxes) South Carolina Corporation has one temporary difference at the end of 2004 that will reverse and cause taxable amounts of $55,000 in 2005, $60,000 in 2006, and $65,000 in 2007. South Carolina's pretax financial income for 2004 is $300,000, and the tax rate is 30% for all years. There are no deferred taxes at the beginning of 2004.

Instructions

(a) Compute taxable income and income taxes payable for 2004.

(b) Prepare the journal entry to record income tax expense, deferred income taxes, and income taxes payable for 2004.

(c) Prepare the income tax expense section of the income statement for 2004, beginning with the line "Income before income taxes."

E19-2 (Two Differences, No Beginning Deferred Taxes, Tracked through 2 Years) The following information is available for Wenger Corporation for 2003.

1. Excess of tax depreciation over book depreciation, $40,000. This $40,000 difference will reverse equally over the years 2004–2007.
2. Deferral, for book purposes, of $20,000 of rent received in advance. The rent will be earned in 2004.
3. Pretax financial income, $300,000.
4. Tax rate for all years, 40%.

Instructions

(a) Compute taxable income for 2003.
(b) Prepare the journal entry to record income tax expense, deferred income taxes, and income taxes payable for 2003.
(c) Prepare the journal entry to record income tax expense, deferred income taxes, and income taxes payable for 2004, assuming taxable income of $325,000.

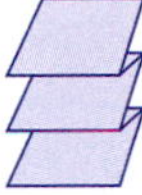

E19-3 (One Temporary Difference, Future Taxable Amounts, One Rate, Beginning Deferred Taxes) Bandung Corporation began 2004 with a $92,000 balance in the Deferred Tax Liability account. At the end of 2004, the related cumulative temporary difference amounts to $350,000, and it will reverse evenly over the next 2 years. Pretax accounting income for 2004 is $525,000, the tax rate for all years is 40%, and taxable income for 2004 is $405,000.

Instructions

(a) Compute income taxes payable for 2004.
(b) Prepare the journal entry to record income tax expense, deferred income taxes, and income taxes payable for 2004.
(c) Prepare the income tax expense section of the income statement for 2004 beginning with the line "Income before income taxes."

E19-4 (Three Differences, Compute Taxable Income, Entry for Taxes) Zurich Company reports pretax financial income of $70,000 for 2004. The following items cause taxable income to be different than pretax financial income.

1. Depreciation on the tax return is greater than depreciation on the income statement by $16,000.
2. Rent collected on the tax return is greater than rent earned on the income statement by $22,000.
3. Fines for pollution appear as an expense of $11,000 on the income statement.

Zurich's tax rate is 30% for all years, and the company expects to report taxable income in all future years. There are no deferred taxes at the beginning of 2004.

Instructions

(a) Compute taxable income and income taxes payable for 2004.
(b) Prepare the journal entry to record income tax expense, deferred income taxes, and income taxes payable for 2004.
(c) Prepare the income tax expense section of the income statement for 2004, beginning with the line "Income before income taxes."
(d) Compute the effective income tax rate for 2004.

E19-5 (Two Temporary Differences, One Rate, Beginning Deferred Taxes) The following facts relate to Krung Thep Corporation.

1. Deferred tax liability, January 1, 2004, $40,000.
2. Deferred tax asset, January 1, 2004, $0.
3. Taxable income for 2004, $95,000.
4. Pretax financial income for 2004, $200,000.
5. Cumulative temporary difference at December 31, 2004, giving rise to future taxable amounts, $240,000.
6. Cumulative temporary difference at December 31, 2004, giving rise to future deductible amounts, $35,000.
7. Tax rate for all years, 40%.
8. The company is expected to operate profitably in the future.

Instructions

(a) Compute income taxes payable for 2004.

(b) Prepare the journal entry to record income tax expense, deferred income taxes, and income taxes payable for 2004.
(c) Prepare the income tax expense section of the income statement for 2004, beginning with the line "Income before income taxes."

E19-6 (Identify Temporary or Permanent Differences) Listed below are items that are commonly accounted for differently for financial reporting purposes than they are for tax purposes.

Instructions

For each item below, indicate whether it involves:

(1) A temporary difference that will result in future deductible amounts and, therefore, will usually give rise to a deferred income tax asset.
(2) A temporary difference that will result in future taxable amounts and, therefore, will usually give rise to a deferred income tax liability.
(3) A permanent difference.

Use the appropriate number to indicate your answer for each.

(a) ___2___ The MACRS depreciation system is used for tax purposes, and the straight-line depreciation method is used for financial reporting purposes for some plant assets.
(b) ___1___ A landlord collects some rents in advance. Rents received are taxable in the period when they are received.
(c) ___3___ Expenses are incurred in obtaining tax-exempt income.
(d) ___1___ Costs of guarantees and warranties are estimated and accrued for financial reporting purposes.
(e) ___2___ Installment sales of investments are accounted for by the accrual method for financial reporting purposes and the installment method for tax purposes.
(f) ___2___ For some assets, straight-line depreciation is used for both financial reporting purposes and tax purposes but the assets' lives are shorter for tax purposes.
(g) ___3___ Interest is received on an investment in tax-exempt municipal obligations.
(h) ___3___ Proceeds are received from a life insurance company because of the death of a key officer. (The company carries a policy on key officers.)
(i) ___3___ The tax return reports a deduction for 80% of the dividends received from U.S. corporations. The cost method is used in accounting for the related investments for financial reporting purposes.
(j) ___1___ Estimated losses on pending lawsuits and claims are accrued for books. These losses are tax deductible in the period(s) when the related liabilities are settled.

E19-7 (Terminology, Relationships, Computations, Entries)

Instructions

Complete the following statements by filling in the blanks.

(a) In a period in which a taxable temporary difference reverses, the reversal will cause taxable income to be _______ (less than, greater than) pretax financial income.
(b) If a $76,000 balance in Deferred Tax Asset was computed by use of a 40% rate, the underlying cumulative temporary difference amounts to $__190K__.
(c) Deferred taxes ________ (are, are not) recorded to account for permanent differences.
(d) If a taxable temporary difference originates in 2004, it will cause taxable income for 2004 to be ________ (less than, greater than) pretax financial income for 2004.
(e) If total tax expense is $50,000 and deferred tax expense is $65,000, then the current portion of the expense computation is referred to as current tax _______ (expense, benefit) of $__15,000__.
(f) If a corporation's tax return shows taxable income of $100,000 for Year 2 and a tax rate of 40%, how much will appear on the December 31, Year 2, balance sheet for "Income tax payable" if the company has made estimated tax payments of $36,500 for Year 2? $__3,500__.
(g) An increase in the Deferred Tax Liability account on the balance sheet is recorded by a _______ (debit, credit) to the Income Tax Expense account.
(h) An income statement that reports current tax expense of $82,000 and deferred tax benefit of $23,000 will report total income tax expense of $__59,000__.
(i) A valuation account is needed whenever it is judged to be _______ that a portion of a deferred tax asset _______ (will be, will not be) realized.
(j) If the tax return shows total taxes due for the period of $75,000 but the income statement shows total income tax expense of $55,000, the difference of $20,000 is referred to as deferred tax _______ (expense, benefit).

E19-8 (Two Temporary Differences, One Rate, 3 Years) Button Company has two temporary differences between its income tax expense and income taxes payable. The following information is available.

	2004	2005	2006
Pretax financial income	$840,000	$910,000	$945,000
Excess of depreciation expense on tax return	(30,000)	(40,000)	(10,000)
Excess of warranty expense on financial income	20,000	10,000	8,000
Taxable income	$830,000	$880,000	$943,000

The income tax rate for all years is 40%.

Instructions

(a) Prepare the journal entry to record income tax expense, deferred income taxes, and income tax payable for 2004, 2005, and 2006.

(b) Assuming there were no temporary differences prior to 2004, indicate how deferred taxes will be reported on the 2006 balance sheet. Button's product warranty is for 12 months.

(c) Prepare the income tax expense section of the income statement for 2006, beginning with the line "Pretax financial income."

E19-9 (Carryback and Carryforward of NOL, No Valuation Account, No Temporary Differences) The pretax financial income (or loss) figures for Jenny Spangler Company are as follows.

1999	$160,000
2000	250,000
2001	80,000
2002	(160,000)
2003	(380,000)
2004	120,000
2005	100,000

Pretax financial income (or loss) and taxable income (loss) were the same for all years involved. Assume a 45% tax rate for 1999 and 2000 and a 40% tax rate for the remaining years.

Instructions

Prepare the journal entries for the years 2001 to 2005 to record income tax expense and the effects of the net operating loss carrybacks and carryforwards assuming Jenny Spangler Company uses the carryback provision. All income and losses relate to normal operations. (In recording the benefits of a loss carryforward, assume that no valuation account is deemed necessary.)

E19-10 (2 NOLs, No Temporary Differences, No Valuation Account, Entries and Income Statement) Felicia Rashad Corporation has pretax financial income (or loss) equal to taxable income (or loss) from 1996 through 2004 as follows.

	Income (Loss)	Tax Rate
1996	$29,000	30%
1997	40,000	30%
1998	17,000	35%
1999	48,000	50%
2000	(150,000)	40%
2001	90,000	40%
2002	30,000	40%
2003	105,000	40%
2004	(60,000)	45%

Pretax financial income (loss) and taxable income (loss) were the same for all years since Rashad has been in business. Assume the carryback provision is employed for net operating losses. In recording the benefits of a loss carryforward, assume that it is more likely than not that the related benefits will be realized.

Instructions

(a) What entry(ies) for income taxes should be recorded for 2000?

(b) Indicate what the income tax expense portion of the income statement for 2000 should look like. Assume all income (loss) relates to continuing operations.

(c) What entry for income taxes should be recorded in 2001?

(d) How should the income tax expense section of the income statement for 2001 appear?

(e) What entry for income taxes should be recorded in 2004?

(f) How should the income tax expense section of the income statement for 2004 appear?

E19-11 (Three Differences, Classify Deferred Taxes) At December 31, 2003, Surya Bonilay Company had a net deferred tax liability of $375,000. An explanation of the items that compose this balance is as follows.

Temporary Differences	Resulting Balances in Deferred Taxes
1. Excess of tax depreciation over book depreciation	$200,000
2. Accrual, for book purposes, of estimated loss contingency from pending lawsuit that is expected to be settled in 2004. The loss will be deducted on the tax return when paid.	(50,000)
3. Accrual method used for book purposes and installment method used for tax purposes for an isolated installment sale of an investment.	225,000
	$375,000

In analyzing the temporary differences, you find that $30,000 of the depreciation temporary difference will reverse in 2004, and $120,000 of the temporary difference due to the installment sale will reverse in 2004. The tax rate for all years is 40%.

Instructions

Indicate the manner in which deferred taxes should be presented on Surya Bonilay Company's December 31, 2003, balance sheet.

E19-12 (Two Temporary Differences, One Rate, Beginning Deferred Taxes, Compute Pretax Financial Income) The following facts relate to Sabrina Duncan Corporation.

1. Deferred tax liability, January 1, 2004, $60,000.
2. Deferred tax asset, January 1, 2004, $20,000.
3. Taxable income for 2004, $105,000.
4. Cumulative temporary difference at December 31, 2004, giving rise to future taxable amounts, $230,000.
5. Cumulative temporary difference at December 31, 2004, giving rise to future deductible amounts, $95,000.
6. Tax rate for all years, 40%. No permanent differences exist.
7. The company is expected to operate profitably in the future.

Instructions

(a) Compute the amount of pretax financial income for 2004.
(b) Prepare the journal entry to record income tax expense, deferred income taxes, and income taxes payable for 2004.
(c) Prepare the income tax expense section of the income statement for 2004, beginning with the line "Income before income taxes."
(d) Compute the effective tax rate for 2004.

E19-13 (One Difference, Multiple Rates, Effect of Beginning Balance versus No Beginning Deferred Taxes) At the end of 2003, Lucretia McEvil Company has $180,000 of cumulative temporary differences that will result in reporting future taxable amounts as follows.

2004	$ 60,000
2005	50,000
2006	40,000
2007	30,000
	$180,000

Tax rates enacted as of the beginning of 2002 are:

2002 and 2003	40%
2004 and 2005	30%
2006 and later	25%

McEvil's taxable income for 2003 is $320,000. Taxable income is expected in all future years.

Instructions

(a) Prepare the journal entry for McEvil to record income taxes payable, deferred income taxes, and income tax expense for 2003, assuming that there were no deferred taxes at the end of 2002.
(b) Prepare the journal entry for McEvil to record income taxes payable, deferred income taxes, and income tax expense for 2003, assuming that there was a balance of $22,000 in a Deferred Tax Liability account at the end of 2002.

E19-14 (Deferred Tax Asset with and without Valuation Account) Jennifer Capriati Corp. has a deferred tax asset account with a balance of $150,000 at the end of 2003 due to a single cumulative temporary difference of $375,000. At the end of 2004 this same temporary difference has increased to a cumulative amount of $450,000. Taxable income for 2004 is $820,000. The tax rate is 40% for all years. No valuation account related to the deferred tax asset is in existence at the end of 2003.

Instructions

(a) Record income tax expense, deferred income taxes, and income taxes payable for 2004, assuming that it is more likely than not that the deferred tax asset will be realized.

(b) Assuming that it is more likely than not that $30,000 of the deferred tax asset will not be realized, prepare the journal entry at the end of 2004 to record the valuation account.

E19-15 (Deferred Tax Asset with Previous Valuation Account) Assume the same information as E19-14, except that at the end of 2003, Jennifer Capriati Corp. had a valuation account related to its deferred tax asset of $45,000.

Instructions

(a) Record income tax expense, deferred income taxes, and income taxes payable for 2004, assuming that it is more likely than not that the deferred tax asset will be realized in full.

(b) Record income tax expense, deferred income taxes, and income taxes payable for 2004, assuming that it is more likely than not that none of the deferred tax asset will be realized.

E19-16 (Deferred Tax Liability, Change in Tax Rate, Prepare Section of Income Statement) Jana Novotna Inc.'s only temporary difference at the beginning and end of 2003 is caused by a $3 million deferred gain for tax purposes for an installment sale of a plant asset, and the related receivable (only one-half of which is classified as a current asset) is due in equal installments in 2004 and 2005. The related deferred tax liability at the beginning of the year is $1,200,000. In the third quarter of 2003, a new tax rate of 34% is enacted into law and is scheduled to become effective for 2005. Taxable income for 2003 is $5,000,000, and taxable income is expected in all future years.

Instructions

(a) Determine the amount reported as a deferred tax liability at the end of 2003. Indicate proper classification(s).

(b) Prepare the journal entry (if any) necessary to adjust the deferred tax liability when the new tax rate is enacted into law.

(c) Draft the income tax expense portion of the income statement for 2003. Begin with the line "Income before income taxes." Assume no permanent differences exist.

E19-17 (Two Temporary Differences, Tracked through 3 Years, Multiple Rates) Taxable income and pretax financial income would be identical for Anke Huber Co. except for its treatments of gross profit on installment sales and estimated costs of warranties. The following income computations have been prepared.

Taxable income	2003	2004	2005
Excess of revenues over expenses (excluding two temporary differences)	$160,000	$210,000	$90,000
Installment gross profit collected	8,000	8,000	8,000
Expenditures for warranties	(5,000)	(5,000)	(5,000)
Taxable income	$163,000	$213,000	$93,000

Pretax financial income	2003	2004	2005
Excess of revenues over expenses (excluding two temporary differences)	$160,000	$210,000	$90,000
Installment gross profit earned	24,000	–0–	–0–
Estimated cost of warranties	(15,000)	–0–	–0–
Income before taxes	$169,000	$210,000	$90,000

The tax rates in effect are: 2003, 40%; 2004 and 2005, 45%. All tax rates were enacted into law on January 1, 2003. No deferred income taxes existed at the beginning of 2003. Taxable income is expected in all future years.

Instructions

Prepare the journal entry to record income tax expense, deferred income taxes, and income tax payable for 2003, 2004, and 2005.

E19-18 (Three Differences, Multiple Rates, Future Taxable Income) During 2004, Anna Nicole Smith Co.'s first year of operations, the company reports pretax financial income at $250,000. Smith's enacted tax rate is 45% for 2004 and 40% for all later years. Smith expects to have taxable income in each of the next 5 years. The effects on future tax returns of temporary differences existing at December 31, 2004, are summarized below.

	Future Years					
	2005	2006	2007	2008	2009	Total
Future taxable (deductible) amounts:						
Installment sales	$32,000	$32,000	$32,000			$ 96,000
Depreciation	6,000	6,000	6,000	$6,000	$6,000	30,000
Unearned rent	(50,000)	(50,000)				(100,000)

Instructions

(a) Complete the schedule below to compute deferred taxes at December 31, 2004.
(b) Compute taxable income for 2004.
(c) Prepare the journal entry to record income tax payable, deferred taxes, and income tax expense for 2004.

			December 31, 2004	
	Future Taxable		Deferred Tax	
Temporary Difference	(Deductible) Amounts	Tax Rate	(Asset)	Liability
Installment sales	$ 96,000			
Depreciation	30,000			
Unearned rent	(100,000)			
Totals	$			

E19-19 (Two Differences, One Rate, Beginning Deferred Balance, Compute Pretax Financial Income) Sharon Stone Co. establishes a $100 million liability at the end of 2004 for the estimated costs of closing two of its manufacturing facilities. All related closing costs will be paid and deducted on the tax return in 2005. Also, at the end of 2004, the company has $50 million of temporary differences due to excess depreciation for tax purposes, $7 million of which will reverse in 2005.

The enacted tax rate for all years is 40%, and the company pays taxes of $64 million on $160 million of taxable income in 2004. Stone expects to have taxable income in 2005.

Instructions

(a) Determine the deferred taxes to be reported at the end of 2004.
(b) Indicate how the deferred taxes computed in (a) are to be reported on the balance sheet.
(c) Assuming that the only deferred tax account at the beginning of 2004 was a deferred tax liability of $10,000,000, draft the income tax expense portion of the income statement for 2004, beginning with the line "Income before income taxes." (*Hint:* You must first compute (1) the amount of temporary difference underlying the beginning $10,000,000 deferred tax liability, then (2) the amount of temporary differences originating or reversing during the year, then (3) the amount of pretax financial income.)

E19-20 (Two Differences, No Beginning Deferred Taxes, Multiple Rates) Teri Hatcher Inc., in its first year of operations, has the following differences between the book basis and tax basis of its assets and liabilities at the end of 2003.

	Book Basis	Tax Basis
Equipment (net)	$400,000	$340,000
Estimated warranty liability	$200,000	$ –0–

It is estimated that the warranty liability will be settled in 2004. The difference in equipment (net) will result in taxable amounts of $20,000 in 2004, $30,000 in 2005, and $10,000 in 2006. The company has taxable income of $520,000 in 2003. As of the beginning of 2003, the enacted tax rate is 34% for 2003–2005, and 30% for 2006. Hatcher expects to report taxable income through 2006.

Instructions

(a) Prepare the journal entry to record income tax expense, deferred income taxes, and income tax payable for 2003.
(b) Indicate how deferred income taxes will be reported on the balance sheet at the end of 2003.

E19-21 (Two Temporary Differences, Multiple Rates, Future Taxable Income) Svetlana Boginskaya Inc. has two temporary differences at the end of 2003. The first difference stems from installment sales, and the second one results from the accrual of a loss contingency. Boginskaya's accounting department has developed a schedule of future taxable and deductible amounts related to these temporary differences as follows.

	2004	2005	2006	2007
Taxable amounts	$40,000	$50,000	$60,000	$80,000
Deductible amounts		(15,000)	(19,000)	
	$40,000	$35,000	$41,000	$80,000

As of the beginning of 2003, the enacted tax rate is 34% for 2003 and 2004, and 38% for 2005–2008. At the beginning of 2003, the company had no deferred income taxes on its balance sheet. Taxable income for 2003 is $500,000. Taxable income is expected in all future years.

Instructions

(a) Prepare the journal entry to record income tax expense, deferred income taxes, and income taxes payable for 2003.

(b) Indicate how deferred income taxes would be classified on the balance sheet at the end of 2003.

E19-22 (Two Differences, One Rate, First Year) The differences between the book basis and tax basis of the assets and liabilities of JoAnn Castle Corporation at the end of 2003 are presented below.

	Book Basis	Tax Basis
Accounts receivable	$50,000	$–0–
Litigation liability	30,000	–0–

It is estimated that the litigation liability will be settled in 2004. The difference in accounts receivable will result in taxable amounts of $30,000 in 2004 and $20,000 in 2005. The company has taxable income of $350,000 in 2003 and is expected to have taxable income in each of the following 2 years. Its enacted tax rate is 34% for all years. This is the company's first year of operations. The operating cycle of the business is 2 years.

Instructions

(a) Prepare the journal entry to record income tax expense, deferred income taxes, and income tax payable for 2003.

(b) Indicate how deferred income taxes will be reported on the balance sheet at the end of 2003.

E19-23 (NOL Carryback and Carryforward, Valuation Account versus No Valuation Account) Spamela Hamderson Inc. reports the following pretax income (loss) for both financial reporting purposes and tax purposes. (Assume the carryback provision is used for a net operating loss.)

Year	Pretax Income (Loss)	Tax Rate
2002	$120,000	34%
2003	90,000	34%
2004	(280,000)	38%
2005	220,000	38%

The tax rates listed were all enacted by the beginning of 2002.

Instructions

(a) Prepare the journal entries for the years 2002–2005 to record income tax expense (benefit) and income tax payable (refundable) and the tax effects of the loss carryback and carryforward, assuming that at the end of 2004 the benefits of the loss carryforward are judged more likely than not to be realized in the future.

(b) Using the assumption in (a), prepare the income tax section of the 2004 income statement beginning with the line "Operating loss before income taxes."

(c) Prepare the journal entries for 2004 and 2005, assuming that based on the weight of available evidence, it is more likely than not that one-fourth of the benefits of the loss carryforward will not be realized.

(d) Using the assumption in (c), prepare the income tax section of the 2004 income statement beginning with the line "Operating loss before income taxes."

E19-24 (NOL Carryback and Carryforward, Valuation Account Needed) Denise Beilman Inc. reports the following pretax income (loss) for both book and tax purposes. (Assume the carryback provision is used where possible for a net operating loss.)

Year	Pretax Income (Loss)	Tax Rate
2002	$120,000	40%
2003	90,000	40%
2004	(280,000)	45%
2005	120,000	45%

The tax rates listed were all enacted by the beginning of 2002.

Instructions

(a) Prepare the journal entries for years 2002–2005 to record income tax expense (benefit) and income tax payable (refundable), and the tax effects of the loss carryback and loss carryforward, assuming that based on the weight of available evidence, it is more likely than not that one-half of the benefits of the loss carryforward will not be realized.

(b) Prepare the income tax section of the 2004 income statement beginning with the line "Operating loss before income taxes."

(c) Prepare the income tax section of the 2005 income statement beginning with the line "Income before income taxes."

E19-25 (NOL Carryback and Carryforward, Valuation Account Needed) Meyer reported the following pretax financial income (loss) for the years 2002–2006.

2002	$240,000
2003	350,000
2004	120,000
2005	(570,000)
2006	180,000

Pretax financial income (loss) and taxable income (loss) were the same for all years involved. The enacted tax rate was 34% for 2002 and 2003, and 40% for 2004–2006. Assume the carryback provision is used first for net operating losses.

Instructions

(a) Prepare the journal entries for the years 2004–2006 to record income tax expense, income tax payable (refundable), and the tax effects of the loss carryback and loss carryforward, assuming that based on the weight of available evidence, it is more likely than not that one-fifth of the benefits of the loss carryforward will not be realized.

(b) Prepare the income tax section of the 2005 income statement beginning with the line "Income (loss) before income taxes."

PROBLEMS

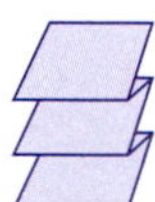

P19-1 (Three Differences, No Beginning Deferred Taxes, Multiple Rates) The following information is available for Swanson Corporation for 2003.

1. Depreciation reported on the tax return exceeded depreciation reported on the income statement by $100,000. This difference will reverse in equal amounts of $25,000 over the years 2004–2007.
2. Interest received on municipal bonds was $10,000.
3. Rent collected in advance on January 1, 2003, totaled $60,000 for a 3-year period. Of this amount, $40,000 was reported as unearned at December 31, for book purposes.
4. The tax rates are 40% for 2003 and 35% for 2004 and subsequent years.
5. Income taxes of $360,000 are due per the tax return for 2003.
6. No deferred taxes existed at the beginning of 2003.

Instructions

(a) Compute taxable income for 2003.

(b) Compute pretax financial income for 2003.

(c) Prepare the journal entries to record income tax expense, deferred income taxes, and income taxes payable for 2003 and 2004. Assume taxable income was $980,000 in 2004.

(d) Prepare the income tax expense section of the income statement for 2003, beginning with "Income before income taxes."

P19-2 (One Temporary Difference, Tracked for 4 Years, One Permanent Difference, Change in Rate) The pretax financial income of Kristal Parker-Gregory Company differs from its taxable income throughout each of 4 years as follows.

Year	Pretax Financial Income	Taxable Income	Tax Rate
2004	$280,000	$180,000	35%
2005	320,000	225,000	40%
2006	350,000	270,000	40%
2007	420,000	580,000	40%

Pretax financial income for each year includes a nondeductible expense of $30,000 (never deductible for tax purposes). The remainder of the difference between pretax financial income and taxable income in each period is due to one depreciation temporary difference. No deferred income taxes existed at the beginning of 2004.

Instructions

(a) Prepare journal entries to record income taxes in all 4 years. Assume that the change in the tax rate to 40% was not enacted until the beginning of 2005.

(b) Draft the income tax section of the income statement for 2005.

P19-3 (Second Year of Depreciation Difference, Two Differences, Single Rate, Extraordinary Item) The following information has been obtained for the Tracy Kerdyk Corporation.

1. Prior to 2003, taxable income and pretax financial income were identical.
2. Pretax financial income is $1,700,000 in 2003 and $1,400,000 in 2004.
3. On January 1, 2003, equipment costing $1,000,000 is purchased. It is to be depreciated on a straight-line basis over 5 years for tax purposes and over 8 years for financial reporting purposes. (*Hint:* Use the half-year convention for tax purposes, as discussed in Appendix 11A.)
4. Interest of $60,000 was earned on tax-exempt municipal obligations in 2004.
5. Included in 2004 pretax financial income is an extraordinary gain of $200,000, which is fully taxable.
6. The tax rate is 35% for all periods.
7. Taxable income is expected in all future years.

Instructions

(a) Compute taxable income and income tax payable for 2004.

(b) Prepare the journal entry to record 2004 income tax expense, income tax payable, and deferred taxes.

(c) Prepare the bottom portion of Kerdyk's 2004 income statement, beginning with "Income before income taxes and extraordinary item."

(d) Indicate how deferred income taxes should be presented on the December 31, 2004, balance sheet.

P19-4 (Permanent and Temporary Differences, One Rate) The accounting records of Anderson Inc. show the following data for 2004.

1. Life insurance expense on officers was $9,000.
2. Equipment was acquired in early January for $200,000. Straight-line depreciation over a 5-year life is used, with no salvage value. For tax purposes, Anderson used a 30% rate to calculate depreciation.
3. Interest revenue on State of New York bonds totaled $4,000.
4. Product warranties were estimated to be $60,000 in 2004. Actual repair and labor costs related to the warranties in 2004 were $10,000. The remainder is estimated to be incurred evenly in 2005 and 2006.
5. Sales on an accrual basis were $100,000. For tax purposes, $75,000 was recorded on the installment sales method.
6. Fines incurred for pollution violations were $4,200.
7. Pretax financial income was $850,000. The tax rate is 30%.

Instructions

(a) Prepare a schedule starting with pretax financial income and ending with taxable income.

(b) Prepare the journal entry for 2004 income tax payable and expense.

P19-5 (Actual NOL without Valuation Account) Mark O'Meara Inc. reported the following pretax income (loss) and related tax rates during the years 1999–2005.

	Pretax Income (loss)	Tax Rate
1999	$ 40,000	30%
2000	25,000	30%
2001	60,000	30%
2002	80,000	40%
2003	(200,000)	45%
2004	70,000	40%
2005	90,000	35%

Pretax financial income (loss) and taxable income (loss) were the same for all years since O'Meara began business. The tax rates from 2002–2005 were enacted in 2002.

Instructions

(a) Prepare the journal entries for the years 2003–2005 to record income tax payable (refundable), income tax expense (benefit), and the tax effects of the loss carryback and carryforward. Assume that O'Meara elects the carryback provision where possible and expects to realize the benefits of any loss carryforward in the year that immediately follows the loss year.

(b) Indicate the effect the 2003 entry(ies) has on the December 31, 2003, balance sheet.

(c) Indicate how the bottom portion of the income statement, starting with "Operating loss before income taxes," would be reported in 2003.

(d) Indicate how the bottom portion of the income statement, starting with "Income before income taxes," would be reported in 2004.

P19-6 (Two Differences, Two Rates, Future Income Expected) Presented below are two independent situations related to future taxable and deductible amounts resulting from temporary differences existing at December 31, 2003.

1. Pirates Co. has developed the following schedule of future taxable and deductible amounts.

	2004	2005	2006	2007	2008
Taxable amounts	$300	$300	$300	$ 300	$300
Deductible amount	—	—	—	(1,400)	—

2. Eagles Co. has the following schedule of future taxable and deductible amounts.

	2004	2005	2006	2007
Taxable amounts	$300	$300	$ 300	$300
Deductible amount	—	—	(2,000)	—

Both Pirates Co. and Eagles Co. have taxable income of $3,000 in 2003 and expect to have taxable income in all future years. The tax rates enacted as of the beginning of 2003 are 30% for 2003–2006 and 35% for years thereafter. All of the underlying temporary differences relate to noncurrent assets and liabilities.

Instructions

For each of these two situations, compute the net amount of deferred income taxes to be reported at the end of 2003, and indicate how it should be classified on the balance sheet.

P19-7 (One Temporary Difference, Tracked 3 Years, Change in Rates, Income Statement Presentation) Gators Corp. sold an investment on an installment basis. The total gain of $60,000 was reported for financial reporting purposes in the period of sale. The company qualifies to use the installment sales method for tax purposes. The installment period is 3 years; one-third of the sale price is collected in the period of sale. The tax rate was 35% in 2003, and 30% in 2004 and 2005. The 30% tax rate was not enacted in law until 2004. The accounting and tax data for the 3 years is shown below.

	Financial Accounting	Tax Return
2003 (35% tax rate)		
Income before temporary difference	$ 70,000	$70,000
Temporary difference	60,000	20,000
Income	$130,000	$90,000
2004 (30% tax rate)		
Income before temporary difference	$ 70,000	$70,000
Temporary difference	–0–	20,000
Income	$ 70,000	$90,000
2005 (30% tax rate)		
Income before temporary difference	$ 70,000	$70,000
Temporary difference	–0–	20,000
Income	$ 70,000	$90,000

Instructions

(a) Prepare the journal entries to record the income tax expense, deferred income taxes, and the income tax payable at the end of each year. No deferred income taxes existed at the beginning of 2003.

(b) Explain how the deferred taxes will appear on the balance sheet at the end of each year. (Assume the Installment Accounts Receivable is classified as a current asset.)

(c) Draft the income tax expense section of the income statement for each year, beginning with "Income before income taxes."

P19-8 (Two Differences, 2 Years, Compute Taxable Income and Pretax Financial Income) The following information was disclosed during the audit of Thomas Muster Inc.

1.

Year	Amount Due per Tax Return
2003	$140,000
2004	112,000

2. On January 1, 2003, equipment costing $400,000 is purchased. For financial reporting purposes, the company uses straight-line depreciation over a 5-year life. For tax purposes, the company uses the elective straight-line method over a 5-year life. (*Hint:* For tax purposes, the half-year convention as discussed in Appendix 11A must be used.)

3. In January 2004, $225,000 is collected in advance rental of a building for a 3-year period. The entire $225,000 is reported as taxable income in 2004, but $150,000 of the $225,000 is reported as unearned revenue in 2004 for financial reporting purposes. The remaining amount of unearned revenue is to be earned equally in 2005 and 2006.

4. The tax rate is 40% in 2003 and all subsequent periods. (*Hint:* To find taxable income in 2003 and 2004, the related income tax payable amounts will have to be grossed up.)

5. No temporary differences existed at the end of 2002. Muster expects to report taxable income in each of the next 5 years.

Instructions

(a) Determine the amount to report for deferred income taxes at the end of 2003, and indicate how it should be classified on the balance sheet.

(b) Prepare the journal entry to record income taxes for 2003.

(c) Draft the income tax section of the income statement for 2003 beginning with "Income before income taxes." (*Hint:* You must compute taxable income and then combine that with changes in cumulative temporary differences to arrive at pretax financial income.)

(d) Determine the deferred income taxes at the end of 2004, and indicate how they should be classified on the balance sheet.

(e) Prepare the journal entry to record income taxes for 2004.

(f) Draft the income tax section of the income statement for 2004, beginning with "Income before income taxes."

P19-9 (Five Differences, Compute Taxable Income and Deferred Taxes, Draft Income Statement) Martha King Company began operations at the beginning of 2004. The following information pertains to this company.

1. Pretax financial income for 2004 is $100,000.

2. The tax rate enacted for 2004 and future years is 40%

3. Differences between the 2004 income statement and tax return are listed below:

- **(a)** Warranty expense accrued for financial reporting purposes amounts to $5,000. Warranty deductions per the tax return amount to $2,000.
- **(b)** Gross profit on construction contracts using the percentage-of-completion method for books amounts to $92,000. Gross profit on construction contracts for tax purposes amounts to $62,000.
- **(c)** Depreciation of property, plant, and equipment for financial reporting purposes amounts to $60,000. Depreciation of these assets amounts to $80,000 for the tax return.
- **(d)** A $3,500 fine paid for violation of pollution laws was deducted in computing pretax financial income.
- **(e)** Interest revenue earned on an investment in tax-exempt municipal bonds amounts to $1,400.

(Assume (a) is short-term in nature; assume (b) and (c) are long-term in nature.)

4. Taxable income is expected for the next few years.

Instructions

(a) Compute taxable income for 2004.

(b) Compute the deferred taxes at December 31, 2004, that relate to the temporary differences described above. Clearly label them as deferred tax asset or liability.

(c) Prepare the journal entry to record income tax expense, deferred taxes, and income taxes payable for 2004.

(d) Draft the income tax expense section of the income statement beginning with "Income before income taxes."

CONCEPTUAL CASES

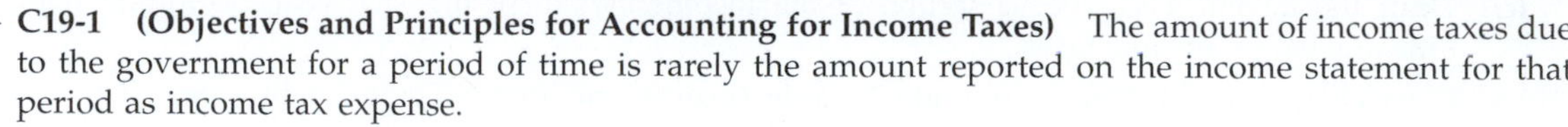

C19-1 (Objectives and Principles for Accounting for Income Taxes) The amount of income taxes due to the government for a period of time is rarely the amount reported on the income statement for that period as income tax expense.

Instructions

(a) Explain the objectives of accounting for income taxes in general purpose financial statements.
(b) Explain the basic principles that are applied in accounting for income taxes at the date of the financial statements to meet the objectives discussed in (a).
(c) List the steps in the annual computation of deferred tax liabilities and assets.

C19-2 (Basic Accounting for Temporary Differences) Iva Majoli Company appropriately uses the asset-liability method to record deferred income taxes. Iva Majoli reports depreciation expense for certain machinery purchased this year using the modified accelerated cost recovery system (MACRS) for income tax purposes and the straight-line basis for financial reporting purposes. The tax deduction is the larger amount this year.

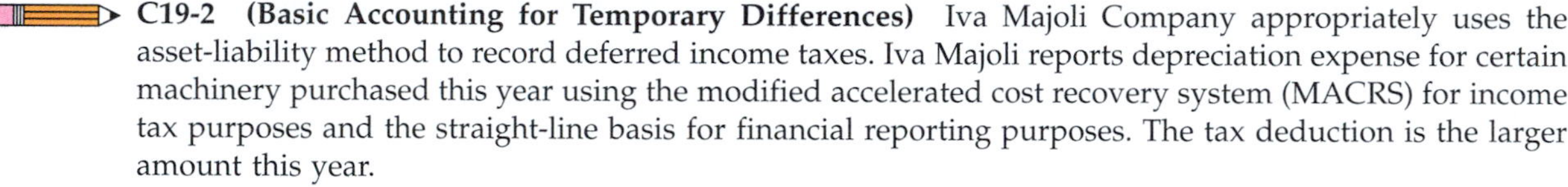

Iva Majoli received rent revenues in advance this year. These revenues are included in this year's taxable income. However, for financial reporting purposes, these revenues are reported as unearned revenues, a current liability.

Instructions

(a) What are the principles of the asset-liability approach?
(b) How would Majoli account for the temporary differences?
(c) How should Majoli classify the deferred tax consequences of the temporary differences on its balance sheet?

C19-3 (Identify Temporary Differences and Classification Criteria) The asset-liability approach for recording deferred income taxes is an integral part of generally accepted accounting principles.

Instructions

(a) Indicate whether each of the following independent situations should be treated as a temporary difference or as a permanent difference and explain why.
  (1) Estimated warranty costs (covering a 3-year warranty) are expensed for financial reporting purposes at the time of sale but deducted for income tax purposes when paid.
  (2) Depreciation for book and income tax purposes differs because of different bases of carrying the related property, which was acquired in a trade-in. The different bases are a result of different rules used for book and tax purposes to compute the basis of property acquired in a trade-in.
  (3) A company properly uses the equity method to account for its 30% investment in another company. The investee pays dividends that are about 10% of its annual earnings.
  (4) A company reports a gain on an involuntary conversion of a nonmonetary asset to a monetary asset. The company elects to replace the property within the statutory period using the total proceeds so the gain is not reported on the current year's tax return.
(b) Discuss the nature of the deferred income tax accounts and possible classifications in a company's balance sheet. Indicate the manner in which these accounts are to be reported.

C19-4 (Accounting and Classification of Deferred Income Taxes)

Part A

This year Lindsay Davenport Company has each of the following items in its income statement.

1. Gross profits on installment sales.
2. Revenues on long-term construction contracts.
3. Estimated costs of product warranty contracts.
4. Premiums on officers' life insurance with Davenport as beneficiary.

Instructions

(a) Under what conditions would deferred income taxes need to be reported in the financial statements?
(b) Specify when deferred income taxes would need to be recognized for each of the items above, and indicate the rationale for such recognition.

Part B
Davenport Company's president has heard that deferred income taxes can be classified in different ways in the balance sheet.

Instructions
Identify the conditions under which deferred income taxes would be classified as a noncurrent item in the balance sheet. What justification exists for such classification?

(AICPA adapted)

C19-5 (Explain Computation of Deferred Tax Liability for Multiple Tax Rates) At December 31, 2004, Martina Hingis Corporation has one temporary difference which will reverse and cause taxable amounts in 2005. In 2004 a new tax act set taxes equal to 45% for 2004, 40% for 2005, and 34% for 2006 and years thereafter.

Instructions
Explain what circumstances would call for Martina Hingis to compute its deferred tax liability at the end of 2004 by multiplying the cumulative temporary difference by:

(a) 45%.
(b) 40%.
(c) 34%.

C19-6 (Explain Future Taxable and Deductible Amounts, How Carryback and Carryforward Affects Deferred Taxes) Mary Joe Fernandez and Meredith McGrath are discussing accounting for income taxes. They are currently studying a schedule of taxable and deductible amounts that will arise in the future as a result of existing temporary differences. The schedule is as follows.

	Current Year	Future Years			
	2004	2005	2006	2007	2008
Taxable income	$850,000				
Taxable amounts		$375,000	$375,000	$ 375,000	$375,000
Deductible amounts				(2,400,000)	
Enacted tax rate	50%	45%	40%	35%	30%

Instructions
(a) Explain the concept of future taxable amounts and future deductible amounts as illustrated in the schedule.
(b) How do the carryback and carryforward provisions affect the reporting of deferred tax assets and deferred tax liabilities?

C19-7 (Deferred Taxes, Income Effects) Henrietta Aguirre, CPA, is the newly hired director of corporate taxation for Mesa Incorporated, which is a publicly traded corporation. Ms. Aguirre's first job with Mesa was the review of the company's accounting practices on deferred income taxes. In doing her review, she noted differences between tax and book depreciation methods that permitted Mesa to realize a sizable deferred tax liability on its balance sheet. As a result, Mesa did not have to report current income tax expenses.

Aguirre also discovered that Mesa has an explicit policy of selling off fixed assets before they reversed in the deferred tax liability account. This policy, coupled with the rapid expansion of its fixed asset base, allowed Mesa to "defer" all income taxes payable for several years, even though it always has reported positive earnings and an increasing EPS. Aguirre checked with the legal department and found the policy to be legal, but she's uncomfortable with the ethics of it.

Instructions
Answer the following questions.

(a) Why would Mesa have an explicit policy of selling fixed assets before the temporary differences reversed in the deferred tax liability account?
(b) What are the ethical implications of Mesa's "deferral" of income taxes?
(c) Who could be harmed by Mesa's ability to "defer" income taxes payable for several years, despite positive earnings?
(d) In a situation such as this, what are Ms. Aguirre's professional responsibilities as a CPA?

USING YOUR JUDGMENT

FINANCIAL REPORTING PROBLEM

3M Company

The financial statements of 3M are presented in Appendix 5B or can be accessed on the Take Action! CD.

Instructions

Refer to 3M's financial statements and the accompanying notes to answer the following questions.

(a) What amounts relative to income taxes does 3M report in its:

(1) 2001 income statement?

(2) December 31, 2001, balance sheet?

(3) 2001 statement of cash flows?

(b) 3M's provision for income taxes in 1999, 2000, and 2001 was computed at what effective tax rates? (See notes to the financial statements.)

(c) How much of 3M's 2001 total provision for income taxes was current tax expense, and how much was deferred tax expense?

(d) What did 3M report as the significant components (the details) of its December 31, 2001, deferred tax assets and liabilities?

FINANCIAL STATEMENT ANALYSIS CASE

Homestake Mining Company

Homestake Mining Company is a 120-year-old international gold mining company with substantial gold mining operations and exploration in the United States, Canada, and Australia. At year-end, Homestake reported the following items related to income taxes (thousands of dollars).

Total current taxes	$ 26,349
Total deferred taxes	(39,436)
Total income and mining taxes (the provision for taxes per its income statement)	(13,087)
Deferred tax liabilities	$303,050
Deferred tax assets, net of valuation allowance of $207,175	95,275
Net deferred tax liability	$207,775

Note 6: The classification of deferred tax assets and liabilities is based on the related asset or liability creating the deferred tax. Deferred taxes not related to a specific asset or liability are classified based on the estimated period of reversal.

Tax loss carryforwards (U.S., Canada, Australia, and Chile)	$71,151
Tax credit carryforwards	$12,007

Instructions

(a) What is the significance of Homestake's disclosure of "Current taxes" of $26,349 and "Deferred taxes" of $(39,436)?

(b) Explain the concept behind Homestake's disclosure of gross deferred tax liabilities (future taxable amounts) and gross deferred tax assets (future deductible amounts).

(c) Homestake reported tax loss carryforwards of $71,151 and tax credit carryforwards of $12,007. How do the carryback and carryforward provisions affect the reporting of deferred tax assets and deferred tax liabilities?

COMPARATIVE ANALYSIS CASE

The Coca-Cola Company and PepsiCo, Inc.

Instructions

Go to the Take Action! CD and use information found there to answer the following questions related to The Coca-Cola Company and PepsiCo, Inc.

(a) What are the amounts of Coca-Cola's and PepsiCo's provision for income taxes for the year 2001? Of each company's 2001 provision for income taxes, what portion is current expense and what portion is deferred expense?

(b) What amount of cash was paid in 2001 for income taxes by Coca-Cola and by PepsiCo?

(c) What was the U.S. federal statutory tax rate in 2001? What was the effective tax rate in 2001 for Coca-Cola and PepsiCo? Why might their effective tax rates differ?

(d) For the year-end 2001, what amounts were reported by Coca-Cola and PepsiCo as (a) gross deferred tax assets and (b) gross deferred tax liabilities?

(e) Do either Coca-Cola or PepsiCo disclose any net operating loss carrybacks and/or carryforwards at year-end 2001? What are the amounts, and when do the carryforwards expire?

RESEARCH CASES

Case 1

As discussed in the chapter, companies must consider all positive and negative information in determining whether a deferred tax asset valuation allowance is needed.

Instructions

Examine the balance sheets and income tax footnotes for two companies that have recorded deferred tax assets, and answer the following questions with regard to each company.

(a) What is the gross amount of the deferred tax asset recorded by the company? Express this amount as a percentage of total assets.

(b) Did the company record a valuation allowance? How large was the allowance?

(c) What evidence, if any, did the company cite with regard to the need for a valuation allowance? Do you consider the company's disclosure to be adequate?

Case 2

The deferred tax liability requires special considerations for financial statement readers.

Instructions

Obtain a recent edition of a financial statement analysis textbook, read the section related to the deferred tax liability, and answer the following questions.

(a) What are the major analytical issues associated with deferred tax liabilities?

(b) What type of adjustments to deferred tax liabilities do analysts make when examining financial statements?

INTERNATIONAL REPORTING CASE

Tomkins PLC

Tomkins PLC is a British company that operates in four business sectors: industrial and automotive engineering; construction components; food manufacturing; and professional, garden, and leisure products. Tomkins prepares its accounts in accordance with United Kingdom (U.K.) accounting standards. Like U.S. reporting, U.K. financial reporting is investor-oriented. As a result, British companies report different income amounts for tax and financial reporting purposes. British companies receive different tax treatment for such items as depreciation (capital allowances), and they receive tax credits for operating losses. Tomkins reported income of £305 million in a recent year and reported total shareholders' funds of £2,221 million at year-end. Tomkins provided the following disclosures related to taxes in its annual report.

If Tomkins had used U.S. GAAP for deferred taxes, its income would have been lower by £8.2 million in the current year. Stockholders' equity at year-end would have been £87.5 million higher if Tompkins had applied U.S. GAAP.

TOMKINS

Principal Accounting Policies—Tax

The tax charge is based on the profit for the year and takes into account tax deferred due to timing differences between the treatment of certain items for tax and accounting purposes. Deferred tax is calculated under the liability method and it is considered probable that all liabilities will crystallise. Deferred tax assets are not recognized in respect of provision for post-retirement benefits.

Note 5: Tax on Profit on Ordinary Activities

	Current Year £ million	Prior Year £ million
Corporation tax at 31%	56.6	69.6
Overseas tax	85.5	95.8
Deferred tax–UK (see note 16)	5.1	(7.1)
–Overseas (see note 16)	7.3	9.2
Associated undertakings' tax	0.7	3.0
	155.2	170.5

The tax charge on exceptional items in 1999 and 1998 is £nil.

Note 16: Provisions for Liabilities and Charges

	Current Year £ million	Prior Year £ million
The deferred tax provision comprises:	98.5	102.9
Excess of capital allowances over depreciation charged	40.8	25.5
Other timing differences	—	(30.3)
Advance corporation tax recoverable	139.3	98.1

Results Under U.S. Accounting Principles

The consolidated financial statements are prepared in conformity with accounting principles generally accepted in the UK (UK GAAP) which differ in certain respects from those generally accepted in the United States (US GAAP). The significant areas of difference affecting the Tomkins consolidated financial statements are described below:

Deferred Income Tax. In Tomkins consolidated financial statements, deferred tax is calculated under the liability method and it is considered probable that all liabilities will crystallise. Deferred tax assets are not recognised in respect of provision for post-retirement benefits. Under US GAAP, deferred taxes are provided for all temporary differences on a full liability basis. Deferred tax assets are also recognized to the extent that their realisation is more likely than not.

Instructions

Use the information in the Tomkins disclosure to answer the following.

(a) Prepare the journal entry that would be required to reconcile Tomkins' income to U.S. GAAP for the differences in deferred taxes under U.S. and U.K. accounting standards.

(b) Prepare the journal entry that would be required to reconcile Tomkins' shareholders' equity to U.S. GAAP for the differences in deferred taxes under U.S. and U.K. accounting standards at the end of the current year.

(c) In light of the information disclosed under "Principal Accounting Policies—Tax," explain why you think Tomkins' equity under U.S. GAAP would be higher at year-end in the current year.

(d) Tomkins indicates that "Deferred tax is calculated under the liability method and it is considered probable that all (deferred tax) liabilities will crystallise [be realized]." Does this approach cause any problems in comparing the financial statements of U.S. and U.K. companies? Explain.

PROFESSIONAL SIMULATION

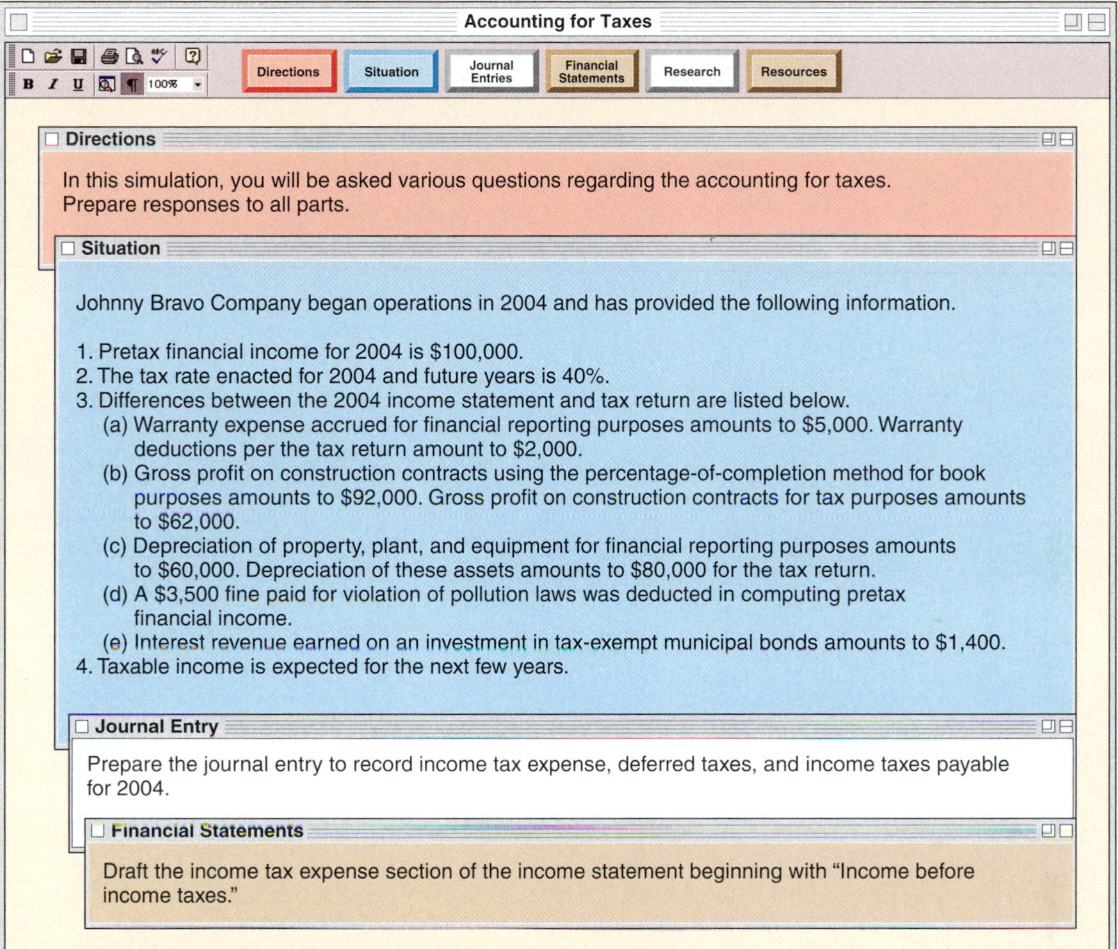

Accounting for Taxes

Directions | Situation | Journal Entries | Financial Statements | Research | Resources

Directions

In this simulation, you will be asked various questions regarding the accounting for taxes. Prepare responses to all parts.

Situation

Johnny Bravo Company began operations in 2004 and has provided the following information.

1. Pretax financial income for 2004 is $100,000.
2. The tax rate enacted for 2004 and future years is 40%.
3. Differences between the 2004 income statement and tax return are listed below.
   (a) Warranty expense accrued for financial reporting purposes amounts to $5,000. Warranty deductions per the tax return amount to $2,000.
   (b) Gross profit on construction contracts using the percentage-of-completion method for book purposes amounts to $92,000. Gross profit on construction contracts for tax purposes amounts to $62,000.
   (c) Depreciation of property, plant, and equipment for financial reporting purposes amounts to $60,000. Depreciation of these assets amounts to $80,000 for the tax return.
   (d) A $3,500 fine paid for violation of pollution laws was deducted in computing pretax financial income.
   (e) Interest revenue earned on an investment in tax-exempt municipal bonds amounts to $1,400.
4. Taxable income is expected for the next few years.

Journal Entry

Prepare the journal entry to record income tax expense, deferred taxes, and income taxes payable for 2004.

Financial Statements

Draft the income tax expense section of the income statement beginning with "Income before income taxes."

Remember to check the **Take Action! CD** and the book's **companion Web site** to find additional resources for this chapter.

CHAPTER 20

Accounting for Pensions and Postretirement Benefits

Pension Fund a Likely Drain

General Motors Corp. (GM) said it expects to meet its annual earnings per share target of $10 by mid-decade despite rising pension costs, but the company warned that its pension liabilities will likely drain cash flow. During a conference call, Eric Feldstein, GM's vice president of finance, said that fixing GM's underfunded pension fund will likely consume a considerable amount of cash. At the end of 2001, GM's pension was underfunded by $9.1 billion. A zero percent pension asset return this year, with no further pension contribution, would result in the pension being underfunded by $12.7 billion. However, GM said the return on the company's pension assets was negative 3 percent through the first half of the year.

Despite its large pension liabilities, GM should be able to offset higher pension expenses by cost cutting and further pension contributions. While a challenge, Mr. Feldstein said GM's pension funding obligations are manageable considering the company's current and future cash flow and given that the company has faced tougher pension problems in the past. GM's pension fund, for example, was underfunded by $18.5 billion in 1993, compared with the pension being underfunded by $9.1 billion in 2001. "We were able to work our way out of '93," Mr. Feldstein said. GM was able to fix the problem with $25 billion in pension contributions between 1993 and 1995. Favorable stock market returns at that time—asset returns were about 14.6 percent on average—also helped the pension fund.

Some U.S. companies are facing large pension liabilities because they have invested in the stock market, which has been weak for the past several months. About 35 to 40 percent of GM's fund is invested in U.S. equities, and 15 to 20 percent is invested in international equities. But GM faces a disadvantage compared with other auto makers because of its ratio of retirees to active employees. GM has 459,000 retirees, more than double the number of active employees. Due to the sagging stock market, GM's pension expense is expected to increase next year. Assuming no further contributions, a 5 percent pension asset return this year would lead to a $1.3 billion pretax increase in pension expense in 2003. Assuming a zero percent return, pension expense could rise to $1.7 billion pretax in 2003. A negative 5 percent asset return this year would increase expense to $2.1 billion pretax next year.[1]

Given the dismal prospects for the effects of GM's and other companies' pension plans on their operating results, it is easy to see why investors demand accounting information on pensions.

[1]Jocelyn Parker, "GM Says Underfunded Pension Fund Will Likely Drain Cash Flow," *Dow Jones Business News* (August 21, 2002).

LEARNING OBJECTIVES

After studying this chapter, you should be able to:

1. **Distinguish between accounting for the employer's pension plan and accounting for the pension fund.**
2. **Identify types of pension plans and their characteristics.**
3. **Explain alternative measures for valuing the pension obligation.**
4. **Identify the components of pension expense.**
5. **Utilize a work sheet for employer's pension plan entries.**
6. **Describe the amortization of unrecognized prior service costs.**
7. **Explain the accounting procedure for recognizing unexpected gains and losses.**
8. **Explain the corridor approach to amortizing unrecognized gains and losses.**
9. **Explain the recognition of a minimum liability.**
10. **Describe the reporting requirements for pension plans in financial statements.**

PREVIEW OF CHAPTER 20

As the opening story indicates, **General Motors** as well as other companies are facing large pension liabilities because of poor investment returns. As a result, these liabilities will have a significant impact on the cash flow of companies. The purpose of this chapter is to discuss the accounting issues related to pension plans. The content and organization of the chapter are as follows.

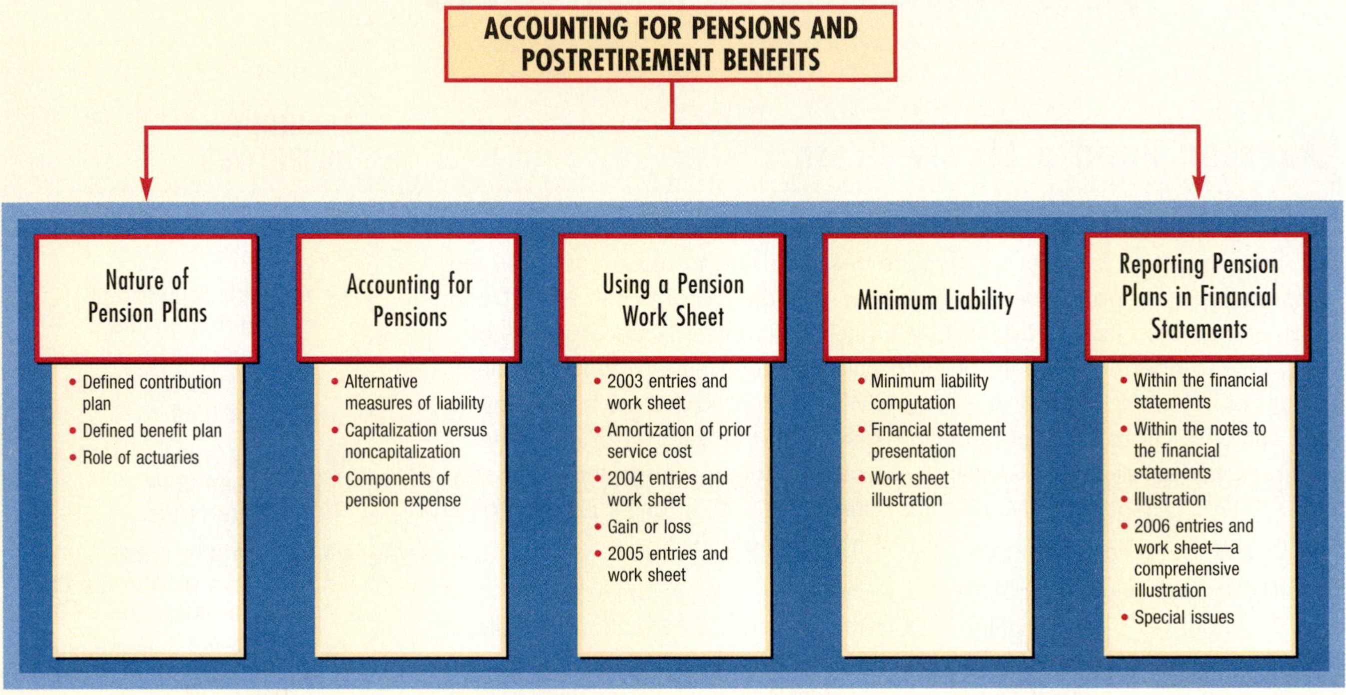

NATURE OF PENSION PLANS

OBJECTIVE 1
Distinguish between accounting for the employer's pension plan and accounting for the pension fund.

A **pension plan** is an arrangement whereby an employer provides benefits (payments) to employees after they retire for services they provided while they were working. Pension accounting may be divided and separately treated as **accounting for the employer** and **accounting for the pension fund**. The company or employer is the organization sponsoring the pension plan. It incurs the cost and makes contributions to the pension fund. The fund or plan is the entity that receives the contributions from the employer, administers the pension assets, and makes the benefit payments to the pension recipients (retired employees). Illustration 20-1 shows the three entities involved in a pension plan and indicates the flow of cash among them.

ILLUSTRATION 20-1
Flow of Cash among Pension Plan Participants

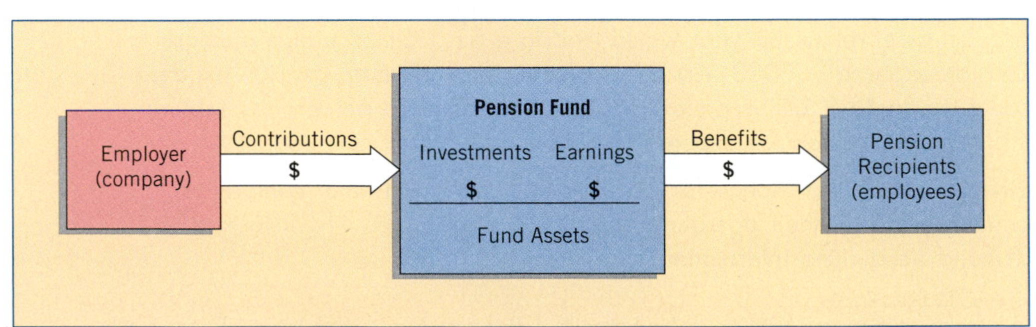

The pension plan in Illustration 20-1 is being **funded**.[2] That is, the employer (company) sets funds aside for future pension benefits by making payments to a funding agency that is responsible for accumulating the assets of the pension fund and for making payments to the recipients as the benefits become due.

Some plans are **contributory**. In these, the employees bear part of the cost of the stated benefits or voluntarily make payments to increase their benefits. Other plans are **noncontributory**. In these, the employer bears the entire cost. Companies generally design **qualified pension plans** in accord with federal income tax requirements that permit **deductibility of the employer's contributions to the pension fund and tax-free status of earnings from pension fund assets**.

The fund should be a separate legal and accounting entity for which a set of books is maintained and financial statements are prepared. Maintaining books and records and preparing financial statements for the fund, known as "accounting for employee benefit plans," is not the subject of this chapter.[3] Instead this chapter is devoted to the pension accounting and reporting problems of **the employer** as the sponsor of a pension plan. The two most common types of pension plans are **defined contribution plans** and **defined benefit plans**.

THESE FUNDS ARE HUGE

WHAT DO THE NUMBERS MEAN?

The need for proper administration of, and sound accounting for, pension funds becomes apparent when one appreciates the size of these funds. Listed below are the pension fund assets and pension expenses of seven major companies.

Company ($ in millions)	Size of Pension Fund	2001 Pension Expense	Pension Expense as % of Operating Profit
General Motors	$73,662	$550	7.8%
Goodyear Tire	4,176	138	49.3
Adolph Coors	527	12	7.9
Hewlett-Packard	2,409	226	15.7
Coca-Cola	1,492	62	1.1
John Deere	5,951	85	–*
Merck	2,865	148	1.5

*Reported an operating loss in 2001.

As indicated, pension expense is a substantial percentage of total profit for many companies.[4]

[2]When used as a verb, **fund** means to pay to a funding agency (as to fund future pension benefits or to fund pension cost). Used as a noun, it refers to assets accumulated in the hands of a funding agency (trustee) for the purpose of meeting pension benefits when they become due.

[3]The FASB issued a separate standard covering the accounting and reporting for employee benefit plans. "Accounting and Reporting by Defined Benefit Pension Plans," *Statement of Financial Accounting Standards No. 35* (Stamford, Conn.: FASB, 1979).

[4]Some have suggested that pension funds are the new owners of America's giant corporations. One study indicated that during the 1990s, pension funds (private and public) held or owned approximately 25 percent of the market value of corporate stock outstanding and accounted for 32 percent of the daily trading volume on the New York Stock Exchange. The enormous size (and the social significance) of these funds is staggering.

Defined Contribution Plan

OBJECTIVE 2
Identify types of pension plans and their characteristics.

In a **defined contribution plan** the employer agrees to contribute to a pension trust a certain sum each period based on a formula. This formula may consider such factors as age, length of employee service, employer's profits, and compensation level. **Only the employer's contribution is defined**; no promise is made regarding the ultimate benefits paid out to the employees.

The size of the pension benefits that the employee finally collects under the plan depends on the amounts originally contributed to the pension trust, the income accumulated in the trust, and the treatment of forfeitures of funds caused by early terminations of other employees. The amounts originally contributed are usually turned over to an **independent third-party trustee** who acts on behalf of the beneficiaries—the participating employees. The trustee assumes ownership of the pension assets and is accountable for their investment and distribution. The trust is separate and distinct from the employer.

The accounting for a defined contribution plan is straightforward. The employee gets the benefit of gain or the risk of loss from the assets contributed to the pension plan. The employer's responsibility is simply to make a contribution each year based on the formula established in the plan. As a result, the employer's annual cost (pension expense) is just the amount that it is obligated to contribute to the pension trust. A liability is reported on the employer's balance sheet only if the contribution has not been made in full, and an asset is reported only if more than the required amount has been contributed.

Disclosures for Defined Contribution Plans

In addition to pension expense, the only disclosures required by the employer under a defined contribution plan are a plan description, including employee groups covered, the basis for determining contributions, and the nature and effect of significant matters affecting comparability from period to period.[5]

WHAT DO THE NUMBERS MEAN?

THE DANGERS OF NOT DIVERSIFYING

The defined contribution plan is very popular with employees. A recent report by **Fidelity Investments** noted that approximately three-quarters of eligible employees contribute to a defined contribution plan. Participants are saving an average of 7 percent of their gross incomes for retirement. However, most investors tend to concentrate their funds in just a few investments, as shown below.

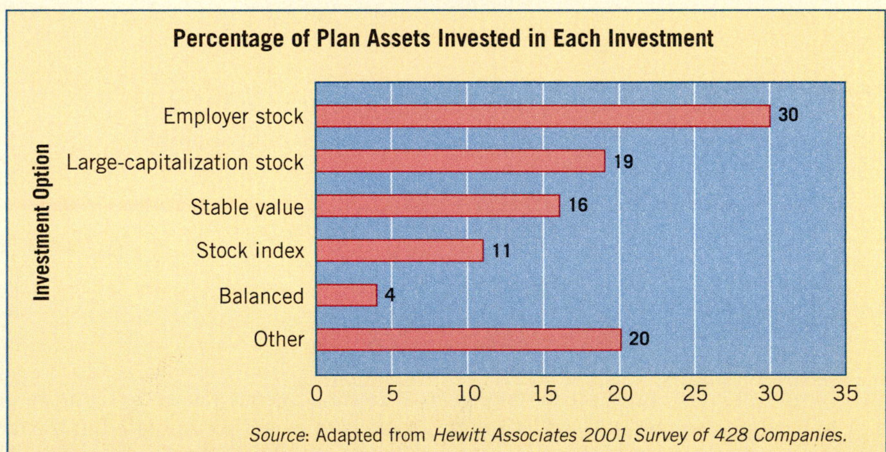

Source: Adapted from *Hewitt Associates 2001 Survey of 428 Companies.*

As the graph shows, a significant percentage of participants invest in their company's stock. However, the dangers of having all your retirement assets in one stock are considerable. For example, **Enron** matched employee's contributions with company stock, ensuring that employee plans were not diversified. As a result, when Enron collapsed these employees lost not only their jobs but a major part of their pension as well.

[5] "Employers' Accounting for Pension Plans," *Statement of Financial Accounting Standards No. 87* (Stamford, Conn.: FASB, 1985), pars. 63–66.

Defined Benefit Plan

A **defined benefit plan** defines the benefits that the employee will receive at the time of retirement. The formula that is typically used provides for the benefits to be a function of the employee's years of service and the employee's compensation level when he or she nears retirement. It is necessary to determine what the contribution should be today to meet the pension benefit commitments that will arise at retirement. Many different contribution approaches could be used. Whatever funding method is employed, it should provide enough money at retirement to meet the benefits defined by the plan.

The **employees** are the beneficiaries of a **defined contribution trust**, but the **employer** is the beneficiary of a **defined benefit trust**. The trust's primary purpose under a defined benefit plan is to safeguard assets and to invest them so that there will be enough to pay the employer's obligation to the employees when they retire. **In form**, the trust is a separate entity; **in substance**, the trust assets and liabilities belong to the employer. That is, **as long as the plan continues, the employer is responsible for the payment of the defined benefits (without regard to what happens in the trust)**. Any shortfall in the accumulated assets held by the trust must be made up by the employer. Any excess accumulated in the trust can be recaptured by the employer, either through reduced future funding or through a reversion of funds.

INTERNATIONAL INSIGHT

Outside the U.S., private pension plans are less common because many other nations tend to rely on government-sponsored pension plans. Consequently, accounting for defined benefit pension plans is typically a less important issue elsewhere.

The accounting for a defined benefit plan is complex. Because the benefits are defined in terms of uncertain future variables, an appropriate funding pattern must be established to ensure that enough funds will be available at retirement to provide the benefits promised. This funding level depends on a number of factors such as turnover, mortality, length of employee service, compensation levels, and interest earnings.

Employers are at risk with defined benefit plans because they must be sure to make enough contributions to meet the cost of benefits that are defined in the plan. The expense recognized each period is not necessarily equal to the cash contribution. Similarly, the liability is controversial because its measurement and recognition relate to unknown future variables. Unfortunately, the accounting issues related to this type of plan are complex. **Our discussion in the following sections primarily deals with defined benefit plans.**[6]

The Role of Actuaries in Pension Accounting

Because the problems associated with pension plans involve complicated actuarial considerations, **actuaries** are engaged to ensure that the plan is appropriate for the employee group covered.[7] Actuaries are individuals who are trained through a long and

[6]One survey found that 356 companies in the S&P 500 and 11 companies in the Nasdaq 100 offer defined benefit plans. (The other companies usually offer 401(K) plans, which are defined contribution plans.) Jane B. Adams, "A Pension Primer," Credit Suisse First Boston, Volume 2, Issue 4 (June 13, 2001).

The recordkeeping requirements for the defined benefit plans are onerous and, therefore, companies have become more reluctant to use these plans. Also, the benefits in a defined contribution plan are easier for the employee to understand; employees tend to prefer them over the defined benefit plan. In terms of total assets, recent Federal Reserve statistics (2001) indicate that assets in private defined benefit and contribution plans were more than $1.8 and $2.4 trillion respectively. In many cases, a defined contribution plan is offered in combination with a defined benefit plan.

[7]An actuary's primary purpose is to ensure that the company has established an appropriate funding pattern to meet its pension obligations. This computation entails the development of a set of assumptions and continued monitoring of these assumptions to ensure their realism. That the general public has little understanding of what an actuary does is illustrated by the following excerpt from the *Wall Street Journal:* "A polling organization once asked the general public what an actuary was and received among its more coherent responses the opinion that it was a place where you put dead actors."

rigorous certification program to assign probabilities to future events and their financial effects. The insurance industry employs actuaries to assess risks and to advise on the setting of premiums and other aspects of insurance policies. Employers rely heavily on actuaries for assistance in developing, implementing, and funding pension plans.

It is actuaries who make predictions (called actuarial assumptions) of mortality rates, employee turnover, interest and earnings rates, early retirement frequency, future salaries, and any other factors necessary to operate a pension plan. They assist by computing the various pension measures that affect the financial statements, such as the pension obligation, the annual cost of servicing the plan, and the cost of amendments to the plan. In summary, accounting for defined benefit pension plans is highly reliant upon information and measurements provided by actuaries.

ACCOUNTING FOR PENSIONS

OBJECTIVE 3
Explain alternative measures for valuing the pension obligation.

In accounting for a company's pension plan, two questions arise: (1) What is the pension obligation that should be reported in the financial statements? (2) What is the pension expense for the period? Attempting to answer the first question has produced much controversy.

Alternative Measures of the Liability

Most agree that an employer's **pension obligation** is the deferred compensation obligation it has to its employees for their service under the terms of the pension plan, but there are alternative ways of measuring it.[8] One measure of the obligation is to base it only on the benefits vested to the employees. **Vested benefits** are those that the employee is entitled to receive even if the employee renders no additional services under the plan. Under most pension plans, a certain minimum number of years of service to the employer is required before an employee achieves vested benefits status. The **vested benefit obligation** is computed using current salary levels and includes only vested benefits.

VBO

INTERNATIONAL INSIGHT

Japan is the most rapidly aging nation in the developed world, with 24 percent of the population expected to be over 65 by the year 2015, compared with 17 percent in Europe and 15 percent in the U.S. Aging populations will affect pension liabilities in these countries.

Another measure of the obligation is to base the computation of the deferred compensation amount on all years of service performed by employees under the plan—both vested and nonvested—using **current salary levels**. This measurement of the pension obligation is called the **accumulated benefit obligation**.

A third measure bases the computation of the deferred compensation amount on both vested and nonvested service **using future salaries**. This measurement of the pension obligation is called the **projected benefit obligation.** Because future salaries are expected to be higher than current salaries, this approach results in the largest measurement of the pension obligation.

The choice between these measures is critical because it affects the amount of the pension liability and the annual pension expense reported. The diagram in Illustration 20-2 presents the differences in these three measurements. Regardless of the approach used, the estimated future benefits to be paid are discounted to present value.

Minor changes in the interest rate used to discount pension benefits can dramatically affect the measurement of the employer's obligation. For example, a 1 percent decrease in the discount rate can increase pension liabilities 15 percent. Discount rates used to measure the pension liability are required to be changed at each measurement date to reflect current interest rates.

---

[8]One measure of the pension obligation is to determine the amount that the **Pension Benefit Guaranty Corporation** would require the employer to pay if it defaulted. (This amount is limited to 30 percent of the employer's net worth.) The accounting profession rejected this approach for financial reporting because it is too hypothetical and ignores the going concern concept.

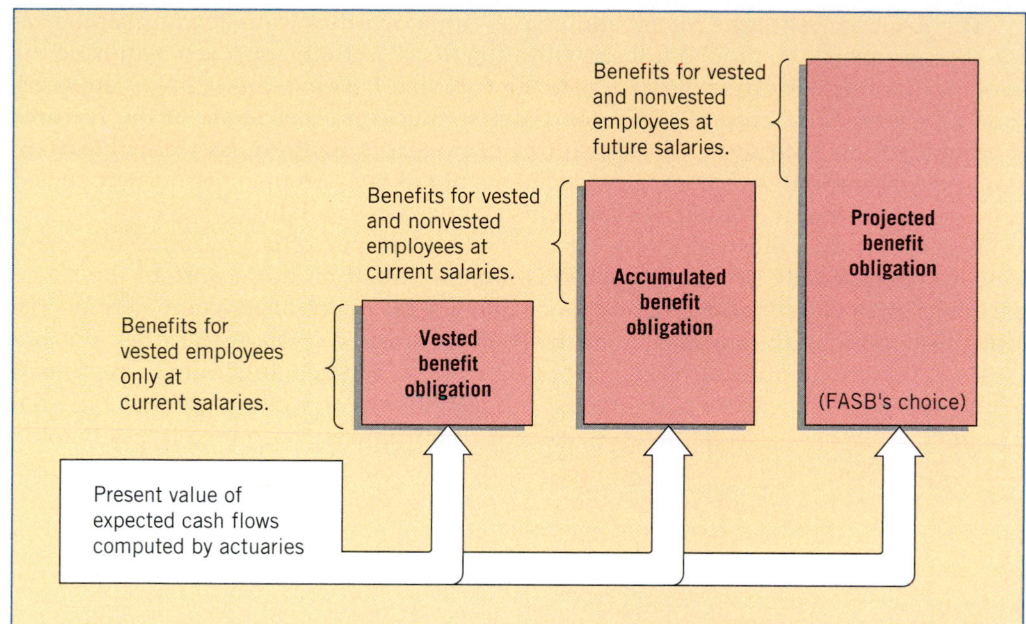

ILLUSTRATION 20-2
Different Measures of the Pension Obligation

Which of these approaches did the profession adopt? **In general, the profession adopted the projected benefit obligation, which is the present value of vested and nonvested benefits accrued to date based on employees' future salary levels.**[9] As you will learn later, however, the profession uses the accumulated benefit obligation in certain situations.

Those critical of the projected benefit obligation argue that using future salary levels is tantamount to adding future obligations to existing ones. Those in favor of the projected benefit obligation contend that a promise by an employer to pay benefits based on a percentage of the employees' future salary is far different from a promise to pay a percentage of their current salary, and such a difference should be reflected in the pension liability and pension expense.

INTERNATIONAL INSIGHT

Whereas the U.S. requires companies to base pension expense on estimated future compensation levels, Germany and Japan do not.

Capitalization versus Noncapitalization

Prior to issuance of *FASB Statement No. 87*, accounting for pension plans followed a **noncapitalization approach**. Noncapitalization, often referred to as **off-balance-sheet financing**, was achieved because the balance sheet reported an asset or liability for the pension plan arrangement only if the amount actually funded during the year by the employer was different from the amount reported by the employer as pension expense for the year.

The accounting profession has been tending toward a **capitalization approach**, which means measuring and reporting in the financial statements a fair representation of the employers' pension assets and liabilities. Capitalization focuses on the **economic substance** of the pension plan arrangement over its legal form. Under this view, the employer has a liability for pension benefits that it has promised to pay for employee services already performed. As pension expense is incurred—as the employees work—the employer's liability increases. Funding the plan has no effect on the amount of the liability; only the employer's promises and the employee's services affect the liability. The pension liability is reduced through the payment of benefits to retired employees.

[9]When the term "present value of benefits" is used throughout this chapter, it really means the actuarial present value of benefits. Actuarial present value is the amount payable adjusted to reflect the time value of money **and** the probability of payment (by means of decrements for events such as death, disability, withdrawals, or retirement) between the present date and the expected date of payment. For simplicity, we will use the term "present value" instead of "actuarial present value" in our discussion.

The FASB in *Statement No. 87* adopted an approach that leans toward capitalization. But, proposals to adopt a full capitalization (total accrual) approach, requiring the recognition of balance sheet items where none existed before, were strongly opposed. *FASB Statement No. 87* **represents a compromise that combines some of the features of capitalization with some of the features of noncapitalization**. As we will learn in more detail later in this chapter, some elements of the pension plan are not recognized in the accounts and the financial statements (that is, not capitalized).

Because of this, the accounting for pensions is not perfectly logical, totally complete, or conceptually sound. The FASB is not entirely at fault. Because of the financial complexity of defined benefit pensions, many well-intentioned, competent people could not agree on the economic substance of such plans. As a result, they did not agree on how to account for them. Because of the difficulties in gaining a consensus among the Board members and support from preparers as well as users of financial statements, *Statement No. 87* involves several compromises that make it less than an ideal application of the capitalization method. In its defense, however, *Statement No. 87* is a great improvement over previous accounting pronouncements and represents a first step toward a conceptually sound approach to employers' accounting for pension plans.

Components of Pension Expense

OBJECTIVE 4
Identify the components of pension expense.

There is broad agreement that pension cost should be accounted for on the **accrual basis**.[10] The profession recognizes that **accounting for pension plans requires measurement of the cost and its identification with the appropriate time periods**. The determination of pension cost, however, is extremely complicated because it is a function of the following components.

1. **Service Cost.** Service cost is the expense caused by the increase in pension benefits payable (the projected benefit obligation) to employees because of their services rendered during the current year. Actuaries compute **service cost** as the present value of the new benefits earned by employees during the year.

UNDERLYING CONCEPTS

The matching concept and the definition of a liability justify accounting for pension cost on the accrual basis. This requires recording an expense when the future benefits are earned by the employees and recognizing an existing obligation to pay pensions later based on current services received.

2. **Interest on the Liability.** Because a pension is a deferred compensation arrangement, there is a time value of money factor. As a result, it is recorded on a discounted basis. **Interest expense accrues each year on the projected benefit obligation just as it does on any discounted debt.** The accountant receives help from the actuary in selecting the interest rate, referred to as the **settlement rate**.
3. **Actual Return on Plan Assets.** The return earned by the accumulated pension fund assets in a particular year is relevant in measuring the net cost to the employer of sponsoring an employee pension plan. Therefore, **annual pension expense should be adjusted for interest and dividends that accumulate within the fund as well as increases and decreases in the market value of the fund assets**.
4. **Amortization of Unrecognized Prior Service Cost.** Pension plan amendments (including initiation of a pension plan) often include provisions to increase benefits (in rare situations, to decrease benefits) for employee service provided in prior years. Because plan amendments are granted with the expectation that the employer will realize economic benefits in future periods, **the cost (prior service cost) of providing these retroactive benefits is allocated to pension expense in the future, specifically to the remaining service-years of the affected employees**.

---

[10]Until the mid-1960s, with few exceptions, companies applied the **cash basis** of accounting to pension plans by recognizing the amount paid in a particular accounting period as the pension expense for the period. The problem was that the amount paid or funded in a fiscal period depended on financial management and was too often discretionary. For example, funding could be based on the availability of cash, the level of earnings, or other factors unrelated to the requirements of the plan. Application of the cash basis made it possible to manipulate the amount of pension expense appearing in the income statement simply by varying the cash paid to the pension fund.

5 **Gain or Loss.** Volatility in pension expense can be caused by sudden and large changes in the market value of plan assets and by changes in the projected benefit obligation (which changes when actuarial assumptions are modified or when actual experience differs from expected experience). Two items comprise this gain or loss: (1) the difference between the actual return and the expected return on plan assets and (2) amortization of the unrecognized net gain or loss from previous periods. This computation is complex and will be discussed later in the chapter.

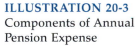

The **components of pension expense** and their effect on total pension expense (increase or decrease) are shown in Illustration 20-3.

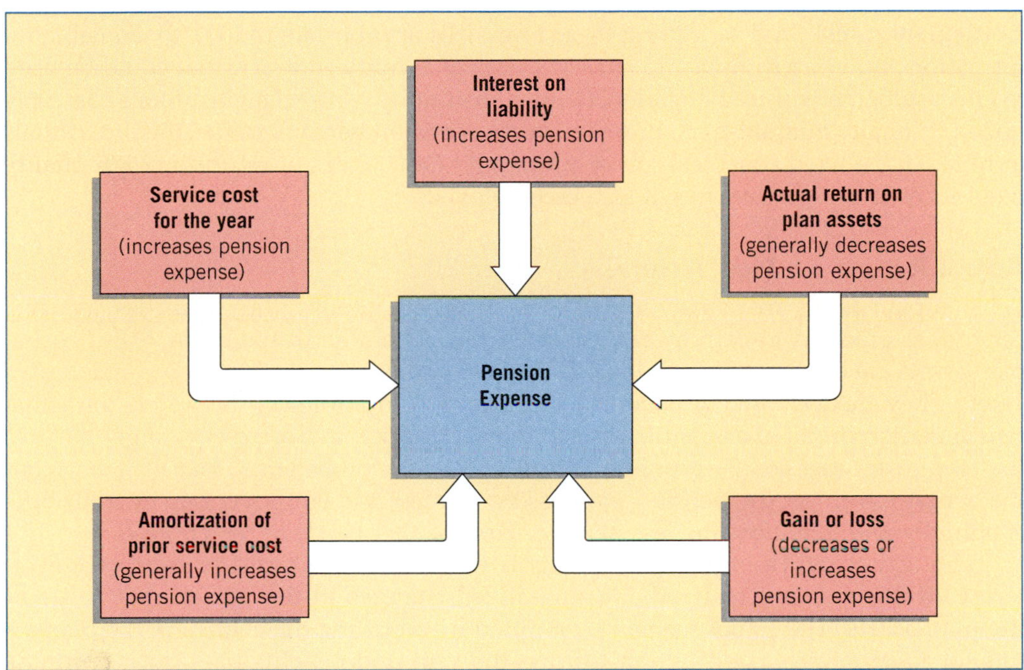

ILLUSTRATION 20-3
Components of Annual Pension Expense

Service Cost

In *FASB Statement No. 87*, the Board states that the **service cost** component recognized in a period **should be determined as the actuarial present value of benefits attributed by the pension benefit formula to employee service during the period**. That is, the actuary predicts the additional benefits that must be paid under the plan's benefit formula as a result of the employees' current year's service and then discounts the cost of those future benefits back to their present value.

The Board concluded that **future compensation levels had to be considered in measuring the present obligation and periodic pension expense if the plan benefit formula incorporated them**. In other words, the present obligation resulting from a promise to pay a benefit of 1 percent of an employee's **final pay** is different from an employer's promise to pay 1 percent of **current pay**. To ignore this fact would be to ignore an important aspect of pension expense. Thus, the **benefits/years-of-service actuarial method** is the approach adopted by the FASB.

Some object to this determination, arguing that a company should have more freedom to select an expense recognition pattern. Others believe that incorporating future salary increases into current pension expense is accounting for events that have not happened yet. They argue that if the plan were terminated today, only liabilities for accumulated benefits would have to be paid. **Nevertheless the Board indicates that the projected benefit obligation provides a more realistic measure on a going concern basis of the employer's obligation under the plan and, therefore, should be used as the basis for determining service cost.**

Interest on the Liability

The second component of pension expense is **interest on the liability**, or **interest expense**. As indicated earlier, a pension is a deferred compensation arrangement under which this element of wages is deferred and a liability is created. Because the liability is not paid until maturity, it is recorded on a discounted basis and accrues interest over the life of the employee. **The interest component is the interest for the period on the projected benefit obligation outstanding during the period.** The FASB did not address the question of how often to compound the interest cost. To simplify our illustrations and problem materials, we use a simple interest computation, applying it to the beginning-of-the-year balance of the projected benefit liability.

How is the interest rate determined? The Board states that the assumed discount rate should **reflect the rates at which pension benefits could be effectively settled (settlement rates)**. In determining these rates, it is appropriate to look to available information about rates implicit in current prices of annuity contracts that could be used to effect settlement of the obligation. (Under an annuity contract an insurance company unconditionally guarantees to provide specific pension benefits to specific individuals in return for a fixed consideration or premium.) Other rates of return on high-quality fixed-income investments might also be employed.

Actual Return on Plan Assets

Pension plan assets are usually investments in stocks, bonds, other securities, and real estate that are held to earn a reasonable return, generally at minimum risk. Pension plan assets are increased by employer contributions and actual returns on pension plan assets. They are decreased by benefits paid to retired employees. As indicated, the actual return earned on these assets increases the fund balance and correspondingly reduces the employer's net cost of providing employees' pension benefits. That is, the higher the actual return on the pension plan assets, the less the employer has to contribute eventually and, therefore the less pension expense that needs to be reported.

The actual return on the plan assets is the increase in pension funds from interest, dividends, and realized and unrealized changes in the fair market value of the plan assets. The actual return is computed by adjusting the change in the plan assets for the effects of contributions during the year and benefits paid out during the year. The following equation, or a variation thereof, can be used to compute the actual return.

ILLUSTRATION 20-4
Equation for Computing Actual Return

$$\text{Actual Return} = \left(\begin{array}{c}\text{Plan Assets}\\\text{Ending Balance}\end{array} - \begin{array}{c}\text{Plan Assets}\\\text{Beginning Balance}\end{array}\right) - (\text{Contributions} - \text{Benefits Paid})$$

Stated another way, the actual return on plan assets is the difference between the **fair value of the plan assets** at the beginning of the period and at the end of the period, adjusted for contributions and benefit payments. Computation of the actual return on the basis of the equation above is illustrated below using some assumed amounts.

ILLUSTRATION 20-5
Computation of Actual Return on Plan Assets

Fair value of plan assets at end of period		$5,000,000
Deduct: Fair value of plan assets at beginning of period		4,200,000
Increase in fair value of plan assets		800,000
Deduct: Contributions to plan during period	$500,000	
Less benefits paid during period	300,000	200,000
Actual return on plan assets		$ 600,000

If the actual return on the plan assets is positive (a gain) during the period, it is subtracted in the computation of pension expense. If the actual return is negative (a loss) during the period, it is added in the computation of pension expense.[11]

USING A PENSION WORK SHEET

Before covering in detail the other pension expense components (amortization of unrecognized prior service cost and gains and losses) which seem to get progressively more complex, we will illustrate the basic accounting entries for the first three components: (1) service cost, (2) interest on the liability, and (3) actual return on plan assets.

Important to accounting for pensions under *Statement No. 87* is the fact that **several significant items of the pension plan are unrecognized in the accounts and in the financial statements**. Among the compromises the FASB made in issuing *Statement No. 87* was the nonrecognition (noncapitalization) of the following pension items:

1. Projected benefit obligation.
2. Pension plan assets.
3. Unrecognized prior service costs.
4. Unrecognized net gain or loss.

As discussed later, the employer is required to **disclose in notes** to the financial statements all of these four noncapitalized items, but they are not recognized in the body of the financial statements. In addition, the exact amount of these items must be known at all times because they are used in the computation of annual pension expense. Therefore, **memo entries and accounts have to be maintained outside the formal general ledger accounting system in order to track these off-balance-sheet pension items**. A work sheet unique to pension accounting will be utilized to record both the formal entries and the memo entries to keep track of all the employer's relevant pension plan items and components.[12]

OBJECTIVE 5
Utilize a work sheet for employer's pension plan entries.

The format of the **pension work sheet** is shown below.

ILLUSTRATION 20-6
Basic Format of Pension Work Sheet

Pension Work Sheet

	General Journal Entries			Memo Record	
Items	Annual Pension Expense	Cash	Prepaid/ Accrued Cost	Projected Benefit Obligation	Plan Assets

The left-hand "General Journal Entries" columns of the work sheet record entries in the formal general ledger accounts. The right-hand "Memo Record" columns maintain balances on the unrecognized (noncapitalized) pension items. On the first line of the work sheet, the beginning balances (if any) are recorded. Subsequently, transactions and events related to the pension plan are recorded, using debits and credits and using both sets of records as if they were one for recording the entries. For each transaction or event, the debits must equal the credits. The balance in the Prepaid/Accrued Cost column should equal the net balance in the memo record.

---

[11]At this point, we are using the actual rate of return. As shown later, for purposes of computing pension expense, the expected rate of return is used.

[12]The use of this pension entry work sheet is recommended and illustrated by Paul B. W. Miller, "The New Pension Accounting (Part 2)," *Journal of Accountancy* (February 1987), pp. 86–94.

2003 Entries and Work Sheet

To illustrate the use of a work sheet and how it helps in accounting for a pension plan, assume that on January 1, 2003, Zarle Company adopts *FASB Statement No. 87* to account for its defined benefit pension plan. The following facts apply to the pension plan for the year 2003.

Plan assets, January 1, 2003, are $100,000.

Projected benefit obligation, January 1, 2003, is $100,000.

Annual service cost is $9,000.

Settlement rate is 10 percent.

Actual return on plan assets is $10,000.

Contributions (funding) are $8,000.

Benefits paid to retirees during the year are $7,000.

Using the data presented above, the work sheet in Illustration 20-7 presents the beginning balances and all of the pension entries recorded by Zarle Company in 2003. The beginning balances for the projected benefit obligation and the pension plan assets are recorded on the first line of the work sheet in the memo record. They are not recorded in the formal general journal and, therefore, are not reported as a liability and an asset in the financial statements of Zarle Company. These two significant pension items are off-balance-sheet amounts that affect pension expense but are not recorded as assets and liabilities in the employer's books.

ILLUSTRATION 20-7
Pension Work Sheet—2003

	General Journal Entries			Memo Record	
Items	Annual Pension Expense	Cash	Prepaid/Accrued Cost	Projected Benefit Obligation	Plan Assets
Balance, Jan. 1, 2003			—	100,000 Cr.	100,000 Dr.
(a) Service cost	9,000 Dr.			9,000 Cr.	
(b) Interest cost	10,000 Dr.			10,000 Cr.	
(c) Actual return	10,000 Cr.				10,000 Dr.
(d) Contributions		8,000 Cr.			8,000 Dr.
(e) Benefits				7,000 Dr.	7,000 Cr.
Journal entry for 2003	9,000 Dr.	8,000 Cr.	1,000 Cr.*		
Balance, Dec. 31, 2003			1,000 Cr.**	112,000 Cr.	111,000 Dr.

*$9,000 − $8,000 = $1,000.
**$112,000 − $111,000 = $1,000.

Entry (a) records the service cost component, which increases pension expense $9,000 and increases the liability (projected benefit obligation) $9,000. Entry (b) accrues the interest expense component, which increases both the liability and the pension expense by $10,000 (the beginning projected benefit obligation multiplied by the settlement rate of 10%). Entry (c) records the actual return on the plan assets, which increases the plan assets and decreases the pension expense. Entry (d) records Zarle Company's contribution (funding) of assets to the pension fund; cash is decreased $8,000 and plan assets are increased $8,000. Entry (e) records the benefit payments made to retirees, which results in equal $7,000 decreases to the plan assets and the projected benefit obligation.

The "formal journal entry" on December 31, which is the entry made to formally record the pension expense in 2003, is as follows.

2003		
Pension Expense	9,000	
Cash		8,000
Prepaid/Accrued Pension Cost		1,000

The credit to Prepaid/Accrued Pension Cost for $1,000 represents the difference between the 2003 pension expense of $9,000 and the amount funded of $8,000. Prepaid/Accrued Pension Cost (credit) is a liability because the plan is underfunded by $1,000. The Prepaid/Accrued Pension Cost account balance of $1,000 also equals the net of the balances in the memo accounts. This reconciliation of the off-balance-sheet items with the prepaid/accrued pension cost reported in the balance sheet is shown in Illustration 20-8.

Projected benefit obligation (Credit)	$(112,000)
Plan assets at fair value (Debit)	111,000
Prepaid/accrued pension cost (Credit)	(1,000)

ILLUSTRATION 20-8
Pension Reconciliation Schedule—December 31, 2003

If the net of the memo record balances is a credit, the reconciling amount in the prepaid/accrued cost column will be a credit equal in amount. If the net of the memo record balances is a debit, the prepaid/accrued cost amount will be a debit equal in amount. The work sheet is designed to produce this reconciling feature, which will be useful later in the preparation of the required notes related to pension disclosures.

In this illustration, the debit to Pension Expense exceeds the credit to Cash, resulting in a credit to Prepaid/Accrued Pension Cost—the recognition of a liability. If the credit to Cash exceeded the debit to Pension Expense, Prepaid/Accrued Pension Cost would be debited—the recognition of an asset.

Amortization of Unrecognized Prior Service Cost (PSC)

OBJECTIVE 6
Describe the amortization of unrecognized prior service costs.

When a defined benefit plan is either initiated (adopted) or amended, credit is often given to employees for years of service provided before the date of initiation or amendment. As a result of prior service credits, the projected benefit obligation is usually greater than it was before. In many cases, the increase in the projected benefit obligation is substantial. One question that arises is whether an expense and related liability for these **prior service costs (PSC)** should be fully reported at the time a plan is initiated or amended. The FASB has taken the position that no expense for these costs and in some cases no liability should be recognized at the time of the plan's adoption or amendment. The Board's rationale is that the employer would not provide credit for past years of service unless it expected to receive benefits in the future. As a result, **the retroactive benefits should not be recognized as pension expense entirely in the year of amendment but should be recognized during the service periods of those employees who are expected to receive benefits under the plan (the remaining service life of the covered active employees).**

The cost of the retroactive benefits (including benefits that are granted to existing retirees) is the increase in the projected benefit obligation at the date of the amendment. The amount of the prior service cost is computed by an actuary. Amortization of the unrecognized prior service cost is an accounting function performed with the assistance of an actuary.

INTERNATIONAL INSIGHT

In the U.S., prior service cost is generally amortized over the average remaining service life of employees. In Germany, prior service cost is recognized immediately. In the Netherlands, prior service cost may either be recognized immediately or directly charged to shareholders' equity.

The Board prefers a **years-of-service** amortization method that is similar to a units-of-production computation. First, the total number of service-years to be worked by all of the participating employees is computed. Second, the unrecognized prior service cost is divided by the total number of service-years, to obtain a cost per service-year (the unit cost). Third, the number of service-years consumed each year is multiplied by the cost per service-year, to obtain the annual amortization charge.

To illustrate the amortization of the unrecognized prior service cost under the years-of-service method, assume that Zarle Company's defined benefit pension plan covers 170 employees. In its negotiations with its employees, Zarle Company amends its pension plan on January 1, 2004, and grants $80,000 of prior service costs to its employees. The employees are grouped according to expected years of retirement, as shown on page 1030.

Group	Number of Employees	Expected Retirement on Dec. 31
A	40	2004
B	20	2005
C	40	2006
D	50	2007
E	20	2008
	170	

The computation of the service-years per year and the total service-years is shown in Illustration 20-9.

ILLUSTRATION 20-9
Computation of Service-Years

	Service-Years					
Year	A	B	C	D	E	Total
2004	40	20	40	50	20	170
2005		20	40	50	20	130
2006			40	50	20	110
2007				50	20	70
2008					20	20
	40	40	120	200	100	500

Computed on the basis of a prior service cost of $80,000 and a total of 500 service-years for all years, the cost per service-year is $160 ($80,000 ÷ 500). The annual amount of amortization based on a $160 cost per service-year is computed as follows.

ILLUSTRATION 20-10
Computation of Annual Prior Service Cost Amortization

Year	Total Service-Years	×	Cost per Service-Year	=	Annual Amortization
2004	170		$160		$27,200
2005	130		160		20,800
2006	110		160		17,600
2007	70		160		11,200
2008	20		160		3,200
	500				$80,000

FASB Statement No. 87 allows an alternative method of computing amortization of unrecognized prior service cost: **Employers may use straight-line amortization over the average remaining service life of the employees.** In this case, with 500 service years and 170 employees, the average would be 2.94 years (500 ÷ 170). Using this method, the $80,000 cost would be charged to expense at $27,211 ($80,000 ÷ 2.94) in 2004, $27,211 in 2005, and $25,578 ($27,211 × .94) in 2006.

If the Board had adopted full capitalization of all elements of the pension plan, the prior service cost would have been capitalized as an intangible asset—pension goodwill—and amortized over its useful life. The intangible asset (goodwill) comes from the assumption that the cost of additional pension benefits increases loyalty and productivity (and reduces turnover) among the affected employees. However, prior service cost is accounted for off-balance-sheet and is called **unrecognized prior service cost**. Although not recognized on the balance sheet, prior service cost is a factor in computing pension expense.

2004 Entries and Work Sheet

Continuing the Zarle Company illustration into 2004, we note that a January 1, 2004, amendment to the pension plan grants to employees prior service benefits having a present value of $80,000. The annual amortization amounts, as computed in the previous section using the years-of-service approach ($27,200 for 2004), are employed in this illustration. The following facts apply to the pension plan for the year 2004.

On January 1, 2004, Zarle Company grants prior service benefits having a present value of $80,000.

Annual service cost is $9,500.

Settlement rate is 10 percent.

Actual return on plan assets is $11,100.

Annual contributions (funding) are $20,000.

Benefits paid to retirees during the year are $8,000.

Amortization of prior service cost (PSC) using the years-of-service method is $27,200.

The following work sheet presents all of the pension entries and information recorded by Zarle Company in 2004.

ILLUSTRATION 20-11
Pension Work Sheet—2004

	General Journal Entries			Memo Record		
Items	Annual Pension Expense	Cash	Prepaid/ Accrued Cost	Projected Benefit Obligation	Plan Assets	Unrecognized Prior Service Cost
Balance, Dec. 31, 2003			1,000 Cr.	112,000 Cr.	111,000 Dr.	
(f) Prior service cost				80,000 Cr.		80,000 Dr.
Balance, Jan. 1, 2004			1,000 Cr.	192,000 Cr.	111,000 Dr.	80,000 Dr.
(g) Service cost	9,500 Dr.			9,500 Cr.		
(h) Interest cost	19,200 Dr.[a]			19,200 Cr.		
(i) Actual return	11,100 Cr.				11,100 Dr.	
(j) Amortization of PSC	27,200 Dr.					27,200 Cr.
(k) Contributions		20,000 Cr.			20,000 Dr.	
(l) Benefits				8,000 Dr.	8,000 Cr.	
Journal entry for 2004	44,800 Dr.	20,000 Cr.	24,800 Cr.			
Balance, Dec. 31, 2004			25,800 Cr.	212,700 Cr.	134,100 Dr.	52,800 Dr.

[a]$19,200 = $192,000 × 10%.

The first line of the work sheet shows the beginning balances of the Prepaid/Accrued Pension Cost account and the memo accounts. Entry (f) records Zarle Company's granting of prior service cost by adding $80,000 to the projected benefit obligation and to the unrecognized (noncapitalized) prior service cost. Entries (g), (h), (i), (k), and (l) are similar to the corresponding entries in 2003. Entry (j) records the 2004 amortization of unrecognized prior service cost by debiting Pension Expense by $27,200 and crediting the new Unrecognized Prior Service Cost account by the same amount.

The journal entry on December 31 to formally record the pension expense—the sum of the annual pension expense column—for 2004 is as follows.

2004		
Pension Expense	44,800	
Cash		20,000
Prepaid/Accrued Pension Cost		24,800

Because the expense exceeds the funding, the Prepaid/Accrued Pension Cost account is credited for the $24,800 difference and is a liability. In 2004, as in 2003, the balance of the Prepaid/Accrued Pension Cost account ($25,800) is equal to the net of the balances in the memo accounts as shown in Illustration 20-12.

ILLUSTRATION 20-12
Pension Reconciliation Schedule—December 31, 2004

Projected benefit obligation (Credit)	$(212,700)
Plan assets at fair value (Debit)	134,100
Funded status	(78,600)
Unrecognized prior service cost (Debit)	52,800
Prepaid/accrued pension cost (Credit)	$ (25,800)

The reconciliation is the formula that makes the work sheet work. It relates the components of pension accounting, recorded and unrecorded, to one another.

Gain or Loss

OBJECTIVE 7
Explain the accounting procedure for recognizing unexpected gains and losses.

Of great concern to companies that have pension plans are the uncontrollable and unexpected swings in pension expense that could be caused by (1) sudden and large changes in the market value of plan assets and (2) changes in actuarial assumptions that affect the amount of the projected benefit obligation. If these gains or losses were to impact fully the financial statements in the period of realization or incurrence, substantial fluctuations in pension expense would result. Therefore, the FASB decided to reduce the volatility associated with pension expense by using **smoothing techniques** that dampen and in some cases fully eliminate the fluctuations.

Smoothing Unexpected Gains and Losses on Plan Assets

One component of pension expense—actual return on plan assets—reduces pension expense (assuming the actual return is positive). A large change in the actual return can substantially affect pension expense for a given year. Assume a company has a 40 percent return in the stock market for the year. Should this substantial, and perhaps one-time, event affect current pension expense?

Actuaries ignore current fluctuations when they develop a funding pattern to pay expected benefits in the future. They develop an **expected rate of return** and multiply it by an asset value weighted over a reasonable period of time to arrive at an **expected return on plan assets**. This return is then used to determine its funding pattern.

The FASB adopted the actuary's approach to dampen wide swings that might occur in the actual return. That is, the expected return on the plan assets is to be included as a component of pension expense, not the actual return in a given year. To achieve this goal, the expected rate of return (the actuary's rate) is multiplied by the fair value of the plan assets or a market-related asset value of the plan assets. (Throughout our Zarle Company illustrations, market-related value and fair value of plan assets are assumed equal.) The **market-related asset value is a calculated value that recognizes changes in fair value in a systematic and rational manner over not more than 5 years.**[13]

What happens to the difference between the expected return and the actual return, often referred to as the **unexpected gain or loss**—also called **asset gains and losses** by the FASB? Asset gains (occurring when actual return is greater than expected return)

[13]Different ways of calculating market-related value may be used for different classes of assets. (For example, an employer might use fair value for bonds and a 5-year-moving-average for equities.) But the manner of determining market-related value should be applied consistently from year to year for each asset class.

and asset losses (occurring when actual return is less than expected return) are recorded in an Unrecognized Net Gain or Loss account and combined with unrecognized gains and losses accumulated in prior years.

To illustrate the computation of an unexpected asset gain or loss and its related accounting, assume that Shierer Company in 2005 has an actual return on plan assets of $16,000 when the expected return is $13,410 (the expected rate of return of 10% times the beginning-of-the-year plan assets). The unexpected asset gain of $2,590 ($16,000 − $13,410) is credited to Unrecognized Net Gain or Loss and debited to Pension Expense.

PENSION COSTS UPS AND DOWNS

WHAT DO THE NUMBERS MEAN?

For some companies, having a pension plan had become a real profit generator in the late 1990s. The income generated in those plans was so strong that the plans not only paid for themselves but also increased earnings. This happens when the expected returns on pension assets are greater than the company's annual costs. At **Norfolk Southern**, pension income amounted to 12 percent of operating profit, and it tallied 11 percent of such profit at **Lucent Technologies**, **Coastal Corp.**, and **Unisys Corp.** The issue is important because in these cases management is not driving the operating income—pension income is. And as a result, income can change quickly.

Unfortunately, the stock market has stopped booming, and now pension expense for many companies has increased substantially. The reason: Expected return on a smaller asset base no longer is sufficient to offset pension service costs and interest on the projected benefit obligation. As a result, many companies are finding it difficult to meet their estimated earnings numbers.

Smoothing Unexpected Gains and Losses on the Pension Liability

In estimating the projected benefit obligation (the liability), actuaries make assumptions about such items as mortality rate, retirement rate, turnover rate, disability rate, and salary amounts. Any change in these actuarial assumptions changes the amount of the projected benefit obligation. Seldom does actual experience coincide exactly with the actuarial predictions. These unexpected gains or losses from changes in the projected benefit obligation are called **liability gains and losses**.

Liability gains (resulting from unexpected decreases in the liability balance) and liability losses (resulting from unexpected increases) are deferred (unrecognized). The liability gains and losses are combined in the same Unrecognized Net Gain or Loss account used for asset gains and losses. They are accumulated from year to year, off-balance-sheet, in a memo record account.

Corridor Amortization

OBJECTIVE 8
Explain the corridor approach to amortizing unrecognized gains and losses.

Because the asset gains and losses and the liability gains and losses can be offsetting, the accumulated total unrecognized net gain or loss may not grow very large. But, it is possible that no offsetting will occur and that the balance in the Unrecognized Net Gain or Loss account will continue to grow. To limit its growth, the FASB invented the **corridor approach** for amortizing the accumulated balance in the Unrecognized Gain or Loss account when it gets too large. **The unrecognized net gain or loss balance is considered too large and must be amortized when it exceeds the arbitrarily selected FASB criterion of 10 percent of the larger of the beginning balances of the projected benefit obligation or the market-related value of the plan assets.**

To illustrate the corridor approach, assume data on the projected benefit obligation and the plan assets over a period of 6 years as shown in Illustration 20-13.

ILLUSTRATION 20-13
Computation of the Corridor

Beginning-of-the-Year Balances	Projected Benefit Obligation	Market-Related Asset Value	Corridor* +/− 10%
2002	$1,000,000	$ 900,000	$100,000
2003	1,200,000	1,100,000	120,000
2004	1,300,000	1,700,000	170,000
2005	1,500,000	2,250,000	225,000
2006	1,700,000	1,750,000	175,000
2007	1,800,000	1,700,000	180,000

*The corridor becomes 10% of the larger (in colored type) of the projected benefit obligation or the market-related plan asset value.

How the corridor works becomes apparent when the data above are portrayed graphically as in the diagram in Illustration 20-14.

ILLUSTRATION 20-14
Graphic Illustration of the Corridor

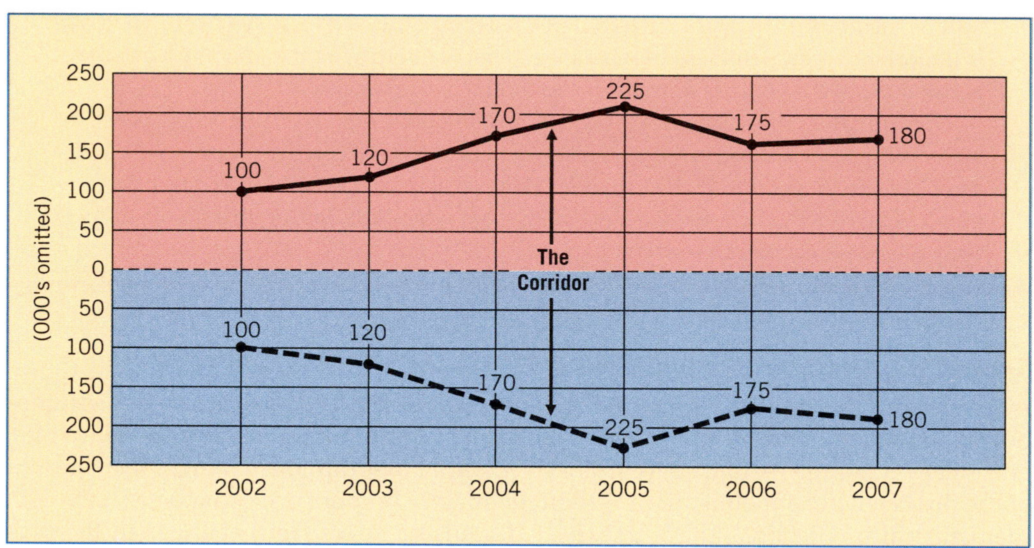

If the balance of the Unrecognized Net Gain or Loss account stays within the upper and lower limits of the corridor, no amortization is required—the unrecognized net gain or loss balance is carried forward unchanged.

If amortization is required, the minimum amortization shall be the excess divided by the average remaining service period of active employees expected to receive benefits under the plan. Any systematic method of amortization of unrecognized gains and losses may be used in lieu of the minimum, provided it is greater than the minimum, is used consistently for both gains and losses, and is disclosed.

Illustration of Unrecognized Gains/Losses

In applying the corridor, the Board decided that amortization of the excess unrecognized net gain or loss should be included as a component of pension expense only if, at the **beginning of the year**, the unrecognized net gain or loss exceeded the corridor. That is, if no unrecognized net gain or loss exists at the beginning of the period, no recognition of gains or losses can result in that period.

To illustrate the amortization of unrecognized net gains and losses, assume the following information for Soft-White, Inc.

	2003	2004	2005
	(beginning of the year)		
Projected benefit obligation	$2,100,000	$2,600,000	$2,900,000
Market-related asset value	2,600,000	2,800,000	2,700,000
Unrecognized net loss	–0–	400,000	300,000

If the average remaining service life of all active employees is 5.5 years, the schedule to amortize the unrecognized net loss is as follows.

ILLUSTRATION 20-15
Corridor Test and Gain/Loss Amortization Schedule

Year	Projected Benefit Obligation[a]	Plan Assets[a]	Corridor[b]	Cumulative Unrecognized Net Loss[a]	Minimum Amortization of Loss (For Current Year)
2003	$2,100,000	$2,600,000	$260,000	$ –0–	$ –0–
2004	2,600,000	2,800,000	280,000	400,000	21,818[c]
2005	2,900,000	2,700,000	290,000	678,182[d]	70,579[d]

[a]All as of the beginning of the period.
[b]10% of the greater of projected benefit obligation or plan assets market-related value.
[c]$400,000 − $280,000 = $120,000; $120,000 ÷ 5.5 = $21,818
[d]$400,000 − $21,818 + $300,000 = $678,182; $678,182 − $290,000 = $388,182; $388,182 ÷ 5.5 = $70,579.

As indicated from Illustration 20-15, the loss recognized in 2004 increased pension expense by $21,818. This amount is small in comparison with the total loss of $400,000. It indicates that the corridor approach dampens the effects (reduces volatility) of these gains and losses on pension expense. The rationale for the corridor is that gains and losses result from refinements in estimates as well as real changes in economic value and that over time some of these gains and losses will offset one another. It therefore seems reasonable that gains and losses should not be recognized fully as a component of pension expense in the period in which they arise.

However, gains and losses that arise from a single occurrence not directly related to the operation of the pension plan and not in the ordinary course of the employer's business should be recognized immediately. For example, a gain or loss that is directly related to a plant closing, a disposal of a component, or a similar event that greatly affects the size of the employee work force, shall be recognized as a part of the gain or loss associated with that event.

At one time, **Bethlehem Steel** reported a third-quarter loss of $477 million. A great deal of this loss was attributable to future estimated benefits payable to workers who were permanently laid off. In this situation, the loss should be treated as an adjustment to the gain or loss on the plant closing and should not affect pension cost for the current or future periods.

Summary of Calculations for Asset Gain or Loss

The difference between the actual return on plan assets and the expected return on plan assets is the unexpected (deferred) asset gain or loss component. This component defers the difference between the actual return and expected return on plan assets in computing current year pension expense. Thus, after considering this component, **it is really the expected return on plan assets (not the actual return) that determines current pension expense.**

The amortized net gain or loss is determined by amortizing the unrecognized gain or loss at the beginning of the year subject to the corridor limitation. In other words, **if the unrecognized gain or loss is greater than the corridor, these net gains and losses are subject to amortization.** This minimum amortization is computed by dividing the net gains or losses subject to amortization by the average remaining service period. When the unexpected gain or loss is combined with the amortization of prior years' actuarial gains and losses, the net amortized and unexpected gains and losses is determined (often referred to simply as gain or loss). This summary is illustrated graphically below.

ILLUSTRATION 20-16
Graphic Summary of Gain or Loss Computation

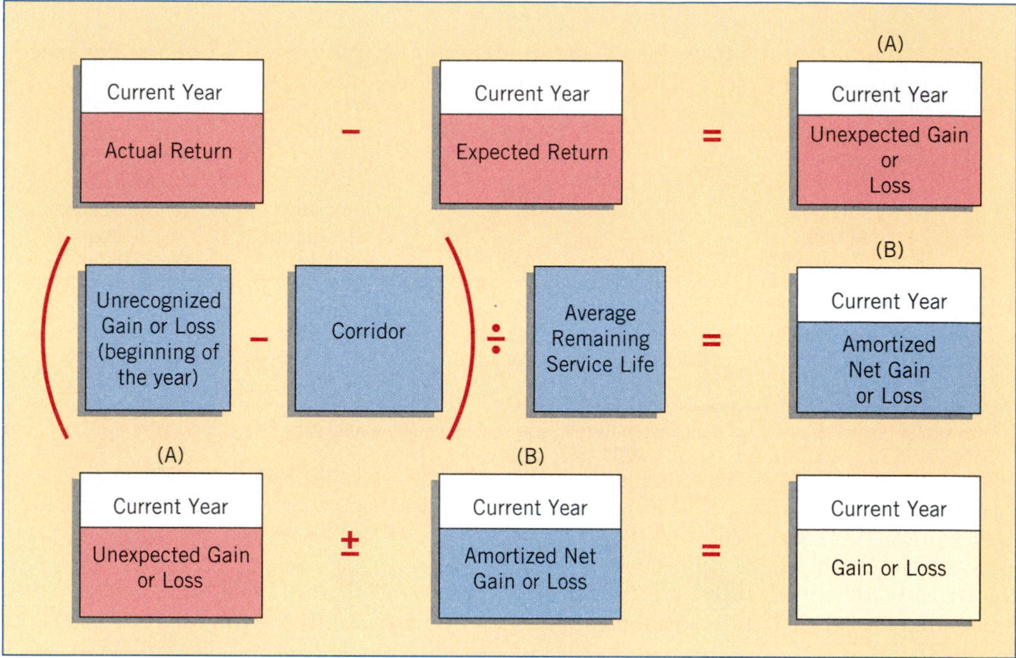

In essence, these gains and losses are subject to triple smoothing. That is, the asset gain or loss is smoothed by using the expected return. Then the unrecognized gain or loss at the beginning of the year is not amortized unless it is greater than the corridor. Finally, the excess is spread over the remaining service life of existing employees.

2005 Entries and Work Sheet

Continuing the Zarle Company illustration, the following facts apply to the pension plan for 2005.

Annual service cost is $13,000.

Settlement rate is 10 percent; expected earnings rate is 10 percent.

Actual return on plan assets is $12,000.

Amortization of prior service cost (PSC) is $20,800.

Annual contributions (funding) are $24,000.

Benefits paid to retirees during the year are $10,500.

Changes in actuarial assumptions establish the end-of-year projected benefit obligation at $265,000.

The work sheet shown in Illustration 20-17 presents all of the pension entries and information recorded by Zarle Company in 2005. On the first line of the work sheet are recorded the beginning balances that relate to the pension plan. In this case, the beginning balances for Zarle Company are the ending balances from the 2004 Zarle Company pension work sheet in Illustration 20-11.

	General Journal Entries			Memo Record			
Items	Annual Pension Expense	Cash	Prepaid/ Accrued Cost	Projected Benefit Obligation	Plan Assets	Unrecognized Prior Service Cost	Unrecognized Net Gain or Loss
Bal., December 31, 2004			25,800 Cr.	212,700 Cr.	134,100 Dr.	52,800 Dr.	
(m) Service cost	13,000 Dr.			13,000 Cr.			
(n) Interest cost	21,270 Dr.			21,270 Cr.			
(o) Actual return	12,000 Cr.				12,000 Dr.		
(p) Unexpected loss	1,410 Cr.						1,410 Dr.
(q) Amortization of PSC	20,800 Dr.					20,800 Cr.	
(r) Contributions		24,000 Cr.			24,000 Dr.		
(s) Benefits				10,500 Dr.	10,500 Cr.		
(t) Liability increase				28,530 Cr.			28,530 Dr.
Journal entry for 2005	41,660 Dr.	24,000 Cr.	17,660 Cr.				
Bal., December 31, 2005			43,460 Cr.	265,000 Cr.	159,600 Dr.	32,000 Dr.	29,940 Dr.

ILLUSTRATION 20-17
Pension Work Sheet—2005

Entries (m), (n), (o), (q), (r), and (s) are similar to the corresponding entries previously explained in 2003 or 2004. Entries (o) and (p) are related. Recording the actual return in entry (o) has been illustrated in both 2003 and 2004; it is recorded similarly in 2005. In both 2003 and 2004 it was assumed that the actual return on plan assets was equal to the expected return on plan assets. In 2005, the expected return of $13,410 (the expected rate of return of 10 percent times the beginning-of-the-year plan assets balance of $134,100) is higher than the actual return of $12,000. To smooth pension expense, the unexpected loss of $1,410 ($13,410 − $12,000) is deferred by debiting the Unrecognized Net Gain or Loss account and crediting Pension Expense. **As a result of this adjustment, the expected return on the plan assets is the amount actually used to compute pension expense.**

Entry (t) records the change in the projected benefit obligation resulting from a change in actuarial assumptions. As indicated, the actuary has now computed the ending balance to be $265,000. Given that the memo record balance at December 31 is $236,470 ($212,700 + $13,000 + $21,270 − $10,500), a difference of $28,530 ($265,000 − $236,470) is indicated. This $28,530 increase in the employer's liability is an unexpected loss that is deferred by debiting it to the Unrecognized Net Gain or Loss account.

The journal entry on December 31 to formally record pension expense for 2005 is as follows.

2005		
Pension Expense	41,660	
Cash		24,000
Prepaid/Accrued Pension Cost		17,660

As illustrated in the work sheets of 2003 and 2004, the balance of the Prepaid/Accrued Pension Cost account at December 31, 2005, of $43,460 is equal to the net of the balances in the memo accounts as shown below.

Projected benefit obligation (Credit)	$(265,000)
Plan assets at fair value (Debit)	159,600
Funded status	(105,400)
Unrecognized prior service cost (Debit)	32,000
Unrecognized net loss (Debit)	29,940
Prepaid/accrued pension cost (Credit)	$ (43,460)

ILLUSTRATION 20-18
Pension Reconciliation Schedule—December 31, 2005

MINIMUM LIABILITY

OBJECTIVE 9
Explain the recognition of a minimum liability.

If the FASB had decided to capitalize pension plan assets and liabilities, Zarle Company in our previous illustration would have reported on December 31, 2005, a liability of $265,000, plan assets of $159,600, and unrecognized prior service cost (goodwill) of $32,000 plus an unrecognized net loss of $29,940. Instead it reports only accrued pension cost of $43,460 as a liability. The Board was well aware of this discrepancy. It believed that an employer with a projected benefit obligation in excess of the fair value of pension plan assets has a liability and that an employer with a fair value of plan assets in excess of projected benefit obligation has an asset. However, when the Board was faced with the final decision on this matter, it decided that to require the reporting of these amounts in the financial statements would be too great a change in practice, because up to then none of these amounts had been reported in the balance sheet.

UNDERLYING CONCEPTS

Recognizing the smaller benefit obligation ignores the going concern concept. A going concern would not expect to settle the obligation today at current salaries and wages. A going concern would expect to settle the obligation based upon future salary levels.

The Board, therefore, developed a compromise approach that requires immediate recognition of a liability—referred to as the minimum liability—when the accumulated benefit obligation exceeds the fair value of plan assets. The purpose of this minimum liability requirement is to assure that if a significant plan amendment or actuarial loss occurs, a liability will be recognized at least to the extent of the unfunded portion of the accumulated benefit obligation.

Note that the plan assets are compared to the smaller **accumulated** benefit obligation instead of the larger projected benefit obligation. The rationale for using the accumulated benefit obligation is that if the liability were settled today, it would be settled on the basis of current salary rates, not future salary rates. Therefore, it is argued that the accumulated benefit obligation should be used, not the projected benefit obligation. Although the compromise approach frequently ignores a portion of the liability, it does help to report some balance sheet effects when a plan amendment or a large loss occurs. **The Board does not permit the recording of an additional asset if the fair value of the pension plan exceeds the accumulated benefit obligation.**

Minimum Liability Computation

INTERNATIONAL INSIGHT

Only the U.S. requires companies to revalue their pension plan obligations each year. Other nations tend to require revaluation at approximately 3-year intervals.

If a liability for accrued pension cost is already reported, only an additional liability to equal the required minimum liability (unfunded accumulated benefit) is recorded. To illustrate, assume that Largent Inc. amends its pension plan on December 31, 2003, giving retroactive benefits to its employees, as follows.

Projected benefit obligation	$8,000,000
Accumulated benefit obligation	7,000,000
Plan assets (at fair value)	5,000,000
Market-related asset value	4,900,000
Unrecognized prior service cost	2,500,000
Accrued pension cost	500,000

The unfunded accumulated benefit is computed as follows.

ILLUSTRATION 20-19
Computation of Unfunded Accumulated Benefit Obligation (Minimum Liability)

Accumulated benefit obligation	$7,000,000
Plan assets (at fair value)	5,000,000
Unfunded accumulated benefit obligation (minimum liability)	$2,000,000

Note that the fair value of the plan assets is used, not the market-related asset value, to compute the unfunded accumulated benefit obligation. In this case, an additional $1,500,000 is required to be recorded as a liability and reported on the financial statements. The computation of the **additional liability** is shown in Illustration 20-20.

Unfunded accumulated benefit obligation (minimum liability)	$2,000,000
Accrued pension cost (balance at December 31, 2003)	500,000
Additional liability required	$1,500,000

ILLUSTRATION 20-20
Computation of Additional Liability Required—Accrued Pension Cost Balance

Largent Inc. would combine the **accrued pension cost** and the additional liability into one amount and report it in the balance sheet as accrued pension cost or pension liability in the amount of $2,000,000.

If Largent Inc. had a **prepaid pension cost** of $300,000 instead of an accrued pension cost of $500,000, an additional liability of $2,300,000 would be recorded as follows.

Unfunded accumulated benefit obligation (minimum liability)	$2,000,000
Prepaid pension cost	300,000
Additional liability required	$2,300,000

ILLUSTRATION 20-21
Computation of Additional Liability Required—Prepaid Pension Cost Balance

The existing balance in the prepaid pension cost (debit) is **combined** with the additional liability (credit) into one amount and reported as accrued pension cost or pension liability in the net amount of $2,000,000.

Financial Statement Presentation

When it is necessary to adjust the accounts to recognize a minimum liability, the debit should be to an intangible asset that is called Intangible Asset—Deferred Pension Cost. The entry to record the liability and related intangible asset for Largent Inc. (first case) is:

Intangible Asset—Deferred Pension Cost	1,500,000	
Additional Pension Liability		1,500,000

INTERNATIONAL INSIGHT

IASB standards do not account for a minimum liability.

One exception to the general rule of reporting an intangible asset is when the **additional liability exceeds the amount of unrecognized prior service cost**. In this case, the excess is debited to Excess of Additional Pension Liability Over Unrecognized Prior Service Cost. When the additional liability exceeds the unrecognized prior service cost, the excess must have resulted from an actuarial loss, such as an increase in the benefit obligation due to an increase in retiree longevity. The justification for recognizing an intangible asset up to the amount of the unrecognized prior service cost is that an amendment to an existing plan increases goodwill with employees and therefore benefits the company in the future. Such is not the case when the additional liability exceeds the unrecognized prior service cost.

When this excess develops, it should be reported as a reduction of other comprehensive income. In addition, its cumulative balance is reported as a component of accumulated other comprehensive income on the balance sheet. Because the excess of additional pension liability over unrecognized prior service cost reduces stockholders' equity, it is often referred to as a contra equity account. To illustrate, assume that Largent Inc. has common stock, with a total par value of $1,000,000, additional paid-in capital of $400,000, and retained earnings of $700,000. In addition, it has an additional liability that exceeds the unrecognized prior service cost by $200,000. A condensed version of Largent's stockholders' equity section is provided in Illustration 20-22.[14]

[14]This treatment is similar to the reporting of the unrealized holding loss on available-for-sale securities discussed in earlier chapters. Note that the components of accumulated other comprehensive income must be shown in the stockholders' equity section of the balance sheet, or in the notes, or in the statement of stockholders' equity.

ILLUSTRATION 20-22
Balance Sheet Presentation of Excess of Additional Pension Liability

Stockholders' Equity Section	
Common stock	$1,000,000
Additional paid-in capital	400,000
Total paid-in capital	1,400,000
Retained earnings	700,000
Accumulated other comprehensive income	(200,000)
Total stockholders' equity	$1,900,000

The amount of the additional liability required should be evaluated each reporting period along with the related intangible asset or contra equity account. At each reporting date, these items may be increased, decreased, or totally eliminated. Neither the intangible asset nor the contra equity account is amortized from period to period; the balances are merely adjusted up or down.

The minimum liability approach for the Zarle Company pension plan for all three years 2003, 2004, and 2005 is illustrated in the following schedule (values are assumed for the accumulated benefit obligation).

ILLUSTRATION 20-23
Minimum Liability Computations

	December 31		
	2003	2004	2005
Accumulated benefit obligation	$(80,000)	$(164,000)	$(240,600)
Plan assets at fair value	111,000	134,100	159,600
Unfunded accumulated benefit obligation (minimum liability)	$ –0–	(29,900)	(81,000)
Accrued pension cost	1,000	25,800	43,460
Additional liability	$ –0–	(4,100)	(37,540)
Unrecognized prior service cost*		52,800	32,000
Excess of additional pension liability over unrecognized prior service cost**		$ –0–	$ (5,540)

*Maximum intangible asset recognizable.
**Reported as contra equity.

In 2003, the fair value of the plan assets exceeds the accumulated benefit obligation. Therefore, no additional liability need be reported. **The Board does not permit the recognition of a net investment in the pension plan when the plan assets exceed the pension obligation.**

In 2004, the minimum liability amount ($29,900) exceeds the accrued pension cost liability already recorded ($25,800), so an additional liability of $4,100 ($29,900 − $25,800) is recorded as follows.

December 31, 2004		
Intangible Asset—Deferred Pension Cost	4,100	
Additional Pension Liability		4,100

In 2005, the minimum liability ($81,000) exceeds the accrued pension cost liability ($43,460), so an additional liability of $37,540 must be reported at the end of 2005. Since a balance of $4,100 already exists in the Additional Pension Liability account, it is credited for $33,440 ($37,540 − $4,100). Also, since the additional liability exceeds the unrecognized prior service cost by $5,540, the excess is debited to the contra equity account, Excess of Additional Pension Liability over Unrecognized Prior Service Cost. The remaining $27,900 ($33,440 − $5,540) is debited to the Intangible Asset—Deferred Pension Cost. The entry on December 31, 2005, to adjust the minimum liability is shown on the next page.

December 31, 2005

Intangible Asset—Deferred Pension Cost	27,900	
Excess of Additional Pension Liability over Unrecognized Prior Service Cost	5,540	
Additional Pension Liability		33,440

As the additional liability changes, the combined debit balance of the intangible asset and contra equity accounts fluctuates by the same amount.

Work Sheet Illustration

To illustrate how the pension work sheet is affected by the minimum liability computation, a revised version of the 2005 work sheet of Zarle Company is shown in Illustration 20-24. The boldface items [entry (u)] relate to adjustments caused by recognition of the minimum liability at the end of 2004 and 2005.

ILLUSTRATION 20-24
Revised Pension Work Sheet—2005, Revised to Include Minimum Liability Computation

	General Journal Entries					
Items	Annual Pension Expense	Cash	Prepaid/ Accrued Cost	Additional Liability	Pension Intangible	Contra Equity
Balance, Dec. 31, 2004			25,800 Cr.	4,100 Cr.	4,100 Dr.	
(m) Service cost	13,000 Dr.					
(n) Interest cost	21,270 Dr.					
(o) Actual return	12,000 Cr.					
(p) Unexpected loss	1,410 Cr.					
(q) Amortization of PSC	20,800 Dr.					
(r) Contributions		24,000 Cr.				
(s) Benefits						
(t) Liability change (Incr.)						
(u) Minimum liab. adj.				33,440 Cr.	27,900 Dr.	5,540 Dr.
Journal entry for 2005	41,660 Dr.	24,000 Cr.	17,660 Cr.			
Balance, Dec. 31, 2005			43,460 Cr.	37,540 Cr.	32,000 Dr.	5,540 Dr.

	Memo Record			
Items	Projected Benefit Obligation	Plan Assets	Unrecognized Prior Service Cost	Unrecognized Net Gain or Loss
Balance, Dec. 31, 2004	212,700 Cr.	134,100 Dr.	52,800 Dr.	
(m) Service cost	13,000 Cr.			
(n) Interest cost	21,270 Cr.			
(o) Actual return		12,000 Dr.		
(p) Unexpected loss				1,410 Dr.
(q) Amortization of PSC			20,800 Cr.	
(r) Contributions		24,000 Dr.		
(s) Benefits	10,500 Dr.	10,500 Cr.		
(t) Liability increase	28,530 Cr.			28,530 Dr.
(u) Minimum liab. adj.				
Journal entry for 2005				
Balance, Dec. 31, 2005	265,000 Cr.	159,600 Dr.	32,000 Dr.	29,940 Dr.

As illustrated in prior work sheets, the balance in the Prepaid/Accrued Pension Cost account ($43,460) equals the net of the balances in the memo accounts ($265,000 − [$159,600 + $32,000 + $29,940]). In this case, the Additional Liability is combined with the Prepaid/Accrued Pension Cost to determine the minimum pension liability in the balance sheet. This computation is shown in Illustration 20-25.

ILLUSTRATION 20-25
Reconciliation Schedule—2005, Revised to Show Additional Pension Liability

Projected benefit obligation (Credit)	$(265,000)
Plan assets at fair value (Debit)	159,600
Funded status	(105,400)
Unrecognized prior service cost (Debit)	32,000
Unrecognized net loss (Debit)	29,940
Prepaid/accrued pension cost (Credit)	(43,460)
Additional liability (Credit)	(37,540)
Accrued pension cost liability recognized in the balance sheet (minimum liability)	$ (81,000)

REPORTING PENSION PLANS IN FINANCIAL STATEMENTS

OBJECTIVE 10
Describe the reporting requirements for pension plans in financial statements.

One might suspect that a phenomenon as significant and complex as pensions would involve extensive reporting and disclosure requirements. We will cover these requirements in two categories: (1) those within the financial statements, and (2) those within the notes to the financial statements.

Within the Financial Statements

If the amount funded (credit to Cash) by the employer to the pension trust is **less than the annual expense** (debit to Pension Expense), a credit balance accrual of the difference arises in the long-term liabilities section. It might be described as Accrued Pension Cost, Liability for Pension Expense Not Funded, or Pension Liability. A liability is classified as current when it requires the disbursement of cash within the next year.

If the amount funded to the pension trust during the period is **greater than the amount charged to expense**, an asset equal to the difference arises. This asset is reported as Prepaid Pension Cost, Deferred Pension Expense, or Prepaid Pension Expense in the current assets section if it is current in nature, and in the other assets section if it is long-term in nature.

If the **accumulated benefit obligation exceeds the fair value of pension plan assets**, an additional liability is recorded. The debit is either to an Intangible Asset—Deferred Pension Cost or to a contra account to stockholders' equity entitled Excess of Additional Pension Liability Over Unrecognized Prior Service Cost. If the debit is less than unrecognized prior service cost, it is reported as an intangible asset. If the debit is greater than unrecognized prior service cost, the excess debit is reported as part of other comprehensive income and the accumulated balance as a component of accumulated other comprehensive income.

Within the Notes to the Financial Statements

Pension plans are frequently important to an understanding of financial position, results of operations, and cash flows of a company. Therefore, the following information, if not disclosed in the body of the financial statements, should be disclosed in the notes.[15]

1. A schedule showing all the major components of pension expense should be reported.
   Rationale: Information provided about the components of pension expense helps users better understand how pension expense is determined and is useful in forecasting a company's net income.

[15]"Employers' Disclosure about Pensions and Other Postretirement Benefits," *Statement of Financial Accounting Standards No. 132* (Stamford, Conn.: FASB, 1998). This statement modifies the disclosure requirements of *SFAS No. 87*. In our view, these disclosure requirements are easier to understand and more streamlined than the disclosure requirements mandated prior to *SFAS No. 132*.

2. A **reconciliation** showing how the projected benefit obligation and the fair value of the plan assets changed from the beginning to the end of the period is required.
Rationale: Disclosing the projected benefit obligation, the fair value of the plan assets, and changes in them should help users understand the economics underlying the obligations and resources of these plans. The Board believes that explaining the changes in the projected benefit obligation and fair value of plan assets in the form of a reconciliation provides a more complete disclosure and makes the financial statements more understandable.

3. The **funded status** of the plan (difference between the projected benefit obligation and fair value of the plan assets) and the amounts recognized and not recognized in the financial statements must be disclosed.
Rationale: Providing a reconciliation of the plan's funded status to the amount reported in the balance sheet highlights the difference between the funded status and the balance sheet presentation.[16]

4. A disclosure of the rates used in measuring the benefit amounts (discount rate, expected return on plan assets, rate of compensation increases) should be disclosed.
Rationale: Disclosure of these rates permits the reader to determine the reasonableness of the assumptions applied in measuring the pension liability and pension expense.

In summary, the disclosure requirements are extensive, and purposely so. One factor that has been a challenge for useful pension reporting in the past has been the lack of consistency in terminology. Furthermore, a substantial amount of offsetting is inherent in the measurement of pension expense and the pension liability. These disclosures are designed to address these concerns and take some of the mystery out of pension reporting.

Illustration of Pension Note Disclosure

In the following sections we provide illustrations and explain the key pension disclosure elements.

Components of Pension Expense

The FASB requires disclosure of the individual pension expense components—(1) service cost, (2) interest cost, (3) expected return on assets, (4) other deferrals and amortization—so that more sophisticated readers can understand how pension expense is determined. Providing information on the components should also be useful in predicting future pension expense. Using the information from the Zarle Company illustration—specifically, the expense component information taken from the left-hand column of the work sheet in Illustration 20-24—an example of this part of the disclosure in presented in the following schedule.

ILLUSTRATION 20-26
Summary of Expense Components—2003, 2004, 2005

ZARLE COMPANY

	2003	2004	2005
Components of Net Periodic Pension Expense			
Service cost	$ 9,000	$ 9,500	$13,000
Interest cost	10,000	19,200	$21,270
Expected return on plan assets	(10,000)	(11,100)	(13,410)*
Amortization of prior service cost	–0–	27,200	20,800
Net periodic pension expense	$ 9,000	$44,800	$41,660

*Note that the expected return must be disclosed, not the actual. In 2005, the expected return is $13,410, which is the actual gain ($12,000) adjusted by the unrecognized loss ($1,410).

[16]The vested benefit obligation does not need to be disclosed, since it is not used in the accounting for the fund. If the accumulated benefit obligation is greater than the fair value of the plan assets, it must be disclosed, to inform readers how the minimum liability was computed.

Reconciliation and Funded Status of Plan

A reconciliation of the changes in the assets and liabilities from the beginning of the year to the end of the year is provided to enable statement readers to better understand the underlying economics of the plan. In essence, this disclosure (reconciliation) contains the information in the pension work sheet for the projected benefit obligation and plan asset columns.

UNDERLYING CONCEPTS

This represents another compromise between relevance and reliability. The disclosure of the unrecognized items attempts to balance these objectives.

In addition, the FASB also requires a disclosure of the funded status of the plan. That is, the off-balance-sheet assets, liabilities, and unrecognized gains and losses must be reconciled with the on-balance-sheet liability or asset. Many believe this is the key to understanding the accounting for pensions. Why is such a disclosure important? The FASB acknowledged that the delayed recognition of some pension elements may exclude the most current and the most relevant information about the pension plan from the financial statements. This important information, however, is provided within this disclosure.

Using the information for Zarle Company, the following schedule provides an example of the reconciliation.

ILLUSTRATION 20-27
Pension Disclosure for Zarle Company—2003, 2004, 2005

ZARLE COMPANY
PENSION DISCLOSURE

	2003	2004	2005
Change in benefit obligation			
Benefit obligation at beginning of year	$100,000	$112,000	$212,700
Service cost	9,000	9,500	13,000
Interest cost	10,000	19,200	21,270
Amendments (Prior service cost)	–0–	80,000	–0–
Actuarial loss	–0–	–0–	28,530
Benefits paid	(7,000)	(8,000)	(10,500)
Benefit obligation at end of year	112,000	212,700	265,000
Change in plan assets			
Fair value of plan assets at beginning of year	100,000	111,000	134,100
Actual return on plan assets	10,000	11,100	12,000
Contributions	8,000	20,000	24,000
Benefits paid	(7,000)	(8,000)	(10,500)
Fair value of plan assets at end of year	111,000	134,100	159,600
Funded status	(1,000)	(78,600)	(105,400)
Unrecognized net actuarial loss	–0–	–0–	29,940
Unrecognized prior service cost	–0–	52,800	32,000
Prepaid (accrued) benefit cost	**(1,000)**	**(25,800)**	**(43,460)**
Minimum liability adjustment included in:			
Intangible assets	–0–	(4,100)	(32,000)
Stockholders' equity	–0–	–0–	(5,540)
Accrued pension cost liability in the balance sheet	$ (1,000)	$ (29,900)	$ (81,000)

UNDERLYING CONCEPTS

Does it make a difference to users of financial statements whether pension information is recognized in the financial statements or disclosed only in the notes? The FASB was not sure, so in accord with the full disclosure principle, it decided to provide extensive pension plan disclosures.

The 2003 column reveals that the projected benefit obligation is underfunded by $1,000. The 2004 column reveals that the underfunded liability of $78,600 is reported in the balance sheet at $29,900, due to the unrecognized prior service cost of $52,800 and the $4,100 additional liability. Finally, the 2005 column indicates that underfunded liability of $105,400 is recognized in the balance sheet at only $81,000 because of $32,000 in unrecognized prior service costs, $29,940 of unrecognized net loss, and $37,540 additional liability (with $5,540 of the minimum liability recorded in stockholders' equity).

Illustration 20-28 provides the complete postretirement benefit disclosure for Gillette Company.[17] This disclosure shows how companies are providing information on the rates used in measuring the benefit amounts.

[17]Note that the Gillette disclosure combines the disclosures for pensions and other postretirement benefits in one disclosure. This is one way the new standard streamlined the reporting on benefit plans. The accounting for other postretirement benefits is discussed in Appendix 20A.

ILLUSTRATION 20-28
Gillette Company Pension Disclosure

Gillette Company

Pensions and Other Retiree Benefits. The Company has various retirement programs, including defined benefit, defined contribution, and other plans, that cover most employees worldwide. Other retiree benefits are health care and life insurance benefits provided to eligible retired employees, principally in the United States. The components of defined benefit expense for continuing operations follow.

	Pensions			Other Retiree Benefits		
Years ended December 31, (millions)	2001	2000	1999	2001	2000	1999
Components of net benefit expense:						
Service cost-benefits earned	$ 61	$ 64	$ 67	$ 6	$ 6	$ 6
Interest cost on benefit obligation	130	122	112	18	19	16
Estimated return on assets	(166)	(171)	(159)	(4)	(4)	(4)
Net amortization	9	5	13	(5)	(7)	(7)
Plan curtailments and other	—	(3)	(7)	—	—	—
	34	17	26	15	14	11
Other	12	9	9	–	—	—
Net defined benefit expense	$ 46	$ 26	$ 35	$15	$14	$11

The funded status of the Company's principal defined benefit and other retiree benefit plans and the amounts recognized in the balance sheet follow.

	Pension Benefits		Other Retiree Benefits	
Years ended December 31, (millions)	2001	2000	2001	2000
Change in benefit obligation:				
Balance at beginning of year	$1,961	$1,956	$ 259	$ 261
Benefit payments	(113)	(111)	(21)	(17)
Service and interest costs	191	185	24	24
Amendments	12	26	(14)	—
Actuarial (gains) losses	(57)	78	135	(7)
Plan curtailments	(3)	(33)	—	—
Divestitures	—	(71)	—	—
Currency translation adjustment	(41)	(69)	(3)	(2)
Balance at end of year	$1,950	$1,961	$ 380	$ 259
Change in fair value of plan assets:				
Balance at beginning of year	$1,878	$2,052	$ 40	$ 41
Actual return on plan assets	(168)	42	(2)	(1)
Employer contribution	35	31	—	—
Benefit payments	(92)	(91)	—	—
Divestitures	—	(87)	—	—
Currency translation adjustment	(35)	(69)	—	—
Balance at end of year	$1,618	$1,878	$ 38	$ 40
Benefit obligations in excess of plan assets	$ (332)	$ (83)	$(342)	$(219)
Unrecognized prior service cost and transition obligation	41	44	2	18
Unrecognized net loss (gain)	399	128	57	(90)
Minimum liability adjustment included in:				
Intangible assets	(12)	(6)	—	—
Stockholders' equity	(87)	(34)	—	—
Net prepaid (accrued) benefit cost	$ 9	$ 49	$(283)	$(291)

Additional Postretirement Benefit Disclosures

The values for pension plans with accumulated benefit obligations in excess of plan assets follow.

At December 31, (millions)	2001	2000
Projected benefit obligation	$550	$513
Accumulated benefit obligation	490	445
Fair value of plan assets	276	277

The weighted average assumptions used in determining related obligations of pension benefit plans are shown below.

At December 31, (percent)	2001	2000	1999
Discount rate	6.8	7.0	6.8
Long-term rate of return on assets	8.6	9.1	9.1
Rate of compensation increases	4.2	4.7	4.7

The weighted average assumptions used in determining related obligations of other retiree benefit plans are shown below.

At December 31, (percent)	2001	2000	1999
Discount rate	7.2	7.2	7.5
Long-term rate of return on assets	9.0	10.0	10.0

The assumed health care cost trend rate for 2002 is 12%, decreasing to 5% by 2007. A one percentage point increase in the trend rate would have increased the accumulated postretirement benefit obligation by 14%, and interest and service cost by 21%. A one percentage point decrease in the trend rate would have decreased the accumulated postretirement benefit obligation by 12%, and interest and service cost by 17%. . . . In addition to the defined benefit and other retiree benefit plans, the Company also sponsors defined contribution plans, primarily covering U.S. employees. The Company's expense for defined contribution plans in 2001, 2000 and 1999 totaled $34 million, $35 million and $36 million, respectively.

2006 Entries and Work Sheet—A Comprehensive Illustration

Incorporating the corridor computation, the minimum liability recognition, and the required disclosures, the Zarle Company pension plan accounting is continued based on the following facts for 2006.

Service cost is $16,000.

Settlement rate is 10 percent; expected rate of return is 10 percent.

Actual return on plan assets is $22,000.

Amortization of unrecognized prior service cost is $17,600.

Annual contributions (funding) are $27,000.

Benefits paid to retirees during the year are $18,000.

Accumulated benefit obligation is $263,000 at the end of 2006.

Average service life of all covered employees is 20 years.

To facilitate accumulation and recording of the components of pension expense and maintenance of the unrecognized amounts related to the pension plan, the following work sheet is prepared from the basic data presented above. Beginning-of-the-year 2006 account balances are the December 31, 2005, balances from the revised 2005 pension work sheet of Zarle Company in Illustration 20-24.

ILLUSTRATION 20-29
Comprehensive Pension Work Sheet—2006

	General Journal Entries					
Items	Annual Pension Expense	Cash	Prepaid/ Accrued Cost	Additional Liability	Pension Intangible	Contra Equity
Balance, Dec. 31, 2005			43,460 Cr.	37,540 Cr.	32,000 Dr.	5,540 Dr.
(aa) Service cost	16,000 Dr.					
(bb) Interest cost	26,500 Dr.					
(cc) Actual return	22,000 Cr.					
(dd) Unexpected gain	6,040 Dr.					
(ee) Amortization of PSC	17,600 Dr.					
(ff) Contributions		27,000 Cr.				
(gg) Benefits						
(hh) Unrecog. loss amort.	172 Dr.					
(ii) Minimum liab. adj.				25,912 Dr.	20,372 Cr.	5,540 Cr.
Journal entry for 2006	44,312 Dr.	27,000 Cr.	17,312 Cr.			
Balance Dec. 31, 2006			60,772 Cr.	11,628 Cr.	11,628 Dr.	–0–

	Memo Record			
Items	Projected Benefit Obligation	Plan Assets	Unrecognized Prior Service Cost	Unrecognized Net Gain or Loss
Balance, Dec. 31, 2005	265,000 Cr.	159,600 Dr.	32,000 Dr.	29,940 Dr.
(aa) Service cost	16,000 Cr.			
(bb) Interest cost	26,500 Cr.			
(cc) Actual return		22,000 Dr.		
(dd) Unexpected gain				6,040 Cr.
(ee) Amortization of PSC			17,600 Cr.	
(ff) Contributions		27,000 Dr.		
(gg) Benefits	18,000 Dr.	18,000 Cr.		
(hh) Unrecog. loss amort.				172 Cr.
(ii) Minimum liab. adj.				
Journal entry for 2006				
Balance Dec. 31, 2006	289,500 Cr.	190,600 Dr.	14,400 Dr.	23,728 Dr.

Work Sheet Explanations and Entries

Entries (aa) through (gg) are similar to the corresponding entries previously explained in the prior years' work sheets with the exception of entry (dd). In 2005 the expected return on plan assets exceeded the actual return producing an unexpected loss. In 2006 the actual return of $22,000 exceeds the expected return of $15,960 ($159,600 × 10%), resulting in an unexpected gain of $6,040, entry (dd). By netting the gain of $6,040 against the actual return of $22,000, pension expense is affected only by the expected return of $15,960.

A new entry (hh) in Zarle Company's work sheet results from application of the corridor test on the accumulated balance of unrecognized net gain or loss. Zarle Company begins 2006 with a balance in the unrecognized net loss account of $29,940. The corridor criterion must be applied in 2006 to determine whether the balance is excessive and should be amortized. In 2006 the corridor is 10 percent of the larger of the beginning-of-the-year projected benefit obligation of $265,000 or the plan asset's market-related asset value (assumed to be fair market value) of $159,600. The corridor for 2006, thus, is $26,500 ($265,000 × 10%). Because the balance in the Unrecognized Net Loss account is $29,940, the excess (outside the corridor) is $3,440 ($29,940 − $26,500). The $3,440 excess is amortized over the average remaining service life of all employees. Using an average remaining service life of 20 years, the amortization in 2006 is $172 ($3,440 ÷ 20). In the 2006 pension work sheet, the $172 is recorded as a debit to Pension Expense and a credit to the Unrecognized Net Loss account. A schedule showing the computation of the $172 amortization charge is presented below.

ILLUSTRATION 20-30
Computation of 2006 Amortization Charge (Corridor Test)

2006 Corridor Test	
Unrecognized net (gain) or loss at beginning of year	$29,940
10% of larger of PBO or market-related asset value of plan assets	26,500
Amortizable amount	$ 3,440
Average service life of all employees	20 years
2006 amortization ($3,440 ÷ 20 years)	$172

The journal entry to formally record pension expense for 2006 is as follows.

2006		
Pension Expense	44,312	
Cash		27,000
Prepaid/Accrued Pension Cost		17,312

The minimum liability, additional liability, and the amount reported as a contra equity charge at the end of 2006 are computed as follows.

ILLUSTRATION 20-31
Minimum Liability Computation—2006

	December 31, 2006
Accumulated benefit obligation (ABO)	$(263,000)
Plan assets at fair value	190,600
Unfunded accumulated benefit obligation (minimum liability)	(72,400)
Accrued pension cost	60,772
Additional liability	(11,628)
Unrecognized prior service cost	14,400
Contra equity charge	$ -0-

As indicated in the above computation, the additional liability balance on December 31, 2006, is $11,628. The balance of $37,540 of additional liability carried over from 2005 requires a downward adjustment of $25,912 ($37,540 − $11,628). The balance in the pension intangible account should also be $11,628. It is, therefore, credited for $20,372 to reduce the balance of $32,000 to the desired amount of $11,628. Because the unrecognized prior service cost balance exceeds the additional liability, no contra equity charge is required. The entry to adjust the minimum liability (the three accounts related thereto) at December 31, 2006, is as follows.

2006		
Additional Pension Liability	25,912	
Intangible Asset—Deferred Pension Cost		20,372
Excess of Additional Pension Liability over Unrecognized Prior Service Cost		5,540

Financial Statement Presentation

The financial statements of Zarle Company at December 31, 2006, present the following items relative to its pension plan.

ILLUSTRATION 20-32
Balance Sheet Presentation of Pension Costs—2006

ZARLE COMPANY
BALANCE SHEET
AS OF DECEMBER 31, 2006

Assets		Liabilities	
Intangible assets		Long-term liabilities	
Deferred pension cost	$11,628	Accrued pension cost	$72,400

The prepaid/accrued pension cost balance of $60,772 and the additional liability balance of $11,628 on the work sheet are combined and reported as one pension liability of $72,400 in the balance sheet.

ILLUSTRATION 20-33
Income Statement Presentation of Pension Expense—2006

ZARLE COMPANY
INCOME STATEMENT
FOR THE YEAR ENDED DECEMBER 31, 2006

Operating expenses	
Pension expense*	$44,312

*Pension expense is frequently reported as "Employee benefits."

ILLUSTRATION 20-34
Statement of Cash Flows Presentation of Pension Liability

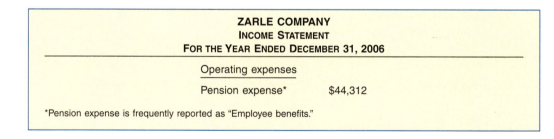

ZARLE COMPANY
STATEMENT OF CASH FLOWS
FOR THE YEAR ENDED DECEMBER 31, 2006

Cash flow from operating activities		
Net income (assumed)		$905,000
Adjustments to reconcile net income to net cash provided by operating activities:		
Increase in accrued pension liability	$17,312	

Note: Significant noncash investing and financing activities
Decrease of $20,372 in intangible asset and decrease of $5,540 in contra equity due to decrease of $25,912 in minimum liability.

Note Disclosure

The minimum note disclosure by Zarle Company of the pension plan for 2006 is shown in Illustration 20-35. Note that in the reconciliation schedule in Illustration 20-35, the adjustment required to recognize the minimum liability of $11,628 is included in order to reconcile to the $72,400 accrued pension cost reported in the balance sheet.

ILLUSTRATION 20-35
Minimum Note Disclosure of Pension Plan, Zarle Company, 2006

ZARLE COMPANY
NOTES TO THE FINANCIAL STATEMENTS

Note D. The company has a pension plan covering substantially all of its employees. The plan is noncontributory and provides pension benefits that are based on the employee's compensation during the three years immediately preceding retirement. The pension plan's assets consist of cash, stocks, and bonds. The company's funding policy is consistent with the relevant government (ERISA) and tax regulations.

Net pension expense for 2006 is comprised of the following components of pension cost.

Service cost	$16,000
Interest on projected benefit obligation	26,500
Expected return on plan assets	(15,960)
Net other components of pension expense[18]	17,772
Net pension expense	$44,312

The following schedule reports changes in the benefit obligation and plan assets during the year and reconciles the funded status of the plan with amounts reported in the company's balance sheet at December 31, 2006:

Change in benefit obligation	
Benefit obligation at beginning of year	$265,000
Service cost	16,000
Interest cost	26,500
Amendments (Prior service cost)	–0–
Actuarial gain	–0–
Benefits paid	(18,000)
Benefit obligation at end of year	289,500
Change in plan assets	
Fair value of plan assets at beginning of year	159,600
Actual return on plan assets	22,000
Contributions	27,000
Benefits paid	(18,000)
Fair value of plan assets at end of year	190,600
Funded status	(98,900)
Unrecognized net actuarial loss	23,728
Unrecognized prior service cost	14,400
Prepaid (accrued) benefit cost	**(60,772)**
Minimum liability adjustment included in:	
Intangible assets	(11,628)
Stockholders' equity	–0–
Accrued pension cost liability in the balance sheet	$(72,400)

The weighted-average discount rate used in determining the 2006 projected benefit obligation was 10 percent. The rate of increase in future compensation levels used in computing the 2006 projected benefit obligation was 4.5 percent. The weighted-average expected long-term rate of return on the plan's assets was 10 percent.

Special Issues

The Pension Reform Act of 1974

The Employee Retirement Income Security Act of 1974—**ERISA**—affects virtually every private retirement plan in the United States. It attempts to safeguard employees' pension rights by mandating many pension plan requirements, including minimum funding, participation, and vesting.

[18]"Net other components of pension expense" in this example is comprised of amortization of prior service cost ($17,600) plus amortization of the unrecognized loss ($172). Amortization of prior service cost and amortization of the unrecognized net gain or loss are combined when reporting the components of pension expense.

Many plans are underfunded but still quite viable. For example, similar to **GM** in the opening story, at one time **Loews Corp.** had a $159 million shortfall. But Loews had earnings of $594 million and a good net worth. Thus, the going concern assumption permits us to ignore these pension underfundings in many cases because in the long run they are not significant.

These requirements can influence the employers' costs significantly. Under this legislation, annual funding is no longer discretionary; an employer must fund the plan in accordance with an actuarial funding method that over time will be sufficient to pay for all pension obligations. If funding is not carried out in a reasonable manner, fines may be imposed and tax deductions denied.

Plan administrators are required to publish a comprehensive description and summary of their plans and detailed annual reports accompanied by many supplementary schedules and statements. ERISA further mandates that the required reports, statements, and supplementary schedules be subjected to audit by qualified independent public accountants.

Another important provision of the Act is the creation of the Pension Benefit Guaranty Corporation (PBGC). **The PBGC's purpose is to administer terminated plans** and to impose liens on the employer's assets for certain unfunded pension liabilities. If a plan is terminated, the PBGC can effectively impose a lien against the employer's assets for the excess of the present value of guaranteed vested benefits over the pension fund assets. This lien generally has had the status of a tax lien and, therefore, takes priority over most other creditorship claims. This section of the Act gives the PBGC the power to force an involuntary termination of a pension plan whenever the risks related to nonpayment of the pension obligation seem too great. Because ERISA restricts to 30 percent of net worth the lien that the PBGC can impose, the PBGC must monitor all plans to ensure that net worth is sufficient to meet the pension benefit obligations.[19]

A large number of terminated plans have caused the PBGC to pay out substantial benefits. Currently the PBGC receives its funding from employers, who contribute a certain dollar amount for each employee covered under the plan.

An interesting accounting problem relates to the manner of disclosing the possible termination of a plan. When, for example, should a contingent liability be disclosed, if a company is experiencing financial difficulty and may not be able to meet its pension obligations if its plan is terminated? At present this issue is unresolved, and considerable judgment would be needed to analyze a company with these contingent liabilities.[20]

Pension Terminations

A congressman at one time noted that "employers are simply treating their employee pension plans like company piggy banks, to be raided at will." What this congressman was referring to is the practice by some companies that have pension plan assets in excess of projected benefit obligations of paying off the obligation and pocketing the difference. ERISA prevents companies from recapturing excess assets unless they pay participants what is owed to them and then terminate the plan. As a result, companies are buying annuities to pay off the pension claimants and using the excess funds for other corporate purposes.[21]

For example, pension plan terminations netted $363 million for **Occidental Petroleum Corp.**, $95 million for **Stroh's Brewery Co.**, $58 million for **Kellogg Co.**, and $29 million for **Western Airlines**. Since 1980, many large companies have terminated their

[19]The major problems in underfunding are occurring in four labor-intensive industries—steel, autos, rubber, and airlines. **General Motors**' plan at one time was 92 percent funded but still had a deficit of over $6 billion.

[20]**Pan American** is a good illustration of how difficult it is to assess when to terminate. When Pan Am filed for bankruptcy in 1991, it had a pension liability of $900 million. From 1983 to 1991, the IRS gave it six waivers so it did not have to make contributions. When the plan was terminated, there was little net worth upon which a lien could be imposed.

[21]A real question exists as to whose money it is. Some argue that the excess funds belong to the employees, not the employer. In addition, given that the funds have been reverting to the employer, critics charge that cost-of-living increases and the possibility of other increased benefits are reduced, because companies will be reluctant to use those excess funds to pay for such increases.

pension plans and captured billions in surplus assets. All of this is quite legal, but is it ethical? It should be noted that federal legislation requires the company to pay an excise tax of anywhere from 20 percent to 50 percent on the gains.

The accounting issue that arises from these terminations is whether a gain should be recognized by the corporation when these assets revert back to the company (often called **asset reversion** transactions). The issue is complex because, in some cases, a new defined benefit plan is started after the old one has been eliminated. Therefore some contend that there has been no change in substance, but merely one in form.

Up to this point the profession has required that these gains be reported if the companies switched from a defined benefit plan to a defined contribution plan. Otherwise, the gain is deferred and amortized over at least 10 years in the future. Many questioned this reporting treatment. As a result the FASB issued *FASB Statement No. 88* that requires recognition in earnings of a new gain or loss when the employer settles a pension obligation either by lump-sum cash payments to participants or by purchasing nonparticipating annuity contracts.[22]

Cash-Balance Pension Plans

Recently, some companies have adopted hybrid pension plans, which combine features of defined benefit and defined contribution plans. These **cash-balance plans** allow employees to transfer their pension benefits when they change employers. This portability-of-benefit feature is popular with younger workers who, unlike earlier generations of workers, expect to change employers several times during their working lives. Such plans are controversial because the change to a cash-balance plan often reduces benefits to older workers. Consequently, the introduction of these plans has drawn the attention of Congress and the IRS to ensure their fairness to all workers.[23]

From an accounting standpoint, cash-balance plans are accounted for similar to a defined benefit plan. This is because employers bear the investment risk in cash-balance plans. Interestingly, when an employer adopts a cash-balance plan, the measurement of the future benefit obligation to employees generally is lower, compared to a traditional defined benefit plan. As a result, when a defined benefit plan is converted to a cash-balance plan, the employer many times will record a negative prior service cost adjustment. The amortization of this prior service cost results in a reduction in pension expense.[24]

Concluding Observation

Hardly a day goes by without the financial press analyzing in depth some issues related to pension plans in the United States. This is hardly surprising, since U.S. pension funds now hold over $5 trillion in assets. As should be obvious by now, the accounting issues related to pension plans are complex. *FASB Statement No. 87* clarifies many of these issues and should help users understand the financial implications of a company's pension plans on its financial position, results of operations, and cash flows.

Critics still argue, however, that much remains to be done. One issue in particular relates to the delayed recognition of certain events. Changes in pension plan obligations and changes in the value of plan assets are not recognized immediately but are systematically incorporated over subsequent periods.

---

[22]"Employers' Accounting for Settlements and Curtailments of Defined Benefit Pension Plans and for Termination Benefits," *Statement of Financial Accounting Standards No. 88* (Stamford, Conn.: FASB, 1985). Some companies have established pension poison pills as an antitakeover measure. These plans require asset reversions from termination of a plan to benefit employees and retirees rather than the acquiring company. For a discussion of pension poison pills, see Eugene E. Comiskey and Charles W. Mulford, "Interpreting Pension Disclosures: A Guide for Lending Officers," *Commercial Lending Review* (Winter 1993–94), Vol. 9, No. 1.

[23]E. Schultz, "IRS Set to Continue to Give Green Light on Pension Plan," *Wall Street Journal* (September 2, 1999), p. A2.

[24]See A. T. Arcady and F. Mellors, "Cash-Balance Conversions," *Journal of Accountancy* (February 2000), pp. 22–28.

SUMMARY OF LEARNING OBJECTIVES

1 Distinguish between accounting for the employer's pension plan and accounting for the pension fund. The company or employer is the organization sponsoring the pension plan. It incurs the cost and makes contributions to the pension fund. The fund or plan is the entity that receives the contributions from the employer, administers the pension assets, and makes the benefit payments to the pension recipients (retired employees). The fund should be a separate legal and accounting entity for which a set of books is maintained and financial statements are prepared.

2 Identify types of pension plans and their characteristics. The two most common types of pension arrangements are: (1) *Defined contribution plans:* The employer agrees to contribute to a pension trust a certain sum each period based on a formula. This formula may consider such factors as age, length of employee service, employer's profits, and compensation level. Only the employer's contribution is defined; no promise is made regarding the ultimate benefits paid out to the employees. (2) *Defined benefit plans:* These plans define the benefits that the employee will receive at the time of retirement. The formula typically used provides for the benefits to be a function of the employee's years of service and the employer's compensation level when he or she nears retirement.

3 Explain alternative measures for valuing the pension obligation. One measure of the pension obligation bases it only on the benefits vested to the employees. Vested benefits are those that the employee is entitled to receive even if the employee renders no additional services under the plan. The *vested benefits pension obligation* is computed using current salary levels and includes only vested benefits. Another measure of the obligation, called the *accumulated benefit obligation*, bases the computation of the deferred compensation amount on all years of service performed by employees under the plan—both vested and nonvested—using current salary levels. A third measure, called the *projected benefit obligation*, bases the computation of the deferred compensation amount on both vested and nonvested service using future salaries.

4 Identify the components of pension expense. Pension expense is a function of the following components: (1) service cost, (2) interest on the liability, (3) return on plan assets, (4) amortization of unrecognized prior service cost, and (5) gain or loss.

5 Utilize a work sheet for employer's pension plan entries. A work sheet unique to pension accounting may be utilized to record both the formal entries and the memo entries to keep track of all the employer's relevant pension plan items and components.

6 Describe the amortization of unrecognized prior service costs. The amount of the prior service cost is computed by an actuary. Amortization of the unrecognized prior service cost is an accounting function performed with the assistance of an actuary. The Board prefers a "years-of-service" amortization method that is similar to a units-of-production computation. First, the total estimated number of service-years to be worked by all of the participating employees is computed. Second, the unrecognized prior service cost is divided by the total number of service-years in order to obtain a cost per service-year (the unit cost). And third, the number of service-years consumed each year is multiplied by the cost per service-year to obtain the annual amortization charge.

7 Explain the accounting procedure for recognizing unexpected gains and losses. In estimating the projected benefit obligation (the liability), actuaries make assumptions about such items as mortality rate, retirement rate, turnover rate, disability rate, and salary amounts. Any change in these actuarial assumptions changes the amount of the projected benefit obligation. These unexpected gains or losses from changes in the projected benefit obligation are liability gains and losses. Liability gains (resulting

KEY TERMS

from unexpected decreases in the liability balance) and liability losses (resulting from unexpected increases) are deferred (unrecognized). The liability gains and losses are combined in the same Unrecognized Net Gain or Loss account used for asset gains and losses and are accumulated from year to year, off-balance-sheet, in a memo record account.

8 Explain the corridor approach to amortizing unrecognized gains and losses. The unrecognized net gain or loss balance is considered too large and must be amortized when it exceeds the arbitrarily selected FASB criterion of 10 percent of the larger of the beginning balances of the projected benefit obligation or the market-related value of the plan assets. If the balance of the unrecognized net gain or loss account stays within the upper and lower limits of the corridor, no amortization is required.

9 Explain the recognition of a minimum liability. Immediate recognition of a liability (referred to as the minimum liability) is required when the accumulated benefit obligation exceeds the fair value of plan assets. The purpose of this minimum liability requirement is to ensure that if a significant plan amendment or actuarial loss occurs, a liability will be recognized at least to the extent of the unfunded portion of the accumulated benefit obligation.

10 Describe the reporting requirements for pension plans in financial statements. The current financial statement disclosure requirements for pension plans are as follows: (1) The components of net periodic pension expense for the period. (2) A schedule showing changes in the benefit obligation and plan assets during the year. (3) A schedule reconciling the funded status of the plan with amounts reported in the employer's statement of financial position. (4) The weighted-average assumed discount rate, the rate of compensation increase used to measure the projected benefit obligation, and the weighted-average expected long-term rate of return on plan assets.

settlement rate, *1026*
unexpected gain or loss, *1032*
unrecognized net gain or loss, *1033*
unrecognized prior service cost, *1030*
vested benefit obligation, *1022*
vested benefits, *1022*
years-of-service method, *1029*

APPENDIX **20A**

Accounting for Postretirement Benefits

IBM Corporation's adoption of a new accounting standard on postretirement benefits in March 1991 resulted in a $2.3 billion charge and a historical curiosity—IBM's first-ever quarterly loss. General Electric Co. disclosed that its charge for adoption of the same new FASB standard would be $2.7 billion. In the fourth quarter of 1993, AT&T Co. absorbed a $2.1 billion pretax hit for postretirement benefits. What is this standard, and how could its adoption have so grave an impact on companies' earnings?

ACCOUNTING GUIDANCE

After a decade of study, the FASB in December 1990 issued *Statement No. 106*, "Employers' Accounting for Postretirement Benefits Other Than Pensions." It alone is the cause for those large charges to income. This standard accounts for health care and other welfare benefits provided to retirees, their spouses, dependents, and beneficiaries.[1] These other welfare benefits include life insurance offered outside a pension plan, dental care as well as medical care, eye care, legal and tax services, tuition assistance, day care, and housing assistance.[2] Because health-care benefits are the largest of the other postretirement benefits, this item is used to illustrate accounting for postretirement benefits.

For many employers (about 95 percent) this standard required a change from the predominant practice of accounting for postretirement benefits on a pay-as-you-go (cash) basis to an accrual basis. Similar to pension accounting, the accrual basis necessitates measurement of the employer's obligation to provide future benefits and accrual of the cost during the years that the employee provides service.

One of the reasons companies have not prefunded these benefit plans is that payments to prefund health-care costs, unlike excess contributions to a pension trust, are not tax deductible. Another reason is that postretirement health-care benefits were once perceived to be a low-cost employee benefit that could be changed or eliminated at will and, therefore, not a legal liability. Now, the accounting definition of a liability goes beyond the notion of a legally enforceable claim to encompass equitable or constructive obligations as well, making it clear that the postretirement benefit promise is a liability.[3]

DIFFERENCES BETWEEN PENSION BENEFITS AND HEALTH-CARE BENEFITS

OBJECTIVE 11
Identify the differences between pensions and postretirement health-care benefits.

The FASB used *Statement No. 87* on pensions as a reference for the accounting prescribed in *Statement No. 106* on health care and other nonpension postretirement benefits.[4] Why didn't the FASB cover both types of postretirement benefits in the earlier pension accounting statement? The apparent similarities between the two benefits mask some significant differences. These differences are shown in Illustration 20A-1.[5]

[1] *Accounting Trends and Techniques—2001* reports that of its 600 surveyed companies, 370 report benefit plans that provide postretirement health-care benefits. Surprisingly, such coverage translates into a total health-care liability estimated at more than $400 billion and perhaps as much as $2 trillion, which is largely unfunded. In response to rising health-care costs and higher premiums on health-care insurance, companies are working to get their postretirement benefit costs under control. For example, a recent study of employer health benefit plans indicates that employers are limiting or curtailing postretirement health benefits. Of the companies surveyed, 20 percent have eliminated the plans altogether. And 17 percent indicated they have just about eliminated their liabilities for such benefits by requiring current retirees to pay health-care premiums. In some cases, employees must work longer at a company before they are eligible for these benefits. See Kelly Greene, "Health Benefits for Retirees Continue to Shrink, Study Says," *Wall Street Journal* (September 16, 2002), p. A2.

[2] "OPEB" is the acronym frequently used to describe postretirement benefits covered by *FASB Statement No. 106*. This term came into being before the scope of the statement was narrowed from "other postemployment benefits" to "other postretirement benefits," thereby excluding postemployment benefits related to severance pay or wage continuation to disabled, terminated, or laid-off employees.

[3] "Elements of Financial Statements," *Statement of Financial Accounting Concepts No. 6* (Stamford, Conn.: 1985), p. 13, footnote 21.

[4] In November 1992 the FASB issued *Statement of Financial Accounting Standards No. 112*, "Employers' Accounting for Postemployment Benefits," which covers postemployment benefits that are not accounted for under *SFAS No. 87* (pensions), *SFAS No. 88* (settlements, curtailments, and termination benefits), or *SFAS No. 106* (postretirement benefits other than pensions). *SFAS No. 112* requires an employer to recognize the obligation to provide postemployment benefits in accordance with *SFAS No. 43*, similar to accounting for compensated absences (see Chapter 13). These *SFAS No. 112* benefits include, but are not limited to, salary continuation, disability-related benefits, severance benefits, and continuance of health-care benefits and life insurance for inactive or former (e.g., terminated, disabled, or deceased) employees or their beneficiaries.

[5] D. Gerald Searfoss and Naomi Erickson, "The Big Unfunded Liability: Postretirement Health-Care Benefits," *Journal of Accountancy* (November 1988), pp. 28–39.

ILLUSTRATION 20A-1
Differences between Pensions and Postretirement Health-Care Benefits

Item	Pensions	Health-Care Benefits
Funding	Generally funded.	Generally *NOT* funded.
Benefit	Well-defined and level dollar amount.	Generally uncapped and great variability.
Beneficiary	Retiree (maybe some benefit to surviving spouse).	Retiree, spouse, and other dependents.
Benefit Payable	Monthly.	As needed and used.
Predictability	Variables are reasonably predictable.	Utilization difficult to predict. Level of cost varies geographically and fluctuates over time.

Two of the differences presented in Illustration 20A-1 highlight why measuring the future payments for health-care benefit plans is so much more difficult than for pension plans:

1. Many postretirement plans do not set a limit on health-care benefits. No matter how serious the illness or how long it lasts, the benefits continue to flow. (Even if the employer uses an insurance company plan, the premiums will escalate according to the increased benefits provided.)
2. The level of health-care benefit utilization and health-care costs is difficult to predict. The increased longevity and unexpected illnesses (e.g., AIDS) along with new medical technologies (e.g., MRI scans) and cures (e.g., radiation) cause changes in health-care utilization.

Additionally, although health-care benefits are generally covered by the fiduciary and reporting standards for employee benefit funds under ERISA, the stringent minimum vesting, participation, and funding standards that apply to pensions do not apply to health-care benefits. Nevertheless, as you will learn, many of the basic concepts and much of the accounting terminology and measurement methodology applicable to pensions are applicable to other postretirement benefits accounting. Therefore, throughout the following discussion and illustrations, we point out the similarities and differences in the accounting and reporting for these two types of postretirement benefits.

POSTRETIREMENT BENEFITS ACCOUNTING PROVISIONS

Health-care and other postretirement benefits for current and future retirees and their dependents are forms of deferred compensation earned through employee service and subject to accrual during the years an employee is working. The period of time over which the postretirement benefit cost is accrued, called the **attribution period**, is the period of service during which the employee earns the benefits under the terms of the plan. This attribution period (shown in Illustration 20A-2 on page 1056) generally begins when an employee is hired and ends on the date the employee is eligible to receive the benefits and ceases to earn additional benefits by performing service, the vesting date.[6]

[6]This is a benefit-years-of-service approach (the projected unit credit actuarial cost method). The FASB found no compelling reason to switch from the traditional pension accounting approach. It rejected the employee's full service period (i.e., to the estimated retirement date) because it was unable to identify any approach that would appropriately attribute benefits beyond the date full eligibility for those benefits is attained. Full eligibility is attained by meeting specified age, service, or age and service requirements of the plan.

ILLUSTRATION 20A-2
Range of Possible Attribution Periods

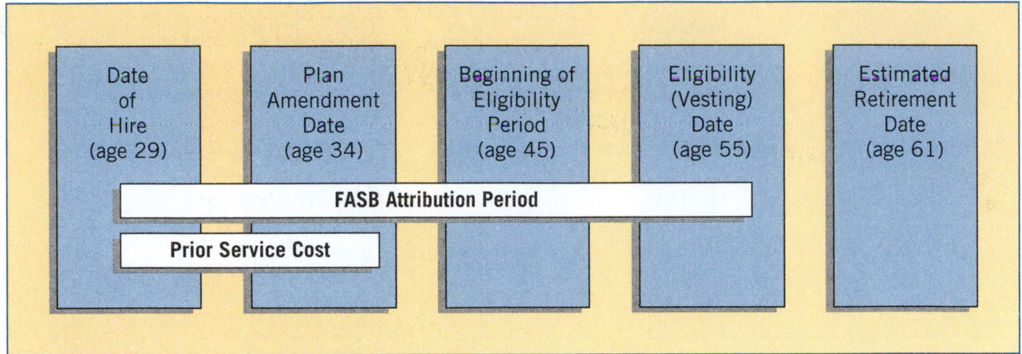

Obligations under Postretirement Benefits

In defining the obligation for postretirement benefits, many concepts similar to pension accounting are maintained, but some new and modified terms are designed specifically for postretirement benefits. Two of the most important are (a) expected postretirement benefit obligation and (b) accumulated postretirement benefit obligation.

Expected Postretirement Benefit Obligation (EPBO). The EPBO is the actuarial present value as of a particular date of **all benefits expected to be paid after retirement to employees and their dependents**. The EPBO is not recorded in the financial statements, but it is used in measuring periodic expense.

Accumulated Postretirement Benefit Obligation (APBO). The APBO is the actuarial present value of **future benefits attributed to employees' services rendered to a particular date**. The APBO is equal to the EPBO for retirees and active employees fully eligible for benefits. Before the date an employee achieves full eligibility, the APBO is only a portion of the EPBO. Or stated another way, the difference between the APBO and the EPBO is the future service costs of active employees who are not yet fully eligible.

Illustration 20A-3 contrasts the EPBO and the APBO.

ILLUSTRATION 20A-3
APBO and EPBO Contrasted

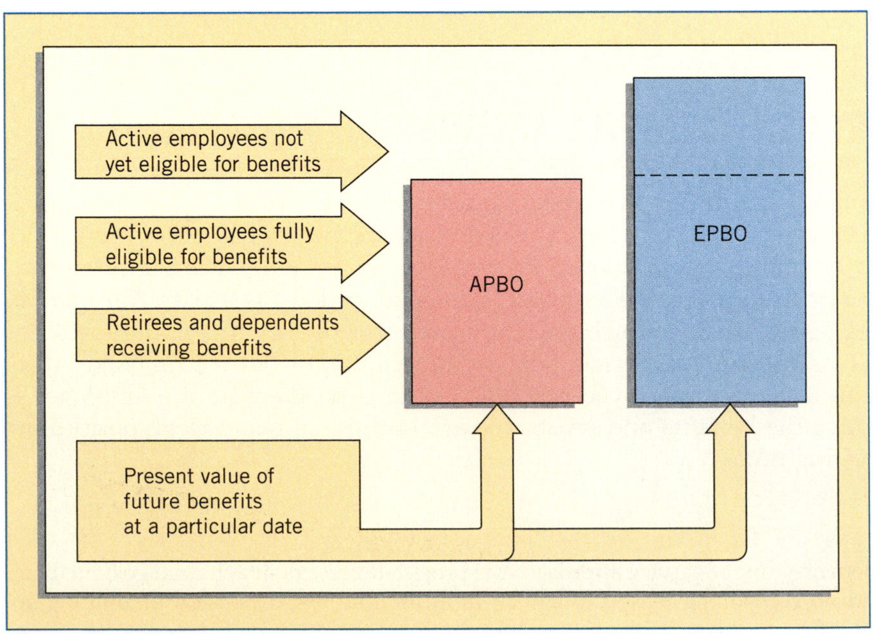

At the date an employee is fully eligible (the end of the attribution period), the APBO and the EPBO relative to that employee are equal.

Postretirement Expense

Postretirement expense, also referred to as **net periodic postretirement benefit cost**, is the employer's annual postretirement benefit expense, which consists of many of the familiar components used to compute annual pension expense. The components of net periodic postretirement benefit cost are as follows.[7]

1. ***Service Cost.*** The portion of the EPBO attributed to employee service during the period.
2. ***Interest Cost.*** The increase in the APBO attributable to the passage of time. It is computed by applying the beginning-of-the-year discount rate to the beginning-of-the-year APBO, adjusted for benefit payments to be made during the period. The discount rate is based on the rates of return on high-quality, fixed-income investments that are currently available.[8]
3. ***Actual Return on Plan Assets.*** The change in the fair value of the plan's assets adjusted for contributions and benefit payments made during the period. Because the postretirement expense is charged or credited for the gain or loss on plan assets (the difference between the actual and the expected return), this component is really expected return.
4. ***Amortization of Prior Service Cost.*** The amortization of the cost of retroactive benefits resulting from plan amendments or a plan initiation that takes place after *Statement No. 106* takes effect. The typical amortization period, beginning at the date of the plan amendment, is the remaining service periods through the full eligibility date.
5. ***Gains and Losses.*** In general, changes in the APBO resulting from changes in assumptions or from experience different from that assumed. For funded plans, this component also includes the difference between actual return and expected return on plan assets (computed the same as for pensions—actual based on fair value and expected based on market-related value). Gains or losses can be recognized immediately or can be based on a "corridor approach" similar to that used for pension accounting.

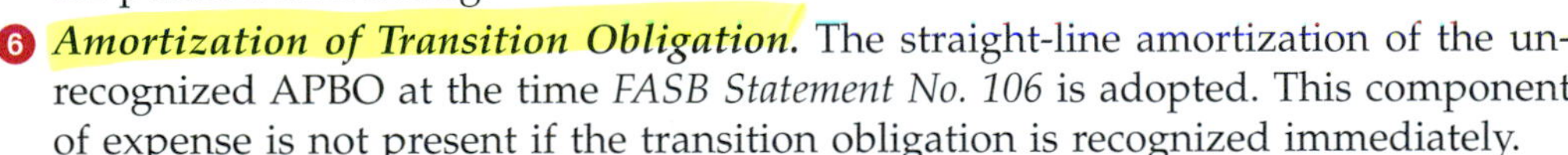

6. ***Amortization of Transition Obligation.*** The straight-line amortization of the unrecognized APBO at the time *FASB Statement No. 106* is adopted. This component of expense is not present if the transition obligation is recognized immediately.

The Transition Amount

At the beginning of the year of adoption of *FASB Statement No. 106*, a **transition amount** (obligation or asset) is computed as the difference between (1) the APBO and (2) the fair value of the plan assets, plus any accrued obligation or less any prepaid cost (asset). Because most plans are unfunded and most employers are accruing postretirement benefit costs for the first time, large transition obligations occur.

The accounting treatment of this transition amount was one of the most controversial issues in postretirement benefit standard setting. The primary concern of many was that an immediate charge to expense for unrecognized past costs, accompanied by recognition of the total unrecognized liability, would have a large negative impact on reported earnings in the year of the change. Of equal concern to others was that the

---

[7]"Employers' Accounting for Postretirement Benefits Other Than Pensions," *Statement of Financial Accounting Standards No. 106* (Norwalk, Conn.: FASB, 1990), paras. 46–66. And, see James R. Wilbert and Kenneth E. Dakdduk, "The New FASB 106: How to Account for Postretirement Benefits," *Journal of Accountancy* (August 1991), pp. 36–41.

[8]The FASB concluded that the discount rate for measuring the present value of the postretirement benefit obligation and the service cost component should be the same as that applied to pension measurements. It chose not to label it the settlement rate, in order to clarify that the objective of the discount rate is to measure the time value of money.

alternative—deferral and amortization of the expense, accompanied by a rapidly increasing liability—would be a drain on reported earnings for many years. And providing the option of immediate write-off or deferral and amortization was also problematic because of the lack of comparability that would result. Nevertheless, the FASB decided to permit employers to choose between the immediate recognition (e.g., the $2.3 billion charge taken by **IBM** in the first quarter of 1991) and deferral and amortization. The two methods work as follows:

> **Immediate recognition**. As an immediate write-off, the transition amount is recognized in the income statement as the "effect of a change in accounting principle" (net of tax)[9] and in the balance sheet as a long-term liability entitled "Postretirement benefit obligation." Restatement of previously issued annual financial statements is not permitted.
>
> **Deferred recognition**. Employers choosing deferred recognition must amortize the transition amount on a straight-line basis over the average remaining service period to expected retirement of the employees in place at the time of transition and expected to receive benefits.[10] If the remaining service period is less than 20 years, the employer may elect a 20-year amortization period. But, the transition amount may not be amortized more slowly than it is paid off (referred to as the "pay-as-you-go constraint").[11]

Once chosen, the method cannot be changed. That is, after once electing to amortize the transition amount, the employer cannot record the remainder of its unamortized transition obligation in a subsequent year under the immediate recognition method.

ILLUSTRATIVE ACCOUNTING ENTRIES

OBJECTIVE 12
Contrast accounting for pensions to accounting for other postretirement benefits.

Like pension accounting, several significant items of the postretirement plan are unrecognized in the accounts and in the financial statements. These off-balance-sheet items are:

1. Expected postretirement benefit obligation (EPBO).
2. Accumulated postretirement benefit obligation (APBO).
3. Postretirement benefit plan assets.
4. Unrecognized transition amount.
5. Unrecognized prior service cost.
6. Unrecognized net gain or loss.

The EPBO is not recognized in the financial statements or disclosed in the notes. It is recomputed each year and used by the actuary in measuring the annual service cost. Because of the numerous assumptions and actuarial complexity involved in measuring annual service cost, we have omitted these computations of the EPBO.

All five of the other off-balance-sheet items listed above must be disclosed by the employer in notes to the financial statements. In addition, as in pension accounting,

---

[9]The FASB uses the term "effect" rather than "cumulative effect," and because of the unique transition provision and calculations involved, the retroactive effects on prior periods are generally not determinable. Therefore pro forma disclosures are not required. The per share effects of the accounting change are required to be shown on the face of the income statement.

[10]For amortization of the transition amount (and for gains and losses as well), the FASB chose the longer "retirement date" as opposed to the "full eligibility date" for pragmatic reasons—the magnitude of the transition amount supports use of a longer amortization period in order to minimize the effect on current financial statements.

[11]In pension accounting, the transition amount must be amortized over the average remaining service life of existing employees or optionally over a 15-year period if the remaining service life is less than 15 years.

the exact amount of these items must be known because they are used in the computation of postretirement expense. Therefore, in order to track these off-balance-sheet postretirement benefit items, the work sheet illustrated in pension accounting will be utilized to record both the formal general journal entries and the memo entries.

2003 Entries and Work Sheet

To illustrate the use of a work sheet in accounting for a postretirement benefits plan, assume that on January 1, 2003, Quest Company adopts *Statement No. 106* to account for its health-care benefit plan. The following facts apply to the postretirement benefits plan for the year 2003.

Plan assets at fair value on January 1, 2003, are zero.
Actual and expected returns on plan assets are zero.
APBO, January 1, 2003, is $400,000.
Service cost is $22,000.
No prior service cost exists.
Discount rate is 8 percent.
Contributions (funding) to plan during the year are $38,000.
Benefit payments to employees from plan are $28,000.
Average remaining service to full eligibility: 21 years.
Average remaining service to expected retirement: 25 years.
Transition amount is to be amortized.

Using the preceding data, the following work sheet presents the beginning balances and all of the postretirement benefit entries recorded by Quest Company in 2003.

ILLUSTRATION 20A-4
Postretirement Benefits Work Sheet—2003

	General Journal Entries			Memo Record		
Items	Annual Postretirement Expense	Cash	Prepaid/ Accrued Cost	APBO	Plan Assets	Unrecognized Transition Amount
Balance, Jan. 1, 2003				400,000 Cr.		400,000 Dr.
(a) Service cost	22,000 Dr.			22,000 Cr.		
(b) Interest cost	32,000 Dr.			32,000 Cr.		
(c) Contributions		38,000 Cr.			38,000 Dr.	
(d) Benefits				28,000 Dr.	28,000 Cr.	
(e) Amortization:						
Transition	16,000 Dr.***					16,000 Cr.
Journal entry for 2003	70,000 Dr.	38,000 Cr.	32,000 Cr.*			
Balance, Dec. 31, 2003			32,000 Cr.**	426,000 Cr.	10,000 Dr.	384,000 Dr.

*$70,000 − $38,000 = $32,000.
**$426,000 − ($10,000 + $384,000) = $32,000
***$400,000 ÷ 25 = $16,000

On the first line of the work sheet, the beginning balances of the APBO and the unrecognized transition amount are recorded in the memo record columns. The transition amount is the difference between the APBO and the fair value of plan assets, in this case $400,000 ($400,000 − $0).

Entry (a) records the service cost component, which increases postretirement expense $22,000 and increases the liability (APBO) $22,000. Entry (b) accrues the interest expense component, which increases both the liability (APBO) and the expense by $32,000 (the beginning APBO multiplied by the discount rate of 8 percent). Entry (c) records Quest Company's contribution (funding) of assets to the postretirement benefit fund; cash is decreased $38,000 and plan assets are increased $38,000. Entry (d) records the benefit payments made to retirees, which results in equal $28,000 decreases to the plan assets and the liability (APBO). Entry (e) records the amortization of the unrecognized transition amount. It is amortized over the average remaining service to expected retirement, 25 years. The amortized amount of $16,000 ($400,000 ÷ 25) increases postretirement expense and decreases the unrecognized transition amount.

The entry on December 31, which is the adjusting entry made to formally record the postretirement expense in 2003, is as follows.

December 31, 2003		
Postretirement Expense	70,000	
Cash		38,000
Prepaid/Accrued Cost		32,000

The credit to Prepaid/Accrued Cost for $32,000 represents the difference between the 2003 postretirement expense of $70,000 and the amount funded of $38,000. The $32,000 credit balance is a liability because the plan is underfunded. The Prepaid/Accrued Cost account balance of $32,000 also equals the net of the balances in the memo accounts. This reconciliation of the off-balance-sheet items with the prepaid/accrued cost reported in the balance sheet is shown below (similar to the pension reconciliation schedule).

ILLUSTRATION 20A-5
Postretirement Benefits Reconciliation Schedule—December 31, 2003

Accumulated postretirement benefit obligation (Credit)	$(426,000)
Plan assets at fair value (Debit)	10,000
Funded status (Credit)	(416,000)
Unrecognized transition amount (Debit)	384,000
Prepaid/accrued cost (Credit)	$ (32,000)

Preparation of this reconciliation schedule is necessary as part of the required note disclosures.

Recognition of Gains and Losses

Gains and losses represent changes in the APBO or the value of plan assets resulting either from actual experience different from that expected or from changes in actuarial assumptions. The FASB noted that "recognizing the effects of revisions in estimates in full in the period in which they occur may produce financial statements that portray more volatility than is inherent in the employer's obligation."[12] Therefore, as in pension accounting, gains and losses are not required to be recognized immediately[13] but may be deferred in the period when they occur and amortized in future years.

The Corridor Approach

Consistent with pension accounting, deferred gains and losses are amortized as a component of net periodic expense if, as of the beginning of the period, they exceed a "corridor." The corridor is defined as the greater of 10 percent of the APBO or 10 percent of the market-related value of plan assets. The **corridor approach** is intended to reduce postretirement expense volatility by providing a reasonable opportunity for gains and losses to offset over time without affecting net periodic expense.

[12]*FASB Statement No. 106,* par. 293.

[13]If an employer adopts a consistent policy of immediately recognizing gains and losses: (1) the amount of any **net gain** in excess of net losses previously recognized in income would first offset any unamortized **transition obligation**; and (2) the amount of any **net loss** in excess of net gains previously recognized in net income would first offset any unamortized **transition asset** (existence of a transition asset, however, is unlikely).

Amortization Methods

If amortization is required, the **minimum amortization amount** is the excess (beyond the corridor) gain or loss divided by the average remaining service life to expected retirement of all active employees. Any systematic method of amortization may be used provided that (1) the amount amortized in any period is equal to or greater than the minimum amount, (2) the method is applied consistently, and (3) the method is applied similarly for both gains and losses.

The amount of unrecognized gain or loss is recomputed each year and amortized over the average remaining service life if the net amount exceeds the "corridor."

2004 Entries and Work Sheet

Continuing the Quest Company illustration into 2004, the following facts apply to the postretirement benefits plan for the year 2004.

Actual return on plan assets is $600.
Expected return on plan assets is $800.
Discount rate is 8 percent.
Increase in APBO due to change in actuarial assumptions is $60,000.
Service cost is $26,000.
Contributions (funding) to plan during the year are $50,000.
Benefit payments to employees during the year are $35,000.
Average remaining service to full eligibility: 21 years.
Average remaining service to expected retirement: 25 years.

The work sheet in Illustration 20A-6 presents all of the postretirement benefit entries and information recorded by Quest Company in 2004. The beginning balances entered on the first line of the Quest Company work sheet are the ending balances from the 2003 Quest Company postretirement benefits work sheet in Illustration 20A-4.

ILLUSTRATION 20A-6
Postretirement Benefits Work Sheet—2004

	General Journal Entries			Memo Record			
Items	Annual Postretirement Expense	Cash	Prepaid/ Accrued Cost	APBO	Plan Assets	Unrecognized Transition Amount	Unrecognized Net Gain or Loss
Balances, Jan. 1, 2004			32,000 Cr.	426,000 Cr.	10,000 Dr.	384,000 Dr.	
(f) Service cost	26,000 Dr.			26,000 Cr.			
(g) Interest cost	34,080 Dr.			34,080 Cr.			
(h) Actual return	600 Cr.				600 Dr.		
(i) Unexpected loss	200 Cr.						200 Dr.
(j) Contributions		50,000 Cr.			50,000 Dr.		
(k) Benefits				35,000 Dr.	35,000 Cr.		
(l) Amortization: Transition	16,000 Dr.					16,000 Cr.	
(m) Inc. in APBO—Loss				60,000 Cr.			60,000 Dr.
Journal entry for 2004	75,280 Dr.	50,000 Cr.	25,280 Cr.*				
Balance, Dec. 31, 2004			57,280 Cr.**	511,080 Cr.	25,600 Dr.	368,000 Dr.	60,200 Dr.

*$75,280 − $50,000 = $25,280
**$511,080 − ($25,600 + $368,000 + $60,200) = $57,280

Entries (f), (g), (j), (k), and (l) are similar to the corresponding entries previously explained in 2003. Entries (h) and (i) are related. The expected return of $800 is higher than the actual return of $600. To smooth postretirement expense, the unexpected loss of $200 ($800 − $600) is deferred by debiting Unrecognized Net Gain or Loss and crediting Postretirement Expense. As a result of this adjustment, the expected return on the plan assets is the amount actually used to compute postretirement expense.

Entry (m) records the change in the APBO resulting from a change in actuarial assumptions. This $60,000 increase in the employer's accumulated liability is an unexpected loss that is deferred by debiting it to Unrecognized Net Gain or Loss.

The journal entry on December 31 to formally record net periodic expense for 2004 is as follows.

December 31, 2004		
Postretirement Expense	75,280	
Cash		50,000
Prepaid/Accrued Cost		25,280

The balance of the Prepaid/Accrued Cost account at December 31, 2004, is $57,280, which is equal to the net of the balances in the memo accounts as shown in the following reconciliation schedule.

ILLUSTRATION 20A-7
Postretirement Benefits Reconciliation Schedule—December 31, 2004

Accumulated postretirement benefit obligation (Credit)	$(511,080)
Plan assets at fair value (Debit)	25,600
Funded status (Credit)	(485,480)
Unrecognized transition amount (Debit)	368,000
Unrecognized net gain or loss (Debit)	60,200
Prepaid/accrued cost (Credit)	$ (57,280)

Amortization of Unrecognized Net Gain or Loss in 2005

Because of the beginning-of-the-year balance in unrecognized net gain or loss, the corridor test for amortization of the balance must be applied at the end of 2005. Illustration 20A-8 shows the computation of the amortization charge for unrecognized net gain or loss.

ILLUSTRATION 20A-8
Computation of Amortization Charge (Corridor Test)—2005

2005 Corridor Test	
Unrecognized net gain or loss at beginning of year	$60,200
10% of greater of APBO or market-related value of plan assets ($511,080 × .10)	51,108
Amortizable amount	$ 9,092
Average remaining service to expected retirement	25 years
2005 amortization of loss ($9,092 ÷ 25)	$364

DISCLOSURES IN NOTES TO THE FINANCIAL STATEMENTS

The disclosures required for other postretirement benefit plans are similar to and just as detailed and extensive as those required for pensions. By recognizing these similarities, under the provisions of *FASB Statement No. 132*, pension and other postretirement benefit disclosures can be combined. This disclosure for **Gillette Company** was provided in Illustration 20-28. As noted there, the following disclosures are required.

1. Postretirement expense for the period, separately identifying all components of that cost.
2. A schedule showing changes in postretirement benefit obligations and plan assets during the year.
3. A schedule reconciling the funded status of the plan with amounts reported in the employer's balance sheet, separately identifying the reconciling items.
4. The assumptions and rates used in computing the EPBO and APBO, including assumed health-care cost trend rates; assumed discount rates; and the effect of a one-percentage-point increase in the assumed health-care cost trend rate on the measurement of the APBO, the service cost, and the interest cost.

ACTUARIAL ASSUMPTIONS AND CONCEPTUAL ISSUES

The measurement of the EPBO and the APBO and the net periodic postretirement benefit cost is involved and complex. Due to the uncertainties in forecasting health-care costs, rates of utilization, changes in government health programs, and the differences employed in nonmedical assumptions (discount rate, employee turnover, rate of pre-65 retirement, spouse-age difference, etc.), estimates of postretirement benefit costs may have a large margin of error. Is the information, therefore, relevant, reliable, or verifiable? The FASB concluded "that the obligation to provide postretirement benefits meets the definition of a liability, is representationally faithful, is relevant to financial statement users, and can be measured with sufficient reliability at a justifiable cost."[14] Failure to accrue an obligation and an expense prior to payment of benefits is considered to be an unfaithful representation of what financial statements purport to represent.[15]

The FASB took a momentous step by requiring the accrual of postretirement benefits as a liability. Many opposed the requirement, warning that the standard would devastate earnings. Others argued that putting "soft" numbers on the balance sheet was inappropriate, and finally, others noted that it would force companies to curtail these benefits to employees.

The authors believe that the FASB deserves special praise for this standard. Because the Board addressed this issue, companies now recognize the magnitude of these costs. This recognition has led to efforts to control escalating health-care costs. As John Ruffle, a former president of the Financial Accounting Foundation noted, "The Board has done American industry a gigantic favor. Over the long term, industry will look back and say thanks."

SUMMARY OF LEARNING OBJECTIVES FOR APPENDIX 20A

11 Identify the differences between pensions and postretirement health-care benefits. Pension plans are generally funded, but health-care benefit plans are not. Pension benefits are generally well-defined and level in amount, but health-care benefits are generally uncapped and variable. Pension benefits are payable monthly, but health-care benefits are paid as needed and used. Pension plan variables are reasonably predictable, whereas health-care plan variables are difficult to predict.

12 Contrast accounting for pensions to accounting for other postretirement benefits. Many of the basic concepts and much of the accounting terminology and measurement methodology applicable to pensions also apply to other postretirement benefit accounting. Because other postretirement benefit plans are unfunded, large transition obligations occur. These may be immediately written off or amortized over 20 years. Two significant concepts peculiar to accounting for other postretirement benefits are (a) expected postretirement benefit obligation (EPBO) and (b) accumulated postretirement benefit obligation (APBO).

KEY TERMS

accumulated postretirement benefit obligation (APBO), *1056*
attribution period, *1055*
corridor approach, *1060*
deferred recognition method, *1058*
expected postretirement benefit obligation (EPBO), *1056*
immediate recognition method, *1058*
minimum amortization amount, *1061*
transition amount, *1057*

[14] *FASB Statement No. 106,* par. 163.

[15] The FASB does not require recognition of a "minimum liability" for postretirement benefit plans. The Board concluded that the postretirement transition provisions that provide for delayed recognition should not be overridden by a requirement to recognize a liability that would accelerate recognition of that obligation in the balance sheet.

Note: All **asterisked** Questions, Brief Exercises, Exercises, Problems, Conceptual Cases, and Using Your Judgment cases relate to material covered in the appendix to the chapter.

QUESTIONS

1. What is a private pension plan? How does a contributory pension plan differ from a noncontributory plan?

2. Differentiate between a defined contribution pension plan and a defined benefit pension plan. Explain how the employer's obligation differs between the two types of plans.

3. Differentiate between "accounting for the employer" and "accounting for the pension fund."

4. The meaning of the term "fund" depends on the context in which it is used. Explain its meaning when used as a noun. Explain its meaning when it is used as a verb.

5. What is the role of an actuary relative to pension plans? What are actuarial assumptions?

6. What factors must be considered by the actuary in measuring the amount of pension benefits under a defined benefit plan?

7. Name three approaches to measuring benefits from a pension plan and explain how they differ.

8. Distinguish between the noncapitalization approach and the capitalization approach with regard to accounting for pension plans. Which approach does *FASB Statement No. 87* adopt?

9. Explain how cash-basis accounting for pension plans differs from accrual-basis accounting for pension plans. Why is cash-basis accounting generally considered unacceptable for pension plan accounting?

10. Identify the five components that comprise pension expense. Briefly explain the nature of each component.

11. What is service cost, and what is the basis of its measurement?

12. In computing the interest component of pension expense, what interest rates may be used?

13. Explain the difference between service cost and prior service cost.

14. What is meant by "prior service cost"? When is prior service cost recognized as pension expense?

15. What are "liability gains and losses," and how are they accounted for?

16. If pension expense recognized in a period exceeds the current amount funded by the employer, what kind of account arises, and how should it be reported in the financial statements? If the reverse occurs—that is, current funding by the employer exceeds the amount recognized as pension expense—what kind of account arises, and how should it be reported?

17. Given the following items and amounts, compute the actual return on plan assets: fair value of plan assets at the beginning of the period $9,200,000; benefits paid during the period $1,400,000; contributions made during the period $1,000,000; and fair value of the plan assets at the end of the period $10,150,000.

18. How does an "asset gain or loss" develop in pension accounting? How does a "liability gain or loss" develop in pension accounting?

19. What is the meaning of "corridor amortization"?

20. Explain when a minimum liability is recognized and how it is reported in the financial statements.

21. Explain the nature of a debit to an intangible asset account when an additional pension liability must be recorded. How does the amount of unrecognized prior service cost influence the amount recognized as an intangible asset?

22. At the end of the current period, Jacob Inc. had an accumulated benefit obligation of $400,000, pension plan assets (at fair value) of $300,000, and a balance in prepaid pension cost of $41,000. Assuming that Jacob Inc. follows *FASB Statement No. 87*, what are the accounts and amounts that will be reported on the company's balance sheet as pension assets or pension liabilities?

23. At the end of the current year, Joshua Co. has unrecognized prior service cost of $9,150,000. In addition, it recognized a minimum liability of $10,500,000 for the year. Where should the unrecognized prior service cost be reported on the balance sheet? Where should the debit related to the establishment of the minimum liability be reported?

24. Determine the meaning of the following terms.

(a) Contributory plan.

(b) Vested benefits.

(c) Retroactive benefits.

(d) Years-of-service method.

25. Of what value to the financial statement reader is the schedule reconciling the funded status of the plan with amounts reported in the employer's balance sheet?

26. A headline in the *Wall Street Journal* stated, "Firms Increasingly Tap Their Pension Funds to Use Excess Assets." What is the accounting issue related to the use of these "excess assets" by companies?

***27.** What are postretirement benefits other than pensions?

***28.** Why didn't the FASB cover both types of postretirement benefits—pensions and health-care—in the earlier pension accounting statement?

***29.** What is the transition amount in postretirement benefit accounting? Why is the accounting for the transition amount so controversial?

***30.** What are the major differences between postretirement health-care benefits and pension benefits?

***31.** What is the difference between the APBO and the EPBO? What are the components of postretirement expense?

BRIEF EXERCISES

BE20-1 The following information is available for **American Airlines** Corporation for 2001 (in millions).

Service cost	$260
Interest on P.B.O.	515
Return on plan assets	539
Amortization of unrecognized prior service cost	11
Amortization of unrecognized net loss	22

Compute American Airlines' 2001 pension expense.

BE20-2 For Becker Corporation, year-end plan assets were $2,000,000. At the beginning of the year, plan assets were $1,680,000. During the year, contributions to the pension fund were $120,000, and benefits paid were $200,000. Compute Becker's actual return on plan assets.

BE20-3 At January 1, 2005, Uddin Company had plan assets of $250,000 and a projected benefit obligation of the same amount. During 2005, service cost was $27,500, the settlement rate was 10%, actual and expected return on plan assets were $25,000, contributions were $20,000, and benefits paid were $17,500. Prepare a pension work sheet for Uddin Company for 2005.

BE20-4 For 2001, **Campbell Soup Company** had pension income of $12 million and contributed $122 million to the pension fund. Prepare **Campbell Soup Company**'s journal entry to record pension income and funding.

BE20-5 Duesbury Corporation amended its pension plan on January 1, 2005, and granted $120,000 of unrecognized prior service costs to its employees. The employees are expected to provide 2,000 service years in the future, with 350 service years in 2005. Compute unrecognized prior service cost amortization for 2005.

BE20-6 At December 31, 2005, Conway Corporation had a projected benefit obligation of $510,000, plan assets of $322,000, unrecognized prior service cost of $127,000, and accrued pension cost of $61,000. Prepare a pension reconciliation schedule for Conway.

BE20-7 Hunt Corporation had a projected benefit obligation of $3,100,000 and plan assets of $3,300,000 at January 1, 2005. Hunt's unrecognized net pension loss was $475,000 at that time. The average remaining service period of Hunt's employees is 7.5 years. Compute Hunt's minimum amortization of pension loss.

BE20-8 Judy O'Neill Corporation provides the following information at December 31, 2004.

Accumulated benefit obligation	$2,800,000
Plan assets at fair value	2,000,000
Accrued pension cost	200,000
Unrecognized prior service cost	1,100,000

Compute the additional liability that O'Neill must record at December 31, 2004.

BE20-9 At December 31, 2005, Judy O'Neill Corporation (see BE20-8) has the following balances.

Accumulated benefit obligation	$3,400,000
Plan assets at fair value	2,420,000
Accrued pension cost	235,000
Unrecognized prior service cost	990,000

O'Neill's Additional Pension Liability was $600,000 at December 31, 2004. Prepare O'Neill's December 31, 2005, entry to adjust Additional Pension Liability.

BE20-10 At December 31, 2004, Jeremiah Corporation was not required to report any additional pension liability. At December 31, 2005, the additional liability required is $600,000, and unrecognized prior service cost was $425,000. Prepare Jeremiah's December 31, 2005, entry to adjust Additional Pension Liability.

***BE20-11** Caleb Corporation has the following information available concerning its postretirement benefit plan for 2005.

Service cost	$40,000
Interest cost	52,400
Actual return on plan assets	26,900
Amortization of unrecognized transition amount	24,600

Compute Caleb's 2005 postretirement expense.

***BE20-12** For 2005, Benjamin Inc. computed its annual postretirement expense as $240,900. Benjamin's contribution to the plan during 2005 was $160,000. Prepare Benjamin's 2005 entry to record postretirement expense.

EXERCISES

E20-1 (Pension Expense, Journal Entries) The following information is available for the pension plan of Kiley Company for the year 2004.

Actual and expected return on plan assets	$ 12,000
Benefits paid to retirees	40,000
Contributions (funding)	95,000
Interest/discount rate	10%
Prior service cost amortization	8,000
Projected benefit obligation, January 1, 2004	500,000
Service cost	60,000

Instructions

(a) Compute pension expense for the year 2004.

(b) Prepare the journal entry to record pension expense and the employer's contribution to the pension plan in 2004.

E20-2 (Computation of Pension Expense) Rebekah Company provides the following information about its defined benefit pension plan for the year 2005.

Service cost	$ 90,000
Contribution to the plan	105,000
Prior service cost amortization	10,000
Actual and expected return on plan assets	64,000
Benefits paid	40,000
Accrued pension cost liability at January 1, 2005	10,000
Plan assets at January 1, 2005	640,000
Projected benefit obligation at January 1, 2005	800,000
Unrecognized prior service cost balance at January 1, 2005	150,000
Interest/discount (settlement) rate	10%

Instructions

Compute the pension expense for the year 2005.

E20-3 (Preparation of Pension Work Sheet with Reconciliation) Using the information in E20-2 prepare a pension work sheet inserting January 1, 2005, balances, showing December 31, 2005, balances and the journal entry recording pension expense.

E20-4 (Basic Pension Work Sheet) The following facts apply to the pension plan of Trudy Borke Inc. for the year 2005.

Plan assets, January 1, 2005	$490,000
Projected benefit obligation, January 1, 2005	490,000
Settlement rate	8.5%
Annual pension service cost	40,000
Contributions (funding)	30,000
Actual return on plan assets	49,700
Benefits paid to retirees	33,400

Instructions

Using the preceding data, compute pension expense for the year 2005. As part of your solution, prepare a pension work sheet that shows the journal entry for pension expense for 2005 and the year-end balances in the related pension accounts.

E20-5 (Application of Years-of-Service Method) Janet Valente Company has five employees participating in its defined benefit pension plan. Expected years of future service for these employees at the beginning of 2005 are as follows.

Employee	Future Years of Service
Ed	3
Paul	4
Mary	6
Dave	6
Caroline	6

On January 1, 2005, the company amended its pension plan increasing its projected benefit obligation by $60,000.

Instructions

Compute the amount of prior service cost amortization for the years 2005 through 2010 using the years-of-service method setting up appropriate schedules.

E20-6 (Computation of Actual Return) James Paul Importers provides the following pension plan information.

Fair value of pension plan assets, January 1, 2005	$2,300,000
Fair value of pension plan assets, December 31, 2005	2,725,000
Contributions to the plan in 2005	250,000
Benefits paid retirees in 2005	350,000

Instructions

From the data above, compute the actual return on the plan assets for 2005.

E20-7 (Basic Pension Work Sheet) The following defined pension data of Doreen Corp. apply to the year 2005.

Projected benefit obligation, 1/1/05 (before amendment)	$560,000
Plan assets, 1/1/05	546,200
Prepaid/accrued pension cost (credit)	13,800
On January 1, 2005, Doreen Corp., through plan amendment, grants prior service benefits having a present value of	100,000
Settlement rate	9%
Annual pension service cost	58,000
Contributions (funding)	55,000
Actual return on plan assets	52,280
Benefits paid to retirees	40,000
Prior service cost amortization for 2005	17,000

Instructions

For 2005, prepare a pension work sheet for Doreen Corp. that shows the journal entry for pension expense and the year-end balances in the related pension accounts.

E20-8 (Application of the Corridor Approach) Dougherty Corp. has beginning-of-the-year present values for its projected benefit obligation and market-related values for its pension plan assets.

	Projected Benefit Obligation	Plan Assets Value
2003	$2,000,000	$1,900,000
2004	2,400,000	2,500,000
2005	2,900,000	2,600,000
2006	3,600,000	3,000,000

The average remaining service life per employee in 2003 and 2004 is 10 years and in 2005 and 2006 is 12 years. The unrecognized net gain or loss that occurred during each year is as follows: 2003, $280,000 loss; 2004, $90,000 loss; 2005, $10,000 loss; and 2006, $25,000 gain. (In working the solution the unrecognized gains and losses must be aggregated to arrive at year-end balances.)

Instructions

Using the corridor approach, compute the amount of unrecognized net gain or loss amortized and charged to pension expense in each of the four years, setting up an appropriate schedule.

E20-9 (Disclosures: Pension Expense and Reconciliation Schedule) Mildred Enterprises provides the following information relative to its defined benefit pension plan.

Balances or Values at December 31, 2005	
Projected benefit obligation	$2,737,000
Accumulated benefit obligation	1,980,000
Vested benefit obligation	1,645,852
Fair value of plan assets	2,278,329
Unrecognized prior service cost	205,000
Unrecognized net loss (1/1/05 balance, –0–)	45,680
Accrued pension cost liability	207,991
Other pension plan data:	
Service cost for 2005	$ 94,000
Unrecognized prior service cost amortization for 2005	45,000
Actual return on plan assets in 2005	130,000
Expected return on plan assets in 2005	175,680
Interest on January 1, 2005, projected benefit obligation	253,000
Contributions to plan in 2005	92,329
Benefits paid	140,000

Instructions

(a) Prepare the note disclosing the components of pension expense for the year 2005.
(b) Reconcile the funded status of the plan with the amount reported in the December 31, 2005, balance sheet.

E20-10 (Pension Work Sheet with Reconciliation Schedule) Tim Buhl Corp. sponsors a defined benefit pension plan for its employees. On January 1, 2005, the following balances relate to this plan.

Plan assets	$480,000
Projected benefit obligation	625,000
Prepaid/accrued pension cost (credit)	45,000
Unrecognized prior service cost	100,000

As a result of the operation of the plan during 2005, the following additional data are provided by the actuary.

Service cost for 2005	$90,000
Settlement rate, 9%	
Actual return on plan assets in 2005	57,000
Amortization of prior service cost	19,000
Expected return on plan assets	52,000
Unexpected loss from change in projected benefit obligation, due to change in actuarial predictions	76,000
Contributions in 2005	99,000
Benefits paid retirees in 2005	85,000

Instructions

(a) Using the data above, compute pension expense for Tim Buhl Corp. for the year 2005 by preparing a pension work sheet that shows the journal entry for pension expense and the year-end balances in the related pension accounts.
(b) At December 31, 2005, prepare a schedule reconciling the funded status of the plan with the pension amount reported on the balance sheet.

E20-11 (Minimum Liability Computation, Entry) The following information is available for McGwire Corporation's defined benefit pension plan for the years 2004 and 2005.

	December 31,	
	2004	2005
Accrued pension cost balance	$ –0–	$ 45,000
Accumulated benefit obligation	260,000	370,000
Fair value of plan assets	255,000	300,000
Prepaid pension cost balance	30,000	–0–
Projected benefit obligation	350,000	455,000
Unrecognized prior service cost	125,000	110,000

Instructions

(a) Compute the amount of additional liability, if any, that McGwire must record at the end of each year.
(b) Prepare the journal entries, if any, necessary to record a minimum liability for 2004 and 2005.

E20-12 (Pension Expense, Journal Entries, Statement Presentation, Minimum Liability) Desiree Griseta Company sponsors a defined benefit pension plan for its employees. The following data relate to the operation of the plan for the year 2004 in which no benefits were paid.

1. The actuarial present value of future benefits earned by employees for services rendered in 2004 amounted to $56,000.
2. The company's funding policy requires a contribution to the pension trustee amounting to $145,000 for 2004.
3. As of January 1, 2004, the company had a projected benefit obligation of $1,000,000, an accumulated benefit obligation of $800,000, and an unrecognized prior service cost of $400,000. The fair value of pension plan assets amounted to $600,000 at the beginning of the year. The market-related asset value was equal to $600,000. The actual and expected return on plan assets was $54,000. The settlement rate was 9%. No gains or losses occurred in 2004 and no benefits were paid.
4. Amortization of unrecognized prior service cost was $40,000 in 2004. Amortization of unrecognized net gain or loss was not required in 2004.

Instructions

(a) Determine the amounts of the components of pension expense that should be recognized by the company in 2004.
(b) Prepare the journal entry or entries to record pension expense and the employer's contribution to the pension trustee in 2004.
(c) Indicate the amounts that would be reported on the income statement and the balance sheet for the year 2004. The accumulated benefit obligation on December 31, 2004, was $830,000.

E20-13 (Pension Expense, Journal Entries, Minimum Liability, Statement Presentation) Nellie Altom Company received the following selected information from its pension plan trustee concerning the operation of the company's defined benefit pension plan for the year ended December 31, 2004.

	January 1, 2004	December 31, 2004
Projected benefit obligation	$2,000,000	$2,077,000
Market-related and fair value of plan assets	800,000	1,130,000
Accumulated benefit obligation	1,600,000	1,720,000
Actuarial (gains) losses (Unrecognized net (gain) or loss)	–0–	(200,000)

The service cost component of pension expense for employee services rendered in the current year amounted to $77,000 and the amortization of unrecognized prior service cost was $115,000. The company's actual funding (contributions) of the plan in 2004 amounted to $250,000. The expected return on plan assets and the actual rate were both 10%; the interest/discount (settlement) rate was 10%. No prepaid/accrued pension cost existed on January 1, 2004. Assume no benefits paid in 2004.

Instructions

(a) Determine the amounts of the components of pension expense that should be recognized by the company in 2004.
(b) Prepare the journal entries to record pension expense and the employer's contribution to the pension plan in 2004.
(c) Indicate the pension-related amounts that would be reported on the income statement and the balance sheet for Nellie Altom Company for the year 2004. (Compute the minimum liability.)

E20-14 (Computation of Actual Return, Gains and Losses, Corridor Test, Prior Service Cost, Minimum Liability, Pension Expense, and Reconciliation) Linda Berstler Company sponsors a defined benefit pension plan. The corporation's actuary provides the following information about the plan.

	January 1, 2005	December 31, 2005
Vested benefit obligation	$1,500	$1,900
Accumulated benefit obligation	1,900	2,730
Projected benefit obligation	2,800	3,645
Plan assets (fair value)	1,700	2,620
Settlement rate and expected rate of return		10%
Prepaid/(accrued) pension cost	–0–	?
Unrecognized prior service cost	1,100	?
Service cost for the year 2005		400
Contributions (funding in 2005)		800
Benefits paid in 2005		200

The average remaining service life per employee is 20 years.

Instructions

(a) Compute the actual return on the plan assets in 2005.
(b) Compute the amount of the unrecognized net gain or loss as of December 31, 2005. (Assume the January 1, 2005, balance was zero.)
(c) Compute the amount of unrecognized net gain or loss amortization for 2005 (corridor approach).
(d) Compute the amount of prior service cost amortization for 2005.
(e) Compute the minimum liability to be reported at December 31, 2005.
(f) Compute pension expense for 2005.
(g) Prepare a schedule reconciling the plan's funded status with the amounts reported in the December 31, 2005, balance sheet.

E20-15 (Work Sheet for E20-14) Using the information in E20-14 about Linda Berstler Company's defined benefit pension plan, prepare a 2005 pension work sheet with supplementary schedules of computations. Prepare the journal entries at December 31, 2005, to record pension expense and any "additional liability." Also, prepare a schedule reconciling the plan's funded status with the pension amounts reported in the balance sheet.

E20-16 (Pension Expense, Minimum Liability, Journal Entries) Walker Company provides the following information related to its defined benefit pension plan for 2004.

Accrued pension cost balance (January 1)	$ 25,000
Accumulated benefit obligation (December 31)	400,000
Actual and expected return on plan assets	15,000
Additional pension liability balance (January 1)	10,000
Contributions (funding) in 2004	150,000
Fair value of plan assets (December 31)	350,000
Settlement rate	10%
Projected benefit obligation (January 1)	700,000
Service cost	90,000

Instructions

(a) Compute pension expense and prepare the journal entry to record pension expense and the employer's contribution to the pension plan in 2004.
(b) Prepare the journal entry to record the minimum liability for 2004.

E20-17 (Pension Expense, Minimum Liability, Statement Presentation) Blum Foods Company obtained the following information from the insurance company that administers the company's employee-defined benefit pension plan.

	For Year Ended December 31		
	2004	2005	2006
Plan assets (at fair value)	$280,000	$398,000	$586,000
Accumulated benefit obligation	378,000	512,000	576,000
Pension expense	95,000	128,000	130,000
Employer's funding contribution	110,000	150,000	125,000
Prior service cost not yet recognized in earnings	494,230	451,365	400,438

Prior to 2004 cumulative pension expense was equal to cumulative contributions. Assume that the market-related asset value is equal to the fair value of plan assets for all three years.

Instructions

(a) Prepare the journal entries to record pension expense, employer's funding contribution, and the adjustment to a minimum pension liability for the years 2004, 2005, and 2006. (Preparation of a pension work sheet is not a requirement of this exercise; insufficient information is given to prepare one.)
(b) Indicate the pension related amounts that would be reported on the company's income statement and balance sheet for 2004, 2005, and 2006.

E20-18 (Minimum Liability, Journal Entries, Balance Sheet Items) Presented on the next page is partial information related to the pension fund of Rose Bryhan Inc.

Funded Status (end of year)	2004	2005	2006
Assets and obligations			
Market-related asset value	$1,300,000	$1,650,000	$1,900,000
Plan assets (at fair value)	1,300,000	1,670,000	1,950,000
Accumulated benefit obligation	1,150,000	1,480,000	2,060,000
Projected benefit obligation	1,600,000	1,910,000	2,500,000
Unfunded accumulated benefits			110,000
Overfunded accumulated benefits	150,000	190,000	
Amounts to be recognized			
(Accrued)/prepaid pension cost at beginning of year	$ –0–	$ 19,000	$ 16,000
Pension expense	(250,000)	(268,000)	(300,000)
Contribution	269,000	265,000	277,000
(Accrued)/prepaid pension cost at end of year	$ 19,000	$ 16,000	$ (7,000)

The company's unrecognized prior service cost is $637,000 at the end of 2006.

Instructions

(a) What pension-related amounts are reported on the balance sheet of Rose Bryhan Inc. for 2004, 2005, and 2006?

(b) What are the journal entries made to record pension expense in 2004, 2005, and 2006?

(c) What journal entries (if any) are necessary to record a minimum liability for 2004, 2005, and 2006?

E20-19 (Reconciliation Schedule, Minimum Liability, and Unrecognized Loss) Presented below is partial information related to Jean Burr Company at December 31, 2004.

Market-related asset value	$700,000
Projected benefit obligation	930,000
Accumulated benefit obligation	865,000
Plan assets (at fair value)	700,000
Vested benefits	200,000
Prior service cost not yet recognized in pension expense	120,000
Gains and losses	–0–

Instructions

(a) Present the schedule reconciling the funded status with the asset/liability reported on the balance sheet. Assume no asset or liability existed at the beginning of period for pensions on Jean Burr Company's balance sheet.

(b) Assume the same facts as in (a) except that Jean Burr Company has an unrecognized loss of $16,000 during 2004.

(c) Explain the rationale for the treatment of the unrecognized loss and the prior service cost not yet recognized in pension expense.

E20-20 (Amortization of Unrecognized Net Gain or Loss [Corridor Approach], Pension Expense Computation) The actuary for the pension plan of Joyce Bush Inc. calculated the following net gains and losses.

Unrecognized Net Gain or Loss	
Incurred during the Year	(Gain) or Loss
2004	$300,000
2005	480,000
2006	(210,000)
2007	(290,000)

Other information about the company's pension obligation and plan assets is as follows.

As of January 1,	Projected Benefit Obligation	Plan Assets (market-related asset value)
2004	$4,000,000	$2,400,000
2005	4,520,000	2,200,000
2006	4,980,000	2,600,000
2007	4,250,000	3,040,000

Joyce Bush Inc. has a stable labor force of 400 employees who are expected to receive benefits under the plan. The total service-years for all participating employees is 5,600. The beginning balance of unrecognized net gain or loss is zero on January 1, 2004. The market-related value and the fair value of plan assets are the same for the 4-year period. Use the average remaining service life per employee as the basis for amortization.

Instructions

(Round to the nearest dollar)

Prepare a schedule which reflects the minimum amount of unrecognized net gain or loss amortized as a component of net periodic pension expense for each of the years 2004, 2005, 2006, and 2007. Apply the "corridor" approach in determining the amount to be amortized each year.

E20-21 (Amortization of Unrecognized Net Gain or Loss [Corridor Approach]) Lowell Company sponsors a defined benefit pension plan for its 600 employees. The company's actuary provided the following information about the plan.

	January 1,	December 31,	
	2004	2004	2005
Projected benefit obligation	$2,800,000	$3,650,000	$4,400,000
Accumulated benefit obligation	1,900,000	2,430,000	2,900,000
Plan assets (fair value and market related asset value)	1,700,000	2,900,000	2,100,000
Unrecognized net (gain) or loss (for purposes of the corridor calculation)	–0–	101,000	(24,000)
Discount rate (current settlement rate)	11%	8%	
Actual and expected asset return rate	10%	10%	

The average remaining service life per employee is 10.5 years. The service cost component of net periodic pension expense for employee services rendered amounted to $400,000 in 2004 and $475,000 in 2005. The unrecognized prior service cost on January 1, 2004, was $1,155,000. No benefits have been paid.

Instructions

(Round to the nearest dollar)

(a) Compute the amount of unrecognized prior service cost to be amortized as a component of net periodic pension expense for each of the years 2004 and 2005.

(b) Prepare a schedule which reflects the amount of net unrecognized gain or loss to be amortized as a component of net periodic pension expense for 2004 and 2005.

(c) Determine the total amount of net periodic pension expense to be recognized by Lowell Company in 2004 and 2005.

***E20-22 (Postretirement Benefit Expense Computation)** Rose Chance Inc. provides the following information related to its postretirement benefits for the year 2006.

Accumulated postretirement benefit obligation at January 1, 2006	$810,000
Actual and expected return on plan assets	34,000
Unrecognized prior service cost amortization	21,000
Amortization of transition amount (loss)	5,000
Discount rate	10%
Service cost	88,000

Instructions

Compute postretirement benefit expense for 2006.

***E20-23 (Postretirement Benefit Expense Computation)** Marvelous Marvin Co. provides the following information about its postretirement benefit plan for the year 2005.

Service cost	$ 90,000
Prior service cost amortization	3,000
Contribution to the plan	16,000
Actual and expected return on plan assets	62,000
Benefits paid	40,000
Plan assets at January 1, 2005	710,000
Accumulated postretirement benefit obligation at January 1, 2005	810,000
Unrecognized prior service cost balance at January 1, 2005	20,000
Amortization of transition amount (Loss)	5,000
Unrecognized transition amount at January 1, 2005	80,000
Discount rate	9%

Instructions

Compute the postretirement benefit expense for 2005.

***E20-24 (Postretirement Benefit Work Sheet)** Using the information in *E20-23 prepare a work sheet inserting January 1, 2005, balances, showing December 31, 2005, balances, and the journal entry recording postretirement benefit expense.

***E20-25 (Postretirement Benefit Reconciliation Schedule)** Presented below is partial information related to Sandra Conley Co. at December 31, 2006.

Accumulated postretirement benefit obligation	$ 950,000
Expected postretirement benefit obligation	1,000,000
Plan assets (at fair value)	650,000
Prior service cost not yet recognized in postretirement expense	60,000
Gain and losses	–0–
Unrecognized transition amount (Loss)	100,000

Instructions

(a) Present the schedule reconciling the funded status with the asset/liability reported on the balance sheet. Assume no asset or liability existed at the beginning of the period for postretirement benefits on Sandra Conley Co.'s balance sheet.

(b) Assume the same facts as in (a) except that Sandra Conley Co. has an unrecognized loss of $20,000 during 2006.

PROBLEMS

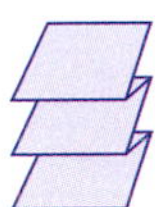

P20-1 (Two-Year Work Sheet and Reconciliation Schedule) On January 1, 2005, Diana Peter Company has the following defined benefit pension plan balances.

Projected benefit obligation	$4,200,000
Fair value of plan assets	4,200,000

The interest (settlement) rate applicable to the plan is 10%. On January 1, 2006, the company amends its pension agreement so that prior service costs of $500,000 are created. Other data related to the pension plan are as follows.

	2005	2006
Service costs	$150,000	$180,000
Unrecognized prior service costs amortization	–0–	90,000
Contributions (funding) to the plan	140,000	185,000
Benefits paid	200,000	280,000
Actual return on plan assets	252,000	260,000
Expected rate of return on assets	6%	8%

Instructions

(a) Prepare a pension work sheet for the pension plan for 2005 and 2006.

(b) As of December 31, 2006, prepare a schedule reconciling the funded status with the reported liability (accrued pension cost).

P20-2 (Three-Year Work Sheet, Journal Entries, and Reconciliation Schedules) Katie Day Company adopts acceptable accounting for its defined benefit pension plan on January 1, 2005, with the following beginning balances: plan assets $200,000; projected benefit obligation $200,000. Other data relating to 3 years' operation of the plan are as follows.

	2005	2006	2007
Annual service cost	$16,000	$ 19,000	$ 26,000
Settlement rate and expected rate of return	10%	10%	10%
Actual return on plan assets	17,000	21,900	24,000
Annual funding (contributions)	16,000	40,000	48,000
Benefits paid	14,000	16,400	21,000
Unrecognized prior service cost (plan amended, 1/1/06)		160,000	
Amortization of unrecognized prior service cost		54,400	41,600
Change in actuarial assumptions establishes a December 31, 2007, projected benefit obligation of:			520,000

Instructions

(a) Prepare a pension work sheet presenting all 3 years' pension balances and activities.
(b) Prepare the journal entries (from the work sheet) to reflect all pension plan transactions and events at December 31 of each year.
(c) At December 31 of each year prepare a schedule reconciling the funded status of the plan with the pension amounts reported in the financial statements.

P20-3 (Pension Expense, Journal Entries, Minimum Pension Liability, Amortization of Unrecognized Loss, Reconciliation Schedule) Paul Dobson Company sponsors a defined benefit plan for its 100 employees. On January 1, 2004, the company's actuary provided the following information.

Unrecognized prior service cost	$150,000
Pension plan assets (fair value and market-related asset value)	200,000
Accumulated benefit obligation	260,000
Projected benefit obligation	350,000

The average remaining service period for the participating employees is 10.5 years. All employees are expected to receive benefits under the plan. On December 31, 2004, the actuary calculated that the present value of future benefits earned for employee services rendered in the current year amounted to $52,000; the projected benefit obligation was $452,000; fair value of pension assets was $276,000; the accumulated benefit obligation amounted to $365,000; and the market-related asset value is $276,000. The expected return on plan assets and the discount rate on the projected benefit obligation were both 10%. The actual return on plan assets is $11,000. The company's current year's contribution to the pension plan amounted to $65,000. No benefits were paid during the year.

Instructions

(Round to the nearest dollar)

(a) Determine the components of pension expense that the company would recognize in 2004. (With only one year involved, you need not prepare a work sheet.)
(b) Prepare the journal entries to record the pension expense and the company's funding of the pension plan in 2004.
(c) Assume Paul Dobson Company elects to recognize the minimum pension liability in its balance sheet for the year ended December 31, 2004. Prepare the journal entry to record the minimum liability.
(d) Compute the amount of the 2004 increase/decrease in unrecognized gains or losses and the amount to be amortized in 2004 and 2005.
(e) Prepare a schedule reconciling the funded status of the plan with the pension amounts reported in the financial statement as of December 31, 2004.

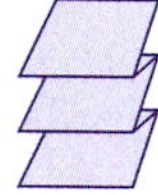

P20-4 (Pension Expense, Minimum Liability, Journal Entries for Two Years) Mantle Company sponsors a defined benefit pension plan. The following information related to the pension plan is available for 2004 and 2005.

	2004	2005
Plan assets (fair value), December 31	$380,000	$465,000
Projected benefit obligation, January 1	600,000	700,000
Prepaid/(accrued) pension cost balance, January 1	(40,000)	?
Unrecognized prior service cost, January 1	250,000	240,000
Service cost	60,000	90,000
Actual and expected return on plan assets	24,000	30,000
Amortization of prior service cost	10,000	12,000
Contributions (funding)	110,000	120,000
Accumulated benefit obligation, December 31	500,000	550,000
Additional pension liability balance, January 1	50,000	?
Interest/settlement rate	9%	9%

Instructions

(a) Compute pension expense for 2004 and 2005.
(b) Prepare the journal entries to record the pension expense and the company's funding of the pension plan for both years.
(c) Compute the minimum liability for 2004 and 2005.
(d) Prepare the journal entries to record the minimum liability for both years.

P20-5 (Computation of Pension Expense, Amortization of Unrecognized Net Gain or Loss [Corridor Approach], Journal Entries for Three Years, and Minimum Pension Liability Computation) Dubel

Toothpaste Company initiates a defined benefit pension plan for its 50 employees on January 1, 2004. The insurance company which administers the pension plan provided the following information for the years 2004, 2005, and 2006.

	For Year Ended December 31,		
	2004	2005	2006
Plan assets (fair value)	$50,000	$ 85,000	$170,000
Accumulated benefit obligation	45,000	165,000	292,000
Projected benefit obligation	55,000	200,000	324,000
Unrecognized net (gain) loss (for purposes of corridor calculation)	–0–	83,950	86,121
Employer's funding contribution (made at end of year)	50,000	60,000	95,000

There were no balances as of January 1, 2004, when the plan was initiated. The actual and expected return on plan assets was 10% over the 3-year period but the settlement rate used to discount the company's pension obligation was 13% in 2004, 11% in 2005, and 8% in 2006. The service cost component of net periodic pension expense amounted to the following: 2004, $55,000; 2005, $85,000; and 2006, $119,000. The average remaining service life per employee is 12 years. No benefits were paid in 2004, $30,000 of benefits were paid in 2005, and $18,500 of benefits were paid in 2006 (all benefits paid at end of year).

Instructions

(Round to the nearest dollar)

(a) Calculate the amount of net periodic pension expense that the company would recognize in 2004, 2005, and 2006.

(b) Prepare the journal entries to record net periodic pension expense, employer's funding contribution, and the adjustment to reflect a minimum pension liability for the years 2004, 2005, and 2006.

P20-6 (Computation of Unrecognized Prior Service Cost Amortization, Pension Expense, Journal Entries, Net Gain or Loss, and Reconciliation Schedule) Ekedahl Inc. has sponsored a noncontributory-defined benefit pension plan for its employees since 1984. Prior to 2004, cumulative net pension expense recognized equaled cumulative contributions to the plan. Other relevant information about the pension plan on January 1, 2004, is as follows.

1. The company has 200 employees. All these employees are expected to receive benefits under the plan. The average remaining service life per employee is 13 years.
2. The projected benefit obligation amounted to $5,000,000 and the fair value of pension plan assets was $3,000,000. The market-related asset value was also $3,000,000. Unrecognized prior service cost was $2,000,000.

On December 31, 2004, the projected benefit obligation and the accumulated benefit obligation were $4,750,000 and $4,025,000, respectively. The fair value of the pension plan assets amounted to $3,900,000 at the end of the year. The market-related asset value was $3,790,000. A 10% settlement rate and a 10% expected asset return rate were used in the actuarial present value computations in the pension plan. The present value of benefits attributed by the pension benefit formula to employee service in 2004 amounted to $200,000. The employer's contribution to the plan assets amounted to $575,000 in 2004. This problem assumes no payment of pension benefits.

Instructions

(Round all amounts to the nearest dollar)

(a) Prepare a schedule, based on the average remaining life per employee, showing the unrecognized prior service cost that would be amortized as a component of pension expense for 2004, 2005, and 2006.

(b) Compute pension expense for the year 2004.

(c) Prepare the journal entries required to report the accounting for the company's pension plan for 2004.

(d) Compute the amount of the 2004 increase/decrease in unrecognized net gains or losses and the amount to be amortized in 2004 and 2005.

(e) Prepare a schedule reconciling the funded status of the plan with the pension amounts reported in the financial statements as of December 31, 2004.

P20-7 (Pension Work Sheet, Minimum Liability) Farrey Corp. sponsors a defined benefit pension plan for its employees. On January 1, 2006, the following balances related to this plan.

Plan assets (fair value)	$520,000
Projected benefit obligation	725,000
Prepaid/accrued pension cost (credit)	33,000
Unrecognized prior service cost	81,000
Unrecognized net gain or loss (debit)	91,000

As a result of the operation of the plan during 2006, the actuary provided the following additional data at December 31, 2006.

Service cost for 2006	$108,000
Settlement rate, 9%; expected return rate, 10%	
Actual return on plan assets in 2006	48,000
Amortization of prior service cost	25,000
Market-related asset value at 1/1/06	550,000
Contributions in 2006	138,000
Benefits paid retirees in 2006	85,000
Average remaining service life of active employees	10 years
Accumulated benefit obligation at 12/31/06	671,000

Instructions

Using the preceding data, compute pension expense for Farrey Corp. for the year 2006 by preparing a pension work sheet that shows the journal entry for pension expense and any additional pension liability. (The minimum pension liability must be computed and the corridor approach must be applied to the unrecognized gain or loss.) Use the market-related asset value to compute the expected return.

P20-8 (Comprehensive 2-Year Work Sheet) Glesen Company sponsors a defined benefit pension plan for its employees. The following data relate to the operation of the plan for the years 2005 and 2006.

	2005	2006
Projected benefit obligation, January 1	$650,000	
Plan assets (fair value and market related value), January 1	410,000	
Prepaid/accrued pension cost (credit), January 1	80,000	
Additional pension liability, January 1	12,300	
Intangible asset-deferred pension cost, January 1	12,300	
Unrecognized prior service cost, January 1	160,000	
Service cost	40,000	$ 59,000
Settlement rate	10%	10%
Expected rate of return	10%	10%
Actual return on plan assets	36,000	61,000
Amortization of prior service cost	70,000	55,000
Annual contributions	72,000	81,000
Benefits paid retirees	31,500	54,000
Increase in projected benefit obligation due to changes in actuarial assumptions	87,000	–0–
Accumulated benefit obligation at December 31	721,800	789,000
Average service life of all employees		20 years
Vested benefit obligation at December 31		464,000

Instructions

(a) Prepare a pension work sheet presenting both years 2005 and 2006 and accompanying computations including the computation of the minimum liability (2005 and 2006) and amortization of the unrecognized loss (2006) using the corridor approach.

(b) Prepare the journal entries (from the work sheet) to reflect all pension plan transactions and events at December 31 of each year.

(c) At December 31, 2006, prepare a schedule reconciling the funded status of the pension plan with the pension amounts reported in the financial statements.

P20-9 (Comprehensive 2-Year Work Sheet) Ingrid Mount Co. has the following defined benefit pension plan balances on January 1, 2003.

Projected benefit obligation	$4,500,000
Fair value of plan assets	4,500,000

The interest (settlement) rate applicable to the plan is 10%. On January 1, 2004, the company amends its pension agreement so that prior service costs of $600,000 are created. Other data related to the pension plan are:

	2003	2004
Service costs	$150,000	$170,000
Unrecognized prior service costs amortization	–0–	90,000
Contributions (funding) to the plan	150,000	184,658
Benefits paid	220,000	280,000
Actual return on plan assets	252,000	250,000
Expected rate of return on assets	6%	8%

Instructions

(a) Prepare a pension work sheet for the pension plan in 2003.

(b) Prepare any journal entries related to the pension plan that would be needed at December 31, 2003.

(c) Prepare a pension work sheet for 2004 and any journal entries related to the pension plan as of December 31, 2004.

(d) As of December 31, 2004, prepare a schedule reconciling the funded status with the reported liability (accrued pension cost).

***P20-10 (Postretirement Benefit Work Sheet with Reconciliation)** Dusty Hass Foods Inc. sponsors a postretirement medical and dental benefit plan for its employees. The company adopts the provisions of *Statement No. 106* beginning January 1, 2005. The following balances relate to this plan on January 1, 2005.

Plan assets	$ 200,000
Expected postretirement benefit obligation	1,420,000
Accumulated postretirement benefit obligation	882,000
No prior service costs exist.	

As a result of the plan's operation during 2005, the following additional data are provided by the actuary.

Service cost for 2005 is $70,000
Discount rate is 9%
Contributions to plan in 2005 are $60,000
Expected return on plan assets is $9,000
Actual return on plan assets is $15,000
Benefits paid to employees from plan are $44,000
Average remaining service to full eligibility: 20 years
Average remaining service to expected retirement: 22 years
Transition amount to be amortized: ?

Instructions

(a) Using the preceding data, compute the net periodic postretirement benefit cost for 2005 by preparing a work sheet that shows the journal entry for postretirement expense and the year-end balances in the related postretirement benefit memo accounts. (Assume that contributions and benefits are paid at the end of the year.)

(b) At December 31, 2005, prepare a schedule reconciling the funded status of the plan with the postretirement amount reported on the balance sheet.

CONCEPTUAL CASES

C20-1 (Pension Terminology and Theory) Many business organizations have been concerned with providing for the retirement of employees since the late 1800s. During recent decades a marked increase in this concern has resulted in the establishment of private pension plans in most large companies and in many medium- and small-sized ones.

The substantial growth of these plans, both in numbers of employees covered and in amounts of retirement benefits, has increased the significance of pension cost in relation to the financial position, results of operations, and cash flows of many companies. In examining the costs of pension plans, a CPA encounters certain terms. The components of pension costs that the terms represent must be dealt with appropriately if generally accepted accounting principles are to be reflected in the financial statements of entities with pension plans.

Instructions

(a) Define a private pension plan. How does a contributory pension plan differ from a noncontributory plan?

(b) Differentiate between "accounting for the employer" and "accounting for the pension fund."
(c) Explain the terms "funded" and "pension liability" as they relate to:
    (1) The pension fund.
    (2) The employer.
(d) (1) Discuss the theoretical justification for accrual recognition of pension costs.
    (2) Discuss the relative objectivity of the measurement process of accrual versus cash (pay-as-you-go) accounting for annual pension costs.
(e) Distinguish among the following as they relate to pension plans.
    (1) Service cost.
    (2) Prior service costs.
    (3) Vested benefits.

C20-2 (Pension Terminology) The following items appear on Hollingsworth Company's financial statements.

1. Under the caption Assets:
   Prepaid pension cost.
   Intangible asset—Deferred pension cost.
2. Under the caption Liabilities:
   Accrued pension cost.
3. Under the caption Stockholders' Equity:
   Excess of additional pension liability over unrecognized prior service cost as a component of Accumulated Other Comprehensive Income.
4. On the income statement:
   Pension expense.

Instructions

Explain the significance of each of the items above on corporate financial statements. (*Note:* All items set forth above are not necessarily to be found on the statements of a single company.)

C20-3 (Basic Terminology) In examining the costs of pension plans, Leah Hutcherson, CPA, encounters certain terms. The components of pension costs that the terms represent must be dealt with appropriately if generally accepted accounting principles are to be reflected in the financial statements of entities with pension plans.

Instructions

(a) (1) Discuss the theoretical justification for accrual recognition of pension costs.
    (2) Discuss the relative objectivity of the measurement process of accrual versus cash (pay-as-you-go) accounting for annual pension costs.
(b) Explain the following terms as they apply to accounting for pension plans.
    (1) Market-related asset value.
    (2) Projected benefit obligation.
    (3) Corridor approach.
(c) What information should be disclosed about a company's pension plans in its financial statements and its notes?

(AICPA adapted)

C20-4 (Major Pension Concepts) Lyons Corporation is a medium-sized manufacturer of paperboard containers and boxes. The corporation sponsors a noncontributory, defined benefit pension plan that covers its 250 employees. Spring Meissner has recently been hired as president of Lyons Corporation. While reviewing last year's financial statements with Sara Montgomery, controller, Meissner expressed confusion about several of the items in the footnote to the financial statements relating to the pension plan. In part, the footnote reads as follows.

> **Note J.** The company has a defined benefit pension plan covering substantially all of its employees. The benefits are based on years of service and the employee's compensation during the last four years of employment. The company's funding policy is to contribute annually the maximum amount allowed under the federal tax code. Contributions are intended to provide for benefits expected to be earned in the future as well as those earned to date.

Effective for the year ending December 31, 2004, Lyons Corporation adopted the provisions of *Statement of Financial Accounting Standard No. 87*—Employer's Accounting for Pensions. The net periodic pension expense on Lyons Corporation's comparative Income Statement was $72,000 in 2005 and $57,680 in 2004.

The following are selected figures from the plan's funded status and amounts recognized in the Lyons Corporation's Statement of Financial Position at December 31, 2005 ($000 omitted).

Actuarial present value of benefit obligations:	
Accumulated benefit obligation	
(including vested benefits of $636)	$ (870)
Projected benefit obligation	$(1,200)
Plan assets at fair value	1,050
Projected benefit obligation in excess of plan assets	$ (150)

Given that Lyons Corporation's work force has been stable for the last 6 years, Meissner could not understand the increase in the net periodic pension expense. Montgomery explained that the net periodic pension expense consists of several elements, some of which may increase or decrease the net expense.

Instructions

(a) The determination of the net periodic pension expense is a function of five elements. List and briefly describe each of the elements.

(b) Describe the major difference and the major similarity between the accumulated benefit obligation and the projected benefit obligation.

(c) **(1)** Explain why pension gains and losses are not recognized on the income statement in the period in which they arise.

(2) Briefly describe how pension gains and losses are recognized.

(d) Under what conditions must Lyons recognize an additional minimum liability?

(CMA adapted)

C20-5 (Implications of *FASB Statement No. 87*) Ruth Moore and Carl Nies have to do a class presentation on the pension pronouncement "Employers' Accounting for Pension Plans." In developing the class presentation, they decided to provide the class with a series of questions related to pensions and then discuss the answers in class. Given that the class has all read *FASB Statement No. 87*, they felt this approach would provide a lively discussion. Here are the situations:

1. In an article in *Business Week* prior to *FASB No. 87*, it was reported that the discount rates used by the largest 200 companies for pension reporting ranged from 5% to 11%. How can such a situation exist, and does the pension pronouncement alleviate this problem?
2. An article indicated that when *FASB Statement No. 87* was issued, it caused an increase in the liability for pensions for approximately 20% of companies. Why might this situation occur?
3. A recent article noted that while "smoothing" is not necessarily an accounting virtue, pension accounting has long been recognized as an exception—an area of accounting in which at least some dampening of market swings is appropriate. This is because pension funds are managed so that their performance is insulated from the extremes of short-term market swings. A pension expense that reflects the volatility of market swings might, for that reason, convey information of little relevance. Are these statements true?
4. Companies as diverse as **American Hospital Supply**, **Ashland Oil**, **Digital Equipment**, **GTE**, **Ralston Purina**, and **Signal Cos.** held assets twice as large as they needed to fund their pension plans at one time. Are these assets reported on the balance sheet of these companies per the pension pronouncement? If not, where are they reported?
5. Understanding the impact of the changes required in pension reporting requires detailed information about its pension plan(s) and an analysis of the relationship of many factors, particularly:
   (a) the type of plan(s) and any significant amendments.
   (b) the plan participants.
   (c) the funding status.
   (d) the actuarial funding method and assumptions currently used.
   What impact does each of these items have on financial statement presentation?
6. An article noted "You also need to decide whether to amortize gains and losses using the corridor method, or to use some other systematic method. Under the corridor approach, only gains and losses in excess of 10% of the greater of the projected benefit obligation or the plan assets would have to be amortized." What is the corridor method and what is its purpose?
7. Some companies may have to establish an intangible asset-deferred pension cost if the plan assets at fair value are less than the accumulated benefit obligation. What is the nature of this intangible asset and how is it amortized each period?
8. In its exposure draft on pensions, the Board required a note that discussed the sensitivity of pension expense to changes in the interest rate and the salary progression assumption. This note might read as follows:

At December 31, 2004, the weighted-average discount rate and rate of increase in future compensation levels used in determining the actuarial present value of the projected benefit obligation were 9% and 6%, respectively. Those assumptions can have a significant effect on the amounts reported. To illustrate, increasing the discount rate assumption to 10% would have decreased the projected benefit obligation and net periodic pension expense by $340,000 and $50,000, respectively, for the year ended December 31, 2004. Increasing the rate of change of future compensation levels to 7% would have increased the projected benefit obligation and net periodic pension cost by $180,000 and $30,000, respectively, for the year ended December 31, 2004.

Why do you believe this disclosure was eliminated from the final pronouncement?

Instructions

What answers do you believe Ruth and Carl gave to each of these questions?

C20-6 (Unrecognized Gains and Losses, Corridor Amortization) Rachel Avery, accounting clerk in the personnel office of Clarence G. Avery Corp., has begun to compute pension expense for 2004 but is not sure whether or not she should include the amortization of unrecognized gains/losses. She is currently working with the following beginning-of-the-year present values for the projected benefit obligation and market-related values for the pension plan:

	Projected Benefit Obligation	Plan Assets Value
2001	$2,200,000	$1,900,000
2002	2,400,000	2,600,000
2003	2,900,000	2,600,000
2004	3,900,000	3,000,000

The average remaining service life per employee in 2001 and 2002 is 10 years and in 2003 and 2004 is 12 years. The unrecognized net gain or loss that occurred during each year is as follows.

2001	$280,000 loss
2002	90,000 loss
2003	12,000 loss
2004	25,000 gain

(In working the solution, you must aggregate the unrecognized gains and losses to arrive at year-end balances.)

Instructions

You are the manager in charge of accounting. Write a memo to Rachel Avery, explaining why in some years she must amortize some of the unrecognized net gains and losses and in other years she does not need to. In order to explain this situation fully, you must compute the amount of unrecognized net gain or loss that is amortized and charged to pension expense in each of the 4 years listed above. Include an appropriate amortization schedule, referring to it whenever necessary.

C20-7 (Nonvested Employees—An Ethical Dilemma) Cardinal Technology recently merged with College Electronix, a computer graphics manufacturing firm. In performing a comprehensive audit of CE's accounting system, Richard Nye, internal audit manager for Cardinal Technology, discovered that the new subsidiary did not capitalize pension assets and liabilities, subject to the requirements of *FASB Statement No. 87*.

The net present value of CE's pension assets was $15.5 million, the vested benefit obligation was $12.9 million, and the projected benefit obligation was $17.4 million. Nye reported this audit finding to Renée Selma, the newly appointed controller of CE. A few days later Selma called Nye for his advice on what to do. Selma started her conversation by asking, "Can't we eliminate the negative income effect of our pension dilemma simply by terminating the employment of nonvested employees before the end of our fiscal year?"

Instructions

How should Nye respond to Selma's remark about firing nonvested employees?

USING YOUR JUDGMENT

FINANCIAL REPORTING PROBLEM

3M Company

The financial statements of 3M are presented in Appendix 5B or can be accessed on the Take Action! CD.

Instructions

Refer to 3M's financial statements and the accompanying notes to answer the following questions.

(a) What kind of pension plan does 3M provide its employees in the United States?

(b) What was 3M's pension expense for 2001, 2000, and 1999 for the United States?

(c) What is the impact of 3M's pension plans for 2001 on its financial statements?

*FINANCIAL STATEMENT ANALYSIS CASE

General Electric

A *Wall Street Journal* article discussed a $1.8 billion charge to income made by General Electric for postretirement benefit costs. It was attributed to previously unrecognized health-care and life insurance cost. As financial vice president and controller for Peake, Inc., you found this article interesting because the president recently expressed concern about the company's rising health costs. The president, Martha Beyerlein, was particularly concerned with health care cost premiums being paid for retired employees. She wondered what charge Peake, Inc. will have to take for its postretirement benefit program.

Instructions

As financial vice president and controller of Peake, Inc., explain what the charge was that General Electric made against income. What are the options for Peake, Inc. in accounting for and reporting any transition amount when it adopts *FASB Statement No. 106*?

COMPARATIVE ANALYSIS CASE

The Coca-Cola Company versus PepsiCo, Inc.

Instructions

Go to the Take Action! CD, and use information found there to answer the following questions related to The Coca-Cola Company and PepsiCo, Inc.

(a) What kind of pension plans do Coca-Cola and PepsiCo provide their employees?

(b) What net periodic pension expense (cost) did Coca-Cola and PepsiCo report in 2001?

(c) What is the year-end 2001 funded status of Coca-Cola's and PepsiCo's U.S. plans?

(d) What relevant rates were used by Coca-Cola and PepsiCo in computing their pension amounts?

INTERNATIONAL REPORTING CASE

Volvo, a Swedish company that operates in the automotive and transport equipment industry, prepares its financial statements in accordance with Swedish accounting standards. Volvo's shares trade on the Nasdaq in the United States (and on several European stock exchanges as well). Volvo sponsors a pension plan for its employees in Sweden and the U.S. Volvo provided a disclosure related to its pension provisions in the notes to its financial statements, as well as an additional disclosure on the differences in accounting for its pension plans under U.S. and Swedish accounting standards. If Volvo had applied U.S. GAAP to its pensions, income would have been 40 million SEK lower in 2001. These disclosures about pension accounting are shown on the next page.

The Volvo Group

Note 22 Provisions for post-employment benefits

	1999	2000	2001
Provisions for pensions	1,002	1,294	3,632
Provisions for other post-employment benefits	1,128	1,338	11,015
Total	2,130	2,632	14,647

The amounts shown for Provisions for post-employment benefits correspond to the actuarially calculated value of obligations not insured with a third party or secured through transfers of funds to pension foundations. The amount of pensions falling due within one year is included. The Swedish Group companies have insured their pension obligations with third parties.

Group pension costs in 2001 amounted to 3,332 (1,548; 1,541). The greater part of pension costs consist of continuing payments to independent organizations that administer defined-contribution pension plans.The pension costs in 2000 was reduced by Alecta (previously SPP) surplus funds of 683.

Significant Differences between Swedish and U.S. accounting principles

Note H: *Provision for pensions and other post-employment benefits.* The greater part of the Volvo Group's pension commitments are defined contribution plans in which regular payments are made to independent authorities or bodies that administer pension plans. There is no difference between U.S. and Swedish accounting principles in accounting for these pension plans.

Other pension commitments are defined-benefit plans; that is, the employee is entitled to receive a certain level of pension benefits, usually related to the employee's final salary. In these cases the annual pension cost is calculated based on the current value of future pension payments. In Volvo's consolidated accounts, provisions for pensions and pension costs for the year in the individual companies are calculated based on local rules and directives. In accordance with U.S. GAAP, provisions for pensions and pension costs for the year should always be calculated as specified in SFAS 87, "Employers Accounting for Pensions." The difference lies primarily in the choice of discount rates and the fact that U.S. calculations of pension benefit obligations, in contrast to Swedish calculations, are based on salaries calculated at the time of retirement. In addition, under U.S. GAAP, the value of pension assets in excess of the pension obligation is accounted for.

Instructions

Use the information on Volvo to respond to the following requirements.

(a) What are the key differences in accounting for pensions under U.S. and Swedish standards?

(b) Briefly explain how differences in U.S. and Swedish standards for pensions would affect the amounts reported in the financial statements.

(c) In light of the differences identified above, what are the likely reason(s) that Volvo's income and equity would be higher under U.S. GAAP than under Swedish accounting standards?

RESEARCH CASES

Case 1

Instructions

Examine the pension footnotes of three companies of your choice and answer the following questions.

(a) For each company, identify the following three assumptions: (1) the weighted-average discount rate, (2) the rate of compensation increase used to measure the projected benefit obligation, and (3) the weighted-average expected long-run rate of return on plan assets.

(b) Comment on any significant differences between the assumptions used by each company.

(c) Did any of the companies change their assumptions during the period covered by the footnote? If so, what was the effect on the financial statements?

Case 2

The June 15, 1999, *Wall Street Journal* included an article by Ellen E. Schultz entitled "Companies Reap a Gain off Fat Pension Plans." (Subscribers to **Business Extra** can access the article at that site.)

Instructions

Read the article and answer the following questions.

(a) Explain how the high investment returns earned on pension plan assets in the late 1990s affected pension expense and net income. Given the recent bear market, what do you believe might happen to many companies' pension expense in the future?

(b) Explain what effect an overfunded pension plan can have on decisions made by management regarding various benefit costs.

(c) What is a major disadvantage of getting a pension plan too overfunded?

(d) What ethical issues are raised at the end of this article?

PROFESSIONAL SIMULATIONS

Simulation 1

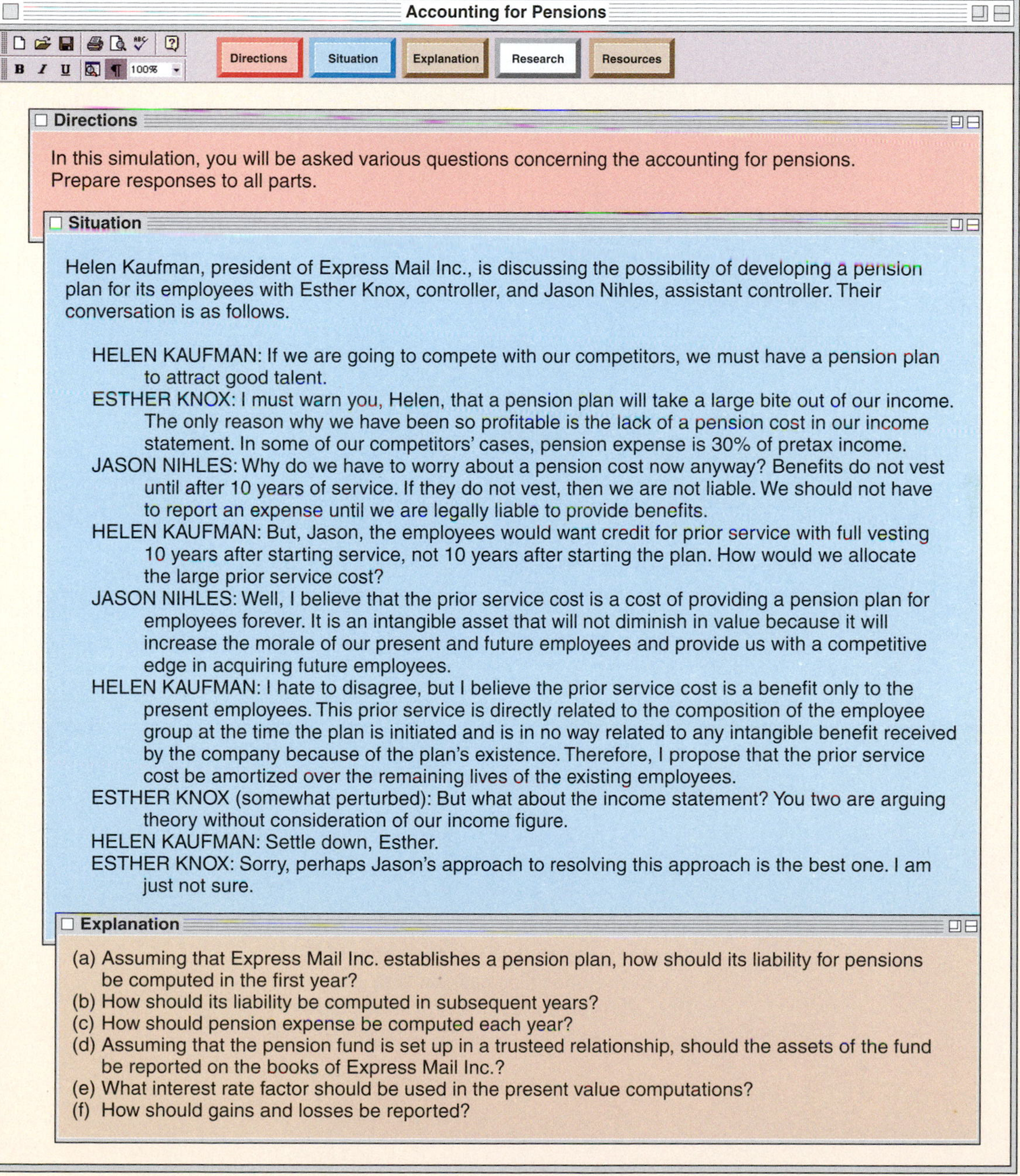

Directions

In this simulation, you will be asked various questions concerning the accounting for pensions. Prepare responses to all parts.

Situation

Helen Kaufman, president of Express Mail Inc., is discussing the possibility of developing a pension plan for its employees with Esther Knox, controller, and Jason Nihles, assistant controller. Their conversation is as follows.

HELEN KAUFMAN: If we are going to compete with our competitors, we must have a pension plan to attract good talent.

ESTHER KNOX: I must warn you, Helen, that a pension plan will take a large bite out of our income. The only reason why we have been so profitable is the lack of a pension cost in our income statement. In some of our competitors' cases, pension expense is 30% of pretax income.

JASON NIHLES: Why do we have to worry about a pension cost now anyway? Benefits do not vest until after 10 years of service. If they do not vest, then we are not liable. We should not have to report an expense until we are legally liable to provide benefits.

HELEN KAUFMAN: But, Jason, the employees would want credit for prior service with full vesting 10 years after starting service, not 10 years after starting the plan. How would we allocate the large prior service cost?

JASON NIHLES: Well, I believe that the prior service cost is a cost of providing a pension plan for employees forever. It is an intangible asset that will not diminish in value because it will increase the morale of our present and future employees and provide us with a competitive edge in acquiring future employees.

HELEN KAUFMAN: I hate to disagree, but I believe the prior service cost is a benefit only to the present employees. This prior service is directly related to the composition of the employee group at the time the plan is initiated and is in no way related to any intangible benefit received by the company because of the plan's existence. Therefore, I propose that the prior service cost be amortized over the remaining lives of the existing employees.

ESTHER KNOX (somewhat perturbed): But what about the income statement? You two are arguing theory without consideration of our income figure.

HELEN KAUFMAN: Settle down, Esther.

ESTHER KNOX: Sorry, perhaps Jason's approach to resolving this approach is the best one. I am just not sure.

Explanation

(a) Assuming that Express Mail Inc. establishes a pension plan, how should its liability for pensions be computed in the first year?

(b) How should its liability be computed in subsequent years?

(c) How should pension expense be computed each year?

(d) Assuming that the pension fund is set up in a trusteed relationship, should the assets of the fund be reported on the books of Express Mail Inc.?

(e) What interest rate factor should be used in the present value computations?

(f) How should gains and losses be reported?

Simulation 2

Accounting for Pensions

Directions | Situation | Journal Entries | Measurement | Research | Resources

Directions

In this simulation, you will be asked various questions concerning the accounting for pensions. Prepare responses to all parts.

Situation

Melanie Vail Corp. sponsors a defined benefit pension plan for its employees. On January 1, 2004, the following balances relate to this plan.

Plan assets	$480,000
Projected benefit obligation	625,000
Prepaid/accrued pension cost (credit)	45,000
Unrecognized prior service cost	100,000

As a result of the operation of the plan during 2004, the following additional data are provided by the actuary.

Service cost for 2004	$90,000
Settlement rate	9%
Actual return on plan assets in 2004	57,000
Amortization of prior service cost	19,000
Expected return on plan assets	52,000
Unexpected loss from change in projected benefit obligation, due to change in actuarial predictions	76,000
Contributions in 2004	99,000
Benefits paid retirees in 2004	85,000

Resources

(a) Use a computer spreadsheet to prepare a pension work sheet. On the pension work sheet, compute pension expense, prepaid/accrued cost, projected benefit obligation, plan assets, unrecognized prior service cost, and unrecognized net gain or loss.

(b) Compute the same items as in (a), assuming that the settlement rate is now 7% and the expected rate of return is 10%.

Journal Entry

Prepare the journal entry to record pension expense in 2004.

Measurement

Prepare a schedule reconciling the funded status of the plan with the pension amount reported on the balance sheet.

Remember to check the **Take Action! CD** and the book's **companion Web site** to find additional resources for this chapter.

CHAPTER 21

Accounting for Leases

More Companies Ask, "Why Buy?"

Leasing has grown tremendously in popularity and today is the fastest-growing form of capital investment. Instead of borrowing money to buy an airplane, a computer, a nuclear core, or a satellite, a company makes periodic payments to lease the asset. Even the gambling casinos lease their slot machines. Airlines and railroads lease huge amounts of equipment; many hotel and motel chains lease their facilities; and most retail chains lease the bulk of their retail premises and warehouses. The popularity of leasing is evidenced in the fact that 558 of 600 companies surveyed by the AICPA in 2001 disclosed lease data.[1]

A classic example is the airline industry. Many travelers on airlines such as **United**, **Delta**, and **Southwest** believe the planes they are flying are owned by these airlines. But in many cases, nothing could be further from the truth. Here are recent lease percentages for the major U.S. airlines.

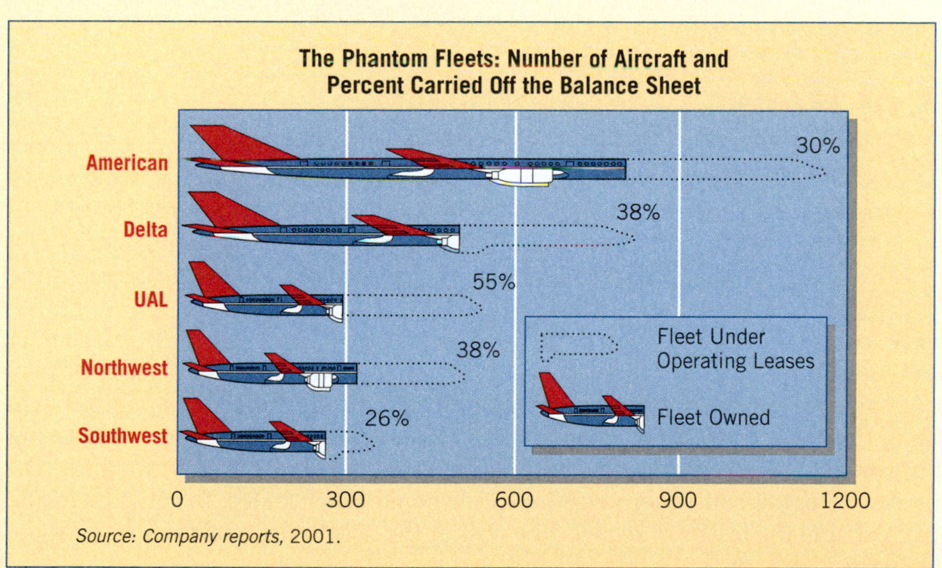

Source: Company reports, 2001.

Why do airline companies lease many of their airplanes? One reason is the favorable accounting treatment that airlines receive if they lease rather than purchase. By not reporting the airplane and related borrowing on their balance sheets, companies lower their debt to equity ratios. In addition, companies that lease often report higher net income in the earlier years of the life of the airplane.

[1]AICPA, *Accounting Trends and Techniques—2001.*

LEARNING OBJECTIVES

After studying this chapter, you should be able to:

1. **Explain the nature, economic substance, and advantages of lease transactions.**
2. **Describe the accounting criteria and procedures for capitalizing leases by the lessee.**
3. **Contrast the operating and capitalization methods of recording leases.**
4. **Identify the classifications of leases for the lessor.**
5. **Describe the lessor's accounting for direct-financing leases.**
6. **Identify special features of lease arrangements that cause unique accounting problems.**
7. **Describe the effect of residual values, guaranteed and unguaranteed, on lease accounting.**
8. **Describe the lessor's accounting for sales-type leases.**
9. **Describe the disclosure requirements for leases.**

PREVIEW OF CHAPTER 21

Because of the increased significance and prevalence of lease arrangements indicated in the opening story, the need for uniform accounting and complete informative reporting of these transactions has intensified. In this chapter, we will look at the accounting issues related to leasing.

The content and organization of this chapter are as follows.

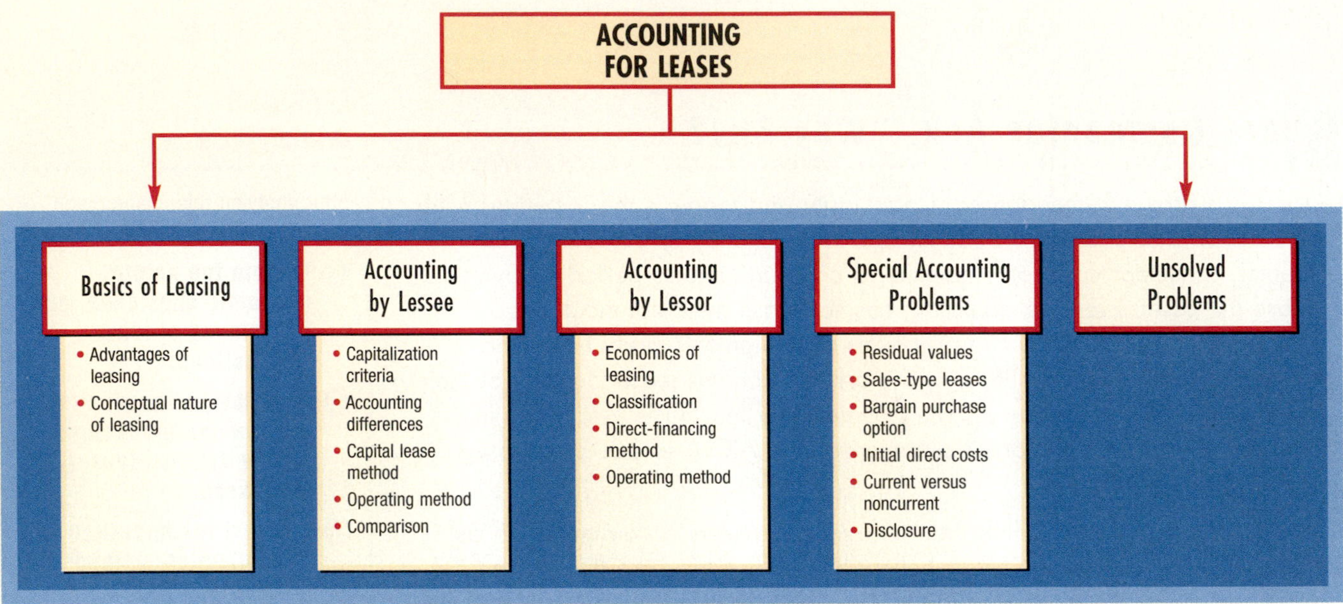

BASICS OF LEASING

OBJECTIVE 1
Explain the nature, economic substance, and advantages of lease transactions.

A **lease** is a contractual agreement between a **lessor** and a **lessee** that gives the lessee the right to use specific property, owned by the lessor, for a specified period of time in return for stipulated, and generally periodic, cash payments (rents). An essential element of the lease agreement is that the lessor conveys less than the total interest in the property.

Because a lease is a contract, the provisions agreed to by the lessor and lessee may vary widely and may be limited only by their ingenuity. The **duration—lease term—** of the lease may be anything from a short period of time to the entire expected economic life of the asset. The **rental payments** may be level from year to year, increasing in amount, or decreasing. They may be predetermined or may vary with sales, the prime interest rate, the consumer price index, or some other factor. In most cases the rent is set to enable the lessor to recover the cost of the asset plus a fair return over the life of the lease.

The **obligations for taxes, insurance, and maintenance** (executory costs) may be assumed by either the lessor or the lessee, or they may be divided. **Restrictions** comparable to bond indentures may limit the lessee's activities regarding dividend payments or the incurrence of further debt and lease obligations in order to protect the lessor from default on the rents. The lease contract may be **noncancelable**, or it may grant the right to **early termination** on payment of a set scale of prices plus a penalty. In case of **default**, the lessee may be liable for all future payments at once, receiving title to the property in exchange. Alternatively, in case of default, the lessor may have the right to sell to a third party and collect from the lessee all or a portion of the difference between the sale price and the lessor's unrecovered cost.

Different treatments for the lessee at termination of the lease may range from none to the right to purchase the leased asset at the fair market value or the right to renew or buy at a nominal price.

Advantages of Leasing

Although leasing is not without its disadvantages, the growth in its use suggests that it often has a genuine advantage over owning property. Some of the commonly discussed advantages to the lessee of leasing are:

1. ***100% Financing at Fixed Rates.*** Leases are often signed without requiring any money down from the lessee, which helps the lessee to conserve scarce cash—an especially desirable feature for new and developing companies. In addition, lease payments often remain fixed, which protects the lessee against inflation and increases in the cost of money. The following comment regarding a conventional loan is typical: "Our local bank finally came up to 80 percent of the purchase price but wouldn't go any higher, and they wanted a floating interest rate. We just couldn't afford the down payment and we needed to lock in a final payment rate we knew we could live with."
2. ***Protection against Obsolescence.*** Leasing equipment reduces the risk of obsolescence to the lessee, and in many cases passes the risk of residual value to the lessor. For example, **Merck** (a pharmaceutical maker) leases computers. Merck is permitted under the lease agreement to turn in an old computer for a new model at any time, canceling the old lease and writing a new one. The cost of the new lease is added to the balance due on the old lease, less the old computer's trade-in value. As one treasurer remarked, "Our instinct is to purchase." But if a new computer comes along in a short time, "then leasing is just a heck of a lot more convenient than purchasing."
3. ***Flexibility.*** Lease agreements may contain less restrictive provisions than other debt agreements. Innovative lessors can tailor a lease agreement to the lessee's special needs. For instance, rental payments can be structured to meet the timing of cash revenues generated by the equipment so that payments are made when the equipment is productive.
4. ***Less Costly Financing.*** Some companies find leasing cheaper than other forms of financing. For example, start-up companies in depressed industries or companies in low tax brackets may lease as a way of claiming tax benefits that might otherwise be lost. Depreciation deductions offer no benefit to companies that have little, if any, taxable income. Through leasing, these tax benefits are used by the leasing companies or financial institutions, which can pass some of the tax benefits back to the user of the asset in the form of lower rental payments.
5. ***Tax Advantages.*** In some cases, companies can "have their cake and eat it too." That is, companies do not report an asset or a liability for the lease arrangement for financial reporting purposes. However, for tax purposes, the asset is capitalized and depreciated. As a result, the company takes deductions earlier rather than later and also saves on its taxes. A common vehicle for this type transaction is a "synthetic lease" arrangement. An expanded discussion of a synthetic lease used by **Krispy Kreme** is on page 1098.
6. ***Off-Balance-Sheet Financing.*** Certain leases do not add debt on a balance sheet or affect financial ratios, and they may add to borrowing capacity.[2] Such **off-balance-sheet financing** is critical to some companies.

INTERNATIONAL INSIGHT

Some companies "double dip" on the international level too. That is, the leasing rules of the lessor's and lessee's countries may be different, permitting both parties to be an owner of the asset. Thus, both lessor and lessee receive the tax benefits related to depreciation.

[2]As demonstrated later in this chapter, certain types of lease arrangements are not capitalized on the balance sheet. The liabilities section is thereby relieved of large future lease commitments that, if recorded, would adversely affect the debt to equity ratio. The reluctance to record lease obligations as liabilities is one of the primary reasons capitalized lease accounting is resisted.

WHAT DO THE NUMBERS MEAN?

OFF-BALANCE-SHEET FINANCING

As shown in our opening story, the airlines use lease arrangements extensively, which results in a great deal of off-balance-sheet financing. The following chart indicates that debt levels are understated by a substantial amount for many airlines that lease aircraft.

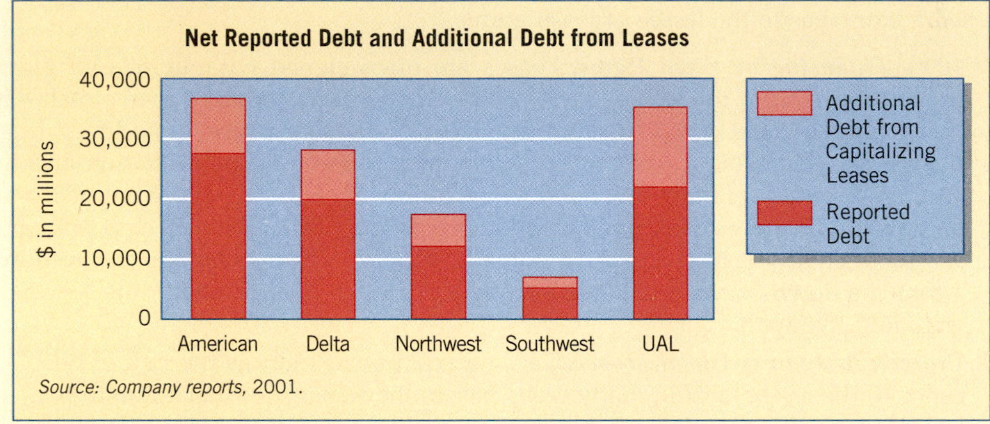

Source: Company reports, 2001.

Analysts must adjust reported debt levels for the effects of non-capitalized leases. For example, the estimates for additional debt in the chart above were derived by taking the present value of each airline's future operating lease payments, as disclosed in the lease note in the company's annual report (as shown in Illustration 21-32).

A methodology for making this adjustment is discussed in Eugene A. Imhoff, Jr., Robert C. Lipe, and David W. Wright, "Operating Leases: Impact of Constructive Capitalization," *Accounting Horizons* (March 1991).

Conceptual Nature of a Lease

If **United Airlines** borrows $47 million on a 10-year note from National City Bank to purchase a Boeing 757 jet plane, it is clear that an asset and related liability should be reported on United's balance sheet at that amount. If United purchases the 757 for $47,000,000 directly from **Boeing** through an installment purchase over 10 years, it is equally clear that an asset and related liability should be reported (i.e., the installment transaction should be "capitalized"). However, if United **leases** the Boeing 757 for 10 years through a noncancelable lease transaction with payments of the same amount as the installment purchase transaction, differences of opinion start to develop over how this transaction should be reported. The various views on **capitalization of leases** are as follows.

1. ***Do Not Capitalize Any Leased Assets.*** In this view, because the lessee does not have ownership of the property, capitalization is considered inappropriate. Furthermore, a lease is an **"executory" contract** requiring continuing performance by both parties. Because other executory contracts (such as purchase commitments and employment contracts) are not capitalized at present, leases should not be capitalized either.
2. ***Capitalize Leases That Are Similar to Installment Purchases.*** In this view, transactions should be reported in accordance with their economic substance. Therefore, if installment purchases are capitalized, so also should leases that have similar characteristics. For example, United Airlines is committed to the same payments over a 10-year period for either a lease or an installment purchase; lessees make rental

payments, whereas owners make mortgage payments. Why shouldn't the financial statements report these transactions in the same manner?

3. ***Capitalize All Long-Term Leases.*** Under this approach, the only requirement for capitalization is the long-term right to use the property. This property-rights approach capitalizes all long-term leases.[3]
4. ***Capitalize Firm Leases Where the Penalty for Nonperformance Is Substantial.*** A final approach is to capitalize only "firm" (noncancelable) contractual rights and obligations. "Firm" means that it is unlikely that performance under the lease can be avoided without a severe penalty.[4]

UNDERLYING CONCEPTS

The issue of how to report leases is the classic case of substance versus form. Although legal title does not technically pass in lease transactions, the benefits from the use of the property do transfer.

In short, the various viewpoints range from no capitalization to capitalization of all leases. The FASB apparently agrees with the capitalization approach when the lease is similar to an installment purchase, noting that **a lease that transfers substantially all of the benefits and risks of property ownership should be capitalized**. Transfer of ownership can be assumed only if there is a high degree of performance to the transfer—that is, if the lease is noncancelable. **Noncancelable** means that the lease contract is cancelable only upon the outcome of some remote contingency, or that the cancellation provisions and penalties of the contract are so costly to the lessee that cancellation probably will not occur. Only noncancelable leases may be capitalized.

This viewpoint leads to three basic conclusions: (1) The characteristics that indicate that substantially all of the benefits and risks of ownership have been transferred must be identified. (2) The same characteristics should apply consistently to the lessee and the lessor. (3) Those leases that **do not** transfer substantially all the benefits and risks of ownership are operating leases. They should not be capitalized but rather accounted for as rental payments and receipts.

ACCOUNTING BY LESSEE

OBJECTIVE 2
Describe the accounting criteria and procedures for capitalizing leases by the lessee.

If a lessee **capitalizes** a lease, the **lessee** records an asset and a liability generally equal to the present value of the rental payments. The **lessor**, having transferred substantially all the benefits and risks of ownership, recognizes a sale by removing the asset from the balance sheet and replacing it with a receivable. The typical journal entries for the lessee and the lessor, assuming equipment is leased and is capitalized, appear as follows.

ILLUSTRATION 21-1
Journal Entries for Capitalized Lease

Lessee			Lessor		
Leased Equipment	XXX		Lease Receivable	XXX	
Lease Liability		XXX	Equipment		XXX

Having capitalized the asset, the lessee records the depreciation. The lessor and lessee treat the lease rental payments as consisting of interest and principal.

If the lease is not capitalized, no asset is recorded by the lessee and no asset is removed from the lessor's books. When a lease payment is made, the lessee records rental expense and the lessor recognizes rental revenue.

For a lease to be recorded as a **capital lease**, the lease must be noncancelable and must meet one or more of the following four criteria.

---

[3]The property rights approach was originally recommended in a research study by the AICPA: John H. Myers, "Reporting of Leases in Financial Statements," *Accounting Research Study No. 4* (New York: AICPA, 1964), pp. 10–11. Recently, this view has received additional support. See Peter H. Knutson, "Financial Reporting in the 1990s and Beyond," Position Paper (Charlottesville, Va.: AIMR, 1993), and Warren McGregor, "Accounting for Leases: A New Approach," Special Report (Norwalk, Conn.: FASB, 1996).

[4]Yuji Ijiri, *Recognition of Contractual Rights and Obligations*, Research Report (Stamford, Conn.: FASB, 1980).

ILLUSTRATION 21-2
Capitalization Criteria for Lessee

Capitalization Criteria (Lessee)

- The lease transfers ownership of the property to the lessee.
- The lease contains a bargain purchase option.[5]
- The lease term is equal to 75 percent or more of the estimated economic life of the leased property.
- The present value of the minimum lease payments (excluding executory costs) equals or exceeds 90 percent of the fair value of the leased property.[6]

Leases that **do not meet any of the four criteria** are classified and accounted for by the lessee as **operating leases**. Illustration 21-3 shows that a lease meeting any one of the four criteria results in the lessee having a capital lease.

ILLUSTRATION 21-3
Diagram of Lessee's Criteria for Lease Classification

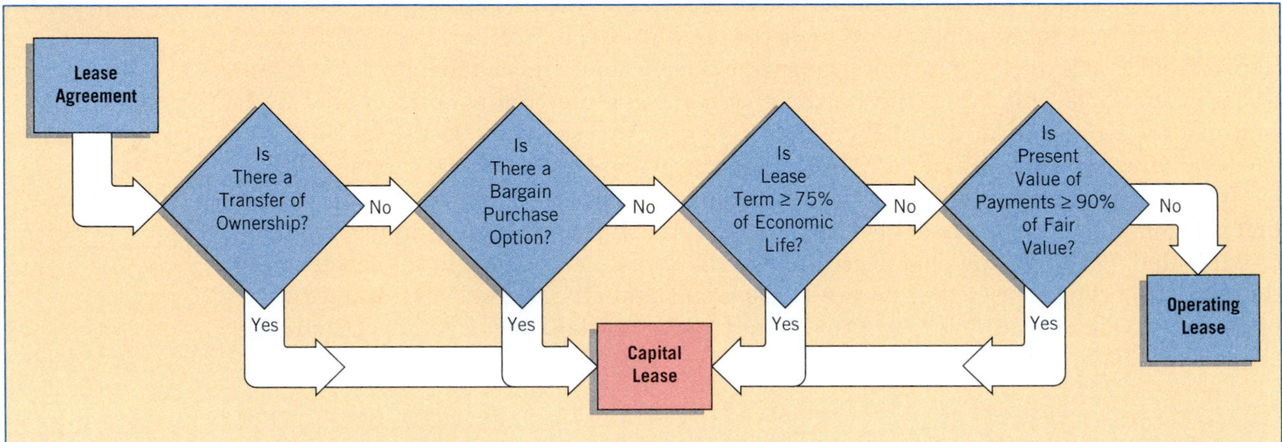

In keeping with the FASB's reasoning that a significant portion of the value of the asset is consumed in the first 75 percent of its life, neither the third nor the fourth criterion is to be applied when the inception of the lease occurs during the last 25 percent of the life of the asset.

Capitalization Criteria

The four **capitalization criteria** that apply to lessees are controversial and can be difficult to apply in practice. They are discussed in detail in the following pages.

Transfer of Ownership Test

If the lease transfers ownership of the asset to the lessee, it is a capital lease. This criterion is not controversial and is easily implemented in practice.

UNDERLYING CONCEPTS

Capitalization of leases illustrates the necessity for good definitions. The lease fits the definition of an asset, as it gives the lessee the economic benefits that flow from the possession or the use of the asset.

Bargain Purchase Option Test

A **bargain purchase option** is a provision allowing the lessee to purchase the leased property for a price that is **significantly lower** than the property's expected fair value at the date the option becomes exercisable. At the inception of the lease, the difference between the option price and the expected fair market value must be large enough to make exercise of the option reasonably assured.

For example, assume that you were to lease a **Honda** Accord for $599 per month for 40 months with an option to purchase for $100 at the end of the 40-month period. If the estimated fair value of the Honda Accord is $3,000 at the end of the 40 months,

[5]A bargain purchase option is defined in the next section.

[6]"Accounting for Leases," *FASB Statement No. 13* as amended and interpreted through May 1980 (Stamford, Conn.: FASB, 1980), par. 7.

the $100 option to purchase is clearly a bargain, and therefore capitalization is required. In other cases, the criterion may not be as easy to apply, and determining *now* that a certain *future* price is a bargain can be difficult.

Economic Life Test (75% Test)

If the lease period equals or exceeds 75 percent of the asset's economic life, most of the risks and rewards of ownership are transferred to the lessee, and capitalization is therefore appropriate. However, determining the lease term and the economic life of the asset can be troublesome.

The lease term is generally considered to be the fixed, noncancelable term of the lease. However, this period can be extended if a bargain renewal option is provided in the lease agreement. A **bargain renewal option** is a provision allowing the lessee to renew the lease for a rental that is lower than the expected fair rental at the date the option becomes exercisable. At the inception of the lease, the difference between the renewal rental and the expected fair rental must be great enough to make exercise of the option to renew reasonably assured.

INTERNATIONAL INSIGHT

In some nations (e.g., Italy, Japan) accounting principles do not specify criteria for capitalization of leases. In others (e.g., Sweden, Switzerland) such criteria exist, but capitalization of the leases is optional.

For example, if a **Dell** PC is leased for 2 years at a rental of $100 per month and subsequently can be leased for $10 per month for another 2 years, it clearly is a bargain renewal option, and the lease term is considered to be 4 years. However, with bargain renewal options, as with bargain purchase options, it is sometimes difficult to determine what is a bargain.[7]

Determining estimated economic life can also pose problems, especially if the leased item is a specialized item or has been used for a significant period of time. For example, determining the economic life of a nuclear core is extremely difficult because it is subject to much more than normal "wear and tear." The FASB takes the position that if the lease starts during the last 25 percent of the life of the asset, the economic-life test cannot be used as a basis to classify a lease as a capital lease.

Recovery of Investment Test (90% Test)

If the present value of the minimum lease payments equals or exceeds 90 percent of the fair market value of the asset, then the leased asset should be capitalized. The rationale for this test is that if the present value of the minimum lease payments is reasonably close to the market price of the asset, the asset is effectively being purchased.

In determining the present value of the minimum lease payments, three important concepts are involved: (1) minimum lease payments, (2) executory costs, and (3) discount rate.

Minimum Lease Payments. **Minimum lease payments** are payments the lessee is obligated to make or can be expected to make in connection with the leased property. They include the following.

1. *Minimum Rental Payments*—These are minimum payments the lessee is obligated to make to the lessor under the lease agreement. In some cases, the minimum rental payments may be equal to the minimum lease payments. However, the minimum lease payments also may include a guaranteed residual value (if any), penalty for failure to renew, or a bargain purchase option (if any), as noted on the next page.

[7]The original lease term is also extended for leases having the following: substantial penalties for nonrenewal; periods for which the lessor has the option to renew or extend the lease; renewal periods preceding the date a bargain purchase option becomes exercisable; and renewal periods in which any lessee guarantees of the lessor's debt are expected to be in effect or in which there will be a loan outstanding from the lessee to the lessor. The lease term, however, can never extend beyond the time a bargain purchase option becomes exercisable. "Accounting for Leases: Sale-Leaseback Transactions Involving Real Estate; Sales-Type Leases of Real Estate; Definition of the Lease Term; Initial Direct Costs of Direct Financing Leases," *Statement of Financial Accounting Standards No. 98* (Stamford, Conn.: FASB, 1988).

2. ***Guaranteed Residual Value***—The residual value is the estimated fair (market) value of the leased property at the end of the lease term. The lessor often transfers the risk of loss to the lessee or to a third party through a guarantee of the estimated residual value. The **guaranteed residual value** is (1) the certain or determinable amount at which the lessor has the right to require the lessee to purchase the asset or (2) the amount the lessee or the third-party guarantor guarantees the lessor will realize. If it is not guaranteed in full, the **unguaranteed residual value** is the estimated residual value exclusive of any portion guaranteed.[8]
3. ***Penalty for Failure to Renew or Extend the Lease***—This is the amount payable that is required of the lessee if the agreement specifies that the lease must be extended or renewed and the lessee fails to do so.
4. ***Bargain Purchase Option***—As indicated earlier (on page 1090), this is an option given to the lessee to purchase the equipment at the end of the lease term at a price that is fixed sufficiently below the expected fair value, so that, at the inception of the lease, purchase appears to be reasonably assured.

Executory costs (defined below) are not included in the lessee's computation of the present value of the minimum lease payments.

Executory Costs. Like most assets, leased tangible assets require the incurrence of insurance, maintenance, and tax expenses—called **executory costs**—during their economic life. If the lessor retains responsibility for the payment of these "ownership-type costs," a portion of each lease payment that represents executory costs **should be excluded** in computing the present value of the minimum lease payments, because it does not represent payment on or reduction of the obligation. If the portion of the minimum lease payments that represents executory costs is not determinable from the provisions of the lease, an estimate of such amount must be made. Many lease agreements, however, specify that executory costs be paid to the appropriate third parties directly by the lessee. In these cases, the rental payment can be used **without adjustment** in the present value computation.

Discount Rate. The lessee computes the present value of the minimum lease payments using the **lessee's incremental borrowing rate.** This rate is defined as, "The rate that, at the inception of the lease, the lessee would have incurred to borrow the funds necessary to buy the leased asset on a secured loan with repayment terms similar to the payment schedule called for in the lease."[9] Assume, for example, that Mortenson Inc. decides to lease computer equipment for a 5-year period at a cost of $10,000 a year. To determine whether the present value of these payments is less than 90 percent of the fair market value of the property, the lessee discounts the payments using its incremental borrowing rate. Determining that rate will often require judgment because it is based on a hypothetical purchase of the property.

However, there is one exception to this rule: If (1) the lessee knows the **implicit interest rate computed by the lessor** and (2) it is less than the lessee's incremental borrowing rate, then the **lessee must use the lessor's implicit rate**. The **interest rate implicit in the lease** is the discount rate that, when applied to the minimum lease payments and any unguaranteed residual value accruing to the lessor, causes the aggregate present value to be equal to the fair value of the leased property to the lessor.[10]

---

[8]A lease provision requiring the lessee to make up a residual value deficiency that is attributable to damage, extraordinary wear and tear, or excessive usage is not included in the minimum lease payments. Such costs are recognized as period costs when incurred. "Lessee Guarantee of the Residual Value of Leased Property," *FASB Interpretation No. 19* (Stamford, Conn.: FASB, 1977), par. 3.

[9]*FASB Statement No. 13*, op. cit., par. 5 (l).

[10]Ibid., par. 5 (k).

The purpose of this exception is twofold: First, the implicit rate of the lessor is generally a **more realistic rate** to use in determining the amount (if any) to report as the asset and related liability for the lessee. Second, the guideline is provided to ensure that the lessee **does not use an artificially high incremental borrowing rate** that would cause the present value of the minimum lease payments to be less than 90 percent of the fair market value of the property—and thus make it possible to avoid capitalization of the asset and related liability. The lessee may argue that it cannot determine the implicit rate of the lessor and therefore the higher rate should be used. However, in many cases, the implicit rate used by the lessor can be approximated. The determination of whether or not a reasonable estimate could be made will require judgment, particularly where the result from using the incremental borrowing rate comes close to meeting the 90 percent test. Because **the lessee may not capitalize the leased property at more than its fair value** (as discussed later), the lessee is prevented from using an excessively low discount rate.

Asset and Liability Accounted for Differently

In a capital lease transaction, the lessee is using the lease as a source of financing. The lessor finances the transaction (provides the investment capital) through the leased asset, and the lessee makes rent payments, which actually are installment payments. Therefore, over the life of the property rented, **the rental payments to the lessor constitute a payment of principal plus interest**.

Asset and Liability Recorded

Under the capital lease method, the lessee treats the lease transaction as if an asset were being purchased in a financing transaction in which an asset is acquired and an obligation created. Therefore, the lessee records a capital lease as an asset and a liability at the lower of (1) the present value of the minimum lease payments (excluding executory costs) or (2) the fair market value of the leased asset at the inception of the lease. The rationale for this approach is that the leased asset should not be recorded for more than its fair market value.

Depreciation Period

One troublesome aspect of accounting for the depreciation of the capitalized leased asset relates to the period of depreciation. If the lease agreement transfers ownership of the asset to the lessee (criterion 1) or contains a bargain purchase option (criterion 2)—the leased asset is depreciated in a manner consistent with the lessee's normal depreciation policy for owned assets, **using the economic life of the asset**. On the other hand, if the lease does not transfer ownership or does not contain a bargain purchase option, then it is depreciated over the **term of the lease**. In this case, the leased asset reverts to the lessor after a certain period of time.

Effective-Interest Method

Throughout the term of the lease, the **effective-interest method** is used to allocate each lease payment between principal and interest. This method produces a periodic interest expense equal to a constant percentage of the carrying value of the lease obligation.

The discount rate used by the lessee to determine the present value of the minimum lease payments must be used by the lessee when applying the effective-interest method to capital leases.

Depreciation Concept

Although the amounts initially capitalized as an asset and recorded as an obligation are computed at the same present value, the **depreciation of the asset and the discharge of the obligation are independent accounting processes** during the term of the lease. The lessee should depreciate the leased asset by applying conventional depreciation methods: straight-line, sum-of-the-years'-digits, declining-balance, units-of-production, etc.

The FASB uses the term "amortization" more frequently than "depreciation" to recognize intangible leased property rights. The authors prefer "depreciation" to describe the write-off of a tangible asset's expired services.

Capital Lease Method (Lessee)

Assume that Lessor Company and Lessee Company sign a lease agreement dated January 1, 2005, that calls for Lessor Company to lease equipment to Lessee Company beginning January 1, 2005. The terms and provisions of the lease agreement and other pertinent data are as follows.

1. The term of the lease is 5 years, and the lease agreement is noncancelable, requiring equal rental payments of $25,981.62 at the beginning of each year (annuity-due basis).
2. The equipment has a fair value at the inception of the lease of $100,000, an estimated economic life of 5 years, and no residual value.
3. Lessee Company pays all of the executory costs directly to third parties except for the property taxes of $2,000 per year, which are included in the annual payments to the lessor.
4. The lease contains no renewal options, and the equipment reverts to Lessor Company at the termination of the lease.
5. Lessee Company's incremental borrowing rate is 11 percent per year.
6. Lessee Company depreciates on a straight-line basis similar equipment that it owns.
7. Lessor Company set the annual rental to earn a rate of return on its investment of 10 percent per year. This fact is known to Lessee Company.[11]

The lease meets the criteria for classification as a capital lease for the following reasons: (1) The lease term of 5 years, being equal to the equipment's estimated economic life of 5 years, satisfies the 75 percent test. (2) The present value of the minimum lease payments ($100,000 as computed below) exceeds 90 percent of the fair value of the property ($100,000).

The minimum lease payments are $119,908.10 ($23,981.62 × 5). The amount capitalized as leased assets is computed as the present value of the minimum lease payments (excluding executory costs—property taxes of $2,000) as follows.

ILLUSTRATION 21-4
Computation of Capitalized Lease Payments

Capitalized amount = ($25,981.62 − $2,000) × Present value of an annuity due of 1 for 5 periods at 10% (Table 6-5)
= $23,981.62 × 4.16986
= $100,000

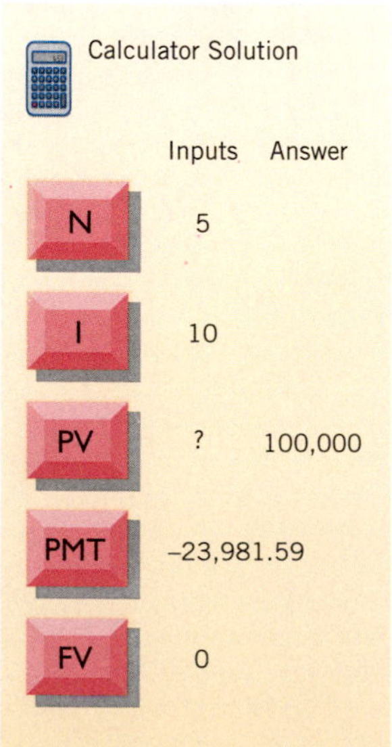

Calculator Solution
Inputs
Answer
N
5
I
10
PV
?
100,000
PMT
-23,981.59
FV
0

The lessor's implicit interest rate of 10 percent is used instead of the lessee's incremental borrowing rate of 11 percent because (1) it is lower and (2) the lessee has knowledge of it.

The entry to record the capital lease on Lessee Company's books on January 1, 2005, is:

Leased Equipment under Capital Leases	100,000	
Lease Liability		100,000

Note that the preceding entry records the obligation at the net amount of $100,000 (the present value of the future rental payments) rather than at the gross amount of $119,908.10 ($23,981.62 × 5).

[11]If Lessee Company had an incremental borrowing rate of, say, 9 percent (lower than the 10 percent rate used by Lessor Company) and it did not know the rate used by Lessor Company, the present value computation would have yielded a capitalized amount of $101,675.35 ($23,981.62 × 4.23972). And, because this amount exceeds the $100,000 fair value of the equipment, Lessee Company would have had to capitalize the $100,000 and use 10 percent as its effective rate for amortization of the lease obligation.

The journal entry to record the **first lease payment on January 1, 2005,** is:

Property Tax Expense	2,000.00	
Lease Liability	23,981.62	
Cash		25,981.62

Each lease payment of $25,981.62 consists of three elements: (1) a reduction in the lease liability (obligation), (2) a financing cost (interest expense), and (3) executory costs (property taxes). The total financing cost (interest expense) over the term of the lease is $19,908.10, which is the difference between the present value of the lease payments ($100,000) and the actual cash disbursed, net of executory costs ($119,908.10). Therefore, the annual interest expense, applying the effective-interest method, is a function of the outstanding liability (obligation), as shown in Illustration 21-5.

ILLUSTRATION 21-5
Lease Amortization Schedule for Lessee—Annuity-Due Basis

LESSEE COMPANY
LEASE AMORTIZATION SCHEDULE
(ANNUITY-DUE BASIS)

Date	Annual Lease Payment	Executory Costs	Interest (10%) on Liability	Reduction of Lease Liability	Lease Liability
	(a)	(b)	(c)	(d)	(e)
1/1/05					$100,000.00
1/1/05	$ 25,981.62	$ 2,000	$ -0-	$ 23,981.62	76,018.38
1/1/06	25,981.62	2,000	7,601.84	16,379.78	59,638.60
1/1/07	25,981.62	2,000	5,963.86	18,017.76	41,620.84
1/1/08	25,981.62	2,000	4,162.08	19,819.54	21,801.30
1/1/09	25,981.62	2,000	2,180.32*	21,801.30	-0-
	$129,908.10	$10,000	$19,908.10	$100,000.00	

(a) Lease payment as required by lease.
(b) Executory costs included in rental payment.
(c) Ten percent of the preceding balance of (e) except for 1/1/05; since this is an annuity due, no time has elapsed at the date of the first payment and no interest has accrued.
(d) (a) minus (b) and (c).
(e) Preceding balance minus (d).
*Rounded by 19 cents.

At the end of Lessee Company's fiscal year, December 31, 2005, **accrued interest** is recorded as follows.

Interest Expense	7,601.84	
Interest Payable		7,601.84

Depreciation of the leased equipment over its lease term of 5 years, applying Lessee Company's normal depreciation policy (straight-line method), results in the following entry on December 31, 2005.

Depreciation Expense—Capital Leases	20,000	
Accumulated Depreciation—Capital Leases		20,000
($100,000 ÷ 5 years)		

At December 31, 2005, the assets recorded under capital leases are separately identified on the lessee's balance sheet. Similarly, the related liabilities are separately identified. The portion due within one year or the operating cycle, whichever is longer, is classified with current liabilities and the rest with noncurrent liabilities. For example, the current portion of the December 31, 2005, total liability of $76,018.38 in the lessee's amortization schedule is the amount of the reduction in the liability in 2006, or $16,379.78. The liabilities section as it relates to lease transactions at December 31, 2005, would appear as shown in Illustration 21-6.

ILLUSTRATION 21-6
Reporting Current and Noncurrent Lease Liabilities

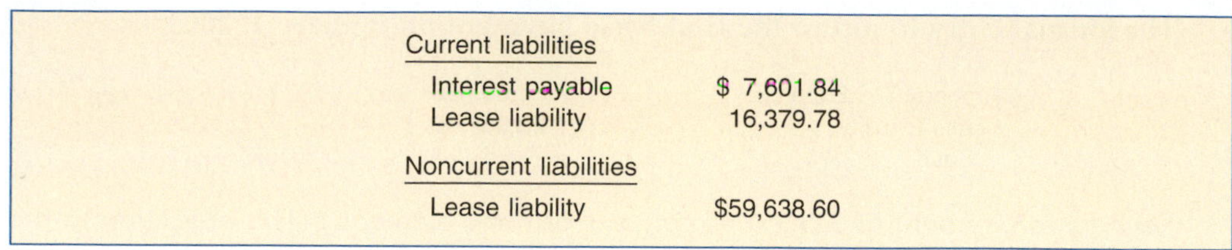

Current liabilities	
Interest payable	$ 7,601.84
Lease liability	16,379.78
Noncurrent liabilities	
Lease liability	$59,638.60

The journal entry to record the lease payment of January 1, 2006, is as follows.

Property Tax Expense	2,000.00	
Interest Payable	7,601.84	
Lease Liability	16,379.78	
Cash		25,981.62

Entries through 2009 would follow the pattern above. Other executory costs (insurance and maintenance) assumed by Lessee Company would be recorded in a manner similar to that used to record any other operating costs incurred on assets owned by Lessee Company.

Upon expiration of the lease, the amount capitalized as leased equipment is fully amortized, and the lease obligation is fully discharged. If not purchased, the equipment would be returned to the lessor, and the leased equipment and related accumulated depreciation accounts would be removed from the books.[12] If the equipment is purchased at termination of the lease at a price of $5,000 and the estimated life of the equipment is changed from 5 to 7 years, the following entry might be made.

Equipment ($100,000 + $5,000)	105,000	
Accumulated Depreciation—Capital Leases	100,000	
Leased Equipment under Capital Leases		100,000
Accumulated Depreciation—Equipment		100,000
Cash		5,000

Operating Method (Lessee)

Under the **operating method**, rent expense (and the associated liability) accrues day by day to the lessee as the property is used. **The lessee assigns rent to the periods benefiting from the use of the asset and ignores, in the accounting, any commitments to make future payments.** Appropriate accruals or deferrals are made if the accounting period ends between cash payment dates.

For example, assume that the capital lease illustrated in the previous section did not qualify as a capital lease and was therefore to be accounted for as an operating lease. The first-year charge to operations would have been $25,981.62, the amount of the rental payment. The journal entry to record this payment on January 1, 2005, would be as follows.

Rent Expense	25,981.62	
Cash		25,981.62

The rented asset, as well as any long-term liability for future rental payments, is not reported on the balance sheet. Rent expense would be reported on the income statement. In addition, **note disclosure is required for all operating leases that have noncancelable lease terms in excess of one year**. Illustration of the type of note disclosure required for an operating lease (as well as other types of leases) is provided in Illustrations 21-30 to 21-33 later in this chapter.

---

[12]If the lessee purchases a leased asset **during the term of a "capital lease,"** it is accounted for like a renewal or extension of a capital lease: "Any difference between the purchase price and the carrying amount of the lease obligation shall be recorded as an adjustment of the carrying amount of the asset." See "Accounting for Purchase of a Leased Asset by the Lessee During the Term of the Lease," *FASB Interpretation No. 26* (Stamford, Conn.: FASB, 1978), par. 5.

Comparison of Capital Lease with Operating Lease

OBJECTIVE 3
Contrast the operating and capitalization methods of recording leases.

As indicated on the previous page, if the lease had been accounted for as an operating lease, the first-year charge to operations would have been $25,981.62, the amount of the rental payment. Treating the transaction as a capital lease, however, resulted in a first-year charge of $29,601.84: depreciation of $20,000 (assuming straight-line), interest expense of $7,601.84 (per Illustration 21-7), and executory costs of $2,000. Illustration 21-7 shows that **while the total charges to operations are the same over the lease term whether the lease is accounted for as a capital lease or as an operating lease, under the capital-lease treatment the charges are higher in the earlier years and lower in the later years.**[13]

ILLUSTRATION 21-7
Comparison of Charges to Operations—Capital vs. Operating Leases

LESSEE COMPANY
SCHEDULE OF CHARGES TO OPERATIONS
CAPITAL LEASE VERSUS OPERATING LEASE

	Capital Lease					
Year	Depreciation	Executory Costs	Interest	Total Charge	Operating Lease Charge	Difference
2005	$ 20,000	$ 2,000	$ 7,601.84	$ 29,601.84	$ 25,981.62	$3,620.22
2006	20,000	2,000	5,963.86	27,963.86	25,981.62	1,982.24
2007	20,000	2,000	4,162.08	26,162.08	25,981.62	180.46
2008	20,000	2,000	2,180.32	24,180.32	25,981.62	(1,801.30)
2009	20,000	2,000	—	22,000.00	25,981.62	(3,981.62)
	$100,000	$10,000	$19,908.10	$129,908.10	$129,908.10	$ -0-

If an accelerated method of depreciation is used, the differences between the amounts charged to operations under the two methods would be even larger in the earlier and later years.

In addition, using the capital-lease approach would have resulted in an asset and related liability of $100,000 initially reported on the balance sheet. No such asset or liability would be reported under the operating method. Therefore, the following differences occur if a capital lease instead of an operating lease is employed:

1. an increase in the amount of reported debt (both short-term and long-term),
2. an increase in the amount of total assets (specifically long-lived assets), and
3. a lower income early in the life of the lease and, therefore, lower retained earnings.

Thus, many companies believe that capital leases have a detrimental impact on their reported financial position: Their debt to total equity ratio increases and their rate of return on total assets decreases. As a result, the business community resists capitalizing leases.

Whether this resistance is well founded is a matter of debate. From a cash flow point of view, the company is in the same position whether the lease is accounted for as an operating or a capital lease. The reason why managers often argue against capitalization is that it can more easily lead to **violation of loan covenants**; it can affect the **amount of compensation received** by managers (for example, a stock compensation plan tied to earnings); and finally, it can **lower rates of return** and **increase debt to**

[13]The higher charges in the early years is one reason lessees are reluctant to adopt the capital-lease accounting method. Lessees (especially those of real estate) claim that it is really no more costly to operate the leased asset in the early years than in the later years. Thus, they advocate an even charge similar to that provided by the operating method.

equity relationships, thus making the company less attractive to present and potential investors.[14]

WHAT DO THE NUMBERS MEAN?

DOLLARS TO DONUTS

Krispy Kreme, a chain of 217 donut shops, has caught the attention—some good, some bad—of Wall Street. On the good side, investors are impressed by the company's ability to grow rapidly on a relatively small bit of capital. For the first 9 months of fiscal 2002, the company's capital expenditures fell to $38 million, from $59 million the year before. Yet Krispy Kreme expanded along with its customers' waistlines during the same period: Its earnings rose 73 percent, to $18 million, on sales that were up 27 percent to $277 million.

That's an impressive feat if you care about return on capital. But there's a hole in this donut. Amid much hoopla, the company announced in 2001 that it would spend $30 million on a new 187,000 square foot mixing plant and warehouse in Effingham, Illinois. Yet the investments and obligations associated with that $30 million are not apparent in the financial statements.

By financing through a synthetic lease, Krispy Kreme can keep the investment and obligation off the books. In a synthetic lease, a financial institution like **Bank of America** sets up a *special purpose entity* (SPE) that borrows money to build the plant and then leases it to Krispy Kreme. For accounting purposes, Krispy Kreme reports an operating lease, but for tax purposes the company is considered the owner of the asset and gets depreciation tax deductions.

In response to negative publicity about the use of SPEs to get favorable financial reporting and tax benefits, Krispy Kreme announced it was going to change its method of financing construction of its dough-making plant.

Source: Adapted from Seth Lubore and Elizabeth MacDonald, "Debt? Who, Me?" *Forbes* (February 18, 2002), p. 56.

ACCOUNTING BY LESSOR

INTERNATIONAL INSIGHT

In some countries, such as Germany, all leases can be off-balance-sheet.

Earlier in this chapter we discussed leasing's advantages to the lessee. Three important benefits are available to the lessor:

1. ***Interest Revenue.*** Leasing is a form of financing; therefore, financial institutions and leasing companies find leasing attractive because it provides competitive interest margins.
2. ***Tax Incentives.*** In many cases, companies that lease cannot use the tax benefit, but leasing provides them with an opportunity to transfer such tax benefits to another party (the lessor) in return for a lower rental rate on the leased asset. To illustrate, **Boeing** at one time sold one of its 767 jet planes to a wealthy investor who didn't need the plane but could use the tax benefit. The investor then leased the plane to a foreign airline, for whom the tax benefit was of no use. Everyone gained: Boeing

[14]One study indicates that management's behavior did change as a result of *FASB No. 13*. For example, many companies restructure their leases to avoid capitalization; others increase their purchases of assets instead of leasing; and others, faced with capitalization, postpone their debt offerings or issue stock instead. However, it is interesting to note that the study found no significant effect on stock or bond prices as a result of capitalization of leases. A. Rashad Abdel-khalik, "The Economic Effects on Lessees of *FASB Statement No. 13*, Accounting for Leases," Research Report (Stamford, Conn.: FASB, 1981).

was able to sell its 767, the investor received the tax benefits, and the foreign airline found a cheaper way to acquire a 767.[15]

3. ***High Residual Value.*** Another advantage to the lessor is the return of the property at the end of the lease term. Residual values can produce very large profits. Citicorp at one time assumed that the commercial aircraft it was leasing to the airline industry would have a residual value of 5 percent of their purchase price. It turned out that they were worth 150 percent of their cost—a handsome profit. However, 3 years later these same planes slumped to 80 percent of their cost, but still far more than 5 percent.

Economics of Leasing

The lessor determines the amount of the rental, basing it on the rate of return—the implicit rate—needed to justify leasing the asset. The key factors considered in establishing the rate of return are the credit standing of the lessee, the length of the lease, and the status of the residual value (guaranteed versus unguaranteed). In the Lessor Company/Lessee Company example on pages 1094–1096, the implicit rate of the lessor was 10 percent, the cost of the equipment to the lessor was $100,000 (also fair market value), and the estimated residual value was zero. Lessor Company determined the amount of the lease payment in the following manner.

ILLUSTRATION 21-8
Computation of Lease Payments

Fair market value of leased equipment	$100,000.00
Less: Present value of the residual value	–0–
Amount to be recovered by lessor through lease payments	$100,000.00
Five beginning-of-the-year lease payments to yield a 10% return ($100,000 ÷ 4.16986[a])	$ 23,981.62

[a]PV of an annuity due of 1 for 5 years at 10% (Table 6-5)

If a residual value were involved (whether guaranteed or not), the lessor would not have to recover as much from the lease payments. Therefore, the lease payments would be less. (This situation is shown in Illustration 21-15.)

Classification of Leases by the Lessor

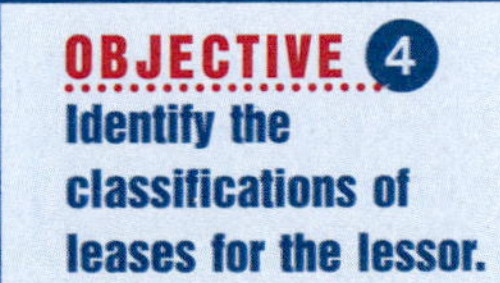

OBJECTIVE 4
Identify the classifications of leases for the lessor.

From the standpoint of the **lessor**, all leases may be classified for accounting purposes as one of the following:

(a) Operating leases.
(b) Direct-financing leases.
(c) Sales-type leases.

Referring to Illustration 21-9 (on page 1100), if at the date of the lease agreement (inception) the lessor is party to a lease that meets **one or more** of the Group I criteria (1, 2, 3, and 4) and **both** of the Group II criteria (1 and 2), the lessor shall classify and account for the arrangement as a direct-financing lease or as a sales-type lease.[16] (Note that the Group I criteria are identical to the criteria that must be met in order for a lease to be classified as a capital lease by a lessee, as shown in Illustration 21-2.)

[15]Some would argue that there is a loser—the U.S. government. The tax benefits enable the profitable investor to reduce or eliminate taxable income.

[16]*FASB Statement No. 13*, op. cit., pars. 6, 7, and 8.

ILLUSTRATION 21-9
Capitalization Criteria for Lessor

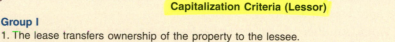

Capitalization Criteria (Lessor)

Group I

1. The lease transfers ownership of the property to the lessee.
2. The lease contains a bargain purchase option.
3. The lease term is equal to 75 percent or more of the estimated economic life of the leased property.
4. The present value of the minimum lease payments (excluding executory costs) equals or exceeds 90 percent of the fair value of the leased property.

Group II

1. Collectibility of the payments required from the lessee is reasonably predictable.
2. No important uncertainties surround the amount of unreimbursable costs yet to be incurred by the lessor under the lease (lessor's performance is substantially complete or future costs are reasonably predictable).

INTERNATIONAL INSIGHT

U.S. GAAP is consistent with *International Standard No. 17* (Accounting for Leases). However, the international standard is a relatively simple statement of basic principles, whereas the U.S. rules on leases are more prescriptive and detailed.

Why the Group II requirements? The answer is that the profession wants to make sure that the lessor has really transferred the risks and benefits of ownership. If collectibility of payments is not predictable or if performance by the lessor is incomplete, then the criteria for revenue recognition have not been met, and the lease should be accounted for as an operating lease.

For example, computer leasing companies at one time used to buy IBM equipment, lease it, and remove the leased assets from their balance sheets. In leasing the asset, the computer lessors stated that they would be willing to substitute new IBM equipment if obsolescence occurred. However, when IBM introduced a new computer line, IBM refused to sell it to the computer leasing companies. As a result, a number of the lessors could not meet their contracts with their customers and were forced to take back the old equipment. What the computer leasing companies had taken off the books now had to be reinstated. Such a case demonstrates one reason for the Group II requirements.

The distinction for the lessor between a direct-financing lease and a sales-type lease is the presence or absence of a manufacturer's or dealer's profit (or loss): A sales-type lease involves a manufacturer's or dealer's profit, and a direct-financing lease does not. The profit (or loss) to the lessor is evidenced by the difference between the fair value of the leased property at the inception of the lease and the lessor's cost or carrying amount (book value). Normally, sales-type leases arise when manufacturers or dealers use leasing as a means of marketing their products. For example, a computer manufacturer will lease its computer equipment to businesses and institutions. Direct-financing leases generally result from arrangements with lessors that are primarily engaged in financing operations, such as lease-finance companies, banks, insurance companies, and pension trusts. However, a lessor need not be a manufacturer or dealer to recognize a profit (or loss) at the inception of a lease that requires application of sales-type lease accounting.

All leases that do not qualify as direct-financing or sales-type leases are classified and accounted for by the lessors as operating leases. Illustration 21-10 shows the circumstances under which a lease is classified as operating, direct-financing, or sales-type for the lessor.

ILLUSTRATION 21-10
Diagram of Lessor's Criteria for Lease Classification

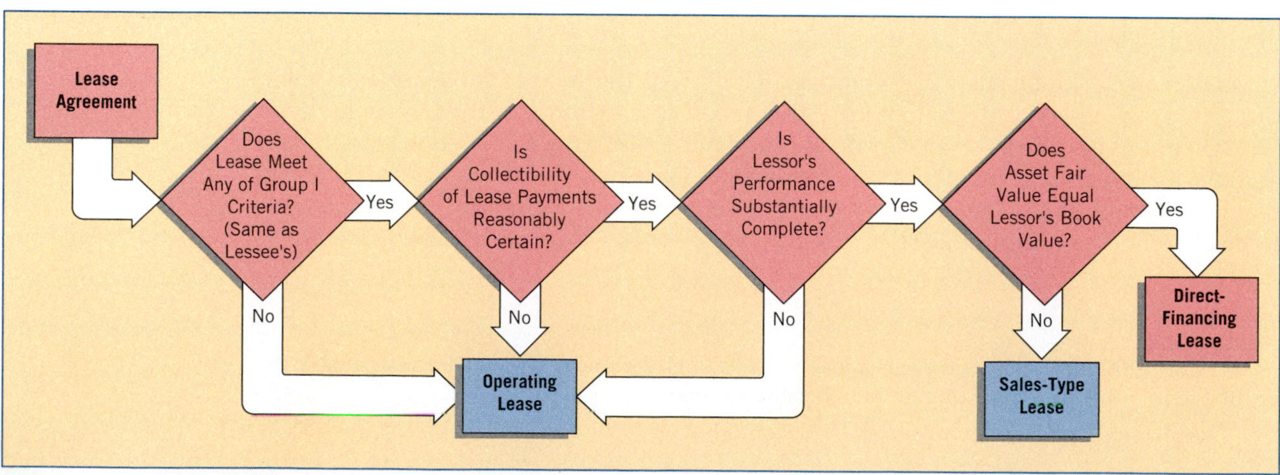

As a consequence of the additional Group II criteria for lessors, it may be that a lessor, having not met both criteria, will classify a lease as an **operating** lease but the lessee will classify the same lease as a **capital** lease. In such an event, both the lessor and lessee will carry the asset on their books, and both will depreciate the capitalized asset.

For purposes of comparison with the lessee's accounting, only the operating and direct-financing leases will be illustrated in the following section. The more complex sales-type lease will be discussed later in the chapter.

Direct-Financing Method (Lessor)

OBJECTIVE 5
Describe the lessor's accounting for direct-financing leases.

Leases that are in substance the financing of an asset purchase by the lessee are called **direct-financing leases**. In this type of lease, the lessor records a **lease receivable** instead of a leased asset. The lease receivable is the present value of the minimum lease payments, plus the present value of the unguaranteed residual value. Remember that "minimum lease payments" for the lessee includes:

1. Rental payments (excluding executory costs).
2. Bargain purchase option (if any).
3. Guaranteed residual value (if any).
4. Penalty for failure to renew (if any).

Thus, the lessor records the residual value, whether guaranteed or not. Also, recall that if the lessor pays any executory costs, then the rental payment should be reduced by that amount for purposes of computing minimum lease payments.

The following presentation, utilizing the data from the preceding Lessor Company/Lessee Company illustration on pages 1094–1096, illustrates the accounting treatment accorded a direct-financing lease. The information relevant to Lessor Company in accounting for this lease transaction is repeated as follows.

1. The term of the lease is 5 years beginning January 1, 2005, is noncancelable, and requires equal rental payments of $25,981.62 at the beginning of each year. Payments include $2,000 of executory costs (property taxes).
2. The equipment has a cost of $100,000 to Lessor Company, a fair value at the inception of the lease of $100,000, an estimated economic life of 5 years, and no residual value.
3. No initial direct costs were incurred in negotiating and closing the lease transaction.
4. The lease contains no renewable options and the equipment reverts to Lessor Company at the termination of the lease.
5. Collectibility is reasonably assured, and no additional costs (with the exception of the property taxes being collected from the lessee) are to be incurred by Lessor Company.
6. Lessor Company set the annual lease payments to ensure a rate of return of 10 percent (implicit rate) on its investment as follows.

ILLUSTRATION 21-11
Computation of Lease Payments

Fair market value of leased equipment	$100,000.00
Less: Present value of residual value	–0–
Amount to be recovered by lessor through lease payments	$100,000.00
Five beginning-of-the-year lease payments to yield a 10% return ($100,000 ÷ 4.16986[a])	$ 23,981.62

[a]PV of an annuity due of 1 for 5 years at 10% (Table 6-5).

The lease meets the criteria for classification as a direct-financing lease because (1) the lease term exceeds 75 percent of the equipment's estimated economic life, (2) the present value of the minimum lease payments exceeds 90 percent of the equipment's fair value, (3) collectibility of the payments is reasonably assured, and (4) there are no further costs to be incurred by Lessor Company. It is not a sales-type lease because there is no difference between the fair value ($100,000) of the equipment and the lessor's cost ($100,000).

The Lease Receivable is the present value of the minimum lease payments (excluding executory costs minus property taxes of $2,000) and is computed as follows.

ILLUSTRATION 21-12
Computation of Lease Receivable

Lease receivable = ($25,981.62 − $2,000) × Present value of an annuity due of 1 for 5 periods at 10% (Table 6-5)
= $23,981.62 × 4.16986
= $100,000

The lease of the asset and the resulting receivable are recorded January 1, 2005 (the inception of the lease), as follows.

Lease Receivable	100,000	
Equipment		100,000

The lease receivable is often **reported** in the balance sheet as "Net investment in capital leases." It is classified either as current or noncurrent, depending upon when the net investment is to be recovered.[17]

The leased equipment with a cost of $100,000, which represents Lessor Company's investment, is replaced with a lease receivable. In a manner similar to the lessee's treatment of interest, Lessor Company applies the effective-interest method and recognizes interest revenue as a function of the lease receivable balance, as shown in Illustration 21-13.

ILLUSTRATION 21-13
Lease Amortization Schedule for Lessor—Annuity-Due Basis

LESSOR COMPANY
LEASE AMORTIZATION SCHEDULE
(ANNUITY-DUE BASIS)

Date	Annual Lease Payment	Executory Costs	Interest (10%) on Lease Receivable	Lease Receivable Recovery	Lease Receivable
	(a)	(b)	(c)	(d)	(e)
1/1/05					$100,000.00
1/1/05	$ 25,981.62	$ 2,000.00	$ –0–	$ 23,981.62	76,018.38
1/1/06	25,981.62	2,000.00	7,601.84	16,379.78	59,638.60
1/1/07	25,981.62	2,000.00	5,963.86	18,017.76	41,620.84
1/1/08	25,981.62	2,000.00	4,162.08	19,819.54	21,801.30
1/1/09	25,981.62	2,000.00	2,180.32*	21,801.30	–0–
	$129,908.10	$10,000.00	$19,908.10	$100,000.00	

(a) Annual rental that provides a 10% return on net investment.
(b) Executory costs included in rental payment.
(c) Ten percent of the preceding balance of (e) except for 1/1/05.
(d) (a) minus (b) and (c).
(e) Preceding balance minus (d).
*Rounded by 19 cents.

On January 1, 2005, the journal entry to record receipt of the first year's lease payment is shown on page 1103.

[17]In the notes to the financial statements (see Illustration 21-33), the lease receivable is reported at its gross amount (minimum lease payments plus the unguaranteed residual value). In addition, the total unearned interest related to the lease is also reported. As a result, some lessors record lease receivables on a gross basis and record the unearned interest in a separate account. The net approach is illustrated here, which is consistent with the accounting for the lessee.

Cash	25,981.62	
Lease Receivable		23,981.62
Property Tax Expense/Property Taxes Payable		2,000.00

On December 31, 2005, the interest revenue earned during the first year is recognized through the following entry.

Interest Receivable	7,601.84	
Interest Revenue		7,601.84

At December 31, 2005, the lease receivable is reported in the lessor's balance sheet among current assets or noncurrent assets, or both. The portion due within one year or the operating cycle, whichever is longer, is classified as a current asset, and the rest with noncurrent assets.

The assets section as it relates to lease transactions at December 31, 2005, would appear as follows.

ILLUSTRATION 21-14
Reporting Lease Transactions by Lessor

Current assets	
Interest receivable	$ 7,601.84
Lease receivable	16,379.78
Noncurrent assets (investments)	
Lease receivable	$59,638.60

The following entries record receipt of the second year's lease payment and recognition of the interest earned.

January 1, 2006

Cash	25,981.62	
Lease Receivable		16,379.78
Interest Receivable		7,601.84
Property Tax Expense/Property Taxes Payable		2,000.00

December 31, 2006

Interest Receivable	5,963.86	
Interest Revenue		5,963.86

Journal entries through 2009 would follow the same pattern except that no entry would be recorded in 2009 (the last year) for earned interest. Because the receivable is fully collected by January 1, 2009, no balance (investment) is outstanding during 2009 to which Lessor Company could attribute any interest. **Lessor Company recorded no depreciation.** If the equipment is sold to Lessee Company for $5,000 upon expiration of the lease, Lessor Company would recognize disposition of the equipment as follows.

Cash	5,000	
Gain on Sale of Leased Equipment		5,000

Operating Method (Lessor)

Under the **operating method** each rental receipt by the lessor is recorded as rental revenue. The **leased asset is depreciated in the normal manner**, with the depreciation expense of the period matched against the rental revenue. The amount of revenue recognized in each accounting period is a level amount (straight-line basis) regardless of the lease provisions, unless another systematic and rational basis is more representative of the time pattern in which the benefit is derived from the leased asset. In addition to the depreciation charge, maintenance costs and the cost of any other services rendered under the provisions of the lease that pertain to the current accounting period are charged to expense. Costs paid to independent third parties, such as appraisal fees, finder's fees, and costs of credit checks, are amortized over the life of the lease.

To illustrate the operating method, assume that the direct-financing lease shown on page 1101 did not qualify as a capital lease and was therefore to be accounted for as an operating lease. The entry to record the cash rental receipt, assuming the $2,000 was for property tax expense, would be as follows.

Cash	25,981.62	
Rental Revenue		25,981.62

Depreciation is recorded by the lessor as follows (assuming a straight-line method, a cost basis of $100,000, and a 5-year life).

Depreciation Expense—Leased Equipment	20,000	
Accumulated Depreciation—Leased Equipment		20,000

If property taxes, insurance, maintenance, and other operating costs during the year are the obligation of the lessor, they are recorded as expenses chargeable against the gross rental revenues.

If the lessor owned plant assets that it used in addition to those leased to others, **the leased equipment and accompanying accumulated depreciation would be separately classified** in an account such as "Equipment leased to others" or "Investment in leased property." If significant in amount or in terms of activity, the rental revenues and accompanying expenses are separated from sales revenue and cost of goods sold in the income statement.

SPECIAL ACCOUNTING PROBLEMS

OBJECTIVE 6
Identify special features of lease arrangements that cause unique accounting problems.

The features of lease arrangements that cause unique accounting problems are:

1. Residual values.
2. Sales-type leases (lessor).
3. Bargain purchase options.
4. Initial direct costs.
5. Current versus noncurrent.
6. Disclosure.

Residual Values

Up to this point, we have generally ignored discussion of residual values in order that the basic accounting issues related to lessee and lessor accounting could be developed. Accounting for residual values is complex and will probably provide you with the greatest challenge in understanding lease accounting.

Meaning of Residual Value

The residual value is the **estimated fair value** of the leased asset at the end of the lease term. Frequently, a significant residual value exists at the end of the lease term, especially when the economic life of the leased asset exceeds the lease term. If title does not pass automatically to the lessee (criterion 1) and a bargain purchase option does not exist (criterion 2), the lessee returns physical custody of the asset to the lessor at the end of the lease term.[18]

Guaranteed versus Unguaranteed

The residual value may be unguaranteed or guaranteed by the lessee. If the lessee agrees to make up any deficiency below a stated amount that the lessor realizes in

[18]When the lease term and the economic life are not the same, the residual value and the salvage value of the asset will probably differ. For simplicity, we will assume that residual value and salvage value are the same, even when the economic life and lease term vary.

residual value at the end of the lease term, that stated amount is the **guaranteed residual value**.

The guaranteed residual value is employed in lease arrangements for two reasons. The first is a business reason: It protects the lessor against any loss in estimated residual value, thereby ensuring the lessor of the desired rate of return on investment. The second reason is an accounting benefit that you will learn from the discussion at the end of this chapter.

Lease Payments

A guaranteed residual value—by definition—has more assurance of realization than does an unguaranteed residual value. As a result, the lessor may adjust lease payments because the certainty of recovery has been increased. After this rate is established, however, it makes no difference from an accounting point of view whether the residual value is guaranteed or unguaranteed. The net investment to be recorded by the lessor (once the rate is set) will be the same.

Assume the same data as in the Lessee Company/Lessor Company illustrations except that a residual value of $5,000 is estimated at the end of the 5-year lease term. In addition, a 10 percent return on investment (ROI) is assumed,[19] whether the residual value is guaranteed or unguaranteed. Lessor Company would compute the amount of the lease payments as follows.

ILLUSTRATION 21-15
Lessor's Computation of Lease Payments

LESSOR'S COMPUTATION OF LEASE PAYMENTS (10% ROI)
GUARANTEED OR UNGUARANTEED RESIDUAL VALUE
(ANNUITY-DUE BASIS, INCLUDING RESIDUAL VALUE)

Fair market value of leased asset to lessor	$100,000.00
Less: Present value of residual value ($5,000 × .62092, Table 6-2)	3,104.60
Amount to be recovered by lessor through lease payments	$ 96,895.40
Five periodic lease payments ($96,895.40 ÷ 4.16986, Table 6-5)	$ 23,237.09

Contrast the foregoing lease payment amount to the lease payments of $23,981.62 as computed in Illustration 21-8, where no residual value existed. The payments are less, because the lessor's total recoverable amount of $100,000 is reduced by the present value of the residual value.

Lessee Accounting for Residual Value

Whether the estimated residual value is guaranteed or unguaranteed has both economic and accounting consequence to the lessee. The accounting difference is that the **minimum lease payments**, the basis for capitalization, includes the guaranteed residual value but excludes the unguaranteed residual value.

OBJECTIVE 7
Describe the effect of residual values, guaranteed and unguaranteed, on lease accounting.

Guaranteed Residual Value (Lessee Accounting). A guaranteed residual value affects the lessee's computation of minimum lease payments and, therefore, the amounts capitalized as a leased asset and a lease obligation. In effect, **it is an additional lease payment that will be paid in property or cash, or both, at the end of the lease term**. Using the rental payments as computed by the lessor in Illustration 21-15, the minimum lease payments are $121,185.45 ([$23,237.09 × 5] + $5,000). The capitalized present value of the minimum lease payments (excluding executory costs) is computed as shown in Illustration 21-16.

[19]Technically, the rate of return demanded by the lessor would be different depending upon whether the residual value was guaranteed or unguaranteed. To simplify the illustrations, we are ignoring this difference in subsequent sections.

ILLUSTRATION 21-16
Computation of Lessee's Capitalized Amount—Guaranteed Residual Value

LESSEE'S CAPITALIZED AMOUNT (10% RATE) (ANNUITY-DUE BASIS, INCLUDING GUARANTEED RESIDUAL VALUE)	
Present value of five annual rental payments ($23,237.09 × 4.16986, Table 6-5)	$ 96,895.40
Present value of guaranteed residual value of $5,000 due five years after date of inception: ($5,000 × .62092, Table 6-2)	3,104.60
Lessee's capitalized amount	$100,000.00

Lessee Company's schedule of interest expense and amortization of the $100,000 lease liability that produces a $5,000 final guaranteed residual value payment at the end of 5 years is shown in Illustration 21-17.

ILLUSTRATION 21-17
Lease Amortization Schedule for Lessee—Guaranteed Residual Value

LESSEE COMPANY
LEASE AMORTIZATION SCHEDULE
(ANNUITY-DUE BASIS, GUARANTEED RESIDUAL VALUE—GRV)

Date	Lease Payment Plus GRV	Executory Costs	Interest (10%) on Liability	Reduction of Lease Liability	Lease Liability
	(a)	(b)	(c)	(d)	(e)
1/1/05					$100,000.00
1/1/05	$ 25,237.09	$ 2,000	–0–	$ 23,237.09	76,762.91
1/1/06	25,237.09	2,000	$ 7,676.29	15,560.80	61,202.11
1/1/07	25,237.09	2,000	6,120.21	17,116.88	44,085.23
1/1/08	25,237.09	2,000	4,408.52	18,828.57	25,256.66
1/1/09	25,237.09	2,000	2,525.67	20,711.42	4,545.24
12/31/09	5,000.00*		454.76**	4,545.24	–0–
	$131,185.45	$10,000	$21,185.45	$100,000.00	

(a) Annual lease payment as required by lease.
(b) Executory costs included in rental payment.
(c) Preceding balance of (e) × 10%, except 1/1/05.
(d) (a) minus (b) and (c).
(e) Preceding balance minus (d).

*Represents the guaranteed residual value.
**Rounded by 24 cents.

The journal entries (Illustration 21-22 on page 1108) to record the leased asset and liability, depreciation, interest, property tax, and lease payments are then made on the basis that the residual value is guaranteed. The format of these entries is the same as illustrated earlier, although the amounts are different because of the guaranteed residual value. The leased asset is recorded at $100,000 and is depreciated over 5 years. To compute depreciation, the guaranteed residual value is subtracted from the cost of the leased asset. Assuming that the straight-line method is used, the depreciation expense each year is $19,000 ([$100,000 − $5,000] ÷ 5 years).

At the end of the lease term, before the lessee transfers the asset to the lessor, the lease asset and liability accounts have the following balances.

ILLUSTRATION 21-18
Account Balances on Lessee's Books at End of Lease Term—Guaranteed Residual Value

Leased equipment under capital leases	$100,000.00	Interest payable	$ 454.76
Less: Accumulated depreciation—capital leases	95,000.00	Lease liability	4,545.24
	$ 5,000.00		$5,000.00

If, at the end of the lease, the fair market value of the residual value is less than $5,000, Lessee Company will have to record a loss. Assume that Lessee Company depreciated the leased asset down to its residual value of $5,000 but that the fair market value of the residual value at December 31, 2009, was $3,000. In this case, the Lessee Company would have to report a loss of $2,000. The following journal entry would be made, assuming cash was paid to make up the residual value deficiency.

Loss on Capital Lease	2,000.00	
Interest Expense (or Interest Payable)	454.76	
Lease Liability	4,545.24	
Accumulated Depreciation—Capital Leases	95,000.00	
Leased Equipment under Capital Leases		100,000.00
Cash		2,000.00

If the fair market value exceeds $5,000, a gain may be recognized. Gains on guaranteed residual values may be apportioned to the lessor and lessee in whatever ratio the parties initially agree.

If the lessee depreciated the total cost of the asset ($100,000), a misstatement would occur. That is, the carrying amount of the asset at the end of the lease term would be zero, but the liability under the capital lease would be stated at $5,000. Thus, if the asset was worth $5,000, the lessee would end up reporting a gain of $5,000 when it transferred the asset to the lessor. As a result, depreciation would be overstated and net income understated in 2005–2008, but in the last year (2009) net income would be overstated.

Unguaranteed Residual Value (Lessee Accounting). An **unguaranteed residual value** from the lessee's viewpoint is the same as no residual value in terms of its effect upon the lessee's method of computing the minimum lease payments and the capitalization of the leased asset and the lease liability.

Assume the same facts as those above except that the $5,000 residual value is **unguaranteed instead of guaranteed**. The amount of the annual lease payments would be the same—$23,237.09. Whether the residual value is guaranteed or unguaranteed, Lessor Company's amount to be recovered through lease rentals is the same—that is, $96,895.40. The minimum lease payments are $116,185.45 ($23,237.09 × 5). Lessee Company would capitalize the following amount.

ILLUSTRATION 21-19
Computation of Lessee's Capitalized Amount—Unguaranteed Residual Value

LESSEE'S CAPITALIZED AMOUNT (10% RATE)
(ANNUITY-DUE BASIS, INCLUDING **UNGUARANTEED** RESIDUAL VALUE)

Present value of 5 annual rental payments of $23,237.09 × 4.16986 (Table 6-5)	$96,895.40
Unguaranteed residual value of $5,000 (not capitalized by lessee)	–0–
Lessee's capitalized amount	$96,895.40

The Lessee Company's schedule of interest expense and amortization of the lease liability of $96,895.40, assuming an unguaranteed residual value of $5,000 at the end of 5 years, is shown in Illustration 21-20.

ILLUSTRATION 21-20
Lease Amortization Schedule for Lessee—Unguaranteed Residual Value

LESSEE COMPANY
LEASE AMORTIZATION SCHEDULE (10%)
(ANNUITY-DUE BASIS, **UNGUARANTEED** RESIDUAL VALUE)

Date	Annual Lease Payments	Executory Costs	Interest (10%) on Liability	Reduction of Lease Liability	Lease Liability
	(a)	(b)	(c)	(d)	(e)
1/1/05					$96,895.40
1/1/05	$ 25,237.09	$ 2,000	–0–	$23,237.09	73,658.31
1/1/06	25,237.09	2,000	$ 7,365.83	15,871.26	57,787.05
1/1/07	25,237.09	2,000	5,778.71	17,458.38	40,328.67
1/1/08	25,237.09	2,000	4,032.87	19,204.22	21,124.45
1/1/09	25,237.09	2,000	2,112.64*	21,124.45	–0–
	$126,185.45	$10,000	$19,290.05	$96,895.40	

(a) Annual lease payment as required by lease.
(b) Executory costs included in rental payment.
(c) Preceding balance of (e) × 10%.
(d) (a) minus (b) and (c).
(e) Preceding balance minus (d).
*Rounded by 19 cents.

The journal entries (Illustration 21-22 below) to record the leased asset and liability, depreciation, interest, property tax, and payments on the lease liability are then made on the basis that the residual value is unguaranteed. The format of these entries is the same as illustrated earlier. Note that the leased asset is recorded at $96,895.40 and is depreciated over 5 years. Assuming that the straight-line method is used, the depreciation expense each year is $19,379.08 ($96,895.40 ÷ 5 years). At the end of the lease term, before the lessee transfers the asset to the lessor, the following balances in the accounts result, as illustrated below.

ILLUSTRATION 21-21
Account Balances on Lessee's Books at End of Lease Term—Unguaranteed Residual Value

Leased equipment under capital leases	$96,895	Lease liability	$–0–
Less: Accumulated depreciation—capital leases	96,895		
	$ –0–		

Assuming that the leased asset has been fully depreciated and that the lease liability has been fully amortized, no entry is required at the end of the lease term, except to remove the asset from the books.

If the lessee depreciated the asset down to its unguaranteed residual value, a misstatement would occur. That is, the carrying amount of the leased asset would be $5,000 at the end of the lease, but the liability under the capital lease would be stated at zero before the transfer of the asset. Thus, the lessee would end up reporting a loss of $5,000 when it transferred the asset to the lessor. Depreciation would be understated and net income overstated in 2005–2008, but in the last year (2009) net income would be understated because of the recorded loss.

ILLUSTRATION 21-22
Comparative Entries for Guaranteed and Unguaranteed Residual Values, Lessee Company

Lessee Entries Involving Residual Values. The entries by Lessee Company for both a guaranteed and an unguaranteed residual value are shown in Illustration 21-22, in comparative form.

Guaranteed Residual Value			Unguaranteed Residual Value		
			Capitalization of Lease 1/1/05:		
Leased Equipment under Capital Leases	100,000.00		Leased Equipment under Capital Leases	96,895.40	
Lease Liability		100,000.00	Lease Liability		96,895.40
			First Payment 1/1/05:		
Property Tax Expense	2,000.00		Property Tax Expense	2,000.00	
Lease Liability	23,237.09		Lease Liability	23,237.09	
Cash		25,237.09	Cash		25,237.09
			Adjusting Entry for Accrued Interest 12/31/05:		
Interest Expense	7,676.29		Interest Expense	7,365.83	
Interest Payable		7,676.29	Interest Payable		7,365.83
			Entry to Record Depreciation 12/31/05:		
Depreciation Expense—Capital Leases	19,000.00		Depreciation Expense—Capital Leases	19,379.08	
Accumulated Depreciation—Capital Leases ([$100,000 − $5,000] ÷ 5 years)		19,000.00	Accumulated Depreciation—Capital Leases ($96,895.40 ÷ 5 years)		19,379.08
			Second Payment 1/1/06:		
Property Tax Expense	2,000.00		Property Tax Expense	2,000.00	
Lease Liability	15,560.80		Lease Liability	15,871.26	
Interest Expense (or Interest Payable)	7,676.29		Interest Expense (or Interest Payable)	7,365.83	
Cash		25,237.09	Cash		25,237.09

Lessor Accounting for Residual Value

As indicated earlier, the net investment to be recovered by the lessor is the same whether the residual value is guaranteed or unguaranteed. The lessor works on the assumption that **the residual value will be realized at the end of the lease term whether guaranteed or unguaranteed**. The lease payments required by the lessor to earn a certain return on investment are the same (e.g., $23,237.09 in our example) whether the residual value is guaranteed or unguaranteed.

Using the Lessee Company/Lessor Company data and assuming a residual value (either guaranteed or unguaranteed) of $5,000 and classification of the lease as a direct financing lease, the lessor determines the payments as follows.

ILLUSTRATION 21-23
Computation of Direct Financing Lease Payments

Fair market value of leased equipment	$100,000.00
Less: Present value of residual value ($5,000 × .62092, Table 6-2)	3,104.60
Amount to be recovered by lessor through lease payments	$ 98,895.40
Five beginning-of-the-year lease payments to yield a 10% return ($100,000 ÷ 4.16986, Table 6-5)	$ 23,237.09

The schedule for amortization with guaranteed or unguaranteed residual value is the same, as shown in Illustration 21-24.

ILLUSTRATION 21-24
Lease Amortization Schedule, for Lessor—Guaranteed or Unguaranteed Residual Value

LESSOR COMPANY
LEASE AMORTIZATION SCHEDULE
(ANNUITY-DUE BASIS, **GUARANTEED** OR **UNGUARANTEED** RESIDUAL VALUE)

Date	Annual Lease Payment Plus Residual Value	Executory Costs	Interest (10%) on Lease Receivable	Lease Receivable Recovery	Lease Receivable
	(a)	(b)	(c)	(d)	(e)
1/1/05					$100,000.00
1/1/05	$ 25,237.09	$ 2,000.00	$ –0–	$ 23,237.09	76,762.91
1/1/06	25,237.09	2,000.00	7,676.29	15,560.80	61,202.11
1/1/07	25,237.09	2,000.00	6,120.21	17,116.88	44,085.23
1/1/08	25,237.09	2,000.00	4,408.52	18,828.57	25,256.66
1/1/09	25,237.09	2,000.00	2,525.67	20,711.42	4,545.24
12/31/09	5,000.00	–0–	454.76*	4,545.24	–0–
	$131,185.45	$10,000.00	$21,185.45	$100,000.00	

(a) Annual lease payment as required by lease.
(b) Executory costs included in rental payment.
(c) Preceding balance of (e) × 10%, except 1/1/05.
(d) (a) minus (b) and (c).
(e) Preceding balance minus (d).
*Rounded by 24 cents.

Using the amounts computed above, the following entries would be made by Lessor Company during the first year for this direct financing lease. Note the similarity to the lessee's entries in Illustration 21-22.

ILLUSTRATION 21-25
Entries for Either Guaranteed or Unguaranteed Residual Value, Lessor Company

Inception of Lease 1/1/05:		
Lease Receivable	100,000.00	
Equipment		100,000.00
First Payment Received 1/1/05:		
Cash	25,237.09	
Lease Receivable		23,237.09
Property Tax Expense/Property Taxes Payable		2,000.00
Adjusting Entry for Accrued Interest 12/31/05:		
Interest Receivable	7,676.29	
Interest Revenue		7,676.29

Sales-Type Leases (Lessor)

As already indicated, the primary difference between a direct-financing lease and a **sales-type lease** is the manufacturer's or dealer's gross profit (or loss). A diagram illustrating these relationships is shown in Illustration 21-26 below.

ILLUSTRATION 21-26
Direct-Financing versus Sales-Type Leases

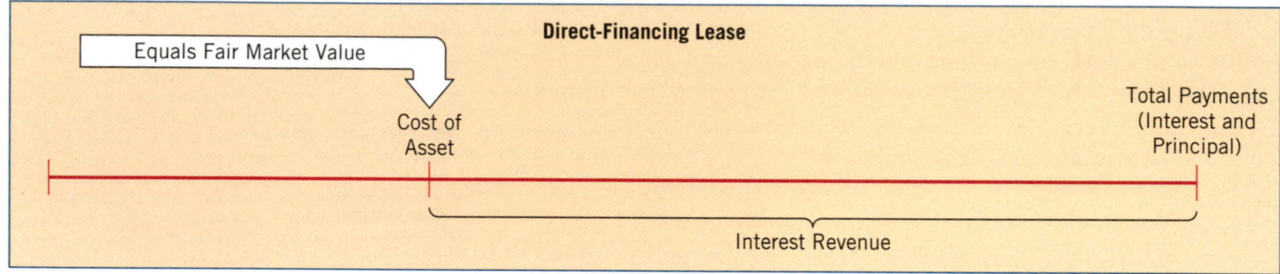

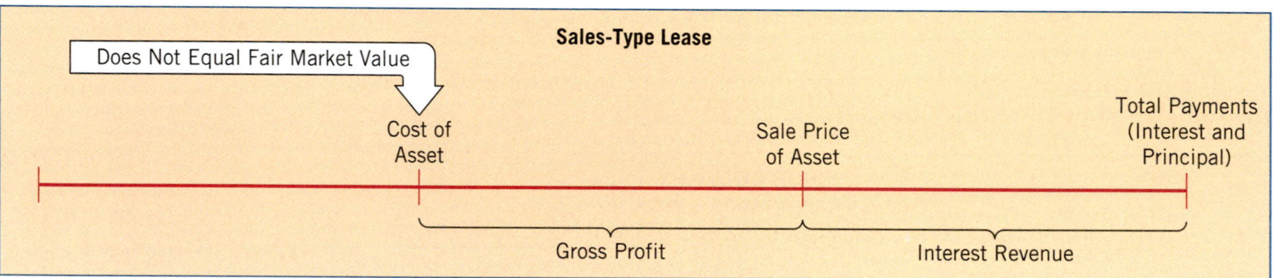

The information necessary to record the sales-type lease is as follows.

SALES-TYPE LEASE TERMS

LEASE RECEIVABLE (also NET INVESTMENT). The present value of the minimum lease payments plus the present value of any unguaranteed residual value. The lease receivable therefore includes the present value of the residual value, whether guaranteed or not.

SALES PRICE OF THE ASSET. The present value of the minimum lease payments.

COST OF GOODS SOLD. The cost of the asset to the lessor, less the present value of any unguaranteed residual value.

OBJECTIVE 8
Describe the lessor's accounting for sales-type leases.

When recording sales revenue and cost of goods sold, there is a difference in the accounting for guaranteed and unguaranteed residual values. The guaranteed residual value can be considered part of sales revenue because the lessor knows that the entire asset has been sold. But there is less certainty that the unguaranteed residual portion of the asset has been "sold" (i.e., will be realized). Therefore, sales and cost of goods sold are recognized only for the portion of the asset for which realization is assured. However, **the gross profit amount on the sale of the asset is the same whether a guaranteed or unguaranteed residual value is involved**.

To illustrate a sales-type lease with a guaranteed residual value and a sales-type lease with an unguaranteed residual value, assume the same facts as in the preceding direct-financing lease situation (pages 1101–1103). The estimated residual value is $5,000 (the present value of which is $3,104.60), and the leased equipment has an $85,000 cost to the dealer, Lessor Company. Assume that the fair market value of the residual value is $3,000 at the end of the lease term.

The amounts relevant to a sales-type lease are computed as shown in Illustration 21-27.

ILLUSTRATION 21-27
Computation of Lease Amounts by Lessor Company—Sales-Type Lease

	Sales-Type Lease	
	Guaranteed Residual Value	Unguaranteed Residual Value
Lease Receivable	$100,000 [$23,237.09 × 4.16986 (Table 6-5) + $5,000 × .62092 (Table 6-2)]	Same
Sales price of the asset	$100,000	$96,895.40 ($100,000 − $3,104.60)
Cost of goods sold	$85,000	$81,895.40 ($85,000 − $3,104.60)
Gross profit	$15,000 ($100,000 − $85,000)	$15,000 ($96,895.40 − $81,895.40)

The profit recorded by Lessor Company at the point of sale is the same ($15,000) whether the residual value is guaranteed or unguaranteed, **but the sales revenue and cost of goods sold amounts are different**. The present value of the unguaranteed residual value is deducted from sales revenue and cost of goods sold for two reasons: (1)The criteria for revenue recognition have not been met, and (2) matching expense against revenue not yet recognized is improper. The revenue recognition criteria have not been met **because of the uncertainty surrounding the realization of the unguaranteed residual value**.

The entries to record this transaction on January 1, 2005, and the receipt of the residual value at the end of the lease term are presented below.

ILLUSTRATION 21-28
Entries for Guaranteed and Unguaranteed Residual Values, Lessor Company—Sales-Type Lease

Guaranteed Residual Value			Unguaranteed Residual Value		
To record sales-type lease at inception (January 1, 2005):					
Cost of Goods Sold	85,000.00		Cost of Goods Sold	81,895.40	
Lease Receivable	100,000.00		Lease Receivable	100,000.00	
Sales Revenue		100,000.00	Sales Revenue		96,895.40
Inventory		85,000.00	Inventory		85,000.00
To record receipt of the first lease payment (January 1, 2005):					
Cash	25,237.09		Cash	25,237.09	
Lease Receivable		23,237.09	Lease Receivable		23,237.09
Prop. Tax Exp./Prop. Tax Pay.		2,000.00	Property Tax Exp./Pay.		2,000.00
To recognize interest revenue earned during the first year (December 31, 2005):					
Interest Receivable	7,676.29		Interest Receivable	7,676.29	
Interest Revenue		7,676.29	Interest Revenue		7,676.29
(See lease amortization schedule, Illustration 21-24 on page 1109.)					
To record receipt of the second lease payment (January 1, 2006):					
Cash	25,237.09		Cash	25,237.09	
Interest Receivable		7,676.29	Interest Receivable		7,676.29
Lease Receivable		15,560.80	Lease Receivable		15,560.80
Property Tax Exp./Pay.		2,000.00	Property Tax Exp./Pay.		2,000.00
To recognize interest revenue earned during the second year (December 31, 2006):					
Interest Receivable	6,120.21		Interest Receivable	6,120.21	
Interest Revenue		6,120.21	Interest Revenue		6,120.21
To record receipt of residual value at end of lease term (December 31, 2009):					
Inventory	3,000		Inventory	3,000	
Cash	2,000		Loss on Capital Lease	2,000	
Lease Receivable		5,000	Lease Receivable		5,000

The **estimated unguaranteed residual value in a sales-type lease** (and a direct financing-type lease) **must be reviewed periodically**. If the estimate of the unguaranteed residual value declines, the accounting for the transaction must be revised using the changed estimate. The decline represents a reduction in the lessor's lease receivable (net investment) and is recognized as a loss in the period in which the residual estimate is reduced. Upward adjustments in estimated residual value are not recognized.

WHAT DO THE NUMBERS MEAN?

XEROX TAKES ON THE SEC

Much of **Xerox**'s income is derived from leasing equipment. Reporting such leases as sales leases, Xerox records a lease contract as a sale, with income therefore being recognized immediately. One problem is that each lease receipt was comprised of payments for various items such as supplies, services, financing, and equipment.

The SEC *accused* Xerox of inappropriately allocating lease receipts, which affects the timing of income that is reported. If SEC guidelines were applied, income would be reported in different time periods. Xerox contended that its methods were correct and also noted that when the lease term is up, the bottom line is the same using either the SEC's recommended allocation method or the method used by Xerox.

Although Xerox can refuse to change its method, the SEC has the right to prevent a company from selling stock or bonds to the public if filings of the company have been rejected by the agency.

Apparently, having access to public markets is very valuable to Xerox. The company agreed to change its accounting according to SEC wishes, and paid a fine of $10 million due to its past accounting practices.

Source: Adapted from "Xerox Takes on the SEC," *Accounting Web* (January 9, 2002) (www.accountingweb.com).

Bargain Purchase Option (Lessee)

A bargain purchase option allows the lessee to purchase the leased property for a future price that is substantially lower than the property's expected future fair value. The price is so favorable at the lease's inception that the future exercise of the option appears to be reasonably assured. If a bargain purchase option exists, **the lessee must increase the present value of the minimum lease payments by the present value of the option price**.

For example, assume that Lessee Company in the illustration on page 1106 had an option to buy the leased equipment for $5,000 at the end of the 5-year lease term when the fair value is expected to be $18,000. The significant difference between the option price and the fair value creates a bargain purchase option, the exercise of which is reasonably assured. Four computations are affected by a bargain purchase option in the same manner that they are by a guaranteed residual value: (1) the amount of the five lease payments necessary for the lessor to earn a 10 percent return on the lease receivable, (2) the amount of the minimum lease payments, (3) the amount capitalized as leased assets and lease liability, and (4) the amortization of the lease liability. Therefore, the computations, amortization schedule, and entries that would be prepared for this $5,000 bargain purchase option are identical to those shown for the $5,000 guaranteed residual value.

The only difference between the accounting treatment for a bargain purchase option and a guaranteed residual value of identical amounts and circumstances is in the **computation of the annual depreciation**. In the case of a guaranteed residual value, the lessee depreciates the asset over the lease term, whereas in the case of a bargain purchase option, the lessee uses the **economic life** of the asset.

Initial Direct Costs (Lessor)

Initial direct costs are of two types.[20] The first, **incremental direct costs**, are costs paid to independent third parties, incurred in originating a lease arrangement. Examples would include the cost of independent appraisal of collateral used to secure a lease, the cost of an outside credit check of the lessee, or a broker's fee for finding the lessee.

[20]"Accounting for Nonrefundable Fees and Costs Associated with Originating or Acquiring Loans and Initial Direct Costs of Leases," *Statement of Financial Accounting Standards No. 91* (Stamford: Conn.: FASB, 1987).

The second type, **internal direct costs**, are the costs directly related to specified activities performed **by the lessor** on a given lease. Examples are evaluating the prospective lessee's financial condition; evaluating and recording guarantees, collateral, and other security arrangements; negotiating lease terms and preparing and processing lease documents; and closing the transaction. The costs directly related to an employee's time spent on a specific lease transaction are also considered initial direct costs.

On the other hand, initial direct costs should **not** include **internal indirect costs** related to activities performed by the lessor for advertising, servicing existing leases, and establishing and monitoring credit policies. Nor should they include costs for supervision and administration. In addition, expenses such as rent and depreciation are not considered initial direct costs.

For **operating leases**, the lessor should defer initial direct costs and **allocate them over the lease term** in proportion to the recognition of rental income. In a **sales-type lease** transaction, the lessor expenses the initial direct costs in the year of incurrence. That is, they are **expensed in the period** in which the profit on the sale is recognized.

In a **direct-financing lease**, however, initial direct costs are added to the net investment in the lease and **amortized over the life of the lease as a yield adjustment**. In addition, the unamortized deferred initial direct costs that are part of the lessor's investment in the direct-financing lease must be disclosed. If the carrying value of the asset in the lease is $4,000,000 and the lessor incurs initial direct costs of $35,000, then the lease receivable (net investment in the lease) would be $4,035,000. The yield would be adjusted to ensure proper amortization of this amount over the life of the lease and would be lower than the initial rate of return.

Current versus Noncurrent

The classification of the lease liability/receivable was presented earlier in an annuity-due situation. As indicated in Illustration 21-6, the lessee's current liability is the payment of $23,981.62 (excluding $2,000 of executory costs) to be made on January 1 of the next year. Similarly, as shown in Illustration 21-14, the lessor's current asset is the amount to be collected of $23,981.62 (excluding $2,000 of executory costs) on January 1 of the next year. In both of these annuity-due instances, the balance sheet date is December 31 and the due date of the lease payment is January 1 (less than one year), so the present value ($23,981.62) of the payment due the following January 1 is the same as the rental payment ($23,981.62).

What happens if the situation is an ordinary-annuity rather than an annuity-due situation? For example, assume that the rent is to be paid at the **end of the year** (December 31) rather than at the beginning (January 1). *FASB Statement No. 13* does not indicate how to measure the current and noncurrent amounts. It requires that for the lessee the "obligations shall be separately identified on the balance sheet as obligations under capital leases and shall be subject to the same considerations as other obligations in classifying them with current and noncurrent liabilities in classified balance sheets."[21] **The most common method of measuring the current liability portion in ordinary annuity leases is the change in the present value method.**[22]

To illustrate the change in the present value method, assume an ordinary-annuity situation with the same facts as the Lessee Company/Lessor Company case, excluding the $2,000 of executory costs. Because the rents are paid at the end of the period instead of at the beginning, the five rents are set at $26,379.73 to have an effective interest rate of 10 percent. The ordinary-annuity amortization schedule is shown in Illustration 21-29.

---

[21]"Accounting for Leases," op. cit., par. 16.

[22]For additional discussion on this approach and possible alternatives, see R. J. Swieringa, "When Current Is Noncurrent and Vice Versa!" *The Accounting Review* (January 1984), pp. 123–30, and A. W. Richardson, "The Measurement of the Current Portion of the Long-Term Lease Obligations—Some Evidence from Practice," *The Accounting Review* (October 1985), pp. 744–52.

ILLUSTRATION 21-29
Lease Amortization Schedule—Ordinary-Annuity Basis

LESSEE COMPANY/LESSOR COMPANY
LEASE AMORTIZATION SCHEDULE
(ORDINARY-ANNUITY BASIS)

Date	Annual Lease Payment	Interest 10%	Reduction of Lease Liability/Receivable	Balance of Lease Liability/Receivable
1/1/05				$100,000.00
12/31/05	$ 26,379.73	$10,000.00	$ 16,379.73	83,620.27
12/31/06	26,379.73	8,362.03	18,017.70	65,602.57
12/31/07	26,379.73	6,560.26	19,819.47	45,783.10
12/31/08	26,379.73	4,578.31	21,801.42	23,981.68
12/31/09	26,379.73	2,398.05*	23,981.68	–0–
	$131,898.65	$31,898.65	$100,000.00	

*Rounded by 12 cents.

The current portion of the lease liability/receivable under the **change in the present value method** as of December 31, 2005, would be $18,017.70 ($83,620.27 − $65,602.57). As of December 31, 2006, it would be $19,819.47 ($65,602.57 − $45,783.10). The portion of the lease liability/receivable that is not current is classified as such. That is, $65,602.57 is the noncurrent portion at December 31, 2005.

Thus, both the annuity-due and the ordinary-annuity situations report the reduction of principal for the next period as a current liability/current asset. In the annuity-due situation, interest is accrued during the year but is not paid until the next period. As a result, **a current liability/current asset arises for both the lease liability/receivable reduction and the interest** that was incurred/earned in the preceding period.

In the ordinary-annuity situation, the interest accrued during the period is also paid in the same period. Consequently, only the principal reduction is shown as a current liability/current asset.

OBJECTIVE 9
Describe the disclosure requirements for leases.

Disclosing Lease Data

Disclosures Required of the Lessee

The FASB requires that the following information with respect to leases be disclosed in the **lessee's** financial statements or in the notes.[23]

ILLUSTRATION 21-30
Lessee's Disclosures

(a) For capital leases:
  i. The gross amount of assets at each balance sheet date categorized by nature or function. This information may be combined with comparable information for owned assets.
  ii. Future *minimum lease payments* as of the latest balance sheet date, in the aggregate and for each of 5 succeeding fiscal years. Separate deductions for *executory costs* included in the *minimum lease payments* and for the amount of imputed interest necessary to reduce net *minimum lease payments* to present value.
  iii. Total noncancelable minimum sublease rentals to be received in the future, as of the latest balance sheet date.
  iv. Total *contingent rentals.*
  v. Assets recorded under capital leases and the accumulated amortization thereon shall be separately identified in the lessee's balance sheet or notes. Likewise, related obligations shall be separately identified as obligations under capital leases. Depreciation on capitalized leased assets should be separately disclosed.

(b) For operating leases having initial or remaining noncancelable *lease terms* in excess of one year:
  i. Future minimum rental payments required as of the latest balance sheet date, in the aggregate and for each of the 5 succeeding fiscal years.
  ii. Total minimum rentals to be received in the future under noncancelable subleases as of the latest balance sheet date.

(c) For all operating leases, rental expense for each period with separate amounts for minimum rentals, *contingent rentals*, and sublease rentals. Rental payments under leases with *terms* of a month or less that were not renewed need not be included.

(d) A general description of the lessee's arrangements including, but not limited to:
  i. The basis on which *contingent rental* payments are determined.
  ii. The existence and terms of renewal or purchase options and escalation clauses.
  iii. Restrictions imposed by lease agreements, such as those concerning dividends, additional debt, and further leasing.

[23]"Accounting for Leases," *FASB Statement No. 13*, as amended and interpreted through May 1980 (Stamford, Conn.: FASB, 1980), par. 16.

Disclosures Required of the Lessor

The FASB requires that **lessors** disclose in the financial statements or in the notes the following information when leasing "is a significant part of the lessor's business activities in terms of revenue, net income, or assets."[24]

ILLUSTRATION 21-31
Lessor's Disclosures

(a) For sales-type and direct-financing leases:
   i. The components of the net investment in sales-type and direct-financing leases as of each balance sheet date:
      a. Future *minimum lease payments* to be received, with separate deductions for
         (i) *executory costs* and (ii) the accumulated allowance for uncollectible *minimum lease payments* receivable.
      b. The *unguaranteed residual values* accruing to the lessor.
      c. Unearned revenue.
   ii. Future *minimum lease payments* to be received for each of the 5 succeeding fiscal years.
   iii. The amount of unearned revenue included in income to offset *initial direct costs* charged against income for each period for which an income statement is presented. (For direct financing leases only.)
   iv. Total *contingent rentals* included in income for each period for which an income statement is presented.

(b) For operating leases:
   i. The cost and carrying amount, if different, of leased property according to nature or function, and total amount of accumulated depreciation.
   ii. Minimum future rentals on noncancelable leases as of the latest balance sheet date, in aggregate and for each of 5 succeeding fiscal years.
   iii. Total *contingent rentals* included in income for each period for which an income statement is presented.

(c) A general description of the lessor's leasing arrangements.

Disclosures Illustrated

The financial statement excerpts from the 2001 Annual Report of **Penn Traffic Company** in Illustration 21-32 present the statement and note disclosures typical of a **lessee** having both capital leases and operating leases.

ILLUSTRATION 21-32
Disclosure of Leases by Lessee

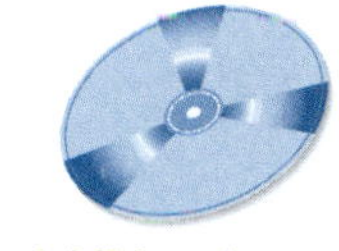

Additional Lease Disclosures

Penn Traffic Company
(dollar amounts in thousands)

Capital Leases (Note 12)	2001	2000
Capital leases	$60,405	$66,119
Less: Accumulated amortization	(9,593)	(5,052)
	50,812	61,067
Current Liabilities		
Current portion of obligations under capital leases (Note 12)	$ 7,878	$ 9,667
Noncurrent Liabilities		
Obligations under capital leases (Note 12)	73,396	82,537

Note 12: Leases (in part)

The Company principally operates in leased store facilities with terms of up to 20 years with renewable options for additional periods. The Company follows the provisions of Statement of Financial Accounting Standards No. 13, "Accounting for Leases" ("SFAS 13"), in determining the criteria for capital leases. Leases that do not meet such criteria are classified as operating leases and related rentals are charged to expense in the year incurred. In addition to minimum rentals, substantially all store leases provide for the Company to pay real estate taxes and other expenses. The majority of store leases also provide for the Company to pay contingent rentals based on a percentage of the store's sales in excess of stipulated amounts.

For 2001, 2000, and 1999, capital lease amortization expense was $7.6 million, $9.0 million, and $11.8 million, respectively.

The following is a summary by year of future minimum rental payments for capitalized leases and for operating leases that have initial or remaining noncancelable terms in excess of one year as of February 3, 2001:

continued on next page

[24]Ibid., par. 23.

Fiscal Years Ending	Total	Operating	Capital
	(in thousands of dollars)		
2002	$ 50,392	$ 33,460	$ 16,932
2003	47,866	32,092	15,774
2004	42,818	29,279	13,539
2005	40,443	27,237	13,206
2006	38,381	25,509	12,872
Later years	243,463	179,614	63,849
Total minimum lease payments	$463,363	$327,191	136,172
Less: Estimated amount representing interest			(54,898)
Present value of net minimum capital lease payments			81,274
Less: Current portion			(7,878)
Long-term obligations under capital leases at February 3, 2001			$ 73,396

Minimum rental payments for operating leases, including contingent rentals and net of sublease payments in 2001, 2000, and 1999 were $30,604, $30,036, and $35,832, respectively.

The following note from the 2001 Annual Report of **Dana Corporation** illustrates the disclosures of a **lessor**.

ILLUSTRATION 21-33
Disclosure of Leases by Lessor

Dana Corporation

Notes to Financial Statements
(in millions)

Note 1 (In Part): Summary of Significant Accounting Policies
Lease Financing

Lease financing consists of direct financing leases, leveraged leases and equipment on operating leases. Income on direct financing leases is recognized by a method which produces a constant periodic rate of return on the outstanding investment in the lease. Income on leveraged leases is recognized by a method which produces a constant rate of return on the outstanding net investment in the lease, net of the related deferred tax liability, in the years in which the net investment is positive. Initial direct costs are deferred and amortized using the interest method over the lease period. Equipment under operating leases is recorded at cost, net of accumulated depreciation. Income from operating leases is recognized ratably over the term of the leases.

The components of the net investment in direct financing leases are as follows:

	December 31 2000	2001
Total minimum lease payments	$154	$125
Residual values	42	38
Deferred initial direct costs	2	2
	198	165
Less: Unearned income	57	47
	$141	$118

The following is a schedule, by year, of total minimum lease payments receivable on direct financing and operating leases as of December 31, 2001:

Year Ending December 31:	Direct Financing	Operating
2002	$ 23	$20
2003	21	16
2004	18	12
2005	16	10
2006	12	8
Later years	35	15
Total minimum lease payments receivable	$125	$81

LEASE ACCOUNTING—UNSOLVED PROBLEMS

As indicated at the beginning of this chapter, lease accounting is a much abused area in which strenuous efforts are being made to circumvent *Statement No. 13*. In practice, the accounting rules for capitalizing leases have been rendered partially ineffective by the strong desires of lessees to resist capitalization. Leasing generally involves large dollar amounts that, when capitalized, materially increase reported liabilities and adversely affect the debt-to-equity ratio. Lease capitalization is also resisted because charges to expense made in the early years of the lease term are higher under the capital-lease method than under the operating method, frequently without tax benefit. As a consequence, "let's beat *Statement No. 13*" is one of the most popular games in town.[25]

To avoid leased asset capitalization, lease agreements are designed, written, and interpreted so that none of the four capitalized lease criteria are satisfied from the lessee's viewpoint. Devising lease agreements in such a way has not been too difficult when the following specifications have been met.

1. Make certain that the lease does not specify the transfer of title of the property to the lessee.
2. Do not write in a bargain purchase option.
3. Set the lease term at something less than 75 percent of the estimated economic life of the leased property.
4. Arrange for the present value of the minimum lease payments to be less than 90 percent of the fair value of the leased property.

The real challenge lies in disqualifying the lease as a capital lease to the lessee while having the same lease qualify as a capital (sales or financing) lease to the lessor. Unlike lessees, lessors try to avoid having lease arrangements classified as operating leases.[26]

Avoiding the first three criteria is relatively simple, but it takes a little ingenuity to avoid the "90 percent recovery test" for the lessee while satisfying it for the lessor. Two of the factors involved in this effort are (1) the use of the incremental borrowing rate by the lessee when it is higher than the implicit interest rate of the lessor, by making information about the implicit rate unavailable to the lessee; and (2) residual-value guarantees.

The lessee's use of the higher interest rate is probably the more popular subterfuge. While lessees are knowledgeable about the fair value of the leased property and, of course, the rental payments, they generally are not aware of the estimated residual value used by the lessor. Therefore the lessee who does not know exactly the lessor's implicit interest rate might use a different incremental borrowing rate.

The residual-value guarantee is the other unique, yet popular, device used by lessees and lessors. In fact, a whole new industry has emerged to circumvent symmetry between the lessee and the lessor in accounting for leases. The residual-value guarantee has spawned numerous companies whose principal, or even sole, function is to guarantee the residual value of leased assets. These **third-party guarantors** (insurers), for a fee, assume the risk of deficiencies in leased-asset residual value.

Because the guaranteed residual value is included in the minimum lease payments for the lessor, the 90 percent recovery of fair market value test is satisfied. The lease is a nonoperating lease to the lessor. But because the residual value is guaranteed by a third party, the minimum lease payments of the lessee do not include the guarantee. Thus, by merely transferring some of the risk to a third party, lessees can alter sub-

[25]Richard Dieter, "Is Lessee Accounting Working?" *The CPA Journal* (August 1979), pp. 13–19. This article provides interesting examples of abuses of *Statement No. 13*, discusses the circumstances that led to the current situation, and proposes a solution.

[26]The reason is that most lessors are financial institutions and do not want these types of assets on their balance sheets. In fact, banks and savings and loans are not permitted to report these assets on their balance sheets except for relatively short periods of time. Furthermore, the capital-lease transaction from the lessor's standpoint provides higher income flows in the earlier periods of the lease.

stantially the accounting treatment by converting what would otherwise be capital leases to operating leases.[27]

WHAT DO THE NUMBERS MEAN?

SWAP MEET

Telecommunication companies have developed one of the more innovative and controversial uses of leases. In order to provide fiber-optic service to their customers in areas where they did not have networks installed, telecommunication companies such as **Global Crossing**, **Qwest Communications International**, and **Cable and Wireless** entered into agreements to swap some of their unused network capacity in exchange for the use of another company's fiber-optic cables. Here's how it works:

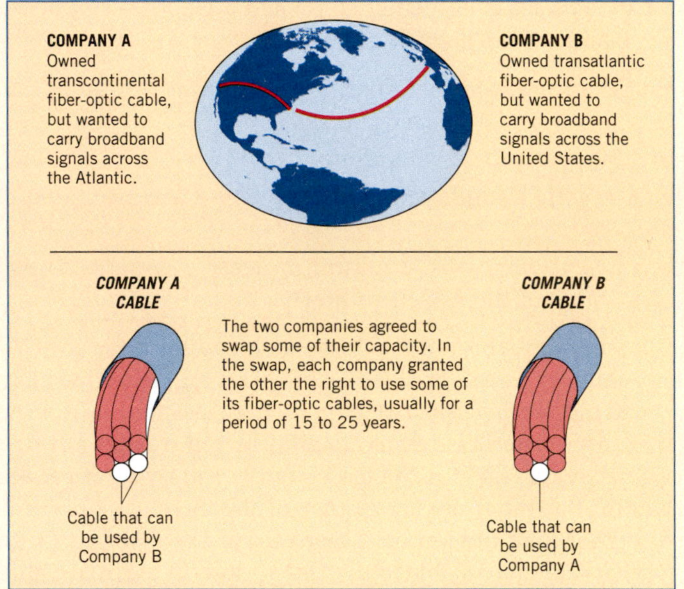

Such trades seem like a good way to make efficient use of telecommunication assets. What got some telecommunications companies in trouble, though, was how they did the accounting for the swap. The most conservative accounting for the capacity trades is to treat the swap as an exchange of assets, which does not affect the income statement. However, Global Crossing got into trouble with the SEC when it structured some of its capacity swaps as leases—the legal right to use capacity. Global Crossing was recognizing as revenue the payments received for the outgoing transfer of capacity, while payments for the incoming cable capacity were treated as capital expenditures, and therefore not expensed. As a result, Global Crossing was showing strong profits from its capacity swaps. However, the company's investors got an unpleasant surprise when the market for bandwidth cooled off and there was no longer demand for its broadband capacity or its long-term leasing arrangements.

Source: Simon Romero and Seth Schiesel, "The Fiber-Optic Fantasy Slips Away," *New York Times on the Web* (February 17, 2002). By permission.

[27]As an aside, third-party guarantors have experienced some difficulty. **Lloyd's of London**, at one time, insured the fast-growing U.S. computer-leasing industry in the amount of $2 billion against revenue losses and losses in residual value if leases were canceled. Because of "overnight" technological improvements and the successive introductions of more efficient and less expensive computers by computer manufacturers, lessees in abundance canceled their leases. As the market for second-hand computers became flooded and residual values plummeted, third-party guarantor Lloyd's of London projected a loss of $400 million. Much of the third-party guarantee business was stimulated by the lessees' and lessors' desire to circumvent *FASB Statement No. 13.*

Much of this circumvention is encouraged by the nature of the criteria, which stem from weaknesses in the basic objective of *Statement No. 13*. Accounting standards-setting bodies continue to have poor experience with arbitrary break points or other size and percentage criteria—that is, rules like "90 percent of," "75 percent of," etc. Some believe that a more workable solution would be to require capitalization of all leases that extend for some defined period (such as one year). The basis for this treatment is that the lessee has acquired an asset (a property right) and a corresponding liability in contrast to the basis that the lease transfers substantially all the risks and rewards of ownership.

Three years after it issued *Statement No. 13*, a majority of the FASB expressed "the tentative view that, if *Statement 13* were to be reconsidered, they would support a property-right approach in which all leases are included as 'rights to use property' and as 'lease obligations' in the lessee's balance sheet."[28] Recently, the FASB and other international standards setters have issued a report on lease accounting that proposes the capitalization of more leases.[29]

SUMMARY OF LEARNING OBJECTIVES

1 Explain the nature, economic substance, and advantages of lease transactions. A lease is a contractual agreement between a lessor and a lessee that conveys to the lessee the right to use specific property (real or personal), owned by the lessor, for a specified period of time. In return for this right, the lessee agrees to make periodic cash payments (rents) to the lessor. The advantages of lease transactions are: (1) 100 percent financing; (2) protection against obsolescence, (3) flexibility, (4) less costly financing, (5) possible tax advantages, and (6) off-balance-sheet financing.

2 Describe the accounting criteria and procedures for capitalizing leases by the lessee. A lease is a capital lease if one or more of the following criteria (Group I criteria) are met: (1) The lease transfers ownership of the property to the lessee; (2) the lease contains a bargain purchase option; (3) the lease term is equal to 75 percent or more of the estimated economic life of the leased property; (4) the present value of the minimum lease payments (excluding executory costs) equals or exceeds 90 percent of the fair value of the leased property. For a capital lease, the lessee records an asset and a liability at the lower of (1) the present value of the minimum lease payments or (2) the fair market value of the leased asset at the inception of the lease.

3 Contrast the operating and capitalization methods of recording leases. The total charges to operations are the same over the lease term whether the lease is accounted for as a capital lease or as an operating lease. Under the capital lease treatment, the charges are higher in the earlier years and lower in the later years. If an accelerated method of depreciation is used, the differences between the amounts charged to operations under the two methods would be even larger in the earlier and later years. The following occurs if a capital lease instead of an operating lease is employed: (1) an increase in the amount of reported debt (both short-term and long-term), (2) an increase in the amount of total assets (specifically long-lived assets), and (3) lower income early in the life of the lease and, therefore, lower retained earnings.

4 Identify the classifications of leases for the lessor. From the standpoint of the lessor, all leases may be classified for accounting purpose as follows: (1) operating leases, (2) direct-financing leases, (3) sales-type leases. The lessor should classify and account for an arrangement as a direct-financing lease or a sales-type lease if, at the date of

KEY TERMS

bargain purchase option, *1090*
bargain renewal option, *1091*
capital lease, *1089*
capitalization criteria, *1090*
capitalization of leases, *1088*
direct-financing lease, *1101*
effective-interest method, *1093*
executory costs, *1092*
guaranteed residual value, *1092*
implicit interest rate, *1092*
incremental borrowing rate, *1092*
initial direct costs, *1112*
lease, *1086*
lease receivable, *1101, 1110*
lease term, *1086*
lessee, *1086*
lessor, *1086*
manufacturer's or dealer's profit, *1100*
minimum lease payments, *1091*
noncancelable, *1089*
off-balance-sheet financing, *1087*
operating lease, *1090*
sales-type lease, *1110*
third-party guarantors, *1117*
unguaranteed residual value, *1107*

[28]"Is Lessee Accounting Working?" op. cit., p. 19.

[29]H. Nailor and A. Lennard, "Capital Leases: Implementation of a New Approach," *Financial Accounting Series No. 206A* (Norwalk, Conn.: FASB, 2000).

the lease agreement, one or more of the Group I criteria (as shown in learning objective 2 for lessees) are met and both of the following Group II criteria are met. *Group II*: (1) Collectibility of the payments required from the lessee is reasonably predictable; and (2) no important uncertainties surround the amount of unreimbursable costs yet to be incurred by the lessor under the lease. All leases that fail to meet the criteria are classified and accounted for by the lessor as operating leases.

5 **Describe the lessor's accounting for direct-financing leases.** Leases that are in substance the financing of an asset purchase by a lessee require the lessor to substitute a "lease receivable" for the leased asset. "Lease receivable" is defined as the present value of the minimum lease payments plus the present value of the unguaranteed residual value. Therefore the residual value, whether guaranteed or unguaranteed, is included as part of lease receivable.

6 **Identify special features of lease arrangements that cause unique accounting problems.** The features of lease arrangements that cause unique accounting problems are: (1) residual values; (2) sales-type leases (lessor); (3) bargain purchase options; (4) initial direct costs; (5) current versus noncurrent; and (6) disclosures.

7 **Describe the effect of residual values, guaranteed and unguaranteed, on lease accounting.** Whether the estimated residual value is guaranteed or unguaranteed is of both economic and accounting consequence to the lessee. The accounting difference is that the minimum lease payments, the basis for capitalization, includes the guaranteed residual value but excludes the unguaranteed residual value. A guaranteed residual value affects the lessee's computation of minimum lease payments and, therefore, the amounts capitalized as a leased asset and a lease obligation. In effect, it is an additional lease payment that will be paid in property or cash, or both, at the end of the lease term. An unguaranteed residual value from the lessee's viewpoint is the same as no residual value in terms of its effect upon the lessee's method of computing the minimum lease payments and the capitalization of the leased asset and the lease liability.

8 **Describe the lessor's accounting for sales-type leases.** Sales-type leases are distinguished from direct-financing leases by the difference in the cost and fair value of the leased asset, which results in gross profit. Lease receivable and interest revenue are the same whether a guaranteed or an unguaranteed residual value is involved. When recording sales revenue and cost of goods sold, there is a difference in the accounting for guaranteed and unguaranteed residual values. The guaranteed residual value can be considered part of sales revenue because the lessor knows that the entire asset has been sold. There is less certainty that the unguaranteed residual portion of the asset has been "sold"; therefore, sales and cost of goods sold are recognized only for the portion of the asset for which realization is assured. However, the gross profit amount on the sale of the asset is the same whether a guaranteed or unguaranteed residual value is involved.

Expanded Discussion of Real Estate Leases and Leveraged Leases

9 **Describe the disclosure requirements for leases.** The disclosure requirements for the **lessee** are classified as follows: (1) capital leases; (2) operating leases having initial or remaining noncancelable lease terms in excess of one year; (3) all operating leases; and (4) a general description of the lessee's arrangements. The disclosure requirements for the **lessor** are classified as follows: (1) sales-type and direct-financing leases; (2) operating leases; and (3) a general description of the lessor's leasing arrangements.

APPENDIX 21A

Illustrations of Lease Arrangements

OBJECTIVE 10
Understand and apply lease accounting concepts to various lease arrangements.

To illustrate concepts discussed in this chapter, assume that Morgan Bakeries is involved in four different lease situations. Each of these leases is noncancelable, and in no case does Morgan receive title to the properties leased during or at the end of the lease term. All leases start on January 1, 2005, with the first rental due at the beginning of the year. The additional information is shown in Illustration 21A-1.

ILLUSTRATION 21A-1
Illustrative Lease Situations, Lessors

	Harmon, Inc.	Arden's Oven Co.	Mendota Truck Co.	Appleland Computer
Type of property	Cabinets	Oven	Truck	Computer
Yearly rental	\$6,000	\$15,000	\$5,582.62	\$3,557.25
Lease term	20 years	10 years	3 years	3 years
Estimated economic life	30 years	25 years	7 years	5 years
Purchase option	None	\$75,000 at end of 10 years \$4,000 at end of 15 years	None	\$3,000 at end of 3 years, which approximates fair market value
Renewal option	None	5-year renewal option at \$15,000 per year	None	1 year at \$1,500; no penalty for nonrenewal; standard renewal clause
Fair market value at inception of lease	\$60,000	\$120,000	\$20,000	\$10,000
Cost of asset to lessor	\$60,000	\$120,000	\$15,000	\$10,000
Residual value				
Guaranteed	–0–	–0–	\$7,000	–0–
Unguaranteed	\$5,000	–0–	–0–	\$3,000
Incremental borrowing rate of lessee	12%	12%	12%	12%
Executory costs paid by	*Lessee* \$300 per year	*Lessee* \$1,000 per year	*Lessee* \$500 per year	*Lessor* Estimated to be \$500 per year
Present value of minimum lease payments				
Using incremental borrowing rate of lessee	\$50,194.68	\$115,153.35	\$20,000	\$8,224.16
Using implicit rate of lessor	Not known	Not known	Not known	Known by lessee, \$8,027.48
Estimated fair market value at end of lease	\$5,000	\$80,000 at end of 10 years \$60,000 at end of 15 years	Not available	\$3,000

HARMON, INC.

The following is an analysis of the Harmon, Inc. lease.

1. **Transfer of title?** No.
2. **Bargain purchase option?** No.
3. **Economic life test (75% test).** The lease term is 20 years and the estimated economic life is 30 years. Thus it **does not** meet the 75 percent test.
4. **Recovery of investment test (90% test):**

Fair market value	$60,000	Rental payments	$ 6,000
Rate	90%	PV of annuity due for 20 years at 12%	× 8.36578
90% of fair market value	$54,000	PV of rental payments	$50,194.68

Because the present value of the minimum lease payments is less than 90 percent of the fair market value, the 90 percent test is not met.

Both Morgan and Harmon should account for this lease as an operating lease, as indicated by the January 1, 2005, entries shown below.

ILLUSTRATION 21A-2
Comparative Entries for Operating Lease

Morgan Bakeries (Lessee)			Harmon, Inc. (Lessor)		
Rent Expense	6,000		Cash	6,000	
Cash		6,000	Rental Revenue		6,000

ARDEN'S OVEN CO.

The following is an analysis of the Arden's Oven Co. lease.

1. **Transfer of title?** No.
2. **Bargain purchase option?** The $75,000 option at the end of 10 years does not appear to be sufficiently lower than the expected fair value of $80,000 to make it reasonably assured that it will be exercised. However, the $4,000 at the end of 15 years when the fair value is $60,000 does appear to be a bargain. From the information given, criterion 2 is therefore met. Note that both the guaranteed and the unguaranteed residual values are assigned zero values because the lessor does not expect to repossess the leased asset.
3. **Economic life test (75% test):** Given that a bargain purchase option exists, the lease term is the initial lease period of 10 years plus the 5-year renewal option since it precedes a bargain purchase option. Even though the lease term is now considered to be 15 years, this test is still not met because 75 percent of the economic life of 25 years is 18.75 years.
4. **Recovery of investment test (90% test):**

Fair market value	$120,000	Rental payments	$ 15,000.00
Rate	90%	PV of annuity due for 15 years at 12%	× 7.62817
90% of fair market value	$108,000	PV of rental payments	$114,422.55

PV of bargain purchase option: $= \$4{,}000 \times (PVF_{15,12\%}) = \$4{,}000 \times .18270 = \$730.80$

PV of rental payments	$114,422.55
PV of bargain purchase option	730.80
PV of minimum lease payments	$115,153.35

The present value of the minimum lease payments is greater than 90% of the fair market value; therefore, the 90% test is met.

Morgan Bakeries should account for this as a capital lease because both criterion 2 and criterion 4 are met. Assuming that Arden's implicit rate is the same as Morgan's incremental borrowing rate, the following entries are made on January 1, 2005.

ILLUSTRATION 21A-3
Comparative Entries for Capital Lease—Bargain Purchase Option

Morgan Bakeries (Lessee)			Arden's Oven Co. (Lessor)		
Leased Asset—Oven	115,153.35		Lease Receivable	120,000	
Lease Liability		115,153.35	Asset—Oven		120,000

Morgan Bakeries would depreciate the leased asset over its economic life of 25 years, given the bargain purchase option. Arden's Oven Co. does not use sales-type accounting because the fair market value and the cost of the asset are the same at the inception of the lease.

MENDOTA TRUCK CO.

The following is an analysis of the Mendota Truck Co. lease.

1. **Transfer of title?** No.
2. **Bargain purchase option?** No.
3. **Economic life test (75% test):** The lease term is 3 years and the estimated economic life is 7 years. Thus it **does not** meet the 75 percent test.
4. **Recovery of investment test (90% test):**

Fair market value	$20,000	Rental payments	$ 5,582.62
Rate	90%	PV of annuity due for 3 years at 12%	× 2.69005
90% of fair market value	$18,000	PV of rental payments	$15,017.54
		(Note: adjusted for $0.01 due to rounding)	

PV of guaranteed residual value: = $7,000 × ($PVF_{3,12\%}$) = $7,000 × .71178 = $4,982.46

PV of rental payments	$15,017.54
PV of guaranteed residual value	4,982.46
PV of minimum lease payments	$20,000.00

The present value of the minimum lease payments is greater than 90 percent of the fair market value; therefore, the 90% test is met.

Assuming that Mendota's implicit rate is the same as Morgan's incremental borrowing rate, the following entries are made on January 1, 2005.

ILLUSTRATION 21A-4
Comparative Entries for Capital Lease

Morgan Bakeries (Lessee)			Mendota Truck Co. (Lessor)		
Leased Asset—Truck	20,000		Lease Receivable	20,000	
Lease Liability		20,000	Cost of Goods Sold	15,000	
			Inventory—Truck		15,000
			Sales		20,000

The leased asset is depreciated by Morgan over 3 years to its guaranteed residual value.

APPLELAND COMPUTER

The following is an analysis of the Appleland Computer lease.

1. **Transfer of title?** No.
2. **Bargain purchase option?** No. The option to purchase at the end of 3 years at approximate fair market value is clearly not a bargain.

3. **Economic life test (75% test):** The lease term is 3 years, and no bargain renewal period exists. Therefore the 75 percent test **is not** met.
4. **Recovery of investment test (90% test):**

Fair market value	$10,000	Rental payments	$3,557.25
Rate	90%	Less executory costs	500.00
90% of fair market value	$ 9,000		3,057.25
		PV of annuity due factor for 3 years at 12%	× 2.69005
		PV of minimum lease payments using incremental borrowing rate	$8,224.16

The present value of the minimum lease payments using the incremental borrowing rate is $8,224.16; using the implicit rate, it is $8,027.48 (see Illustration 21A-1). The implicit rate of the lessor is, therefore, higher than the incremental borrowing rate. Given this situation, the lessee uses the $8,224.16 (lower interest rate when discounting) when comparing with the 90% of fair market value. Because the present value of the minimum lease payments is lower than 90 percent of the fair market value, the recovery of investment test **is not** met.

The following entries are made on January 1, 2005, indicating an operating lease.

ILLUSTRATION 21A-5
Comparative Entries for Operating Lease

Morgan Bakeries (Lessee)			Appleland Computer (Lessor)		
Rent Expense	3,557.25		Cash	3,557.25	
Cash		3,557.25	Rental Revenue		3,557.25

If the lease payments had been $3,557.25 with no executory costs involved, this lease arrangement would have qualified for capital-lease accounting treatment.

SUMMARY OF LEARNING OBJECTIVE FOR APPENDIX 21A

10 **Understand and apply lease accounting concepts to various lease arrangements.** The classification of leases by lessees and lessors is based on criteria that assess whether substantially all of the risks and benefits of ownership of the asset have been transferred from the lessor to the lessee. In addition, lessors assess two additional criteria to ensure that payment is assured and that there are not uncertainties about lessor's future costs. Lessees capitalize leases that meet any of the criteria, recording a lease asset and related lease liability. For leases that are in substance a financing of an asset purchase, lessors substitute a lease receivable for the leased asset. In a sales-type lease, the fair value of the leased asset is greater than the cost, and lessors record gross profit. Leases that do not meet capitalization criteria are classified as operating leases, on which rent expense (revenue) is recognized by lessees (lessors) for lease payments.

APPENDIX 21B

Sale-Leasebacks

OBJECTIVE 11
Describe the lessee's accounting for sale-leaseback transactions.

The term **sale-leaseback** describes a transaction in which the owner of the property (seller-lessee) sells the property to another and simultaneously leases it back from the new owner. The use of the property is generally continued without interruption.

Sale-leasebacks are common. Financial institutions (e.g., **Bank of America** and **First Chicago**) have used this technique for their administrative offices, public utilities (**Ohio Edison** and **Pinnacle West Corporation**) for their generating plants, and airlines (**Continental** and **Alaska Airlines**) for their aircraft. The advantages of a sale-leaseback from the seller's viewpoint usually involve two primary considerations:

1. *Financing*—If the purchase of equipment has already been financed, a sale-leaseback can allow the seller to refinance at lower rates, assuming rates have dropped. In addition, a sale-leaseback can provide another source of working capital, particularly when liquidity is tight.
2. *Taxes*—At the time a company purchased equipment, it may not have known that it would be subject to a minimum tax and that ownership might increase its minimum tax liability. By selling the property, the seller-lessee may deduct the entire lease payment, which is not subject to minimum tax considerations.

DETERMINING ASSET USE

To the extent the **seller-lessee's use** of the asset sold continues after the sale, the sale-leaseback is really a form of financing, and therefore **no gain or loss should be recognized** on the transaction. In short, the seller-lessee is simply borrowing funds. On the other hand, if the **seller-lessee gives up the right to the use** of the asset sold, the transaction is in substance a sale, and **gain or loss recognition** is appropriate. Trying to ascertain when the lessee has given up the use of the asset is difficult, however, and complex rules have been formulated to identify this situation.[1] To understand the profession's position in this area, the basic accounting for the lessee and lessor are discussed below.

UNDERLYING CONCEPTS

A sale-leaseback is similar in substance to the parking of inventories discussed in Chapter 8. The ultimate economic benefits remain under the control of the "seller," thus satisfying the definition of an asset.

Lessee

If the lease meets one of the four criteria for treatment as a capital lease (see Illustration 21-2), the **seller-lessee accounts for the transaction as a sale and the lease as a capital lease**. Any profit or loss experienced by the seller-lessee from the sale of the assets that are leased back under a capital lease should be **deferred and amortized over the lease term** (or the economic life if either criterion 1 or 2 is satisfied) in proportion to the amortization of the leased assets. For example, if Lessee, Inc. sells equipment having a book value of $580,000 and a fair value of $623,110 to Lessor, Inc. for $623,110 and leases the equipment back for $50,000 a year for 20 years, the profit of $43,110

[1]Sales and leasebacks of real estate are often accounted for differently. A discussion of the issues related to these transactions is beyond the scope of this textbook. See *Statement of Financial Accounting Standards No. 98,* op. cit.

should be amortized over the 20-year period at the same rate that the $623,110 is depreciated.[2] The $43,110 is credited to "**Unearned Profit on Sale-Leaseback.**"

If none of the capital lease criteria are satisfied, **the seller-lessee accounts for the transaction as a sale and the lease as an operating lease**. Under an operating lease, such profit or loss should be deferred and amortized in proportion to the rental payments over the period of time the assets are expected to be used by the lessee.

There are exceptions to these two general rules. They are:

1. ***Losses Recognized***—The profession requires that, when the fair value of the asset is **less than the book value** (carrying amount), a loss must be recognized immediately up to the amount of the difference between the book value and fair value. For example, if Lessee, Inc. sells equipment having a book value of $650,000 and a fair value of $623,110, the difference of $26,890 should be charged to a loss account.[3]
2. ***Minor Leaseback***—Leasebacks in which the present value of the rental payments are 10 percent or less of the fair value of the asset are defined as **minor leasebacks**. In this case, the seller-lessee gives up most of the rights to the use of the asset sold. Therefore, the transaction is a sale, and full gain or loss recognition is appropriate. It is not a financing transaction because the risks of ownership have been transferred.[4]

Lessor

If the lease meets one of the criteria in Group I and both of the criteria in Group II (see Illustration 21-9), the **purchaser-lessor** records the transaction as a purchase and a direct-financing lease. If the lease does not meet the criteria, the purchaser-lessor records the transaction as a purchase and an operating lease.

SALE-LEASEBACK ILLUSTRATION

To illustrate the accounting treatment accorded a sale-leaseback transaction, assume that Lessee Corp. on January 1, 2005, sells a used Boeing 767 having a carrying amount on its books of $75,500,000 to Lessor Corp. for $80,000,000 and immediately leases the aircraft back under the following conditions:

1. The term of the lease is 15 years, noncancelable, and requires equal rental payments of $10,487,443 at the beginning of each year.
2. The aircraft has a fair value of $80,000,000 on January 1, 2005, and an estimated economic life of 15 years.
3. Lessee Corp. pays all executory costs.
4. Lessee Corp. depreciates similar aircraft that it owns on a straight-line basis over 15 years.
5. The annual payments assure the lessor a 12 percent return.
6. The incremental borrowing rate of Lessee Corp. is 12 percent.

This lease is a capital lease to Lessee Corp. because the lease term exceeds 75 percent of the estimated life of the aircraft and because the present value of the lease payments exceeds 90 percent of the fair value of the aircraft to the lessor. Assuming that col-

[2]*Statement of Financial Accounting Standards No. 28*, "Accounting for Sales with Leasebacks" (Stamford, Conn.: FASB, 1979).

[3]There can be two types of losses in sale-leaseback arrangements. One is a **real economic loss** that results when the carrying amount of the asset is higher than the fair market value of the asset. In this case, the loss should be recognized. An **artificial loss** results when the sale price is below the carrying amount of the asset but the fair market value is above the carrying amount. In this case the loss is more in the form of prepaid rent and should be deferred and amortized in the future.

[4]In some cases the seller-lessee retains more than a minor part but less than substantially all. The computations to arrive at these values are complex and beyond the scope of this textbook.

lectibility of the lease payments is reasonably predictable and that no important uncertainties exist in relation to unreimbursable costs yet to be incurred by the lessor, Lessor Corp. should classify this lease as a direct-financing lease.

The typical journal entries to record the transactions relating to this lease for both Lessee Corp. and Lessor Corp. for the first year are presented below.

ILLUSTRATION 21B-1
Comparative Entries for Sale-Leaseback for Lessee and Lessor

Lessee Corp.			Lessor Corp.		
Sale of Aircraft by Lessee to Lessor Corp., January 1, 2005:					
Cash	80,000,000		Aircraft	80,000,000	
Aircraft		75,500,000	Cash		80,000,000
Unearned Profit on Sale-Leaseback		4,500,000	Lease Receivable	80,000,000	
Leased Aircraft under Capital Leases	80,000,000		Aircraft		80,000,000
Lease Liability		80,000,000			
First Lease Payment, January 1, 2005:					
Lease Liability	10,487,443		Cash	10,487,443	
Cash		10,487,443	Lease Receivable		10,487,443
Incurrence and Payment of Executory Costs by Lessee Corp. throughout 2005:					
Insurance, Maintenance, Taxes, etc.	XXX		(No entry)		
Cash or Accounts Payable		XXX			
Depreciation Expense on the Aircraft, December 31, 2005:					
Depreciation Expense	5,333,333		(No entry)		
Accumulated Depr.—Capital Leases ($80,000,000 ÷ 15)		5,333,333			
Amortization of Profit on Sale-Leaseback by Lessee Corp., December 31, 2005:					
Unearned Profit on Sale-Leaseback	300,000		(No entry)		
Depreciation Expense ($4,500,000 ÷ 15)		300,000			
Note: A case might be made for crediting Revenue instead of Depreciation Expense.					
Interest for 2005, December 31, 2005:					
Interest Expense	8,341,507[a]		Interest Receivable	8,341,507	
Interest Payable		8,341,507	Interest Revenue		8,341,507[a]

[a]Partial Lease Amortization Schedule:

Date	Annual Rental Payment	Interest 12%	Reduction of Balance	Balance
1/1/05				$80,000,000
1/1/05	$10,487,443	$ –0–	$10,487,443	69,512,557
1/1/06	10,487,443	8,341,507	2,145,936	67,366,621

SUMMARY OF LEARNING OBJECTIVE FOR APPENDIX 21B

11 **Describe the lessee's accounting for sale-leaseback transactions.** If the lease meets one of the four criteria for treatment as a capital lease, the seller-lessee accounts for the transaction as a sale and the lease as a capital lease. Any profit experienced by the seller-lessee from the sale of the assets that are leased back under a capital lease should be deferred and amortized over the lease term (or the economic life if either criterion 1 or 2 is satisfied) in proportion to the amortization of the leased assets. If none of the capital lease criteria are satisfied, the seller-lessee accounts for the transaction as a

KEY TERMS

minor leaseback, *1126*
sale-leaseback, *1125*

sale and the lease as an operating lease. Under an operating lease, such profit should be deferred and amortized in proportion to the rental payments over the period of time the assets are expected to be used by the lessee.

Note: All **asterisked** Questions, Brief Exercises, Exercises, and Conceptual Cases relate to material contained in the appendix to the chapter.

QUESTIONS

1. Jackie Remmers Co. is expanding its operations and is in the process of selecting the method of financing this program. After some investigation, the company determines that it may (1) issue bonds and with the proceeds purchase the needed assets or (2) lease the assets on a long-term basis. Without knowing the comparative costs involved, answer these questions:

(a) What might be the advantages of leasing the assets instead of owning them?

(b) What might be the disadvantages of leasing the assets instead of owning them?

(c) In what way will the balance sheet be differently affected by leasing the assets as opposed to issuing bonds and purchasing the assets?

2. Mildred Natalie Corp. is considering leasing a significant amount of assets. The president, Joan Elaine Robinson, is attending an informal meeting in the afternoon with a potential lessor. Because her legal advisor cannot be reached, she has called on you, the controller, to brief her on the general provisions of lease agreements to which she should give consideration in such preliminary discussions with a possible lessor. Identify the general provisions of the lease agreement that the president should be told to include in her discussion with the potential lessor.

3. Identify the two recognized lease accounting methods for lessees and distinguish between them.

4. Wayne Higley Company rents a warehouse on a month-to-month basis for the storage of its excess inventory. The company periodically must rent space whenever its production greatly exceeds actual sales. For several years the company officials have discussed building their own storage facility, but this enthusiasm wavers when sales increase sufficiently to absorb the excess inventory. What is the nature of this type of lease arrangement, and what accounting treatment should be accorded it?

5. Distinguish between minimum rental payments and minimum lease payments, and indicate what is included in minimum lease payments.

6. Explain the distinction between a direct-financing lease and a sales-type lease for a lessor.

7. Outline the accounting procedures involved in applying the operating method by a lessee.

8. Outline the accounting procedures involved in applying the capital-lease method by a lessee.

9. Identify the lease classifications for lessors and the criteria that must be met for each classification.

10. Outline the accounting procedures involved in applying the direct-financing method.

11. Outline the accounting procedures involved in applying the operating method by a lessor.

12. Joan Elbert Company is a manufacturer and lessor of computer equipment. What should be the nature of its lease arrangements with lessees if the company wishes to account for its lease transactions as sales-type leases?

13. Gordon Graham Corporation's lease arrangements qualify as sales-type leases at the time of entering into the transactions. How should the corporation recognize revenues and costs in these situations?

14. Joann Skabo, M.D. (lessee) has a noncancelable 20-year lease with Cheryl Countryman Realty, Inc. (lessor) for the use of a medical building. Taxes, insurance, and maintenance are paid by the lessee in addition to the fixed annual payments, of which the present value is equal to the fair market value of the leased property. At the end of the lease period, title becomes the lessee's at a nominal price. Considering the terms of the lease described above, comment on the nature of the lease transaction and the accounting treatment that should be accorded it by the lessee.

15. The residual value is the estimated fair value of the leased property at the end of the lease term.

(a) Of what significance is (1) an unguaranteed and (2) a guaranteed residual value in the lessee's accounting for a capitalized-lease transaction?

(b) Of what significance is (1) an unguaranteed and (2) a guaranteed residual value in the lessor's accounting for a direct-financing lease transaction?

16. How should changes in the estimated residual value be handled by the lessor?

17. Describe the effect of a "bargain purchase option" on accounting for a capital-lease transaction by a lessee.

18. What are "initial direct costs" and how are they accounted for?

19. What disclosures should be made by a lessee if the leased assets and the related obligation are not capitalized?

***20.** What is the nature of a "sale-leaseback" transaction?

BRIEF EXERCISES

BE21-1 Assume that **Best Buy** leased equipment from Photon Company. The lease term is 5 years and requires equal rental payments of $30,000 at the beginning of each year. The equipment has a fair value at the inception of the lease of $138,000, an estimated useful life of 8 years, and no residual value. Best Buy pays all executory costs directly to third parties. Photon set the annual rental to earn a rate of return of 10%, and this fact is known to Best Buy. The lease does not transfer title or contain a bargain purchase option. How should Best Buy classify this lease?

BE21-2 Waterworld Company leased equipment from Costner Company. The lease term is 4 years and requires equal rental payments of $37,283 at the beginning of each year. The equipment has a fair value at the inception of the lease of $130,000, an estimated useful life of 4 years, and no salvage value. Waterworld pays all executory costs directly to third parties. The appropriate interest rate is 10%. Prepare Waterworld's January 1, 2005, journal entries at the inception of the lease.

BE21-3 Rick Kleckner Corporation recorded a capital lease at $200,000 on January 1, 2005. The interest rate is 12%. Kleckner Corporation made the first lease payment of $35,947 on January 1, 2005. The lease requires eight annual payments. The equipment has a useful life of 8 years with no salvage value. Prepare Kleckner Corporation's December 31, 2005, adjusting entries.

BE21-4 Use the information for Rick Kleckner Corporation from BE21-3. Assume that at December 31, 2005, Kleckner made an adjusting entry to accrue interest expense of $19,686 on the lease. Prepare Kleckner's January 1, 2006, journal entry to record the second lease payment of $35,947.

BE21-5 Jana Kingston Corporation enters into a lease on January 1, 2005, that does not transfer ownership or contain a bargain purchase option. It covers 3 years of the equipment's 8-year useful life, and the present value of the minimum lease payments is less than 90% of the fair market value of the asset leased. Prepare Jana Kingston's journal entry to record its January 1, 2005, annual lease payment of $37,500.

BE21-6 Assume that **IBM** leased equipment that was carried at a cost of $150,000 to Sharon Swander Company. The term of the lease is 6 years beginning January 1, 2005, with equal rental payments of $30,677 at the beginning of each year. All executory costs are paid by Swander directly to third parties. The fair value of the equipment at the inception of the lease is $150,000. The equipment has a useful life of 6 years with no salvage value. The lease has an implicit interest rate of 9%, no bargain purchase option, and no transfer of title. Collectibility is reasonably assured with no additional cost to be incurred by Henkel. Prepare IBM's January 1, 2005, journal entries at the inception of the lease.

BE21-7 Use the information for **IBM** from BE21-6. Assume the direct-financing lease was recorded at a present value of $150,000. Prepare IBM's December 31, 2005, entry to record interest.

BE21-8 Jennifer Brent Corporation owns equipment that cost $72,000 and has a useful life of 8 years with no salvage value. On January 1, 2005, Jennifer Brent leases the equipment to Donna Havaci Inc. for one year with one rental payment of $15,000 on January 1. Prepare Jennifer Brent Corporation's 2005 journal entries.

BE21-9 Indiana Jones Corporation enters into a 6-year lease of equipment on January 1, 2005, which requires 6 annual payments of $30,000 each, beginning January 1, 2005. In addition, Indiana Jones guarantees the lessor a residual value of $20,000 at lease-end. The equipment has a useful life of 6 years. Prepare Indiana Jones' January 1, 2005, journal entries assuming an interest rate of 10%.

BE21-10 Use the information for Indiana Jones Corporation from BE21-9. Assume that for Lost Ark Company, the lessor, collectibility is reasonably predictable, there are no important uncertainties concerning costs, and the carrying amount of the machinery is $155,013. Prepare Lost Ark's January 1, 2005, journal entries.

BE21-11 Starfleet Corporation manufactures replicators. On January 1, 2005, it leased to Ferengi Company a replicator that had cost $110,000 to manufacture. The lease agreement covers the 5-year useful life of the replicator and requires 5 equal annual rentals of $45,400 each. An interest rate of 12% is implicit in the lease agreement. Collectibility of the rentals is reasonably assured, and there are no important uncertainties concerning costs. Prepare Starfleet's January 1, 2005, journal entries.

***BE21-12** On January 1, 2005, Acme Animation sold a truck to Coyote Finance for $35,000 and immediately leased it back. The truck was carried on Acme's books at $28,000. The term of the lease is 5 years, and title transfers to Acme at lease-end. The lease requires five equal rental payments of $9,233 at the end of each year. The appropriate rate of interest is 10%, and the truck has a useful life of 5 years with no salvage value. Prepare Acme's 2005 journal entries.

EXERCISES

E21-1 (Lessee Entries; Capital Lease with Unguaranteed Residual Value) On January 1, 2004, Burke Corporation signed a 5-year noncancelable lease for a machine. The terms of the lease called for Burke to make annual payments of $8,668 at the beginning of each year, starting January 1, 2004. The machine has an estimated useful life of 6 years and a $5,000 unguaranteed residual value. The machine reverts back to the lessor at the end of the lease term. Burke uses the straight-line method of depreciation for all of its plant assets. Burke's incremental borrowing rate is 10%, and the Lessor's implicit rate is unknown.

Instructions

(a) What type of lease is this? Explain.
(b) Compute the present value of the minimum lease payments.
(c) Prepare all necessary journal entries for Burke for this lease through January 1, 2005.

E21-2 (Lessee Computations and Entries; Capital Lease with Guaranteed Residual Value) Pat Delaney Company leases an automobile with a fair value of $8,725 from John Simon Motors, Inc., on the following terms:

1. Noncancelable term of 50 months.
2. Rental of $200 per month (at end of each month). (The present value at 1% per month is $7,840.)
3. Estimated residual value after 50 months is $1,180. (The present value at 1% per month is $715.) Delaney Company guarantees the residual value of $1,180.
4. Estimated economic life of the automobile is 60 months.
5. Delaney Company's incremental borrowing rate is 12% a year (1% a month). Simon's implicit rate is unknown.

Instructions

(a) What is the nature of this lease to Delaney Company?
(b) What is the present value of the minimum lease payments?
(c) Record the lease on Delaney Company's books at the date of inception.
(d) Record the first month's depreciation on Delaney Company's books (assume straight-line).
(e) Record the first month's lease payment.

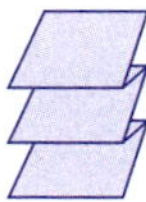

E21-3 (Lessee Entries; Capital Lease with Executory Costs and Unguaranteed Residual Value) Assume that on January 1, 2005, **Kimberly-Clark Corp.** signs a 10-year noncancelable lease agreement to lease a storage building from Sheffield Storage Company. The following information pertains to this lease agreement.

1. The agreement requires equal rental payments of $72,000 beginning on January 1, 2005.
2. The fair value of the building on January 1, 2005 is $440,000.
3. The building has an estimated economic life of 12 years, with an unguaranteed residual value of $10,000. Kimberly-Clark depreciates similar buildings on the straight-line method.
4. The lease is nonrenewable. At the termination of the lease, the building reverts to the lessor.
5. Kimberly-Clark's incremental borrowing rate is 12% per year. The lessor's implicit rate is not known by Kimberly-Clark.
6. The yearly rental payment includes $2,470.51 of executory costs related to taxes on the property.

Instructions

Prepare the journal entries on the lessee's books to reflect the signing of the lease agreement and to record the payments and expenses related to this lease for the years 2005 and 2006. Kimberly-Clark's corporate year end is December 31.

E21-4 (Lessor Entries; Direct-Financing Lease with Option to Purchase) Castle Leasing Company signs a lease agreement on January 1, 2005, to lease electronic equipment to Jan Way Company. The term of the noncancelable lease is 2 years, and payments are required at the end of each year. The following information relates to this agreement:

1. Jan Way Company has the option to purchase the equipment for $16,000 upon the termination of the lease.
2. The equipment has a cost and fair value of $160,000 to Castle Leasing Company. The useful economic life is 2 years, with a salvage value of $16,000.
3. Jan Way Company is required to pay $5,000 each year to the lessor for executory costs.
4. Castle Leasing Company desires to earn a return of 10% on its investment.
5. Collectibility of the payments is reasonably predictable, and there are no important uncertainties surrounding the costs yet to be incurred by the lessor.

Instructions

(a) Prepare the journal entries on the books of Castle Leasing to reflect the payments received under the lease and to recognize income for the years 2005 and 2006.

(b) Assuming that Jan Way Company exercises its option to purchase the equipment on December 31, 2006, prepare the journal entry to reflect the sale on Castle's books.

E21-5 (Type of Lease; Amortization Schedule) Mike Maroscia Leasing Company leases a new machine that has a cost and fair value of $95,000 to Maggie Sharrer Corporation on a 3-year noncancelable contract. Maggie Sharrer Corporation agrees to assume all risks of normal ownership including such costs as insurance, taxes, and maintenance. The machine has a 3-year useful life and no residual value. The lease was signed on January 1, 2005. Mike Maroscia Leasing Company expects to earn a 9% return on its investment. The annual rentals are payable on each December 31.

Instructions

(a) Discuss the nature of the lease arrangement and the accounting method that each party to the lease should apply.

(b) Prepare an amortization schedule that would be suitable for both the lessor and the lessee and that covers all the years involved.

E21-6 (Lessor Entries; Sales-Type Lease) Crosley Company, a machinery dealer, leased a machine to Dexter Corporation on January 1, 2004. The lease is for an 8-year period and requires equal annual payments of $35,013 at the beginning of each year. The first payment is received on January 1, 2004. Crosley had purchased the machine during 2003 for $160,000. Collectibility of lease payments is reasonably predictable, and no important uncertainties surround the amount of costs yet to be incurred by Crosley. Crosley set the annual rental to ensure an 11% rate of return. The machine has an economic life of 10 years with no residual value and reverts to Crosley at the termination of the lease.

Instructions

(a) Compute the amount of the lease receivable.

(b) Prepare all necessary journal entries for Crosley for 2004.

E21-7 (Lessee-Lessor Entries; Sales-Type Lease) On January 1, 2004, Bensen Company leased equipment to Flynn Corporation. The following information pertains to this lease.

1. The term of the noncancelable lease is 6 years, with no renewal option. The equipment reverts to the lessor at the termination of the lease.
2. Equal rental payments are due on January 1 of each year, beginning in 2004.
3. The fair value of the equipment on January 1, 2004, is $150,000, and its cost is $120,000.
4. The equipment has an economic life of 8 years, with an unguaranteed residual value of $10,000. Flynn depreciates all of its equipment on a straight-line basis.
5. Bensen set the annual rental to ensure an 11% rate of return. Flynn's incremental borrowing rate is 12%, and the implicit rate of the lessor is unknown.
6. Collectibility of lease payments is reasonably predictable, and no important uncertainties surround the amount of costs yet to be incurred by the lessor.

Instructions

(a) Discuss the nature of this lease to Bensen and Flynn.

(b) Calculate the amount of the annual rental payment.

(c) Prepare all the necessary journal entries for Flynn for 2004.

(d) Prepare all the necessary journal entries for Bensen for 2004.

E21-8 (Lessee Entries with Bargain Purchase Option) The following facts pertain to a noncancelable lease agreement between Mike Mooney Leasing Company and Denise Rode Company, a lessee.

Inception date:	May 1, 2004
Annual lease payment due at the beginning of each year, beginning with May 1, 2004	$21,227.65
Bargain purchase option price at end of lease term	$ 4,000.00
Lease term	5 years
Economic life of leased equipment	10 years
Lessor's cost	$65,000.00
Fair value of asset at May 1, 2004	$91,000.00
Lessor's implicit rate	10%
Lessee's incremental borrowing rate	10%

The collectibility of the lease payments is reasonably predictable, and there are no important uncertainties surrounding the costs yet to be incurred by the lessor. The lessee assumes responsibility for all executory costs.

Instructions

(Round all numbers to the nearest cent.)

(a) Discuss the nature of this lease to Rode Company.
(b) Discuss the nature of this lease to Mooney Company.
(c) Prepare a lease amortization schedule for Rode Company for the 5-year lease term.
(d) Prepare the journal entries on the lessee's books to reflect the signing of the lease agreement and to record the payments and expenses related to this lease for the years 2004 and 2005. Rode's annual accounting period ends on December 31. Reversing entries are used by Rode.

E21-9 (Lessor Entries with Bargain Purchase Option) A lease agreement between Mooney Leasing Company and Rode Company is described in E21-8.

Instructions

(Round all numbers to the nearest cent.)
Refer to the data in E21-8 and do the following for the lessor.

(a) Compute the amount of the lease receivable at the inception of the lease.
(b) Prepare a lease amortization schedule for Mooney Leasing Company for the 5-year lease term.
(c) Prepare the journal entries to reflect the signing of the lease agreement and to record the receipts and income related to this lease for the years 2004, 2005, and 2006. The lessor's accounting period ends on December 31. Reversing entries are not used by Mooney.

E21-10 (Computation of Rental; Journal Entries for Lessor) Morgan Marie Leasing Company signs an agreement on January 1, 2004, to lease equipment to Cole William Company. The following information relates to this agreement.

1. The term of the noncancelable lease is 6 years with no renewal option. The equipment has an estimated economic life of 6 years.
2. The cost of the asset to the lessor is $245,000. The fair value of the asset at January 1, 2004, is $245,000.
3. The asset will revert to the lessor at the end of the lease term at which time the asset is expected to have a residual value of $43,622, none of which is guaranteed.
4. Cole William Company assumes direct responsibility for all executory costs.
5. The agreement requires equal annual rental payments, beginning on January 1, 2004.
6. Collectibility of the lease payments is reasonably predictable. There are no important uncertainties surrounding the amount of costs yet to be incurred by the lessor.

Instructions

(Round all numbers to the nearest cent.)

(a) Assuming the lessor desires a 10% rate of return on its investment, calculate the amount of the annual rental payment required. Round to the nearest dollar.
(b) Prepare an amortization schedule that would be suitable for the lessor for the lease term.
(c) Prepare all of the journal entries for the lessor for 2004 and 2005 to record the lease agreement, the receipt of lease payments, and the recognition of income. Assume the lessor's annual accounting period ends on December 31.

E21-11 (Amortization Schedule and Journal Entries for Lessee) Laura Potts Leasing Company signs an agreement on January 1, 2004, to lease equipment to Janet Plote Company. The following information relates to this agreement.

1. The term of the noncancelable lease is 5 years with no renewal option. The equipment has an estimated economic life of 5 years.
2. The fair value of the asset at January 1, 2004, is $80,000.
3. The asset will revert to the lessor at the end of the lease term, at which time the asset is expected to have a residual value of $7,000, none of which is guaranteed.
4. Plote Company assumes direct responsibility for all executory costs, which include the following annual amounts: (1) $900 to Rocky Mountain Insurance Company for insurance and (2) $1,600 to Laclede County for property taxes.
5. The agreement requires equal annual rental payments of $18,142.95 to the lessor, beginning on January 1, 2004.

6. The lessee's incremental borrowing rate is 12%. The lessor's implicit rate is 10% and is known to the lessee.
7. Plote Company uses the straight-line depreciation method for all equipment.
8. Plote uses reversing entries when appropriate.

Instructions

(Round all numbers to the nearest cent.)

(a) Prepare an amortization schedule that would be suitable for the lessee for the lease term.

(b) Prepare all of the journal entries for the lessee for 2004 and 2005 to record the lease agreement, the lease payments, and all expenses related to this lease. Assume the lessee's annual accounting period ends on December 31.

E21-12 (Accounting for an Operating Lease) On January 1, 2004, Doug Nelson Co. leased a building to Patrick Wise Inc. The relevant information related to the lease is as follows.

1. The lease arrangement is for 10 years.
2. The leased building cost $4,500,000 and was purchased for cash on January 1, 2004.
3. The building is depreciated on a straight-line basis. Its estimated economic life is 50 years.
4. Lease payments are $275,000 per year and are made at the end of the year.
5. Property tax expense of $85,000 and insurance expense of $10,000 on the building were incurred by Nelson in the first year. Payment on these two items was made at the end of the year.
6. Both the lessor and the lessee are on a calendar-year basis.

Instructions

(a) Prepare the journal entries that Nelson Co. should make in 2004.

(b) Prepare the journal entries that Wise Inc. should make in 2004.

(c) If Nelson paid $30,000 to a real estate broker on January 1, 2004, as a fee for finding the lessee, how much should be reported as an expense for this item in 2004 by Nelson Co.?

E21-13 (Accounting for an Operating Lease) On January 1, 2005, a machine was purchased for $900,000 by Tom Young Co. The machine is expected to have an 8-year life with no salvage value. It is to be depreciated on a straight-line basis. The machine was leased to St. Leger Inc. on January 1, 2005, at an annual rental of $210,000. Other relevant information is as follows.

1. The lease term is for 3 years.
2. Tom Young Co. incurred maintenance and other executory costs of $25,000 in 2005 related to this lease.
3. The machine could have been sold by Tom Young Co. for $940,000 instead of leasing it.
4. St. Leger is required to pay a rent security deposit of $35,000 and to prepay the last month's rent of $17,500.

Instructions

(a) How much should Tom Young Co. report as income before income tax on this lease for 2005?

(b) What amount should St. Leger Inc. report for rent expense for 2005 on this lease?

E21-14 (Operating Lease for Lessee and Lessor) On February 20, 2004, Barbara Brent Inc., purchased a machine for $1,500,000 for the purpose of leasing it. The machine is expected to have a 10-year life, no residual value, and will be depreciated on the straight-line basis. The machine was leased to Chuck Rudy Company on March 1, 2004, for a 4-year period at a monthly rental of $19,500. There is no provision for the renewal of the lease or purchase of the machine by the lessee at the expiration of the lease term. Brent paid $30,000 of commissions associated with negotiating the lease in February 2004:

Instructions

(a) What expense should Chuck Rudy Company record as a result of the facts above for the year ended December 31, 2004? Show supporting computations in good form.

(b) What income or loss before income taxes should Brent record as a result of the facts above for the year ended December 31, 2004? (*Hint:* Amortize commissions over the life of the lease.)

(AICPA adapted)

***E21-15 (Sale and Leaseback)** Assume that on January 1, 2004, **Elmer's Restaurants** sells a computer system to Liquidity Finance Co. for $680,000 and immediately leases the computer system back. The relevant information is as follows.

1. The computer was carried on Elmer's books at a value of $600,000.
2. The term of the noncancelable lease is 10 years; title will transfer to Elmer.
3. The lease agreement requires equal rental payments of $110,666.81 at the end of each year.

4. The incremental borrowing rate for Elmer is 12%. Elmer is aware that Liquidity Finance Co. set the annual rental to insure a rate of return of 10%.
5. The computer has a fair value of $680,000 on January 1, 2004, and an estimated economic life of 10 years.
6. Elmer pays executory costs of $9,000 per year.

Instructions

Prepare the journal entries for both the lessee and the lessor for 2004 to reflect the sale and leaseback agreement. No uncertainties exist, and collectibility is reasonably certain.

***E21-16 (Lessee-Lessor, Sale-Leaseback)** Presented below are four independent situations.

(a) On December 31, 2005, Nancy Zarle Inc. sold computer equipment to Erin Daniell Co. and immediately leased it back for 10 years. The sales price of the equipment was $520,000, its carrying amount is $400,000, and its estimated remaining economic life is 12 years. Determine the amount of deferred revenue to be reported from the sale of the computer equipment on December 31, 2005.

(b) On December 31, 2005, Linda Wasicsko Co. sold a machine to Cross Co. and simultaneously leased it back for one year. The sale price of the machine was $480,000, the carrying amount is $420,000, and it had an estimated remaining useful life of 14 years. The present value of the rental payments for the one year is $35,000. At December 31, 2005, how much should Linda Wasicsko report as deferred revenue from the sale of the machine?

(c) On January 1, 2005, Joe McKane Corp. sold an airplane with an estimated useful life of 10 years. At the same time, Joe McKane leased back the plane for 10 years. The sales price of the airplane was $500,000, the carrying amount $379,000, and the annual rental $73,975.22. Joe McKane Corp. intends to depreciate the leased asset using the sum-of-the-years'-digits depreciation method. Discuss how the gain on the sale should be reported at the end of 2005 in the financial statements.

(d) On January 1, 2005, Dick Sondgeroth Co. sold equipment with an estimated useful life of 5 years. At the same time, Dick Sondgeroth leased back the equipment for 2 years under a lease classified as an operating lease. The sales price (fair market value) of the equipment was $212,700, the carrying amount is $300,000, the monthly rental under the lease is $6,000, and the present value of the rental payments is $115,753. For the year ended December 31, 2005, determine which items would be reported on its income statement for the sale-leaseback transaction.

PROBLEMS

P21-1 (Lessee-Lessor Entries; Sales-Type Lease) Stine Leasing Company agrees to lease machinery to Potter Corporation on January 1, 2004. The following information relates to the lease agreement.

1. The term of the lease is 7 years with no renewal option, and the machinery has an estimated economic life of 9 years.
2. The cost of the machinery is $420,000, and the fair value of the asset on January 1, 2004, is $560,000.
3. At the end of the lease term the asset reverts to the lessor. At the end of the lease term the asset is expected to have a guaranteed residual value of $80,000. Potter depreciates all of its equipment on a straight-line basis.
4. The lease agreement requires equal annual rental payments, beginning on January 1, 2004.
5. The collectibility of the lease payments is reasonably predictable, and there are no important uncertainties surrounding the amount of costs yet to be incurred by the lessor.
6. Stine desires a 10% rate of return on its investments. Potter's incremental borrowing rate is 11%, and the lessor's implicit rate is unknown.

Instructions

(a) Discuss the nature of this lease for both the lessee and the lessor.
(b) Calculate the amount of the annual rental payment required.
(c) Compute the present value of the minimum lease payments.
(d) Prepare the journal entries Potter would make in 2004 and 2005 related to the lease arrangement.
(e) Prepare the journal entries Stine would make in 2004 and 2005.

P21-2 (Lessee-Lessor Entries; Operating Lease) Synergetics Inc. leased a new crane to M. K. Gumowski Construction under a 5-year noncancelable contract starting January 1, 2005. Terms of the lease require payments of $22,000 each January 1, starting January 1, 2005. Synergetics will pay insurance, taxes, and maintenance charges on the crane, which has an estimated life of 12 years, a fair value of $160,000, and a cost to Synergetics of $160,000. The estimated fair value of the crane is expected to be $45,000 at the end of the lease term. No bargain purchase or renewal options are included in the contract. Both Synergetics and Gumowski adjust and close books annually at December 31. Collectibility of the lease payments is reasonably certain, and no uncertainties exist relative to unreimbursable lessor costs. Gumowski's incremental borrowing rate is 10%, and Synergetics' implicit interest rate of 9% is known to Gumowski.

Instructions

(a) Identify the type of lease involved and give reasons for your classification. Discuss the accounting treatment that should be applied by both the lessee and the lessor.

(b) Prepare all the entries related to the lease contract and leased asset for the year 2005 for the lessee and lessor, assuming the following amounts.

- **(1)** Insurance $500.
- **(2)** Taxes $2,000.
- **(3)** Maintenance $650.
- **(4)** Straight-line depreciation and salvage value $10,000.

(c) Discuss what should be presented in the balance sheet, the income statement, and the related notes of both the lessee and the lessor at December 31, 2005.

P21-3 (Lessee-Lessor Entries, Balance Sheet Presentation; Sales-Type Lease) Cascade Industries and Barbara Hardy Inc. enter into an agreement that requires Barbara Hardy Inc. to build three diesel-electric engines to Cascade's specifications. Upon completion of the engines, Cascade has agreed to lease them for a period of 10 years and to assume all costs and risks of ownership. The lease is noncancelable, becomes effective on January 1, 2005, and requires annual rental payments of $620,956 each January 1, starting January 1, 2005.

Cascade's incremental borrowing rate is 10%, and the implicit interest rate used by Barbara Hardy Inc. and known to Cascade is 8%. The total cost of building the three engines is $3,900,000. The economic life of the engines is estimated to be 10 years, with residual value set at zero. Cascade depreciates similar equipment on a straight-line basis. At the end of the lease, Cascade assumes title to the engines. Collectibility of the lease payments is reasonably certain, and no uncertainties exist relative to unreimbursable lessor costs.

Instructions

(Round all numbers to the nearest dollar.)

(a) Discuss the nature of this lease transaction from the viewpoints of both lessee and lessor.

(b) Prepare the journal entry or entries to record the transaction on January 1, 2005, on the books of Cascade Industries.

(c) Prepare the journal entry or entries to record the transaction on January 1, 2005, on the books of Barbara Hardy Inc.

(d) Prepare the journal entries for both the lessee and lessor to record the first rental payment on January 1, 2005.

(e) Prepare the journal entries for both the lessee and lessor to record interest expense (revenue) at December 31, 2005. (Prepare a lease amortization schedule for 2 years.)

(f) Show the items and amounts that would be reported on the balance sheet (not notes) at December 31, 2005, for both the lessee and the lessor.

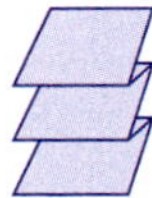

P21-4 (Balance Sheet and Income Statement Disclosure—Lessee) The following facts pertain to a noncancelable lease agreement between Ben Alschuler Leasing Company and John McKee Electronics, a lessee, for a computer system.

Inception date	October 1, 2004
Lease term	6 years
Economic life of leased equipment	6 years
Fair value of asset at October 1, 2004	$200,255
Residual value at end of lease term	–0–
Lessor's implicit rate	10%
Lessee's incremental borrowing rate	10%
Annual lease payment due at the beginning of each year, beginning with October 1, 2004	$41,800

The collectibility of the lease payments is reasonably predictable, and there are no important uncertainties surrounding the costs yet to be incurred by the lessor. The lessee assumes responsibility for all executory costs, which amount to $5,500 per year and are to be paid each October 1, beginning October 1, 2004. (This $5,500 is not included in the rental payment of $41,800.) The asset will revert to the lessor at the end of the lease term. The straight-line depreciation method is used for all equipment.

The following amortization schedule has been prepared correctly for use by both the lessor and the lessee in accounting for this lease. The lease is to be accounted for properly as a capital lease by the lessee and as a direct-financing lease by the lessor.

Date	Annual Lease Payment/ Receipt	Interest (10%) on Unpaid Liability/Receivable	Reduction of Lease Liability/Receivable	Balance of Lease Liability/Receivable
10/01/04				$200,255
10/01/04	$ 41,800		$ 41,800	158,455
10/01/05	41,800	$15,846	25,954	132,501
10/01/06	41,800	13,250	28,550	103,951
10/01/07	41,800	10,395	31,405	72,546
10/01/08	41,800	7,255	34,545	38,001
10/01/09	41,800	3,799*	38,001	–0–
	$250,800	$50,545	$200,255	

*Rounding error is $1.

Instructions

(Round all numbers to the nearest cent.)

(a) Assuming the lessee's accounting period ends on September 30, answer the following questions with respect to this lease agreement.
  (1) What items and amounts will appear on the lessee's income statement for the year ending September 30, 2005?
  (2) What items and amounts will appear on the lessee's balance sheet at September 30, 2005?
  (3) What items and amounts will appear on the lessee's income statement for the year ending September 30, 2006?
  (4) What items and amounts will appear on the lessee's balance sheet at September 30, 2006?

(b) Assuming the lessee's accounting period ends on December 31, answer the following questions with respect to this lease agreement.
  (1) What items and amounts will appear on the lessee's income statement for the year ending December 31, 2004?
  (2) What items and amounts will appear on the lessee's balance sheet at December 31, 2004?
  (3) What items and amounts will appear on the lessee's income statement for the year ending December 31, 2005?
  (4) What items and amounts will appear on the lessee's balance sheet at December 31, 2005?

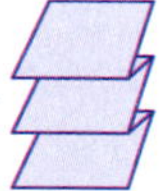

P21-5 (Balance Sheet and Income Statement Disclosure—Lessor) Assume the same information as in P21-4.

Instructions

(Round all numbers to the nearest cent.)

(a) Assuming the lessor's accounting period ends on September 30, answer the following questions with respect to this lease agreement.
  (1) What items and amounts will appear on the lessor's income statement for the year ending September 30, 2005?
  (2) What items and amounts will appear on the lessor's balance sheet at September 30, 2005?
  (3) What items and amounts will appear on the lessor's income statement for the year ending September 30, 2006?
  (4) What items and amounts will appear on the lessor's balance sheet at September 30, 2006?

(b) Assuming the lessor's accounting period ends on December 31, answer the following questions with respect to this lease agreement.
  (1) What items and amounts will appear on the lessor's income statement for the year ending December 31, 2004?
  (2) What items and amounts will appear on the lessor's balance sheet at December 31, 2004?
  (3) What items and amounts will appear on the lessor's income statement for the year ending December 31, 2005?
  (4) What items and amounts will appear on the lessor's balance sheet at December 31, 2005?

P21-6 (Lessee Entries with Residual Value) The following facts pertain to a noncancelable lease agreement between Frank Voris Leasing Company and Tom Zarle Company, a lessee.

Inception date	January 1, 2004
Annual lease payment due at the beginning of each year, beginning with January 1, 2004	$81,365
Residual value of equipment at end of lease term, guaranteed by the lessee	$50,000
Lease term	6 years
Economic life of leased equipment	6 years
Fair value of asset at January 1, 2004	$400,000
Lessor's implicit rate	12%
Lessee's incremental borrowing rate	12%

The lessee assumes responsibility for all executory costs, which are expected to amount to $4,000 per year. The asset will revert to the lessor at the end of the lease term. The lessee has guaranteed the lessor a residual value of $50,000. The lessee uses the straight-line depreciation method for all equipment.

Instructions

(Round all numbers to the nearest cent.)

(a) Prepare an amortization schedule that would be suitable for the lessee for the lease term.

(b) Prepare all of the journal entries for the lessee for 2004 and 2005 to record the lease agreement, the lease payments, and all expenses related to this lease. Assume the lessee's annual accounting period ends on December 31 and reversing entries are used when appropriate.

P21-7 (Lessee Entries and Balance Sheet Presentation; Capital Lease) Hilary Brennan Steel Company as lessee signed a lease agreement for equipment for 5 years, beginning December 31, 2004. Annual rental payments of $32,000 are to be made at the beginning of each lease year (December 31). The taxes, insurance, and the maintenance costs are the obligation of the lessee. The interest rate used by the lessor in setting the payment schedule is 10%; Brennan's incremental borrowing rate is 12%. Brennan is unaware of the rate being used by the lessor. At the end of the lease, Brennan has the option to buy the equipment for $1, considerably below its estimated fair value at that time. The equipment has an estimated useful life of 7 years, with no salvage value. Brennan uses the straight-line method of depreciation on similar owned equipment.

Instructions

(Round all numbers to the nearest dollar.)

(a) Prepare the journal entry or entries, with explanations, that should be recorded on December 31, 2004, by Brennan. (Assume no residual value.)

(b) Prepare the journal entry or entries, with explanations, that should be recorded on December 31, 2005, by Brennan. (Prepare the lease amortization schedule for all five payments.)

(c) Prepare the journal entry or entries, with explanations, that should be recorded on December 31, 2006, by Brennan.

(d) What amounts would appear on Brennan's December 31, 2006, balance sheet relative to the lease arrangement?

P21-8 (Lessee Entries and Balance Sheet Presentation; Capital Lease) On January 1, 2005, Charlie Doss Company contracts to lease equipment for 5 years, agreeing to make a payment of $94,732 (including the executory costs of $6,000) at the beginning of each year, starting January 1, 2005. The taxes, the insurance, and the maintenance, estimated at $6,000 a year, are the obligations of the lessee. The leased equipment is to be capitalized at $370,000. The asset is to be amortized on a double-declining-balance basis, and the obligation is to be reduced on an effective-interest basis. Doss's incremental borrowing rate is 12%, and the implicit rate in the lease is 10%, which is known by Doss. Title to the equipment transfers to Doss when the lease expires. The asset has an estimated useful life of 5 years and no residual value.

Instructions

(Round all numbers to the nearest dollar.)

(a) Explain the probable relationship of the $370,000 amount to the lease arrangement.

(b) Prepare the journal entry or entries that should be recorded on January 1, 2005, by Charlie Doss Company.

(c) Prepare the journal entry to record depreciation of the leased asset for the year 2005.

(d) Prepare the journal entry to record the interest expense for the year 2005.

(e) Prepare the journal entry to record the lease payment of January 1, 2006, assuming reversing entries are not made.

(f) What amounts will appear on the lessee's December 31, 2005, balance sheet relative to the lease contract?

P21-9 (Lessee Entries, Capital Lease with Monthly Payments) John Roesch Inc. was incorporated in 2003 to operate as a computer software service firm with an accounting fiscal year ending August 31. Roesch's primary product is a sophisticated online inventory-control system; its customers pay a fixed fee plus a usage charge for using the system.

Roesch has leased a large, Alpha-3 computer system from the manufacturer. The lease calls for a monthly rental of $50,000 for the 144 months (12 years) of the lease term. The estimated useful life of the computer is 15 years.

Each scheduled monthly rental payment includes $4,000 for full-service maintenance on the computer to be performed by the manufacturer. All rentals are payable on the first day of the month beginning with August 1, 2004, the date the computer was installed and the lease agreement was signed.

The lease is noncancelable for its 12-year term, and it is secured only by the manufacturer's chattel lien on the Alpha-3 system. Roesch can purchase the Alpha-3 system from the manufacturer at the end of the 12-year lease term for 75% of the computer's fair value at that time.

This lease is to be accounted for as a capital lease by Roesch, and it will be depreciated by the straight-line method with no expected salvage value. Borrowed funds for this type of transaction would cost Roesch 12% per year (1% per month). Following is a schedule of the present value of $1 for selected periods discounted at 1% per period when payments are made at the beginning of each period.

Periods (months)	Present Value of $1 per Period Discounted at 1% per Period
1	1.000
2	1.990
3	2.970
143	76.658
144	76.899

Instructions

Prepare, in general journal form, all entries Roesch should have made in its accounting records during August 2004 relating to this lease. Give full explanations and show supporting computations for each entry. Remember, August 31, 2004, is the end of Roesch's fiscal accounting period and it will be preparing financial statements on that date. Do not prepare closing entries.

(AICPA adapted)

P21-10 (Lessor Computations and Entries; Sales-Type Lease with Unguaranteed RV) Thomas Hanson Company manufactures a computer with an estimated economic life of 12 years and leases it to Flypaper Airlines for a period of 10 years. The normal selling price of the equipment is $210,482, and its unguaranteed residual value at the end of the lease term is estimated to be $20,000. Flypaper will pay annual payments of $30,000 at the beginning of each year and all maintenance, insurance, and taxes. Hanson incurred costs of $135,000 in manufacturing the equipment and $4,000 in negotiating and closing the lease. Hanson has determined that the collectibility of the lease payments is reasonably predictable, that no additional costs will be incurred, and that the implicit interest rate is 10%.

Instructions

(Round all numbers to the nearest dollar.)

(a) Discuss the nature of this lease in relation to the lessor and compute the amount of each of the following items.
  (1) Lease receivable.
  (2) Sales price.
  (3) Cost of sales.

(b) Prepare a 10-year lease amortization schedule.

(c) Prepare all of the lessor's journal entries for the first year.

P21-11 (Lessee Computations and Entries; Capital Lease with Unguaranteed Residual Value) Assume the same data as in P21-10 with Flypaper Airlines Co. having an incremental borrowing rate of 10%.

Instructions

(Round all numbers to the nearest dollar.)

(a) Discuss the nature of this lease in relation to the lessee, and compute the amount of the initial obligation under capital leases.

(b) Prepare a 10-year lease amortization schedule.

(c) Prepare all of the lessee's journal entries for the first year.

P21-12 (Basic Lessee Accounting with Difficult PV Calculation) In 2002 Judy Yin Trucking Company negotiated and closed a long-term lease contract for newly constructed truck terminals and freight storage facilities. The buildings were erected to the company's specifications on land owned by the company. On January 1, 2003, Judy Yin Trucking Company took possession of the lease properties. On January 1, 2003 and 2004, the company made cash payments of $1,048,000 that were recorded as rental expenses.

Although the terminals have a composite useful life of 40 years, the noncancelable lease runs for 20 years from January 1, 2003, with a bargain purchase option available upon expiration of the lease.

The 20-year lease is effective for the period January 1, 2003, through December 31, 2022. Advance rental payments of $900,000 are payable to the lessor on January 1 of each of the first 10 years of the lease term. Advance rental payments of $320,000 are due on January 1 for each of the last 10 years of the lease. The company has an option to purchase all of these leased facilities for $1 on December 31, 2022. It also must make annual payments to the lessor of $125,000 for property taxes and $23,000 for insurance. The lease was negotiated to assure the lessor a 6% rate of return.

Instructions

(Round all numbers to the nearest dollar.)

(a) Prepare a schedule to compute for Judy Yin Trucking Company the discounted present value of the terminal facilities and related obligation at January 1, 2003.

(b) Assuming that the discounted present value of terminal facilities and related obligation at January 1, 2003, was $8,400,000, prepare journal entries for Judy Yin Trucking Company to record the:

(1) Cash payment to the lessor on January 1, 2005.

(2) Amortization of the cost of the leased properties for 2005 using the straight-line method and assuming a zero salvage value.

(3) Accrual of interest expense at December 31, 2005.

Selected present value factors are as follows:

Periods	For an Ordinary Annuity of $1 at 6%	For $1 at 6%
1	.943396	.943396
2	1.833393	.889996
8	6.209794	.627412
9	6.801692	.591898
10	7.360087	.558395
19	11.158117	.330513
20	11.469921	.311805

(AICPA adapted)

P21-13 (Lessor Computations and Entries; Sales-Type Lease with Guaranteed Residual Value) Laura Jennings Inc. manufactures an X-ray machine with an estimated life of 12 years and leases it to Craig Gocker Medical Center for a period of 10 years. The normal selling price of the machine is $343,734, and its guaranteed residual value at the end of the lease term is estimated to be $15,000. The hospital will pay rents of $50,000 at the beginning of each year and all maintenance, insurance, and taxes. Laura Jennings Inc. incurred costs of $210,000 in manufacturing the machine and $14,000 in negotiating and closing the lease. Laura Jennings Inc. has determined that the collectibility of the lease payments is reasonably predictable, that there will be no additional costs incurred, and that the implicit interest rate is 10%.

Instructions

(Round all numbers to the nearest dollar.)

(a) Discuss the nature of this lease in relation to the lessor and compute the amount of each of the following items.

(1) Lease receivable at inception of the lease.

(2) Sales price.

(3) Cost of sales.

(b) Prepare a 10-year lease amortization schedule.

(c) Prepare all of the lessor's journal entries for the first year.

P21-14 (Lessee Computations and Entries; Capital Lease with Guaranteed Residual Value) Assume the same data as in P21-13 and that Craig Gocker Medical Center has an incremental borrowing rate of 10%.

Instructions

(Round all numbers to the nearest dollar.)

(a) Discuss the nature of this lease in relation to the lessee, and compute the amount of the initial obligation under capital leases.

(b) Prepare a 10-year lease amortization schedule.

(c) Prepare all of the lessee's journal entries for the first year.

P21-15 (Operating Lease vs. Capital Lease) You are auditing the December 31, 2003, financial statements of Sarah Shamess, Inc., manufacturer of novelties and party favors. During your inspection of the company garage, you discovered that a 2002 Shirk automobile not listed in the equipment subsidiary ledger is parked in the company garage. You ask Sally Straub, plant manager, about the vehicle, and she tells you that the company did not list the automobile because the company was only leasing it. The lease agreement was entered into on January 1, 2003, with Jack Hayes New and Used Cars.

You decide to review the lease agreement to ensure that the lease should be afforded operating lease treatment, and you discover the following lease terms.

1. Noncancelable term of 50 months.
2. Rental of $180 per month (at the end of each month). (The present value at 1% per month is $7,055.)
3. Estimated residual value after 50 months is $1,100. (The present value at 1% per month is $699.) Shamess guarantees the residual value of $1,100.
4. Estimated economic life of the automobile is 60 months.
5. Shamess's incremental borrowing rate is 12% per year (1% per month).

Instructions

You are a senior auditor writing a memo to your supervisor, the audit partner in charge of this audit, to discuss the above situation. Be sure to include **(a)** why you inspected the lease agreement, **(b)** what you determined about the lease, and **(c)** how you advised your client to account for this lease. Explain every journal entry that you believe is necessary to record this lease properly on the client's books. (It is also necessary to include the fact that you communicated this information to your client.)

P21-16 (Lessee-Lessor Accounting for Residual Values) Jodie Lanier Dairy leases its milking equipment from Steve Zeff Finance Company under the following lease terms.

1. The lease term is 10 years, noncancelable, and requires equal rental payments of $25,250 due at the beginning of each year starting January 1, 2004.
2. The equipment has a fair value and cost at the inception of the lease (January 1, 2004) of $185,078, an estimated economic life of 10 years, and a residual value (which is guaranteed by Lanier Dairy) of $20,000.
3. The lease contains no renewable options, and the equipment reverts to Steve Zeff Finance Company upon termination of the lease.
4. Lanier Dairy's incremental borrowing rate is 9% per year. The implicit rate is also 9%.
5. Lanier Dairy depreciates similar equipment that it owns on a straight-line basis.
6. Collectibility of the payments is reasonably predictable, and there are no important uncertainties surrounding the costs yet to be incurred by the lessor.

Instructions

(a) Evaluate the criteria for classification of the lease, and describe the nature of the lease. In general, discuss how the lessee and lessor should account for the lease transaction.

(b) Prepare the journal entries for the lessee and lessor at January 1, 2004, and December 31, 2004 (the lessee's and lessor's year-end). Assume no reversing entries.

(c) What would have been the amount capitalized by the lessee upon the inception of the lease if:

(1) The residual value of $20,000 had been guaranteed by a third party, not the lessee?

(2) The residual value of $20,000 had not been guaranteed at all?

(d) On the lessor's books, what would be the amount recorded as the Net Investment (Lease Receivable) at the inception of the lease, assuming:

(1) The residual value of $20,000 had been guaranteed by a third party?

(2) The residual value of $20,000 had not been guaranteed at all?

(e) Suppose the useful life of the milking equipment is 20 years. How large would the residual value have to be at the end of 10 years in order for the lessee to qualify for the operating method? (Assume that the residual value would be guaranteed by a third party.) (*Hint:* The lessee's annual payments will be appropriately reduced as the residual value increases.)

CONCEPTUAL CASES

C21-1 (Lessee Accounting and Reporting) On January 1, 2005, Sandy Hayes Company entered into a noncancelable lease for a machine to be used in its manufacturing operations. The lease transfers ownership of the machine to Yen Quach by the end of the lease term. The term of the lease is 8 years. The minimum lease payment made by Yen Quach on January 1, 2005, was one of eight equal annual payments. At the inception of the lease, the criteria established for classification as a capital lease by the lessee were met.

Instructions

(a) What is the theoretical basis for the accounting standard that requires certain long-term leases to be capitalized by the lessee? Do not discuss the specific criteria for classifying a specific lease as a capital lease.

(b) How should Hayes account for this lease at its inception and determine the amount to be recorded?

(c) What expenses related to this lease will Hayes incur during the first year of the lease, and how will they be determined?

(d) How should Hayes report the lease transaction on its December 31, 2005, balance sheet?

C21-2 (Lessor and Lessee Accounting and Disclosure) Laurie Gocker Inc. entered into a lease arrangement with Nathan Morgan Leasing Corporation for a certain machine. Morgan's primary business is leasing; it is not a manufacturer or dealer. Gocker will lease the machine for a period of 3 years, which is 50% of the machine's economic life. Morgan will take possession of the machine at the end of the initial 3-year lease and lease it to another, smaller company that does not need the most current version of the machine. Gocker does not guarantee any residual value for the machine and will not purchase the machine at the end of the lease term.

Gocker's incremental borrowing rate is 15%, and the implicit rate in the lease is 14%. Gocker has no way of knowing the implicit rate used by Morgan. Using either rate, the present value of the minimum lease payments is between 90% and 100% of the fair value of the machine at the date of the lease agreement.

Gocker has agreed to pay all executory costs directly, and no allowance for these costs is included in the lease payments.

Morgan is reasonably certain that Gocker will pay all lease payments, and because Gocker has agreed to pay all executory costs, there are no important uncertainties regarding costs to be incurred by Morgan. Assume that no indirect costs are involved.

Instructions

(a) With respect to Gocker (the lessee), answer the following.

- **(1)** What type of lease has been entered into? Explain the reason for your answer.
- **(2)** How should Gocker compute the appropriate amount to be recorded for the lease or asset acquired?
- **(3)** What accounts will be created or affected by this transaction, and how will the lease or asset and other costs related to the transaction be matched with earnings?
- **(4)** What disclosures must Gocker make regarding this leased asset?

(b) With respect to Morgan (the lessor), answer the following:

- **(1)** What type of leasing arrangement has been entered into? Explain the reason for your answer.
- **(2)** How should this lease be recorded by Morgan, and how are the appropriate amounts determined?
- **(3)** How should Morgan determine the appropriate amount of earnings to be recognized from each lease payment?
- **(4)** What disclosures must Morgan make regarding this lease?

(AICPA adapted)

C21-3 (Lessee Capitalization Criteria) On January 1, Melanie Shinault Company, a lessee, entered into three noncancelable leases for brand-new equipment, Lease L, Lease M, and Lease N. None of the three leases transfers ownership of the equipment to Melanie Shinault at the end of the lease term. For each of the three leases, the present value at the beginning of the lease term of the minimum lease payments, excluding that portion of the payments representing executory costs such as insurance, maintenance, and taxes to be paid by the lessor, is 75% of the fair value of the equipment.

The following information is peculiar to each lease.

1. Lease L does not contain a bargain purchase option. The lease term is equal to 80% of the estimated economic life of the equipment.
2. Lease M contains a bargain purchase option. The lease term is equal to 50% of the estimated economic life of the equipment.
3. Lease N does not contain a bargain purchase option. The lease term is equal to 50% of the estimated economic life of the equipment.

Instructions

(a) How should Melanie Shinault Company classify each of the three leases above, and why? Discuss the rationale for your answer.

(b) What amount, if any, should Melanie Shinault record as a liability at the inception of the lease for each of the three leases above?

(c) Assuming that the minimum lease payments are made on a straight-line basis, how should Melanie Shinault record each minimum lease payment for each of the three leases above?

(AICPA adapted)

C21-4 (Comparison of Different Types of Accounting by Lessee and Lessor)

Part 1

Capital leases and operating leases are the two classifications of leases described in FASB pronouncements from the standpoint of the **lessee**.

Instructions

(a) Describe how a capital lease would be accounted for by the lessee both at the inception of the lease and during the first year of the lease, assuming the lease transfers ownership of the property to the lessee by the end of the lease.

(b) Describe how an operating lease would be accounted for by the lessee both at the inception of the lease and during the first year of the lease, assuming equal monthly payments are made by the lessee at the beginning of each month of the lease. Describe the change in accounting, if any, when rental payments are not made on a straight-line basis.

Do **not** discuss the criteria for distinguishing between capital leases and operating leases.

Part 2

Sales-type leases and direct financing leases are two of the classifications of leases described in FASB pronouncements from the standpoint of the **lessor**.

Instructions

Compare and contrast a sales-type lease with a direct financing lease as follows.

(a) Lease receivable.
(b) Recognition of interest revenue.
(c) Manufacturer's or dealer's profit.

Do **not** discuss the criteria for distinguishing between the leases described above and operating leases.
(AICPA adapted)

C21-5 (Lessee Capitalization of Bargain Purchase Option) Brad Hayes Corporation is a diversified company with nationwide interests in commercial real estate developments, banking, copper mining, and metal fabrication. The company has offices and operating locations in major cities throughout the United States. Corporate headquarters for Brad Hayes Corporation is located in a metropolitan area of a midwestern state, and executives connected with various phases of company operations travel extensively. Corporate management is currently evaluating the feasibility of acquiring a business aircraft that can be used by company executives to expedite business travel to areas not adequately served by commercial airlines. Proposals for either leasing or purchasing a suitable aircraft have been analyzed, and the leasing proposal was considered to be more desirable.

The proposed lease agreement involves a twin-engine turboprop Viking that has a fair market value of $1,000,000. This plane would be leased for a period of 10 years beginning January 1, 2005. The lease agreement is cancelable only upon accidental destruction of the plane. An annual lease payment of $141,780 is due on January 1 of each year; the first payment is to be made on January 1, 2005. Maintenance operations are strictly scheduled by the lessor, and Brad Hayes Corporation will pay for these services as they are performed. Estimated annual maintenance costs are $6,900. The lessor will pay all insurance premiums and local property taxes, which amount to a combined total of $4,000 annually and are included in the annual lease payment of $141,780. Upon expiration of the 10-year lease, Brad Hayes Corporation can purchase the Viking for $44,440. The estimated useful life of the plane is 15 years, and its salvage value in the used plane market is estimated to be $100,000 after 10 years. The salvage value probably will never be less than $75,000 if the engines are overhauled and maintained as prescribed by the manufacturer. If the purchase option is not exercised, possession of the plane will revert to the lessor, and there is no provision for renewing the lease agreement beyond its termination on December 31, 2014.

Brad Hayes Corporation can borrow $1,000,000 under a 10-year term loan agreement at an annual interest rate of 12%. The lessor's implicit interest rate is not expressly stated in the lease agreement, but this rate appears to be approximately 8% based on ten net rental payments of $137,780 per year and the initial market value of $1,000,000 for the plane. On January 1, 2005, the present value of all net rental payments and the purchase option of $44,440 is $888,890 using the 12% interest rate. The present value of all net rental payments and the $44,440 purchase option on January 1, 2005, is $1,022,226 using the 8% interest rate implicit in the lease agreement. The financial vice-president of Brad Hayes Corporation has established that this lease agreement is a capital lease as defined in *Statement of Financial Accounting Standards No. 13,* "Accounting for Leases."

Instructions

(a) What is the appropriate amount that Brad Hayes Corporation should recognize for the leased aircraft on its balance sheet after the lease is signed?

(b) Without prejudice to your answer in part (a), assume that the annual lease payment is $141,780 as stated in the question, that the appropriate capitalized amount for the leased aircraft is $1,000,000 on January 1, 2005, and that the interest rate is 9%. How will the lease be reported in the December 31, 2005, balance sheet and related income statement? (Ignore any income tax implications.)

(CMA adapted)

C21-6 (Lease Capitalization, Bargain Purchase Option) Cuby Corporation entered into a lease agreement for 10 photocopy machines for its corporate headquarters. The lease agreement qualifies as an operating lease in all terms except there is a bargain purchase option. After the 5-year lease term, the corporation can purchase each copier for $1,000, when the anticipated market value is $2,500.

Glenn Beckert, the financial vice president, thinks the financial statements must recognize the lease agreement as a capital lease because of the bargain purchase agreement. The controller, Donna Kessinger, disagrees: "Although I don't know much about the copiers themselves, there is a way to avoid recording the lease liability." She argues that the corporation might claim that copier technology advances rapidly and that by the end of the lease term the machines will most likely not be worth the $1,000 bargain price.

Instructions

Answer the following questions.

(a) What ethical issue is at stake?
(b) Should the controller's argument be accepted if she does not really know much about copier technology? Would it make a difference if the controller were knowledgeable about the pace of change in copier technology?
(c) What should Beckert do?

***C21-7 (Sale-Leaseback)** On January 1, 2004, Laura Dwyer Company sold equipment for cash and leased it back. As seller-lessee, Laura Dwyer retained the right to substantially all of the remaining use of the equipment.

The term of the lease is 8 years. There is a gain on the sale portion of the transaction. The lease portion of the transaction is classified appropriately as a capital lease.

Instructions

(a) What is the theoretical basis for requiring lessees to capitalize certain long-term leases? **Do not discuss the specific criteria for classifying a lease as a capital lease.**
(b) **(1)** How should Laura Dwyer account for the sale portion of the sale-leaseback transaction at January 1, 2004?
(2) How should Laura Dwyer account for the leaseback portion of the sale-leaseback transaction at January 1, 2004?
(c) How should Laura Dwyer account for the gain on the sale portion of the sale-leaseback transaction during the first year of the lease? Why?

(AICPA adapted)

***C21-8 (Sale-Leaseback)** On December 31, 2004, Laura Truttman Co. sold 6-month old equipment at fair value and leased it back. There was a loss on the sale. Laura Truttman pays all insurance, maintenance, and taxes on the equipment. The lease provides for eight equal annual payments, beginning December 31, 2005, with a present value equal to 85% of the equipment's fair value and sales price. The lease's term is equal to 80% of the equipment's useful life. There is no provision for Laura Truttman to reacquire ownership of the equipment at the end of the lease term.

Instructions

(a) **(1)** Why is it important to compare an equipment's fair value to its lease payments' present value and its useful life to the lease term?
(2) Evaluate Laura Truttman's leaseback of the equipment in terms of each of the four criteria for determination of a capital lease.
(b) How should Laura Truttman account for the sale portion of the sale-leaseback transaction at December 31, 2004?
(c) How should Laura Truttman report the leaseback portion of the sale-leaseback transaction on its December 31, 2005, balance sheet?

USING YOUR JUDGMENT

FINANCIAL REPORTING PROBLEM

3M Company

The financial statements of **3M** are presented in Appendix 5B or can be accessed on the Take Action! CD.

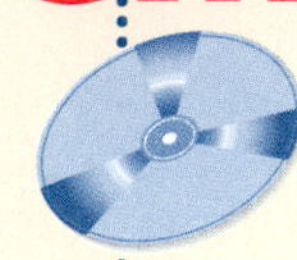

Instructions

Refer to 3M's financial statements and the accompanying notes to answer the following questions.

(a) What types of leases are used by 3M?

(b) What amount of rental expense was reported by 3M in 1999, 2000, and 2001?

(c) What minimum annual rental commitments under all noncancelable leases at December 31, 2001, did 3M disclose?

FINANCIAL STATEMENT ANALYSIS CASE

Penn Traffic Company

Presented in Illustration 21-32 are the financial statement disclosures from the 2001 Annual Report of **Penn Traffic Company**.

Instructions

Answer the following questions related to these disclosures.

(a) What is the total obligation under capital leases at February 3, 2001, for Penn Traffic?

(b) What is the book value of the assets under capital lease at February 3, 2001, for Penn Traffic? Explain why there is a difference between the amounts reported for assets and liabilities under capital leases.

(c) What is the total rental expense reported for leasing activity for the year ended February 3, 2001, for Penn Traffic?

(d) Estimate the off-balance-sheet liability due to Penn Traffic's operating leases at fiscal year-end 2001.

COMPARATIVE ANALYSIS CASE

UAL, Inc. and Southwest Airlines

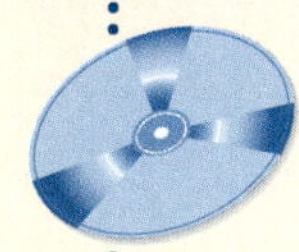

Instructions

Go to the Take Action! CD and use information found there to answer the following questions related to **UAL, Inc.** and **Southwest Airlines**.

(a) What types of leases are used by Southwest and on what assets are these leases primarily used?

(b) How long-term are some of Southwest's leases? What are some of the characteristics or provisions of Southwest's (as lessee) leases?

(c) What did Southwest report in 2001 as its future minimum annual rental commitments under noncancelable leases?

(d) At year-end 2001, what was the present value of the minimum rental payments under Southwest's capital leases? How much imputed interest was deducted from the future minimum annual rental commitments to arrive at the present value?

(e) What were the amounts and details reported by Southwest for rental expense in 2001, 2000, and 1999?

(f) How does UAL's use of leases compare with Southwest's?

RESEARCH CASES

Case 1

The accounting for operating leases is a controversial issue. Many contend that firms employing operating leases are utilizing significantly more assets and are more highly leveraged than indicated by the balance sheet alone. As a result, analysts often use footnote disclosures to "constructively capitalize" operating lease obligations. One way to do so is to increase a firm's assets and liabilities by the present value of all future minimum rental payments.

Instructions

(a) Obtain the most recent annual report for a firm that relies heavily on operating leases. (Firms in the airline and retail industries are good candidates.) The schedule of future minimum rental payments is usually included in the "Commitments and Contingencies" footnote. Use the schedule to determine the present value of future minimum rental payments, assuming a discount rate of 10%.

(b) Calculate the company's debt-to-total-assets ratio with and without the present value of operating lease payments. Is there a significant difference?

Case 2

The January 7, 2002, edition of the *Wall Street Journal* includes an article by Judith Burns and Michael Schroeder, entitled "Accounting Firms Ask SEC for Post-**Enron** Guide." (Subscribers to **Business Extra** can access the article at that site.)

Instructions

Read the article and answer the following questions.

(a) Why are the Big 5 firms asking the SEC to issue new guidance for disclosure?

(b) One of the areas the Big 5 suggest needs improving is reporting of lease obligations. How are off-balance-sheet lease obligations currently reported?

(c) One of the suggestions the Big 5 firms make for improving lease reporting is that firms should have to describe why these obligations aren't reported in the financial statements. Why aren't these obligations reported in the financial statements as liabilities?

INTERNATIONAL REPORTING CASE

As discussed in the chapter, U.S. GAAP accounting for leases allows companies to use off-balance-sheet financing for the purchase of operating assets. International accounting standards are similar to U.S. GAAP in that under these rules, companies can keep leased assets and obligations off their balance sheets. However, under *International Accounting Standard No. 17 (IAS 17)*, leases are capitalized based on the subjective evaluation of whether the risks and rewards of ownership are transferred in the lease. In Japan, virtually all leases are treated as operating leases. Furthermore, unlike U.S. and IAS standards, the Japanese rules do not require disclosure of future minimum lease payments.

Presented below are recent financial data for three major airlines that lease some part of their aircraft fleet. **American Airlines** prepares its financial statements under U.S. GAAP and leases approximately 27% of its fleet. **KLM Royal Dutch Airlines** and **Japan Airlines (JAL)** present their statements in accordance with their home country GAAP (Netherlands and Japan respectively). KLM leases about 22% of its aircraft, and JAL leases approximately 50% of its fleet.

Financial Statement Data	American Airlines (millions of dollars)	KLM Royal Dutch Airlines (millions of guilders)	Japan Airlines (millions of yen)
As-reported			
Assets	20,915	19,205	2,042,761
Liabilities	14,699	13,837	1,857,800
Income	985	606	4,619
Estimated impact of capitalizing operating leases on:[1]			
Assets	5,897	1,812	244,063
Liabilities	6,886	1,776	265,103
Income	(143)	24	(9,598)

[1]Based on *Apples to Apples: Global Airlines: Flight to Quality* (New York: N.Y.: Morgan Stanley Dean Witter, October 1998).

Instructions

(a) Using the as-reported data for each of the airlines, compute the rate of return on assets and the debt to assets ratio. Compare these companies on the basis of this analysis.

(b) Adjust the as-reported numbers of the three companies for the effects of non-capitalization of leases, and then redo the analysis in part (a).

(c) The following statement was overheard in the library: "Non-capitalization of operating leases is not that big a deal for profitability analysis based on rate of return on assets, since the operating lease payments (under operating lease accounting) are about the same as the sum of the interest and depreciation expense under capital lease treatment." Do you agree? Explain.

(d) Since the accounting for leases worldwide is similar, does your analysis above suggest there is a need for an improved accounting standard for leases? (*Hint:* Reflect on comparability of information about these companies' leasing activities, when leasing is more prevalent in one country than in others.)

PROFESSIONAL SIMULATIONS

Simulation 1

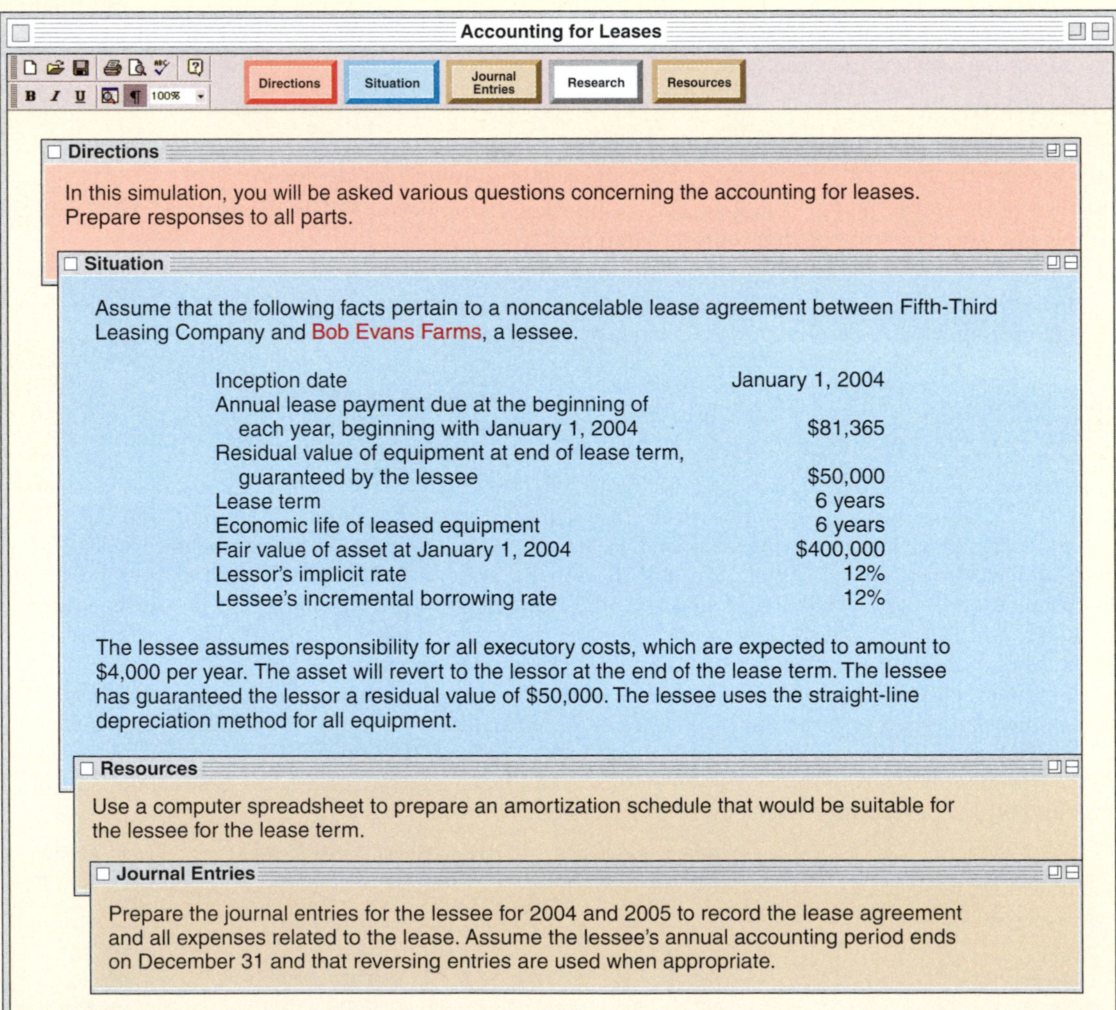

Directions

In this simulation, you will be asked various questions concerning the accounting for leases. Prepare responses to all parts.

Situation

Assume that the following facts pertain to a noncancelable lease agreement between Fifth-Third Leasing Company and Bob Evans Farms, a lessee.

Inception date	January 1, 2004
Annual lease payment due at the beginning of each year, beginning with January 1, 2004	$81,365
Residual value of equipment at end of lease term, guaranteed by the lessee	$50,000
Lease term	6 years
Economic life of leased equipment	6 years
Fair value of asset at January 1, 2004	$400,000
Lessor's implicit rate	12%
Lessee's incremental borrowing rate	12%

The lessee assumes responsibility for all executory costs, which are expected to amount to $4,000 per year. The asset will revert to the lessor at the end of the lease term. The lessee has guaranteed the lessor a residual value of $50,000. The lessee uses the straight-line depreciation method for all equipment.

Resources

Use a computer spreadsheet to prepare an amortization schedule that would be suitable for the lessee for the lease term.

Journal Entries

Prepare the journal entries for the lessee for 2004 and 2005 to record the lease agreement and all expenses related to the lease. Assume the lessee's annual accounting period ends on December 31 and that reversing entries are used when appropriate.

Simulation 2

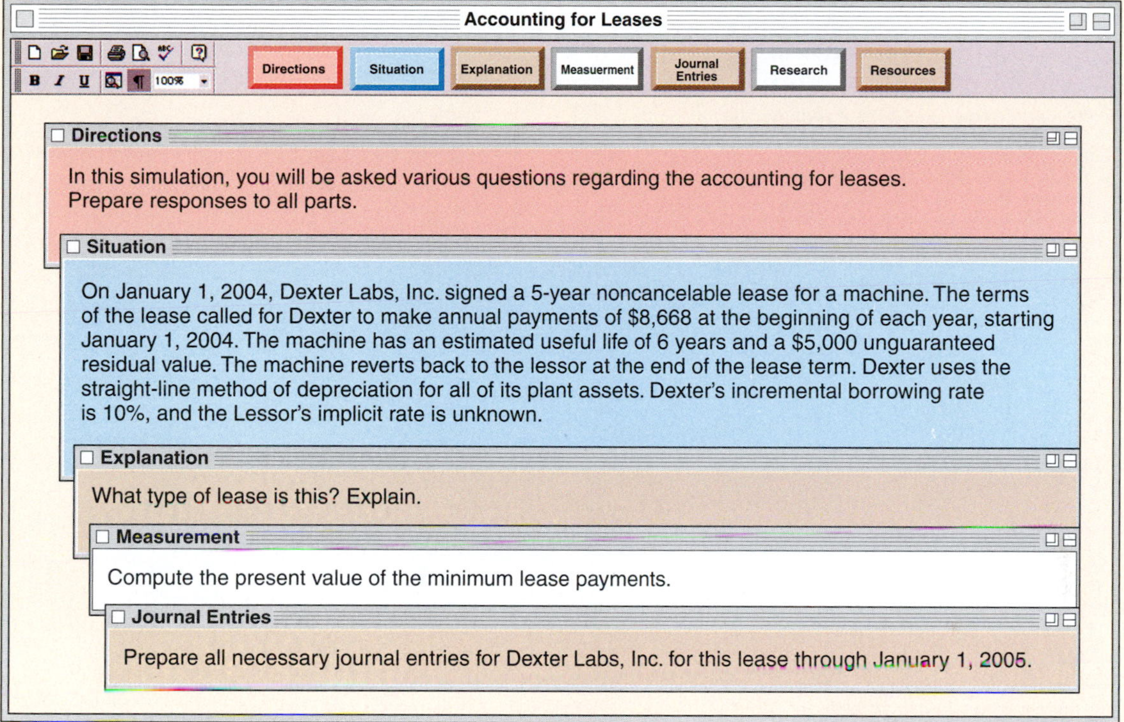

Accounting for Leases
Directions
Situation
Explanation
Measuerment
Journal Entries
Research
Resources
Directions
In this simulation, you will be asked various questions regarding the accounting for leases. Prepare responses to all parts.
Situation
On January 1, 2004, Dexter Labs, Inc. signed a 5-year noncancelable lease for a machine. The terms of the lease called for Dexter to make annual payments of $8,668 at the beginning of each year, starting January 1, 2004. The machine has an estimated useful life of 6 years and a $5,000 unguaranteed residual value. The machine reverts back to the lessor at the end of the lease term. Dexter uses the straight-line method of depreciation for all of its plant assets. Dexter's incremental borrowing rate is 10%, and the Lessor's implicit rate is unknown.
Explanation
What type of lease is this? Explain.
Measurement
Compute the present value of the minimum lease payments.
Journal Entries
Prepare all necessary journal entries for Dexter Labs, Inc. for this lease through January 1, 2005.

Remember to check the **Take Action! CD** and the book's **companion Web site** to find additional resources for this chapter.

CHAPTER 22

Accounting Changes and Error Analysis

Can I Get My Money Back?

Recently investors have lost money when companies report restatements. Restatements arise when companies discover errors or irregularities in their prior years' accounting reports. For example, in 2000 **Microstrategy** restated previously reported revenue amounts such that profits for 1998 and 1999 turned into losses. And in 2001 **Enron** restated its results for the gains on the sale of assets to one of its subsidiaries, which were improperly recorded. In both cases, the company's stock price took a beating when the market discovered that the prior periods' numbers were in error. Microstrategy's stock dropped from $227 to $87. Enron's shares dropped from over $80 to under $1 per share, and the firm declared bankruptcy shortly after.

What are investors to do if a company misleads them by misstating its financial results? Join other investors in a class action suit against the company and in some cases, the auditor. In the Microstrategy case, investors laid claim to a $155 million settlement. Class action activity has picked up in recent years, with 307 class action suits in 2000, up from 196 in 1996.

Though the settlements can be large (a total of over $4.3 billion in 2000), only about half of investors who are eligible join a class action suit. To find out about class actions, investors can go online to see if they are eligible to join any class actions. Below are some recent examples.

Company	Settlement Amount	Contact for Claim
Econnect	$ 400,000	www.dberdon.com
Olston	24,100,000	www.dberdon.com
Quaker Oats	10,400,000	www.gilardi.com
Smart Choice Automotive	2,500,000	www.gilardi.com
Sunbeam	110,000,000	www.gilardi.com

The amounts reported are before attorney's fees, which can range from 15 to 30 percent of the total. And there can be taxes owed if the settlement results in a capital gain on the investment. Thus, investors can get back some of the money they lost due to restatements, but they should be prepared to pay an attorney and the "tax man" first.[1]

LEARNING OBJECTIVES

After studying this chapter, you should be able to:

1. **Identify the types of accounting changes.**
2. **Describe the accounting for changes in accounting principles.**
3. **Understand how to account for cumulative-effect accounting changes.**
4. **Understand how to account for retroactive accounting changes.**
5. **Understand how to account for changes to LIFO.**
6. **Describe the accounting for changes in estimates.**
7. **Identify changes in a reporting entity.**
8. **Describe the accounting for correction of errors.**
9. **Identify economic motives for changing accounting methods.**
10. **Analyze the effect of errors.**

[1]Adapted from C. Coolidge, "Lost and Found," *Forbes* (October 1, 2001), 124–125.

PREVIEW OF CHAPTER 22

As the opening story indicates, investors can be affected adversely by misstatements of financial information. When misstatements occur, companies must follow specific accounting and reporting requirements. In addition, to ensure comparability among companies, the reporting of accounting changes and accounting estimates has been standardized to help investors better understand a company's financial condition. The content and organization of the chapter are as follows.

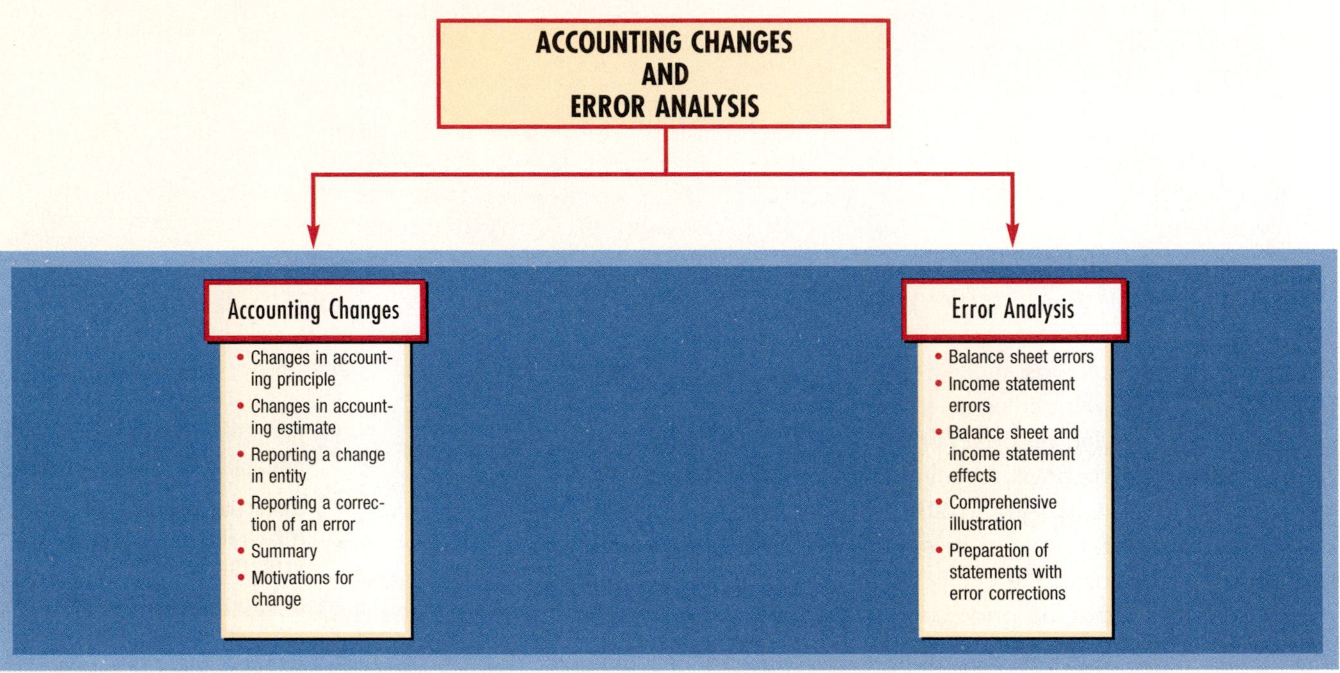

SECTION 1 ACCOUNTING CHANGES

OBJECTIVE 1
Identify the types of accounting changes.

When accounting alternatives exist, comparability of the statements between periods and between companies is diminished and useful historical trend data are obscured. The first step in this area, then, was to establish categories for the different types of changes and corrections that occur in practice.[2] The three types of accounting changes are:

1. *Change in Accounting Principle*. A change from one generally accepted accounting principle to another generally accepted accounting principle. Example: a change in the method of depreciation from double-declining to straight-line depreciation of plant assets.
2. *Change in Accounting Estimate*. A change that occurs as the result of new information or as additional experience is acquired. Example: a change in the estimate of the useful lives of depreciable assets.

While the qualitative characteristic of *usefulness* may be enhanced by changes in accounting, the characteristics of *comparability* and *consistency* may be adversely affected.

[2]"Accounting Changes," *Opinions of the Accounting Principles Board No. 20* (New York: AICPA, 1971).

3 *Change in Reporting Entity*. A change from reporting as one type of entity to another type of entity. Example: changing specific subsidiaries that constitute the group of companies for which consolidated financial statements are prepared.[3]

A fourth category necessitates changes in the accounting, though it is not classified as an accounting change.

4 ***Errors in Financial Statements.*** Errors occur as a result of mathematical mistakes, mistakes in the application of accounting principles, or oversight or misuse of facts that existed at the time financial statements were prepared. Example: the incorrect application of the retail inventory method for determining the final inventory value.

Changes are classified in these four categories because the individual characteristics of each category necessitate different methods of recognizing these changes in the financial statements. Each of these items is discussed separately, to investigate its unusual characteristics and to determine how each item should be reported in the accounts and how the information should be disclosed in comparative statements.

CHANGES IN ACCOUNTING PRINCIPLE

OBJECTIVE 2
Describe the accounting for changes in accounting principles.

A change in accounting principle involves a change from one generally accepted accounting principle to another. For example, a company might change the basis of inventory pricing from average cost to LIFO. Or it might change the method of depreciation on plant assets from accelerated to straight-line, or vice versa. Yet another change might be from the completed-contract to percentage-of-completion method of accounting for construction contracts.

A careful examination must be made in each circumstance to ensure that a change in principle has actually occurred. **A change in accounting principle is not considered to result from the adoption of a new principle in recognition of events that have occurred for the first time or that were previously immaterial.** For example, when a depreciation method that is adopted for **newly** acquired plant assets is different from the method or methods used for **previously recorded** assets of a similar class, a change in accounting principle has **not occurred**. As another example, certain marketing expenditures that were previously immaterial and expensed in the period incurred may become material and acceptably deferred and amortized without a change in accounting principle occurring.

Finally, **if the accounting principle previously followed was not acceptable, or if the principle was applied incorrectly, a change to a generally accepted accounting principle is considered a correction of an error**. A switch from the cash or income tax basis of accounting to the accrual basis is considered a correction of an error. If the company deducted salvage value when computing double-declining depreciation on plant assets and later recomputed depreciation without deduction of estimated salvage value, an error is corrected.

Three approaches have been suggested for reporting changes in accounting principles in the accounts:

---

[3]*Accounting Trends and Techniques—2001* in its survey of 600 annual reports identified the following specific types of accounting changes reported.

Revenue recognition	92	Reporting entity	8
Software development costs	13	Derivatives and hedging	6
Start-up costs	9	Depreciable lives	3
Inventories	9	Other	42

Retroactively. The cumulative effect of the use of the new method on the financial statements at the beginning of the period is computed. A **retroactive adjustment** of the financial statements is then made, recasting the financial statements of prior years on a basis consistent with the newly adopted principle. Advocates of this position argue that only by restatement of prior periods can changes in accounting principles lead to comparable financial statements. If this approach is not used, the year previous to the change will be on the old method; the year of the change will report the entire cumulative adjustment in income; and the following year will present financial statements on the new basis without the cumulative effect of the change. Consistency is considered essential in providing meaningful earnings-trend data and other financial relationships necessary to evaluate the business.

Currently. The cumulative effect of the use of the new method on the financial statements at the beginning of the period is computed. This adjustment is then reported in the current year's income statement as a **special item** between the captions "Extraordinary items" and "Net income." Advocates of this position argue that restating financial statements for prior years results in a loss of confidence by investors in financial reports. How will a present or prospective investor react when told that the earnings computed 5 years ago are now entirely different? Restatement, if permitted, also might upset many contractual and other arrangements that were based on the old figures. For example, profit-sharing arrangements computed on the old basis might have to be recomputed and completely new distributions made, which might create numerous legal problems. Many practical difficulties also exist; the cost of restatement may be excessive, or restatement may be impossible on the basis of data available.

Prospectively (in the future). Previously reported results remain; no change is made. Opening balances are not adjusted, and no attempt is made to allocate charges or credits for prior events. Advocates of this position argue that once management presents financial statements based on acceptable accounting principles, they are final; management cannot change prior periods by adopting a new principle. According to this line of reasoning, the cumulative adjustment in the current year is not appropriate, because such an approach includes amounts that have little or no relationship to the current year's income or economic events.

Before the adoption of *APB Opinion No. 20*, all three of the approaches above were used. *APB Opinion No. 20*, however, settled this issue by establishing guidelines for changes depending on the type of change in accounting principle involved. We have classified these changes in accounting principle into three categories:

1. Cumulative-effect accounting change.
2. Retroactive-effect accounting change.
3. Change to the LIFO method of inventory.

Cumulative-Effect Accounting Change

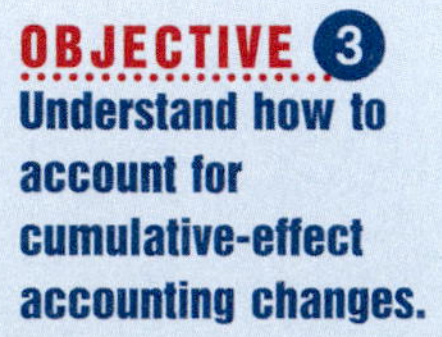

The general requirement established by the profession was that the **current, or "catch-up," method should be used to account for changes in accounting principles**. The general requirements are as follows:

1. The current or catch-up approach should be employed. The **cumulative effect** of the adjustment for prior periods should be reported in the income statement between the captions "Extraordinary items" and "Net income."
2. Financial statements for prior periods included for comparative purposes should not be restated.

3 Income before extraordinary items and net income, computed on a **pro forma (as if)** basis should be shown on the face of the income statement for all periods. They are presented **as if the newly adopted principle had been applied during all periods affected**. Related earnings per share data should also be reported. The reader, then, has some understanding of how restated financial statements appear.[4]

Illustration

Assume that Lang Inc. decided at the beginning of 2005 to change from the sum-of-the-years'-digits method of depreciation to the straight-line method for financial reporting for its buildings. For tax purposes, the company has employed the straight-line method and will continue to do so. The assets originally cost $120,000 in 2003 and have an estimated useful life of 15 years. The data assumed for this illustration are as follows.

ILLUSTRATION 22-1
Data for Change in Depreciation Method

Year	Sum-of-the-Years'-Digits Depreciation	Straight-Line Depreciation	Difference	Tax Effect 40%	Effect on Income (net of tax)
2003	$15,000[a]	$ 8,000[b]	$ 7,000	$2,800	$4,200
2004	14,000	8,000	6,000	2,400	3,600
	$29,000	$16,000	$13,000	$5,200	$7,800

[a] $\$120,000 \times \frac{15}{120} = \$15,000$ [b] $\$120,000 \div 15 = \$8,000$

Lang Inc. has income before extraordinary items and cumulative effect of changes in accounting principle of $130,000 in 2005 and $111,000 in 2004. Also, Lang Inc. has an extraordinary loss (net of tax) of $30,000 in 2005 and an extraordinary gain (net of tax) of $10,000 in 2004.

Journal Entry

Although the journal entry can be made any time during the year, it is effective **as of the beginning of the year**. The entry made to record this change to straight-line depreciation in 2005 should be:

Accumulated Depreciation	13,000	
Deferred Tax Asset		5,200
Cumulative Effect of Change in Accounting Principle—Depreciation		7,800

The debit of $13,000 to Accumulated Depreciation is the excess of the sum-of-the-years'-digits depreciation over the straight-line depreciation. The credit to the Deferred Tax Asset of $5,200 is recorded to eliminate this account from the financial statements. Prior to the change in accounting principle, sum-of-the-years'-digits was used for book but not tax purposes, which gave rise to a debit balance in the Deferred Tax Asset account of $5,200. The cumulative effect on income resulting from the difference between sum-of-the-years'-digits depreciation and straight-line depreciation is reduced by the tax effect on that difference. Now that the company intends to use the straight-line method for both tax and book purposes, no deferred income taxes related to depreciation should exist, and the Deferred Tax Asset account should be eliminated.

Income Statement Presentation

The cumulative effect of the change in accounting principle should be reported on the income statement between the captions "Extraordinary items" and "Net income." The cumulative effect is not an extraordinary item but is reported on a net-of-tax basis similar to that used for extraordinary items. This information is shown in Illustration 22-2.

[4]Ibid., par. 21.

ILLUSTRATION 22-2
Income Statement without Pro-Forma Amounts

	2005	2004
Income before extraordinary item and cumulative effect of a change in accounting principles	$130,000	$111,000
Extraordinary item, net of tax	(30,000)	10,000
Cumulative effect on prior years of retroactive application of new depreciation method, net of tax	7,800	
Net income	$107,800	$121,000
Per share amounts		
Earnings per share (10,000 shares)		
Income before extraordinary item and cumulative effect of a change in accounting principle	$13.00	$11.10
Extraordinary item	(3.00)	1.00
Cumulative effect on prior years of retroactive application of new depreciation method	0.78	
Net income	$10.78	$12.10

Note that depreciation expense for 2005 is computed on the straight-line basis.

The pro forma treatment attempts to restore the comparability of the income statements.

Pro Forma Amounts

Pro forma amounts permit financial statements users to determine the net income that **would have been shown** if the newly adopted principle had been in effect in earlier periods. In other words, how would Lang Inc.'s income be reported if the straight-line method had been used in 2004? To determine this amount, the prior year (2004) is restated, assuming that the straight-line method is used. The computation is as follows.

ILLUSTRATION 22-3
Computation of Pro Forma Income, 2004

Income before extraordinary item (2004) not restated	$111,000
Excess of sum-of-the-years-digits depreciation over straight-line depreciation	3,600
Pro forma income before extraordinary item (2004)	$114,600

This and other information is shown on the face of the income statement as follows.

ILLUSTRATION 22-4
Income Statement with Pro Forma Amounts

Pro forma (as if) amounts, assuming retroactive application of new depreciation method:

	2005	2004
Income before extraordinary item	$130,000	$114,600
Earnings per common share	$13.00	$11.46
Net income	$100,000[a]	$124,600[b]
Earnings per common share	$10.00	$12.46

[a]($130,000 − $30,000 = $100,000)
[b]($114,600 + $10,000 = $124,600)

The $130,000 of 2005 income before extraordinary item needs no restatement like the 2004 income because the new straight-line method of depreciation is used in 2005.

Pro forma information is useful to individuals interested in assessing the trend of earnings over a period of time. Pro forma information, which is only shown as supplementary information, may be reported in the income statement, in a separate schedule, or in the notes to the financial statements.

The pro forma amounts should include both (1) the direct effects of a change, and (2) nondiscretionary adjustments in items based on income before taxes or net income (such as profit-sharing expense and certain royalties) that would have been recognized if the newly adopted principle had been followed in prior periods. Related income tax effects should be recognized for both (1) and (2). If an income statement is presented for the current period only, the actual and pro forma amounts (including earnings per share) for the immediately preceding period should be disclosed.

Summary Illustration

Illustration 22-5 indicates how this information is presented on the income statement.[5] The appropriate note disclosure is also provided.

ILLUSTRATION 22-5
Cumulative-Effect-Type Accounting Change, Reporting the Change in 2-Year Comparative Statements

LANG INC.
INCOME STATEMENT

	2005	2004
Income before extraordinary item and cumulative effect of a change in accounting principles	$130,000	$111,000
Extraordinary item, net of tax	(30,000)	10,000
Cumulative effect on prior years of retroactive application of new depreciation method, net of tax (Note A)	7,800	
Net income	$107,800	$121,000
Per share amounts		
Earnings per share (10,000 shares)		
Income before extraordinary item and cumulative effect of a change in accounting principle	$13.00	$11.10
Extraordinary item	(3.00)	1.00
Cumulative effect on prior years of rectroactive application of new depreciation method	0.78	
Net income	$10.78	$12.10

Pro forma (as if) amounts, assuming retroactive application of new depreciation method:

	2005	2004
Income before extraordinary item	$130,000	$114,600
Earnings per common share	$13.00	$11.46
Net income	$100,000	$124,600
Earnings per common share	$10.00	$12.46

Note A: Change in Depreciation Method for Plant Assets. In 2005 depreciation of plant assets is computed by use of the straight-line method. In prior years, beginning in 2003, depreciation of buildings was computed by the sum-of-the-years'-digits method. The new method of depreciation was adopted in recognition of . . . [state justification for the change of depreciation method] . . . and has been applied retroactively to building acquisitions of prior years to determine the cumulative effect. The effect of the change in 2005 was to increase income before extraordinary item by approximately $3,000 (or 30 cents per share). The adjustment necessary for retroactive application of the new method, amounting to $7,800, is included in income of 2005. The pro forma amounts shown on the income statement have been adjusted for the effect of retroactive application on depreciation, and the pro forma effect for related income taxes.

Retroactive-Effect Accounting Change

OBJECTIVE 4
Understand how to account for retroactive accounting changes.

In certain circumstances, a change in accounting principle may be handled retroactively. Under the retroactive treatment, the cumulative effect of the new method on the financial statements at the beginning of the period is computed. A retroactive adjustment of the financial statements presented is made by **recasting the statements of prior**

[5]In practice, 3-year comparative income statements are prepared. For reasons of simplicity, we have presented 2-year comparatives.

years on a basis consistent with the newly adopted principle. Any part of the cumulative effect attributable to years prior to those presented is treated as an adjustment of beginning retained earnings of the earliest year presented. In such situations, the nature of and justification for the change and the effect on net income and related per share amounts should be disclosed for each period presented. The five situations that require the restatement of all prior period financial statements are:

1. A change from the LIFO inventory valuation method to another method.
2. A change in the method of accounting for long-term construction-type contracts.
3. A change to or from the "full-cost" method of accounting in the extractive industries.
4. Issuance of financial statements by a company for the first time to obtain additional equity capital, to effect a business combination, or to register securities. (This procedure may be used only by closely held companies and then only once.)
5. A professional pronouncement recommends that a change in accounting principle be treated retroactively. For example, *FASB No. 11* requires that retroactive treatment be given for changes in "Accounting for Contingencies" and *FASB Statement No. 73* requires retroactive treatment for a change from retirement-replacement-betterment accounting to depreciation accounting.[6]

INTERNATIONAL INSIGHT

IAS 8 generally requires restatement of prior years for accounting changes. However, *IAS 8* permits the cumulative-effect method or prospective method if the amounts to restate prior periods are not reasonably determinable.

Why did the profession provide for these exceptions? Though the reasons are varied, the major one is that reporting the cumulative adjustment in the period of the change might have such a large effect on net income that the income figure would be misleading. A perfect illustration is the experience of **Chrysler Corporation** (now **DaimlerChrysler**) when it changed its inventory accounting from LIFO to FIFO. If the change had been handled correctly, Chrysler would have had to report a $53,500,000 adjustment to net income, which would have resulted in net income of $45,900,000 instead of a net loss of $7,600,000.

As another illustration, in the early 1980s the railroad industry switched from the retirement-replacement method of depreciating railroad equipment to a more generally used method such as straight-line depreciation. Cumulative-effect treatment meant that a substantial adjustment would be made to income in the period of change. Many in the railroad industry argued that the adjustment was so large that to include the cumulative effect in the current year instead of restating prior years would distort the information and make it less useful. Such situations lend support to restatement so that comparability is not seriously affected.

Illustration

To illustrate the retroactive method, assume that Denson Construction Co. has accounted for its income from long-term construction contracts using the completed-contract method. In 2005 the company changed to the percentage-of-completion method because management believes that this approach provides a more appropriate measure of the income earned. For tax purposes (assume a 40 percent enacted tax rate), the company has employed the completed-contract method and plans to continue using this method in the future.

Illustration 22-6 provides the information for analysis.

[6] "Accounting for Contingencies—Transition Method," *Statement of the Financial Accounting Standards Board No. 11* (Stamford, Conn.: FASB, 1975); "Reporting a Change in Accounting for Railroad Track Structures," *Statement of the Financial Accounting Standards Board No. 73* (Stamford, Conn.: FASB, 1983). Note that the FASB standard on "Accounting for Income Taxes" permits the company to use either the cumulative-effect approach or the retroactive method in changing from the deferred method to the asset-liability method. In addition, if the company elects the cumulative-effect approach, pro forma amounts are not required because of the cost and difficulty of developing this information.

ILLUSTRATION 22-6
Data for Change in Accounting for Long-Term Construction Contracts

Year	Pretax Income from Percentage-of-Completion	Pretax Income from Completed-Contract	Difference in Income: Difference	Difference in Income: Tax Effect 40%	Difference in Income: Income Effect (net of tax)
Prior to 2004	$600,000	$400,000	$200,000	$80,000	$120,000
In 2004	180,000	160,000	20,000	8,000	12,000
Total at beginning of 2005	$780,000	$560,000	$220,000	$88,000	$132,000
Total in 2005	$200,000	$190,000	$ 10,000	$ 4,000	$ 6,000

The entry to record the change in 2005 would be:

Construction in Process	220,000	
Deferred Tax Liability		88,000
Retained Earnings		132,000

The Construction in Process account is increased by $220,000. This amount represents the adjustment in prior years' income of $132,000 and the adjustment in prior years' tax expense of $88,000. The Deferred Tax Liability account is used to recognize a tax liability for future taxable amounts. That is, in future periods taxable income will be higher than book income as a result of current temporary differences, and therefore a deferred tax liability must be reported in the current year.

Income Statement Presentation

The bottom portion of the income statement for Denson Construction Co., **before giving effect to the retroactive change in accounting principle**, would be as follows.

ILLUSTRATION 22-7
Income Statement before Retroactive Change

Income Statement	2005	2004
Net income	$114,000[a]	$96,000[a]
Per Share Amounts		
Earnings per share (100,000 shares)	$1.14	$.96

[a]The net income for the two periods is computed as follows:
2005 $190,000 − .40($190,000) = $114,000
2004 $160,000 − .40($160,000) = $96,000

The bottom portion of the income statement for Denson Construction Co., **after giving effect to the retroactive change in accounting principle**, would be as follows.

ILLUSTRATION 22-8
Income Statement after Retroactive Change

Income Statement	2005	2004
Net income	$120,000[a]	$108,000[a]
Per Share Amounts		
Earnings per share (100,000 shares)	$1.20	$1.08

[a]The net income for the two periods is computed as follows:
2005 $200,000 − .40($200,000) = $120,000
2004 $180,000 − .40($180,000) = $108,000

The 2-year comparative income statement (Illustration 22-8) has a major difference from the earlier 2-year comparative income statement for Lang Inc. (Illustration 22-5):

No pro forma information is necessary when changes in accounting principles are handled retroactively, because the income numbers for previous periods are restated.

Retained Earnings Statement

Assuming a retained earnings balance of $1,600,000 at the beginning of 2004, the retained earnings statement **before giving effect to the retroactive change in accounting principle**, would appear as follows.

ILLUSTRATION 22-9
Retained Earnings Statement before Retroactive Change

RETAINED EARNINGS STATEMENT

	2005	2004
Balance at beginning of year	$1,696,000	$1,600,000
Net income	114,000	96,000
Balance at end of year	$1,810,000	$1,696,000

A comparative retained earnings statement, **after giving effect to the retroactive change in accounting principle**, would be as follows.

ILLUSTRATION 22-10
Retained Earnings Statement after Retroactive Change

RETAINED EARNINGS STATEMENT

	2005	2004
Balance at beginning of year, as previously reported	$1,696,000	$1,600,000
Add: Adjustment for the cumulative effect on prior years of applying retroactively the new method of accounting for long-term contracts (Note A)	132,000	120,000
Balance at beginning of year, as adjusted	1,828,000	1,720,000
Net income	120,000	108,000
Balance at end of year	$1,948,000	$1,828,000

Note A: Change in Method of Accounting for Long-Term Contracts. The company has accounted for revenue and costs for long-term construction contracts by the percentage-of-completion method in 2005, whereas in all prior years revenue and costs were determined by the completed-contract method. The new method of accounting for long-term contracts was adopted to recognize . . . [state justification for change in accounting principle] . . . and financial statements of prior years have been restated to apply the new method retroactively. For income tax purposes, the completed-contract method has been continued. The effect of the accounting change on income of 2005 was an increase of $6,000 net of related taxes and on income of 2004 as previously reported was an increase of $12,000 net of related taxes. The balances of retained earnings for 2004 and 2005 have been adjusted for the effect of applying retroactively the new method of accounting.

An expanded retained earnings statement is included in this 2-year comparative presentation to indicate the type of adjustment that is needed to restate the beginning balance of retained earnings. In 2004, the beginning balance was adjusted for the excess of the percentage-of-completion income over the completed-contract income prior to 2004 ($120,000). In 2005, the beginning balance was adjusted for the $120,000 cumulative difference plus the additional $12,000 for 2004.

No such adjustments are necessary when the current or catch-up method is employed, because the cumulative effect of the change on net income is reported in the income statement of the current year and no prior period reports are restated. It is ordinarily appropriate to prepare a retained earnings or stockholders' equity statement when presenting comparative statements regardless of what type of accounting change is involved; an illustration was provided for the retroactive method only to explain the additional computations required.

CHANGE MANAGEMENT

WHAT DO THE NUMBERS MEAN?

The recent experience at **Halliburton** offers a case study in the importance of good reporting of an accounting change. Recall from Chapter 18 that Halliburton uses percentage-of-completion accounting for its long-term construction services contracts. Recently, the SEC questioned the company about its change in accounting for disputed claims.

Prior to 1998 Halliburton took a very conservative approach to its accounting for disputed claims. That is, the company waited until all disputes were resolved before recognizing associated revenues. In contrast, in 1998 the company recognized revenue for disputed claims before their resolution, using estimates of amounts expected to be recovered. Such revenue and its related profit are more tentative and subject to possible later adjustment. The accounting method in 1998 is more aggressive than the company's former policy but is still within the boundaries of GAAP.

It appears that the problem with Halliburton's accounting stems more from the way it handled its accounting change than from the new accounting method itself. That is, an overt reference to the company's change in accounting method was not provided in its 1998 annual report. In fact, rather than stating its new policy, the company simply deleted the sentence that described how it accounted for disputed claims. Then later, in its 1999 annual report, the new accounting policy was stated.

When such changes in accounting are made, investors need to be apprised of them and their effects on the company's financial results and position. With such information, current results can be compared with those of prior periods and a more informed assessment can be made about the company's future prospects.

Source: Adapted from "Accounting Ace Charles Mulford Answers Accounting Questions," *Wall Street Journal Online* (June 7, 2002).

Change to LIFO Method

OBJECTIVE 5
Understand how to account for changes to LIFO.

As indicated, the cumulative effect of any accounting change should be shown in the income statement between "Extraordinary items" and "Net income," except for the conditions mentioned in the preceding section. In addition, this rule does not apply when a company changes to the LIFO method of inventory valuation. In such a situation, **the base-year inventory for all subsequent LIFO calculations is the opening inventory in the year the method is adopted. There is no restatement of prior years' income because it is just too impractical.** A restatement to LIFO would be subject to assumptions as to the different years that the layers were established, and these assumptions would ordinarily result in the computation of a number of different earnings figures. The only adjustment necessary may be to restate the beginning inventory to a cost basis from a lower of cost or market approach.

Disclosure then is limited to showing the effect of the change on the results of operations in the period of change. Also, the reasons for omitting the computations of the cumulative effect and the pro forma amounts for prior years should be explained. Finally, the company should disclose the justification for the change to LIFO. As shown in Illustration 22-11 on the next page, the Annual Report of **Quaker Oats Company** indicates the type of disclosure necessary.

In practice, many companies defer the formal adoption of LIFO until year-end. Management thus has an opportunity to assess the impact that a change to LIFO will have on the financial statements and to evaluate the desirability of a change for tax purposes. As indicated in Chapter 8, many companies use LIFO because of the advantages of this inventory valuation method in a period of inflation.

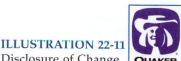

ILLUSTRATION 22-11
Disclosure of Change to LIFO

The Quaker Oats Company

Note 1 (In Part): Summary of Significant Accounting Policies

Inventories. Inventories are valued at the lower of cost or market, using various cost methods, and include the cost of raw materials, labor and overhead. The percentage of year-end inventories valued using each of the methods is as follows:

June 30	1989	1988	1987
Average quarterly cost	21%	54%	52%
Last-in, first-out (LIFO)	65%	29%	31%
First-in, first-out (FIFO)	14%	17%	17%

Effective July 1, 1988, the Company adopted the LIFO cost flow assumption for valuing the majority of remaining U.S. Grocery Products inventories. The Company believes that the use of the LIFO method better matches current costs with current revenues. The cumulative effect of this change on retained earnings at the beginning of the year is not determinable, nor are the pro-forma effects of retroactive application of LIFO to prior years. The effect of this change on fiscal 1989 was to decrease net income by $16.0 million, or $.20 per share.

If the LIFO method of valuing certain inventories were not used, total inventories would have been $60.1 million, $24.0 million and $14.6 million higher than reported at June 30, 1989, 1988, and 1987, respectively.

CHANGES IN ACCOUNTING ESTIMATE

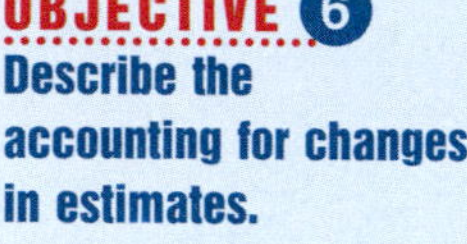
OBJECTIVE 6
Describe the accounting for changes in estimates.

The preparation of financial statements requires estimating the effects of future conditions and events. The following are examples of items that require estimates:

1. Uncollectible receivables.
2. Inventory obsolescence.
3. Useful lives and salvage values of assets.
4. Periods benefited by deferred costs.
5. Liabilities for warranty costs and income taxes.
6. Recoverable mineral reserves.

Future conditions and events and their effects cannot be perceived with certainty; therefore, estimating requires the exercise of judgment. Accounting estimates will change as new events occur, as more experience is acquired, or as additional information is obtained.

Changes in estimates must be handled prospectively. That is, no changes should be made in previously reported results. Opening balances are not adjusted, and no attempt is made to "catch-up" for prior periods. Financial statements of prior periods are not restated, and pro forma amounts for prior periods are not reported. Instead, the effects of all changes in estimate are accounted for in (1) the period of change if the change affects that period only, or (2) the period of change and future periods if the change affects both. As a result, changes in estimates are viewed as **normal recurring corrections and adjustments**, the natural result of the accounting process. Retroactive treatment is prohibited.

INTERNATIONAL INSIGHT

In most nations, changes in accounting estimates are treated prospectively. International differences occur in the degree of disclosure required.

The circumstances related to a change in estimate are different from those surrounding a change in accounting principle. If changes in estimates were handled on a retroactive basis, or on a cumulative-effect basis, continual adjustments of prior years' income would occur. It seems proper to accept the view that because new conditions or circumstances exist, the revision fits the new situation and should be handled in the current and future periods.

To illustrate, Underwriters Labs Inc. purchased a building for $300,000 which was originally estimated to have a useful life of 15 years and no salvage value. Depreciation has been recorded for 5 years on a straight-line basis. On January 1, 2005, the estimate of the useful life is revised so that the asset is considered to have a total life of 25 years. Assume that the useful life for financial reporting and tax purposes is the same. The accounts at the beginning of the sixth year are as follows.

ILLUSTRATION 22-12
Book Value after 5 Years' Depreciation

Building	$300,000
Less: Accumulated depreciation—building (5 × $20,000)	100,000
Book value of building	$200,000

The entry to record depreciation for the year 2005 is:

Depreciation Expense	10,000	
Accumulated Depreciation—Building		10,000

The $10,000 depreciation charge is computed as follows.

ILLUSTRATION 22-13
Depreciation after Change in Estimate

$$\text{Depreciation charge} = \frac{\text{Book value of asset}}{\text{Remaining service live}} = \frac{\$200{,}000}{25\text{ years} - 5\text{ years}} = \$10{,}000$$

The disclosure of a change in estimated useful lives appeared in the Annual Report of **Ampco–Pittsburgh Corporation**.

ILLUSTRATION 22-14
Disclosure of Change in Estimated Useful Lives

Ampco–Pittsburgh Corporation

Note 11: Change in Accounting Estimate. The Corporation revised its estimate of the useful lives of certain machinery and equipment. Previously, all machinery and equipment, whether new when placed in use or not, were in one class and depreciated over 15 years. The change principally applies to assets purchased new when placed in use. Those lives are now extended to 20 years. These changes were made to better reflect the estimated periods during which such assets will remain in service. The change had the effect of reducing depreciation expense and increasing net income by approximately $991,000 ($.10 per share).

Differentiating between a change in an estimate and a change in an accounting principle is sometimes difficult. Is it a change in principle or a change in estimate when a company changes from deferring and amortizing certain marketing costs to recording them as an expense as incurred because future benefits of these costs have become doubtful? In such a case, **whenever it is impossible to determine whether a change in principle or a change in estimate has occurred, the change should be considered a change in estimate**.

A similar problem occurs in differentiating between a change in estimate and a correction of an error, although the answer is more clear cut. How do we determine whether the information was overlooked in earlier periods (an error) or whether the information is now available for the first time (change in estimate)? Proper classification is important because corrections of errors have a different accounting treatment from that given changes in estimates. The general rule is that **careful estimates that later prove to be incorrect should be considered changes in estimate**. Only when the estimate was obviously computed incorrectly because of lack of expertise or in bad faith should the adjustment be considered an error. There is no clear demarcation line here, and good judgment must be used in light of all the circumstances.[7]

[7]In evaluating reasonableness, the auditor should use one or a combination of the following approaches:

(a) Review and test the process used by management to develop the estimate.
(b) Develop an independent expectation of the estimate to corroborate the reasonableness of management's estimate.
(c) Review subsequent events or transactions occurring prior to completion of fieldwork.

"Auditing Accounting Estimates," *Statement on Auditing Standards No. 57* (New York: AICPA, 1988).

REPORTING A CHANGE IN ENTITY

OBJECTIVE 7
Identify changes in a reporting entity.

An accounting change that results in financial statements that are actually the statements of a different entity should be reported by **restating the financial statements of all prior periods presented**, to show the financial information for the new reporting entity for all periods.

Examples of a change in reporting entity are:

1. Presenting consolidated statements in place of statements of individual companies.
2. Changing specific subsidiaries that constitute the group of companies for which consolidated financial statements are presented.
3. Changing the companies included in combined financial statements.
4. Accounting for a pooling of interests.
5. A change in the cost, equity, or consolidation method of accounting for subsidiaries and investments.[8] A change in the reporting entity does not result from creation, cessation, purchase, or disposition of a subsidiary or other business unit.

The financial statements of the year in which the change in reporting entity is made should disclose the nature of the change and the reason for it. The effect of the change on income before extraordinary items, net income, and earnings per share amounts should be reported for all periods presented. These disclosures need not be repeated in subsequent periods' financial statements. The Annual Report of **Hewlett-Packard Company** illustrates a note disclosing a change in reporting entity.

ILLUSTRATION 22-15
Disclosure of Change in Reporting Entity

Hewlett-Packard Company

Note: Accounting and Reporting Changes (In Part)

Consolidation of Hewlett-Packard Finance Company. The company implemented *Statement of Financial Accounting Standards No. 94 (SFAS 94)*, "Consolidation of All Majority-owned Subsidiaries." With the adoption of *SFAS 94*, the company consolidated the accounts of Hewlett-Packard Finance Company (HPFC), a wholly owned subsidiary previously accounted for under the equity method, with those of the company. The change resulted in an increase in consolidated assets and liabilities but did not have a material effect on the company's financial position. Since HPFC was previously accounted for under the equity method, the change did not affect net earnings. Prior years' consolidated financial information has been restated to reflect this change for comparative purposes.

REPORTING A CORRECTION OF AN ERROR

OBJECTIVE 8
Describe the accounting for correction of errors.

APB Opinion No. 20 also discussed how a **correction of an error** should be handled in the financial statements. (No authoritative guidelines existed previously.) The conclusions of *APB Opinion No. 20* were reaffirmed in *FASB Statement No. 16*.[9] No business, large or small, is immune from errors. The risk of material errors, however, may be reduced through the installation of good internal control and the application of sound accounting procedures.

The following are examples of accounting errors:

1. A change from an accounting principle that is **not** generally accepted to an accounting principle that is acceptable. The rationale adopted is that the prior periods were incorrectly presented because of the application of an improper

---

[8]Exceptions to retroactive treatment may occur when changing from the equity method. An illustration of the accounting for a change from and to the equity method is provided in Appendix 22A.

[9]"Prior Period Adjustments," *Statement of Financial Accounting Standards No. 16* (Stamford, Conn.: FASB, 1977), p. 5.

accounting principle. Example: a change from the cash or income tax basis of accounting to the accrual basis.

2. Mathematical mistakes that result from adding, subtracting, and so on. Example: the totaling of the inventory count sheets incorrectly in computing the inventory value.
3. Changes in estimate that occur because the estimates are not prepared in good faith. Example: the adoption of a clearly unrealistic depreciation rate.
4. An oversight, such as the failure to accrue or defer certain expenses and revenues at the end of the period.
5. A misuse of facts, such as the failure to use salvage value in computing the depreciation base for the straight-line approach.
6. The incorrect classification of a cost as an expense instead of an asset and vice versa.

As soon as they are discovered, errors must be corrected by proper entries in the accounts and reported in the financial statements. **Corrections of errors are treated as prior period adjustments.** They are recorded in the year in which the error was discovered and are reported in the financial statements as an adjustment to the beginning balance of retained earnings. If comparative statements are presented, the prior statements affected should be restated to correct for the error. The disclosures need not be repeated in the financial statements of subsequent periods.

RESTATEMENTS EVERYWHERE

WHAT DO THE NUMBERS MEAN?

To say that restatements have been on the rise would be an understatement. As shown in the following chart, over the past 5 years, the number of companies announcing restatements doubled—and this was in a period when there are fewer public companies due to the slowdown in the stock market.

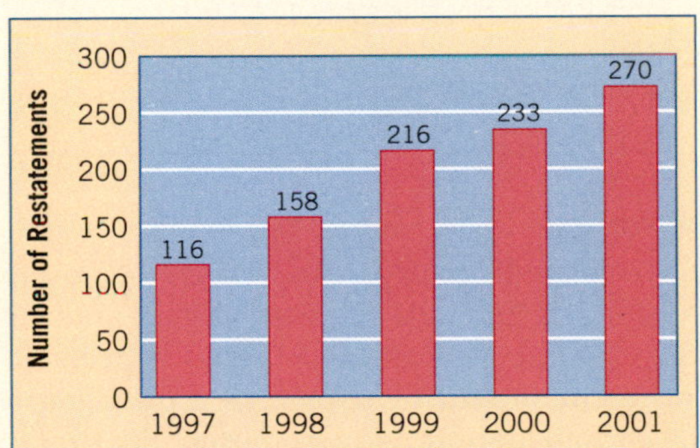

These restatements arise from over 16 different accounting areas. Restatements related to revenue recognition are the most common type of restatement, comprising over 20 percent of the restatements during this period. As noted in the opening story, restatements can lead to negative market reactions and possible shareholder lawsuits, highlighting the need for transparent reporting.

Source: "A Study of Restatement Matters for the Five Years Ended December 31, 2001," Huron Consulting Group Web site (www.huronconsultinggroup.com, June 11, 2002).

Illustration

To illustrate, in 2005 the bookkeeper for Selectric Company discovered that in 2004 the company failed to record in the accounts $20,000 of depreciation expense on a newly constructed building. The depreciation is correctly included in the tax return. Because of numerous temporary differences, reported net income for 2004 was $150,000 and taxable income was $110,000. The following entry was made for income taxes (assume a 40 percent effective tax rate in 2004).

Income Tax Expense	60,000	
Income Tax Payable		44,000
Deferred Tax Liability		16,000

As a result of the $20,000 omission error in 2004:

Depreciation expense (2004) **was** understated	$20,000
Accumulated depreciation **is** understated	20,000
Income tax expense (2004) **was** overstated ($20,000 × 40%)	8,000
Net income (2004) **was** overstated	12,000
Deferred tax liability **is** overstated ($20,000 × 40%)	8,000

The entry made in 2005 to correct the omission of $20,000 of depreciation in 2004 would be:

2005 Correcting Entry

Retained Earnings	12,000	
Deferred Tax Liability	8,000	
Accumulated Depreciation—Buildings		20,000

The journal entry to record the correction of the error is the same whether single-period or comparative financial statements are prepared. However, presentation on the financial statements will differ. If single-period (noncomparative) statements are presented (see Illustration 22-16), the error should be reported as an adjustment to the opening balance of retained earnings of the period in which the error is discovered.

ILLUSTRATION 22-16
Reporting an Error—Single-Period Financial Statement

Retained earnings, January 1, 2005		
As previously reported		$350,000
Correction of an error (depreciation)	$20,000	
Less: Applicable income tax reduction	8,000	(12,000)
Adjusted balance of retained earnings, January 1, 2005		338,000
Add: Net income 2005		400,000
Retained earnings, December 31, 2005		$738,000

Comparative Statements

If comparative financial statements are prepared, adjustments should be made to correct the amounts for all affected accounts reported in the statements for all periods reported. The data for each year being presented should be restated to the correct basis, and any **catch-up adjustment should be shown as a prior period adjustment to retained earnings for the earliest period being reported**. For example, in the case of Selectric Company, the error of omitting the depreciation of $20,000 in 2004, which was discovered in 2005, results in the restatement of the 2004 financial statements when presented in comparison with those of 2005. The following accounts in the 2004 financial statements (presented in comparison with those of 2005) would have been restated.

ILLUSTRATION 22-17
Reporting an Error—Comparative Financial Statements

In the balance sheet:	
Accumulated depreciation—buildings	$20,000 increase
Deferred tax liability	$ 8,000 decrease
Retained earnings, ending balance	$12,000 decrease
In the income statement:	
Depreciation expense—buildings	$20,000 increase
Tax expense	$ 8,000 decrease
Net income	$12,000 decrease
In the retained earnings statement:	
Retained earnings, ending balance (due to lower net income for the period)	$12,000 decrease

The 2005 financial statements in comparative form with those of 2004 are prepared as if the error had not occurred. At a minimum, such comparative statements in 2005 would include a note in the financial statements calling attention to restatement of the 2004 statements and disclosing the effect of the correction on income before extraordinary items, net income, and the related per share amounts.

SUMMARY OF ACCOUNTING CHANGES AND CORRECTIONS OF ERRORS

The development of guidelines in reporting accounting changes and corrections has helped resolve several long-standing accounting problems. Yet, because of diversity in situations and characteristics of the items encountered in practice, the application of professional judgment is of paramount importance. In applying these guidelines, the primary objective is to serve the user of the financial statements. Achieving such service requires accuracy, full disclosure, and an absence of misleading inferences. The principal distinction and treatments presented in the earlier discussion are summarized in Illustration 22-18.

ILLUSTRATION 22-18
Summary of Guidelines for Accounting Changes and Errors

- **Changes in accounting principle.**

  General Rule:
  Employ the current or catch-up approach by:
  a. Reporting current results on the new basis.
  b. Reporting the cumulative effect of the adjustment in the current income statement between the captions "Extraordinary items" and "Net income."
  c. Presenting prior period financial statements as previously reported.
  d. Presenting pro forma data on income and earnings per share for all prior periods presented.
  Exceptions:
  Employ the retroactive approach by:
  a. Restating the financial statements of all prior periods presented.
  b. Disclosing in the year of the change the effect on net income and earnings per share for all prior periods presented.
  c. Reporting an adjustment to the beginning retained earnings balance in the statement of retained earnings.
  Employ the change to LIFO approach by:
  a. Not restating prior years' income.
  b. Using opening inventory in the year the method is adopted as the base-year inventory for all subsequent LIFO computations.
  c. Disclosing the effect of the change on the current year, and the reasons for omitting the computation of the cumulative effect and pro forma amounts for prior years.
- **Changes in accounting estimate.**
  Employ the current and prospective approach by:
  a. Reporting current and future financial statements on the new basis.
  b. Presenting prior period financial statements as previously reported.
  c. Making no adjustments to current-period opening balances for purposes of catch-up and making no pro forma presentations.
- **Changes in reporting entity.**
  Employ the retroactive approach by:
  a. Restating the financial statements of all prior periods presented.
  b. Disclosing in the year of change the effect on net income and earnings per share data for all prior periods presented.
- **Changes due to error.**
  Employ the retroactive approach by:
  a. Correcting all prior period statements presented.
  b. Restating the beginning balance of retained earnings for the first period presented when the error effects occur in a period prior to that one.

Changes in accounting principle are considered appropriate only when the enterprise demonstrates that the alternative generally accepted accounting principle that is adopted is **preferable** to the existing one. Preferability among accounting principles

UNDERLYING CONCEPTS

This is an example of two widely accepted concepts conflicting. Which is more important, matching (emphasis on the income statement) or qualitative characteristic of representational faithfulness (emphasis on the balance sheet)?

should be determined on the basis of whether the new principle constitutes an **improvement in financial reporting**, not on the basis of the income tax effect alone.[10]

But it is not always easy to determine what is an improvement in financial reporting. **How does one measure preferability or improvement?** Quaker Oats Company, for example argues that a change in accounting principle to LIFO inventory valuation "better matches current costs with current revenues" (see Illustration 22-11, page 1160). Conversely, another enterprise might change from LIFO to FIFO because it wishes to report a more realistic ending inventory. How do you determine which is the better of these two arguments? The auditor must have some "standard" or "objective" as a basis for determining the preferable method. Because no universal standard or objective is generally accepted, the problem of determining preferability continues to be a difficult one.

Initially the SEC took the position that the auditor should indicate whether a change in accounting principle was preferable. The SEC has since modified this approach, noting that greater reliance may be placed on management's judgment in assessing preferability. Even though the criterion of preferability is difficult to apply, the general guidelines established have acted as a deterrent to capricious changes in accounting principles.[11] **If an FASB standard creates a new principle or expresses preference for or rejects a specific accounting principle, a change is considered clearly acceptable.** Similarly, other authoritative documents, such as AcSEC's statements of position and AICPA industry audit guides, are considered preferable accounting when a change in accounting principles is contemplated.

MOTIVATIONS FOR CHANGE

OBJECTIVE 9
Identify economic motives for changing accounting methods.

Difficult as it is to determine which accounting standards have the strongest conceptual support, other complications make the process even more complex. These complications stem from the fact that managers (and others) have a self-interest in how the financial statements make the company look. Managers naturally wish to show their financial performance in the best light. A **favorable profit picture** can influence investors, and a strong liquidity position can influence creditors. **Too favorable a profit picture**, however, can provide union negotiators and government regulators with ammunition during bargaining talks. Hence, managers might have varying profit motives depending on economic times and whom they seek to impress.

Research has provided additional insight into why companies may prefer certain accounting methods. Some of these reasons are as follows:

1. ***Political Costs.*** As companies become larger and more politically visible, politicians and regulators devote more attention to them. Many suggest that politicians and regulators can "feather their own nests" by imposing regulations on these organizations for the benefit of their own constituents. Thus the larger the firm, the more likely it is to become subject to regulation such as antitrust and the more likely it is to be required to pay higher taxes. Therefore, companies that are politically visible may attempt to report income numbers that are low, to avoid the

[10]A change in accounting principle, a change in the reporting entity (special type of change in accounting principle), and a correction of an error involving a change in accounting principle require an explanatory paragraph in the auditor's report discussing lack of consistency from one period to the next. A change in accounting estimate does not affect the auditor's opinion relative to consistency; however, if the change in estimate has a material effect on the financial statements, disclosure may still be required. Error correction not involving a change in accounting principle does not require disclosure relative to consistency.

[11]If management has not provided reasonable justification for the change in accounting principle, the auditor should express a qualified opinion or, if the effect of the change is sufficiently material, the auditor should express an adverse opinion on the financial statements. "Reports on Audited Financial Statements," *Statement on Auditing Standards No. 58* (New York: AICPA, 1988).

scrutiny of regulators. Companies thus hope to reduce their exposure to the perception of monopoly power. In addition, other constituents such as labor unions may be less willing to ask for wage increases if reported income is low. Researchers have found that the larger the company, the more likely it is to adopt income decreasing approaches in selecting accounting methods.[12]

2 ***Capital Structure.*** A number of studies have indicated that the capital structure of the company can affect the selection of accounting methods. For example, a company with a high debt-to-equity ratio is more likely to be constrained by debt covenants. That is, a company may have a debt covenant that indicates that it cannot pay any dividends if retained earnings fall below a certain level. As a result, such a company is more likely to select accounting methods that will increase net income. For example, one group of writers indicated that a company's capital structure affected its decision whether to expense or capitalize interest.[13] Others indicated that full cost accounting was selected instead of successful efforts by companies that have high debt-to-equity ratios.[14]

3 ***Bonus Payments.*** If bonus payments paid to management are tied to income, it has been found that management will select accounting methods that maximize their bonus payments. Thus, in selecting accounting methods, management does concern itself with the effect of accounting income changes on their compensation plans.[15]

4 ***Smooth Earnings.*** Substantial increases in earnings attract the attention of politicians, regulators, and competitors. In addition, large increases in income create problems for management because the same results are difficult to achieve the following year. Executive compensation plans would use these higher numbers as a baseline and make it difficult for management to earn bonuses in subsequent years. Conversely, large decreases in earnings might be viewed as a signal that the company is in financial trouble. Furthermore, substantial decreases in income raise concerns on the part of stockholders, lenders, and other interested parties about the competency of management. Thus, companies have an incentive to "manage" or "smooth" earnings. Management therefore believes that a steady 10 percent growth a year is much better than a 30 percent growth one year and a 10 percent decline the next.[16] In other words, management usually prefers a gradually increasing income report (often referred to as "income smoothers") and sometimes changes accounting methods to ensure such a result.

Management pays careful attention to the accounting it follows and often changes accounting methods not for conceptual reasons, but for economic reasons. As indicated throughout this textbook, such arguments have come to be known as "economic consequences arguments," since they focus on the supposed impact of the accounting

---

[12]Ross L. Watts and Jerold L. Zimmerman, "Positive Accounting Theory: A Ten-Year Perspective," *The Accounting Review* (January 1990).

[13]R. M. Bowen, E. W. Noreen, and J. M. Lacy, "Determinants of the Corporate Decision to Capitalize Interest," *Journal of Accounting and Economics* (August 1981).

[14]See, for example, Dan S. Dhaliwal, "The Effect of the Firm's Capital Structure on the Choice of Accounting Methods," *The Accounting Review* (January 1980); and W. Bruce Johnson and Ramachandran Ramanan, "Discretionary Accounting Changes from 'Successful Efforts' to 'Full Cost' Methods: 1970–1976," *The Accounting Review* (January 1988). The latter study found that firms that changed to full cost were more likely to exhibit higher levels of financial risk (leverage) than firms that retained successful efforts.

[15]See, for example, Mark Zmijewski and Robert Hagerman, "An Income Strategy Approach to the Positive Theory of Accounting Standard Setting/Choice," *Journal of Accounting and Economics* (1985).

[16]O. Douglas Moses, "Income Smoothing and Incentives: Empirical Tests Using Accounting Changes," *The Accounting Review* (April 1987). Findings provide evidence that smoothers are associated with firm size, the existence of bonus plans, and the divergence of actual earnings from expectations.

method on the behavior of investors, creditors, competitors, governments, or managers of the reporting companies themselves.[17]

To counter these pressures, standards setters such as the FASB have declared, as part of their conceptual framework, that they will assess the merits of proposed standards from a position of neutrality. That is, the soundness of standards should not be evaluated on the grounds of their possible impact on behavior. It is not the FASB's place to choose standards according to the kinds of behavior they wish to promote and the kinds they wish to discourage. At the same time, it must be admitted that some standards **will** often have the effect of influencing behavior. Yet their justification should be conceptual, and not viewed in terms of their impact.

WHAT DO THE NUMBERS MEAN?

WHY CHANGE?

Why do companies change accounting methods or estimates? As indicated earlier, many changes are implemented because the FASB or SEC mandates them in a new rule. For example, in 2000, many companies adopted new revenue recognition rules as required by the SEC and so recorded cumulative effect adjustments that reduced earnings. **Alcoa Co.**, **Mead Corporation**, and **Murphy Oil**, for example, reported earnings decreases of up to 3 percent in adopting these new rules.

Other accounting changes are voluntary. **Goodyear Tire and Rubber** changed from LIFO to FIFO and reported a $44.4 million increase in income in 2000. Conceptually, such voluntary changes have merit if the revised methods result in more representative reporting of financial results. However, observing negative earnings effects for mandatory changes but positive earnings effects from voluntary changes raises concerns that managers' voluntary changes are implemented in order to present their financial performance in the most favorable light. Such reporting could help managers achieve compensation targets or relax debt restrictions, which are based on reported earnings.

SECTION 2 ERROR ANALYSIS

OBJECTIVE 10
Analyze the effect of errors.

As indicated earlier, material errors are unusual in large corporations because internal control procedures coupled with the diligence of the accounting staff are ordinarily sufficient to find any major errors in the system. Smaller businesses may face a different problem. These enterprises may not be able to afford an internal audit staff or to implement the necessary control procedures to ensure that accounting data are always recorded accurately.[18]

In practice, firms do not correct for errors discovered that do not have a significant effect on the presentation of the financial statements. For example, the failure to record accrued wages of $5,000 when the total payroll for the year is $1,750,000 and net income is $940,000 is not considered significant, and no correction is made. Obviously, defining materiality is difficult, and experience and judgment must be used to determine whether adjustment is necessary for a given error. **All errors discussed in this**

[17]Lobbyists use economic consequences arguments—and there are many of them—to put pressure on standards setters. We have seen examples of these arguments in the oil and gas industry about successful efforts versus full cost, in the technology area with the issue of mandatory expensing of research and developmental costs, and so on.

[18]See Mark L. DeFord and James Jiambalvo, "Incidence and Circumstances of Accounting Errors," *The Accounting Review* (July 1991), for examples of different types of errors and why these errors might have occurred.

section are assumed to be material and to require adjustment. Also, all tax effects are ignored in this section.

Three questions must be answered in error analysis:

1. What type of error is involved?
2. What entries are needed to correct for the error?
3. How are financial statements to be restated once the error is discovered?

As indicated earlier, errors are **treated as prior period adjustments and reported in the current year as adjustments to the beginning balance of Retained Earnings**. If comparative statements are presented, the prior statements affected should be restated to correct for the error.

Three types of errors can occur. Because each type has its own peculiarities, it is important to differentiate among them.

BALANCE SHEET ERRORS

Balance sheet errors affect only the presentation of an asset, liability, or stockholders' equity account. Examples are the classification of a short-term receivable as part of the investment section, the classification of a note payable as an account payable, and the classification of plant assets as inventory. Reclassification of the item to its proper position is needed when the error is discovered. If comparative statements that include the error year are prepared, the balance sheet for the error year is restated correctly.

INCOME STATEMENT ERRORS

Income statement errors affect only the presentation of the nominal accounts in the income statement. These errors involve the improper classification of revenues or expenses, such as recording interest revenue as part of sales, purchases as bad debt expense, and depreciation expense as interest expense. An income statement classification error has no effect on the balance sheet and no effect on net income. A reclassification entry is needed when the error is discovered, if it is discovered in the year it is made. If the error occurred in prior periods, no entry is needed at the date of discovery because the accounts for the current year are correctly stated. If comparative statements that include the error year are prepared, the income statement for the error year is restated correctly.

BALANCE SHEET AND INCOME STATEMENT EFFECTS

The third type of error involves both the balance sheet and income statement. For example, assume that accrued wages payable were overlooked by the bookkeeper at the end of the accounting period. The effect of this error is to understate expenses, understate liabilities, and overstate net income for that period of time. This type of error affects both the balance sheet and the income statement and is classified in one of two ways—counterbalancing or noncounterbalancing.

Counterbalancing errors are errors that will be offset or corrected over two periods. For example, the failure to record accrued wages is considered a counterbalancing error because over a 2-year period the error will no longer be present. In other words the failure to record accrued wages in the previous period means: (1) net income for the first period is overstated; (2) accrued wages payable (a liability) is understated, and (3) wages expense is understated. In the next period, net income is understated; accrued wages payable (a liability) is correctly stated; and wages expense is overstated. For the **2 years combined**: (1) net income is correct; (2) wages expense is correct; and (3) accrued wages payable at the end of the second year is correct. Most errors in accounting that affect both the balance sheet and income statement are counterbalancing errors.

Noncounterbalancing errors are errors that are not offset in the next accounting period. An example would be the failure to capitalize equipment that has a useful life of 5 years. If we expense this asset immediately, expenses will be overstated in the first period but understated in the next four periods. At the end of the second period, the effect of the error is not fully offset. Net income is correct in the aggregate only at the end of 5 years, because the asset is fully depreciated at this point. Thus, **noncounterbalancing errors are those that take longer than two periods to correct themselves.**

Only in rare instances is an error never reversed—for example, when land is initially expensed. Because land is not depreciable, theoretically the error is never offset unless the land is sold.

Counterbalancing Errors

The usual types of counterbalancing errors are illustrated on the following pages. In studying these illustrations, keep in mind a number of points: First, determine whether or not the books have been closed for the period in which the error is found:

1. **If the books have been closed:**
   - **a.** If the error is already counterbalanced, no entry is necessary.
   - **b.** If the error is not yet counterbalanced, an entry is necessary to adjust the present balance of retained earnings.
2. **If the books have not been closed:**
   - **a.** If the error is already counterbalanced and the company is in the second year, an entry is necessary to correct the current period and to adjust the beginning balance of Retained Earnings.
   - **b.** If the error is not yet counterbalanced, an entry is necessary to adjust the beginning balance of Retained Earnings and correct the current period.

Second, if comparative statements are presented, restatement of the amounts for comparative purposes is necessary. **Restatement is necessary even if a correcting journal entry is not required.** To illustrate, assume that Sanford's Cement Co. failed to accrue revenue in 2002 when earned, but recorded the revenue in 2003 when received. The error was discovered in 2005. No entry is necessary to correct for this error because the effects have been counterbalanced by the time the error is discovered in 2005. However, if comparative financial statements for 2002 through 2005 are presented, the accounts and related amounts for the years 2002 and 2003 should be restated correctly for financial reporting purposes.

Failure to Record Accrued Wages

On December 31, 2004, Hurley Enterprises did not accrue wages in the amount of $1,500. The entry in 2005 to correct this error, assuming that the books have not been closed for 2005, is:

Retained Earnings	1,500	
Wages Expense		1,500

The rationale for this entry is as follows: (1) When the accrued wages of 2004 are paid in 2005 an additional debit of $1,500 is made to 2005 Wages Expense. (2) Wages Expense—2005 is overstated by $1,500. (3) Because 2004 accrued wages were not recorded as Wages Expense—2004, the net income for 2004 was overstated by $1,500. (4) Because 2004 net income is overstated by $1,500, the Retained Earnings account is overstated by $1,500 because net income is closed to Retained Earnings.

If the books have been closed for 2005, no entry is made because the error is counterbalanced.

Failure to Record Prepaid Expenses

In January 2004 Hurley Enterprises purchased a 2-year insurance policy costing $1,000. Insurance Expense was debited, and Cash was credited. No adjusting entries were made at the end of 2004.

The entry on December 31, 2005, to correct this error, assuming that the books have not been closed for 2005, is:

Insurance Expense	500	
Retained Earnings		500

If the books have been closed for 2005, no entry is made because the error is counterbalanced.

Understatement of Unearned Revenue

On December 31, 2004, Hurley Enterprises received $50,000 as a prepayment for renting certain office space for the following year. The entry made at the time of receipt of the rent payment was a debit to Cash and a credit to Rent Revenue. No adjusting entry was made as of December 31, 2004. The entry on December 31, 2005, to correct for this error, assuming that the books have not been closed for 2005, is:

Retained Earnings	50,000	
Rent Revenue		50,000

If the books have been closed for 2005, no entry is made because the error is counterbalanced.

Overstatement of Accrued Revenue

On December 31, 2004, Hurley Enterprises accrued as interest revenue $8,000 that applied to 2005. The entry made on December 31, 2004, was to debit Interest Receivable and credit Interest Revenue. The entry on December 31, 2005, to correct for this error, assuming that the books have not been closed for 2005, is:

Retained Earnings	8,000	
Interest Revenue		8,000

If the books have been closed for 2005, no entry is made because the error is counterbalanced.

Overstatement of Purchases

Hurley Enterprises' accountant recorded a purchase of merchandise for $9,000 in 2004 that applied to 2005. The physical inventory for 2004 was correctly stated. The company uses the periodic inventory method. The entry on December 31, 2005, to correct for this error, assuming that the books have not been closed for 2005, is:

Purchases	9,000	
Retained Earnings		9,000

If the books have been closed for 2005, no entry is made because the error is counterbalanced.

Noncounterbalancing Errors

Because such errors do not counterbalance over a 2-year period, the entries for noncounterbalancing errors are more complex, and correcting entries are needed, even if the books have been closed.

Failure to Record Depreciation

Assume that on January 1, 2004, Hurley Enterprises purchased a machine for $10,000 that had an estimated useful life of 5 years. The accountant incorrectly expensed this machine in 2004. The error was discovered in 2005. If we assume that the company desires to use straight-line depreciation on this asset, the entry on December 31, 2005, to correct for this error, given that the books have not been closed, is:

Machinery	10,000	
Depreciation Expense	2,000	
Retained Earnings		8,000[a]
Accumulated Depreciation (20% × $10,000 × 2)		4,000

[a]Computations:

Retained Earnings	
Overstatement of expense in 2004	$10,000
Proper depreciation for 2004 (20% × $10,000)	(2,000)
Retained earnings understated as of Dec. 31, 2004	$ 8,000

If the books have been closed for 2005, the entry is:

Machinery	10,000	
Retained Earnings		6,000[a]
Accumulated Depreciation		4,000

[a]Computations:

Retained Earnings

Retained earnings understated as of Dec. 31, 2004	$ 8,000
Proper depreciation for 2005 (20% × $10,000)	(2,000)
Retained earnings understated as of Dec. 31, 2005	$ 6,000

Failure to Adjust for Bad Debts

Companies sometimes use a specific charge-off method in accounting for bad debt expense when a percentage of sales is more appropriate. Adjustments are often made to change from the specific writeoff to some type of allowance method. For example, assume that Hurley Enterprises has recognized bad debt expense when the debts have actually become uncollectible as follows.

	2004	2005
From 2004 sales	$550	$690
From 2005 sales		700

Hurley estimates that an additional $1,400 will be charged off in 2006, of which $300 is applicable to 2004 sales and $1,100 to 2005 sales. The entry on December 31, 2005, assuming that the **books have not been closed for 2005**, is:

Bad Debt Expense	410[a]	
Retained Earnings	990[a]	
Allowance for Doubtful Accounts		1,400

[a]Computations:

Allowance for doubtful accounts: Additional $300 for 2004 sales and $1,100 for 2005 sales.

Bad debts and retained earnings balance:

	2004	2005
Bad debts charged for	$1,240[b]	$ 700
Additional bad debts anticipated in 2006	300	1,100
Proper bad debt expense	1,540	1,800
Charges currently made to each period	(550)	(1,390)
Bad debt adjustment	$ 990	$ 410

[b]$550 + $690 = $1,240

If the **books have been closed for 2005**, the entry is:

Retained Earnings	1,400	
Allowance for Doubtful Accounts		1,400

COMPREHENSIVE ILLUSTRATION: NUMEROUS ERRORS

In some circumstances a combination of errors occurs. A work sheet is therefore prepared to facilitate the analysis. The following problem demonstrates the use of a work sheet. The mechanics of the work sheet preparation should be obvious from the solution format.

The income statements of Hudson Company for the years ended December 31, 2003, 2004, and 2005 indicate the following net incomes.

2003	$17,400
2004	20,200
2005	11,300

An examination of the accounting records of Hudson Company for these years indicates that several errors were made in arriving at the net income amounts reported. The following errors were discovered:

1. Wages earned by workers but not paid at December 31 were consistently omitted from the records. The amounts omitted were:

December 31, 2003	$1,000
December 31, 2004	$1,400
December 31, 2005	$1,600

These amounts were recorded as expenses when paid in the year following that in which they were earned.

2. The merchandise inventory on December 31, 2003, was overstated by $1,900 as the result of errors made in the footings and extensions on the inventory sheets.
3. Unexpired insurance of $1,200, applicable to 2005, was expensed on December 31, 2004.
4. Interest receivable in the amount of $240 was not recorded on December 31, 2004.
5. On January 2, 2004, a piece of equipment costing $3,900 was sold for $1,800. At the date of sale the equipment had accumulated depreciation of $2,400. The cash received was recorded as Miscellaneous Income in 2004. In addition, depreciation was recorded for this equipment in both 2004 and 2005 at the rate of 10 percent of cost.

The first step in preparing the work sheet is to prepare a schedule showing the corrected net income amounts for the years ended December 31, 2003, 2004, and 2005. Each correction of the amount originally reported is clearly labeled. The next step is to indicate the balance sheet accounts affected as of December 31, 2005. The completed work sheet for Hudson Company is as follows.

ILLUSTRATION 22-19
Work Sheet to Correct Income and Balance Sheet Errors

HUDSON COMPANY
Work Sheet to Correct Income and Balance Sheet Errors

	A	B	C	D	E	F	G	H
1		Work Sheet Analysis of Changes in Net Income				Balance Sheet Correction at December 31, 2005		
2		2003	2004	2005	Totals	Debit	Credit	Account
3	Net income as reported	$17,400	$20,200	$11,300	$48,900			
4	Wages unpaid, 12/31/03	(1,000)	1,000		–0–			
5	Wages unpaid, 12/31/04		(1,400)	1,400	–0–			
6	Wages unpaid, 12/31/05			(1,600)	(1,600)		$1,600	Wages Payable
7	Inventory overstatement, 12/31/03	(1,900)	1,900		–0–			
8	Unexpired insurance, 12/31/04		1,200	(1,200)	–0–			
9	Interest receivable, 12/31/04		240	(240)	–0–			
10	Correction for entry made upon sale of equipment, 1/2/04[a]		(1,500)		(1,500)	$2,400	3,900	Accumulated Depreciation Machinery
11	Overcharge of depreciation, 2004		390		390	390		Accumulated Depreciation
12	Overcharge of depreciation, 2005			390	390	390		Accumulated Depreciation
13	Corrected net income	$14,500	$22,030	$10,050	$46,580			
14	[a]Cost	$ 3,900						
15	Accumulated depreciation	2,400						
16	Book value	1,500						
17	Proceeds from sale	1,800						
18	Gain on sale	300						
19	Income reported	(1,800)						
20	Adjustment	$(1,500)						

Sheet1 / Sheet2 / Sheet3

Correcting entries **if the books have not been closed** on December 31, 2005, are:

Retained Earnings	1,400	
Wages Expense		1,400
(To correct improper charge to Wages Expense for 2005)		
Wages Expense	1,600	
Wages Payable		1,600
(To record proper wages expense for 2005)		
Insurance Expense	1,200	
Retained Earnings		1,200
(To record proper insurance expense for 2005)		
Interest Revenue	240	
Retained Earnings		240
(To correct improper credit to Interest Revenue in 2005)		
Retained Earnings	1,500	
Accumulated Depreciation	2,400	
Machinery		3,900
(To record writeoff of machinery in 2004 and adjustment of Retained Earnings)		
Accumulated Depreciation	780	
Depreciation Expense		390
Retained Earnings		390
(To correct improper charge for depreciation expense in 2004 and 2005)		

If the books have been closed for 2005, the correcting entries are:

Retained Earnings	1,600	
Wages Payable		1,600
(To record proper wage expense for 2005)		
Retained Earnings	1,500	
Accumulated Depreciation	2,400	
Machinery		3,900
(To record writeoff of machinery in 2004 and adjustment of Retained Earnings)		
Accumulated Depreciation	780	
Retained Earnings		780
(To correct improper charge for depreciation expense in 2004 and 2005)		

PREPARATION OF FINANCIAL STATEMENTS WITH ERROR CORRECTIONS

Up to now, our discussion of error analysis has been concerned with the identification of the type of error involved and the accounting for its correction in the accounting records. The correction of the error should be presented on comparative financial statements. In addition, 5- or 10-year summaries are given for the interested financial reader. The following situation illustrates how a typical year's financial statements are restated given many different errors.

Dick & Wally's Outlet is a small retail outlet in the town of Holiday. Lacking expertise in accounting, the company does not keep adequate records. As a result, numerous errors occurred in recording accounting information. The errors are listed below.

1. The bookkeeper inadvertently failed to record a cash receipt of $1,000 on the sale of merchandise in 2005.
2. Accrued wages expense at the end of 2004 was $2,500; at the end of 2005, $3,200. The company does not accrue for wages; all wages are charged to Administrative Expenses.
3. No allowance had been set up for estimated uncollectible receivables. Dick and Wally decided to set up such an allowance for the estimated probable losses as of

December 31, 2005 for 2004 accounts of $700, and for 2005 accounts of $1,500. They also decided to correct the charge against each year so that it shows the losses (actual and estimated) relating to that year's sales. Accounts have been written off to bad debt expense (selling expense) as follows.

	In 2004	In 2005
2004 accounts	$400	$2,000
2005 accounts		1,600

4. Unexpired insurance not recorded at the end of 2004 was $600, and at the end of 2005, $400. All insurance is charged to Administrative Expenses.
5. An account payable of $6,000 should have been a note payable.
6. During 2004, an asset that cost $10,000 and had a book value of $4,000 was sold for $7,000. At the time of sale Cash was debited and Miscellaneous Income was credited for $7,000.
7. As a result of the last transaction, the company overstated depreciation expense (an administrative expense) in 2004 by $800 and in 2005 by $1,200.

A work sheet that begins with the unadjusted trial balance of Dick & Wally's Outlet is presented in Illustration 22-20. The correcting entries and their effect on the financial statements can be determined by examining the work sheet.

ILLUSTRATION 22-20
Work Sheet to Analyze Effect of Errors in Financial Statements

DICK & WALLY'S OUTLET
Work Sheet Analysis to Adjust Financial Statements for the Year 2005

	A	B		C	D	E	F	G	H	I	J
1		Trial Balance Unadjusted		Adjustments				Income Statement Adjusted		Balance Sheet Adjusted	
2		Debit	Credit		Debit		Credit	Debit	Credit	Debit	Credit
3	Cash	3,100		(1)	1,000					4,100	
4	Accounts Receivable	17,600								17,600	
5	Notes Receivable	8,500								8,500	
6	Inventory	34,000								34,000	
7	Property, Plant, and Equipment	112,000				(6)	10,000[a]			102,000	
8	Accumulated Depreciation		83,500	(6)	6,000[a]						75,500
9				(7)	2,000						
10	Investments	24,300								24,300	
11	Accounts Payable		14,500	(5)	6,000						8,500
12	Notes Payable		10,000			(5)	6,000				16,000
13	Capital Stock		43,500								43,500
14	Retained Earnings		20,000	(3)	2,700[b]						
15				(6)	4,000[a]	(4)	600				
16				(2)	2,500	(7)	800				12,200
17	Sales		94,000			(1)	1,000		95,000		
18	Cost of Goods Sold	21,000						21,000			
19	Selling Expenses	22,000				(3)	500[b]	21,500			
20	Administrative Expenses	23,000		(2)	700	(4)	400	22,700			
21				(4)	600	(7)	1,200				
22	Totals	265,500	265,500								
23	Wages Payable					(2)	3,200				3,200
24	Allowance for Doubtful Accounts					(3)	2,200[b]				2,200
25	Unexpired Insurance			(4)	400					400	
26	Net Income							29,800			29,800
27	Totals				25,900		25,900	95,000	95,000	190,900	190,900

Sheet1 / Sheet2 / Sheet3

Computations:

[a]Machinery

Proceeds from sale	$7,000
Book value of machinery	4,000
Gain on sale	3,000
Income credited	7,000
Retained earnings adjustment	$4,000

[b]Bad Debts

	2004	2005
Bad debts charged for	$2,400	$1,600
Additional bad debts anticipated	700	1,500
	3,100	3,100
Charges currently made to each year	(400)	(3,600)
Bad debt adjustment	$2,700	$ (500)

SUMMARY OF LEARNING OBJECTIVES

1 Identify the types of accounting changes. The three different types of accounting changes are: (1) *Change in accounting principle:* a change from one generally accepted accounting principle to another generally accepted accounting principle. (2) *Change in accounting estimate:* a change that occurs as the result of new information or as additional experience is acquired. (3) *Change in reporting entity:* a change from reporting as one type of entity to another type of entity.

2 Describe the accounting for changes in accounting principles. A change in accounting principle involves a change from one generally accepted accounting principle to another. A change in accounting principle is not considered to result from the adoption of a new principle in recognition of events that have occurred for the first time or that were previously immaterial. If the accounting principle previously followed was not acceptable or if the principle was applied incorrectly, a change to a generally accepted accounting principle is considered a correction of an error.

3 Understand how to account for cumulative-effect accounting changes. The general requirement for changes in accounting principle is that the cumulative effect of the change (net of tax) be shown at the bottom of the current year's income statement and that pro forma net income and earnings per share amounts be reported for all prior periods presented.

4 Understand how to account for retroactive accounting changes. A number of accounting principle changes are handled in a retroactive manner. That is, prior years' financial statements are recast on a basis consistent with the newly adopted principle, and any part of the effect attributable to years prior to those presented is treated as an adjustment of the earliest retained earnings presented.

5 Understand how to account for changes to LIFO. In changing to LIFO, the base year inventory for all subsequent LIFO calculations is the opening inventory in the year the method is adopted. There is no restatement of prior years' income because it is just too impractical to do so.

6 Describe the accounting for changes in estimates. Changes in estimates must be handled prospectively. That is, no changes should be made in previously reported results. Opening balances are not adjusted, and no attempt is made to "catch up" for prior periods. Financial statements of prior periods are not restated, and pro forma amounts for prior periods are not reported.

7 Identify changes in a reporting entity. An accounting change that results in financial statements that are actually the statements of a different entity should be reported by restating the financial statements of all prior periods presented, to show the financial information for the new reporting entity for all periods.

8 Describe the accounting for correction of errors. As soon as they are discovered, errors must be corrected by proper entries in the accounts and reported in the financial statements. Corrections of errors are treated as prior period adjustments and are recorded in the year in which the error was discovered. They are reported in the financial statements as an adjustment to the beginning balance of retained earnings. If comparative statements are presented, the prior statements affected should be restated to correct for the error. The disclosures need not be repeated in the financial statements of subsequent periods.

9 Identify economic motives for changing accounting methods. Managers might have varying profit motives depending on economic times and whom they seek to impress. Some of the reasons for changing accounting methods are: (1) political costs, (2) capital structure, (3) bonus payments, and (4) smooth earnings.

KEY TERMS

change in accounting estimate, *1150*
change in accounting principle, *1150*
change in reporting entity, *1151*
correction of an error, *1162*
counterbalancing errors, *1169*
cumulative effect changes, *1152*
current changes, *1152*
noncounterbalancing errors, *1170*
pro forma, *1153*
prospective changes, *1152*
retroactive changes, *1152*

⑩ **Analyze the effect of errors.** Three types of errors can occur: (1) *Balance sheet errors*, which affect only the presentation of an asset, liability, or stockholders' equity account. (2) *Income statement errors*, which affect only the presentation of the nominal accounts in the income statement. (3) *Balance sheet and income statement effects*, which involve both the balance sheet and income statement. Errors are classified into two types: (1) *Counterbalancing errors* will be offset or corrected over two periods. (2) *Noncounterbalancing errors* are not offset in the next accounting period and take longer than two periods to correct themselves.

APPENDIX 22A

Changing from and to the Equity Method

As noted in the chapter, an accounting change that results in financial statements for a different entity should be reported by **restating the financial statements of all prior periods presented**. An example of a change in reporting entity is when a company's level of ownership or influence changes, such that it should change from or to the equity method. We present illustrations for these changes in entity in the following two sections.

CHANGE FROM THE EQUITY METHOD

OBJECTIVE ⑪
Make the computations and prepare the entries necessary to record a change from or to the equity method of accounting.

If the investor level of influence or ownership falls below that necessary for continued use of the equity method, a change must be made to the fair value method. The earnings or losses that were previously recognized by the investor under the equity method should **remain as part of the carrying amount** of the investment with no retroactive restatement to the new method.

When a change is made **from the equity method to the fair value method, the cost basis for accounting purposes is the carrying amount of the investment at the date of the change**. In addition, amortizing the excess of acquisition price over the proportionate share of book value acquired attributable to undervalued depreciable assets ceases when the change of methods occurs. In other words, the new method is applied in its entirety once the equity method is no longer appropriate. At the next reporting date, the investor should record the unrealized holding gain or loss to recognize the difference between the carrying amount and fair value.

Dividends in Excess of Earnings

To the extent that dividends received by the investor company in subsequent periods exceed its share of the investee's earnings for such periods (all periods following the change in method), they should be accounted for as a **reduction of the investment carrying amount**, rather than as revenue.

To illustrate, assume that on January 1, 2002, Investor Company purchased 250,000 shares of Investee Company's 1,000,000 shares of outstanding stock for $8,500,000. Investor correctly accounted for this investment using the equity method. After accounting for dividends received and investee net income, in 2002, Investor reported its investment in Investee Company at $8,780,000 at December 31, 2002. On January 2, 2003, Investee Company sold 1,500,000 additional shares of its own common stock to the public, thereby reducing Investor Company's ownership from 25 percent to 10 percent. The net income (or loss) and dividends of Investee Company for the years 2003 through 2005 are as shown below.

ILLUSTRATION 22A-1
Income Earned and Dividends Received

Year		Investor's Share of Investee Income (Loss)	Investee Dividends Received by Investor
2003		$600,000	$ 400,000
2004		350,000	400,000
2005		–0–	210,000
	Totals	$950,000	$1,010,000

Assuming a change from the equity method to the fair value method as of January 2, 2003, Investor Company's reported investment in Investee Company and its reported income would be as shown below.

ILLUSTRATION 22A-2
Impact on Investment Carrying Amount

Year	Dividend Revenue Recognized	Cumulative Excess of Share of Earnings Over Dividends Received	Investment at December 31
2003	$400,000	$200,000[a]	$8,780,000
2004	400,000	150,000[b]	8,780,000
2005	150,000	(60,000)[c]	8,780,000 − $60,000 = $8,720,000

[a]$600,000 − $400,000 = $200,000
[b]($350,000 − $400,000) + $200,000 = $150,000
[c]$150,000 − $210,000 = $(60,000)

The following entries would be recorded by Investor Company to recognize the above dividends and earnings data for the 3 years subsequent to the change in methods.

2003 and 2004

Cash	400,000	
Dividend Revenue		400,000
(To record dividend received from Investee Company)		

2005

Cash	210,000	
Available-for-Sale Securities		60,000
Dividend Revenue		150,000
(To record dividend revenue from Investee Company in 2005 and to recognize cumulative excess of dividends received over share of Investee earnings in periods subsequent to change from equity method)		

CHANGE TO THE EQUITY METHOD

When converting to the equity method, a retroactive adjustment is necessary. Such a change involves **adjusting retroactively the carrying amount of the investment, results of current and prior operations, and retained earnings of the investor as if the**

equity method has been in effect during all of the previous periods in which this investment was held.[1] When changing from the fair value method to the equity method, it is also necessary to eliminate any balances in the Unrealized Holding Gain or Loss—Equity account and the Securities Fair Value Adjustment account. In addition, the available-for-sale classification for this investment is eliminated, and the investment in stock under the equity method is recorded.

For example, on January 2, 2004, Amsted Corp. purchased, for $500,000 cash, 10 percent of the outstanding shares of Cable Company common stock. On that date, the net assets of Cable Company had a book value of $3,000,000. The excess of cost over the underlying equity in net assets of Cable Company is attributed to goodwill. On January 2, 2006, Amsted Corp. purchased an additional 20 percent of Cable Company's stock for $1,200,000 cash when the book value of Cable's net assets was $4,000,000. The excess of cost over book value related to this additional investment is attributed to goodwill. Now having a 30 percent interest, Amsted Corp. must use the equity method. From January 2, 2004, to January 2, 2006, Amsted Corp. used the fair value method and categorized these securities as available-for-sale. At January 2, 2006, Amsted has a credit balance of $92,000 in its Unrealized Holding Gain or Loss—Equity account and a debit balance in its Securities Fair Value Adjustment account of the same amount. Assume that this adjustment was made on December 31, 2004. The net income reported by Cable Company and the Cable Company dividends received by Amsted during the period 2004 through 2006 were as follows.

ILLUSTRATION 22A-3
Income Earned and Dividends Received

Year	Cable Company Net Income	Cable Co. Dividends Paid to Amsted
2004	$ 500,000	$ 20,000
2005	1,000,000	30,000
2006	1,200,000	120,000

The journal entries recorded from January 2, 2004, through December 31, 2006, relative to Amsted Corp.'s investment in Cable Company, reflecting the data above and a change from the fair value method to the equity method, are as follows.[2]

January 2, 2004

Available-for-Sale Securities	500,000	
Cash		500,000
(To record the purchase of a 10% interest in Cable Company)		

December 31, 2004

Cash	20,000	
Dividend Revenue		20,000
(To record the receipt of cash dividends from Cable Company)		
Securities Fair Value Adjustment (Available-for-Sale)	92,000	
Unrealized Holding Gain or Loss—Equity		92,000
(To record increase in fair value of securities)		

December 31, 2005

Cash	30,000	
Dividend Revenue		30,000
(To record the receipt of cash dividends from Cable Company)		

[1]"The Equity Method of Accounting for Investments in Common Stock," *Opinions of the Accounting Principles Board No. 18* (New York: AICPA, 1971), par. 17.

[2]Adapted from Paul A. Pacter, "Applying APB Opinion No. 18—Equity Method," *Journal of Accountancy* (September 1971), pp. 59–60.

January 2, 2006

Investment in Cable Stock	1,300,000	
Cash		1,200,000
Retained Earnings		100,000
(To record the purchase of an additional interest in Cable Company and to reflect retroactively a change from the fair value method to the equity method of accounting for the investment. The $100,000 adjustment is computed as follows:		

	2004	2005	Total
Amsted Corp. equity in earnings of Cable Company (10%)	$50,000	$100,000	$150,000
Dividend received	(20,000)	(30,000)	(50,000)
Prior period adjustment	$30,000	$ 70,000	$100,000

January 2, 2006

Investment in Cable Stock	500,000	
Available-for-Sale Securities		500,000
(To reclassify initial 10% interest to equity method)		

January 2, 2006

Unrealized Holding Gain or Loss—Equity	92,000	
Securities Fair Value Adjustment (Available-for-Sale)		92,000
(To eliminate fair value accounts for change to equity method)		

December 31, 2006

Investment in Cable Stock	360,000	
Revenue from Investment		360,000
[To record equity in earnings of Cable Company (30% of $1,200,000)]		
Cash	120,000	
Investment in Cable Stock		120,000
(To record the receipt of cash dividends from Cable Company)		

Changing to the equity method is accomplished by placing the accounts related to and affected by the investment on the same basis as if the equity method had always been the basis of accounting for that investment. Thus, the effects of this accounting change are reported using the retroactive approach.

SUMMARY OF LEARNING OBJECTIVE FOR APPENDIX 22A

⑪ **Make the computations and prepare the entries necessary to record a change from or to the equity method of accounting.** When changing from the equity method to the fair value method, the cost basis for accounting purposes is the carrying amount used for the investment at the date of change. The new method is applied in its entirety once the equity method is no longer appropriate. When changing to the equity method, a retroactive adjustment of the carrying amount, of results of current and past operations, and of retained earnings is necessary to make the accounts as if the equity method has been in effect during all of the periods in which the investment was held.

Note: All **asterisked** Brief Exercises, Exercises, and Problems relate to material contained in the appendix to the chapter.

QUESTIONS

1. In recent years, the *Wall Street Journal* has indicated that many companies have changed their accounting principles. What are the major reasons why companies change accounting methods?

2. State how each of the following items is reflected in the financial statements.

(a) Change from straight-line method of depreciation to sum-of-the-years'-digits.

(b) Change from FIFO to LIFO method for inventory valuation purposes.

(c) Charge for failure to record depreciation in a previous period.

(d) Litigation won in current year, related to prior period.

(e) Change in the realizability of certain receivables.

(f) Writeoff of receivables.

(g) Change from the percentage-of-completion to the completed-contract method for reporting net income.

3. What are the advantages of employing the current or catch-up method for handling changes in accounting principle?

4. Explain when pro forma amounts are reported and why these amounts are useful to financial statement readers.

5. Define a change in estimate and provide an illustration. When is a change in accounting estimate affected by a change in accounting principle?

6. Sandwich State Bank has followed the practice of capitalizing certain marketing costs and amortizing these costs over their expected life. In the current year, the bank determined that the future benefits from these costs were doubtful. Consequently, the bank adopted the policy of expensing these costs as incurred. How should this accounting change be reported in the comparative financial statements?

7. Indicate how the following items are recorded in the accounting records in the current year of Tami Agler Co.

(a) Large writeoff of goodwill.

(b) A change in depreciating plant assets from accelerated to the straight-line method.

(c) Large writeoff of inventories because of obsolescence.

(d) Change from the cash basis to accrual basis of accounting.

(e) Change from LIFO to FIFO method for inventory valuation purposes.

(f) Change in the estimate of service lives for plant assets.

8. R. M. Andrews Construction Co. had followed the practice of expensing all materials assigned to a construction job without recognizing any salvage inventory. On December 31, 2004, it was determined that salvage inventory should be valued at $62,000. Of this amount, $29,000 arose during the current year. How does this information affect the financial statements to be prepared at the end of 2004?

9. E. A. Basler Inc. wishes to change from the sum-of-the-years'-digits to the straight-line depreciation method for financial reporting purposes. The auditor indicates that a change would be permitted only if it is to a preferable method. What difficulties develop in assessing preferability?

10. Discuss how a change to the LIFO method of inventory valuation is handled.

11. How should consolidated financial statements be reported this year when statements of individual companies were presented last year?

12. Karen Beers controlled four domestic subsidiaries and one foreign subsidiary. Prior to the current year, Beers had excluded the foreign subsidiary from consolidation. During the current year, the foreign subsidiary was included in the financial statements. How should this change in accounting principle be reflected in the financial statements?

13. Clara Beverage Co., a closely held corporation, is in the process of preparing financial statements to accompany an offering of its common stock. The company at this time has decided to switch from the accelerated depreciation method to the straight-line method of depreciation to better present its financial operations. How should this change in accounting principle be reported in the financial statements?

14. Distinguish between counterbalancing and noncounterbalancing errors. Give an example of each.

15. Discuss and illustrate how a correction of an error in previously issued financial statements should be handled.

16. Prior to 2005, Mary Boudreau Inc. excluded manufacturing overhead costs from work in process and finished goods inventory. These costs have been expensed as incurred. In 2005, the company decided to change its accounting methods for manufacturing inventories to full costing by including these costs as product costs. Assuming that these costs are material, how should this change be reflected in the financial statements for 2004 and 2005?

17. Lou Brady Corp. failed to record accrued salaries for 2002, $2,000; 2003, $2,100; and 2004, $3,900. What is the amount of the overstatement or understatement of Retained Earnings at December 31, 2005?

18. In January 2004, installation costs of $8,000 on new machinery were charged to Repair Expense. Other costs of this machinery of $30,000 were correctly recorded and have been depreciated using the straight-line method with an estimated life of 10 years and no salvage value. At December 31, 2005, it is decided that the machinery has a useful life of 20 years, starting with January 1, 2005. What entry(ies) should be made in 2005 to correctly record transactions related to machinery, assuming the machinery has no salvage value? The books have not been closed for 2005 and depreciation expense has not yet been recorded for 2005.

19. On January 2, 2004, $100,000 of 11%, 20-year bonds were issued for $97,000. The $3,000 discount was charged to Interest Expense. The bookkeeper, John Castle, records interest only on the interest payment dates of January 1 and July 1. What is the effect on reported net income for 2004 of this error, assuming straight-line amortization of the discount? What entry is necessary to correct for this error, assuming that the books are not closed for 2004?

20. An account payable of $13,000 for merchandise purchased on December 23, 2004, was recorded in January 2005. This merchandise was not included in inventory at December 31, 2004. What effect does this error have on reported net income for 2004? What entry should be made to correct for this error, assuming that the books are not closed for 2004?

21. Equipment was purchased on January 2, 2004, for $18,000, but no portion of the cost has been charged to depreciation. The corporation wishes to use the straight-line method for these assets, which have been estimated to have a life of 10 years and no salvage value. What effect does this error have on net income in 2004. What entry is necessary to correct for this error, assuming that the books are not closed for 2004?

BRIEF EXERCISES

BE22-1 Larry Beaty Corporation decided at the beginning of 2005 to change from double-declining balance depreciation to straight-line depreciation for financial reporting. The company will continue to use MACRS for tax purposes. For years prior to 2005, depreciation expense under the two methods was as follows: double-declining balance $128,000, and straight-line $80,000. The tax rate is 35%. Prepare Beaty's 2005 journal entry to record the change in accounting principle.

BE22-2 Bruce Bickner Company changed depreciation methods in 2005 from straight-line to double-declining balance, resulting in a cumulative-effect adjustment of $84,000. The 2005 income before the change was $250,000. Bickner had 10,000 shares of common stock outstanding all year. Prepare Bickner's 2005 income statement beginning with income before cumulative effect.

BE22-3 Robert Boey, Inc., changed from the LIFO cost flow assumption to the FIFO cost flow assumption in 2005. The increase in the prior year's income before taxes is $1,000,000. The tax rate is 40%. Prepare Boey's 2005 journal entry to record the change in accounting principle.

BE22-4 Nancy Castle Company purchased a computer system for $60,000 on January 1, 2003. It was depreciated based on a 7-year life and an $18,000 salvage value. On January 1, 2005, Castle revised these estimates to a total useful life of 4 years and a salvage value of $10,000. Prepare Castle's entry to record 2005 depreciation expense.

BE22-5 In 2005, John Hiatt Corporation discovered that equipment purchased on January 1, 2003, for $75,000 was expensed at that time. The equipment should have been depreciated over 5 years, with no salvage value. The effective tax rate is 30%. Prepare Hiatt's 2005 journal entry to correct the error.

BE22-6 At January 1, 2005, William R. Monat Company reported retained earnings of $2,000,000. In 2005, Monat discovered that 2004 depreciation expense was understated by $500,000. In 2005, net income was $900,000 and dividends declared were $250,000. The tax rate is 40%. Prepare a 2005 retained earnings statement for William R. Monat Company.

BE22-7 Indicate the effect—**U**nderstate, **O**verstate, **N**o **E**ffect—that each of the following errors has on 2004 net income and 2005 net income.

	2004	2005
(a) Wages payable were not recorded at 12/31/04.	____	____
(b) Equipment purchased in 2003 was expensed.	____	____
(c) Equipment purchased in 2004 was expensed.	____	____
(d) 2004 ending inventory was overstated.	____	____
(e) Patent amortization was not recorded in 2005.	____	____

***BE22-8** Robocop Corporation owns stock of Terminator, Inc. Prior to 2005, the investment was accounted for using the equity method. In early 2005, Robocop sold part of its investment in Terminator, and began using the fair value method. In 2005, Terminator earned net income of $80,000 and paid dividends of

$95,000. Prepare Robocop's entries related to Terminator's net income and dividends, assuming Robocop now owns 8% of Terminator's stock.

***BE22-9** Rocket Corporation has owned stock of Knight Corporation since 2001. At December 31, 2004, its balances related to this investment were:

Available-for-Sale Securities	$185,000
Securities Fair Value Adj (AFS)	34,000 Dr.
Unrealized Holding Gain or Loss—Equity	34,000 Cr.

On January 1, 2005, Rocket purchased additional stock of Knight Company for $445,000 and now has significant influence over Knight. If the equity method had been used in 2001–2004, income would have been $33,000 greater than dividends received. Prepare Rocket's journal entries to record the purchase of the investment and the change to the equity method.

EXERCISES

E22-1 (Error and Change in Principle—Depreciation) Joy Cunningham Co. purchased a machine on January 1, 2002, for $550,000. At that time it was estimated that the machine would have a 10-year life and no salvage value. On December 31, 2005, the firm's accountant found that the entry for depreciation expense had been omitted in 2003. In addition, management has informed the accountant that the company plans to switch to straight-line depreciation, starting with the year 2005. At present, the company uses the sum-of-the-years'-digits method for depreciating equipment.

Instructions

Prepare the general journal entries the accountant should make at December 31, 2005. (Ignore tax effects.)

E22-2 (Change in Principle and Change in Estimate—Depreciation) Kathleen Cole Inc. acquired the following assets in January of 2002.

Equipment, estimated service life, 5 years; salvage value, $15,000	$525,000
Building, estimated service life, 30 years; no salvage value	$693,000

The equipment has been depreciated using the sum-of-the-years'-digits method for the first 3 years for financial reporting purposes. In 2005, the company decided to change the method of computing depreciation to the straight-line method for the equipment, but no change was made in the estimated service life or salvage value. It was also decided to change the total estimated service life of the building from 30 years to 40 years, with no change in the estimated salvage value. The building is depreciated on the straight-line method.

The company has 100,000 shares of capital stock outstanding. Results of operations for 2005 and 2004 are shown below.

	2005	2004
Income before cumulative effect of change in computing depreciation for 2005: depreciation for 2005 has been computed on the straight-line basis for both the equipment and building[a]	$385,000	$380,000
Income per share before cumulative effect of change in computing depreciation for 2005	$3.85	$3.80

[a]The computation for depreciation expense for 2005 and 2004 for the building was based on the original estimate of service life for 30 years.

Instructions

(a) Compute the cumulative effect of the change in accounting principle to be reported in the income statement for 2005, and prepare the journal entry to record the change. (Ignore tax effects.)

(b) Present comparative data for the years 2004 and 2005, starting with income before cumulative effect of accounting change. Prepare pro-forma data. Do not prepare the footnote. (Ignore tax effects.)

E22-3 (Change in Principle and Change in Estimated Depreciation) On January 1, 2001, Jackson Company purchased a building and equipment that have the following useful lives, salvage values, and costs.

Building, 40-year estimated useful life, $50,000 salvage value, $800,000 cost
Equipment, 12-year estimated useful life, $10,000 salvage value, $100,000 cost

The building has been depreciated under the double-declining balance method through 2004. In 2005, the company decided to switch to the straight-line method of depreciation. Jackson also decided to change the total useful life of the equipment to 9 years, with a salvage value of $5,000 at the end of that time. The equipment is depreciated using the straight-line method.

Instructions

(a) Compute the cumulative effect of the change in accounting principle for 2005.
(b) Prepare the journal entry(ies) necessary to record the changes made in 2005.
(c) Compute depreciation expense on the equipment for 2005.

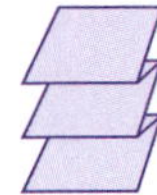

E22-4 (Change in Estimate—Depreciation) Peter M. Dell Co. purchased equipment for $510,000 which was estimated to have a useful life of 10 years with a salvage value of $10,000 at the end of that time. Depreciation has been entered for 7 years on a straight-line basis. In 2005, it is determined that the total estimated life should be 15 years with a salvage value of $5,000 at the end of that time.

Instructions

(a) Prepare the entry (if any) to correct the prior years' depreciation.
(b) Prepare the entry to record depreciation for 2005.

E22-5 (Change in Principle—Depreciation) Gerald Englehart Industries changed from the double-declining balance to the straight-line method in 2005 on all its plant assets. For tax purposes, assume that the amount of tax depreciation is higher than the double-declining balance depreciation for each of the 3 years. The appropriate information related to this change is as follows.

Year	Double-Declining Balance Depreciation	Straight-Line Depreciation	Difference
2003	$250,000	$125,000	$125,000
2004	225,000	125,000	100,000
2005	202,500	125,000	77,500

Net income for 2004 was reported at $270,000. Net income for 2005 was reported at $300,000, excluding any adjustment for the cumulative effect of a change in depreciation methods. The straight-line method of depreciation was employed in computing net income for 2005.

Instructions

(a) Assuming a tax rate of 34%, what is the amount of the cumulative effect adjustment in 2005?
(b) Prepare the journal entry(ies) to record the cumulative effect adjustment in the accounting records.
(c) Starting with income before cumulative effect of change in accounting principle, prepare the remaining portion of the income statement for 2004 and 2005. Indicate the pro forma net income that should be reported. Ignore per share computations and note disclosures.

E22-6 (Change in Principle—Depreciation) At the end of fiscal 2005, management of Carol Dilbeck Manufacturing Company has decided to change its depreciation method from the double-declining balance method to the straight-line method for financial reporting purposes. For federal income taxes the company will continue to use the MACRS method. The income tax rate for all years is 30%. At the end of fiscal 2005, the company has 200,000 common shares issued and outstanding. Information regarding depreciation expense and income after income taxes is as follows.

Depreciation expense to date under:

	MACRS	Straight-Line	Double-Declining Balance
Pre-2004	$1,000,000	$400,000	$950,000
2004	300,000	150,000	260,000
2005	280,000	140,000	250,000

Reported income after income taxes:

2004	$1,200,000
2005	1,400,000

Instructions

(a) Prepare the journal entries to record the change in accounting method in 2005 and indicate how the change in depreciation method would be reported in the income statement of 2005. Also indicate how earnings per share would be disclosed. (*Hint:* Adjust Deferred Tax Liability account.)
(b) Show the amount of depreciation expense to be reported in 2005.

E22-7 (Change in Principle—Long-term Contracts) Pam Erickson Construction Company changed from the completed-contract to the percentage-of-completion method of accounting for long-term construction contracts during 2005. For tax purposes, the company employs the completed-contract method and will continue this approach in the future. (*Hint:* Adjust all tax consequences through the Deferred Tax Liability account.) The appropriate information related to this change is as follows.

	Pretax Income from:		
	Percentage-of-Completion	Completed-Contract	Difference
2004	$780,000	$590,000	$190,000
2005	700,000	480,000	220,000

Instructions

(a) Assuming that the tax rate is 35%, what is the amount of net income that would be reported in 2005?

(b) What entry(ies) are necessary to adjust the accounting records for the change in accounting principle?

E22-8 (Various Changes in Principle—Inventory Methods) Below is the net income of Anita Ferreri Instrument Co., a private corporation, computed under the three inventory methods using a periodic system.

	FIFO	Average Cost	LIFO
2002	$26,000	$24,000	$20,000
2003	30,000	25,000	21,000
2004	28,000	27,000	24,000
2005	34,000	30,000	26,000

Instructions

(Ignore tax considerations.)

(a) Assume that in 2005 Ferreri decided to change from the FIFO method to the average cost method of pricing inventories. Prepare the journal entry necessary for the change that took place during 2005, and show all the appropriate information needed for reporting on a comparative basis.

(b) Assume that in 2005 Ferreri, which had been using the LIFO method since incorporation in 2002, changed to the FIFO method of pricing inventories. Prepare the journal entry necessary for the change, and show all the appropriate information needed for reporting on a comparative basis.

E22-9 (Change in Principle—Inventory Methods) Holder-Webb Company began operations on January 1, 2002, and uses the average cost method of pricing inventory. Management is contemplating a change in inventory methods for 2005. The following information is available for the years 2002–2004.

	Net Income Computed Using		
	Average Cost Method	FIFO Method	LIFO Method
2002	$15,000	$19,000	$12,000
2003	18,000	23,000	14,000
2004	20,000	25,000	17,000

Instructions

(a) Prepare the journal entry necessary to record a change from the average cost method to the FIFO method in 2005.

(b) Show the comparative income statements for 2004 and 2005, starting with income before the cumulative effect of change in accounting principle. Assume net income for 2005 was $32,000.

(c) Assume Holder-Webb Company used the LIFO method instead of the average cost method during the years 2002–2004. In 2005, Holder-Webb changed to the FIFO method. Prepare the journal entry necessary to record the change in principle.

E22-10 (Error Correction Entries) The first audit of the books of Bruce Gingrich Company was made for the year ended December 31, 2005. In examining the books, the auditor found that certain items had been overlooked or incorrectly handled in the last 3 years. These items are:

1. At the beginning of 2003, the company purchased a machine for $510,000 (salvage value of $51,000) that had a useful life of 6 years. The bookkeeper used straight-line depreciation, but failed to deduct the salvage value in computing the depreciation base for the 3 years.
2. At the end of 2004, the company failed to accrue sales salaries of $45,000.
3. A tax lawsuit that involved the year 2003 was settled late in 2005. It was determined that the company owed an additional $85,000 in taxes related to 2003. The company did not record a liability in 2003 or 2004 because the possibility of loss was considered remote, and charged the $85,000 to a loss account in 2005.
4. Gingrich Company purchased a copyright from another company early in 2003 for $45,000. Gingrich had not amortized the copyright because its value had not diminished. The copyright has a useful life at purchase of 20 years.

5. In 2005, the company changed its basis of inventory pricing from FIFO to LIFO. The cumulative effect of this change was to decrease net income by $71,000. The company debited this cumulative effect to Retained Earnings. LIFO was used in computing income for 2005.
6. In 2005, the company wrote off $87,000 of inventory considered to be obsolete; this loss was charged directly to Retained Earnings.

Instructions

Prepare the journal entries necessary in 2005 to correct the books, assuming that the books have not been closed. Disregard effects of corrections on income tax.

E22-11 (Change in Principle and Error; Financial Statements) Presented below are the comparative statements for Denise Habbe Inc.

	2005	2004
Sales	$340,000	$270,000
Cost of sales	200,000	142,000
Gross profit	140,000	128,000
Expenses	88,000	50,000
Net income	$ 52,000	$ 78,000
Retained earnings (Jan. 1)	$125,000	$ 72,000
Net income	52,000	78,000
Dividends	(30,000)	(25,000)
Retained earnings (Dec. 31)	$147,000	$125,000

The following additional information is provided:

1. In 2005, Denise Habbe Inc. decided to switch its depreciation method from sum-of-the-years'-digits to the straight-line method. The expense for the two depreciation methods for the assets involved is:

	2005	2004
Sum-of-the-years'-digits	$30,000[a]	$40,000
Straight-line	25,000	25,000

[a]The 2005 income statement contains depreciation expense of $30,000.

2. In 2005, the company discovered that the ending inventory for 2004 was overstated by $24,000; ending inventory for 2005 is correctly stated.

Instructions

(a) Prepare the revised income and retained earnings statement for 2004 and 2005, assuming comparative statements. (Ignore income tax effects.) Do not prepare footnotes or pro forma amounts.

(b) Prepare the revised income and retained earnings statement for 2005, assuming a noncomparative presentation. (Ignore income tax effects.) Do not prepare footnotes or pro forma amounts.

E22-12 (Error Analysis and Correcting Entry) You have been engaged to review the financial statements of Linette Gottschalk Corporation. In the course of your examination you conclude that the bookkeeper hired during the current year is not doing a good job. You notice a number of irregularities as follows.

1. Year-end wages payable of $3,400 were not recorded because the bookkeeper thought that "they were immaterial."
2. Accrued vacation pay for the year of $31,100 was not recorded because the bookkeeper "never heard that you had to do it."
3. Insurance for a 12-month period purchased on November 1 of this year was charged to insurance expense in the amount of $2,640 because "the amount of the check is about the same every year."
4. Reported sales revenue for the year is $2,120,000. This includes all sales taxes collected for the year. The sales tax rate is 6%. Because the sales tax is forwarded to the state's Department of Revenue, the Sales Tax Expense account is debited. The bookkeeper thought that "the sales tax is a selling expense." At the end of the current year, the balance in the Sales Tax Expense account is $103,400.

Instructions

Prepare the necessary correcting entries, assuming that Gottschalk uses a calendar-year basis.

E22-13 (Error Analysis and Correcting Entry) The reported net incomes for the first 2 years of Sandra Gustafson Products, Inc., were as follows: 2004, $147,000; 2005, $185,000. Early in 2006, the following errors were discovered.

1. Depreciation of equipment for 2004 was overstated $17,000.
2. Depreciation of equipment for 2005 was understated $38,500.
3. December 31, 2004, inventory was understated $50,000.
4. December 31, 2005, inventory was overstated $16,200.

Instructions

Prepare the correcting entry necessary when these errors are discovered. Assume that the books are closed. (Ignore income tax considerations.)

E22-14 (Error Analysis) Peter Henning Tool Company's December 31 year-end financial statements contained the following errors.

	December 31, 2004	December 31, 2005
Ending inventory	$9,600 understated	$8,100 overstated
Depreciation expense	$2,300 understated	—

An insurance premium of $66,000 was prepaid in 2004 covering the years 2004, 2005, and 2006. The entire amount was charged to expense in 2004. In addition, on December 31, 2005, fully depreciated machinery was sold for $15,000 cash, but the entry was not recorded until 2006. There were no other errors during 2004 or 2005, and no corrections have been made for any of the errors. (Ignore income tax considerations.)

Instructions

(a) Compute the total effect of the errors on 2005 net income.
(b) Compute the total effect of the errors on the amount of Henning's working capital at December 31, 2005.
(c) Compute the total effect of the errors on the balance of Henning's retained earnings at December 31, 2005.

E22-15 (Error Analysis; Correcting Entries) A partial trial balance of Julie Hartsack Corporation is as follows on December 31, 2005.

	Dr.	Cr.
Supplies on hand	$ 2,700	
Accrued salaries and wages		$ 1,500
Interest receivable on investments	5,100	
Prepaid insurance	90,000	
Unearned rent		–0–
Accrued interest payable		15,000

Additional adjusting data:

1. A physical count of supplies on hand on December 31, 2005, totaled $1,100.
2. Through oversight, the Accrued Salaries and Wages account was not changed during 2005. Accrued salaries and wages on December 31, 2005, amounted to $4,400.
3. The Interest Receivable on Investments account was also left unchanged during 2005. Accrued interest on investments amounts to $4,350 on December 31, 2005.
4. The unexpired portions of the insurance policies totaled $65,000 as of December 31, 2005.
5. $28,000 was received on January 1, 2005 for the rent of a building for both 2005 and 2006. The entire amount was credited to rental income.
6. Depreciation for the year was erroneously recorded as $5,000 rather than the correct figure of $50,000.
7. A further review of depreciation calculations of prior years revealed that depreciation of $7,200 was not recorded. It was decided that this oversight should be corrected by a prior period adjustment.

Instructions

(a) Assuming that the books have not been closed, what are the adjusting entries necessary at December 31, 2005? (Ignore income tax considerations.)
(b) Assuming that the books have been closed, what are the adjusting entries necessary at December 31, 2005? (Ignore income tax considerations.)

E22-16 (Error Analysis) The before-tax income for Lonnie Holdiman Co. for 2004 was $101,000 and $77,400 for 2005. However, the accountant noted that the following errors had been made:

1. Sales for 2004 included amounts of $38,200 which had been received in cash during 2004, but for which the related products were delivered in 2005. Title did not pass to the purchaser until 2005.
2. The inventory on December 31, 2004, was understated by $8,640.

3. The bookkeeper in recording interest expense for both 2004 and 2005 on bonds payable made the following entry on an annual basis.

Interest Expense	15,000	
Cash		15,000

The bonds have a face value of $250,000 and pay a stated interest rate of 6%. They were issued at a discount of $15,000 on January 1, 2004, to yield an effective interest rate of 7%. (Assume that the effective-yield method should be used.)

4. Ordinary repairs to equipment had been erroneously charged to the Equipment account during 2004 and 2005. Repairs in the amount of $8,500 in 2004 and $9,400 in 2005 were so charged. The company applies a rate of 10% to the balance in the Equipment account at the end of the year in its determination of depreciation charges.

Instructions

Prepare a schedule showing the determination of corrected income before taxes for 2004 and 2005.

E22-17 (Error Analysis) When the records of Debra Hanson Corporation were reviewed at the close of 2005, the errors listed below were discovered. For each item indicate by a check mark in the appropriate column whether the error resulted in an overstatement, an understatement, or had no effect on net income for the years 2004 and 2005.

	2004			2005		
Item	Over-statement	Under-statement	No Effect	Over-statement	Under-statement	No Effect
1. Failure to record amortization of patent in 2005.						
2. Failure to record the correct amount of ending 2004 inventory. The amount was understated because of an error in calculation.						
3. Failure to record merchandise purchased in 2004. Merchandise was also omitted from ending inventory in 2004 but was not yet sold.						
4. Failure to record accrued interest on notes payable in 2004; that amount was recorded when paid in 2005.						
5. Failure to reflect supplies on hand on balance sheet at end of 2004.						

E22-18 (Accounting for Accounting Changes and Errors) Listed below are various types of accounting changes and errors.

_____ 1. Change in a plant asset's salvage value.
_____ 2. Change due to overstatement of inventory.
_____ 3. Change from sum-of-the-years'-digits to straight-line method of depreciation.
_____ 4. Change from presenting unconsolidated to consolidated financial statements.
_____ 5. Change from LIFO to FIFO inventory method.
_____ 6. Change in the rate used to compute warranty costs.
_____ 7. Change from an unacceptable accounting principle to an acceptable accounting principle.
_____ 8. Change in a patent's amortization period.
_____ 9. Change from completed-contract to percentage-of-completion method on construction contracts.
_____ 10. Change from FIFO to average-cost inventory method.

Instructions

For each change or error, indicate how it would be accounted for using the following code letters:

a. Accounted for currently.
b. Accounted for prospectively.
c. Accounted for retroactively.
d. None of the above.

***E22-19 (Change from Fair Value to Equity)** On January 1, 2004, Barbra Streisand Co. purchased 25,000 shares (a 10% interest) in Elton John Corp. for $1,400,000. At the time, the book value and the fair value of John's net assets were $13,000,000.

On July 1, 2005, Streisand paid $3,040,000 for 50,000 additional shares of John common stock, which represented a 20% investment in John. The fair value of John's identifiable assets net of liabilities was equal to their carrying amount of $14,200,000. As a result of this transaction, Streisand owns 30% of John and can exercise significant influence over John's operating and financial policies. Any excess fair value is attributed to goodwill.

John reported the following net income and declared and paid the following dividends.

	Net Income	Dividend per Share
Year ended 12/31/04	$700,000	None
Six months ended 6/30/05	500,000	None
Six months ended 12/31/05	815,000	$1.55

Instructions

Determine the ending balance that Streisand Co. should report as its investment in John Corp. at the end of 2005.

***E22-20 (Change from Equity to Fair Value)** Dan Aykroyd Corp. was a 30% owner of John Belushi Company, holding 210,000 shares of Belushi's common stock on December 31, 2003. The investment account had the following entries.

Investment in Belushi

1/1/02 Cost	$3,180,000	12/6/02 Dividend received	$150,000
12/31/02 Share of income	390,000	12/5/03 Dividend received	240,000
12/31/03 Share of income	510,000		

On January 2, 2004, Aykroyd sold 126,000 shares of Belushi for $3,440,000, thereby losing its significant influence. During the year 2004 Belushi experienced the following results of operations and paid the following dividends to Aykroyd.

	Belushi Income (Loss)	Dividends Paid to Aykroyd
2004	$300,000	$50,400

At December 31, 2004, the fair value of Belushi shares held by Aykroyd is $1,570,000. This is the first reporting date since the January 2 sale.

Instructions

(a) What effect does the January 2, 2004, transaction have upon Aykroyd's accounting treatment for its investment in Belushi?
(b) Compute the carrying amount in Belushi as of December 31, 2004.
(c) Prepare the adjusting entry on December 31, 2004, applying the fair value method to Aykroyd's long-term investment in Belushi Company securities.

PROBLEMS

P22-1 (Change in Estimate, Principle, and Error Correction) Brueggen Company is in the process of having its financial statements audited for the first time as of December 31, 2004. The auditor has found the following items that occurred in previous years:

1. Brueggen purchased equipment on January 2, 2001, for $65,000. At that time, the equipment had an estimated useful life of 10 years with a $5,000 salvage value. The equipment is depreciated on a straight-line basis. On January 2, 2004, as a result of additional information, the company determined that the equipment had a total estimated useful life of 7 years with a $3,000 salvage value.

2. During 2004 Brueggen changed from the double-declining balance method for its building to the straight-line method. The auditor provided the following computations which present depreciation on both bases.

	2004	2003	2002
Straight-line	$27,000	$27,000	$27,000
Declining-balance	48,600	54,000	60,000

3. Brueggen purchased a machine on July 1, 2002, at a cost of $80,000. The machine has a salvage value of $8,000 and a useful life of 8 years. Brueggen's bookkeeper recorded straight-line depreciation during each year but failed to consider the salvage value.

Instructions

(a) Prepare the necessary journal entries to record each of the preceding changes or errors. The books for 2004 have not been closed.
(b) Compute the 2004 depreciation expense on the equipment.
(c) Show the comparative statements for 2003 and 2004, starting with income before the cumulative effect of change in accounting principle. Income before depreciation expense was $300,000 in 2004, and net income was $210,000 in 2003.

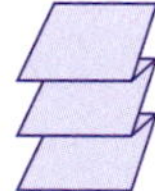

P22-2 (Comprehensive Accounting Change and Error Analysis Problem) On December 31, 2005, before the books were closed, the management and accountants of Eloise Keltner Inc. made the following determinations about three depreciable assets.

1. Depreciable asset A was purchased January 2, 2002. It originally cost $495,000 and, for depreciation purposes, the straight-line method was originally chosen. The asset was originally expected to be useful for 10 years and have a zero salvage value. In 2005, the decision was made to change the depreciation method from straight-line to sum-of-the-years'-digits, and the estimates relating to useful life and salvage value remained unchanged.
2. Depreciable asset B was purchased January 3, 2001. It originally cost $120,000 and, for depreciation purposes, the straight-line method was chosen. The asset was originally expected to be useful for 15 years and have a zero salvage value. In 2005, the decision was made to shorten the total life of this asset to 9 years and to estimate the salvage value at $3,000.
3. Depreciable asset C was purchased January 5, 2001. The asset's original cost was $140,000, and this amount was entirely expensed in 2001. This particular asset has a 10-year useful life and no salvage value. The straight-line method was chosen for depreciation purposes.

Additional data:

1. Income in 2005 before depreciation expense amounted to $400,000.
2. Depreciation expense on assets other than A, B, and C totaled $55,000 in 2005.
3. Income in 2004 was reported at $370,000.
4. Ignore all income tax effects.
5. 100,000 shares of common stock were outstanding in 2004 and 2005.

Instructions

(a) Prepare all necessary entries in 2005 to record these determinations.
(b) Prepare comparative income statements for Eloise Keltner Inc. for 2004 and 2005, starting with income before the cumulative effects of any change in accounting principle.
(c) Prepare comparative retained earnings statements for Eloise Keltner Inc. for 2004 and 2005. The company had retained earnings of $200,000 at December 31, 2003.

P22-3 (Comprehensive Accounting Change and Error Analysis Problem) Larry Kingston Inc. was organized in late 2002 to manufacture and sell hosiery. At the end of its fourth year of operation, the company has been fairly successful, as indicated by the following reported net incomes.

2002	$140,000[a]	2004	$205,000
2003	160,000[b]	2005	276,000

[a]Includes a $12,000 increase because of change in bad debt experience rate.
[b]Includes extraordinary gain of $40,000.

The company has decided to expand operations and has applied for a sizable bank loan. The bank officer has indicated that the records should be audited and presented in comparative statements to facilitate analysis by the bank. Larry Kingston Inc. therefore hired the auditing firm of Check & Doublecheck Co. and has provided the following additional information.

1. In early 2003, Larry Kingston Inc. changed its estimate from 2% to 1% on the amount of bad debt expense to be charged to operations. Bad debt expense for 2002, if a 1% rate had been used, would have been $12,000. The company therefore restated its net income for 2002.
2. In 2005, the auditor discovered that the company had changed its method of inventory pricing from LIFO to FIFO. The effect on the income statements for the previous years is as follows.

	2002	2003	2004	2005
Net income unadjusted—LIFO basis	$140,000	$160,000	$205,000	$276,000
Net income unadjusted—FIFO basis	155,000	165,000	215,000	260,000
	$ 15,000	$ 5,000	$ 10,000	($ 16,000)

3. In 2003, the company changed its method of depreciation from the accelerated method to the straight-line approach. The company used the straight-line method in 2003. The effect on the income statement for the previous year is as follows.

	2002
Net income unadjusted—accelerated method	$140,000
Net income unadjusted—straight-line method	147,000
	$ 7,000

4. In 2005, the auditor discovered that:
   a. The company incorrectly overstated the ending inventory by $11,000 in 2004.
   b. A dispute developed in 2003 with the Internal Revenue Service over the deductibility of entertainment expenses. In 2002, the company was not permitted these deductions, but a tax settlement was reached in 2005 that allowed these expenses. As a result of the court's finding, tax expenses in 2005 were reduced by $60,000.

Instructions

(a) Indicate how each of these changes or corrections should be handled in the accounting records. Ignore income tax considerations.

(b) Present comparative income statements for the years 2002 to 2005, starting with income before extraordinary items. Do not prepare pro-forma amounts. Ignore income tax considerations.

P22-4 (Change in Principle—LIFO to Average Cost; Income Statements—Periodic) The management of Scott Kreiter Instrument Company had concluded, with the concurrence of its independent auditors, that results of operations would be more fairly presented if Kreiter changed its method of pricing inventory from last-in, first-out (LIFO) to average cost in 2004. Given below is the 5-year summary of income and a schedule of what the inventories might have been if stated on the average cost method.

SCOTT KREITER INSTRUMENT COMPANY
STATEMENT OF INCOME AND RETAINED EARNINGS
FOR THE YEARS ENDED MAY 31

	2000	2001	2002	2003	2004
Sales—net	$13,964	$15,506	$16,673	$18,221	$18,898
Cost of goods sold					
Beginning inventory	1,000	1,100	1,000	1,115	1,237
Purchases	13,000	13,900	15,000	15,900	17,100
Ending inventory	(1,100)	(1,000)	(1,115)	(1,237)	(1,369)
Total	12,900	14,000	14,885	15,778	16,968
Gross profit	1,064	1,506	1,788	2,443	1,930
Administrative expenses	700	763	832	907	989
Income before taxes	364	743	956	1,536	941
Income taxes (50%)	182	372	478	768	471
Net income	182	371	478	768	470
Retained earnings—beginning	1,206	1,388	1,759	2,237	3,005
Retained earnings—ending	$ 1,388	$ 1,759	$ 2,237	$ 3,005	$ 3,475
Earnings per share	$1.82	$3.71	$4.78	$7.68	$4.70

Schedule of Inventory Balances Using Average Cost Method
Year Ended May 31

1999	2000	2001	2002	2003	2004
$950	$1,124	$1,091	$1,270	$1,480	$1,699

Instructions

Prepare comparative statements for the 5 years, assuming that Kreiter changed its method of inventory pricing to average cost. Indicate the effects on net income and earnings per share for the years involved. (All amounts except EPS are rounded up to the nearest dollar.)

P22-5 (Error Corrections) You have been assigned to examine the financial statements of Vickie L. Lemke Company for the year ended December 31, 2005. You discover the following situations.

1. Depreciation of $3,200 for 2005 on delivery vehicles was not recorded.
2. The physical inventory count on December 31, 2004, improperly excluded merchandise costing $19,000 that had been temporarily stored in a public warehouse. Lemke uses a periodic inventory system.
3. The physical inventory count on December 31, 2005, improperly included merchandise with a cost of $8,500 that had been recorded as a sale on December 27, 2005, and held for the customer to pick up on January 4, 2006.
4. A collection of $5,600 on account from a customer received on December 31, 2005, was not recorded until January 2, 2006.
5. In 2005, the company sold for $3,700 fully depreciated equipment that originally cost $22,000. The company credited the proceeds from the sale to the Equipment account.
6. During November 2005, a competitor company filed a patent-infringement suit against Lemke claiming damages of $220,000. The company's legal counsel has indicated that an unfavorable verdict is probable and a reasonable estimate of the court's award to the competitor is $125,000. The company has not reflected or disclosed this situation in the financial statements.
7. Lemke has a portfolio of trading securities. No entry has been made to adjust to market. Information on cost and market value is as follows.

	Cost	Market
December 31, 2004	$95,000	$95,000
December 31, 2005	$84,000	$82,000

8. At December 31, 2005, an analysis of payroll information shows accrued salaries of $12,200. The Accrued Salaries Payable account had a balance of $16,000 at December 31, 2005, which was unchanged from its balance at December 31, 2004.
9. A large piece of equipment was purchased on January 3, 2005, for $32,000 and was charged to Repairs Expense. The equipment is estimated to have a service life of 8 years and no residual value. Lemke normally uses the straight-line depreciation method for this type of equipment.
10. A $15,000 insurance premium paid on July 1, 2004, for a policy that expires on June 30, 2007, was charged to insurance expense.
11. A trademark was acquired at the beginning of 2004 for $50,000. No amortization has been recorded since its acquisition. The maximum allowable amortization period is 10 years.

Instructions

Assume the trial balance has been prepared but the books have not been closed for 2005. Assuming all amounts are material, prepare journal entries showing the adjustments that are required. (Ignore income tax considerations.)

P22-6 (Error Corrections and Changes in Principle) Patricia Voga Company is in the process of adjusting and correcting its books at the end of 2005. In reviewing its records, the following information is compiled.

1. Voga has failed to accrue sales commissions payable at the end of each of the last 2 years, as follows.

December 31, 2004	$4,000
December 31, 2005	$2,500

2. In reviewing the December 31, 2005, inventory, Voga discovered errors in its inventory-taking procedures that have caused inventories for the last 3 years to be incorrect, as follows.

December 31, 2003	Understated	$16,000
December 31, 2004	Understated	$21,000
December 31, 2005	Overstated	$ 6,700

Voga has already made an entry that established the incorrect December 31, 2005, inventory amount.

3. At December 31, 2005, Voga decided to change the depreciation method on its office equipment from double-declining balance to straight-line. Assume that tax depreciation is higher than the double-declining depreciation taken for each period. The following information is available. (The tax rate is 40%.)

	Double-Declining Balance	Straight-Line	Pretax Difference	Tax Effect	Difference, Net of Tax
Prior to 2005	$70,000	$40,000	$30,000	$12,000	$18,000
2005	12,000	10,000	2,000	800	1,200

Voga has already recorded the 2005 depreciation expense using the double-declining balance method.

4. Before 2005, Voga accounted for its income from long-term construction contracts on the completed-contract basis. Early in 2005, Voga changed to the percentage-of-completion basis for both accounting and tax purposes. Income for 2005 has been recorded using the percentage-of-completion method. The income tax rate is 40%. The following information is available.

	Pretax Income	
	Percentage-of-Completion	Completed-Contract
Prior to 2005	$150,000	$95,000
2005	60,000	20,000

Instructions

Prepare the journal entries necessary at December 31, 2005, to record the above corrections and changes. The books are still open for 2005. Voga has not yet recorded its 2005 income tax expense and payable amounts so current year-tax effects may be ignored. Prior-year tax effects must be considered in items 3 and 4.

P22-7 (Change in Principle) Plato Corporation performs year-end planning in November of each year before their calendar year ends in December. The preliminary estimated net income is $3 million. The CFO, Mary Sheets, meets with the company president, S. A. Plato, to review the projected numbers. She presents the following projected information.

PLATO CORPORATION
PROJECTED INCOME STATEMENT
FOR THE YEAR ENDED DECEMBER 31, 2004

Sales		$29,000,000
Cost of goods sold	$14,000,000	
Depreciation	2,600,000	
Operating expenses	6,400,000	23,000,000
Income before income taxes		$ 6,000,000
Provision for income taxes		3,000,000
Net income		$ 3,000,000

PLATO CORPORATION
SELECTED BALANCE SHEET INFORMATION
AT DECEMBER 31, 2004

Estimated cash balance	$ 5,000,000
Available-for-sale securities (at cost)	10,000,000
Security fair value adjustment account (1/1/04)	200,000

Estimated market value at December 31, 2004:

Security	Cost	Estimated Market
A	$ 2,000,000	$ 2,200,000
B	4,000,000	3,900,000
C	3,000,000	3,000,000
D	1,000,000	2,800,000
Total	$10,000,000	$11,900,000

Other information at December 31, 2004:

Equipment	$3,000,000
Accumulated depreciation (5-year SL)	1,200,000
New robotic equipment (purchased 1/1/04)	5,000,000
Accumulated depreciation (5-year DDB)	2,000,000

The corporation has never used robotic equipment before, and Sheets assumed an accelerated method because of the rapidly changing technology in robotic equipment. The company normally uses straight-line depreciation for production equipment.

Plato explains to Sheets that it is important for the corporation to show an $8,000,000 net income before taxes because Plato receives a $1,000,000 bonus if the income before taxes and bonus reaches $8,000,000. He also cautions that he will not pay more than $3,000,000 in income taxes to the government.

Instructions

(a) What can Sheets do within GAAP to accommodate the president's wishes to achieve $8,000,000 income before taxes and bonus? Present the revised income statement based on your decision.

(b) Are the actions ethical? Who are the stakeholders in this decision, and what effect does Sheets' actions have on their interests?

P22-8 (Comprehensive Error Analysis) On March 5, 2005, you were hired by Gretchen Hollenbeck Inc., a closely held company, as a staff member of its newly created internal auditing department. While reviewing the company's records for 2004 and 2005, you discover that no adjustments have yet been made for the items listed below.

Items

1. Interest income of $14,100 was not accrued at the end of 2003. It was recorded when received in February 2004.
2. A computer costing $8,000 was expensed when purchased on July 1, 2003. It is expected to have a 4-year life with no salvage value. The company typically uses straight-line depreciation for all fixed assets.
3. Research and development costs of $33,000 were incurred early in 2003. They were capitalized and were to be amortized over a 3-year period. Amortization of $11,000 was recorded for 2003 and $11,000 for 2004.
4. On January 2, 2003, Hollenbeck leased a building for 5 years at a monthly rental of $8,000. On that date, the company paid the following amounts, which were expensed when paid.

Security deposit	$25,000
First month's rent	8,000
Last month's rent	8,000
	$41,000

5. The company received $30,000 from a customer at the beginning of 2003 for services that it is to perform evenly over a 3-year period beginning in 2003. None of the amount received was reported as unearned revenue at the end of 2003.
6. Merchandise inventory costing $18,200 was in the warehouse at December 31, 2003, but was incorrectly omitted from the physical count at that date. The company uses the periodic inventory method.

Instructions

Indicate the effect of any errors on the net income figure reported on the income statement for the year ending December 31, 2003, and the retained earnings figure reported on the balance sheet at December 31, 2004. Assume all amounts are material, and ignore income tax effects. Using the following format, enter the appropriate dollar amounts in the appropriate columns. Consider each item independent of the other items. It is not necessary to total the columns on the grid.

	Net Income for 2003		Retained Earnings at 12/31/04	
Item	Understated	Overstated	Understated	Overstated

(CIA adapted)

P22-9 (Error Analysis) Mary Keeton Corporation has used the accrual basis of accounting for several years. A review of the records, however, indicates that some expenses and revenues have been handled on a cash basis because of errors made by an inexperienced bookkeeper. Income statements prepared by the bookkeeper reported $29,000 net income for 2004 and $37,000 net income for 2005. Further examination of the records reveals that the following items were handled improperly.

1. Rent was received from a tenant in December 2004. The amount, $1,300, was recorded as income at that time even though the rental pertained to 2005.
2. Wages payable on December 31 have been consistently omitted from the records of that date and have been entered as expenses when paid in the following year. The amounts of the accruals recorded in this manner were:

December 31, 2003	$1,100
December 31, 2004	1,500
December 31, 2005	940

3. Invoices for office supplies purchased have been charged to expense accounts when received. Inventories of supplies on hand at the end of each year have been ignored, and no entry has been made for them.

December 31, 2003	$1,300
December 31, 2004	740
December 31, 2005	1,420

Instructions

Prepare a schedule that will show the corrected net income for the years 2004 and 2005. All items listed should be labeled clearly. (Ignore income tax considerations.)

P22-10 (Error Analysis and Correcting Entries) You have been asked by a client to review the records of Larry Landers Company, a small manufacturer of precision tools and machines. Your client is interested in buying the business, and arrangements have been made for you to review the accounting records. Your examination reveals the following.

1. Landers Company commenced business on April 1, 2002, and has been reporting on a fiscal year ending March 31. The company has never been audited, but the annual statements prepared by the bookkeeper reflect the following income before closing and before deducting income taxes.

Year Ended March 31	Income Before Taxes
2003	$ 71,600
2004	111,400
2005	103,580

2. A relatively small number of machines have been shipped on consignment. These transactions have been recorded as ordinary sales and billed as such. On March 31 of each year, machines billed and in the hands of consignees amounted to:

2003	$6,500
2004	none
2005	5,590

Sales price was determined by adding 30% to cost. Assume that the consigned machines are sold the following year.

3. On March 30, 2004, two machines were shipped to a customer on a C.O.D. basis. The sale was not entered until April 5, 2004, when cash was received for $6,100. The machines were not included in the inventory at March 31, 2004. (Title passed on March 30, 2004.)
4. All machines are sold subject to a 5-year warranty. It is estimated that the expense ultimately to be incurred in connection with the warranty will amount to ½ of 1% of sales. The company has charged an expense account for warranty costs incurred.

   Sales per books and warranty costs were as follows.

		Warranty Expense for Sales Made In			
Year Ended March 31	Sales	2003	2004	2005	Total
2003	$ 940,000	$760			$ 760
2004	1,010,000	360	$1,310		1,670
2005	1,795,000	320	1,620	$1,910	3,850

5. A review of the corporate minutes reveals the manager is entitled to a bonus of ½ of 1% of the income before deducting income taxes and the bonus. The bonuses have never been recorded or paid.
6. Bad debts have been recorded on a direct writeoff basis. Experience of similar enterprises indicates that losses will approximate ¼ of 1% of sales. Bad debts written off were:

	Bad Debts Incurred on Sales Made In			
	2003	2004	2005	Total
2003	$750			$ 750
2004	800	$ 520		1,320
2005	350	1,800	$1,700	3,850

7. The bank deducts 6% on all contracts financed. Of this amount, ½% is placed in a reserve to the credit of Landers Company that is refunded to Landers as finance contracts are paid in full. The reserve established by the bank has not been reflected in the books of Landers. The excess of credits over debits (net increase) to the reserve account with Landers on the books of the bank for each fiscal year were as follows.

2003	$ 3,000
2004	3,900
2005	5,100
	$12,000

8. Commissions on sales have been entered when paid. Commissions payable on March 31 of each year were as follows.

2003	$1,400
2004	800
2005	1,120

Instructions

(a) Present a schedule showing the revised income before income taxes for each of the years ended March 31, 2003, 2004, and 2005. Make computations to the nearest whole dollar.

(b) Prepare the journal entry or entries you would give the bookkeeper to correct the books. Assume the books have not yet been closed for the fiscal year ended March 31, 2004. Disregard correction of income taxes.

(AICPA adapted)

***P22-11 (Fair Value to Equity Method with Goodwill)** On January 1, 2003, Latoya Inc. paid $700,000 for 10,000 shares of Jones Company's voting common stock, which was a 10% interest in Jones. At that date the net assets of Jones totaled $6,000,000. The fair values of all of Jones' identifiable assets and liabilities were equal to their book values. Latoya does not have the ability to exercise significant influence over the operating and financial policies of Jones. Latoya received dividends of $2.00 per share from Jones on October 1, 2003. Jones reported net income of $500,000 for the year ended December 31, 2003.

On July 1, 2004, Latoya paid $2,325,000 for 30,000 additional shares of Jones Company's voting common stock which represents a 30% investment in Jones. The fair values of all of Jones' identifiable assets net of liabilities were equal to their book values of $6,550,000. As a result of this transaction, Latoya has the ability to exercise significant influence over the operating and financial policies of Jones. Latoya received dividends of $2.00 per share from Jones on April 1, 2004, and $2.50 per share on October 1, 2004. Jones reported net income of $650,000 for the year ended December 31, 2004, and $400,000 for the 6 months ended December 31, 2004.

Instructions

(a) Prepare a schedule showing the income or loss before income taxes for the year ended December 31, 2003, that Latoya should report from its investment in Jones in its income statement issued in March 2004.

(b) During March 2005, Latoya issues comparative financial statements for 2003 and 2004. Prepare schedules showing the income or loss before income taxes for the years ended December 31, 2003 and 2004, that Latoya should report from its investment in Jones.

(AICPA adapted)

***P22-12 (Change from Fair Value to Equity Method)** On January 3, 2002, Calvin Company purchased for $500,000 cash a 10% interest in Coolidge Corp. On that date the net assets of Coolidge had a book value of $3,750,000. The excess of cost over the underlying equity in net assets is attributable to undervalued depreciable assets having a remaining life of 10 years from the date of Calvin's purchase.

The fair value of Calvin's investment in Coolidge securities is as follows: December 31, 2002, $570,000, and December 31, 2003, $515,000.

On January 2, 2003, Calvin purchased an additional 30% of Coolidge's stock for $1,545,000 cash when the book value of Coolidge's net assets was $4,150,000. The excess was attributable to depreciable assets having a remaining life of 8 years.

During 2002, 2003, and 2004 the following occurred.

	Coolidge Net Income	Dividends Paid by Coolidge to Calvin
2002	$350,000	$15,000
2003	400,000	20,000
2004	550,000	70,000

Instructions

On the books of Calvin Company prepare all journal entries in 2002, 2003, and 2004 that relate to its investment in Coolidge Corp., reflecting the data above and a change from the fair value method to the equity method.

CONCEPTUAL CASES

C22-1 (Analysis of Various Accounting Changes and Errors) Erin Kramer Inc. has recently hired a new independent auditor, Jodie Larson, who says she wants "to get everything straightened out." Consequently, she has proposed the following accounting changes in connection with Erin Kramer Inc.'s 2005 financial statements.

1. At December 31, 2004, the client had a receivable of $820,000 from Holly Michael Inc. on its balance sheet. Holly Michael Inc. has gone bankrupt, and no recovery is expected. The client proposes to write off the receivable as a prior period item.
2. The client proposes the following changes in depreciation policies.
   - **(a)** For office furniture and fixtures it proposes to change from a 10-year useful life to an 8-year life. If this change had been made in prior years, retained earnings at December 31, 2004, would have been $250,000 less. The effect of the change on 2005 income alone is a reduction of $60,000.
   - **(b)** For its manufacturing assets the client proposes to change from double-declining balance depreciation to straight-line. If straight-line depreciation had been used for all prior periods, retained earnings would have been $380,800 greater at December 31, 2004. The effect of the change on 2005 income alone is a reduction of $48,800.
   - **(c)** For its equipment in the leasing division the client proposes to adopt the sum-of-the-years'-digits depreciation method. The client had never used SYD before. The first year the client operated a leasing division was 2005. If straight-line depreciation were used, 2005 income would be $110,000 greater.
3. In preparing its 2004 statements, one of the client's bookkeepers overstated ending inventory by $235,000 because of a mathematical error. The client proposes to treat this item as a prior period adjustment.
4. In the past, the client has spread preproduction costs in its furniture division over 5 years. Because its latest furniture is of the "fad" type, it appears that the largest volume of sales will occur during the first 2 years after introduction. Consequently, the client proposes to amortize preproduction costs on a per-unit basis, which will result in expensing most of such costs during the first 2 years after the furniture's introduction. If the new accounting method had been used prior to 2005, retained earnings at December 31, 2004, would have been $375,000 less.
5. For the nursery division the client proposes to switch from FIFO to LIFO inventories because it believes that LIFO will provide a better matching of current costs with revenues. The effect of making this change on 2005 earnings will be an increase of $320,000. The client says that the effect of the change on December 31, 2004, retained earnings cannot be determined.
6. To achieve a better matching of revenues and expenses in its building construction division, the client proposes to switch from the completed-contract method of accounting to the percentage-of-completion method. Had the percentage-of-completion method been employed in all prior years, retained earnings at December 31, 2004, would have been $1,175,000 greater.

Instructions

- **(a)** For each of the changes described above decide whether:
  - **(1)** The change involves an accounting principle, accounting estimate, or correction of an error.
  - **(2)** Restatement of opening retained earnings is required.
- **(b)** Do any of the changes require presentation of pro forma amounts?
- **(c)** What would be the proper adjustment to the December 31, 2004, retained earnings? What would be the "cumulative effect" shown separately in the 2005 income statement?

C22-2 (Analysis of Various Accounting Changes and Errors) Various types of accounting changes can affect the financial statements of a business enterprise differently. Assume that the following list describes changes that have a material effect on the financial statements for the current year of your business enterprise.

1. A change from the completed-contract method to the percentage-of-completion method of accounting for long-term construction-type contracts.
2. A change in the estimated useful life of previously recorded fixed assets as a result of newly acquired information.
3. A change from deferring and amortizing preproduction costs to recording such costs as an expense when incurred because future benefits of the costs have become doubtful. The new accounting method was adopted in recognition of the change in estimated future benefits.
4. A change from including the employer share of FICA taxes with Payroll Tax Expenses to including it with "Retirement benefits" on the income statement.
5. Correction of a mathematical error in inventory pricing made in a prior period.
6. A change from prime costing to full absorption costing for inventory valuation.
7. A change from presentation of statements of individual companies to presentation of consolidated statements.
8. A change in the method of accounting for leases for tax purposes to conform with the financial accounting method. As a result, both deferred and current taxes payable changed substantially.
9. A change from the FIFO method of inventory pricing to the LIFO method of inventory pricing.

Instructions

Identify the type of change that is described in each item above and indicate whether the prior year's financial statements should be restated when presented in comparative form with the current year's statements. Ignore possible pro forma effects.

C22-3 (Analysis of Three Accounting Changes and Errors) Listed below are three independent, unrelated sets of facts relating to accounting changes.

Situation 1

Penelope Millhouse Company is in the process of having its first audit. The company's policy with regard to recognition of revenue is to use the installment method. However, *APB No. 10* states that the installment method of revenue recognition is not a generally accepted accounting principle except in certain circumstances, which are not present here. Millhouse president, A. G. Shumway, is willing to change to an acceptable method.

Situation 2

Cheri Nestor Co. decides in January 2005 to adopt the straight-line method of depreciation for plant equipment. The straight-line method will be used for new acquisitions as well as for previously acquired plant equipment for which depreciation had been provided on an accelerated basis.

Situation 3

Laura Osmund Co. determined that the depreciable lives of its fixed assets are too long at present to fairly match the cost of the fixed assets with the revenue produced. The company decided at the beginning of the current year to reduce the depreciable lives of all of its existing fixed assets by 5 years.

Instructions

For each of the situations described, provide the information indicated below.

(a) Type of accounting change.
(b) Manner of reporting the change under current generally accepted accounting principles including a discussion, where applicable, of how amounts are computed.
(c) Effect of the change on the balance sheet and income statement.

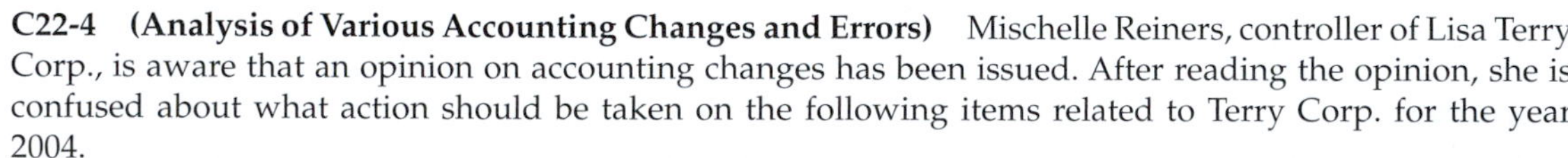

C22-4 (Analysis of Various Accounting Changes and Errors) Mischelle Reiners, controller of Lisa Terry Corp., is aware that an opinion on accounting changes has been issued. After reading the opinion, she is confused about what action should be taken on the following items related to Terry Corp. for the year 2004.

1. In 2004, Terry decided to change its policy on accounting for certain marketing costs. Previously, the company had chosen to defer and amortize all marketing costs over at least 5 years because Terry believed that a return on these expenditures did not occur immediately. Recently, however, the time differential has considerably shortened, and Terry is now expensing the marketing costs as incurred.
2. In 2004, the company examined its entire policy relating to the depreciation of plant equipment. Plant equipment had normally been depreciated over a 15-year period, but recent experience has indicated that the company was incorrect in its estimates and that the assets should be depreciated over a 20-year period.
3. One division of Terry Corp., Ralph Rosentiel Co., has consistently shown an increasing net income from period to period. On closer examination of their operating statement, it is noted that bad debt

expense and inventory obsolescence charges are much lower than in other divisions. In discussing this with the controller of this division, it has been learned that the controller has increased his net income each period by knowingly making low estimates related to the writeoff of receivables and inventory.

4. In 2004, the company purchased new machinery that should increase production dramatically. The company has decided to depreciate this machinery on an accelerated basis, even though other machinery is depreciated on a straight-line basis.
5. All equipment sold by Terry is subject to a 3-year warranty. It has been estimated that the expense ultimately to be incurred on these machines is 1% of sales. In 2004, because of a production breakthrough, it is now estimated that ½ of 1% of sales is sufficient. In 2002 and 2003, warranty expense was computed as $64,000 and $70,000, respectively. The company now believes that these warranty costs should be reduced by 50%.
6. In 2004, the company decided to change its method of inventory pricing from average cost to the FIFO method. The effect of this change on prior years is to increase 2002 income by $65,000 and increase 2003 income by $20,000.

Instructions

Mischelle Reiners has come to you, as her CPA, for advice about the situations above. Prepare a memorandum to Reiners, indicating the appropriate accounting treatment that should be given each of these situations.

C22-5 (Comprehensive Accounting Changes and Error Analysis) Charlene Rydell Manufacturing Co. is preparing its year-end financial statements. The controller, Kimbria Shumway, is confronted with several decisions about statement presentation with regard to the following items.

1. The vice president of sales had indicated that one product line has lost its customer appeal and will be phased out over the next 3 years. Therefore, a decision has been made to lower the estimated lives on related production equipment from the remaining 5 years to 3 years.
2. Estimating the lives of new products in the Leisure Products Division has become very difficult because of the highly competitive conditions in this market. Therefore, the practice of deferring and amortizing preproduction costs has been abandoned in favor of expensing such costs as they are incurred.
3. The Hightone Building was converted from a sales office to offices for the Accounting Department at the beginning of this year. Therefore, the expense related to this building will now appear as an administrative expense rather than a selling expense on the current year's income statement.
4. When the year-end physical inventory adjustment was made for the current year, the controller discovered that the prior year's physical inventory sheets for an entire warehouse were mislaid and excluded from last year's count.
5. The method of accounting used for financial reporting purposes for certain receivables has been approved for tax purposes during the current tax year by the Internal Revenue Service. This change for tax purposes will cause both deferred and current taxes payable to change substantially.
6. Management has decided to switch from the FIFO inventory valuation method to the LIFO inventory valuation method for all inventories.
7. Rydell's Custom Division manufactures large-scale, custom-designed machinery on a contract basis. Management decided to switch from the completed-contract method to the percentage-of-completion method of accounting for long-term contracts.

Instructions

(a) *APB Opinion No. 20*, "Accounting Changes," identifies four types of accounting changes—changes in accounting principle, changes in estimates, changes in entity, and changes due to error. For each of these four types of accounting changes:

   (1) Define the type of change.

   (2) Explain the general accounting treatment required according to *APB Opinion No. 20* with respect to the current year and prior years' financial statements.

(b) For each of the seven changes Rydell Manufacturing Co. has made in the current year, identify and explain whether the change is a change in accounting principle, in estimate, in entity, or due to error. If any of the changes is not one of these four types, explain why.

(CMA adapted)

C22-6 (Change in Principle, Estimate) As a certified public accountant, you have been contacted by Ben Thinken, CEO of Sports-Pro Athletics, Inc., a manufacturer of a variety of athletic equipment. He has asked you how to account for the following changes.

1. Sports-Pro appropriately changed its depreciation method for its production machinery from the double-declining balance method to the production method effective January 1, 2004.

2. Effective January 1, 2004, Sports-Pro appropriately changed the salvage values used in computing depreciation for its office equipment.
3. On December 31, 2004, Sports-Pro appropriately changed the specific subsidiaries constituting the group of companies for which consolidated financial statements are presented.

Instructions

Write a 1–1.5 page letter to Ben Thinken explaining how each of the above changes should be presented in the December 31, 2004, financial statements.

C22-7 (Change in Estimates) Andy Frain is an audit senior of a large public accounting firm who has just been assigned to the Usher Corporation's annual audit engagement. Usher has been a client of Frain's firm for many years. Usher is a fast-growing business in the commercial construction industry. In reviewing the fixed asset ledger, Frain discovered a series of unusual accounting changes, in which the useful lives of assets, depreciated using the straight-line method, were substantially lowered near the midpoint of the original estimate. For example, the useful life of one dump truck was changed from 10 to 6 years during its fifth year of service. Upon further investigation, Andy was told by Vince Lloyd, Usher's accounting manager, "I don't really see your problem. After all, it's perfectly legal to change an accounting estimate. Besides, our CEO likes to see big earnings!"

Instructions

Answer the following questions.

(a) What are the ethical issues concerning Usher's practice of changing the useful lives of fixed assets?
(b) Who could be harmed by Usher's unusual accounting changes?
(c) What should Frain do in this situation?

USING YOUR JUDGMENT

FINANCIAL REPORTING PROBLEM

3M Company

The financial statements of 3M are provided in Appendix 5B or can be accessed on the Take Action! CD.

Instructions

Refer to 3M financial statements and the accompanying notes to answer the following questions.

(a) Were there changes in accounting principles reported by 3M during the three years covered by its income statements (1999–2001)? If so, describe the nature of the change and the year of change.

(b) For each change in accounting principle identify, if possible, the effect of each change on prior years and the effect on operating results in the year of change.

(c) Were any changes in estimates made by 3M in 2001?

COMPARATIVE ANALYSIS CASE

The Coca-Cola Company and PepsiCo, Inc.

Instructions

Go to the Take Action! CD and use information found there to answer the following questions related to The Coca-Cola Company and PepsiCo Inc.

(a) Identify the changes in accounting principles reported by Coca-Cola during the 3 years covered by its income statements (1999–2001). Describe the nature of the change and the year of change.

(b) Identify the changes in accounting principles reported by PepsiCo during the 3 years covered by its income statements (1999–2001). Describe the nature of the change and the year of change.

(c) For each change in accounting principle by Coca-Cola and PepsiCo, identify, if possible, the cumulative effect, the pro forma effect of each change on prior years and the effect on operating results in the year of change.

RESEARCH CASES

Case 1

Instructions

Use an appropriate source to identify two firms that recently reported a *voluntary* change in accounting principle. Answer the following questions with regard to each of the companies.

(a) What is the name of the company? What source did you use to identify the company?

(b) How did the change impact current earnings?

(c) How will the change impact future earnings?

(d) What rationale did the firm's management offer for the change? Do you agree with their stated reasons?

Case 2

The May 7, 2002 edition of the *Wall Street Journal* includes an article by James Bandler and Mark Maremont entitled "KPMG's Work With Xerox Sets Up a New Test for SEC." (Subscribers to **Business Extra** can access the article at that site.)

Instructions

Read the article and answer the following questions.

(a) A change in estimated residual value is usually reported as a change in estimate. What distinguishes a change in estimate from an error correction?

(b) How does the reporting of a change in estimate differ from reporting of an error correction? Why would Xerox prefer to report the change in residual value as an error correction?

(c) The SEC says accounting rules ban any upward adjustments of residual value. Is the SEC correct? Justify your answer, providing citations from generally accepted accounting principles.

PROFESSIONAL SIMULATION

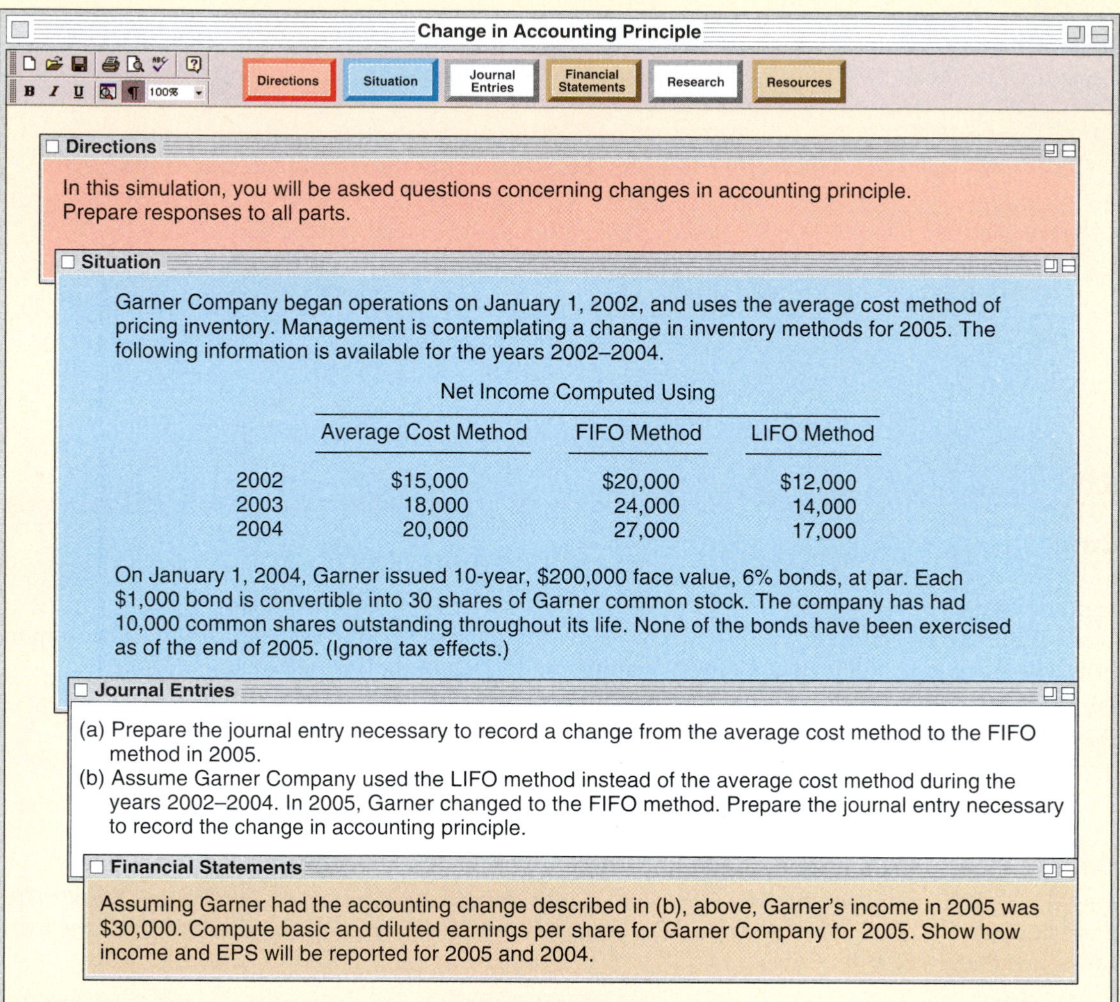

Change in Accounting Principle

Directions | Situation | Journal Entries | Financial Statements | Research | Resources

Directions

In this simulation, you will be asked questions concerning changes in accounting principle. Prepare responses to all parts.

Situation

Garner Company began operations on January 1, 2002, and uses the average cost method of pricing inventory. Management is contemplating a change in inventory methods for 2005. The following information is available for the years 2002–2004.

	Net Income Computed Using		
	Average Cost Method	FIFO Method	LIFO Method
2002	$15,000	$20,000	$12,000
2003	18,000	24,000	14,000
2004	20,000	27,000	17,000

On January 1, 2004, Garner issued 10-year, $200,000 face value, 6% bonds, at par. Each $1,000 bond is convertible into 30 shares of Garner common stock. The company has had 10,000 common shares outstanding throughout its life. None of the bonds have been exercised as of the end of 2005. (Ignore tax effects.)

Journal Entries

(a) Prepare the journal entry necessary to record a change from the average cost method to the FIFO method in 2005.

(b) Assume Garner Company used the LIFO method instead of the average cost method during the years 2002–2004. In 2005, Garner changed to the FIFO method. Prepare the journal entry necessary to record the change in accounting principle.

Financial Statements

Assuming Garner had the accounting change described in (b), above, Garner's income in 2005 was $30,000. Compute basic and diluted earnings per share for Garner Company for 2005. Show how income and EPS will be reported for 2005 and 2004.

Remember to check the **Take Action! CD** and the book's **companion Web site** to find additional resources for this chapter

CHAPTER 23

Statement of Cash Flows

Don't Take Cash Flow for Granted

Investors usually look to net income as a key indicator of a company's financial health and future prospects. The following graph shows the net income of one company over a 7-year period.

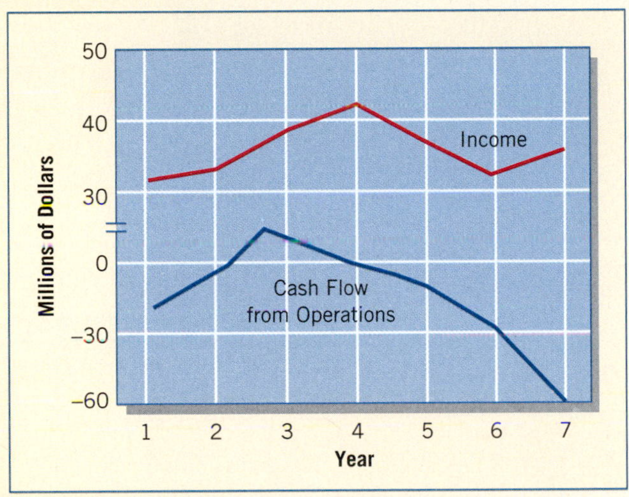

The company showed a pattern of consistent profitability and even some periods of income growth. Between years 1 and 4, net income for this company grew by 32 percent, from $31 million to $41 million. Does this company look like a good investment? Would you expect its profitability to continue? The company had consistently paid dividends and interest. Would you expect it to continue to do so? Investors answered "yes" to all three of these questions, by buying the company's stock.

Eighteen months later, this company—**W. T. Grant**—filed for bankruptcy, in what was then the largest bankruptcy filing in the United States. As indicated by the second line in the graph, the company had experienced several years of negative cash flow from its operations, even though it reported profits. How could this happen? It was partly because the sales that W. T. Grant reported on the income statement were made on credit, and the company was having trouble collecting the receivables from the sales, causing cash flow to be less than the net income. Analysis of the cash flows would have provided an early warning signal of W. T. Grant's operating problems.[1]

[1]Adapted from James A. Largay III and Clyde P. Stickney, "Cash Flows, Ratio Analysis, and the W. T. Grant Company Bankruptcy," *Financial Analysts Journal* (July–August 1980), p. 51.

LEARNING OBJECTIVES

After studying this chapter, you should be able to:

1. **Describe the purpose of the statement of cash flows.**
2. **Identify the major classifications of cash flows.**
3. **Differentiate between net income and net cash flows from operating activities.**
4. **Contrast the direct and indirect methods of calculating net cash flow from operating activities.**
5. **Determine net cash flows from investing and financing activities.**
6. **Prepare a statement of cash flows.**
7. **Identify sources of information for a statement of cash flows.**
8. **Identify special problems in preparing a statement of cash flows.**
9. **Explain the use of a work sheet in preparing a statement of cash flows.**

PREVIEW OF CHAPTER 23

As indicated in the opening story, an examination of **W. T. Grant**'s cash flow provided by operations would have shown the significant lack of liquidity and financial inflexibility that eventually caused the company's bankruptcy. The purpose of this chapter is to explain the main components of a statement of cash flows and the types of information it provides. The content and organization of the chapter are as follows.

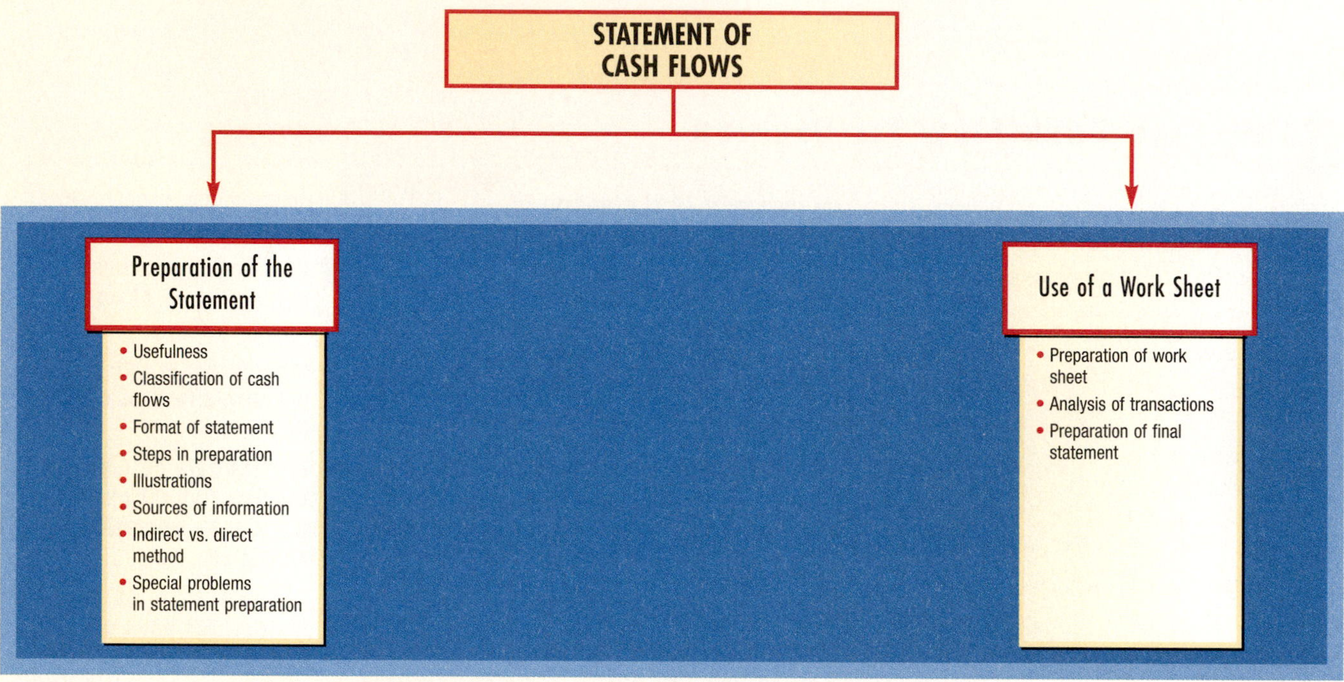

SECTION 1 *PREPARATION OF THE STATEMENT OF CASH FLOWS*

OBJECTIVE 1
Describe the purpose of the statement of cash flows.

The primary purpose of the **statement of cash flows** is to provide information about an entity's cash receipts and cash payments during a period. A secondary objective is to provide information on a cash basis about its operating, investing, and financing activities. **The statement of cash flows therefore reports cash receipts, cash payments, and net change in cash resulting from operating, investing, and financing activities of an enterprise during a period, in a format that reconciles the beginning and ending cash balances.**

USEFULNESS OF THE STATEMENT OF CASH FLOWS

The information in a statement of cash flows should help investors, creditors, and others assess the following:[2]

1. ***The entity's ability to generate future cash flows.*** A primary objective of financial reporting is to provide information that makes it possible to predict the amounts,

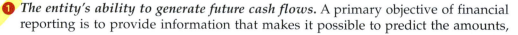

[2]"The Statement of Cash Flows," *Statement of Financial Accounting Standards No. 95* (Stamford, Conn.: FASB, 1987), pars. 4 and 5.

timing, and uncertainty of future cash flows. By examining relationships between items such as sales and net cash flow from operating activities, or net cash flow from operating activities and increases or decreases in cash, it is possible to make better predictions of the amounts, timing, and uncertainty of future cash flows than is possible using accrual basis data.

2 ***The entity's ability to pay dividends and meet obligations.*** Simply put, cash is essential. If a company does not have adequate cash, employees cannot be paid, debts cannot be settled, dividends cannot be paid, and equipment cannot be acquired. A statement of cash flows indicates how cash is used and where it comes from. Employees, creditors, stockholders, and customers should be particularly interested in this statement, because it alone shows the flows of cash in a business.

3 ***The reasons for the difference between net income and net cash flow from operating activities.*** The net income number is important, because it provides information on the success or failure of a business enterprise from one period to another. But some people are critical of accrual-basis net income because estimates must be made to arrive at it. As a result, the reliability of the number is often challenged. Such is not the case with cash. Thus, as illustrated in the opening story, readers of the financial statements benefit from knowing the reasons for the difference between net income and net cash flow from operating activities. Then they can assess for themselves the reliability of the income number.

4 ***The cash and noncash investing and financing transactions during the period.*** By examining a company's investing activities (purchase and sales of assets other than its products) and its financing transactions (borrowings and repayments of borrowings, investments by owners and distributions to owners), a financial statement reader can better understand why assets and liabilities increased or decreased during the period. For example, the following questions might be answered:

How did cash increase when there was a net loss for the period?
How were the proceeds of the bond issue used?
How was the expansion in plant and equipment financed?
Why were dividends not increased?
How was the retirement of debt accomplished?
How much money was borrowed during the year?
Is cash flow greater or less than net income?

CLASSIFICATION OF CASH FLOWS

OBJECTIVE 2
Identify the major classifications of cash flows.

The statement of cash flows classifies cash receipts and cash payments by operating, investing, and financing activities.[3] Transactions and other events characteristic of each kind of activity are as follows.

 **Operating activities** involve the cash effects of transactions that enter into the determination of net income, such as cash receipts from sales of goods and services

[3]The basis recommended by the FASB for the statement of cash flows is actually "cash and cash equivalents." **Cash equivalents** are short-term, highly liquid investments that are both: (a) readily convertible to known amounts of cash, and (b) so near their maturity that they present insignificant risk of changes in interest rates. Generally, only investments with original maturities of 3 months or less qualify under this definition. Examples of cash equivalents are Treasury bills, commercial paper, and money market funds purchased with cash that is in excess of immediate needs.

Although we use the term "cash" throughout our discussion and illustrations in this chapter, we mean cash and cash equivalents when reporting the cash flows and the net increase or decrease in cash.

and cash payments to suppliers and employees for acquisitions of inventory and expenses.

2. **Investing activities** generally involve long-term assets and include (a) making and collecting loans and (b) acquiring and disposing of investments and productive long-lived assets.

3. **Financing activities** involve liability and stockholders' equity items and include (a) obtaining cash from creditors and repaying the amounts borrowed and (b) obtaining capital from owners and providing them with a return on, and a return of, their investment.

Illustration 23-1 classifies the typical cash receipts and payments of a business enterprise according to operating, investing, and financing activities.

ILLUSTRATION 23-1
Classification of Typical Cash Inflows and Outflows

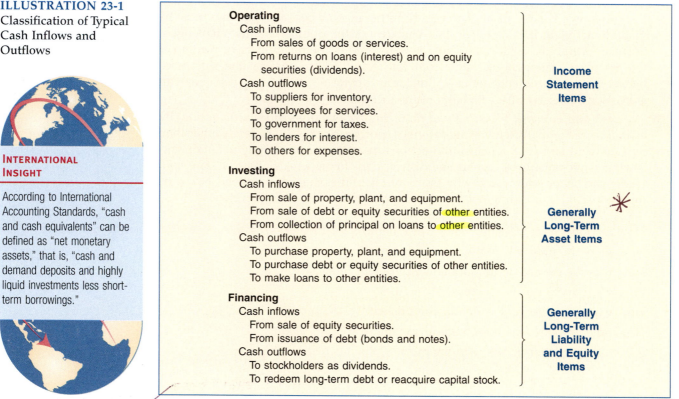

Operating Cash inflows From sales of goods or services. From returns on loans (interest) and on equity securities (dividends). Cash outflows To suppliers for inventory. To employees for services. To government for taxes. To lenders for interest. To others for expenses.	**Income Statement Items**
Investing Cash inflows From sale of property, plant, and equipment. From sale of debt or equity securities of other entities. From collection of principal on loans to other entities. Cash outflows To purchase property, plant, and equipment. To purchase debt or equity securities of other entities. To make loans to other entities.	**Generally Long-Term Asset Items**
Financing Cash inflows From sale of equity securities. From issuance of debt (bonds and notes). Cash outflows To stockholders as dividends. To redeem long-term debt or reacquire capital stock.	**Generally Long-Term Liability and Equity Items**

INTERNATIONAL INSIGHT

According to International Accounting Standards, "cash and cash equivalents" can be defined as "net monetary assets," that is, "cash and demand deposits and highly liquid investments less short-term borrowings."

Some cash flows relating to investing or financing activities are classified as operating activities.[4] For example, receipts of investment income (interest and dividends) and payments of interest to lenders are classified as operating activities. Conversely, some cash flows relating to operating activities are classified as investing or financing activities. For example, the cash received from the sale of property, plant, and equipment at a gain, although reported in the income statement, is classified as an investing activity, and the effects of the related gain would not be included in net cash flow from

[4] For exceptions to the treatment of purchases and sales of loans and securities by banks and brokers, see *Statement of Financial Accounting Standards No. 102* (February 1989) and "Relevance Gained: FASB Modifies Cash Flow Statement Requirements for Banks," by James Don Edwards and Cynthia D. Heagy in *Journal of Accountancy* (June 1991). Banks and brokers are required to classify cash flows from purchases and sales of loans and securities specifically for resale and carried at market value **as operating activities**. This requirement recognizes that for these firms these assets are similar to inventory in other businesses.

operating activities. Likewise, a gain or loss on the payment (extinguishment) of debt would generally be part of the cash outflow related to the repayment of the amount borrowed, and therefore it is a financing activity.

HOW'S MY CASH FLOW?

WHAT DO THE NUMBERS MEAN?

Evaluation of overall cash flow requires examination of the alternative sources of cash flows and of where in the product life cycle a company is. Generally, companies move through several stages of development, which have implications for an evaluation of cash flow. As shown in the graph below, the pattern of cash flows from operating, financing, and investing activities will vary depending on the stage of the product life cycle.

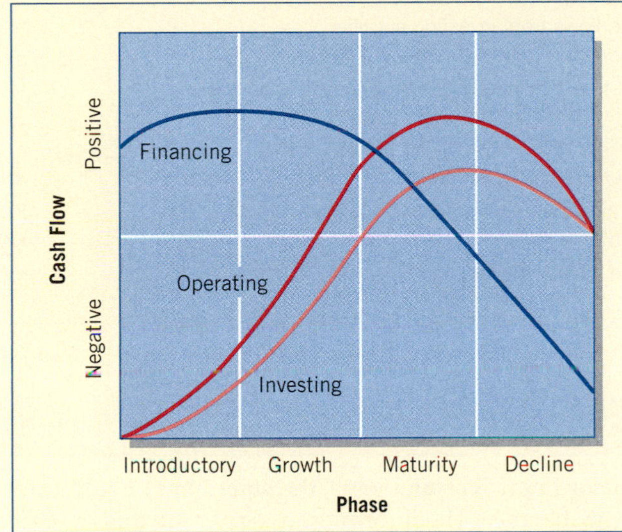

In the introductory phase, the product is likely not generating much revenue (operating cash flow is negative). However, because the company is making heavy investments to get a product off the ground (and paid for with borrowed money), cash flow from investment is negative, and financing cash flows are positive. As the product moves to the growth and maturity phases, these cash flow relationships reverse. The product generates more cash flow from operations, which can be used to cover investments needed to support the product, and less cash is needed from financing. So is a negative operating cash flow bad? Not always. It depends on the product life cycle.

Source: Adapted from Paul D. Kimmel, Jerry J. Weygandt, and Donald E. Kieso, *Financial Accounting: Tools for Business Decision Making*, 2nd ed. (New York: John Wiley & Sons, 2000), p. 602.

FORMAT OF THE STATEMENT OF CASH FLOWS

The three activities discussed in the preceding paragraphs constitute the general format of the statement of cash flows. The cash flows from operating activities section always appears first, followed by the investing section and then the financing activities section. The individual inflows and outflows from investing and financing activities are reported separately. That is, they are reported gross, not netted against one another. Thus, cash outflow from the purchase of property is reported separately from the cash inflow from the sale of property. Similarly, the cash inflow from the issuance of debt is reported separately from the cash outflow from its retirement. The net increase or decrease in cash reported during the period should reconcile the beginning and ending cash balances as reported in the comparative balance sheets.

The skeleton format of the statement of cash flows is presented in Illustration 23-2.

ILLUSTRATION 23-2
Format of the Statement of Cash Flows

COMPANY NAME
STATEMENT OF CASH FLOWS
PERIOD COVERED

Cash flows from operating activities		
Net income		XXX
Adjustments to reconcile net income to net cash provided by operating activities:		
(List of individual items)	XX	XX
Net cash flow from operating activities		XXX
Cash flows from investing activities		
(List of individual inflows and outflows)	XX	
Net cash provided (used) by investing activities		XXX
Cash flows from financing activities		
(List of individual inflows and outflows)	XX	
Net cash provided (used) by financing activities		XXX
Net increase (decrease) in cash		XXX
Cash at beginning of period		XXX
Cash at end of period		XXX

STEPS IN PREPARATION

Unlike the other major financial statements, the statement of cash flows is not prepared from the adjusted trial balance. The information to prepare this statement usually comes from three sources:

Comparative balance sheets provide the amount of the changes in assets, liabilities, and equities from the beginning to the end of the period.

Current income statement data help the reader determine the amount of cash provided by or used by operations during the period.

Selected transaction data from the general ledger provide additional detailed information needed to determine how cash was provided or used during the period.

Preparing the statement of cash flows from the data sources above involves three major steps:

Step 1. Determine the change in cash. This procedure is straightforward because the difference between the beginning and the ending cash balance can be easily computed from an examination of the comparative balance sheets.

Step 2. Determine the net cash flow from operating activities. This procedure is complex: It involves analyzing not only the current year's income statement but also comparative balance sheets and selected transaction data.

Step 3. Determine net cash flows from investing and financing activities. All other changes in the balance sheet accounts must be analyzed to determine their effects on cash.

On the following pages we work through these three steps in the process of preparing the statement of cash flows for a company over several years.

FIRST ILLUSTRATION—2003

To illustrate a statement of cash flows, we will use the **first year of operations** for Tax Consultants Inc. The company started on January 1, 2003, when it issued 60,000 shares of $1 par value common stock for $60,000 cash. The company rented its office space and furniture and equipment, and it performed tax consulting services throughout the first year. The comparative balance sheets at the beginning and end of the year 2003 appear as follows.

ILLUSTRATION 23-3
Comparative Balance Sheets, Tax Consultants Inc., Year 1

TAX CONSULTANTS INC.
COMPARATIVE BALANCE SHEETS

Assets	Dec. 31, 2003	Jan. 1, 2003	Change Increase/Decrease
Cash	$49,000	$–0–	$49,000 Increase
Accounts receivable	36,000	–0–	36,000 Increase
Total	$85,000	$–0–	
Liabilities and Stockholders' Equity			
Accounts payable	$ 5,000	$–0–	$ 5,000 Increase
Common stock ($1 par)	60,000	–0–	60,000 Increase
Retained earnings	20,000	–0–	20,000 Increase
Total	$85,000	$–0–	

The income statement and additional information for Tax Consultants Inc. are as follows.

ILLUSTRATION 23-4
Income Statement, Tax Consultants Inc., Year 1

TAX CONSULTANTS INC.
INCOME STATEMENT
FOR THE YEAR ENDED DECEMBER 31, 2003

Revenues	$125,000
Operating expenses	85,000
Income before income taxes	40,000
Income tax expense	6,000
Net income	$ 34,000

Additional Information
Examination of selected data indicates that a dividend of $14,000 was paid during the year.

Step 1: Determine the Change in Cash

To prepare a statement of cash flows, the first step—**determining the change in cash**—is a simple computation. Tax Consultants Inc. had no cash on hand at the beginning of the year 2003, but $49,000 was on hand at the end of 2003. Thus, the change in cash for 2003 was an increase of $49,000.

The other two steps are more complex and involve additional analysis.

OBJECTIVE 3
Differentiate between net income and net cash flows from operating activities.

Step 2: Determine Net Cash Flow from Operating Activities

A useful starting point in **determining net cash flow from operating activities**[5] is to understand why net income must be converted. Under generally accepted accounting principles, most companies must use the accrual basis of accounting, requiring that

[5]"Net cash flow from operating activities" is a generic phrase, which is replaced in the statement of cash flows with either "Net cash **provided by** operating activities" if operations increase cash or by "Net cash **used by** operating activities" if operations decrease cash.

revenue be recorded when earned and that expenses be recorded when incurred. Net income may include credit sales that have not been collected in cash and expenses incurred that may not have been paid in cash. Thus, under the accrual basis of accounting, net income will not indicate the net cash flow from operating activities.

To arrive at net cash flow from operating activities, it is necessary to report revenues and expenses on a **cash basis. This is done by eliminating the effects of income statement transactions that did not result in a corresponding increase or decrease in cash.** The relationship between net income and net cash flow from operating activities is graphically depicted as follows.

ILLUSTRATION 23-5
Net Income versus Net Cash Flow from Operating Activities

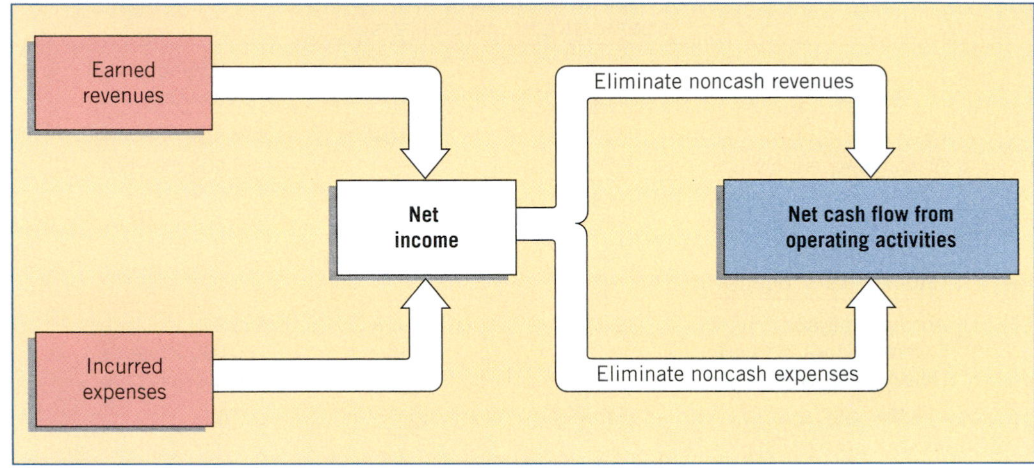

In this chapter, we use the term net income to refer to accrual-based net income.

The conversion of net income to net cash flow from operating activities may be done through either a direct method or an indirect method as explained in the following discussion.

Direct Method

OBJECTIVE 4
Contrast the direct and indirect methods of calculating net cash flow from operating activities.

The **direct method** (also called the income statement method) reports cash receipts and cash disbursements from operating activities. The difference between these two amounts is the net cash flow from operating activities. In other words, the direct method deducts from operating cash receipts the operating cash disbursements. The direct method results in the presentation of a condensed cash receipts and cash disbursements statement.

As indicated from the accrual-based income statement, Tax Consultants Inc. reported revenues of $125,000. However, because the company's accounts receivable increased during 2003 by $36,000, only $89,000 ($125,000 − $36,000) in cash was collected on these revenues. Similarly, Tax Consultants Inc. reported operating expenses of $85,000, but accounts payable increased during the period by $5,000. Assuming that these payables related to operating expenses, cash operating expenses were $80,000 ($85,000 − $5,000). Because no taxes payable exist at the end of the year, the $6,000 income tax expense for 2003 must have been paid in cash during the year. Then the computation of net cash flow from operating activities is as follows.

ILLUSTRATION 23-6
Computation of Net Cash Flow from Operating Activities, Year 1—Direct Method

Cash collected from revenues	$89,000
Cash payments for expenses	80,000
Income before income taxes	9,000
Cash payments for income taxes	6,000
Net cash provided by operating activities	$ 3,000

"Net cash provided by operating activities" is the equivalent of cash-basis net income. ("Net cash used by operating activities" would be equivalent to cash-basis net loss.)

Indirect Method

The **indirect method** (or reconciliation method) starts with net income and converts it to net cash flow from operating activities. In other words, **the indirect method adjusts net income for items that affected reported net income but did not affect cash.** To compute net cash flow from operating activities, noncash charges in the income statement are added back to net income, and noncash credits are deducted. Explanations for the two adjustments to net income in this example—namely, the increases in accounts receivable and accounts payable—are as follows.

Increase in Accounts Receivable—Indirect Method. When accounts receivable increase during the year, revenues on an accrual basis are higher than revenues on a cash basis because goods sold on account are reported as revenues. In other words, operations of the period led to increased revenues, but not all of these revenues resulted in an increase in cash. Some of the increase in revenues resulted in an increase in accounts receivable. To convert net income to net cash flow from operating activities, the increase of $36,000 in accounts receivable must be deducted from net income.

Increase in Accounts Payable—Indirect Method. When accounts payable increase during the year, expenses on an accrual basis are higher than they are on a cash basis because expenses are incurred for which payment has not taken place. To convert net income to net cash flow from operating activities, the increase of $5,000 in accounts payable must be added to net income.

As a result of the accounts receivable and accounts payable adjustments, net cash provided by operating activities is determined to be $3,000 for the year 2003. This computation is shown as follows.

Net income		$34,000
Adjustments to reconcile net income to net cash provided by operating activities:		
Increase in accounts receivable	$(36,000)	
Increase in accounts payable	5,000	(31,000)
Net cash provided by operating activities		$ 3,000

ILLUSTRATION 23-7
Computation of Net Cash Flow from Operating Activities, Year 1—Indirect Method

Note that net cash provided by operating activities is the same whether the direct or the indirect method is used.

PUMPING UP CASH

WHAT DO THE NUMBERS MEAN?

Due to recent concerns about a decline in the quality of earnings, some investors have been focusing on cash flow. And management has an incentive to make operating cash flow look good, because Wall Street has paid a premium for companies that generate a lot of cash from operations, rather than through borrowings. However, similar to earnings, companies have ways to pump up cash flow from operations.

One way that companies can boost their operating cash flow is by securitizing receivables. Recall from Chapter 7 that companies can speed up cash collections by selling their receivables. For example, in 2001 **Oxford Industries**, an apparel company, reported a $74 million increase in cash flow from operations. This seems impressive until you read the fine print, which indicates that a big part of the increase was due to the sale of receivables. As discussed in this section, decreases in accounts receivable increase cash flow from operations. So while it appears that Oxford's core operations have improved, the company really did little more than accelerate collections of its receivables. In fact, without the cash flow boost from the securitizations, Oxford's operating cash flow would have been negative. Thus, just like earnings, cash flow can be of high or low quality.

Source: Adapted from Ann Tergesen, "Cash Flow Hocus Pocus," *Business Week* (July 16, 2002), pp. 130–131.

Step 3: Determine Net Cash Flows from Investing and Financing Activities

OBJECTIVE 5
Determine net cash flows from investing and financing activities.

Once the net cash flow from operating activities is computed, the next step is to determine whether any other changes in balance sheet accounts caused an increase or decrease in cash.

For example, an examination of the remaining balance sheet accounts for Tax Consultants Inc. shows that both common stock and retained earnings have increased. The common stock increase of $60,000 resulted from the issuance of common stock for cash. The issuance of common stock is a receipt of cash from a financing activity and is reported as such in the statement of cash flows. The retained earnings increase of $20,000 is caused by two items:

1. Net income of $34,000 increased retained earnings.
2. Dividends declared of $14,000 decreased retained earnings.

Net income has been converted into net cash flow from operating activities, as explained earlier. The additional data indicate that the dividend was paid. Thus, the dividend payment on common stock is reported as a cash outflow, classified as a financing activity.

Statement of Cash Flows—2003

OBJECTIVE 6
Prepare a statement of cash flows.

We are now ready to prepare the statement of cash flows. The statement starts with the operating activities section. Either the direct or indirect method may be used to report net cash flow from operating activities. The FASB **encourages** the use of the direct method over the indirect method. If the direct method of reporting net cash flow from operating activities is used, the FASB **requires** that the reconciliation of net income to net cash flow from operating activities be provided in a separate schedule. If the indirect method is used, the reconciliation may be either reported within the statement of cash flows or provided in a separate schedule, with the statement of cash flows reporting only the **net** cash flow from operating activities.[6] Therefore, the indirect method, which is also used more extensively in practice,[7] is used throughout this chapter. In doing homework assignments, you should follow instructions for use of either the direct or indirect method. The advantages and disadvantages of these two methods are discussed later in this chapter.

The statement of cash flows for Tax Consultants Inc. is as follows.

ILLUSTRATION 23-8
Statement of Cash Flows, Tax Consultants Inc., Year 1

TAX CONSULTANTS INC.
STATEMENT OF CASH FLOWS
FOR THE YEAR ENDED DECEMBER 31, 2003
INCREASE (DECREASE) IN CASH

Cash flows from operating activities		
Net income		$34,000
Adjustments to reconcile net income to net cash provided by operating activities:		
Increase in accounts receivable	$(36,000)	
Increase in accounts payable	5,000	(31,000)
Net cash provided by operating activities		3,000
Cash flows from financing activities		
Issuance of common stock	60,000	
Payment of cash dividends	(14,000)	
Net cash provided by financing activities		46,000
Net increase in cash		49,000
Cash, January 1, 2003		–0–
Cash, December 31, 2003		$49,000

[6]"The Statement of Cash Flows," pars. 27 and 30.

[7]*Accounting Trends and Techniques—2001* reports that out of its 600 surveyed companies, 593 (approximately 99%) used the indirect method, while only 7 used the direct method.

As indicated, the $60,000 increase in common stock results in a cash inflow from a financing activity. The payment of $14,000 in cash dividends is classified as a use of cash from a financing activity. The $49,000 increase in cash reported in the statement of cash flows agrees with the increase of $49,000 shown as the change in the cash account in the comparative balance sheets.

SECOND ILLUSTRATION—2004

Tax Consultants Inc. continued to grow and prosper during its second year of operations. Land, building, and equipment were purchased, and revenues and earnings increased substantially over the first year. Information related to the second year of operations for Tax Consultants Inc. is presented in Illustrations 23-9 and 23-10.

ILLUSTRATION 23-9
Comparative Balance Sheets, Tax Consultants Inc., Year 2

TAX CONSULTANTS INC.
COMPARATIVE BALANCE SHEETS
DECEMBER 31

Assets	2004	2003	Change Increase/Decrease
Cash	$ 37,000	$49,000	$12,000 Decrease
Accounts receivable	26,000	36,000	10,000 Decrease
Prepaid expenses	6,000	–0–	6,000 Increase
Land	70,000	–0–	70,000 Increase
Building	200,000	–0–	200,000 Increase
Accumulated depreciation—building	(11,000)	–0–	11,000 Increase
Equipment	68,000	–0–	68,000 Increase
Accumulated depreciation—equipment	(10,000)	–0–	10,000 Increase
Total	$386,000	$85,000	
Liabilities and Stockholders' Equity			
Accounts payable	$ 40,000	$ 5,000	$ 35,000 Increase
Bonds payable	150,000	–0–	150,000 Increase
Common stock ($1 par)	60,000	60,000	–0–
Retained earnings	136,000	20,000	116,000 Increase
Total	$386,000	$85,000	

ILLUSTRATION 23-10
Income Statement, Tax Consultants Inc., Year 2

TAX CONSULTANTS INC.
INCOME STATEMENT
FOR THE YEAR ENDED DECEMBER 31, 2004

Revenues		$492,000
Operating expenses (excluding depreciation)	$269,000	
Depreciation expense	21,000	290,000
Income from operations		202,000
Income tax expense		68,000
Net income		$134,000

Additional Information
(a) In 2004, the company paid an $18,000 cash dividend.
(b) The company obtained $150,000 cash through the issuance of long-term bonds.
(c) Land, building, and equipment were acquired for cash.

Step 1: Determine the Change in Cash

To prepare a statement of cash flows from the available information, the first step is to determine the change in cash. As indicated from the information presented, cash decreased $12,000 ($49,000 − $37,000).

Step 2: Determine Net Cash Flow from Operating Activities—Indirect Method

Using the indirect method, we adjust net income of $134,000 on an accrual basis to arrive at net cash flow from operating activities. Explanations for the adjustments to net income are as follows.

Decrease in Accounts Receivable

When accounts receivable decrease during the period, revenues on a cash basis are higher than revenues on an accrual basis, because cash collections are higher than revenues reported on an accrual basis. To convert net income to net cash flow from operating activities, the decrease of $10,000 in accounts receivable must be added to net income.

Increase in Prepaid Expenses

When prepaid expenses (assets) increase during a period, expenses on an accrual-basis income statement are lower than they are on a cash-basis income statement. Expenditures (cash payments) have been made in the current period, but expenses (as charges to the income statement) have been deferred to future periods. To convert net income to net cash flow from operating activities, the increase of $6,000 in prepaid expenses must be deducted from net income. An increase in prepaid expenses results in a decrease in cash during the period.

Increase in Accounts Payable

Like the increase in 2003, the 2004 increase of $35,000 in accounts payable must be added to net income to convert to net cash flow from operating activities. A greater amount of expense was incurred than cash disbursed.

Depreciation Expense (Increase in Accumulated Depreciation)

The purchase of depreciable assets is shown as a use of cash in the investing section in the year of acquisition. The depreciation expense of $21,000 (also represented by the increase in accumulated depreciation) is a noncash charge that is added back to net income to arrive at net cash flow from operating activities. The $21,000 is the sum of the depreciation on the building of $11,000 and the depreciation on the equipment of $10,000.

Other charges to expense for a period that do not require the use of cash, such as the amortization of intangible assets and depletion expense, are treated in the same manner as depreciation. Depreciation and similar noncash charges are frequently listed in the statement as the first adjustments to net income.

As a result of the foregoing items, net cash provided by operating activities is $194,000 as shown in Illustration 23-11.

ILLUSTRATION 23-11
Computation of Net Cash Flow from Operating Activities, Year 2—Indirect Method

Net income		$134,000
Adjustments to reconcile net income to		
net cash provided by operating activities:		
Depreciation expense	$21,000	
Decrease in accounts receivable	10,000	
Increase in prepaid expenses	(6,000)	
Increase in accounts payable	35,000	60,000
Net cash provided by operating activities		$194,000

Step 3: Determine Net Cash Flows from Investing and Financing Activities

After you have determined the items affecting net cash provided by operating activities, the next step involves analyzing the remaining changes in balance sheet accounts. The following accounts were analyzed.

Increase in Land

As indicated from the change in the land account, land of $70,000 was purchased during the period. This transaction is an investing activity that is reported as a use of cash.

Increase in Building and Related Accumulated Depreciation

As indicated in the additional data, and from the change in the building account, an office building was acquired using cash of $200,000. This transaction is a cash outflow reported in the investing section. The accumulated depreciation account increase of $11,000 is fully explained by the depreciation expense entry for the period. As indicated earlier, the reported depreciation expense has no effect on the amount of cash.

Increase in Equipment and Related Accumulated Depreciation

An increase in equipment of $68,000 resulted because equipment was purchased for cash. This transaction should be reported as an outflow of cash from an investing activity. The increase in Accumulated Depreciation—Equipment was explained by the depreciation expense entry for the period.

Increase in Bonds Payable

The bonds payable account increased $150,000. Cash received from the issuance of these bonds represents an inflow of cash from a financing activity.

Increase in Retained Earnings

Retained earnings increased $116,000 during the year. This increase can be explained by two factors: (1) Net income of $134,000 increased retained earnings, and (2) dividends of $18,000 decreased retained earnings. Payment of the dividends is a financing activity that involves a cash outflow.

Statement of Cash Flows—2004

Combining the foregoing items, we get a statement of cash flows for 2004 for Tax Consultants Inc., using the indirect method to compute net cash flow from operating activities.

ILLUSTRATION 23-12
Statement of Cash Flows, Tax Consultants Inc., Year 2

TAX CONSULTANTS INC.
STATEMENT OF CASH FLOWS
FOR THE YEAR ENDED DECEMBER 31, 2004
INCREASE (DECREASE) IN CASH

Cash flows from operating activities		
Net income		$134,000
Adjustments to reconcile net income to net cash provided by operating activities:		
Depreciation expense	$ 21,000	
Decrease in accounts receivable	10,000	
Increase in prepaid expenses	(6,000)	
Increase in accounts payable	35,000	60,000
Net cash provided by operating activities		194,000
Cash flows from investing activities		
Purchase of land	(70,000)	
Purchase of building	(200,000)	
Purchase of equipment	(68,000)	
Net cash used by investing activities		(338,000)
Cash flows from financing activities		
Issuance of bonds	150,000	
Payment of cash dividends	(18,000)	
Net cash provided by financing activities		132,000
Net decrease in cash		(12,000)
Cash, January 1, 2004		49,000
Cash, December 31, 2004		$ 37,000

THIRD ILLUSTRATION—2005

Our third illustration covering the 2005 operations of Tax Consultants Inc. is slightly more complex. It again uses the indirect method to compute and present net cash flow from operating activities.

Tax Consultants Inc. experienced continued success in 2005 and expanded its operations to include the sale of selected lines of computer software that are used in tax return preparation and tax planning. Thus, inventories is one of the new assets appearing in its December 31, 2005, balance sheet. The comparative balance sheets, income statements, and selected data for 2005 are shown in Illustrations 23-13 and 23-14.

ILLUSTRATION 23-13
Comparative Balance Sheets, Tax Consultants Inc., Year 3

TAX CONSULTANTS INC.
COMPARATIVE BALANCE SHEETS
DECEMBER 31

Assets	2005	2004	Change Increase/Decrease
Cash	$ 54,000	$ 37,000	$ 17,000 Increase
Accounts receivable	68,000	26,000	42,000 Increase
Inventories	54,000	–0–	54,000 Increase
Prepaid expenses	4,000	6,000	2,000 Decrease
Land	45,000	70,000	25,000 Decrease
Buildings	200,000	200,000	–0–
Accumulated depreciation—buildings	(21,000)	(11,000)	10,000 Increase
Equipment	193,000	68,000	125,000 Increase
Accumulated depreciation—equipment	(28,000)	(10,000)	18,000 Increase
Totals	$569,000	$386,000	
Liabilities and Stockholders' Equity			
Accounts payable	$ 33,000	$ 40,000	$ 7,000 Decrease
Bonds payable	110,000	150,000	40,000 Decrease
Common stock ($1 par)	220,000	60,000	160,000 Increase
Retained earnings	206,000	136,000	70,000 Increase
Totals	$569,000	$386,000	

ILLUSTRATION 23-14
Income Statement, Tax Consultants Inc., Year 3

TAX CONSULTANTS INC.
INCOME STATEMENT
FOR THE YEAR ENDED DECEMBER 31, 2005

Revenues		$890,000
Cost of goods sold	$465,000	
Operating expenses	221,000	
Interest expense	12,000	
Loss on sale of equipment	2,000	700,000
Income from operations		190,000
Income tax expense		65,000
Net income		$125,000

Additional Information

(a) Operating expenses include depreciation expense of $33,000 and amortization of prepaid expenses of $2,000.
(b) Land was sold at its book value for cash.
(c) Cash dividends of $55,000 were paid in 2005.
(d) Interest expense of $12,000 was paid in cash.
(e) Equipment with a cost of $166,000 was purchased for cash. Equipment with a cost of $41,000 and a book value of $36,000 was sold for $34,000 cash.
(f) Bonds were redeemed at their book value for cash.
(g) Common stock ($1 par) was issued for cash.

Step 1: Determine the Change in Cash

The first step in the preparation of the statement of cash flows is to determine the change in cash. As is shown in the comparative balance sheet, cash increased $17,000 in 2005. The second and third steps are discussed below and on the following pages.

Step 2: Determine Net Cash Flow from Operating Activities—Indirect Method

Explanations of the adjustments to net income of $125,000 are as follows.

Increase in Accounts Receivable

The increase in accounts receivable of $42,000 represents recorded accrual-basis revenues in excess of cash collections in 2005. The increase is deducted from net income to convert from the accrual basis to the cash basis.

Increase in Inventories

The increase in inventories of $54,000 represents an operating use of cash for which an expense was not incurred. This amount is therefore deducted from net income to arrive at cash flow from operations. In other words, when inventory purchased exceeds inventory sold during a period, cost of goods sold on an accrual basis is lower than on a cash basis.

Decrease in Prepaid Expenses

The decrease in prepaid expenses of $2,000 represents a charge to the income statement for which there was no cash outflow in the current period. The decrease is added back to net income to arrive at net cash flow from operating activities.

Decrease in Accounts Payable

When accounts payable decrease during the year, cost of goods sold and expenses on a cash basis are higher than they are on an accrual basis, because on a cash basis the goods and expenses are recorded as expense when paid. To convert net income to net cash flow from operating activities, the decrease of $7,000 in accounts payable must be deducted from net income.

Depreciation Expense (Increase in Accumulated Depreciation)

Accumulated Depreciation—Buildings increased $10,000 ($21,000 − $11,000). The Buildings account did not change during the period, which means that $10,000 of depreciation was recorded in 2005.

Accumulated Depreciation—Equipment increased by $18,000 ($28,000 − $10,000) during the year. But Accumulated Depreciation—Equipment was decreased by $5,000 as a result of the sale during the year. Thus, depreciation for the year was $23,000. The reconciliation of Accumulated Depreciation—Equipment is as follows.

Beginning balance	$10,000
Add: Depreciation for 2005	23,000
	33,000
Deduct: Sale of equipment	5,000
Ending balance	$28,000

The total depreciation of $33,000 ($10,000 + $23,000) charged to the income statement must be added back to net income to determine net cash flow from operating activities.

Loss on Sale of Equipment

Equipment having a cost of $41,000 and a book value of $36,000 was sold for $34,000. As a result, the company reported a loss of $2,000 on its sale. To arrive at net cash flow from operating activities, it is necessary to add back to net income the loss on the sale of the equipment. The reason is that the loss is a noncash charge to the income statement. It did not reduce cash, but it did reduce net income.

From the foregoing items, the operating activities section of the statement of cash flows is prepared as shown in Illustration 23-15.

ILLUSTRATION 23-15
Operating Activities Section of Cash Flows Statement

Cash flows from operating activities		
Net income		$125,000
Adjustments to reconcile net income to net cash provided by operating activities:		
Depreciation expense	$33,000	
Increase in accounts receivable	(42,000)	
Increase in inventories	(54,000)	
Decrease in prepaid expenses	2,000	
Decrease in accounts payable	(7,000)	
Loss on sale of equipment	2,000	(66,000)
Net cash provided by operating activities		59,000

Step 3: Determine Net Cash Flows from Investing and Financing Activities

By analyzing the remaining changes in the balance sheet accounts, we can identify cash flows from investing and financing activities.

Land

Land decreased $25,000 during the period. As indicated from the information presented, land was sold for cash at its book value. This transaction is an investing activity reported as a $25,000 source of cash.

Equipment

An analysis of the equipment account indicates the following.

Beginning balance	$ 68,000
Purchase of equipment	166,000
	234,000
Sale of equipment	41,000
Ending balance	$193,000

Equipment with a fair value of $166,000 was purchased for cash—an investing transaction reported as a cash outflow. The sale of the equipment for $34,000 is also an investing activity, but one that generates a cash inflow.

Bonds Payable

Bonds payable decreased $40,000 during the year. As indicated from the additional information, bonds were redeemed at their book value. This financing transaction used cash of $40,000.

Common Stock

The common stock account increased $160,000 during the year. As indicated from the additional information, common stock of $160,000 was issued at par. This is a financing transaction that provided cash of $160,000.

Retained Earnings

Retained earnings changed $70,000 ($206,000 − $136,000) during the year. The $70,000 change in retained earnings is the result of net income of $125,000 from operations and the financing activity of paying cash dividends of $55,000.

Statement of Cash Flows—2005

The statement of cash flows as shown in Illustration 23-16 is prepared by combining the foregoing items.

ILLUSTRATION 23-16
Statement of Cash Flows, Tax Consultants Inc., Year 3

TAX CONSULTANTS INC.
STATEMENT OF CASH FLOWS
FOR THE YEAR ENDED DECEMBER 31, 2005
INCREASE (DECREASE) IN CASH

Cash flows from operating activities		
Net income		$125,000
Adjustments to reconcile net income to net cash provided by operating activities:		
Depreciation expense	$ 33,000	
Increase in accounts receivable	(42,000)	
Increase in inventories	(54,000)	
Decrease in prepaid expenses	2,000	
Decrease in accounts payable	(7,000)	
Loss on sale of equipment	2,000	(66,000)
Net cash provided by operating activities		59,000
Cash flows from investing activities		
Sale of land	25,000	
Sale of equipment	34,000	
Purchase of equipment	(166,000)	
Net cash used by investing activities		(107,000)
Cash flows from financing activities		
Redemption of bonds	(40,000)	
Sale of common stock	160,000	
Payment of dividends	(55,000)	
Net cash provided by financing activities		65,000
Net increase in cash		17,000
Cash, January 1, 2005		37,000
Cash, December 31, 2005		$ 54,000

SOURCES OF INFORMATION FOR THE STATEMENT OF CASH FLOWS

OBJECTIVE 7
Identify sources of information for a statement of cash flows.

Important points to remember in the preparation of the statement of cash flows are as follows.

1. Comparative balance sheets provide the basic information from which the report is prepared. Additional information obtained from analyses of specific accounts is also included.
2. An analysis of the Retained Earnings account is necessary. The net increase or decrease in Retained Earnings without any explanation is a meaningless amount in the statement, because it might represent the effect of net income, dividends declared, or prior period adjustments.
3. The statement includes all changes that have passed through cash or have resulted in an increase or decrease in cash.
4. Writedowns, amortization charges, and similar "book" entries, such as depreciation of plant assets, are considered as neither inflows nor outflows of cash because

they have no effect on cash. To the extent that they have entered into the determination of net income, however, they must be added back to or subtracted from net income to arrive at net cash flow from operating activities.

NET CASH FLOW FROM OPERATING ACTIVITIES—INDIRECT VERSUS DIRECT METHOD

As we discussed previously, the two different methods available to adjust income from operations on an accrual basis to net cash flow from operating activities are the indirect (reconciliation) method and the direct (income statement) method.

The FASB encourages use of the direct method and permits use of the indirect method. Yet, if the direct method is used, the Board requires that a reconciliation of net income to net cash flow from operating activities be provided in a separate schedule. Therefore, under either method the indirect (reconciliation) method must be prepared and reported.

Indirect Method

For consistency and comparability and because it is the most widely used method in practice, we used the indirect method in the illustrations just presented. We determined net cash flows from operating activities by adding back to or deducting from net income those items that had no effect on cash. The following diagram presents more completely the common types of adjustments that are made to net income to arrive at net cash flow from operating activities.

ILLUSTRATION 23-17
Adjustments Needed to Determine Net Cash Flow from Operating Activities—Indirect Method

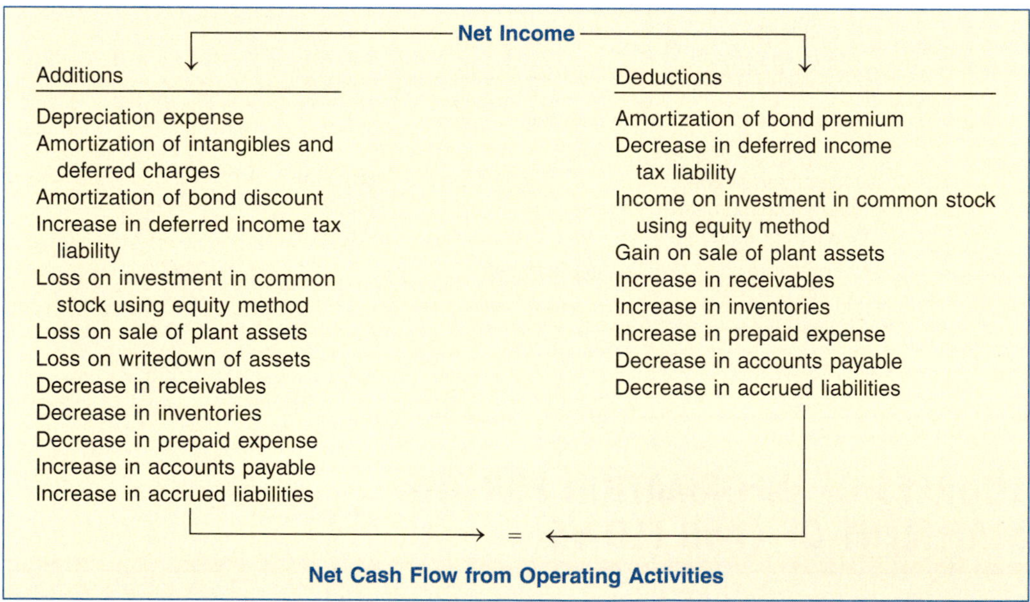

The additions and deductions listed above reconcile net income to net cash flow from operating activities, illustrating the reason for referring to the indirect method as the reconciliation method.

Direct Method—An Illustration

Under the direct method the statement of cash flows reports net cash flow from operating activities as major classes of operating cash receipts (e.g., cash collected from customers and cash received from interest and dividends) and cash disbursements (e.g., cash paid to suppliers for goods, to employees for services, to creditors for interest, and to government authorities for taxes).

The direct method is illustrated here in more detail to help you understand the difference between accrual-based income and net cash flow from operating activities and to illustrate the data needed to apply the direct method. Emig Company, which began business on January 1, 2005, has the following selected balance sheet information.

ILLUSTRATION 23-18
Balance Sheet Accounts, Emig Co.

	December 31	
	2005	2004
Cash	$159,000	–0–
Accounts receivable	15,000	–0–
Inventory	160,000	–0–
Prepaid expenses	8,000	–0–
Property, plant, and equipment (net)	90,000	–0–
Accounts payable	60,000	–0–
Accrued expenses payable	20,000	–0–

Emig Company's December 31, 2005, income statement and additional information are:

ILLUSTRATION 23-19
Income Statement, Emig Co.

Revenues from sales		$780,000
Cost of goods sold		450,000
Gross profit		330,000
Operating expenses	$160,000	
Depreciation	10,000	170,000
Income before income taxes		160,000
Income tax expense		48,000
Net income		$112,000

Additional Information:
(a) Dividends of $70,000 were declared and paid in cash.
(b) The accounts payable increase resulted from the purchase of merchandise.
(c) Prepaid expenses and accrued expenses payable relate to operating expenses.

Under the **direct method**, net cash provided by operating activities is computed by **adjusting each item in the income statement** from the accrual basis to the cash basis. To simplify and condense the operating activities section, only major classes of operating cash receipts and cash payments are reported. The difference between these major classes of cash receipts and cash payments is the net cash provided by operating activities as shown in Illustration 23-20.

ILLUSTRATION 23-20
Major Classes of Cash Receipts and Payments

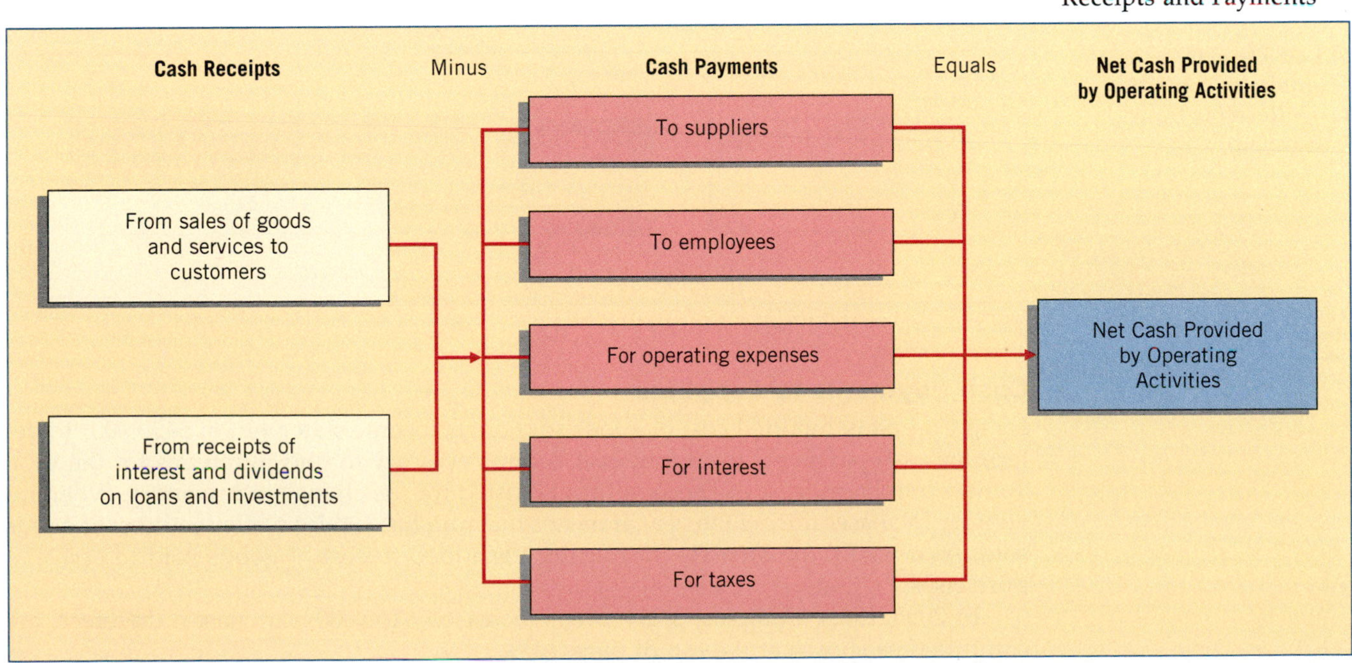

An efficient way to apply the direct method is to analyze the revenues and expenses reported in the income statement in the order in which they are listed. Cash receipts and cash payments related to these revenues and expenses should then be determined. The direct method adjustments for Emig Company in 2005 to determine net cash provided by operating activities are presented in the following sections.

Cash Receipts from Customers

The income statement for Emig Company reported revenues from customers of $780,000. To determine cash receipts from customers, it is necessary to consider the change in accounts receivable during the year. When accounts receivable increase during the year, revenues on an accrual basis are higher than cash receipts from customers. In other words, operations led to increased revenues, but not all of these revenues resulted in cash receipts. To determine the amount of increase in cash receipts, deduct the amount of the increase in accounts receivable from the total sales revenues. Conversely, a decrease in accounts receivable is added to sales revenues, because cash receipts from customers then exceed sales revenues.

For Emig Company, accounts receivable increased $15,000. Thus, cash receipts from customers were $765,000, computed as follows.

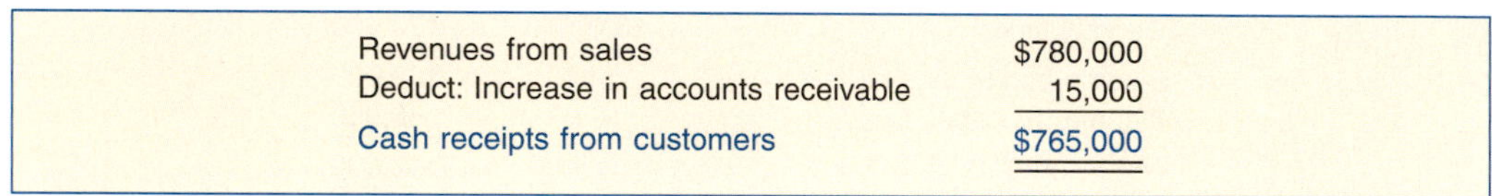

Revenues from sales	$780,000
Deduct: Increase in accounts receivable	15,000
Cash receipts from customers	$765,000

Cash receipts from customers may also be determined from an analysis of the Accounts Receivable account as shown below.

Accounts Receivable

1/1/05	Balance	–0–	Receipts from customers	765,000
	Revenue from sales	780,000		
12/31/05	Balance	15,000		

The relationships between cash receipts from customers, revenues from sales, and changes in accounts receivable are shown in Illustration 23-21.

ILLUSTRATION 23-21
Formula to Compute Cash Receipts from Customers

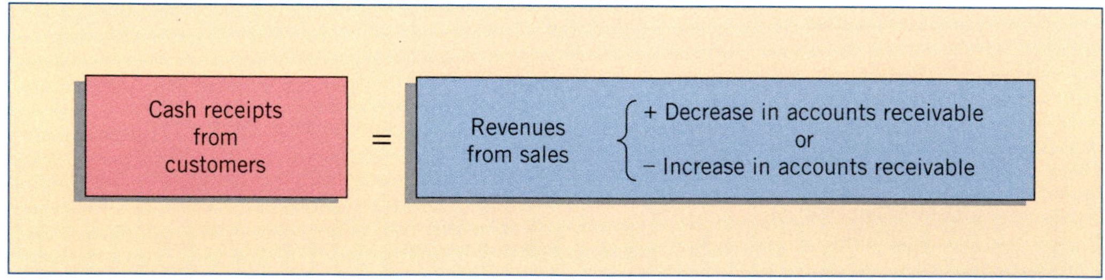

Cash Payments to Suppliers

Emig Company reported cost of goods sold on its income statement of $450,000. To determine cash payments to suppliers, it is first necessary to find purchases for the year. To find purchases, cost of goods sold is adjusted for the change in inventory. When inventory increases during the year, it means that purchases this year exceed cost of goods sold. As a result, the increase in inventory is added to cost of goods sold to arrive at purchases.

In 2005, Emig Company's inventory increased $160,000. Purchases, therefore, are computed as shown at the top of page 1223.

Cost of goods sold	$450,000
Add: Increase in inventory	160,000
Purchases	$610,000

After purchases are computed, cash payments to suppliers are determined by adjusting purchases for the change in accounts payable. When accounts payable increase during the year, purchases on an accrual basis are higher than they are on a cash basis. As a result, an increase in accounts payable is deducted from purchases to arrive at cash payments to suppliers. Conversely, a decrease in accounts payable is added to purchases because cash payments to suppliers exceed purchases. Cash payments to suppliers were $550,000, computed as follows.

Purchases	$610,000
Deduct: Increase in accounts payable	60,000
Cash payments to suppliers	$550,000

Cash payments to suppliers may also be determined from an analysis of the Accounts Payable account as shown below.

Accounts Payable

Payments to suppliers	550,000	1/1/05	Balance	–0–
			Purchases	610,000
		12/31/05	Balance	60,000

The relationships between cash payments to customers, cost of goods sold, changes in inventory, and changes in accounts payable are shown in Illustration 23-22.

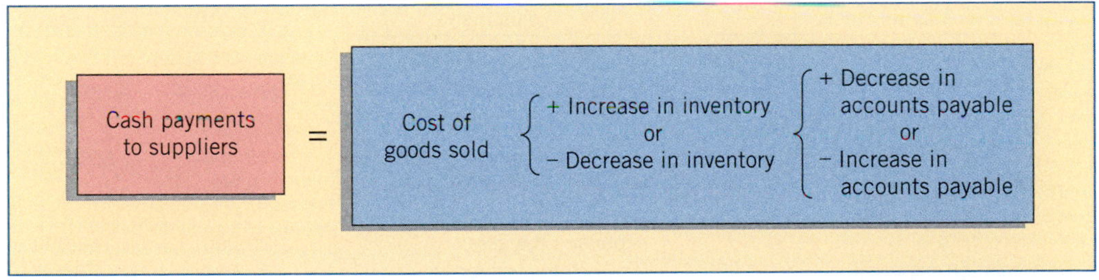

ILLUSTRATION 23-22
Formula to Compute Cash Payments to Suppliers

Cash Payments for Operating Expenses

Operating expenses of $160,000 were reported on Emig's income statement. To determine the cash paid for operating expenses, this amount must be adjusted for any changes in prepaid expenses and accrued expenses payable. For example, when prepaid expenses increased $8,000 during the year, cash paid for operating expenses was $8,000 higher than operating expenses reported on the income statement. To convert operating expenses to cash payments for operating expenses, the increase of $8,000 must be added to operating expenses. Conversely, if prepaid expenses decrease during the year, the decrease must be deducted from operating expenses.

Operating expenses must also be adjusted for changes in accrued expenses payable. When accrued expenses payable increase during the year, operating expenses on an accrual basis are higher than they are on a cash basis. As a result, an increase in accrued expenses payable is deducted from operating expenses to arrive at cash payments for operating expenses. Conversely, a decrease in accrued expenses payable is added to operating expenses because cash payments exceed operating expenses.

Emig Company's cash payments for operating expenses were $148,000, computed as shown at the top of page 1224.

Operating expenses	$160,000
Add: Increase in prepaid expenses	8,000
Deduct: Increase in accrued expenses payable	(20,000)
Cash payments for operating expenses	$148,000

The relationships among cash payments for operating expenses, changes in prepaid expenses, and changes in accrued expenses payable are shown in the following formula.

ILLUSTRATION 23-23
Formula to Compute Cash Payments for Operating Expenses

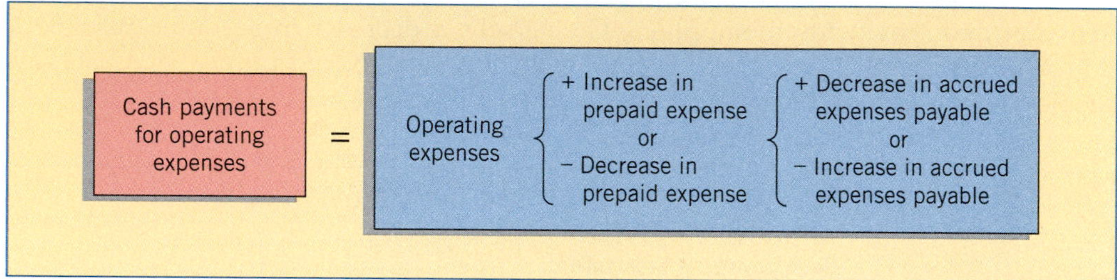

Note that depreciation expense was not considered because it is a noncash charge.

Cash Payments for Income Taxes

The income statement for Emig shows income tax expense of $48,000. This amount equals the cash paid because the comparative balance sheet indicated no income taxes payable at either the beginning or end of the year.

Summary of Net Cash Flow from Operating Activities—Direct Method

The computations illustrated above are summarized in the following schedule.

ILLUSTRATION 23-24
Accrual Basis to Cash Basis

Accrual Basis			Adjustment	Add (Subtract)	Cash Basis
Revenues from sales	$780,000	−	Increase in accounts receivable	$(15,000)	$765,000
Cost of goods sold	450,000	+	Increase in inventory	160,000	
		−	Increase in accounts payable	(60,000)	550,000
Operating expenses	160,000	+	Increase in prepaid expenses	8,000	
		−	Increase in accrued expenses payable	(20,000)	148,000
Depreciation expense	10,000	−	Depreciation expense	(10,000)	–0–
Income tax expense	48,000				48,000
Total expense	668,000				746,000
Net income	$112,000		Net cash provided by operating activities		$ 19,000

Presentation of the direct method for reporting net cash flow from operating activities takes the following form for the Emig Company illustration.

ILLUSTRATION 23-25
Operating Activities Section—Direct Method, 2005

EMIG COMPANY
STATEMENT OF CASH FLOWS (PARTIAL)

Cash flows from operating activities		
Cash received from customers		$765,000
Cash payments:		
To suppliers	$ 550,000	
For operating expenses	148,000	
For income taxes	48,000	746,000
Net cash provided by operating activities		$ 19,000

If Emig Company uses the direct method to present the net cash flows from operating activities, it must provide in a separate schedule the reconciliation of net income to net cash provided by operating activities. The reconciliation assumes the identical form and content of the indirect method of presentation as shown below.

ILLUSTRATION 23-26
Reconciliation of Net Income to Net Cash Provided by Operating Activities

EMIG COMPANY RECONCILIATION		
Net income		$112,000
Adjustments to reconcile net income to net cash provided by operating activities:		
Depreciation expense	$ 10,000	
Increase in accounts receivable	(15,000)	
Increase in inventory	(160,000)	
Increase in prepaid expenses	(8,000)	
Increase in accounts payable	60,000	
Increase in accrued expense payable	20,000	(93,000)
Net cash provided by operating activities		$ 19,000

The reconciliation may be presented at the bottom of the statement of cash flows when the direct method is used or in a separate schedule.

Direct Versus Indirect Controversy

The most contentious decision that the FASB faced in issuing *Statement No. 95* was choosing between the direct method and the indirect method of determining net cash flow from operating activities. Companies lobbied against the direct method, urging adoption of the indirect method. Commercial lending officers expressed a strong preference to the FASB that the direct method be required.

In Favor of the Direct Method

The principal advantage of the direct method is that **it shows operating cash receipts and payments**. That is, it is more consistent with the objective of a statement of cash flows—to provide information about cash receipts and cash payments—than the indirect method, which does not report operating cash receipts and payments.

Supporters of the direct method contend that knowledge of the specific sources of operating cash receipts and the purposes for which operating cash payments were made in past periods is useful in estimating future operating cash flows. Furthermore, information about amounts of major classes of operating cash receipts and payments is more useful than information only about their arithmetic sum (the net cash flow from operating activities). Such information is more revealing of an enterprise's ability (1) to generate sufficient cash from operating activities to pay its debts, (2) to reinvest in its operations, and (3) to make distributions to its owners.[8]

Many companies indicate that they do not currently collect information in a manner that allows them to determine amounts such as cash received from customers or cash paid to suppliers directly from their accounting systems. But supporters of the direct method contend that the incremental cost of assimilating such operating cash receipts and payments data is not significant.

In Favor of the Indirect Method

The principal advantage of the indirect method is that **it focuses on the differences between net income and net cash flow from operating activities**. That is, it provides a useful link between the statement of cash flows and the income statement and balance sheet.

[8]"Statement of Cash Flows," pars. 107 and 111.

Many companies contend that it is less costly to adjust net income to net cash flow from operating activities (indirect) than it is to report gross operating cash receipts and payments (direct). Supporters of the indirect method also state that the direct method, which effectively reports income statement information on a cash rather than an accrual basis, may erroneously suggest that net cash flow from operating activities is as good as, or better than, net income as a measure of performance.

Special Rules Applying to Direct and Indirect Methods

Companies that use the direct method are required, at a minimum, to report separately the following classes of operating cash receipts and payments:

Receipts

1. Cash collected from customers (including lessees, licensees, etc.).
2. Interest and dividends received.
3. Other operating cash receipts, if any.

INTERNATIONAL INSIGHT

Consolidated statements of cash flows may be of limited use to analysts evaluating multinational companies. Without disaggregation, users of such statements are not able to determine "where in the world" the funds are sourced and used.

Payments

1. Cash paid to employees and suppliers of goods or services (including suppliers of insurance, advertising, etc.).
2. Interest paid.
3. Income taxes paid.
4. Other operating cash payments, if any.

Companies are encouraged to provide further breakdowns of operating cash receipts and payments that they consider meaningful.

Companies using the indirect method are required to disclose separately changes in inventory, receivables, and payables in order to reconcile net income to net cash flow from operating activities. In addition, interest paid (net of amount capitalized) and income taxes paid must be disclosed elsewhere in the financial statements or accompanying notes.[9] The FASB requires these separate and additional disclosures so that users may approximate the direct method. Also, an acceptable alternative presentation of the indirect method is to report net cash flow from operating activities as a single line item in the statement of cash flows and to present the reconciliation details elsewhere in the financial statements.

WHAT DO THE NUMBERS MEAN?

NOT WHAT IT SEEMS

The controversy over direct and indirect methods highlights the importance that the market attributes to operating cash flow. By showing an improving cash flow, a company can give a favorable impression of its ongoing operations. For example, **WorldCom** was able to conceal declines in its operations by capitalizing certain operating expenses—to the tune of $3.8 billion! This practice not only juiced up income but also made it possible to report the cash payments in the investing section of the cash flow statement rather than as a deduction from operating cash flow. So while the overall cash flow—from operations, investing, and financing—remained the same, the company's operating cash flow looked better than it really was.

Source: Peter Elstrom, "How to Hide $3.8 Billion in Expenses," *BusinessWeek Online* (July 8, 2002).

[9] *Accounting Trends and Techniques—2001* reports that of the 600 companies surveyed, 315 disclosed interest paid in notes to the financial statements, 233 disclosed interest at the bottom of the statement of cash flows, 20 disclosed interest within the statement of cash flows, and 32 reported no separate amount. Income taxes paid during the year were disclosed in a manner similar to interest payments.

SPECIAL PROBLEMS IN STATEMENT PREPARATION

Some of the special problems related to preparing the statement of cash flows were discussed in connection with the preceding illustrations. Other problems that arise with some frequency in the preparation of this statement may be categorized as follows:

OBJECTIVE 8
Identify special problems in preparing a statement of cash flows.

1. Adjustments similar to depreciation.
2. Accounts receivable (net).
3. Other working capital changes.
4. Net losses.
5. Gains.
6. Stock options.
7. Postretirement benefit costs.
8. Extraordinary items.
9. Significant noncash transactions.

Adjustments Similar to Depreciation

Depreciation expense is the most common adjustment to net income that is made to arrive at net cash flow from operating activities. But there are numerous other noncash expense or revenue items. Examples of expense items that must be added back to net income are the **amortization of intangible assets** such as trademarks and patents, and the **amortization of deferred costs** such as bond issue costs. These charges to expense involve expenditures made in prior periods that are being amortized currently and reduce net income without affecting cash in the current period.

Also, **amortization of bond discount or premium** on long-term bonds payable affects the amount of interest expense, but neither changes cash. As a result, amortization of these items should be added back to (discount) or subtracted from (premium) net income to arrive at net cash flow from operating activities.

In a similar manner, **changes in deferred income taxes** affect net income but have no effect on cash. For example, **Kroger Co.** at one time experienced an increase in its liability for deferred taxes of approximately $42 million. Tax expense was increased and net income was decreased by this amount, but cash was not affected; therefore, $42 million was added back to net income on a statement of cash flows. Conversely, **General Electric Company** at one time had a decrease in its liability for deferred taxes of $171 million. Tax expense decreased and net income increased by this amount, but cash flow was unaffected. Therefore, GE subtracted this amount from net income to arrive at net cash flow from operating activities.

Another common adjustment to net income is **a change related to an investment in common stock** when income or loss is accrued under the equity method. Recall that under the equity method, the investor (1) debits the investment account and credits revenue for its share of the investee's net income and (2) credits dividends received to the investment account. Therefore, the net increase in the investment account does not affect cash flow and must be deducted from net income in arriving at net cash flow from operating activities. To illustrate, assume that Victor Co. owns 40 percent of Milo Inc., and during the year Milo Inc. reports net income of $100,000 and pays a cash dividend of $30,000. This information is reported in Victor Co.'s statement of cash flows as a deduction from net income in the following manner—Equity in earnings of Milo Inc., net of dividends, $28,000.

If the fair value method is used, income of the investee is not recognized, and any cash dividend received is recorded as revenue. In this case, no adjustment to net income in the statement of cash flows is necessary for any cash dividend received.

Accounts Receivable (Net)

Up to this point, we have assumed that no allowance for doubtful accounts—a contra account—was needed to offset accounts receivable. However, if an allowance for doubtful accounts is needed, how does it affect the determination of net cash flow from operating activities? For example, assume that Redmark Co. reports net income of $40,000 and has the following balances related to accounts receivable.

ILLUSTRATION 23-27
Accounts Receivable Balances, Redmark Co.

	2005	2004	Change Increase/Decrease
Accounts receivable	$105,000	$90,000	$15,000 Increase
Allowance for doubtful accounts	(10,000)	(4,000)	6,000 Increase
Accounts receivable (net)	$ 95,000	$86,000	9,000 Increase

The proper reporting treatment using the indirect and direct methods is illustrated in the following sections.

Indirect Method

Because an increase in the Allowance for Doubtful Accounts is caused by a charge to bad debts expense, an increase in the Allowance for Doubtful Accounts should be added back to net income to arrive at net cash flow from operating activities. One method for presenting this information in a statement of cash flows is as follows.

ILLUSTRATION 23-28
Presentation of Allowance for Doubtful Accounts—Indirect Method

REDMARK CO.
STATEMENT OF CASH FLOWS (PARTIAL)
FOR THE YEAR 2005

Cash flows from operating activities		
Net income		$40,000
Adjustments to reconcile net income to net cash provided by operating activities:		
Increase in accounts receivable	$(15,000)	
Increase in allowance for doubtful accounts	6,000	(9,000)
		$31,000

As indicated, the increase in the Allowance for Doubtful Accounts balance is caused by a charge to bad debt expense for the year. Because bad debt expense is a noncash charge, it must be added back to net income in arriving at net cash flow from operating activities.

Instead of separately analyzing the allowance account, a short-cut approach is to net the allowance balance against the receivable balance and compare the change in accounts receivable on a net basis. This presentation would be as follows.

ILLUSTRATION 23-29
Net Approach to Allowance for Doubtful Accounts—Indirect Method

REDMARK CO.
STATEMENT OF CASH FLOWS (PARTIAL)
FOR THE YEAR 2005

Cash flows from operating activities	
Net income	$40,000
Adjustments to reconcile net income to net cash provided by operating activities:	
Increase in accounts receivable (net)	(9,000)
	$31,000

This short-cut procedure works also if the change in the allowance account was caused by a writeoff of accounts receivable. In this case, both the Accounts Receivable and the Allowance for Doubtful Accounts are reduced, and no effect on cash flows occurs. Because of its simplicity, you should use the net approach on your homework assignments.

Direct Method

If the direct method is used, the Allowance for Doubtful Accounts should **not be netted against the Accounts Receivable**. To illustrate, assume that Redmark Co.'s net income of $40,000 comprised the following items.

ILLUSTRATION 23-30
Income Statement, Redmark Co.

REDMARK CO. INCOME STATEMENT FOR THE YEAR 2005		
Sales		$100,000
Expenses		
Salaries	$46,000	
Utilities	8,000	
Bad debts	6,000	60,000
Net income		$ 40,000

If the $9,000 increase in accounts receivable (net) is deducted from sales for the year, cash sales would be reported at $91,000 ($100,000 − $9,000) and cash payments for operating expenses at $60,000. Both items are misstated because cash sales should be reported at $85,000 ($100,000 − $15,000), and total cash payments for operating expenses should be reported at $54,000 ($60,000 − $6,000). The proper presentation is as follows.

ILLUSTRATION 23-31
Bad Debts—Direct Method

REDMARK CO. STATEMENT OF CASH FLOWS (PARTIAL) FOR THE YEAR 2005		
Cash flows from operating activities		
Cash received from customers		$85,000
Salaries paid	$46,000	
Utilities paid	8,000	54,000
Net cash provided by operating activities		$31,000

An added complication develops when accounts receivable are written off. Simply adjusting sales for the change in accounts receivable will not provide the proper amount of cash sales. The reason is that the writeoff of the accounts receivable is not a cash collection. Thus an additional adjustment is necessary.

Other Working Capital Changes

Up to this point, all of the changes in working capital items (current asset and current liability items) have been handled as adjustments to net income in determining net cash flow from operating activities. You must be careful, however, because **some changes in working capital, although they affect cash, do not affect net income**. Generally, these are investing or financing activities of a current nature. For example, the purchase of **short-term available-for-sale securities** for $50,000 cash has no effect on net income, but it does cause a $50,000 decrease in cash.[10] This transaction is reported as a cash flow from investing activities and reported gross as shown on page 1230.[11]

[10]If the basis of the statement of cash flows is cash **and cash equivalents** and the short-term investment is considered a cash equivalent, then nothing would be reported in the statement because the balance of cash and cash equivalents does not change as a result of this transaction.

[11]"Accounting for Certain Investments in Debt and Equity Securities," *Statement of Financial Accounting Standards No. 115* (Norwalk, Conn.: 1993), par. 118.

Cash flows from investing activities	
Purchase of short-term available-for-sale securities	$(50,000)

Another example is the issuance of a $10,000 **short-term nontrade note payable** for cash. This change in a working capital item has no effect on income from operations but it increases cash $10,000. It is reported in the statement of cash flows as follows.

Cash flows from financing activities	
Issuance of short-term note	$10,000

Another change in a working capital item that has no effect on income from operations or on cash is a **cash dividend payable**. Although the cash dividends when paid will be reported as a financing activity, the declared but unpaid dividend is not reported on the statement of cash flows.

Because **trading securities** are bought and held principally for the purpose of selling them in the near term, the cash flows from purchases and sales of trading securities should be classified as cash flows from **operating activities**.[12]

Net Losses

If an enterprise reports a net loss instead of a net income, the net loss must be adjusted for those items that do not result in a cash inflow or outflow. The net loss after adjusting for the charges or credits not affecting cash may result in a negative **or** a positive cash flow from operating activities. For example, if the net loss was $50,000 and the total amount of charges to be added back was $60,000, then net cash provided by operating activities is $10,000, as shown in the computation below.

ILLUSTRATION 23-32
Computation of Net Cash Flow from Operating Activities—Cash Inflow

Net loss		$(50,000)
Adjustments to reconcile net income to net cash provided by operating activities:		
Depreciation of plant assets	$55,000	
Amortization of patents	5,000	60,000
Net cash provided by operating activities		$ 10,000

If the company experiences a net loss of $80,000 and the total amount of the charges to be added back is $25,000, the presentation appears as follows.

ILLUSTRATION 23-33
Computation of Net Cash Flow from Operating Activities—Cash Outflow

Net loss	$(80,000)
Adjustments to reconcile net income to net cash used by operating activities:	
Depreciation of plant assets	25,000
Net cash used by operating activities	$(55,000)

Although it is not illustrated in this chapter, a negative cash flow may result even if the company reports a net income.

Gains

In the third illustration (2005) of Tax Consultants Inc., the company experienced a loss of $2,000 from the sale of equipment. This loss was added to net income to compute net cash flow from operating activities because **the loss is a noncash charge in the income statement**. If a gain from a sale of equipment is experienced, it too requires that net income be adjusted. Because the gain is reported in the statement of cash flows as part of the cash proceeds from the sale of equipment under investing activities, **the**

[12]Ibid., par. 118.

gain is deducted from net income to avoid double counting—once as part of net income and again as part of the cash proceeds from the sale.

Stock Options

If a company has a stock option plan, compensation expense will be recorded during the period(s) in which the employee performs the services. Although compensation expense is debited, stockholders' equity (the paid-in capital accounts) is credited, and cash remains unaffected by the amount of the expense. **Therefore, net income has to be increased by the amount of compensation expense from stock options in computing net cash flow from operating activities.**

Postretirement Benefit Costs

If a company has postretirement costs such as an employee pension plan, chances are that the pension expense recorded during a period will either be higher than the cash funded (when there is an unfunded liability) or lower than the cash funded (when there is a deferred or prepaid pension cost). When the expense is higher or lower than the cash paid, **net income must be adjusted by the difference between cash paid and the expense reported** in computing net cash flow from operating activities.

Extraordinary Items

Cash flows from extraordinary transactions and other events whose effects are included in net income, but which are not related to operations, should be reported **either as investing activities or as financing activities**. For example, assume that Tax Consultants had land with a carrying value of $200,000, which was condemned by the state of Maine for a highway project. The condemnation proceeds received were $205,000, resulting in a gain of $5,000 less $2,000 of taxes. In the statement of cash flows (indirect method), the $5,000 gain would be deducted from net income in the operating activities section, and the $205,000 cash inflow from the condemnation would be reported as an investing activity, as follows.

Cash flows from investing activities	
Condemnation of land	$205,000

Note that for Tax Consultants the gain is handled at its gross amount ($5,000), not net of tax. The cash received in the condemnation is reported as an investing activity at $205,000, also exclusive of the tax effect. The FASB requires that **all income taxes paid be classified as operating cash outflows**. Some suggested that income taxes paid be allocated to investing and financing transactions. But, the Board decided that allocation of income taxes paid to operating, investing, and financing activities would be so complex and arbitrary that the benefits, if any, would not justify the costs involved. Under both the direct method and the indirect method the total amount of income taxes paid must be disclosed.[13]

By rejecting the requirement to allocate taxes to the various activities, the Board invoked the cost-benefit constraint. The information would be beneficial, but the cost of providing such information would exceed the benefits of providing the information.

[13]For an insightful article on some weaknesses and limitations in the statement of cash flows caused by implementation of *FASB Statement No. 95*, see Hugo Nurnberg, "Inconsistencies and Ambiguities in Cash Flow Statements Under *FASB Statement No. 95*," *Accounting Horizons* (June 1993), pp. 60–73. Nurnberg identifies the inconsistencies caused by the three-way classification of all cash receipts and cash payments, gross versus net of tax, the ambiguous disclosure requirements for noncash investing and financing transactions, and the ambiguous presentation of third-party financing transactions. See also Paul R. Bahnson, Paul B. W. Miller, and Bruce P. Budge, "Nonarticulation in Cash Flow Statements and Implications for Education, Research, and Practice," *Accounting Horizons* (December 1996), pp. 1–15.

Significant Noncash Transactions

Because the statement of cash flows reports only the effects of operating, investing, and financing activities in terms of cash flows, some **significant noncash transactions** and other events that are investing or financing activities are omitted from the body of the statement. Among the more common of these noncash transactions that should be reported or disclosed in some manner are the following.

Examples of Cash Flow Statements

1. Acquisition of assets by assuming liabilities (including capital lease obligations) or by issuing equity securities.
2. Exchanges of nonmonetary assets.
3. Refinancing of long-term debt.
4. Conversion of debt or preferred stock to common stock.
5. Issuance of equity securities to retire debt.

These noncash items are not to be incorporated in the statement of cash flows. If material in amount, these disclosures may be either narrative or summarized in a separate schedule at the bottom of the statement, or they may appear in a separate note or supplementary schedule to the financial statements. The presentation of these significant noncash transactions or other events in a separate schedule at the bottom of the statement of cash flows is shown as follows.

ILLUSTRATION 23-34
Schedule Presentation of Noncash Investing and Financing Activities

Net increase in cash	$3,717,000
Cash at beginning of year	5,208,000
Cash at end of year	$8,925,000
Noncash investing and financing activities	
Purchase of land and building through issuance of 250,000 shares of common stock	$1,750,000
Exchange of Steadfast, NY, land for Bedford, PA, land	$2,000,000
Conversion of 12% bonds to 50,000 shares of common stock	$ 500,000

Or, these noncash transactions might be presented in a separate note as follows.

ILLUSTRATION 23-35
Note Presentation of Noncash Investing and Financing Activities

Note G: Significant noncash transactions. During the year the company engaged in the following significant noncash investing and financing transactions:

Issued 250,000 shares of common stock to purchase land and building	$1,750,000
Exchanged land in Steadfast, NY, for land in Bedford, PA	$2,000,000
Converted 12% bonds due 2004 to 50,000 shares of common stock	$ 500,000

Certain other significant noncash transactions or other events are generally not reported in conjunction with the statement of cash flows. Examples of these types of transactions are **stock dividends and stock splits**. These items, neither financing nor investing activities, are generally reported in conjunction with the statement of stockholders' equity or schedules and notes pertaining to changes in capital accounts.

CASH FLOW TOOL

WHAT DO THE NUMBERS MEAN?

By understanding the relationship between cash flow and income measures, analysts can gain better insights into company performance. Because earnings altered through creative accounting practices generally do not change operating cash flows, the relationship between earnings and operating cash flow can be used to detect suspicious accounting practices. Also, by monitoring the ratio between cash flow from operations and operating income, the analyst can get a clearer picture of developing problems in a company. The chart below plots the ratio of operating cash flows to earnings for **Xerox Corp.** in the years leading up to the SEC singling it out in 2000 for aggressive revenue recognition practices on its leases.

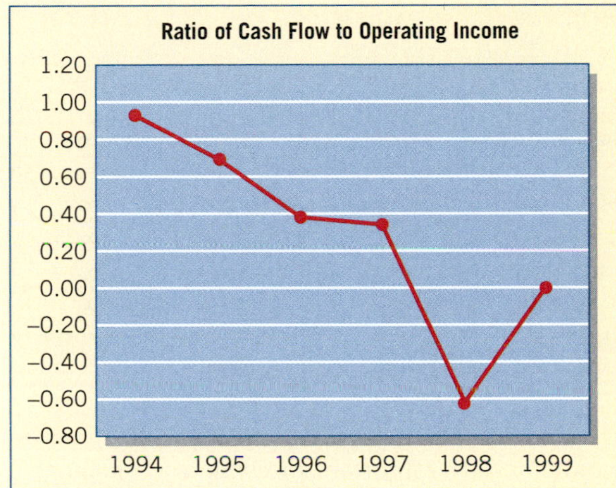

Similar to **W. T. Grant** in our opening story, Xerox was reporting earnings growth in the years leading up to its financial breakdown in 2000 but teetering near bankruptcy in 2001. However, Xerox's cash flow to earnings ratio showed a declining trend and became negative well before its revenue recognition practices were revealed. The trend revealed in the graph should have given any analyst reason to investigate Xerox further. As one analyst noted, "Earnings growth that exceeds the growth in operating cash flow cannot continue for extended periods and should be investigated."

Source: Adapted from Charles Mulford and Eugene Comiskey, *The Financial Numbers Game: Detecting Creative Accounting Practices* (New York: John Wiley & Sons, 2002), Chapter 11, by permission.

USE OF A WORK SHEET

SECTION 2

OBJECTIVE 9
Explain the use of a work sheet in preparing a statement of cash flows.

When numerous adjustments are necessary or other complicating factors are present, **a work sheet is often used to assemble and classify the data that will appear on the statement of cash flows**. The work sheet (a **spreadsheet** when using computer software) is merely a device that aids in the preparation of the statement. Its use is optional. The skeleton format of the work sheet for preparation of the statement of cash flows using the indirect method is shown in Illustration 23-26 on the next page.

XYZ COMPANY
Statement of Cash Flows For the Year Ended...

	A	B	C	D	E
			Reconciling Items		
1	Balance Sheet Accounts	End of Prior Year Balances	Debits	Credits	End of Current Year Balances
2	Debit balance accounts	XX	XX	XX	XX
3		XX	XX	XX	XX
4	Totals	XXX			XXX
5	Credit balance accounts	XX	XX	XX	XX
6		XX	XX	XX	XX
7	Totals	XXX			XXX
8	Statement of Cash Flows Effects				
9	Operating activities				
10	Net income		XX		
11	Adjustments		XX	XX	
12	Investing activities				
13	Receipts and payments		XX	XX	
14	Financing activities				
15	Receipts and payments		XX	XX	
16	Totals		XXX	XXX	
17	Increase (decrease) in cash		(XX)	XX	
18	Totals		XXX	XXX	

Sheet1 / Sheet2 / Sheet3

ILLUSTRATION 23-36
Format of Work Sheet for Preparation of Statement of Cash Flows

The following guidelines are important in using a work sheet.

1. In the balance sheet accounts section, **accounts with debit balances are listed separately from those with credit balances**. This means, for example, that Accumulated Depreciation is listed under credit balances and not as a contra account under debit balances. The beginning and ending balances of each account are entered in the appropriate columns. The transactions that caused the change in the account balance during the year are entered as reconciling items in the two middle columns. After all reconciling items have been entered, each line pertaining to a balance sheet account should foot across. That is, the beginning balance plus or minus the reconciling item(s) must equal the ending balance. When this agreement exists for all balance sheet accounts, all changes in account balances have been reconciled.

2. The bottom portion of the work sheet consists of the operating, investing, and financing activities sections. Accordingly, it provides the information necessary to prepare the formal statement of cash flows. **Inflows of cash are entered as debits in the reconciling columns, and outflows of cash are entered as credits in the reconciling columns.** Thus, in this section, the sale of equipment for cash at book value is entered as a debit under inflows of cash from investing activities. Similarly, the purchase of land for cash is entered as a credit under outflows of cash from investing activities.

3. **The reconciling items shown in the work sheet are not entered in any journal or posted to any account.** They do not represent either adjustments or corrections of the balance sheet accounts. They are used only to facilitate the preparation of the statement of cash flows.

PREPARATION OF THE WORK SHEET

The preparation of a work sheet involves a series of prescribed steps. The steps in this case are shown on the next page.

Step 1. Enter the balance sheet accounts and their beginning and ending balances in the balance sheet accounts section.

Step 2. Enter the data that explain the changes in the balance sheet accounts (other than cash) and their effects on the statement of cash flows in the reconciling columns of the work sheet.

Step 3. Enter the increase or decrease in cash on the cash line and at the bottom of the work sheet. This entry should enable the totals of the reconciling columns to be in agreement.

To illustrate the preparation and use of a work sheet and to illustrate the reporting of some of the special problems discussed in the prior section, the following comprehensive illustration is presented for Satellite Corporation. Again, the indirect method serves as the basis for the computation of net cash provided by operating activities. The financial statements and other data related to Satellite Corporation are presented with the balance sheet and the statement of income and retained earnings shown on the following pages. Additional explanations related to the preparation of the work sheet are provided throughout the discussion that follows the financial statements.

ILLUSTRATION 23-37
Comparative Balance Sheet, Satellite Corporation

SATELLITE CORPORATION
Comparative Balance Sheet–December 31, 2005 and 2004

	A	B	C	D
1		2005	2004	Increase or (Decrease)
2	Assets			
3	Cash	$ 59,000	$ 66,000	$ (7,000)
4	Accounts receivable (net)	104,000	51,000	53,000
5	Inventories	493,000	341,000	152,000
6	Prepaid expenses	16,500	17,000	(500)
7	Investments in stock of Porter Co. (equity method)	18,500	15,000	3,500
8	Land	131,500	82,000	49,500
9	Equipment	187,000	142,000	45,000
10	Accumulated depreciation—equipment	(29,000)	(31,000)	(2,000)
11	Buildings	262,000	262,000	—
12	Accumulated depreciation—buildings	(74,100)	(71,000)	3,100
13	Trademark	7,600	10,000	(2,400)
14	Total assets	$1,176,000	$884,000	
15	Liabilities			
16	Accounts payable	$ 132,000	$ 131,000	1,000
17	Accrued liabilities	43,000	39,000	4,000
18	Income tax payable	3,000	16,000	(13,000)
19	Notes payable (long-term)	60,000	—	60,000
20	Bonds payable	100,000	100,000	—
21	Premium on bonds payable	7,000	8,000	(1,000)
22	Deferred tax liability (long-term)	9,000	6,000	3,000
23	Total liabilities	354,000	300,000	
24	Stockholders' Equity			
25	Common stock ($1 par)	60,000	50,000	10,000
26	Additional paid-in capital	187,000	38,000	149,000
27	Retained earnings	592,000	496,000	96,000
28	Treasury stock	(17,000)	—	17,000
29	Total stockholders' equity	822,000	584,000	
30	Total liabilities and stockholders' equity	$1,176,000	$884,000	

Sheet1 / Sheet2 / Sheet3

ILLUSTRATION 23-38
Income and Retained Earnings Statements, Satellite Corporation

SATELLITE CORPORATION
COMBINED STATEMENT OF INCOME AND RETAINED EARNINGS
FOR THE YEAR ENDED DECEMBER 31, 2005

Net sales		$526,500
Other revenue		3,500
Total revenues		530,000
Expense		
Cost of goods sold		310,000
Selling and administrative expenses		47,000
Other expenses and losses		12,000
Total expenses		369,000
Income before income tax and extraordinary item		161,000
Income tax		
Current	$47,000	
Deferred	3,000	50,000
Income before extraordinary item		111,000
Gain on condemnation of land (net of $2,000 tax)		6,000
Net income		117,000
Retained earnings, January 1		496,000
Less:		
Cash dividends	6,000	
Stock dividend	15,000	21,000
Retained earnings, December 31		$592,000
Per share:		
Income before extraordinary item		$2.02
Extraordinary item		.11
Net income		$2.13

Additional Information

(a) Other income of $3,500 represents Satellite's equity share in the net income of Porter Co., an equity investee. Satellite owns 22% of Porter Co.

(b) An analysis of the equipment account and related accumulated depreciation indicates the following:

	Equipment Dr./(Cr.)	Accum. Dep. Dr./(Cr.)	Gain or (Loss)
Balance at end of 2004	$142,000	$(31,000)	
Purchases of equipment	53,000		
Sale of equipment	(8,000)	2,500	$(1,500)
Depreciation for the period		(11,500)	
Major repair charged to accumulated depreciation		11,000	
Balance at end of 2005	$187,000	$(29,000)	

(c) Land in the amount of $60,000 was purchased through the issuance of a long-term note; in addition, certain parcels of land costing $10,500 were condemned. The state government paid Satellite $18,500, resulting in an $8,000 gain which has a $2,000 tax effect.

(d) The change in the accumulated depreciation—buildings, trademark, and premium on bonds payable accounts resulted from depreciation and amortization entries.

(e) An analysis of the paid-in capital accounts in stockholders' equity discloses the following:

	Common Stock	Additional Paid-In Capital
Balance at end of 2004	$50,000	$ 38,000
Issuance of 2% stock dividend	1,000	14,000
Sale of stock for cash	9,000	135,000
Balance at end of 2005	$60,000	$187,000

(f) Interest paid (net of amount capitalized) is $9,000; income taxes paid is $62,000.

ANALYSIS OF TRANSACTIONS

The following discussion provides an explanation of the individual adjustments that appear on the work sheet in Illustration 23-39 (page 1241). Because cash is the basis for the analysis, the cash account is reconciled last. Because income is the first item that appears on the statement of cash flows, it is handled first.

Change in Retained Earnings

Net income for the period is $117,000. The entry for it on the work sheet is as follows.

(1)

Operating—Net Income	117,000	
Retained Earnings		117,000

Net income is reported on the bottom section of the work sheet and **is the starting point for preparation of the statement of cash flows (under the indirect method).**

Retained earnings was also affected by a stock dividend and a cash dividend. The retained earnings statement reports a stock dividend of $15,000. The work sheet entry for this transaction is as follows.

(2)

Retained Earnings	15,000	
Common Stock		1,000
Additional Paid-in Capital		14,000

The issuance of stock dividends is not a cash operating, investing, or financing item. Therefore, **although this transaction is entered on the work sheet for reconciling purposes, it is not reported in the statement of cash flows.**

The cash dividends paid of $6,000 represents a financing activity cash outflow. The following work sheet entry is made:

(3)

Retained Earnings	6,000	
Financing—Cash Dividends		6,000

The beginning and ending balances of retained earnings are reconciled by the entry of the three items above.

Accounts Receivable (Net)

The increase in accounts receivable (net) of $53,000 represents adjustments that did not result in cash inflows during 2005. As a result, the increase of $53,000 would be deducted from net income. The following work sheet entry is made.

(4)

Accounts Receivable (net)	53,000	
Operating—Increase in Accounts Receivable (net)		53,000

Inventories

The increase in inventories of $152,000 represents an operating use of cash. The incremental investment in inventories during the year reduces cash without increasing the cost of goods sold. The work sheet entry is made as follows.

(5)

Inventories	152,000	
Operating—Increase in Inventories		152,000

Prepaid Expense

The decrease in prepaid expenses of $500 represents a charge in the income statement for which there was no cash outflow in the current period. It should be added back to net income through the entry shown on the next page.

(6)

Operating—Decrease in Prepaid Expenses	500	
Prepaid Expenses		500

Investment in Stock

The investment in the stock of Porter Co. increased $3,500, which reflects Satellite's share of the income earned by its equity investee during the current year. Although revenue, and therefore income per the income statement, was increased $3,500 by the accounting entry that recorded Satellite's share of Porter Co.'s net income, no cash (dividend) was provided. The following work sheet entry is made.

(7)

Investment in Stock of Porter Co.	3,500	
Operating—Equity in Earnings of Porter Co.		3,500

Land

Land in the amount of $60,000 was purchased through the issuance of a long-term note payable. This transaction did not affect cash. It is considered a significant noncash investing/financing transaction that would be disclosed either in a separate schedule below the statement of cash flows or in the accompanying notes. The following entry is made to reconcile the work sheet.

(8)

Land	60,000	
Notes Payable		60,000

In addition to the noncash transaction involving the issuance of a note to purchase land, the Land account was decreased by the condemnation proceedings. The work sheet entry to record the receipt of $18,500 for land having a book value of $10,500 is as follows.

(9)

Investing—Proceeds from Condemnation of Land	18,500	
Land		10,500
Operating—Gain on Condemnation of Land		8,000

The extraordinary gain of $8,000 is deducted from net income in reconciling net income to net cash flow from operating activities because the transaction that gave rise to the gain is an item whose cash effect is already classified as an investing cash inflow. The Land account is now reconciled.

Equipment and Accumulated Depreciation

An analysis of Equipment and Accumulated Depreciation shows that a number of transactions have affected these accounts. Equipment in the amount of $53,000 was purchased during the year. The entry to record this transaction on the work sheet is as follows.

(10)

Equipment	53,000	
Investing—Purchase of Equipment		53,000

In addition, equipment with a book value of $5,500 was sold at a loss of $1,500. The entry to record this transaction on the work sheet is as follows.

(11)

Investing—Sale of Equipment	4,000	
Operating—Loss on Sale of Equipment	1,500	
Accumulated Depreciation—Equipment	2,500	
Equipment		8,000

The proceeds from the sale of the equipment provided cash of $4,000. In addition, the loss on the sale of the equipment has reduced net income, but did not affect cash.

Therefore, it is added back to net income to report accurately cash provided by operating activities.

Depreciation on the equipment was reported at $11,500 and is presented on the work sheet in the following manner.

(12)

Operating—Depreciation Expense—Equipment	11,500	
Accumulated Depreciation—Equipment		11,500

The depreciation expense is added back to net income because it reduced income but did not affect cash.

Finally, a major repair to the equipment in the amount of $11,000 was charged to Accumulated Depreciation—Equipment. Because this expenditure required cash, the following work sheet entry is made.

(13)

Accumulated Depreciation—Equipment	11,000	
Investing—Major Repairs of Equipment		11,000

The balances in the Equipment and related Accumulated Depreciation accounts are reconciled after adjustment for the foregoing items.

Building Depreciation and Amortization of Trademark

Depreciation expense on the buildings of $3,100 and amortization of trademark of $2,400 are both expenses in the income statement that reduced net income but did not require cash outflows in the current period. The following work sheet entry is made.

(14)

Operating—Depreciation Expense—Buildings	3,100	
Operating—Amortization of Trademark	2,400	
Accumulated Depreciation—Buildings		3,100
Trademark		2,400

Other Noncash Charges or Credits

An analysis of the remaining accounts indicates that changes in the Accounts Payable, Accrued Liabilities, Income Tax Payable, Premium on Bonds Payable, and Deferred Tax Liability balances resulted from charges or credits to net income that did not affect cash. Each of these items should be individually analyzed and entered in the work sheet. We have summarized in the following compound entry to the work sheet these noncash, income-related items.

(15)

Income Tax Payable	13,000	
Premium on Bonds Payable	1,000	
Operating—Increase in Accounts Payable	1,000	
Operating—Increase in Accrued Liabilities	4,000	
Operating—Increase in Deferred Tax Liability	3,000	
Operating—Decrease in Income Tax Payable		13,000
Operating—Amortization of Bond Premium		1,000
Accounts Payable		1,000
Accrued Liabilities		4,000
Deferred Tax Liability		3,000

Common Stock and Related Accounts

A comparison of the common stock balances and the additional paid-in capital balances shows that transactions during the year affected these accounts. First, a stock dividend of 2 percent was issued to stockholders. As indicated in the discussion of work sheet entry (2), no cash was provided or used by the stock dividend transaction. In addition to the shares issued via the stock dividend, Satellite sold shares of common stock at $16 per share. The work sheet entry to record this transaction is as follows.

(16)

Financing—Sale of Common Stock	144,000	
Common Stock		9,000
Additional Paid-in Capital		135,000

Also, the company purchased shares of its common stock in the amount of $17,000. The work sheet entry to record this transaction is as follows.

(17)

Treasury Stock	17,000	
Financing—Purchase of Treasury Stock		17,000

Final Reconciling Entry

The final entry to reconcile the change in cash and to balance the work sheet is shown below.

(18)

Decrease in Cash	7,000	
Cash		7,000

The $7,000 amount is the difference between the beginning and ending cash balance.

Once it has been determined that the differences between the beginning and ending balances per the work sheet columns have been accounted for, the reconciling transactions columns can be totaled, and they should balance. The statement of cash flows can be prepared entirely from the items and amounts that appear at the bottom of the work sheet under "Statement of Cash Flows Effects," as shown in Illustration 23-39.

ILLUSTRATION 23-39
Completed Work Sheet for Preparation of Statement of Cash Flows, Satellite Corporation

SATELLITE CORPORATION
Work Sheet for Preparation of Statement of Cash Flows For the Year Ended December 31, 2005

	A	B	C	D	E	F	G
			Reconciling Items–2005				
1		Balance 12/31/04		Debits		Credits	Balance 12/31/05
2	Debits						
3	Cash	$ 66,000			(18)	7,000	$ 59,000
4	Accounts receivable (net)	51,000	(4)	$ 53,000			104,000
5	Inventories	341,000	(5)	152,000			493,000
6	Prepaid expenses	17,000			(6)	500	16,500
7	Investment (equity method)	15,000	(7)	3,500			18,500
8	Land	82,000	(8)	60,000	(9)	10,500	131,500
9	Equipment	142,000	(10)	53,000	(11)	8,000	187,000
10	Building	262,000					262,000
11	Trademark	10,000			(14)	2,400	7,600
12	Treasury stock		(17)	17,000			17,000
13	Total debits	$986,000					$1,296,100
14	Credits						
15	Accum. depr.–equipment	$ 31,000	(11)	2,500	(12)	11,500	
16			(13)	11,000			$ 29,000
17	Accum. depr.–building	71,000			(14)	3,100	74,100
18	Accounts payable	131,000			(15)	1,000	132,000
19	Accrued liabilities	39,000			(15)	4,000	43,000
20	Income tax payable	16,000	(15)	13,000			3,000
21	Notes payable	-0-			(8)	60,000	60,000
22	Bonds payable	100,000					100,000
23	Premium on bonds payable	8,000	(15)	1,000			7,000
24	Deferred tax liability	6,000			(15)	3,000	9,000
25	Common stock	50,000			(2)	1,000	
26					(16)	9,000	60,000
27	Additional paid-in capital	38,000			(2)	14,000	
28					(16)	135,000	187,000
29	Retained earnings	496,000	(2)	15,000	(1)	117,000	
30			(3)	6,000			592,000
31	Total credits	$986,000					$1,296,100
32	Statement of Cash Flows Effects						
33	Operating activities						
34	Net income		(1)	117,000			
35	Increase in accounts receivable (net)				(4)	53,000	
36	Increase in inventories				(5)	152,000	
37	Decrease in prepaid expenses		(6)	500			
38	Equity in earnings of Porter Co.				(7)	3,500	
39	Gain on condemnation of land				(9)	8,000	
40	Loss on sale of equipment		(11)	1,500			
41	Depr. expense–equipment		(12)	11,500			
42	Depr. expense–building		(14)	3,100			
43	Amortization of trademark		(14)	2,400			
44	Increase in accounts payable		(15)	1,000			
45	Increase in accrued liabilities		(15)	4,000			
46	Increase in deferred tax liability		(15)	3,000			
47	Decrease in income tax payable				(15)	13,000	
48	Amortization of bond premium				(15)	1,000	
49	Investing activities						
50	Proceeds from condemnation of land		(9)	18,500			
51	Purchase of equipment				(10)	53,000	
52	Sale of equipment		(11)	4,000			
53	Major repairs of equipment				(13)	11,000	
54	Financing activities						
55	Payment of cash dividend				(3)	6,000	
56	Issuance of common stock		(16)	144,000			
57	Purchase of treasury stock				(17)	17,000	
58	Totals			697,500		704,500	
59	Decrease in cash		(18)	7,000			
60	Totals			$704,500		$704,500	

Sheet1 / Sheet2 / Sheet3

PREPARATION OF FINAL STATEMENT

Presented below is a formal statement of cash flows prepared from the data compiled in the lower portion of the work sheet.

ILLUSTRATION 23-40
Statement of Cash Flows, Satellite Corporation

SATELLITE CORPORATION
STATEMENT OF CASH FLOWS
FOR THE YEAR ENDED DECEMBER 31, 2005
INCREASE (DECREASE) IN CASH

Cash flows from operating activities		
Net income		$117,000
Adjustments to reconcile net income to net cash used by operating activities:		
Depreciation expense	$ 14,600	
Amortization of trademark	2,400	
Amortization of bond premium	(1,000)	
Equity in earnings of Porter Co.	(3,500)	
Gain on condemnation of land	(8,000)	
Loss on sale of equipment	1,500	
Increase in deferred tax liability	3,000	
Increase in accounts receivable (net)	(53,000)	
Increase in inventories	(152,000)	
Decrease in prepaid expenses	500	
Increase in accounts payable	1,000	
Increase in accrued liabilities	4,000	
Decrease in income tax payable	(13,000)	(203,500)
Net cash used by operating activities		(86,500)
Cash flows from investing activities		
Proceeds from condemnation of land	18,500	
Purchase of equipment	(53,000)	
Sale of equipment	4,000	
Major repairs of equipment	(11,000)	
Net cash used by investing activities		(41,500)
Cash flows from financing activities		
Payment of cash dividend	(6,000)	
Issuance of common stock	144,000	
Purchase of treasury stock	(17,000)	
Net cash provided by financing activities		121,000
Net decrease in cash		(7,000)
Cash, January 1, 2005		66,000
Cash, December 31, 2005		$ 59,000

Supplemental Disclosures of Cash Flow Information:

Cash paid during the year for:	
Interest (net of amount capitalized)	$ 9,000
Income taxes	$ 62,000

Supplemental Schedule of Noncash Investing and Financing Activities:
Purchase of land for $60,000 in exchange for a $60,000 long-term note.

Discussion of the T-account Approach to Preparation of the Statement of Cash Flows

SUMMARY OF LEARNING OBJECTIVES

1 Describe the purpose of the statement of cash flows. The primary purpose of the statement of cash flows is to provide information about cash receipts and cash payments of an entity during a period. A secondary objective is to report the entity's operating, investing, and financing activities during the period.

2 Identify the major classifications of cash flows. The cash flows are classified as: (1) *Operating activities*—transactions that result in the revenues, expenses, gains, and losses that determine net income. (2) *Investing activities*—lending money and collecting on those loans, and acquiring and disposing of investments, plant assets, and intangible assets. (3) *Financing activities*—obtaining cash from creditors and repaying loans, issuing and reacquiring capital stock, and paying cash dividends.

3 Differentiate between net income and net cash flows from operating activities. Net income on an accrual basis must be adjusted to determine net cash flow from operating activities because some expenses and losses do not cause cash outflows and some revenues and gains do not provide cash inflows.

4 Contrast the direct and indirect methods of calculating net cash flow from operating activities. Under the direct approach, major classes of operating cash receipts and cash disbursements are calculated. The computations are summarized in a schedule of changes from the accrual to the cash-basis income statement. Presentation of the direct approach of reporting net cash flow from operating activities takes the form of a condensed cash-basis income statement. The indirect method adds back to net income the noncash expenses and losses and subtracts the noncash revenues and gains.

5 Determine net cash flows from investing and financing activities. Once the net cash flow from operating activities is computed, the next step is to determine whether any other changes in balance sheet accounts caused an increase or decrease in cash. Net cash flows from investing and financing activities can be determined by examining the changes in noncurrent balance sheet accounts.

6 Prepare a statement of cash flows. Preparing the statement involves three major steps: (1) *Determine the change in cash.* This is the difference between the beginning and the ending cash balance shown on the comparative balance sheets. (2) *Determine the net cash flow from operating activities.* This procedure is complex; it involves analyzing not only the current year's income statement but also the comparative balance sheets and the selected transaction data. (3) *Determine cash flows from investing and financing activities.* All other changes in the balance sheet accounts must be analyzed to determine the effects on cash.

7 Identify sources of information for a statement of cash flows. The information to prepare the statement usually comes from three sources: (1) *Comparative balance sheets.* Information in these statements indicate the amount of the changes in assets, liabilities, and equities during the period. (2) *Current income statement.* Information in this statement is used in determining the cash provided by operations during the period. (3) *Selected transaction data.* These data from the general ledger provide additional detailed information needed to determine how cash was provided or used during the period.

8 Identify special problems in preparing a statement of cash flows. These special problems are: (1) adjustments similar to depreciation; (2) accounts receivable (net); (3) other working capital changes; (4) net losses; (5) gains; (6) stock options; (7) postretirement benefit costs; (8) extraordinary items; and (9) significant noncash transactions.

9 Explain the use of a work sheet in preparing a statement of cash flows. When numerous adjustments are necessary, or other complicating factors are present, a work sheet is often used to assemble and classify the data that will appear on the statement of cash flows. The work sheet is merely a device that aids in the preparation of the statement. Its use is optional.

KEY TERMS

cash equivalents, *1205n*
direct method, *1210*
financing activities, *1206*
indirect method, *1211*
investing activities, *1206*
operating activities, *1205*
significant noncash transactions, *1232*
statement of cash flows, *1204*

QUESTIONS

1. What is the purpose of the statement of cash flows? What information does it provide?
2. Of what use is the statement of cash flows?
3. Differentiate between investing activities, financing activities, and operating activities.
4. What are the major sources of cash (inflows) in a statement of cash flows? What are the major uses (outflows) of cash?
5. Identify and explain the major steps involved in preparing the statement of cash flows.
6. Identify the following items as (1) operating, (2) investing, or (3) financing activities: purchase of land; payment of dividends; cash sales; and purchase of treasury stock.
7. Unlike the other major financial statements, the statement of cash flows is not prepared from the adjusted trial balance. From what sources does the information to prepare this statement come, and what information does each source provide?
8. Why is it necessary to convert accrual-based net income to a cash basis when preparing a statement of cash flows?
9. Differentiate between the direct method and the indirect method by discussing each method.
10. Bonnie Raitt Company reported net income of $3.5 million in 2005. Depreciation for the year was $520,000; accounts receivable increased $500,000; and accounts payable increased $350,000. Compute net cash flow from operating activities using the indirect method.
11. Sophie B. Hawkins Co. reported sales on an accrual basis of $100,000. If accounts receivable increased $30,000, and the allowance for doubtful accounts increased $9,000 after a writeoff of $4,000, compute cash sales.
12. Your roommate is puzzled. During the last year, the company in which she is a stockholder reported a net loss of $675,000, yet its cash increased $321,000 during the same period of time. Explain to your roommate how this situation could occur.
13. The board of directors of Kenny G Corp. declared cash dividends of $260,000 during the current year. If dividends payable was $85,000 at the beginning of the year and $70,000 at the end of the year, how much cash was paid in dividends during the year?
14. Explain how the amount of cash payments to suppliers is computed under the direct method.
15. The net income for Silverchair Company for 2005 was $320,000. During 2005, depreciation on plant assets was $114,000, amortization of patent was $40,000, and the company incurred a loss on sale of plant assets of $21,000. Compute net cash flow from operating activities.
16. Each of the following items must be considered in preparing a statement of cash flows for Frogstomp Inc. for the year ended December 31, 2005. State where each item is to be shown in the statement, if at all.
    - **(a)** Plant assets that had cost $20,000 6½ years before and were being depreciated on a straight-line basis over 10 years with no estimated scrap value were sold for $4,000.
    - **(b)** During the year, 10,000 shares of common stock with a stated value of $20 a share were issued for $41 a share.
    - **(c)** Uncollectible accounts receivable in the amount of $22,000 were written off against the Allowance for Doubtful Accounts.
    - **(d)** The company sustained a net loss for the year of $50,000. Depreciation amounted to $22,000, and a gain of $9,000 was realized on the sale of available-for-sale securities for $38,000 cash.
17. Classify the following items as (1) operating, (2) investing, (3) financing, or (4) significant noncash investing and financing activities, using the direct method.
    - **(a)** Purchase of equipment.
    - **(b)** Redemption of bonds.
    - **(c)** Sale of building.
    - **(d)** Cash payments to suppliers.
    - **(e)** Exchange of equipment for furniture.
    - **(f)** Issuance of capital stock.
    - **(g)** Cash received from customers.
    - **(h)** Purchase of treasury stock.
    - **(i)** Issuance of bonds for land.
    - **(j)** Payment of dividends.
    - **(k)** Cash payments to employees.
    - **(l)** Cash payments for operating expenses.
18. Clay Walker and David Ball were discussing the presentation format of the statement of cash flows of Martina McBride Co. At the bottom of McBride's statement of cash flows was a separate section entitled "Noncash investing and financing activities." Give three examples of significant noncash transactions that would be reported in this section.
19. During 2005, Bryan Adams Company redeemed $2,000,000 of bonds payable for $1,780,000 cash. Indicate how this transaction would be reported on a statement of cash flows, if at all.
20. What are some of the arguments in favor of using the indirect (reconciliation) method as opposed to the direct method for reporting a statement of cash flows?
21. Why is it desirable to use a work sheet when preparing a statement of cash flows? Is a work sheet required to prepare a statement of cash flows?

BRIEF EXERCISES

BE23-1 American Gladhanders Corporation had the following activities in 2005.

Sale of land $130,000
Purchase of inventory $845,000
Purchase of treasury stock $72,000
Purchase of equipment $415,000
Issuance of common stock $320,000
Purchase of available-for-sale securities $59,000

Compute the amount American Gladhanders should report as net cash provided (used) by investing activities in its statement of cash flows.

BE23-2 Chrono Trigger Corporation had the following activities in 2005.

Payment of accounts payable $770,000
Issuance of common stock $250,000
Payment of dividends $300,000
Collection of note receivable $100,000
Issuance of bonds payable $510,000
Purchase of treasury stock $46,000

Compute the amount Chrono Trigger should report as net cash provided (used) by financing activities in its 2005 statement of cash flows.

BE23-3 Ryker Corporation is preparing its 2005 statement of cash flows, using the indirect method. Presented below is a list of items that may affect the statement. Using the code below, indicate how each item will affect Ryker's 2005 statement of cash flows.

Code Letter	Effect
A	Added to net income in the operating section
D	Deducted from net income in the operating section
R-I	Cash receipt in investing section
P-I	Cash payment in investing section
R-F	Cash receipt in financing section
P-F	Cash payment in financing section
N	Noncash investing and/or financing activity

Items

____ **(a)** Increase in accounts receivable.
____ **(b)** Decrease in accounts receivable.
____ **(c)** Issuance of stock.
____ **(d)** Depreciation expense.
____ **(e)** Sale of land at book value.
____ **(f)** Sale of land at a gain.
____ **(g)** Payment of dividends.
____ **(h)** Purchase of land and building.
____ **(i)** Purchase of available-for-sale investment.
____ **(j)** Increase in accounts payable.
____ **(k)** Decrease in accounts payable.
____ **(l)** Loan from bank by signing note.
____ **(m)** Purchase of equipment using a note.
____ **(n)** Increase in inventory.
____ **(o)** Issuance of bonds.
____ **(p)** Retirement of bonds.
____ **(q)** Sale of equipment at a loss.
____ **(r)** Purchase of treasury stock.

BE23-4 Azure Corporation had the following 2005 income statement.

Sales	$200,000
Cost of goods sold	120,000
Gross profit	80,000

Operating expenses (includes depreciation of $21,000)	50,000
Net income	$ 30,000

The following accounts increased during 2005: accounts receivable $17,000; inventory $11,000; accounts payable $13,000. Prepare the cash flows from operating activities section of Azure's 2005 statement of cash flows using the direct method.

BE23-5 Use the information from BE23-4 for Azure Corporation. Prepare the cash flows from operating activities section of Azure's 2005 statement of cash flows using the indirect method.

BE23-6 At January 1, 2005, Cyberslider Inc. had accounts receivable of $72,000. At December 31, 2005, accounts receivable is $59,000. Sales for 2005 is $420,000. Compute Cyberslider's 2005 cash receipts from customers.

BE23-7 Donkey Kong Corporation had January 1 and December 31 balances as follows.

	1/1/05	12/31/05
Inventory	$90,000	$113,000
Accounts payable	61,000	69,000

For 2005, cost of goods sold was $500,000. Compute Donkey Kong's 2005 cash payments to suppliers.

BE23-8 In 2005, Fieval Corporation had net cash provided by operating activities of $531,000; net cash used by investing activities of $963,000; and net cash provided by financing activities of $585,000. At January 1, 2005, the cash balance was $333,000. Compute December 31, 2005, cash.

BE23-9 Tool Time Corporation had the following 2005 income statement.

Revenues	$100,000
Expenses	60,000
	$ 40,000

In 2005, Tool Time had the following activity in selected accounts.

Accounts Receivable

1/1/05	20,000		
Revenues	100,000	1,000	Writeoffs
		90,000	Collections
12/31/05	29,000		

Allowance for Doubtful Accounts

		1,200	1/1/05
Writeoffs	1,000	1,540	Bad debt expense
		1,740	12/31/05

Prepare Tool Time's cash flows from operating activities section of the statement of cash flows using (a) the direct method and (b) the indirect method.

BE23-10 Red October Corporation reported net income of $50,000 in 2005. Depreciation expense was $17,000. The following working capital accounts changed.

Accounts receivable	$11,000 increase
Available-for-sale securities	16,000 increase
Inventory	7,400 increase
Nontrade note payable	15,000 decrease
Accounts payable	9,300 increase

Compute net cash provided by operating activities.

BE23-11 In 2005, Izzy Corporation reported a net loss of $70,000. Izzy's only net income adjustments were depreciation expense $84,000, and increase in accounts receivable $8,100. Compute Izzy's net cash provided (used) by operating activities.

BE23-12 In 2005, Mufosta Inc. issued 1,000 shares of $10 par value common stock for land worth $50,000.

(a) Prepare Mufosta's journal entry to record the transaction.
(b) Indicate the effect the transaction has on cash.
(c) Indicate how the transaction is reported on the statement of cash flows.

BE23-13 Indicate in general journal form how the items below would be entered in a work sheet for the preparation of the statement of cash flows.

(a) Net income is $317,000.
(b) Cash dividends declared and paid totaled $120,000.

(c) Equipment was purchased for $114,000.
(d) Equipment that originally cost $40,000 and had accumulated depreciation of $32,000 was sold for $13,000.

EXERCISES

E23-1 (Classification of Transactions) Red Hot Chili Peppers Co. had the following activity in its most recent year of operations.

(a) Purchase of equipment.
(b) Redemption of bonds.
(c) Sale of building.
(d) Depreciation.
(e) Exchange of equipment for furniture.
(f) Issuance of capital stock.
(g) Amortization of intangible assets.
(h) Purchase of treasury stock.
(i) Issuance of bonds for land.
(j) Payment of dividends.
(k) Increase in interest receivable on notes receivable.
(l) Pension expense exceeds amount funded.

Instructions

Classify the items as (1) operating—add to net income; (2) operating—deduct from net income; (3) investing; (4) financing; or (5) significant noncash investing and financing activities. Use the indirect method.

E23-2 (Statement Presentation of Transactions—Indirect Method) Each of the following items must be considered in preparing a statement of cash flows (indirect method) for Turbulent Indigo Inc. for the year ended December 31, 2004.

(a) Plant assets that had cost $20,000 6 years before and were being depreciated on a straight-line basis over 10 years with no estimated scrap value were sold for $5,300.
(b) During the year, 10,000 shares of common stock with a stated value of $10 a share were issued for $43 a share.
(c) Uncollectible accounts receivable in the amount of $27,000 were written off against the Allowance for Doubtful Accounts.
(d) The company sustained a net loss for the year of $50,000. Depreciation amounted to $22,000, and a gain of $9,000 was realized on the sale of land for $39,000 cash.
(e) A 3-month U.S. Treasury bill was purchased for $100,000. The company uses a cash and cash-equivalent basis for its cash flow statement.
(f) Patent amortization for the year was $20,000.
(g) The company exchanged common stock for a 70% interest in Tabasco Co. for $900,000.
(h) During the year, treasury stock costing $47,000 was purchased.

Instructions

State where each item is to be shown in the statement of cash flows, if at all.

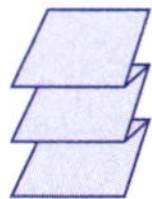

E23-3 (Preparation of Operating Activities Section—Indirect Method, Periodic Inventory) The income statement of Vince Gill Company is shown below.

VINCE GILL COMPANY
INCOME STATEMENT
FOR THE YEAR ENDED DECEMBER 31, 2005

Sales		$6,900,000
Cost of goods sold		
Beginning inventory	$1,900,000	
Purchases	4,400,000	
Goods available for sale	6,300,000	
Ending inventory	1,600,000	
Cost of goods sold		4,700,000
Gross profit		2,200,000
Operating expenses		
Selling expenses	450,000	
Administrative expenses	700,000	1,150,000
Net income		$1,050,000

Additional information:

1. Accounts receivable decreased $360,000 during the year.
2. Prepaid expenses increased $170,000 during the year.
3. Accounts payable to suppliers of merchandise decreased $275,000 during the year.
4. Accrued expenses payable decreased $100,000 during the year.
5. Administrative expenses include depreciation expense of $60,000.

Instructions

Prepare the operating activities section of the statement of cash flows for the year ended December 31, 2005, for Vince Gill Company, using the indirect method.

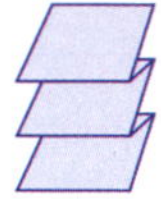

E23-4 (Preparation of Operating Activities Section—Direct Method) Data for the Vince Gill Company are presented in E23-3.

Instructions

Prepare the operating activities section of the statement of cash flows using the direct method.

E23-5 (Preparation of Operating Activities Section—Direct Method) Alison Krauss Company's income statement for the year ended December 31, 2004, contained the following condensed information.

Revenue from fees		$840,000
Operating expenses (excluding depreciation)	$624,000	
Depreciation expense	60,000	
Loss on sale of equipment	26,000	710,000
Income before income taxes		130,000
Income tax expense		40,000
Net income		$ 90,000

Krauss's balance sheet contained the following comparative data at December 31.

	2004	2003
Accounts receivable	$37,000	$54,000
Accounts payable	41,000	31,000
Income taxes payable	4,000	8,500

(Accounts payable pertains to operating expenses.)

Instructions

Prepare the operating activities section of the statement of cash flows using the direct method.

E23-6 (Preparation of Operating Activities Section—Indirect Method) Data for Alison Krauss Company are presented in E23-5.

Instructions

Prepare the operating activities section of the statement of cash flows using the indirect method.

E23-7 (Computation of Operating Activities—Direct Method) Presented below are two independent situations.

Situation A:

Annie Lennox Co. reports revenues of $200,000 and operating expenses of $110,000 in its first year of operations, 2005. Accounts receivable and accounts payable at year-end were $71,000 and $29,000, respectively. Assume that the accounts payable related to operating expenses. Ignore income taxes.

Instructions

Using the direct method, compute net cash provided by operating activities.

Situation B:

The income statement for Blues Traveler Company shows cost of goods sold $310,000 and operating expenses (exclusive of depreciation) $230,000. The comparative balance sheet for the year shows that inventory increased $26,000, prepaid expenses decreased $8,000, accounts payable (related to merchandise) decreased $17,000, and accrued expenses payable increased $11,000.

Instructions

Compute (a) cash payments to suppliers and (b) cash payments for operating expenses.

E23-8 (Schedule of Net Cash Flow from Operating Activities—Indirect Method) Glen Ballard Co. reported $145,000 of net income for 2005. The accountant, in preparing the statement of cash flows, noted several items occurring during 2005 that might affect cash flows from operating activities. These items are listed on page 1249.

1. Ballard purchased 100 shares of treasury stock at a cost of $20 per share. These shares were then resold at $25 per share.
2. Ballard sold 100 shares of IBM common at $200 per share. The acquisition cost of these shares was $145 per share. This investment was shown on Ballard's December 31, 2004, balance sheet as an available-for-sale security.
3. Ballard changed from the straight-line method to the double-declining balance method of depreciation for its machinery. The total cumulative effect was for $14,600.
4. Ballard revised its estimate for bad debts. Before 2005, Ballard's bad debt expense was 1% of its net sales. In 2005, this percentage was increased to 2%. Net sales for 2005 were $500,000, and net accounts receivable decreased by $12,000 during 2005.
5. Ballard issued 500 shares of its $10 par common stock for a patent. The market value of the shares on the date of the transaction was $23 per share.
6. Depreciation expense is $39,000.
7. Ballard Co. holds 40% of the Nirvana Company's common stock as a long-term investment. Nirvana Company reported $27,000 of net income for 2005.
8. Nirvana Company paid a total of $2,000 of cash dividends to all investees in 2005.
9. Ballard declared a 10% stock dividend. One thousand shares of $10 par common stock were distributed. The market price at date of issuance was $20 per share.

Instructions

Prepare a schedule that shows the net cash flow from operating activities using the indirect method. Assume no items other than those listed above affected the computation of 2005 net cash flow from operating activities.

E23-9 (SCF—Direct Method) Los Lobos Corp. uses the direct method to prepare its statement of cash flows. Los Lobos's trial balances at December 31, 2004 and 2003, are as follows.

	December 31	
	2004	2003
Debits		
Cash	$ 35,000	$ 32,000
Accounts receivable	33,000	30,000
Inventory	31,000	47,000
Property, plant, & equipment	100,000	95,000
Unamortized bond discount	4,500	5,000
Cost of goods sold	250,000	380,000
Selling expenses	141,500	172,000
General and administrative expenses	137,000	151,300
Interest expense	4,300	2,600
Income tax expense	20,400	61,200
	$756,700	$976,100
Credits		
Allowance for doubtful accounts	$ 1,300	$ 1,100
Accumulated depreciation	16,500	15,000
Trade accounts payable	25,000	15,500
Income taxes payable	21,000	29,100
Deferred income taxes	5,300	4,600
8% callable bonds payable	45,000	20,000
Common stock	50,000	40,000
Additional paid-in capital	9,100	7,500
Retained earnings	44,700	64,600
Sales	538,800	778,700
	$756,700	$976,100

Additional information:

1. Los Lobos purchased $5,000 in equipment during 2004.
2. Los Lobos allocated one-third of its depreciation expense to selling expenses and the remainder to general and administrative expenses.
3. Bad debt expense for 2004 was $5,000, and writeoffs of uncollectible accounts totaled $4,800.

Instructions

Determine what amounts Los Lobos should report in its statement of cash flows for the year ended December 31, 2004, for the following items shown on page 1250.

1. Cash collected from customers.
2. Cash paid to suppliers.
3. Cash paid for interest.
4. Cash paid for income taxes.
5. Cash paid for selling expenses.

E23-10 (Classification of Transactions) Following are selected balance sheet accounts of Allman Bros. Corp. at December 31, 2005 and 2004, and the increases or decreases in each account from 2004 to 2005. Also presented is selected income statement information for the year ended December 31, 2005, and additional information.

Selected balance sheet accounts	2005	2004	Increase (Decrease)
Assets			
Accounts receivable	$ 34,000	$ 24,000	$ 10,000
Property, plant, and equipment	277,000	247,000	30,000
Accumulated depreciation	(178,000)	(167,000)	(11,000)
Liabilities and stockholders' equity			
Bonds payable	49,000	46,000	3,000
Dividends payable	8,000	5,000	3,000
Common stock, $1 par	22,000	19,000	3,000
Additional paid-in capital	9,000	3,000	6,000
Retained earnings	104,000	91,000	13,000
Selected income statement information for the year ended December 31, 2005			
Sales revenue	$155,000		
Depreciation	33,000		
Gain on sale of equipment	14,500		
Net income	31,000		

Additional information:

1. During 2005, equipment costing $45,000 was sold for cash.
2. Accounts receivable relate to sales of merchandise.
3. During 2005, $20,000 of bonds payable were issued in exchange for property, plant, and equipment. There was no amortization of bond discount or premium.

Instructions

Determine the category (operating, investing, or financing) and the amount that should be reported in the statement of cash flows for the following items.

1. Payments for purchase of property, plant, and equipment.
2. Proceeds from the sale of equipment.
3. Cash dividends paid.
4. Redemption of bonds payable.

E23-11 (SCF—Indirect Method) Condensed financial data of Pat Metheny Company for 2005 and 2004 are presented below.

PAT METHENY COMPANY
COMPARATIVE BALANCE SHEET
AS OF DECEMBER 31, 2005 AND 2004

	2005	2004
Cash	$1,800	$1,150
Receivables	1,750	1,300
Inventory	1,600	1,900
Plant assets	1,900	1,700
Accumulated depreciation	(1,200)	(1,170)
Long-term investments (Held-to-maturity)	1,300	1,420
	$7,150	$6,300
Accounts payable	$1,200	$ 900
Accrued liabilities	200	250
Bonds payable	1,400	1,550
Capital stock	1,900	1,700
Retained earnings	2,450	1,900
	$7,150	$6,300

PAT METHENY COMPANY
INCOME STATEMENT
FOR THE YEAR ENDED DECEMBER 31, 2005

Sales	$6,900
Cost of goods sold	4,700
Gross margin	2,200
Selling and administrative expense	930
Income from operations	1,270
Other revenues and gains	
Gain on sale of investments	80
Income before tax	1,350
Income tax expense	540
Net income	810
Cash dividends	260
Income retained in business	$ 550

Additional information:

During the year, $70 of common stock was issued in exchange for plant assets. No plant assets were sold in 2005.

Instructions

Prepare a statement of cash flows using the indirect method.

E23-12 (SCF—Direct Method) Data for Pat Metheny Company are presented in E23-11.

Instructions

Prepare a statement of cash flows using the direct method. (Do not prepare a reconciliation schedule.)

E23-13 (SCF—Direct Method) Brecker Inc., a greeting card company, had the following statements prepared as of December 31, 2005.

BRECKER INC.
COMPARATIVE BALANCE SHEET
AS OF DECEMBER 31, 2005 AND 2004

	12/31/05	12/31/04
Cash	$ 6,000	$ 7,000
Accounts receivable	62,000	51,000
Short-term investments (Available-for-sale)	35,000	18,000
Inventories	40,000	60,000
Prepaid rent	5,000	4,000
Printing equipment	154,000	130,000
Accumulated depr.—equipment	(35,000)	(25,000)
Copyrights	46,000	50,000
Total assets	$313,000	$295,000
Accounts payable	$ 46,000	$ 40,000
Income taxes payable	4,000	6,000
Wages payable	8,000	4,000
Short-term loans payable	8,000	10,000
Long-term loans payable	60,000	69,000
Common stock, $10 par	100,000	100,000
Contributed capital, common stock	30,000	30,000
Retained earnings	57,000	36,000
Total liabilities & equity	$313,000	$295,000

BRECKER INC.
INCOME STATEMENT
FOR THE YEAR ENDING DECEMBER 31, 2005

Sales	$338,150
Cost of goods sold	175,000
Gross margin	163,150
Operating expenses	120,000
Operating income	43,150

Interest expense	$11,400	
Gain on sale of equipment	2,000	9,400
Income before tax		33,750
Income tax expense		6,750
Net income		$ 27,000

Additional information:

1. Dividends in the amount of $6,000 were declared and paid during 2005.
2. Depreciation expense and amortization expense are included in operating expenses.
3. No unrealized gains or losses have occurred on the investments during the year.
4. Equipment that had a cost of $20,000 and was 70% depreciated was sold during 2005.

Instructions

Prepare a statement of cash flows using the direct method. (Do not prepare a reconciliation schedule.)

E23-14 (SCF—Indirect Method) Data for Brecker Inc. are presented in E23-13.

Instructions

Prepare a statement of cash flows using the indirect method.

E23-15 (SCF—Indirect Method) Presented below are data taken from the records of Antonio Brasileiro Company.

	December 31, 2005	December 31, 2004
Cash	$ 15,000	$ 8,000
Current assets other than cash	85,000	60,000
Long-term investments	10,000	53,000
Plant assets	335,000	215,000
	$445,000	$336,000
Accumulated depreciation	$ 20,000	$ 40,000
Current liabilities	40,000	22,000
Bonds payable	75,000	–0–
Capital stock	254,000	254,000
Retained earnings	56,000	20,000
	$445,000	$336,000

Additional information:

1. Held-to-maturity securities carried at a cost of $43,000 on December 31, 2004, were sold in 2005 for $34,000. The loss (not extraordinary) was incorrectly charged directly to Retained Earnings.
2. Plant assets that cost $50,000 and were 80% depreciated were sold during 2005 for $8,000. The loss (not extraordinary) was incorrectly charged directly to Retained Earnings.
3. Net income as reported on the income statement for the year was $57,000.
4. Dividends paid amounted to $10,000.
5. Depreciation charged for the year was $20,000.

Instructions

Prepare a statement of cash flows for the year 2005 using the indirect method.

E23-16 (Cash Provided by Operating, Investing, and Financing Activities) The balance sheet data of Brown Company at the end of 2004 and 2003 follow.

	2004	2003
Cash	$ 30,000	$ 35,000
Accounts receivable (net)	55,000	45,000
Merchandise inventory	65,000	45,000
Prepaid expenses	15,000	25,000
Equipment	90,000	75,000
Accumulated depreciation—equipment	(18,000)	(8,000)
Land	70,000	40,000
Totals	$307,000	$257,000

Accounts payable	$ 65,000	$ 52,000
Accrued expenses	15,000	18,000
Notes payable—bank, long-term	–0–	23,000
Bonds payable	30,000	–0–
Common stock, $10 par	189,000	159,000
Retained earnings	8,000	5,000
	$307,000	$257,000

Land was acquired for $30,000 in exchange for common stock, par $30,000, during the year; all equipment purchased was for cash. Equipment costing $10,000 was sold for $3,000; book value of the equipment was $6,000. Cash dividends of $10,000 were declared and paid during the year.

Instructions

Compute net cash provided (used) by:

(a) operating activities.
(b) investing activities.
(c) financing activities.

E23-17 (SCF—Indirect Method and Balance Sheet) Jobim Inc., had the following condensed balance sheet at the end of operations for 2004.

JOBIM INC.
BALANCE SHEET
DECEMBER 31, 2004

Cash	$ 8,500	Current liabilities	$ 15,000
Current assets other than cash	29,000	Long-term notes payable	25,500
Investments	20,000	Bonds payable	25,000
Plant assets (net)	67,500	Capital stock	75,000
Land	40,000	Retained earnings	24,500
	$165,000		$165,000

During 2005 the following occurred.

1. A tract of land was purchased for $9,000.
2. Bonds payable in the amount of $15,000 were retired at par.
3. An additional $10,000 in capital stock was issued at par.
4. Dividends totaling $9,375 were paid to stockholders.
5. Net income was $35,250 after allowing depreciation of $13,500.
6. Land was purchased through the issuance of $22,500 in bonds.
7. Jobim Inc. sold part of its investment portfolio for $12,875. This transaction resulted in a gain of $2,000 for the company. The company classifies the investments as available-for-sale.
8. Both current assets (other than cash) and current liabilities remained at the same amount.

Instructions

(a) Prepare a statement of cash flows for 2005 using the indirect method.
(b) Prepare the condensed balance sheet for Jobim Inc. as it would appear at December 31, 2005.

E23-18 (Partial SCF—Indirect Method) The accounts below appear in the ledger of Anita Baker Company.

	Retained Earnings	Dr.	Cr.	Bal.
Jan. 1, 2005	Credit Balance			$ 42,000
Aug. 15	Dividends (cash)	$15,000		27,000
Dec. 31	Net Income for 2005		$40,000	67,000

	Machinery	Dr.	Cr.	Bal.
Jan. 1, 2005	Debit Balance			$140,000
Aug. 3	Purchase of Machinery	$62,000		202,000
Sept. 10	Cost of Machinery Constructed	48,000		250,000
Nov. 15	Machinery Sold		$56,000	194,000

	Accumulated Depreciation—Machinery	Dr.	Cr.	Bal.
Jan. 1, 2005	Credit Balance			$ 84,000
Apr. 8	Extraordinary Repairs	$21,000		63,000
Nov. 15	Accum. Depreciation on Machinery Sold	25,200		37,800
Dec. 31	Depreciation for 2005		$16,800	54,600

Instructions

From the postings in the accounts above, indicate how the information is reported on a statement of cash flows by preparing a partial statement of cash flows using the indirect method. The loss on sale of equipment (November 15) was $5,800.

E23-19 (Work Sheet Analysis of Selected Accounts) Data for Anita Baker Company are presented in E23-18.

Instructions

Prepare entries in journal form for all adjustments that should be made on a work sheet for a statement of cash flows.

E23-20 (Work Sheet Analysis of Selected Transactions) The transactions below took place during the year 2005.

1. Convertible bonds payable with a par value of $300,000 were exchanged for unissued common stock with a par value of $300,000. The market price of both types of securities was par.
2. The net income for the year was $410,000.
3. Depreciation charged on the building was $90,000.
4. Some old office equipment was traded in on the purchase of some dissimilar office equipment and the following entry was made.

Office Equipment	50,000	
Accum. Depreciation—Office Equipment	30,000	
Office Equipment		40,000
Cash		34,000
Gain on Disposal of Plant Assets		6,000

   The Gain on Disposal of Plant Assets was credited to current operations as ordinary income.
5. Dividends in the amount of $123,000 were declared. They are payable in January of next year.

Instructions

Show by journal entries the adjustments that would be made on a work sheet for a statement of cash flows.

E23-21 (Work Sheet Preparation) Below is the comparative balance sheet for Stevie Wonder Corporation.

	Dec. 31, 2005	Dec. 31, 2004
Cash	$ 16,500	$ 21,000
Short-term investments	25,000	19,000
Accounts receivable	43,000	45,000
Allowance for doubtful accounts	(1,800)	(2,000)
Prepaid expenses	4,200	2,500
Inventories	81,500	65,000
Land	50,000	50,000
Buildings	125,000	73,500
Accumulated depreciation—buildings	(30,000)	(23,000)
Equipment	53,000	46,000
Accumulated depreciation—equipment	(19,000)	(15,500)
Delivery equipment	39,000	39,000
Accumulated depreciation—delivery equipment	(22,000)	(20,500)
Patents	15,000	–0–
	$379,400	$300,000

	Dec. 31, 2005	Dec. 31, 2004
Accounts payable	$ 26,000	$ 16,000
Short-term notes payable	4,000	6,000
Accrued payables	3,000	4,600
Mortgage payable	73,000	53,400
Bonds payable	50,000	62,500
Capital stock	140,000	102,000
Additional paid-in capital	10,000	4,000
Retained earnings	73,400	51,500
	$379,400	$300,000

Dividends in the amount of $15,000 were declared and paid in 2005.

Instructions

From this information, prepare a work sheet for a statement of cash flows. Make reasonable assumptions as appropriate. The short-term investments are considered available-for-sale and no unrealized gains or losses have occurred on these securities.

PROBLEMS

P23-1 (SCF—Indirect Method) The following is Method Man Corp.'s comparative balance sheets accounts work sheet at December 31, 2005 and 2004, with a column showing the increase (decrease) from 2004 to 2005.

COMPARATIVE BALANCE SHEETS

	2005	2004	Increase (Decrease)
Cash	$ 807,500	$ 700,000	$107,500
Accounts receivable	1,128,000	1,168,000	(40,000)
Inventories	1,850,000	1,715,000	135,000
Property, plant and equipment	3,307,000	2,967,000	340,000
Accumulated depreciation	(1,165,000)	(1,040,000)	(125,000)
Investment in Blige Co.	305,000	275,000	30,000
Loan receivable	262,500	—	262,500
Total assets	$6,495,000	$5,785,000	$710,000
Accounts payable	$1,015,000	$ 955,000	$ 60,000
Income taxes payable	30,000	50,000	(20,000)
Dividends payable	80,000	100,000	(20,000)
Capital lease obligation	400,000	—	400,000
Capital stock, common, $1 par	500,000	500,000	—
Additional paid-in capital	1,500,000	1,500,000	—
Retained earnings	2,970,000	2,680,000	290,000
Total liabilities and stockholders' equity	$6,495,000	$5,785,000	$710,000

Additional information:

1. On December 31, 2004, Method Man acquired 25% of Blige Co.'s common stock for $275,000. On that date, the carrying value of Blige's assets and liabilities, which approximated their fair values, was $1,100,000. Blige reported income of $120,000 for the year ended December 31, 2005. No dividend was paid on Blige's common stock during the year.
2. During 2005, Method Man loaned $300,000 to TLC Co., an unrelated company. TLC made the first semi-annual principal repayment of $37,500, plus interest at 10%, on December 31, 2005.
3. On January 2, 2005, Method Man sold equipment costing $60,000, with a carrying amount of $35,000, for $40,000 cash.
4. On December 31, 2005, Method Man entered into a capital lease for an office building. The present value of the annual rental payments is $400,000, which equals the fair value of the building. Method Man made the first rental payment of $60,000 when due on January 2, 2006.
5. Net income for 2005 was $370,000.
6. Method Man declared and paid cash dividends for 2005 and 2004 as shown on page 1256.

	2005	2004
Declared	December 15, 2005	December 15, 2004
Paid	February 28, 2006	February 28, 2005
Amount	$80,000	$100,000

Instructions

Prepare a statement of cash flows for Method Man, Corp. for the year ended December 31, 2005, using the indirect method.

(AICPA adapted)

P23-2 (SCF—Indirect Method) The comparative balance sheets for Shenandoah Corporation show the following information.

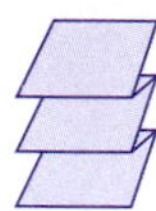

	December 31	
	2005	2004
Cash	$ 38,500	$13,000
Accounts receivable	12,250	10,000
Inventory	12,000	9,000
Investments	–0–	3,000
Building	–0–	29,750
Equipment	40,000	20,000
Patent	5,000	6,250
Totals	$107,750	$91,000
Allowance for doubtful accounts	3,000	4,500
Accumulated depreciation on equipment	2,000	4,500
Accumulated depreciation on building	–0–	6,000
Accounts payable	5,000	3,000
Dividends payable	–0–	5,000
Notes payable, short-term (nontrade)	3,000	4,000
Long-term notes payable	31,000	25,000
Common stock	43,000	33,000
Retained earnings	20,750	6,000
	$107,750	$91,000

Additional data related to 2005 are as follows.

1. Equipment that had cost $11,000 and was 30% depreciated at time of disposal was sold for $2,500.
2. $10,000 of the long-term note payable was paid by issuing common stock.
3. Cash dividends paid were $5,000.
4. On January 1, 2005, the building was completely destroyed by a flood. Insurance proceeds on the building were $30,000 (net of $2,000 taxes).
5. Investments (available-for-sale) were sold at $3,700 above their cost. The company has made similar sales and investments in the past.
6. Cash of $15,000 was paid for the acquisition of equipment.
7. A long-term note for $16,000 was issued for the acquisition of equipment.
8. Interest of $2,000 and income taxes of $6,500 were paid in cash.

Instructions

Prepare a statement of cash flows using the indirect method. Flood damage is unusual and infrequent in that part of the country.

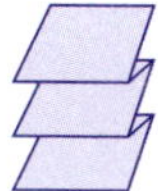

P23-3 (SCF—Direct Method) Mardi Gras Company has not yet prepared a formal statement of cash flows for the 2005 fiscal year. Comparative balance sheets as of December 31, 2004 and 2005, and a statement of income and retained earnings for the year ended December 31, 2005, are presented below.

MARDI GRAS COMPANY
STATEMENT OF INCOME AND RETAINED EARNINGS
YEAR ENDED DECEMBER 31, 2005
($000 OMITTED)

Sales		$3,800
Expenses		
Cost of goods sold	$1,200	
Salaries and benefits	725	

Heat, light, and power	75	
Depreciation	80	
Property taxes	19	
Patent amortization	25	
Miscellaneous expenses	10	
Interest	30	2,164
Income before income taxes		1,636
Income taxes		818
Net income		818
Retained earnings—Jan. 1, 2005		310
		1,128
Stock dividend declared and issued		600
Retained earnings—Dec. 31, 2005		$ 528

MARDI GRAS COMPANY
COMPARATIVE BALANCE SHEETS
DECEMBER 31
($000 OMITTED)

Assets	2005	2004
Current assets		
Cash	$ 383	$ 100
U.S. Treasury notes (Available-for-sale)	–0–	50
Accounts receivable	740	500
Inventory	720	560
Total current assets	1,843	1,210
Long-term assets		
Land	150	70
Buildings and equipment	910	600
Accumulated depreciation	(200)	(120)
Patents (less amortization)	105	130
Total long-term assets	965	680
Total assets	$2,808	$1,890
Liabilities and Stockholders' Equity		
Current liabilities		
Accounts payable	$ 420	$ 340
Income taxes payable	40	20
Notes payable	320	320
Total current liabilities	780	680
Long-term notes payable—due 2007	200	200
Total liabilities	980	880
Stockholders' equity		
Common stock	1,300	700
Retained earnings	528	310
Total stockholders' equity	1,828	1,010
Total liabilities and stockholders' equity	$2,808	$1,890

Instructions

Prepare a statement of cash flows using the direct method. Changes in accounts receivable and accounts payable relate to sales and cost of goods sold. Do not prepare a reconciliation schedule.

(CMA adapted)

P23-4 (SCF—Direct Method) Ashley Cleveland Company had available at the end of 2004 the information on page 1258.

ASHLEY CLEVELAND COMPANY
COMPARATIVE BALANCE SHEETS
AS OF DECEMBER 31, 2004 AND 2003

	2004	2003
Cash	$ 15,000	$ 4,000
Accounts receivable	17,500	12,950
Short-term investments	20,000	30,000
Inventory	42,000	35,000
Prepaid rent	3,000	12,000
Prepaid insurance	2,100	900
Office supplies	1,000	750
Land	125,000	175,000
Building	350,000	350,000
Accumulated depreciation	(105,000)	(87,500)
Equipment	525,000	400,000
Accumulated depreciation	(130,000)	(112,000)
Patent	45,000	50,000
Total assets	$910,600	$871,100
Accounts payable	$ 27,000	$ 32,000
Taxes payable	5,000	4,000
Wages payable	5,000	3,000
Short-term notes payable	10,000	10,000
Long-term notes payable	60,000	70,000
Bonds payable	400,000	400,000
Premium on bonds payable	20,303	25,853
Common stock	240,000	220,000
Paid-in capital in excess of par	20,000	17,500
Retained earnings	123,297	88,747
Total liabilities and equity	$910,600	$871,100

ASHLEY CLEVELAND COMPANY
INCOME STATEMENT
FOR THE YEAR ENDED DECEMBER 31, 2004

Sales revenue		$1,160,000
Cost of goods sold		(748,000)
		412,000
Gross margin		
Operating expenses		
Selling expenses	$ 79,200	
Administrative expenses	156,700	
Depreciation/Amortization expense	40,500	
Total operating expenses		(276,400)
Income from operations		135,600
Other revenues/expenses		
Gain on sale of land	8,000	
Gain on sale of short-term investment	4,000	
Dividend revenue	2,400	
Interest expense	(51,750)	(37,350)
Income before taxes		98,250
Income tax expense		(39,400)
Net income		58,850
Dividends to common stockholders		(24,300)
To retained earnings		$ 34,550

Instructions

Prepare a statement of cash flows for Ashley Cleveland Company using the direct method accompanied by a reconciliation schedule. Assume the short-term investments are available-for-sale securities.

P23-5 (SCF—Indirect Method) You have completed the field work in connection with your audit of Shirley Caesar Corporation for the year ended December 31, 2005. The following schedule shows the balance sheet accounts at the beginning and end of the year.

	Dec. 31, 2005	Dec. 31, 2004	Increase or (Decrease)
Cash	$ 267,900	$ 298,000	($30,100)
Accounts receivable	479,424	353,000	126,424
Inventory	741,700	610,000	131,700
Prepaid expenses	12,000	8,000	4,000
Investment in subsidiary	110,500	–0–	110,500
Cash surrender value of life insurance	2,304	1,800	504
Machinery	207,000	190,000	17,000
Buildings	535,200	407,900	127,300
Land	52,500	52,500	–0–
Patents	69,000	64,000	5,000
Copyright	40,000	50,000	(10,000)
Bond discount and expense	4,502	–0–	4,502
	$2,522,030	$2,035,200	$486,830
Accrued taxes payable	$ 90,250	$ 79,600	$ 10,650
Accounts payable	299,280	280,000	19,280
Dividends payable	70,000	–0–	70,000
Bonds payable—8%	125,000	–0–	125,000
Bonds payable—12%	–0–	100,000	(100,000)
Allowance for doubtful accounts	35,300	40,000	(4,700)
Accumulated depreciation—buildings	424,000	400,000	24,000
Accumulated depreciation—machinery	173,000	130,000	43,000
Premium on bonds payable	–0–	2,400	(2,400)
Capital stock—no par	1,176,200	1,453,200	(277,000)
Additional paid-in capital	109,000	–0–	109,000
Retained earnings—unappropriated	20,000	(450,000)	470,000
	$2,522,030	$2,035,200	$486,830

Statement of Retained Earnings

January 1, 2005	Balance (deficit)	$(450,000)
March 31, 2005	Net income for first quarter of 2005	25,000
April 1, 2005	Transfer from paid-in capital	425,000
	Balance	–0–
December 31, 2005	Net income for last three quarters of 2005	90,000
	Dividend declared—payable January 21, 2006	(70,000)
	Balance	$ 20,000

Your working papers contain the following information:

1. On April 1, 2005, the existing deficit was written off against paid-in capital created by reducing the stated value of the no-par stock.
2. On November 1, 2005, 29,600 shares of no-par stock were sold for $257,000. The board of directors voted to regard $5 per share as stated capital.
3. A patent was purchased for $15,000.
4. During the year, machinery that had a cost basis of $16,400 and on which there was accumulated depreciation of $5,200 was sold for $7,000. No other plant assets were sold during the year.
5. The 12%, 20-year bonds were dated and issued on January 2, 1993. Interest was payable on June 30 and December 31. They were sold originally at 106. These bonds were retired at 102 (net of $100 tax) plus accrued interest on March 31, 2005.
6. The 8%, 40-year bonds were dated January 1, 2005, and were sold on March 31 at 97 plus accrued interest. Interest is payable semiannually on June 30 and December 31. Expense of issuance was $839.
7. Shirley Caesar Corporation acquired 70% control in Amarillo Company on January 2, 2005, for $100,000. The income statement of Amarillo Company for 2005 shows a net income of $15,000.
8. Extraordinary repairs to buildings of $7,200 were charged to Accumulated Depreciation—Buildings.
9. Interest paid in 2005 was $10,500 and income taxes paid were $34,000.

Instructions

From the information given, prepare a statement of cash flows using the indirect method. A work sheet is not necessary, but the principal computations should be supported by schedules or skeleton ledger accounts.

P23-6 (SCF—Indirect Method, and Net Cash Flow from Operating Activities, Direct Method) Comparative balance sheet accounts of Jon Secada Inc. are presented below.

JON SECADA INC.
COMPARATIVE BALANCE SHEET ACCOUNTS
DECEMBER 31, 2005 AND 2004

	December 31	
Debit Accounts	2005	2004
Cash	$ 45,000	$ 33,750
Accounts Receivable	67,500	60,000
Merchandise Inventory	30,000	24,000
Investments (available-for-sale)	22,250	38,500
Machinery	30,000	18,750
Buildings	67,500	56,250
Land	7,500	7,500
Totals	$269,750	$238,750
Credit Accounts		
Allowance for Doubtful Accounts	$ 2,250	$ 1,500
Accumulated Depreciation—Machinery	5,625	2,250
Accumulated Depreciation—Buildings	13,500	9,000
Accounts Payable	30,000	24,750
Accrued Payables	3,375	2,625
Long-Term Note Payable	26,000	31,000
Common Stock, no par	150,000	125,000
Retained Earnings	39,000	42,625
Total	$269,750	$238,750

Additional data (ignoring taxes):

1. Net income for the year was $42,500.
2. Cash dividends declared during the year were $21,125.
3. A 20% stock dividend was declared during the year. $25,000 of retained earnings was capitalized.
4. Investments that cost $20,000 were sold during the year for $23,750.
5. Machinery that cost $3,750, on which $750 of depreciation had accumulated, was sold for $2,200.

Jon Secada's 2005 income statement follows (ignoring taxes).

Sales		$540,000
Less: Cost of goods sold		380,000
Gross margin		160,000
Less: Operating expenses (includes $8,625 depreciation and $5,400 bad debts)		120,450
Income from operations		39,550
Other: Gain on sale of investments	$3,750	
Loss on sale of machinery	(800)	2,950
Net income		$ 42,500

Instructions

(a) Compute net cash flow from operating activities using the direct method.
(b) Prepare a statement of cash flows using the indirect method.

P23-7 (SCF—Direct and Indirect Methods from Comparative Financial Statements) George Winston Company, a major retailer of bicycles and accessories, operates several stores and is a publicly traded company. The comparative statement of financial position and income statement for Winston as of May 31, 2005, are shown on the next page. The company is preparing its statement of cash flows.

GEORGE WINSTON COMPANY
COMPARATIVE STATEMENT OF FINANCIAL POSITION
AS OF MAY 31,

	2005	2004
Current assets		
Cash	$ 33,250	$ 20,000
Accounts receivable	80,000	58,000
Merchandise inventory	210,000	250,000
Prepaid expenses	9,000	7,000
Total current assets	332,250	335,000
Plant assets		
Plant assets	600,000	502,000
Less: Accumulated depreciation	150,000	125,000
Net plant assets	450,000	377,000
Total assets	$782,250	$712,000
Current liabilities		
Accounts payable	$123,000	$115,000
Salaries payable	47,250	72,000
Interest payable	27,000	25,000
Total current liabilities	197,250	212,000
Long-term debt		
Bonds payable	70,000	100,000
Total liabilities	267,250	312,000
Shareholders' equity		
Common stock, $10 par	370,000	280,000
Retained earnings	145,000	120,000
Total shareholders' equity	515,000	400,000
Total liabilities and shareholders' equity	$782,250	$712,000

GEORGE WINSTON COMPANY
INCOME STATEMENT
FOR THE YEAR ENDED MAY 31, 2005

Sales	$1,255,250
Cost of merchandise sold	722,000
Gross profit	533,250
Expenses	
Salary expense	252,100
Interest expense	75,000
Other expenses	8,150
Depreciation expense	25,000
Total expenses	360,250
Operating income	173,000
Income tax expense	43,000
Net income	$ 130,000

The following is additional information concerning Winston's transactions during the year ended May 31, 2005.

1. All sales during the year were made on account.
2. All merchandise was purchased on account, comprising the total accounts payable account.
3. Plant assets costing $98,000 were purchased by paying $48,000 in cash and issuing 5,000 shares of stock.
4. The "other expenses" are related to prepaid items.
5. All income taxes incurred during the year were paid during the year.
6. In order to supplement its cash, Winston issued 4,000 shares of common stock at par value.
7. There were no penalties assessed for the retirement of bonds.
8. Cash dividends of $105,000 were declared and paid at the end of the fiscal year.

Instructions

(a) Compare and contrast the direct method and the indirect method for reporting cash flows from operating activities.

(b) Prepare a statement of cash flows for Winston Company for the year ended May 31, 2005, using the direct method. Be sure to support the statement with appropriate calculations. (A reconciliation of net income to net cash provided is not required.)

(c) Using the indirect method, calculate only the net cash flow from operating activities for Winston Company for the year ended May 31, 2005.

P23-8 (SCF—Direct and Indirect Methods) Comparative balance sheet accounts of Jensen Company are presented below.

JENSEN COMPANY
COMPARATIVE BALANCE SHEET ACCOUNTS
DECEMBER 31,

Debit Balances	2004	2003
Cash	$ 80,000	$ 51,000
Accounts Receivable	145,000	130,000
Merchandise Inventory	75,000	61,000
Investments (Available-for-sale)	55,000	85,000
Equipment	70,000	48,000
Buildings	145,000	145,000
Land	40,000	25,000
Totals	$610,000	$545,000
Credit Balances		
Allowance for Doubtful Accounts	$ 10,000	$ 8,000
Accumulated Depreciation—Equipment	21,000	14,000
Accumulated Depreciation—Building	37,000	28,000
Accounts Payable	70,000	60,000
Income Taxes Payable	12,000	10,000
Long-Term Notes Payable	62,000	70,000
Common Stock	310,000	260,000
Retained Earnings	88,000	95,000
Totals	$610,000	$545,000

Additional data:

1. Equipment that cost $10,000 and was 40% depreciated was sold in 2004.
2. Cash dividends were declared and paid during the year.
3. Common stock was issued in exchange for land.
4. Investments that cost $35,000 were sold during the year.

Jensen's 2004 income statement is as follows.

Sales		$950,000
Less: Cost of goods sold		600,000
Gross profit		350,000
Less: Operating expenses (includes depreciation and bad debt expense)		250,000
Income from operations		100,000
Other revenues and expenses		
Gain on sale of investments	$15,000	
Loss on sale of equipment	(3,000)	12,000
Income before taxes		112,000
Income taxes		45,000
Net income		$ 67,000

Instructions

(a) Compute net cash provided by operating activities under the direct method.

(b) Prepare a statement of cash flows using the indirect method.

P23-9 (Indirect SCF) Seneca Corporation has contracted with you to prepare a statement of cash flows. The controller has provided the following information.

	December 31	
	2004	2003
Cash	$ 43,500	$13,000
Accounts receivable	12,250	10,000
Inventory	12,000	10,000
Investments	–0–	3,000
Building	–0–	29,750
Equipment	35,000	20,000
Copyright	5,000	5,250
Totals	$107,750	$91,000
Allowance for doubtful accounts	$ 3,000	$ 4,500
Accumulated depreciation on equipment	2,000	4,500
Accumulated depreciation on building	–0–	6,000
Accounts payable	5,000	4,000
Dividends payable	–0–	5,000
Notes payable, short-term (nontrade)	3,000	4,000
Long-term notes payable	36,000	25,000
Common stock	38,000	33,000
Retained earnings	20,750	5,000
	$107,750	$91,000

Additional data related to 2004 are as follows.

1. Equipment that had cost $11,000 and was 40% depreciated at time of disposal was sold for $2,500.
2. $5,000 of the long-term note payable was paid by issuing common stock.
3. Cash dividends paid were $5,000.
4. On January 1, 2004, the building was completely destroyed by a flood. Insurance proceeds on the building were $33,000 (net of $4,000 taxes).
5. Investments (available-for-sale) were sold at $2,500 above their cost. The company has made similar sales and investments in the past.
6. Cash of $10,000 was paid for the acquisition of equipment.
7. A long-term note for $16,000 was issued for the acquisition of equipment.
8. Interest of $2,000 and income taxes of $5,000 were paid in cash.

Instructions

(a) Use the indirect method to analyze the above information and prepare a statement of cash flows for Seneca. Flood damage is unusual and infrequent in that part of the country.

(b) What would you expect to observe in the operating, investing, and financing sections of a statement of cash flows of:

(1) a severely financially troubled firm?

(2) a recently formed firm which is experiencing rapid growth?

CONCEPTUAL CASES

C23-1 (Analysis of Improper SCF) The following statement was prepared by Abriendo Corporation's accountant.

ABRIENDO CORPORATION
STATEMENT OF SOURCES AND APPLICATION OF CASH
FOR THE YEAR ENDED SEPTEMBER 30, 2005

Sources of cash	
Net income	$ 95,000
Depreciation and depletion	70,000
Increase in long-term debt	179,000
Common stock issued under employee option plans	16,000
Changes in current receivables and inventories, less current liabilities (excluding current maturities of long-term debt)	14,000
	$374,000
Application of cash	
Cash dividends	$ 60,000
Expenditure for property, plant, and equipment	214,000
Investments and other uses	20,000
Change in cash	80,000
	$374,000

The following additional information relating to Abriendo Corporation is available for the year ended September 30, 2005.

1. The corporation received $16,000 in cash from its employees on its employee stock option plans, and wage and salary expense attributable to the option plans was an additional $22,000.
2. | | |
   |---|---|
   | Expenditures for property, plant, and equipment | $250,000 |
   | Proceeds from retirements of property, plant, and equipment | 36,000 |
   | Net expenditures | $214,000 |
3. A stock dividend of 10,000 shares of Abriendo Corporation common stock was distributed to common stockholders on April 1, 2005, when the per-share market price was $7 and par value was $1.
4. On July 1, 2005, when its market price was $6 per share, 16,000 shares of Abriendo Corporation common stock were issued in exchange for 4,000 shares of preferred stock.
5. | | |
   |---|---|
   | Depreciation expense | $ 65,000 |
   | Depletion expense | 5,000 |
   | | $ 70,000 |
6. | | |
   |---|---|
   | Increase in long-term debt | $620,000 |
   | Retirement of debt | 441,000 |
   | Net increase | $179,000 |

Instructions

(a) In general, what are the objectives of a statement of the type shown above for Abriendo Corporation? Explain.

(b) Identify the weaknesses in the form and format of Abriendo Corporation's statement of cash flows without reference to the additional information. (Assume adoption of the indirect method.)

(c) For each of the six items of additional information for the statement of cash flows, indicate the preferable treatment and explain why the suggested treatment is preferable.

(AICPA adapted)

C23-2 (SCF Theory and Analysis of Improper SCF) Gloria Estefan and Flaco Jimenez are examining the following statement of cash flows for Tropical Clothing Store's first year of operations.

TROPICAL CLOTHING STORE
STATEMENT OF CASH FLOWS
FOR THE YEAR ENDED JANUARY 31, 2005

Sources of cash	
From sales of merchandise	$ 362,000
From sale of capital stock	400,000
From sale of investment	120,000
From depreciation	80,000
From issuance of note for truck	30,000
From interest on investments	8,000
Total sources of cash	1,000,000
Uses of cash	
For purchase of fixtures and equipment	340,000
For merchandise purchased for resale	253,000
For operating expenses (including depreciation)	170,000
For purchase of investment	85,000
For purchase of truck by issuance of note	30,000
For purchase of treasury stock	10,000
For interest on note	3,000
Total uses of cash	891,000
Net increase in cash	$ 109,000

Gloria claims that Tropical's statement of cash flows is an excellent portrayal of a superb first year, with cash increasing $109,000. Flaco replies that it was not a superb first year—that the year was an operating failure, the statement was incorrectly presented, and $109,000 is not the actual increase in cash.

Instructions

(a) With whom do you agree, Gloria or Flaco? Explain your position.

(b) Using the data provided, prepare a statement of cash flows in proper indirect method form. The only noncash items in income are depreciation and the gain from the sale of the investment (purchase and sale are related).

C23-3 (SCF Theory and Analysis of Transactions) John Lee Hooker Company is a young and growing producer of electronic measuring instruments and technical equipment. You have been retained by Hooker to advise it in the preparation of a statement of cash flows using the indirect method. For the fiscal year ended October 31, 2005, you have obtained the following information concerning certain events and transactions of Hooker.

1. The amount of reported earnings for the fiscal year was $800,000, which included a deduction for an extraordinary loss of $110,000 (see item 5 below).
2. Depreciation expense of $315,000 was included in the income statement.
3. Uncollectible accounts receivable of $40,000 were written off against the allowance for doubtful accounts. Also, $51,000 of bad debt expense was included in determining income for the fiscal year, and the same amount was added to the allowance for doubtful accounts.
4. A gain of $9,000 was realized on the sale of a machine. It originally cost $75,000, of which $30,000 was undepreciated on the date of sale.
5. On April 1, 2005, lightning caused an uninsured building loss of $110,000 ($180,000 loss, less reduction in income taxes of $70,000). This extraordinary loss was included in determining income as indicated in 1 above.
6. On July 3, 2005, building and land were purchased for $700,000. Hooker gave in payment $75,000 cash, $200,000 market value of its unissued common stock, and signed a $425,000 mortgage note payable.
7. On August 3, 2005, $800,000 face value of Hooker's 10% convertible debentures were converted into $150,000 par value of its common stock. The bonds were originally issued at face value.

Instructions

Explain whether each of the seven numbered items above is a source or use of cash, and explain how it should be disclosed in John Lee Hooker's statement of cash flows for the fiscal year ended October 31, 2005. If any item is neither a source nor a use of cash, explain why it is not, and indicate the disclosure, if any, that should be made of the item in John Lee Hooker's statement of cash flows for the fiscal year ended October 31, 2005.

C23-4 (Analysis of Transactions' Effect on SCF) Each of the following items must be considered in preparing a statement of cash flows for Buddy Guy Fashions Inc. for the year ended December 31, 2005.

1. Fixed assets that had cost $20,000 6½ years before and were being depreciated on a 10-year basis, with no estimated scrap value, were sold for $5,250.
2. During the year, goodwill of $15,000 was considered impaired and was completely written off to expense.
3. During the year, 500 shares of common stock with a stated value of $25 a share were issued for $34 a share.
4. The company sustained a net loss for the year of $2,100. Depreciation amounted to $2,000 and patent amortization was $400.
5. Uncollectible accounts receivable in the amount of $2,000 were written off against the Allowance for Doubtful Accounts.
6. Investments (available-for-sale) that cost $12,000 when purchased 4 years earlier were sold for $10,600. The loss was considered ordinary.
7. Bonds payable with a par value of $24,000 on which there was an unamortized bond premium of $2,000 were redeemed at 103. The gain was credited to ordinary income.

Instructions

For each item, state where it is to be shown in the statement and then how you would present the necessary information, including the amount. Consider each item to be independent of the others. Assume that correct entries were made for all transactions as they took place.

C23-5 (Purpose and Elements of SCF) In 1961 the AICPA recognized the importance of the funds statement by publishing *Accounting Research Study No. 2*, "'Cash Flow' Analysis and the Funds Statement." Prior to this time, accountants had prepared funds statements primarily as management reports. The Accounting Principles Board responded by issuing *APB Opinion No. 3*, "The Statement of Source and Application of Funds," which recommended that a statement of source and application of funds be presented on a supplementary basis. Because of the favorable response of the business community to this pronouncement, the APB issued *Opinion No. 19*, "Reporting Changes in Financial Position" in 1971. This opinion required that a statement of changes in financial position be presented as a basic financial statement and be covered by the auditor's report.

In 1981 the Financial Accounting Standards Board reconsidered funds flow issues as part of the conceptual framework project. At this time, the FASB decided that cash flow reporting issues should be considered at the standards level. Subsequent deliberations resulted in *Statement of Financial Accounting Standards (SFAS) No. 95*, "Statement of Cash Flows."

Instructions

(a) Explain the purposes of the statement of cash flows.
(b) List and describe the three categories of activities that must be reported in the statement of cash flows.
(c) Identify and describe the two methods that are allowed for reporting cash flows from operations.
(d) Describe the financial statement presentation of noncash investing and financing transactions. Include in your description an example of a noncash investing and financing transaction.

C23-6 (Cash Flow Reporting) Durocher Guitar Company is in the business of manufacturing top-quality, steel-string folk guitars. In recent years the company has experienced working capital problems resulting from the procurement of factory equipment, the unanticipated buildup of receivables and inventories, and the payoff of a balloon mortgage on a new manufacturing facility. The founder and president of the company, Laraine Durocher, has attempted to raise cash from various financial institutions, but to no avail because of the company's poor performance in recent years. In particular, the company's lead bank, First Financial, is especially concerned about Durocher's inability to maintain a positive cash position. The commercial loan officer from First Financial told Laraine, "I can't even consider your request for capital financing unless I see that your company is able to generate positive cash flows from operations."

Thinking about the banker's comment, Laraine came up with what she believes is a good plan: With a more attractive statement of cash flows, the bank might be willing to provide long-term financing. To "window dress" cash flows, the company can sell its accounts receivables to factors and liquidate its raw material inventories. These rather costly transactions would generate lots of cash. As the chief accountant for Durocher Guitar, it is your job to tell Laraine what you think of her plan.

Instructions

Answer the following questions.

(a) What are the ethical issues related to Laraine Durocher's idea?
(b) What would you tell Laraine Durocher?

USING YOUR JUDGMENT

FINANCIAL REPORTING PROBLEM

3M Company

The financial statements of 3M are presented in Appendix 5B or can be accessed on the Take Action! CD.

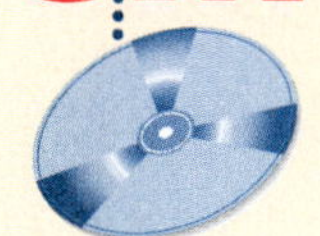

Instructions

Refer to 3M's financial statements and the accompanying notes to answer the following questions.

(a) Which method of computing net cash provided by operating activities does 3M use? What were the amounts of cash provided by operations for the years 1999, 2000, and 2001? Which two items were most responsible for the increase in cash provided by operating activities in 2001?
(b) What was the most significant item in the cash flows used for the investing activities section in 2001? What was the most significant item in the cash flows used for the financing activities section in 2001?
(c) Where is "deferred taxes" reported in 3M's statement of cash flows? Why does it appear in that section of the statement of cash flows?
(d) Where is depreciation reported in 3M's statement of cash flows? Why is depreciation added to net income in the statement of cash flows?

FINANCIAL STATEMENT ANALYSIS CASE

Vermont Teddy Bear Co.

Founded in the early 1980s, the **Vermont Teddy Bear Co.** designs and manufactures American-made teddy bears and markets them primarily as gifts called Bear-Grams or Teddy Bear-Grams. Bear-Grams are personalized teddy bears delivered directly to the recipient for special occasions such as birthdays and anniversaries. The Shelburne, Vermont, company's primary markets are New York, Boston, and Chicago. Sales have jumped dramatically in recent years. Such dramatic growth has significant implications for cash flows. Provided below are the cash flow statements for two recent years for the company.

	Current Year	Prior Year
Cash flows from operating activities:		
Net income	$ 17,523	$ 838,955
Adjustments to reconcile net income to net cash provided by operating activities		
Deferred income taxes	(69,524)	(146,590)
Depreciation and amortization	316,416	181,348
Changes in assets and liabilities:		
Accounts receivable, trade	(38,267)	(25,947)
Inventories	(1,599,014)	(1,289,293)
Prepaid and other current assets	(444,794)	(113,205)
Deposits and other assets	(24,240)	(83,044)
Accounts payable	2,017,059	(284,567)
Accrued expenses	61,321	170,755
Accrued interest payable, debentures	—	(58,219)
Other	—	(8,960)
Income taxes payable	—	117,810
Net cash provided by (used for) operating activities	236,480	(700,957)
Net cash used for investing activities	(2,102,892)	(4,422,953)
Net cash (used for) provided by financing activities	(315,353)	9,685,435
Net change in cash and cash equivalents	(2,181,765)	4,561,525

Other information:

	Current Year	Prior Year
Current liabilities	$ 4,055,465	$ 1,995,600
Total liabilities	4,620,085	2,184,386
Net sales	20,560,566	17,025,856

Instructions

(a) Note that net income in the current year was only $17,523 compared to prior-year income of $838,955, but cash flow from operations was $236,480 in the current year and a negative $700,957 in the prior year. Explain the causes of this apparent paradox.

(b) Evaluate Vermont Teddy Bear's liquidity, solvency, and profitability for the current year using cash flow-based ratios.

COMPARATIVE ANALYSIS CASE

The Coca-Cola Company and PepsiCo, Inc.

Instructions

Go to the Take Action! CD and use information found there to answer the following questions related to **The Coca-Cola Company** and **PepsiCo, Inc.**

(a) What method of computing net cash provided by operating activities does Coca-Cola use? What method does PepsiCo use? What were the amounts of cash provided by operating activities reported by Coca-Cola and PepsiCo in 2001?

(b) What was the most significant item reported by Coca-Cola and PepsiCo in 2001 in their investing activities sections? What is the most significant item reported by Coca-Cola and PepsiCo in 2001 in their financing activities sections?

(c) What were these two companies' trends in net cash provided by operating activities over the period 1999 to 2001?

(d) Where is "depreciation and amortization" reported by Coca-Cola and PepsiCo in their statements of cash flows? What is the amount and why does it appear in that section of the statement of cash flows?

(e) Based on the information contained in Coca-Cola's and PepsiCo's financial statements, compute the following 2001 ratios for each company. These ratios require the use of statement of cash flows data. (These ratios were covered in Chapter 5.)

(1) Current cash debt coverage ratio.

(2) Cash debt coverage ratio.

(f) What conclusions concerning the management of cash can be drawn from the ratios computed in (e)?

RESEARCH CASE

The March 5, 2002, edition of the *Wall Street Journal* included an article by Mark Maremont entitled "How Is **Tyco** Accounting for Its Cash Flow?—Its Touted Measure of Strength Leaves Room for Interpretation." (Subscribers to **Business Extra** can access the article at that site.)

Instructions

Read the article and answer the following questions.

(a) Many analysts believe that cash flow is not as susceptible to "reporting manipulation" as income. What "complications" discussed in this article make that belief questionable?

(b) What is "free cash flow"? How was Tyco manipulating its reporting of "free cash flow"?

(c) Under U.S. GAAP, how is free cash flow determined?

(d) How is Tyco "buying earnings and operating cash flow"? Why is this practice risky for investors?

INTERNATIONAL REPORTING CASE

As noted in the chapter, there is international diversity in the preparation of the statement of cash flows. For example, under International Accounting Standards companies may choose how to classify dividends and interest in the cash flow statement. In some countries, like Brazil, a cash flow statement is not required. **Embraer**, a Brazilian aircraft manufacturer, prepared a statement of changes in financial position, rather than a statement of cash flows.

Instructions

Refer to Embraer's 2000 Statement of Changes in Financial Position on page 1269 to answer the following questions.

(a) Briefly discuss at least two similarities between Embraer's statement of changes in financial position and a statement of cash flows prepared according to U.S. GAAP.

(b) Briefly discuss at least two differences between Embraer's statement of changes in financial position and a statement of cash flows prepared according to U.S. GAAP.

Embraer

Consolidated Statement of Changes in Financial Position
for the Year Ended December 31, 2000
(in thousands of Brazilian reals)

Sources of Funds	2000
Provided by operations	
Net income	645,179
Items not affecting working capital—Depreciation, amortization, gains and losses	214,996
Long-term deferred income and social contribution taxes	9,751
Provision for contingencies	15,471
Funds provided by operations	885,397
From shareholders	
Capital increase	439,824
From third parties	
Increase in long-term liabilities	444,991
Transfer to current assets	52,194
Increase in minority interest	10,690
Funds provided by third parties	507,875
Total sources	1,833,096
Applications of Funds	
Increase in noncurrent assets	17,903
Increase in permanent assets	
Investments; property, plant, and equipment; other	301,798
Transfer to current liabilities	308,608
Dividends	187,042
Interest on capital	100,698
Total applications	916,049
Increase in working capital	917,047
Working capital—end of year	
Current assets	4,053,088
Current liabilities	2,668,783
	1,384,305
Working capital—beginning of year	467,258
Increase in working capital	917,047

PROFESSIONAL SIMULATION

Statement of Cash Flows

Directions | Situation | Financial Statements | Explanation | Research | Resources

Directions

In this simulation, you will be asked questions concerning the statement of cash flows. Prepare responses to all parts.

Situation

Ellwood House, Inc. had the following condensed balance sheet at the end of 2003.

ELLWOOD HOUSE, INC.
Balance Sheet
December 31, 2003

Cash	$ 10,000	Current liabilities	$ 14,500
Current assets (noncash)	34,000	Long-term notes payable	30,000
Investments (available-for-sale)	40,000	Bonds payable	32,000
Plant assets	57,500	Capital stock	80,000
Land	38,500	Retained earnings	23,500
	$180,000		$180,000

During 2004 the following occurred.

1. Ellwood House, Inc., sold part of its investment portfolio for $15,500, resulting in a gain of $500 for the firm. The company often sells and buys securities of this nature.
2. Dividends totaling $19,000 were paid to stockholders.
3. A parcel of land was purchased for $5,500.
4. $20,000 of capital stock was issued at par.
5. $10,000 of bonds payable were retired at par.
6. Heavy equipment was purchased through the issuance of $32,000 of bonds.
7. Net income for 2004 was $42,000 after allowing depreciation of $13,550.
8. Both current assets (other than cash) and current liabilities remained at the same amount.

Financial Statements

Prepare a statement of cash flows for 2004, using the indirect method.

Explanation

Draft a one-page letter to Gerald Brauer, president of Ellwood House, Inc., briefly explaining the changes within each major cash flow category. Refer to your cash flow statement whenever necessary.

Remember to check the **Take Action! CD** and the book's **companion Web site** to find additional resources for this chapter

CHAPTER 24

Full Disclosure in Financial Reporting

LEARNING OBJECTIVES

After studying this chapter, you should be able to:

1. **Review the full disclosure principle and describe problems of implementation.**
2. **Explain the use of notes in financial statement preparation.**
3. **Describe the disclosure requirements for major segments of a business.**
4. **Describe the accounting problems associated with interim reporting.**
5. **Identify the major disclosures found in the auditor's report.**
6. **Understand management's responsibilities for financials.**
7. **Identify issues related to financial forecasts and projections.**
8. **Describe the profession's response to fraudulent financial reporting.**

High-Quality Financial Reporting—It's a Necessity

Here are excerpts from leading experts regarding the importance of high-quality financial reporting:[1]

Warren E. Buffett, Chairman and Chief Executive Officer, **Berkshire Hathaway Inc.**:

> Financial reporting for Berkshire Hathaway, and for me personally, is the beginning of every decision that we make around here in terms of capital. I'm punching out 10-Ks and 10-Qs every single day. We look at the numbers and try to evaluate the quality of the financial reporting, and then we try to figure out what that means for the bonds and stocks that we're looking at, and thinking of either buying or selling.

Abby Joseph Cohen, Chair, Investment Policy Committee, **Goldman, Sachs & Co.**:

> High-quality financial reporting is perhaps the most important thing we can expect from companies. For investors to make good decisions—whether those investors are buying stocks or bonds or making private investments—they need to know the truth. And we think that when information is as clear as possible and is reported as frequently as makes sense, investors can do their jobs as best they can.

Jeffrey E. Garton, Dean of the Yale School of Management and former Under Secretary of Commerce for International Trade:

> . . . The integrity of the whole society is undermined if financial information is misrepresented, or if it isn't accurate or understandable. Because we live in a market society—and increasingly, the world does—unless the markets can be trusted, then you have widespread corruption . . . and a market economy that doesn't function.

Judy C. Lewent, Executive Vice President and Chief Financial Officer, **Merck & Co., Inc.**:

> . . . Higher standards, when properly implemented, drive excellence. I can make a parallel to the pharmaceutical industry. If you look around the world at where innovations come from, economists have studied and seen that where regulatory standards are the highest is where innovation is also the highest.

Floyd Norris, Chief Financial Correspondent, the **New York Times**:

> We are in a situation now in our society where the temptations to provide "bad" financial reporting are probably greater than they used to be. The need to get the stock price up, or to keep it up, is intense. So, the temptation to play games, the temptation to manage earnings—some of which can be legitimate and some of which cannot be—is probably greater than it used to be.

In short, the comments of these respected individuals illustrate why high-quality financial reporting is important to companies, to investors, and to the capital markets. At the heart of high-quality financial reporting is full disclosure.

[1]Excerpts taken from video entitled "Financially Correct with Ben Stein," Financial Accounting Standards Board (Norwalk, Conn.: FASB, 2002). By permission.

PREVIEW OF CHAPTER 24

As indicated in the opening story, without transparent, complete, and truthful reporting of financial performance our markets will not function properly. That is why it is so important that all aspects of financial reporting—the financial statements, the notes, the president's letter, and management's discussion and analysis—be read and understood. In this chapter, we cover the full disclosure principle in more detail and examine disclosures that must accompany financial statements so that they are not misleading. The content and organization of this chapter are as follows.

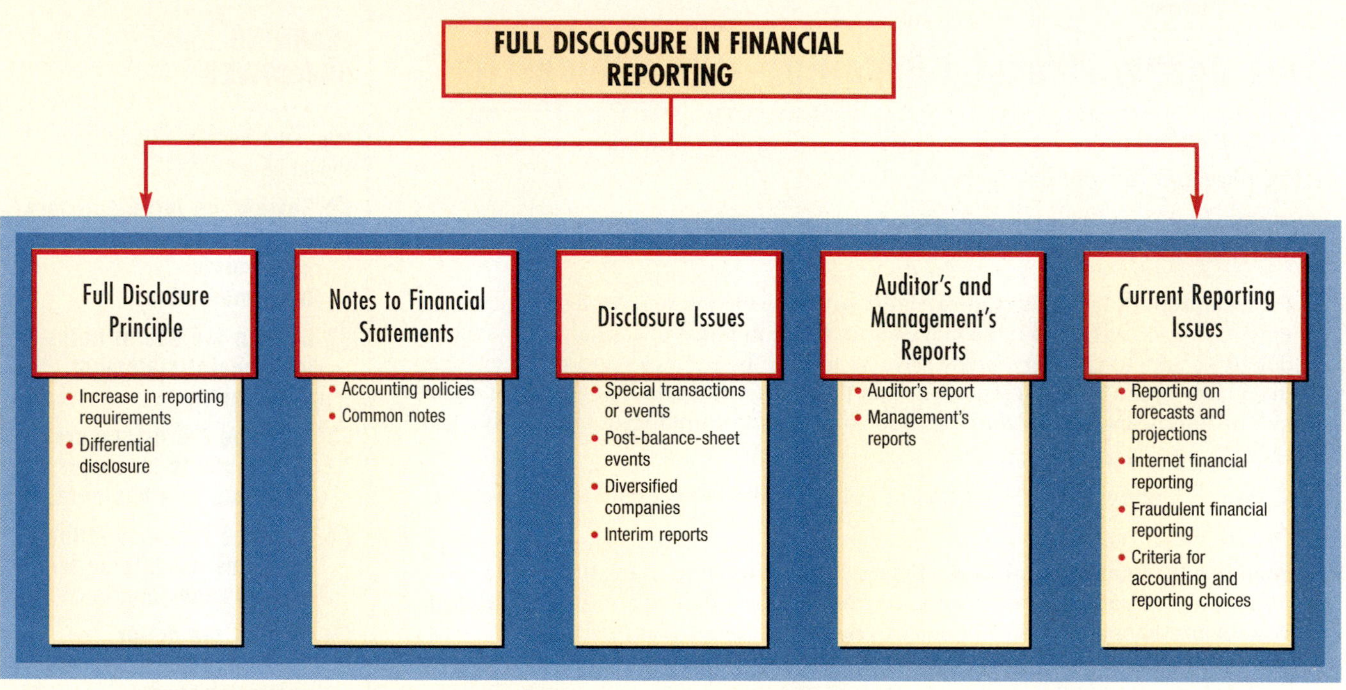

FULL DISCLOSURE PRINCIPLE

FASB Concepts Statement No. 1 notes that some useful information is better provided in the financial statements, and some is better provided by means of financial reporting other than in financial statements. For example, earnings and cash flows are readily available in financial statements—but investors might do better to look at comparisons to other companies in the same industry, found in news articles or brokerage house reports.

OBJECTIVE 1
Review the full disclosure principle and describe problems of implementation.

Financial statements, notes to the financial statements, and supplementary information are areas directly affected by FASB standards. Other types of information found in the annual report, such as management's discussion and analysis, are not subject to FASB standards. Illustration 24-1 indicates the types of financial information presented.

As indicated in Chapter 2, the profession has adopted a **full disclosure principle** that calls for financial reporting of **any financial facts significant enough to influence the judgment of an informed reader**. In some situations, the benefits of disclosure may be apparent but the costs uncertain. In other instances, the costs may be certain but the benefits of disclosure not as apparent.

Here is a good example of the trade-off between the cost/benefit constraint and the full disclosure principle.

For example, the SEC increased the amount of information financial institutions must disclose about their foreign lending practices. With some foreign countries in economic straits, the benefits of increased disclosure about the risk of uncollectibility are fairly obvious to the investing public. The exact costs of disclosure in these situations cannot be quantified, though they would appear to be relatively small.

ILLUSTRATION 24-1 Types of Financial Information

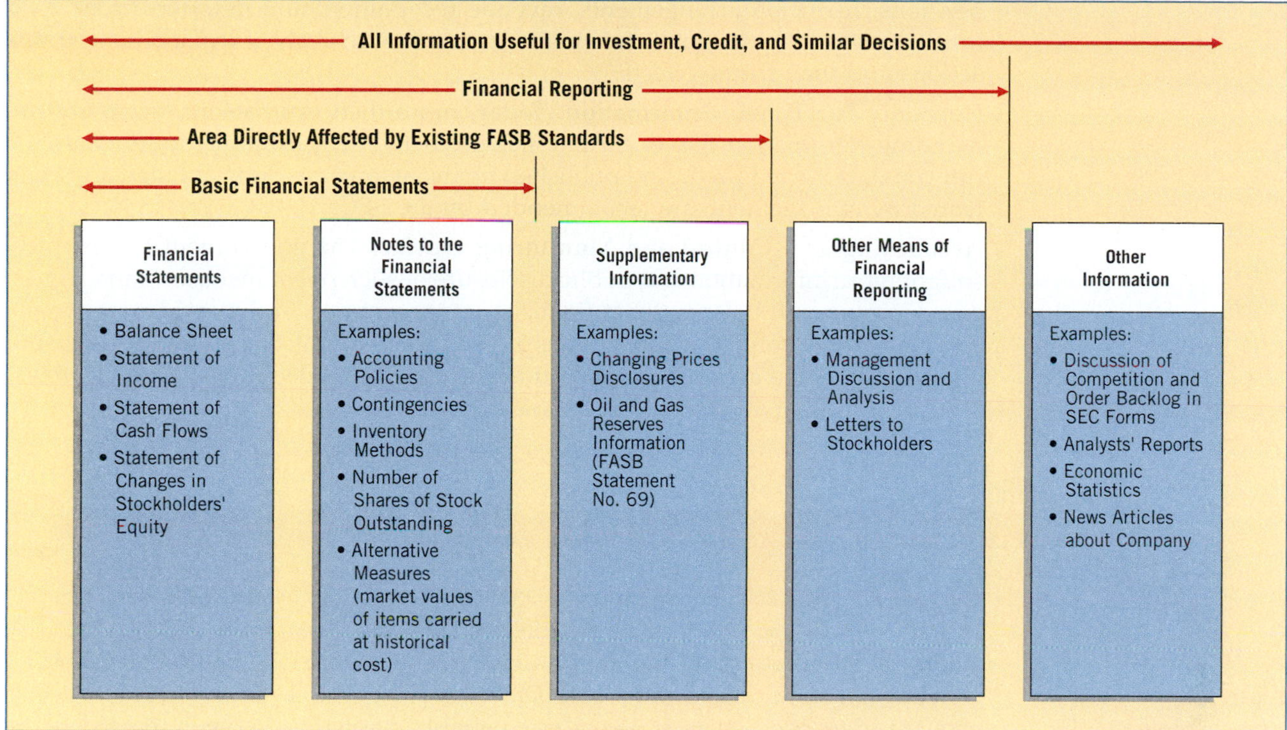

On the other hand, the cost of disclosure can be substantial in some cases and the benefits difficult to assess. For example, the *Wall Street Journal* reported that, at one time, if segment reporting were adopted, a company like **Fruehauf** would have had to increase its accounting staff 50 percent, from 300 to 450 individuals. In this case, the cost of disclosure is apparent, but the benefits are less well defined. Some would even argue that the reporting requirements are so detailed and substantial that users will have a difficult time absorbing the information. These critics charge the profession with engaging in **information overload**.

The AICPA's Special Committee on Financial Reporting notes that business reporting is not free, and improving it requires considering the relative costs and benefits of information, just as costs and benefits are key to determining the features included in any product. Undisciplined expansion of mandated reporting could result in large and needless costs.

The difficulty of implementing the full disclosure principle is highlighted by such financial disasters as **Enron**, **PharMor**, **WorldCom**, and **Global Crossing**. Why were investors not aware of potential problems—Was the information presented about these companies not comprehensible? Was it buried? Was it too technical? Was it properly presented and fully disclosed as of the financial statement date, but the situation later deteriorated? Or was it simply not there?

Increase in Reporting Requirements

Disclosure requirements have increased substantially. One survey showed that in a sample of 25 large, well-known companies over a recent 10-year period, the average number of pages of notes to the financial statements increased from 9 to 17 pages, and the average number of pages for management's discussion and analysis grew from 7 to 12 pages. This result is not surprising because as illustrated throughout this textbook, the FASB has issued many standards in the last 10 years that have substantial disclosure provisions.[2] The reasons for this increase in disclosure requirements are varied. Some of them are:

Complexity of the Business Environment. The difficulty of distilling economic events into summarized reports has been magnified by the increasing complexity

[2]The survey results were taken from Ray J. Groves, "Financial Disclosure: When More Is Not Better," *Financial Executive* (May/June 1994).

of business operations in such areas as derivatives, leasing, business combinations, pensions, financing arrangements, revenue recognition, and deferred taxes. As a result, **notes to the financial statements** are used extensively to explain these transactions and their future effects.

Necessity for Timely Information. Today, more than ever before, users are demanding information that is current and predictive. For example, more complete **interim data** are required. And published financial forecasts, long avoided and even feared by management, are recommended by the SEC.

Accounting as a Control and Monitoring Device. The government has recently sought more information and public disclosure of such phenomena as management compensation, off-balance-sheet financing arrangements, and related party transactions. An "Enronitis" concern is expressed in many of these newer disclosure requirements, and accountants and auditors have been selected as the agents to assist in controlling and monitoring these concerns.

WHAT DO THE NUMBERS MEAN?

SUPERSIZE THAT, PLEASE!

General Electric's 2001 annual report is 93 pages and has 30 percent more financial information than the year before. Primarily GE provided more specific data about 26 individual businesses, including its industrial units as well as GE Capital, compared with just 12 business segments for 2000. Other companies such as **International Business Machines** and **Sun Trust Banks** have promised greater disclosure in reports, as investors seem now to want more corporate nitty-gritty, hoping it will protect them from **Enron**-like surprises. **Williams Companies**, a natural gas and energy trading company, may take the prize for having the largest annual report—it's 1,234 pages, three times as large as the previous year!

Source: Rachel Emma Silverman, "GE's Annual Report Bulges With Data in Bid to Address Post-Enron Concerns," *Wall Street Journal* (March 11, 2002).

Differential Disclosure

UNDERLYING CONCEPTS

The AICPA Special Committee on Financial Reporting indicated that users differ in their needs for information, and that not all companies should report all elements of information. Rather, companies should report only information that users and preparers agree is needed in the particular circumstances.

A trend toward **differential disclosure** is also occurring. For example, the SEC requires that certain substantive information be reported to it that is not found in annual reports to stockholders. And the FASB, recognizing that certain disclosure requirements are costly and unnecessary for certain companies, has eliminated reporting requirements for nonpublic enterprises in such areas as fair value of financial instruments and segment reporting.[3]

Some still complain that the FASB has not gone far enough. They note that certain types of companies (small or nonpublic) should not have to follow complex GAAP requirements such as deferred income taxes, leases, or pensions. This issue, often referred to as **Big GAAP versus Little GAAP**, continues to be controversial. The FASB takes the position that one set of GAAP should be used, except in unusual situations.

NOTES TO THE FINANCIAL STATEMENTS

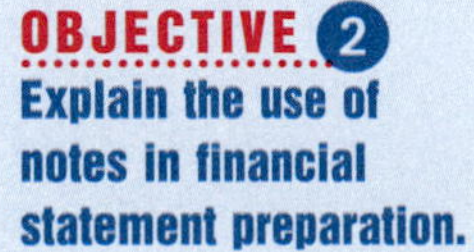

OBJECTIVE 2
Explain the use of notes in financial statement preparation.

As you know from your study of this textbook, notes are an integral part of the financial statements of a business enterprise. However, they are often overlooked because they are highly technical and often appear in small print. **Notes are the means of am-**

[3]The FASB has had a disclosure-effectiveness project. The revised pension and postretirement benefit disclosures discussed in Chapter 20 (*FASB Statement No. 132*) are one example of how disclosures can be streamlined and made more useful.

plifying or explaining the items presented in the main body of the statements. Information pertinent to specific financial statement items can be explained in qualitative terms, and supplementary data of a quantitative nature can be provided to expand the information in the financial statements. Restrictions imposed by financial arrangements or basic contractual agreements also can be explained in notes. Although notes may be technical and difficult to understand, they provide meaningful information for the user of the financial statements.

Accounting Policies

Accounting policies of a given entity are the specific accounting principles and methods currently employed and considered most appropriate to present fairly the financial statements of the enterprise. *APB Opinion No. 22*, "Disclosure of Accounting Policies," concluded that information about the accounting policies adopted and followed by a reporting entity is essential for financial statement users in making economic decisions. It recommended that a **statement identifying the accounting policies adopted and followed by the reporting entity should also be presented as an integral part of the financial statements**. The disclosure should be given as the initial note or in a separate Summary of Significant Accounting Policies section preceding the notes to the financial statements. The Summary of Significant Accounting Policies answers such questions as: What method of depreciation is used on plant assets? What valuation method is employed on inventories? What amortization policy is followed in regard to intangible assets? How are marketing costs handled for financial reporting purposes?

Refer to Appendix 5B, pages 202–228, for an illustration of note disclosure of accounting policies (Note 1) and other notes accompanying the audited financial statements of **3M Company**. An illustration from **OshKosh B'Gosh, Inc.** is provided in Illustration 24-2.

ILLUSTRATION 24-2
Note Disclosure of Accounting Policies

OshKosh B'Gosh, Inc. and Subsidiaries
(Dollars in thousands, except per share amounts)

Note 1. Significant Accounting Policies

Business
OshKosh B'Gosh, Inc. and its wholly-owned subsidiaries (the Company) are engaged primarily in the design, sourcing, and marketing of apparel to wholesale customers and through Company-owned retail stores.

Principles of consolidation
The consolidated financial statements include the accounts of all wholly-owned subsidiaries. All significant intercompany accounts and transactions have been eliminated in consolidation.

Cash and cash equivalents
Cash equivalents consist of highly liquid debt instruments such as money market accounts and commercial paper with original maturities of three months or less and other financial instruments that can be readily liquidated. The Company's policy is to invest cash in conservative instruments as part of its cash management program and to evaluate the credit exposure of any investment. Cash equivalents are stated at cost, which approximates market value.

Investments
Investments are classified as available-for-sale securities and are highly liquid debt instruments. These investments are stated at cost, which approximates market value.

Financial instruments
The fair value of financial instruments, primarily accounts receivable and debt, do not materially differ from their carrying value.

Inventories
Inventories are stated at the lower of cost or market. Inventories stated on the last-in, first-out (LIFO) basis represent 99.4% of total 2001 and 99.6% of total 2000 inventories. Remaining inventories are valued using the first-in, first-out (FIFO) method.

Property, plant and equipment
Property, plant and equipment are carried at cost or at management's estimate of fair market value if considered impaired under the provisions of Statement of Financial Accounting Standards (SFAS) No. 121, "Accounting for the Impairment of Long-Lived Assets and for Long-Lived Assets to be Disposed of," less accumulated depreciation. Expenditures for improvements that increase asset values and extend usefulness are capitalized. Expenditures for maintenance and repairs are expensed as incurred. Depreciation and amortization for financial reporting purposes are calculated using the straight-line method based on the following useful lives:

	Years
Land improvements	10 to 15
Buildings	10 to 40
Leasehold improvements	5 to 10
Machinery and equipment	3 to 10

Revenue recognition
Revenue within wholesale operations is recognized at the time merchandise is shipped and title is transferred to customers. Retail store revenues are recognized at the time of sale.

Use of estimates
The preparation of financial statements in conformity with accounting principles generally accepted in the United States requires management to make estimates and assumptions that affect the amounts reported in the financial statements and accompanying notes. Actual results could differ from those estimates.

Advertising
Advertising costs are expensed as incurred and totaled $14,896, $16,318 and $13,803 in 2001, 2000 and 1999, respectively.

Earnings per share
The numerator for the calculation of basic and diluted earnings per share is net income. The denominator is computed as follows (in thousands):

	2001	2000	1999
Denominator for basic earnings per share—weighted average shares	**12,191**	12,321	16,112
Employee stock options (treasury stock method)	**390**	157	208
Denominator for diluted earnings per share	**12,581**	12,478	16,320

The Company had 26,500, 639,450 and 361,000 employee stock options that were anti-dilutive in 2001, 2000 and 1999, respectively, and, accordingly, are not included in the diluted earnings per share calculations.

Fiscal year
The Company's fiscal year is a 52/53 week year ending on the Saturday closest to December 31. Fiscal 2001 ended on December 29, 2001, fiscal 2000 ended on December 30, 2000 and fiscal 1999 ended on January 1, 2000, all of which were 52 week years. All references to years in this report refer to the fiscal years described above.

Comprehensive income
Comprehensive income equaled net income in 2001, 2000 and 1999.

Reclassifications
Certain prior year amounts have been reclassified to conform with the current year presentation.

UNDERLYING CONCEPTS

The AICPA's Special Committee on Financial Reporting states that to meet users' changing needs, business reporting must: (1) Provide more forward-looking information about plans, opportunities, risks, and uncertainties. (2) Focus more on the factors that create longer-term value, including nonfinancial measures indicating how key business processes are performing. (3) Better align information reported externally with the information reported internally.

Analysts examine carefully the summary of accounting policies section to determine whether the company is using conservative or liberal accounting practices. For example, depreciating plant assets over an unusually long period of time is considered liberal. On the other hand, using LIFO inventory valuation in a period of inflation is generally viewed as following a conservative practice.

Companies that fail to adopt high-quality reporting policies are now being heavily penalized by the market. For example, when **IBM** disclosed that it had used the gain on sale of one of its businesses to lower reported expenses, its shares were slammed in the market. Investors felt that IBM was trying to look better than it really was. In short, its quality of earnings was viewed as low.

Common Notes

Many of the **notes to the financial statements** have been discussed throughout this textbook. Others will be discussed more fully in this chapter. The more common are as follows.

MAJOR DISCLOSURES

Inventory. The basis upon which inventory amounts are stated (lower of cost or market) and the method used in determining cost (LIFO, FIFO, average cost, etc.) should be reported. Manufacturers should report the inventory composition (finished goods, work in process, raw materials) either in the balance sheet or in a separate schedule in the notes. Unusual or significant financing arrangements relating to inventories that may require disclosure include transactions with related parties, product financing arrangements, firm purchase commitments, involuntary liquidation of LIFO inventories, and pledging of inventories as collateral. Chapter 9 (pages 441–442) illustrates these disclosures.

Property, Plant, and Equipment. The basis of valuation for property, plant, and equipment should be stated. It is usually historical cost. Pledges, liens, and other commitments related to these assets should be disclosed. In the presentation of depreciation, the following disclosures should be made in the financial statements or in the notes: (1) depreciation expense for the period; (2) balances of major classes of depreciable assets, by nature and function, at the balance sheet date; (3) accumulated depreciation, either by major classes of depreciable assets or in total, at the balance sheet date; and (4) a general description of the method or methods used in computing depreciation with respect to major classes of depreciable assets. Any major impairments should be explained. Chapter 11 (pages 541–542) illustrates these disclosures.

Credit Claims. An investor normally finds it extremely useful to determine the nature and cost of creditorship claims. However, the liabilities section in the balance sheet can provide the major types of liabilities outstanding only in the aggregate. Note schedules regarding such obligations provide additional information about how the company is financing its operations, the costs that will have to be borne in future periods, and the timing of future cash outflows. Financial statements must disclose for each of the 5 years following the date of the financial statements the aggregate amount of maturities and sinking fund requirements for all long-term borrowings. Chapter 14 (pages 691–692) illustrates these disclosures.

Equity Holders' Claims. Many companies present in the body of the balance sheet the number of shares authorized, issued, and outstanding and the par value for each type of equity security. Such data may also be presented in a note. Beyond that, the most common type of equity note disclosure relates to contracts and senior securities outstanding that might affect the various claims of the residual equity holders—for example, the existence of outstanding stock options, outstanding convertible debt, redeemable preferred stock, and convertible preferred stock. In addition, it is necessary to disclose to equity claimants certain types of restrictions currently in force. Generally, these types of restrictions involve the amount of earnings available for dividend distribution. Examples of these types of disclosures are illustrated in Chapter 15 (pages 747–749) and Chapter 16 (pages 799–800).

Contingencies and Commitments. An enterprise may have gain or loss contingencies that are not disclosed in the body of the financial statements. These contingencies include litigation, debt and other guarantees, possible tax assessments, renegotiation of government contracts, sales of receivables with recourse, and so on. In addition, commitments that relate to dividend restrictions, purchase agreements (through-put and take-or-pay), hedge contracts, and employment contracts are also disclosed. Disclosures of items of this nature are illustrated in Chapter 7 (pages 337–338), Chapter 9 (pages 430–432), and Chapter 13 (pages 640–643).

UNDERLYING CONCEPTS

The AICPA Special Committee on Financial Reporting notes that standards setters should address disclosures and accounting requirements for off-balance-sheet financial arrangements to ensure that business reporting faithfully reports the risks, opportunities, resources, and obligations that result from those arrangements, consistent with users' needs for information.

Deferred Taxes, Pensions, and Leases. Extensive disclosure is required in these three areas. Chapter 19 (pages 980–983), Chapter 20 (pages 1043–1045), and Chapter 21 (pages 1114–1116) discuss each of these disclosures in detail. It should be emphasized that notes to the financial statements should be given a careful reading for information about off-balance-sheet commitments, future financing needs, and the quality of a company's earnings.

Changes in Accounting Principles. The profession defines various types of accounting changes and establishes guides for reporting each type. Either in the summary of significant accounting policies or in the other notes, changes in accounting principles (as well as material changes in estimates and corrections of errors) are discussed. See Chapter 22 (pages 1154–1158 and 1162–1165).

Additional Examples of Major Disclosures

The disclosures listed above have been discussed in earlier chapters. Four additional disclosures of significance—special transactions or events, subsequent events, segment reporting, and interim reporting—are illustrated in the following sections of this chapter.

WHAT DO THE NUMBERS MEAN?

MORE PAGES, BUT BETTER?

The biggest overall change in annual reports recently is that companies are now disclosing debt-rating triggers buried in their financing arrangements. These triggers can require a company to pay off a loan immediately if the debt rating folds; they are one of the reasons Enron crumbled so quickly. But few Enron stockholders knew about them until the gun had gone off. Companies are also telling more about their bank credit lines, liquidity, and any special purpose entities, which were major villains in the Enron drama.

Source: Gretchen Morgenson, "Annual Reports: More Pages, But Better?" *New York Times* (March 17, 2002).

DISCLOSURE ISSUES

Disclosure of Special Transactions or Events

Related party transactions, errors and irregularities, and illegal acts pose especially sensitive and difficult problems. The accountant/auditor who has responsibility for reporting on these types of transactions has to be extremely careful that the rights of the reporting company and the needs of users of the financial statements are properly balanced.

Related party transactions arise when a business enterprise engages in transactions in which one of the transacting parties has the ability to influence significantly the policies of the other, or in which a nontransacting party has the ability to influence the policies of the two transacting parties.[4] Transactions involving related parties cannot be presumed to be carried out on an "arm's-length" basis because the requisite conditions of competitive, free-market dealings may not exist. Transactions such as borrowing or lending money at abnormally low or high interest rates, real estate sales at amounts that differ significantly from appraised value, exchanges of nonmonetary assets, and transactions involving enterprises that have no economic substance ("shell corporations") suggest that related parties may be involved.

INTERNATIONAL INSIGHT

In Switzerland there are no requirements to disclose related party transactions. In Italy and Germany related parties do not include a company's directors.

The economic substance rather than the legal form of these transactions should be reported in order to make adequate disclosures. *FASB Statement No. 57* requires the following disclosures of material related party transactions.

1. The nature of the relationship(s) involved.
2. A description of the transactions (including transactions to which no amounts or nominal amounts were ascribed) for each of the periods for which income statements are presented.
3. The dollar amounts of transactions for each of the periods for which income statements are presented.
4. Amounts due from or to related parties as of the date of each balance sheet presented.

Illustration 24-3 is an example of the disclosure of related party transactions taken from the annual report of **Tyler Technologies, Inc.**

Tyler Technologies, Inc.

(4) (in part): Related Party Transactions
On September 29, 2000, the Company sold for cash certain net assets of Kofile and another subsidiary, the Company's interest in a certain intangible work product, and a building and related building improvements to investment entities beneficially owned by a principal shareholder of the Company, who was also a director at the time (See Note 3).

ILLUSTRATION 24-3
Disclosure of Related Party Transactions

Errors are defined as unintentional mistakes, whereas **irregularities** are intentional distortions of financial statements.[5] As indicated in this textbook, when errors are discovered, the financial statements should be corrected. The same treatment should be

[4]Examples of related party transactions include transactions between (a) a parent company and its subsidiaries; (b) subsidiaries of a common parent; (c) an enterprise and trusts for the benefit of employees (controlled or managed by the enterprise); and (d) an enterprise and its principal owners, management, or members of immediate families, and affiliates. Two classic cases of related party transactions were **Enron**, with its misuse of special purpose entities, and **Tyco International**, with its forgiving of loans to its management team.

[5]"The Auditor's Responsibility to Detect and Report Errors and Irregularities," *Statement on Auditing Standards No. 53* (New York, AICPA, 1988).

given irregularities. The discovery of irregularities, however, gives rise to a whole different set of suspicions, procedures, and responsibilities on the part of the accountant/auditor.[6]

Illegal acts encompass such items as illegal political contributions, bribes, kickbacks, and other violations of laws and regulations.[7] In these situations, the accountant/auditor must evaluate the adequacy of disclosure in the financial statements. For example, if revenue is derived from an illegal act that is considered material in relation to the financial statements, this information should be disclosed. To deter these illegal acts, Congress recently enacted the Sarbanes-Oxley Act of 2002. This acts adds significant fines and longer jail time for those who improperly sign off on the correctness of financial statements that actually include willing and knowing misstatements.

Many companies are involved in related party transactions; errors and irregularities, and illegal acts, however, are the exception rather than the rule. Disclosure plays a very important role in these areas because the transaction or event is more qualitative than quantitative and involves more subjective than objective evaluation. The users of the financial statements must be provided with some indication of the existence and nature of these transactions where material, through disclosures, modifications in the auditor's report, or reports of changes in auditors.

Post-Balance-Sheet Events (Subsequent Events)

Notes to the financial statements should explain any significant financial events that took place after the formal balance sheet date, but before it is finally issued. These events are referred to as **post-balance-sheet events**, events subsequent to the balance sheet date, or just plain **subsequent events**. The subsequent events period is time-diagrammed as shown in Illustration 24-4.

ILLUSTRATION 24-4
Time Periods for Subsequent Events

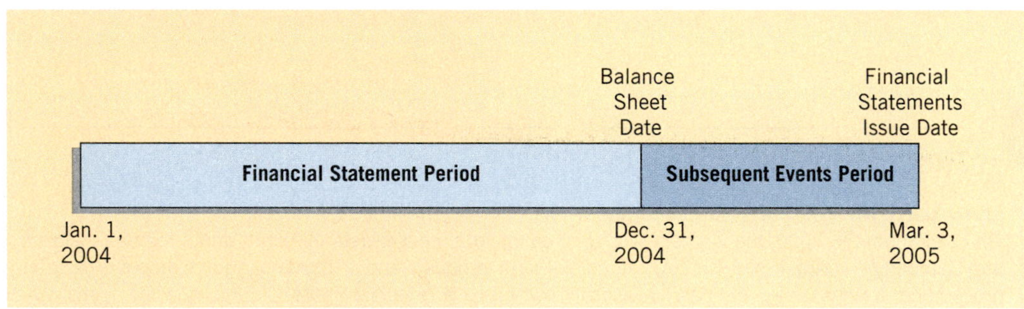

A period of several weeks, and sometimes months, may elapse after the end of the year before the financial statements are issued. Taking and pricing the inventory, reconciling subsidiary ledgers with controlling accounts, preparing necessary adjusting entries, ensuring that all transactions for the period have been entered, obtaining an audit of the financial statements by independent certified public accountants, and printing the annual report all take time. During the period between the balance sheet date and its distribution to stockholders and creditors, important transactions or other events may occur that materially affect the company's financial position or operating situation.

[6]The profession became so concerned with certain management frauds that affect financial statements that it established a National Commission on Fraudulent Financial Reporting. The major purpose of this organization was to determine how fraudulent reporting practices can be constrained. Fraudulent financial reporting is discussed later in this chapter.

[7]"Illegal Acts by Clients," *Statement on Auditing Standards No. 54* (New York, AICPA, 1988).

Many who read a recent balance sheet believe the balance sheet condition is constant and they project it into the future. However, readers must be told if the company has sold one of its plants, acquired a subsidiary, suffered extraordinary losses, settled significant litigation, or experienced any other important event in the post-balance-sheet period. Without an explanation in a note, the reader might be misled and draw inappropriate conclusions.

Two types of events or transactions occurring after the balance sheet date may have a material effect on the financial statements or may need to be considered to interpret these statements accurately:

UNDERLYING CONCEPTS

The periodicity or time period assumption implies that economic activities of an enterprise can be divided into artificial time periods for purpose of analysis.

1. **Events that provide additional evidence about conditions that existed at the balance sheet date, affect the estimates used in preparing financial statements, and therefore result in needed adjustments:** All information available prior to the issuance of the financial statements is used to evaluate estimates previously made. To ignore these subsequent events is to pass up an opportunity to improve the accuracy of the financial statements. This first type encompasses information that would have been recorded in the accounts had it been known at the balance sheet date.

   For example, if a loss on an account receivable results from a customer's bankruptcy subsequent to the balance sheet date, the financial statements are adjusted before their issuance. The bankruptcy stems from the customer's poor financial health existing at the balance sheet date.

   The same criterion applies to settlements of litigation. The financial statements must be adjusted if the events that gave rise to the litigation, such as personal injury or patent infringement, took place prior to the balance sheet date. If the event giving rise to the claim took place subsequent to the balance sheet date, no adjustment is necessary, but disclosure is. To illustrate, a loss resulting from a customer's fire or flood after the balance sheet date is not indicative of conditions existing at that date. Thus, adjustment of the financial statements is not necessary.

2. **Events that provide evidence about conditions that did not exist at the balance sheet date but arise subsequent to that date and do not require adjustment of the financial statements:** Some of these events may have to be disclosed to keep the financial statements from being misleading. These disclosures take the form of notes, supplemental schedules, or even pro forma ("as if") financial data prepared as if the event had occurred on the balance sheet date. Below are examples of such events that require disclosure (but do not result in adjustment):

   (a) Sale of bonds or capital stock; stock splits or stock dividends.

   (b) Business combination pending or effected.

   (c) Settlement of litigation when the event giving rise to the claim took place subsequent to the balance sheet date.

   (d) Loss of plant or inventories from fire or flood.

   (e) Losses on receivables resulting from conditions (such as customer's major casualty) arising subsequent to the balance sheet date.

   (f) Gains or losses on certain marketable securities.[8]

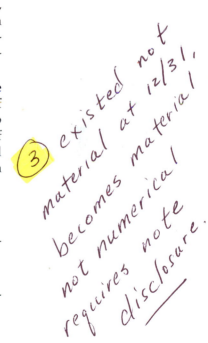

An example of subsequent events disclosure, excerpted from the Annual Report of **Krispy Kreme Doughnuts, Inc.** is presented in Illustration 24-5.

[8]"Subsequent Events," *Statement on Auditing Standards No. 1* (New York: AICPA, 1973), pp. 123–124. *Accounting Trends and Techniques—2001* listed the following types of subsequent events and their frequency of occurrence among the 600 companies surveyed: debt incurred, reduced, or refinanced, 72; business combinations pending or effected, 63; discontinued operations, 33; litigation, 31; and capital stock issued or repurchased, 16.

ILLUSTRATION 24-5
Disclosure of Subsequent Events

Krispy Kreme Doughnuts, Inc.

Note 21. Subsequent Events
In February 2001, the Company completed a follow-on public offering of 5,200,000 shares of common stock at a price of $33.50 per share with the net proceeds totaling $31.83 per share after underwriters' commissions. The 5,200,000 shares included a 600,000 share over-allotment option exercised by the underwriters. Of the 5,200,000 shares, 4,656,650 were sold by selling shareholders and 543,350 were sold by the Company. Net proceeds to the Company were $17,295,000.

On February 2, 2001, the Company acquired the assets of Digital Java, Inc., a Chicago-based coffee company for a purchase price of $389,500 plus an earn-out not to exceed $775,000. Digital Java, Inc. is a sourcer and micro-roaster of premium quality coffees and offers a broad line of coffee-based and non-coffee beverages.

On February 5, 2001, the Company purchased a 104,000 square foot manufacturing facility in Winston-Salem for approximately $3.3 million. The Company will relocate its equipment manufacturing and training facilities from its current location in Winston-Salem to this new facility.

Many subsequent events or developments are not likely to require either adjustment of or disclosure in the financial statements. Typically, these are nonaccounting events or conditions that managements normally communicate by other means. These events include legislation, product changes, management changes, strikes, unionization, marketing agreements, and loss of important customers.

Reporting for Diversified (Conglomerate) Companies

OBJECTIVE 3
Describe the disclosure requirements for major segments of a business.

In the last several decades business enterprises at times have had a tendency to diversify their operations. Take the case of conglomerate GenCorp. whose products at one time had included tires, Penn tennis balls, parts for the MX missile, and linings for disposable diapers. Its RKO subsidiary owned radio and television stations, made movies, bottled soda pop, ran hotels, and held a big stake in an airline. As a result of such diversification efforts, investors and investment analysts have sought more information concerning the details behind conglomerate financial statements. Particularly, they want income statement, balance sheet, and cash flow information on the **individual** segments that compose the **total** business income figure.

An illustration of **segmented** (disaggregated) financial information is presented in the following example of an office equipment and auto parts company.

ILLUSTRATION 24-6
Segmented Income Statement

OFFICE EQUIPMENT AND AUTO PARTS COMPANY
INCOME STATEMENT DATA
(IN MILLIONS)

	Consolidated	Office Equipment	Auto Parts
Net sales	$78.8	$18.0	$60.8
Manufacturing costs			
Inventories, beginning	12.3	4.0	8.3
Materials and services	38.9	10.8	28.1
Wages	12.9	3.8	9.1
Inventories, ending	(13.3)	(3.9)	(9.4)
	50.8	14.7	36.1
Selling and administrative expense	12.1	1.6	10.5
Total operating expenses	62.9	16.3	46.6
Income before taxes	15.9	1.7	14.2
Income taxes	(9.3)	(1.0)	(8.3)
Net income	$ 6.6	$ 0.7	$ 5.9

If only the consolidated figures are available to the analyst, much information regarding the composition of these figures is hidden in aggregated totals. There is no way to tell from the consolidated data the extent to which the differing product lines **contribute to the company's profitability, risk, and growth potential**. For example, in Illustration 24-6, if the office equipment segment is deemed a risky venture, then segmented reporting provides useful information for purposes of making an informed investment decision regarding the whole company.

A classic situation that demonstrates the need for segmented data involved **Caterpillar, Inc.** Caterpillar was cited by the SEC because it failed to tell investors that nearly a quarter of its income in 1989 came from a Brazilian unit. This income was nonrecurring in nature. The company knew that different economic policies in the next year would probably greatly affect earnings of the Brazilian unit. But Caterpillar presented its financial results on a consolidated basis, not disclosing the Brazilian's operations. The SEC stated that Caterpillar's failure to include information about Brazil left investors with an incomplete picture of the company's financial results and denied investors the opportunity to see the company "through the eyes of management."

Companies have always been somewhat hesitant to disclose segmented data for various reasons:

1. Without a thorough knowledge of the business and an understanding of such important factors as the competitive environment and capital investment requirements, the investor may find the segmented information meaningless or may even draw improper conclusions about the reported earnings of the segments.
2. Additional disclosure may harm reporting firms because it may be helpful to competitors, labor unions, suppliers, and certain government regulatory agencies.
3. Additional disclosure may discourage management from taking intelligent business risks because segments reporting losses or unsatisfactory earnings may cause stockholder dissatisfaction with management.
4. The wide variation among firms in the choice of segments, cost allocation, and other accounting problems limits the usefulness of segmented information.
5. The investor is investing in the company as a whole and not in the particular segments, and it should not matter how any single segment is performing if the overall performance is satisfactory.
6. Certain technical problems, such as classification of segments and allocation of segment revenues and costs (especially "common costs"), are formidable.

On the other hand, the advocates of segmented disclosures offer these reasons in support of the practice:

1. Segmented information is needed by the investor to make an intelligent investment decision regarding a diversified company.
   - **(a)** Sales and earnings of individual segments are needed to forecast consolidated profits because of the differences between segments in growth rate, risk, and profitability.
   - **(b)** Segmented reports disclose the nature of a company's businesses and the relative size of the components as an aid in evaluating the company's investment worth.
2. The absence of segmented reporting by a diversified company may put its unsegmented, single product-line competitors at a competitive disadvantage because the conglomerate may obscure information that its competitors must disclose.

The advocates of segmented disclosures appear to have a much stronger case. Many users indicate that segmented data are the most useful financial information provided, aside from the basic financial statements. As a result, the FASB has issued extensive reporting guidelines in this area.

Objective of Reporting Segmented Information

The objective of reporting segmented financial data is to provide information about the **different types of business activities** in which an enterprise engages and the **different economic environments** in which it operates, in order to help users of financial statements do the following.

(a) Better understand the enterprise's performance.
(b) Better assess its prospects for future net cash flows.
(c) Make more informed judgments about the enterprise as a whole.

Basic Principles

A company might meet the segmented reporting objective by providing complete sets of financial statements that are disaggregated in several ways. For example, financial statements can be disaggregated by products or services, by geography, by legal entity, or by type of customer. However, it is not feasible to provide all of that information in every set of financial statements. *FASB Statement No. 131* requires that general purpose financial statements include selected information on a single basis of segmentation. The method chosen is referred to as the **management approach**.[9] **The management approach is based on the way that management segments the company for making operating decisions.** Consequently, the segments are evident from the company's organization structure. It focuses on information about components of the business that management uses to make decisions about operating matters. These components are called **operating segments**.

Identifying Operating Segments

An **operating segment** is a component of an enterprise:

(a) That engages in business activities from which it earns revenues and incurs expenses.
(b) Whose operating results are regularly reviewed by the company's chief operating decision maker to assess segment performance and allocate resources to the segment.
(c) For which discrete financial information is available that is generated by or based on the internal financial reporting system.

Information about two or more operating segments may be aggregated only if the segments have the same basic characteristics in each of the following areas.

(a) The nature of the products and services provided.
(b) The nature of the production process.
(c) The type or class of customer.
(d) The methods of product or service distribution.
(e) If applicable, the nature of the regulatory environment.

After the company decides on the segments for possible disclosure, a quantitative materiality test is made to determine whether the segment is significant enough to warrant actual disclosure. An operating segment is regarded as significant and therefore identified as a reportable segment if it satisfies **one or more** of the following quantitative thresholds.

1 Its **revenue** (including both sales to external customers and intersegment sales or transfers) is 10 percent or more of the combined revenue of all the enterprise's operating segments.

[9]"Disclosures about Segments of an Enterprise and Related Information," *Statement of Financial Accounting Standards No. 131* (Norwalk, Conn.: FASB, 1997).

2. The absolute amount of its **profit or loss** is 10 percent or more of the greater, in absolute amount, of

   (a) the combined operating profit of all operating segments that did not incur a loss, or

   (b) the combined loss of all operating segments that did report a loss.

3. Its **identifiable assets** are 10 percent or more of the combined assets of all operating segments.

In applying these tests, two additional factors must be considered. First, segment data must explain a significant portion of the company's business. Specifically, the segmented results must equal or exceed 75 percent of the combined sales to unaffiliated customers for the entire enterprise. This test prevents a company from providing limited information on only a few segments and lumping all the rest into one category.

Second, the profession recognizes that reporting too many segments may overwhelm users with detailed information. The FASB decided that 10 is a reasonable upper limit for the number of segments that a company should be required to disclose.

To illustrate these requirements, assume a company has identified six possible reporting segments (000 omitted):

ILLUSTRATION 24-7
Data for Different Possible Reporting Segments

Segments	Total Revenue (Unaffiliated)	Operating Profit (Loss)	Identifiable Assets
A	$ 100	$10	$ 60
B	50	2	30
C	700	40	390
D	300	20	160
E	900	18	280
F	100	(5)	50
	$2,150	$85	$970

The respective tests may be applied as follows:

Revenue test: 10% × $2,150 = $215; C, D, and E meet this test.

Operating profit (loss) test: 10% × $90 = $9 (note that the $5 loss is ignored); A, C, D, and E meet this test.

Identifiable assets tests: 10% × $970 = $97; C, D, and E meet this test.

The segments are therefore A, C, D, and E, assuming that these four segments have enough sales to meet the 75 percent of combined sales test. The 75 percent test is computed as follows.

75% of combined sales test: 75% × $2,150 = $1,612.50. The sales of A, C, D, and E total $2,000 ($100 + $700 + $300 + $900); therefore, the 75% test is met.

UNDERLYING CONCEPTS

The AICPA Special Committee on Financial Reporting notes that multi-segment companies operate diverse businesses that are subject to different opportunities and risks. Many users view business segments as the engines that generate future earnings or cash flows and thereby drive returns on investments. Segment information provides additional insight about the opportunities and risks of investments and sharpens predictions. Because of its predictive value, improving segment reporting is of the highest priority.

Measurement Principles

The accounting principles to be used for segment disclosure need not be the same as the principles used to prepare the consolidated statements. This flexibility may at first appear inconsistent. But, preparing segment information in accordance with generally accepted accounting principles would be difficult because some principles are not expected to apply at a segment level. Examples are accounting for the cost of companywide employee benefit plans, accounting for income taxes in a company that files a consolidated tax return, and accounting for inventory on a LIFO basis if the pool includes items in more than one segment.

Allocations of joint, common, or company-wide costs solely for external reporting purposes are not required. **Common costs** are those incurred for the benefit of more than one segment and whose interrelated nature prevents a completely objective division of costs among segments. For example, the company president's salary is difficult to allocate to various segments. Allocations of common costs are inherently arbitrary and may not be meaningful if they are not used for internal management purposes. There is a presumption that allocations to segments are either directly attributable or reasonably allocable.

Segmented Information Reported

The FASB requires that an enterprise report the following.

1. ***General information about its operating segments.*** This includes factors that management considers most significant in determining the company's operating segments, and the types of products and services from which each operating segment derives its revenues.

2. ***Segment profit and loss and related information.*** Specifically, the following information about each operating segment must be reported if the amounts are included in the determination of segment profit or loss.
   - **(a)** Revenues from transactions with external customers.
   - **(b)** Revenues from transactions with other operating segments of the same enterprise.
   - **(c)** Interest revenue.
   - **(d)** Interest expense.
   - **(e)** Depreciation, depletion, and amortization expense.
   - **(f)** Unusual items.
   - **(g)** Equity in the net income of investees accounted for by the equity method.
   - **(h)** Income tax expense or benefit.
   - **(i)** Extraordinary items.
   - **(j)** Significant noncash items other than depreciation, depletion, and amortization expense.

3. ***Segment assets.*** An enterprise must report each operating segment's total assets.

4. ***Reconciliations.*** An enterprise must provide a reconciliation of the total of the segments' revenues to total revenues, a reconciliation of the total of the operating segments' profits and losses to its income before income taxes, and a reconciliation of the total of the operating segments' assets to total assets.

5. ***Information about products and services and geographic areas.*** For each operating segment that has not been determined based on geography, the enterprise must report (unless it is impracticable): (1) revenues from external customers, (2) long-lived assets, and (3) expenditures during the period for long-lived assets. This information, if material, must be reported (a) in the enterprise's country of domicile and (b) in each other country.

6. ***Major customers.*** If 10 percent or more of the revenues is derived from a single customer, the enterprise must disclose the total amount of revenues from each such customer by segment.

Illustration of Disaggregated Information

The segment disclosure for **Johnson & Johnson** is shown in Illustration 24-8.

ILLUSTRATION 24-8
Segment Disclosure

Johnson & Johnson

Johnson & Johnson
(Notes excluded)
Segments of Business

(dollars in millions)	Sales to Customers 2001	2000	1999
Consumer—Domestic	$ 3,789	$ 3,760	$ 3,670
International	3,173	3,144	3,194
Total	6,962	6,904	6,864
Pharmaceutical—Domestic	10,240	8,441	6,955
International	4,611	4,220	4,275
Total	14,851	12,661	11,230
Medical Devices & Diagnostics—Domestic	6,175	5,506	5,296
International	5,016	4,775	4,617
Total	11,191	10,281	9,913
Worldwide total	$33,004	$29,846	$28,007

(dollars in millions)	Operating Profit 2001	2000	1999	Identifiable Assets 2001	2000	1999
Consumer	$ 1,004	$ 867	$ 683	$ 4,209	$ 4,761	$ 4,901
Pharmaceutical	4,928	4,394	3,735	11,568	9,209	8,797
Medical Devices & Diagnostics	2,001	1,696	1,632	13,645	12,745	12,458
Segments total	7,933	6,957	6,050	29,422	26,715	26,156
Expenses not allocated to segments	(35)	(89)	(173)			
General corporate				9,066	7,530	4,908
Worldwide total	$ 7,898	$ 6,868	$ 5,877	$38,488	$34,245	$31,064

(dollars in millions)	Additions to Property, Plant & Equipment 2001	2000	1999	Depreciation and Amortization 2001	2000	1999
Consumer	$ 230	$ 336	$ 412	$ 263	$ 275	$ 277
Pharmaceutical	749	627	760	492	474	407
Medical Devices & Diagnostics	621	665	576	801	801	786
Segments total	1,600	1,628	1,748	1,556	1,550	1,470
General corporate	131	61	74	49	42	40
Worldwide total	$ 1,731	$ 1,689	$ 1,822	$ 1,605	$ 1,592	$ 1,510

Geographic Areas

(dollars in millions)	Sales to Customers 2001	2000	1999	Long-Lived Assets 2001	2000	1999
United States	$20,204	$17,707	$15,921	$11,922	$10,043	$10,033
Europe	6,853	6,365	6,711	3,632	3,551	3,698
Western Hemisphere excluding U.S.	2,142	2,084	2,023	640	653	550
Asia-Pacific, Africa	3,805	3,690	3,352	433	427	439
Segments total	33,004	29,846	28,007	16,627	14,674	14,720
General corporate				319	255	282
Other non long-lived assets				21,542	19,316	16,062
Worldwide total	$33,004	$29,846	$28,007	$38,488	$34,245	$31,064

Interim Reports

One further source of information for the investor is interim reports. As noted earlier, **interim reports** are those reports that cover periods of less than one year. At one time, interim reports were referred to as the "forgotten reports"; this is no longer the case.

OBJECTIVE 4
Describe the accounting problems associated with interim reporting.

The stock exchanges, the SEC, and the accounting profession have taken an active role in developing guidelines for the presentation of interim information.

The SEC mandates that certain companies file a Form 10-Q, which requires a company to disclose quarterly data similar to that disclosed in the annual report. It also requires those companies to disclose selected quarterly information in notes to the annual financial statements. Illustration 24-9 presents the disclosure of selected quarterly data for **Tootsie Roll Industries, Inc.** In addition to this requirement, the APB issued *Opinion No. 28*, which attempted to narrow the reporting alternatives related to interim reports.[10]

ILLUSTRATION 24-9
Disclosure of Selected Quarterly Data

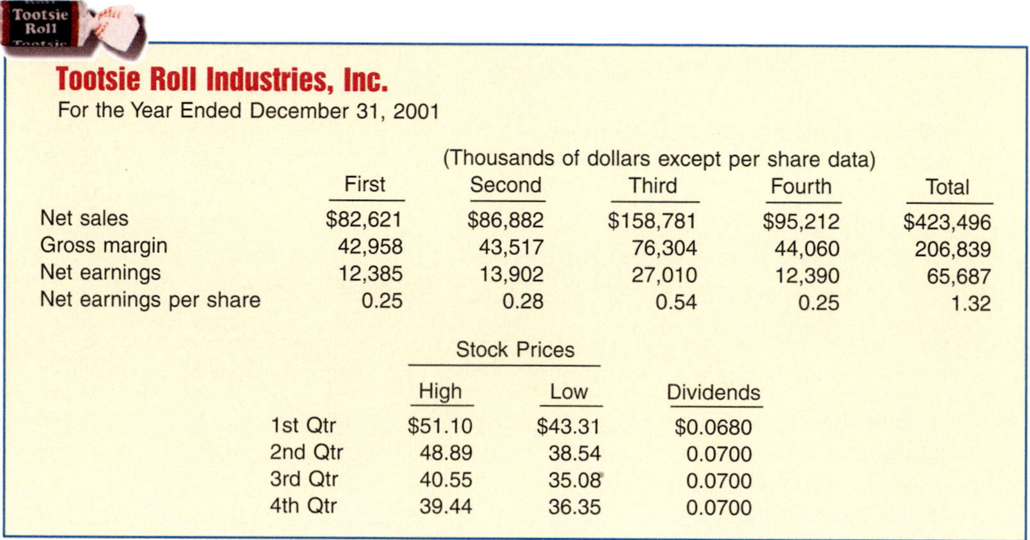

Tootsie Roll Industries, Inc.
For the Year Ended December 31, 2001

(Thousands of dollars except per share data)

	First	Second	Third	Fourth	Total
Net sales	$82,621	$86,882	$158,781	$95,212	$423,496
Gross margin	42,958	43,517	76,304	44,060	206,839
Net earnings	12,385	13,902	27,010	12,390	65,687
Net earnings per share	0.25	0.28	0.54	0.25	1.32

	Stock Prices		
	High	Low	Dividends
1st Qtr	$51.10	$43.31	$0.0680
2nd Qtr	48.89	38.54	0.0700
3rd Qtr	40.55	35.08	0.0700
4th Qtr	39.44	36.35	0.0700

UNDERLYING CONCEPTS

For information to be relevant, it must be available to decision makers before it loses its capacity to influence their decisions (timeliness). Interim reporting is an excellent example of this concept.

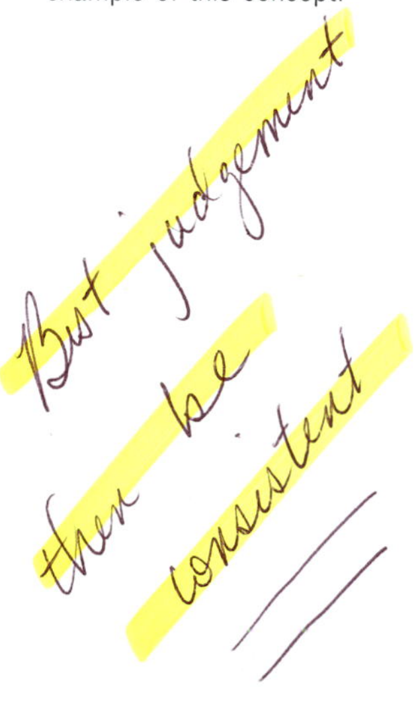

Because of the short-term nature of the information in these reports, however, there is considerable controversy as to the general approach that should be employed. One group, which holds the **discrete view**, believes that each interim period should be treated as a separate accounting period; deferrals and accruals would therefore follow the principles employed for annual reports. In this view, accounting transactions should be reported as they occur, and expense recognition should not change with the period of time covered. Another group, which holds the **integral view**, believes that the interim report is an integral part of the annual report and that deferrals and accruals should take into consideration what will happen for the entire year. In this approach, estimated expenses are assigned to parts of a year on the basis of sales volume or some other activity base. At present, many companies follow the discrete approach for certain types of expenses and the integral approach for others, because the standards currently employed in practice are vague and lead to differing interpretations.

Interim Reporting Requirements

Generally, the same accounting principles used for annual reports should be employed for interim reports. Revenues should be recognized in interim periods on the same basis as they are for annual periods. For example, if the installment-sales method is used as the basis for recognizing revenue on an annual basis, then the installment basis should be applied to interim reports as well. Also, costs directly associated with revenues (product costs), such as materials, labor and related fringe benefits, and manufacturing overhead, should be treated in the same manner for interim reports as for annual reports.

[10]"Interim Financial Reporting," *Opinions of the Accounting Principles Board No. 28* (New York: AICPA, 1973).

Companies should use the same inventory pricing methods (FIFO, LIFO, etc.) for interim reports that they use for annual reports. However, the following exceptions are appropriate at interim reporting periods.

1. Companies may use the gross profit method for interim inventory pricing, but disclosure of the method and adjustments to reconcile with annual inventory are necessary.
2. When LIFO inventories are liquidated at an interim date and are expected to be replaced by year-end, cost of goods sold should include the expected cost of replacing the liquidated LIFO base and not give effect to the interim liquidation.
3. Inventory market declines should not be deferred beyond the interim period unless they are temporary and no loss is expected for the fiscal year.
4. Planned variances under a standard cost system which are expected to be absorbed by year-end ordinarily should be deferred.

Costs and expenses other than product costs, often referred to as **period costs**, are often charged to the interim period as incurred. But they may be allocated among interim periods on the basis of an estimate of time expired, benefit received, or activity associated with the periods. Considerable latitude is exercised in accounting for these costs in interim periods, and many believe more definitive guidelines are needed.

Regarding disclosure, the following interim data should be reported as a minimum.

1. Sales or gross revenues, provision for income taxes, extraordinary items, cumulative effect of a change in accounting principles or practices, and net income.
2. Basic and diluted earnings per share where appropriate.
3. Seasonal revenue, cost, or expenses.
4. Significant changes in estimates or provisions for income taxes.
5. Disposal of a component of a business and extraordinary, unusual, or infrequently occurring items.
6. Contingent items.
7. Changes in accounting principles or estimates.
8. Significant changes in financial position.

Companies are encouraged but not required to publish a balance sheet and a statement of cash flows. When this information is not presented, significant changes in such items as liquid assets, net working capital, long-term liabilities, and stockholders' equity should be disclosed.

Unique Problems of Interim Reporting

In *APB Opinion No. 28*, the Board indicated that it favored the integral approach. However, within this broad guideline, a number of unique reporting problems develop related to the following items.

Advertising and Similar Costs. The general guidelines are that costs such as advertising should be **deferred in an interim period if the benefits extend beyond that period; otherwise they should be expensed as incurred**. But such a determination is difficult, and even if they are deferred, how should they be allocated between quarters? Because of the vague guidelines in this area, accounting for advertising varies widely. At one time, some companies in the food industry, such as **RJR Nabisco** and **Pillsbury**, charged advertising costs as a percentage of sales and adjusted to actual at year-end, whereas **General Foods** and **Kellogg** expensed these costs as incurred.

The same type of problem relates to such items as Social Security taxes, research and development costs, and major repairs. For example, should the company expense Social Security costs (payroll taxes) on highly paid personnel early in the year, or allocate and spread them to subsequent quarters? Should a major repair that occurs later in the year be anticipated and allocated proportionately to earlier periods?

Expenses Subject to Year-End Adjustment. Bad debts, executive bonuses, pension costs, and inventory shrinkage are often not known with a great deal of certainty until year-end. **These costs should be estimated and allocated in the best possible way to interim periods.** Companies use a variety of allocation techniques to accomplish this objective.

Income Taxes. Not every dollar of corporate taxable income is assessed at the same rate; the tax rate is progressive. This aspect of business income taxes poses a problem in preparing **interim financial statements**. Should the income to date be annualized and the proportionate income tax accrued for the period to date **(annualized approach)**? Or should the first amount of income earned be taxed at the lower rate of tax applicable to such income **(marginal principle approach)**? At one time, companies generally followed the latter approach and accrued the tax applicable to each additional dollar of income.

The marginal principle was especially applicable to businesses having a seasonal or uneven income pattern, because the interim accrual of tax was based on the actual results to date. The profession now, however, uses the annualized approach requiring that "at the end of each interim period the company should make its best estimate of the effective tax rate expected to be applicable for the full fiscal year. The rate so determined should be used in providing for income taxes on income for the quarter."[11]

Because businesses did not uniformly apply this guideline in accounting for similar situations, the FASB issued *Interpretation No. 18*. This interpretation requires that the **estimated annual effective tax rate** be applied to the year-to-date "ordinary" income at the end of each interim period to compute the year-to-date tax. Further, the **interim period tax** related to "ordinary" income shall be the difference between the amount so computed and the amounts reported for previous interim periods of the fiscal period.[12]

Extraordinary Items. Extraordinary items consist of unusual and nonrecurring material gains and losses. In the past, they were handled in interim reports in one of three ways: (1) absorbed entirely in the quarter in which they occurred; (2) prorated over the four quarters; or (3) disclosed only by note. **The required approach is to charge or credit the loss or gain in the quarter that it occurs instead of attempting some arbitrary multiple-period allocation.** This approach is consistent with the way in which extraordinary items are currently handled on an annual basis. No attempt is made to prorate the extraordinary items over several years.

Some favor the omission of extraordinary items from the quarterly net income. They believe that inclusion of extraordinary items that may be large in proportion to interim results distorts the predictive value of interim reports. Many, however, consider such an omission inappropriate because it deviates from actual results.

Changes in Accounting. What happens if a company decides to change an accounting principle in the third quarter of a fiscal year? Should the cumulative effect adjustment be charged or credited to that quarter? Presentation of a cumulative effect in the third quarter may be misleading because of the inherent subjectivity associated with the first two quarters' reported income. In addition, a question arises as to whether such a change might not be used to manipulate a given quarter's income.

As a result, *FASB Statement No. 3* was issued, indicating that **if a cumulative effect change occurs in other than the first quarter, no cumulative effect should be recog-**

---

[11]"Interim Financial Reporting," *Opinions of the Accounting Principles Board No. 28* (New York: AICPA, 1973), par. 19. The estimated annual effective tax rate should reflect anticipated tax credits, foreign tax rates, percentage depletion, capital gains rates, and other available tax planning alternatives.

[12]"Accounting for Income Taxes in Interim Periods," *FASB Interpretation No. 18* (Stamford, Conn.: FASB, March 1977), par. 9. "Ordinary" income (or loss) refers to "income (or loss) from continuing operations before income taxes (or benefits)" excluding extraordinary items, discontinued operations, and cumulative effects of changes in accounting principles.

nized in those quarters.[13] **Rather, the cumulative effect at the beginning of the year should be computed and the first quarter restated.** Subsequent quarters would not report a cumulative effect adjustment.

Earnings per Share. Interim reporting of earnings per share has all the problems inherent in computing and presenting annual earnings per share, and then some. If shares are issued in the third period, EPS for the first two periods will not be indicative of year-end EPS. If an extraordinary item is present in one period and new equity shares are sold in another period, the EPS figure for the extraordinary item will change for the year. On an annual basis only one EPS figure is associated with an extraordinary item and that figure does not change; the interim figure is subject to change. **For purposes of computing earnings per share and making the required disclosure determinations, each interim period should stand alone. That is, all applicable tests should be made for that single period.**

Seasonality. **Seasonality** occurs when sales are compressed into one short period of the year while certain costs are fairly evenly spread throughout the year. For example, the natural gas industry has its heavy sales in the winter months. In contrast, the beverage industry has its heavy sales in the summer months.

The problem of seasonality is related to the matching concept in accounting. Expenses should be matched against the revenues they create. In a seasonal business, wide fluctuations in profits occur because off-season sales do not absorb the company's fixed costs (for example, manufacturing, selling, and administrative costs that tend to remain fairly constant regardless of sales or production).

To illustrate why seasonality is a problem, assume the following information.

Develop your own set of rules.

ILLUSTRATION 24-10
Data for Seasonality Example

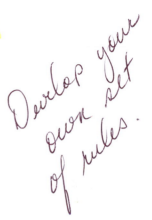

Selling price per unit	$1
Annual sales for the period (projected and actual)	
100,000 units @ $1	$100,000
Manufacturing costs	
Variable	10¢ per unit
Fixed	20¢ per unit or $20,000 for the year
Nonmanufacturing costs	
Variable	10¢ per unit
Fixed	30¢ per unit or $30,000 for the year

Sales for four quarters and the year (projected and actual) were:

ILLUSTRATION 24-11
Sales Data for Seasonality Example

		Percent of Sales
1st Quarter	$ 20,000	20%
2nd Quarter	5,000	5
3rd Quarter	10,000	10
4th Quarter	65,000	65
Total for the year	$100,000	100%

Under the present accounting framework, the income statements for the quarters might be shown as in Illustration 24-12.

[13]"Reporting Accounting Changes in Interim Financial Statements," *Statement of the Financial Accounting Standards Board No. 3* (Stamford, Conn.: FASB, 1974). This standard also provides guidance related to a LIFO change and accounting changes made in the fourth quarter of a fiscal year in which interim data are not presented.

ILLUSTRATION 24-12
Interim Net Income for Seasonal Business—Discrete Approach

	1st Qtr	2nd Qtr	3rd Qtr	4th Qtr	Year
Sales	$20,000	$ 5,000	$10,000	$65,000	$100,000
Manufacturing costs					
Variable	(2,000)	(500)	(1,000)	(6,500)	(10,000)
Fixed[a]	(4,000)	(1,000)	(2,000)	(13,000)	(20,000)
	14,000	3,500	7,000	45,500	70,000
Nonmanufacturing costs					
Variable	(2,000)	(500)	(1,000)	(6,500)	(10,000)
Fixed[b]	(7,500)	(7,500)	(7,500)	(7,500)	(30,000)
Net income	$ 4,500	$(4,500)	$ (1,500)	$31,500	$ 30,000

[a]The fixed manufacturing costs are inventoried, so that equal amounts of fixed costs do not appear during each quarter.
[b]The fixed nonmanufacturing costs are not inventoried, so equal amounts of fixed costs appear during each quarter.

An investor who uses the first quarter's results can be misled. If the first quarter's earnings are $4,500, should this figure be multiplied by four to predict annual earnings of $18,000? Or, as the analysis suggests, inasmuch as $20,000 in sales is 20 percent of the predicted sales for the year, net income for the year should be $22,500 ($4,500 × 5). Either figure is obviously wrong, and after the second quarter's results occur, the investor may become even more confused.

The problem with the conventional approach is that the fixed nonmanufacturing costs are not charged in proportion to sales. Some enterprises have adopted a way of avoiding this problem by making all fixed nonmanufacturing costs follow the sales pattern, as shown in Illustration 24-13.

ILLUSTRATION 24-13
Interim Net Income for Seasonal Business—Integral Approach

	1st Qtr	2nd Qtr	3rd Qtr	4th Qtr	Year
Sales	$20,000	$ 5,000	$10,000	$65,000	$100,000
Manufacturing costs					
Variable	(2,000)	(500)	(1,000)	(6,500)	(10,000)
Fixed	(4,000)	(1,000)	(2,000)	(13,000)	(20,000)
	14,000	3,500	7,000	45,500	70,000
Nonmanufacturing costs					
Variable	(2,000)	(500)	(1,000)	(6,500)	(10,000)
Fixed	(6,000)	(1,500)	(3,000)	(19,500)	(30,000)
Net income	$ 6,000	$ 1,500	$ 3,000	$19,500	$ 30,000

INTERNATIONAL INSIGHT

IASB GAAP requires that interim financial statements use the discrete method, except for the tax charge.

This approach solves some of the problems of interim reporting: Sales in the first quarter are 20 percent of total sales for the year, and net income in the first quarter is 20 percent of total income. In this case, as in the previous example, the investor cannot rely on multiplying any given quarter by four, but can use comparative data or rely on some estimate of sales in relation to income for a given period.

The greater the degree of seasonality experienced by a company, the greater the possibility of distortion. Because no definitive guidelines are available for handling such items as the fixed nonmanufacturing costs, variability in income can be substantial. To alleviate this problem, the profession recommends that companies subject to material seasonal variations disclose the seasonal nature of their business and consider supplementing their interim reports with information for 12-month periods ended at the interim date for the current and preceding years.

The two illustrations above highlight the difference between the **discrete** and **integral** viewpoints. The fixed nonmanufacturing expenses are expensed as incurred under the discrete viewpoint. They are charged to expense on the basis of some measure of activity under the integral method.

Continuing Controversy. The profession has developed some standards for interim reporting, but much still has to be done. As yet, it is unclear whether the discrete, integral, or some combination of these two methods will be settled on.

Discussion also persists concerning the independent auditor's involvement in interim reports. Many auditors are reluctant to express an opinion on interim financial information, arguing that the data are too tentative and subjective. Conversely, an increasing number of individuals advocate some type of examination of interim reports. A compromise may be a limited review of interim reports that provides some assurance that an examination has been conducted by an outside party and that the published information appears to be in accord with generally accepted accounting principles.[14]

UNDERLYING CONCEPTS

The AICPA Special Committee on Financial Reporting indicates that users would benefit from separate fourth-quarter reporting, including management's analysis of fourth-quarter activities and events. Also, quarterly segment reporting was demanded. Under *FASB Statement No. 131*, companies now provide quarterly segment data.

Analysts want financial information as soon as possible, before it's old news. We may not be far from a continuous database system in which corporate financial records can be accessed via the Internet. Investors might be able to access a company's financial records whenever they wish and put the information in the format they need. Thus, they could learn about sales slippage, cost increases, or earnings changes as they happen, rather than waiting until after the quarter has ended.[15]

A steady stream of information from the company to the investor could be very positive because it might alleviate management's continual concern with short-run interim numbers. Today many contend that U.S. management is too short-run oriented. The truth of this statement is echoed by the words of the president of a large company who decided to retire early: "I wanted to look forward to a year made up of four seasons rather than four quarters."

I WANT IT FASTER

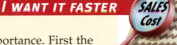

WHAT DO THE NUMBERS MEAN?

The SEC has decided that timeliness of information is of extreme importance. First the SEC has said that public companies will have only 60 days to complete their annual reports, down from 90 days. And quarterly reports must be done within 35 days of the close of the quarter, instead of 45. In addition, corporate executives and shareholders with more than 10 percent of a company's outstanding stock will have 2 days to disclose their sale or purchase of stock.

Also, in a bid to encourage Internet disclosure, the SEC encourages companies to post current, quarterly, and annual reports on their Web sites—or explain why they don't. The Internet postings would have to be made by the day the company submits the information to the SEC, rather than within 24 hours as current rules allow.

AUDITOR'S AND MANAGEMENT'S REPORTS

Auditor's Report

OBJECTIVE 5
Identify the major disclosures found in the auditor's report.

Another important source of information that is often overlooked is the **auditor's report**. An **auditor** is an accounting professional who conducts an independent examination of the accounting data presented by a business enterprise. If the auditor is satisfied that the financial statements present the financial position, results of operations, and cash

[14]The AICPA has been involved in developing guidelines for the review of interim reports. "Limited Review of Interim Financial Statements," *Statement on Auditing Standards No. 24* (New York: AICPA, 1979) sets standards for the review of interim reports.

[15]A step in this direction is the SEC's mandate for companies to file their financial statements electronically with the SEC. The system, called EDGAR (electronic data gathering and retrieval) provides interested parties with computer access to financial information such as periodic filings, corporate prospectuses, and proxy materials.

flows fairly in accordance with generally accepted accounting principles, an **unqualified opinion** is expressed, as shown in Illustration 24-14.[16]

ILLUSTRATION 24-14
Auditor's Report

Boeing Company

Independent Auditors' Report

Board of Directors and Shareholders, The Boeing Company:

We have audited the accompanying consolidated statements of financial position of The Boeing Company and subsidiaries (the "Company") as of December 31, 2001 and 2000, and the related consolidated statements of operations, shareholders' equity, and cash flows for each of the three years in the period ended December 31, 2001. These financial statements are the responsibility of the Company's management. Our responsibility is to express an opinion on these financial statements based on our audits.

We conducted our audits in accordance with auditing standards generally accepted in the United States of America. Those standards require that we plan and perform the audit to obtain reasonable assurance about whether the financial statements are free of material misstatement. An audit includes examining, on a test basis, evidence supporting the amounts and disclosures in the financial statements. An audit also includes assessing the accounting principles used and significant estimates made by management, as well as evaluating the overall financial statement presentation. We believe that our audits provide a reasonable basis for our opinion.

In our opinion, the financial statements referred to above present fairly, in all material respects, the financial position of The Boeing Company and subsidiaries as of December 31, 2001 and 2000, and the results of their operations and their cash flows for each of the three years in the period ended December 31, 2001, in conformity with accounting principles generally accepted in the United States of America.

As discussed in Note 23 to the consolidated financial statements, in 2001 the Company changed its method of accounting for derivative financial statements to confirm to Statement of Financial Accounting Standards No. 133, *Accounting for Derivative Financial Instruments and Hedging Activities*, as amended.

Deloitte & Touche LLP
Chicago, Illinois
January 28, 2002

INTERNATIONAL INSIGHT

In Germany, auditors' opinions address whether the statements have been prepared in accordance with German law—a statutory audit.

In preparing this report, the auditor follows these reporting standards.

1. The report shall state whether the financial statements are presented in accordance with generally accepted accounting principles.
2. The report shall identify those circumstances in which such principles have not been consistently observed in the current period in relation to the preceding period.
3. Informative disclosures in the financial statements are to be regarded as reasonably adequate unless otherwise stated in the report.
4. The report shall contain either an expression of opinion regarding the financial statements taken as a whole or an assertion to the effect that an opinion cannot be expressed. When an overall opinion cannot be expressed, the reasons why should be stated. In all cases where an auditor's name is associated with financial statements, the report should contain a clear-cut indication of the character of the auditor's examination, if any, and the degree of responsibility being taken.

In most cases, the auditor issues a standard **unqualified** or **clean opinion**. That is, the auditor expresses the opinion that the financial statements present fairly, in all material respects, the financial position, results of operations, and cash flows of the en-

[16]This auditor's report is in exact conformance with the specifications contained in "Reports on Audited Financial Statements," *Statement on Auditing Standards No. 58* (New York: AICPA, 1988).

tity in conformity with generally accepted accounting principles. Certain circumstances, although they do not affect the auditor's unqualified opinion, may require the auditor to add an explanatory paragraph to the audit report. Some of the more important circumstances are as follows.

1. ***Uncertainties.*** A matter involving an **uncertainty** is one that is expected to be resolved at a future date, at which time sufficient evidence concerning its outcome is expected to become available. In deciding whether an explanatory paragraph is needed, the auditor should consider the likelihood of a material loss resulting from the contingency. If, for example, the possibility that a loss will be incurred is remote, then an explanatory paragraph is not warranted. If the loss is probable but not estimable, or is reasonably possible and material, then an explanatory paragraph is warranted.
2. ***Lack of Consistency.*** If there has been a change in accounting principles or in the method of their application that has a material effect on the comparability of the company's financial statements, the auditor should refer to the change in an explanatory paragraph of the report. Such an explanatory paragraph should identify the nature of the change and refer the reader to the note in the financial statements that discusses the change in detail. The auditor's concurrence with a change is implicit unless exception to the change is taken in expressing the auditor's opinion as to fair presentation of the financial statements in conformity with generally accepted accounting principles.
3. ***Emphasis of a Matter.*** The auditor may wish to emphasize a matter regarding the financial statements, but nevertheless intends to express an unqualified opinion. For example, the auditor may wish to emphasize that the entity is a component of a larger business enterprise or that it has had significant transactions with related parties. Such explanatory information should be presented in a separate paragraph of the auditor's report.

In some situations, however, the auditor is required to (1) express a **qualified** opinion, (2) express an **adverse** opinion, or (3) **disclaim** an opinion. A **qualified opinion** contains an exception to the standard opinion. Ordinarily the exception is not of sufficient magnitude to invalidate the statements as a whole; if it were, an adverse opinion would be rendered. The usual circumstances in which the auditor may deviate from the standard unqualified short-form report on financial statements are as follows.

1. The scope of the examination is limited or affected by conditions or restrictions.
2. The statements do not fairly present financial position or results of operations because of:
   - **(a)** Lack of conformity with generally accepted accounting principles and standards.
   - **(b)** Inadequate disclosure.

If the auditor is confronted with one of the situations noted above, the opinion must be qualified. A qualified opinion states that, except for the effects of the matter to which the qualification relates, the financial statements present fairly, in all material respects, the financial position, results of operations, and cash flows in conformity with generally accepted accounting principles.

An **adverse opinion** is required in any report in which the exceptions to fair presentation are so material that in the independent auditor's judgment a qualified opinion is not justified. In such a case, the financial statements taken as a whole are not presented in accordance with generally accepted accounting principles. Adverse opinions are rare, because most enterprises change their accounting to conform with the auditor's desires.

A **disclaimer of an opinion** is appropriate when the auditor has gathered so little information on the financial statements that no opinion can be expressed.

An example of a report in which the opinion is qualified because of the use of an accounting principle at variance with generally accepted accounting principles is shown in Illustration 24-15 (assuming the effects are such that the auditor has concluded that an adverse opinion is not appropriate).

ILLUSTRATION 24-15
Qualified Auditor's Report

Helio Company

Independent Auditor's Report

(Same first paragraph as the standard report)

Helio Company has excluded, from property and debt in the accompanying balance sheets, certain lease obligations that, in our opinion, should be capitalized in order to conform with generally accepted accounting principles. If these lease obligations were capitalized, property would be increased by $1,500,000 and $1,300,000, long-term debt by $1,400,000 and $1,200,000, and retained earnings by $100,000 and $50,000 as of December 31, in the current and prior year, respectively. Additionally, net income would be decreased by $40,000 and $30,000 and earnings per share would be decreased by $.06 and $.04, respectively, for the years then ended.

In our opinion, except for the effects of not capitalizing certain lease obligations as discussed in the preceding paragraph, the financial statements referred to above present fairly, in all material respects, the financial position of Helio Company, and the results of its operations and its cash flows for the years then ended in conformity with generally accepted accounting principles.

The profession also requires the auditor to evaluate whether there is substantial doubt about the entity's **ability to continue as a going concern** for a reasonable period of time (not to exceed one year beyond the date of the financial statements). If the auditor concludes that substantial doubt exists, an explanatory note to the auditor's report would be added describing the potential problem.[17]

The audit report should provide useful information to the investor. One investment banker noted, "Probably the first item to check is the auditor's opinion to see whether or not it is a clean one—'in conformity with generally accepted accounting principles'—or is qualified in regard to differences between the auditor and company management in the accounting treatment of some major item, or in the outcome of some major litigation."

Management's Reports

Management's Discussion and Analysis

Management's discussion and analysis (MD&A) section covers three financial aspects of an enterprise's business—liquidity, capital resources, and results of operations. **It requires management to highlight favorable or unfavorable trends and to identify significant events and uncertainties that affect these three factors.** This approach obviously involves a number of subjective estimates, opinions, and soft data. However, the SEC, which has mandated this disclosure, believes the relevance of this information exceeds the potential lack of reliability.

[17]"The Auditor's Consideration of an Entity's Ability to Continue as a Going Concern," *Statement on Auditing Standards No. 59* (New York: AICPA, 1988).

The MD&A section (2001 outlook only) of **Eastman Kodak**'s Annual Report is presented in Illustration 24-16.

Eastman Kodak Company

Outlook

The Company expects 2002 to be another difficult economic year, with full year revenues level with 2001 and some earnings improvement in the second half of 2002. We do not expect to see any real upturn in the economy until 2003, with a very gradual return to consumer spending habits and behavior that will positively affect our business growth. The Company will continue to take actions to minimize the financial impact of this slowdown. These actions include efforts to better manage production and inventory levels and reduce capital spending, while at the same time reducing discretionary spending to further hold down costs. The Company will also complete the implementation of the restructuring programs announced in 2001 to make its operations more cost competitive and improve margins, particularly in its health imaging and consumer digital camera businesses.

During 2000, the Company completed an ongoing program of real estate divestitures and portfolio rationalization that contributed to other income (charges) reaching an annual average of $100 million over the past three years. Now that this program is largely complete, the other income (charges) category is expected to run in the negative $50 million to negative $100 million range annually.

The Company expects its effective tax rate to approximate 29% in 2002. The lower rate is attributable to favorable tax benefits from the elimination of goodwill amortization and expected increased earnings from operations in certain lower-taxed jurisdictions outside the U.S.

From a liquidity and capital resource perspective, the Company expects to generate $6 billion in cash flow after dividends during the next six years, with approximately $400 million of this being achieved in 2002. This will enable the Company to maintain its dividend, pay down debt and make acquisitions that promote profitable growth. Cash flow is defined as net cash flows (after dividends), excluding the impacts from debt and transactions in the Company's own equity, such as stock repurchases and proceeds from the exercise of stock options.

ILLUSTRATION 24-16
Management's Discussion and Analysis

UNDERLYING CONCEPTS

FASB Concepts Statement No. 1 notes that management knows more about the enterprise than users and therefore can increase the usefulness of financial information by identifying significant transactions that affect the enterprise and by explaining their financial impact.

The MD&A section also must provide information concerning the effects of inflation and changing prices if material to financial statement trends. No specific numerical computations are specified, and companies have provided little analysis on changing prices.

How this section of the annual report can be made even more effective is the subject of continuing questions such as:

Expanded Discussion of Accounting for Changing Prices

1. Is sufficient forward-looking information being disclosed under current MD&A requirements?
2. Should MD&A disclosures be changed to become more of a risk analysis?
3. Should the MD&A be audited by independent auditors?

Management's Responsibilities for Financial Statements

OBJECTIVE 6
Understand management's responsibilities for financials.

Some companies already present a report on management's responsibilities, including its responsibilities for, and assessment of, the internal control system. The Sarbanes-Oxley Act requires the SEC to develop guidelines for providing this information for all publicly traded companies. An example of the type of disclosure that some companies are now making is shown in Illustration 24-17.

ILLUSTRATION 24-17
Report on Management's Responsibilities

AMR Corporation

Report of Management

The management of AMR Corporation is responsible for the integrity and objectivity of the Company's financial statements and related information. The financial statements have been prepared in conformity with accounting principles generally accepted in the United States and reflect certain estimates and judgments of management as to matters set forth therein.

AMR maintains a system of internal controls designed to provide reasonable assurance, at reasonable cost, that its financial records can be relied upon in the preparation of financial statements and that its assets are safeguarded against loss or unauthorized use. An important element of the Company's control systems is the ongoing program to promote control consciousness throughout the organization. Management's commitment to the program is evidenced by organizational arrangements that provide for divisions of responsibility, effective communication of policies and procedures, selection of competent financial managers and development and maintenance of financial planning and reporting systems.

Management continually monitors the system for compliance. AMR maintains a strong internal auditing program that independently assesses the effectiveness of the internal controls and recommends possible improvements. Ernst & Young, independent auditors, is engaged to audit the Company's financial statements. Ernst & Young obtains and maintains an understanding of the internal control structure and conducts such tests and other auditing procedures considered necessary in the circumstances to render the opinion on the financial statements contained in their report.

The Audit Committee of the Board of Directors, composed entirely of independent directors, meets regularly with the independent auditors, management and internal auditors to review their work and confirm that they are properly discharging their responsibilities. In addition, the independent auditors and the internal auditors meet periodically with the Audit Committee, without the presence of management, to discuss the results of their work and other relevant matters.

Donald J. Carty
Chairman, President and Chief Executive Officer

Thomas W. Horton
Senior Vice President and Chief Financial Officer

CURRENT REPORTING ISSUES

Reporting on Financial Forecasts and Projections

In recent years, the investing public's demand for more and better information has focused on disclosure of corporate expectations for the future.[18] These disclosures take one of two forms:[19]

[18]Some areas in which companies are using financial information about the future are equipment lease-versus-buy analysis, analysis of a company's ability to successfully enter new markets, and examining merger and acquisition opportunities. In addition, forecasts and projections are also prepared for use by third parties in public offering documents (requiring financial forecasts), tax-oriented investments, and financial feasibility studies. Use of forward-looking data has been enhanced by the increased capability of the microcomputer to analyze, compare, and manipulate large quantities of data.

[19]"Guide for Prospective Financial Information," *Audit and Accounting Guide* (New York: AICPA, May 1999), pars. 3.04 and 3.05.

OBJECTIVE 7
Identify issues related to financial forecasts and projections.

Financial Forecast. Prospective financial statements that present, to the best of the responsible party's knowledge and belief, an entity's expected financial position, results of operations, and cash flows. A financial forecast is based on the responsible party's assumptions reflecting conditions it expects to exist and the course of action it expects to take.

Financial Projection. Prospective financial statements that present, to the best of the responsible party's knowledge and belief, given one or more hypothetical assumptions, an entity's expected financial position, results of operations, and cash flows. A financial projection is based on the responsible party's assumptions reflecting conditions it expects would exist and the course of action it expects would be taken, given one or more hypothetical assumptions.

The difference between a financial forecast and a financial projection is that a forecast attempts to provide information on what is **expected** to happen, whereas a projection may provide information on what is not necessarily expected to happen, but **might** take place.

Financial forecasts are the subject of intensive discussion with journalists, corporate executives, the SEC, financial analysts, accountants, and others. Predictably, there are strong arguments on either side. Listed below are some of the arguments.

Arguments for requiring published forecasts:

1. Investment decisions are based on future expectations. Therefore information about the future facilitates better decisions.
2. Forecasts are already circulated informally, but are uncontrolled, frequently misleading, and not available equally to all investors. This confused situation should be brought under control.
3. Circumstances now change so rapidly that historical information is no longer adequate for prediction.

Arguments against requiring published forecasts:

1. No one can foretell the future. Therefore forecasts, while conveying an impression of precision about the future, will inevitably be wrong.
2. Organizations will strive only to meet their published forecasts, not to produce results that are in the stockholders' best interest.
3. When forecasts are not proved to be accurate, there will be recriminations and probably legal actions.[20]
4. Disclosure of forecasts will be detrimental to organizations, because forecasts will fully inform not only investors but also competitors (foreign and domestic).

UNDERLYING CONCEPTS

The AICPA's Special Committee on Financial Reporting indicates that the current legal environment discourages companies from disclosing forward-looking information. Companies should not have to expand reporting of forward-looking information until there are more effective deterrents to unwarranted litigation.

The AICPA has issued a statement on standards for accountants' services on prospective financial information. This statement establishes guidelines for the preparation and presentation of financial forecasts and projections.[21] It requires accountants to provide (1) a summary of significant assumptions used in the forecast or projection and (2) guidelines for minimum presentation.

To encourage management to disclose this type of information, the SEC has a **safe harbor rule**. This rule provides protection to an enterprise that presents an erroneous forecast as long as the forecast is prepared on a reasonable basis and is disclosed in

[20]The issue is serious. Over a recent 3-year period, 8 percent of the companies on the NYSE were sued because of an alleged lack of financial disclosure. Companies complain that they are subject to lawsuits whenever the stock price drops. And as one executive noted, "You can even be sued if the stock price goes up—because you did not disclose the good news fast enough."

[21]"Guide for Prospective Financial Information," op. cit., par. 1.02.

good faith.[22] However, many companies note that the safe harbor rule does not work in practice, since it does not cover oral statements, nor has it kept them out of court.

Experience in Great Britain

Great Britain has permitted financial forecasts for years, and the results have been fairly successful. Some significant differences exist between the English and the American business and legal environment,[23] but probably none that could not be overcome if influential interests in this country cooperated to produce an atmosphere conducive to quality forecasting. A typical British forecast adapted from a construction company's report to support a public offering of stock is as follows.

ILLUSTRATION 24-18
Financial Forecast of a British Company

Profits have grown substantially over the past 10 years and directors are confident of being able to continue this expansion. . . . While the rate of expansion will be dependent on the level of economic activity in Ireland and England, the group is well structured to avail itself of opportunities as they arise, particularly in the field of property development, which is expected to play an increasingly important role in the group's future expansion.

Profits before taxation for the half year ended 30th June 1999 were 402,000 pounds. On the basis of trading experiences since that date and the present level of sales and completions, the directors expect that in the absence of unforeseen circumstances, the group's profits before taxation for the year to 31st December 1999 will be not less than 960,000 pounds.

No dividends will be paid in respect of the year December 31, 1999. In a full financial year, on the basis of above forecasts (not including full year profits) it would be the intention of the board, assuming current rates of tax, to recommend dividends totaling 40% (of after-tax profits), of which 15% payable would be as an interest dividend in November 2000 and 25% as a final dividend in June 2001.

A general narrative-type forecast issued by a U.S. corporation might appear as follows.

ILLUSTRATION 24-19
Financial Forecast for an American Company

On the basis of promotions planned by the company for the second half of fiscal 2002, net earnings for that period are expected to be approximately the same as those for the first half of fiscal 2002, with net earnings for the third quarter expected to make the predominant contribution to net earnings for the second half of fiscal 2002.

Questions of Liability

What happens if a company does not meet its forecasts? Are the company and the auditor going to be sued? If a company, for example, projects an earnings increase of 15 percent and achieves only 5 percent, should stockholders be permitted to have some judicial recourse against the company?

One court case involving **Monsanto Chemical Corporation** has provided some guidelines. In this case, Monsanto predicted that sales would increase 8 to 9 percent and that earnings would rise 4 to 5 percent. In the last part of the year, the demand for Monsanto's products dropped as a result of a business turndown. Therefore, instead of increasing, the company's earnings declined. The company was sued because the projected earnings figure was erroneous, but the judge dismissed the suit because the forecasts were the best estimates of qualified people whose intents were honest.

[22]"Safe-Harbor Rule for Projections," *Release No. 5993* (Washington: SEC, 1979). The Private Securities Litigation Reform Act of 1995 recognizes that some information that is useful to investors is inherently subject to less certainty or reliability than other information. By providing safe harbor for forward-looking statements, Congress has sought to facilitate access to this information by investors.

[23]The British system, for example, does not permit litigation on forecasted information, and the solicitor (lawyer) is not permitted to work on a contingent fee basis. See "A Case for Forecasting—The British Have Tried It and Find That It Works," *World* (New York: Peat, Marwick, Mitchell & Co., Autumn 1978), pp. 10–13.

As indicated earlier, the SEC's safe harbor rules are intended to protect enterprises that provide good-faith projections. However, much concern exists as to how the SEC and the courts will interpret such terms as "good faith" and "reasonable assumptions" when erroneous forecasts mislead users of this information.

Internet Financial Reporting

How can companies improve the usefulness of their financial reporting practices? Many companies are using the power and reach of the Internet to provide more useful information to financial statement readers. Recent surveys indicate that most large companies have Internet sites, and a large proportion of these companies' Web sites contain links to their financial statements and other disclosures.[24] The increased popularity of such reporting is not surprising, since the costs of printing and disseminating paper reports could be reduced with the use of Internet reporting.

How does Internet financial reporting improve the overall usefulness of a company's financial reports? First, dissemination of reports via the Web can allow firms **to communicate with more users** than is possible with traditional paper reports. In addition, **Internet reporting allows users to take advantage of tools** such as search engines and hyperlinks to quickly find information about the firm and, sometimes, to download the information for analysis, perhaps in computer spreadsheets. Finally, **Internet reporting can help make financial reports more relevant** by allowing companies to report expanded disaggregated data and more timely data than is possible through paper-based reporting. For example, some companies voluntarily report weekly sales data and segment operating data on their Web sites.

Given these benefits and ever-improving Internet tools, will it be long before electronic reporting replaces paper-based financial disclosure? The main obstacles to achieving complete electronic reporting are related to equality of access to electronic financial reporting and the reliability of the information distributed via the Internet. Although companies may practice Internet financial reporting, they must still prepare traditional paper reports because some investors may not have access to the Internet. These investors would receive differential (less) information relative to other "wired" investors if companies were to eliminate paper reports. In addition, at present, Internet financial reporting is a voluntary means of reporting. As a result, there are no standards as to the completeness of reports on the Internet, nor is there the requirement that these reports be audited. One concern in this regard is that computer "hackers" could invade a company's Web site and corrupt the financial information contained therein.

Thus, although Internet financial reporting is gaining in popularity, until issues related to differential access to the Internet and the reliability of information disseminated via the Web are solved, we will continue to see traditional paper-based reporting.

Fraudulent Financial Reporting

OBJECTIVE 8
Describe the profession's response to fraudulent financial reporting.

Fraudulent financial reporting is defined as **"intentional or reckless conduct, whether act or omission, that results in materially misleading financial statements."** Fraudulent reporting can involve gross and deliberate distortion of corporate records (such as inventory count tags), or misapplication of accounting principles (failure to disclose material transactions).[25] Although frauds are unusual, recent events involving such well-known companies as **Enron**, **WorldCom**, **Adelphia Communications**, and **Tyco International** indicate that more must be done to address this issue.

[24]The FASB has issued a report on electronic dissemination of financial reports. This report summarizes current practice and research conducted on Internet financial reporting. See Business Reporting Research Project, "Electronic Distribution of Business Reporting Information" (Norwalk, Conn.: FASB, 2000).

[25]"Report of the National Commission on Fraudulent Financial Reporting" (Washington, D.C., 1987), page 2. Unintentional errors as well as corporate improprieties (such as tax fraud, employee embezzlements, and so on) which do not cause the financial statements to be misleading are excluded from the definition of fraudulent financial reporting.

WHAT DO THE NUMBERS MEAN?

HERE'S A FRAUD

The case of **ESM Government Securities, Inc. (ESM)** exemplifies the seriousness of these frauds. ESM was a Fort Lauderdale securities dealer entrusted with monies to invest by municipalities from Toledo, Ohio to Beaumont, Texas. The cities provided the cash to ESM which they thought was collateralized with government securities. Examination of ESM's balance sheet indicated that the company owed about as much as it expected to collect. Unfortunately, the amount it expected to collect was from insolvent affiliates which, in effect, meant that ESM was bankrupt. In fact, ESM had been bankrupt for more than 6 years, and the fraud was discovered only because a customer questioned a note to the balance sheet! More than $300 million of losses had been disguised.

Source: For an expanded discussion of this case, see Robert J. Sack and Robert Tangreti, "ESM: Implications for the Profession," *Journal of Accountancy* (April 1987).

Causes of Fraudulent Financial Reporting

Fraudulent financial reporting usually occurs because of conditions in the internal or external environment.[26] Influences in the **internal environment** relate to poor systems of internal control, management's poor attitude toward ethics, or perhaps a company's liquidity or profitability. Those in the **external environment** may relate to industry conditions, overall business environment, or legal and regulatory considerations.

General incentives for fraudulent financial reporting are the desire to obtain a higher stock price or debt offering, to avoid default on a loan covenant, or to make a personal gain of some type (additional compensation, promotion). Situational pressures on the company or an individual manager also may lead to fraudulent financial reporting. Examples of these situational pressures include:

1. Sudden decreases in revenue or market share. A single company or an entire industry can experience these decreases.
2. Unrealistic budget pressures, particularly for short-term results. These pressures may occur when headquarters arbitrarily determines profit objectives and budgets without taking actual conditions into account.
3. Financial pressure resulting from bonus plans that depend on short-term economic performance. This pressure is particularly acute when the bonus is a significant component of the individual's total compensation.

Opportunities for fraudulent financial reporting are present in circumstances when the fraud is easy to commit and when detection is difficult. Frequently these opportunities arise from:

1. ***The absence of a board of directors or audit committee*** that vigilantly oversees the financial reporting process.
2. ***Weak or nonexistent internal accounting controls.*** This situation can occur, for example, when a company's revenue system is overloaded as a result of a rapid expansion of sales, an acquisition of a new division, or the entry into a new, unfamiliar line of business.
3. ***Unusual or complex transactions*** such as the consolidation of two companies, the divestiture or closing of a specific operation, and agreements to buy or sell government securities under a repurchase agreement.
4. ***Accounting estimates, requiring significant subjective judgment*** by company management, such as reserves for loan losses and the yearly provision for warranty expense.

[26]The discussion in this section is based on the Report of the National Commission on Fraudulent Financial Reporting, pp. 23–24.

5 *Ineffective internal audit staffs* resulting from inadequate staff size and severely limited audit scope.

A weak corporate ethical climate contributes to these situations. Opportunities for fraudulent financial reporting also increase dramatically when the accounting principles followed in reporting transactions are nonexistent, evolving, or subject to varying interpretations.

The Auditing Standards Board of the AICPA has issued numerous auditing standards in response to concerns expressed by the accounting profession, by the media, and by the public.[27] For example, the Board issued a new standard that "raises the bar" on the performance of financial statement audits by explicitly requiring auditors to assess the risk of material financial misstatement due to fraud.[28] As indicated earlier, the Sarbanes-Oxley Act of 2002 now raises the penalty substantially for executives who are involved in fraudulent financial reporting.

Criteria for Making Accounting and Reporting Choices

Throughout this textbook, we have stressed the need to provide information that is useful to predict the amounts, timing, and uncertainty of future cash flows. To achieve this objective, judicious choices between alternative accounting concepts, methods, and means of disclosure must be made. You are probably surprised by the large number of choices that exist among acceptable alternatives.

You should recognize, however, as indicated in Chapter 1, that accounting is greatly influenced by its environment. Because it does not exist in a vacuum, it seems unrealistic to assume that alternative presentations of certain transactions and events will be eliminated entirely. Nevertheless, we are hopeful that the profession, through the development of a conceptual framework, will be able to focus on the needs of financial statement users and eliminate diversity where appropriate. The profession must continue its efforts to develop a sound foundation upon which financial standards and practice can be built. As Aristotle said: "The correct beginning is more than half the whole."

The FASB concept statements on objectives of financial reporting, elements of financial statements, qualitative characteristics of accounting information, and recognition and measurement are important steps in the right direction.

SUMMARY OF LEARNING OBJECTIVES

1 **Review the full disclosure principle and describe problems of implementation.** The full disclosure principle calls for financial reporting of any financial facts significant enough to influence the judgment of an informed reader. Implementing the full disclosure principle is difficult, because the cost of disclosure can be substantial and the benefits difficult to assess. Disclosure requirements have increased because of (1) the growing complexity of the business environment, (2) the necessity for timely information, and (3) the use of accounting as a control and monitoring device.

2 **Explain the use of notes in financial statement preparation.** Notes are the accountant's means of amplifying or explaining the items presented in the main body of the statements. Information pertinent to specific financial statement items can be explained in qualitative terms, and supplementary data of a quantitative nature can be

KEY TERMS

accounting policies, *1275*
adverse opinion, *1295*
auditor, *1293*
auditor's report, *1293*
common costs, *1286*
differential disclosure, *1274*
disclaimer of an opinion, *1295*
discrete view, *1288*

[27]Because the profession believes that the role of the auditor is not well understood outside the profession, much attention has been focused on the expectation gap. The **expectation gap** is the gap between (1) the expectation of financial statement users concerning the level of assurance they believe the independent auditor provides and (2) the assurance that the independent auditor actually does provide under generally accepted auditing standards.

[28]"Consideration of Fraud in a Financial Statement Audit," *Statement on Auditing Standards No. 99* (New York: AICPA, 2002).

provided to expand the information in the financial statements. Common note disclosures relate to such items as the following: accounting policies; inventories; property, plant, and equipment; credit claims; contingencies and commitments; and subsequent events.

3 Describe the disclosure requirements for major segments of a business. If only the consolidated figures are available to the analyst, much information regarding the composition of these figures is hidden in aggregated figures. There is no way to tell from the consolidated data the extent to which the differing product lines contribute to the company's profitability, risk, and growth potential. As a result, segment information is required by the profession in certain situations.

4 Describe the accounting problems associated with interim reporting. Interim reports cover periods of less than one year. Two viewpoints exist regarding interim reports. One view (discrete view) holds that each interim period should be treated as a separate accounting period. Another view (integral view) is that the interim report is an integral part of the annual report and that deferrals and accruals should take into consideration what will happen for the entire year.

The same accounting principles used for annual reports should be employed for interim reports. A number of unique reporting problems develop related to the following items: (1) advertising and similar costs, (2) expenses subject to year-end adjustment, (3) income taxes, (4) extraordinary items, (5) changes in accounting, (6) earnings per share, and (7) seasonality.

5 Identify the major disclosures found in the auditor's report. If the auditor is satisfied that the financial statements present the financial position, results of operations, and cash flows fairly in accordance with generally accepted accounting principles, an unqualified opinion is expressed. A qualified opinion contains an exception to the standard opinion; ordinarily the exception is not of sufficient magnitude to invalidate the statements as a whole.

An adverse opinion is required in any report in which the exceptions to fair presentation are so material that a qualified opinion is not justified. A disclaimer of an opinion is appropriate when the auditor has gathered so little information on the financial statements that no opinion can be expressed.

6 Understand management's responsibilities for financials. Management's discussion and analysis section covers three financial aspects of an enterprise's business: liquidity, capital resources, and results of operations. Management has primary responsibility for the financial statements, and this responsibility is often indicated in a letter to stockholders in the annual report.

7 Identify issues related to financial forecasts and projections. The SEC has indicated that companies are permitted (not required) to include profit forecasts in reports filed with that agency. To encourage management to disclose this type of information, the SEC has issued a "safe harbor" rule. The safe harbor rule provides protection to an enterprise that presents an erroneous forecast as long as the projection was prepared on a reasonable basis and was disclosed in good faith. However, the safe harbor rule has not worked well in practice.

8 Describe the profession's response to fraudulent financial reporting. Fraudulent financial reporting is intentional or reckless conduct, whether act or omission, that results in materially misleading financial statements. Fraudulent financial reporting usually occurs because of poor internal control, management's poor attitude toward ethics, and so on. The recently enacted Sarbanes-Oxley Act has numerous provisions intended to help prevent fraudulent financial reporting.

APPENDIX 24A

Basic Financial Statement Analysis

What would be important to you in studying a company's financial statements? The answer depends on your particular interest—whether you are a creditor, stockholder, potential investor, manager, government agency, or labor leader. For example, **short-term creditors** such as banks are primarily interested in the ability of the firm to pay its currently maturing obligations. In that case, you would examine the current assets and their relation to short-term liabilities to evaluate the short-run solvency of the firm. **Bondholders**, on the other hand, look more to long-term indicators, such as the enterprise's capital structure, past and projected earnings, and changes in financial position. **Stockholders**, present or prospective, also are interested in many of the features considered by a long-term creditor. As a stockholder, you would focus on the earnings picture, because changes in it greatly affect the market price of your investment. You also would be concerned with the financial position of the firm, because it affects indirectly the stability of earnings.

The **management** of a company is concerned about the composition of its capital structure and about the changes and trends in earnings. This financial information has a direct influence on the type, amount, and cost of external financing that the company can obtain. In addition, the company finds financial information useful on a day-to-day operating basis in such areas as capital budgeting, breakeven analysis, variance analysis, gross margin analysis, and for internal control purposes.

PERSPECTIVE ON FINANCIAL STATEMENT ANALYSIS

OBJECTIVE 9
Understand the approach to financial statement analysis.

Information from financial statements can be gathered by examining relationships between items on the statements and identifying trends in these relationships. The relationships are expressed numerically in ratios and percentages, and trends are identified through comparative analysis.

A problem with learning how to analyze statements is that the means may become an end in itself. There are thousands of possible relationships that could be calculated and trends that could be identified. If one knows only how to calculate ratios and trends without understanding how such information can be used, little is accomplished. Therefore, a logical approach to financial statement analysis is necessary. Such an approach may consist of the following steps.

1. ***Know the questions for which you want to find answers.*** As indicated at the beginning of this chapter, various groups have different types of interest in a company.
2. ***Know the questions that particular ratios and comparisons are able to help answer.*** These will be discussed in this appendix.
3. ***Match 1 and 2 above.*** By such a matching, the statement analysis will have a logical direction and purpose.

Because financial statements report on the past, they emphasize the *qualitative characteristic of feedback value.* This feedback value is useful because it can be used to better achieve the *qualitative characteristic of predictive value.*

INTERNATIONAL INSIGHT

Some companies outside the U.S. provide "convenience" financial statements for U.S. readers. These financial statements have been translated into English, and they may also translate the currency units into U.S. dollars. However, the statements are *not restated* using U.S. accounting principles, and financial statement analysis needs to take this fact into account.

Several caveats must be mentioned. **Financial statements report on the past.** As such, analysis of these data is an examination of the past. Whenever such information is incorporated into a decision-making (future-oriented) process, a critical assumption is that the past is a reasonable basis for predicting the future. This is usually a reasonable approach, but the limitations associated with it should be recognized. Also, ratio and trend analyses will help identify present strengths and weaknesses of a company. They may serve as "red flags" indicating problem areas. In many cases, however, such analyses will not reveal **why** things are as they are. Finding answers about "why" usually requires an in-depth analysis and an awareness of many factors about a company that are not reported in the financial statements—for instance, the impact of inflation, actions of competitors, technological developments, a strike at a major supplier's or buyer's operations, and so on.

Another caveat is that a **single ratio by itself is not likely to be very useful**. For example, a current ratio of 2 to 1 (current assets are twice current liabilities) may be viewed as satisfactory. However, if the industry average is 3 to 1, such a conclusion may be questioned. Even given this industry average, one may conclude that the particular company is doing well if one knows the previous year's ratio was 1.5 to 1. Consequently, to derive meaning from ratios, some standard against which to compare them is needed. Such a standard may come from industry averages, past years' amounts, a particular competitor, or planned levels.

Finally, **awareness of the limitations of accounting numbers used in an analysis** is important. We will discuss some of these limitations and their consequences later in this appendix.

RATIO ANALYSIS

OBJECTIVE 10
Identify major analytic ratios and describe their calculation.

Various devices are used in the analysis of financial statement data to bring out the comparative and relative significance of the financial information presented. These devices include ratio analysis, comparative analysis, percentage analysis, and examination of related data. No one device is more useful than another. Every situation faced by the investment analyst is different, and the answers needed are often obtained only upon close examination of the interrelationships among all the data provided. Ratio analysis is the starting point in developing the information desired by the analyst.

Ratios can be classified as follows.

MAJOR TYPES OF RATIOS

LIQUIDITY RATIOS. Measures of the enterprise's short-run ability to pay its maturing obligations.

ACTIVITY RATIOS. Measures of how effectively the enterprise is using the assets employed.

PROFITABILITY RATIOS. Measures of the degree of success or failure of a given enterprise or division for a given period of time.

COVERAGE RATIOS. Measures of the degree of protection for long-term creditors and investors.[1]

[1]Other terms may be used to categorize these ratios. For example, liquidity ratios are sometimes referred to as solvency ratios; activity ratios as turnover or efficiency ratios; and coverage ratios as leverage or capital structure ratios.

Discussions and illustrations about the computation and use of these financial ratios have been integrated throughout this book. Illustration 24A-1 summarizes all of the ratios presented in the book and identifies the specific chapters in which ratio coverage has been presented.

ILLUSTRATION 24A-1
Summary of Financial Ratios

SUMMARY OF RATIOS PRESENTED IN EARLIER CHAPTERS

Ratio	Formula for Computation	Reference
I. Liquidity		
1. **Current ratio**	Current assets / Current liabilities	Chapter 13, p. 643
2. **Quick or acid-test ratio**	Cash, marketable securities, and net receivables / Current liabilities	Chapter 13, p. 644
3. **Current cash debt ratio**	Net cash provided by operating activities / Average current liabilities	Chapter 5, p. 196
II. Activity		
4. **Receivables turnover**	Net sales / Average trade receivables (net)	Chapter 7, p. 338
5. **Inventory turnover**	Cost of goods sold / Average inventory	Chapter 9, p. 442
6. **Asset turnover**	Net sales / Average total assets	Chapter 11, p. 543
III. Profitability		
7. **Profit margin on sales**	Net income / Net sales	Chapter 11, p. 543
8. **Rate of return on assets**	Net income / Average total assets	Chapter 11, p. 543
9. **Rate of return on common stock equity**	Net income minus preferred dividends / Average common stockholders' equity	Chapter 15, p. 749
10. **Earnings per share**	Net income minus preferred dividends / Weighted shares outstanding	Chapter 16, p. 801
11. **Payout ratio**	Cash dividends / Net income	Chapter 15, p. 750
IV. Coverage		
12. **Debt to total assets ratio**	Debt / Total assets or equities	Chapter 14, p. 692
13. **Times interest earned**	Income before interest charges and taxes / Interest charges	Chapter 14, p. 693
14. **Cash debt coverage ratio**	Net cash provided by operating activities / Average total liabilities	Chapter 5, p. 197
15. **Book value per share**	Common stockholders' equity / Outstanding shares	Chapter 15, p. 750

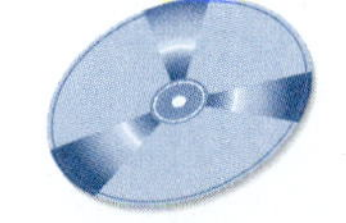

Financial Analysis Primer

Supplemental coverage of these ratios, accompanied with assignment material, is contained on the Take Action! CD. This supplemental coverage takes the form of a comprehensive case adapted from the annual report of a large international chemical company that we have disguised under the name of Anetek Chemical Corporation.

Limitations of Ratio Analysis

OBJECTIVE 11
Explain the limitations of ratio analysis.

The reader of financial statements must understand the basic limitations associated with ratio analysis. As analytical tools, ratios are attractive because they are simple and convenient. But too frequently, decisions are based on only these simple computations. The ratios are only as good as the data upon which they are based and the information with which they are compared.

One important limitation of ratios is that they generally are **based on historical cost, which can lead to distortions in measuring performance**. By failing to incorporate changing price information, many believe that inaccurate assessments of the enterprise's financial condition and performance result.

Also, investors must remember that **where estimated items (such as depreciation and amortization) are significant, income ratios lose some of their credibility**. Income recognized before the termination of the life of the business is an approximation. In analyzing the income statement, the user should be aware of the uncertainty surrounding the computation of net income. As one writer aptly noted, "The physicist has long since conceded that the location of an electron is best expressed by a probability curve. Surely an abstraction like earnings per share is even more subject to the rules of probability and risk."[2]

UNDERLYING CONCEPTS

Consistency and comparability are important concepts when financial statement analysis is performed. If the principles and assumptions used to prepare the financial statements are continually changing, it becomes difficult to make accurate assessments of a company's progress.

Probably the greatest criticism of ratio analysis is the **difficult problem of achieving comparability among firms in a given industry**. Achieving comparability among firms requires that the analyst (1) identify basic differences existing in their accounting principles and procedures and (2) adjust the balances to achieve comparability.

Basic differences in accounting usually involve one of the following areas.

1. Inventory valuation (FIFO, LIFO, average cost).
2. Depreciation methods, particularly the use of straight-line versus accelerated depreciation.
3. Capitalization versus expense of certain costs.
4. Pooling versus purchase in accounting for business combinations.
5. Capitalization of leases versus noncapitalization.
6. Investments in common stock carried at equity versus fair value.
7. Differing treatments of postretirement benefit costs.
8. Questionable practices of defining discontinued operations, impairments, and extraordinary items.

The use of these different alternatives can make quite a significant difference in the ratios computed. For example, in the brewing industry, at one time **Anheuser-Busch** noted that if it had used average cost for inventory valuation instead of LIFO, inventories would have increased approximately $33,000,000. Such an increase would have a substantive impact on the current ratio. Several studies have analyzed the impact of different accounting methods on financial statement analysis. The differences in income that can develop are staggering in some cases. The average investor may find it difficult to grasp all these differences, but investors must be aware of the potential pitfalls if they are to be able to make the proper adjustments.

Finally, it must be recognized that a **substantial amount of important information** is not included in a company's financial statements. Events involving such things as industry changes, management changes, competitors' actions, technological developments, government actions, and union activities are often critical to a company's successful operation. These events occur continuously, and information about them must come from careful analysis of financial reports in the media and other sources. Indeed many argue, under what is known as the **efficient market hypothesis**, that financial statements contain "no surprises" to those engaged in market activities. They contend that the effect of these events is known in the marketplace—and the price of the company's stock adjusts accordingly—well before the issuance of such reports.

[2]Richard E. Cheney, "How Dependable Is the Bottom Line?" *The Financial Executive* (January 1971), p. 12.

COMPARATIVE ANALYSIS

In **comparative analysis** the same information is presented for two or more different dates or periods so that like items may be compared. Ratio analysis provides only a single snapshot, the analysis being for one given point or period in time. In a comparative analysis, an investment analyst can concentrate on a given item and determine whether it appears to be growing or diminishing year by year and the proportion of such change to related items. Generally, companies present comparative financial statements.[3]

OBJECTIVE 12
Describe techniques of comparative analysis.

In addition, many companies include in their annual reports 5- or 10-year summaries of pertinent data that permit the reader to examine and analyze trends. *ARB No. 43* concluded that "the presentation of comparative financial statements in annual and other reports enhances the usefulness of such reports and brings out more clearly the nature and trends of current changes affecting the enterprise." An illustration of a 5-year condensed statement with additional supporting data as presented by Anetek Chemical Corporation is presented in Illustration 24A-2.

ILLUSTRATION 24A-2
Condensed Comparative Financial Information

ANETEK CHEMICAL CORPORATION
CONDENSED COMPARATIVE STATEMENTS
(000,000 OMITTED)

	2004	2003	2002	2001	2000	10 Years Ago 1994	20 Years Ago 1984
Sales and other revenue:							
Net sales	$1,600.0	$1,350.0	$1,309.7	$1,176.2	$1,077.5	$636.2	$170.7
Other revenue	75.0	50.0	39.4	34.1	24.6	9.0	3.7
Total	1,675.0	1,400.0	1,349.1	1,210.3	1,102.1	645.2	174.4
Costs and other charges:							
Cost of sales	1,000.0	850.0	827.4	737.6	684.2	386.8	111.0
Depreciation and amortization	150.0	150.0	122.6	115.6	98.7	82.4	14.2
Selling and administrative expenses	225.0	150.0	144.2	133.7	126.7	66.7	10.7
Interest expense	50.0	25.0	28.5	20.7	9.4	8.9	1.8
Taxes on income	100.0	75.0	79.5	73.5	68.3	42.4	12.4
Total	1,525.0	1,250.0	1,202.2	1,081.1	987.3	587.2	150.1
Net income for the year	$ 150.0	$ 150.0	$ 146.9	$ 129.2	$ 114.8	$ 58.0	$ 24.3
Other Statistics							
Earnings per share on common stock (in dollars)[a]	$ 5.00	$ 5.00	$ 4.90	$ 3.58	$ 3.11	$ 1.66	$ 1.06
Cash dividends per share on common stock (in dollars)[a]	2.25	2.15	1.95	1.79	1.71	1.11	0.25
Cash dividends declared on common stock	67.5	64.5	58.5	64.6	63.1	38.8	5.7
Stock dividend at approximate market value				46.8		27.3	
Taxes (major)	144.5	125.9	116.5	105.6	97.8	59.8	17.0
Wages paid	389.3	325.6	302.1	279.6	263.2	183.2	48.6
Cost of employee benefits	50.8	36.2	32.9	28.7	27.2	18.4	4.4
Number of employees at year end (thousands)	47.4	36.4	35.0	33.8	33.2	26.6	14.6
Additions to property	306.3	192.3	241.5	248.3	166.1	185.0	49.0

[a]Adjusted for stock splits and stock dividends.

[3]All 600 companies surveyed in *Accounting Trends and Techniques—2001* presented comparative 2000 amounts in their 2001 balance sheets and presented comparative 1999 and 2000 amounts in their 2001 income statements.

PERCENTAGE (COMMON-SIZE) ANALYSIS

OBJECTIVE 13
Describe techniques of percentage analysis.

Analysts also use percentage analysis to help them evaluate and compare companies. **Percentage analysis** consists of reducing a series of related amounts to a series of percentages of a given base. All items in an income statement are frequently expressed as a percentage of sales or sometimes as a percentage of cost of goods sold. A balance sheet may be analyzed on the basis of total assets. This analysis facilitates comparison and is helpful in evaluating the relative size of items or the relative change in items. A conversion of absolute dollar amounts to percentages may also facilitate comparison between companies of different size.

To illustrate, here is a comparative analysis of the expense section of Anetek for the last 2 years.

ILLUSTRATION 24A-3
Horizontal Percentage Analysis

ANETEK CHEMICAL CORPORATION
HORIZONTAL COMPARATIVE ANALYSIS
(000,000 OMITTED)

	2004	2003	Difference	% Change Inc. (Dec.)
Cost of sales	$1,000.0	$850.0	$150.0	17.6%
Depreciation and amortization	150.0	150.0	0	0
Selling and administrative expenses	225.0	150.0	75.0	50.0
Interest expense	50.0	25.0	25.0	100.0
Taxes	100.0	75.0	25.0	33.3

This approach, normally called **horizontal analysis**, indicates the proportionate change over a period of time. It is especially useful in evaluating a trend situation, because absolute changes are often deceiving.

Another approach, called **vertical analysis**, is the proportional expression of each item on a financial statement in a given period to a base figure. For example, Anetek Chemical's income statement using this approach appears below.

ILLUSTRATION 24A-4
Vertical Percentage Analysis

ANETEK CHEMICAL CORPORATION
INCOME STATEMENT
(000,000 OMITTED)

	Amount	Percentage of Total Revenue
Net sales	$1,600.0	96%
Other revenue	75.0	4
Total revenue	1,675.0	100
Less:		
Cost of goods sold	1,000.0	60
Depreciation and amortization	150.0	9
Selling and administrative expenses	225.0	13
Interest expense	50.0	3
Income tax	100.0	6
Total expenses	1,525.0	91
Net income	$ 150.0	9%

Reducing all the dollar amounts to a percentage of a base amount is frequently called **common-size analysis** because all of the statements and all of the years are reduced to a common size. That is, all of the elements within each statement are expressed in percentages of some common number and always add up to 100 percent. Common-size (percentage) analysis is the analysis of the composition of each of the financial statements.

In the analysis of the balance sheet, common-size analysis answers such questions as: What is the distribution of equities between current liabilities, long-term debt, and owners' equity? What is the mix of assets (percentage-wise) with which the enterprise has chosen to conduct its business? What percentage of current assets are in inventory, receivables, and so forth?

The income statement lends itself to common-size analysis because each item in it is related to a common amount, usually sales. It is instructive to know what proportion of each sales dollar is absorbed by various costs and expenses incurred by the enterprise.

Common-size statements may be used for comparing one company's statements from different years to detect trends not evident from the comparison of absolute amounts. Also, common-size statements provide intercompany comparisons regardless of size because the financial statements can be recast into a comparable common-size format.

SUMMARY OF LEARNING OBJECTIVES FOR APPENDIX 24A

9 **Understand the approach to financial statement analysis.** Basic financial statement analysis involves examining relationships between items on the statements (ratio and percentage analysis) and identifying trends in these relationships (comparative analysis). Analysis is used to predict the future, but ratio analysis is limited because the data are from the past. Also, ratio analysis identifies present strengths and weaknesses of a company, but it may not reveal why they are as they are. Although single ratios are helpful, they are not conclusive; they must be compared with industry averages, past years, planned amounts, and the like for maximum usefulness.

10 **Identify major analytic ratios and describe their calculation.** Ratios are classified as liquidity ratios, activity ratios, profitability ratios, and coverage ratios: (1) *Liquidity ratio analysis* measures the short-run ability of the enterprise to pay its currently maturing obligations. (2) *Activity ratio analysis* measures how effectively the enterprise is using its assets. (3) *Profitability ratio analysis* measures the degree of success or failure of an enterprise to generate revenues adequate to cover its costs of operation and provide a return to the owners. (4) *Coverage ratio analysis* measures the degree of protection afforded long-term creditors and investors.

11 **Explain the limitations of ratio analysis.** One important limitation of ratios is that they are based on historical cost, which can lead to distortions in measuring performance. Also, where estimated items (such as depreciation and amortization) are significant, income ratios lose some of their credibility. In addition, difficult problems of comparability exist because firms use different accounting principles and procedures. Finally, it must be recognized that a substantial amount of important information is not included in a company's financial statements.

12 **Describe techniques of comparative analysis.** Companies present comparative data, which generally includes 2 years of balance sheet information and 3 years of income statement information. In addition, many companies include in their annual reports 5- to 10-year summaries of pertinent data that permit the reader to examine and analyze trends.

13 **Describe techniques of percentage analysis.** Percentage analysis consists of reducing a series of related amounts to a series of percentages of a given base. Two approaches are often used: *Horizontal analysis* indicates the proportionate change in financial statement items over a period of time; such analysis is most helpful in evaluating trends. *Vertical analysis* (common-size analysis) is a proportional expression of

KEY TERMS

acid-test ratio, *1307*
activity ratios, *1306*
asset turnover, *1307*
book value per share, *1307*
cash debt coverage ratio, *1307*
common-size analysis, *1310*
comparative analysis, *1309*
coverage ratios, *1306*
current cash debt ratio, *1307*
current ratio, *1307*
debt to total assets ratio, *1307*
earnings per share, *1307*
horizontal analysis, *1310*
inventory turnover, *1307*
liquidity ratios, *1306*
payout ratio, *1307*
percentage analysis, *1310*
profit margin on sales, *1307*
profitability ratios, *1306*
quick ratio, *1307*
rate of return on assets, *1307*
rate of return on common stock equity, *1307*
receivables turnover, *1307*
times interest earned, *1307*
vertical analysis, *1310*

each item on the financial statements in a given period to a base amount. It analyzes the composition of each of the financial statements from different years (a) to detect trends not evident from the comparison of absolute amounts and (b) to make intercompany comparisons of different sized enterprises.

Note: All **asterisked** Questions, Brief Exercises, Exercises, Problems, and Conceptual Cases relate to materials contained in the appendix to the chapter.

QUESTIONS

1. What are the major advantages of notes to the financial statements? What types of items are usually reported in notes?

2. What is the full disclosure principle in accounting? Why has disclosure increased substantially in the last 10 years?

3. The FASB requires a reconciliation between the effective tax rate and the federal government's statutory rate. Of what benefit is such a disclosure requirement?

4. At the beginning of 2004, Beausoleil Inc. entered into an 8-year nonrenewable lease agreement. Provisions in the lease require the client to make substantial reconditioning and restoration expenditures at the end of the lease. What type of disclosure do you believe is necessary for this type of situation?

5. What type of disclosure or accounting do you believe is necessary for the following items?

(a) Because of a general increase in the number of labor disputes and strikes, both within and outside the industry, there is an increased likelihood that a company will suffer a costly strike in the near future.

(b) A company reports an extraordinary item (net of tax) correctly on the income statement. No other mention is made of this item in the annual report.

(c) A company expects to recover a substantial amount in connection with a pending refund claim for a prior year's taxes. Although the claim is being contested, counsel for the company has confirmed the client's expectation of recovery.

6. The following information was described in a note of Cebar Packing Co.

"During August, A. Belew Products Corporation purchased 311,003 shares of the Company's common stock which constitutes approximately 35% of the stock outstanding. A. Belew has since obtained representation on the Board of Directors."

"An affiliate of A. Belew Products Corporation acts as a food broker for the Company in the greater New York City marketing area. The commissions for such services after August amounted to approximately $20,000."

Why is this information disclosed?

7. What are the major types of subsequent events? Indicate how each of the following "subsequent events" would be reported.

(a) Collection of a note written off in a prior period.

(b) Issuance of a large preferred stock offering.

(c) Acquisition of a company in a different industry.

(d) Destruction of a major plant in a flood.

(e) Death of the company's chief executive officer (CEO).

(f) Additional wage costs associated with settlement of a four-week strike.

(g) Settlement of a federal income tax case at considerably more tax than anticipated at year-end.

(h) Change in the product mix from consumer goods to industrial goods.

8. What are diversified companies? What accounting problems are related to diversified companies?

9. What quantitative materiality test is applied to determine whether a segment is significant enough to warrant separate disclosure?

10. Identify the segment information that is required to be disclosed by *FASB Statement No. 131*.

11. What is an operating segment, and when can information about two operating segments be aggregated?

12. The controller for Chang Lee Inc. recently commented, "If I have to disclose our segments individually, the only people who will gain are our competitors and the only people that will lose are our present stockholders." Evaluate this comment.

13. An article in the financial press entitled "Important Information in Annual Reports This Year" noted that annual reports include a management discussion and analysis section. What would this section contain?

14. "The financial statements of a company are management's, not the accountant's." Discuss the implications of this statement.

15. Olga Conrad, a financial writer, noted recently, "There are substantial arguments for including earnings projections in annual reports and the like. The most compelling is that it would give anyone interested something now available to only a relatively select few—like large stockholders, creditors, and attentive bartenders."

Identify some arguments against providing earnings projections.

16. The following comment appeared in the financial press: "Inadequate financial disclosure, particularly with respect to how management views the future and its role in the marketplace, has always been a stone in the shoe. After all, if you don't know how a company views the future, how can you judge the worth of its corporate strategy?" What are some arguments for reporting earnings forecasts?

17. What are interim reports? Why are balance sheets often not provided with interim data?

18. What are the accounting problems related to the presentation of interim data?

19. Mysteries Inc., a closely held corporation, has decided to go public. The controller, C. Keene, is concerned with presenting interim data when a LIFO inventory valuation is used. What problems are encountered with LIFO inventories when quarterly data are presented?

20. What approaches have been suggested to overcome the seasonality problem related to interim reporting?

21. What is the difference between a CPA's unqualified opinion or "clean" opinion and a qualified one?

22. Mary Beidler and Lee Pannebecker are discussing the recent fraud that occurred at LowRental Leasing, Inc. The fraud involved the improper reporting of revenue to ensure that the company would have income in excess of $1 million. What is fraudulent financial reporting, and how does it differ from an embezzlement of company funds?

***23.** "The significance of financial statement data is not in the amount alone." Discuss the meaning of this statement.

***24.** A close friend of yours, who is a history major and who has not had any college courses or any experience in business, is receiving the financial statements from companies in which he has minor investments (acquired for him by his now-deceased father). He asks you what he needs to know to interpret and to evaluate the financial statement data that he is receiving. What would you tell him?

***25.** Distinguish between ratio analysis and percentage analysis relative to the interpretation of financial statements. What is the value of these two types of analysis?

***26.** In calculating inventory turnover, why is cost of goods sold used as the numerator? As the inventory turnover increases, what increasing risk does the business assume?

***27.** What is the relationship of the asset turnover ratio to the rate of return on assets?

***28.** Explain the meaning of the following terms: (a) common-size analysis, (b) vertical analysis, (c) horizontal analysis, (d) percentage analysis.

***29.** Presently, the profession requires that earnings per share be disclosed on the face of the income statement. What are some disadvantages of reporting ratios on the financial statements?

BRIEF EXERCISES

BE24-1 An annual report of D. Robillard Industries states, "The company and its subsidiaries have long-term leases expiring on various dates after December 31, 2004. Amounts payable under such commitments, without reduction for related rental income, are expected to average approximately $5,711,000 annually for the next 3 years. Related rental income from certain subleases to others is estimated to average $3,094,000 annually for the next 3 years." What information is provided by this note?

BE24-2 An annual report of **Ford Motor Corporation** states, "Net income a share is computed based upon the average number of shares of capital stock of all classes outstanding. Additional shares of common stock may be issued or delivered in the future on conversion of outstanding convertible debentures, exercise of outstanding employee stock options, and for payment of defined supplemental compensation. Had such additional shares been outstanding, net income a share would have been reduced by 10¢ in the current year and 3¢ in the previous year. . . . As a result of capital stock transactions by the company during the current year (primarily the purchase of Class A Stock from Ford Foundation), net income a share was increased by 6¢." What information is provided by this note?

BE24-3 Linden Corporation is preparing its December 31, 2003, financial statements. Two events that occurred between December 31, 2003, and March 10, 2004, when the statements were issued, are described below.

1. A liability, estimated at $150,000 at December 31, 2003, was settled on February 26, 2004, at $170,000.
2. A flood loss of $80,000 occurred on March 1, 2004.

What effect do these subsequent events have on 2003 net income?

BE24-4 Bess Marvin, a student of intermediate accounting, was heard to remark after a class discussion on diversified reporting, "All this is very confusing to me. First we are told that there is merit in presenting the consolidated results, and now we are told that it is better to show segmental results. I wish they would make up their minds." Evaluate this comment.

BE24-5 Roder Corporation has seven industry segments with total revenues as follows.

Genso	$600	Sergei	$225
Konami	650	Takuhi	200
RPG	250	Nippon	700
Red Moon	375		

Based only on the revenues test, which industry segments are reportable?

BE24-6 Operating profits and losses for the seven industry segments of Roder Corporation are:

Genso	$ 90	Sergei	$ (20)
Konami	(40)	Takuhi	34
RPG	25	Nippon	100
Red Moon	50		

Based only on the operating profit (loss) test, which industry segments are reportable?

BE24-7 Identifiable assets for the seven industry segments of Roder Corporation are:

Genso	$500	Sergei	$200
Konami	550	Takuhi	150
RPG	400	Nippon	475
Red Moon	400		

Based only on the identifiable assets test, which industry segments are reportable?

***BE24-8** Answer each of the questions in the following unrelated situations.

(a) The current ratio of a company is 5:1 and its acid-test ratio is 1:1. If the inventories and prepaid items amount to $600,000, what is the amount of current liabilities?

(b) A company had an average inventory last year of $200,000 and its inventory turnover was 5. If sales volume and unit cost remain the same this year as last and inventory turnover is 8 this year, what will average inventory have to be during the current year?

(c) A company has current assets of $90,000 (of which $40,000 is inventory and prepaid items) and current liabilities of $30,000. What is the current ratio? What is the acid-test ratio? If the company borrows $15,000 cash from a bank on a 120-day loan, what will its current ratio be? What will the acid-test ratio be?

(d) A company has current assets of $600,000 and current liabilities of $240,000. The board of directors declares a cash dividend of $180,000. What is the current ratio after the declaration but before payment? What is the current ratio after the payment of the dividend?

***BE24-9** Aston Martin Company's budgeted sales and budgeted cost of goods sold for the coming year are $144,000,000 and $90,000,000 respectively. Short-term interest rates are expected to average 10%. If Aston Martin can increase inventory turnover from its present level of 9 times a year to a level of 12 times per year, compute its expected cost savings for the coming year.

***BE24-10** Ferrari Company's net accounts receivable were $1,000,000 at December 31, 2003, and $1,200,000 at December 31, 2004. Net cash sales for 2004 were $400,000. The accounts receivable turnover for 2004 was 5.0. Determine Ferrari's total net sales for 2004.

EXERCISES

E24-1 (Post-Balance-Sheet Events) Madrasah Corporation issued its financial statements for the year ended December 31, 2005, on March 10, 2006. The following events took place early in 2006.

(a) On January 10, 10,000 shares of $5 par value common stock were issued at $66 per share.

(b) On March 1, Madrasah determined after negotiations with the Internal Revenue Service that income taxes payable for 2005 should be $1,270,000. At December 31, 2005, income taxes payable were recorded at $1,100,000.

Instructions

Discuss how the preceding post-balance sheet events should be reflected in the 2005 financial statements.

E24-2 (Post-Balance-Sheet Events) For each of the following subsequent (post-balance-sheet) events, indicate whether a company should (a) adjust the financial statements, (b) disclose in notes to the financial statements, or (c) neither adjust nor disclose.

_____ **1.** Settlement of federal tax case at a cost considerably in excess of the amount expected at year-end.
_____ **2.** Introduction of a new product line.
_____ **3.** Loss of assembly plant due to fire.
_____ **4.** Sale of a significant portion of the company's assets.
_____ **5.** Retirement of the company president.
_____ **6.** Prolonged employee strike.
_____ **7.** Loss of a significant customer.
_____ **8.** Issuance of a significant number of shares of common stock.
_____ **9.** Material loss on a year-end receivable because of a customer's bankruptcy.
_____ **10.** Hiring of a new president.
_____ **11.** Settlement of prior year's litigation against the company.
_____ **12.** Merger with another company of comparable size.

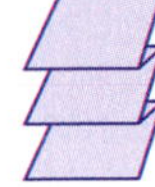

E24-3 (Segmented Reporting) Carlton Company is involved in four separate industries. The following information is available for each of the four industries.

Operating Segment	Total Revenue	Operating Profit (Loss)	Identifiable Assets
W	$ 60,000	$15,000	$167,000
X	10,000	3,000	83,000
Y	23,000	(2,000)	21,000
Z	9,000	1,000	19,000
	$102,000	$17,000	$290,000

Instructions

Determine which of the operating segments are reportable based on the:

(a) Revenue test.
(b) Operating profit (loss) test.
(c) Identifiable assets test.

***E24-4 (Ratio Computation and Analysis; Liquidity)** As loan analyst for Utrillo Bank, you have been presented the following information.

	Toulouse Co.	Lautrec Co.
Assets		
Cash	$ 120,000	$ 320,000
Receivables	220,000	302,000
Inventories	570,000	518,000
Total current assets	910,000	1,140,000
Other assets	500,000	612,000
Total assets	$1,410,000	$1,752,000
Liabilities and Stockholders' Equity		
Current liabilities	$ 305,000	$ 350,000
Long-term liabilities	400,000	500,000
Capital stock and retained earnings	705,000	902,000
Total liabilities and stockholders' equity	$1,410,000	$1,752,000
Annual sales	$ 930,000	$1,500,000
Rate of gross profit on sales	30%	40%

Each of these companies has requested a loan of $50,000 for 6 months with no collateral offered. Inasmuch as your bank has reached its quota for loans of this type, only one of these requests is to be granted.

Instructions

Which of the two companies, as judged by the information given above, would you recommend as the better risk and why? Assume that the ending account balances are representative of the entire year.

***E24-5 (Analysis of Given Ratios)** Picasso Company is a wholesale distributor of professional equipment and supplies. The company's sales have averaged about $900,000 annually for the 3-year period 2003–2005. The firm's total assets at the end of 2005 amounted to $850,000.

The president of Picasso Company has asked the controller to prepare a report that summarizes the financial aspects of the company's operations for the past 3 years. This report will be presented to the board of directors at their next meeting.

In addition to comparative financial statements, the controller has decided to present a number of relevant financial ratios which can assist in the identification and interpretation of trends. At the request of the controller, the accounting staff has calculated the following ratios for the 3-year period 2003–2005.

	2003	2004	2005
Current ratio	1.80	1.89	1.96
Acid-test (quick) ratio	1.04	0.99	0.87
Accounts receivable turnover	8.75	7.71	6.42
Inventory turnover	4.91	4.32	3.42
Percent of total debt to total assets	51	46	41
Percent of long-term debt to total assets	31	27	24
Sales to fixed assets (fixed asset turnover)	1.58	1.69	1.79
Sales as a percent of 2003 sales	1.00	1.03	1.07
Gross margin percentage	36.0	35.1	34.6
Net income to sales	6.9%	7.0%	7.2%
Return on total assets	7.7%	7.7%	7.8%
Return on stockholders' equity	13.6%	13.1%	12.7%

In preparation of the report, the controller has decided first to examine the financial ratios independent of any other data to determine if the ratios themselves reveal any significant trends over the 3-year period.

Instructions

(a) The current ratio is increasing while the acid-test (quick) ratio is decreasing. Using the ratios provided, identify and explain the contributing factor(s) for this apparently divergent trend.

(b) In terms of the ratios provided, what conclusion(s) can be drawn regarding the company's use of financial leverage during the 2003–2005 period?

(c) Using the ratios provided, what conclusion(s) can be drawn regarding the company's net investment in plant and equipment?

***E24-6 (Ratio Analysis)** Edna Millay Inc. is a manufacturer of electronic components and accessories with total assets of $20,000,000. Selected financial ratios for Millay and the industry averages for firms of similar size are presented below.

	Edna Millay			2004 Industry Average
	2002	2003	2004	
Current ratio	2.09	2.27	2.51	2.24
Quick ratio	1.15	1.12	1.19	1.22
Inventory turnover	2.40	2.18	2.02	3.50
Net sales to stockholders' equity	2.71	2.80	2.99	2.85
Net income to stockholders' equity	0.14	0.15	0.17	0.11
Total liabilities to stockholders' equity	1.41	1.37	1.44	0.95

Millay is being reviewed by several entities whose interests vary, and the company's financial ratios are a part of the data being considered. Each of the parties listed below must recommend an action based on its evaluation of Millay's financial position.

Archibald MacLeish Bank. The bank is processing Millay's application for a new 5-year term note. Archibald MacLeish has been Millay's banker for several years but must reevaluate the company's financial position for each major transaction.

Robert Lowell Company. Lowell is a new supplier to Millay and must decide on the appropriate credit terms to extend to the company.

Robert Penn Warren. A brokerage firm specializing in the stock of electronics firms that are sold over-the-counter, Robert Penn Warren must decide if it will include Millay in a new fund being established for sale to Robert Penn Warren's clients.

Working Capital Management Committee. This is a committee of Millay's management personnel chaired by the chief operating officer. The committee is charged with the responsibility of periodically reviewing the company's working capital position, comparing actual data against budgets, and recommending changes in strategy as needed.

Instructions

(a) Describe the analytical use of each of the six ratios presented above.

(b) For each of the four entities described above, identify two financial ratios, from those ratios presented in Illustration 24A-1 (on page 1307), that would be most valuable as a basis for its decision regarding Millay.

(c) Discuss what the financial ratios presented in the question reveal about Millay. Support your answer by citing specific ratio levels and trends as well as the interrelationships between these ratios.

(CMA adapted)

PROBLEMS

P24-1 (Subsequent Events) Your firm has been engaged to examine the financial statements of Sabrina Corporation for the year 2005. The bookkeeper who maintains the financial records has prepared all the unaudited financial statements for the corporation since its organization on January 2, 1999. The client provides you with the information below.

SABRINA CORPORATION
BALANCE SHEET
AS OF DECEMBER 31, 2005

Assets		Liabilities	
Current assets	$1,881,100	Current liabilities	$ 962,400
Other assets	5,171,400	Long-term liabilities	1,439,500
		Capital	4,650,600
	$7,052,500		$7,052,500

An analysis of current assets discloses the following.

Cash (restricted in the amount of $400,000 for plant expansion)	$ 571,000
Investments in land	185,000
Accounts receivable less allowance of $30,000	480,000
Inventories (LIFO flow assumption)	645,100
	$1,881,100

Other assets include:

Prepaid expenses	$ 47,400
Plant and equipment less accumulated depreciation of $1,430,000	4,130,000
Cash surrender value of life insurance policy	84,000
Unamortized bond discount	49,500
Notes receivable (short-term)	162,300
Goodwill	252,000
Land	446,200
	$5,171,400

Current liabilities include:

Accounts payable	$ 510,000
Notes payable (due 2007)	157,400
Estimated income taxes payable	145,000
Premium on common stock	150,000
	$ 962,400

Long-term liabilities include:

Unearned revenue	$ 489,500
Dividends payable (cash)	200,000
8% bonds payable (due May 1, 2010)	750,000
	$1,439,500

Capital includes:

Retained earnings	$2,810,600
Capital stock, par value $10; authorized 200,000 shares, 184,000 shares issued	1,840,000
	$4,650,600

The supplementary information below is also provided.

1. On May 1, 2005, the corporation issued at 93.4, $750,000 of bonds to finance plant expansion. The long-term bond agreement provided for the annual payment of interest every May 1. The existing plant was pledged as security for the loan. Use straight-line method for discount amortization.
2. The bookkeeper made the following mistakes.

(a) In 2003, the ending inventory was overstated by $183,000. The ending inventories for 2004 and 2005 were correctly computed.
(b) In 2005, accrued wages in the amount of $275,000 were omitted from the balance sheet and these expenses were not charged on the income statement.
(c) In 2005, a gain of $175,000 (net of tax) on the sale of certain plant assets was credited directly to retained earnings.

3. A major competitor has introduced a line of products that will compete directly with Sabrina's primary line, now being produced in a specially designed new plant. Because of manufacturing innovations, the competitor's line will be of comparable quality but priced 50% below Sabrina's line. The competitor announced its new line on January 14, 2006. Sabrina indicates that the company will meet the lower prices that are high enough to cover variable manufacturing and selling expenses, but permit recovery of only a portion of fixed costs.
4. You learned on January 28, 2006, prior to completion of the audit, of heavy damage because of a recent fire to one of Sabrina's two plants; the loss will not be reimbursed by insurance. The newspapers described the event in detail.

Instructions

Analyze the above information to prepare a corrected balance sheet for Sabrina in accordance with proper accounting and reporting principles. Prepare a description of any notes that might need to be prepared. The books are closed and adjustments to income are to be made through retained earnings.

P24-2 (Segmented Reporting) Friendly Corporation is a diversified company that operates in five different industries: A, B, C, D, and E. The following information relating to each segment is available for 2004.

	A	B	C	D	E
Sales	$40,000	$ 80,000	$580,000	$35,000	$55,000
Cost of goods sold	19,000	50,000	270,000	19,000	30,000
Operating expenses	10,000	40,000	235,000	12,000	18,000
Total expenses	29,000	90,000	505,000	31,000	48,000
Operating profit (loss)	$11,000	$(10,000)	$ 75,000	$ 4,000	$ 7,000
Identifiable assets	$35,000	$ 60,000	$500,000	$65,000	$50,000

Sales of segments B and C included intersegment sales of $20,000 and $100,000, respectively.

Instructions

(a) Determine which of the segments are reportable based on the:
  (1) Revenue test.
  (2) Operating profit (loss) test.
  (3) Identifiable assets test.
(b) Prepare the necessary disclosures required by *FASB No. 131*.

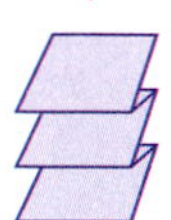

***P24-3 (Ratio Computations and Additional Analysis)** Carl Sandburg Corporation was formed 5 years ago through a public subscription of common stock. Robert Frost, who owns 15% of the common stock, was one of the organizers of Sandburg and is its current president. The company has been successful, but it currently is experiencing a shortage of funds. On June 10, Robert Frost approached the Spokane National Bank, asking for a 24-month extension on two $35,000 notes, which are due on June 30, 2004, and September 30, 2004. Another note of $6,000 is due on December 31, 2005, but he expects no difficulty in paying this note on its due date. Frost explained that Sandburg's cash flow problems are due primarily to the company's desire to finance a $300,000 plant expansion over the next 2 fiscal years through internally generated funds.

The Commercial Loan Officer of Spokane National Bank requested financial reports for the last 2 fiscal years. These reports are reproduced below.

CARL SANDBURG CORPORATION
STATEMENT OF FINANCIAL POSITION
MARCH 31

Assets	2004	2003
Cash	$ 18,200	$ 12,500
Notes receivable	148,000	132,000
Accounts receivable (net)	131,800	125,500
Inventories (at cost)	95,000	50,000
Plant & equipment (net of depreciation)	1,449,000	1,420,500
Total assets	$1,842,000	$1,740,500

Liabilities and Owners' Equity		
Accounts payable	$ 69,000	$ 91,000
Notes payable	76,000	61,500
Accrued liabilities	9,000	6,000
Common stock (130,000 shares, $10 par)	1,300,000	1,300,000
Retained earnings[a]	388,000	282,000
Total liabilities and owners' equity	$1,842,000	$1,740,500

[a]Cash dividends were paid at the rate of $1 per share in fiscal year 2003 and $2 per share in fiscal year 2004.

CARL SANDBURG CORPORATION
INCOME STATEMENT
FOR THE FISCAL YEARS ENDED MARCH 31

	2004	2003
Sales	$3,000,000	$2,700,000
Cost of goods sold[a]	1,530,000	1,425,000
Gross margin	$1,470,000	$1,275,000
Operating expenses	860,000	780,000
Income before income taxes	$ 610,000	$ 495,000
Income taxes (40%)	244,000	198,000
Net income	$ 366,000	$ 297,000

[a]Depreciation charges on the plant and equipment of $100,000 and $102,500 for fiscal years ended March 31, 2003 and 2004, respectively, are included in cost of goods sold.

Instructions

(a) Compute the following items for Carl Sandburg Corporation.

(1) Current ratio for fiscal years 2003 and 2004.

(2) Acid-test (quick) ratio for fiscal years 2003 and 2004.

(3) Inventory turnover for fiscal year 2004.

(4) Return on assets for fiscal years 2003 and 2004. (Assume total assets were $1,688,500 at 3/31/02.)

(5) Percentage change in sales, cost of goods sold, gross margin, and net income after taxes from fiscal year 2003 to 2004.

(b) Identify and explain what other financial reports and/or financial analyses might be helpful to the commercial loan officer of Spokane National Bank in evaluating Robert Frost's request for a time extension on Sandburg's notes.

(c) Assume that the percentage changes experienced in fiscal year 2004 as compared with fiscal year 2003 for sales and cost of goods sold will be repeated in each of the next 2 years. Is Sandburg's desire to finance the plant expansion from internally generated funds realistic? Discuss.

(d) Should Spokane National Bank grant the extension on Sandburg's notes considering Robert Frost's statement about financing the plant expansion through internally generated funds? Discuss.

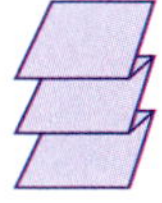

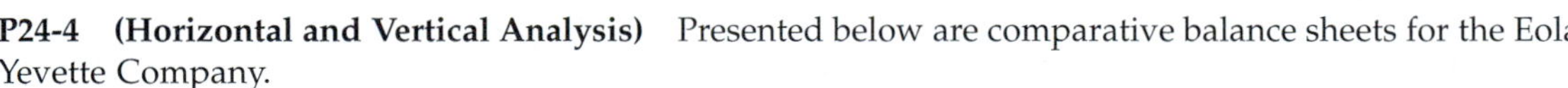

***P24-4 (Horizontal and Vertical Analysis)** Presented below are comparative balance sheets for the Eola Yevette Company.

EOLA YEVETTE COMPANY
COMPARATIVE BALANCE SHEET
DECEMBER 31, 2004 AND 2003

	December 31	
	2004	2003
Assets		
Cash	$ 180,000	$ 275,000
Accounts receivable (net)	220,000	155,000
Short-term investments	270,000	150,000
Inventories	960,000	980,000
Prepaid expense	25,000	25,000
Fixed assets	2,685,000	1,950,000
Accumulated depreciation	(1,000,000)	(750,000)
	$3,340,000	$2,785,000

Liabilities and Stockholders' Equity		
Accounts payable	$ 50,000	$ 75,000
Accrued expenses	170,000	200,000
Bonds payable	500,000	190,000
Capital stock	2,100,000	1,770,000
Retained earnings	520,000	550,000
	$3,340,000	$2,785,000

Instructions

(a) Prepare a comparative balance sheet of Yevette Company showing the percent each item is of the total assets or total liabilities and stockholders' equity.

(b) Prepare a comparative balance sheet of Yevette Company showing the dollar change and the percent change for each item.

(c) Of what value is the additional information provided in part (a)?

(d) Of what value is the additional information provided in part (b)?

***P24-5 (Dividend Policy Analysis)** Dawna Remmers Inc. went public 3 years ago. The board of directors will be meeting shortly after the end of the year to decide on a dividend policy. In the past, growth has been financed primarily through the retention of earnings. A stock or a cash dividend has never been declared. Presented below is a brief financial summary of Dawna Remmers Inc. operations.

			($000 omitted)		
	2004	2003	2002	2001	2000
Sales	$20,000	$16,000	$14,000	$6,000	$4,000
Net income	2,900	1,600	800	900	250
Average total assets	22,000	19,000	11,500	4,200	3,000
Current assets	8,000	6,000	3,000	1,200	1,000
Working capital	3,600	3,200	1,200	500	400
Common shares:					
Number of shares outstanding (000)	2,000	2,000	2,000	20	20
Average market price	$9	$6	$4	—	—

Instructions

(a) Suggest factors to be considered by the board of directors in establishing a dividend policy.

(b) Compute the rate of return on assets, profit margin on sales, earnings per share, price-earnings ratio, and current ratio for each of the 5 years for Dawna Remmers Inc.

(c) Comment on the appropriateness of declaring a cash dividend at this time, using the ratios computed in part (b) as a major factor in your analysis.

CONCEPTUAL CASES

C24-1 (General Disclosures, Inventories, Property, Plant, and Equipment) Dan D. Lion Corporation is in the process of preparing its annual financial statements for the fiscal year ended April 30, 2004. Because all of Lion's shares are traded intrastate, the company does not have to file any reports with the Securities and Exchange Commission. The company manufactures plastic, glass, and paper containers for sale to food and drink manufacturers and distributors.

Lion Corporation maintains separate control accounts for its raw materials, work-in-process, and finished goods inventories for each of the three types of containers. The inventories are valued at the lower of cost or market.

The company's property, plant, and equipment are classified in the following major categories: land, office buildings, furniture and fixtures, manufacturing facilities, manufacturing equipment, and leasehold improvements. All fixed assets are carried at cost. The depreciation methods employed depend upon the type of asset (its classification) and when it was acquired.

Lion Corporation plans to present the inventory and fixed asset amounts in its April 30, 2004, balance sheet as shown below.

Inventories	$4,814,200
Property, plant, and equipment (net of depreciation)	6,310,000

Instructions

What information regarding inventories and property, plant, and equipment must be disclosed by Dan D. Lion Corporation in the audited financial statements issued to stockholders, either in the body or the notes, for the 2003–2004 fiscal year?

(CMA adapted)

C24-2 (Disclosures Required in Various Situations) Rem Inc. produces electronic components for sale to manufacturers of radios, television sets, and digital sound systems. In connection with her examination of Rem's financial statements for the year ended December 31, 2004, Maggie Zeen, CPA, completed field work 2 weeks ago. Ms. Zeen now is evaluating the significance of the following items prior to preparing her auditor's report. Except as noted, none of these items have been disclosed in the financial statements or notes.

Item 1

A 10-year loan agreement, which the company entered into 3 years ago, provides that dividend payments may not exceed net income earned after taxes subsequent to the date of the agreement. The balance of retained earnings at the date of the loan agreement was $420,000. From that date through December 31, 2004, net income after taxes has totaled $570,000 and cash dividends have totaled $320,000. On the basis of these data, the staff auditor assigned to this review concluded that there was no retained earnings restriction at December 31, 2004.

Item 2

Recently Rem interrupted its policy of paying cash dividends quarterly to its stockholders. Dividends were paid regularly through 2003, discontinued for all of 2004 to finance purchase of equipment for the company's new plant, and resumed in the first quarter of 2005. In the annual report dividend policy is to be discussed in the president's letter to stockholders.

Item 3

A major electronics firm has introduced a line of products that will compete directly with Rem's primary line, now being produced in the specially designed new plant. Because of manufacturing innovations, the competitor's line will be of comparable quality but priced 50% below Rem's line. The competitor announced its new line during the week following completion of field work. Ms. Zeen read the announcement in the newspaper and discussed the situation by telephone with Rem executives. Rem will meet the lower prices that are high enough to cover variable manufacturing and selling expenses but will permit recovery of only a portion of fixed costs.

Item 4

The company's new manufacturing plant building, which cost $2,400,000 and has an estimated life of 25 years, is leased from Ancient National Bank at an annual rental of $600,000. The company is obligated to pay property taxes, insurance, and maintenance. At the conclusion of its 10-year noncancellable lease, the company has the option of purchasing the property for $1. In Rem's income statement the rental payment is reported on a separate line.

Instructions

For each of the items above discuss any additional disclosures in the financial statements and notes that the auditor should recommend to her client. (The cumulative effect of the four items should not be considered.)

C24-3 (Disclosures Required in Various Situations) You have completed your audit of Keesha Inc. and its consolidated subsidiaries for the year ended December 31, 2004, and were satisfied with the results of your examination. You have examined the financial statements of Keesha for the past 3 years. The corporation is now preparing its annual report to stockholders. The report will include the consolidated financial statements of Keesha and its subsidiaries and your short-form auditor's report. During your audit the following matters came to your attention.

1. A vice president who is also a stockholder resigned on December 31, 2004, after an argument with the president. The vice president is soliciting proxies from stockholders and expects to obtain sufficient proxies to gain control of the board of directors so that a new president will be appointed. The president plans to have a note prepared that would include information of the pending proxy fight, management's accomplishments over the years, and an appeal by management for the support of stockholders.
2. The corporation decides in 2004 to adopt the straight-line method of depreciation for plant equipment. The straight-line method will be used for new acquisitions as well as for previously acquired plant equipment for which depreciation had been provided on an accelerated basis.

3. The Internal Revenue Service is currently examining the corporation's 2001 federal income tax return and is questioning the amount of a deduction claimed by the corporation's domestic subsidiary for a loss sustained in 2001. The examination is still in process, and any additional tax liability is indeterminable at this time. The corporation's tax counsel believes that there will be no substantial additional tax liability.

Instructions

(a) Prepare the notes, if any, that you would suggest for the items listed above.

(b) State your reasons for not making disclosure by note for each of the listed items for which you did not prepare a note.

(AICPA adapted)

C24-4 (Disclosures, Conditional and Contingent Liabilities) Presented below are three independent situations.

Situation 1

A company offers a one-year warranty for the product that it manufactures. A history of warranty claims has been compiled, and the probable amounts of claims related to sales for a given period can be determined.

Situation 2

Subsequent to the date of a set of financial statements, but prior to the issuance of the financial statements, a company enters into a contract that will probably result in a significant loss to the company. The amount of the loss can be reasonably estimated.

Situation 3

A company has adopted a policy of recording self-insurance for any possible losses resulting from injury to others by the company's vehicles. The premium for an insurance policy for the same risk from an independent insurance company would have an annual cost of $4,000. During the period covered by the financial statements, there were no accidents involving the company's vehicles that resulted in injury to others.

Instructions

Discuss the accrual or type of disclosure necessary (if any) and the reason(s) why such disclosure is appropriate for each of the three independent sets of facts above.

(AICPA adapted)

C24-5 (Post-Balance Sheet Events) At December 31, 2004, Joni Brandt Corp. has assets of $10,000,000, liabilities of $6,000,000, common stock of $2,000,000 (representing 2,000,000 shares of $1 par common stock), and retained earnings of $2,000,000. Net sales for the year 2004 were $18,000,000, and net income was $800,000. As auditors of this company, you are making a review of subsequent events on February 13, 2005, and you find the following.

1. On February 3, 2005, one of Brandt's customers declared bankruptcy. At December 31, 2004, this company owed Brandt $300,000, of which $40,000 was paid in January, 2005.
2. On January 18, 2005, one of the three major plants of the client burned.
3. On January 23, 2005, a strike was called at one of Brandt's largest plants, which halted 30% of its production. As of today (February 13) the strike has not been settled.
4. A major electronics enterprise has introduced a line of products that would compete directly with Brandt's primary line, now being produced in a specially designed new plant. Because of manufacturing innovations, the competitor has been able to achieve quality similar to that of Brandt's products, but at a price 50% lower. Brandt officials say they will meet the lower prices, which are high enough to cover variable manufacturing and selling costs but which permit recovery of only a portion of fixed costs.
5. Merchandise traded in the open market is recorded in the company's records at $1.40 per unit on December 31, 2004. This price had prevailed for 2 weeks, after release of an official market report that predicted vastly enlarged supplies; however, no purchases were made at $1.40. The price throughout the preceding year had been about $2, which was the level experienced over several years. On January 18, 2005, the price returned to $2, after public disclosure of an error in the official calculations of the prior December, correction of which destroyed the expectations of excessive supplies. Inventory at December 31, 2004, was on a lower of cost or market basis.
6. On February 1, 2005, the board of directors adopted a resolution accepting the offer of an investment banker to guarantee the marketing of $1,200,000 of preferred stock.

Instructions

State in each case how the 2004 financial statements would be affected, if at all.

C24-6 (Segment Reporting) You are compiling the consolidated financial statements for Vender Corporation International. The corporation's accountant, Vincent Price, has provided you with the following segment information.

Note 7: Major Segments of Business

VCI conducts funeral service and cemetery operations in the United States and Canada. Substantially all revenues of VCI's major segments of business are from unaffiliated customers. Segment information for fiscal 2004, 2003, and 2002 follows.

	Funeral	Floral	Cemetery	(thousands) Corporate	Dried Whey	Limousine	Consolidated
Revenues							
2004	$302,000	$10,000	$ 83,000	$ —	$7,000	$14,000	$416,000
2003	245,000	6,000	61,000	—	4,000	8,000	324,000
2002	208,000	3,000	42,000	—	1,000	6,000	260,000
Operating Income							
2004	79,000	1,500	18,000	(36,000)	500	2,000	65,000
2003	64,000	200	12,000	(28,000)	200	400	48,800
2002	54,000	150	6,000	(21,000)	100	350	39,600
Capital Expenditures[a]							
2004	26,000	1,000	9,000	400	300	1,000	37,700
2003	28,000	2,000	60,000	1,500	100	700	92,300
2002	14,000	25	8,000	600	25	50	22,700
Depreciation and Amortization							
2004	13,000	100	2,400	1,400	100	200	17,200
2003	10,000	50	1,400	700	50	100	12,300
2002	8,000	25	1,000	600	25	50	9,700
Identifiable Assets							
2004	334,000	1,500	162,000	114,000	500	8,000	620,000
2003	322,000	1,000	144,000	52,000	1,000	6,000	526,000
2002	223,000	500	78,000	34,000	500	3,500	339,500

[a]Includes $4,520,000, $111,480,000, and $1,294,000 for the years ended April 30, 2004, 2003, and 2002, respectively, for purchases of businesses.

Instructions

Determine which of the above segments must be reported separately and which can be combined under the category "Other." Then, write a one-page memo to the company's accountant, Vincent Price, explaining the following.

(a) What segments must be reported separately and what segments can be combined.
(b) What criteria you used to determine reportable segments.
(c) What major items for each must be disclosed.

C24-7 (Segment Reporting—Theory) Presented below is an excerpt from the financial statements of **H. J. Heinz Company**.

Segment and Geographic Data

The company is engaged principally in one line of business—processed food products—which represents over 90% of consolidated sales. Information about the business of the company by geographic area is presented in the table below.

There were no material amounts of sales or transfers between geographic areas or between affiliates, and no material amounts of United States export sales.

(in thousands of U.S. dollars)	Domestic	Foreign: United Kingdom	Canada	Western Europe	Other	Total	Worldwide
Sales	$2,381,054	$547,527	$216,726	$383,784	$209,354	$1,357,391	$3,738,445
Operating income	246,780	61,282	34,146	29,146	25,111	149,685	396,465
Identifiable assets	1,362,152	265,218	112,620	294,732	143,971	816,541	2,178,693
Capital expenditures	72,712	12,262	13,790	8,253	4,368	38,673	111,385
Depreciation expense	42,279	8,364	3,592	6,355	3,606	21,917	64,196

Instructions

(a) Why does H. J. Heinz not prepare segment information on its products or services?
(b) What are export sales, and when should they be disclosed?
(c) Why are sales by geographical area important to disclose?

C24-8 (Segment Reporting—Theory) The following article appeared in the *Wall Street Journal*.

> WASHINGTON—The Securities and Exchange Commission staff issued guidelines for companies grappling with the problem of dividing up their business into industry segments for their annual reports.
>
> An industry segment is defined by the Financial Accounting Standards Board as a part of an enterprise engaged in providing a product or service or a group of related products or services primarily to unaffiliated customers for a profit.
>
> Although conceding that the process is a "subjective task" that "to a considerable extent, depends on the judgment of management," the SEC staff said companies should consider . . . various factors . . . to determine whether products and services should be grouped together or reported as segments. . . .

Instructions

(a) What does financial reporting for segments of a business enterprise involve?
(b) Identify the reasons for requiring financial data to be reported by segments.
(c) Identify the possible disadvantages of requiring financial data to be reported by segments.
(d) Identify the accounting difficulties inherent in segment reporting.

C24-9 (Interim Reporting) J. J. Kersee Corporation, a publicly traded company, is preparing the interim financial data which it will issue to its stockholders and the Securities and Exchange Commission (SEC) at the end of the first quarter of the 2003–2004 fiscal year. Kersee's financial accounting department has compiled the following summarized revenue and expense data for the first quarter of the year.

Sales	$60,000,000
Cost of goods sold	36,000,000
Variable selling expenses	2,000,000
Fixed selling expenses	3,000,000

Included in the fixed selling expenses was the single lump sum payment of $2,000,000 for television advertisements for the entire year.

Instructions

(a) J. J. Kersee Corporation must issue its quarterly financial statements in accordance with generally accepted accounting principles regarding interim financial reporting.
  (1) Explain whether Kersee should report its operating results for the quarter as if the quarter were a separate reporting period in and of itself or as if the quarter were an integral part of the annual reporting period.
  (2) State how the sales, cost of goods sold, and fixed selling expenses would be reflected in Kersee Corporation's quarterly report prepared for the first quarter of the 2003–2004 fiscal year. Briefly justify your presentation.
(b) What financial information, as a minimum, must Kersee Corporation disclose to its stockholders in its quarterly reports?

(CMA adapted)

C24-10 (Treatment of Various Interim Reporting Situations) The following statement is an excerpt from Paragraphs 9 and 10 of *Accounting Principles Board (APB) Opinion No. 28*, "Interim Financial Reporting."

> Interim financial information is essential to provide investors and others with timely information as to the progress of the enterprise. The usefulness of such information rests on the relationship that it has to the annual results of operations. Accordingly, the Board has concluded that each interim period should be viewed primarily as an integral part of an annual period.
>
> In general, the results for each interim period should be based on the accounting principles and practices used by an enterprise in the preparation of its latest annual financial statements unless a change in an accounting practice or policy has been adopted in the current year. The Board has concluded, however, that certain accounting principles and practices followed for annual reporting purposes may require modification at interim reporting dates so that the reported results for the interim period may better relate to the results of operations for the annual period.

Instructions

Listed below are six independent cases on how accounting facts might be reported on an individual company's interim financial reports. For each of these cases, state whether the method proposed to be used for interim reporting would be acceptable under generally accepted accounting principles applicable to interim financial data. Support each answer with a brief explanation.

- **(a)** B. J. King Company takes a physical inventory at year-end for annual financial statement purposes. Inventory and cost of sales reported in the interim quarterly statements are based on estimated gross profit rates, because a physical inventory would result in a cessation of operations. King Company does have reliable perpetual inventory records.
- **(b)** Florence Chadwick Company is planning to report one-fourth of its pension expense each quarter.
- **(c)** N. Lopez Company wrote inventory down to reflect lower of cost or market in the first quarter. At year-end the market exceeds the original acquisition cost of this inventory. Consequently, management plans to write the inventory back up to its original cost as a year-end adjustment.
- **(d)** K. Witt Company realized a large gain on the sale of investments at the beginning of the second quarter. The company wants to report one-third of the gain in each of the remaining quarters.
- **(e)** Alice Marble Company has estimated its annual audit fee. They plan to prorate this expense equally over all four quarters.
- **(f)** Lori McNeil Company was reasonably certain it would have an employee strike in the third quarter. As a result, it shipped heavily during the second quarter but plans to defer the recognition of the sales in excess of the normal sales volume. The deferred sales will be recognized as sales in the third quarter when the strike is in progress. McNeil Company management thinks this is more nearly representative of normal second- and third-quarter operations.

C24-11 (Financial Forecasts) An article in *Barron's* noted the following.

> Okay. Last fall, someone with a long memory and an even longer arm reached into that bureau drawer and came out with a moldy cheese sandwich and the equally moldy notion of corporate forecasts. We tried to find out what happened to the cheese sandwich—but, rats!, even recourse to the Freedom of Information Act didn't help. However, the forecast proposal was dusted off, polished up and found quite serviceable. The SEC, indeed, lost no time in running it up the old flagpole—but no one was very eager to salute. Even after some of the more objectionable features—compulsory corrections and detailed explanations of why the estimates went awry—were peeled off the original proposal.
>
> Seemingly, despite the Commission's smiles and sweet talk, those craven corporations were still afraid that an honest mistake would lead them down the primrose path to consent decrees and class action suits. To lay to rest such qualms, the Commission last week approved a "Safe Harbor" rule that, providing the forecasts were made on a reasonable basis and in good faith, protected corporations from litigation should the projections prove wide of the mark (as only about 99% are apt to do).

Instructions

- **(a)** What are the arguments for preparing profit forecasts?
- **(b)** What is the purpose of the "safe harbor" rule?
- **(c)** Why are corporations concerned about presenting profit forecasts?

C24-12 (Disclosure of Estimates—Ethics) Patty Gamble, the financial vice-president, and Victoria Maher, the controller, of Castle Manufacturing Company are reviewing the financial ratios of the company for the years 2003 and 2004. The financial vice president notes that the profit margin on sales ratio has increased from 6% to 12%, a hefty gain for the 2-year period. Gamble is in the process of issuing a media release that emphasizes the efficiency of Castle Manufacturing in controlling cost. Victoria Maher knows that the difference in ratios is due primarily to an earlier company decision to reduce the estimates of warranty and bad debt expense for 2004. The controller, not sure of her supervisor's motives, hesitates to suggest to Gamble that the company's improvement is unrelated to efficiency in controlling cost. To complicate matters, the media release is scheduled in a few days.

Instructions

- **(a)** What, if any, is the ethical dilemma in this situation?
- **(b)** Should Maher, the controller, remain silent? Give reasons.
- **(c)** What stakeholders might be affected by Gamble's media release?
- **(d)** Give your opinion on the following statement and cite reasons: "Because Gamble, the vice president, is most directly responsible for the media release, Maher has no real responsibility in this matter."

C24-13 (Reporting of Subsequent Event—Ethics) In June 2004, the board of directors for Holtzman Enterprises Inc. authorized the sale of $10,000,000 of corporate bonds. Michelle Collins, treasurer for Holtzman Enterprises Inc., is concerned about the date when the bonds are issued. The company really needs the cash, but she is worried that if the bonds are issued before the company's year-end (December 31, 2004) the additional liability will have an adverse effect on a number of important ratios. In July, she explains to company president Kenneth Holtzman that if they delay issuing the bonds until after December 31 the bonds will not affect the ratios until December 31, 2005. They will have to report the issuance as a subsequent event which requires only footnote disclosure. Collins expects that with expected improved financial performance in 2005 ratios should be better.

Instructions

(a) What are the ethical issues involved?
(b) Should Holtzman agree to the delay?

***C24-14 (Effect of Transactions on Financial Statements and Ratios)** The transactions listed below relate to Botticelli Inc. You are to assume that on the date on which each of the transactions occurred the corporation's accounts showed only common stock ($100 par) outstanding, a current ratio of 2.7:1, and a substantial net income for the year to date (before giving effect to the transaction concerned). On that date the book value per share of stock was $151.53.

Each numbered transaction is to be considered completely independent of the others, and its related answer should be based on the effect(s) of that transaction alone. Assume that all numbered transactions occurred during 2004 and that the amount involved in each case is sufficiently material to distort reported net income if improperly included in the determination of net income. Assume further that each transaction was recorded in accordance with generally accepted accounting principles and, where applicable, in conformity with the all-inclusive concept of the income statement.

For each of the numbered transactions you are to decide whether it:

a. Increased the corporation's 2004 net income.
b. Decreased the corporation's 2004 net income.
c. Increased the corporation's total retained earnings directly (i.e., not via net income).
d. Decreased the corporation's total retained earnings directly.
e. Increased the corporation's current ratio.
f. Decreased the corporation's current ratio.
g. Increased each stockholder's proportionate share of total owner's equity.
h. Decreased each stockholder's proportionate share of total owner's equity.
i. Increased each stockholder's equity per share of stock (book value).
j. Decreased each stockholder's equity per share of stock (book value).
k. Had none of the foregoing effects.

Instructions

List the numbers 1 through 10. Select as many letters as you deem appropriate to reflect the effect(s) of each transaction as of the date of the transaction by printing beside the transaction number the letter(s) that identifies that transaction's effect(s).

Transactions

____ **1.** Treasury stock originally repurchased and carried at $127 per share was sold for cash at $153 per share.

____ **2.** The corporation sold at a profit land and a building that had been idle for some time. Under the terms of the sale, the corporation received a portion of the sales price in cash immediately, the balance maturing at 6 month intervals.

____ **3.** In January the board directed the writeoff of certain patent rights that had suddenly and unexpectedly become worthless.

____ **4.** The corporation wrote off all of the unamortized discount and issue expense applicable to bonds that it refinanced in 2004.

____ **5.** The board of directors authorized the writeup of certain fixed assets to values established in a competent appraisal.

____ **6.** The corporation called in all its outstanding shares of stock and exchanged them for new shares on a 2-for-1 basis, reducing the par value at the same time to $50 per share.

____ **7.** The corporation paid a cash dividend that had been recorded in the accounts at time of declaration.

____ **8.** Litigation involving Botticelli Inc. as defendant was settled in the corporation's favor, with the plaintiff paying all court costs and legal fees. In 2001 the corporation had appropriately established a special contingency for this court action. (Indicate the effect of reversing the contingency only.)

____ **9.** The corporation received a check for the proceeds of an insurance policy from the company with which it is insured against theft of trucks. No entries concerning the theft had been made previously, and the proceeds reduce but do not cover completely the loss.

____ **10.** Treasury stock, which had been repurchased at and carried at $127 per share, was issued as a stock dividend. In connection with this distribution, the board of directors of Botticelli Inc. had authorized a transfer from retained earnings to permanent capital of an amount equal to the aggregate market value ($153 per share) of the shares issued. No entries relating to this dividend had been made previously.

(AICPA adapted)

USING YOUR JUDGMENT

FINANCIAL REPORTING PROBLEM

3M Company

In response to the investing public's demand for greater disclosure of corporate expectations for the future, safe-harbor rules and legislation have been passed to encourage and protect corporations that issue financial forecasts and projections. Review 3M's Analysis of Financial Condition and Results of Operations—Future Outlook and Forward-Looking Statements sections in Appendix 5B or on the Take Action! CD.

Instructions

Refer to 3M's financial statements and the accompanying notes to answer the following questions.

(a) What initiatives has 3M launched in 2001 that will help meet its economic challenges?

(b) What does 3M estimate its earnings per share will be for 2002?

(c) What caveats or other statements that temper its forecasts does 3M make?

(d) What is the difference between a financial forecast and a financial projection?

*FINANCIAL STATEMENT ANALYSIS CASE

Twin Ricky Inc. (TRI) manufactures a variety of consumer products. The company's founders have run the company for 30 years and are now interested in retiring. Consequently, they are seeking a purchaser who will continue its operations, and a group of investors, Donna Inc., is looking into the acquisition of TRI. To evaluate its financial stability and operating efficiency, TRI was requested to provide the latest financial statements and selected financial ratios. Summary information provided by TRI is presented on the next page.

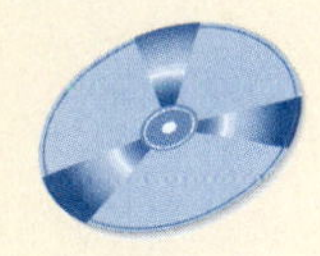

Additional Financial Statement Analysis Problems

TRI
INCOME STATEMENT
FOR THE YEAR ENDED NOVEMBER 30, 2004
(IN THOUSANDS)

Sales (net)	$30,500
Interest income	500
Total revenue	31,000
Costs and expenses	
Cost of goods sold	17,600
Selling and administrative expense	3,550
Depreciation and amortization expense	1,890
Interest expense	900
Total costs and expenses	23,940
Income before taxes	7,060
Income taxes	2,900
Net income	$ 4,160

TRI
STATEMENT OF FINANCIAL POSITION
AS OF NOVEMBER 30
(IN THOUSANDS)

	2004	2003
Cash	$ 400	$ 500
Marketable securities (at cost)	500	200
Accounts receivable (net)	3,200	2,900
Inventory	5,800	5,400
Total current assets	9,900	9,000
Property, plant, & equipment (net)	7,100	7,000
Total assets	$17,000	$16,000
Accounts payable	$ 3,700	$ 3,400
Income taxes payable	900	800
Accrued expenses	1,700	1,400
Total current liabilities	6,300	5,600
Long-term debt	2,000	1,800
Total liabilities	8,300	7,400
Common stock ($1 par value)	2,700	2,700
Paid-in capital in excess of par	1,000	1,000
Retained earnings	5,000	4,900
Total shareholders' equity	8,700	8,600
Total liabilities and shareholders' equity	$17,000	$16,000

Selected Financial Ratios

	TRI 2003	TRI 2002	Current Industry Average
Current ratio	1.61	1.62	1.63
Acid-test ratio	.64	.63	.68
Times interest earned	8.55	8.50	8.45
Profit margin on sales	13.2%	12.1%	13.0%
Total debt to net worth	.86	1.02	1.03
Asset turnover	1.84	1.83	1.84
Inventory turnover	3.17	3.21	3.18

Instructions

(a) Calculate a new set of ratios for the fiscal year 2004 for TRI based on the financial statements presented.

(b) Explain the analytical use of each of the seven ratios presented, describing what the investors can learn about TRI's financial stability and operating efficiency.

(c) Identify two limitations of ratio analysis.

(CMA adapted)

COMPARATIVE ANALYSIS CASE

The Coca-Cola Company versus PepsiCo, Inc.

Instructions

Go to the Take Action! CD and use information found there to answer the following questions related to **The Coca-Cola Company** and **PepsiCo, Inc.**

(a) **(1)** What specific items does Coca-Cola discuss in its **Note 1—Accounting Policies**? (Prepare a list of the headings only.)

(2) What specific items does PepsiCo discuss in its **Note 1—Summary of Significant Accounting Policies**? (Prepare a list of the headings only.)

(3) Note the similarities and differences between Coca-Cola's and PepsiCo's lists.

(b) For what lines of business or segments do Coca-Cola and PepsiCo present segmented information?

(c) Note and comment on the similarities and differences between the auditors' reports submitted by the independent auditors of Coca-Cola and PepsiCo for the year 2001.

RESEARCH CASES

Case 1

Read the article entitled "FASB Is Criticized for Inaction on Off-Balance-Sheet Debt Issue," by Steve Liesman, Jonathan Weil, and Scott Paltrow in the January 18, 2002, *Wall Street Journal*. (Subscribers to **Business Extra** can access the article at that site.)

Instructions

Answer the following questions.

(a) Why has the FASB not set better rules for when a firm should be allowed to keep debt off its balance sheet?

(b) Who is helped (in the short term and the long term) by a firm's being able to keep debt off its balance sheet? Who is hurt (short term and long term)?

(c) According to the article, when the FASB proposes new rules that would hurt them, "corporate America and its allies invoke portents of doom as to why we shouldn't have honest accounting treatment" of what's being proposed. How does this affect the usefulness of financial reporting for investors and creditors?

(d) Who has Congress favored in the past in similar situations? Why has Congress favored them?

(e) One of the groups criticizing the FASB for moving too slowly is the Financial Executives International (FEI), which opposed requiring firms to consolidate the results of all their entities. The FEI also opposed the FASB's proposal to require firms to expense executive stock options. Based on this, would you consider FEI "part of the solution" or "part of the problem"? Justify your answer.

Case 2

Companies registered with the Securities and Exchange Commission are required to file a quarterly report on Form 10-Q within 45 days of the end of the first three fiscal quarters.

Instructions

Use EDGAR or some other source to examine the most recent 10-Q for the company of your choice and answer the following questions.

(a) What financial information is included in Part I?

(b) Read the notes to the financial statements and identify any departures from the "integral approach."

(c) Does the 10-Q include any information under Part II? Describe the nature of the information.

*PROFESSIONAL SIMULATION

Financial Statement Analysis

Directions | Situation | Analysis | Explanation | Research | Resources

Directions

In this simulation, you will be asked to evaluate a company's solvency and going-concern potential. You will be asked to analyze a set of ratios and indicate possible limitations of ratio analysis.
Prepare responses to all parts.

Situation

As the CPA for Packard Clipper, Inc., you have been requested to develop some key ratios from the comparative financial statements. This information is to be used to convince creditors that Packard Clipper, Inc. is solvent and to support the use of going-concern valuation procedures in the financial statements.

The data requested and the computations developed from the financial statements follow:

	2004	2003
Current ratio	2.6 times	2.1 times
Acid-test ratio	.8 times	1.3 times
Property, plant, and equipment to stockholders' equity	2.5 times	2.2 times
Sales to stockholders' equity	2.4 times	2.7 times
Net income	Up 32%	Down 9%
Earnings per share	$3.30	$2.50
Book value per share	Up 6%	Up 9%

Analysis

Packard Clipper asks you to prepare a list of brief comments stating how each of these items supports the solvency and going-concern potential of the business. The company wishes to use these comments to support its presentation of data to its creditors. You are to prepare the comments as requested, giving the implications and the limitations of each item separately, and then the collective inference that may be drawn from them about Packard Clipper's solvency and going-concern potential.

Explanation

Having done as the client requested in the Analysis section above, prepare a brief listing of additional ratio-analysis-type data for this client which you think its creditors are going to ask for to supplement the analytical data you provided. Explain why you think the additional data will be helpful to these creditors in evaluating the client's solvency. What warnings should you offer these creditors about the limitations of ratio analysis for the purposes stated here?

Remember to check the **Take Action! CD** and the book's **companion Web site** to find additional resources for this chapter.

The following time value of money tables are also presented at the end of Chapter 6, "Accounting and the Time Value of Money," in Volume I (pages 302–311). They are presented here to facilitate your use of Volume II.

TABLE 6-1 FUTURE VALUE OF 1 (FUTURE VALUE OF A SINGLE SUM)

$FVF_{n,i} = (1 + i)^n$

(n) Periods	2%	2½%	3%	4%	5%	6%
1	1.02000	1.02500	1.03000	1.04000	1.05000	1.06000
2	1.04040	1.05063	1.06090	1.08160	1.10250	1.12360
3	1.06121	1.07689	1.09273	1.12486	1.15763	1.19102
4	1.08243	1.10381	1.12551	1.16986	1.21551	1.26248
5	1.10408	1.13141	1.15927	1.21665	1.27628	1.33823
6	1.12616	1.15969	1.19405	1.26532	1.34010	1.41852
7	1.14869	1.18869	1.22987	1.31593	1.40710	1.50363
8	1.17166	1.21840	1.26677	1.36857	1.47746	1.59385
9	1.19509	1.24886	1.30477	1.42331	1.55133	1.68948
10	1.21899	1.28008	1.34392	1.48024	1.62889	1.79085
11	1.24337	1.31209	1.38423	1.53945	1.71034	1.89830
12	1.26824	1.34489	1.42576	1.60103	1.79586	2.01220
13	1.29361	1.37851	1.46853	1.66507	1.88565	2.13293
14	1.31948	1.41297	1.51259	1.73168	1.97993	2.26090
15	1.34587	1.44830	1.55797	1.80094	2.07893	2.39656
16	1.37279	1.48451	1.60471	1.87298	2.18287	2.54035
17	1.40024	1.52162	1.65285	1.94790	2.29202	2.69277
18	1.42825	1.55966	1.70243	2.02582	2.40662	2.85434
19	1.45681	1.59865	1.75351	2.10685	2.52695	3.02560
20	1.48595	1.63862	1.80611	2.19112	2.65330	3.20714
21	1.51567	1.67958	1.86029	2.27877	2.78596	3.39956
22	1.54598	1.72157	1.91610	2.36992	2.92526	3.60354
23	1.57690	1.76461	1.97359	2.46472	3.07152	3.81975
24	1.60844	1.80873	2.03279	2.56330	3.22510	4.04893
25	1.64061	1.85394	2.09378	2.66584	3.38635	4.29187
26	1.67342	1.90029	2.15659	2.77247	3.55567	4.54938
27	1.70689	1.94780	2.22129	2.88337	3.73346	4.82235
28	1.74102	1.99650	2.28793	2.99870	3.92013	5.11169
29	1.77584	2.04641	2.35657	3.11865	4.11614	5.41839
30	1.81136	2.09757	2.42726	3.24340	4.32194	5.74349
31	1.84759	2.15001	2.50008	3.37313	4.53804	6.08810
32	1.88454	2.20376	2.57508	3.50806	4.76494	6.45339
33	1.92223	2.25885	2.65234	3.64838	5.00319	6.84059
34	1.96068	2.31532	2.73191	3.79432	5.25335	7.25103
35	1.99989	2.37321	2.81386	3.94609	5.51602	7.68609
36	2.03989	2.43254	2.89828	4.10393	5.79182	8.14725
37	2.08069	2.49335	2.98523	4.26809	6.08141	8.63609
38	2.12230	2.55568	3.07478	4.43881	6.38548	9.15425
39	2.16474	2.61957	3.16703	4.61637	6.70475	9.70351
40	2.20804	2.68506	3.26204	4.80102	7.03999	10.28572

TABLE 6-1 FUTURE VALUE OF 1

8%	9%	10%	11%	12%	15%	(n) Periods
1.08000	1.09000	1.10000	1.11000	1.12000	1.15000	1
1.16640	1.18810	1.21000	1.23210	1.25440	1.32250	2
1.25971	1.29503	1.33100	1.36763	1.40493	1.52088	3
1.36049	1.41158	1.46410	1.51807	1.57352	1.74901	4
1.46933	1.53862	1.61051	1.68506	1.76234	2.01136	5
1.58687	1.67710	1.77156	1.87041	1.97382	2.31306	6
1.71382	1.82804	1.94872	2.07616	2.21068	2.66002	7
1.85093	1.99256	2.14359	2.30454	2.47596	3.05902	8
1.99900	2.17189	2.35795	2.55803	2.77308	3.51788	9
2.15892	2.36736	2.59374	2.83942	3.10585	4.04556	10
2.33164	2.58043	2.85312	3.15176	3.47855	4.65239	11
2.51817	2.81267	3.13843	3.49845	3.89598	5.35025	12
2.71962	3.06581	3.45227	3.88328	4.36349	6.15279	13
2.93719	3.34173	3.79750	4.31044	4.88711	7.07571	14
3.17217	3.64248	4.17725	4.78459	5.47357	8.13706	15
3.42594	3.97031	4.59497	5.31089	6.13039	9.35762	16
3.70002	4.32763	5.05447	5.89509	6.86604	10.76126	17
3.99602	4.71712	5.55992	6.54355	7.68997	12.37545	18
4.31570	5.14166	6.11591	7.26334	8.61276	14.23177	19
4.66096	5.60441	6.72750	8.06231	9.64629	16.36654	20
5.03383	6.10881	7.40025	8.94917	10.80385	18.82152	21
5.43654	6.65860	8.14028	9.93357	12.10031	21.64475	22
5.87146	7.25787	8.95430	11.02627	13.55235	24.89146	23
6.34118	7.91108	9.84973	12.23916	15.17863	28.62518	24
6.84847	8.62308	10.83471	13.58546	17.00000	32.91895	25
7.39635	9.39916	11.91818	15.07986	19.04007	37.85680	26
7.98806	10.24508	13.10999	16.73865	21.32488	43.53532	27
8.62711	11.16714	14.42099	18.57990	23.88387	50.06561	28
9.31727	12.17218	15.86309	20.62369	26.74993	57.57545	29
10.06266	13.26768	17.44940	22.89230	29.95992	66.21177	30
10.86767	14.46177	19.19434	25.41045	33.55511	76.14354	31
11.73708	15.76333	21.11378	28.20560	37.58173	87.56507	32
12.67605	17.18203	23.22515	31.30821	42.09153	100.69983	33
13.69013	18.72841	25.54767	34.75212	47.14252	115.80480	34
14.78534	20.41397	28.10244	38.57485	52.79962	133.17552	35
15.96817	22.25123	30.91268	42.81808	59.13557	153.15185	36
17.24563	24.25384	34.00395	47.52807	66.23184	176.12463	37
18.62528	26.43668	37.40434	52.75616	74.17966	202.54332	38
20.11530	28.81598	41.14479	58.55934	83.08122	232.92482	39
21.72452	31.40942	45.25926	65.00087	93.05097	267.86355	40

TABLE 6-2 PRESENT VALUE OF 1 (PRESENT VALUE OF A SINGLE SUM)

$$PVF_{n,i} = \frac{1}{(1+i)^n} = (1+i)^{-n}$$

(n) Periods	2%	2½%	3%	4%	5%	6%
1	.98039	.97561	.97087	.96154	.95238	.94340
2	.96117	.95181	.94260	.92456	.90703	.89000
3	.94232	.92860	.91514	.88900	.86384	.83962
4	.92385	.90595	.88849	.85480	.82270	.79209
5	.90573	.88385	.86261	.82193	.78353	.74726
6	.88797	.86230	.83748	.79031	.74622	.70496
7	.87056	.84127	.81309	.75992	.71068	.66506
8	.85349	.82075	.78941	.73069	.67684	.62741
9	.83676	.80073	.76642	.70259	.64461	.59190
10	.82035	.78120	.74409	.67556	.61391	.55839
11	.80426	.76214	.72242	.64958	.58468	.52679
12	.78849	.74356	.70138	.62460	.55684	.49697
13	.77303	.72542	.68095	.60057	.53032	.46884
14	.75788	.70773	.66112	.57748	.50507	.44230
15	.74301	.69047	.64186	.55526	.48102	.41727
16	.72845	.67362	.62317	.53391	.45811	.39365
17	.71416	.65720	.60502	.51337	.43630	.37136
18	.70016	.64117	.58739	.49363	.41552	.35034
19	.68643	.62553	.57029	.47464	.39573	.33051
20	.67297	.61027	.55368	.45639	.37689	.31180
21	.65978	.59539	.53755	.43883	.35894	.29416
22	.64684	.58086	.52189	.42196	.34185	.22751
23	.63416	.56670	.50669	.40573	.32557	.26180
24	.62172	.55288	.49193	.39012	.31007	.24698
25	.60953	.53939	.47761	.37512	.29530	.23300
26	.59758	.52623	.46369	.36069	.28124	.21981
27	.58586	.51340	.45019	.34682	.26785	.20737
28	.57437	.50088	.43708	.33348	.25509	.19563
29	.56311	.48866	.42435	.32065	.24295	.18456
30	.55207	.47674	.41199	.30832	.23138	.17411
31	.54125	.46511	.39999	.29646	.22036	.16425
32	.53063	.45377	.38834	.28506	.20987	.15496
33	.52023	.44270	.37703	.27409	.19987	.14619
34	.51003	.43191	.36604	.26355	.19035	.13791
35	.50003	.42137	.35538	.25342	.18129	.13011
36	.49022	.41109	.34503	.24367	.17266	.12274
37	.48061	.40107	.33498	.23430	.16444	.11579
38	.47119	.39128	.32523	.22529	.15661	.10924
39	.46195	.38174	.31575	.21662	.14915	.10306
40	.45289	.37243	.30656	.20829	.14205	.09722

TABLE 6-2 PRESENT VALUE OF 1

8%	9%	10%	11%	12%	15%	(n) Periods
.92593	.91743	.90909	.90090	.89286	.86957	1
.85734	.84168	.82645	.81162	.79719	.75614	2
.79383	.77218	.75132	.73119	.71178	.65752	3
.73503	.70843	.68301	.65873	.63552	.57175	4
.68058	.64993	.62092	.59345	.56743	.49718	5
.63017	.59627	.56447	.53464	.50663	.43233	6
.58349	.54703	.51316	.48166	.45235	.37594	7
.54027	.50187	.46651	.43393	.40388	.32690	8
.50025	.46043	.42410	.39092	.36061	.28426	9
.46319	.42241	.38554	.35218	.32197	.24719	10
.42888	.38753	.35049	.31728	.28748	.21494	11
.39711	.35554	.31863	.28584	.25668	.18691	12
.36770	.32618	.28966	.25751	.22917	.16253	13
.34046	.29925	.26333	.23199	.20462	.14133	14
.31524	.27454	.23939	.20900	.18270	.12289	15
.29189	.25187	.21763	.18829	.16312	.10687	16
.27027	.23107	.19785	.16963	.14564	.09293	17
.25025	.21199	.17986	.15282	.13004	.08081	18
.23171	.19449	.16351	.13768	.11611	.07027	19
.21455	.17843	.14864	.12403	.10367	.06110	20
.19866	.16370	.13513	.11174	.09256	.05313	21
.18394	.15018	.12285	.10067	.08264	.04620	22
.17032	.13778	.11168	.09069	.07379	.04017	23
.15770	.12641	.10153	.08170	.06588	.03493	24
.14602	.11597	.09230	.07361	.05882	.03038	25
.13520	.10639	.08391	.06631	.05252	.02642	26
.12519	.09761	.07628	.05974	.04689	.02297	27
.11591	.08955	.06934	.05382	.04187	.01997	28
.10733	.08216	.06304	.04849	.03738	.01737	29
.09938	.07537	.05731	.04368	.03338	.01510	30
.09202	.06915	.05210	.03935	.02980	.01313	31
.08520	.06344	.04736	.03545	.02661	.01142	32
.07889	.05820	.04306	.03194	.02376	.00993	33
.07305	.05340	.03914	.02878	.02121	.00864	34
.06763	.04899	.03558	.02592	.01894	.00751	35
.06262	.04494	.03235	.02335	.01691	.00653	36
.05799	.04123	.02941	.02104	.01510	.00568	37
.05369	.03783	.02674	.01896	.01348	.00494	38
.04971	.03470	.02430	.01708	.01204	.00429	39
.04603	.03184	.02210	.01538	.01075	.00373	40

TABLE 6-3 FUTURE VALUE OF AN ORDINARY ANNUITY OF 1

$$FVF\text{-}OA_{n,i} = \frac{(1+i)^n - 1}{i}$$

(n) Periods	2%	2½%	3%	4%	5%	6%
1	1.00000	1.00000	1.00000	1.00000	1.00000	1.00000
2	2.02000	2.02500	2.03000	2.04000	2.05000	2.06000
3	3.06040	3.07563	3.09090	3.12160	3.15250	3.18360
4	4.12161	4.15252	4.18363	4.24646	4.31013	4.37462
5	5.20404	5.25633	5.30914	5.41632	5.52563	5.63709
6	6.30812	6.38774	6.46841	6.63298	6.80191	6.97532
7	7.43428	7.54743	7.66246	7.89829	8.14201	8.39384
8	8.58297	8.73612	8.89234	9.21423	9.54911	9.89747
9	9.75463	9.95452	10.15911	10.58280	11.02656	11.49132
10	10.94972	11.20338	11.46338	12.00611	12.57789	13.18079
11	12.16872	12.48347	12.80780	13.48635	14.20679	14.97164
12	13.41209	13.79555	14.19203	15.02581	15.91713	16.86994
13	14.68033	15.14044	15.61779	16.62684	17.71298	18.88214
14	15.97394	16.51895	17.08632	18.29191	19.59863	21.01507
15	17.29342	17.93193	18.59891	20.02359	21.57856	23.27597
16	18.63929	19.38022	20.15688	21.82453	23.65749	25.67253
17	20.01207	20.86473	21.76159	23.69751	25.84037	28.21288
18	21.41231	22.38635	23.41444	25.64541	28.13238	30.90565
19	22.84056	23.94601	25.11687	27.67123	30.53900	33.75999
20	24.29737	25.54466	26.87037	29.77808	33.06595	36.78559
21	25.78332	27.18327	28.67649	31.96920	35.71925	39.99273
22	27.29898	28.86286	30.53678	34.24797	38.50521	43.39229
23	28.84496	30.58443	32.45288	36.61789	41.43048	46.99583
24	30.42186	32.34904	34.42647	39.08260	44.50200	50.81558
25	32.03030	34.15776	36.45926	41.64591	47.72710	54.86451
26	33.67091	36.01171	38.55304	44.31174	51.11345	59.15638
27	35.34432	37.91200	40.70963	47.08421	54.66913	63.70577
28	37.05121	39.85980	42.93092	49.96758	58.40258	68.52811
29	38.79223	41.85630	45.21885	52.96629	62.32271	73.63980
30	40.56808	43.90270	47.57542	56.08494	66.43885	79.05819
31	42.37944	46.00027	50.00268	59.32834	70.76079	84.80168
32	44.22703	48.15028	52.50276	62.70147	75.29883	90.88978
33	46.11157	50.35403	55.07784	66.20953	80.06377	97.34316
34	48.03380	52.61289	57.73018	69.85791	85.06696	104.18376
35	49.99448	54.92821	60.46208	73.65222	90.32031	111.43478
36	51.99437	57.30141	63.27594	77.59831	95.83632	119.12087
37	54.03425	59.73395	66.17422	81.70225	101.62814	127.26812
38	56.11494	62.22730	69.15945	85.97034	107.70955	135.90421
39	58.23724	64.78298	72.23423	90.40915	114.09502	145.05846
40	60.40198	67.40255	75.40126	95.02552	120.79977	154.76197

TABLE 6-3 FUTURE VALUE OF AN ORDINARY ANNUITY OF 1

8%	9%	10%	11%	12%	15%	(n) Periods
1.00000	1.00000	1.00000	1.00000	1.00000	1.00000	1
2.08000	2.09000	2.10000	2.11000	2.12000	2.15000	2
3.24640	3.27810	3.31000	3.34210	3.37440	3.47250	3
4.50611	4.57313	4.64100	4.70973	4.77933	4.99338	4
5.86660	5.98471	6.10510	6.22780	6.35285	6.74238	5
7.33592	7.52334	7.71561	7.91286	8.11519	8.75374	6
8.92280	9.20044	9.48717	9.78327	10.08901	11.06680	7
10.63663	11.02847	11.43589	11.85943	12.29969	13.72682	8
12.48756	13.02104	13.57948	14.16397	14.77566	16.78584	9
14.48656	15.19293	15.93743	16.72201	17.54874	20.30372	10
16.64549	17.56029	18.53117	19.56143	20.65458	24.34928	11
18.97713	20.14072	21.38428	22.71319	24.13313	29.00167	12
21.49530	22.95339	24.52271	26.21164	28.02911	34.35192	13
24.21492	26.01919	27.97498	30.09492	32.39260	40.50471	14
27.15211	29.36092	31.77248	34.40536	37.27972	47.58041	15
30.32428	33.00340	35.94973	39.18995	42.75328	55.71747	16
33.75023	36.97371	40.54470	44.50084	48.88367	65.07509	17
37.45024	41.30134	45.59917	50.39593	55.74972	75.83636	18
41.44626	46.01846	51.15909	56.93949	63.43968	88.21181	19
45.76196	51.16012	57.27500	64.20283	72.05244	102.44358	20
50.42292	56.76453	64.00250	72.26514	81.69874	118.81012	21
55.45676	62.87334	71.40275	81.21431	92.50258	137.63164	22
60.89330	69.53194	79.54302	91.14788	104.60289	159.27638	23
66.76476	76.78981	88.49733	102.17415	118.15524	184.16784	24
73.10594	84.70090	98.34706	114.41331	133.33387	212.79302	25
79.95442	93.32398	109.18177	127.99877	150.33393	245.71197	26
87.35077	102.72314	121.09994	143.07864	169.37401	283.56877	27
95.33883	112.96822	134.20994	159.81729	190.69889	327.10408	28
103.96594	124.13536	148.63093	178.39719	214.58275	377.16969	29
113.28321	136.30754	164.49402	199.02088	241.33268	434.74515	30
123.34587	149.57522	181.94343	221.91317	271.29261	500.95692	31
134.21354	164.03699	201.13777	247.32362	304.84772	577.10046	32
145.95062	179.80032	222.25154	275.52922	342.42945	644.66553	33
158.62667	196.98234	245.47670	306.83744	384.52098	765.36535	34
172.31680	215.71076	271.02437	341.58955	431.66350	881.17016	35
187.10215	236.12472	299.12681	380.16441	484.46312	1014.34568	36
203.07032	258.37595	330.03949	422.98249	543.59869	1167.49753	37
220.31595	282.62978	364.04343	470.51056	609.83053	1343.62216	38
238.94122	309.06646	401.44778	523.26673	684.01020	1546.16549	39
259.05652	337.88245	442.59256	581.82607	767.09142	1779.09031	40

TABLE 6-4 PRESENT VALUE OF AN ORDINARY ANNUITY OF 1

$$PVF\text{-}OA_{n,i} = \frac{1 - \dfrac{1}{(1+i)^n}}{i}$$

(n) Periods	2%	2½%	3%	4%	5%	6%
1	.98039	.97561	.97087	.96154	.95238	.94340
2	1.94156	1.92742	1.91347	1.88609	1.85941	1.83339
3	2.88388	2.85602	2.82861	2.77509	2.72325	2.67301
4	3.80773	3.76197	3.71710	3.62990	3.54595	3.46511
5	4.71346	4.64583	4.57971	4.45182	4.32948	4.21236
6	5.60143	5.50813	5.41719	5.24214	5.07569	4.91732
7	6.47199	6.34939	6.23028	6.00205	5.78637	5.58238
8	7.32548	7.17014	7.01969	6.73274	6.46321	6.20979
9	8.16224	7.97087	7.78611	7.43533	7.10782	6.80169
10	8.98259	8.75206	8.53020	8.11090	7.72173	7.36009
11	9.78685	9.51421	9.25262	8.76048	8.30641	7.88687
12	10.57534	10.25776	9.95400	9.38507	8.86325	8.38384
13	11.34837	10.98319	10.63496	9.98565	9.39357	8.85268
14	12.10625	11.69091	11.29607	10.56312	9.89864	9.29498
15	12.84926	12.38138	11.93794	11.11839	10.37966	9.71225
16	13.57771	13.05500	12.56110	11.65230	10.83777	10.10590
17	14.29187	13.71220	13.16612	12.16567	11.27407	10.47726
18	14.99203	14.35336	13.75351	12.65930	11.68959	10.82760
19	15.67846	14.97889	14.32380	13.13394	12.08532	11.15812
20	16.35143	15.58916	14.87747	13.59033	12.46221	11.46992
21	17.01121	16.18455	15.41502	14.02916	12.82115	11.76408
22	17.65805	16.76541	15.93692	14.45112	13.16300	12.04158
23	18.29220	17.33211	16.44361	14.85684	13.48857	12.30338
24	18.91393	17.88499	16.93554	15.24696	13.79864	12.55036
25	19.52346	18.42438	17.41315	15.62208	14.09394	12.78336
26	20.12104	18.95061	17.87684	15.98277	14.37519	13.00317
27	20.70690	19.46401	18.32703	16.32959	14.64303	13.21053
28	21.28127	19.96489	18.76411	16.66306	14.89813	13.40616
29	21.84438	20.45355	19.18845	16.98371	15.14107	13.59072
30	22.39646	20.93029	19.60044	17.29203	15.37245	13.76483
31	22.93770	21.39541	20.00043	17.58849	15.59281	13.92909
32	23.46833	21.84918	20.38877	17.87355	15.80268	14.08404
33	23.98856	22.29188	20.76579	18.14765	16.00255	14.23023
34	24.49859	22.72379	21.13184	18.41120	16.19290	14.36814
35	24.99862	23.14516	21.48722	18.66461	16.37419	14.49825
36	25.48884	23.55625	21.83225	18.90828	16.54685	14.62099
37	25.96945	23.95732	22.16724	19.14258	16.71129	14.73678
38	26.44064	24.34860	22.49246	19.36786	16.86789	14.84602
39	26.90259	24.73034	22.80822	19.58448	17.01704	14.94907
40	27.35548	25.10278	23.11477	19.79277	17.15909	15.04630

TABLE 6-4 PRESENT VALUE OF AN ORDINARY ANNUITY OF 1

8%	9%	10%	11%	12%	15%	(n) Periods
.92593	.91743	.90909	.90090	.89286	.86957	1
1.78326	1.75911	1.73554	1.71252	1.69005	1.62571	2
2.57710	2.53130	2.48685	2.44371	2.40183	2.28323	3
3.31213	3.23972	3.16986	3.10245	3.03735	2.85498	4
3.99271	3.88965	3.79079	3.69590	3.60478	3.35216	5
4.62288	4.48592	4.35526	4.23054	4.11141	3.78448	6
5.20637	5.03295	4.86842	4.71220	4.56376	4.16042	7
5.74664	5.53482	5.33493	5.14612	4.96764	4.48732	8
6.24689	5.99525	5.75902	5.53705	5.32825	4.77158	9
6.71008	6.41766	6.14457	5.88923	5.65022	5.01877	10
7.13896	6.80519	6.49506	6.20652	5.93770	5.23371	11
7.53608	7.16073	6.81369	6.49236	6.19437	5.42062	12
7.90378	7.48690	7.10336	6.74987	6.42355	5.58315	13
8.24424	7.78615	7.36669	6.98187	6.62817	5.72448	14
8.55948	8.06069	7.60608	7.19087	6.81086	5.84737	15
8.85137	8.31256	7.82371	7.37916	6.97399	5.95424	16
9.12164	8.54363	8.02155	7.54879	7.11963	6.04716	17
9.37189	8.75563	8.20141	7.70162	7.24967	6.12797	18
9.60360	8.95012	8.36492	7.83929	7.36578	6.19823	19
9.81815	9.12855	8.51356	7.96333	7.46944	6.25933	20
10.01680	9.29224	8.64869	8.07507	7.56200	6.31246	21
10.20074	9.44243	8.77154	8.17574	7.64465	6.35866	22
10.37106	9.58021	8.88322	8.26643	7.71843	6.39884	23
10.52876	9.70661	8.98474	8.34814	7.78432	6.43377	24
10.67478	9.82258	9.07704	8.42174	7.84314	6.46415	25
10.80998	9.92897	9.16095	8.48806	7.89566	6.49056	26
10.93516	10.02658	9.23722	8.54780	7.94255	6.51353	27
11.05108	10.11613	9.30657	8.60162	7.98442	6.53351	28
11.15841	10.19828	9.36961	8.65011	8.02181	6.55088	29
11.25778	10.27365	9.42691	8.69379	8.05518	6.56598	30
11.34980	10.34280	9.47901	8.73315	8.08499	6.57911	31
11.43500	10.40624	9.52638	8.76860	8.11159	6.59053	32
11.51389	10.46444	9.56943	8.80054	8.13535	6.60046	33
11.58693	10.51784	9.60858	8.82932	8.15656	6.60910	34
11.65457	10.56682	9.64416	8.85524	8.17550	6.61661	35
11.71719	10.61176	9.67651	8.87859	8.19241	6.62314	36
11.77518	10.65299	9.70592	8.89963	8.20751	6.62882	37
11.82887	10.69082	9.73265	8.91859	8.22099	6.63375	38
11.87858	10.72552	9.75697	8.93567	8.23303	6.63805	39
11.92461	10.75736	9.77905	8.95105	8.24378	6.64178	40

TABLE 6-5 PRESENT VALUE OF AN ANNUITY DUE OF 1

$$PVF\text{-}AD_{n,i} = 1 + \frac{1 - \frac{1}{(1+i)^{n-1}}}{i}$$

(n) Periods	2%	2½%	3%	4%	5%	6%
1	1.00000	1.00000	1.00000	1.00000	1.00000	1.00000
2	1.98039	1.97561	1.97087	1.96154	1.95238	1.94340
3	2.94156	2.92742	2.91347	2.88609	2.85941	2.83339
4	3.88388	3.85602	3.82861	3.77509	3.72325	3.67301
5	4.80773	4.76197	4.71710	4.62990	4.54595	4.46511
6	5.71346	5.64583	5.57971	5.45182	5.32948	5.21236
7	6.60143	6.50813	6.41719	6.24214	6.07569	5.91732
8	7.47199	7.34939	7.23028	7.00205	6.78637	6.58238
9	8.32548	8.17014	8.01969	7.73274	7.46321	7.20979
10	9.16224	8.97087	8.78611	8.43533	8.10782	7.80169
11	9.98259	9.75206	9.53020	9.11090	8.72173	8.36009
12	10.78685	10.51421	10.25262	9.76048	9.30641	8.88687
13	11.57534	11.25776	10.95400	10.38507	9.86325	9.38384
14	12.34837	11.98319	11.63496	10.98565	10.39357	9.85268
15	13.10625	12.69091	12.29607	11.56312	10.89864	10.29498
16	13.84926	13.38138	12.93794	12.11839	11.37966	10.71225
17	14.57771	14.05500	13.56110	12.65230	11.83777	11.10590
18	15.29187	14.71220	14.16612	13.16567	12.27407	11.47726
19	15.99203	15.35336	14.75351	13.65930	12.68959	11.82760
20	16.67846	15.97889	15.32380	14.13394	13.08532	12.15812
21	17.35143	16.58916	15.87747	14.59033	13.46221	12.46992
22	18.01121	17.18455	16.41502	15.02916	13.82115	12.76408
23	18.65805	17.76541	16.93692	15.45112	14.16300	13.04158
24	19.29220	18.33211	17.44361	15.85684	14.48857	13.30338
25	19.91393	18.88499	17.93554	16.24696	14.79864	13.55036
26	20.52346	19.42438	18.41315	16.62208	15.09394	13.78336
27	21.12104	19.95061	18.87684	16.98277	15.37519	14.00317
28	21.70690	20.46401	19.32703	17.32959	15.64303	14.21053
29	22.28127	20.96489	19.76411	17.66306	15.89813	14.40616
30	22.84438	21.45355	20.18845	17.98371	16.14107	14.59072
31	23.39646	21.93029	20.60044	18.29203	16.37245	14.76483
32	23.93770	22.39541	21.00043	18.58849	16.59281	14.92909
33	24.46833	22.84918	21.38877	18.87355	16.80268	15.08404
34	24.98856	23.29188	21.76579	19.14765	17.00255	15.23023
35	25.49859	23.72379	22.13184	19.41120	17.19290	15.36814
36	25.99862	24.14516	22.48722	19.66461	17.37419	15.49825
37	26.48884	24.55625	22.83225	19.90828	17.54685	15.62099
38	26.96945	24.95732	23.16724	20.14258	17.71129	15.73678
39	27.44064	25.34860	23.49246	20.36786	17.86789	15.84602
40	27.90259	25.73034	23.80822	20.58448	18.01704	15.94907

TABLE 6-5 PRESENT VALUE OF AN ANNUITY DUE OF 1

8%	9%	10%	11%	12%	15%	(n) Periods
1.00000	1.00000	1.00000	1.00000	1.00000	1.00000	1
1.92593	1.91743	1.90909	1.90090	1.89286	1.86957	2
2.78326	2.75911	2.73554	2.71252	2.69005	2.62571	3
3.57710	3.53130	3.48685	3.44371	3.40183	3.28323	4
4.31213	4.23972	4.16986	4.10245	4.03735	3.85498	5
4.99271	4.88965	4.79079	4.69590	4.60478	4.35216	6
5.62288	5.48592	5.35526	5.23054	5.11141	4.78448	7
6.20637	6.03295	5.86842	5.71220	5.56376	5.16042	8
6.74664	6.53482	6.33493	6.14612	5.96764	5.48732	9
7.24689	6.99525	6.75902	6.53705	6.32825	5.77158	10
7.71008	7.41766	7.14457	6.88923	6.65022	6.01877	11
8.13896	7.80519	7.49506	7.20652	6.93770	6.23371	12
8.53608	8.16073	7.81369	7.49236	7.19437	6.42062	13
8.90378	8.48690	8.10336	7.74987	7.42355	6.58315	14
9.24424	8.78615	8.36669	7.98187	7.62817	6.72448	15
9.55948	9.06069	8.60608	8.19087	7.81086	6.84737	16
9.85137	9.31256	8.82371	8.37916	7.97399	6.95424	17
10.12164	9.54363	9.02155	8.54879	8.11963	7.04716	18
10.37189	9.75563	9.20141	8.70162	8.24967	7.12797	19
10.60360	9.95012	9.36492	8.83929	8.36578	7.19823	20
10.81815	10.12855	9.51356	8.96333	8.46944	7.25933	21
11.01680	10.29224	9.64869	9.07507	8.56200	7.31246	22
11.20074	10.44243	9.77154	9.17574	8.64465	7.35866	23
11.37106	10.58021	9.88322	9.26643	8.71843	7.39884	24
11.52876	10.70661	9.98474	9.34814	8.78432	7.43377	25
11.67478	10.82258	10.07704	9.42174	8.84314	7.46415	26
11.80998	10.92897	10.16095	9.48806	8.89566	7.49056	27
11.93518	11.02658	10.23722	9.54780	8.94255	7.51353	28
12.05108	11.11613	10.30657	9.60162	8.98442	7.53351	29
12.15841	11.19828	10.36961	9.65011	9.02181	7.55088	30
12.25778	11.27365	10.42691	9.69379	9.05518	7.56598	31
12.34980	11.34280	10.47901	9.73315	9.08499	7.57911	32
12.43500	11.40624	10.52638	9.76860	9.11159	7.59053	33
12.51389	11.46444	10.56943	9.80054	9.13535	7.60046	34
12.58693	11.51784	10.60858	9.82932	9.15656	7.60910	35
12.65457	11.56682	10.64416	9.85524	9.17550	7.61661	36
12.71719	11.61176	10.67651	9.87859	9.19241	7.62314	37
12.77518	11.65299	10.70592	9.89963	9.20751	7.62882	38
12.82887	11.69082	10.73265	9.91859	9.22099	7.63375	39
12.87858	11.72552	10.75697	9.93567	9.23303	7.63805	40

Logo Credits

The following companies have granted permission for their logos to be included in this text.

3M Company

Alterra Healthcare Corporation

Anchor BanCorp Wisconsin Inc.

Avon Rubber p.l.c. The Avon logo is a registered trademark supplied by kind permission of Avon Rubber p.l.c.

Brown Shoe Company, Inc.

The Coca-Cola Company

The Walt Disney Company

Gateway, Inc.

The Gillette Company

Johnson & Johnson

Kellogg Company. KELLOGG'S™ is a trademark of Kellogg Company. All rights reserved. Used with permission.

Mack Trucks, Inc.

Mattel, Inc. Mattel logo courtesy of Mattel, Inc.

Merck & Co. Inc.

Occidental Petroleum Corporation

PepsiCo, Inc. © 2002 PepsiCo, Inc. All rights reserved. Used with permission.

Quaker Oats Company. The Quaker name and Quaker Oats logo are registered trademarks of the Quaker Oats Company.

Southwest Airlines

Tompkins PLC

Tootsie Roll Industries, Inc.

Union Planters Corporation

Uniroyal Technology Corporation

Westinghouse Electric Corporation

Index

OFFICIAL ACCOUNTING PRONOUNCEMENTS

The following list of official accounting pronouncements constitutes the major part of *generally accepted accounting principles* (GAAP) and represents the authoritative source documents for much of the discussion contained in this book.

Accounting Research Bulletins (ARB's), Committee on Accounting Procedures, AICPA (1953–1959)

Date Issued		No.	Title
June	1953	No. 43	Restatement and Revision of Accounting Research Bulletins Nos. 1–42, and Accounting Terminology Bulletin No. 1 (originally issued 1939–1953)
Oct.	1954	No. 44	Declining-Balance Depreciation; Revised July, 1958 (amended)
Oct.	1955	No. 45	Long-term Construction-type Contracts (unchanged)
Feb.	1956	No. 46	Discontinuance of Dating Earned Surplus (unchanged)
Sept.	1956	No. 47	Accounting for Costs of Pension Plans (superseded)
Jan.	1957	No. 48	Business Combinations (superseded)
April	1958	No. 49	Earnings Per Share (superseded)
Oct.	1958	No. 50	Contingencies (superseded)
Aug.	1959	No. 51	Consolidated Financial Statements (amended and partially superseded)

Accounting Terminology Bulletins, Committee on Terminology, AICPA

Aug.	1953	No. 1	Review and Résumé (of the eight original terminology bulletins) (amended)
Mar.	1955	No. 2	Proceeds, Revenue, Income, Profit, and Earnings (amended)
Aug.	1956	No. 3	Book Value (unchanged)
July	1957	No. 4	Cost, Expense, and Loss (amended)

Accounting Principles Board (APB) Opinions, AICPA (1962–1973)

Nov.	1962	No. 1	New Depreciation Guidelines and Rules (amended)
Dec.	1962	No. 2	Accounting for the "Investment Credit" (amended)
Oct.	1963	No. 3	The Statement of Source and Application of Funds (superseded)
Mar.	1964	No. 4	Accounting for the "Investment Credit" (Amending No. 2)
Sept.	1964	No. 5	Reporting of Leases in Financial Statements of Lessee (superseded)
Oct.	1965	No. 6	Status of Accounting Research Bulletins (partially superseded)
May	1966	No. 7	Accounting for Leases in Financial Statements of Lessors (superseded)
Nov.	1966	No. 8	Accounting for the Cost of Pension Plans (superseded)
Dec.	1966	No. 9	Reporting the Results of Operations (amended and partially superseded)
Dec.	1966	No. 10	Omnibus Opinion—1966 (amended and partially superseded)
Dec.	1967	No. 11	Accounting for Income Taxes (superseded)
Dec.	1967	No. 12	Omnibus Opinion—1967 (partially superseded)
Mar.	1969	No. 13	Amending Paragraph 6 of APB Opinion No. 9, Application to Commercial Banks (unchanged)
Mar.	1969	No. 14	Accounting for Convertible Debt and Debt Issued with Stock Purchase Warrants (unchanged)
May	1969	No. 15	Earnings per Share (superseded)
Aug.	1970	No. 16	Business Combinations (superseded)
Aug.	1970	No. 17	Intangible Assets (superseded)
Mar.	1971	No. 18	The Equity Method of Accounting for Investments in Common Stock (amended)
Mar.	1971	No. 19	Reporting Changes in Financial Position (amended)
July	1971	No. 20	Accounting Changes (amended)
Aug.	1971	No. 21	Interest on Receivables and Payables (amended)
April	1972	No. 22	Disclosure of Accounting Policies (amended)
April	1972	No. 23	Accounting for Income Taxes—Special Areas (superseded)
April	1972	No. 24	Accounting for Income Taxes—Equity Method Investments (unchanged)
Oct.	1972	No. 25	Accounting for Stock Issued to Employees (unchanged)
Oct.	1972	No. 26	Early Extinguishment of Debt (amended)
Nov.	1972	No. 27	Accounting for Lease Transactions by Manufacturer or Dealer Lessors (superseded)
May	1973	No. 28	Interim Financial Reporting (amended and partially superseded)
May	1973	No. 29	Accounting for Nonmonetary Transactions (amended)
June	1973	No. 30	Reporting the Results of Operations (amended)
June	1973	No. 31	Disclosure of Lease Commitments by Lessees (superseded)

Financial Accounting Standards Board (FASB), Statements of Financial Accounting Standards (1973–2002)

Dec.	1973	No. 1	Disclosure of Foreign Currency Translation Information (superseded)
Oct.	1974	No. 2	Accounting for Research and Development Costs (amended)
Dec.	1974	No. 3	Reporting Accounting Changes in Interim Financial Statements
Mar.	1975	No. 4	Reporting Gains and Losses from Extinguishment of Debt (superseded)
Mar.	1975	No. 5	Accounting for Contingencies (amended)
May	1975	No. 6	Classification of Short-term Obligations Expected to be Refinanced
June	1975	No. 7	Accounting and Reporting by Development Stage Enterprises
Oct.	1975	No. 8	Accounting for the Translation of Foreign Currency Transactions and Foreign Financial Statements (superseded)

Date Issued		No.	Title
Oct.	1975	No. 9	Accounting for Income Taxes—Oil and Gas Producing Companies (superseded)
Oct.	1975	No. 10	Extension of "Grandfather" Provisions for Business Combinations (superseded)
Dec.	1975	No. 11	Accounting for Contingencies—Transition Method
Dec.	1975	No. 12	Accounting for Certain Marketable Securities (superseded)
Nov.	1976	No. 13	Accounting for Leases (amended, interpreted, and partially superseded)
Dec.	1976	No. 14	Financial Reporting for Segments of a Business Enterprise (amended)
June	1977	No. 15	Accounting by Debtors and Creditors for Troubled Debt Restructurings (amended)
June	1977	No. 16	Prior Period Adjustments (amended)
Nov.	1977	No. 17	Accounting for Leases—Initial Direct Costs
Nov.	1977	No. 18	Financial Reporting for Segments of a Business Enterprise—Interim Financial Statements
Dec.	1977	No. 19	Financial Accounting and Reporting by Oil and Gas Producing Companies (amended)
Dec.	1977	No. 20	Accounting for Forward Exchange Contracts (superseded)
April	1978	No. 21	Suspension of the Reporting of Earnings per Share and Segment Information by Nonpublic Enterprises (amended)
June	1978	No. 22	Changes in the Provisions of Lease Agreements Resulting from Refundings of Tax-Exempt Debt (amended)
Aug.	1978	No. 23	Inception of the Lease
Dec.	1978	No. 24	Reporting Segment Information in Financial Statements That Are Presented in Another Enterprise's Financial Report
Feb.	1979	No. 25	Suspension of Certain Accounting Requirements for Oil and Gas Producing Companies
April	1979	No. 26	Profit Recognition on Sales-Type Leases of Real Estate
May	1979	No. 27	Classification of Renewals or Extensions of Existing Sales-Type or Direct Financing Leases
May	1979	No. 28	Accounting for Sales with Leasebacks
June	1979	No. 29	Determining Contingent Rentals
Aug.	1979	No. 30	Disclosure of Information about Major Customers
Sept.	1979	No. 31	Accounting for Tax Benefits Related to U.K. Tax Legislation Concerning Stock Relief
Sept.	1979	No. 32	Specialized Accounting and Reporting Principles and Practices in AICPA Statements of Position and Guides on Accounting and Auditing Matters (amended and partially superseded)
Sept.	1979	No. 33	Financial Reporting and Changing Prices (amended and partially superseded)
Oct.	1979	No. 34	Capitalization of Interest Cost (amended)
Mar.	1980	No. 35	Accounting and Reporting by Defined Benefit Pension Plans (amended)
May	1980	No. 36	Disclosure of Pension Information (superseded)
July	1980	No. 37	Balance Sheet Classification of Deferred Income Taxes (amended)
Sept.	1980	No. 38	Accounting for Preacquisition Contingencies of Purchased Enterprises (superseded)
Oct.	1980	No. 39	Financial Reporting and Changing Prices: Specialized Assets—Mining and Oil and Gas
Nov.	1980	No. 40	Financial Reporting and Changing Prices: Specialized Assets—Timberlands and Growing Timber
Nov.	1980	No. 41	Financial Reporting and Changing Prices: Specialized Assets—Income-Producing Real Estate
Nov.	1980	No. 42	Determining Materiality for Capitalization of Interest Cost
Nov.	1980	No. 43	Accounting for Compensated Absences (amended)
Dec.	1980	No. 44	Accounting for Intangible Assets of Motor Carriers (superseded)
Mar.	1981	No. 45	Accounting for Franchise Fee Revenue (amended)
Mar.	1981	No. 46	Financial Reporting and Changing Prices: Motion Picture Films
Mar.	1981	No. 47	Disclosure of Long-Term Obligations (amended)
June	1981	No. 48	Revenue Recognition When Right of Return Exists
June	1981	No. 49	Accounting for Product Financing Arrangements
Nov.	1981	No. 50	Financial Reporting in the Record and Music Industry
Nov.	1981	No. 51	Financial Reporting by Cable Television Companies (amended)
Dec.	1981	No. 52	Foreign Currency Translation (amended)
Dec.	1981	No. 53	Financial Reporting by Producers and Distributors of Motion Picture Films (superseded)
Jan.	1982	No. 54	Financial Reporting and Changing Prices: Investment Companies (superseded)
Feb.	1982	No. 55	Determining Whether a Convertible Security is a Common Stock Equivalent (superseded)
Feb.	1982	No. 56	Designation of AICPA Guide and SOP 81-1 on Contractor Accounting and SOP 81-2 on Hospital-Related Organizations as Preferable for Applying APB Opinion 20 (superseded)
Mar.	1982	No. 57	Related Party Disclosures
April	1982	No. 58	Capitalization of Interest Cost in Financial Statements that Include Investments Accounted for by the Equity Method
April	1982	No. 59	Deferral of the Effective Date of Certain Accounting Requirements for Revision Plans of State and Local Governmental Units
June	1982	No. 60	Accounting and Reporting by Insurance Enterprises (amended)
June	1982	No. 61	Accounting for Title Plant (amended)
June	1982	No. 62	Capitalization of Interest Cost in Situations Involving Certain Tax-Exempt Borrowings and Certain Gifts and Grants
June	1982	No. 63	Financial Reporting by Broadcasters (amended)

Date Issued		No.	Title
Sept.	1982	No. 64	Extinguishment of Debt Made to Satisfy Sinking-Fund Requirements (superseded)
Sept.	1982	No. 65	Accounting for Certain Mortgage Bank Activities (amended)
Oct.	1982	No. 66	Accounting for Sales of Real Estate (amended)
Oct.	1982	No. 67	Accounting for Costs and Initial Rental Operations of Real Estate Projects (amended)
Oct.	1982	No. 68	Research and Development Arrangements (amended)
Nov.	1982	No. 69	Disclosures about Oil and Gas Producing Activities
Dec.	1982	No. 70	Financial Reporting and Changing Prices: Foreign Currency Translation
Dec.	1982	No. 71	Accounting for the Effects of Certain Types of Regulation (amended)
Feb.	1983	No. 72	Accounting for Certain Acquisitions of Banking or Thrift Institutions (amended)
Aug.	1983	No. 73	Reporting a Change in Accounting for Railroad Track Structures
Aug.	1983	No. 74	Accounting for Special Termination Benefits Paid to Employees
Nov.	1983	No. 75	Deferral of the Effective Date of Certain Accounting Requirements for Pension Plans of State and Local Governmental Units (superseded)
Nov.	1983	No. 76	Extinguishment of Debt (superseded)
Dec.	1983	No. 77	Reporting by Transferors for Transfers of Receivables with Recourse (superseded)
Dec.	1983	No. 78	Classifications of Obligations that Are Callable by the Creditor
Feb.	1984	No. 79	Elimination of Certain Disclosures for Business Combinations by Nonpublic Enterprises (superseded)
Aug.	1984	No. 80	Accounting for Futures Contracts (superseded)
Nov.	1984	No. 81	Disclosure of Postretirement Health Care and Life Insurance Benefits
Nov.	1984	No. 82	Financial Reporting and Changing Prices: Elimination of Certain Disclosures
Mar.	1985	No. 83	Designation of AICPA Guides and Statement of Position on Accounting by Brokers and Dealers in Securities, by Employee Benefit Plans, and by Banks as Preferable for Purposes of Applying APB Opinion 20
Mar.	1985	No. 84	Induced Conversions of Convertible Debt
Mar.	1985	No. 85	Yield Test for Determining Whether a Convertible Security Is a Common Stock Equivalent (superseded)
Aug.	1985	No. 86	Accounting for the Costs of Computer Software to be Sold, Leased, or Otherwise Marketed
Dec.	1985	No. 87	Employers' Accounting for Pensions (amended)
Dec.	1985	No. 88	Employers' Accounting for Settlements and Curtailments of Defined Benefit Pension Plans and for Termination Benefits (amended)
Dec.	1986	No. 89	Financial Reporting and Changing Prices (amended)
Dec.	1986	No. 90	Regulated Enterprises—Accounting for Abandonments and Disallowances of Plant Costs
Dec.	1986	No. 91	Accounting for Nonrefundable Fees and Costs Associated with Originating or Acquiring Loans and Initial Direct Costs of Leases
Aug.	1987	No. 92	Regulated Enterprises—Accounting for Phase-in Plans
Aug.	1987	No. 93	Recognition of Depreciation by Not-for-Profit Organizations
Oct.	1987	No. 94	Consolidation of All Majority-Owned Subsidiaries
Nov.	1987	No. 95	Statement of Cash Flows (amended)
Dec.	1987	No. 96	Accounting for Income Taxes (superseded)
Dec.	1987	No. 97	Accounting and Reporting by Insurance Enterprises for Certain Long-Duration Contracts and for Realized Gains and Losses from the Sale of Investments
June	1988	No. 98	Accounting for Leases; Sale-Leaseback Transactions Involving Real Estate; Sales-Type Leases of Real Estate; Definition of the Lease Term; Initial Direct Costs of Direct Financing Leases
Sept.	1988	No. 99	Deferral of the Effective Date of Recognition of Depreciation by Not-for-Profit Organizations
Dec.	1988	No. 100	Accounting for Income Taxes—Deferral of the Effective Date of FASB Statement No. 96
Dec.	1988	No. 101	Regulated Enterprises—Accounting for the Discontinuation of Application of FASB Statement No. 71 (amended)
Feb.	1989	No. 102	Statement of Cash Flows—Exemption of Certain Enterprises and Classification of Cash Flows from Certain Securities Acquired for Resale (amended)
Dec.	1989	No. 103	Accounting for Income Taxes—Deferral of the Effective Date of FASB Statement No. 96
Dec.	1989	No. 104	Statement of Cash Flows—Net Reporting of Certain Cash Receipts and Cash Payments and Classification of Cash Flows from Hedging Transactions
Mar.	1990	No. 105	Disclosure of Information About Financial Instruments with Off-Balance-Sheet Risk and Financial Instruments with Concentrations of Credit Risk (superseded)
Dec.	1990	No. 106	Employers' Accounting for Postretirement Benefits Other Than Pensions (amended)
Dec.	1991	No. 107	Disclosures about Fair Value of Financial Instruments (amended)
Dec.	1991	No. 108	Accounting for Income Taxes—Deferral of the Effective Date of FASB Statement No. 96
Feb.	1992	No. 109	Accounting for Income Taxes (amended)
Aug.	1992	No. 110	Reporting by Defined Benefit Pension Plans of Investment Contracts
Nov.	1992	No. 111	Rescission of FASB Statement No. 32 and Technical Corrections
Nov.	1992	No. 112	Employers' Accounting for Postemployment Benefits
Dec.	1992	No. 113	Accounting and Reporting for Reinsurance of Short-Duration and Long-Duration Contracts
May	1993	No. 114	Accounting by Creditors for Impairment of a Loan (amended)
May	1993	No. 115	Accounting for Certain Investments in Debt and Equity Securities (amended)

Date Issued		No.	Title
June	1993	No. 116	Accounting for Contributions Received and Contributions Made
June	1993	No. 117	Financial Statements of Not-for-Profit Organizations (amended)
Oct.	1994	No. 118	Accounting by Creditors for Impairments of a Loan—Income Recognition and Disclosures
Oct.	1994	No. 119	Disclosure about Derivative Financial Instruments and Fair Value of Financial Instruments (superseded)
Jan.	1995	No. 120	Accounting and Reporting by Mutual Life Insurance Enterprises
Mar.	1995	No. 121	Accounting for the Impairment of Long-Lived Assets (superseded)
May	1995	No. 122	Accounting for Mortgage Servicing Rights (superseded)
Oct.	1995	No. 123	Accounting for Stock-Based Compensation (amended)
Nov.	1995	No. 124	Accounting for Certain Investments Held by Not-for-Profit Organizations
June	1996	No. 125	Accounting for Transfers and Servicing of Financial Assets and Extinguishment of Liabilities (amended)
Dec.	1996	No. 126	Exemption from Certain Required Disclosures about Financial Instruments for Certain Nonpublic Entities
Dec.	1996	No. 127	Deferral of the Effective Date of Certain Provisions of FASB Statement No. 125
Feb.	1997	No. 128	Earnings per Share (amended)
Feb.	1997	No. 129	Disclosure of Information about Capital Structure
June	1997	No. 130	Reporting Comprehensive Income
June	1997	No. 131	Reporting Disaggregated Information about a Business Enterprise
Feb.	1998	No. 132	Employers' Disclosures about Pensions and Other Postretirement Benefits an amendment of FASB Statements No. 87, 88, and 106
June	1998	No. 133	Accounting for Derivative Instruments and Hedging Activities (amended)
Oct.	1998	No. 134	Accounting for Mortgage-Backed Securities Retained after the Securitization of Mortgage Loans Held for Sale by a Mortgage Banking Enterprise (an amendment of FASB Statement No. 65)
Feb.	1999	No. 135	Rescission of FASB Statement No. 75 and Technical Corrections (amended)
June	1999	No. 136	Transfers of Assets to a Not-for-Profit Organization or Charitable Trust That Raises or Holds Contributions for Others (amended)
June	1999	No. 137	Accounting for Derivative Instruments and Hedging Activities—Deferral of the Effective Date for FASB Statement No. 133 (an amendment of Statement No. 133)
June	2000	No. 138	Accounting for Certain Derivative Instruments and Certain Hedging Activities (an amendment of FASB Statement No. 133)
June	2000	No. 139	Rescission of FASB Statement No. 53 and amendments to FASB Statements No. 63, 89, and 121
Sept.	2000	No. 140	Accounting for Transfers and Servicing of Financial Assets and Extinguishments of Liabilities (a replacement of FASB Statement 125)
June	2001	No. 141	Business Combinations (amended)
June	2001	No. 142	Goodwill and Other Intangible Assets (amended)
June	2001	No. 143	Accounting for Asset Retirement Obligations (amended)
Aug.	2001	No. 144	Accounting for the Impairment or Disposal of Long-Lived Assets (amended)
April	2002	No. 145	Rescission of FASB Statements No. 4, 44, and 64, Amendment of FASB Statement No. 13, and Technical Corrections
June	2002	No. 146	Accounting for Costs Associated with Exit or Disposal Activities
Oct.	2002	No. 147	Acquisitions of Certain Financial Institutions, an Amendment of FASB Statements No. 72 and 144 and FASB Interpretation No. 9
Dec.	2002	No. 148	Accounting for Stock-Based Compensation—Transition and Disclosure
Feb.	2003	No. 149	Accounting for Certain Financial Instruments with Characteristics of Liabilities and Equity

Financial Accounting Standards Board (FASB), Interpretations (1974–2002)

June	1974	No. 1	Accounting Changes Related to the Cost of Inventory (APB Opinion No. 20)
June	1974	No. 2	Imputing Interest on Debt Arrangements Made Under the Federal Bankruptcy Act (APB Opinion No. 21) (superseded)
Dec.	1974	No. 3	Accounting for the Cost of Pension Plans Subject to the Employee Retirement Income Security Act of 1974 (APB Opinion No. 8)
Feb.	1975	No. 4	Applicability of FASB Statement No. 2 to Purchase Business Combinations (amended)
Feb.	1975	No. 5	Applicability of FASB St. No. 2 to Development Stage Enterprises (superseded)
Feb.	1975	No. 6	Applicability of FASB Statement No. 2 to Computer Software
Oct.	1975	No. 7	Applying FASB Statement No. 7 in Statements of Established Enterprises
Jan.	1976	No. 8	Classification of a Short-Term Obligation Repaid Prior to Being Replaced by a Long-Term Security (FASB Std. No. 6)
Feb.	1976	No. 9	Applying APB Opinion No. 16 and 17 when a Savings and Loan or Similar Institution is Acquired in a Purchase Business Combination (APB Op. No. 16 & 17) (amended)
Sept.	1976	No. 10	Application of FASB Statement No. 12 to Personal Financial Statements (FASB Std. No. 12)
Sept.	1976	No. 11	Changes in Market Value after the Balance Sheet Date (FASB Std. No. 12)
Sept.	1976	No. 12	Accounting for Previously Established Allowance Accounts (FASB Std. No. 12)
Sept.	1976	No. 13	Consolidation of a Parent and Its Subsidiaries Having Different Balance Sheet Dates (FASB Std. No. 12)
Sept.	1976	No. 14	Reasonable Estimation of the Amount of a Loss (FASB Std. No. 5)

Date Issued		No.	Title
Sept.	1976	No. 15	Translation of Unamortized Policy Acquisition Costs by Stock Life Insurance Company (FASB Std. No. 8) (amended and partially superseded)
Feb.	1977	No. 16	Clarification of Definitions and Accounting for Marketable Equity Securities That Become Nonmarketable (FASB Std. No. 12)
Feb.	1977	No. 17	Applying the Lower of Cost or Market Rule in Translated Financial Statements (FASB Std. No. 8) (superseded)
Mar.	1977	No. 18	Accounting for Income Taxes in Interim Periods (APB Op. No. 28) (amended)
Oct.	1977	No. 19	Lessee Guarantee of the Residual Value of Leased Property (FASB Std. No. 13)
Nov.	1977	No. 20	Reporting Accounting Changes under AICPA Statements of Position (APB Op. No. 20)
April	1978	No. 21	Accounting for Leases in a Business Combination (FASB Std. No. 13) (amended)
April	1978	No. 22	Applicability of Indefinite Reversal Criteria to Timing Differences (APB Op. No. 11 and 23)
Aug.	1978	No. 23	Leases of Certain Property Owned by a Governmental Unit or Authority (FASB Std. No. 13)
Sept.	1978	No. 24	Leases Involving Only Part of a Building (FASB Std. No. 13)
Sept.	1978	No. 25	Accounting for an Unused Investment Tax Credit (APB Op. No. 2, 4, 11, and 16)
Sept.	1978	No. 26	Accounting for Purchase of a Leased Asset by the Lessee During the Term of the Lease (FASB Std. No. 13)
Nov.	1978	No. 27	Accounting for a Loss on a Sublease (FASB Std. No. 13 and APB Op. No. 30) (amended)
Dec.	1978	No. 28	Accounting for Stock Appreciation Rights and Other Variable Stock Option or Award Plans (APB Op. No. 15 and 25) (amended)
Feb.	1979	No. 29	Reporting Tax Benefits Realized on Disposition of Investments in Certain Subsidiaries and Other Investees (APB Op. No. 23 and 24)
Sept.	1979	No. 30	Accounting for Involuntary Conversions of Nonmonetary Assets to Monetary Assets (APB Op. No. 29)
Feb.	1980	No. 31	Treatment of Stock Compensation Plans in EPS Computations (APB Op. No. 15 and Interp. 28) (superseded)
Mar.	1980	No. 32	Application of Percentage Limitations in Recognizing Investment Tax Credit (APB Op. No. 2, 4, and 11)
Aug.	1980	No. 33	Applying FASB Statement No. 34 to Oil and Gas Producing Operations (FASB Std. No. 34)
Mar.	1981	No. 34	Disclosure of Indirect Guarantees of Indebtedness of Others (FASB Std. No. 5)
May	1981	No. 35	Criteria for Applying the Equity Method of Accounting for Investments in Common Stock (APB Op. No. 18)
Oct.	1981	No. 36	Accounting for Exploratory Wells in Progress at the End of a Period
July	1983	No. 37	Accounting for Translation Adjustments upon Sale of Part of an Investment in a Foreign Entity (Interprets FASB Statement No. 52)
Aug.	1984	No. 38	Determining the Measurement Date for Stock Option, Purchase, and Award Plans Involving Junior Stock (Interprets APB Opinion No. 25)
Mar.	1992	No. 39	Offsetting of Amounts Related to Certain Contracts (Interprets APB Opinion No. 10 and FASB Statement No. 105) (amended)
Apr.	1993	No. 40	Applicability of Generally Accepted Accounting Principles to Mutual Life Insurance and Other Enterprises (Interprets FASB Statements No. 12, 60, 97, and 113)
Dec.	1994	No. 41	Offsetting of Amounts Related to Certain Repurchase and Reverse Repurchase Agreements
Sept.	1996	No. 42	Accounting for Transfers of Assets in Which a Not-for-Profit Organization is Granted Variance Power
June	1999	No. 43	Real Estate Sales (Interprets FASB Statement No. 66) (amended)
		No. 44	Accounting for Certain Transactions involving Stock Compensation (an interpretation of APB Opinion No. 25) (amended)
Nov.	2002	No. 45	Guarantor's Accounting and Disclosure Requirements for Guarantees, Including Indirect Guarantees of Indebtedness of Others
Jan.	2003	No. 46	Consolidation of Variable Interest Entities (an interpretation of ARB No. 51)

Financial Accounting Standards Board (FASB), Technical Bulletins (1979–2002)

Date Issued		No.	Title
Dec.	1979	No. 79-1	Purpose and Scope of FASB Technical Bulletins and Procedures for Issuance
Dec.	1979	No. 79-2	Computer Software Costs
Dec.	1979	No. 79-3	Subjective Acceleration Clauses in Long-Term Debt Agreements
Dec.	1979	No. 79-4	Segment Reporting of Puerto Rican Operations
Dec.	1979	No. 79-5	Meaning of the Term 'Customer' as it Applies to Health Care Facilities under FASB Statement No. 14
Dec.	1979	No. 79-6	Valuation Allowances Following Debt Restructuring
Dec.	1979	No. 79-7	Recoveries of a Previous Writedown under a Troubled Debt Restructuring Involving a Modification of Terms
Dec.	1979	No. 79-8	Applicability of FASB Statements 21 and 33 to Certain Brokers and Dealers in Securities
Dec.	1979	No. 79-9	Accounting in Interim Periods for Changes in Income Tax Rates
Dec.	1979	No. 79-10	Fiscal Funding Clauses in Lease Agreements
Dec.	1979	No. 79-11	Effect of a Penalty on the Term of a Lease
Dec.	1979	No. 79-12	Interest Rate Used in Calculating the Present Value of Minimum Lease Payments
Dec.	1979	No. 79-13	Applicability of FASB Statement No. 13 to Current Value Financial Statements
Dec.	1979	No. 79-14	Upward Adjustment of Guaranteed Residual Values
Dec.	1979	No. 79-15	Accounting for Loss on a Sublease Not Involving the Disposal of a Segment
Dec.	1979	No. 79-16	Effect on a Change in Income Tax Rate on the Accounting for Leveraged Leases

Date Issued		No.	Title
Dec.	1979	No. 79-17	Reporting Cumulative Effect Adjustment from Retroactive Application of FASB No. 13
Dec.	1979	No. 79-18	Transition Requirements of Certain FASB Amendments and Interpretations of FASB Statement No. 13
Dec.	1979	No. 79-19	Investor's Accounting for Unrealized Losses on Marketable Securities Owned by an Equity Method Investee
Dec.	1980	No. 80-1	Early Extinguishment of Debt through Exchange for Common or Preferred Stock (amended)
Dec.	1980	No. 80-2	Classification of Debt Restructuring by Debtors and Creditors
Feb.	1981	No. 81-1	Disclosure of Interest Rate Futures Contracts and Forward and Standby Contracts
Feb.	1981	No. 81-2	Accounting for Unused Investment Tax Credits Acquired in a Business Combination Accounted for by the Purchase Method
Feb.	1981	No. 81-3	Multiemployer Pension Plan Amendments Act of 1980
Feb.	1981	No. 81-4	Classification as Monetary or Nonmonetary Items
Feb.	1981	No. 81-5	Offsetting Interest Cost to be Capitalized with Interest Income
Nov.	1981	No. 81-6	Applicability of Statement 15 to Debtors in Bankruptcy Situations
Jan.	1982	No. 82-1	Disclosure of the Sale or Purchase of Tax Benefits through Tax Leases (amended)
Mar.	1982	No. 82-2	Accounting for the Conversion of Stock Options into Incentive Stock Options as a Result of the Economic Recovery Tax Act of 1981
July	1983	No. 83-1	Accounting for the Reduction in the Tax Basis of an Asset Caused by the Investment Tax Credit (ITC)
Mar.	1984	No. 84-1	Accounting for Stock Issued to Acquire the Results of a Research and Development Arrangement (amended)
June	1984	No. 79-1	Purpose and Scope of FASB Technical Bulletins and Procedures for Issuance (Revised)
Sept.	1984	No. 84-2	Accounting for the Effects of the Tax Reform Act of 1984 on Deferred Income Taxes Relating to Domestic International Sales Corporations
Sept.	1984	No. 84-3	Accounting for the Effects of the Tax Reform Act of 1984 on Deferred Income Taxes of Stock Life Insurance Enterprises
Oct.	1984	No. 84-4	In-Substance Defeasance of Debt
Mar.	1985	No. 85-1	Accounting for the Receipt of Federal Home Loan Mortgage Corporation Participating Preferred Stock
Mar.	1985	No. 85-2	Accounting for Collateralized Mortgage Obligations (CMOs) (superseded)
Nov.	1985	No. 85-3	Accounting for Operating Leases with Scheduled Rent Increases
Nov.	1985	No. 85-4	Accounting for Purchases of Life Insurance (superseded)
Dec.	1985	No. 85-5	Issues Relating to Accounting for Business Combinations (amended)
Dec.	1985	No. 85-6	Accounting for a Purchase of Treasury Shares
Oct.	1986	No. 86-1	Accounting for Certain Effects of the Tax Reform Act of 1986
Dec.	1986	No. 86-2	Accounting for an Interest in the Residual Value of a Leased Asset (amended)
April	1987	No. 87-1	Accounting for a Change in Method of Accounting for Certain Postretirement Benefits
Dec.	1987	No. 87-2	Computation of a Loss on an Abandonment
Dec.	1987	No. 87-3	Accounting for Mortgage Servicing Fees and Rights (amended)
Dec.	1988	No. 88-1	Issues Relating to Accounting for Leases
Dec.	1988	No. 88-2	Definition of a Right of Setoff
Dec.	1990	No. 90-1	Accounting for Separately Priced Extended Warranty and Product Maintenance Contracts
Apr.	1994	No. 94-1	Application of Statement 115 to Debt Securities Restructured in a Troubled Debt Restructuring
Dec.	1997	No. 97-1	Accounting under Statement 123 for Certain Employee Stock Purchase Plans with a Look-Back Option
July	2001	No. 01-1	Effective Date for Certain Financial Institutions of Certain Provisions of Statement No. 140 Related to the Isolation of Transferred Financial Assets

Financial Accounting Standards Board (FASB), Statements of Financial Accounting Concepts (1978–2002)

Nov.	1978	No. 1	Objectives of Financial Reporting by Business Enterprises
May	1980	No. 2	Qualitative Characteristics of Accounting Information
Dec.	1980	No. 3	Elements of Financial Statements of Business Enterprises
Dec.	1980	No. 4	Objectives of Financial Reporting by Nonbusiness Organizations
Dec.	1984	No. 5	Recognition and Measurement in Financial Statements of Business Enterprises
Dec.	1985	No. 6	Elements of Financial Statements
Feb.	2000	No. 7	Using Cash Flow Information and Present Value in Accounting Measurements

NATIONAL ACCOUNTING BOARDS AND ORGANIZATIONS

American Accounting Association (AAA)
5717 Bessie Drive
Sarasota, FL 34233
(941) 921-7747
www.aaa-edu.org

American Institute of Certified Public Accountants (AICPA)
1211 Avenue of the Americas
New York, NY 10036
(212) 596-6200
www.aicpa.org

Association of Government Accountants (AGA)
2208 Mount Vernon Ave.
Alexandria, VA 22301
(703) 684-6931
www.agacgfm.org

Financial Accounting Standards Board (FASB)
401 Merritt 7
P.O. Box 5116
Norwalk, CT 06856
(203) 847-0700
www.fasb.org

Financial Executives Institute (FEI)
10 Madison Ave.
P.O. Box 1938
Morristown, NJ 07962-1938
(973) 898-4600
www.fei.org

Governmental Accounting Standards Board (GASB)
401 Merritt 7
P.O. Box 5116
Norwalk, CT 06856
(203) 847-0700
www.fasb.org

International Accounting Standards Board (IASB)
30 Cannon Street
London EC4M 6XH, United Kingdom
Telephone: +44 (0)20 7246 6410
e-mail: iasb@iasb.org.uk

Institute of Certified Management Accountants
10 Paragon Drive
Montvale, NJ 07645-1718
(201) 573-9000
www.imanet.org

Institute of Internal Auditors (IIA)
249 Maitland Avenue, P.O. Box 1119
Altamonte Springs, FL 32701
(407) 830-7600
www.theiia.org

Institute of Management Accountants (IMA)
10 Paragon Drive
Montvale, NJ 07645-1718
(201) 573-9000
www.imanet.org

Securities and Exchange Commission (SEC)
450 Fifth Street NW
Washington, DC 20549
(202) 942-7040
www.sec.gov